Masterpieces of the Drama

Alexander W. Allison   The University of Michigan

Arthur J. Carr   Williams College

Arthur M. Eastman   Carnegie-Mellon University

Masterpieces of the Drama

THIRD EDITION

MACMILLAN PUBLISHING CO., INC.

New York

Macmillan Publishing Co., Inc.
866 Third Avenue
New York, New York 10022

Collier-Macmillan Canada, Ltd.

Library of Congress Cataloging in Publication Data

Allison, Alexander Ward, ed.
    Masterpieces of the drama.

        1. Drama—Collections. I. Carr, Arthur Japheth, (date) joint ed.
II. Eastman, Arthur M., (date) joint ed. III. Title.
PN6112.A44   1974   808'.82   73-1042
ISBN 0-02-301890-9

Printing: 1 2 3 4 5 6 7 8   Year: 4 5 6 7 8 9 0

We sorrowfully dedicate this edition
to the memory of our dear friends
ALEXANDER and NANCY DEAN ALLISON

Preface

The third edition of *Masterpieces of the Drama* contains twice the number of plays in the previous edition. In all but one instance the process of revision has been a process of augmentation; the earlier contents have not been jostled to make room for the new. The freedom of a more generous length has been devoted to representing each dramatic period by more masterpieces from it.

Courses in drama that can accommodate a study of twenty-eight plays are rare. However, by offering more than enough in this edition of *Masterpieces of the Drama,* we hope to provide a satisfactory selection of plays for many different uses, to reduce the number of books necessary to one course, and to give the reader easy access to works related to those he studies. Because the word "masterpieces" in the title has been taken as literally as possible in making selections for the anthology, we trust that browsing in the volume will waste no reader's application. At the same time, it must be acknowledged that recent and contemporary works are included or excluded not in accordance with unfettered literary decisions, but by a compromise between them and the vagaries of publishers' permission-to-reprint policies.

A. W. A.
A. J. C.
A. M. E.

Contents

Masterpieces
of the Drama

Introduction

This introduction details some matters of fact and some articles of theory that it is hoped students will find serviceable and teachers less than meddlesome.

A play is a work of literary fiction enacted by living persons before the eyes of an audience. A literary study of the drama postulates an ideal performance of each work, assuming that the mind's eye will apprehend living persons and the mind's ear the intonations of speech. If one wants to appeal more particularly than this to the plays as theater pieces, as it will profit him to do from time to time, he must distinguish different kinds of theatrical performance.

One may conceive of the Greek plays in this book as they were performed—in a large outdoor amphitheater before the façade of a supposed palace or temple. This stage had no curtain; the actors either came out of the palace gates or entered in plain sight from the sides. They wore masks accentuating the dominant traits of the characters they portrayed and high-soled boots that increased their stature. In front of the stage, in the focal area of the semicircular theater, was the circular "orchestra" or dancing place, and in the center of that, at the theater's focal point, stood an altar to Dionysus, the god in whose honor the plays were given. A chorus of fifteen men entered the orchestra during the first ode ("párodos") and remained there until the end of the play. This ode and the others they chanted melodically, supporting their chant by the motions and poses of a highly stylized form of dancing. Sometimes they would divide into semichoruses of seven and seven and chant responsively, their leader performing sometimes with the rest of them and sometimes singly. At times he might take part in spoken interchanges with the actors. At times, also, one or more of the actors might chant responsively with the chorus. Taken together, the absence of particular setting and the stylized character of the whole performance kept the Greek plays from seeming representative of any special time

1

and place, leaving their audience free to consider their universal implications.

The medieval *Second Shepherds' Play,* one of a cycle of plays based on biblical history, was perhaps performed on and before a movable stage called a pageant—a two-story wagon with a curtained dressing room beneath and a canopied stage above. (A procession of pageants would bring the individual plays of a cycle to a number of locations within a town on the day or days of a religious festival.) But pageants, being expensive, were often dispensed with; *The Second Shepherds' Play* was more likely performed in an open area such as a marketplace or field, where one or more stages or booths had been set up to accommodate the several plays of the cycle to which it belonged. The scholar C. G. Childs very plausibly conceived of a performance of it on a Yorkshire moor at the edge of the town of Wakefield, with open moor on one side of the acting area, Mak's house on the other side, and a stable for the Nativity in the center. Costumes and properties for the biblical cycles were simple but sometimes spectacular. And although the plays treated more explicitly religious themes than the ancient Greek dramas did, they devolved into a naturalism alien to the Athenian stage. Because there was no barrier separating the actors from the audience, the parts of the plays acted on the ground in front of the pageants or booths allowed interchange and even horseplay between actors and spectators.

Elizabethan plays (*Volpone* and *The Duchess of Malfi*) were commonly performed in the courtyard of a three-tiered theater, on a stage jutting out into the courtyard. Spectators sat in the three tiers of balconies or stood around the stage. There was no curtain; actors began scenes by walking on and ended them by walking off. Set into the wall behind the stage, however, were two small curtained acting areas, one at stage level and the other in the theater's second story. The lower one of these usually represented a ground-floor interior (e.g., Volpone's or the Duchess of Malfi's bedchamber); the upper, an upstairs room or balcony; the whole backdrop, the front of a house. All major features of the Elizabethan theater were built into it and hence remained constant, but stage properties and costumes were changed. In general, theatrical performances of the time were not severely formal; but neither were they literally representative.

The subsequent plays in this volume were written, with few exceptions, for a stage of which three essential features are familiar to us all: it is recessed into one wall of an indoor theater, it is curtained, and it is illuminated by footlights. This proscenium-arch stage, as it is called, lends itself to a very literal form of illusion. As the curtain rises, the audience may imagine that the fourth wall of a room has been removed, revealing real people within. Molière's *The Miser* and Sheridan's *The Rivals,* to be sure, were still written with highly artificial stage conventions in view. But the plays immediately following these show to the audience for the most part the physical face of external reality. The construction of the modern theater, like the constitution of the modern mind in one of its aspects, fosters somewhat literal representations of life as it is illuminated by the light of common day.

In another of its aspects, the modern mind harbors doubts as to whether any reality beyond itself can be confidently distinguished: whether, in particular, the order of things apparent in a work of dramatic fiction answers to any order in the world "out there" or is solely a figment of the playwright's imagination.

These questions are raised by Strindberg's bold and seminal *Ghost Sonata,* and they supply an explicit theme of Pirandello's still more seminal *Six Characters in Search of an Author.* The great majority of recent playwrights deviate from so-called fourth-wall realism into at least some form of suggestive representation—their imaginations supplying symbolic or allegorical or absurd versions of the reality assumed by common sense.

There has been an attendant and consequent reaction against the physical features of the proscenium-arch stage: against the formal curtain, the recessed acting area, and the bank of footlights separating actors from audience. The use of a dawning light in lieu of an opening curtain eliminates one barrier; a central or "arena" stage, uncurtained and with entrances and exits effected through the aisles, can eliminate almost all. And performances in small and (frequently) improvised theaters can be as flexible and informal as cabaret entertainment. From a historical perspective, such expedients are seen to recapture features of the medieval and Elizabethan stage. Because they are not yet codified, however (except perhaps for the arena stage), they lend themselves less well to simple and neutral description. It will perhaps suffice to generalize that recent drama invites fluid and fanciful and rather casual theatrical performance—in keeping with the tentativeness of modern beliefs.

It is possible, moreover, to abstract the whole body of plays in this volume or any other from their differing modes of performance and to examine them for the features they have in common. They obey the laws that govern all literary fictions: ideally each one is single and complete, each is free from any sort of irrelevance, each traces a necessary or probable sequence of events.

The most rigid dramatic theory actually prescribes a single structure to which all plays must conform; and although no intelligent students of drama find exclusive virtue in this pattern, almost all of them grant its generality of application and use at least some of the terms it has made current. According to this strict theory, the audience is first given enough general information so that it will be able to understand the action that follows; this initial imparting of knowledge is called the *exposition.* Then the leading character (*protagonist*) becomes involved in an action that will materially affect his future well-being; this involvement is called the *complication.* There presently follows in the natural course a happening that predicts whether the whole action will turn out well or ill; this critical happening is called the *crisis.* The play then moves toward its inevitable conclusion, variously called the *denouement* ("unraveling") or the *catastrophe*—the latter word being now reserved for an adverse outcome.

There is, finally, a general recognition of two sharply opposed dramatic kinds, tragedy and comedy, and a partly independent body of theory for each of these. The most influential body of tragic theory remains Aristotle's *Poetics*, and the section of it most often alluded to reads as follows:

A perfect tragedy should imitate actions which excite pity and fear, this being the distinctive function of tragic imitation. It follows plainly, in the first place, that the change of fortune presented must not be the spectacle of a virtuous man brought from prosperity to adversity, for this moves neither pity nor fear; it merely shocks us. Nor, again, that of a bad man passing from adversity to prosperity, for nothing can be more alien to the spirit of Tragedy; it possesses no single tragic quality; it neither satisfies the moral sense nor calls forth pity or fear. Nor, again, should the downfall of an utter villain be exhibited. A plot of this kind would doubtless satisfy the moral sense, but it would inspire neither pity nor fear; for pity is aroused by unmerited misfortune, fear by the misfortune of a man like ourselves. Such an event, therefore, will be neither pitiful nor terrible. There remains, then, the character between these two extremes—that of a man who is not eminently good and just, yet whose misfortune is brought about not by vice or depravity, but by some error or frailty. He must be one who is highly renowned and prosperous —a personage like Oedipus, Thyestes, or other illustrious men of such families. (Trans. S. H. Butcher)

Aristotle's theory strongly emphasizes the sense of release ("purgation") that the audience experiences upon the completion of a tragedy. Variants of this theory substitute admiration for fear as a component of the tragic emotion and emphasize the hero's ethical growth as a result of his misfortune.

There is no single theory of comedy as widely accepted, even with qualification, as is Aristotle's theory of tragedy. But there is considerable agreement on the nature of comedy at its most frankly satiric. It is agreed that a chief source of humor is incongruity and that in satiric comedy some norm of just and reasonable behavior is assumed, departures from which impress us as incongruous and therefore amusing. To respond to satire, it logically follows, we must retain a measure of detachment. And no comedy asks for either the kind or the degree of emotional commitment that tragedy demands.

It is, however, hard to generalize concerning comedy or any other literary form—both hard and less than wholly rewarding. One of the delights of literary study, indeed, is the discovery that although great works conform in part to the same great patterns, each one also takes a shape distinctively its own.

A NOTE ON ANNOTATION

Notes are supplied to forestall misunderstanding or to present information that is not common knowledge. Annotation is generally avoided when the pertinent information can be found in the standard college dictionaries.

Aeschylus

525–456 B.C.

Agamemnon

458 B.C.

Based on Homeric myth yet profoundly imbued with the spirit of fifth-century Athens, *Agamemnon* stands among those "monuments of unageing intellect" celebrated by Yeats. Yet only in retrospect does it appear monumental, massive, and serene. When confronted directly in the text or in the theater, it involves us in a torsion of thought and feeling mounting through a sequence of scenes and choric odes unmatched for eloquence and economy of dramatic means.

One of the oldest known Greek dramas, and the first part of the only surviving complete trilogy—the *Oresteia*—*Agamemnon* is itself a perfected tragedy yet points consistently forward to its sequels. In the second play, *The Libation Bearers,* Orestes and his sister Electra must avenge their father's murder and so in turn claim the life of their mother, Clytemnestra. In the third, *The Eumenides,* Apollo and Athena themselves descend to earth to ajudicate the otherwise unending blood-feud and bless the advent of a society under the benign rule of a court of law dispensing both human and divine justice. The last play concludes with a procession celebrating the founding of Athens.

As usual in Greek tragedy the action on stage is austerely simple, and its significance is repeatedly pondered in choric odes rich in metaphor and cadence. To some degree the chorus functions as an on-stage audience, responding to events that it can neither control nor fully understand. Because the chorus is constantly remembering the dreadful past and hoping to foresee a less dreadful future, it endows the movement of time with special significance. Events do not simply unfold in sequence: they recapitulate and inform the past; they foreordain the future. The sense of deeply contemplated causality springs directly from the interplay between the brief scenes of dialogue and action and the soaring meditations of the odes. In few dramas are we given so keen an impression of being carried through visible and audible surfaces to deeper levels of meaning. Nightmarish scenes and terrifying possibilities of evil are confronted by the humane and fallible chorus, endowed by Aeschylus with aspirations to both wisdom and courage.

The theme of *Agamemnon,* as of the entire trilogy, is the entanglement of justice with injustice and the painful evolution of the ideal of civic justice in human consciousness. *Dikê,* the Greek word that is on the lips and conscience of every character in the play, does not translate readily: it means that which is right, that which is ordained, not to be exceeded or opposed, something enforced obscurely yet adamantly by fates, furies, or *daimons,* by memories and curses. In the mythic time in which these dramas are laid, *dikê* operates without explicit laws, without tribunal, and without appeal. The sacramental founding of an Athenian court— the Areopagus—brings justice out of primeval shadows into the light of Hellenic history.

Aeschylus presents this struggle toward justice against the background of the contention between two "houses"—that of Priam (Troy) just fallen and that of Atreus (representing Greece) apparently triumphant in Agamemnon's victory. Yet the house of Atreus is deeply torn by a series of ancestral crimes perpetuated by the requirements of vengeance. The as-yet unwritten law—*dikê* —broken by one murder demands satisfaction by another, in the interminable and merciless reciprocity of the blood-feud. Crime requires justice; justice requires crime. Hence the ineluctable Aeschylean irony everywhere manifest in *Agamemnon,* in explicit pronouncements and, more significantly, in the dramatic conception of the play as it moves through a single symbolic day. *That* day, "born from the womb" of a ten-year-long night, is signaled by a beacon kindled at the burning of Troy. That day witnesses the return of triumphant Agamemnon to the house and household that he has both avenged and desecrated. In his

train is the enslaved Trojan princess, Cassandra, whose presence as his concubine manifests his victory. Her presence also aggravates the fury of Clytemnestra's determination to sacrifice her husband at the household altar that he had profaned when, on the way to Troy, he sacrificed their daughter, Iphigeneia, to advance the war. This long-awaited day recalls and reenacts the foulest crimes, and Agamemnon's high noon of splendor, as he reenters his house—treading with naked feet tapestries appropriate only for the gods— is the hour of his sacrificial murder.

That hour is the crest of the action and is prolonged almost intolerably. When Agamemnon has solemnly entered his palace, Clytemnestra closes the doors. The scene that follows, a *kommos,* a mixture of choric lament and of dialogue between Cassandra and the chorus of elders, is the crest and—at length—the breaking point. At first in obscure prophetic lamentations, but at last forthrightly, Cassandra evokes the old crimes of the house of Atreus and then the evil about to engulf Agamemnon and herself. The chorus is paralyzed with misgivings and doubts, pity and fear. Cassandra enters the palace and the doors shut again. For yet another minute the crest hangs suspended as the chorus meditates. Then Agamemnon's cries are heard:

ōmoi, peplēgmai kairian plēgēn esō.
("Oh! I am struck a mortal blow—within!")

The crest breaks, and the dark hour of Clytemnestra's victory begins.

Clytemnestra alone of the characters has more than a single scene, and the double meanings of theme and action all center in her. But no character is free of entangling and divided purposes. All seem wound in an ever-lengthening chain of crime and necessary retribution, itself impure. Yet through this darkness shines in each character some nobility of purpose matched by the electric instancy of the dramatic action. Nothing is accidental, nothing tangential or abstract. The "unageing intellect" does not intellectualize. It is present in every pulsation of the action and in the opulent, dense, and enigmatic style that challenges our understanding.

Agamemnon

AESCHYLUS

Translated by Louis MacNeice

CHARACTERS (IN ORDER OF APPEARANCE)

A WATCHMAN
CHORUS OF OLD MEN
CLYTEMNESTRA   *the Queen, wife of
    Agamemnon*
A HERALD
AGAMEMNON   *King of Argos and son of Atreus*
CASSANDRA   *daughter of Priam, the King of
    Troy*
AEGISTHUS   *son of Thyestes, who was a
    brother of Atreus*
SOLDIERS OF THE PALACE GUARD

PROLOGUE°

[SCENE. *A space in front of the palace of Agamemnon in Argos. Night. A* WATCHMAN *on the
roof of the palace.*]

WATCHMAN. The gods it is I ask to release me
                                [from this watch   5

Prologue this play consists of a prologue, a párodos, five scenes—each accompanied by an ode or a kommos (a dialogue between a character and the chorus in which are mingled lyrical measures of choral lament)—and an éxodos. The **párodos** is the ode sung by the chorus as it enters the orchestra, where it remains throughout the play; the **éxodus** is that part of the play that follows the last ode or kommos. The play, then, is composed of a beginning (prologue and parodos) in which the situation is defined and explored; a middle (the five scenes with their odes or kommoi) in which the plot develops, with choral commentary, to the catastrophe; and an end (the éxodos) in which the consequences of the catastrophe are explored, and in part, realized.

Reprinted by permission of Faber and Faber Ltd.

A year's length now, spending my nights like a
[dog,
Watching on my elbow on the roof of the sons
[of Atreus°
5 So that I have come to know the assembly of
[the nightly stars
Those which bring storm and those which bring
[summer to men,
The shining Masters riveted in the sky—
10 I know the decline and rising of those stars.
And now I am waiting for the sign of the
[beacon,
The flame of fire that will carry the report from
[Troy,
15 News of her taking. Which task has been
[assigned me
By a woman of sanguine heart but a man's
[mind.
Yet when I take my restless rest in the soaking
20 [dew,
My night not visited with dreams—
For fear stands by me in the place of sleep
That I cannot firmly close my eyes in sleep—
Whenever I think to sing or hum to myself
25 As an antidote to sleep, then every time I groan
And fall to weeping for the fortunes of this
[house
Where not as before are things well ordered
[now.
30 But now may a good chance fall, escape from
[pain,
The good news visible in the midnight fire.
[*Pause. A light appears, gradually increasing,
the light of the beacon.*]
35 Ha! I salute you, torch of the night whose light
Is like the day, an earnest of many dances
In the city of Argos, celebration of Peace.
I call to Agamemnon's wife; quickly to rise

Out of her bed and in the house to raise
Clamor of joy in answer to this torch   40
For the city of Troy is taken—
Such is the evident message of the beckoning
[flame.
And I myself will dance my solo first
For I shall count my master's fortune mine   45
Now that this beacon has thrown me a lucky
[throw.
And may it be when he comes, the master of
[this house,
That I grasp his hand in my hand.   50
As to the rest, I am silent. A great ox, as they
[say,
Stands on my tongue. The house itself, if it
[took voice,
Could tell the case most clearly. But I will only 55
[speak
To those who know. For the others I remember
[nothing.

PARODOS

[*Enter* CHORUS OF OLD MEN. *During the fol-
lowing chorus the day begins to dawn.*]   60
   CHORUS. The tenth year it is since Priam's
[high
Adversary, Menelaus the king
And Agamemnon, the double-throned and
[sceptered 65
Yoke of the sons of Atreus
Ruling in fee from God,
From this land gathered an Argive army
On a mission of war a thousand ships,
Their hearts howling in boundless bloodlust   70
In eagles' fashion who in lonely
Grief for nestlings above their homes hang
Turning in cycles
Beating the air with the oars of their wings,
   Now to no purpose   75
      Their love and task of attention.

But above there is One,
Maybe Pan, maybe Zeus or Apollo,
Who hears the harsh cries of the birds
Guests in his kingdom,   80
Wherefore, though late, in requital
He sends the Avenger.

---

sons of Atreus specifically, Agamemnon and Menelaus; but the "house" of Atreus also includes the
descendants of Pelops, the father of Atreus, and
connotes the acts of fratricide, incest, and child-
murder that mark the successive royal generations,
particularly the relationship between Atreus and his
brother Thyestes. Agamemnon married Clytemnestra,
daughter of Tyndareus and Leda; Menelaus married
Helen, daughter of Leda and Zeus. Her abduction
by Paris incited the ten-year-long Trojan War.

Thus Zeus our master
Guardian of guest and of host
Sent against Paris the sons of Atreus
For a woman of many men,
5 Many the dog-tired wrestlings
Limbs and knees in the dust pressed—
    For both the Greeks and Trojans
    An overture of breaking spears.

Things are where they are, will finish
10 In the manner fated and neither
Fire beneath nor oil above can soothe
The stubborn anger of the unburnt offering.
As for us, our bodies are bankrupt,
The expedition left us behind
15 And we wait supporting on sticks
Our strength—the strength of a child;
For the marrow that leaps in a boy's body
Is no better than that of the old
For the War God is not in his body;
20 While the man who is very old
And his leaf withering away
Goes on the three-foot way°
No better than a boy, and wanders
A dream in the middle of the day.

25 But you, daughter of Tyndareus,
Queen Clytemnestra,
What is the news, what is the truth, what have
                    [you learnt,
On the strength of whose word have you thus
30 Sent orders for sacrifice round?
All the gods, the gods of the town,
Of the worlds of Below and Above,
By the door, in the square,
Have their altars ablaze with your gifts,
35 From here, from there, all sides, all corners,
Sky-high leap the flame-jets fed
By gentle and undeceiving
Persuasion of sacred unguent,
Oil from the royal stores.
40 Of these things tell
That which you can, that which you may,
Be healer of this our trouble
Which at times torments with evil
Though at times by propitiations

A shining hope repels   45
The insatiable thought upon grief
Which is eating away our hearts.
Of the omen which powerfully speeded
That voyage of strong men, by God's grace
                    [even I   50
Can tell, my age can still
Be galvanized to breathe the strength of song,
To tell how the kings of all the youth of Greece
Two-throned but one in mind
Were launched with pike and punitive hand   55
Against the Trojan shore by angry birds.
Kings of the birds to our kings came,
One with a white rump, the other black,
Appearing near the palace on the spear-arm
                    [side   60
Where all could see them,
Tearing a pregnant hare with the unborn young
Foiled of their courses.
    Cry, cry upon Death; but may the good
                    [prevail.   65

But the diligent prophet of the army seeing the
                    [sons
Of Atreus twin in temper knew
That the hare-killing birds were the two
Generals, explained it thus—   70
"In time this expedition sacks the town
Of Troy before whose towers
By Fate's force the public
Wealth will be wasted.
Only let not some spite from the gods benight 75
                    [the bulky battalions,
The bridle of Troy,° nor strike them untimely;
For the goddess feels pity, is angry
With the winged dogs of her father
Who killed the cowering hare with her unborn   80
                    [young;
Artemis° hates the eagles' feast."

bridle of Troy   the Greek army, likened to horse tamers
Artemis   sister of Apollo and protectress of flocks and
    young animals; because she favored the Trojans and
    because Agamemnon killed one of her sacred an-
    imals, she caused the Greek ships to be bound in
    the harbor of Aulis by adverse winds. To appease her
    Agamemnon sacrificed his daughter Iphigeneia, thus
    continuing the series of crimes blighting the "house"
    of Atreus.

three-foot way   on two legs and a staff

Cry, cry upon Death; but may the good
[prevail.

"But though you are so kind, goddess,
To the little cubs of lions
5 And to all the sucking young of roving beasts
In whom your heart delights,
Fulfil us the signs of these things,
The signs which are good but open to blame,
And I call on Apollo the Healer
10 That his sister raise not against the Greeks
Unremitting gales to balk their ships,
Hurrying on another kind of sacrifice, with no
[feasting,
Barbarous building of hates and disloyalties
15 Grown on the family. For anger grimly returns
Cunningly haunting the house, avenging the
[death of a child, never forgetting its due."
So cried the prophet—evil and good together,
Fate that the birds foretold to the king's house.
20 In tune with this
Cry, cry upon Death; but may the good
[prevail.

Zeus, whoever He is, if this
Be a name acceptable,
25 By this name I will call him.
There is no one comparable
When I reckon all of the case
Excepting Zeus, if ever I am to jettison
The barren care which clogs my heart.

30 Not He who° formerly was great
With brawling pride and mad for broils
Will even be said to have been.
And He° who was next has met
His match and is seen no more,
35 But Zeus is the name to cry in your triumph-
[song
And win the prize for wisdom.

Who setting us on the road
Made this a valid law—
40 "That men must learn by suffering."

Drop by drop in sleep upon the heart
Falls the laborious memory of pain,
Against one's will comes wisdom;
The grace of the gods is forced on us
Throned inviolably.   45

So at that time the elder
Chief of the Greek ships
Would not blame any prophet
Nor face the flail of fortune;
For unable to sail, the people°   50
Of Greece were heavy with famine,
Waiting in Aulis where the tides
Flow back, opposite Chalcis.°

But the winds that blew from the Strymon,°
Bringing delay, hunger, evil harborage,   55
Crazing men, rotting ships and cables,
By drawing out the time
Were shredding into nothing the flower of
[Argos,
When the prophet screamed a new   60
Cure for that bitter tempest
And heavier still for the chiefs,
Pleading the anger of Artemis so that the sons
[of Atreus
Beat the ground with their scepters and shed   65
[tears.

Then the elder king found voice and answered:
"Heavy is my fate, not obeying,
And heavy it is if I kill my child, the delight of
[my house, 70
And with a virgin's blood upon the altar
Make foul her father's hands.
Either alternative is evil.
How can I betray the fleet
And fail the allied army?   75
It is right they should passionately cry for the
[winds to be lulled
By the blood of a girl. So be it. May it be well."

But when he had put on the halter of Necessity

He who   Uranus, first of the great king-gods
And He   Cronos, who dispossessed him and was in
  turn overthrown by Zeus

people   army
Chalchis . . . Strymon   a town and a river in Asia
  Minor, across the straits from Aulis where the Greeks
  were anchored

Breathing in his heart a veering wind of evil
Unsanctioned, unholy, from that moment
                                    [forward
He changed his counsel, would stop at nothing.
5 For the heart of man is hardened by infatuation,
A faulty adviser, the first link of sorrow.
Whatever the cause, he brought himself to slay
His daughter, an offering to promote the voyage
To a war for a runaway wife.

10 Her prayers and her cries of father,
Her life of a maiden,
Counted for nothing with those militarists;
But her father, having duly prayed, told the
                                    [attendants
15 To lift her, like a goat, above the altar
With her robes falling about her,
To lift her boldly, her spirit fainting,
And hold back with a gag upon her lovely
                                    [mouth
20 By the dumb force of a bridle
The cry which would curse the house.
Then dropping on the ground her saffron dress,
Glancing at each of her appointed
Sacrificers a shaft of pity,
25 Plain as in a picture she wished
To speak to them by name, for often
At her father's table where men feasted
She had sung in celebration for her father
With a pure voice, affectionately, virginally,
30 The hymn for happiness at the third libation.
The sequel to this I saw not and tell not
But the crafts of Calchas gained their object.
To learn by suffering is the equation of Justice;
                                    [the Future
35 Is known when it comes, let it go till then.
To know in advance is to sorrow in advance.
The facts will appear with the shining of the
                                    [dawn.

SCENE I

[*Enter* CLYTEMNESTRA.]
40 But may good, at the least, follow after
As the queen here wishes, who stands
Nearest the throne, the only
Defense of the land of Argos.
    LEADER OF THE CHORUS. I have come,

[Clytemnestra, reverencing your authority.   45
For it is right to honor our master's wife
When the man's own throne is empty.
But you, if you have heard good news for
                                    [certain, or if
You sacrifice on the strength of flattering   50
                                    [hopes,
I would gladly hear. Though I cannot cavil at
                                    [silence.
    CLYTEMNESTRA. Bearing good news, as the
                        [proverb says, may Dawn 55
Spring from her mother Night.
You will hear something now that was beyond
                                    [your hopes.
The men of Argos have taken Priam's city.
    LEADER. What! I cannot believe it. It escapes 60
                                    [me.
    CLYT. Troy in the hands of the Greeks. Do I
                                    [speak plain?
    LEADER. Joy creeps over me, calling out my
                                    [tears. 65
    CLYT. Yes. Your eyes proclaim your loyalty.
    LEADER. But what are your grounds? Have
                        [you a proof of it?
    CLYT. There is proof indeed—unless God has
                                    [cheated us. 70
    LEADER. Perhaps you believe the inveigling
                        [shapes of dreams?
    CLYT. I would not be credited with a dozing
                                    [brain!
    LEADER. Or are you puffed up by Rumor, the 75
                        [wingless flyer?
    CLYT. You mock my common sense as if I
                        [were a child.
    LEADER. But at what time was the city given
                                    [to sack? 80
    CLYT. In this very night that gave birth to this
                                    [day.
    LEADER. What messenger could come so fast?
    CLYT. Hephaestus,° launching a fine flame
                        [from Ida,° 85
Beacon forwarding beacon, despatch-riders of
                                    [fire,

Hephaestus god of fire
Ida a mountain overlooking the Trojan plain and from
which the gods beheld the battles. The place names
that follow trace a course that would send a series
of beacon flares to Argos in peninsular Greece.

Ida relayed to Hermes' cliff in Lemnos
And the great glow from the island was taken
          [over third
By the height of Athos that belongs to Zeus,
5 And towering then to straddle over the sea
The might of the running torch joyfully tossed
The gold gleam forward like another sun,
Herald of light to the heights of Mount
          [Macistus,
10 And he without delay, nor carelessly by sleep
Encumbered, did not shirk his intermediary
          [role,
His farflung ray reached the Euripus' tides
And told Messapion's watchers, who in turn
15 Sent on the message further
Setting a stack of dried-up heather on fire.
And the strapping flame, not yet enfeebled,
          [leapt
Over the plain of Asopus like a blazing moon
20 And woke on the crags of Cithaeron
Another relay in the chain of fire.
The light that was sent from far was not
          [declined
By the look-out men, who raised a fiercer yet,
25 A light which jumped the water of Gorgopis
And to Mount Aegiplanctus duly come
Urged the reveille of the punctual fire.
So then they kindle it squanderingly and launch
A beard of flame big enough to pass
30 The headland that looks down upon the Saronic
          [gulf,
Blazing and bounding till it reached at length
The Arachnaean steep, our neighboring
          [heights;
35 And leaps in the latter end on the roof of the
          [sons of Atreus
Issue and image of the fire on Ida.
Such was the assignment of my torch-racers,
The task of each fulfilled by his successor,
And victor is he who ran both first and last.
40 Such is the proof I offer you, the sign
My husband sent me out of Troy.
    LEADER. To the gods, queen, I shall give
          [thanks presently.
45 But I would like to hear this story further,
To wonder at it in detail from your lips.
    CLYT. The Greeks hold Troy upon this day.
The cries in the town I fancy do not mingle.

Pour oil and vinegar into the same jar,
You would say they stand apart unlovingly;   50
Of those who are captured and those who have
          [conquered
Distinct are the sounds of their diverse
          [fortunes,
For *these* having flung themselves about the 55
          [bodies
Of husbands and brothers, or sons upon the
          [bodies
Of aged fathers from a throat no longer
Free, lament the fate of their most loved.   60
But *those* a night's marauding after battle
Sets hungry to what breakfast the town offers
Not billeted duly in any barracks order
But as each man has drawn his lot of luck.
So in the captive homes of Troy already   65
They take their lodging, free of the frosts
And dews of the open. Like happy men
They will sleep all night without sentry.
But if they respect duly the city's gods,
Those of the captured land and the sanctuaries 70
          [of the gods,
They need not, having conquered, fear
          [reconquest.
But let no lust fall first upon the troops
To plunder what is not right, subdued by gain, 75
For they must still, in order to come home safe,
Get round the second lap of the doubled course.
So if they return without offense to the gods
The grievance of the slain may learn at last
A friendly talk—unless some fresh wrong falls. 80
Such are the thoughts you hear from me, a
          [woman.
But may the good prevail for all to see.
We have much good. I only ask to enjoy it.
    LEADER. Woman, you speak with sense like 85
          [a prudent man.
I, who have heard your valid proofs, prepare
To give the glory to God.
Fair recompense is brought us for our troubles.
    [CLYTEMNESTRA *goes back into the palace.*] 90

ODE I

CHORUS. O Zeus our king and Night our
          [friend
Donor of glories,

Night who cast on the towers of Troy
A close-clinging net so that neither the grown
Nor any of the children can pass
The enslaving and huge
5   Trap of all-taking destruction.
Great Zeus, guardian of host and guest,
I honor who has done his work and taken
A leisured aim at Paris so that neither
Too short nor yet over the stars
10   He might shoot to no purpose.

From Zeus is the blow they can tell of,
This at least can be established,
They have fared according to his ruling. For
[some
15   Deny that the gods deign to consider those
[among men
Who trample on the grace of inviolate things;
It is the impious man says this,
For Ruin is revealed the child
20   Of not to be attempted actions
When men are puffed up unduly
And their houses are stuffed with riches.
Measure is the best. Let danger be distant,
This should suffice a man
25   With a proper part of wisdom.
For a man has no protection
Against the drunkenness of riches
Once he has spurned from his sight
The high altar of Justice.

30   Somber Persuasion compels him,
Intolerable child of calculating Doom;
All cure is vain, there is no glozing it over
But the mischief shines forth with a deadly light
And like bad coinage
35   By rubbings and frictions
He stands discolored and black
Under the test—like a boy
Who chases a winged bird.
He has branded his city for ever.
40   His prayers are heard by no god.
Who makes such things his practice
The gods destroy him.
This way came Paris
To the house of the sons of Atreus
45   And outraged the table of friendship
Stealing the wife of his host.

Leaving to her countrymen clanging of
Shields and of spears and
Launching of warships
And bringing instead of a dowry destruction to   50
[Troy
Lightly she was gone through the gates daring
Things undared. Many the groans
Of the palace spokesmen on this theme—
"O the house, the house, and its princes,   55
O the bed and the imprint of her limbs;
One can see him crouching in silence
Dishonored and unreviling."
Through desire for her who is overseas, a ghost
Will seem to rule the household.   60
And now her husband hates
The grace of shapely statues;
In the emptiness of their eyes
All their appeal is departed.

But appearing in dreams persuasive   65
Images come bringing a joy that is vain,
Vain for when in fancy he looks to touch her—
Slipping through his hands the vision
Rapidly is gone
Following on wings the walks of sleep.   70
Such are his griefs in his house on his hearth,
Such as these and worse than these,
But everywhere through the land of Greece
[which men have left
Are mourning women with enduring hearts   75
To be seen in all houses; many
Are the thoughts which stab their hearts;
For those they sent to war
They know, but in place of men
That which comes home to them   80
Is merely an urn and ashes.

But the money-changer War, changer of bodies,
Holding his balance in the battle
Home from Troy refined by fire
Sends back to friends the dust   85
That is heavy with tears, stowing
A man's worth of ashes
In an easily handled jar.
And they wail speaking well of the men how
[that one   90
Was expert in battle, and one fell well in the
[carnage—

But for another man's wife.
Muffled and muttered words;
And resentful grief creeps up against the sons
Of Atreus and their cause.
5   But others there by the wall
Entombed in Trojan ground
Lie, handsome of limb,
Holding and hidden in enemy soil.

Heavy is the murmur of an angry people
10   Performing the purpose of a public curse;
There is something cowled in the night
That I anxiously wait to hear.
For the gods are not blind to the
Murderers of many and the black
15   Furies in time
When a man prospers in sin
By erosion of life reduce him to darkness,
Who, once among the lost, can no more
Be helped. Over-great glory
20   Is a sore burden. The high peak
Is blasted by the eyes of Zeus.
      I prefer an unenvied fortune,
      Not to be a sacker of cities
      Nor to find myself living at another's
25   Ruling, myself a captive.

AN OLD MAN. From the good news' beacon
                          [a swift
Rumor is gone through the town.
Who knows if it be true
30   Or some deceit of the gods?
      ANOTHER O.M. Who is so childish or broken
                          [in wit
To kindle his heart at a new-fangled message
                          [of flame
35   And then be downcast
At a change of report?
      ANOTHER O.M. It fits the temper of a woman
To give her assent to a story before it is proved.
      ANOTHER O.M. The over-credulous passion
40   [of women expands
In swift conflagration but swiftly declining is
                          [gone
The news that a woman announced.
      LEADER OF THE CHORUS. Soon we shall know
45   [about the illuminant torches,

The beacons and the fiery relays,
Whether they were true or whether like dreams
That pleasant light came here and hoaxed our
                          [wits.
Look: I see, coming from the beach, a herald   50
Shadowed with olive shoots; the dust upon
                          [him,
Mud's thirsty sister and colleague, is my
                          [witness
That he will not give dumb news nor news by   55
                          [lighting
A flame of fire with the smoke of mountain
                          [timber;
In words he will either corroborate our joy—
But the opposite version I reject with horror.   60
To the good appeared so far may good be
                          [added.
ANOTHER SPEAKER. Whoever makes other
                          [prayers for this our city,
May he reap himself the fruits of his wicked   65
                          [heart.

SCENE II

[*Enter the* HERALD, *who kisses the ground before speaking.*]
      HERALD. Earth of my fathers, O the earth of
                          [Argos,   70
In the light of the tenth year I reach you thus
After many shattered hopes achieving one,
For never did I dare to think that here in Argive
                          [land
I should win a grave in the dearest soil of home;   75
But now hail, land, and hail, light of the sun,
And Zeus high above the country and the
                          [Pythian king—°
May he no longer shoot his arrows at us
(Implacable long enough beside Scamander)°   80
But now be savior to us and be healer,
King Apollo. And all the Assembly's gods
I call upon, and him my patron, Hermes,
The dear herald whom all heralds adore,
And the Heroes who sped our voyage, again   95
                          [with favor
Take back the army that has escaped the spear.

Pythian king   Apollo, who favored the Trojan cause
Scamander   river flowing beside Troy

O cherished dwelling, palace of royalty,
O august thrones and gods facing the sun,
If ever before, now with your bright eyes
Gladly receive your king after much time,
5 Who comes bringing light to you in the night
                              [time,
And to all these as well—King Agamemnon.
Give him a good welcome as he deserves,
Who with the axe of judgment-awarding God
10 Has smashed Troy and levelled the Trojan
                              [land;
The altars are destroyed, the seats of the gods,
And the seed of all the land is perished from it.
Having cast this halter round the neck of Troy
15 The King, the elder son of Atreus, a blessed
                              [man,
Comes, the most worthy to have honor of all
Men that are now. Paris nor his guilty city
Can boast that the crime was greater than the
20   [atonement.
Convicted in a suit for rape and robbery
He has lost his stolen goods and with
                        [consummate ruin
Mowed down the whole country and his
25   [father's house.
The sons of Priam have paid their account
                        [with interest.
LEADER OF THE CHORUS. Hail and be glad,
                    [herald of the Greek army.
30 HERALD. Yes. Glad indeed! So glad that at the
                        [gods' demand
I should no longer hesitate to die.
LEADER. Were you so harrowed by desire for
                        [home?
35 HERALD. Yes. The tears come to my eyes for
                        [joy.
LEADER. Sweet then is the fever which afflicts
                        [you.
HERALD. What do you mean? Let me learn
40   [your drift.
LEADER. Longing for those whose love came
                        [back in echo.
HERALD. Meaning the land was homesick for
                        [the army?
45 LEADER. Yes. I would often groan from a
                        [darkened heart.
HERALD. This sullen hatred—how did it
                        [fasten on you?

LEADER. I cannot say. Silence is my stock
                    [prescription. 50
HERALD. What? In your masters' absence
                    [were there some you feared?
LEADER. Yes. In your phrase, death would
                    [now be a gratification.
HERALD. Yes, for success is ours. These   55
                    [things have taken time.
Some of them we could say have fallen well,
While some we blame. Yet who except the gods
Is free from pain the whole duration of life?
If I were to tell of our labors, our hard lodging, 60
The sleeping on crowded decks, the scanty
                    [blankets,
Tossing and groaning, rations that never
                    [reached us—
And the land too gave matter for more disgust, 65
For our beds lay under the enemy's walls.
Continuous drizzle from the sky, dews from the
                    [marshes,
Rotting our clothes, filling our hair with lice.
And if one were to tell of the bird-destroying 70
                    [winter
Intolerable from the snows of Ida
Or of the heat when the sea slackens at noon
Waveless and dozing in a depressed calm—
But why make these complaints? The weariness 75
                    [is over;
Over indeed for some who never again
Need even trouble to rise.
Why make a computation of the lost?
Why need the living sorrow for the spites of 80
                    [fortune?
I wish to say a long goodbye to disasters.
For us, the remnant of the troops of Argos,
The advantage remains, the pain can not
                    [outweigh it; 85
So we can make our boast to this sun's light,
Flying on words above the land and sea:
"Having taken Troy the Argive expedition
Has nailed up throughout Greece in every
                    [temple 90
These spoils, these ancient trophies."
Those who hear such things must praise the city
And the generals. And the grace of God be
                    [honored
Which brought these things about. You have 95
                    [the whole story.

LEADER. I confess myself convinced by your
                                        [report.
Old men are always young enough to learn.
[*Enter* CLYTEMNESTRA *from the palace.*]
5 This news belongs by right first to the house
And Clytemnestra—though I am enriched also.
    CLYT. Long before this I shouted at joy's
                                        [command
At the coming of the first night-messenger of
10   [fire
Announcing the taking and capsizing of Troy.
And people reproached me saying, "Do mere
                                        [beacons
Persuade you to think that Troy is already
15   [down?
Indeed a woman's heart is easily exalted."
Such comments made me seem to be wandering
                                        [but yet
I began my sacrifices and in the women's
20   [fashion
Throughout the town they raised triumphant
                                        [cries
And in the gods' enclosures
Lulling the fragrant, incense-eating flame.
25 And now what need is there for you to tell me
                                        [more?
From the King himself I shall learn the whole
                                        [story.
But how the best to welcome my honored lord
30 I shall take pains when he comes back—For
                                        [what
Is a kinder light for a woman to see than this,
To open the gates to her man come back from
                                        [war
35 When God has saved him? Tell this to my
                                        [husband,
To come with all speed, the city's darling;
May he returning find a wife as loyal
As when he left her, watchdog of the house,
40 Good to *him* but fierce to the ill-intentioned,
And in all other things as ever, having
                                        [destroyed
No seal or pledge at all in the length of time.
I know no pleasure with another man, no
45   [scandal,
More than I know how to dye metal red.
Such is my boast, bearing a load of truth,

A boast that need not disgrace a noble wife.
[*Exit.*]
    LEADER. Thus has she spoken; if you take her 50
                                        [meaning,
Only a specious tale to shrewd interpreters.
But do you, herald, tell me; I ask after Menelaus
Whether he will, returning safe preserved,
Come back with you, our land's loved master. 55
    HERALD. I am not able to speak the lovely
                                        [falsehood
To profit you, my friends, for any stretch of
                                        [time.
    LEADER. But if only the true tidings could be 60
                                        [also good!
It is hard to hide a division of good and true.
    HERALD. The prince is vanished out of the
                                        [Greek fleet,
Himself and ship. I speak no lie. 65
    LEADER. Did he put forth first in the sight of
                                        [all from Troy,
Or a storm that troubled all sweep him apart?
    HERALD. You have hit the target like a master
                                        [archer, 70
Told succinctly a long tale of sorrow.
    LEADER. Did the rumors current among the
                                        [remaining ships
Represent him as alive or dead?
    HERALD. No one knows so as to tell for sure 75
Except the sun who nurses the breeds of earth.
    LEADER. Tell me how the storm came on the
                                        [host of ships
Through the divine anger, and how it ended.
    HERALD. Day of good news should not be 80
                                        [fouled by tongue
That tells ill news. To each god his season.
When, despair in his face, a messenger brings
                                        [to a town
The hated news of a fallen army— 85
One general wound to the city and many men
Outcast, outcursed, from many homes
By the double whip which War is fond of,
Doom with a bloody spear in either hand,
One carrying such a pack of grief could well 90
Recite this hymn of the Furies at your asking.
But when our cause is saved and a messenger of
                                        [good
Comes to a city glad with festivity,

How am I to mix good news with bad,
                [recounting
The storm that meant God's anger on the
                [Greeks?
5 For they swore together, those inveterate
                [enemies,
Fire and sea, and proved their alliance,
                [destroying
The unhappy troops of Argos.
10 In night arose ill-waved evil,
Ships on each other the blasts from Thrace
Crashed colliding, which butting with horns in
                [the violence
Of big wind and rattle of rain were gone
15 To nothing, whirled all ways by a wicked
                [shepherd.
But when there came up the shining light of
                [the sun
We saw the Aegean sea flowering with corpses
20 Of Greek men and their ships' wreckage.
But for us, our ship was not damaged,
Whether someone snatched it away or begged
                [it off,
Some god, not a man, handling the tiller;
25 And Saving Fortune was willing to sit upon our
                [ship
So that neither at anchor we took the tilt of
                [waves
Nor ran to splinters on the crag-bound coast.
30 But then having thus escaped death on the sea,
In the white day, not trusting our fortune,
We pastured this new trouble upon our
                [thoughts,
The fleet being battered, the sailors weary,
35 And now if any of *them* still draw breath,
They are thinking no doubt of us as being lost
And we are thinking of them as being lost.
May the best happen. As for Menelaus
The first guess and most likely is a disaster.
40 But still—if any ray of sun detects him
Alive, with living eyes, by the plan of Zeus
Not yet resolved to annul the race completely,
There is some hope then that he will return
                [home.
45 So much you have heard. Know that it is the
                [truth.
    [*Exit.*]

ODE II

CHORUS. Who was it named her thus
In all ways appositely
Unless it was Someone whom we do not see, 50
Fore-knowing fate
And plying an accurate tongue?
Helen, bride of spears and conflict's
Focus, who as was befitting
Proved a hell° to ships and men, 55
Hell to her country, sailing
Away from delicately-sumptuous curtains,
Away on the wind of a giant Zephyr,
And shielded hunters mustered many
On the vanished track of the oars, 60
Oars beached on the leafy
Banks of a Trojan river
For the sake of bloody war.

But on Troy was thrust a marring marriage
By the Wrath that working to an end exacts 65
In time a price from guests
Who dishonored their host
And dishonored Zeus of the Hearth,
From those noisy celebrants
Of the wedding hymn which fell 70
To the brothers of Paris
To sing upon that day.
But learning this, unlearning that,
Priam's ancestral city now
Continually mourns, reviling 75
Paris the fatal bridegroom.
The city has had much sorrow,
Much desolation in life,
From the pitiful loss of her people.

So in his house a man might rear 80
A lion's cub caught from the dam
In need of suckling,
In the prelude of its life
Mild, gentle with children,
For old men a playmate, 85
Often held in the arms
Like a new-born child,

hell in Greek the name *Helen* can be punned on a
verb meaning *to destroy*

Wheedling the hand,
Fawning at belly's bidding.

But matured by time he showed
The temper of his stock and paid
5 Thanks for his fostering
With disaster of slaughter of sheep
Making an unbidden banquet
And now the house is a shambles,
Irremediable grief to its people,
10 Calamitous carnage:
For the pet they had fostered was sent
By God as a priest of Ruin.

So I would say there came
To the city of Troy
15 A notion of windless calm,
Delicate adornment of riches,
Soft shooting of the eyes and flower
Of desire that stings the fancy.
But swerving aside she achieved
20 A bitter end to her marriage,
Ill guest and ill companion,
Hurled upon Priam's sons, convoyed
By Zeus, patron of guest and host,
Dark angel dowered with tears.

25 Long current among men an old saying
Runs that a man's prosperity
When grown to greatness
Comes to the birth, does not die childless—
His good luck breeds for his house
30 Distress that shall not be appeased.
I only, apart from the others,
Hold that the unrighteous action
Breeds true to its kind,
Leaves its own children behind it.
35 But the lot of a righteous house
Is a fair offspring always.

Ancient self-glory is accustomed
To bear to light in the evil sort of men
A new self-glory and madness,
40 Which sometime or sometime finds
The appointed hour for its birth,
And born therewith is the Spirit, intractable,
[unholy, irresistible,
The reckless lust that brings black Doom upon
45 [the house,

A child that is like its parents.

But Honest Dealing is clear
Shining in smoky homes,
Honors the god-fearing life.
Mansions gilded by filth of hands she leaves, 50
Turns her eyes elsewhere, visits the innocent
[house,
Not respecting the power
Of wealth mis-stamped with approval,
But guides all to the goal. 55

SCENE III

[*Enter* AGAMEMNON *and* CASSANDRA *on char-iots.*]
CHORUS. Come then my King, stormer of
[Troy,
Offspring of Atreus, 60
How shall I hail you, how give you honor
Neither overshooting nor falling short
Of the measure of homage?
There are many who honor appearance too
[much 65
Passing the bounds that are right.
To condole with the unfortunate man
Each one is ready but the bite of the grief
Never goes through to the heart.
And they join in rejoicing, affecting to share it, 70
Forcing their face to a smile.
But he who is shrewd to shepherd his sheep
Will fail not to notice the eyes of a man
Which seem to be loyal but lie,
Fawning with watery friendship. 75
Even you, in my thought, when you marshalled
[the troops
For Helen's sake, I will not hide it,
Made a harsh and ugly picture,
Holding badly the tiller of reason, 80
Paying with the death of men
Ransom for a willing whore.
But now, not unfriendly, not superficially,
I offer my service, well-doers' welcome.
In time you will learn by inquiry 85
Who has done rightly, who transgressed
In the work of watching the city.
AGAMEMNON. First to Argos and the country's
[gods
My fitting salutations, who have aided me 90

To return and in the justice which I exacted
From Priam's city. Hearing the unspoken case
The gods unanimously had cast their vote
Into the bloody urn for the massacre of Troy;
5   But to the opposite urn
Hope came, dangled her hand, but did no more.
Smoke marks even now the city's capture.
Whirlwinds of doom are alive, the dying ashes
Spread on the air the fat savor of wealth.
10   For these things we must pay some memorable
                              [return
To Heaven, having exacted enormous
                              [vengeance
For wife-rape; for a woman
15   The Argive monster ground a city to powder,
Sprung from a wooden horse°, shield-
                              [wielding folk,
Launching a leap at the setting of the Pleiads,
Jumping the ramparts, a ravening lion,
20   Lapped its fill of the kingly blood.
To the gods I have drawn out this overture
But as for your concerns, I bear them in my
                              [mind
And say the same, you have me in agreement.
25   To few of men does it belong by nature
To congratulate their friends unenviously,
For a sullen poison fastens on the heart,
Doubling the pain of a man with this disease;
He feels the weight of his own griefs and when
30   He sees another's prosperity he groans.
I speak with knowledge, being well acquainted
With the mirror of comradeship—ghost of a
                              [shadow
Were those who seemed to be so loyal to me.
35   Only Odysseus, who sailed against his will,
Proved, when yoked with me, a ready
                              [tracehorse;
I speak of him not knowing if he is alive.
But for what concerns the city and the gods
40   Appointing public debates in full assembly
We shall consult. That which is well already
We shall take steps to ensure it remain well.
But where there is need of medical remedies,
By applying benevolent cautery or surgery
45   We shall try to deflect the dangers of disease.

But now, entering the halls where stands my
                              [hearth,
First I shall make salutation to the gods
Who sent me a far journey and have brought
                              [me back.   50
And may my victory not leave my side.
[*Enter* CLYTEMNESTRA, *followed by women
slaves carrying purple tapestries.*]
   CLYT. Men of the city, you the aged of Argos,
I shall feel no shame to describe to you my love   55
Towards my husband. Shyness in all of us
Wears thin with time. Here are the facts first
                              [hand.
I will tell you of my own unbearable life
I led so long as this man was at Troy.   60
For first that the woman separate from her man
Should sit alone at home is extreme cruelty,
Hearing so many malignant rumors—First
Comes one, and another comes after, bad news
                              [to worse,   65
Clamor of grief to the house. If Agamemnon
Had had so many wounds as those reported
Which poured home through the pipes of
                              [hearsay, then—
Then he would be gashed fuller than a net has   70
                              [holes!
And if only he had died . . . as often as rumor
                              [told us,
He would be like the giant° in the legend,
Three-bodied. Dying once for every body,   75
He should have by now three blankets of earth
                              [above him—
All that above him; I care not how deep the
                              [mattress under!
Such are the malignant rumors thanks to which   80
They have often seized me against my will and
                              [undone
The loop of a rope° from my neck.
And this is why our son is not standing here,
The guarantee of your pledges and mine,   85
As he should be, Orestes.° Do not wonder;
He is being brought up by a friendly ally and
                              [host,

---

horse   the great wooden horse in which Greek soldiers
    hid themselves; when it was conveyed inside the
    citadel of Troy, they captured it

giant   Geryon, said to have three heads or three
    bodies
rope   with which, she implies, she tried to hang herself
    in despair
Orestes   who in the next play of the trilogy returns
    and avenges his father

Strophius the Phocian, who warned me in
[advance
Of dubious troubles, both your risks at Troy
And the anarchy of shouting mobs that might
5 Overturn policy, for it is born in men
To kick the man who is down.
This is not a disingenuous excuse.
For me the outrushing wells of weeping are
[dried up,
10 There is no drop left in them.
My eyes are sore from sitting late at nights
Weeping for you and for the baffled beacons,
Never lit up. And, when I slept, in dreams
I have been waked by the thin whizz of a
15 [buzzing
Gnat, seeing more horrors fasten on you
Than could take place in the mere time of my
[dream
Having endured all this, now, with unsorrowed
20 [heart
I would hail this man as the watchdog of the
[farm,
Forestay that saves the ship, pillar that props
The lofty roof, appearance of an only son
25 To a father or of land to sailors past their hope,
The loveliest day to see after the storm,
Gush of well-water for the thirsty traveller.
Such are the metaphors I think befit him,
But envy be absent. Many misfortunes already
30 We have endured. But now, dear head, come
[down
Out of that car, not placing upon the ground
Your foot, O King, the foot that trampled Troy.
Why are you waiting, slaves, to whom the task
35 [is assigned
To spread the pavement of his path with
[tapestries?
At once, at once let his way be strewn with
[purple
40 That Justice lead him toward his unexpected
[home.
The rest a mind, not overcome by sleep
Will arrange rightly, with God's help, as
[destined.
45 AGAM. Daughter of Leda, guardian of my
[house,
You have spoken in proportion to my absence.
You have drawn your speech out long. Duly to
[praise me,
That is a duty to be performed by others. 50
And further—do not by women's methods
[make me
Effeminate nor in barbarian fashion
Gape ground-grovelling acclamations at me
Nor strewing my path with cloths make it 55
[invidious.
It is the gods should be honored in this way.
But being mortal to tread embroidered beauty
For me is no way without fear.
I tell you to honor me as a man, not god. 60
Footcloths are very well—Embroidered stuffs
Are stuff for gossip. And not to think unwisely
Is the greatest gift of God. Call happy only him
Who has ended his life in sweet prosperity.
I have spoken. This thing I could not do with 65
[confidence.
 CLYT. Tell me now, according to your
[judgment.
 AGAM. I tell you you shall not override my
[judgment. 70
 CLYT. Supposing you had feared
[something . . .
Could you have vowed to God to do this thing?
 AGAM. Yes. If an expert had prescribed that
[vow. 75
 CLYT. And how would Priam have acted in
[your place?
 AGAM. He would have trod the cloths, I
[think, for certain.
 CLYT. Then do not flinch before the blame of 80
[men.
 AGAM. The voice of the multitude is very
[strong.
 CLYT. But the man none envy is not enviable.
 AGAM. It is not a woman's part to love 85
[disputing.
 CLYT. But it is a conqueror's part to yield
[upon occasion.
 AGAM. You think such victory worth fighting
[for? 90
 CLYT. Give way. Consent to let me have the
[mastery.
 AGAM. Well, if such is your wish, let
[someone quickly loose
My vassal sandals, underlings of my feet, 95
And stepping on these sea-purples may no god

Shoot me from far with the envy of his eye.
Great shame it is to ruin my house and spoil
The wealth of costly weavings with my feet.
But of this matter enough. This stranger woman
5   [here
Take in with kindness. The man who is a
                     [gentle master
God looks on from far off complacently.
For no one of his will bears the slave's yoke.
10 This woman, of many riches being the chosen
Flower, gift of the soldiers, has come with me.
But since I have been prevailed on by your
                     [words
I will go to my palace home, treading on
15   [purples.
[*He dismounts from the chariot and begins
to walk up the tapestried path. During the fol-
lowing speech he enters the palace.*]
CLYT. There is the sea and who shall drain
20   [it dry? It breeds
Its wealth in silver of plenty of purple gushing
And ever-renewed, the dyeings of our
                   [garments.
The house has its store of these by God's grace,
25   [King.
This house is ignorant of poverty
And I would have vowed a pavement of many
                   [garments
Had the palace oracle enjoined that vow
30 Thereby to contrive a ransom for his life.
For while there is root, foliage comes to the
                   [house
Spreading a tent of shade against the Dog
                   [Star.°
35 So now that you have reached your hearth and
                   [home
You prove a miracle—advent of warmth in
                   [winter;
And further this—even in the time of heat
40 When God is fermenting wine from the bitter
                   [grape,
Even then it is cool in the house if only
Its master walk at home, a grown man, ripe.
O Zeus the Ripener, ripen these my prayers;
45 Your part it is to make the ripe fruit fall.
[*She enters the palace.*]

Dog Star Sirius, associated with hot summer weather

ODE III

CHORUS. Why, why at the doors
Of my fore-seeing heart
Does this terror keep beating its wings?
And my song play the prophet   50
Unbidden, unhired—
Which I cannot spit out
Like the enigmas of dreams
Nor plausible confidence
Sit on the throne of my mind?   55
It is long time since
The cables let down from the stern
Were chafed by the sand when the seafaring
           [army started for Troy.

And I learn with my eyes   60
And witness myself their return;
But the hymn without lyre goes up,
The dirge of the Avenging Fiend,°
In the depths of my self-taught heart
Which has lost its dear   65
Possession of the strength of hope.
But my guts and my heart
Are not idle which seethe with the waves
Of trouble nearing its hour.
But I pray that these thoughts   70
May fall out not as I think
    And not be fulfilled in the end.

Truly when health grows much
It respects not limit; for disease,
Its neighbor in the next door room,   75
Presses upon it.
A man's life, crowding sail,
Strikes on the blind reef:
But if caution in advance
Jettison part of the cargo   80
With the derrick of due proportion,
The whole house does not sink,
Though crammed with a weight of woe
The hull does not go under.
The abundant bounty of God   85

Fiend here, as in later references to "demons,"
"black Spirit," and "Evil Genius," the concept is that
of Furies, or certain *daimons*, or Erinyes, all dark
and fearful divinities who mercilessly punish crimes
against hearth and home

And his gifts from the year's furrows
Drive the famine back.

But when upon the ground there has fallen
[once
5 The black blood of a man's death,
Who shall summon it back by incantations?
Even Asclepius° who had the art
To fetch the dead to life, even to him
Zeus put a provident end.
10 But, if of the heaven-sent fates
One did not check the other,
Cancel the other's advantage,
My heart would outrun my tongue
In pouring out these fears.
15 But now it mutters in the dark,
Embittered, no way hoping
To unravel a scheme in time
    From a burning mind.

SCENE IV

[CLYTEMNESTRA appears in the door of the
20 palace.]
    CLYT. Go in too, you; I speak to you,
[Cassandra,
Since God in his clemency has put you in this
[house
25 To share our holy water, standing with many
[slaves
Beside the altar that protects the house,
Step down from the car there, do not be
[overproud.
30 Heracles° himself they say was once
Sold, and endured to eat the bread of slavery.
But should such a chance inexorably fall,
There is much advantage in masters who have
[long been rich.
35 Those who have reaped a crop they never
[expected

Asclepius a god of medicine and healing, whom Zeus
    is said to have killed lest he give immortality to
    mortals
Heracles (or Hercules) the godlike athlete who in a
    spasm of madness killed his friend and was sen-
    tenced by the Delphic Oracle to work three years as
    a servant. In an earlier fit of madness he had mur-
    dered his own children.

Are in all things hard on their slaves and
[overstep the line.
From us you will have the treatment of
[tradition. 40
LEADER OF CHORUS. You, it is you she has
[addressed, and clearly.
Caught as you are in these predestined toils
Obey her if you can. But should you disobey . . .
    CLYT. If she has more than the gibberish of 45
[the swallow,
An unintelligible barbaric speech,
I hope to read her mind, persuade her reason.
    LEADER. As things now stand for you, she
[says the best. 50
Obey her; leave that car and follow her.
    CLYT. I have no leisure to waste out here,
[outside the door.
Before the hearth in the middle of my house
The victims stand already, wait the knife. 55
You, if you will obey me, waste no time.
But if you cannot understand my language—
[To CHORUS LEADER.]
You make it plain to her with the brute and
[voiceless hand. 60
    LEADER. The stranger seems to need a clear
[interpreter.
She bears herself like a wild beast newly
[captured.
    CLYT. The fact is she is mad, she listens to evil 65
[thoughts,
Who has come here leaving a city newly
[captured
Without experience how to bear the bridle
So as not to waste her strength in foam and 70
[blood.
I will not spend more words to be ignored.
[She re-enters the palace.]

KOMMOS I

CHORUS. But I, for I pity her, will not be
[angry. 75
Obey, unhappy woman. Leave this car.
Yield to your fate. Put on the untried yoke.
    CASS. Apollo! Apollo!
    CHORUS. Why do you cry like this upon
[Apollo? 80
He is not the kind of god that calls for dirges.

CASS. Apollo! Apollo!

CHORUS. Once more her funereal cries invoke
[the god
Who has no place at the scene of lamentation.

5 CASS. Apollo! Apollo!
God of the Ways! My destroyer!
Destroyed again—and this time utterly!

CHORUS. She seems about to predict her own
[misfortunes.
10 The gift of the god endures, even in a slave's
[mind.

CASS. Apollo! Apollo!
God of the Ways! My destroyer!
Where? To what house? Where, where have
15 [you brought me?

CHORUS. To the house of the sons of Atreus.
[If you do not know it,
I will tell you so. You will not find it false.

CASS. No, no, but to a god-hated, but to an
20 [accomplice
In much kin-killing, murdering nooses,
Man-shambles, a floor asperged with blood.

CHORUS. The stranger seems like a hound
[with a keen scent,
25 Is picking up a trail that leads to murder.

CASS. Clues! I have clues! Look! They are
[these.
These wailing, these children, butchery of
[children;°
30 Roasted flesh, a father sitting to dinner.

CHORUS. Of your prophetic fame we have
[heard before
But in this matter prophets are not required.

CASS. What is she doing? What is she
35 [planning?
What is this new great sorrow?
Great crime . . . within here . . . planning
Unendurable to his folk, impossible
Ever to be cured. For help
40 Stands far distant.

CHORUS. This reference I cannot catch. But
[the children

---

children two brothers of Aegisthus, and sons of Thyestes, the brother of Atreus. Thyestes committed adultery with Atreus' wife. In revenge Atreus secretly slaughtered Thyestes' elder sons and served their flesh to their father at the banquet described in Aegisthus' first speech (p. 30, ll. 15–60).

I recognized; that refrain is hackneyed.

CASS. Damned, damned, bringing this work
[to completion— 45
Your husband who shared your bed
To bathe him, to cleanse him, and then—
How shall I tell of the end?
Soon, very soon, it will fall.
The end comes hand over hand 50
Grasping in greed.

CHORUS. Not yet do I understand. After her
[former riddles
Now I am baffled by these dim
[pronouncements. 55

CASS. Ah God, the vision! God, God, the
[vision!
A net, is it? Net of Hell!
But herself is the net; shared bed; shares
[murder. 60
O let the pack ever-hungering after the family
Howl for the unholy ritual, howl for the victim.

CHORUS. What black Spirit is this you call
[upon the house—
To raise aloft her cries? Your speech does not 65
[lighten me.
Into my heart runs back the blood
Yellow as when for men by the spear fallen
The blood ebbs out with the rays of the setting
[life 70
And death strides quickly.

CASS. Quick! Be on your guard! The bull—
Keep him clear of the cow.
Caught with a trick, the black horn's point,
She strikes. He falls; lies in the water. 75
Murder; a trick in a bath. I tell what I see.

CHORUS. I would not claim to be expert in
[oracles
But these, as I deduce, portend disaster.
Do men ever get a good answer from oracles? 80
No. It is only through disaster
That their garrulous craft brings home
The meaning of the prophet's panic.

CASS. And for me also, for me, chance
[ill-destined! 85
My own now I lament, pour into the cup my
[own.
Where is this you have brought me in my
[misery?
Unless to die as well. What else is meant? 90

CHORUS. You are mad, mad, carried away by
                      [the god,
Raising the dirge, the tuneless
Tune, for yourself. Like the tawny
5 Unsatisfied singer from her luckless heart
Lamenting "Itys, Itys," ° the nightingale
Lamenting a life luxuriant with grief.
    CASS. Oh the lot of the songful nightingale!
The gods enclosed her in a winged body,
10 Gave her a sweet and tearless passing,
But for me remains the two-edged cutting
                      [blade.
    CHORUS. From whence these rushing and
                      [God-inflicted
15 Profitless pains?
Why shape with your sinister crying
The piercing hymn—fear-piercing?
How can you know the evil-worded landmarks
    On the prophetic path?
20   CASS. Oh the wedding, the wedding of Paris
                  [—death to his people!
O river Scamander, water drunk by my fathers!
When I was young, alas, upon your beaches
I was brought up and cared for.
25 But now it is the River of Wailing and the
                      [banks of Hell
That shall hear my prophecy soon.
    CHORUS. What is this clear speech, too clear?
A child could understand it.
30 I am bitten with fangs that draw blood
By the misery of your cries,
Cries harrowing the heart.
    CASS. Oh trouble on trouble of a city lost,
                      [lost utterly!
35 My father's sacrifices before the towers,
Much killing of cattle and sheep,
No cure—availed not at all
To prevent the coming of what came to Troy,
And I, my brain on fire, shall soon enter the
40   [trap.
    CHORUS. This speech accords with the
                      [former.
What god, malicious, over-heavy, persistently
                      [pressing,

"Itys" the traditional lamenting bird-call of Philomela,
who was transformed by the gods into a nightingale
after she had been raped by her brother-in-law
Tereus. Like Thyestes, Tereus was deceived into
eating the flesh of his son, Itys.

Drives you to chant of these lamentable   45
Griefs with death their burden?
But I cannot see the end.

SCENE V

[CASSANDRA *now steps down from the car.*]
    CASS. The oracle now no longer from behind
                      [veils   50
Will be peeping forth like a newly-wedded
                      [bride;
But I can feel it like a fresh wind swoop
And rush in the face of the dawn and, wave-
                  [like, wash   55
Against the sun a vastly greater grief
Than this one. I shall speak no more
                    [conundrums.
And bear me witness, pacing me, that I
Am trailing on the scent of ancient wrongs.   60
For this house here a choir never deserts,
Chanting together ill. For they mean ill,
And to puff up their arrogance they have drunk
Men's blood, this band of revellers that haunts
                  [the house,   65
Hard to be rid of, fiends that attend the family.
Established in its rooms they hymn their hymn
Of that original sin, abhor in turn
The adultery that proved a brother's ruin.
A miss? Or do my arrows hit the mark?   70
Or am I a quack prophet who knocks at doors,
                  [a babbler?
Give me your oath, confess I have the facts,
The ancient history of this house's crimes.
    LEADER. And how could an oath's assurance,   75
                  [however finely assured,
Turn out a remedy? I wonder, though, that you
Being brought up overseas, of another tongue,
Should hit on the whole tale as if you had been
                  [standing by.   80
    CASS. Apollo the prophet set me to prophesy.
    LEADER. Was he, although a god, struck by
                  [desire?
    CASS. Till now I was ashamed to tell that
                  [story.   85
    LEADER. Yes. Good fortune keeps us all
                  [fastidious.
    CASS. He wrestled hard upon me, panting
                  [love.

LEADER. And did you come, as they do, to
           [child-getting?
CASS. No. I agreed to him. And I cheated
           [him.
5 LEADER. Were you already possessed by the
           [mystic art?
CASS. Already I was telling the townsmen all
           [their future suffering.
LEADER. Then how did you escape the doom
10   [of Apollo's anger?
CASS. I did not escape. No one ever believed
           [me.
LEADER. Yet to us your words seem worthy of
           [belief.
15 CASS. Oh misery, misery!
Again comes on me the terrible labor of true
Prophecy, dizzying prelude; distracts . . .
Do you see these who sit before the house,
Children, like the shapes of dreams?
20 Children who seem to have been killed by their
           [kinsfolk,
Filling their hands with meat, flesh of
           [themselves,
Guts and entrails, handfuls of lament—
25 Clear what they hold—the same their father
           [tasted.
For this I declare someone is plotting
           [vengeance—
A lion? Lion but coward, that lurks in bed,
30 Good watchdog truly against the lord's
           [return—
My lord, for I must bear the yoke of serfdom.
Leader of the ships, overturner of Troy,
He does not know what plots the accursed
35   [hound
With the licking tongue and the pricked-up ear
           [will plan
In the manner of a lurking doom, in an evil
40   [hour.
A daring criminal! Female murders male.
What monster could provide her with a title?
An amphisbaena or hag of the sea who dwells
In rocks to ruin sailors—
A raving mother of death who breathes against
45   [her folk
War to the finish. Listen to her shout of
           [triumph,
Who shirks no horrors, like men in a rout of
           [battle.

And yet she poses as glad at their return. 50
If you distrust my words, what does it matter?
That which will come will come. You too will
           [soon stand here
And admit with pity that I spoke too truly.
LEADER. Thyestes' dinner of his children's 55
           [meat
I understood and shuddered, and fear grips me
To hear the truth, not framed in parables.
But hearing the rest I am thrown out of my
           [course. 60
CASS. It is Agamemnon's death I tell you you
           [shall witness.
LEADER. Stop! Provoke no evil. Quiet your
           [mouth!
CASS. The god who gives me words is here 65
           [no healer.
LEADER. Not if this shall be so. But may some
           [chance avert it.
CASS. *You* are praying. But others are busy
           [with murder. 70
LEADER. What man is he promotes this
           [terrible thing?
CASS. Indeed you have missed my drift by a
           [wide margin!
LEADER. But I do not understand the 75
           [assassin's method.
CASS. And yet too well I know the speech of
           [Greece!
LEADER. So does Delphi° but the replies are
           [hard. 80
CASS. Ah what a fire it is! It comes upon me.
Apollo, Wolf-Destroyer, pity, pity . . .
It is the two-foot lioness who beds
Beside a wolf, the noble lion away,
It is she will kill me. Brewing a poisoned cup 85
She will mix my punishment too in the angry
           [draught
And boasts, sharpening the dagger for her
           [husband,
To pay back murder for my bringing here. 90
Why then do I wear these mockeries of myself,
The wand and the prophet's garland round my
           [neck?
My hour is coming—but you shall perish first.
Destruction! Scattered thus you give me my 95
           [revenge;

Delphi the oracle of Apollo

Go and enrich some other woman with ruin.
See: Apollo himself is stripping me
Of my prophetic gear, who has looked on
When in this dress I have been a laughing-
5   [stock
To friends and foes alike, and to no purpose;
They called me crazy, like a fortune-teller,
A poor starved beggar-woman—and I bore it.
And now the prophet undoing his prophetess
10 Has brought me to this final darkness.
Instead of my father's altar the executioner's
                                              [block
Waits me the victim, red with my hot blood.
But the gods will not ignore me as I die.
15 One will come after to avenge my death,
A matricide, a murdered father's champion.
Exile and tramp and outlaw he will come back
To gable the family house of fatal crime;
His father's outstretched corpse shall lead him
20   [home.
Why need I then lament so pitifully?
For now that I have seen the town of Troy
Treated as she was treated, while her captors
Come to their reckoning thus by the gods'
25   [verdict,
I will go in and have the courage to die.
Look, these gates are the gates of Death. I greet
                                            [them.
And I pray that I may meet a deft and mortal
30   [stroke
So that without a struggle I may close
My eyes and my blood ebb in easy death.
    LEADER. Oh woman very unhappy and very
                                            [wise,
35 Your speech was long. But if in sober truth
You know your fate, why like an ox that the
                                            [gods
Drive, do you walk so bravely to the altar?
    CASS. There is no escape, strangers. No; not
40   [by postponement.
    LEADER. But the last moment has the privilege
                                        [of hope.
    CASS. The day is here. Little should I gain by
                                        [flight.
45 LEADER. This patience of yours comes from a
                                      [brave soul.
    CASS. A happy man is never paid that
                                    [compliment.

LEADER. But to die with credit graces a mortal
                                      [man. 50
    CASS. Oh my father! You and your noble
                                      [sons!
[She approaches the door, then suddenly
recoils.]
    LEADER. What is it? What is the fear that   55
                                [drives you back?
    CASS. Faugh.
    LEADER. Why faugh? Or is this some
                            [hallucination?
    CASS. These walls breathe out a death that   60
                            [drips with blood.
    LEADER. Not so. It is only the smell of the
                                [sacrifice.
    CASS. It is like a breath out of a charnel-
                                [house. 65
    LEADER. You think our palace burns odd
                                [incense then!
    CASS. But I will go to lament among the dead
My lot and Agamemnon's. Enough of life!
Strangers,   70
I am not afraid like a bird afraid of a bush
But witness you my words after my death
When a woman dies in return for me a woman
And a man falls for a man with a wicked wife.
I ask this service, being about to die.   75
    LEADER. Alas, I pity you for the death you
                                [have foretold.
    CASS. One more speech I have; I do not wish
                                [to raise
The dirge for my own self. But to the sun I pray 80
In face of his last light that my avengers
May make my murderers pay for this my death,
Death of a woman slave, an easy victim.
    [She enters the palace.]

CHORAL INTERLUDE

LEADER. Ah the fortunes of men! When they   85
                                [go well
A shadow sketch would match them, and in
                                [ill-fortune
The dab of a wet sponge destroys the drawing.
It is not myself but the life of man I pity.   90
    CHORUS. Prosperity in all men cries
For more prosperity. Even the owner

Of the finger-pointed-at palace never shuts
His door against her, saying "Come no more."
So to our king the blessed gods had granted
To take the town of Priam, and heaven-favored
5 He reaches home. But now if for former
                [bloodshed
  He must pay blood
And dying for the dead shall cause
  Other deaths in atonement
10 What man could boast he was born
  Secure, who heard this story?
  AGAM. [*within*]. Oh! I am struck a mortal
                [blow—within!
  LEADER. Silence! Listen. Who calls out,
15   [wounded with a mortal stroke?
  AGAM. Again—the second blow—I am
                [struck again.
  LEADER. You heard the king cry out. I think
                [the deed is done.
20 Let us see if we can concert some sound
                [proposal.
  2ND OLD MAN. Well, I will tell you my
                [opinion—
Raise an alarm, summon the folk to the palace.
25   3RD OLD MAN. I say burst in with all speed
                [possible,
Convict them of the deed while still the sword
                [is wet.
  4TH OLD MAN. And I am partner to some
30   [such suggestion.
I am for taking some course. No time to
                [dawdle.
  5TH OLD MAN. The case is plain. This is but
                [the beginning.
35 They are going to set up dictatorship in the
                [state.
  6TH OLD MAN. We are wasting time. The
          [assassins tread to earth
The decencies of delay and give their hands no
40   [sleep.
  7TH OLD MAN. I do not know what plan I
          [could hit on to propose.
The man who acts is in the position to plan.
  8TH OLD MAN. So I think, too, for I am at a
45   [loss
To raise the dead man up again with words.
  9TH OLD MAN. Then to stretch out our life
                [shall we yield thus

To the rule of these profaners of the house?
  10TH OLD MAN. It is not to be endured. To die 50
                [is better.
Death is more comfortable than tyranny.
  11TH OLD MAN. And are we on the evidence
              [of groans
Going to give oracle that the prince is dead? 55
  12TH OLD MAN. We must know the facts for
           [sure and *then* be angry.
Guesswork is not the same as certain
                [knowledge.
  LEADER. Then all of you back me and approve 60
             [this plan—
To ascertain how it is with Agamemnon.
[*The doors of the palace open, revealing the
bodies of* AGAMEMNON *and* CASSANDRA. CLY-
TEMNESTRA *stands above them.*] 65
  CLYT. Much having been said before to fit the
                [moment,
To say the opposite now will not outface me.
How else could one serving hate upon the
                [hated, 70
Thought to be friends, hang high the nets of
                [doom
To preclude all leaping out?
For me I have long been training for this match,
I tried a fall and won—a victory overdue. 75
I stand here where I struck, above my victims;
So I contrived it—this I will not deny—
That he could neither fly nor ward off death;
Inextricable like a net for fishes
I cast about him a vicious wealth of raiment 80
And struck him twice and with two groans he
                [loosed
His limbs beneath him, and upon him fallen
I deal him the third blow to the God beneath
              [the earth, 85
To the safe keeper of the dead a votive gift,
And with that he spits his life out where he lies
And smartly spouting blood he sprays me with
The somber drizzle of bloody dew and I
Rejoice no less than in God's gift of rain. 90
The crops are glad when the ear of corn gives
                [birth.
These things being so, you, elders of Argos,
Rejoice if rejoice you will. Mine is the glory.
And if I could pay this corpse his due libation 95
I should be right to pour it and more than right;

With so many horrors this man mixed and
                [filled
The bowl—and, coming home, has drained the
                [draught himself.
5   LEADER. Your speech astonishes us. This
                [brazen boast
Above the man who was your king and
                [husband!
CLYT. You challenge me as a woman without
10   [foresight
But I with unflinching heart to you who know
Speak. And you, whether you will praise or
                [blame,
It makes no matter. Here lies Agamemnon,
15   My husband, dead, the work of this right hand,
An honest workman. There you have the facts.

KOMMOS II

CHORUS. Woman, what poisoned
Herb of the earth have you tasted
Or potion of the flowing sea
20   To undertake this killing and the people's
                [curses?
You threw down, you cut off—The people will
                [cast you out,
Black abomination to the town.
25   CLYT. Now your verdict—in my case—is
                [exile
And to have the people's hatred, the public
                [curses,
Though then in no way you opposed this man
30   Who carelessly, as if it were a head of sheep
Out of the abundance of his fleecy flocks,
Sacrificed his own daughter, to me the dearest
Fruit of travail, charm for the Thracian winds.
He was the one to have banished from this
35   [land,
Pay off the pollution. But when you hear what I
Have done, you judge severely. But I warn
                [you—
Threaten me on the understanding that I am
40   [ready
For two alternatives—Win by force the right
To rule me, but, if God brings about the
                [contrary,
Late in time you will have to learn self-
45   [discipline.

CHORUS. You are high in the thoughts,
You speak extravagant things,
After the soiling murder your crazy heart
Fancies your forehead with a smear of blood.
Unhonored, unfriended, you must   50
Pay for a blow with a blow.
CLYT. Listen then to this—the sanction of my
                [oaths:
By the Justice totting up my child's atonement,
By the Avenging Doom and Fiend to whom I   55
                [killed this man,
For me hope walks not in the rooms of fear
So long as my fire is lit upon my hearth
By Aegisthus, loyal to me as he was before.
The man who outraged me lies here,   60
The darling of each courtesan at Troy,
And here with him is the prisoner clairvoyante,
The fortune-teller that he took to bed,
Who shares his bed as once his bench on
              [shipboard, 65
A loyal mistress. Both have their deserts.
He lies so; and she who like a swan
Sang her last dying lament
Lies his lover, and the sight contributes
An appetizer to my own bed's pleasure.   70
   CHORUS. Ah would some quick death come
              [not overpainful,
Not overlong on the sickbed,
Establishing in us the ever-
Lasting unending sleep now that our guardian 75
Has fallen, the kindest of men,
Who suffering much for a woman
By a woman has lost his life.
   O Helen, insane, being one
   One to have destroyed so many   80
   And many souls under Troy,
   Now is your work complete, blossomed not
            [for oblivion,
   Unfading stain of blood. Here now, if in any
            [home, 85
   Is Discord, here is a man's deep-rooted ruin.
   CLYT. Do not pray for the portion of death
Weighed down by these things, do not turn
Your anger on Helen as destroyer of men,
One woman destroyer of many   90
Lives of Greek men,
   A hurt that cannot be healed.
   CHORUS. O Evil Spirit, falling on the family,

On the two sons of Atreus and using
Two sisters in heart as your tools,
A power that bites to the heart—
See on the body
5 Perched like a raven he gloats
Harshly croaking his hymn.
    CLYT. Ah, now you have amended your lips'
                        [opinion,
Calling upon this family's three times gorged
10 Genius—demon who breeds
Blood-hankering lust in the belly:
Before the old sore heals, new pus collects.
    CHORUS. It is a great spirit—great—
You tell of, harsh in anger,
15 A ghastly tale, alas,
Of unsatisfied disaster
Brought by Zeus, by Zeus,
Cause and worker of all.
For without Zeus what comes to pass among us?
20 Which of these things is outside Providence?
    O my king, my king,
    How shall I pay you in tears,
    Speak my affection in words?
    You lie in that spider's web,
25 In a desecrating death breathe out your life,
Lie ignominiously
Defeated by a crooked death
And the two-edged cleaver's stroke.
    CLYT. You say this is *my* work—mine?
30 Do not cozen yourself that I am Agamemnon's
                        [wife.
Masquerading as the wife
Of the corpse there the old sharp-witted Genius
Of Atreus who gave the cruel banquet
35 Has paid with a grown man's life
The due for children dead.
    CHORUS. That you are not guilty of
This murder who will attest?
No, but you may have been abetted
40 By some ancestral Spirit of Revenge.
Wading a millrace of the family's blood
The black Manslayer forces a forward path
To make the requital at last
For the eaten children, the blood-clot cold with
45   [time.
    O my king, my king,
    How shall I pay you in tears,
    Speak my affection in words?

    You lie in that spider's web,
    In a desecrating death breathe out your life, 50
Lie ignominiously
Defeated by a crooked death
And the two-edged cleaver's stroke.
    CLYT. Did he not, too, contrive a crooked
Horror for the house? My child by him, 55
Shoot that I raised, much-wept-for Iphigeneia,
He treated her like this;
So suffering like this he need not make
Any great brag in Hell having paid with death
Dealt by the sword for work of his own 60
                        [beginning.
    CHORUS. I am at a loss for thought, I lack
All nimble counsel as to where
To turn when the house is falling.
I fear the house-collapsing crashing 65
Blizzard of blood—of which these drops are
                        [earnest.
Now is Destiny sharpening her justice
On other whetstones for a new infliction.
    O earth, earth, if only you had received me 70
    Before I saw this man lie here as if in bed
        In a bath lined with silver.
Who will bury him? Who will keen him?
Will you, having killed your own husband,
Dare now to lament him 75
And after great wickedness make
       Unamending amends to his ghost?
And who above this godlike hero's grave
Pouring praises and tears
    Will grieve with a genuine heart? 80
    CLYT. It is not your business to attend to that.
By my hand he fell low, lies low and dead,
And I shall bury him low down in the earth,
And his household need not weep him
For Iphigeneia his daughter 85
Tenderly, as is right,
Will meet her father at the rapid ferry of
                        [sorrows,
Put her arms round him and kiss him!
    CHORUS. Reproach answers reproach, 90
It is hard to decide,
The catcher is caught, the killer pays for his kill.
But the law abides while Zeus abides enthroned
That the wrongdoer suffers. That is established.
Who could expel from the house the seed of the 95
                        [Curse?

The race is soldered in sockets of Doom and
[Vengeance.
CLYT. In this you say what is right and the
[will of God.
5 But for my part I am ready to make a contract
With the Evil Genius of the House of Atreus
To accept what has been till now, hard though
[it is,
But that for the future he shall leave this house
10 And wear away some other stock with deaths
Imposed among themselves. Of my possessions
A small part will suffice if only I
Can rid these walls of the mad exchange of
[murder.

ÉXODOS

15 [*Enter* AEGISTHUS, *followed by soldiers.*]
AEG. O welcome light of a justice-dealing
[day!
From now on I will say that the gods, avenging
[men,
20 Look down from above on the crimes of earth,
Seeing as I do in woven robes of the Furies
This man lying here—a sight to warm my
[heart—
Paying for the crooked violence of his father.
25 For his father Atreus, when he ruled the
[country,
Because his power was challenged, hounded
[out
From state and home his own brother Thyestes.
30 My father—let me be plain—was this Thyestes,
Who later came back home a suppliant,
There, miserable, found so much asylum
As not to die on the spot, stain the ancestral
[floor.
35 But to show his hospitality godless Atreus
Gave him an eager if not a loving welcome,
Pretending a day of feasting and rich meats
Served my father with his children's flesh.
The hands and feet, fingers and toes, he hid
40 At the bottom of the dish. My father sitting
[apart
Took unknowing the unrecognizable portion
And ate of a dish that has proved, as you see,
[expensive.

But when he knew he had eaten worse than   45
[poison
He fell back groaning, vomiting their flesh,
And invoking a hopeless doom on the sons of
[Pelops
Kicked over the table to confirm his curse—   50
So may the whole race perish!
Result of this—you see this man lie here.
I stitched this murder together; it was my title.
Me the third son he left, an unweaned infant,
To share the bitterness of my father's exile.   55
But I grew up and Justice brought me back,
I grappled this man while still beyond his door,
Having pieced together the program of his ruin.
So now would even death be beautiful to me
Having seen Agamemnon in the nets of Justice. 60
LEADER. Aegisthus. I cannot respect brutality
[in distress.
You claim that you deliberately killed this
[prince
And that you alone planned this pitiful murder. 65
Be sure that in your turn your head shall not
[escape
The people's volleyed curses mixed with
[stones.
AEG. Do you speak so who sit at the lower   70
[oar
While those on the upper bench control the
[ship?
Old as you are, you will find it is a heavy load
To go to school when old to learn the lesson of 75
[tact.
For old age, too, jail and hunger are fine
Instructors in wisdom, second-sighted doctors.
You have eyes. Cannot you see?
Do not kick against the pricks. The blow will   80
[hurt you.
LEADER. You woman° waiting in the house
[for those who return from battle
While you seduce their wives! Was it you
[devised   85
The death of a master of armies?

woman whereas Clytemnestra is said to have "a man's
mind" because of her audacity, Aegisthus is here
called "woman" because he skulked at home instead
of going to the war

AEG. And these words, too, prepare the way
[for tears.
Contrast your voice with the voice of Orpheus:
[he
5 Led all things after him bewitched with joy, but
[you
Having stung me with your silly yelps shall be
Led off yourself, to prove more mild when
[mastered.
10 LEADER. Indeed! So you are now to be king
[of Argos,
You who, when you had plotted the king's
[death,
Did not even dare to do that thing yourself!
15 AEG. No. For the trick of it was clearly
[woman's work.
I was suspect, an enemy of old.
But now I shall try with Agamemnon's wealth
To rule the people. Any who is disobedient
20 I will harness in a heavy yoke, no tracehorse
[work for him
Like barley-fed colt, but hateful hunger lodging
Beside him in the dark will see his temper
[soften.
25 LEADER. Why with your cowardly soul did
[you yourself
Not strike this man but left that work to a
[woman
Whose presence pollutes our country and its
30 [gods?
But Orestes—does he somewhere see the light
That he may come back here by favor of
[fortune
And kill this pair and prove the final victor?
35 AEG. [*summoning his guards*]. Well, if such
[is your design in deeds and words, you
[will quickly learn—
Here my friends, here my guards, there is
[work for you at hand.
40 LEADER. Come then, hands on hilts, be each
[and all of us prepared.
[*The old men and the guards threaten each
other.*]
AEG. Very well! I too am ready to meet death
45 [with sword in hand.
LEADER. We are glad you speak of dying. We
[accept your words for luck.

CLYT. No, my dearest, do not so. Add no
[more to the train of wrong.
To reap these many present wrongs is harvest 50
[enough of misery.
Enough of misery. Start no more. Our hands
[are red.
But do you, and you old men, go home and
[yield to fate in time, 55
In time before you suffer. We have acted as we
[had to act.
If only our afflictions now could prove enough,
[we should agree—
We who have been so hardly mauled in the 60
[heavy claws of the evil god.
So stands my word, a woman's, if any man
[thinks fit to hear.
AEG. But to think that these should thus
[pluck the blooms of an idle tongue 65
And should throw out words like these, giving
[the evil god his chance,
And should miss the path of prudence and
[insult their master so!
LEADER. It is not the Argive way to fawn 70
[upon a cowardly man.
AEG. Perhaps. But I in later days will take
[further steps with you.
LEADER. Not if the god who rules the family
[guides Orestes to his home. 75
AEG. Yes. I know that men in exile feed
[themselves on barren hopes.
LEADER. Go on, grow fat defiling justice . . .
[while you have your hour.
AEG. Do not think you will not pay me a 80
[price for your stupidity.
LEADER. Boast on in your self-assurance, like
[a cock beside his hen.
CLYT. Pay no heed, Aegisthus, to these futile
[barkings. 85
You and I,
Masters of this house, from now shall order all
[things well.

[*They enter the palace.*]

Sophocles

496?–406 B.C.

Oedipus Rex

430 B.C.

In *Oedipus Rex* Sophocles endows the figures of a legend with such distinctive yet universal traits that we seem to know them as well as our own acquaintances. We recognize his Oedipus as a mighty and benevolent man who turns rashly tyrannical when crossed, who out of pride and a need for self-assertion imposes his own character on his community, and who from an honesty more compelling than pride destroys himself in a quest for truth. "I am on the brink of dreadful speech!" says the shepherd, and Oedipus replies, "And I of dreadful hearing. Yet I must hear."

Sophocles develops his plot with the same profound fidelity to universal human experience that governs his characterization. From Oedipus' opening assertion of authority to Creon's final rebuff ("Think no longer That you are in command here"), we witness a sequence of events recognizably true in even their smallest elements to the motives, feelings, and temperaments of the characters involved. We understand, for example, why Oedipus responds to Teiresias' silence with irritation mounting to wrath, why Teiresias finally tells his secret, and why Oedipus cannot begin to apprehend it. The importance of plot rendered thus true to human experience is that it gives intelligible form to that experience. As we understand merely one character or another, one act or another, we understand only the accidents of human nature, the unrelated particulars of life. But when we see one act lead naturally to another and that to another, as in Sophocles' linked chain of causation from glorious beginning to hideous end, we have seen through accident to form, through experience to the laws that govern experience.

To understand Oedipus and the laws that govern him, we must understand more than psychology. We must apprehend the world in which he acts and reacts. This world, as the religious festival that gives the play its occasion suggests, is one that the gods govern. And the gods, be it said, are no mere collection of superstitious oddities. They are the embodiments of a profound conviction that the universe, however mysterious, is governed by an agency that takes moral cognizance of man. The play begins in religious supplication; Teiresias speaks with supernatural authority; the chorus repeatedly prays to the gods; and when Oedipus makes his final discovery, it is that he and his parents, in their desperate efforts to escape the oracles, have lived out, against their own wills, the wills of the gods.

This conflict between Oedipus and the oracles, between the pride of self-sufficient man and the authority of divine law, gives the play its form, which is based on a separation between human will and divine will, a separation rhythmically narrowing with each accession of knowledge until the two merge. The units of rhythm are the individual scenes, each of which shows an Oedipus who is convinced of his own innocence seeking a knowledge that, as he approaches it, turns ironically into an evidence of his own guilt.

The irony of the play deserves particular mention. That it informs the plot is already evident. It also throws its oblique light on every character. Teiresias means to keep his secret but tells it; Iocastê cheers Oedipus with her tale of a false oracle that turns out to be deadly true; the messenger brings good news but finds it most evil. Even the shepherd thought to save a child but committed him to an unspeakable destiny. The irony enters, too, into scores of lines that mean one thing to the speaker, another to the audience. "Poor children," says Oedipus, "I know that you are deathly sick; and yet, Sick as you are, not one is as sick as I." The importance of this pervading irony is that it gives us a dual vision, a view of things as seen by mortal man and a view of the same things under the aspect of eternity. It catches in its duality the play's conflict and the play's theme.

Oedipus and the chorus ultimately discover what the irony keeps making us see—that the individual mind, self-sufficient in its ignorance, responds in fact to control beyond its ken, gives unknown allegiance to a will that unites the infinity of the world's separate wills into a single harmony. Before that greater will man can only do what Creon does—submit himself—and say with the chorus:

Let me be reverent in the ways of right,
Lowly the paths I journey on;
Let all my words and actions keep
The laws of the pure universe
From highest Heaven handed down.

Oedipus Rex

SOPHOCLES

*An English Version
by Dudley Fitts and Robert Fitzgerald*

CHARACTERS

OEDIPUS   *King of Thebes*
A PRIEST
CREON   *brother of Iocastê*
TEIRESIAS   *a blind seer*
IOCASTÊ   *the Queen, wife of Oedipus*
MESSENGER
SHEPHERD OF LAÏOS
SECOND MESSENGER
CHORUS OF THEBAN ELDERS

   SCENE. *Before the palace of Oedipus, King of Thebes. A central door and two lateral doors open onto a platform which runs the length of the façade. On the platform, right and left, are*
5 *altars; and three steps lead down into the orchestra, or chorus-ground. At the beginning of the action these steps are crowded by suppliants who have brought branches and chaplets of olive leaves and who lie in various attitudes*
10 *of despair.* OEDIPUS *enters.*

PROLOGUE°

OEDIPUS. My children, generations of the
         [living
In the line of Kadmos,° nursed at his ancient
         [hearth:
Why have you strewn yourselves before these 15
         [altars
In supplication, with your boughs and
         [garlands?
The breath of incense rises from the city
With a sound of prayer and lamentation. 20
         Children,
I would not have you speak through
         [messengers,
And therefore I have come myself to hear
         [you— 25
I, Oedipus, who bear the famous name.
 [*To a* PRIEST.]
You, there, since you are eldest in the company,
Speak for them all, tell me what preys upon
         [you, 30
Whether you come in dread, or crave some
         [blessing:
Tell me, and never doubt that I will help you
In every way I can; I should be heartless
Were I not moved to find you suppliant here. 35
 PRIEST. Great Oedipus, O powerful King of
         [Thebes!
You see how all the ages of our people
Cling to your altar steps: here are boys
Who can barely stand alone, and here are 40
         [priests
By weight of age, as I am a priest of God,
And young men chosen from those yet
         [unmarried;
As for the others, all that multitude, 45
They wait with olive chaplets in the squares,
At the two shrines of Pallas, and where Apollo
Speaks in the glowing embers.
       Your own eyes
Must tell you: Thebes is in her extremity 50

Prologue see p. 7. Although it lacks the kommoi and is a scene shorter, *Oedipus Rex* has the same essential structure as *Agamemnon*.
Kadmos founder of Thebes, great-great-grandfather of Oedipus. Cf. p. 39, ll. 71–72.

And can not lift her head from the surge of
[death.
A rust consumes the buds and fruits of the
[earth;
5 The herds are sick; children die unborn,
And labor is vain. The god of plague and pyre
Raids like detestable lightning through the city,
And all the house of Kadmos is laid waste,
All emptied, and all darkened: Death alone
10 Battens upon the misery of Thebes.

You are not one of the immortal gods, we
[know;
Yet we have come to you to make our prayer
As to the man of all men best in adversity
15 And wisest in the ways of God. You saved us
From the Sphinx,° that flinty singer, and the
[tribute
We paid to her so long; yet you were never
Better informed than we, nor could we teach
20 [you:
It was some god breathed in you to set us free.

Therefore, O mighty King, we turn to you:
Find us our safety, find us a remedy,
Whether by counsel of the gods or men.
25 A king of wisdom tested in the past
Can act in a time of troubles, and act well.
Noblest of men, restore
Life to your city! Think how all men call you
Liberator for your triumph long ago;
30 Ah, when your years of kingship are
[remembered,
Let them not say We rose, but later fell—
Keep the State from going down in the storm!
Once, years ago, with happy augury,
35 You brought us fortune; be the same again!
No man questions your power to rule the land:
But rule over men, not over a dead city!
Ships are only hulls, citadels are nothing,
When no life moves in the empty passageways.

Sphinx monster that settled near Thebes and slew all
  passers-by who failed to solve the riddle she asked
  of them: "What being has four feet in the morning,
  two at noon, and three at night?" Years before the
  play's opening Oedipus had rescued Thebes by
  solving the riddle ("Man"), whereupon the Sphinx
  killed herself, and the Thebans made Oedipus their
  king.

OEDIPUS. Poor children! You may be sure I   40
[know
All that you longed for in your coming here.
I know that you are deathly sick; and yet,
Sick as you are, not one is as sick as I.
Each of you suffers in himself alone   45
His anguish, not another's; but my spirit
Groans for the city, for myself, for you.

I was not sleeping, you are not waking me.
No, I have been in tears for a long while
And in my restless thought walked many ways.   50
In all my search, I found one helpful course,
And that I have taken: I have sent Creon,
Son of Menoikeus, brother of the Queen,
To Delphi, Apollo's place of revelation,
To learn there, if he can,   55
What act or pledge of mine may save the city.
I have counted the days, and now, this very
[day,
I am troubled, for he has overstayed his time.
What is he doing? He has been gone too long.   60
Yet whenever he comes back, I should do ill
To scant whatever hint the god may give.
    PRIEST. It is a timely promise. At this instant
They tell me Creon is here.
    OEDIPUS.   O Lord Apollo!   65
May his news be fair as his face is radiant!
    PRIEST. It could not be otherwise: he is
[crowned with bay,°
The chaplet is thick with berries.
    OEDIPUS.   We shall soon know;   70
He is near enough to hear us now.
    [Enter CREON.]

                        O Prince:
Brother: son of Menoikeus:
What answer do you bring us from the god?   75
    CREON. It is favorable. I can tell you, great
[afflictions
Will turn out well, if they are taken well.
    OEDIPUS. What was the oracle? These vague
[words   80
Leave me still hanging between hope and fear.
    CREON. Is it your pleasure to hear me with all
[these
Gathered around us? I am prepared to speak,

bay the laurel, sacred to Apollo and, when worn in
  wreaths or crowns, symbolic of victory

But should we not go in?
OEDIPUS.   Let them all hear it.
It is for them I suffer, more than for myself.
CREON. Then I will tell you what I heard at
5   [Delphi.

In plain words
The god commands us to expel from the land
                              [of Thebes
An old defilement that it seems we shelter.
10 It is a deathly thing, beyond expiation.
We must not let it feed upon us longer.
OEDIPUS. What defilement? How shall we rid
                              [ourselves of it?
CREON. By exile or death, blood for blood. It
15   [was
Murder that brought the plague-wind on the
                              [city.
OEDIPUS. Murder of whom? Surely the god
                              [has named him?
20 CREON. My lord: long ago Laïos was our
                              [king,
Before you came to govern us.
OEDIPUS.   I know;
I learned of him from others; I never saw him.
25 CREON. He was murdered; and Apollo
                              [commands us now
To take revenge upon whoever killed him.
OEDIPUS. Upon whom? Where are they?
                              [Where shall we find a clue
30 To solve that crime, after so many years?
CREON. Here in this land, he said.
                              If we make enquiry,
We may touch things that otherwise escape us.
OEDIPUS. Tell me: Was Laïos murdered in his
35   [house,
Or in the fields, or in some foreign country?
CREON. He said he planned to make a
                              [pilgrimage.
He did not come home again.
40 OEDIPUS.   And was there no one,
No witness, no companion, to tell what
                              [happened?
CREON. They were all killed but one, and he
                              [got away
45 So frightened that he could remember one
                              [thing only.
OEDIPUS. What was that one thing? One may
                              [be the key

To everything, if we resolve to use it.
CREON. He said that a band of highwaymen   50
                              [attacked them,
Outnumbered them, and overwhelmed the
                              [King.
OEDIPUS. Strange, that a highwayman should
                              [be so daring—   55
Unless some faction here bribed him to do it.
CREON. We thought of that. But after Laïos'
                              [death
New troubles arose and we had no avenger.
OEDIPUS. What troubles could prevent your   60
                              [hunting down the killers?
CREON. The riddling Sphinx's song
Made us deaf to all mysteries but her own.
OEDIPUS. Then once more I must bring what
                              [is dark to light.   65
It is most fitting that Apollo shows,
As you do, this compunction for the dead.
You shall see how I stand by you, as I should,
To avenge the city and the city's god,
And not as though it were for some distant   70
                              [friend,
But for my own sake, to be rid of evil.
Whoever killed King Laïos might—who
                              [knows?—
Decide at any moment to kill me as well.   75
By avenging the murdered king I protect
                              [myself.

Come, then, my children: leave the altar steps,
Lift up your olive boughs!
                    One of you go   80
And summon the people of Kadmos to gather
                              [here.
I will do all that I can; you may tell them that.
[*Exit a* PAGE.]
So, with the help of God,°   85
We shall be saved—or else indeed we are lost.
PRIEST. Let us rise, children. It was for this
                              [we came,
And now the King has promised it himself.
Phoibos has sent us an oracle; may he descend 90
Himself to save us and drive out the plague.

God Apollo, god of music, archery, healing, light
(**Phoibos,** as he is called at l. 90, means *light* or
pure), and truth. Through his oracle he mediates
between man and the gods.

[*Exeunt* OEDIPUS *and* CREON *into the palace by the central door. The* PRIEST *and the* SUPPLIANTS *disperse R. and L. After a short pause the* CHORUS *enters the orchestra.*]

PÁRODOS

Strophe 1

5   CHORUS. What is the god singing in his
                                [profound
Delphi of gold and shadow?
What oracle for Thebes, the sunwhipped city?

Fear unjoints me, the roots of my heart tremble.

10 Now I remember, O Healer, your power, and
                                [wonder:
Will you send doom like a sudden cloud, or
                                [weave it
Like nightfall of the past?

15 Ah no: be merciful, issue of holy sound:
Dearest to our expectancy: be tender!

Antistrophe 1

Let me pray to Athenê, the immortal daughter
                                [of Zeus,
And to Artemis her sister
20 Who keeps her famous throne in the market
                                [ring,
And to Apollo, bowman at the far butts of
                                [heaven—

O gods, descend! Like three streams leap
                                [against
25 The fires of our grief, the fires of darkness;
Be swift to bring us rest!

As in the old time from the brilliant house
Of air you stepped to save us, come again!

Strophe 2

30 Now our afflictions have no end.
Now all our stricken host lies down
And no man fights off death with his mind;

The noble plowland bears no grain,
And groaning mothers can not bear—

See, how our lives like birds take wing,   35
Like sparks that fly when a fire soars,
To the shore of the god of evening.

Antistrophe 2

The plague burns on, it is pitiless, .
Though pallid children laden with death
Lie unwept in the stony ways,   40

And old gray women by every path
Flock to the strand about the altars

There to strike their breasts and cry
Worship of Zeus in wailing prayers:
Be kind, God's golden child!°   45

Strophe 3

There are no swords in this attack by fire,
No shields, but we are ringed with cries.

Send the besieger plunging from our homes
Into the vast sea-room of the Atlantic
Or into the waves that foam eastward of   50
                                [Thrace—

For the day ravages what the night spares—

Destroy our enemy, lord of the thunder!
Let him be riven by lightning from heaven!

Antistrophe 3

Phoibos Apollo, stretch the sun's bowstring,   55
That golden cord, until it sing for us,
Flashing arrows in heaven!
                    Artemis, Huntress,
Race with flaring lights upon our mountains!

O scarlet° god, O golden-banded brow,   60
O Theban° Bacchos in a storm of Maenads,
                [*Enter* OEDIPUS, *center.*]
Whirl upon Death, that all the Undying hate!
Come with blinding cressets, come in joy!

God's golden child Athena, daughter of Zeus
scarlet flushed with wine
Theban born in Thebes and descended on his mortal
    side from Kadmos

SCENE I

OEDIPUS. Is this your prayer? It may be
                              [answered. Come,
Listen to me, act as the crisis demands,
And you shall have relief from all these evils.

5 Until now I was a stranger to this tale,
As I had been a stranger to the crime.
Could I track down the murderer without a
                              [clue?
But now, friends,
10 As one who became a citizen after the murder,
I make this proclamation to all Thebans:
If any man knows by whose hands Laïos, son of
                              [Labdakos,
Met his death, I direct that man to tell me
15   [everything,
No matter what he fears for having so long
                              [withheld it.
Let it stand as promised that no further trouble
Will come to him, but he may leave the land in
20   [safety.

Moreover: If anyone knows the murderer to
                              [be foreign,
Let him not keep silent: he shall have his
                              [reward from me.
25 However, if he does conceal it, if any man
Fearing for his friend or for himself disobeys
                              [this edict,
Hear what I propose to do:

I solemnly forbid the people of this country,
30 Where power and throne are mine, ever to
                              [receive that man
Or speak to him, no matter who he is, or let
                              [him
Join in sacrifice, lustration, or in prayer.
35 I decree that he be driven from every house,
Being, as he is, corruption itself to us: the
                              [Delphic
Voice of Zeus has pronounced this revelation.
Thus I associate myself with the oracle
40 And take the side of the murdered king.

As for the criminal, I pray to God—
Whether it be a lurking thief, or one of a
                              [number—
I pray that that man's life be consumed in evil
                              [and wretchedness. 45
And as for me, this curse applies no less
If it should turn out that the culprit is my guest
                              [here,
Sharing my hearth.
                    You have heard the penalty. 50
I lay it on you now to attend to this
For my sake, for Apollo's, for the sick
Sterile city that heaven has abandoned.
Suppose the oracle had given you no command:
Should this defilement go uncleansed for ever? 55
You should have found the murderer: your
                              [king,
A noble king, had been destroyed!
                              Now I,
Having the power that he held before me, 60
Having his bed, begetting children there
Upon his wife, as he would have, had he
                              [lived—
Their son would have been my children's
                              [brother, 65
If Laïos had had luck in fatherhood!
(But surely ill luck rushed upon his reign)—
I say I take the son's part, just as though
I were his son, to press the fight for him
And see it won! I'll find the hand that brought 70
Death to Labdakos' and Polydoros' child,
Heir of Kadmos' and Agenor's line.°
And as for those who fail me,
May the gods deny them the fruit of the earth,
Fruit of the womb, and may they rot utterly! 75
Let them be wretched as we are wretched, and
                              [worse!

For you, for loyal Thebans, and for all
Who find my actions right, I pray the favor
Of justice, and of all the immortal gods. 80
LEADER OF THE CHORUS. Since I am under
                              [oath, my lord, I swear
I did not do the murder, I can not name
The murderer. Might not the oracle

Labdakos' . . . line the child is Laïos, whose male ancestry Oedipus traces back: Laïos-Labdakos-Poly-
  doros-Kadmos-Agenor

That has ordained the search tell where to find
[him?
OEDIPUS. An honest question. But no man in
[the world
5 Can make the gods do more than the gods will.
LEADER. There is one last expedient—
OEDIPUS.   Tell me what it is.
Though it seem slight, you must not hold it
[back.
10   LEADER. A lord clairvoyant to the lord Apollo,
As we all know, is the skilled Teiresias.
One might learn much about this from him,
[Oedipus.
OEDIPUS. I am not wasting time:
15 Creon spoke of this and I have sent for him—
Twice, in fact; it is strange that he is not here.
LEADER. The other matter—that old report—
[seems useless.
OEDIPUS. Tell me. I am interested in all
20   [reports.
LEADER. The King was said to have been
[killed by highwaymen.
OEDIPUS. I know. But we have no witnesses
[to that.
25   LEADER. If the killer can feel a particle of
[dread,
Your curse will bring him out of hiding!
OEDIPUS.   No.
The man who dared that act will fear no curse.
30 [Enter the blind seer TEIRESIAS led by a PAGE.]
LEADER. But there is one man who may detect
[the criminal.
This is Teiresias, this is the holy prophet
In whom, alone of all men, truth was born.
35   OEDIPUS. Teiresias: seer: student of
[mysteries,
Of all that's taught and all that no man tells,
Secrets of Heaven and secrets of the earth:
Blind though you are, you know the city lies
40 Sick with plague; and from this plague, my
[lord,
We find that you alone can guard or save us.

Possibly you did not hear the messengers?
Apollo, when we sent to him,
45 Sent us back word that this great pestilence
Would lift, but only if we established clearly
The identity of those who murdered Laïos.

They must be killed or exiled.
                          Can you use
Birdflight or any art of divination   50
To purify yourself, and Thebes, and me
From this contagion? We are in your hands.
There is no fairer duty
Than that of helping others in distress.
TEIRESIAS. How dreadful knowledge of the   55
[truth can be
When there's no help in truth! I knew this well,
But did not act on it: else I should not have
[come.
OEDIPUS. What is troubling you? Why are   60
[your eyes so cold?
TEIRESIAS. Let me go home. Bear your own
[fate, and I'll
Bear mine. It is better so: trust what I say.
OEDIPUS. What you say is ungracious and   65
[unhelpful
To your native country. Do not refuse to speak.
TEIRESIAS. When it comes to speech, your
[own is neither temperate
Nor opportune. I wish to be more prudent.   70
OEDIPUS. In God's name, we all beg you—
TEIRESIAS.   You are all ignorant.
No; I will never tell you what I know.
Now it is my misery; then, it would be yours.
OEDIPUS. What! You do know something,   75
[and will not tell us?
You would betray us all and wreck the State?
TEIRESIAS. I do not intend to torture myself,
[or you.
Why persist in asking? You will not persuade   80
[me.
OEDIPUS. What a wicked old man you are!
[You'd try a stone's
Patience! Out with it! Have you no feeling at
[all? 85
TEIRESIAS. You call me unfeeling. If you
[could only see
The nature of your own feelings . . .
OEDIPUS.   Why,
Who would not feel as I do? Who could endure 90
Your arrogance toward the city?
TEIRESIAS.   What does it matter!
Whether I speak or not, it is bound to come.
OEDIPUS. Then, if "it" is bound to come, you
[are bound to tell me. 95

TEIRESIAS. No, I will not go on. Rage as you
[please.
  OEDIPUS. Rage? Why not!
         And I'll tell you what I think:
5 You planned it, you had it done, you all but
Killed him with your own hands: if you had
[eyes,
I'd say the crime was yours, and yours alone.
  TEIRESIAS. So? I charge you, then,
10 Abide by the proclamation you have made:
From this day forth
Never speak again to these men or to me;
You yourself are the pollution of this country.
  OEDIPUS. You dare say that! Can you
15 [possibly think you have
Some way of going free, after such insolence?
  TEIRESIAS. I have gone free. It is the truth
[sustains me.
  OEDIPUS. Who taught you shamelessness?
20 [It was not your craft.
  TEIRESIAS. You did. You made me speak. I
[did not want to.
  OEDIPUS. Speak what? Let me hear it again
[more clearly.
25   TEIRESIAS. Was it not clear before? Are you
[tempting me?
  OEDIPUS. I did not understand it. Say it again.
  TEIRESIAS. I say that you are the murderer
[whom you seek.
30   OEDIPUS. Now twice you have spat out
[infamy. You'll pay for it!
  TEIRESIAS. Would you care for more? Do you
[wish to be really angry?
  OEDIPUS. Say what you will. Whatever you
35 [say is worthless.
  TEIRESIAS. I say that you live in hideous love
[with her
Who is nearest you in blood. You are blind to
[the evil.
40   OEDIPUS. It seems you can go on mouthing
[like this for ever.
  TEIRESIAS. I can, if there is power in truth.
  OEDIPUS.   There is:
But not for you, not for you,
45 You sightless, witless, senseless, mad old man!
  TEIRESIAS. You are the madman. There is no
[one here
Who will not curse you soon, as you curse me.

  OEDIPUS. You child of endless night! You
[can not hurt me 50
Or any other man who sees the sun.
  TEIRESIUS. True: it is not from me your fate
[will come.
That lies within Apollo's competence,
As it is his concern. 55
  OEDIPUS.   Tell me:
Are you speaking for Creon, or for yourself?
  TEIRESIUS. Creon is no threat. You weave
[your own doom.
  OEDIPUS. Wealth, power, craft of 60
[statesmanship!
Kingly position, everywhere admired!
What savage envy is stored up against these,
If Creon, who I trusted, Creon my friend,
For this great office which the city once 65
Put in my hands unsought—if for this power
Creon desires in secret to destroy me!

He has bought this decrepit fortune-teller, this
Collector of dirty pennies, this prophet fraud—
Why, he is no more clairvoyant than I am! 70
                                 Tell us:
Has your mystic mummery ever approached
[the truth?
When that hellcat the Sphinx was performing
[here, 75
What help were you to these people?
Her magic was not for the first man who came
[along:
It demanded a real exorcist. Your birds—
What good are they? or the gods, for the matter 80
[of that?
But I came by,
Oedipus, the simple man, who knows
[nothing—
I thought it out for myself, no birds helped me! 85
And this is the man you think you can destroy,
That you may be close to Creon when he's king!
Well, you and your friend Creon, it seems to me,
Will suffer most. If you were not an old man,
You would have paid already for your plot. 90
  LEADER OF THE CHORUS. We can not see that
[his words or yours
Have been spoken except in anger, Oedipus,
And of anger we have no need. How can God's
[will 95

Be accomplished best? That is what most
[concerns us.
TEIRESIAS. You are a king. But where
[argument's concerned
5 I am your man, as much a king as you.
I am not your servant, but Apollo's.
I have no need of Creon to speak for me.

Listen to me. You mock my blindness, do you?
But I say that you, with both your eyes, are
10 [blind:
You can not see the wretchedness of your life,
Nor in whose house you live, no, nor with
[whom.
Who are your father and mother? Can you tell
15 [me?
You do not even know the blind wrongs
That you have done them, on earth and in the
[world below.
But the double lash of your parents' curse will
20 [whip you
Out of this land some day, with only night
Upon your precious eyes.
Your cries then—where will they not be heard?
What fastness of Kithairon° will not echo
25 [them?
And that bridal-descant of yours—you'll know
[it then,
The song they sang when you came here to
[Thebes
30 And found your misguided berthing.
All this, and more, that you can not guess at
[now,
Will bring you to yourself among your
[children.

35 Be angry then. Curse Creon. Curse my words.
I tell you, no man that walks upon the earth
Shall be rooted out more horribly than you.
OEDIPUS. Am I to bear this from him?—
[Damnation
40 Take you! Out of this place! Out of my sight!
TEIRESIAS. I would not have come at all if you
[had not asked me.
OEDIPUS. Could I have told that you'd talk

Kithairon mountain near Thebes where the infant
Oedipus was left to die. Cf. pp. 46–47, ll. 86–2.

[nonsense, that
You'd come here to make a fool of yourself, 45
[and of me?
TEIRESIAS. A fool? Your parents thought me
[sane enough.
OEDIPUS. My parents again!—Wait: who
[were my parents? 50
TEIRESIAS. This day will give you a father,
[and break your heart.
OEDIPUS. Your infantile riddles! Your
[damned abracadabra!
TEIRESIAS. You were a great man once at 55
[solving riddles.
OEDIPUS. Mock me with that if you like; you
[will find it true.
TEIRESIAS. It was true enough. It brought
[about your ruin. 60
OEDIPUS. But if it saved this town?
TEIRESIAS [to the PAGE]. Boy, give me your
[hand.
OEDIPUS. Yes, boy; lead him away.
—While you are here 65
We can do nothing. Go; leave us in peace.
TEIRESIAS. I will go when I have said what I
[have to say.
How can you hurt me? And I tell you again:
The man you have been looking for all this 70
[time,
The damned man, the murderer of Laïos,
That man is in Thebes. To your mind he is
[foreign-born,
But it will soon be shown that he is a Theban, 75
A revelation that will fail to please.
A blind man,
Who has his eyes now; a penniless man, who
[is rich now;
And he will go tapping the strange earth with 80
[his staff.
To the children with whom he lives now he
[will be
Brother and father—the very same; to her
Who bore him, son and husband—the very 85
[same
Who came to his father's bed, wet with his
[father's blood.

Enough. Go think that over.
If later you find error in what I have said, 90

You may say that I have no skill in prophecy.
[*Exit* TEIRESIAS, *led by his* PAGE. OEDIPUS *goes
into the palace.*]

ODE I

Strophe 1
CHORUS. The Delphic stone of prophecies°
5 Remembers ancient regicide
And a still bloody hand.
That killer's hour of flight has come.
He must be stronger than riderless
Coursers of untiring wind,
10 For the son of Zeus° armed with his father's
[thunder
Leaps in lightning after him;
And the Furies follow him, the sad Furies.

Antistrophe 1
Holy Parnassos'° peak of snow
15 Flashes and blinds that secret man,
That all shall hunt him down:
Though he may roam the forest shade
Like a bull gone wild from pasture
To rage through glooms of stone.
20 Doom comes down on him; flight will not avail
[him;
For the world's heart calls him desolate,
And the immortal Furies follow, for ever
[follow.

Strophe 2
25 But now a wilder thing is heard
From the old man skilled at hearing Fate in the
[wingbeat of a bird.
Bewildered as a blown bird, my soul hovers and
[can not find
30 Foothold in this debate, or any reason or rest
[of mind.
But no man ever brought—none can bring
Proof of strife between Thebes' royal house,
Labdakos' line, and the son of Polybos;°

Delphic stone of prophecies platform of rock on
which stood the temple of the Delphic oracle
son of Zeus Apollo
Parnassos mountain, sacred to Apollo, on the side of
which Delphi and its oracle stood
son of Polybos Oedipus. Cf. pp. 47–48, ll. 94–1.

And never until now has any man brought   35
[word
Of Laïos' dark death staining Oedipus the
[King.

Antistrophe 2
Divine Zeus and Apollo hold
Perfect intelligence alone of all tales ever told; 40
And well though this diviner works, he works
[in his own night;
No man can judge that rough unknown or trust
[in second sight,
For wisdom changes hands among the wise.   45
Shall I believe my great lord criminal
At a raging word that a blind old man let fall?
I saw him, when the carrion woman faced him
[of old,
Prove his heroic mind! These evil words are   50
[lies.

SCENE II

CREON. Men of Thebes:
I am told that heavy accusations
Have been brought against me by King
[Oedipus. 55

I am not the kind of man to bear this tamely.

If in these present difficulties
He holds me accountable for any harm to him
Through anything I have said or done—why,
[then, 60
I do not value life in this dishonor.
It is not as though this rumor touched upon
Some private indiscretion. The matter is grave.
The fact is that I am being called disloyal
To the State, to my fellow citizens, to my   65
[friends.
LEADER OF THE CHORUS. He may have spoken
[in anger, not from his mind.
CREON. But did you hear him say I was the
[one 70
Who seduced the old prophet into lying?
LEADER. The thing was said; I do not know
[how seriously.
CREON. But you were watching him! Were
[his eyes steady? 75

Did he look like a man in his right mind?
    LEADER.   I do not know.
I can not judge the behavior of great men.
But here is the King himself.
5   [*Enter* OEDIPUS.]
    OEDIPUS.   So you dared come back.
Why? How brazen of you to come to my house,
You murderer!
                Do you think I do not know
10 That you plotted to kill me, plotted to steal my
                          [throne?
Tell me, in God's name: am I coward, a fool,
That you should dream you could accomplish
                          [this?
15 A fool who could not see your slippery game?
A coward, not to fight back when I saw it?
You are the fool, Creon, are you not? hoping
Without support or friends to get a throne?
Thrones may be won or bought: you could do
20   [neither.
    CREON. Now listen to me. You have talked;
                    [let me talk, too.
You can not judge unless you know the facts.
    OEDIPUS. You speak well: there is one fact;
25   [but I find it hard
To learn from the deadliest enemy I have.
    CREON. That above all I must dispute with
                        [you.
    OEDIPUS. That above all I will not hear you
30   [deny.
    CREON. If you think there is anything good in
                    [being stubborn
Against all reason, then I say you are wrong.
    OEDIPUS. If you think a man can sin against
35   [his own kind
And not be punished for it, I say you are mad.
    CREON. I agree. But tell me: what have I done
                     [to you?
    OEDIPUS. You advised me to send for that
40   [wizard, did you not?
    CREON. I did. I should do it again.
    OEDIPUS.   Very well. Now tell me:
How long has it been since Laïos—
    CREON.   What of Laïos?
45 OEDIPUS. Since he vanished in that onset by
                   [the road?
    CREON. It was long ago, a long time.
    OEDIPUS.   And this prophet,

Was he practicing here then?
    CREON.   He was; and with honor, as now.   50
    OEDIPUS. Did he speak of me at that time?
    CREON.   He never did;
At least, not when I was present.
    OEDIPUS.   But . . . the enquiry?
I suppose you held one?   55
    CREON.   We did, but we learned nothing.
    OEDIPUS. Why did the prophet not speak
                  [against me then?
    CREON. I do not know; and I am the kind of
                  [man 60
Who holds his tongue when he has no facts to
                  [go on.
    OEDIPUS. There's one fact that you know,
              [and you could tell it.
    CREON. What fact is that? If I know it, you   65
                 [shall have it.
    OEDIPUS. If he were not involved with you,
                 [he could not say
That it was I who murdered Laïos.
    CREON. If he says that, you are the one that   70
                [knows it?—
But now it is my turn to question you.
    OEDIPUS. Put your questions. I am no
                [murderer.
    CREON. First, then: You married my sister?   75
    OEDIPUS.   I married your sister.
    CREON. And you rule the kingdom equally
               [with her?
    OEDIPUS. Everything that she wants she has
              [from me. 80
    CREON. And I am the third, equal to both of
               [you?
    OEDIPUS. That is why I call you a bad friend.
    CREON. No. Reason it out, as I have done.
Think of this first: Would any sane man prefer   85
Power, with all a king's anxieties,
To that same power and the grace of sleep?
Certainly not I.
I have never longed for the king's power—only
              [his rights. 90
Would any wise man differ from me in this?
As matters stand, I have my way in everything
With your consent, and no responsibilities.
If I were king, I should be a slave to policy.

How could I desire a scepter more   95

Than what is now mine—untroubled influence?
No, I have not gone mad; I need no honors,
Except those with the perquisites I have now.
I am welcome everywhere; every man salutes

5   [me,
And those who want your favor seek my ear,
Since I know how to manage what they ask.
Should I exchange this ease for that anxiety?
Besides, no sober mind is treasonable.

10 I hate anarchy
And never would deal with any man who likes
                                                    [it.

Test what I have said. Go to the priestess
At Delphi, ask if I quoted her correctly.

15 And as for this other thing: if I am found
Guilty of treason with Teiresias,
Then sentence me to death! You have my word
It is a sentence I should cast my vote for—
But not without evidence!

20   You do wrong
When you take good men for bad, bad men for
                                                  [good.
A true friend thrown aside—why, life itself
Is not more precious!

25   In time you will know this well:
For time, and time alone, will show the just
                                                   [man,
Though scoundrels are discovered in a day.
LEADER. This is well said, and a prudent man

30   [would ponder it.
Judgments too quickly formed are dangerous.
OEDIPUS. But is he not quick in his duplicity?
And shall I not be quick to parry him?
Would you have me stand still, hold my peace,

35   [and let
This man win everything, through my inaction?
CREON. And you want—what is it, then? To
                                                  [banish me?
OEDIPUS. No, not exile. It is your death I

40   [want,
So that all the world may see what treason
                                                   [means.
CREON. You will persist, then? You will not
                                                  [believe me?

45 OEDIPUS. How can I believe you?
CREON.   Then you are a fool.
OEDIPUS. To save myself?

CREON.   In justice, think of me.
OEDIPUS. You are evil incarnate.
CREON.   But suppose that you are wrong?   50
OEDIPUS. Still I must rule.
CREON.   But not if you rule badly.
OEDIPUS. O city, city!
CREON.   It is my city, too!
LEADER. Now, my lords, be still. I see the   55
                                                 [Queen,
Iocastê, coming from her palace chambers;
And it is time she came, for the sake of you
                                                  [both.
This dreadful quarrel can be resolved through   60
                                                   [her.

[*Enter* IOCASTÊ.]
IOCASTÊ. Poor foolish men, what wicked din
                                                 [is this?
With Thebes sick to death, is it not shameful   65
That you should rake some private quarrel up?
    [*To* OEDIPUS.]
Come into the house.
                              —And you, Creon, go now:
Let us have no more of this tumult over   70
                                                 [nothing.
CREON. Nothing? No, sister: what your
                                          [husband plans for me
Is one of two great evils: exile or death.
OEDIPUS. He is right.   75
        Why, woman I have caught him squarely
Plotting against my life.
CREON.   No! Let me die.
Accurst if ever I have wished you harm!
IOCASTÊ. Ah, believe it, Oedipus!   80
In the name of the gods, respect this oath of his
For my sake, for the sake of these people here!

Strophe 1
LEADER. Open your mind to her, my lord. Be
                                          [ruled by her, I beg you!
OEDIPUS. What would you have me do?   85
LEADER. Respect Creon's word He has never
                                          [spoken like a fool,
And now he has sworn an oath.
OEDIPUS.   You know what you ask?
LEADER.   I do.   90
OEDIPUS.   Speak on, then.
LEADER. A friend so sworn should not be
                                                 [baited so,

In blind malice, and without final proof.
OEDIPUS. You are aware, I hope, that what
[you say
Means death for me, or exile at the least.

Strophe 2

5 LEADER. No, I swear by Helios,° first in
[Heaven!
May I die friendless and accurst,
The worst of deaths, if ever I meant that!
It is the withering fields
10   That hurt my sick heart:
Must we bear all these ills,
      And now your bad blood as well?
OEDIPUS. Then let him go. And let me die,
[if I must,
15 Or be driven by him in shame from the land of
[Thebes.
It is your unhappiness, and not his talk,
That touches me.
      As for him—
20 Wherever he is, I will hate him as long as I live.
CREON. Ugly in yielding, as you were ugly in
[rage!
Natures like yours chiefly torment themselves.
OEDIPUS. Can you not go? Can you not leave
25 [me?
CREON.   I can.
You do not know me; but the city knows me,
And in its eyes I am just, if not in yours.
[*Exit* CREON.]

Antistrophe 1

30 LEADER. Lady Iocastê, did you not ask the
[King to go to his chambers?
IOCASTÊ. First tell me what has happened.
LEADER. There was suspicion without
[evidence; yet it rankled
35 As even false charges will.
IOCASTÊ.   On both sides?
LEADER.   On both.
IOCASTÊ.   But what was said?
LEADER. Oh let it rest, let it be done with!
40 Have we not suffered enough?
OEDIPUS. You see to what your decency has
[brought you:

Helios the sun-god

You have made difficulties where my heart saw
[none.

Antistrophe 2

LEADER. Oedipus, it is not once only I have   45
[told you—
You must know I should count myself unwise
To the point of madness, should I now forsake
[you—
You, under whose hand,   50
    In the storm of another time,
Our dear land sailed out free.
    But now stand fast at the helm!
IOCASTÊ. In God's name, Oedipus, inform
[your wife as well: 55
Why are you so set in this hard anger?
OEDIPUS. I will tell you, for none of these
[men deserves
My confidence as you do. It is Creon's work,
His treachery, his plotting against me.   60
IOCASTÊ. Go on, if you can make this clear to
[me.
OEDIPUS. He charges me with the murder of
[Laïos.
IOCASTÊ. Has he some knowledge? Or does he   65
[speak from hearsay?
OEDIPUS. He would not commit himself to
[such a charge,
But he has brought in that damnable soothsayer
To tell his story.   70
IOCASTÊ.   Set your mind at rest.
If it is a question of soothsayers, I tell you
That you will find no man whose craft gives
[knowledge
Of the unknowable.   75
    Here is my proof:

An oracle was reported to Laïos once
(I will not say from Phoibos himself, but from
His appointed ministers, at any rate)
That his doom would be death at the hands of   80
[his own son—
His son, born of his flesh and of mine!
Now, you remember the story: Laïos was killed
By marauding strangers where three highways
[meet;   85
But his child had not been three days in this
[world

Before the King had pierced the baby's ankles
And had him left to die on a lonely mountain.

Thus, Apollo never caused that child
To kill his father, and it was not Laïos' fate
5 To die at the hands of his son, as he had feared.
This is what prophets and prophecies are
                              [worth!
Have no dread of them.
                    It is God himself
10 Who can show us what he wills, in his own
                              [way.
    OEDIPUS. How strange a shadowy memory
                          [crossed my mind,
Just now while you were speaking; it chilled
15   [my heart.
    IOCASTÊ. What do you mean? What memory
                          [do you speak of?
    OEDIPUS. If I understand you, Laïos was
                              [killed
20 At a place where three roads meet.
    IOCASTÊ.   So it was said;
We have no later story.
    OEDIPUS.   Where did it happen?
    IOCASTÊ. Phokis, it is called: at a place where
25   [the Theban Way
Divides into the roads toward Delphi and
                              [Daulia.
    OEDIPUS. When?
    IOCASTÊ.   We had the news not long
30   [before you came
And proved the right to your succession here.
    OEDIPUS. Ah, what net has God been weaving
                              [for me?
    IOCASTÊ. Oedipus! Why does this trouble
35   [you?
    OEDIPUS.   Do not ask me yet.
First, tell me how Laïos looked, and tell me
How old he was.
    IOCASTÊ.   He was tall, his hair just touched
40 With white; his form was not unlike your own.
    OEDIPUS. I think that I myself may be accurst
By my own ignorant edict.
    IOCASTÊ.   You speak strangely.
It makes me tremble to look at you, my King.
45 OEDIPUS. I am not sure that the blind man can
                              [not see.
But I should know better if you were to tell

                              [me—
    IOCASTÊ. Anything—though I dread to hear
                          [you ask it. 50
    OEDIPUS. Was the King lightly escorted, or
                          [did he ride
With a large company, as a ruler should?
    IOCASTÊ. There were five men with him in all:
                          [one was a herald; 55
And a single chariot, which he was driving.
    OEDIPUS. Alas, that makes it plain enough!
                          But who—
Who told you how it happened?
    IOCASTÊ.   A household servant, 60
The only one to escape.
    OEDIPUS.   And is he still
A servant of ours?
    IOCASTÊ.   No; for when he came back at
                          [last 65
And found you enthroned in the place of the
                          [dead king,
He came to me, touched my hand with his, and
                          [begged
That I would send him away to the frontier 70
                          [district
Where only the shepherds go—
As far away from the city as I could send him.
I granted his prayer; for although the man was
                          [a slave, 75
He had earned more than this favor at my
                          [hands.
    OEDIPUS. Can he be called back quickly?
    IOCASTÊ.   Easily.
But why? 80
    OEDIPUS.   I have taken too much upon
                          [myself
Without enquiry; therefore I wish to consult
                          [him.
    IOCASTÊ. Then he shall come. 85
                    But am I not one also
To whom you might confide these fears of
                          [yours?
    OEDIPUS. That is your right; it will not be
                          [denied you, 90
Now least of all; for I have reached a pitch
Of wild foreboding. Is there anyone
To whom I should sooner speak?

Polybos of Corinth is my father.

My mother is a Dorian: Meropê.
I grew up chief among the men of Corinth
Until a strange thing happened—
Not worth my passion, it may be, but strange.

5　At a feast, a drunken man maundering in his
　　　　　　　　　　　　　　　　　[cups
Cries out that I am not my father's son!

I contained myself that night, though I felt
　　　　　　　　　　　　　　　　　[anger
10　And a sinking heart. The next day I visited
My father and mother, and questioned them.
　　　　　　　　　　　　　　　[They stormed,
Calling it all the slanderous rant of a fool;
And this relieved me. Yet the suspicion
15　Remained always aching in my mind;
I knew there was talk; I could not rest;
And finally, saying nothing to my parents,
I went to the shrine at Delphi.

The god dismissed my question without reply;
20　He spoke of other things.
　　　　　　　　　　　　Some were clear,
Full of wretchedness, dreadful, unbearable:
As, that I should lie with my own mother, breed
Children from whom all men would turn their
25　　　　　　　　　　　　　　　　[eyes;
And that I should be my father's murderer.

I heard all this, and fled. And from that day
Corinth to me was only in the stars
Descending in that quarter of the sky,
30　As I wandered farther and farther on my way
To a land where I should never see the evil
Sung by the oracle. And I came to this country
Where, so you say, King Laïos was killed.

I will tell you all that happened there, my lady.

35　There were three highways
Coming together at a place I passed;
And there a herald came towards me, and a
　　　　　　　　　　　　　　　　[chariot
Drawn by horses, with a man such as you
40　　　　　　　　　　　　　　　[describe
Seated in it. The groom leading the horses
Forced me off the road at his lord's command;

But as this charioteer lurched over towards me
I struck him in my rage. The old man saw me
And brought his double goad down upon my　45
　　　　　　　　　　　　　　　　[head
As I came abreast.
　　　　　　　　He was paid back, and more!
Swinging my club in this right hand I knocked
　　　　　　　　　　　　　　　[him　50
Out of his car, and he rolled on the ground.
　　　　　　　　　　　　　I killed him.

I killed them all.
Now if that stranger and Laïos were—kin,
Where is a man more miserable than I?　55
More hated by the gods? Citizen and alien alike
Must never shelter me or speak to me—
I must be shunned by all.
　　　　　　　　　　　And I myself
Pronounced this malediction upon myself!　60
Think of it: I have touched you with these
　　　　　　　　　　　　　　　[hands,
These hands that killed your husband. What
　　　　　　　　　　　　　　[defilement!

Am I all evil, then? It must be so,　65
Since I must flee from Thebes, yet never again
See my own countrymen, my own country,
For fear of joining my mother in marriage
And killing Polybos, my father.
　　　　　　　　　　　　　Ah,　70
If I was created so, born to this fate,
Who could deny the savagery of God?

O holy majesty of heavenly powers!
May I never see that day! Never!
Rather let me vanish from the race of men　75
Than know the abomination destined me!
　　LEADER. We too, my lord, have felt dismay at
　　　　　　　　　　　　　　　[this.
But there is hope: you have yet to hear the
　　　　　　　　　　　　　　[shepherd.　80
　　OEDIPUS. Indeed, I fear no other hope is left
　　　　　　　　　　　　　　　[me.
　　IOCASTÊ. What do you hope for him when
　　　　　　　　　　　　　　[he comes?
　　OEDIPUS.　　This much:　85
If his account of the murder tallies with yours,
Then I am cleared.

IOCASTÊ.   What was it that I said
Of such importance?
  OEDIPUS.   Why, "marauders," you said,
Killed the King, according to this man's story.
5 If he maintains that still, if there were several,
Clearly the guilt is not mine: I was alone.
But if he says one man, singlehanded, did it,
Then the evidence all points to me.
  IOCASTÊ. You may be sure that he said there
10   [were several;
And can he call back that story now? He can
          [not.
The whole city heard it as plainly as I.
But suppose he alters some detail of it:
15 He can not ever show that Laïos' death
Fulfilled the oracle: for Apollo said
My child was doomed to kill him; and my
         [child—
Poor baby!—it was my child that died first.
20 No. From now on, where oracles are concerned,
I would not waste a second thought on any.
  OEDIPUS. You may be right.
      But come: let someone go
For the shepherd at once. This matter must be
25   [settled.
  IOCASTÊ. I will send for him.
I would not wish to cross you in anything,
And surely not in this.—Let us go in.
  [*Exeunt into the palace.*]

ODE II

Strophe 1
30 CHORUS. Let me be reverent in the ways of
         [right,
Lowly the paths I journey on;
Let all my words and actions keep
The laws of the pure universe
35 From highest Heaven handed down.
For Heaven is their bright nurse,
Those generations of the realms of light;
Ah, never of mortal kind were they begot,
Nor are they slaves of memory, lost in sleep:
40 Their Father is greater than Time, and ages not.

Antistrophe 1
The tyrant is a child of Pride
Who drinks from his great sickening cup

Recklessness and vanity,
Until from his high crest headlong
He plummets to the dust of hope.   45
That strong man is not strong.
But let no fair ambition be denied;
May God protect the wrestler for the State
In government, in comely policy,
Who will fear God, and on His ordinance wait.   50

Strophe 2
Haughtiness and the high hand of disdain
Tempt and outrage God's holy law;
And any mortal who dares hold
No immortal Power in awe
Will be caught up in a net of pain: 55
The price for which his levity is sold.
Let each man take due earnings, then,
And keep his hands from holy things,
And from blasphemy stand apart—
Else the crackling blast of heaven   60
Blows on his head, and on his desperate heart;
Though fools will honor impious men,
In their cities no tragic poet sings.

Antistrophe 2
Shall we lose faith in Delphi's obscurities,
We who have heard the world's core   65
Discredited, and the sacred wood
Of Zeus at Elis praised no more?
The deeds and the strange prophecies
Must make a pattern yet to be understood.
Zeus, if indeed you are lord of all,   70
Throned in light over night and day,
Mirror this in your endless mind:
Our masters call the oracle
Words on the wind, and the Delphic vision
        [blind! 75
Their hearts no longer know Apollo,
And reverence for the gods has died away.

SCENE III

[*Enter* IOCASTÊ.]
IOCASTÊ. Princes of Thebes, it has occurred to
        [me 80
To visit the altars of the gods, bearing
These branches as a suppliant, and this incense.
Our King is not himself: his noble soul

Is overwrought with fantasies of dread,
Else he would consider
The new prophecies in the light of the old.
He will listen to any voice that speaks disaster,
5 And my advice goes for nothing.
    [*She approaches the altar, R.*]
                         To you, then, Apollo,
Lycean lord,° since you are nearest, I turn in
                         [prayer.
10 Receive these offerings, and grant us
                         [deliverance
From defilement. Our hearts are heavy with
                         [fear
When we see our leader distracted, as helpless
15   [sailors
Are terrified by the confusion of their
                         [helmsman.
    [*Enter* MESSENGER.]
    MESSENGER. Friends, no doubt you can direct
20   [me:
Where shall I find the house of Oedipus,
Or, better still, where is the King himself?
    LEADER. It is this very place, stranger; he is
                         [inside.
25 This is his wife and mother of his children.
    MESSENGER. I wish her happiness in a happy
                         [house,
Blest in all the fulfillment of her marriage.
    IOCASTÊ. I wish as much for you: your
30   [courtesy
Deserves a like good fortune. But now, tell me:
Why have you come? What have you to say to
                         [us?
    MESSENGER. Good news, my lady, for your
35   [house and your husband.
    IOCASTÊ. What news? Who sent you here?
    MESSENGER.   I am from Corinth.
The news I bring ought to mean joy for you,
Though it may be you will find some grief in it.
40   IOCASTÊ. What is it? How can it touch us in
                         [both ways?
    MESSENGER. The people of Corinth, they say,
Intend to call Oedipus to be their king.
    IOCASTÊ. But old Polybos—is he not reigning
45   [still?
    MESSENGER. No. Death holds him in his

                         [sepulchre.
    IOCASTÊ. What are you saying? Polybos is
                         [dead?
    MESSENGER. If I am not telling the truth, may 50
                         [I die myself.
    IOCASTÊ [*to a* MAID-SERVANT]. Go in, go
                         [quickly; tell this to your master.

O riddlers of God's will, where are you now!
This was the man whom Oedipus, long ago, 55
Feared so, fled so, in dread of destroying him—
But it was another fate by which he died.
    [*Enter* OEDIPUS, *center.*]
    OEDIPUS. Dearest Iocastê, why have you sent
                         [for me? 60
    IOCASTÊ. Listen to what this man says, and
                         [then tell me
What has become of the solemn prophecies.
    OEDIPUS. Who is this man? What is his news
                         [for me? 65
    IOCASTÊ. He has come from Corinth to
                         [announce your father's death!
    OEDIPUS. Is it true, stranger? Tell me in your
                         [own words.
    MESSENGER. I can not say it more clearly: the 70
                         [King is dead.
    OEDIPUS. Was it by treason? Or by an attack
                         [of illness?
    MESSENGER. A little thing brings old men to
                         [their rest. 75
    OEDIPUS. It was sickness, then?
    MESSENGER.   Yes, and his many years.
    OEDIPUS. Ah!
Why should a man respect the Pythian hearth,°
                         [or 80
Give heed to the birds that jangle above his
                         [head?
They prophesied that I should kill Polybos,
Kill my own father; but he is dead and buried,
And I am here—I never touched him, never, 85
Unless he died of grief for my departure,
And thus, in a sense, through me. No. Polybos
Has packed the oracles off with him
                         [underground.
They are empty words. 90

IOCASTÊ.   Had I not told you so?
OEDIPUS. You had; it was my faint heart that
[betrayed me.
IOCASTÊ. From now on never think of those
5   [things again.
OEDIPUS. And yet—must I not fear my
[mother's bed?
IOCASTÊ. Why should anyone in this world be
[afraid,
10 Since Fate rules us and nothing can be foreseen?
A man should live only for the present day.

Have no more fear of sleeping with your
[mother:
How many men, in dreams, have lain with
15   [their mothers!
No reasonable man is troubled by such things.
     OEDIPUS. That is true; only—
If only my mother were not still alive!
But she is alive. I can not help my dread.
20   IOCASTÊ. Yet this news of your father's death
[is wonderful.
OEDIPUS. Wonderful. But I fear the living
[woman.
MESSENGER. Tell me, who is this woman that
25   [you fear?
OEDIPUS. It is Meropê, man; the wife of King
[Polybos.
MESSENGER. Meropê? Why should you be
[afraid of her?
30 OEDIPUS. An oracle of the gods, a dreadful
[saying.
MESSENGER. Can you tell me about it or are
[you sworn to silence?
OEDIPUS. I can tell you, and I will.
35 Apollo said through his prophet that I was the
[man
Who should marry his own mother, shed his
[father's blood
With his own hands. And so, for all these years
40 I have kept clear of Corinth, and no harm has
[come—
Though it would have been sweet to see my
[parents again.
MESSENGER. And is this the fear that drove
45   [you out of Corinth?
OEDIPUS. Would you have me kill my father?
MESSENGER.   As for that

You must be reassured by the news I gave you.
OEDIPUS. If you could reassure me, I would
[reward you. 50
MESSENGER. I had that in mind, I will confess:
[I thought
I could count on you when you returned to
[Corinth.
OEDIPUS. No: I will never go near my parents 55
[again.
MESSENGER. Ah, son, you still do not know
[what you are doing—
OEDIPUS. What do you mean? In the name of
[God tell me! 60
MESSENGER. —If these are your reasons for
[not going home.
OEDIPUS. I tell you, I fear the oracle may
[come true.
MESSENGER. And guilt may come upon you 65
[through your parents?
OEDIPUS. That is the dread that is always in
[my heart.
MESSENGER. Can you not see that all your
[fears are groundless? 70
OEDIPUS. How can you say that? They are
[my parents, surely?
MESSENGER. Polybos was not your father.
OEDIPUS.   Not my father?
MESSENGER. No more your father than the 75
[man speaking to you.
OEDIPUS. But you are nothing to me!
MESSENGER.   Neither was he.
OEDIPUS. Then why did he call me son?
MESSENGER.   I will tell you: 80
Long ago he had you from my hands, as a gift.
OEDIPUS. Then how could he love me so, if I
[was not his?
MESSENGER. He had no children, and his heart
[turned to you. 85
OEDIPUS. What of you? Did you buy me?
[Did you find me by chance?
MESSENGER. I came upon you in the crooked
[pass of Kithairon.
OEDIPUS. And what were you doing there? 90
MESSENGER.   Tending my flocks.
OEDIPUS. A wandering shepherd?
MESSENGER.   But your savior, son, that
[day.
OEDIPUS. From what did you save me? 95

MESSENGER.   Your ankles should tell you
                                          [that.
OEDIPUS. Ah, stranger, why do you speak of
                          [that childhood pain?
5   MESSENGER. I cut the bonds that tied your
                              [ankles together.
OEDIPUS. I have had the mark as long as I
                              [can remember.
MESSENGER. That was why you were given
10   [the name you bear.°
OEDIPUS. God! Was it my father or my
                          [mother who did it?
Tell me!
MESSENGER. I do not know. The man who
15   [gave you to me
Can tell you better than I.
OEDIPUS. It was not you that found me, but
                              [another?
MESSENGER. It was another shepherd gave
20   [you to me.
OEDIPUS. Who was he? Can you tell me who
                              [he was?
MESSENGER. I think he was said to be one of
                              [Laïos' people.
25   OEDIPUS. You mean the Laïos who was king
                              [here years ago?
MESSENGER. Yes; King Laïos, and the man
                      [was one of his herdsmen.
OEDIPUS. Is he still alive? Can I see him?
30   MESSENGER.   These men here
Know best about such things.
OEDIPUS.   Does anyone here
Know this shepherd that he is talking about?
Have you seen him in the fields, or in the town?
35   If you have, tell me. It is time things were made
                              [plain.
LEADER. I think the man he means is that
                              [same shepherd
You have already asked to see. Iocastê perhaps
40   Could tell you something.
OEDIPUS.   Do you know anything
About him, Lady? Is he the man we have
                              [summoned?
Is that the man this shepherd means?
45   IOCASTÊ.   Why think of him?
Forget this herdsman. Forget it all.
This talk is a waste of time.

the name you bear   *Oedipus* means *swollen-foot*

OEDIPUS.   How can you say that,
When the clues to my true birth are in my
                          [hands?   50
IOCASTÊ. For God's love, let us have no more
                          [questioning!
Is your life nothing to you?
My own is pain enough for me to bear.
OEDIPUS. You need not worry. Suppose my   55
                          [mother a slave,
And born of slaves: no baseness can touch you.
IOCASTÊ. Listen to me, I beg you: do not do
                          [this thing!
OEDIPUS. I will not listen; the truth must be   60
                          [made known.
IOCASTÊ. Everything that I say is for your
                          [own good!
OEDIPUS.   My own good
Snaps my patience, then; I want none of it.   65
IOCASTÊ. You are fatally wrong! May you
                          [never learn who you are!
OEDIPUS. Go, one of you, and bring the
                          [shepherd here.
Let us leave this woman to brag of her royal   70
                          [name.
IOCASTÊ. Ah, miserable!
That is the only word I have for you now.
That is the only word I can ever have.
[*Exit into the palace.*]   75
LEADER. Why has she left us, Oedipus? Why
                          [has she gone
In such a passion of sorrow? I fear this silence:
Something dreadful may come of it.
OEDIPUS.   Let it come!   80
However base my birth, I must know about it.
The Queen, like a woman, is perhaps ashamed
To think of my low origin. But I
Am a child of Luck; I cannot be dishonored.
Luck is my mother; the passing months, my   85
                          [brothers,
Have seen me rich and poor.
                          If this is so,
How could I wish that I were someone else?
How could I not be glad to know my birth?   90

ODE III

Strophe

CHORUS. If ever the coming time were known
To my heart's pondering,

Kithairon, now by Heaven I see the torches
At the festival of the next full moon,
And see the dance, and hear the choir sing
A grace to your gentle shade:
5 Mountain where Oedipus was found,
O mountain guard of a noble race!
May the god who heals us lend his aid,
And let that glory come to pass
For our king's cradling-ground.°

Antistrophe
10 Of the nymphs that flower beyond the years,
Who bore you, royal child,
To Pan of the hills or the timberline Apollo,
Cold in delight where the upland clears,
Or Hermês for whom Kyllenê's° heights are
15   [piled?
Or flushed as evening cloud,
Great Dionysos, roamer of mountains,
He—was it he who found you there,
And caught you up in his own proud
20 Arms from the sweet god-ravisher°
Who laughed by the Muses' fountains?°

SCENE IV

OEDIPUS. Sirs: though I do not know the man,
I think I see him coming, this shepherd we
                 [want:
25 He is old, like our friend here, and the men
Bringing him seem to be servants of my house.
But you can tell, if you have ever seen him.
  [*Enter* SHEPHERD *escorted by servants.*]
LEADER. I know him, he was Laïos' man. You
30   [can trust him.
OEDIPUS. Tell me first, you from Corinth: is
                [this the shepherd
We were discussing?
MESSENGER.   This is the very man.
35 OEDIPUS [*to* SHEPHERD]. Come here. No, look

And let that glory . . . cradling-ground i.e., let this
wonderful thing which I prophesy come true for
Kithairon
Kyllenê highest mountain in the Peloponnesus, sacred
to Hermes
god-ravisher nymph whom the chorus conjecture to
have been Oedipus' mother
Muses' fountains springs of Helicon, sacred to Apollo
and the Muses

               [at me. You must answer
Everything I ask.—You belonged to Laïos?
SHEPHERD. Yes: born his slave, brought up in
                [his house.
OEDIPUS. Tell me: what kind of work did you   40
                [do for him?
SHEPHERD. I was a shepherd of his, most of
                [my life.
OEDIPUS. Where mainly did you go for
              [pasturage?   45
SHEPHERD. Sometimes Kithairon, sometimes
              [the hills near-by.
OEDIPUS. Do you remember ever seeing this
              [man out there?
SHEPHERD. What would he be doing there?   50
               [This man?
OEDIPUS. This man standing here. Have you
             [ever seen him before?
SHEPHERD. No. At least, not to my
             [recollection.   55
MESSENGER. And that is not strange, my
             [lord. But I'll refresh
His memory: he must remember when we two
Spent three whole seasons together, March to
            [September,   60
On Kithairon or thereabouts. He had two
             [flocks;
I had one. Each autumn I'd drive mine home
And he would go back with his to Laïos'
           [sheepfold.—   65
Is this not true, just as I have described it?
SHEPHERD. True, yes; but it was all so long
             [ago.
MESSENGER. Well, then: do you remember,
           [back in those days,   70
That you gave me a baby boy to bring up as my
            [own?
SHEPHERD. What if I did? What are you
           [trying to say?
MESSENGER. King Oedipus was once that   75
           [little child.
SHEPHERD. Damn you, hold your tongue!
OEDIPUS.   No more of that!
It is your tongue needs watching, not this
            [man's.   80
SHEPHERD. My King, my Master, what is it I
           [have done wrong?
OEDIPUS. You have not answered his question
           [about the boy.

SHEPHERD. He does not know . . . He is only
               [making trouble . . .
OEDIPUS. Come, speak plainly, or it will go
               [hard with you.
5   SHEPHERD. In God's name, do not torture an
               [old man!
OEDIPUS. Come here, one of you; bind his
               [arms behind him.
SHEPHERD. Unhappy king! What more do you
10   [wish to learn?
OEDIPUS. Did you give this man the child he
               [speaks of?
SHEPHERD.   I did.
And I would to God I had died that very day.
15   OEDIPUS. You will die now unless you speak
               [the truth.
SHEPHERD. Yet if I speak the truth, I am
               [worse than dead.
OEDIPUS. Very well; since you insist upon
20   [delaying—
SHEPHERD. No! I have told you already that I
               [gave him the boy.
OEDIPUS. Where did you get him? From your
             [house? From somewhere else?
25   SHEPHERD. Not from mine, no. A man gave
               [him to me.
OEDIPUS. Is that man here? Do you know
             [whose slave he was?
SHEPHERD. For God's love, my King, do not
30   [ask me any more!
OEDIPUS. You are a dead man if I have to
             [ask you again.
SHEPHERD. Then . . . Then the child was from
             [the palace of Laïos.
35   OEDIPUS. A slave child? or a child of his own
             [line?
SHEPHERD. Ah, I am on the brink of dreadful
             [speech!
OEDIPUS. And I of dreadful hearing. Yet I
40   [must hear.
SHEPHERD. If you must be told, then . . .
       They say it was Laïos' child;
But it is your wife who can tell you about that.
OEDIPUS. My wife!—Did she give it to you?
45   SHEPHERD.   My lord, she did.
OEDIPUS. Do you know why?
SHEPHERD.   I was told to get rid of it.
OEDIPUS. An unspeakable mother!

SHEPHERD.   There had been prophecies . . .
OEDIPUS. Tell me.   50
SHEPHERD.   It was said that the boy would
             [kill his own father.
OEDIPUS. Then why did you give him over
            [to this old man?
SHEPHERD. I pitied the baby, my King,   55
And I thought that this man would take him
           [far away
To his own country.
        He saved him—but for what a fate!
For if you are what this man says you are,   60
No man living is more wretched than Oedipus.
    OEDIPUS. Ah God!
It was true!
        All the prophecies!
                —Now,   65
O Light, may I look on you for the last time!
I, Oedipus,
Oedipus, damned in his birth, in his marriage
           [damned,
Damned in the blood he shed with his own   70
           [hand!

[*He rushes into the palace.*]

ODE IV

Strophe 1
CHORUS. Alas for the seed of men.

What measure shall I give these generations
That breathe on the void and are void   75
And exist and do not exist?

Who bears more weight of joy
Than mass of sunlight shifting in images,
Or who shall make his thought stay on
That down time drifts away?   80

Your splendor is all fallen.

O naked brow of wrath and tears,
O change of Oedipus!
I who saw your days call no man blest—
Your great days like ghosts gone.   85

Antistrophe 1
That mind was a strong bow.

Deep, how deep you drew it then, hard archer,
At a dim fearful range,
And brought dear glory down!

You overcame the stranger—
5   The virgin with her hooking lion claws—
And though death sang, stood like a tower
To make pale Thebes take heart.

Fortress against our sorrow!

Divine king, giver of laws,
10 Majestic Oedipus!
No prince in Thebes had ever such renown,
No prince won such grace of power.

Strophe 2
And now of all men ever known
Most pitiful is this man's story:
15 His fortunes are most changed, his state
Fallen to a low slave's
Ground under bitter fate.

O Oedipus, most royal one!
The great door that expelled you to the light
20 Gave at night—ah, gave night to your glory:
As to the father, to the fathering son.

All understood too late.

How could that queen whom Laïos won,
The garden that he harrowed at his height,
25 Be silent when that act was done?

Antistrophe 2
But all eyes fail before time's eye,
All actions come to justice there.
Though never willed, though far down the deep
[past,
30 Your bed, your dread sirings,
Are brought to book at last.

Child by Laïos doomed to die,
Then doomed to lose that fortunate little death,
Would God you never took breath in this air
35 That with my wailing lips I take to cry:

For I weep the world's outcast.

Blind I was, and cannot tell why;
Asleep, for you had given ease of breath;
A fool, while the false years went by.

ÉXODOS

[*Enter, from the palace,* SECOND MESSENGER.]   40
2ND MESSENGER. Elders of Thebes, most
[honored in this land,
What horrors are yours to see and hear, what
[weight
Of sorrow to be endured, if, true to your birth,   45
You venerate the line of Labdakos!
I think neither Istros nor Phasis,° those great
[rivers,
Could purify this place of the corruption
It shelters now, or soon must bring to light—   50
Evil not done unconsciously, but willed.

The greatest griefs are those we cause
[ourselves.
LEADER. Surely, friend, we have grief enough
[already;   55
What new sorrow do you mean?
2ND MESSENGER.   The Queen is dead.
LEADER. Iocastê? Dead? But at whose hand?
2ND MESSENGER.   Her own.
The full horror of what happened you cannot   60
[know,
For you did not see it: but I, who did, will tell
[you
As clearly as I can how she met her death.

When she had left us,   65
In passionate silence, passing through the court,
She ran to her apartment in the house,
Her hair clutched by the fingers of both hands.
She closed the doors behind her; then, by that
[bed   70
Where long ago the fatal son was conceived—
That son who should bring about his father's
[death—
We heard her call upon Laïos, dead so many
[years,   75

Istros . . . Phasis the Danube and the Rion, conventional types of great rivers

And heard her wail for the double fruit of her
[marriage,
A husband by her husband, children by her
[child.
5 Exactly how she died I do not know:
For Oedipus burst in moaning and would not
[let us
Keep vigil to the end: it was by him
As he stormed about the room that our eyes
10 [were caught.
From one to another of us he went, begging a
[sword,
Cursing the wife who was not his wife, the
[mother
15 Whose womb had carried his own children and
[himself.
I do not know: it was none of us aided him,
But surely one of the gods was in control!
For with a dreadful cry
20 He hurled his weight, as though wrenched out
[of himself,
At the twin doors: the bolts gave, and he rushed
[in.
And there we saw her hanging, her body
25 [swaying
From the cruel cord she had noosed about her
[neck.
A great sob broke from him, heartbreaking to
[hear,
30 As he loosed the rope and lowered her to the
[ground.

I would blot out from my mind what happened
[next!
For the King ripped from her gown the golden
35 [brooches
That were her ornament, and raised them, and
[plunged them down
Straight into his own eyeballs, crying, "No
[more,
40 No more shall you look on the misery about
[me,
The horrors of my own doing! Too long you
[have known
The faces of those whom I should never have
45 [seen,
Too long been blind to those for whom I was
[searching!

From this hour, go in darkness!"And as he
[spoke,
He struck at his eyes—not once, but many   50
[times;
And the blood spattered his beard,
Bursting from his ruined sockets like red hail.
So from the unhappiness of two this evil has
[sprung,   55
A curse on the man and woman alike. The old
Happiness of the house of Labdakos
Was happiness enough: where is it today?
It is all wailing and ruin, disgrace, death—all
The misery of mankind that has a name—   60
And it is wholly and for ever theirs.
        LEADER. Is he in agony still? Is there no rest
[for him?
        2ND MESSENGER. He is calling for someone to
[lead him to the gates   65
So that all the children of Kadmos may look
[upon
His father's murderer, his mother's—no,
I can not say it!
                        And then he will leave Thebes,   70
Self-exiled, in order that the curse
Which he himself pronounced may depart from
[the house.
He is weak, and there is none to lead him,
So terrible is his suffering.   75
                        But you will see:
Look, the doors are opening; in a moment
You will see a thing that would crush a heart
[of stone.
        [*The central door is opened;* OEDIPUS, *blind-*   80
ed, is led in.]
        LEADER. Dreadful indeed for men to see.
Never have my own eyes
Looked on a sight so full of fear.

Oedipus!   85
What madness came upon you, what daemon
Leaped on your life with heavier
Punishment than a mortal man can bear?
No: I cannot even
Look at you, poor ruined one.   90
And I would speak, question, ponder,
If I were able. No.
You make me shudder.
        OEDIPUS. God.   God.

Is there a sorrow greater?
Where shall I find harbor in this world?
My voice is hurled far on a dark wind.
What has God done to me?
5   LEADER. Too terrible to think of, or to see.

Strophe 1
OEDIPUS. O cloud of night,
Never to be turned away: night coming on,
I can not tell how: night like a shroud!

My fair winds brought me here.
10   O God. Again
The pain of the spikes where I had sight,
The flooding pain
Of memory, never to be gouged out.
    LEADER. This is not strange.
15   You suffer it all twice over, remorse in pain,
Pain in remorse.

Antistrophe 1
OEDIPUS. Ah dear friend
Are you faithful even yet, you alone?
Are you still standing near me, will you stay
20   [here,
Patient, to care for the blind?
                  The blind man!
Yet even blind I know who it is attends me,
By the voice's tone—
25   Though my new darkness hide the comforter.
    LEADER. Oh fearful act!
What god was it drove you to rake black
Night across your eyes?

Strophe 2
OEDIPUS. Apollo. Apollo. Dear
30   Children, the god was Apollo.
He brought my sick, sick fate upon me.
But the blinding hand was my own!
How could I bear to see
When all my sight was horror everywhere?
35   LEADER. Everywhere; that is true.
    OEDIPUS. And now what is left?
Images? Love? A greeting even,
Sweet to the senses? Is there anything?
Ah, no, friends: lead me away.
40   Lead me away from Thebes.
              Lead the great wreck

And hell of Oedipus, whom the gods hate.
    LEADER. Your fate is clear, you are not blind
                  [to that.
Would God you had never found it out!   45

Antistrophe 2
OEDIPUS. Death take the man who unbound
My feet on that hillside
And delivered me from death to life! What life?
If only I had died,
This weight of monstrous doom   50
Could not have dragged me and my darlings
                  [down.
    LEADER. I would have wished the same.
    OEDIPUS. Oh never to have come here
With my father's blood upon me! Never   55
To have been the man they call his mother's
                  [husband!
Oh accurst! Oh child of evil,
To have entered that wretched bed—
              the selfsame one! 60
More primal than sin itself, this fell to me.
    LEADER. I do not know how I can answer you.
You were better dead than alive and blind.
    OEDIPUS. Do not counsel me any more. This
               [punishment 65
That I have laid upon myself is just.
If I had eyes,
I do not know how I could bear the sight
Of my father, when I came to the house of
                  [Death, 70
Or my mother: for I have sinned against them
                  [both
So vilely that I could not make my peace
By strangling my own life.
           Or do you think my children, 75
Born as they were born, would be sweet to my
                  [eyes?
Ah never, never! Nor this town with its high
                  [walls,
Nor the holy images of the gods.   80
              For I,
Thrice miserable!—Oedipus, noblest of all the
                  [line
Of Kadmos, have condemned myself to enjoy
These things no more, by my own malediction 85
Expelling that man whom the gods declared
To be a defilement in the house of Laïos.

After exposing the rankness of my own guilt,
How could I look men frankly in the eyes?
No, I swear it,
If I could have stifled my hearing at its source,
5 I would have done it and made all this body
A tight cell of misery, blank to light and sound:
So I should have been safe in a dark agony
Beyond all recollection.
                                    Ah Kithairon!
10 Why did you shelter me? When I was cast upon
                                              [you,
Why did I not die? Then I should never
Have shown the world my execrable birth.

Ah Polybos! Corinth, city that I believed
15 The ancient seat of my ancestors: how fair
I seemed, your child! And all the while this evil
Was cancerous within me!
                                    For I am sick
In my daily life, sick in my origin.

20 O three roads, dark ravine, woodland and way
Where three roads met: you, drinking my
                                        [father's blood,
My own blood, spilled by my own hand: can
                                        [you remember
25 The unspeakable things I did there, and the
                                              [things
I went on from there to do?
                              O marriage, marriage!
The act that engendered me, and again the act
30 Performed by the son in the same bed—
                                        Ah, the net
Of incest, mingling fathers, brothers, sons,
With brides, wives, mothers: the last evil
That can be known by men: no tongue can say
35 How evil!
              No. For the love of God, conceal me
Somewhere far from Thebes; or kill me; or hurl
                                              [me
Into the sea, away from men's eyes for ever.

40 Come, lead me. You need not fear to touch me.
Of all men, I alone can bear this guilt.
    [Enter CREON.]
    LEADER. We are not the ones to decide; but
                                        [Creon here
45 May fitly judge of what you ask. He only
Is left to protect the city in your place.

OEDIPUS. Alas, how can I speak to him? What
                                        [right have I
To beg his courtesy whom I have deeply
                                        [wronged? 50
    CREON. I have not come to mock you,
                                        [Oedipus,
Or to reproach you, either.
    [To ATTENDANTS.]—You, standing there:
If you have lost all respect for man's dignity, 55
At least respect the flame of Lord Helios:
Do not allow this pollution to show itself
Openly here, an affront to the earth
And Heaven's rain and the light of day. No,
                                        [take him 60
Into the house as quickly as you can.
For it is proper
That only the close kindred see his grief.
    OEDIPUS. I pray you in God's name, since
                                        [your courtesy 65
Ignores my dark expectation, visiting
With mercy this man of all men most execrable:
Give me what I ask—for your good, not for
                                        [mine.
    CREON: And what is it that you would have 70
                                        [me do?
    OEDIPUS. Drive me out of this country as
                                        [quickly as may be
To a place where no human voice can ever
                                        [greet me. 75
    CREON. I should have done that before now—
                                        [only,
God's will had not been wholly revealed to me.
    OEDIPUS. But his command is plain: the
                                        [parricide 80
Must be destroyed. I am that evil man.
    CREON. That is the sense of it, yes; but as
                                        [things are,
We had best discover clearly what is to be done.
    OEDIPUS. You would learn more about a man 85
                                        [like me?
    CREON. You are ready now to listen to the
                                        [god.
    OEDIPUS. I will listen. But it is to you
That I must turn for help. I beg you, hear me. 90

The woman in there—
Give her whatever funeral you think proper:
She is your sister.
                    —But let me go, Creon!

Let me purge my father's Thebes of the
                              [pollution
Of my living here, and go out to the wild hills,
To Kithairon, that has won such fame with me,
5   The tomb my mother and father appointed for
                              [me,
And let me die there, as they willed I should.
And yet I know
Death will not ever come to me through
10   [sickness
Or in any natural way: I have been preserved
For some unthinkable fate. But let that be.

As for my sons, you need not care for them.
They are men, they will find some way to live.
15 But my poor daughters, who have shared my
                              [table,
Who never before have been parted from their
                              [father—
Take care of them, Creon; do this for me.
20 And will you let me touch them with my hands
A last time, and let us weep together?
Be kind, my lord,
Great prince, be kind!
                    Could I but touch them,
25 They would be mine again, as when I had my
                              [eyes.
    [*Enter* ANTIGONE *and* ISMENE, *attended.*]
Ah, God!
Is it my dearest children I hear weeping?
30 Has Creon pitied me and sent my daughters?
        CREON. Yes, Oedipus: I knew that they were
                              [dear to you
In the old days, and know you must love them
                              [still.
35 OEDIPUS. May God bless you for this—and
                              [be a friendlier
Guardian to you than he has been to me!

Children, where are you?
Come quickly to my hands; they are your
40   [brother's—
Hands that have brought your father's once
                              [clear eyes
To this way of seeing—
                    Ah dearest ones,
45 I had neither sight nor knowledge then, your
                              [father
By the woman who was the source of his own
                              [life!
And I weep for you—having no strength to see
                              [you—, 50
I weep for you when I think of the bitterness
That men will visit upon you all your lives.
What homes, what festivals can you attend
Without being forced to depart again in tears?
And when you come to marriageable age,   55
Where is the man, my daughters, who would
                              [dare
Risk the bane that lies on all my children?
Is there any evil wanting? Your father killed
His father; sowed the womb of her who bore   60
                              [him;
Engendered you at the fount of his own
                              [existence!

That is what they will say of you.

                    Then, whom   65
Can you ever marry? There are no bridegrooms
                              [for you,
And your lives must wither away in sterile
                              [dreaming.

O Creon, son of Menoikeus!   70
You are the only father my daughters have,
Since we, their parents, are both of us gone for
                              [ever.
They are your own blood: you will not let them
Fall into beggary and loneliness;   75
You will keep them from the miseries that are
                              [mine!
Take pity on them; see, they are only children,
Friendless except for you. Promise me this,
Great Prince, and give me your hand in token   80
                              [of it.
    [CREON *clasps his right hand.*]
Children:
I could say much, if you could understand me,
But as it is, I have only this prayer for you: 85
Live where you can, be as happy as you can—
Happier, please God, than God has made your
                              [father!
    CREON. Enough. You have wept enough. Now
                              [go within. 90
    OEDIPUS. I must; but it is hard.
    CREON.   Time eases all things.
    OEDIPUS. But you must promise—

CREON.   Say what you desire.
OEDIPUS. Send me from Thebes!
CREON.   God grant that I may!
OEDIPUS. But since God hates me . . .
5   CREON.   No, he will grant your wish.
OEDIPUS. You promise?
CREON.   I can not speak beyond my
                              [knowledge.
OEDIPUS. Then lead me in.
10   CREON.   Come now, and leave your
                              [children.
OEDIPUS. No! Do not take them from me!
CREON.   Think no longer
That you are in command here, but rather think
15 How, when you were, you served your own
                              [destruction.

[*Exeunt into the house all but the* CHORUS;
the LEADER *chants directly to the audience.*]
    LEADER. Men of Thebes: look upon Oedipus.
20 This is the king who solved the famous riddle
And towered up, most powerful of men.
No mortal eyes but looked on him with envy,
Yet in the end ruin swept over him.

Let every man in mankind's frailty
25 Consider his last day; and let none
Presume on his good fortune until he find
Life, at his death, a memory without pain.

Aristophanes

447?–385? B.C.

Lysistrata

411 B.C.

Produced in the twentieth year of the Peloponnesian War, in which Athens at the ultimate sacrifice of her democracy and her sovereignty attempted to dominate the other city-states of Greece, *Lysistrata* is one of the most remarkable peace plays in world literature. It avails itself of neither pathos nor moral indignation, the stocks-in-trade of its genre. It mentions neither material nor spiritual cost. About death it is silent. Instead it deals broadly, explicitly, and always comically with sex—with full breasts, rounded buttocks, frankly admired vulvas (hairless in the high Greek fashion), then increasingly with phalluses monstrously, persistently, and futilely erect. For the women of Greece, all Greece, have joined the energetic and farsighted Lysistrata in a marital strike to end the war. The state of Greece, so runs the unspoken argument, should be one as husbands and wives should be one. If the men in their folly force divisions in the political sphere, then to bring them to their senses women will force divisions in the domestic sphere. In the end there will be reconciliation, and bodies both political and domestic will be reunited.

Lysistrata is a feminist play as well as a pacifist play, treating the masculine establishment with visible derision. On stage the women invariably best the men. Sprightly old women beat their doddering male coevals, the female battalions beat back the magistrate's policemen, and Lysistrata and her followers transform the irascible magistrate first into a woman, then into a corpse.

These feminine conquests, moreover, are as just as they are amusing. From start to finish the men are little better than overgrown adolescents, warring first because they have the money to afford it—as though war were some leisure-class sport—and secondly because they have, like idlers on a street corner, a positive instinct for trouble. ("We go to Sparta when we're sober," an Athenian says, "and look around to stir up trouble. And then we don't hear what they say—and as for what they *don't* say, we have all sorts of suspicions.") They like to dress in armor and visit the marketplace to clank and jangle and frighten the old marketwomen. Listening to the homely analogy in which Lysistrata likens statecraft to washing, carding, and blending a fleece of wool (an analogy comparable in imaginative force to those of the garden in Shakespeare's *Richard II* and of the hive in *Henry V*), they are conscious only of its lowly domesticity, not at all of its cogency. And it is perhaps just to see in their final capitulation a continuation of the frivolity of which the play has indicted them all along: the ambassadors are lured into peace at the sight of the naked statue of the goddess Reconciliation, coveting her anatomical territory as warriors covet geographical territory.

The women, to be sure, are not without frailty. The tipsy Calonice finds it almost impossible to keep the vow of abstinence ("O Lysistrata, I feel so weak in the knees"), and after five days the pact threatens to fall apart as the ladies backslide and desert in increasing numbers. Collectively, however, with Lysistrata's moral force to strengthen them, they hold out long enough for victory.

Structurally the play is remarkably tight, its parts balanced and interlocked, its different veins of comedy counterpointing one another. The plot is symmetrical, with the first part, the rising action that sets in motion the combined marital strike and the women's occupation of the Acropolis (site of the treasury), being about equal in length to the progress toward the conclusion. The play has, furthermore, formal and thematic unity from prologue through éxodos; the interactions between principal characters alternate with lively choral passages, and the whole elides from the tension of the posing of the problem to the calm of its resolution.

Perhaps the most notable aspect of the play is the high and happy religious solemnity of the éxodos. Gone now are the broad humor and the horseplay, the exposures of masculine and feminine frailty, the divisions within families and states. Now in the mood of reconciliation, Spartans and Athenians, husbands and wives, celebrate their unity, call on the gods to witness "peace and bonds of harmonious love," and leave the stage singing and dancing.

This is how wars and efforts to end wars may in fantasy be concluded. And Aristophanes, that very bawdy and very moral playwright, comes close to demonstrating that this is how they could end in fact.

Lysistrata

ARISTOPHANES

Translated into English Prose and Verse by Charles T. Murphy

CHARACTERS°

LYSISTRATA ⎫
CALONICE ⎬ *Athenian women*
MYRRHINE ⎭
LAMPITO   *a Spartan woman*
LEADER OF THE CHORUS OF OLD MEN
CHORUS OF OLD MEN
LEADER OF THE CHORUS OF OLD WOMEN
CHORUS OF OLD WOMEN
ATHENIAN MAGISTRATE
THREE ATHENIAN WOMEN
CINESIAS   *an Athenian, husband of* MYRRHINE
SPARTAN HERALD
SPARTAN AMBASSADORS
ATHENIAN AMBASSADORS
TWO ATHENIAN CITIZENS
CHORUS OF ATHENIANS
CHORUS OF SPARTANS

characters "As is usual in ancient comedy, the leading characters have significant names. Lysistrata is 'She who disbands the armies'; Myrrhine's name is chosen to suggest *myrton*, a Greek word meaning *pudenda muliebria*; Lampito is a celebrated Spartan name; Cinesias, although a real name in Athens, is chosen to suggest a Greek verb *kinein*, to move, then *to make love, to have intercourse;* and the name of his deme, Paionidai, suggests the verb *paiein*, which has about the same significance." [Translator's note.]

SCENE. *In Athens, beneath the Acropolis. In the center of the stage is the Propylaea, or gateway to the Acropolis; to one side is a small grotto, sacred to Pan. The Orchestra represents a slope leading up to the gate-way. It is early in the morning.* LYSISTRATA *is pacing impatiently up and down.*   5

PROLOGUE°

LYS. If they'd been summoned to worship the God of Wine, or Pan, or to visit the Queen of Love, why, you couldn't have pushed your way 10 through the streets for all the timbrels. But now there's not a single woman here—except my neighbor; here she comes. [*Enter* CALONICE.] Good day to you, Calonice.

CAL. And to you, Lysistrata. [*Noticing* LY- 15 SISTRATA'S *impatient air.*] But what ails you? Don't scowl, my dear; it's not becoming to you to knit your brows like that.

LYS. [*sadly*]. Ah, Calonice, my heart aches; I'm so annoyed at us women. For among men 20 we have a reputation for sly trickery—

CAL. And rightly too, on my word!

LYS. —but when they were told to meet here to consider a matter of no small importance, they lie abed and don't come.   25

CAL. Oh, they'll come all right, my dear. It's not easy for a woman to get out, you know. One is working on her husband, another is getting up the maid, another has to put the baby to bed, or wash and feed it.   30

LYS. But after all, there are other matters more important than all that.

CAL. My dear Lysistrata, just what is this matter you've summoned us women to consider? What's up? Something big?   35

LYS. Very big.

CAL. [*interested*]. Is it stout, too?

LYS. [*smiling*]. Yes indeed—both big and stout.

prologue the division of the text into its constituent parts—prologue, párodos, scenes, choral episodes, and éxodos—follows Dudley Fitts, *Aristophanes' Lysistrata: An English Version*, Harcourt Brace Jovanovich, Inc., 1954, 1962

CAL. What? And the women still haven't come?

LYS. It's not what you suppose; they'd come soon enough for *that*. But I've worked up some-
5 thing, and for many a sleepless night I've turned it this way and that.

CAL. [*in mock disappointment*]. Oh, I guess it's pretty fine and slender, if you've turned it this way and that.

10 LYS. So fine that the safety of the whole of Greece lies in us women.

CAL. In us women? It depends on a very slender reed then.

LYS. Our country's fortunes are in our hands;
15 and whether the Spartans shall perish—

CAL.: Good! Let them perish, by all means.

LYS. —and the Boeotians shall be completely annihilated.

CAL. Not completely! Please spare the eels.°

20 LYS. As for Athens, I won't use any such unpleasant words. But you understand what I mean. But if the women will meet here—the Spartans, the Boeotians, and we Athenians— then all together we will save Greece.

25 CAL. But what could women do that's clever or distinguished? We just sit around all dolled up in silk robes, looking pretty in our sheer gowns and evening slippers.

LYS. These are just the things I hope will save
30 us: these silk robes, perfumes, evening slippers, rouge, and our chiffon blouses.

CAL. How so?

LYS. So never a man alive will lift a spear against the foe—

35 CAL. I'll get a silk gown at once.

LYS. —or take up his shield—

CAL. I'll put on my sheerest gown!

LYS. —or sword.

CAL. I'll buy a pair of evening slippers.

40 LYS. Well then, shouldn't the women have come?

CAL. Come? Why, they should have *flown* here.

LYS. Well, my dear, just watch: they'll act in
45 true Athenian fashion—everything too late!

And now there's not a woman here from the shore or from Salamis.

CAL. They're coming, I'm sure; at daybreak they were laying—to their oars to cross the straits. 50

LYS. And those I expected would be the first to come—the women of Acharnae—they haven't arrived.

CAL. Yet the wife of Theagenes means to come: she consulted Hecate about it. [*Seeing* 55 *a group of women approaching.*] But look! Here come a few. And there are some more over here. Hurrah! Where do they come from?

LYS. From Anagyra.

CAL. Yes indeed! We've raised up quite a 60 stink from Anagyra° anyway.

[*Enter* MYRRHINE *in haste, followed by several other women.*]

MYR. [*breathlessly*]. Have we come in time, Lysistrata? What do you say? Why so quiet? 65

LYS. I can't say much for you, Myrrhine, coming at this hour on such important business.

MYR. Why, I had trouble finding my girdle in the dark. But if it's so important, we're here now; tell us. 70

LYS. No. Let's wait a little for the women from Boeotia and the Peloponnesus.

MYR. That's a much better suggestion. Look! Here comes Lampito now.

[*Enter* LAMPITO *with two other women.*] 75

LYS. Greetings, my dear Spartan friend. How pretty you look, my dear. What a smooth com- plexion and well-developed figure. You could throttle an ox.

LAM. Faith, yes, I think I could. I take exer- 80 cises and kick my heels against my bum. [*She demonstrates with a few steps of the Spartan "bottom-kicking" dance.*]

LYS. And what splendid breasts you have.

LAM. La! You handle me like a prize steer. 85

LYS. And who is this young lady with you?

LAM. Faith, she's an Ambassadress from Boeotia.

---

eels Boeotia was noted for its seafood, especially its eels

stink from Anagyra a punning reference to a prover- bial phrase. The deme or township of Anagyra took its name from an ill-smelling plant, to stir which meant, colloquially, to raise a stink.

Lys. Oh yes, a Boeotian, and blooming like a garden too.

Cal. [*lifting up her skirt*]. My word! How neatly her garden's weeded!°

5 Lys. And who is the other girl?

Lam. Oh, she's a Corinthian swell.

Myr. [*after a rapid examination*]. Yes indeed. She swells very nicely [*pointing*] here and here.

Lam. Who has gathered together this com-
10 pany of women?

Lys. I have.

Lam. Speak up, then. What do you want?

Myr. Yes, my dear, do tell us what this important matter is.

15 Lys. Very well, I'll tell you. But before I speak, let me ask you a little question.

Myr. Anything you like.

Lys. [*earnestly*]. Tell me: don't you yearn for the fathers of your children, who are away at
20 the wars? I know you all have husbands abroad.

Cal. Why, yes; mercy me! my husband's been away for five months in Thrace keeping guard on—Eucrates.°

Myr. And mine for seven whole months in
25 Pylus.

Lam. And mine, as soon as ever he returns from the fray, readjusts his shield and flies out of the house again.

Lys. And as for lovers, there's not even a
30 ghost of one left. Since the Milesians revolted from us,° I've not even seen an eight-inch dingus to be a leather consolation for us widows. Are you willing, if I can find a way, to help me end the war?

35 Myr. Goodness, yes! I'd do it, even if I had to pawn my dress and—get drunk on the spot!

Cal. And I, even if I had to let myself be split in two like a flounder.

Lam. I'd climb up Mt. Taygetus° if I could
40 catch a glimpse of peace.

Lys. I'll tell you, then, in plain and simple

words. My friends, if we are going to force our men to make peace, we must do without—

Myr. Without what? Tell us.

Lys. Will you do it? 45

Myr. We'll do it, if it kills us.

Lys. Well then, we must do without sex altogether. [*General consternation.*] Why do you turn away? Where go you? Why turn so pale? Why those tears? Will you do it or not? 50
What means this hesitation?

Myr. I won't do it! Let the war go on.

Cal. Nor I! Let the war go on.

Lys. So, my little flounder? Didn't you say just now you'd split yourself in half? 55

Cal. Anything else you like. I'm willing, even if I have to walk through fire. Anything rather than sex. There's nothing like it, my dear.

Lys. [*to* Myrrhine]. What about you? 60

Myr. [*sullenly*]. I'm willing to walk through fire, too.

Lys. Oh vile and cursed breed! No wonder they make tragedies about us: we're naught but "love-affairs and bassinets."° But you, my dear 65
Spartan friend, if you alone are with me, our enterprise might yet succeed. Will you vote with me?

Lam. 'Tis cruel hard, by my faith, for a woman to sleep alone without her nooky; but 70
for all that, we certainly do need peace.

Lys. O my dearest friend! You're the only real woman here.

Cal. [*wavering*]. Well, if we do refrain from —[*shuddering*] what you say (God forbid!), 75
would that bring peace?

Lys. My goodness, yes! If we sit at home all rouged and powdered, dressed in our sheerest gowns, and neatly depilated, our men will get excited and want to take us; but if you don't 80
come to them and keep away, they'll soon make a truce.

Lam. Aye; Menelaus caught sight of Helen's

---

weeded i.e., depilated

Eucrates an Athenian general who, according to un-verified tradition, was mercenary and traitorous

Milesians . . . us Milesia was recognized for its leather goods among which, apparently, were dildos, the lack of which Lysistrata here laments

Mt. Taygetus a mountain range looming over Sparta

"love-affairs and bassinets" Lysistrata's point seems to be that although women have passionate and ten-der experiences, which are the material of tragedy, they lack character, resolution, fortitude

naked breast and dropped his sword,° they say.

CAL. What if the men give us up?

LYS. "Flay a skinned dog," as Pherecrates°
5 says.

CAL. Rubbish! These make-shifts are no good. But suppose they grab us and drag us into the bedroom?

LYS. Hold on to the door.

10 CAL. And if they beat us?

LYS. Give in with a bad grace. There's no pleasure in it for them when they have to use violence. And you must torment them in every possible way. They'll give up soon enough; a
15 man gets no joy if he doesn't get along with his wife.

MYR. If this is your opinion, we agree.

LAM. As for our own men, we can persuade them to make a just and fair peace; but what
20 about the Athenian rabble? Who will persuade them not to start any more monkey-shines?

LYS. Don't worry. We guarantee to convince them.

LAM. Not while their ships are rigged so well
25 and they have that mighty treasure in the temple of Athene.

LYS. We've taken good care for that too: we shall seize the Acropolis today. The older women have orders to do this, and while we are
30 making our arrangements, they are to pretend to make a sacrifice and occupy the Acropolis.

LAM. All will be well then. That's a very fine idea.

LYS. Let's ratify this, Lampito, with the most
35 solemn oath.

LAM. Tell us what oath we shall swear.

LYS. All right? Where's our Policewoman? [To a Scythian slave.] What are you gaping at?

Set a shield upside-down here in front of me, and give me the sacred meats.   40

CAL. Lysistrata, what sort of an oath are we to take?

LYS. What oath? I'm going to slaughter a sheep over the shield, as they do in Aeschylus.°

CAL. Don't, Lysistrata! No oaths about peace 45
over a shield.

LYS. What shall the oath be, then?

CAL. How about getting a white horse somewhere and cutting out its entrails for the sacrifice?   50

LYS. White horse indeed!

CAL. Well then, how shall we swear?

MYR. I'll tell you: let's place a large black bowl upside-down and then slaughter—a flask of Thasian wine. And then let's swear—not to 55
pour in a single drop of water.

LAM. Lord! How I like that oath!

LYS. Someone bring out a bowl and a flask. [A slave brings the utensils for the sacrifice.]

CAL. Look, my friends! What a big jar! Here's 60
a cup that 'twould give me joy to handle. [She picks up the bowl.]

LYS. Set it down and put your hands on our victim. [As CALONICE places her hands on the flask.] O Lady of Persuasion and dear Loving 65
Cup, graciously vouchsafe to receive this sacrifice from us women. [She pours the wine into the bowl.]

CAL. The blood has a good color and spurts out nicely.   70

LAM. Faith, it has a pleasant smell, too.

MYR. Oh, let me be the first to swear, ladies!

CAL. No, by my Lady! Not unless you're alloted the first turn.

LYS. Place all your hands on the cup, and one 75
of you repeat on behalf of all what I say. Then all will swear and ratify the oath. *I will suffer no man, be he husband or lover,*

CAL. *I will suffer no man, be he husband or lover,*   80

LYS. *To approach me all hot and horny.* [As CALONICE hesitates.] Say it!

CAL. [slowly and painfully]. *To approach me*

Menelaus . . . sword in Euripides' *Andromache*, "Menelaus, about to stab his faithless wife, is overcome by her beauty and drops his sword." [Fitts's note.]

Pherecrates a comic writer none of whose work is extant. The quoted phrase seems tantamount to "carrying coals to Newcastle," but most translators assume that Aristophanes is twisting it ironically. One reads: "We'll have to take things into our own hands"; another: "We'd have to fall back on ourselves."

Aeschylus "In the *Seven against Thebes*." [Translator's note.]

all hot and horny. O Lysistrata, I feel so weak
in the knees!

Lys. *I will remain at home unmated,*

Cal. *I will remain at home unmated,*

5 Lys. *Wearing my sheerest gown and carefully
adorned,*

Cal. *Wearing my sheerest gown and carefully adorned,*

Lys. *That my husband may burn with desire*
10 *for me.*

Cal. *That my husband may burn with desire
for me.*

Lys. *And if he takes me by force against my
will,*

15 Cal. *And if he takes me by force against my
will,*

Lys. *I shall do it badly and keep from moving.*

Cal. *I shall do it badly and keep from mov-*
20 *ing.*

Lys. *I will not stretch my slippers toward the
ceiling,*

Cal. *I will not stretch my slippers toward the
ceiling,*

25 Lys. *Nor will I take the posture of the lioness
on the knife-handle.*°

Cal. *Nor will I take the posture of the lioness
on the knife-handle.*

Lys. *If I keep this oath, may I be permitted to*
30 *drink from this cup,*

Cal. *If I keep this oath, may I be permitted to
drink from this cup,*

Lys. *But if I break it, may the cup be filled
with water.*

35 Cal. *But if I break it, may the cup be filled
with water.*

Lys. Do you all swear to this?

All. I do, so help me!

Lys. Come then, I'll just consummate this
40 offering. [*She takes a long drink from the cup.*]

Cal. [*snatching the cup away*]. Shares, my
dear! Let's drink to our continued friendship.

[*A shout is heard from off-stage.*]

Lam. What's that shouting?

45 Lys. That's what I was telling you: the
women have just seized the Acropolis. Now,
Lampito, go home and arrange matters in Sparta; and leave these two ladies here as hostages.
We'll enter the Acropolis to join our friends
and help them lock the gates.   50

Cal. Don't you suppose the men will come
to attack us?

Lys. Don't worry about them. Neither threats
nor fire will suffice to open the gates, except
on the terms we've stated.   55

Cal. I should say not! Else we'd belie our
reputation as unmanageable pests.

[Lampito *leaves the stage, The other women
retire and enter the Acropolis through the
Propylaea.*]   60

[*Enter the* Chorus of Old Men, *carrying
fire-pots and a load of heavy sticks.*]

PÁRODOS

Leader of Men. Onward, Draces, step by
[step, though your shoulder's aching.
Cursèd logs of olive-wood, what a load you're   65
[making!
1st Semi-chorus of Old Men [*singing*].
Aye, many surprises await a man who lives to a
[ripe old age;
For who could suppose, Strymodorus my lad,   70
[that the women we've nourished (alas!),
Who sat at home to vex our days,
Would seize the holy image here,
And occupy this sacred shrine.
With bolts and bars, with fell design,   75
To lock the Propylaea?
Leader. Come with speed, Philourgus, come!
[to the temple hast'ning.
There we'll heap these logs about in a circle
[round them,   80
And whoever has conspired, raising this
[rebellion,
Shall be roasted, scorched, and burnt, all
[without exception,
Doomed by one unanimous vote—but first the   85
[wife of Lycon.°

---

posture . . . knife-handle i.e., on all fours

wife of Lycon Rhodia, the wife of the demagogue,
much lampooned for the laxness of her morality

2ND SEMI-CHORUS [singing].
No, no! by Demeter, while I'm alive, no woman
           [shall mock at me.
Not even the Spartan Cleomenes,° our citadel
5   [first to seize,
Got off unscathed; for all his pride
And haughty Spartan arrogance,
He left his arms and sneaked away,
Stripped to his shirt, unkempt, unshav'd,
10 With six years' filth still on him.
    LEADER. I besieged that hero bold, sleeping
           [at my station,
Marshalled at these holy gates sixteen deep
           [against him.
15 Shall I not these cursèd pests punish for their
           [daring,
Burning these Euripides-and-God-detested
           [women?
Aye! Or else may Marathon overturn my
20   [trophy.
    1ST SEMI-CHORUS [singing]. There remains of
           [my road
Just this brow of the hill;
There I speed on my way.
25 Drag the logs up the hill, though we've got no
           [ass to help.
(God! my shoulder's bruised and sore!)
Onward still must we go.
Blow the fire! Don't let it go out
30 Now we're near the end of our road.
    ALL [blowing on the fire-pots]. Whew!
           [Whew! Drat the smoke!
    2ND SEMI-CHORUS [singing]. Lord, what
           [smoke rushing forth
35 From the pot, like a dog
Running mad, bites my eyes!
This must be Lemnos-fire.° What a sharp and
           [stinging smoke!
Rushing onward to the shrine
40 Aid the gods. Once for all

Cleomenes a Spartan king who occupied the Acropolis for two days (not six years!) almost a hundred
years before the incidents of the play. The men of
the chorus would seem either extraordinarily old or
invested with a communal but unreliable memory.

Lemnos-fire according to Fitts, a bad pun, the Greek
words for Lemnos (an island in the Aegean) and for
sore eyes being similar

Show your mettle, Laches my boy!
To the rescue hastening all!
    ALL [blowing on the fire-pots]. Whew!
           [Whew! Drat the smoke!
[The chorus has now reached the edge of the 45
orchestra nearest the stage, in front of the
Propylaea. They begin laying their logs and
fire-pots on the ground.]
    LEADER. Thank heaven, this fire is still alive.
Now let's first put down these logs here and 50
place our torches in the pots to catch; then let's
make a rush for the gates with a battering-
ram. If the women don't unbar the gate at our
summons, we'll have to smoke them out.
    Let me put down my load. Ouch! That hurts! 55
[To the audience.] Would any of the generals
in Samos° like to lend a hand with this log?
[Throwing down a log.] Well, that won't break
my back any more, at any rate. [Turning to his
fire-pot.] Your job, my little pot, is to keep 60
those coals alive and furnish me shortly with a
red-hot torch.
    O mistress Victory, be my ally and grant me
to rout these audacious women in the Acropolis.
[While the men are busy with their logs and 65
fires, the CHORUS OF OLD WOMEN enters, carry-
ing pitchers of water.]
    LEADER OF WOMEN. What's this I see? Smoke
           [and flames? Is that a fire ablaze?
Let's rush upon them. Hurry up! They'll find 70
           [us women ready.
    1ST SEMI-CHORUS OF OLD WOMEN [singing].
With wingèd foot onward I fly,
Ere the flames consume Neodice;
Lest Critylla be overwhelmed 75
By a lawless, accurst herd of old men.
I shudder with fear. Am I too late to aid them?
At break of the day filled we our jars with water
Fresh from the spring, pushing our way straight
           [through the crowds. Oh, what a din! 80
Mid crockery crashing, jostled by slave-girls,
Sped we to save them, aiding our neighbors,
Bearing this water to put out the flames.
    2ND SEMI-CHORUS OF OLD WOMEN [singing].
Such news I've heard: doddering fools 85

Samos an island in the Aegean that was still allied to
Athens

Come with logs, like furnace-attendants,
Loaded down with three hundred pounds
Breathing many a vain, blustering threat,
That all these abhorred sluts will be burnt to
5   [charcoal.
O goddess, I pray never may they be kindled;
Grant them to save Greece and our men;
           [madness and war help them to end.
With this as our purpose, golden-plumed
10   [Maiden,°
Guardian of Athens, seized we thy precinct.
Be my ally, Warrior-maiden,
'Gainst these old men, bearing water with me.

[*The women have now reached their position*
15 *in the orchestra, and their* LEADER *advances*
toward the LEADER OF THE MEN.]

L. WOM. Hold on there! What's this, you utter scoundrels? No decent, God-fearing citizens would act like this.

20 L. MEN. Oho! Here's something unexpected: a swarm of women have come out to attack us.

L. WOM. What, do we frighten you? Surely you don't think we're too many for you. And yet there are ten thousand times more of us
25 whom you haven't even seen.

L. MEN. What say, Phaedria? Shall we let these women wag their tongues? Shan't we take our sticks and break them over their backs?

L. WOM. Let's set our pitchers on the ground;
30 then if anyone lays a hand on us, they won't get in our way.

L. MEN. By God! If someone gave them two or three smacks on the jaw, like Bupalus,° they wouldn't talk so much!

35 L. WOM. Go on, hit me, somebody! Here's my jaw! But no other bitch will bite a piece out of you before me.

L. MEN. Silence! or I'll knock out your— senility!

40 L. WOM. Just lay one finger on Stratyllis, I dare you!

L. MEN. Suppose I dust you off with this fist? What will you do?

---

golden-plumed Maiden Athene
Bupalus according to the poet Hipponax, Bupalus was the recipient, not the bestower, of smacks on the jaw

L. WOM. I'll tear the living guts out of you with my teeth.   45

L. MEN. No poet is more clever than Euripedes: "There is no beast so shameless as a woman."

L. WOM. Let's pick up our jars of water, Rhodippe.   50

L. MEN. Why have you come here with water, you detestable slut?

L. WOM. And why have you come with fire, you funeral vault? To cremate yourself?

L. MEN. To light a fire and singe your friends.   55

L. WOM. And I've brought water to put out your fire.

L. MEN. What? You'll put out my fire?

L. WOM. Just try and see!

L. MEN. I wonder: shall I scorch you with   60 this torch of mine?

L. WOM. If you've got any soap, I'll give you a bath.

L. MEN. Give *me* a bath, you stinking hag?

L. WOM. Yes—a bridal bath!   65

L. MEN. Just listen to her! What crust!

L. WOM. Well, I'm a free citizen.

L. MEN. I'll put an end to your bawling. [*The men pick up their torches.*]

L. WOM. You'll never do jury-duty again.   70 [*The women pick up their pitchers.*]

L. MEN. Singe her hair for her!

L. WOM. Do your duty, water! [*The women empty their pitchers on the men.*]

L. MEN. Ow! Ow! For heaven's sake!   75

L. WOM. Is it too hot?

L. MEN. What do you mean "hot"? Stop! What are you doing?

L. WOM. I'm watering you, so you'll be fresh and green.   80

L. MEN. But I'm all withered up with shaking.

L. WOM. Well, you've got a fire; why don't you dry yourself?

SCENE I

[*Enter an Athenian* MAGISTRATE, *accompanied by four Scythian policemen.*]   85

MAG. Have these wanton women flared up again with their timbrels and their continual

worship of Sabazius?° Is this another Adonis-
dirge upon the roof-tops—which we heard not
long ago in the Assembly? That confounded
Demostratus was urging us to sail to Sicily,
5 and the whirling women shouted, "Woe for
Adonis!"° And then Demostratus said we'd
best enroll the infantry from Zacynthus, and a
tipsy woman on the roof shrieked, "Beat your
breasts for Adonis!" And that vile and filthy
10 lunatic forced his measure through. Such license
do our women take.

L. MEN. What if you heard of the insolence
of these women here? Besides their other violent acts, they threw water all over us, and
15 we have to shake out our clothes just as if we'd
leaked in them.

MAG. And rightly too, by God! For we ourselves lead the women astray and teach them to
play the wanton; from these roots such notions
20 blossom forth. A man goes into the jeweler's
shop and says, "About that necklace you made
for my wife, goldsmith: last night, while she
was dancing, the fastening-bolt slipped out of
the hole. I have to sail over to Salamis today;
25 if you're free, do come around tonight and fit
in a new bolt for her." Another goes to the
shoe-maker, a strapping young fellow with
manly parts, and says, "See here, cobbler, the
sandal-strap chafes my wife's little—toe; it's so
30 tender. Come around during the siesta and
stretch it a little, so she'll be more comfortable."
Now we see the results of such treatment: here
I'm a special Councillor and need money to
procure oars for the galleys; and I'm locked
35 out of the Treasury by these women.

But this is no time to stand around. Bring up
crow-bars there! I'll put an end to their insolence. [*To one of the policemen.*] What are
you gaping at, you wretch? What are you star-
40 ing at? Got an eye out for a tavern, eh? Set your
crow-bars here to the gates and force them

open. [*Retiring to a safe distance.*] I'll help
from over here.

[*The gates are thrown open and* LYSISTRATA
comes out followed by several other women.] 45

LYS. Don't force the gates; I'm coming out
of my own accord. We don't need crow-bars
here; what we need is good sound commonsense.

MAG. Is that so, you strumpet? Where's my 50
policeman? Officer, arrest her and tie her arms
behind her back.

LYS. By Artemis, if he lays a finger on me,
he'll pay for it, even if he is a public servant.

[*The policeman retires in terror.*] 55

MAG. You there, are you afraid? Seize her
round the waist—and you, too. Tie her up,
both of you!

1ST WOMAN [*as the second policeman approaches* LYSISTRATA]. By Pandrosus,° if you 60
but touch her with your hand, I'll kick the
stuffings out of you.

[*The second policeman retires in terror.*]

MAG. Just listen to that: "kick the stuffings
out." Where's another policeman? Tie *her* up 65
first, for her chatter.

2ND WOMAN. By the Goddess of the Light,° if
you lay the tip of your finger on her, you'll
soon need a doctor.

[*The third policemen retires in terror.*] 70

MAG. What's this? Where's my policeman?
Seize *her* too. I'll soon stop your sallies.

3RD WOMAN. By the Goddess of Tauros,°
if you go near her, I'll tear out your hair until
it shrieks with pain. 75

[*The fourth policeman retires in terror.*]

MAG. Oh, damn it all! I've run out of policemen. But women must never defeat us. Officers,
let's charge them all together. Close up your
ranks! 80

Sabazius a Thracian and Phrygian deity whom the
   Greeks usually identified with Dionysus
Demostratus . . . Adonis Demostratus took a leading
   part in selling the disastrous Sicilian expedition to
   the Athenian assembly. Plutarch records the women's
   dirge for Adonis as among the evil omens precedent
   to the expedition.

Pandrosus goddess of the dew. Parker wonders if
   pandrosus (all-bedewing) may not have been another
   epithet for Artemis, "classical antiquity's best-at-
   tested virgin, who is otherwise invoked here in three
   out of the four instances"—Aristophanes, *Lysistrata*,
   Douglass Parker, trans., The Complete Greek Comedy, William Arrowsmith, ed. (Ann Arbor: The University of Michigan Press, 1964).
Goddess of the Light Artemis
Goddess of Tauros Artemis. Tauros is the Crimea.

[*The policemen rally for a mass attack.*]

LYS. By heaven, you'll soon find out that we have four companies of warrior-women, all fully equipped within!

5 MAG. [*advancing*]. Twist their arms off, men!

LYS. [*shouting*]. To the rescue, my valiant women!
O sellers-of-barley-green-stuffs-and-eggs,
O sellers-of-garlic, ye keepers-of-taverns, and
10 [vendors-of-bread,
Grapple! Smite! Smash!
Won't you heap filth on them? Give them a
[tongue-lashing!

[*The women beat off the policemen.*]

15 Halt! Withdraw! No looting on the field.

MAG. Damn it! My police-force has put up a very poor show.

LYS. What did you expect? Did you think you were attacking slaves? Didn't you know that
20 women are filled with passion?

MAG. Aye, passion enough—for a good
[strong drink!

L. MEN. O chief and leader of this land, why
[spend your words in vain?
25 Don't argue with these shameless beasts. You
[know not how we've fared:
A soapless bath they've given us; our clothes
[are soundly soaked.

L. WOM. Poor fool! You never should attack
30 [or strike a peaceful girl.
But if you do, your eyes must swell. For I am
[quite content
To sit unmoved, like modest maids, in peace
[and cause no pain;
35 But let a man stir up my hive, he'll find me
[like a wasp.

CHORUS OF MEN [*singing*].
O God, whatever shall we do with creatures like
[Womankind?
40 This can't be endured by any man alive.
[Question them!
Let us try to find out what this means.
To what end have they seized on this shrine,
This steep and rugged, high and holy,
45 Undefiled Acropolis?

L. MEN. Come, put your questions; don't
[give in, and probe her every statement.

For base and shameful it would be to leave this
[plot untested.

MAG. Well then, first of all I wish to ask her 50 this: for what purpose have you barred us from the Acropolis?

LYS. To keep the treasure safe, so you won't make war on account of it.

MAG. What? Do we make war on account of 55 the treasure?

LYS. Yes, and you cause all our other troubles for it, too. Peisander° and those greedy office-seekers keep things stirred up so they can find occasions to steal. Now let them do what they 60 like: they'll never again make off with any of this money.

MAG. What will you do?

LYS. What a question! We'll administer it
[ourselves. 65

MAG. *You* will administer the treasure?

LYS. What's so strange in that? Don't we administer the household money for you?

MAG. That's different.

LYS. How is it different? 70

MAG. We've got to make war with this money.

LYS. But that's the very first thing: you mustn't make war.

MAG. How else can we be saved? 75

LYS. We'll save you.

MAG. *You?*

LYS. Yes, we!

MAG. God forbid!

LYS. We'll save you, whether you want it or 80 not.

MAG. Oh! This is terrible!

LYS. You don't like it, but we're going to do it none the less.

MAG. Good God! it's illegal! 85

LYS. We *will* save you, my little man!

MAG. Suppose I don't want you to?

LYS. That's all the more reason.

MAG. What business have you with war and peace? 90

Peisander "Engineer of the oligarchic revolt which overthrew the Athenian constitution in May 411 and set up the Council of Four Hundred." [Parker's note.]

LYS. I'll explain.

MAG. [*shaking his fist*]. Speak up, or you'll smart for it.

LYS. Just listen, and try to keep your hands
5 still.

MAG. I can't. I'm so mad I can't stop them.

FIRST WOMAN. Then you'll be the one to smart for it.

MAG. Croak to yourself, old hag! [*To LY-*
10 *SISTRATA.*] Now then, speak up.

LYS. Very well. Formerly we endured the war for a good long time with our usual restraint, no matter what you men did. You wouldn't let us say "boo," although nothing you did suited
15 us. But we watched you well, and though we stayed at home we'd often hear of some terribly stupid measure you'd proposed. Then, though grieving at heart, we'd smile sweetly and say, "What was passed in the Assembly
20 today about writing on the treaty-stone?" "What's that to you?" my husband would say. "Hold your tongue!" And I held my tongue.

1ST WOMAN. But I wouldn't have—not I!

MAG. You'd have been soundly smacked, if
25 you hadn't kept still.

LYS. So I kept still at home. Then we'd hear of some plan still worse than the first; we'd say, "Husband, how could you pass such a stupid proposal?" He'd scowl at me and say,
30 "If you don't mind your spinning, your head will be sore for weeks. *War shall be the concern of Men.*"°

MAG. And he was right, upon my word!

LYS. Why right, you confounded fool, when
35 your proposals were so stupid and we weren't allowed to make suggestions?

"There's not a *man* left in the country," says one. "No, not one," says another. Therefore all we women have decided in council to make a
40 common effort to save Greece. How long should we have waited? Now, if you're willing to listen to our excellent proposals and keep silence for us in your turn, we still may save you.

MAG. We men keep silence for you? That's
45 terrible; I won't endure it!

LYS. Silence!

War ... Men   Homer, *Iliad* vi. 492. [Translator's note.]

MAG. Silence for *you*, you wench, when you're wearing a snood?° I'd rather die!

LYS. Well, if that's all that bothers you— here! take my snood and tie it round your head.   50 [*During the following words the women dress up the* MAGISTRATE *in women's garments.*] And *now* keep quiet! Here, take this spinning-basket, too, and card your wool with robes tucked up, munching on beans. *War shall be the con-*   55 *cern of Women!*

L. WOM. Arise and leave your pitchers, girls;
            [no time is this to falter.
We too must aid our loyal friends; our turn has
            [come for action.   60
CHORUS OF WOMEN [*singing*].
I'll never tire of aiding them with song and
            [dance; never may
Faintness keep my legs from moving to and fro
            [endlessly.   65
For I yearn to do all for my friends;
They have charm, they have wit, they have
            [grace,
With courage, brains, and best of virtues—
Patriotic sapience.   70

L. WOM. Come, child of manliest ancient
            [dames, offspring of stinging nettles,
Advance with rage unsoftened; for fair
            [breezes speed you onward.

LYS. If only sweet Eros and the Cyprian   75 Queen of Love° shed charm over our breasts and limbs and inspire our men with amorous longing and priapic spasms, I think we may soon be called Peacemakers among the Greeks.

MAG. What will you do?   80

LYS. First of all, we'll stop those fellows who run madly about the Marketplace in arms.

1ST WOM. Indeed we shall, by the Queen of Paphos.°

snood   the Greek word is variously translated *snood*, *fillet, wimple.* To the magistrate it signifies female inferiority.
Cyprian ... Love   Aphrodite
Queen of Paphos   Aphrodite, who was believed to have risen from the sea near Paphos in western Cyprus

LYS. For now they roam about the market, amid the pots and greenstuffs, armed to the teeth like Corybantes.

MAG. That's what manly fellows ought to do!

5 LYS. But it's so silly: a chap with a Gorgon-emblazoned shield buying pickled herring.

1ST WOM. Why, just the other day I saw one of those long-haired dandies who command our cavalry ride up on horseback and pour into his 10 bronze helmet the egg-broth he'd bought from an old dame. And there was a Thracian slinger too, shaking his lance like Tereus; he'd scared the life out of the poor fig-peddler and was gulping down all her ripest fruit.

15 MAG. How can you stop all the confusion in the various states and bring them together?

LYS. Very easily.

MAG. Tell me how.

LYS. Just like a ball of wool, when it's con-20 fused and snarled: we take it thus, and draw out a thread here and a thread there with our spindles; thus we'll unsnarl this war, if no one prevents us, and draw together the various states with embassies here and embassies there.

25 MAG. Do you suppose you can stop this dreadful business with balls of wool and spindles, you nit-wits?

LYS. Why, if *you* had any wits, you'd manage all affairs of state like our wool-working.

30 MAG. How so?

LYS. First you ought to treat the city as we do when we wash the dirt out of a fleece: stretch it out and pluck and thrash out of the city all those prickly scoundrels; aye, and card 35 out those who conspire and stick together to gain office, pulling off their heads. Then card the wool, all of it, into one fair basket of good-will, mingling in the aliens residing here, any loyal foreigners, and anyone who's in debt to 40 the Treasury; and consider that all our colonies lie scattered round about like remnants; from all of these collect the wool and gather it to-gether here, wind up a great ball, and then weave a good stout cloak for the democracy.

45 MAG. Dreadful! Talking about thrashing and winding balls of wool, when you haven't the slightest share in the war!

LYS. Why, you dirty scoundrel, we bear more than twice as much as you. First, we bear chil-dren and send off our sons as soldiers. 50

MAG. Hush! Let bygones be bygones!

LYS. Then, when we ought to be happy and enjoy our youth, we sleep alone because of your expeditions abroad. But never mind us married women: I grieve most for the maids 55 who grow old at home unwed.

MAG. Don't men grow old, too?

LYS. For heaven's sake! That's not the same thing. When a man comes home, no matter how grey he is, he soon finds a girl to marry. 60 But woman's bloom is short and fleeting; if she doesn't grasp her chance, no man is willing to marry her and she sits at home a prey to every fortune-teller.

MAG. [*coarsely*]. But if a man can still get 65 it up—

LYS. See here, you: what's the matter? Aren't you dead yet? There's plenty of room for you. Buy yourself a shroud and I'll bake you a honey-cake. [*Handing him a copper coin for* 70 *his passage across the Styx.*] Here's your fare! Now get yourself a wreath.

[*During the following dialogue the women dress up the* MAGISTRATE *as a corpse.*]

1ST WOM. Here, take these fillets. 75

2ND WOM. Here, take this wreath.

LYS. What do you want? What's lacking? Get moving; off to the ferry! Charon is calling you; don't keep him from sailing.

MAG. Am I to endure these insults? By God! 80 I'm going straight to the magistrates to show them how I've been treated.

LYS. Are you grumbling that you haven't been properly laid out? Well, the day after to-morrow we'll send around all the usual offer- 85 ings early in the morning.

[*The* MAGISTRATE *goes out still wearing his funeral decorations.* LYSISTRATA *and the women retire into the Acropolis.*]

CHORAL EPISODE

L. MEN. Wake, ye sons of freedom, wake! 90
    ['Tis no time for sleeping.
Up and at them, like a man! Let us strip for
    [action.

[*The* CHORUS OF MEN *remove their outer cloaks.*]

CHORUS OF MEN [*singing*].
Surely there is something here greater than
5   [meets the eye;
For without a doubt I smell Hippias' tyranny.°
Dreadful fear assails me lest certain bands of
                [Spartan men,
Meeting here with Cleisthenes,° have inspired
10   [through treachery
All these god-detested women secretly to
                [seize
Athens' treasure in the temple, and to stop that
                [pay
15 Whence I live at my ease.°
    L. MEN. Now isn't it terrible for them to advise the state and chatter about shields, being mere women?
    And they think to reconcile us with the
20 Spartans—men who hold nothing sacred any more than hungry wolves. Surely this is a web of deceit, my friends, to conceal an attempt at tyranny. But they'll never lord it over me; I'll be on my guard and from now on,
25 "The blade I bear   A myrtle spray shall wear."
I'll occupy the market under arms and stand next to Aristogeiton.
    Thus I'll stand beside him. [*He strikes the pose of the famous statue of tyrannicides, with*
30 *one arm raised.*] And here's my chance to take this accurst old hag and—[*striking the* LEADER OF WOMEN] smack her on the jaw!

    L. WOM. You'll go home in such a state your
                [Ma won't recognize you!
35 Ladies all, upon the ground let us place these
                [garments.

Hippias' tyranny Hippias, the last of the Tyrants of Athens, ruled 527–510 B.C.
Cleisthenes a notorious homosexual, also mentioned unmentionably [Fitts's phrase] at l. 8, p. 82.
stop . . . ease this phrase and l. 70, p. 69. ("You'll never do jury-duty again") make it reasonably clear that the basic source of income for the old men of the chorus is jury duty, for which they received three obols a day. The money, says Parker, "would naturally be stored inside the Citadel in the Treasury."

[*The* CHORUS OF WOMEN *remove their outer garments.*]

CHORUS OF WOM. [*singing*]. Citizens of
    [Athens, hear useful words for the state. 40
Rightly; for it nurtured me in my youth
                [royally.
As a child of seven years carried I the sacred
                [box;°
Then I was a Miller-maid, grinding at Athene's 45
                [shrine;
Next I wore the saffron robe and played
                [Brauronia's Bear;
And I walked as Basket-bearer, wearing chains
                [of figs, 50
As a sweet maiden fair.
    L. WOM. Therefore, am I not bound to give good advice to the city?
    Don't take it ill that I was born a woman, if I contribute something better than our present 55 troubles. I pay my share; for I contribute MEN. But you miserable old fools contribute nothing, and after squandering our ancestral treasure, the fruit of the Persian Wars, you make no contribution in return. And now, all on account of 60 you, we're facing ruin.
    What, muttering, are you? If you annoy me, I'll take this hard, rough slipper and—[*striking the* LEADER OF MEN] smack you on the jaw!

CHORUS OF MEN [*singing*]. This is outright 65
    [insolence! Things go from bad to worse.

carried . . . box "Since this passage is frequently cited as primary evidence for the *cursus honorum* of a high-born young girl in fifth-century Athens, here are the steps set forth a bit more explicitly: (1) *arrêphoros* ('relic-bearer') to Athene, one of four little girls who carried the Goddess' sacred objects in Her semi-annual festival of the *Arréphoria;* (2) *aletris* ('mill-girl') to the Founding Mother (doubtless Athene), one of the girls who ground the meal to be made into sacrificial cakes; (3) *arktos* ('she-bear') at the *Brauronia,* a festival of Artemis held every fifth year at Brauron in Attika, centering on a myth which told of the killing of a tame bear sacred to that goddess; and (4) *kanêphoros* ('basket-bearer'), the maiden who bore the sacrificial cake and led the procession at Athens' most important festivals, such as the City Dionysia and the Great Panathenaia." [Parker's note.]

If you're men with any guts, prepare to meet
[the foe.
Let us strip our tunics off! We need the smell
[of male

5 Vigor. And we cannot fight all swaddled up in
[clothes.
[*They strip off their tunics.*]
Come then, my comrades, on to the battle,
[ye who once to Leipsydrion° came;

10 Then ye were MEN. Now call back your
[youthful vigor.
With light, wingèd footstep advance,
Shaking old age from your frame.
L. MEN. If any of us give these wenches the

15 slightest hold, they'll stop at nothing: such is
their cunning.
They will even build ships and sail against us,
like Artemisia.° Or if they turn to mounting,
I count our Knights as done for: a woman's

20 such a tricky jockey when she gets astraddle,
with a good firm seat for trotting. Just look at
those Amazons that Micon painted, fighting on
horseback against men!
But we must throw them all in the pillory—

25 [*seizing and choking the* LEADER OF WOMEN]
grabbing hold of yonder neck!

CHORUS OF WOM. [*singing*]. 'Ware my anger!
[Like a boar 'twill rush upon you men.
Soon you'll bawl aloud for help, you'll be so

30 [soundly trimmed!
Come, my friends, let's strip with speed, and
[lay aside these robes;
Catch the scent of women's rage. Attack with
[tooth and nail!

35 [*They strip off their tunics.*]
Now then, come near me, you miserable man!
[you'll never eat garlic or black beans again.
And if you utter a single hard word, in rage I

[will "nurse" you as once
The beetle requited her foe.° 40
L. WOM. For you don't worry me; no, not so
long as my Lampito lives and our Theban
friend, the noble Ismenia.
You can't do anything, not even if you pass a
dozen—decrees! You miserable fool, all our 45
neighbors hate you. Why, just the other day
when I was holding a festival for Hecate, I invited as a playmate from our neighbors the
Boeotians a charming, well-bred Copaic—eel.
But they refused to send me one on account of 50
your decrees.

And you'll never stop passing decrees until I
grab your foot and—[*tripping up the* LEADER
OF MEN] toss you down and break your neck!

[*Here an interval of five days is supposed to* 55
elapse.]

SCENE II

[LYSISTRATA *comes out from the Acropolis.*]
L. WOM. [*dramatically*]. Empress of this great
[emprise and undertaking,
Why come you forth, I pray, with frowning 60
[brow?
LYS. Ah, these cursèd women! Their deeds
and female notions make me pace up and down
in utter despair.
L. WOM. Ah, what sayest thou? 65
LYS. The truth, alas! the truth.
L. WOM. What dreadful tale hast thou to
tell thy friends?
LYS. 'Tis shame to speak, and not to speak
is hard. 70
L. WOM. Hide not from me whatever woes
we suffer.
LYS. Well then, to put it briefly, we want—
laying!
L. WOM. O Zeus, Zeus! 75
LYS. Why call on Zeus? That's the way things

Leipsydrion a mountain slope north of Athens where,
a century before the time of the play, the exiled
Alkmaionids or Patriots for a time fought off the
the forces of the tyrant Hippias

Artemisia "Queen of Halikarnassos, who, as an ally
of the Persian King Xerxes in his invasion of Greece,
fought with particular distinction at the sea battle
of Salamis in 480." [Parker's note.]

beetle . . . foe Aesop's fable (No. 223), *The Eagle
and the Beetle* [translator's note]. Injured by the
eagle, the beetle retaliated by breaking the eagle's
eggs wherever they were laid—even in the bosom
of Zeus.

are. I can no longer keep them away from the men, and they're all deserting. I caught one wriggling through a hole near the grotto of Pan, another sliding down a rope, another de-
5 serting her post; and yesterday I found one getting on a sparrow's back to fly off to Orsilochus,° and had to pull her back by the hair. They're digging up all sorts of excuses to get home. Look, here comes one of them now. [*A*
10 *woman comes hastily out of the Acropolis.*] Here you! Where are you off to in such a hurry?

1st Wom. I want to go home. My very best wool is being devoured by moths.

Lys. Moths? Nonsense! Go back inside.

15 1st Wom. I'll come back; I swear it. I just want to lay it out on the bed.

Lys. Well, you won't lay it out, and you won't go home, either.

1st Wom. Shall I let my wool be ruined?

20 Lys. If necessary, yes. [*Another woman comes out.*]

2nd Wom. Oh dear! Oh dear! My precious flax! I left it at home all unpeeled.

Lys. Here's another one, going home for her
25 "flax." Come back here!

2nd Wom. But I just want to work it up a little and then I'll be right back.

Lys. No indeed! If you start this, all the other women will want to do the same. [*A third*
30 *woman comes out.*]

3rd Wom. O Eilithyia, goddess of travail, stop my labor till I come to a lawful spot!

Lys. What's this nonsense?

3rd Wom. I'm going to have a baby—right
35 now!

Lys. But you weren't even pregnant yesterday.

3rd Wom. Well, I am today. O Lysistrata, do send me home to see a midwife, right away.

40 Lys. What are you talking about? [*Putting her hand on her stomach.*] What's this hard lump here?

3rd Wom. A little boy.

Lys. My goodness, what have you got there?
45 It seems hollow; I'll just find out. [*Pulling aside her robe.*] Why, you silly goose, you've got

Orsilochus keeper of a brothel

Athene's sacred helmet there. And you said you were having a baby!

3rd Wom. Well, I *am* having one, I swear!

Lys. Then what's this helmet for? 50

3rd Wom. If the baby starts coming while I'm still in the Acropolis, I'll creep into this like a pigeon and give birth to it there.

Lys. Stuff and nonsense! It's plain enough what you're up to. You just wait here for the 55 christening of this—helmet.

3rd Wom. But I can't sleep in the Acropolis since I saw the sacred snake.

1st Wom. And I'm dying for lack of sleep: the hooting of the owls keeps me awake. 60

Lys. Enough of these shams, you wretched creatures. You want your husbands, I suppose. Well, don't you think they want us? I'm sure they're spending miserable nights. Hold out, my friends, and endure for just a little while. 65 There's an oracle that we shall conquer, if we don't split up. [*Producing a roll of paper.*] Here it is.

1st Wom. Tell us what it says.

Lys. Listen. 70
"When in the length of time the Swallows shall
[gather together,
Fleeing the Hoopoe's amorous flight and the
[Cockatoo shunning,
Then shall your woes be ended and Zeus who 75
[thunders in heaven
Set what's below on top—"
1st Wom. What? Are we going to be on top?
Lys. "But if the Swallows rebel and flutter
[away from the temple, 80
Never a bird in the world shall seem more
[wanton and worthless."
1st Wom. That's clear enough, upon my word!

Lys. By all that's holy, let's not give up the 85 struggle now. Let's go back inside. It would be a shame, my dear friends, to disobey the oracle. [*The women all retire to the Acropolis again.*]

CHORAL EPISODE

Chorus of Men [*singing*]. I have a tale to tell, Which I know full well. 90
It was told me

In the nursery.

Once there was a likely lad,
   Melanion they name him;
The thought of marriage made him mad,
5   For which I cannot blame him.

So off he went to mountains fair;
   (No women to upbraid him!)
A mighty hunter of the hare,
   He had a dog to aid him.

10 He never came back home to see
   Detested women's faces.
He showed a shrewd mentality.
   With him I'd fain change places!

ONE OF THE MEN [*to one of the women*].
15 Come here, old dame; give me a kiss.
   WOM. You'll ne'er eat garlic, if you dare!
   MAN. I want to kick you—just like this!
   WOM. Oh, there's a leg with bushy hair!
   MAN. Myronides and Phormio°
20 Were hairy—and they thrashed the foe.

CHORUS OF WOMEN [*singing*]. I have another
                            [tale,
With which to assail
   Your contention
25   'Bout Melanion.

Once upon a time a man
   Named Timon left our city,
To live in some deserted land.
   (We thought him rather witty.)

30 He dwelt alone amidst the thorn;
   In solitude he brooded.
From some grim Fury he was born:
   Such hatred he exuded.

He cursed you men, as scoundrels through
35   And through, till life he ended.
He couldn't stand the sight of YOU!
   But women he befriended.

Myronides and Phormio respectively a victorious
   Athenian general, admiral

WOM. [*to one of the men*]. I'll smash your
                            [face in, if you like.
MAN. Oh no, please don't! You frighten me. 40
WOM. I'll lift my foot—and thus I'll strike.
MAN. Aha! Look there! What's that I see?
WOM. Whate'er you see, you cannot say
That I'm not neatly trimmed today.

SCENE III

[LYSISTRATA *appears on the wall of the Acrop-* 45
olis.]
   LYS. Hello! Hello! Girls, come here quick!
[*Several women appear beside her.*]
   WOM. What is it? Why are you calling?
   LYS. I see a man coming: he's in a dreadful 50
state. He's mad with passion. O Queen of
Cyprus, Cythera, and Paphos, just keep on
this way!
   WOM. Where is the fellow?
   LYS. There, beside the shrine of Demeter. 55
   WOM. Oh yes, so he is. Who is he?
   LYS. Let's see. Do any of you know him?
   MYR. Yes indeed. That's my husband, Cin-
esias.
   LYS. It's up to you, now: roast him, rack him, 60
fool him, love him—and leave him! Do every-
thing, except what our oath forbids.
   MYR. Don't worry; I'll do it.
   LYS. I'll stay here to tease him and warm him
up a bit. Off with you. 65
[*The other women retire from the wall. Enter*
CINESIAS *followed by a slave carrying a baby.*
CINESIAS *is obviously in great pain and distress.*]
   CIN. [*groaning*]. Oh-h! Oh-h-h! This is kill-
ing me! O God, what tortures I'm suffering! 70
   LYS. [*from the wall*]. Who's that within our
lines?
   CIN. Me.
   LYS. A *man*?
   CIN. [*pointing*]. A *man*, indeed! 75
   LYS. Well, go away!
   CIN. Who are you to send me away?
   LYS. The captain of the guard.
   CIN. Oh, for heaven's sake, call out Myrrhine
for me. 80
   LYS. Call Myrrhine? Nonsense! Who are
you?

CIN. Her husband, Cinesias of Paionidai.

LYS. [*appearing much impressed*]. Oh, greetings, friend. Your name is not without honor here among us. Your wife is always talking about you, and whenever she takes an egg or an apple, she says, "Here's to my dear Cinesias!"

CIN. [*quivering with excitement*]. Oh, ye gods in heaven!

LYS. Indeed she does! And whenever our conversations turn to men, your wife immediately says, "All men are mere rubbish compared with Cinesias."

CIN. [*groaning*]. Oh! Do call her for me.

LYS. Why should I? What will you give me?

CIN. Whatever you want. All I have is yours —and you see what I've got!

LYS. Well then, I'll go down and call her. [*She descends.*]

CIN. And hurry up! I've had no joy of life ever since she left home. When I go in the house, I feel awful: everything seems so empty and I can't enjoy my dinner. I'm in such a state all the time!

MYR. [*from behind the wall*]. I *do* love him so. But he won't let me love him. No, no! Don't ask me to see him!

CIN. O my darling, O Myrrhine honey, why do you do this to me? [MYRRHINE *appears on the wall.*] Come down here!

MYR. No, I won't come down.

CIN. Won't you come, Myrrhine, when *I* call you?

MYR. No; you don't want me.

CIN. *Don't want you?* I'm in agony!

MYR. I'm going now.

CIN. Please don't! At least, listen to your baby. [*To the baby.*] Here you, call your mamma! [*Pinching the baby.*]

BABY. Ma-ma! Ma-ma! Ma-ma!

CIN. [*to* MYRRHINE]. What's the matter with you? Have you no pity for your child, who hasn't been washed or fed for five whole days?

MYR. Oh, poor child; your father pays no attention to you.

CIN. Come down then, you heartless wretch, for the baby's sake.

MYR. Oh, what it is to be a mother! I've got

to come down, I suppose. [*She leaves the wall and shortly reappears at the gate.*]

CIN. [*to himself*]. She seems much younger, and she has such a sweet look about her. Oh, the way she teases me! And her pretty, provoking ways make me burn with longing.

MYR. [*coming out of the gate and taking the baby*]. O my sweet little angel. Naughty papa! Here, let Mummy kiss you, Mamma's little sweetheart! [*She fondles the baby lovingly.*]

CIN. [*in despair*]. You heartless creature, why do you do this? Why follow these other women and make both of us suffer so? [*He tries to embrace her.*]

MYR. Don't touch me!

CIN. You're letting all our things at home go to wrack and ruin.

MYR. I don't care.

CIN. You don't care that your wool is being plucked to pieces by the chickens?

MYR. Not in the least.

CIN. And you haven't celebrated the rites of Aphrodite for ever so long. Won't you come home?

MYR. Not on your life, unless you men make a truce and stop the war.

CIN. Well then, if that pleases you, we'll do it.

MYR. Well then, if that pleases *you*, I'll come home—afterwards! Right now I'm on oath not to.

CIN. Then just lie down here with me for a moment.

MYR. No—[*in a teasing voice*] and yet, I won't say I don't love you.

CIN. You love me? Oh, do lie down here, Myrrhine dear!

MYR. What, you silly fool! in front of the baby?

CIN. [*hastily thrusting the baby at the slave*]. Of course not. Here—home! Take him, Manes! [*The slave goes off with the baby.*] See, the baby's out of the way. Now won't you lie down?

MYR. But where, my dear?

CIN. Where? The grotto of Pan's a lovely spot.

MYR. How could I purify myself before returning to the shrine?

CIN. Easily: just wash here in the Clepsydra.

MYR. And then, shall I go back on my oath?

CIN. On my head be it! Don't worry about
5 the oath.

MYR. All right, then. Just let me bring out a
bed.

CIN. No, don't. The ground's all right.

MYR. Heavens, no! Bad as you are, I won't
10 let you lie on the bare ground. [*She goes into
the Acropolis.*]

CIN. Why, she really loves me; it's plain to
see.

MYR. [*returning with a bed*]. There! Now
15 hurry up and lie down. I'll just slip off this
dress. But—let's see: oh yes, I must fetch a
mattress.

CIN. Nonsense! No mattress for me.

MYR. Yes indeed! It's not nice on the bare
20 springs.

CIN. Give me a kiss.

MYR. [*giving him a hasty kiss*]. There! [*She
goes.*]

CIN. [*in mingled distress and delight*]. Oh-h!
25 Hurry back!

MYR. [*returning with a mattress*]. Here's the
mattress; lie down on it. I'm taking my things
off now—but—let's see: you have no pillow.

CIN. I don't *want* a pillow!

30 MYR. But I do. [*She goes.*]

CIN. Cheated again, just like Heracles and his
dinner!°

MYR. [*returning with a pillow*]. Here lift your
head. [*To herself, wondering how else to tease
35 him.*] Is that all?

CIN. Surely that's all! Do come here, precious!

MYR. I'm taking off my girdle. But remember: don't go back on your promise about the
40 truce.

CIN. Hope to die, if I do.

MYR. You don't have a blanket.

CIN. [*shouting in exasperation*]. *I don't want*

one! I WANT TO—

MYR. Sh-h! There, there, I'll be back in a 45
minute. [*She goes.*]

CIN. She'll be the death of me with these bed-
clothes.

MYR. [*returning with a blanket*]. Here, get
up. 50

CIN. I've got *this* up!

MYR. Would you like some perfume?

CIN. Good heavens, no! I won't have it!

MYR. Yes, you shall, whether you want it or
not. [*She goes.*] 55

CIN. O lord! Confound all perfumes anyway!

MYR. [*returning with a flask*]. Stretch out
your hand and put some on.

CIN. [*suspiciously*]. By God, I don't much
like this perfume. It smacks of shilly-shallying, 60
and has no scent of the marriage-bed.

MYR. Oh dear! This is Rhodian perfume I've
brought.

CIN. It's quite all right dear. Never mind.

MYR. Don't be silly! [*She goes out with the* 65
flask.]

CIN. Damn the man who first concocted
perfumes!

MYR. [*returning with another flask*]. Here,
try this flask. 70

CIN. I've got another one all ready for you.
Come, you wretch, lie down and stop bringing
me things.

MYR. All right; I'm taking off my shoes. But,
my dear, see that you vote for peace. 75

CIN. [*absently*]. I'll consider it. [MYRRHINE
runs away to the Acropolis.] I'm ruined! The
wench has skinned me and run away! [*Chanting, in tragic style.*] Alas! Alas! Deceived, deserted by this fairest of women, whom shall I— 80
lay? Ah, my poor child, how shall I nurture
thee? Where's Cynalopex?° I needs must hire
a nurse!

L. MEN. [*chanting*]. Ah, wretched man, in
dreadful wise beguiled, bewrayed, thy soul is 85
sore distressed. I pity thee, alas! alas! What
soul, what loins, what liver could stand this

Heracles . . . dinner "A stock comeay bit wherein the
glutton hero, raving with hunger, is systematically
diddled of his dinner by his hosts." [Parker's note.]

Cynalopex a pimp. The "poor little child" in the preceding line is Cinesias's phallus.

strain? How firm and unyielding he stands,
with naught to aid him of a morning.

CIN. O lord! O Zeus! What tortures I endure!

L. MEN. This is the way she's treated you,
5 that vile and cursèd wanton.

L. WOM. Nay, not vile and cursèd, but sweet
and dear.

L. MEN. Sweet, you say? Nay, hateful, hateful!

10 CIN. Hateful indeed! O Zeus, Zeus!
Seize her and snatch her away,
Like a handful of dust, in a mighty,
Fiery tempest! Whirl her aloft, then let her
                                                    [drop
15 Down to the earth, with a crash, as she falls—
On the point of this waiting
Thingummybob! [*He goes out.*]

SCENE IV

[*Enter a* Spartan HERALD *in an obvious state
of excitement, which he is doing his best to
20 conceal.*]

HER. Where can I find the Senate or the
Prytanes?° I've got an important message. [*The
Athenian* MAGISTRATE *enters.*]

MAG. Say there, are you a man or Priapus?

25 HER. [*in annoyance*]. I'm a herald, you lout!
I've come from Sparta about the truce.

MAG. Is that a spear you've got under your
cloak?

HER. No, of course not!

30 MAG. Why do you twist and turn so? Why
hold your cloak in front of you? Did you rupture yourself on the trip?

HER. By gum, the fellow's an old fool.

MAG. [*pointing*]. Why, you dirty rascal,
35 you're all excited.

HER. Not at all. Stop this tom-foolery.

MAG. Well, what's that I see?

HER. A Spartan message-staff.

MAG. Oh, certainly! That's just the kind of
40 message-staff I've got. But tell me the honest
truth: how are things going in Sparta?

Prytanes   members of the executive committee of the
Senate

HER. All the land of Sparta is up in arms—
and our allies are up, too. We need Pellene.°

MAG. What brought this trouble on you? A
sudden Panic?   45

HER. No, Lampito started it and then all
the other women in Sparta with one accord
chased their husbands out of their beds.

MAG. How do you feel?

HER. Terrible. We walk around the city bent 50
over like men lighting matches in a wind. For
our women won't let us touch them until we all
agree and make peace throughout Greece.

MAG. This is a general conspiracy of the
women; I see it now. Well, hurry back and tell 55
the Spartans to send ambassadors here with full
powers to arrange a truce. And I'll go tell the
Council to choose ambassadors from here; I've
got a little something here that will persuade
them!   60

HER. I'll fly there; for you've made an excellent suggestion.

[*The* HERALD *and the* MAGISTRATE *depart on
opposite sides of the stage.*]

CHORAL EPISODE

L. MEN. No beast or fire is harder than   65
                            [womankind to tame,
Nor is the spotted leopard so devoid of shame.

L. WOM. Knowing this, you dare provoke us
                                        [to attack?
I'd be your steady friend, if you'd but take us 70
                                            [back.

L. MEN. I'll never cease my hatred keen of
                                    [womankind.

L. WOM. Just as you will. But now just let
                            [me help you find 75
That cloak you threw aside. You look so silly
                                            [there
Without your clothes. Here, put it on and don't
                                        [go bare.

Pellene   a petty state allied with Sparta. Commentators
differ as to the point here. Perhaps it's that, after the
string of double entendres, one expects yet another
or the plain truth (they need women) and receives
instead an answer merely military and, given the
relative unimportance of Pellene, comically unsatis-
factory.

L. Men. That's very kind, and shows you're
[not entirely bad.
But I threw off my things when I was good and
[mad.
5 L. Wom. At last you seem a man, and won't
[be mocked, my lad.
If you'd been nice to me, I'd take this little
[gnat
That's in your eye and pluck it out for you,
10 [like that.
L. Men. So that's what's bothered me and bit
[my eye so long!
Please dig it out for me. I own that I've been
[wrong.
15 L. Wom. I'll do so, though you've been a most
[ill-natured brat.
Ye gods! See here! A huge and monstrous little
[gnat!
L. Men. Oh, how that helps! For it was
20 [digging wells in me.
And now it's out, my tears are flowing fast and
[free.
L. Wom. Here, let me wipe them off, although
[you're such a knave,
25 And kiss me.
L. Men.   No!
L. Wom.   Whate'er you say, a kiss I'll
[have. [*She kisses him.*]
L. Men. Oh, confound these women! They've
30 [a coaxing way about them.
He was wise and never spoke a truer word, who
[said,
"We can't live with women, but we cannot live
[without them."
35 Now I'll make a truce with you. We'll fight no
[more; instead
I will not injure you if you do me no wrong.
And now let's join our ranks and then begin
[a song.

40 Combined Chorus [*singing*]. Athenians,
[we're not prepared,
To say a single ugly word
About our fellow-citizens.
Quite the contrary: we desire but to say and to
45 [do
Naught but good. Quite enough are the ills
[now on hand.

Men and women, be advised:
   If anyone requires
Money—minae two or three—,   50
   We've got what he desires.

My purse is yours, on easy terms:
   When Peace shall reappear,
Whate'er you've borrowed will be due.
   So speak up without fear.   55

You needn't pay me back, you see,
If you can get a cent from me!

We're about to entertain
   Some foreign gentlemen;
We've soup and tender, fresh-killed pork.   60
   Come round to dine at ten.

Come early; wash and dress with care,
   And bring the children, too.
Then step right in, no "by your leave."
   We'll be expecting you.   65

Walk in as if you owned the place.
You'll find the door—shut in your face!

SCENE V

[*Enter a group of Spartan* Ambassadors;
*they are in the same desperate condition as the
Herald in the previous scene.*]   70
   Leader of Chorus: Here come the envoys
from Sparta, sprouting long beards and looking
for all the world as if they were carrying pig-
pens in front of them.
   Greetings, gentlemen of Sparta. Tell me, in 75
what state have you come?
   Spartan. Why waste words? You can plainly
see what state we've come in!
   L. Cho. Wow! You're in a pretty high-strung
condition, and it seems to be getting worse.   80
   Spa. It's indescribable. Won't someone please
arrange a peace for us—in any way you like.
   L. Cho. Here come our own, native ambassadors, crouching like wrestlers and holding
their clothes in front of them; this seems an   85
athletic kind of malady.
   [*Enter several Athenian* Ambassadors.]

ATH. Can anyone tell us where Lysistrata is? You see our condition.

L. CHO. Here's another case of the same complaint. Tell me, are the attacks worse in the
5 morning?

ATH. No, we're always afflicted this way. If someone doesn't soon arrange a truce, you'd better not let me get my hands on—Cleisthenes!°

10 L. CHO. If you're smart, you'll arrange your cloaks so none of the fellows who smashed the Hermae° can see you.

ATH. Right you are; a very good suggestion.

SPA. Aye, by all means. Here, let's hitch up
15 our clothes.

ATH. Greetings, Spartan. We've suffered dreadful things.

SPA. My dear fellow, we'd have suffered still worse if one of those fellows had seen us in
20 this condition.

ATH. Well, gentlemen, we must get down to business. What's your errand here?

SPA. We're ambassadors about peace.

ATH. Excellent; so are we. Only Lysistrata
25 can arrange things for us; shall we summon her?

SPA. Aye, and Lysistratus too, if you like.

L. CHO. No need to summon her, it seems. She's coming out of her own accord.

30 [Enter LYSISTRATA accompanied by a statue of a nude female figure, which represents Reconciliation.]

Hail, noblest of women; now must thou be
A judge shrewd and subtle, mild and severe,
35 Be sweet yet majestic: all manners employ.
The leaders of Hellas, caught by thy love-
[charms,
Have come to thy judgment, their charges
[submitting.

40 LYS. This is no difficult task, if one catch them

still in amorous passion, before they've resorted to each other. But I'll soon find out. Where's Reconciliation? Go, first bring the Spartans here, and don't seize them rudely and violently, as our tactless husbands used to do, but as be- 45 fits a woman, like an old, familiar friend; if they won't give you their hands, take them however you can. Then go fetch these Athenians here, taking hold of whatever they offer you. Now then, men of Sparta, stand here beside me, and 50 you Athenians on the other side, and listen to my words.

I am a woman, it is true, but I have a mind; I'm not badly off in native wit, and by listening to my father and my elders, I've had a decent 55 schooling.

Now I intend to give you a scolding which you both deserve. With one common font you worship at the same altars, just like brothers, at Olympia, at Thermopylae, at Delphi—how 60 many more might I name, if time permitted— and the Barbarians stand by waiting with their armies; yet you are destroying the men and towns of Greece.

ATH. Oh, this tension is killing me! 65

LYS. And now, men of Sparta—to turn to you—don't you remember how the Spartan Pericleidas came here once as a suppliant, and sitting at our altar, all pale with fear in his crimson cloak, begged us for an army? For all 70 Messene had attacked you and the god sent an earthquake too? Then Cimon went forth with four thousand hoplites and saved all Lacedaemon. Such was the aid you received from Athens, and now you lay waste the country 75 which once treated you so well.

ATH. [hotly]. They're in the wrong, Lysistrata, upon my word, they are!

SPA. [absently, looking at the statue of Reconciliation]. We're in the wrong. What hips! 80 How lovely they are!

LYS. Don't think I'm going to let you Athenians off. Don't you remember how the Spartans came in arms when you were wearing the rough, sheepskin cloak of slaves and slew 85 the host of Thessalians, the comrades and allies of Hippias? Fighting with you on that day, alone of all the Greeks, they set you free and

Cleisthenes   cf. l. 9, p. 74, and note
fellows . . . Hermae   just before the sailing of the Sicilian expedition vandals smashed off the heads and phalluses of the statues of Hermes that served the Athenians as boundary markers and protectors of houses

instead of a sheepskin gave your folk a handsome robe to wear.

SPA. [*looking at* LYSISTRATA]. I've never seen
a more distinguished woman.

5 ATH. [*looking at Reconciliation*]. I've never
seen a more voluptuous body!

LYS. Why then, with these many noble deeds
to think of, do you fight each other? Why don't
you stop this villainy? Why not make peace?
10 Tell me, what prevents it?

SPA. [*waving vaguely at Reconciliation*].
We're willing, if you're willing to give up your
position on yonder flank.

LYS. What position, my good man?

15 SPA. Pylus; we've been panting for it for ever
so long.

ATH. No, by God! You shan't have it!

LYS. Let them have it, my friend.

ATH. Then what shall we have to rouse things
20 up with?

LYS. Ask for another place in exchange.

ATH. Well, let's see: first of all [*pointing to
various parts of Reconciliation's anatomy*] give
us Echinus here, this Maliac Inlet in back there,
25 and these two Megarian legs.

SPA. No, by heavens! You can't have *everything,* you crazy fool!

LYS. Let it go. Don't fight over a pair of legs.

ATH. [*taking off his cloak*]. I think I'll strip
30 and do a little planting now.

SPA. [*following suit*]. And I'll just do a little
fertilizing, by gosh!

LYS. Wait until the truce is concluded. Now
if you've decided on this course, hold a con-
35 ference and discuss the matter with your allies.

ATH. Allies? Don't be ridiculous! They're in
the same state we are. Won't all our allies want
the same thing we do—to jump in bed with
their women?

40 SPA. Ours will, I know.

ATH. Especially the Carystians, by God!

LYS. Very well. Now purify yourselves, that
your wives may feast and entertain you in the
Acropolis; we've provisions by the basketful.
45 Exchange your oaths and pledges there, and
then each of you may take his wife and go
home.

ATH. Let's go at once.

SPA. Come on, where you will.

ATH. For God's sake, let's hurry! 50
[*They all go into the Acropolis.*]

CHO. [*singing*]. Whate'er I have of coverlets
And robes of varied hue
And golden trinkets,—without stint
I offer them to you. 55

Take what you will and bear it home,
Your children to delight,
Or if your girl's a Basket-maid;
Just choose whate'er's in sight.

There's naught within so well secured 60
You cannot break the seal
And bear it off; just help yourselves;
No hesitation feel.

But you'll see nothing, though you try,
Unless you've sharper eyes than I! 65

If anyone needs bread to feed
A growing family,
I've lots of wheat and full-grown loaves;
So just apply to me.

Let every poor man who desires 70
Come round and bring a sack
To fetch the grain; my slave is there
To load it on his back.

But don't come near my door, I say:
Beware the dog, and stay away! 75

ÉXODOS

[*An* ATHENIAN *enters carrying a torch; he
knocks at the gate.*]

ATH. Open the door! [*To the* CHORUS, *which
is clustered around the gate.*] Make way, won't
you! What are you hanging around for? Want 80
me to singe you with this torch? [*To himself.*]
No; it's a stale trick, I won't do it! [*To the
audience.*] Still, if I've got to do it to please
you, I suppose I'll have to take the trouble.

[*A* SECOND ATHENIAN *comes out of the gate.*] 85
2ND ATH. And I'll help you.

1st Ath. [*waving his torch at the* Chorus]. Get out! Go bawl your heads off! Move on there, so the Spartans can leave in peace when the banquet's over.

5 [*They brandish their torches until the* Chorus *leaves the Orchestra.*]

2nd Ath. I've never seen such a pleasant banquet: the Spartans are charming fellows, indeed they are! And we Athenians are very

10 witty in our cups.

1st Ath. Naturally: for when we're sober we're never at our best. If the Athenians would listen to me, we'd always get a little tipsy on our embassies. As things are now, we go to

15 Sparta when we're sober and look around to stir up trouble. And then we don't hear what they say—and as for what they *don't* say, we have all sorts of suspicions. And then we bring back varying reports about the mission. But

20 this time everything is pleasant; even if a man should sing the Telamon-song when he ought to sing "Cleitagoras," we'd praise him and swear it was excellent.°

[*The two* Choruses *return, as a* Chorus of

25 Athenians *and a* Chorus of Spartans.]

Here they come back again. Go to the devil, you scoundrels!

2nd Ath. Get out, I say! They're coming out from the feast.

30 [*Enter the Spartan and Athenian envoys, followed by* Lysistrata *and all the women.*]

Spa. [*to one of his fellow-envoys*]. My good fellow, take up your pipes; I want to do a fancy two-step and sing a jolly song for the Athe-

35 nians.

Ath. Yes, do take up your pipes, by all means. I'd love to see you dance.

Spa. [*singing and dancing with the* Chorus of Spartans].

40 These youths inspire
To song and dance, O Memory;
Stir up my Muse, to tell how we
And Athens' men, in our galleys clashing

At Artemisium, 'gainst foemen dashing
In godlike ire, 45
Conquered the Persian° and set Greece free.

Leonidas
Led on his valiant warriors
Whetting their teeth like angry boars.
Abundant foam on their lips was flow'ring, 50
A stream of sweat from their limbs was
[show'ring.
The Persian was
Numberless as the sand on the shores.

O Huntress° who slayest the beasts in the 55
[glade,
O Virgin divine, hither come to our truce,
Unite us in bonds which all time will not loose.
Grant us to find in this treaty, we pray,
An unfailing source of true friendship today, 60
And all of our days, helping us to refrain
From weaseling tricks which bring war in their
[train.
Then hither, come hither! O huntress maid.

Lys. Come then, since all is fairly done, men 65
of Sparta, lead away your wives, and you, Athenians, take yours. Let every man stand beside
his wife, and every wife beside her man, and
then, to celebrate our fortune, let's dance. And
in the future, let's take care to avoid these mis- 70
understandings.

Chorus of Athenians [*singing and dancing*].
Lead on the dances, your graces revealing.
Call Artemis hither, call Artemis' twin,
Leader of dances, Apollo the Healing, 75
Kindly God—hither! let's summon him in!

Nysian° Bacchus call,
Who with his Maenads, his eyes flashing fire,
Dances, and last of all
Zeus of the thunderbolt flaming, the Sire, 80

---

swear . . . excellent the reference here is to a song-capping game, common at Athenian banquets, and to the gaffe of failing to follow one's cue

Conquered the Persian Xerxes, at the battle of Salamis

Huntress Artemis

Nysian Nysa was the mountain on which Bacchus was said to have been reared

And Hera in majesty,
Queen of prosperity.

Come, ye Powers who dwell above
Unforgetting, our witnesses be
5 Of Peace with bonds of harmonious love—
The Peace which Cypris° has wrought for me.
   Alleluia! Io Paean!
   Leap in joy—hurrah! hurrah!
   'Tis victory—hurrah! hurrah!
10 Euoi! Euoi! Euai! Euai!

LYS. [*to the Spartans*]. Come now, sing a
new song to cap ours.

CHORUS OF SPARTANS [*singing and dancing*].
Leaving Taygetus fair and renown'd,
15 Muse of Laconia,° hither come:
Amyclae's god in hymns resound,
Athene of the Brazen Home,
And Castor and Pollux, Tyndareus' sons,
Who sport where Eurotas murmuring runs.

20 On with the dance! Heia! Ho!
   All leaping along,
Mantles a-swinging as we go!
   Of Sparta our song.
There the holy chorus ever gladdens,
25 There the beat of stamping feet,
As our winsome fillies, lovely maidens,
Dance, beside Eurotas' banks a-skipping,—
   Nimbly go to and fro
Hast'ning, leaping feet in measures tripping,
30 Like the Bacchae's revels, hair a-streaming.
Leda's child, divine and mild,
Leads the holy dance, her fair face beaming.
On with the dance! as your hand
   Presses the hair
35 Streaming away unconfined.

Leap in the air
Light as the deer; footsteps resound
Aiding our dance, beating the ground.
Praise Athene, Maid divine, unrivalled in her
                                    [might, 40
Dweller in the Brazen Home, unconquered in
                                    [the fight.

[*All go out singing and dancing.*]

Cypris Aphrodite
Laconia the country of which Sparta was the capital.
In the following lines further references to Sparta
appear. Amyclae was a town on the river Eurotas
near to Sparta that had a famous sanctuary and
throne of Apollo. The Brazen Home was a temple on
the Spartan Acropolis. Tyndareus had been a king
of Sparta. His sons, by Leda, were worshipped in
Sparta as the tutelary gods of warlike youth.

Euripides

485?–406? B.C.

The Bacchae

406? B.C.

In a narrow sense, *The Bacchae* is a play about Dionysus' revenge on Thebes for denying his divine paternity and present deity. It is a well-made play and builds unrelentingly to its catastrophe. From the beginning, when Dionysus manifests his identity and purpose, the conclusion is foregone. Pentheus, king of Thebes, *thinks* that he is the hunter, tracking down the stranger to destroy him. We *know,* in a metaphor the play repeats, that the hunter is the hunted, that each step he makes toward the kill is toward his own destruction. We see Pentheus flout Dionysus and plan to destroy the god's converts among the Theban women. We hear, too, that Pentheus' mother, Agauë, one of those who once repudiated the god, has become one of his converts and leads the Theban Bacchae on the side of Mt. Cithaeron. Son and mother, we apprehend with ironic certainty, are moving toward a fatal convergence. And when they come, in their agonies, to the knowledge of what Dionysus has willed for them, they discover indeed that a god insulted does not forgive.

Thus seen, the play has about it the special if chilly gratification that comes from dramas of intrigue, in which the schemer is hoist with his own petard. But Euripides so manipulates the audience's feelings that the promised gratification is not attained. At first we are attracted to Dionysus, the injured deity concerned for his mother's honor and his own. The chorus of Asian women, his devotees who have followed him into this land, compellingly testifies to his power and appeal. Even Cadmus and Teiresias, submitting their withered limbs to the Bacchic dance, add their witness. And Pentheus so fatuously refuses to hear reason, so disgustingly reveals the obscene shape of his own imaginings, that we side with Dionysus and look forward to his revenge. When the god enters Pentheus, however, metamorphosing his blunt masculinity into horrid effeminacy, our pleasure may begin to pall. At length Euripides forces on us the full horror of Pentheus' destruction, the man crying out as his body is torn asunder, "Mother, have mercy; I have sinned, But I am still your own son. Do not take my life!" We are further made to behold Agaüe's agony as her eyes clear and she sees what it is that she has held aloft in ecstatic triumph. So terrible is this suffering, so terrible the god ruthlessly exacting it, that our allegiances shift—from the injured god to the more cruelly injured mortals. In their plight we experience our own.

The Bacchae is about Dionysus, not Apollo. No character raises the great questions, as Oedipus does, or arrives at the great answers. We appear to be in a diminished universe where the gods are gods not because they are wise and good, but because they are powerful. Here there is feeling, not thought, and the Dionysian feeling operates with the ambiguity of wine. Wine frees man from what diminishes him and releases his powers. "Without wine," says the herdsman, "neither love nor any other pleasure would be left for us." The god-intoxicated Theban women sing and decorously dance on the mountain side; they feed the animal young and ride joyful children on their shoulders. Dionysus is genial, benign—a savior. But wine liberates in another way; it rids man of what keeps him human, and surrenders him to his lusts. The Bacchae tear the flesh of heifers, bulls, human beings. They glut themselves with blood and triumph in kindless savagery. Dionysus is violent, brutal—a destroyer.

Euripides visits upon us the meaning of the Dionysian spirit, whether the intoxication be that of grape, religious enthusiasm, or political cult. He preaches no lesson of abstinence, certainly, or even of moderation. But, making Dionysus manifest both to the dying eyes of the Theban king and to the living eyes of the audience, he compels us at once to acknowledge and to fear this ambiguous power, demonic or divine.

The Bacchae

EURIPIDES

CHARACTERS

DIONYSUS
CHORUS   of Oriental women, devotees of Dionysus
TEIRESIAS   a blind seer
CADMUS   founder of Thebes, and formerly king
PENTHEUS   his grandson, now king of Thebes
A GUARD   attending Pentheus
A HERDSMAN
A MESSENGER
AGAÜE   daughter of Cadmus and mother of Pentheus

SCENE. Before the palace of Pentheus in Thebes. At one side of the stage is the monument of Semele; above it burns a low flame, and around it are the remains of ruined and blackened masonry.

5

PROLOGUE°

[DIONYSUS enters on stage right. He has a crown of ivy, a thyrsus° in his hand, and a fawnskin draped over his body. He has long

---

Prologue   see p. 7. Although it lacks the kommoi, The Bacchae has essentially the same structure as Agamemnon.

thyrsus   a light stick of reed or fennel, with fresh strands of ivy twined round it. It was carried by every devotee of Dionysus, and the action of the play illustrates the supernatural power that was held to reside in it. [Translator's note.]

From The Bacchae and Other Plays, translated by Phillip Vellacott. Copyright © Phillip Vellacott. Reprinted by permission of Penguin Books Ltd.

flowing hair and a youthful, almost feminine beauty.]

DIONYSUS. I am Dionysus, son of Zeus. My
[mother was
5 Semele, Cadmus' daughter. From her womb the
[fire
Of a lightning-flash delivered me. I have come
[here
To Thebes and her two rivers, Dirce and
10 [Ismenus,
Veiling my godhead in a mortal shape. I see
Here near the palace my mother's monument,
[that records
Her death by lightning. Here her house stood;
15 [and its ruins
Smoulder with the still living flame of Zeus's
[fire—
The immortal cruelty Hera wreaked upon my
[mother.
20 Cadmus does well to keep this ground
[inviolable,
A precinct consecrated in his daughter's name;
And I have decked it round with sprays of
[young vineleaves.
25 From the fields of Lydia and Phrygia, fertile in
[gold,
I travelled first to the sun-smitten Persian
[plains,
The walled cities of Bactria, the harsh Median
30 [country,
Wealthy Arabia, and the whole tract of the
[Asian coast
Where mingled swarms of Greeks and
[Orientals live
35 In vast magnificent cities; and before reaching
[this,
The first city of Hellas I have visited,
I had already, in all those regions of the east,
Performed my dances and set forth my ritual
40 To make my godhead manifest to mortal men.

The reason why I have chosen Thebes as the
[first place
To raise my Bacchic shout, and clothe all who
[respond
45 In fawnskin habits, and put my thyrsus in their
[hands—
The weapon wreathed with ivy-shoots—my

[reason is this:
My mother's sisters said—what they should
[have been the last 50
To say—that I, Dionysus, was not Zeus's son;
That Semele, being with child—they said—by
[some mortal,
Obeyed her father's prompting, and ascribed to
[Zeus 55
The loss of her virginity; and they loudly
[claimed
That this lie was the sin for which Zeus took
[her life.

Therefore I have driven those same sisters mad, 60
[turned them
All frantic out of doors; their home now is the
[mountain;
Their wits are gone. I have made them bear the
[emblem of 65
My mysteries; the whole female population of
[Thebes,
To the last woman, I have sent raving from
[their homes.
Now, side by side with Cadmus' daughters, 70
[one and all
Sit roofless on the rocks under the silver pines.
For Thebes, albeit reluctantly, must learn in full
This lesson, that my Bacchic worship is a matter
As yet beyond her knowledge and experience; 75
And I must vindicate my mother Semele
By manifesting myself before the human race
As the divine son whom she bore to immortal
[Zeus.

Now Cadmus has made over his throne and 80
[kingly honors
To Pentheus, son of his eldest daughter Agaüe.
[He
Is a fighter against gods, defies me, excludes me
[from 85
Libations, never names me in prayers.
[Therefore I will
Demonstrate to him, and to all Thebes, that I
[am a god.

When I have set all in order here, I will pass on 90
To another place, and manifest myself.
[Meanwhile

If Thebes in anger tries to bring the Bacchants
[home
By force from the mountain, I myself will join
[that army
5 Of women possessed and lead them to battle.
[That is why
I have changed my form and taken the likeness
[of a man.
Come, my band of worshippers, women whom
10 [I have brought

From lands of the east, from Tmolus, bastion
[of Lydia,
To be with me and share my travels! Raise the
[music
15 Of your own country, the Phrygian drums
[invented by
Rhea the Great Mother and by me. Fill
[Pentheus' palace
With a noise to make the city of Cadmus turn
20 [and look!
—And I will go to the folds of Mount
[Cithaeron, where
The Bacchants are, and join them in their holy
[dance.
25 [DIONYSUS *goes out towards the mountain.*
The CHORUS *enter where* DIONYSUS *entered,*
from the road by which they have travelled.]

PÁRODOS

Strophe 1
CHORUS. From far-off lands of Asia,
From Tmolus the holy mountain,
30 We run with the god of laughter;
Labor is joy and weariness is sweet,
And our song resounds to Bacchus!

Antistrophe 1
Who stands in our path?
Make way, make way!
35 Who in the house? Close every lip,
Keep holy silence, while we sing
The appointed hymn to Bacchus!

Strophe 2
Blest is the happy man
Who knows the mysteries the gods ordain,

And sanctifies his life,   40

Joins soul with soul in mystic unity,
And, by due ritual made pure,
Enters the ecstasy of mountain solitudes;
Who observes the mystic rites
Made lawful by Cybele the Great Mother;   45
Who crowns his head with ivy,
And shakes aloft his wand in worship of
[Dionysus.

On, on! Run, dance, delirious, possessed!
Dionysus comes to his own;   50
Bring from the Phrygian hills to the broad
[streets of Hellas
The god, child of a god,
Spirit of revel and rapture, Dionysus!

Antistrophe 2
Once, on the womb that held him   55
The fire-bolt flew from the hand of Zeus;
And pains of child-birth bound his mother fast,
And she cast him forth untimely,
And under the lightning's lash relinquished
[life; 60

And Zeus the son of Cronos
Ensconced him instantly in a secret womb
Chambered within his thigh,
And with golden pins closed him from Hera's
[sight. 65

So, when the Fates had made him ripe for birth,
Zeus bore the bull-horned god
And wreathed his head with wreaths of
[writhing snakes;
Which is why the Maenads catch   70
Wild snakes, nurse them and twine them round
[their hair.

Strophe 3
O Thebes, old nurse that cradled Semele,
Be ivy garlanded, burst into flower
With wreaths of lush bright-berried bryony,   75
Bring sprays of fir, green branches torn from
[oaks,
Fill soul and flesh with Bacchus' mystic power;
Fringe and bedeck your dappled fawnskin
[cloaks 80

With wooly tufts and locks of purest white.
There's a brute wildness in the fennel-wands—
Reverence it well. Soon the whole land will

[dance

5 When the god with ecstatic shout
Leads his companies out
To the mountain's mounting height
Swarming with riotous bands
Of Theban women leaving
10 Their spinning and their weaving
Stung with the maddening trance
Of Dionysus!

Antistrophe 3

O secret chamber the Curetes knew!°
O holy cavern in the Cretan glade
15 Where Zeus was cradled, where for our delight
The triple-crested Corybantes drew
Tight the round drum-skin, till its wild beat

[made

Rapturous rhythm to the breathing sweetness
20 Of Phrygian flutes! Then divine Rhea found
The drum could give her Bacchic airs

[completeness;

From her, the Mother of all,
The crazy Satyrs soon,
25 In their dancing festival
When the second year comes round,
Seized on the timbrel's tune
To play the leading part
In feasts that delight the heart
30 Of Dionysus.

Epode

O what delight is in the mountains!
There the celebrant,° wrapped in his sacred

[fawnskin,

Flings himself on the ground surrendered,
35 While the swift-footed company streams on;
There he hunts for blood, and rapturously
Eats the raw flesh of the slaughtered goat,

Curetes demigods who cared for the infant Zeus
celebrant Dionysus and the Chorus comprise the
typical group of Bacchic worshippers, a male leader
with a devoted band of women and girls. The leader
flings himself on the ground in the climax of ecstasy,
when the power of the god enters into him and he
becomes possessed. [Translator's note.]

Hurrying on to the Phrygian or Lydian

[mountain heights.

Possessed, ecstatic, he leads their happy cries; 40
The earth flows with milk, flows with wine,
Flows with nectar of bees;
The air is thick with a scent of Syrian myrrh.
The celebrant runs entranced, whirling the

[torch 45

That blazes red from the fennel-wand in his

[grasp,

And with shouts he rouses the scattered bands,
Sets their feet dancing,
As he shakes his delicate locks to the wild wind. 50
And amidst the frenzy of song he shouts like

[thunder:

"On, on! Run, dance, delirious, possessed!
You, the beauty and grace of golden Tmolus,
Sing to the rattle of thunderous drums, 55
Sing for joy,
Praise Dionysus, god of joy!
Shout like Phrygians, sing out the tunes you

[know,

While the sacred pure-toned flute 60
Vibrates the air with holy merriment,
In time with the pulse of the feet that flock
To the mountains, to the mountains!"
And, like a foal with its mother at pasture,
Runs and leaps for joy every daughter of 65

[Bacchus.

SCENE I

[*Enter* TEIRESIAS. *Though blind, he makes
his way unaided to the door, and knocks.*]
  TEIRESIAS. Who keeps the gate? Call Cadmus

[out, Agenor's son, 70

Who came from Sidon here to build these walls

[of Thebes.

Go, someone, say Teiresias is looking for him.
He knows why; I'm an old man, and he's older

[still— 75

But we agreed to equip ourselves with Bacchic

[wands

And fawnskin cloaks, and put on wreaths of

[ivy-shoots.

  [*Enter* CADMUS.] 80
  CADMUS. Dear friend, I knew your voice,

[although I was indoors,

As soon as I heard it—the wise voice of a wise
[man.
I am ready. See, I have all that the god
[prescribes.
5 He is my daughter's son; we must do all we can
To exalt and honor him. Where shall we go to
[dance
And take our stand with others, tossing our
[gray heads?
10 You tell me what to do, Teiresias. We're both
[old,
But you're the expert. [*He stumps about, beating his thyrsus on the ground.*] I could drum
[the ground all night
15 And all day too, without being tired. What joy
[it is
To forget one's age!
TEIRESIAS. I feel exactly the same way,
Bursting with youth! I'll try it—I'll dance with
20 [the rest.
CADMUS. You don't think we should go to the
[mountain in a coach?
TEIRESIAS. No, no. That would not show the
[god the same respect.
25 CADMUS. I'll take you there myself then—
[old as we both are.
TEIRESIAS. The god will guide us there, and
[without weariness.
CADMUS. Are we the only Thebans who will
30 [dance to him?
TEIRESIAS. We see things clearly; all the
[others are perverse.
CADMUS. We're wasting time; come, take my
[hand.
35 TEIRESIAS. Here, then; hold tight.
CADMUS. I don't despise religion. I'm a mortal
[man.
TEIRESIAS. We have no use for theological
[subtleties.
40 The beliefs we have inherited, as old as time,
Cannot be overthrown by any argument,
Not by the most inventive ingenuity.
It will be said, I lack the dignity of my age,
To wear this ivy-wreath and set off for the
45 [dance.
No so; the god draws no distinction between
[young
And old, to tell us which should dance and
[which should not.
He desires equal worship from all men; his   50
[claim
To glory is universal; no one is exempt.
CADMUS. Teiresias, I shall be your prophet,
[since you are blind.
Pentheus, to whom I have resigned my rule in   55
[Thebes,
Is hurrying here towards the palace. He appears
Extremely agitated. What news will he bring?
[*Enter* PENTHEUS. *He addresses the audience,
without at first noticing* CADMUS *and* TEIRESIAS,   60
who stand at the opposite side of the stage.]
PENTHEUS. I happen to have been away from
[Thebes; reports
Of this astounding scandal have just been
[brought to me.   65
Our women, it seems, have left their homes on
[some pretense
Of Bacchic worship, and now are gadding about
On the wooded mountain-slopes, dancing in
[honor of   70
This upstart god Dionysus, whoever he may be.
Amidst these groups of worshippers, they tell
[me, stand
Bowls full of wine; and our women go creeping
[off   75
This way and that to lonely places and give
[themselves
To lecherous men. They are Maenad
[priestesses, if you please!
Aphrodite supplants Bacchus in their ritual.   80
Well, those I've caught, my guards are keeping
[safe; we've tied
Their hands, and lodged them at state expense.
[Those still at large
On the mountain I am going to hunt out; and   85
[that
Includes my own mother Agauë and her sisters
Ino and Autonoë. Once they're fast in iron
[fetters,
I'll put a stop to this outrageous Bacchism.   90

They tell me, too, some oriental conjurer
Has come from Lydia, a magician with golden
[hair
Flowing in scented ringlets, his face flushed
[with wine,   95

His eyes lit with the charm of Aphrodite; and
[he
Entices young girls with his Bacchic mysteries,
Spends days and nights consorting with them.
[Once let me
5 Get that fellow inside my walls—I'll cut his
[head
From his shoulders, that will stop him
[drumming with his thyrsus,
10 Tossing his long hair. *He's the one*—this
[foreigner—
Who says Dionysus is a god; who says he was
Sewn up in Zeus's thigh. The truth about
[Dionysus
15 Is that he's dead, burnt to a cinder by lightning
Along with his mother, because she said Zeus
[lay with her.
Whoever the man may be, is not his arrogance
An outrage? Has he not earned a rope around
20 [his neck?
[PENTHEUS *turns to go, and sees* CADMUS *and*
TEIRESIAS.]
Why, look! Another miracle! Here's Teiresias
The prophet—in a fawnskin; and my mother's
25 [father—
A Bacchant with a fennel-wand! Well, there's a
[sight
For laughter! [*But he is raging, not laughing.*]

Sir, I am ashamed to see two men
30 Of your age with so little sense of decency.
Come, you're my grandfather: throw down that
[ivy-wreath,
Get rid of that thyrsus!—*You* persuaded him
[to this,
35 Teiresias. By introducing a new god, you hope
To advance your augurer's business, to collect
[more fees
For inspecting sacrifices. Listen: your gray hairs
Are your protection; otherwise you'd be sitting
40 [now
In prison with all these crazy females, for
[promoting
Pernicious practices. As for women, I tell you
[this:
45 Wherever the sparkle of sweet wine adorns
[their feast,
No good will follow from such Bacchic

[ceremonies.
CHORUS. Have you no reverence, Sir, no
[piety? Do you mock 50
Cadmus, who sowed the dragon-seed of
[earth-born men?°
Do you, Echion's son, dishonor your own race?
TEIRESIAS. When a good speaker has a sound
[case to present, 55
Then eloquence is no great feat. Your fluent
[tongue
Promises wisdom; but the content of your
[speech
Is ignorant. Power and eloquence in a 60
[headstrong man
Spell folly; such a man is a peril to the state.

This new god, whom you ridicule—no words
[of mine
Could well express the ascendency he will 65
[achieve
In Hellas. There are two powers, young man,
[which are supreme
In human affairs: first, Demeter—the same
[goddess 70
Is also Earth; give her which name you please
[—and she
Supplies mankind with solid food. After her
[came
Dionysus, Semele's son; the blessing he 75
[procured
And gave to men is counterpart to that of
[bread:
The clear juice of the grape. When mortals
[drink their fill 80
Of wine, the sufferings of our unhappy race
Are banished, each day's troubles are forgotten
[in sleep.
There is no other cure for sorrow. Dionysus,
Himself a god, is thus poured out in offering 85
To the gods, so that through him come blessings
[on mankind.
And do you scorn this legend, that he was sewn
[up

earth-born men by Athena's advice Cadmus sowed
the teeth of a dragon he had slain; the harvest was
armed men who fought and slew each other until
only five were left—the ancestors of the Theban
nobility

In Zeus's thigh? I will explain the truth to you.
When Zeus snatched Dionysus from the
                              [lightning flame
And took the child up to Olympus as a god,
5   Hera resolved to cast him out of heaven. But
                              [Zeus
Found such means to prevent her as a god will
                              [find.
He took a fragment of the ether that surrounds
10 The earth, fashioned it like a child, presented it
To Hera as a pledge to sooth her jealousy,
And saved Dionysus from her. Thus, in time,
                              [because
The ancient words for "pledge" and "thigh"°
15   [are similar,
People confused them, and the "pledge" Zeus
                              [gave to Hera
Became transformed, as time went on, into the
                              [tale
20 That Dionysus was sewn up in Zeus's thigh.

And this god is a prophet; the Bacchic ecstasy
And frenzy hold a strong prophetic element.
When he fills irresistibly a human body
He gives those so possessed power to foretell
25   [the future.
In Ares' province too Dionysus has his share;
Sometimes an army, weaponed and drawn up
                              [for battle,
Has fled in wild panic before a spear was raised.
30 This too is an insanity sent by Dionysus.

Ay, and the day will come when, on the very
                              [crags
Of Delphi, you shall see him leaping, amidst
                              [the blaze
35 Of torches, over the twin-peaked ridge, waving
                              [aloft
And brandishing his Bacchic staff, while all
                              [Hellas
Exalts him. Pentheus, pay heed to my words.
40   [You rely
On force; but it is not force that governs human

---

the ancient words for "pledge" and "thigh" the
translation necessarily expands the original.
Homeros means *pledge*, and *meros thigh* [Trans-
lator's note.]

                              [affairs.
Do not mistake for wisdom that opinion which
May rise from a sick mind. Welcome this god
                              [to Thebes,   45
Offer libations to him, celebrate his rites,
Put on his garland. Dionysus will not compel
Women to be chaste, since in all matters
                              [self-control
Resides in our own natures. You should   50
                              [consider this;
For in the Bacchic ritual, as elsewhere, a woman
Will be safe from corruption if her mind is
                              [chaste.

Think of this too: when crowds stand at the   55
                              [city gates
And Thebes extols the name of Pentheus, you
                              [rejoice;
So too, I think, the god is glad to receive honor.

Well, I at least, and Cadmus, whom you mock, 60
                              [will wear
The ivy-wreath and join the dancing—we are
                              [a pair
Of gray heads, but this is our duty; and no
                              [words 65
Of yours shall lure me into fighting against
                              [gods.
For a most cruel insanity has warped your
                              [mind;
While drugs may well have caused it, they can 70
                              [bring no cure.
CHORUS. What you have said, Teiresias,
                              [shows no disrespect
To Apollo; at the same time you prove your
                              [judgment sound 75
In honoring Dionysus as a mighty god.
CADMUS. My dear son, Teiresias has given
                              [you good advice.
Don't stray beyond pious tradition; live with
                              [us. 80
Your wits have flown to the winds, your sense
                              [is foolishness.
Even if, as you say, Dionysus is no god,
Let him have *your* acknowledgment; lie royally,
That Semele may get honor as having borne a   85
                              [god,
And credit come to us and to all our family.

Remember, too, Actaeon's miserable fate—
Torn and devoured by hounds which he himself
[had bred,
Because he filled the mountains with the boast
5 [that he
Was a more skillful hunter than Artemis
[herself.
Don't share his fate, my son! Come, let me
[crown your head
10 With a wreath of ivy; join us in worshipping
[this god.
PENTHEUS. Keep your hands off! Go to your
[Bacchic rites, and don't
Wipe off your crazy folly on me. But I will
15 [punish
This man who has been your instructor in
[lunacy.
Go, someone, quickly to his seat of augury,
Smash it with crowbars, topple the walls,
20 [throw all his things
In wild confusion, turn the whole place upside
[down,
Fling out his holy fripperies to the hurricane
[winds!
25 This sacrilege will sting him more than
[anything else.
The rest of you—go, comb the country and
[track down
That effeminate foreigner, who plagues our
30 [women with
This new disease, fouls the whole land with
[lechery;
And once you catch him, tie him up and bring
[him here
35 To me; I'll deal with him. He shall be stoned to
[death.
He'll wish he'd never brought his Bacchic rites
[to Thebes.
[*Exit* PENTHEUS.]
40 TEIRESIAS. Foolhardy man! You do not know
[what you have said.
Before, you were unbalanced; now you are
[insane.
Come, Cadmus; let us go and pray both for
45 [this man,
Brutish as he is, and for our city, and beg the
[god
To show forbearance. Come, now, take your

[ivy staff
And let us go. Try to support me; we will help 50
Each other. It would be scandalous for two old
[men
To fall; still, we must go, and pay our due
[service
To Dionysus, son of Zeus. Cadmus, the name 55
Pentheus means *sorrow*. God grant he may not
[bring sorrow
Upon your house. Do not take that as prophecy;
I judge his acts. Such foolish words bespeak a
[fool. 60

[*Exeunt* TEIRESIAS *and* CADMUS.]

ODE I

Strophe 1
CHORUS. Holiness, Queen of heaven,
Holiness, golden-winged ranging the earth,
Do you hear his blasphemy?
Pentheus dares—do you hear?—to revile the 65
[god of joy,
The son of Semele, who when the gay-crowned
[feast is set
Is named among gods the chief;
Whose gifts are joy and union of soul in 70
[dancing,
Joy in music of flutes,
Joy when sparkling wine at feasts of the gods
Soothes the sore regret,
Banishes every grief, 75
When the reveller rests, enfolded deep
In the cool shade of ivy-shoots,
On wine's soft pillow of sleep.

Antistrophe 1
The brash, unbridled tongue,
The lawless folly of fools, will end in pain. 80
But the life of wise content
Is blest with quietness, escapes the storm
And keeps its house secure.
Though blessed gods dwell in the distant skies,
They watch the ways of men. 85
To know much is not to be wise.
Pride more than mortal hastens life to its end;
And they who in pride pretend
Beyond man's limit, will lose what lay
Close to their hand and sure. 90

I count it madness, and know no cure can mend
The evil man and his evil way.

Strophe 2

O to set foot on Aphrodite's island,
On Cyprus, haunted by the Loves, who enchant
5   Brief life with sweetness; or in that strange land
Whose fertile river carves a hundred channels
To enrich her rainless sand;
Or where the sacred pastures of Olympus slant
Down to Pieria, where the Muses dwell—
10 Take me, O Bromius,° take me and inspire
Laughter and worship! There our holy spell
And ecstasy are welcome; there the gentle band
Of Graces have their home, and sweet Desire.
Dionysus, son of Zeus, delights in banquets;

Antistrophe 2

15 And his dear love is Peace, giver of wealth,
Savior of young men's lives—a goddess rare!
In wine, his gift that charms all griefs away,
Alike both rich and poor may have their part.
His enemy is the man who has no care
20 To pass his years in happiness and health,
His days in quiet and his nights in joy,
Watchful to keep aloof both mind and heart
From men whose pride claims more than
                              [mortals may.
25 The life that wins the poor man's common
                                      [voice,
His creed, his practice—this shall be my choice.

SCENE II

[*Some of the guards whom* PENTHEUS *sent to
arrest* DIONYSUS *now enter with their prisoner.*
30 PENTHEUS *enters from the palace.*]
    GUARD. Pentheus, we've brought the prey
                            [you sent us out to catch;
We hunted him, and here he is. But, Sir, we
                                      [found
35 The beast was gentle; made no attempt to run
                                      [away,
Just held his hands out to be tied; didn't turn
                                      [pale,
But kept his florid color, smiling, telling us

Bromius another name for Dionysus

To tie him up and run him in; gave us no   40
                              [trouble
At all, just waited for us. Naturally I felt
A bit embarrassed. "You'll excuse me, Sir," I
                                      [said,
"I don't want to arrest you; it's the king's   45
                              [command."

Another thing, sir—those women you rounded
                              [up
And put in fetters in the prison, those
                              [Bacchants;   50
Well, they're all gone, turned loose to the glens;
                              [and there they are,
Frisking about, calling on Bromius their god.
The fetters simply opened and fell off their
                              [feet;   55
The bolts shot back, untouched by mortal hand;
                              [the doors
Flew wide. Master, this man has come here
                              [with a load
Of miracles. Well, what happens next is your   60
                              [concern.
    PENTHEUS. Untie this man's hands. (*The*
    [GUARD *does so.*) He's securely in the trap.
He's not so nimble-footed as to escape me now.

Well, friend: your shape is not unhandsome—   65
                              [for the pursuit
Of women, which is the purpose of your
                              [presence here.
You are no wrestler, I can tell from these long
                              [curls   70
Cascading most seductively over your cheek.
Your skin, too, shows a whiteness carefully
                              [preserved;
You keep away from the sun's heat, walk in
                              [the shade,   75
So hunting Aphrodite with your lovely face.

Ah, well; first tell me who you are. What is
                              [your birth?
    DIONYSUS. Your question's easily answered,
                              [it is no secret.   80
Perhaps you have heard of Tmolus, a mountain
                              [decked with flowers.
    PENTHEUS. A range that curves round Sardis?
                              [Yes, I know of it.

DIONYSUS. That is my home. I am a Lydian by
[birth.
PENTHEUS. How comes it that you bring these
[rituals to Hellas?
5 DIONYSUS. Dionysus, son of Zeus, himself
[instructed me.
PENTHEUS. Is there a Lydian Zeus, then, who
[begets new gods?
DIONYSUS. I speak of Zeus who wedded
10 [Semele here in Thebes.
PENTHEUS. Did he possess you in a dream, or
[visibly?
DIONYSUS. Yes, face to face; he gave these
[mysteries to me.
15 PENTHEUS. These mysteries you speak of:
[what form do they take?
DIONYSUS. To the uninitiated that must not
[be told.
PENTHEUS. And those who worship—what
20 [advantage do they gain?
DIONYSUS. It is not for you to learn; yet it is
[worth knowing.
PENTHEUS. You bait your answer well, to
[arouse my eagerness.
25 DIONYSUS. His rituals abhor a man of impious
[life.
PENTHEUS. You say you saw him face to face:
[what was he like?
DIONYSUS. Such as he chose to be. I had no
30 [say in that.
PENTHEUS. Still you side-track my question
[with an empty phrase.
DIONYSUS. Just so. A prudent speech sleeps
[in a foolish ear.
35 PENTHEUS. Is Thebes the first place where
[you have introduced this god?
DIONYSUS. No; every eastern land dances
[these mysteries.
PENTHEUS. No doubt. Their moral standards
40 [fall far below ours.
DIONYSUS. In this they are superior; but their
[customs differ.
PENTHEUS. Do you perform these mysteries
[by night or day?
45 DIONYSUS. Chiefly by night. Darkness
[promotes religious awe.
PENTHEUS. For women darkness is deceptive
[and impure.

DIONYSUS. Impurity can be pursued by
[daylight too. 50
PENTHEUS. You must be punished for your
[foul and slippery tongue.
DIONYSUS. And you for blindness and impiety
[to the god.
PENTHEUS. How bold this Bacchant is! A 55
[practiced pleader too.
DIONYSUS. Tell me my sentence. What dread
[pain will you inflict?
PENTHEUS. I'll start by cutting off your
[delicate long hair. 60
DIONYSUS. My hair is sacred; I preserve it for
[the god.
PENTHEUS. And next, that thyrsus in your
[hand—give to to me.
DIONYSUS. Take it from me yourself; it is the 65
[god's emblem.
PENTHEUS. I'll lock you up in prison and keep
[you there.
DIONYSUS. The god
Himself, whenever I desire, will set me free. 70
PENTHEUS. Of course—when you, with all
[your Bacchants, call to him!
DIONYSUS. He is close at hand here, and sees
[what is done to me.
PENTHEUS. Indeed? Where is he, then? Not 75
[visible to my eyes.
DIONYSUS. Beside me. You, being a
[blasphemer, see nothing.
PENTHEUS [*to the* GUARDS]. Get hold of him;
[he's mocking me and the whole city. 80
DIONYSUS [*to the* GUARDS]. Don't bind me,
[I warn you. [*To* PENTHEUS.] I am sane,
[and you are mad.
PENTHEUS. My word overrules yours. (*To the*
[GUARDS.) I tell you, bind him fast. 85
DIONYSUS. You know not what you are
[saying, what you do, nor who
You are.
PENTHEUS. Who? Pentheus, son of Echion
[and Agauë. 90
DIONYSUS. Your name points to calamity. It
[fits you well.
PENTHEUS. Take him away and shut him in
[my stables, where
He can stay staring at darkness.—You can 95
[dance in there!

As for these women you've brought as your
[accomplices,
I'll either send them to the slave-market to be
[sold,
5 Or keep them in my own household to work
[the looms;
And that will stop their fingers drumming on
[tamborines!
    DIONYSUS. I'll go. Nothing can touch me that
10   [is not ordained.
But I warn you: Dionysus, who you say is dead,
Will come in swift pursuit to avenge this
[sacrilege.
You are putting *him* in prison when you lay
15   [hands on me.
   [GUARDS *take* DIONYSUS *away to the stables;*
PENTHEUS *follows.*]

ODE II

Strophe

    CHORUS. Dirce, sweet and holy maid,
Acheloüs' Theban daughter,
20 Once the child of Zeus was made
Welcome in your welling water,
When the lord of earth and sky
Snatched him from the undying flame,
Laid him safe within his thigh,
25 Calling loud the infant's name:
"Twice-born Dithyrambus! Come,
Enter here your father's womb;
Bacchic child, I now proclaim
This in Thebes shall be your name."
30 Now, divine Dirce, when my head is crowned
And my feet dance in Bacchus' revelry—
Now you reject me from your holy ground.
Why should you fear me? By the purple fruit
That glows in glory on Dionysus' tree,
35 His dread name yet shall haunt your memory!

Antistrophe

Oh, what anger lies beneath
Pentheus' voice and sullen face—
Offspring of the dragon's teeth,
And Echion's earth-born race,
40 Brute with bloody jaws agape,
God-defying, gross and grim,
Slander of his human shape!

Soon he'll chain us limb to limb—
Bacchus' servants! Yes, and more:
Even now our comrade lies   45
Deep on his dark prison floor.
Dionysus! Do your eyes
See us? O son of Zeus, the oppressor's rod
Falls on your worshippers; come, mighty god,
Brandish your golden thyrsus and descend   50
From great Olympus; touch this murderous
[man,
And bring his violence to a sudden end!

Epode

Where are you, Dionysus? Leading your
[dancing bands 55
Over the mountain slopes, past many a wild
[beast's lair,
Or on Corycian crags, with the thyrsus in their
[hands?
Or in the wooded coverts, maybe, of Olympus, 60
[where
Orpheus once gathered the trees and mountain
[beasts,
Gathered them with his lyre, and sang an
[enchanting air. 65
Happy vale of Pieria! Bacchus delights in you;
He will cross the flood and foam of the Axius
[river, and there,
He will bring his whirling Maenads, with
[dancing and with feasts, 70
Cross the father of waters, Lydias, generous
[giver
Of wealth and luck, they say, to the land he
[wanders through,
Whose famous horses graze by the rich and 75
[lovely river.

SCENE III

[*Suddenly a shout is heard from inside the
building—the voice of* DIONYSUS.]
    DIONYSUS. Io,° Io! Do you know my voice,
[do you hear? 80
Worshippers of Bacchus! Io, Io!
    CHORUS. Who is that? Where is he?
The shout of Dionysus is calling us!

Io an ecstatic cry

DIONYSUS. Io, Io! hear me again:
I am the son of Semele, the son of Zeus!
CHORUS. Io, Io, our lord, our lord!
Come, then, come to our company, lord of joy!
5 DIONYSUS. O dreadful earthquake, shake the
[floor of the world!
CHORUS [*with a scream of terror*].
Pentheus' palace is falling, crumbling in
[pieces! [*They continue severally.*]
10 —Dionysus stands in the palace; bow before
[him!
—We bow before him.—See how the roof
[and pillars
Plunge to the ground!—Bromius is with us,
15 He shouts from prison the shout of victory!
[*The flame on Semele's tomb grows and brightens.*]
DIONYSUS. Fan to a blaze the lightning lit;
Kindle the conflagration of Pentheus' palace!
20 CHORUS. Look, look, look!
Do you see, do you see the flame of Semele's
[tomb,
The flame that lived when she died of the
[lightning-stroke?
25 [*A noise of crashing masonry is heard.*]
Down, trembling Maenads! Hurl yourselves to
[the ground.
Your god is wrecking the palace, roof to floor;
He heard our cry—he is coming, the son of
30 [Zeus!
[*The doors open and* DIONYSUS *appears.*]
DIONYSUS. Women of Asia, why do you
[cower thus, prostrate and terrified?
Surely you could hear Dionysus shattering
35 [Pentheus' palace? Come,
Lift yourselves up, take good courage, stop this
[trembling of your limbs!
CHORUS. We are saved! Oh, what a joy to
[hear your Bacchic call ring out!
40 We were all alone, deserted; you have come,
[and we rejoice.
DIONYSUS. Were you comfortless,
[despondent, when I was escorted in,
Helpless, sentenced to be cast in Pentheus'
45 [murky prison-cell?
CHORUS. Who could help it? What protector
[had we, once deprived of you?
Tell us now how you escaped the clutches of

[this wicked man.
DIONYSUS. I alone, at once, unaided,   50
[effortlessly freed myself.
CHORUS. How could that be? Did not
[Pentheus bind your arms with
[knotted ropes?
DIONYSUS. There I made a mockery of him.   55
[He thought he was binding me;
But he neither held nor touched me, save in his
[deluded mind.
Near the mangers where he meant to tie me up,
[he found a bull;   60
And he tied his rope round the bull's knees and
[hooves, panting with rage,
Dripping sweat, biting his lips; while I sat
[quietly by and watched.
It was then that Dionysus shook the building,   65
[made the flame
On his mother's tomb flare up. When Pentheus
[saw this, he supposed
The whole place was burning. He rushed this
[way, that way, calling out   70
To the servants to bring water; every slave
[about the place
Was engaged upon this futile task. He left it
[presently,
Thinking I had escaped; snatched up his   75
[murderous sword, darted indoors.
Thereupon Dionysus—as it seemed to me; I
[merely guess—
Made a phantom hover in the courtyard.
[Pentheus flew at it,   80
Stabbing at the empty sunlight, thinking he
[was killing *me*.
Yet a further humiliation Bacchus next
[contrived for him:
He destroyed the stable buildings. Pentheus   85
[sees my prison now
Lying there, a heap of rubble; and the picture
[grieves his heart.
Now he's dazed and helpless with exhaustion.
[He has dropped his sword.   90
He, a man, dared to take arms against a god. I
[quietly walked
Out of the palace here to join you, giving
[Pentheus not a thought.
But I hear his heavy tread inside the palace.   95
[Soon, I think,

He'll be out here in the forecourt. After what
                    [has happened now,
What will he have to say? For all his rage, he
                    [shall not ruffle *me*.
5   It's a wise man's part to practice a smooth-
                    [tempered self-control.
    [*Enter* PENTHEUS.]
    PENTHEUS. This is outrageous. He has escaped
                    [—that foreigner.
10 Only just now I had him locked up and in
                    [chains.

    [*He sees* DIONYSUS *and gives an excited
    shout.*]
    He's there! Well, what's going on now? How
15   [did you get out?
    How dare you show your face here at my very
                    [door?
    DIONYSUS. Stay where you are. You are
                    [angry; now control yourself.
20 PENTHEUS. You were tied up inside there.
                    [How did you escape?
    DIONYSUS. I said—did you not hear?—that I
                    [should be set free—
    PENTHEUS. By whom? You're always finding
25   [something new to say.
    DIONYSUS. By him who plants for mortals the
                    [rich-clustered vine.
    PENTHEUS. The god who frees his worshippers
                    [from every law.
30 DIONYSUS. Your insult to Dionysus is a
                    [compliment.
    PENTHEUS [*to attendant* GUARDS]. Go round
        [the walls and tell them to close every gate.
    DIONYSUS. And why? Or cannot gods pass
35   [even over walls?
    PENTHEUS. Oh, you know everything—save
                    [what you ought to know.
    DIONYSUS. The things most needful to be
                    [known, those things I know.
40 But listen first to what this man has to report;
    He comes from the mountain, and he has some
                    [news for you.
    I will stay here; I promise not to run away.
    [*Enter a* HERDSMAN.]
45 HERDSMAN. Pentheus, great king of Thebes!
                    [I come from Mount Cithaeron,
    Whose slopes are never free from dazzling
                    [shafts of snow.

PENTHEUS. And what comes next? What
                    [urgent message do you bring?   50
    HERDSMAN. I have seen the holy Bacchae,
                    [who like a flight of spears
    Went streaming bare-limbed, frantic, out of
                    [the city gate.
    I have come with the intention of telling you,   55
                    [my lord,
    And the city, of their strange and terrible
                    [doings—things
    Beyond all wonder. But first I would learn
                    [whether   60
    I may speak freely of what is going on there, or
    If I should trim my words. I fear your hastiness,
    My lord, your anger, your too potent royalty.
    PENTHEUS. From me fear nothing. Say all that
                    [you have to say;   65
    Anger should not grow hot against the
                    [innocent.
    The more dreadful your story of these Bacchic
                    [rites,
    The heavier punishment I will inflict upon   70
    This man who enticed our women to their evil
                    [ways.
    HERDSMAN. At dawn today, when first the
                    [sun's rays warmed the earth,
    My herd of cattle was slowly climbing up   75
                    [towards
    The high pastures; and there I saw three
                    [separate
    Companies of women. The leader of one
                    [company   80
    Was Autonoë, your mother Agauë was at the
                    [head
    Of the second, Ino of the third; and they all lay
    Relaxed and quietly sleeping. Some rested on
                    [beds   85
    Of pine-needles, others had pillows of oak-
                    [leaves.
    They lay just as they had thrown themselves
                    [down on the ground,
    But modestly, not—as you told us—drunk with   90
                    [wine
    Or flute-music, seeking the solitary woods
    For the pursuit of love.
    When your mother Agauë
    Heard the horned cattle bellowing, she stood   95
                    [upright

Among the Bacchae, and called to them to stir
     [themselves
From sleep; and they shook off the strong
     [sleep from their eyes
5 And leapt to their feet. They were a sight to
     [marvel at
For modest comeliness; women both old and
     [young,
Girls still unmarried. First they let their hair fall
10   [free
Over their shoulders; some tied up the
     [fastenings
Of fawnskins they had loosened; round the
     [dappled fur
15 Curled snakes that licked their cheeks. Some
     [would have in their arms
A young gazelle, or wild wolf-cubs, to which
     [they gave
Their own white milk—those of them who had
20   [left at home
Young children newly born, so that their
     [breasts were full.
And they wore wreathes of ivy-leaves, or oak,
     [or flowers
25 Of bryony. One would strike her thyrsus on a
     [rock,
And from the rock a limpid stream of water
     [sprang.
Another dug her wand into the earth, and there
30 The god sent up a fountain of wine. Those who
     [desired
Milk had only to scratch the earth with finger-
     [tips,
And there was the white stream flowing for
35   [them to drink,
While from the thyrsus a sweet ooze of honey
     [dripped.
Oh! if you had been there and seen all this, you
     [would
40 Have offered prayers to this god whom you now
     [condemn.
We herdsmen, then, and shepherds gathered
     [to exchange
Rival reports of these strange and extraordinary
45 Performances; and one, who had knocked about
     [the town,
And had a ready tongue, addressed us: "You
     [who live

On the holy mountain heights," he said, "shall
     [we hunt down 50
Agauë, Pentheus' mother, and bring her back
     [from these
Rituals, and gratify the king? What do you
     [say?"
This seemed a good suggestion; so we hid 55
     [ourselves
In the leafy bushes, waiting. When the set time
     [came,
The women began brandishing their wands,
     [preparing 60
To dance, calling in unison on the son of Zeus,
"Iacchus! Bromius!" And with them the whole
     [mountain,
And all the creatures there, joined in the mystic
     [rite 65
Of Dionysus, and with their motion all things
     [moved.

Now, Agauë as she danced passed close to me;
     [and I
At once leapt out from hiding, bent on 70
     [capturing her.
But she called out, "Oh, my swift-footed
     [hounds, these men
Are hunting us. Come, follow me! Each one of
     [you 75
Arm yourself with the holy thyrsus, and
     [follow me!"

So we fled, and escaped being torn in pieces by
Those possessed women. But our cattle were
     [there, cropping 80
The fresh grass; and the women attacked them,
     [with their bare hands.
You could see one take a full-uddered bellowing
     [young heifer
And hold it by the legs with her two arms 85
     [stretched wide;
Others seized on our cows and tore them limb
     [from limb;
You'd see some ribs, or a cleft hoof, tossed high
     [and low; 90
And rags of flesh hung from pine-branches,
     [dripping blood.
Bulls, which one moment felt proud rage hot
     [in their horns,

The next were thrown bodily to the ground,
                    [dragged down
By hands of girls in thousands; and they
                    [stripped the flesh
5 From the bodies faster than you could wink
                    [your royal eyes.

Then, skimming bird-like over the surface of
                    [the ground,
They scoured the plain which stretches by
10   [Asopus' banks
And yields rich crops for Thebes; and like an
                    [enemy force
They fell on Hysiae and Erythrae, two villages
On the low slopes of Cithaeron, and ransacked
15   [them both;
Snatched babies out of the houses; any plunder
                    [which
They carried on their shoulders stayed there
                    [without straps—
20 Nothing fell to the ground, not bronze or iron;
                    [they carried
Fire on their heads, and yet their soft hair was
                    [not burnt.
The villagers, enraged at being so plundered,
25   [armed
Themselves to resist; and then, my lord, an
                    [amazing sight
Was to be seen. The spears those men were
                    [throwing drew
30 No blood; but the women, hurling a thyrsus
                    [like a spear,
Dealt wounds; in short, those women turned
                    [the men to flight.
There was the power of a god in that. Then
35   [they went back
To the place where they had started from, to
                    [those fountains
The god had caused to flow for them. And they
                    [washed off
40 The blood; and snakes licked clean the stains,
                    [till their cheeks shone.

So, master, whoever this divinity may be,
Receive him in this land. His powers are
                    [manifold;
45 But chiefly, as I hear, he gave to men the vine

To cure their sorrows; and without wine,
                    [neither love
Nor any other pleasure would be left for us.
    CHORUS. I shrink from speaking freely before
                    [the king; yet I   50
Will say it: there is no greater god than
                    [Dionysus.
    PENTHEUS. This Bacchic arrogance advances
                    [on us like
A spreading fire, disgracing us before all Hellas.   55
We must act now. [To the HERDSMAN.] Go
                    [quickly to the Electran gate;
Tell all my men who carry shields, heavy or
                    [light,
All riders on fast horses, all my archers with   60
Their twanging bows, to meet me there in
                    [readiness
For an onslaught on these maniacs. This is
                    [beyond
All bearing, if we must let women so defy us.   65
    DIONYSUS. You refuse, Pentheus, to give heed
                    [to what I say
Or change your ways. Yet still, despite your
                    [wrongs to me,
I warn you: stay here quietly; do not take up   70
                    [arms
Against a god. Dionysus will not tolerate
Attempts to drive his worshippers from their
                    [holy hills.
    PENTHEUS. I'll not have you instruct me. You   75
                    [have escaped your chains;
Now be content—or must I punish you again?
    DIONYSUS. I would control my rage and
                    [sacrifice to him
If I were you, rather than kick against the goad.   80
Can you, a mortal, measure your strength with
                    [a god's?
    PENTHEUS. I'll sacrifice, yes—blood of women,
                    [massacred
Wholesale, as they deserve, among Cithaeron's   85
                    [glens.
    DIONYUS. Your army will be put to flight.
                    [What a disgrace
For bronze shields to be routed by those
                    [women's wands!   90
    PENTHEUS. How can I deal with this
                    [impossible foreigner?
In prison or out, nothing will make him hold

[his tongue.
DIONYSUS. My friend, a happy settlement
[may still be found.
PENTHEUS. How? must I be a slave to my own
5   [slave-women?
DIONYSUS. I will, using no weapons, bring
[those women here.
PENTHEUS. Hear that, for the gods' sake!
[You're playing me some trick.
10 DIONYSUS. What trick?—if I am ready to save
[you by my skill.
PENTHEUS. You've planned this with them,
[so that the rituals can go on.
DIONYSUS. Indeed I have planned this—not
15   [with them, but with the god.
PENTHEUS. Bring out my armor, there!—
[That is enough from you.
DIONYSUS [*with an authoritative shout*].
Wait! [*Then quietly.*] Do you want *to see*
20 Those women, where they sit together, up in
[the hills?
PENTHEUS. Why, yes; for that, I'd give a
[weighty sum of gold.
DIONYSUS. What made you fall into this
25   [great desire to see?
PENTHEUS. It would cause me distress to see
[them drunk with wine.
DIONYSUS. Yet you would gladly witness this
[distressing sight?
30 PENTHEUS. Of course—if I could quietly sit
[under the pines.
DIONYSUS. They'll track you down, even if
[you go there secretly.
PENTHEUS. Openly, then. Yes, what you say
35   [is very true.
DIONYSUS. Then shall I lead you? You will
[undertake to go?
PENTHEUS. Yes, lead me there at once; I am
[impatient.
40 DIONYSUS. Then,
You must first dress yourself in a fine linen
[gown.
PENTHEUS. Why in a linen gown? Must I
[then change my sex?
45 DIONYSUS. In case they kill you, if you are
[seen there as a man.
PENTHEUS. Again you are quite right. How
[you think of everything!

DIONYSUS. It was Dionysus who inspired me
[with that thought. 50
PENTHEUS. Then how can your suggestion
[best be carried out?
DIONYSUS. I'll come indoors with you myself
[and dress you.
PENTHEUS. What? 55
Dress me? In woman's clothes? But I would be
[ashamed.
DIONYSUS. Do you want to watch the
[Maenads? Are you less eager now?
PENTHEUS. What kind of dress did you say 60
[you would put on me?
DIONYSUS. First I'll adorn your head with
[locks of flowing hair.
PENTHEUS. And after that? What style of
[costume shall I have? 65
DIONYSUS. A full-length robe; and on your
[head shall be a snood.
PENTHEUS. Besides these, is there anything
[else you'll put on me?
DIONYSUS. A dappled fawnskin round you, 70
[a thyrsus in your hand.
PENTHEUS. I could not bear to dress myself
[in woman's clothes.
DIONYSUS. If you join battle with the
[Maenads, blood will flow. 75
PENTHEUS. You are right; I must first go to
[spy on them.
DIONYSUS. That way
Is better than inviting force by using it.
PENTHEUS. And how shall I get through the 80
[town without being seen?
DIONYSUS. We'll go by empty streets; I will
[show you the way.
PENTHEUS. The Maenads must not mock me;
[better anything 85
Than that. Now I'll go in, and think how best
[to act.
DIONYSUS. You may do so. My preparations
[are all made.
PENTHEUS. I'll go in, then; and either I'll set 90
[forth at the head
Of my armed men—or else I'll follow your
[advice.
[*Exit* PENTHEUS.]
DIONYSUS. Women, this man is walking into 95
[the net. He will

Visit the Bacchae; and there death shall punish
[him.
Dionysus!—for you are not far distant—all is
[now
5 In your hands. Let us be revenged on him! And
[first
Fill him with wild delusions, drive him out of
[his mind.
While sane, he'll not consent to put on woman's
10   [clothes;
Once free from the curb of reason, he will put
[them on.
I long to set Thebes laughing at him, as he walks
In female garb through all the streets; to
15   [humble him
From the arrogance he showed when first he
[threatened me.
Now I will go, to array Pentheus in the dress
Which he will take down with him to the house
20   [of Death,
Slaughtered by his own mother's hands. And
[he shall know
Dionysus, son of Zeus, in his full nature God,
Most terrible, although most gentle, to
25   [mankind.
[DIONYSUS *follows* PENTHEUS *into the palace.*]

ODE III

Strophe
CHORUS. O for long nights of worship, gay
With the pale gleam of dancing feet,
With head tossed high to the dewy air—
30 Pleasure mysterious and sweet!
O for the joy of a fawn at play
In the fragrant meadow's green delight,
Who has leapt out free from the woven snare,
Away from the terror of chase and flight,
35 And the huntsman's shout, and the straining
[pack,
And skims the sand by the river's brim
With the speed of wind in each aching limb,
To the blessed lonely forest where
40 The soil's unmarked by a human track,
And leaves hang thick and the shades are dim.

Refrain
What prayer should we call wise?

What gift of Heaven should man
Count a more noble prize,
A prayer more prudent, than   45
To stretch a conquering arm
Over the fallen crest
Of those who wished us harm?
And what is noble every heart loves best.

Antistrophe
Slow, yet unfailing, move the Powers   50
Of heaven with the moving hours.
When mind runs mad, dishonors God,
And worships self and senseless pride,
Then Law eternal wields the rod.
Still Heaven hunts down the impious man,   55
Though divine subtlety may hide
Time's creeping foot. No mortal ought
To challenge Time—to overbear
Custom in act, or age in thought.
All men, at little cost, may share   60
The blessing of a pious creed;
Truths more than mortal, which began
In the beginning, and belong
To very nature—these indeed
Reign in our world, are fixed and strong.   65

Refrain
What prayer should we call wise?
What gift of heaven should man
Count a more noble prize,
A prayer more prudent, than
To stretch a conquering arm   70
Over the fallen crest
Of those who wished us harm?
And what is noble every heart loves best.

Epode
Blest is the man who cheats the stormy sea
And safely moors beside the sheltering quay;   75
So, blest is he who triumphs over trial.
One man, by various means, in wealth or
[strength
Outdoes his neighbor; hope in a thousand
[hearts 80
Colors a thousand different dreams; at length
Some find a dear fulfilment, some denial.
    But this I say
    That he who best

Enjoys each passing day
Is truly blest.

SCENE IV

[*Enter* DIONYSUS. *He turns to call* PENTHEUS.]
DIONYSUS. Come, perverse man, greedy for
5   [sights you should not see,
Eager for deeds you should not do—Pentheus!
          [Come out
Before the palace and show yourself to me,
          [wearing
10 The garb of a frenzied Bacchic woman, and
          [prepared
To spy on your mother and all her Bacchic
          [company.
[*Enter* PENTHEUS *dressed as a Bacchic devotee.*
15 *He is dazed and entirely subservient to* DIONY-
SUS.]
You are the very image of one of Cadmus'
          [daughters.
PENTHEUS. Why now! I seem to see two suns;
20   [a double Thebes;
Our city's wall with seven gates appears double.
[DIONYSUS *takes* PENTHEUS *by the hand and
leads him forward.*]
You are a bull I see leading me forward now;
25 A pair of horns seems to have grown upon your
          [head.
Were you a beast before? You have become a
          [bull.
DIONYSUS. The god then did not favor us; he
30   [is with us now,
We have made our peace with him; you see as
          [you should see.
PENTHEUS. How do I look? Tell me, is not the
          [way I stand
35 Like the way Ino stands, or like my mother
          [Agaüe?
DIONYSUS. Looking at you, I think I see them
          [both. Wait, now;
Here is a curl has slipped out of its proper place,
40 Not as I tucked it carefully below your snood.
PENTHEUS. Indoors, as I was tossing my head
          [up and down
Like a Bacchic dancer, I dislodged it from its
          [place.
45 DIONYSUS. Come, then; I am the one who

          [should look after you.
I'll fix it in its place again. There; lift your head.
PENTHEUS. You dress me, please; I have put
          [myself in your hands now.
DIONYSUS. Your girdle has come loose; and   50
          [now your dress does not
Hang, as it should, in even pleats down to the
          [ankle.
PENTHEUS. That's true, I think—at least by
          [the right leg, on this side;   55
But on the other side the gown hangs well to
          [the heel.
DIONYSUS. You'll surely count me chief
          [among your friends, when you
Witness the Maenads' unexpected modesty.   60
PENTHEUS. Ought I to hold my thyrsus in the
          [right hand—so,
Or in the left, to look more like a Bacchanal?
DIONYSUS. In the right hand; and raise it at
          [the same time as   65
Your right foot. I am glad you are so changed
          [in mind.
PENTHEUS. Could I lift up on my own
          [shoulders the whole weight
Of Mount Cithaeron, and all the women   70
          [dancing there?
DIONYSUS. You could, if you so wished. The
          [mind you had before
Was sickly; now your mind is just as it should
          [be.   75
PENTHEUS. Shall we take crowbars? Or shall
          [I put my shoulder under
The rocks, and heave the mountain up with
          [my two arms?
DIONYSUS. Oh, come now! Don't destroy the   80
          [dwellings of the nymphs,
And the quiet places where Pan sits to play his
          [pipes.
PENTHEUS. You are right. We ought not to
          [use force to overcome   85
Those women. I will hide myself among the
          [pines.
DIONYSUS. Hide—yes, you'll hide, and find
          [the proper hiding-place
For one who comes by stealth to spy on Bacchic   90
          [rites.
PENTHEUS. Why, yes! I think they are there
          [now in their hidden nests,

Like birds, all clasped close in the sweet prison
[of love.
DIONYSUS. What you are going to watch for
[is this very thing!
5 Perhaps you will catch them—if you are not
[first caught yourself.
PENTHEUS. Now take me through the central
[streets of Thebes; for I
Am the one man among them all that dares do
10 [this.
DIONYSUS. One man alone, you agonize for
[Thebes; therefore
It is your destined ordeal that awaits you now.
Come with me; I will bring you safely to the
15 [place;
Another shall conduct you back.
PENTHEUS. My mother—yes?
DIONYSUS. A sight for all to witness.
PENTHEUS. To this end I go.
20 DIONYSUS. You will return borne high—
PENTHEUS. Royal magnificence!
DIONYSUS. In your own mother's arms.
PENTHEUS. You insist that I be spoiled.
DIONYSUS One kind of spoiling.
25 PENTHEUS. Yet I win what I deserve.
[Exit PENTHEUS.]
DIONYSUS. Pentheus, you are a man to make
[men fear; fearful
Will be your end—an end that shall lift up your
30 [fame
To the height of heaven.
Agauë, and you her sisters, daughters of
[Cadmus,
Stretch out your hands! See, I am bringing this
35 [young man
To his great battle; and I and Bromius shall be
Victors. What more shall happen, the event will
[show.
[Exit DIONYSUS.]

ODE IV

Strophe
40 CHORUS. Hounds of Madness, fly to the
[mountain, fly
Where Cadmus' daughters are dancing in
[ecstasy!
Madden them like a frenzied herd stampeding,

Against the madman hiding in woman's clothes 45
To spy on the Maenads' rapture!
First his mother shall see him craning his neck
Down from a rounded rock or a sharp crag.
And shout to the Maenads, "Who is the man,
[you Bacchae, 50
Who has come to the mountain, come to the
[mountain spying
On the swift wild mountain—dances of
[Cadmus' daughters?
Which of you is his mother? 55
No, that lad never lay in a woman's womb;
A lioness gave him suck, or a Libyan Gorgon!"

Justice, now be revealed! Now let your sword
Thrust—through and through—to sever the
[throat 60
Of the godless, lawless, shameless son of
[Echion,
Who sprang from the womb of Earth!

Antistrophe
See! With contempt of right, with a reckless
[rage 65
To combat your and your mother's mysteries,
[Bacchus,
With maniac fury out he goes, stark mad,
For a trial of strength against *your* invincible
[arm! 70
His proud purposes death shall discipline.
He who unquestioning gives the gods their due,
And knows that his days are as dust, shall live
[untouched.
I have no wish to grudge the wise their wisdom; 75
But the joys *I* seek are greater, outshine all
[others,
And lead our life to goodness and loveliness:
The joy of the holy heart
That night and day is bent to honor the gods 80
And disown all custom that breaks the bounds
[of right.

Justice, now be revealed! Now let your sword
Thrust—through and through—to sever the
[throat 85
Of the godless, lawless, shameless son of
[Echion,
Who sprang from the womb of Earth!

[*Then with growing excitement, shouting in unison, and dancing to the rhythm of their words.*]

Epode

Come, Dionysus!
5   Come, and appear to us!
Come like a bull or a
Hundred-headed serpent,
Come like a lion snorting
Flame from your nostrils!
10   Swoop down, Bacchus, on the
Hunter of the Bacchae;
Smile at him and snare him;
Then let the stampeding
Herd of the Maenads
15   Throw him and throttle him,
Catch, trip, trample him to death!

SCENE V

[*Enter a* MESSENGER.]
MESSENGER. O house that once shone glorious
               [throughout Hellas, home
20 Of the old Sidonian king who planted in this
               [soil
The dragon's earth-born harvest! How I weep
               [for you!
Slave though I am, I suffer with my master's
25   [fate.
CHORUS. Are you from the mountain, from
               [the Bacchic rites? What news?
MESSENGER. Pentheus, son of Echion, is dead.
CHORUS. Bromius, lord! Your divine power is
30   [revealed!
MESSENGER. What, woman? What was that
               [you said? Do you exult
When such a cruel fate has overtaken the king?
CHORUS. I am no Greek.
35 I sing my joy in a foreign tune.
Not any more do I cower in terror of prison!
MESSENGER. Do you think Thebes has no
               [men left who can take command?
CHORUS. Dionysus commands *me*;
40 Not Thebes, but Dionysus.
MESSENGER. Allowance must be made for
               [you; yet, to rejoice
At the accomplishment of horrors, is not right.

CHORUS. Tell us everything, then: this tyrant
               [king 45
Bent on cruelty—how did he die?
MESSENGER. When we had left behind the
               [outlying parts of Thebes
And crossed the river Asopus, we began to
               [climb 50
Toward the uplands of Cithaeron, Pentheus
               [and I—
I went as his attendant—and the foreigner
Who was our guide to the spectacle we were to
               [see. 55
Well, first we sat down in a grassy glade. We
               [kept
Our footsteps and our talk as quiet as possible,
So as to see without being seen. We found
               [ourselves 60
In a valley full of streams, with cliffs on either
               [side.
There, under the close shade of branching
               [pines, the Maenads
Were sitting, their hands busy at their happy 65
               [tasks;
Some of them twining a fresh crown of ivy-
               [leaves
For a stripped thyrsus; others, gay as fillies
               [loosed 70
From painted yokes, were singing holy Bacchic
               [songs,
Each answering other. But the ill-fated
               [Pentheus saw
None of this; and he said, "My friend, from 75
               [where we stand
My eyes cannot make out these so-called
               [worshippers;
But if I climb a towering pine-tree on the cliff
I would have a clear view of their shameful 80
               [practices."

And then I saw that foreigner do an amazing
               [thing.
He took hold of a pine-tree's soaring, topmost
               [branch, 85
And dragged it down, down to the dark earth.
               [It was bent
In a circle as a bow is bent, as a wheel's curve,
Drawn with a compass, bends the rim to its
               [own shape; 90

The foreigner took that mountain-pine in his
[two hands
And bent it down—a thing no mortal man
[could do.
5 Then seating Pentheus on a high branch, he
[began
To let the tree spring upright, slipping it
[through his hands
Steadily, taking care he should not be flung off.
10 The pine-trunk, straightened, soared into the
[soaring sky,
Bearing my master seated astride, so that he
[was
More visible to the Maenads than they were to
15 [him.
He was just coming into view on his high perch,
When out of the sky a voice—Dionysus, I
[suppose;
That foreigner was nowhere to be seen—pealed
20 [forth:
"Women, here is the man who made a mock of
[you,
And me, and of my holy rites. Now punish
[him."
25 And in the very moment the voice spoke, a
[flash
Of dreadful fire stretched between earth and
[high heaven.

The air fell still. The wooded glade held every
30 [leaf
Still. You could hear no cry of any beast. The
[women,
Not having caught distinctly what the voice
[uttered,
35 Stood up and gazed around. Then came a
[second word
Of command. As soon as Cadmus' daughters
[recognized
The clear bidding of Bacchus, with the speed of
40 [doves
They darted forward, and all the Bacchae after
[them.
Through the torrent-filled valley, over the
[rocks, possessed
45 By the very breath of Bacchus they went
[leaping on.
Then, when they saw my master crouched high
[in the pine,

At first they climbed the cliff which towered
[opposite,   50
And violently flung at him pieces of rocks, or
[boughs
Of pine-trees which they hurled as javelins;
[and some
Aimed with the thyrsus; through the high air   55
[all around
Their wretched target missiles flew. Yet every
[aim
Fell short, the tree's height baffled all their
[eagerness;   60
While Pentheus, helpless in this pitiful trap, sat
[there.
Then, with a force like lightning, they tore
[down branches
Of oak, and with these tried to prize up the   65
[tree's roots.
When all their struggles met with no success,
[Agaué
Cried out, "Come, Maenads, stand in a circle
[round the tree   70
And take hold of it. We must catch this
[climbing beast,
Or he'll disclose the secret dances of Dionysus."
They came; a thousand hands gripped on the
[pine and tore it   75
Out of the ground. Then from his high perch
[plunging, crashing
To the earth Pentheus fell, with one incessant
[scream
As he understood what end was near.   80

His mother first,
As priestess, led the rite of death, and fell upon
[him.
He tore the headband from his hair, that his
[wretched mother   85
Might recognize him and not kill him.
"Mother," he cried,
Touching her cheek, "it is I, your own son
[Pentheus, whom
You bore to Echion. Mother, have mercy; I   90
[have sinned,
But I am still your own son. Do not take my
[life!"

Agaué was foaming at the mouth; her rolling
[eyes   95

Were wild; she was not in her right mind, but
[possessed
By Bacchus, and she paid no heed to him. She
[grasped
5   His right arm between wrist and elbow, set her
[foot
Against his ribs, and tore his arm off by the
[shoulder.
It was no strength of hers that did it, but the
10 [god
Filled her, and made it easy. On the other side
Ino was at him, tearing at his flesh; and now
Autonoë joined them, and the whole maniacal
[horde.
15 A single and continuous yell arose—Pentheus
Shrieking as long as life was left in him, the
[women
Howling in triumph. One of them carried off an
[arm,
20 Another a foot, the boot still laced on it. The
[ribs
Were stripped, clawed clean; and women's
[hands, thick red with blood,
Were tossing, catching, like a plaything,
25 [Pentheus' flesh.

His body lies—no easy task to find—scattered
Under hard rocks, or in the green woods. His
[poor head—
His mother carries it, fixed on her thyrsus-
30 [point,
Openly over Cithaeron's pastures, thinking it
The head of a young mountain-lion. She has
[left her sisters
Dancing among the Maenads, and herself
35 [comes here
Inside the walls, exulting in her hideous prey,
Shouting to Bacchus, calling him her fellow-
[hunter,
Her partner in the kill, comrade in victory.
40 But Bacchus gives her bitter tears for her
[reward.

Now I will go. I must find some place far away
From this horror, before Agauë returns home.
A sound and humble heart that reverences the
45 [gods
Is man's noblest possession; and the same
[virtue

Is wisest too, I think, for those who practice it.
[*Exit the* MESSENGER.]

ODE V

CHORUS. Let us dance a dance to Bacchus,   50
[shout and sing
For the fall of Pentheus, heir of the dragon's
[seed,
Who hid his beard in a woman's gown,
And sealed his death with the holy sign   55
Of ivy wreathing a fennel-reed,
When bull led man to the ritual slaughter-ring.
Frenzied daughters of Cadmus, what renown
Your victory wins you—such a song
As groans must stifle, tears must drown!   60

Emblem of conquest, brave and fine!—
A mother's hand, defiled
With blood and dripping red
Caresses the torn head
Of her own murdered child!   65

But look! I see her—there, running towards the
[palace—
Agauë, Pentheus' mother, her eyes wildly
[rolling.
Come, welcome them—Dionysus' holy   70
[company.

ÉXODOS

AGAUË *appears, frenzied and panting, with*
PENTHEUS' *head held in her hand. The rest of
her band of devotees, whom the* CHORUS *saw
approaching with her, do not enter; but a few* 75
*are seen standing by the entrance, where they
wait until the end of the play.*]
AGAUË. Women of Asia! Worshippers of
[Bacchus!
[AGAUË *tries to show them* PENTHEUS' *head;* 80
they shrink from it.]
CHORUS. Why do you urge me? Oh!
AGAUË. I am bringing home from the
[mountains
A vine-branch freshly cut,   85
For the gods have blessed our hunting.
CHORUS. We see it . . . and welcome you in
[fellowship.

AGAUË. I caught him without a trap,
A lion-cub, young and wild.
Look, you may see him: there!
    CHORUS. Where was it?
5 AGAUË. On Cithaeron;
The wild and empty mountain—
    CHORUS. Cithaeron!
AGAUË. . . . spilt his life-blood.
    CHORUS. Who shot him?
10 AGAUË. I was first;
All the women are singing,
"Honor to great Agauë!"
    CHORUS. And then—who next?
    AGAUË. Why, Cadmus' . . .
15   CHORUS. What—Cadmus?
    AGAUË. Yes, his daughters—
But after me, after me—
Laid their hands to the kill.
Today was a splendid hunt!
20 Come now, join in the feast!
    CHORUS. What, wretched woman? *Feast?*
    AGAUË [*tenderly stroking the head as she
holds it*]. This calf is young: how thickly
The new-grown hair goes crisping
25 Up to his delicate crest!
    CHORUS. Indeed, his long hair makes him
Look like some wild creature.
    AGAUË. The god is a skilled hunter?
And he poised his hunting women,
30 And hurled them at the quarry.
    CHORUS. True, our god is a hunter.
    AGAUË. Do you praise me?
    CHORUS. Yes, we praise you.
    AGAUË. So will the sons of Cadmus . . .
35   CHORUS. And Pentheus too, Agauë?
    AGAUË. Yes he will praise his mother
For the lion-cub she killed.
    CHORUS. Oh, fearful!
    AGAUË. Ay, fearful!
40   CHORUS. You are happy?
    AGAUË. I am enraptured;
Great in the eyes of the world,
Great are the deeds I've done,
And the hunt that I hunted there!
45   CHORUS. Then show it, poor Agauë—this
        [triumphant spoil
You've brought home; show it to all the citizens
        [of Thebes.
AGAUË. Come, all you Thebans living within
        [these towered walls, 50
Come, see the beast we, Cadmus' daughters,
        [caught and killed;
Caught not with nets or thonged Thessalian
        [javelins,
But with our own bare arms and fingers. After 55
        [this
Should huntsmen glory in their exploits, who
        [must buy
Their needless tools from armorers? We with
        [our hands 60
Hunted and took this beast, then tore it limb
        [from limb.

Where is my father? Let old Cadmus come.
        [And where
Is my son Pentheus? Let him climb a strong 65
        [ladder
And nail up on the cornice of the palace wall
This lion's head that I have hunted and brought
        [home.
    [*Enter* CADMUS *with attendants bearing the* 70
body of PENTHEUS.]
    CADMUS. Come, men, bring your sad burden
        [that was Pentheus. Come,
Set him at his own door. By weary, endless
        [search 75
I found his body's remnants scattered far and
        [wide
About Cithaeron's glens, or hidden in thick
        [woods.
I gathered them and brought them here. 80

I had already
Returned with old Teiresias from the Bacchic
        [dance,
And was inside the walls, when news was
        [brought me of 85
My daughters' terrible deed. I turned straight
        [back; and now
Return, bringing my grandson, whom the
        [Maenads killed.
I saw Autonoë, who bore Actaeon to Aristaeus, 90
And Ino with her, there among the trees, still
        [rapt

In their unhappy frenzy; but I understood
That Agauë had come dancing on her way to
[Thebes—
And there indeed she is, a sight for misery!
5   AGAUË. Father! Now you may boast as
[loudly as you will
That you have sired the noblest daughters of
[this age!
I speak of all three, but myself especially.
10   I have left weaving at the loom for greater
[things,
For hunting wild beasts with my bare hands.
[See this prize,
Here in my arms; I won it, and it shall be hung
15   On your palace wall. There, father, take it in
[your hands.
Be proud of my hunting; call your friends to a
[feast; let them
Bless you and envy you for the splendor of my
20   [deed.
      CADMUS. Oh, misery unmeasured, sight
[intolerable!
Oh, bloody deed enacted by most pitiful hands!
What noble prize is this you lay at the gods'
25   [feet,
Calling the city, and me, to a banquet? Your
[wretchedness
Demands the bitterest tears; but mine is next
[to yours.
30   Dionysus has dealt justly, but pursued justice
Too far; born of my blood, he has destroyed
[my house.
      AGAUË. What an ill-tempered creature an old
[man is! How full
35   Of scowls! I wish my son were a great hunter
[like
His mother, hunting beasts with the young men
[of Thebes;
But *he* can only fight with gods. Father, you
40   [must
Correct him.—Will not someone go and call
[him here
To see me, and to share in my great happiness?
      CADMUS. Alas, my daughters! If you come
45   [to understand
What you have done, how terrible your pain
[will be!

If you remain as you are now, though you could
[not
Be happy, at least you will not feel your   50
[wretchedness.
      AGAUË. Why not happy? What cause have I
[for wretchedness?
      CADMUS. Come here. First turn your eyes
[this way. Look at the sky.   55
      AGAUË. I am looking. Why should you want
[me to look at it?
      CADMUS. Does it appear the same to you, or is
[it changed?
      AGAUË. Yes, it is clearer than before, more   60
[luminous.
      CADMUS. And this disturbance of your
[mind—is it still there?
      AGAUË. I don't know what you mean; but—
[yes, I feel a change;   65
My mind is somehow clearer than it was
[before.
      CADMUS. Could you now listen to me and
[give a clear reply?
      AGAUË. Yes, father. I have forgotten what we   70
[said just now.
      CADMUS. When you were married, whose
[house did you go to then?
      AGAUË. You gave me to Echion, of the sown
[race, they said.   75
      CADMUS. Echion had a son born to him. Who
[was he?
      AGAUË. Pentheus. His father lay with me; I
[bore a son.
      CADMUS. Yes, and whose head is that you are   80
[holding in your arms?
      AGAUË. A lion's—so the women said who
[hunted it.
      CADMUS. Then look straight at it. Come, to
[look is no great task.   85
[AGAUË *looks; and suddenly screams.*]
      AGAUË. What am I looking at? What is this
[in my hands?
      CADMUS. Look at it steadily; come closer to
[the truth.   90
      AGAUË. I see—O gods, what horror! Oh,
[what misery!
      CADMUS. Does this appear to you to be a
[lion's head?

AGAUË. No! I hold Pentheus' head in my
[accursed hand.
CADMUS. It is so. Tears have been shed for
[him, before you knew.
5 AGAUË. But who killed him? How did he
[come into my hands?
CADMUS. O cruel hour, that brings a bitter
[truth to light!
AGAUË. Tell me—my heart is bursting, I
10 [must know the rest.
CADMUS. It was you, Agaüë, and your sisters.
[You killed him.
AGAUË. Where was it done? Here in the
[palace? Or where else?
15 CADMUS. Where, long ago, Actaeon was
[devoured by hounds.
AGAUË. Cithaeron, But what evil fate took
[Pentheus there?
CADMUS. He went to mock Dionysus and
20 [your Bacchic rites.
AGAUË. Why were we on Cithaeron? What
[had brought us there.
CADMUS. You were possessed. All Thebes
[was in a Bacchic trance.
25 AGAUË. Dionysus has destroyed us. Now I
[understand.
CADMUS. He was insulted. You refused to call
[him god.
AGAUË. Father, where is the beloved body of
30 [my son?
CADMUS. Here. It was I who brought it, after
[painful search.
AGAUË. And are his limbs now decently
[composed?
35 CADMUS. Not yet.
We came back to the city with all possible
[haste.
AGAUË. How could I touch his body with
[these guilty hands?
40 CADMUS. Your guilt, my daughter, was not
[heavier than his.
AGAUË. What part did Pentheus have, then,
[in my insanity?
CADMUS. He sinned like you, refusing
45 [reverence to a god.
Therefore the god has joined all in one ruin—
[you,
Your sisters, Pentheus—to destroy my house
[and me.

I have no son; and now, my unhappy child, I 50
[see
This son of yours dead by a shameful, hideous
[death.
You were the new hope of our house, its bond
[of strength, 55
Dear grandson. And Thebes feared you; no
[one dared insult
Your old grandfather if he saw you near; you
[would
Teach him his lesson. But now I shall live 60
[exiled,
Dishonored—I, Cadmus the great, who planted
[here,
And reaped, that glorious harvest of the
[Theban race. 65

O dearest son—yes, even in death you shall be
[held
Most dear—you will never touch my beard
[again, and call
Me Grandfather, and put your arm round me 70
[and say,
"Who has wronged you or insulted you? Who
[is unkind,
Or vexes or disturbs you? Tell me, Grandfather,
That I may punish him." Never again. For me 75
All that remains is pain; for you, the pity of
[death;
For your mother, tears; torment for our whole
[family.

If any man derides the unseen world, let him 80
Ponder the death of Pentheus, and believe in
[gods.
CHORUS. I grieve for your fate, Cadmus;
[though your grandson's death
Was justly merited, it falls cruelly on you. 85
AGAUË. Father, you see how one disastrous
[day has shattered
My whole life . . .

[At this point the two MSS on which the
text of this play depends show a lacuna of con- 90
siderable extent; it covers the end of this scene,
in which Agaüë mourns over Pentheus' body,
and the appearance of Dionysus manifested as
a god. The MSS resume in the middle of a
speech by Dionysus. A number of quotations by 95

ancient authors, together with less than 20
lines from *Christus Patiens* (an anonymous
fourth century A.D. work consisting largely of
lines adapted from Greek tragedies), make it
5 possible to attempt a guess at the content of
the missing lines. Because this play is often
performed, it seems worthwhile to provide here
a usable text. In the lines that follow, the words
printed in italics are mere conjecture, and have
10 no value except as a credible completion of the
probable sense; while those in Roman type
represent the sources available from *Christus
Patiens* and elsewhere.—Translator's note.]

... my whole life, *turned my pride to shame,*
15   *[my happiness*
To horror, Now my only wish is to compose
My son's body for burial, and lament for him;
And then die. But this is not lawful; *for my*
                          [hands
20 *Are filthy with pollution of their own making.*
When I have spilt the blood I bore, and torn the
                          [flesh
That grew in my own womb, how can I after
                          [this
25 *Enfold him to my breast, or chant his ritual*
                          [dirge?
And yet, I beg you, pity me, and let me touch
My son, and say farewell to that dear body
                          [which
30 *I cherished, and destroyed unknowing.* It is
                          [right
That you should pity, for your hands are
                          [innocent.
CADMUS. My daughter, you and I and our
35   *[whole house are crushed*
And broken by the anger of this powerful god.
It is not for me to keep you from your son.
                          [Only
Be resolute, and steel your heart against a sight
40 *Which must be fearful to any eyes, but most*
                          [of all
To a mother's. [*To attendants.*] Men, put down
                          [your burden on the ground
Before Agauë, and remove the covering.
45 AGAUË. *Dear child, how cruel, how unnatural*
                          [are these tears,
Which should have fallen from your eyes on my
                          [dead face.

Now I shall die with none to mourn me. This is
                          [just; 50
For in my pride I did not recognize the god,
Nor understand the things I ought to have
                          [understood.
You too are punished for the same impiety;
But which is the more terrible, your fate or 55
                          [mine,
I cannot tell. Since you have suffered too, you
                          [will
Forgive both what I did, not knowing what I
                          [did, 60
And what I do now, touching you with unholy
                          [hands—
At once your cruellest enemy and your dearest
                          [friend.

I place your limbs as they should lie; I kiss the 65
                          [flesh
That my own body nourished and my own
                          [care reared
To manhood. Help me, father; lay his poor
                          [head here. 70
Make all exact and seemly, with what care we
                          [can.
O dearest face, O young fresh cheek? O kingly
                          [eyes,
Your light now darkened! O my Son! See, with 75
                          [this veil
I now cover your head, your torn and
                          [bloodstained limbs.
Take him up, carry him to burial, a king
Lured to a shameful death by the anger of a 80
                          [god.
[*Enter* DIONYSUS.]
CHORUS. But look! Who is this, rising above
                          [the palace door?
It is he—Dionysus comes himself, no more 85
                          [disguised
As mortal, but in the glory of his divinity!
DIONYSUS. Behold me, a god great and
                          [powerful, Dionysus,
The son whom Theban Semele bore to immortal 90
                          [Zeus.
I come to the city of seven gates, to famous
                          [Thebes,
Whose people slighted me, denied my divinity,
Refused my ritual dances. Now they reap the 95
                          [fruit

Of impious folly. The royal house is
                              [overthrown;
The city's streets tremble in guilt, as every
                              [Theban
5 *Repents too late his blindness and his*
                              [blasphemy.
Foremost in sin was Pentheus, who not only
                              [scorned
My claims, but put me in fetters and insulted
10   *[me.*
Therefore death came to him in the most
                              [shameful way,
At his own mother's hands. This fate he justly
                              [earned;
15 *No god can see his worship scorned, and hear*
                              [his name
Profaned, and not take vengeance to the utmost
                              [limit.
Thus men may learn that gods are more
20   *[powerful than they.*
Agauë and her sisters must immediately
Depart from Thebes; their exile will be just
                              [penance
For the pollution which this blood has brought
25   *[on them.*
Never again shall they enjoy their native land;
That such defilement ever should appear before
The city's altars, is an offense to piety.

Now Cadmus, hear what suffering Fate
30   [appoints for you.

[Here the MSS resume.—Translator's note.]

You shall transmute your nature, and become
                              [a serpent.
Your wife Harmonia, whom her father Ares
35   [gave
To you, a mortal, likewise shall assume the
                              [nature
Of beasts, and live a snake. The oracle of Zeus
Foretells that you, at the head of a barbaric
40   [horde,
Shall with your wife drive forth a pair of
                              [heifers yoked,
And with your countless army destroy many
                              [cities;

But when they plunder Loxias' oracle, they shall 45
                              [find
A miserable homecoming. However, Ares shall
At last deliver both you and Harmonia,
And grant you immortal life among the blessed
                              [gods. 50

I who pronounce these fates am Dionysus,
                              [begotten
Not by a mortal father, but by Zeus. If you
Had chosen wisdom, when you would not, you
                              [would have lived 55
In wealth and safety, having the son of Zeus
                              [your friend.
    CADMUS. Have mercy on us, Dionysus. We
                              [have sinned.
    DIONYSUS. You know too late. You did not 60
                              [know me when you should.
    CADMUS. We acknowledge this; but your
                              [revenge is merciless.
    DIONYSUS. And rightly; I am a god, and you
                              [insulted me. 65
    CADMUS. Gods should not be like mortals in
                              [vindictiveness.
    DIONYSUS. All this my father Zeus ordained
                              [from the beginning.
    AGAUË. No hope, father. Our harsh fate is 70
                              [decreed: exile.
    DIONYSUS. Then why put off a fate which is
                              [inevitable?
[*Exit* DIONYSUS.]
    CADMUS. Dear child, what misery has 75
                              [overtaken us all—
You, and your sisters, and your old unhappy
                              [father!
I must set forth from home and live in
                              [barbarous lands; 80
Further than that, it is foretold that I shall lead
A mixed barbarian horde to Hellas. And my
                              [wife,
Harmonia, Ares' daughter, and I too, must take
The brutish form of serpents; and I am to lead 85
                              [her thus
At the head of an armed force, to desecrate the
                              [tombs
And temples of our native land. I am to reach
No respite from this curse; I may not even cross 90

The downward stream of Acheron to find peace
              [in death.
   AGAUË. And I in exile, father, shall live far
               [from you.

5   CADMUS. Poor child, why do you cling to me,
              [as the young swan
Clings fondly to the old, helpless and white
              [with age?
   AGAUË. Where can I turn for comfort,

10   [homeless and exiled?
   CADMUS. I do not know. Your father is little
              [help to you.
   AGAUË. Farewell, my home; farewell the land
              [I know.

15 Exiled, accursed and wretched, now I go
Forth from this door where first I came a bride.
   CADMUS. Go, daughter, find some secret place
              [to hide
Your shame and sorrow.

20   AGAUË. Father, I weep for you.
   CADMUS. I for your suffering, and your
              [sisters' too.
   AGAUË. There is strange tyranny in the god
              [who sent

25 Against your house this cruel punishment.
   CADMUS. Not strange: our citizens despised
              [his claim,
And you, and they, put him to open shame.
   AGAUË. Father, farewell.

30   CADMUS. Poor child! I cannot tell
How you can *fare well*; yet I say, Farewell.
   AGAUË. I go to lead my sisters by the hand
To share my wretchedness in a foreign land.
   [*She turns to the Theban women who have*

35 *been waiting at the edge of the stage.*]
Come, see me forth.
Gods, lead me to some place
Where loath'd Cithaeron may not see my face,
Nor I Cithaeron. I have had my fill

40 Of mountain-ecstasy; now take who will
My holy ivy-wreath, my thyrsus-rod,
All that reminds me how I served this god!
   [*Exit, followed by* CADMUS.]
   CHORUS. Gods manifest themselves in many

45   [forms,
Bring many matters to surprising ends;
The things we thought would happen do not
              [happen;
The unexpected God makes possible:
And that is what has happened here today.   50
   [*Exeunt.*]

Anonymous

The Second Shepherds' Play

Late Fourteenth Century

In the late medieval cycles of plays celebrating human history from the Creation through the Incarnation to the Day of Judgment, there was place for a play about the shepherds to whom came an angel with tidings that a savior was born. In the cycle at Wakefield, in Yorkshire, there were two such plays, called simply *The First* and *The Second Shepherds' Plays*. The latter is the crowning achievement of the author, whom we know only as the Wakefield Master, and perhaps of the religious drama of the Middle Ages.

The world of this play, like that of medieval art generally, comprehends, but is not confined by, particularities of time and space. Although Christ is not yet born in the early scenes, the shepherds call upon His Cross and His name and also upon Christian saints, among them St. Nicholas, who lived more than three centuries after Christ. Also, the shepherds seem firmly grounded near Wakefield, inasmuch as the nearby village of Horbury is referred to; yet when the angel sends them to Bethlehem, they go, arriving before dawn and without crossing water. Such literal impossibilities seem not to have concerned artists who, from the perspective of eternity, saw history as synchronous, space as seamless and unitary. And in their art they captured, both realistically and ritualistically, timely and timeless truths.

The liveried retainers who expropriate to their own use the goods of such underlings as Coll; the feckless and procreant among the lower orders, like Mak and Gill, who cog, shuffle, and filch, with imagination if without much success; and the lowly and oppressed herdsmen who scrabble for a living and find little more than song and the brief charitable impulses of their own hearts to rejoice in— these come to us with remarkable particularity from the Wakefield Master's contemporary experience; yet surely they embody as well the nature and condition of such men as, fourteen centuries before, would have journeyed to the town of

117

Bethlehem or dwelt in the fields nearby, keeping watch over their flocks by night.

Mary and the "little day-star" in her lap, by contrast, are unique as well as typical. To render them vivid as a mother and child, the same kind of particularity that the Wakefield Master had invested in the shepherds was needed. To celebrate them as the transcendent Mother and Child, ritual was called for—in the pageants of communal drama as in the services of the Church. And these modes are handled with a brilliance virtually unexampled.

In the beginning, when the three shepherds lament the political, domestic, and natural causes of their suffering, and when they are joined by the light-fingered and slippery-tongued night-walker Mak, the mode is realistic if anachronistic. Even here, though, we see symbolic elements anticipating the Adoration of the Christ Child. This is the darkness before the dawn, the suffering before the redemption, and the local flood is likened to the Flood of Noah, the antetype of Christ, who preserved a remnant of mankind from destruction and with whom the Lord established an everlasting covenant.

In the play's middle portion realism is again the mode—comic realism now, exploiting the petty irritabilities of the shepherds, the cat-and-dog marriage of Mak and Gill, the theft and discovery of the sheep. Nevertheless, for all the comedy, the symbols gain in intensity. Mak, commending himself to the hands of Pontius Pilate and then casting a spell on the shepherds, looms momentarily as the devil. Gill's device for hiding the sheep is a false nativity, preparing by contrast for the true one to follow. Mak's anticipated meal and his somewhat insistent invitations to the shepherds to eat and drink are clear if oblique reminders of the mass, the eucharistic feast.

In the final scene the realistic detail typifies as before—more powerfully, perhaps; certainly without the former hint of abrasiveness—as the shepherds offer their humble gifts and bestow on the child just such happy affection as men have felt at cradles throughout all ages: "he merries," "he laughs," "darling dear." The element of ritual, anticipated by the earlier symbols, now achieves its fullest expression. No longer allusively but directly the play deals with Mary and her Son. In one of the imposing tableaux of Christian art, the shepherds kneel and are inspired to a litany of grateful praise, uniting worship with natural affection in perfect expression of their faith that God has become man:

> Hail, sovereign savior . . .
> Hail, little tiny mop!

When they depart, singing, to publish their story, the miracle of spirit made flesh and dwelling among mankind has been fully confirmed as a vision at once contemporary and timeless.

The Second Shepherds' Play

ANONYMOUS

Adapted by Arthur M. Eastman from the modernizations of Clarence Griffin Child and Martial Rose

CHARACTERS

COLL   *the first shepherd*
GIB   *the second shepherd*
DAW   *the third shepherd, a boy*
MAK   *the sheep-stealer*
GILL   *Mak's wife*
ANGEL
MARY   *with the baby Jesus*

SCENE I

[*The open fields.*]
COLL. Lord, but this weather is cold, and I
                      [am ill wrapped,
Near numb, were truth told, so long have I
                      [napped; 5
My legs they fold, my fingers are chapped.
It is not as I would, for I am all lapped
   In sorrow.
In storms and tempest,
Now in the east, now in the west, 10
Woe is him has never rest

Modification of The Second Shepherds' Play *of the Towneley Cycle as translated by Clarence Griffin Child, from* Riverside Literature Series Number 191, *copyright © 1910, 1938 by Houghton Mifflin Company. "The Second Shepherds' Play" from the book* The Wakefield Mystery Plays *edited by Martial Rose. Copyright 1961 by Martial Rose. Reprinted by Doubleday & Company, Inc.*

Now or tomorrow.

But we simple shepherds that walk on the moor,
In faith, we are near-hands out of the door.°
No wonder, as it stands, if we be poor, 15
For the tilth° of our lands lies as fallow as the
                      [floor,
   As you ken.°
We are so lamed,
Overtaxed and maimed, 20
We are made hand-tamed,
   By these gentry men.

They rob us of our rest, our Lady them harry!
These men that are lord-fast,° they cause the
                    [plow tarry. 25
That, men say, is for the best; we find it
                    [contrary.
Thus are husbandmen oppressed, in point to
                    [miscarry,
   In life. 30
Thus hold they us under,
Thus bring us to blunder;
It were great wonder,
   If ever we should thrive.

Get a man a liveried sleeve or a brooch, 35
                    [nowadays
Woe is him that him grieves, or once him
                    [gainsays!
No blame may he receive, howe'er grasping
                    [his ways; 40
And yet may no man believe one word that he
                    [says—
   Not a letter.
He can seize what he's lacking,
Boastfully and bragging; 45
And all is through the backing
   Of men who are greater.

There shall come a swain, a proud peacock,
                    [you know;
He must borrow my wain, my plough also; 50

near-hands . . . door nearly homeless
tilth arable part
ken know
lord-fast attached to or retained by lords

These I am full fain to grant ere he go.
Thus live we in pain, anger and woe
   By night and day.
He must have, if he choose,
5 What I must needs lose;
I were better hanged than refuse,
   Than once say him nay.

It does me good, as I walk thus on my own,
Of this world for to talk, and so make my
10   [moan.
To my sheep will I stalk and harken anon,
There abide on a balk° or sit on a stone
   Full soon.
For I trow, pardie,°
15 True men, if they be,
We get more company
   Ere it be noon.

[*He steps aside. Gib enters.*]

   GIB. *Benste and Dominus!*° What may this
20   [mean?
The world faring thus, how oft have we seen?
Lord, this weather works through us, and the
                      [wind is full keen,
And the frosts so hideous they water mine
25   [een—°
   No lie!
Now in dry, now in wet,
Now in snow, now in sleet,
When my shoes freeze to my feet,
30   It's not at all easy.

But as far as I ken, wherever I go,
We poor wedded men suffer much woe;
We have sorrow ever again—it falls often so.
Silly Copple, our hen, both to and fro
35   She cackles;
But begin she to croak
To groan or to cluck,
For our cock it's no joke

For he is in shackles.

These men that are wed have not all their will; 40
When they're full hard bestead,° they sigh
                     [mighty still.
God knows the life they're led is full hard and
                     [full ill;
In bower nor in bed may they speak their will. 45
   This tide°
My part have I found,
Learned my lesson sound:
Woe to him who is bound,
   For he must it abide.   50

But now late in our lives—a marvel to me,
That I think my heart rives such wonders to
                     [see;
That which destiny drives will come to be—
Some men will have two wives, and some men 55
                     [three
   In store.
Some are grieved that have any,
But I'll wager my penny
Woe is him that has many,   60
   For he feels sore!

But, young men, of wooing, for God that you
                     [bought,
Beware well of wedding, and hold well in
                     [thought, 65
"Had I known" is a thing that serves not a jot.
Much constant mourning has wedding home
                     [brought,
   And grief,
With many a sharp shower;°   70
For you may catch in an hour
What shall savor full sour
   As long as you live.

For, as e'er read I Epistle, I have one to my fere°
As sharp as a thistle, as rough as a briar. 75
She is browed like a bristle, with a sour face by
                     [her.

---

balk strip of grassland between plowed fields
trow, pardie believe, by God
Benste . . . Dominus bless us (*benste* is a shortened
   form of *benedicite*) and Lord
een eyes

bestead put to it
tide time
shower pain
fere mate

If she once wets her whistle she can sing full
                    [clear
  Her paternoster.
As great as a whale,
5 She has a gallon of gall.
By him that died for us all,
  I would I'd run till I'd lost her!

  Coll. Gib, look over the row! Full deafly you
                    [stand.
10 Gib. Yea, the devil in your maw, so tarrying!
Did'st see aught of Daw?
  Coll.   Yea, on the lea-land°
I heard him blow.° He comes near at hand,
  Not far.
15 Stand still.
  Gib.   Why?
  Coll. For he comes, think I.
  Gib. He'll beguile us with a lie
Unless we beware.

20 [*Enter* Daw.]
  Daw. Christ's cross me speed, and Saint
                    [Nicholas!
Thereof have I need; it is worse than it was.
Who knows should take heed and let the world
25   [pass;
Ill ever it speeds; it's as brittle as glass,
  And drifts.
But the world never fared so,
And marvels greater grow—
30 Now in weal, now in woe—
  And everything shifts.

Was never since Noah's flood such floodings
                    [seen,
Winds and rains so rude and storms so keen:
35 Some stammered, some stood in doubt,° as I
                    [ween.
Now God turn all to good! I say as I mean,
  For ponder:
These floods they so drown,
40 Both in fields and in town,
  And bear all down;

---

lea-land meadow
blow i.e., his horn
Some . . . doubt i.e., at the time of Noah's flood

And that is a wonder.

We that walk in the nights our cattle to keep,
We see fearful sights when other men sleep.
  [*Catching sight of the others.*]   45
Yet my heart grows light—I see rascals a-peep.
[*Aside.*] You two are tall wights°—I will give
                    [my sheep
  A turn, below
But full ill have I meant;°   50
As I walk on this bent,°
I may lightly repent,
  If I stub my toe.

Ah, sir, God you save, and master mine!
A drink would I have and somewhat to dine.   55
  Coll. Christ's curse, my knave, you're a lazy
                  [hind!
  Gib. What, let the boy rave!—Wait till later
                  [this time.
  We've had our food.   60
Ill luck to your pate!—
Though the knave came late,
Yet he's in a state
  To sup, if he could.

  Daw. Such servants as I, who work and   65
                  [sweat,
Eat our bread full dry, and that makes me fret.
We're oft wet and weary while our masters
                  [sleep yet;
But comes full tardy the food that we get—   70
  And less than our due.
Both our dame and our sire,
When we've run in the mire,
Take a nip at our hire—
  And pay us late, too.   75

But hear the truth, master, for the fare that you
                  [pay
I shall work hereafter—tit for tat is fair play.
I shall do little, sir, but sport as I may,

---

tall wights proper creatures; i.e., a fine pair
But . . . meant Daw reproves himself for the disrespect
  he has just expressed toward his elders, then, in the
  following lines, proposes for himself an easy penance
bent field

For ne'er does my supper my stomach dismay
   In fields.
Why should I threap?°
With my staff can I leap;°
5 Men say, "Bargain cheap
   But a poor return yields."

   COLL. You were an ill lad to go a-wooing
With a master that had but little for spending.
   GIB. Peace, I say, lad. No more jangling,
10 Or I'll make you full sad, by heaven's king!
   Your gauds—°
Where are our sheep, boy?—We scorn.
   DAW. Sir, this same day at morn°
I left them in the corn,
15   When they rang Lauds.°

They have pasture good, they cannot go wrong.
   COLL. That is right. By the rood,° these
                           [nights are long!
Ere we go now, I would someone gave us a
20   [song.
   GIB. So I thought as I stood, to cheer us
                           [along.
DAW.
   I agree.
25 COLL. The tenor I'll try.
   GIB. And I the treble so high.
   DAW. Then the mean° shall be I.
How you chant now, let's see!

   [They sing. Then MAK enters, wearing a
30 cloak.]

   MAK. Now, lord, by thy seven names' spell,
                  [that made the stars on high,
Full more than I can tell, thy will for me lack I.
I'm all at odds, naught's well—that oft my
35   [brains doth try.

Would God I might in heaven dwell, for there
                           [no children cry,
   So shrill.
   COLL. Who is it pipes so poor?
   MAK. Would God you knew of me, sure!   40
Lo, a man that walks on the moor,
   And has not all his will.

   GIB. Mak, whither do you speed? What news
                           [do you bring?
   DAW. Is he come? Then take heed each one to 45
                           [his thing.
[He takes MAK's cloak from him.]
   MAK. I be a yeoman, indeed, under the king,
The self and the same. A lord's message I
                           [bring— 50
   No lie.
Fie on you! Go hence
Out of my presence!
I must have reverence.
   Why, who be I?   55

   COLL. Why play it so quaint? Mak, you do
                           [wrong.
   GIB. Would you play the saint? For that do
                           [you long?
   DAW. With words he can paint—the devil   60
                           [him hang!
   MAK. I'll make a complaint: you'll be flogged
                           [ere long,
   At a word,
And wracked without ruth.   65
   COLL. But, Mak, is that truth?
Now take out that southern tooth,°
   And set in a turd.

   GIB. Mak, the devil in your eye! A blow I'd
                           [fain give you. 70
   DAW. Mak, know you not me? By God, I
                           [could beat you!
   MAK. God keep you all three! Methought I
                           [had seen you.
You're a fair company!   75
   COLL.   Now you remember, do you?

---

threap haggle
With . . . leap i.e., run away
gauds pranks
morn i.e., after midnight
Lauds matins, the church service held at midnight
   (as here) or dawn
rood cross
mean middle part

southern tooth Mak has been speaking in a southern
   dialect

Gib.
   Take heed!
When thus late a man goes,
What will folks suppose?
5   You've a bad name, God knows,
      For stealing of sheep.

   Mak. That I am true as steel no men debate,
But a sickness I feel has brought me to this
                              [state:
10 My belly lacks a meal and suffers ill fate.
      Daw. "Seldom lies the de'il dead by the
                              [gate."°
   Mak.
      Therefore
15 Full sore am I and ill;
   May I turn stone-still
   If I've eaten a morsel
      This month and more.

      Coll. How fares your wife? By my hood,
20   [how fares she?
      Mak. Sprawling, by the rood, at the fire
                              [she'll be,
   And a house full of brood. With the bottle
                              [she's free—
25 For else not much good for aught I can see
      Or do.
   Eats as fast as she can,
   And each year that comes to man
   Adds another to our clan—
30   And some years two.

   Now were I richer and full of purse
   I'd be eaten clear out of home and house.
   She's a foul dear, if look you durst!
   There's none can see her, who knows a worse
35   Than know I.
   Would you see what I'd proffer?
   I'd give all in my coffer
   For her soul might I offer
      A prayer for aye.

40 Gib. I know so wearièd none is in this shire;

I'd sleep though I earnèd less for my hire.
   Daw. I'm cold and naked and long for a fire.
   Coll. I'm weary with walk and am covered
                              [with mire.
   Look to!   45
      Gib. Nay, near shall I lie
For I must sleep soundly.
      Daw. As good a man's son, I,
      As any of you.

[*They lie down.*]   50

But, Mak, come lie here—in between—if you
                              [please.
      Mak. You'll be hindered, I fear, from talking
                              [at ease,
   Indeed.   55
[*He lies among them. They sleep.*]
From my top to my toe,
Manus tuas commendo,
Pontio Pilato.°
      Christ's cross me speed!   60

[*He rises.*]

It is time to strike ere the iron grows cold,
And craftily creep now into the fold,
And nimbly to work, but not be too bold,
For bitter the bargain, if all were told   65
      At the ending.
Time now for haste, truth to tell,
But he needs good counsel
That fain would fare well
      With but little for spending.   70

Put about you a circle as round as the moon,
   [*He draws the circle.*]
Till I have done what I will, until it be noon,
Lie you stone still until I have done
While I summon my skill some magic to croon.   75
   "On high,
Over your heads I raise my hand.
Your sight is lost on sea and land!"
But I must gain much more command

"**Seldom . . . gate**" proverbial: appearances are deceptive

Manus . . . Pilato I commend your hands to Pontius Pilate

To work it right.

Lord, but they sleep hard—as you may all hear.
Never yet was I shepherd, but of that I've no
[fear.
5 If the flock be scared, yet shall I nip near
Hey! Draw hitherward! [*He seizes a sheep.*]
[*Now mends our cheer
From sorrow.
A fat sheep, I dare say,
10 A good fleece, dare I lay.
When I can, I'll repay,
But this will I borrow.

[*He departs with the sheep.*]

SCENE II

[MAK's *cottage.*]
15 MAK [*outside*]. Hey, Gill, are you in? Get us
[some light!
GILL [*within*]. Who makes such a din this
[time of the night?
I've sat down to spin; I doubt that I might
20 Rise a penny to win—I curse them on high!
So fares
A housewife that has been
Fretted 'twixt and between.
Here may no work be seen
25 For such small chores.

MAK. Good wife, open this hatch. See you
[not what I bring?
GILL. I'll let you draw the latch (MAK *opens
[the door.*) Ah, come in, my sweeting.
30 MAK. You care not a scratch for my long
[standing.
GILL. By your naked neck are you like to be
[hanging.
MAK.
35 Away!
I am worth my meat,
For in a fix can I get
More than they that toil and sweat
All the long day.

40 Thus it fell to my lot, Gill! Such luck came my
[way!

GILL. It were a foul blot to be hanged, as you
[may.
MAK. I've oft 'scaped, Gillot, as risky a play.
GILL. "But so long goes the pot to the water," 45
[men say,
"At last
Comes it home broken."
MAK. Well know I the token,
But let it never be spoken! 50
But come and help fast.

I would he were slain, I want so to eat.
Not this year was I so fain to have some sheep's
[meat.
GILL. If they come ere he's slain and hear the 55
[sheep bleat—
MAK. Then might I be ta'en: that were a cold
[sweat!
Go bar
The outer door. 60
GILL.   Yes, Mak,
For if they come at your back—
MAK. Then might I get from the whole pack
The devil, and more.

GILL. A good trick have I spied, since you 65
[think of none:
Here shall we him hide till they be gone.
In my cradle. Abide! Let me alone,
And I shall lie beside, as in childbed, and groan.
MAK. 70
Well said!
And I shall say this night
A boy child saw the light.
GILL. Now bless I that day bright
That saw me born and bred! 75

This is a good device and a far cast.°
Ever a woman's advice helps at the last.
I never know who spies: go you back fast.
MAK. Save I come ere they raise, there'll
[blow a cold blast! 80
I will go sleep.
[*He returns to the shepherds.*]
Still sleeps all this company,
And I shall slip in privily

far cast clever trick

As it had never been I
That carried off their sheep.

SCENE III

[*The open fields.*]

COLL. *Resurrex a mortruus!*° Reach me a
5   [hand!
Judas carnas dominus!° I scarcely can stand:
My foot sleeps, by Jesus; hunger has me
                          [unmanned.
I thought that we laid us full nigh to England.
10   GIB. Verily!
Lord, but I have slept well!
As fresh as an eel,
As light I do feel
    As leaf on a tree.

15   DAW [*disoriented.*] A blessing within!
                   [Whatever is shaking
My heart from my skin, my body thus quaking?
Who's making this din that's set my head
                            [aching?
20 To the door I'll win. Hark, fellows, be waking!
    Four we were—
See you aught of Mak now?
    COLL. We were up ere you.
    GIB. Man, to God I vow,
25   He's yet gone nowhere.

    DAW. Methought he was lapped in a wolf's
                              [skin.
    COLL. So many are wrapped now—namely
                             [within.
30   DAW. When we had long napped, methought
                          [with a gin°
A fat sheep he trapped; but he made no din.
    GIB.
    Be still!
35 Your dream makes you mad;
It's a nightmare you've had.
    COLL. God bring good out of bad,
    If it be his will.

Resurrex a mortruus garbled Latin, referring appar-
    ently to Christ's resurrection from the dead
Judas . . . dominus Judas, lord (in?)carnate
gin snare

GIB. Rise, Mak, for shame! Right long you
                        [do lie.   40
MAK. Now Christ's holy name be with us for
                        [aye!
What's this? By Saint James, I can't move when
                        [I try.
I suppose I'm the same. Aah, my neck's lain   45
                        [awry
Herein.
[*They help him get up.*]
Many thanks! Since yester-even,
Now by Saint Stephen,   50
I was so flayed by a dream
    My heart jumped from my skin.

I thought Gill began to croak and travail full
                        [sad;
Well-nigh at the first cock she bore a young lad   55
To add to our flock. Then will I never be glad.
Of cares I've a stock more than ever I had.
    Ah, my head!
A house full of hunger pains—
The devil knock out their brains!   60
Woe is him has many bairns
    And has but little bread.

I must go home, by your leave, to Gill, as I
                        [thought.
Pray look up my sleeve that I've stolen naught: 65
I am loath you to grieve or from you take
                        [aught.
[*He goes.*]
DAW. Go forth, ill may you thrive! Now
                   [would I we sought   70
This morn
For the sheep in our care.
    COLL. First I shall fare.
Let us meet.
    GIB.   Where?   75
    DAW.
At the crooked thorn.

SCENE IV

[MAK's *cottage.*]
MAK [*outside*]. Undo this door! Who is here?
                   [How long shall I stand?   80

GILL [*within*]. Who makes such a blare?
             [Now walk in the wenyand!°
MAK. Ah, Gill, what cheer? It is I, Mak, your
             [husband.
5   GILL. Then may we see here the devil in a
             [band—°
[*Opening the door.*]
Sir Guile!
Lo, he comes with a croak
10 As though held by the throat.
And I cannot devote
   To my work any while.

MAK. Oh, the fuss that she makes to get an
             [excuse.
15 Naught but pleasure she takes, and curls up
             [her toes.
   GILL. Why, who works and who wakes?
             [Who comes, who goes?
Who brews, who bakes? What makes me thus
20   [hoarse?
   And then
It is sad to behold—
Now in hot, now in cold,
Full woeful the household
25   That wants a woman!

But how have you sped with the shepherds,
             [Mak?
   MAK. The last word that they said when I
             [turned my back,
30 They would count each head of sheep in their
             [pack.
They'll not be pleased, I'm afraid, when they
             [their sheep lack,
   Pardie!
35 But howe'er the game go,
They'll suspect me, I know,
And raise a great bellow,
   And cry out against me.

But now do as you hight.°
40   GILL.   To that I agree.
I'll swaddle him right in the cradle by me.
Were it a greater sleight, yet could I help be.

---

wenyand waning of the moon: an unlucky time
band noose
hight promised

I will lie down straight. Come cover me.
   [*She lies down.* MAK *tucks her in.*]
   Behind!   45
Come Coll and his crew,
They'll pry through and through.
   MAK. For help I'll halloo
   The sheep if they find.

   GILL. Hark now for their call—they will   50
             [come anon.
Come and make ready all, and sing on your
             [own—
Sing lullay° you shall, for I must groan
And cry out by the wall on Mary and John 55
   Full sore.
Sing lullay quite fast
When you hear them at last.
If my part is miscast,
   Trust me no more.   60

SCENE V

[*The crooked thorn.*]
DAW. Ah, Coll, good morn! Why sleep you
             [not?
COLL. Alas that ever I was born! We have a
             [foul blot— 65
A fat wether have we lorn.°
   DAW.   God forbid, say it not!
   GIB. Who should give us this scorn? That's
             [a foul spot.
   COLL.   70
   Some shrew.°
I have searched with my dogs
All Horbury shrogs,°
And with fifteen hogs°
   Found I only the ewe.   75

DAW. Now trust me, if you will, by Saint
             [Thomas of Kent,
Either Mak or Gill had a hand in this event.
   COLL. Peace, man, be still! I saw when he
             [went. 80

---

lullay a lullaby
lorn lost
shrew rascal
shrogs thickets
hogs young sheep

You slander him ill; you ought to repent
  With good speed.
  GIB. Now as ever I might thrive,
As I hope to keep alive,
5 Only Mak could contrive
  To do that same deed.

  DAW. Then off to his homestead, be brisk on
            [our feet.
I shall never eat bread till I know all complete.
10 COLL. Nor have drink in my head till with
            [him I meet.
  GIB. In no place will I bed until I him greet—
My brother!
One vow will I plight,
15 Till I see him in sight,
I will ne'er sleep one night
  Where I do another!

SCENE VI

[MAK's *cottage.*]
[MAK, *hearing the shepherds coming, be-*
20 *gins to sing a lullaby at the top of his voice;*
GILL *groans in concert.*]
  DAW. D'you hear how they croak? Our sire
            [will now croon.
  COLL. Never heard I folk so clean out of tune.
25 Call him.
  GIB.   Mak! Undo your door soon!
  MAK. Who is it that spoke, as if it were noon,
So loud?
Who is it, I say?
30 DAW. Good fellows, were it day!
  MAK. [*as the shepherds enter*]. As far as you
           [may,
  Speak low

Over a sick woman's head, who is not at her
35   [ease;
I had rather be dead than she suffer unease.
  GILL [*as they approach her*]. Get away from
        [my bed! Let me breathe, if you please.
Each step that you tread from my nose to my
40   [knees
  Goes through me.
  COLL. Tell us, Mak, if you may,
How fare you, I say?
  MAK. Are you in town today?

How fare you three?   45

You have run in the mire, and now are all wet.
I shall make you a fire, if you will sit.
A nurse would I hire—remember you yet
My dream, which entire has fulfilled its threat
  In due season?   50
I have bairns, if you knew,
Far more than a few;
But we must drink as we brew,
  And that is but reason.

I would you'd dine ere you went. Methinks 55
           [that you sweat.
  GIB. Our mood won't be mended by drink
           [nor by meat.
  MAK. Is ought then ill sent?
  DAW.   Our loss is great. 60
A sheep stol'n we lament, ta'en while we slept.
  MAK.
  Sirs, drink!
Had I been there
Some should have paid full dear. 65
  COLL. Marry, some trow that you were,
  And that makes us think!

  GIB. Mak, one and another trows it must
           [have been thee.
  DAW. Either you or your spouse, so say we. 70
  MAK. Now if aught suspicion throws on Gill
           [or me,
Come and search our house, and then may you
           [see
  Who had her—   75
If I any sheep got,
Either cow or stot—°
And Gill, my wife, rose not,
  Here since she laid her.

As I am true and leal,° to God, here I say 80
That this be the first meal I shall eat this day.
  COLL. Mak, as hope I for weal, advise you, I
           [say:
"He learned timely to steal that could not say
           [nay." 85

[*They begin to search.*]

cow or stot female or male
leal loyal, honest

GILL.
My death you've dealt!
Out, thieves, nor come again,
You've come to rob us, that's plain.
5   MAK. Hear you not how she groans amain?
    Your hearts should melt!

    GILL. Out, thieves, from my bairn. Go not to
                                [him near.
    MAK. If you knew all she's borne, your hearts
10   [would be sore.
You do wrong, I you warn, thus to come before
A woman that has borne—but I say no more.
    GILL.
    Oh, my middle—I die!
15 I vow to God so mild,
If e'er I you beguiled,
May I eat this child
    That in this cradle lies!

    MAK. Peace, woman, for God's pain, and cry
20   [not so!
You'll burst your brain and fill me with woe.
    GIB. I trow our sheep be slain. What find you
                              [two, though?
Our work's all in vain. We may as well go.
25 Save clothes and such matters
I can find no flesh
Hard or nesh°
Salt nor fresh,
    Save two empty platters.
30 [Gesturing toward the cradle.] No live stock
but this, tame or wild,
None, so may I have bliss, as loud as he°
                                [smelled.
    GILL. No, so God me bless, and give me joy
35   [of my child!
    COLL. We have aimed amiss; I hold us
                                [beguiled.
    GIB.
    Completely, each one!
40 Sir—our Lady him save!—
Is your child a knave?°
    MAK. Any lord might him have,
    This child, for his son.

When he wakes, so he grips, it's a pleasure to
                                [see.   45
    DAW. Good luck to his hips,° and blessing,
                                [say we!
But who were his gossips,° that were so soon
                                [ready?
    MAK. Blest be their lips— [Hesitates, at a   50
                                [loss.]
    COLL.   A lie now, hark ye!
    MAK.
God give them thanks.
Parkin and Gibbon Waller, I say.   55
And gentle John Horn, in good fay—°
He made such droll display
    With his long shanks.

    GIB. Mak, friends will we be, for we are all
                                [one.   60
    MAK. We? Count not on me, for amends get
                                [I none.
Farewell all three! And gladly begone.
[The shepherds leave, speaking outside the
cottage.]   65
    DAW. Fair words there may be, but love there
                                [is none
This year.
    COLL. Gave you the child anything?
    GIB. I trow not one farthing.   70
    DAW. Fast back will I fling.
    Wait for me here.

[He reenters the cottage, COLL and GIB slowly
following.]

    DAW. Mak, I trust you'll not grieve, if I come   75
                                [to your child.
    MAK. Nay, great shame I receive—you have
                                [acted full vile.
    DAW. Your bairn 'twill not grieve, little day-
                                [star so mild.   80
Mak, by your leave, let me give your child
    But sixpence.
    [He goes to the cradle and starts to draw
away the cover.]
    MAK. Nay, stop it—he sleeps!   85

---

nesh   soft
he   i.e., the stolen sheep
knave   boy

to his hips   i.e., to him
gossips   godparents
fay   faith

DAW. Methinks he peeps—
MAK. When he wakens, he weeps.
I pray you go hence.

DAW. Give me leave him to kiss, and lift
5   [up the clout.
[*Lifts the cover.*]
What the devil is this? He has a long snout!
COLL. He's birth-marked amiss. We waste
                 [time hereabout.
10 GIB. A weft that ill-spun is comes ever foul
                 [out.
Aye—so!
He is like to our sheep!
DAW. Ho, Gib, may I peep?
15 COLL. I trow Nature will creep
Where it may not go.°

GIB. This was a quaint gaud and a far cast.
It was a high fraud.
DAW.   Yea, sirs, that was't.
20 Let's burn this bawd and bind her fast.
A false scold, by the Lord, will hang at the last.
So shalt thou!
Do you see how they swaddle
His four feet in the middle?
25 Saw I never in the cradle
A horned lad ere now.

MAK. Peace, I say! What, let be your blare!
It was I him begot and yon woman him bare.
COLL. What devil's name has he got, Mak?—
30   [Lo, God, Mak's heir!
GIB. Come, joke with him not. Now, God
                 [give him care,
I say!
GILL. A pretty child is he
35 As sits on a woman's knee,
A darling, perdie,
To make a man gay.

DAW. I know him by the ear-mark—that's a
                 [good token.
40 MAK. I tell you, sirs, hark! His nose was
                 [broken.
There told me a clerk he'd been forspoken.°

COLL. You deal falsely and dark; I would
                 [fain be wroken.°
Get a weapon!   45
GILL. He was witched by an elf;
I saw it myself.
When the clock struck twelve,
He was misshapen.

GIB. You two are at one, that's plain, in all   50
                 [you've done and said.
COLL. Since their theft they maintain, let's
                 [strike them dead.
MAK. If I trespass again, cut off my head.
At your will I remain.   55
DAW.
Sirs, take my counsel instead.
For this trespass
We'll neither curse nor chide,
Fight nor deride,   60
Nor longer bide,
But toss him in canvas.

[*They toss* MAK *in a blanket.*]

SCENE VII

[*The open fields.*]
COLL. Lord, but I'm sore, ready to burst!   65
In faith, I may no more; therefore will I rest.
GIB. Like a sheep of seven score he weighed
                 [in my fist.
To sleep anywhere I think I'd like best.
DAW.   70
Now I you pray.
On this green let us lie.
COLL. O'er those thieves yet chafe I.
DAW. Let your anger go by.
Come do as I say.   75

[*They sleep. An* ANGEL *sings "Gloria in excelsis," then speaks.*]

ANGEL. Rise, herdsmen gentle, for now is he
                 [born
That shall take from the fiend what Adam had   80
                 [lorn;
That warlock° to end, this night is he born.

---

go   walk; i.e., the truth will out
clerk, forspoken   priest, bewitched

wroken   revenged
warlock   devil

God is made your friend now on this morn.
    Leave your flocks:
To Bethlehem go see
Where he lies so free,
5 In a crib full poorly,
    Between ass and ox.

[*The* ANGEL *goes.*]

COLL. This was a fine voice, even as ever I
                [heard.
10 It's a marvel to dream on, thus with dread to be
                [stirred.
GIB. To God's son from heaven these tidings
                [referred.
All the wood with a lightning methought at his
15   [word
  Shone fair.
  DAW. Of a child did he tell,
In Bethlehem, mark well.
  COLL. Yon star there doth dwell.
20 Let us seek him there.

GIB. Say, what was his song—how it went,
              [did you hear?
Three breves° to a long—
  DAW.   Marry, yes. To my ear
25 There was no crotchet° wrong, nothing lacked,
             [and 'twas clear.
  COLL. To sing it here, us among, as he sang
            [it, full near,
  I know how—
30 GIB. Let's see how you croon.
Can you bark at the moon?
  DAW. Hold your tongues! Have done!
Hark after me now.

[*They sing.*]

35 GIB. To Bethlehem he bade that we should
             [go;
And sure we be mad to tarry so.
  DAW. Be merry and not sad, our mirth may
             [flow.
40 Ever to be glad is the reward we shall know
  And choose.

breves short notes
crotchet note

COLL. Then let us hither hie,
Though we be wet and weary,
To that child and that lady;
    We have no time to lose.   45

GIB. We find by the prophecy—let be your
             [din!—
Of David and Isaiah, and more of their kin—
They prophesied learnedly that in a virgin
Should God come to lie, to atone for our sin,   50
  And take it,
Our nature, from woe.
Isaiah said so.
Ecce virgo
  Concipiet° a child that is naked.   55

DAW. Full glad may we be if we await the
             [day,
That sweet sight to see who all power may
             [sway.
Lord, well were me, now and for aye,   60
Might I kneel on my knee some word for to say
  To that child.
But the angel said
In a crib was he laid;
He was poorly arrayed,   65
  Both meek and mild.

COLL. Patriarchs that have been and prophets
             [of yore
Desired to have seen this child that is born.
They are gone full clean—that they have lorn. 70
We shall see him, I ween, ere it be morn,
  As a token.
When I see him and feel,
I shall know full well,
It is true as steel,   75
  What prophets have spoken:

To so poor as we are that he would appear
First, and declare by his messenger.
  GIB. Go we now, let us fare; the place is us
            [near. 80
  DAW. I am ready and eager. Let's together
            [with cheer
  To that bright one go.

Ecce . . . concipiet Behold, a virgin shall conceive
(Isaiah vii.14)

Lord, if thy will it be—
We are simple all three—
On thy child grant that we
 May some comfort bestow.

SCENE VIII

5 [*The stable in Bethlehem, the shepherds
kneeling before Mary and Jesus.*]
  COLL. Hail, comely and clean! Hail, young
             [child!
Hail creator, I mean, from a maiden so mild!
10 Thou hast cursed, I ween, the warlock so wild:
The beguiler of men, now goes he beguiled.
 Lo, he merries,
Lo, he laughs, my sweeting!
A happy meeting!
15 Here's my promised greeting:
 Have a bob° of cherries.

 GIB. Hail, sovereign savior, for thou hast us
            [sought!
Hail, noble food and flower, that all things hast
20   [wrought!
Hail, full of favor, that made all of naught!
Hail! I kneel and I cower. A bird have I brought,
 Bairn that you are.
Hail, little tiny mop!
25 Of our creed thou art top;
I would drink from thy cup,
 Little day-star.

 DAW. Hail, darling dear, full of godhead!
I pray thee be near when that I have need.
30 Hail, sweet is thy cheer!° My heart would bleed
To see thee sit here in so poor a weed
 With no pennies.
Hail! Put forth thy dall.°
I bring thee but a ball:
35 Take it and play withal,
 And go to the tennis.

 MARY. The father of heaven, God
          [omnipotent,
That made all in days seven—his son has he

             [sent. 40
My name he naměd, in me alighted ere he
             [went.
Conceived I him, even through his might, as he
            [meant;°
 And now is he born.   45
May he keep you from woe!
I shall pray him do so.
Tell of him as you go,
 And remember this morn.

 COLL. Farewell, lady, so fair to behold,   50
With thy child on thy knee.
GIB.   But he lies full cold.
Lord, well is me! Now back to our fold.
 DAW. Forsooth, already it seems to be told
Full oft.   55
 COLL. What grace we have found!
GIB. We are won safe and sound!
DAW. To sing are we bound:
Make it ring then aloft!

[*They depart singing.*]   60

---

bob bunch
cheer countenance
dall hand

meant intended

Ben Jonson

1573?–1637

Volpone, or the Fox

1606

The theater-goer who saw Ben Jonson's new comedy *Volpone, or the Fox* for the first time may well have been reminded of Shakespeare's recent tragedy, *Othello, the Moor of Venice.* Both plays are set against the background of a city noted alike for its magnificence and its vice. Both present characters of "rare ingenious knavery" (Shakespeare's Iago resembling both Volpone and Mosca). And both exhibit the dramatic inventiveness and varied eloquence of the finest Elizabethan drama. At the center of Jonson's satiric comedy, however, there stands not a heroic Othello but Volpone, a genius in crime, incapable of either generosity or self-knowledge. His fall reveals not the mystery of the human lot but the tendency of vice to overreach itself.

Although the satire is ultimately moral, its immediate perspective is largely social and legal. It traces the features of vice under the masks of respectability, exposing the manipulations of the hypocrites without altogether excusing the imperceptiveness of their victims. Against scoundrels cloaked in propriety and skilled in legal dodging, the mainly passive virtuous characters are practically defenseless. Even the good-natured guardians of the law are dull-witted, and the true innocents, Bonario and Celia, finally get free only because the knaves ensnare themselves in their own subtleties. The laws of the state are vindicated, but only at long last and in tones of slightly hollow self-congratulation.

Despite its consistently satiric purpose, *Volpone* at first appears bewilderingly diverse. A seemingly irrelevant academic skit is enacted by a dwarf, a eunuch, and a hermaphrodite. Disguised as a mountebank, Volpone makes a long-winded spiel aimed as much at burlesquing itinerant quacks as at advancing his designs on Celia. The English travelers play out an almost independent farce of their own. And in the unraveling of the main plot Jonson risks anticlimax by launching, as late as the fifth act, a brilliant new series of complications.

Such fertility of dramatic device may well leave an impression of rich disorder.

The play is rich but it is not disordered. Volpone, flanked by the indefatigable Mosca, draws all events and characters into his orbit. Around him circle the lesser predators —a "Vulture," a "Raven," a "Crow"— impelled by avarice and dragging in their train others less guilty, merely foolish, or altogether innocent. Even Sir Politic Would-be, with his little schemes for getting rich, his pretentious misinformation, and his empty suspicions, is in some ways a parody of Volpone and has an equally appropriate comeuppance.

Beyond these adroit elaborations of plot and character a principle of thematic integration is at work. From Volpone's first speech, in idolatry of gold, to the final plainspoken summary of the magistrate, Jonson tirelessly explores the idea of hyprocrisy as the mask of lust and of lust as perversion of human nature. Lust in the guise of avarice is thematically developed in references to possessions, possessing, and—at length—being possessed. That lust is perverse and deceptive is expressed by emphasis on tricks and transformations. The themes interlace. Volpone's lust for gold fires his imagination to feats of deception and rhetoric beyond the reach of his victims. Mosca, touched with the same fire, caters to Volpone's lust for Celia, which in turn leads him to impersonate a mountebank, the very emblem of greed and falsehood. Lust for Volpone's possessions makes a husband eager to prostitute his wife and a father to disown his son. In the oddly relevant academic skit the deformed and mutilated servants of Volpone's household make sport of greed, hypocrisy, and perversion to gratify their master's taste.

Throughout the play the figures of speech and the historical and classical allusions embroider these themes of possession and transformation. They concur most explicitly in Volpone's attempt to transform Celia, the object of his lust, into a prize possession.

That is the turning point of his fortunes. Thereafter his brilliance decays as he becomes more and more visibly what he is. In the last three scenes of the play the word *possession,* echoed by almost every character, attains a culminating definition: *possessed by demons.*

The final transformations reveal the truth. Volpone's last stratagem is to remove his last disguise and to pull all the hypocrites down in his own ruin. Virtue is barely saved as the virtuosity of Ben Jonson triumphs.

Volpone,
or the Fox

JONSON

CHARACTERS°

VOLPONE   *a magnifico*
MOSCA   *his parasite*
VOLTORE   *an advocate*
CORBACCIO   *an old gentleman*
CORVINO   *a merchant*
BONARIO   *a young gentleman*
POLITIC WOULD-BE   *a knight*
PEREGRINE   *a gentleman traveler*
NANO   *a dwarf*
CASTRONE   *a eunuch*
ANDROGYNO   *a hermaphrodite*
GREGE   *mob*
COMMANDADORI   *officers*
MERCATORI   *three merchants*
AVOCATORI   *four magistrates*
NOTARIO   *the register*
SERVITORE   *a servant*
MADAM WOULD-BE   *the knight's wife*
CELIA   *Corvino's wife*
WOMEN

SCENE. *Venice.*

The Argument

V   OLPONE, childless, rich, feigns, sick, despairs,
O   ffers his state to hopes of several heirs,
L   ies languishing; his parasite receives

Characters: Mosca the fly   **Voltore** the vulture
Corbaccio the raven   **Corvino** the crow   **Bonario** the well-favored man   **Politic Would-be** the
professed man of the world   **Celia** the heavenly
one

P   resents of all, assures, deludes; then weaves   5
O   ther cross plots, which ope themselves, are
     told.
N   ew tricks for safety are sought; they thrive:
     when, bold,
E   ach tempts th' other again, and all are sold.°   10

ACT I

Scene i

[*A room in* VOLPONE's *house.*]
[*Enter* VOLPONE *and* MOSCA.]
   VOLPONE. Good morning to the day; and next,
                    [my gold.
Open the shrine, that I may see my saint.—   15
Hail the world's soul, and mine. More glad
                    [than is
The teeming earth to see the long'd-for sun
Peep through the horns of the celestial Ram°,
Am I, to view thy splendor darkening his;   20
That, lying here, amongst my other hoards,
Show'st like a flame by night, or like the day
Struck out of chaos, when all darkness fled
Unto the center.° O thou son of Sol,
But brighter than thy father, let me kiss,   25
With adoration, thee, and every relic
Of sacred treasure in this blessed room.
Well did wise poets, by thy glorious name,
Title that age which they would have the best;
Thou being the best of things, and far   30
                    [transcending
All style of joy, in children, parents, friends,
Or any other waking dream on earth.
Thy looks when they to Venus did ascribe,
They should have giv'n her twenty thousand   35
                    [Cupids;
Such are thy beauties and our loves! Dear saint,

sold   defrauded
Ram   zodiacal sign, Aries, which the sun enters in late
    March
day . . . center   the first day of the Creation, when
    darkness fled to the center of the earth. In this
    speech Volpone also alludes to the Golden Age (that
    age), the golden goddess (**Venus**), the adage that
    Silence is Golden (the dumb god), and the old belief
    that gold ore was imprisoned sunlight and was plen-
    tiful in the soil of hell.

Riches, the dumb god, that giv'st all men
[tongues,
That canst do naught, and yet mak'st men do
[all things;
5 The price of souls; even hell, with thee to boot,
Is made worth Heaven. Thou art virtue, fame,
Honor, and all things else! Who can get thee,
He shall be noble, valiant, honest, wise—
Mosca. And what he will, sir. Riches are in
10 [fortune
A greater good than wisdom is in nature.
Volpone. True, my beloved Mosca. Yet I
[glory
More in the cunning purchase° of my wealth
15 Than in the glad possession, since I gain
No common way; I use no trade, no venture;
I wound no earth with plowshares, fat no
[beasts
To feed the shambles; have no mills for iron,
20 Oil, corn, or men, to grind 'em into powder;
I blow no subtle glass,° expose no ships
To threat'nings of the furrow-faced sea;
I turn no monies in the public bank,
No usure° private—
25 Mosca. No, sir, nor devour
Soft prodigals. You shall ha' some will swallow
A melting heir as glibly as your Dutch
Will pills of butter, and ne'er purge for 't;
Tear forth the fathers of poor families
30 Out of their beds, and coffin them alive
In some kind clasping prison, where their bones
May be forthcoming, when the flesh is rotten.
But your sweet nature doth abhor these courses;
You loathe the widow's or the orphan's tears
35 Should wash your pavements, or their piteous
[cries
Ring in your roofs, and beat the air for
[vengeance.
Volpone. Right, Mosca; I do loathe it.—
40 Mosca. And, besides, sir,
You are not like the thresher that doth stand
With a huge flail, watching a heap of corn,
And, hungry, dares not taste the smallest grain,
But feeds on mallows, and such bitter herbs;

Nor like the merchant, who hath fill'd his 45
[vaults
With Romagnía, rich and Candian wines,
Yet drinks the lees of Lombard's vinegar.
You will not lie in straw, whilst moths and
[worms 50
Feed on your sumptuous hangings and soft
[beds.
You know the use of riches, and dare give now
From that bright heap, to me, your poor
[observer,° 55
Or to your dwarf, or your hermaphrodite,
Your eunuch, or what other household trifle
Your pleasure allows maintenance.—
Volpone. Hold thee, Mosca;
Take of my hand; thou strik'st on truth in all, 60
And they° are envious term thee parasite.
Call forth my dwarf, my eunuch, and my fool,
And let 'em make me sport.
[Exit Mosca.]
What should I do, 65
But cocker up° my genius, and live free
To all delights my fortune calls me to?
I have no wife, no parent, child, ally,
To give my substance to; but whom I make
Must be my heir; and this makes men observe° 70
[me.
This draws new clients daily to my house,
Women and men of every sex and age,
That bring me presents, send me plate, coin,
[jewels, 75
With hope that when I die (which they expect
Each greedy minute) it shall then return
Tenfold upon them; whilst some, covetous
Above the rest, seek to engross me whole,
And counter work the one unto the other, 80
Contend in gifts, as they would seem in love;
All which I suffer, playing with their hopes,
And am content to coin 'em into profit,
And look upon their kindness, and take more,
And look on that; still bearing them in hand, 85
Letting the cherry knock against their lips,
And draw it by their mouths, and back again.—
How now!

purchase acquisition
subtle glass fine Venetian glassware
usure usury

observer servant
they those who
cocker up indulge
observe be attentive to

Scene ii

[*Enter* MOSCA *with* NANO, ANDROGYNO, *and*
CASTRONE.]

NANO. Now, room for fresh gamesters, who
　　　　　　　　　　　　　[do will you to know
5　They do bring you neither play nor university
　　　　　　　　　　　　　　　　　　[show,
And therefore do entreat you that whatsoever
　　　　　　　　　　　　　　　[they rehearse
May not fare a whit the worse for the false
10　　　　　　　　　　　　　　[pace of the verse.
If you wonder at this, you will wonder more ere
　　　　　　　　　　　　　　　　[we pass;
For know, here° is enclos'd the soul of
　　　　　　　　　　　　　　　　[Pythagoras,
15　That juggler divine, as hereafter shall follow,
Which soul, fast and loose, sir, came first from
　　　　　　　　　　　　　　　　　[Apollo,
And was breath'd into Aethalides, Mercurius
　　　　　　　　　　　　　　　　　[his son,
20　Where it had the gift to remember all that ever
　　　　　　　　　　　　　　　　[was done.
From thence it fled forth, and made quick
　　　　　　　　　　　　　　[transmigration
To goldy-lock'd Euphorbus, who was kill'd, in
25　　　　　　　　　　　　　　[good fashion,
At the siege of old Troy, by the cuckold of
　　　　　　　　　　　　　　　　[Sparta.
Hermotimus was next (I find it in my charta);
To whom it did pass, where no sooner it was
30　　　　　　　　　　　　　　[missing,
But with one Pyrrhus of Delos it learn'd to go
　　　　　　　　　　　　　　[a-fishing;

And thence did it enter the sophist of Greece.
From Pythagore, she went into a beautiful
　　　　　　　　　　　　　　[piece,　35
Hight Aspasia, the meretrix; and the next toss
　　　　　　　　　　　　　　　[of her
Was again of a whore—she became a
　　　　　　　　　　　　　　[philosopher,
Crates the cynic, as itself doth relate it.　　　40
Since, kings, knights, and beggars, knaves,
　　　　　　　　　　　　[lords, and fools gat it,
Besides ox and ass, camel, mule, goat, and
　　　　　　　　　　　　　　　[brock,
In all which it hath spoke, as in the cobbler's　45
　　　　　　　　　　　　　　　[cock.
But I came not here to discourse of that matter,
Or his one, two, or three, or his great oath, "By
　　　　　　　　　　　　　[QUATER!"
His musics, his trigon, his golden thigh,°　　50
Or his telling how elements shift; but I
Would ask, how of late thou hast suffered
　　　　　　　　　　　　　　[translation,
And shifted thy coat in these days of
　　　　　　　　　　　　　　[reformation.　55
ANDROGYNO. Like one of the reformed,° a
　　　　　　　　　　　　　[fool, as you see,
Counting all old doctrine heresy.
NANO. But not on thine own forbid meats
　　　　　　　　　　　　[hast thou ventur'd?　60
ANDROGYNO. On fish, when first a Carthusian
　　　　　　　　　　　　　　[I enter'd.
NANO. Why, then thy dogmatical silence°
　　　　　　　　　　　　　　[hath left thee?
ANDROGYNO. Of that an obstreperous lawyer　65
　　　　　　　　　　　　　　[bereft me.
NANO. O wonderful change! When sir lawyer
　　　　　　　　　　　　　　[forsook thee,
For Pythagore's sake, what body then took
　　　　　　　　　　　　　　[thee,　70

---

here in Androgyno, the "man-woman." This scene, in
the style of an academic skit, refers especially to
Lucian's dialogue between a cobbler who longs for
riches and a cock who embodies the soul of the
Greek philosopher, Pythagoras. The soul recounts
its transmigrations through the lives of men and
women famous for the pursuit of wealth (e.g., **Aethalides,** herald of the Argonauts who found the Golden
Fleece; **Aspasia,** the noted courtesan, mistress of
Pericles) and of philosophers who, it is implied,
prostituted their talents. By alluding to the Pythagorean Brotherhood, a mystic society that strictly forbade the eating of flesh and beans and employed an
esoteric symbolism of numbers, Jonson also satirizes
some of the religious extremists of his time.

Or his . . . thigh or of Pythagorean practices and
traditions: the number-symbolism; the oath **By Qua-
ter!** on the "triangle of four"; the abstruse theory of
musical intervals; the symbolic triangular harp (**trigon**); and the legend that the thigh of Pythagoras
was all of gold
reformed extreme Protestants
silence vowed by Pythagoreans as well as, later, by
Carthusians, who were members of a rigorous monastic order

ANDROGYNO. A good dull mule.

NANO.　　And how! by that means
Thou wert brought to allow of the eating of
　　　　　　　　　　　[beans?

5　ANDROGYNO. Yes.

NANO.　　But from the mule into whom
　　　　　　　　　　　[didst thou pass?

ANDROGYNO. Into a very strange beast, by
　　　　　　　　　　　[some writers call'd an ass;

10　By others a precise, pure, illuminate brother°
Of those devour flesh—and sometimes one
　　　　　　　　　　　[another;
And will drop you forth a libel, or a sanctifi'd
　　　　　　　　　　　[lie,

15　Betwixt every spoonful of a nativity-pie.°

NANO. Now quit thee, 'fore Heaven, of that
　　　　　　　　　　　[profane nation;
And gently report thy next transmigration.

ANDROGYNO. To the same that I am.

20　NANO.　　A creature of delight,
And, what is more than a fool,° an
　　　　　　　　　　　[hermaphrodite!
Now, pray thee, sweet soul, in all thy variation,
Which body wouldst thou choose to take up

25　　　　　　　　　　　[thy station?

ANDROGYNO. Troth, this I am in; even here
　　　　　　　　　　　[would I tarry.

NANO. 'Cause here the delight of each sex
　　　　　　　　　　　[thou canst vary?

30　ANDROGYNO. Alas, those pleasures be stale
　　　　　　　　　　　[and forsaken;
No, 'tis your fool wherewith I am so taken,
The only one creature that I can call blessed;
For all other forms I have prov'd most

35　　　　　　　　　　　[distressed.

NANO. Spoke true, as thou wert in Pythagoras
　　　　　　　　　　　[still.
This learned opinion we celebrate will,
Fellow eunuch, as behoves us, with all our wit

40　　　　　　　　　　　[and art,
To dignify that whereof ourselves are so great
　　　　　　　　　　　[and special a part.

VOLPONE. Now, very, very pretty. Mosca,
　　　　　　　　　　　[this
Was thy invention?　　　　　　　　　　45

MOSCA.　　　　If it please my patron,
Not else.

VOLPONE.　　It doth, good Mosca.

MOSCA.　　Then it was, sir.
[Sings.]　　　　　　　　　　　　　50
Fools they are the only nation
Worth men's envy or admiration;
Free from care or sorrow taking,
Selves and others merry making:
All they speak or do is sterling.　　　　55
Your fool he is your great man's dearling,
And your ladies' sport and pleasure;
Tongue and bauble are his treasure.
E'en his face begetteth laughter,
And he speaks truth free from slaughter;°　　60
He's the grace of every feast,
And sometimes the chiefest guest;
Hath his trencher and his stool,
When wit waits upon the fool.
　　O, who would not be　　　　　　　65
　　He, he, he,?
[One knocks without.]

VOLPONE. Who's that? Away! Look, Mosca.

MOSCA.　　Fool, begone!
[Exeunt NANO, CASTRONE, and ANDROGYNO.]　70
'Tis Signior Voltore, the advocate;
I know him by his knock.

VOLPONE.　　　　　　Fetch me my gown,
My furs, and nightcaps; say my couch is
　　　　　　　　　　　[changing,　75
And let him entertain himself awhile
Without, i' th' gallery. [Exit MOSCA.] Now,
　　　　　　　　　　　[now, my clients
Begin their visitation! Vulture, kite,
Raven, and gorcrow, all my birds of prey,　　80
That think me turning carcass, now they come;
I am not for 'em yet.
[Reenter MOSCA, with the gown, etc.]
　　　　　　　　How now! the news?

MOSCA. A piece of plate,° sir.　　　　　85

VOLPONE.　　Of what bigness?

MOSCA.　　　　　　　Huge,

---

precise . . . brother　hair-splitting, self-righteous Puritan who claims to be divinely enlightened

nativity-pie　Christmas pie (another dig at the "precise" Puritan who shrank from saying "Christmas" to avoid the "Popish" reference to "Christ's Mass")

fool　jester, not necessarily a simpleton

slaughter　punishment

plate　dish of gold or silver

Massy, and antique with your name inscrib'd,
And arms engraven.
    VOLPONE.   Good! and not a fox
Stretch'd on the earth, with fine delusive
5   [sleights,
Mocking a gaping crow? ha, Mosca?
    MOSCA.   Sharp, sir.
    VOLPONE. Give me my furs—Why dost thou
                        [laugh so, man?
10   MOSCA. I cannot choose, sir, when I
                        [apprehend
What thoughts he has without now, as he
                        [walks:
That this might be the last gift he should give,
15 That this would fetch you;° if you died today,
And gave him all, what he should be tomorrow;
What large return would come of all his
                        [ventures;
How he should worshipp'd be, and reverenc'd;
20 Ride with his furs and footcloths,° waited on
By herds of fools and clients; have clear way
Made for his mule, as letter'd as himself;
Be call'd the great and learned advocate!
And then concludes there's naught impossible.
25   VOLPONE. Yes, to be learned, Mosca.
    MOSCA.   O, no! rich
Implies it. Hood an ass with reverend purple,
So you can hide his two ambitious ears,
And he shall pass for a cathedral doctor.°
30   VOLPONE. My caps, my caps, good Mosca.
                    [Fetch him in.
    MOSCA. Stay, sir; your ointment for your
                        [eyes.
    VOLPONE.   That's true;
35 Dispatch, dispatch; I long to have possession
Of my new present.
    MOSCA.   That, and thousands more,
I hope to see you lord of.
    VOLPONE.   Thanks, kind Mosca.
40   MOSCA. And that, when I am lost in blended
                        [dust,
And hundred such as I am, in succession—
    VOLPONE. Nay, that were too much, Mosca.
    MOSCA.   You shall live

Still to delude these harpies.   45
    VOLPONE.   Loving Mosca!
'Tis well; my pillow now, and let him enter.
    [*Exit* MOSCA.]
Now, my feign'd cough, my phthisic, and my
                      [gout, 50
My apoplexy, palsy, and catarrhs,
Help, with your forced functions this my
                      [posture,°
Wherein, this three year, I have milk'd their
                      [hopes. 55
He comes; I hear him—Uh, uh, uh, uh!—Oh!

Scene iii

[*Enter* MOSCA *with* VOLTORE.]
    MOSCA. You still are what you were, sir. Only
                      [you,
Of all the rest, are he commands his love,   60
And you do wisely to preserve it thus,
With early visitation and kind notes
Of your good meaning to him, which, I know,
Cannot but come most grateful. Patron! sir!
Here's Signior Voltore is come—   65
    VOLPONE.   What say you?
    MOSCA. Sir, Signior Voltore is come this
                      [morning
To visit you.
    VOLPONE.   I thank him.   70
    MOSCA.   And hath brought
A piece of antique plate, bought of St. Mark,°
With which he here presents you.
    VOLPONE.   He is welcome.
Pray him to come more often.   75
    MOSCA.   Yes.
    VOLTORE.   What says he?
    MOSCA. He thanks you, and desires you see
                      [him often.
    VOLPONE. Mosca.   80
    MOSCA.   My patron!
    VOLPONE.   Bring him near. Where is he?
I long to feel his hand.
    MOSCA.   The plate is here, sir.
    VOLTORE. How fare you, sir?   85
    VOLPONE.   I thank you, Signior Voltore.

---

fetch you   persuade you to make him your heir
footcloths   decorative trappings of a horse
cathedral doctor   university professor

Help . . . posture   help with your simulated actions this
my (im)posture
St. Mark   St. Mark's Square

Where is the plate? mine eyes are bad.

    VOLTORE.   I'm sorry

To see you still thus weak.

    MOSCA [aside].   That he is not weaker.

5   VOLPONE. You are too munificent.

    VOLTORE.   No, sir; would to Heaven

I could as well give health to you, as that plate.

    VOLPONE. You give, sir, what you can. I

                [thank you. Your love

10   Hath taste in this, and shall not be unanswer'd.

I pray you see me often.

    VOLTORE.   Yes, I shall, sir.

    VOLPONE. Be not far from me.

    MOSCA.   Do you observe that, sir?

15   VOLPONE. Harken unto me still; it will

                [concern you.

    MOSCA. You are a happy man, sir; know

                [your good.

    VOLPONE. I cannot now last long—

20   MOSCA [aside].   You are his heir, sir.

    VOLTORE [aside]. Am I?

    VOLPONE. I feel me going—uh, uh, uh, uh!—

I'm sailing to my port—uh, uh, uh, uh!—

And I am glad I am so near my haven.

25   MOSCA. Alas, kind gentleman; well, we must

                [all go—

    VOLTORE. But, Mosca—

    MOSCA.   Age will conquer.

    VOLTORE.   'Pray thee, hear me.

30   Am I inscrib'd his heir, for certain?

    MOSCA.   Are you!

I do beseech you, sir, you will vouchsafe

To write me i' your family.° All my hopes

Depend upon your Worship. I am lost

35   Except the rising sun do shine on me.

    VOLTORE. It shall both shine, and warm thee,

                [Mosca.

    MOSCA.   Sir,

I am a man that hath not done your love

40   All the worst offices; here I wear your keys,

See all your coffers and your caskets lock'd,

Keep the poor inventory of your jewels,

Your plate, and monies; am your steward, sir,

Husband your goods here.

45   VOLTORE.   But am I sole heir?

write . . . family   regard me as a servant of your household

    MOSCA. Without a partner, sir; confirm'd this

                [morning;

The wax is warm yet, and the ink scarce dry

Upon the parchment.

    VOLTORE.   Happy, happy me!   50

By what good chance, sweet Mosca?

    MOSCA.   Your desert, sir;

I know no second cause.

    VOLTORE.   Thy modesty

Is loath to know it; well, we shall requite it.   55

    MOSCA. He ever lik'd your course, sir; that

                [first took him.

I oft have heard him say how he admir'd

Men of your large profession, that could speak

To every cause, and things mere contraries,   60

Till they were hoarse again, yet all be law;

That, with most quick agility, could turn,

And return; make knots, and undo them;

Give forked counsel; take provoking gold°

On either hand, and put it up;° these men,   65

He knew, would thrive with their humility.

And, for his part, he thought he should be blest

To have his heir of such a suffering° spirit,

So wise, so grave, of so perplex'd a tongue,°

And loud withal, that would not wag, nor   70

                [scarce

Lie still, without a fee; when every word

Your Worship but lets fall, is a *cecchine!*°

    [*Another knocks.*]

Who's that? One knocks; I would not have you   75

                [seen, sir.

And yet—pretend you came and went in haste;

I'll fashion an excuse. And, gentle sir,

When you do come to swim in golden lard,

Up to the arms in honey, that your chin   80

Is borne up stiff with fatness of the flood,

Think on your vassal; but remember me:

I ha' not been your worst of clients.

    VOLTORE.   Mosca—

    MOSCA. When will you have your inventory   85

                [brought, sir?

Or see a copy of the will?—Anon.—

provoking gold a legal fee
put it up pocket it
suffering tolerant
so . . . tongue such devious utterance
cecchine gold coin

I'll bring 'em to you, sir. Away, begone,
Put business i' your face.
   [*Exit* VOLTORE.]
VOLPONE.   Excellent Mosca!
5 Come hither, let me kiss thee.
   MOSCA.   Keep you still, sir.
Here is Corbaccio.
   VOLPONE.   Set the plate away.
The vulture's gone, and the old raven's come.

Scene iv

10   [MOSCA *and* VOLPONE *remain*.]
   MOSCA. Betake you to your silence, and your
                          [sleep.—
   [*To the plate*.] Stand there and multiply.—
               [(*Aside*.) Now shall we see
15 A wretch who is indeed more impotent°
Than this can feign to be; yet hopes to hop
Over his grave.—
   [*He admits* CORBACCIO.]
               Signior Corbaccio!
20 You're very welcome, sir.
   CORBACCIO.   How does your patron?
   MOSCA. Troth, as he did, sir; no amends.
   CORBACCIO.   What? mends he?
   MOSCA. No, sir: he is rather worse.
25   CORBACCIO.   That's well. Where is he?
   MOSCA. Upon his couch, sir, newly fall'n
                         [asleep.
   CORBACCIO. Does he sleep well?
   MOSCA.   No wink, sir, all this night,
30 Nor yesterday; but slumbers.°
   CORBACCIO.   Good! he should take
Some counsel of physicians. I have brought
                       [him
An opiate here, from mine own doctor—
35   MOSCA. He will not hear of drugs.
   CORBACCIO.   Why? I myself
Stood by while 'twas made, saw all th'
                      [ingredients,
And know it cannot but most gently work.
40 My life for his, 'tis but to make him sleep.
   VOLPONE [*aside*]. Ay, his last sleep, if he
                     [would take it.
   MOSCA.   Sir,

He has no faith in physic.
   CORBACCIO.   Say you? say you?   45
   MOSCA. He has no faith in physic; he does
                          [think
Most of your doctors are the greater danger,
And worse disease, t' escape. I often have
Heard him protest that your° physician   50
Should never be his heir.
   CORBACCIO.   Not I his heir?
   MOSCA. Not your physician, sir.
   CORBACCIO.   O, no, no, no;
I do not mean it.   55
   MOSCA.   No, sir, nor their fees
He cannot brook; he says they flay a man
Before they kill him.
   CORBACCIO.   Right, I do conceive you.
   MOSCA. And then they do it by experiment;   60
For which the law not only doth absolve 'em,
But gives them great reward; and he is loath
To hire his death so.
   CORBACCIO.   It is true, they kill
With as much license as a judge.   65
   MOSCA.   Nay, more;
For he but kills, sir, where the law condemns,
And these can kill him too.
   CORBACCIO.   Ay, or me,
Or any man. How does his apoplex?   70
Is that strong on him still?
   MOSCA.   Most violent.
His speech is broken, and his eyes are set,
His face drawn longer than 'twas wont—
   CORBACCIO.   How? how?   75
Stronger than he was wont?
   MOSCA.   No, sir; his face
Drawn longer than 'twas wont.
   CORBACCIO.   O good.
   MOSCA.   His mouth   80
Is ever gaping, and his eyelids hang.
   CORBACCIO.   Good.
   MOSCA. A freezing numbness stiffens all his
                         [joints,
And makes the color of his flesh like lead.   85
   CORBACCIO.   'Tis good.
   MOSCA. His pulse beats slow, and dull.
   CORBACCIO.   Good symptoms still.
   MOSCA. And from his brain—

---

impotent infirm
slumbers dozes

your the

CORBACCIO. Ha? How? Not from his
[brain?
MOSCA. Yes, sir, and from his brain—
CORBACCIO. I conceive you; good.
5   MOSCA. Flows a cold sweat, with a continual
[rheum,
Forth the resolved° corners of his eyes.
    CORBACCIO. Is 't possible? Yet I am better, ha!
How does he with the swimming of his head?
10   MOSCA. O, sir, 'tis past the scotomy;° he now
Hath lost his feeling, and hath left° to snort;
You hardly can perceive him, that he breathes.
    CORBACCIO. Excellent, excellent; sure I shall
[outlast him;
15   This makes me young again, a score of years.
    MOSCA. I was a-coming for you, sir.
    CORBACCIO. Has he made his will?
What has he giv'n me?
    MOSCA. No, sir.
20   CORBACCIO. Nothing? ha?
    MOSCA. He has not made his will, sir.
    CORBACCIO. Oh, oh, oh.
What then did Voltore, the lawyer, here?
    MOSCA. He smelt a carcass, sir, when he but
25   [heard
My master was about his testament;°
As I did urge him to it for your good—
    CORBACCIO. He came unto him, did he? I
[thought so.
30   MOSCA. Yes, and presented him this piece of
[plate.
    CORBACCIO. To be his heir?
    MOSCA. I do not know, sir.
    CORBACCIO. True;
35   I know it too.
    MOSCA [aside]. By your own scale, sir.
    CORBACCIO. Well,
I shall prevent° him yet. See, Mosca, look,
Here I have brought a bag of bright cecchines,
40   Will quite weigh down his plate.
    MOSCA. Yea, marry, sir.
This is true physic, this your sacred medicine;
No talk of opiates to this great elixir!

CORBACCIO. 'Tis aurum palpabile, if not
[potabile.° 45
MOSCA. It shall be minister'd to him in his
[bowl!
CORBACCIO. Ay, do, do, do.
MOSCA. Most blessed cordial!
This will recover him.° 50
    CORBACCIO. Yes, do, do, do.
    MOSCA. I think it were not best, sir.
    CORBACCIO. What?
    MOSCA. To recover° him.
    CORBACCIO. O, no, no, no; by no means. 55
    MOSCA. Why, sir, this
Will work some strange effect, if he but feel it.
    CORBACCIO. 'Tis true; therefore forbear. I'll
[take my venture;
Give me 't again. 60
    MOSCA. At no hand;° pardon me,
You shall not do yourself that wrong, sir. I
Will so advise you, you shall have it all.
    CORBACCIO. How?
    MOSCA. All, sir; 'tis your right, your own; 65
[no man
Can claim a part; 'tis yours without a rival,
Decreed by destiny.
    CORBACCIO. How, how, good Mosca?
    MOSCA. I'll tell you, sir. This fit he shall 70
[recover—
    CORBACCIO. I do conceive you.
    MOSCA. And, on first advantage
Of his gain'd sense, will I re-importune him
Unto the making of his testament, 75
And show him this. [Points to the money.]
    CORBACCIO. Good, good.
    MOSCA. 'Tis better yet,
If you will hear, sir.
    CORBACCIO. Yes, with all my heart. 80
    MOSCA. Now would I counsel you, make
[home with speed;
There, frame a will; whereto you shall inscribe
My master your sole heir.
    CORBACCIO. And disinherit 85
My son?

---

resolved decomposing
scotomy giddiness
left ceased
about his testament planning his will
prevent get ahead of

aurum . . . potabile gold tangible, if not drinkable.
    Elixir of gold was an esteemed restorative.
recover him recover his favor
recover cure
At no hand by no means

MOSCA.　　　O, sir, the better; for that color°
Shall make it much more taking.
　　CORBACCIO.　　　　　　　O, but color?
　　MOSCA. This will, sir, you shall send it unto
5　　　　　　　　　　　　　　　　　　　　[me.
Now, when I come to enforce, as I will do,
Your cares, your watchings, and your many
　　　　　　　　　　　　　　　　　[prayers,
Your more than many gifts, your this day's
10　　　　　　　　　　　　　　　　　　[present,
And last, produce your will; where (without
　　　　　　　　　　　　　　　　　[thought
Or least regard unto your proper issue,
A son so brave, and highly meriting)
15 The stream of your diverted love hath thrown
　　　　　　　　　　　　　　　　　　[you
Upon my master, and made him your heir;
He cannot be so stupid or stone-dead,
But, out of conscience and mere gratitude—
20　　CORBACCIO. He must pronounce me his?
　　MOSCA.　　　　'Tis true.
　　CORBACCIO.　　　　　　　This plot
Did I think on before.
　　MOSCA.　　　　　　　I do believe it.
25　　CORBACCIO. Do you not believe it?
　　MOSCA.　　　　　　　　　　　Yes, sir.
　　CORBACCIO.　　　Mine own project.
　　MOSCA. Which, when he hath done, sir—
　　CORBACCIO.　　　Publish'd me his heir?
30　　MOSCA. And you so certain to survive him—
　　CORBACCIO.　　　Ay.
　　MOSCA. Being so lusty a man—
　　CORBACCIO.　　　　　　　　'Tis true.
　　MOSCA.　　　Yes, sir—
35　　CORBACCIO. I thought on that too. See, how
　　　　　　　　　　　　　　　[he should be°
The very organ to express my thoughts!
　　MOSCA. You have not only done yourself a
　　　　　　　　　　　　　　　　　[good—
40　　CORBACCIO. But multiplied it on my son!
　　MOSCA. 'Tis right, sir.
　　CORBACCIO. Still, my invention.
　　MOSCA.　　　'Las, sir! Heaven knows,
It hath been all my study, all my care,
45 (I e'en grow gray withal) how to work things—

color pretense
he should be Mosca is

　　CORBACCIO. I do conceive, sweet Mosca.
　　MOSCA.　　　You are he
For whom I labor here.
　　CORBACCIO.　　　Ay, do, do, do.
I'll straight about it.　　　　　　　　　　50
　　MOSCA [*aside*]. Rook go with you, raven.
　　CORBACCIO. I know thee honest.
　　MOSCA.　　　You do lie, sir—
　　CORBACCIO.　　　　　　　And—
　　MOSCA. Your knowledge is no better than　　55
　　　　　　　　　　　　　　[your ears, sir.
　　CORBACCIO. I do not doubt to be a father to
　　　　　　　　　　　　　　　　　[thee.
　　MOSCA. Nor I to gull my brother of his
　　　　　　　　　　　　　　[blessing.　60
　　CORBACCIO. I may ha' my youth restor'd to
　　　　　　　　　　　　　　[me, why not?
　　MOSCA. Your Worship is a precious ass—
　　CORBACCIO.　　　What say'st thou?
　　MOSCA. I do desire your Worship to make　65
　　　　　　　　　　　　　　[haste,° sir.
　　CORBACCIO. 'Tis done, 'tis done; I go.
[*Exit.*]
　　VOLPONE [*leaping from his couch*]. Oh, I shall
　　　　　　　　　　　　　　[burst!　70
Let out my sides, let out my sides—
　　MOSCA.　　　　　　　　Contain
Your flux of laughter, sir; you know this hope
Is such a bait, it covers any hook.
　　VOLPONE. O, but thy working, and thy　　75
　　　　　　　　　　　　　　[placing it!
I cannot hold; good rascal, let me kiss thee;
I never knew thee in so rare a humor.
　　MOSCA. Alas, sir, I but do as I am taught;
Follow your grave instructions, give 'em words,　80
Pour oil into their ears, and send them hence.
　　VOLPONE. 'Tis true, 'tis true. What a rare
　　　　　　　　　　　　　　[punishment
Is avarice to itself!
　　MOSCA.　　　Ay, with our help, sir.　85
　　VOLPONE. So many cares, so many maladies,
So many fears attending on old age.
Yea, death so often call'd on, as no wish
Can be more frequent with 'em, their limbs
　　　　　　　　　　　　　　[faint,　90
Their senses dull, their seeing, hearing, going,

haste pronounced hasst

All dead before them; yea, their very teeth,
Their instruments of eating, failing them.
Yet this is reckon'd life! Nay, here was one,
Is now gone home, that wishes to live longer!
5 Feels not his gout, nor palsy; feigns himself
Younger by scores of years, flatters his age
With confident belying it, hopes he may
With charms like Aeson° have his youth
                                            [restor'd;
10 And with these thoughts so battens, as if fate
Would be as easily cheated on as he;
And all turns air! Who's that there, now? a
                                            [third?

[*Another knocks.*]

15 MOSCA. Close; to your couch again; I hear
                                            [his voice.
It is Corvino, our spruce merchant.
VOLPONE [*lying down*].   Dead.
MOSCA. Another bout, sir, with your eyes.
20   [(*Anointing them.*)—Who's there?

Scene v

[*Enter* CORVINO.]
Signior Corvino! come most wish'd for! Oh,
How happy were you, if you knew it, now!
CORVINO. Why? what? wherein?
25 MOSCA.   The tardy hour is come, sir.
CORVINO. He is not dead?
MOSCA.   Not dead, sir, but as
                                            [good;
He knows no man.
30 CORVINO.   How shall I do then?
MOSCA.   Why, sir?
CORVINO. I have brought him here a pearl.
MOSCA.   Perhaps he has
So much rembrance left as to know you, sir.
35 He still calls on you; nothing but your name
Is in his mouth. Is your pearl orient, sir?
CORVINO. Venice was never owner of the like.
VOLPONE. Signior Corvino!
MOSCA.   Hark!
40 VOLPONE.   Signior Corvino.
MOSCA. He calls you; step and give it him.—
                                            [H' is here, sir.
And he has brought you a rich pearl.
CORVINO.   How do you do, sir?—
45 Tell him it doubles the twelfth carat.

Aeson a legendary Greek king

MOSCA.   Sir,
He cannot understand: his hearing's gone;
And yet it comforts him to see you—
CORVINO.   Say
I have a diamond for him, too.   50
MOSCA.   Best show 't, sir;
Put it into his hand; 'tis only there
He apprehends; he has his feeling yet.
See, how he grasps it!
CORVINO.   'Las, good gentleman!   55
How pitiful the sight is!
MOSCA.   Tut, forget, sir.
The weeping of an heir should still be laughter
Under a visor.
CORVINO.   Why, am I his heir?   60
MOSCA. Sir, I am sworn, I may not show the
                                            [will
Till he be dead. But here has been Corbaccio,
Here has been Voltore, here were others too—
I cannot number 'em, they were so many—   65
All gaping here for legacies; but I,
Taking the vantage of his naming you,
"Signior Corvino, Signior Corvino," took
Paper, and pen, and ink, and there I ask'd him
Whom he would have his heir! "Corvino."   70
                                            [Who
Should be executor? "Corvino." And
To any question he was silent to,
I still interpreted the nods he made,
Through weakness, for consent; and sent home   75
                                            [th' others,
Nothing bequeath'd them, but to cry and
                                            [curse.
CORVINO. Oh, my dear Mosca. (*They
                    [embrace.*) Does he not perceive us? 80
MOSCA. No more than a blind harper. He
                                            [knows no man,
No face of friend, nor name of any servant,
Who 'twas that fed him last, or gave him drink;
Not those he hath begotten, or brought up,   85
Can he remember.
CORVINO.   Has he children?
MOSCA.   Bastards,
Some dozen, or more, that he begot on beggars,
Gypsies, and Jews, and black-moors, when he   90
                                            [was drunk.
Knew you not that, sir? 'Tis the common fable.
The dwarf, the fool, the eunuch, are all his;
H' is the true father of his family,

In all save me. But he has giv'n 'em nothing.
  CORVINO. That's well, that's well. Art sure
                    [he does not hear us?
  MOSCA. Sure, sir! Why, look you, credit your
5   [own sense. (*Shouts in* VOLPONE'S *ear.*)
The pox approach, and add to your diseases,
If it would send you hence the sooner, sir;
For your incontinence it hath deserv'd it
Throughly and throughly, and the plague to
10   [boot!—
You may come near, sir.—Would you would
                    [once close
Those filthy eyes of yours, that flow with slime
Like two frog-pits; and those same hanging
15   [cheeks,
Cover'd with hide instead of skin—Nay, help,
                    [sir—
That look like frozen dishclouts set on end.
  CORVINO. Or like an old smok'd wall, on
20   [which the rain
Ran down in streaks.
  MOSCA.   Excellent, sir! speak out;
You may be louder yet; a culverin
Discharged in his ear would hardly bore it.
25 CORVINO. His nose is like a common sewer,
                    [still running.
  MOSCA. 'Tis good! And what his mouth?
  CORVINO.   A very draught.
  MOSCA. O, stop it up—
30 CORVINO.   By no means.
  MOSCA.   Pray you, let me;
Faith, I could stifle him rarely° with a pillow
As well as any woman that should keep° him.
  CORVINO. Do as you will; but I'll be gone.
35 MOSCA.   Be so;
It is your presence makes him last so long.
  CORVINO. I pray you use no violence.
  MOSCA.   No, sir? why?
Why should you be thus scrupulous, 'pray you,
40   [sir?
  CORVINO. Nay, at your discretion.
  MOSCA.   Well, good sir, begone.
  CORVINO. I will not trouble him now to take
                    [my pearl?
45 MOSCA. Pooh, nor your diamond. What a
                    [needless care

Is this afflicts you? Is not all here yours?
Am not I here, whom you have made, your
                    [creature,
That owe my being to you?   50
  CORVINO.   Grateful Mosca!
Thou art my friend, my fellow, my companion,
My partner, and shalt share in all my fortunes.
  MOSCA. Excepting one.
  CORVINO.   What's that?   55
  MOSCA.   Your gallant wife, sir.
[*Exit* CORVINO.]
Now is he gone; we had no other means
To shoot him hence but this.
  VOLPONE.   My divine Mosca!   60
Thou hast today outgone thyself. Who's there?
    [*Another knocks.*]
I will be troubled with no more. Prepare
Me music, dances, banquets, all delights;
The Turk is not more sensual in his pleasures   65
Than will Volpone. [*Exit* MOSCA.] Let me see;
                    [a pearl!
A diamond! plate! *cecchines!* Good morning's
                    [purchase.
Why, this is better than rob churches, yet;   70
Or fat, by eating, once a month, a man—
    [*Re-enter* MOSCA.]
Who is 't?
  MOSCA.   The beauteous Lady Would-be,
                    [sir.   75
Wife to the English knight, Sir Politic Would-
                    [be—
This is the style, sir, is directed me—
Hath sent to know how you have slept tonight,
And if you would be visited.   80
  VOLPONE.   Not now.
Some three hours hence—
  MOSCA.   I told the squire so much.
  VOLPONE. When I am high with mirth and
                    [wine; then, then.   85
'Fore Heaven, I wonder at the desperate valor
Of the bold English, that they dare let loose
Their wives to all encounters!
  MOSCA.   Sir, this knight
Had not his name for nothing: he is politic,°   90
And knows, howe'er his wife affect strange
                    [airs,
She hath not yet the face to be dishonest.

---

rarely exceedingly well
keep attend

politic worldly wise, devious and urbane

But had she Signior Corvino's wife's face—
   VOLPONE. Hath she so rare a face?
   MOSCA.   O, sir, the wonder,
The blazing star of Italy! a wench
5 Of the first year! a beauty ripe as harvest!
Whose skin is whiter than a swan, all over!
Than silver, snow, or lilies! a soft lip,
Would tempt you to eternity of kissing!
And flesh that melteth in the touch to blood!
10 Bright as your gold! and lovely as your gold!
   VOLPONE. Why had not I known this before?
   MOSCA.   Alas, sir,
Myself but yesterday discover'd it.
   VOLPONE. How might I see her?
15   MOSCA.   Oh, not possible;
She's kept as warily as is your gold;
Never does come abroad, never takes air
But at a window. All her looks are sweet,
As the first grapes or cherries, and are watch'd
20 As near as they are.
   VOLPONE.   I must see her—
   MOSCA.   Sir,
There is a guard of ten spies thick upon her,
All his whole household; each of which is set
25 Upon his fellow, and have all their charge,
When he goes out, when he comes in, examin'd.
   VOLPONE. I will go see her, though but at her
           [window.
Mosca. In some disguise then.
30   VOLPONE.   That is true; I must
Maintain mine own shape still the same; we'll
           [think.

[*Exeunt.*]

ACT II

Scene i

[*Before* CORVINO's *house in St. Mark's*
35 *Square.*]
   [*Enter* SIR POLITIC WOULD-BE *and* PEREGRINE.]
   POLITIC. Sir, to a wise man, all the world's his
           [soil:
It is not Italy, nor France, nor Europe,
40 That must bound me, if my fates call me forth.
Yet I protest, it is no salt desire
Of seeing countries, shifting a religion,
Nor any disaffection to the state
Where I was bred, and unto which I owe

My dearest plots, hath brought me out; much   45
           [less
That idle, antic, stale, gray-headed project
Of knowing men's minds and manners, with
           [Ulysses!
But a peculiar humor of my wife's   50
Laid for° this height° of Venice, to observe,
To quote,° to learn the language, and so forth—
I hope you travel, sir, with license?°
   PEREGRINE.   Yes.
   POLITIC. I dare the safelier converse.—How   55
           [long, sir,
Since you left England?
   PEREGRINE.   Seven weeks.
   POLITIC.   So lately!
You ha' not been with my Lord Ambassador?   60
   PEREGRINE.   Not yet, sir.
   POLITIC. Pray you, what news, sir, vents our
           [climate?
I heard last night a most strange thing reported
By some of my Lord's followers, and I long   65
To hear how 'twill be seconded!
   PEREGRINE.   What was 't, sir?
   POLITIC. Marry, sir, of a raven° that should
           [build
In a ship royal of the king's.   70
   PEREGRINE [*aside*].   This fellow,
Does he gull me, trow? or is gull'd?—Your
           [name, sir?
   POLITIC. My name is Politic Would-be.
   PEREGRINE [*aside*].   O, that speaks him.—   75
A knight, sir?
   POLITIC.   A poor knight, sir.
   PEREGRINE.   Your lady
Lies here in Venice, for intelligence
Of tires and fashions and behavior,   80
Among the courtesans? The fine Lady Would-
           [be?

Laid for headed for   **height of** highly fashionable
quote note
license government authorization
raven this reference, like the following ones to lion's
   whelps, the new star (a famous nova, of 1604), porpoises, and a whale, indicates both the ready
   credulity of Sir Politic and the widespread interest in
   omens associated with the wars and negotiations
   between the Protestants (of Great Britain and the
   Low Countries) and the Catholics (of Austria, Italy,
   and Spain)

POLITIC. Yes, sir; the spider and the bee
[ofttimes
Suck from one flower.
PEREGRINE.   Good Sir Politic!
5 I cry you mercy; I have heard much of you.
'Tis true, sir, of your raven.
POLITIC.   On your knowledge?
PEREGRINE. Yes, and your lion's whelping in
[the Tower.
10 POLITIC. Another whelp!
PEREGRINE.   Another, sir.
POLITIC.   Now Heaven!
What prodigies be these? The fires° at Berwick!
And the new star! These things concurring,
15   [strange!
And full of omen! Saw you those meteors?
PEREGRINE. I did, sir.
POLITIC.   Fearful! Pray you, sir,
[confirm me,
20 Were there three porpoises seen, above the
[Bridge,
As they give out?
PEREGRINE.   Six, and a sturgeon, sir.
POLITIC. I am astonish'd!
25 PEREGRINE.   Nay, sir, be not so;
I'll tell you a greater prodigy than these—
POLITIC. What should these things portend?
PEREGRINE.   The very day,
Let me be sure, that I put forth from London,
30 There was a whale discover'd in the river,
As high as Woolwich, that had waited there,
Few know how many months, for the
[subversion
Of the Stode fleet.°
35 POLITIC.   Is 't possible? Believe it,
'Twas either sent from Spain, or the
[Archdukes!°
Spinola's° whale, upon my life, my credit!
Will they not leave these projects? Worthy sir,

Some other news.   40
PEREGRINE.   Faith, Stone, the fool, is dead,
And they do lack a tavern fool extremely.
POLITIC. Is Mas' Stone dead?
PEREGRINE.   He's dead, sir; why, I hope
You thought him not immortal?—[*Aside.*] Oh, 45
[this knight,
Were he well known, would be a precious
[thing
To fit our English stage. He that should write
But such a fellow, should be thought to feign 50
Extremely, if not maliciously.
POLITIC.   Stone dead!
PEREGRINE. Dead.—Lord! how deeply, sir,
[you apprehend it!
He was no kinsman to you?   55
POLITIC.   That I know of.
Well! that same fellow was an unknown° fool.
PEREGRINE. And yet you knew him, it seems?
POLITIC.   I did so. Sir,
I knew him one of the most dangerous heads   60
Living within the state, and so I held him.
PEREGRINE. Indeed, sir?
POLITIC.   While he liv'd, in action,
He has receiv'd weekly intelligence,
Upon my knowledge, out of the Low Countries; 65
For all parts of the world, in cabbages;
And those dispens'd again to ambassadors.
In oranges, muskmelons, apricots,
Lemons, pome-citrons, and such like;
[sometimes 70
In Colchester oysters, and your Selsey cockles.
PEREGRINE. You make me wonder!
POLITIC.   Sir, upon my knowledge.
Nay, I have observ'd him, at your public
[ordinary,° 75
Take his advertisement° from a traveller
(A conceal'd statesman) in a trencher of meat;
And instantly, before the meal was done,
Convey an answer in a toothpick.
PEREGRINE.   Strange!   80
How could this be, sir?
POLITIC.   Why, the meat was cut
So like his character, and so laid as he

fires   meteors
Stode fleet   vessels of the English Merchant Adventurers, a trading company with a base at Stade, near Hamburg, Germany
Archdukes   Archduke Albert of Austria and his wife, the Spanish Infanta Isabella, jointly the governors of the Netherlands and titled "the Archdukes"
Spinola   commander of Spanish forces in the Netherlands

unknown   unrecognized
ordinary   tavern
advertisement   information

Must easily read the cipher.
    PEREGRINE.   I have heard
He could not read, sir.
    POLITIC.   So 'twas given out,
5 In polity,° by those that did employ him;
But he could read, and had your languages,
And to 't, as sound a noddle—
    PEREGRINE.   I have heard, sir,
That your baboons were spies, and that they
10   [were
A kind of subtle nation near to China.
    POLITIC. Ay, ay, your Mamaluchi.° Faith,
                          [they had
Their hand in a French plot or two; but they
15 Were so extremely given to women, as
They made discovery of all: yet I
Had my advices here, on Wednesday last,
From one of their own coat, they were return'd,
Made their relations, as the fashion is,
20 And now stand fair for fresh employment.
    PEREGRINE [aside].   Heart!
This Sir Pol will be ignorant of nothing.—
It seems, sir, you know all.
    POLITIC.   Not all, sir. But
25 I have some general notions. I do love
To note and to observe. Though I live out,
Free from the active torrent, yet I'd mark
The currents and the passages of things
For mine own private use; and know the ebbs
30 And flows of state.
    PEREGRINE.   Believe it, sir, I hold
Myself in no small tie unto my fortunes,
For casting me thus luckily upon you,
Whose knowledge, if your bounty equal it,
35 May do me great assistance, in instruction
For my behavior, and my bearing, which
Is yet so rude and raw—
    POLITIC.   Why? came you forth
Empty of rules for travel?
40 PEREGRINE.   Faith, I had
Some common ones, from out that vulgar
                        [grammar,
Which he that cri'd Italian to me, taught me.
    POLITIC. Why, this it is that spoils all our

                      [brave bloods, 45
Trusting our hopeful gentry unto pedants,
Fellows of outside, and mere bark. You seem
To be a gentleman of ingenuous race.—
I not profess it, but my fate hath been
To be where I have been consulted with, 50
In this high kind, touching some great men's
                          [sons,
Persons of blood and honor.—
    PEREGRINE.   Who be these, sir?

Scene ii

[Enter MOSCA and NANO disguised, with 55
workmen who erect a stage.]
    MOSCA. Under that window, there 't must be.
                        [The same.
    POLITIC. Fellows to mount a bank!° Did your
                      [instructor 60
In the dear tongues never discourse to you
Of the Italian mountebanks?
    PEREGRINE.   Yes, sir.
    POLITIC.   Why,
Here shall you see one. 65
    PEREGRINE.   They are quacksalvers,
Fellows that live by venting° oils and drugs!
    POLITIC. Was that the character he gave you
                      [of them?
    PEREGRINE. As I remember. 70
    POLITIC.   Pity his ignorance.
They are the only knowing men of Europe!
Great general scholars, excellent physicians,
Most admir'd statesmen, profess'd favorites
And cabinet counsellors to the greatest princes! 75
The only languag'd men of all the world!
    PEREGRINE. And, I have heard, they are most
                  [lewd° impostors;
Made all of terms and shreds; no less beliers
Of great men's favors, than their own vile 80
                  [med'cines;
Which they will utter° upon monstrous oaths;
Selling that drug for twopence, ere they part,
Which they have valu'd at twelve crowns
                  [before. 85

In polity for political reasons
Mamaluchi Mamelukes, a powerful group of Moham-
  medan white slaves, noted for their machinations

bank a small platform
venting vending
lewd ignorant
utter dispense

POLITIC. Sir, calumnies are answer'd best with
[silence.
Yourself shall judge.—Who is it mounts, my
[friends?
5   MOSCA. Scoto of Mantua, sir.
POLITIC.   Is 't he? Nay, then
I'll proudly promise, sir, you shall behold
Another man than has been phant'sied° to you.
I wonder yet, that he should mount his bank
10   Here in this nook, that has been wont t' appear
In face of the Piazza! Here he comes.
[*Enter* VOLPONE, *disguised as a mountebank
doctor, and followed by a crowd of people.*]
VOLPONE [*to* NANO]. Mount, zany.
15   GREGE. Follow, follow, follow, follow, follow.
POLITIC. See how the people follow him! he's
[a man
May write ten thousand crowns in bank here.
[Note,
20   Mark but his gesture—I do use to observe
The state he keeps in getting up!
PEREGRINE.   'Tis worth it, sir.
VOLPONE. Most noble gentlemen, and my
worthy patrons, it may seem strange that I,
25   your Scoto Mantuano, who was ever wont to
fix my bank in the face of the public Piazza,
near the shelter of the portico to the Procuratia,
should now, after eight months' absence from
this illustrious city of Venice, humbly retire
30   myself into an obscure nook of the Piazza.
POLITIC. Did not I now object the same?
PEREGRINE.   Peace, sir.
VOLPONE. Let me tell you: I am not, as your
Lombard proverb saith, cold on my feet; or
35   content to part with my commodities at a
cheaper rate than I accustomed—look not for it.
Nor that the calumnious reports of that impudent detractor, and shame to our profession
(Alessandro Buttone, I mean), who gave out,
40   in public, I was condemn'd *a' sforzato*° to the
galleys, for poisoning the Cardinal Bembo's
cook, hath at all attached, much less dejected
me. No, no, worthy gentlemen; to tell you true,
I cannot endure to see the rabble of these

ground *ciarlitani*° that spread their cloaks on   45
the pavement, as if they meant to do feats of
activity, and then come in lamely, with their
mouldy tales of Boccaccio, like stale Tabarin,
the fabulist; some of them discoursing their
travels, and of their tedious captivity in the   50
Turk's galleys, when, indeed, were the truth°
known, they were the Christian's galleys, where
very temperately they ate bread, and drunk
water, as a wholesome penance, enjoin'd them
by their confessors, for base pilferies.   55
POLITIC. Note but his bearing, and contempt
of these.
VOLPONE.   These   turdy-facy-nasty-paty-
lousy-fartical rogues, with one poor groat's-
worth of unprepar'd antimony, finely wrapp'd   60
up in several *scartoccios*,° are able, very well,
to kill their twenty a week, and play; yet these
meager, starv'd spirits, who have half stopp'd
the organs of their minds with earthy oppilations,° want not their favorers among your   65
shrivell'd salad-eating artisans, who are over-
joy'd that they may have their half-pe'rth° of
physic; though it purge 'em into another world,
't makes no matter.
POLITIC. Excellent! ha' you heard better lan-   70
guage, sir?
VOLPONE. Well, let 'em go. And, gentlemen,
know that for this time our bank, being thus
remov'd from the clamors of the *canaglia*,° shall
be the scene of pleasure and delight; for I have   75
nothing to sell, little or nothing to sell.
POLITIC. I told you, sir, his end.
PEREGRINE.   You did so, sir.
VOLPONE. I protest I and my six servants are
not able to make of this precious liquor so fast   80
as it is fetch'd away from my lodging by gentlemen of your city, strangers of the terra-firma,
worshipful merchants, ay, and senators, too,
who, ever since my arrival, have detained me to

---

ground ciarlitani   cheap entertainers
the truth   i.e., that they were criminals being properly
       punished rather than slaves of the Turkish infidels
scartoccios   twists of paper
oppilations   obstructions
half-pe'rth   halfpenny's worth
canaglia   rabble

---

phant'sied   represented
a' sforzato   to hard labor

their uses, by their splendidous liberalities. And worthily. For what avails your rich man to have his magazines° stuff'd with *moscadelli*,° or of the purest grape, when his physicians prescribe
5 him, on pain of death, to drink nothing but water cocted with aniseeds? O health! health! the blessing of the rich! the riches of the poor! who can buy thee at too dear a rate, since there is no enjoying this world without thee?
10 Be not then so sparing of your purses, honorable gentlemen, as to abridge the natural course of life—

PEREGRINE. You see his end.
POLITIC.   Ay, is 't not good?
15 VOLPONE. For, when a humid flux, or catarrh, by the mutability of air, falls from your head into an arm or shoulder, or any other part, take you a ducat, or your *cecchine* of gold, and apply to the place affected; see what good effect it
20 can work. No, no; 'tis this blessed *unguento*, this rare extraction, that hath only power to disperse all malignant humors° that proceed either of hot, cold, moist, or windy causes—

PEREGRINE. I would he had put in dry too.
25 POLITIC.   'Pray you, observe.
VOLPONE. To fortify the most indigest and crude stomach, ay, were it of one that, through extreme weakness, vomited blood, applying only a warm napkin to the place, after the unc-
30 tion and fricace;°—for the *vertigine* in the head, putting but a drop into your nostrils, likewise behind the ears, a most sovereign and approv'd remedy; the *mal caduco*, cramps, convulsions, paralyses, epilepsies, *tremor cordia*,
35 retir'd nerves, ill vapors of the spleen, stoppings of the liver, the stone, the strangury, *hernia ventosa*, *iliaca passio*; stops a *dysenteria* immediately; easeth the torsion of the small guts; and cures *melancholia hypochondriaca*, being
40 taken and applied according to my printed re-

ceipt. [*Pointing to his bill and his glass.*] For this is the physician, this the medicine; this counsels, this cures; this gives direction, this works the effect; and, in sum, both together may be term'd an abstract of the theoric and 45 practic in the Aesculapian art. 'Twill cost you eight crowns.—And, Zan Fritada, pray thee sing a verse, extempore, in honor of it.

POLITIC. How do you like him, sir?
PEREGRINE.   Most strangely, I!   50
POLITIC. Is not his language rare?
PEREGRINE.   But° alchemy,
I never heard the like, or Broughton's° books.

NANO [*sings*]. Had old Hippocrates, or Galen,
That to their books put med'cines all in,   55
But known this secret, they had never
(Of which they will be guilty ever)
Been murderers of so much paper,
Or wasted many a hurtless taper;
No Indian drug had e'er been famed,   60
Tobacco, sassafras, not named;
Ne yet of guacum one small stick, sir,
Nor Raymund Lully's great elixir.°
Ne had been known the Danish Gonswart,
Or Paracelsus, with his long-sword.   65

PEREGRINE. All this, yet, will not do; eight crowns is high.

VOLPONE. No more.—Gentlemen, if I had but time to discourse to you the miraculous effects of this my oil, surnamed *oglio del Scoto*, with 70 the countless catalogue of those I have cured of th' aforesaid, and many more diseases; the patents and privileges of all the princes and commonwealths of Christendom; or but the depositions of those that appear'd on my part, 75 before the signiory of the Sanitâ° and most learned College of Physicians; where I was authorized, upon notice taken of the admirable virtues of my medicaments, and mine own excellency in matter of rare and unknown secrets, 80 not only to disperse them publicly in this famous city, but in all the territories that happily joy under the government of the most pious and

magazines storage vaults   moscadelli muscatel
humors in medieval physiology, the four kinds of body-fluid, corresponding to the traditional four elements, that determined both health and temperament
unction and fricace ointment and massage. In the rest of this speech Volpone makes a flourish of medical terminology not to inform but to impress.

But except for
Broughton an eccentric English theologian
great elixir of youth
signiory . . . Sanitâ governors of the hospital

magnificent states of Italy. But may some other gallant fellow say, "Oh, there be divers that make profession to have as good, and as ex-perimented receipts as yours." Indeed, very
5 many have assay'd, like apes, in imitation of that which is really and essentially in me, to make of this oil; bestow'd great cost in fur-naces, stills, alembics, continual fires, and pre-paration of the ingredients (as indeed there
10 goes to it six hundred several simples, besides some quantity of human fat, for the congluti-nation, which we buy of the anatomists); but when these practitioners come to the last de-coction—blow, blow, puff, puff, and all flies in
15 fumo. Ha, ha, ha! Poor wretches! I rather pity their folly and indiscretion, than their loss of time and money; for those may be recovered by industry; but to be a fool born, is a disease in-curable. For myself, I always from my youth
20 have endeavor'd to get the rarest secrets, and book them, either in exchange or for money; I spared nor cost nor labor where anything was worthy to be learned. And, gentlemen, honor-able gentlemen, I will undertake, by virtue of
25 chemical art, out of the honorable hat that covers your head, to extract the four elements; that is to say, the fire, air, water, and earth, and return you your felt without burn or stain. For, whilst others have been at the *balloo*° I have
30 been at my book; and am now past the craggy paths of study, and come to the flow'ry plains of honor and reputation.
    Politic. I do assure you, sir, that is his aim.
    Volpone. But, to our price.
35   Peregrine.   And that withal, Sir Pol.
    Volpone. You all know, honorable gentle-men, I never valu'd this *ampulla*, or vial, at less than eight crowns; but for this time, I am con-tent to be depriv'd of it for six; six crowns is
40 the price, and less in courtesy I know you can-not offer me; take it or leave it, howsoever, both it and I am at your service. I ask you not as the value of the thing, for then I should demand of you a thousand crowns; so the Cardinals Mon-
45 talto, Fernese, the great Duke of Tuscany, my

gossip,° with divers other princes, have given me; but I despise money. Only to show my affection to you, honorable gentlemen, and your illustrious state here, I have neglected the mes-sages of these princes, mine own offices, fram'd 50 my journey hither, only to present you with the fruits of my travels.—Tune your voices once more to the touch of your instruments, and give the honorable assembly some delightful recreation. 55
    Peregrine. What monstrous and most pain-
                     [ful circumstance
Is here, to get some three or four gazets,°
Some threepence i' the whole! for that 'twill
                     [come to. 60
    Nano [*sings*]. You that would last long, list
                     [to my song;
Make no more coil, but buy of this oil.
Would you be ever fair, and young?
Stout of teeth, and strong of tongue? 65
Tart of palate? quick of ear?
Sharp of sight? of nostril clear?
Moist of hand? and light of foot?
Or (I will come nearer to 't)
Would you live free from all diseases? 70
Do the act your mistress pleases,
Yet fright all aches from your bones?
Here's a med'cine for the nones.°
    Volpone. Well, I am in humor, at this time, to make a present of the small quantity my coffer 75 contains; to the rich in courtesy, and to the poor for God's sake. Wherefore now mark: I ask'd you six crowns; and six crowns, at other times, you have paid me; you shall not give me six crowns, nor five, nor four, nor three, nor 80 two, nor one; nor half a ducat; no, nor a *moc-cinigo*.° Sixpence it will cost you, or six hundred pound—expect no lower price, for, by the ban-ner of my front,° I will not bate a bagatine,°— that I will have, only, a pledge of your loves, 85 to carry something from amongst you, to show I am not contemn'd by you. Therefore, now,

gossip close friend
gazets small coins
nones purpose
moccinigo small Venetian coin
banner of my front flag of my profession
bagatine trivial coin

balloo a game of ball

toss your handkerchiefs, cheerfully, cheerfully;
and be advertised, that the first heroic spirit
that deigns to grace me with a handkerchief, I
will give it a little remembrance of something
5 beside, shall please it better than if I had presented it with a double pistolet.°

PEREGRINE. Will you be that heroic spark, Sir
Pol?

[CELIA, *at the window, throws down her*
10 *handkerchief.*]

O, see! the window has prevented you.

VOLPONE. Lady, I kiss your bounty; and, for
this timely grace you have done your poor Scoto
of Mantua, I will return you, over and above
15 my oil, a secret of that high and inestimable
nature, shall make you for ever enamor'd on
that minute wherein your eye first descended
on so mean, yet not altogether to be despis'd an
object. Here is a powder conceal'd in this paper,
20 of which, if I should speak to the worth, nine
thousand volumes were but as one page, that
page as a line, that line as a word; so short is
this pilgrimage of man, which some call life, to
the expressing of it. Would I reflect on the
25 price? Why, the whole world is but as an
empire, that empire as a province, that province
as a bank, that bank as a private purse, to the
purchase of it. I will only tell you: it is the powder that made Venus a goddess, given her by
30 Apollo, that kept her perpetually young, clear'd
her wrinkles, firm'd her gums, fill'd her skin,
color'd her hair; from her deriv'd to Helen, and
at the sack of Troy unfortunately lost; till now,
in this our age, it was as happily recover'd, by a
35 studious antiquary, out of some ruins of Asia,
who sent a moiety of it to the court of France
(but much sophisticated), wherewith the ladies
there now color their hair. The rest, at this present, remains with me, extracted to a quintes-
40 sence; so that, wherever it but touches, in youth
it perpetually preserves, in age restores the
complexion; seats your teeth, did they dance
like virginal jacks,° firm as a wall; makes them
white as ivory, that were black as—

---

pistolet   gold coin
virginal jacks   activating levers, or keys, of a small
    harpsichord

Scene iii

[*Enter* CORVINO.]   45

CORVINO. Spite o' the devil, and my shame!
                    [Come down here;
Come down!—No house but mine to make your
                                    [scene?
Signior Flaminio,° will you down, sir? down?   50
What, is my wife your Franciscina,° sir?
No windows on the whole piazza, here,
To make your properties, but mine? but mine?
    [*He beats away the mountebank, etc.*]
Heart! ere tomorrow I shall be new christen'd, 55
And called the *Pantalone di Bisognosi*°
About the town.

PEREGRINE.   What should this mean, Sir
                                    [Pol?
POLITIC. Some trick of state, believe it; I will   60
                                    [home.
PEREGRINE. It may be some design on you.
POLITIC.   I know not.
I'll stand upon my guard.

PEREGRINE.   It is your best, sir.   65
POLITIC. This three weeks, all my advices, all
                                    [my letters,
They have been intercepted.

PEREGRINE.   Indeed, sir?
Best have a care.   70

POLITIC.   Nay, so I will.

PEREGRINE [*aside*].   This knight.
I may not lose him, for my mirth, till night.
    [*Exeunt.*]

Scene iv

[*A room in* VOLPONE's *house.*]   75
[*Enter* VOLPONE *and* MOSCA.]

VOLPONE. O, I am wounded.

MOSCA.   Where, sir?

VOLPONE.   Not without;
Those blows were nothing; I could bear them   80
                                    [ever.
But angry Cupid, bolting from her eyes,

Signior Flaminio "Mr. Leading Actor"
Franciscina cute little maidservant (a type in the
    Italian popular plays)
Pantalone di Bisognosi the doting old fool (another
    such type)

Hath shot himself into me like a flame;
Where now he flings about his burning heat,
As in a furnace some ambitious fire
Whose vent is stopp'd. The fight is all within
5   [me.
I cannot live, except thou help me, Mosca;
My liver melts, and I, without the hope
Of some soft air from her refreshing breath,
Am but a heap of cinders.
10   Mosca.   'Las, good sir,
Would you had never seen her.
    Volpone.   Nay, would thou
Hadst never told me of her.
    Mosca.   Sir, 'tis true;
15 I do confess I was unfortunate,
And you unhappy; but I am bound in
                          [conscience,
No less than duty, to effect my best
To your release of torment, and I will, sir.
20   Volpone. Dear Mosca, shall I hope?
    Mosca.   Sir, more than dear,
I will not bid you to despair of aught
Within a human compass.
    Volpone.   O, there spoke
25 My better angel. Mosca, take my keys,
Gold, plate, and jewels, all 's at thy devotion;
Employ them how thou wilt—nay, coin me
                          [too—
So thou in this but crown my longings, Mosca!
30   Mosca. Use but your patience.
    Volpone.   So I have.
    Mosca.   I doubt not
To bring success to your desires.
    Volpone.   Nay, then,
35 I not repent me of my late disguise.
    Mosca. If you can horn° him, sir, you need
                         [not.
    Volpone.   True.
Besides, I never meant him for my heir.
40 Is not the color o' my beard and eyebrows
To make me known?
    Mosca.   No jot.
    Volpone.   I did it well.
    Mosca. So well, would I could follow you in
45   [mine,

With half the happiness; and yet I would
Escape your epilogue.
    Volpone.   But were they gull'd
With a belief that I was Scoto?
    Mosca.   Sir,   50
Scoto himself could hardly have distinguish'd!
I have not time to flatter you now; we'll part,
And as I prosper, so applaud my art.
   [*Exeunt.*]

Scene v

[*A room in* Corvino's *house.*]   55
[*Enter* Corvino, *with his sword in his hand,*
dragging in Celia.]
    Corvino. Death of mine honor, with the
                      [city's fool!
A juggling, tooth-drawing, prating   60
                    [mountebank!
And at a public window! where, whilst he,
With his strain'd action, and his dole of faces,
To his drug-lecture draws your itching ears,
A crew of old, unmarried, noted lechers,   65
Stood leering up like satyrs, and you smile
Most graciously! and fan your favors forth,
To give your hot spectators satisfaction!
What, was your mountebank their call? their
                    [whistle?   70
Or were you enamor'd on his copper rings,
His saffron jewel, with the toad-stone in 't,
Or his embroid'red suit, with the cope-stitch,
Made of a hearse cloth, or his old tilt-feather,
Or his starch'd beard? Well! you shall have   75
                    [him, yes.
He shall come home, and minister unto you
The fricace for the mother.° Or, let me see,
I think you'd rather mount! Would you not
                    [mount?   80
Why, if you'll mount, you may; yes, truly, you
                    [may.
And so you may be seen, down to th' foot.
Get you a cittern, Lady Vanity,°
And be a dealer with the virtuous man;   85
Make one. I'll but protest myself a cuckold,
And save your dowry. I am a Dutchman, I!

---

horn cuckold. Folk tradition had it that a deceived
   husband grew horns.

fricace ... mother literally, massage to cure hysteria
Lady Vanity character representing worldly pleasure
   in the old morality plays

For if you thought me an Italian,
You would be damn'd ere you did this, you
                  [whore.
Thou 'dst tremble to imagine that the murder
5 Of father, mother, brother, all thy race,
Should follow, as the subject of my justice!
   CELIA. Good sir, have patience!
   CORVINO.   What couldst thou propose
Less to thyself, than in this heat of wrath,
10 And stung with my dishonor, I should strike
This steel into thee, with as many stabs
As thou wert gaz'd upon with goatish eyes?
   CELIA. Alas, sir, be appeas'd! I could not
                  [think
15 My being at the window should more now
Move your impatience than at other times.
   CORVINO. No? not to seek and entertain a
                  [parley
With a known knave? before a multitude?
20 You were an actor with your handkerchief!
Which he most sweetly kiss'd in the receipt,
And might, no doubt, return it with a letter
And 'point the place where you might meet;
                [your sister's,
25 Your mother's, or your aunt's might serve the
                  [turn.
   CELIA. Why, dear sir, when do I make these
                [excuses,
Or ever stir abroad, but to the church?
30 And that so seldom—
   CORVINO.   Well, it shall be less;
And thy restraint before was liberty,
To what I now decree; and therefore mark me.
First, I will have this bawdy light° damm'd up;
35 And till 't be done, some two or three yards off
I'll chalk a line; o'er which if thou but chance
To set thy desp'rate foot, more hell, more
                [horror,
More wild remorseless rage shall seize on thee
40 Than on a conjuror that had heedless left
His circle's safety ere his devil was laid.
Then here's a lock which I will hang upon thee,
And, now I think on 't, I will keep thee
                [backwards;°
45 Thy lodging shall be backwards, thy walks

light window
backwards in the back rooms of the house

                [backwards,
Thy prospect—all be backwards, and no
                [pleasure,
That thou shalt know but backwards. Nay,
            [since you force 50
My honest nature, know it is your own
Being too open, makes me use you thus.
Since you will not contain your subtle nostrils
In a sweet room, but they must snuff the air
Of rank and sweaty passengers°—(knock   55
            [within) one knocks.
Away, and be not seen, pain of thy life;
Nor look toward the window; if thou dost—
Nay, stay, hear this—let me not prosper,
            [whore, 60
But I will make thee an anatomy,
Dissect thee mine own self, and read a lecture
Upon thee to the city, and in public.
Away!—
   [*Exit* CELIA.]   65
   [*Enter* SERVITORE.]
      Who's there?
   SERVITORE.   'Tis Signior Mosca, sir.

Scene vi

[CORVINO *and* SERVITORE *remain.*]
   CORVINO. Let him come in. [*Exit* SERVITORE.]   70
        [—His master's dead!
There's yet
Some good to help the bad.—[*Enter* MOSCA.]
        [My Mosca, welcome;
I guess your news.   75
   MOSCA.   I fear you cannot, sir.
   CORVINO. Is 't not his death?
   MOSCA.   Rather the contrary.
   CORVINO. Not his recovery?
   MOSCA.   Yes, sir.   80
   CORVINO.   I am curs'd;
I am bewitch'd; my crosses meet to vex me.
How? how? how? how?
   MOSCA.   Why, sir, with Scoto's oil!
Corbaccio and Voltore brought of it,   85
Whilst I was busy in an inner room—
   CORVINO. Death! that damn'd mountebank!
        [but for the law,
Now, I could kill the rascal. 'T cannot be

passengers passers-by

His oil should have that virtue. Ha' not I
Known him a common rogue, come fiddling in
To th' *osteria*,° with a tumbling whore,
And, when he has done all his forc'd tricks,
5   [been glad
Of a poor spoonful of dead wine, with flies
                        [in 't?
It cannot be. All his ingredients
Are a sheep's gall, a roasted bitch's marrow,
10 Some few sod earwigs, pounded caterpillars,
A little capon's grease, and fasting spittle:
I know 'em to a dram.
     MOSCA.   I know not, sir;
But some on 't, there, they pour'd into his ears,
15 Some in his nostrils, and recover'd him;
Applying but the fricace.
       CORVINO.   Pox° o' that fricace.
     MOSCA. And, since, to seem the more officious
And flatt'ring of his health, there, they have
20   [had,
At extreme fees, the college of physicians
Consulting on him, how they might restore
                      [him;
Where one would have a cataplasm of spices,
25 Another a flay'd ape clapp'd to his breast,
A third would ha' it a dog, a fourth an oil,
With wildcats' skins. At last, they all resolv'd
That, to preserve him, was no other means
But some young woman must be straight
30   [sought out,
Lusty, and full of juice, to sleep by him;
And to this service most unhappily,
And most unwillingly, am I now employ'd,
Which here I thought to pre-acquaint you with,
35 For your advice, since it concerns you most;
Because I would not do that thing might cross
Your ends, on whom I have my whole
                    [dependence, sir.
Yet, if I do not they may relate
40 My slackness to my patron, work me out
Of his opinion; and there all your hopes,
Ventures, or whatsoever, are all frustrate.
I do but tell you, sir. Besides, they are all
Now striving who shall first present him.
45   [Therefore—

I could entreat you, briefly, conclude somewhat:
Prevent 'em if you can.
     CORVINO.   Death to my hopes!
This is my villainous fortune! Best to hire
Some common courtesan!   50
     MOSCA.   Ay, I thought on that, sir;
But they are all so subtle, full of art—
And age again doting and flexible,
So as—I cannot tell—we may, perchance,
Light on a quean may cheat us all.   55
     CORVINO.   'Tis true.
     MOSCA. No, no; it must be one that has no
                    [tricks, sir,
Some simple thing, a creature made unto it;
Some wench you may command. Ha' you no   60
                    [kinswoman?
Gods so°—Think, think, think, think, think,
                    [think, think, sir.
One o' the doctors offer'd there his daughter.
     CORVINO. How!   65
     MOSCA.   Yes, Signior Lupo, the physician.
     CORVINO. His daughter!
     MOSCA.   And a virgin, sir. Why, alas,
He knows the state of 's body, what it is:
That naught can warm his blood, sir, but a   70
                    [fever,
Nor any incantation raise his spirit;
A long forgetfulness hath seiz'd that part.
Besides, sir, who shall know it? Some one or
                    [two— 75
     CORVINO. I pray thee give me leave.—
           [(*Stepping aside.*) If any man
But I had had this luck—The thing in 't self,
I know, is nothing.—Wherefore should not I
As well command my blood and my affections   80
As this dull doctor? In the point of honor,
The cases are all one of wife and daughter.
     MOSCA [*aside*]. I hear him coming.
     CORVINO [*aside*].   She shall do 't; 'tis
                    [done. 85
'Slight!° if this doctor, who is not engag'd,
Unless 't be for his counsel, which is nothing,
Offer his daughter, what should I, that am
So deeply in? I will prevent him. Wretch!
Covetous wretch!—Mosca, I have determin'd. 90

---

osteria   hostelry
Pox   a plague

Gods so   on God's oath
'Slight   by God's light

MOSCA. How sir?

CORVINO.   We'll make all sure. The party
                                              [you wot of
Shall be mine own wife, Mosca.

5   MOSCA.   Sir, the thing,
But that I would not seem to counsel you,
I should have motion'd to you, at the first;
And make your count, you have cut all their
                                              [throats.
10   Why! 'tis directly taking a possession!
And in his next fit, we may let him go.
'Tis but to pull the pillow from his head,
And he is throttled; it had been done before
But for your scrupulous doubts.
15   CORVINO.   Ay, a plague on 't;
My conscience fools my wit! Well, I'll be brief,
And so be thou, lest they should be before us.
Go home; prepare him; tell him with what zeal
And willingness I do it. Swear it was
20   On the first hearing, as thou mayst do, truly,
Mine own free motion.
      MOSCA.   Sir, I warrant you,
I'll so possess him with it, that the rest
Of his starv'd clients shall be banish'd all;
25   And only you receiv'd. But come not, sir,
Until I send, for I have something else
To ripen for your good—you must not know 't.
      CORVINO. But do not you forget to send, now.
      MOSCA.   Fear not.
30   [Exit.]

Scene vii

[CORVINO remains.]
CORVINO. Where are you, wife? My Celia!
                                              [Wife!
[Enter CELIA.]
35   —What, blubbering?
Come, dry those tears. I think you thought'st
                                              [me in earnest;
Ha? By this light I talk'd so but to try thee.
Methinks, the lightness of the occasion
40   Should ha' confirmed thee. Come, I am not
                                              [jealous.
      CELIA. No?
      CORVINO. Faith I am not, I, nor never was;
It is a poor, unprofitable humor.
45   Do not I know, if women have a will,
They'll do 'gainst all the watches o' the world,

And that the fiercest spies are tam'd with gold?
Tut, I am confident in thee, thou shalt see 't;
And see I'll give thee cause, too, to believe it.
Come, kiss me.—Go, and make thee ready   50
                                              [straight,
In all thy best attire, thy choicest jewels,
Put 'em all on, and, with 'em, thy best looks:
We are invited to a solemn feast,
At old Volpone's, where it shall appear   55
How far I am free from jealousy or fear.
      [Exeunt.]

ACT III

Scene i

[A street.]
[Enter MOSCA.]
      MOSCA. I fear I shall begin to grow in love   60
With my dear self and my most prosp'rous
                                              [parts;°
They do so spring and burgeon. I can feel
A whimsy i' my blood—I know not how—
Success hath made me wanton. I could skip   65
Out of my skin now, like a subtle snake.
I am so limber. Oh! your parasite
Is a most precious thing, dropp'd from above,
Not bred 'mongst clods and clotpolls,° here on
                                              [earth. 70
I muse the mystery° was not made a science,
It is so liberally profess'd! Almost
All the wise world is little else, in nature,
But parasites or sub-parasites. And yet
I mean not those that have your bare town-art, 75
To know who's fit to feed 'em; have no house,
No family, no care, and therefore mold
Tales for men's ears, to bait that sense; or get
Kitchen-invention, and some stale receipts
To please the belly, and the groin; nor those,   80
With their court dog-tricks, that can fawn and
                                              [fleer,
Make their revenue out of legs and faces,°
Echo my Lord, and lick away a moth:
But your fine, elegant rascal, that can rise   85

parts abilities
clotpolls blockheads
muse the mystery wonder that the trade
legs and faces bows and smiles

And stoop, almost together, like an arrow;
Shoot through the air as nimbly as a star;
Turn short as doth a swallow; and be here,
And there, and here, and yonder, all at once;
5 Present to any humor, all occasion;
And change a visor° swifter than a thought!
This is the creature had the art born with him;
Toils not to learn it, but doth practise it
Out of most excellent nature; and such sparks
10 Are the true parasites, others but their zanies.

Scene ii

[*Enter* BONARIO.]
MOSCA. Who's this? Bonario, old Corbaccio's
                        [son?
The person I was bound to seek. Fair sir,
15 You are happ'ly met.
    BONARIO.   That cannot be by thee.
    MOSCA. Why, sir?
    BONARIO.   Nay, 'pray thee know thy way,
                      [and leave me.
20 I would be loath to interchange discourse
With such a mate as thou art.
    MOSCA.   Courteous sir,
Scorn not my poverty.
    BONARIO.   Not I, by Heaven;
25 But thou shalt give me leave to hate thy
                      [baseness.
    MOSCA. Baseness!
    BONARIO.   Ay; answer me, is not thy sloth
Sufficient argument? thy flattery?
30 Thy means of feeding?
    MOSCA.   Heaven be good to me.
These imputations are too common, sir,
And eas'ly stuck on virtue, when she's poor.
You are unequal° to me, and howe'er
35 Your sentence may be righteous, yet you are
                      [not,
That, ere you know me, thus proceed in
                      [censure.
St. Mark bear witness 'gainst you, 'tis inhuman.
40   [*Weeps.*]
    BONARIO [*aside*]. What! does he weep? the
                    [sign is soft and good!
I do repent me that I was so harsh.

MOSCA. 'Tis true, that, sway'd by strong
                     [necessity, 45
I am enforc'd to eat my careful bread
With too much obsequy;° 'tis true, beside,
That I am fain to spin mine own poor raiment
Out of my mere observance, being not born
To a free fortune; but that I have done   50
Base offices, in rending friends asunder,
Dividing families, betraying counsels,
Whispering false lies, or mining° men with
                    [praises,
Train'd their credulity with perjuries,   55
Corrupted chastity, or am in love
With mine own tender ease, but would not
                    [rather
Prove the most rugged and laborious course,
That might redeem my present estimation, 60
Let me here perish, in all hopes of goodness.
    BONARIO [*aside*]. This cannot be a
                [personated passion!—
I was to blame, so to mistake thy nature;
'Pray thee forgive me; and speak out thy 65
                    [bus'ness.
    MOSCA. Sir, it concerns you; and though I
                  [may seem
At first to make a main offence in manners,
And in my gratitude unto my master,   70
Yet for the pure love which I bear all right,
And hatred of the wrong, I must reveal it.
This very hour your father is in purpose
To disinherit you—
    BONARIO.   How!   75
    MOSCA.   And thrust you forth,
As a mere stranger to his blood; 'tis true, sir.
The work no way engageth me, but as
I claim an interest in the general state
Of goodness and true virtue, which I hear 80
T' abound in you; and for which mere respect,
Without a second aim, sir, I have done it.
    BONARIO. This tale hath lost thee much of the
                [late trust
Thou hadst with me; it is impossible. 85
I know not how to lend it any thought
My father should be so unnatural.
    MOSCA. It is a confidence that well becomes

---

a visor his expression
unequal (1) of superior rank (2) unjust

obsequy obsequiousness
mining undermining

Your piety;° and form'd, no doubt, it is
From your own simple innocence; which makes
Your wrong more monstrous and abhorr'd. But,
                       [sir,
5 I now will tell you more. This very minute,
It is, or will be doing; and if you
Shall be put pleas'd to go with me, I'll bring
                       [you,
I dare not say where you shall be, but where
10 Your ear shall be a witness of the deed;
Hear yourself written bastard, and profess'd
The common issue of the earth.
    BONARIO.   I'm maz'd!
    MOSCA. Sir, if I do it not, draw your just
15   [sword,
And score your vengeance on my front° and
                       [face;
Mark me your villain. You have too much
                       [wrong,
20 And I do suffer for you, sir. My heart
Weeps blood in anguish—
    BONARIO.   Lead. I follow thee.
    [Exeunt.]

Scene iii

[A room in VOLPONE's house.]
25 [Enter VOLPONE, NANO, ANDROGYNO, and
CASTRONE.]
    VOLPONE. Mosca stays long, methinks.—
               [Bring forth your sports,
And help to make the wretched time more
30   [sweet.
    NANO. Dwarf, fool, and eunuch, well met
                  [here we be.
A question it were now, whether of us three,
Being all the known delicates of a rich man,
35 In pleasing him, claim the precedency can?
    CASTRONE. I claim for myself.
    ANDROGYNO.   And so doth the fool.
    NANO. 'Tis foolish indeed; let me set you
                [both to school.
40 First for your dwarf, he's little and witty,
And everything, as it is little, is pretty;
Else why do men say to a creature of my shape,
So soon as they see him, "It's a pretty little

ape"?
And why a pretty ape, but for pleasing   45
                  [imitation
Of greater men's action, in a ridiculous fashion?
Beside, this feat body of mine doth not crave
Half the meat, drink, and cloth, one of your
              [bulks will have. 50
Admit your fool's face be the mother of
              [laughter,
Yet, for his brain, it must always come after;
And though that do feed him, it's a pitiful case,
His body is beholding to such a bad face.   55
    [One knocks.]
    VOLPONE. Who's there? My couch: away!
                [Look, Nano, see.—
    [Exeunt ANDROGYNO and CASTRONE.]
Give me my caps first—go, inquire. (Exit   60
           [NANO.) Now, Cupid
Send it be Mosca, and with fair return.
    [Re-enter NANO.]
    NANO. It is the beauteous Madam—
    VOLPONE.   Would-be—is it?   65
    NANO. The same.
    VOLPONE.   Now torment on me! Squire
               [her in;
For she will enter, or dwell here for ever.
Nay, quickly. (Exit NANO; VOLPONE retires to his 70
           [couch.)—That my fit were past! I fear
A second hell too, that my loathing this
Will quite expel my appetite to the other.
Would she were taking now her tedious leave.
Lord, how it threats me what I am to suffer! 75

Scene iv

[Enter NANO and LADY POLITIC WOULD-BE.]
    LADY. I thank you, good sir. Pray you signify
Unto your patron I am here.—This band
Shows not my neck enough.—I trouble you,
              [sir; 80
Let me request you bid one of my women
Come hither to me. [Exit NANO.]—In good
           [faith, I am dress'd
Most favorably today; it is no matter;
'Tis well enough.   85
    [Re-enter NANO with a WAITING WOMAN.]
           Look, see, these petulant things!
How they have done this!
    VOLPONE [aside].   I do feel the fever

---

piety filial loyalty
front brow

Ent'ring in at mine ears; oh, for a charm
To fright it hence.
    LADY.   Come nearer. Is this curl
In his right place? or this? Why is this higher
5 Than all the rest? You ha' not wash'd your
                               [eyes yet?
Or do they not stand even i' your head?
Where's your fellow? call her.
    [*Exit* WOMAN.]
10 NANO [*aside.*]   Now, St. Mark
Deliver us! anon she'll beat her women,
Because her nose is red.
    [*Re-enter* WOMAN *with another.*]
    LADY.   I pray you view
15 This tire, forsooth. Are all things apt, or no?
    WOMAN. One hair a little here sticks out,
                              [forsooth.
    LADY. Does 't so, forsooth! and where was
                        [your dear sight,
20 When it did so, forsooth? What now! bird-
                                [ey'd?
And you, too? 'Pray you, both approach and
                            [mend it.
Now, by that light I muse you're not asham'd!
25 I, that have preach'd these things so oft unto
                                [you,
Read you the principles, argu'd all the grounds,
Disputed every fitness, every grace,
Call'd you to counsel of so frequent dressings—
30 NANO [*aside*]. More carefully than of your
                        [fame or honor.
    LADY. Made you acquainted what an ample
                           [dowry
The knowledge of these things would be unto
35   [you,
Able alone to get you noble husbands
At your return; and you thus to neglect it!
Besides, you seeing what a curious° nation
Th' Italians are, what will they say of me?
40 "The English lady cannot dress herself."
Here's a fine imputation to our country!
Well, go your ways, and stay i' the next room.
This fucus° was too coarse too; it's no
                              [matter.—
45 Good sir, you'll give 'em entertainment?

---

curious fastidious
fucus rouge

[*Exeunt* NANO *and* WAITING WOMEN.]
VOLPONE [*aside*]. The storm comes toward
                                [me.
LADY [*going to the couch*].   How does my
                            [Volpone? 50
    VOLPONE. Troubled with noise; I cannot
                           [sleep. I dreamt
That a strange Fury ent'red now my house,
And, with the dreadful tempest of her breath,
Did cleave my roof asunder.   55
    LADY.   Believe me, and I
Had the most fearful dream, could I
                          [remember 't—
    VOLPONE [*aside*]. Out on my fate! I ha' giv'n
                         [her the occasion 60
How to torment me: she will tell me hers.
    LADY. Methought the golden mediocrity,°
Polite, and delicate—
    VOLPONE.   O, if you do love me,
No more; I sweat, and suffer, at the mention 65
Of any dream. Feel how I tremble yet.
    LADY. Alas, good soul! the passion of the
                            [heart.°
Seed-pearl were good now, boil'd with syrup of
                            [apples, 70
Tincture of gold, and coral, citron-pills,
Your elecampane root, myrobalans—
    VOLPONE [*aside*]. Ay me, I have ta'en a
                      [grasshopper by the wing!
    LADY. Burnt silk and amber. You have 75
                          [muscadel
Good i' the house—
    VOLPONE.   You will not drink, and part?
    LADY. No, fear not that. I doubt we shall not
                            [get 80
Some English saffron—half a dram would
                             [serve;
Your sixteen cloves, a little musk, dried mints,
Bugloss, and barley meal—
    VOLPONE [*aside*].   She's in again; 85
Before I feign'd diseases—now I have one.
    LADY. And these appli'd with a right scarlet
                           [cloth—

---

the . . . mediocrity a personification of the Golden
  Mean
passion . . . heart a symptom of love-melancholy. A
  catalogue of supposed remedies follows.

VOLPONE [*aside*]. Another flood of words! a
                              [very torrent!
LADY. Shall I, sir, make you a poultice?
VOLPONE.   No, no, no.
5 I am very well; you need prescribe no more.
    LADY. I have studied physic; but now
I'm all for music, save i' the forenoons,
An hour or two for painting. I would have
A lady, indeed, t' have all letters and arts,
10 Be able to discourse, to write, to paint;
But principal, as Plato holds, your music
(And so does wise Pythagoras, I take it)
Is your true rapture, when there is consent°
In face, in voice, and clothes, and is, indeed,
15 Our sex's chiefest ornament.
    VOLPONE.   The poet
As old in time as Plato, and as knowing,
Says that your highest female grace is silence.
    LADY. Which o' your poets? Petrarch, or
20   [Tasso, or Dante?
Guarini? Ariosto? Aretine?
Cieco di Hadria? I have read them all.
    VOLPONE [*aside*]. Is everything a cause to my
                              [destruction?
25 LADY. I think I ha' two or three of 'em about
                              [me.
    VOLPONE [*aside*]. The sun, the sea, will
                              [sooner both stand still
Than her eternal tongue! Nothing can 'scape it.
30 LADY. Here's *Pastor Fido*°—
    VOLPONE [*aside*].   Profess obstinate
                              [silence;
That's now my safest.
    LADY.   All our English writers,
35 I mean such as are happy in th' Italian,
Will deign to steal out of this author, mainly;
Almost as much as from Montagnié:°
He has so modern and facile a vein,
Fitting the time, and catching the court-ear.
40 Your Petrarch is more passionate, yet he,
In days of sonneting, trusted 'em with much.°
Dante is hard, and few can understand him.

But for a desperate° wit, there's Aretine!°
Only, his pictures are a little obscene—
You mark me not!   45
    VOLPONE.   Alas, my mind's perturb'd.
    LADY. Why, in such cases, we must cure
                              [ourselves,
Make use of our philosophy—
    VOLPONE.   Oh, ay me!   50
    LADY. And as we find our passions do rebel,
Encounter 'em with reason, or divert 'em,
By giving scope unto some other humor
Of lesser danger; as, in politic bodies,
There's nothing more doth overwhelm the   55
                              [judgment,
And clouds the understanding, than too much
Settling and fixing, and, as 'twere, subsiding
Upon one object. For the incorporating
Of these same outward things into that part   60
Which we call mental, leaves some certain
                              [faeces
That stop the organs, and, as Plato says,
Assassinates our knowledge.
    VOLPONE [*aside*].   Now, the spirit   65
Of patience help me.
    LADY.   Come, in faith, I must
Visit you more, a' days, and make you well—
Laugh and be lusty.
    VOLPONE [*aside*].   My good angel save   70
                              [me!
    LADY. There was but one sole man in all the
                              [world
With whom I e'er could sympathize; and he
Would lie you, often, three, four hours together 75
To hear me speak; and be sometimes so rapt,
As he would answer me quite from the purpose,
Like you, and you are like him, just. I'll
                              [discourse,
An't be but only, sir, to bring you asleep,   80
How we did spend our time and loves together,
For some six years.
    VOLPONE.   Oh, oh, oh, oh, oh, oh!
    LADY. For we were coaetanei,° and brought
                              [up—   85
    VOLPONE [*aside*]. Some power, some fate,
                              [some fortune rescue me!

---

consent harmony
Pastor Fido Guarini's *Faithful Shepherd*, a pastoral
    tragicomedy then much in vogue as a model of ele-
    gant style and sentiment
Montagnié Montaigne
trusted 'em with much was much copied by English
    sonnet writers

desperate extraordinary   **Aretine** Pietro Aretino,
    author of sonnets based on obscene drawings by
    Giulio Romano
coaetanei of the same age

Scene v

[*Enter* MOSCA.]
MOSCA. God save you, madam.
LADY.   Good sir.
VOLPONE.   Mosca! welcome—
5 [*aside*]. Welcome to my redemption.
    MOSCA [*aside*].   Why, sir?
    VOLPONE [*aside*].   Oh,
Rid me of this my torture, quickly, there;
My madam with the everlasting voice.
10 The bells,° in time of pestilence, ne'er made
Like noise, or were in that perpetual motion—
The cockpit comes not near it. All my house,
But now, steam'd like a bath with her thick
                              [breath,
15 A lawyer could not have been heard; nor scarce
Another woman, such a hail of words
She has let fall. For hell's sake, rid her hence.
    MOSCA. Has she presented?°
    VOLPONE.   Oh, I do not care:
20 I'll take her absence upon any price,
With any loss.
    MOSCA.   Madam—
    LADY.   I ha' brought your patron
A toy, a cap here, of mine own work—
25 MOSCA.   'Tis well.
I had forgot to tell you I saw your knight
Where you'd little think it—
    LADY.   Where?
    MOSCA.   Marry,°
30 Where yet, if you make haste, you may
                              [apprehend him,
Rowing upon the water in a gondola,
With the most cunning courtesan of Venice.
    LADY. Is 't true?
35 MOSCA.   Pursue 'em, and believe your
                              [eyes;
Leave me to make your gift. [*Exit* LADY.]—I
                              [knew 'twould take;
For, lightly, they that use themselves most
40   [license,°
Are still most jealous.

bells which, in time of plague, were tolled almost
    continuously for the dead and dying
presented given a present
Marry indeed
lightly . . . license generally, those who allow them-
    selves most leeway

VOLPONE.   Mosca, hearty thanks
For thy quick fiction, and delivery of me.
Now to my hopes, what say'st thou?
    [*Re-enter* LADY.]   45
    LADY.   But do you hear, sir?—
    VOLPONE [*aside*]. Again! I fear a paroxysm.
    LADY.   Which way
Row'd they together?
    MOSCA.   Toward the Rialto.   50
    LADY. I pray you lend me your dwarf.
    MOSCA.   I pray you take him.
    [*Exit* LADY.]
Your hopes, sir, are like happy blossoms, fair,
And promise timely fruit, if you will stay   55
But the maturing. Keep you at your couch;
Corbaccio will arrive straight, with the will;
When he is gone, I'll tell you more.
    [*Exit.*]
    VOLPONE.   My blood,   60
My spirits are return'd; I am alive;
And, like your wanton gamester at primero,°
Whose thought had whisper'd to him, not go
                              [less,
Methinks I lie, and draw—for an encounter.   65

Scene vi

[*Enter* MOSCA *and* BONARIO.]
MOSCA. Sir, here conceal'd [*opening a door*]
                    [you may hear all. But, pray you,
Have patience, sir; [*one knocks*] the same 's
                    [your father knocks.   70
I am compell'd to leave you.
    [*Exit.*]
    BONARIO.   Do so.—Yet
Cannot my thought imagine this a truth.
    [*Goes in.*]   75

Scene vii

[*Enter* MOSCA, CORVINO, *and* CELIA.]
MOSCA. Death on me! You are come too
                    [soon, What meant you?
Did not I say I would send?
    CORVINO.   Yes, but I fear'd   80
You might forget it, and then they prevent us.
    MOSCA. Prevent!—[*Aside.*] Did e'er man
                    [haste so for his horns?

primero a kind of poker, on the terms of which Vol-
    pone puns as he draws the curtain of his bed

BEN JONSON | Act III, Scene vii

A courtier would not ply it so for a place.—°
Well, now there is no helping it, stay here;
I'll presently return.
    [*Exit.*]
5 CORVINO.   Where are you, Celia?
You know not wherefore I have brought you
                            [hither?
    CELIA. Not well, except you told me.
    CORVINO.   Now I will.
10 Hark hither. [*They retire to one side.*]
    [*Re-enter* MOSCA.]
    MOSCA [*to* BONARIO]. Sir, your father hath
                            [sent word
It will be half an hour ere he come;
15 And therefore, if you please to walk the while
Into the gallery—at the upper end,
There are some books to entertain the time;
And I'll take care no man shall come unto you,
                            [sir.
20 BONARIO. Yes, I will stay there.—[*Aside.*] I
                            [do doubt this fellow.
    [*Exit.*]
    MOSCA [*looking after him*]. There; he is far
                            [enough; he can hear nothing.
25 And for his father, I can keep him off.
    CORVINO [*advancing with* CELIA]. Nay, now,
            [there is no starting back, and therefore,
Resolve upon it; I have so decreed.
It must be done. Nor would I move 't afore,°
30 Because I would avoid all shifts and tricks,
That might deny me.
    CELIA.   Sir, let me beseech you,
Affect not these strange trials; if you doubt
My chastity, why, lock me up for ever;
35 Make me the heir of darkness. Let me live
Where I may please your fears, if not your
                            [trust.
    CORVINO. Believe it, I have no such humor, I.
All that I speak I mean; yet I am not mad;
40 Not horn-mad, see you? Go to, show yourself
Obedient, and a wife.
    CELIA.   O Heaven!
    CORVINO.   I say it,
Do so.
45 CELIA.   Was this the train?°

CORVINO.   I have told you reasons;
What the physicians have set down; how much
It may concern me; what my engagements are;
My means, and the necessity of those means
For my recovery. Wherefore, if you be   50
Loyal, and mine, be won; respect my venture.
    CELIA. Before your honor?
    CORVINO.   Honor! tut, a breath.
There's no such thing in nature; a mere term
Invented to awe fools. What is my gold   55
The worse for touching, clothes for being
                            [look'd on?
Why, this 's no more. An old decrepit wretch,
That has no sense, no sinew; takes his meat
With others' fingers; only knows to gape   60
When you do scald his gums; a voice, a
                            [shadow;
And what can this man hurt you?
    CELIA [*aside*].   Lord! what spirit
Is this hath ent'red him?   65
    CORVINO.   And for your fame,°
That's such a jig;° as if I would go tell it,
Cry it on the Piazza! Who shall know it
But he that cannot speak it, and this fellow,
Whose lips are i' my pocket? Save yourself—   70
If you'll proclaim 't, you may,—I know no
                            [other
Should come to know it.
    CELIA.   Are Heaven and saints then
                            [nothing? 75
Will they be blind or stupid?
    CORVINO.   How?
    CELIA.   Good sir,
Be jealous still, emulate them; and think
What hate they burn with toward every sin.   80
    CORVINO. I grant you; if I thought it were a
                            [sin
I would not urge you. Should I offer this
To some young Frenchman, or hot Tuscan
                            [blood 85
That had read Aretine, conn'd all his prints,
Knew every quirk within lust's labyrinth,
And were profess'd critic in lechery;
And I would look upon him, and applaud him;
This were a sin: but here, 'tis contrary,   90
A pious work, mere charity, for physic,

---

ply ... place try so hard to wangle an official position
move 't afore propose it before now
train trick

fame reputation
jig jest

And honest polity, to assure mine own.
CELIA. O Heaven! canst thou suffer such a
                    [change?
VOLPONE [*aside*]. Thou art mine honor,
5   [Mosca, and my pride,
My joy, my tickling, my delight! Go bring 'em.
MOSCA. Please you draw near, sir.
CORVINO.   Come on, what—
You will not be rebellious? By that light—
10   MOSCA. Sir, Signior Corvino, here, is come to
                    [see you.
VOLPONE. Oh.
MOSCA.   And hearing of the consultation
                    [had,
15 So lately, for your health, is come to offer,
Or rather, sir, to prostitute—
CORVINO.   Thanks, sweet Mosca.
MOSCA. Freely, unask'd, or unentreated—
CORVINO.   Well.
20   MOSCA. As the true fervent instance of his
                    [love,
His own most fair and proper wife, the beauty
Only of price° in Venice—
CORVINO.   'Tis well urg'd.
25   MOSCA. To be your comfortress, and to
                [preserve you.
VOLPONE. Alas, I am past, already! 'Pray you,
                [thank him
For his good care and promptness; but for that,
'Tis a vain labor e'en to fight 'gainst Heaven;
30 Applying fire to a stone—uh, uh, uh, uh!—
Making a dead leaf grow again. I take
His wishes gently, though; and you may tell
                  [him
35 What I have done for him; marry, my state is
                [hopeless!
Will him to pray for me; and t' use his fortune
With reverence when he comes to 't.
MOSCA.   Do you hear, sir?
40 Go to him with your wife.
CORVINO.   Heart of my father!
Wilt thou persist thus? Come, I pray thee, come.
Thou seest 'tis nothing, Celia. By this hand,
I shall grow violent. Come, do 't, I say.
45   CELIA. Sir, kill me, rather. I will take down
                [poison,
Eat burning coals, do anything—

Only of price peerless

CORVINO.   Be damn'd!
Heart, I will drag thee hence home by the hair;
Cry thee a strumpet through the streets; rip up 50
Thy mouth unto thine ears; and slit thy nose,
Like a raw rochet°—Do not tempt me, come;
Yield; I am loath—Death! I will buy some
                [slave
Whom I will kill, and bind thee to him alive, 55
And at my window hang you forth, devising
Some monstrous crime, which I, in capital
                [letters,
Will eat into thy flesh with aqua fortis,
And burning cor'sives,° on this stubborn breast. 60
Now, by the blood thou hast incens'd, I'll do it!
CELIA. Sir, what you please, you may; I am
                [your martyr.
CORVINO. Be not thus obstinate; I ha' not
                [deserv'd it. 65
Think who it is entreats you. 'Pray thee, sweet;
Good faith, thou shalt have jewels, gowns,
                [attires,
What thou wilt think, and ask. Do but go kiss
                [him. 70
Or touch him but. For my sake. At my suit.°
This once. No? not? I shall remember this.
Will you disgrace me thus? Do you thirst my
                [undoing?
MOSCA. Nay, gentle lady, be advis'd. 75
CORVINO.   No, no.
She has watch'd her time. God's precious,° this
                [is scurvy,
'Tis very scurvy; and you are—
MOSCA.   Nay, good sir. 80
CORVINO. An errant locust—by heaven, a
              [locust!—Whore,
Crocodile, that hast thy tears prepar'd,
Expecting how thou'lt bid 'em flow.
MOSCA.   Nay, 'pray you, sir! 85
She will consider.
CELIA.   Would my life would serve
To satisfy—
CORVINO.   'Sdeath!° if she would but
                [speak to him, 90

rochet large-headed fish
cor'sives corrosives
suit plea
God's precious a truncated oath, short for "God's
    precious body" or "bones" or "wounds," etc.
'Sdeath by God's death (the Crucifixion)

And save my reputation, 'twere somewhat;
But spitefully to affect my utter ruin!
   MOSCA [*aside to* CORVINO]. Ay, now you have
                [put your fortune in her hands.
5 Why, i' faith, it is her modesty. I must quit°
                          [her.
If you were absent, she would be more coming;
I know it, and dare undertake for her.
What woman can before her husband? 'Pray
10   [you,
Let us depart and leave her here.
   CORVINO.   Sweet Celia,
Thou mayst redeem all yet; I'll say no more.
If not, esteem yourself as lost.—Nay, stay
15   [there.
   [*Exit with* MOSCA.]
   CELIA. O God, and his good angels! whither,
                  [whither,
Is shame fled human breasts? that with such
20   [ease,
Men dare put off your honors, and their own?
Is that which ever was a cause of life°
Now plac'd beneath the basest circumstance,
And modesty an exile made, for money?
25   VOLPONE. Ay, in Corvino, and such earth-fed
                   [minds,
   [*He leaps off from his couch.*]
That never tasted the true heav'n of love.
Assure thee, Celia, he that would sell thee,
30 Only for hope of gain, and that uncertain,
He would have sold his part of Paradise
For ready money, had he met a copeman.°
Why art thou maz'd to see me thus reviv'd?
Rather applaud thy beauty's miracle;
35 'Tis thy great work, that hath, not now alone,
But sundry times, rais'd me, in several shapes,
And, but this morning, like a mountebank,
To see thee at thy window; ay, before
I would have left my practice° for thy love,
40 In varying figures I would have contended
With the blue Proteus, or the horned flood.°

quit   acquit
cause of life   principle to be defended with life itself
copeman   dealer
left . . . practice   left off my stratagems
contended . . . flood   rivaled the Old Man of the Sea or
   even Acheloüs, Greek legendary figures adept at
   transforming themselves

Now art thou welcome.
   CELIA.   Sir!
   VOLPONE.   Nay, fly me not,   45
Nor let thy false imagination
That I was bedrid, make thee think I am so—
Thou shalt not find it. I am now as fresh,
As hot, as high, and in as jovial plight
As when, in that so celebrated scene,   50
At recitation of our comedy,
For entertainment of the great Valois,°
I acted young Antinoüs,° and attracted
The eyes and ears of all the ladies present,
T' admire each graceful gesture, note, and
                  [footing.   55
   [*Sings.*]
Come, my Celia, let us prove,
While we can, the sports of love.
Time will not be ours for ever,
He, at length, our good will sever.   60
Spend not then his gifts in vain.
Suns that set may rise again;
But if once we lose this light,
'Tis with us perpetual night.
Why should we defer our joys?   65
Fame and rumor are but toys.
Cannot we delude the eyes
Of a few poor household spies?
Or his easier ears beguile,
Thus removed by our wile?   70
'Tis no sin love's fruits to steal,
But the sweet thefts to reveal;
To be taken, to be seen,
These have crimes accounted been.

   CELIA. Some serene° blast me, or dire   75
                  [lightning strike
This my offending face.
   VOLPONE.   Why droops my Celia?
Thou hast, in place of a base husband, found
A worthy lover; use thy fortune well,   80
With secrecy and pleasure. See, behold,
What thou art queen of; not in expectation,
As I feed others, but possess'd and crown'd.

Valois   Henry III of France, who visited Venice in 1574
Antinoüs   a handsome boy beloved by the Roman
   emperor Hadrian
serene   baneful night mist

See, here, a rope of pearl; and each more orient
Than that the brave Egyptian queen carous'd.°
Dissolve and drink 'em. See, a carbuncle,
May put out both the eyes of our St. Mark;°
5 A diamond would have bought Lollia Paulina,°
When she came in like starlight, hid with jewels
That were the spoils of provinces; take these,
And wear and lose 'em; yet remains an earring
To purchase them again, and this whole state.
10 A gem but worth a private patrimony
Is nothing; we will eat such at a meal.
The heads of parrots, tongues of nightingales,
The brains of peacocks and of estriches,
Shall be our food; and, could we get the
15   [phoenix,
Though nature lost her kind, she were our dish.
    CELIA. Good sir, these things might move a
                [mind affected
With such delights; but I, whose innocence
20 Is all I can think wealthy, or worth th' enjoying,
And which, once lost, I have naught to lose
                [beyond it,
Cannot be taken with these sensual baits.
If you have conscience—
25   VOLPONE.   'Tis the beggar's virtue;
If thou hast wisdom, hear me, Celia.
Thy baths shall be the juice of July-flowers,°
Spirit of roses and of violets,
The milk of unicorns, and panthers' breath
30 Gather'd in bags and mix'd with Cretan wines.
Our drink shall be prepared gold and amber,
Which we will take until my roof whirl round
With the vertigo; and my dwarf shall dance,
My eunuch sing, my fool make up the antic,
35 Whilst we, in changed shapes, act Ovid's
              [tales:°
Thou like Europa now, and I like Jove;

Then I like Mars, and thou like Erycine;
So of the rest, till we have quite run through
And wearied all the fables of the gods.   40
Then will I have thee in more modern forms,
Attired like some sprightly dame of France,
Brave Tuscan lady, or proud Spanish beauty;
Sometimes unto the Persian sophy's° wife,
Or the Grand Signior's° mistress; and, for   45
              [change,
To one of our most artful courtesans,
Or some quick Negro, or cold Russian;
And I will meet thee in as many shapes,
Where we may so transfuse our wand'ring   50
              [souls
Out at our lips, and score up sums of pleasures,

That the curious shall not know
How to tell them as they flow;
And the envious, when they find   55
What their number is, be pin'd.

    CELIA. If you have ears that will be pierc'd—
              [or eyes
That can be open'd—a heart, may be touch'd—
Or any part that yet sounds man about you—   60
If you have touch of holy saints, or Heaven,
Do me the grace to let me 'scape. If not,
Be bountiful and kill me. You do know
I am a creature hither ill betray'd
By one whose shame I would forget it were;   65
If you will deign me neither of these graces,
Yet feed your wrath, sir, rather than your lust,
(It is a vice comes nearer manliness)
And punish that unhappy crime of nature,
Which you miscall my beauty; flay my face,   70
Or poison it with ointments for seducing
Your blood to this rebellion. Rub these hands
With what may cause an eating leprosy,
E'en to my bones and marrow, anything
That may disfavor me, save in my honor.   75
And I will kneel to you, pray for you, pay down
A thousand hourly vows, sir, for your health;
Report, and think you virtuous—
    VOLPONE.   Think me cold,
Frozen, and impotent, and so report me!   80

---

that . . . carous'd the pearl that Cleopatra drank in
   a cup of wine (an example of great luxury)
put . . . Mark outshine the jewels in the treasury of
   St. Mark's cathedral
Lollia Paulina a notorious Roman beauty whom the
   emperor Caligula married and divorced
July-flowers gillyflowers
Ovid's tales his *Metamorphoses* ("Transformations")
   relating such stories as that of Europa, a maiden
   abducted by Jove in the shape of a bull, and the
   love-affair of Venus (**Erycine**) and **Mars**

sophy's king's
Grand Signior's Sultan of Turkey's

That I had Nestor's° hernia, thou wouldst
                                    [think.
I do degenerate, and abuse my nation,
To play with opportunity thus long;
5 I should have done the act, and then have
                                    [parley'd.
Yield, or I'll force thee.
    CELIA.   O! just God!
    VOLPONE.   In vain—
10 BONARIO [leaps out from where MOSCA had
placed him]. Forbear, foul ravisher, libidinous
                                    [swine;
Free the forc'd lady, or thou di'st, impostor.
But that I am loath to snatch thy punishment
15 Out of the hand of justice, thou shouldst yet
Be made the timely sacrifice of vengeance,
Before this altar and this dross, thy idol.—
Lady, let's quit the place; it is the den
Of villainy; fear naught: you have a guard;
20 And he ere long shall meet his just reward.
    [Exeunt BONARIO and CELIA.]
    VOLPONE. Fall on me, roof, and bury me in
                                    [ruin;
Become my grave, that wert my shelter. Oh!
25 I am unmask'd, unspirited, undone,
Betray'd to beggary, to infamy—

Scene viii

[Enter MOSCA.]
MOSCA. Where shall I run, most wretched
                                [shame of men,
30 To beat out my unlucky brains?
    VOLPONE.   Here, here.
What! dost thou bleed?
    MOSCA.   O, that his well-driv'n sword
Had been so courteous to have cleft me down
35 Unto the navel, ere I liv'd to see
My life, my hopes, my spirits, my patron, all
Thus desperately engaged, by my error.
    VOLPONE. Woe on thy fortune.
    MOSCA.   And my follies, sir.
40 VOLPONE. Th' hast made me miserable.
    MOSCA.   And myself, sir.
Who would have thought he would have
                                [harken'd so?
    VOLPONE. What shall we do?
45 MOSCA.   I know not; if my heart

Could expiate the mischance, I'd pluck it out.
Will you be pleas'd to hang me, or cut my
                                    [throat?
And I'll requite you, sir. Let's die like Romans,°
Since we have liv'd like Grecians.°   50
    [They knock without.]
    VOLPONE.   Hark! who's there?
I hear some footing; officers, the saffi,°
Come to apprehend us! I do feel the brand
Hissing already at my forehead; now   55
Mine ears are boring.°
    MOSCA.   To your couch, sir, you;
Make that place good, however.
    [VOLPONE lies down as before.]
—[Aside.] Guilty men   60
Suspect what they deserve still.—Signior
                                    [Corbaccio!

Scene ix

[Enter CORBACCIO.]
CORBACCIO. Why, how now, Mosca?
MOSCA.   O, undone, amaz'd, sir.   65
Your son, I know not by what accident,
Acquainted with your purpose to my patron,
Touching your will and making him your heir,
Ent'red our house with violence, his sword
                                    [drawn, 70
Sought for you, call'd you wretch, unnatural,
Vow'd he would kill you.
    CORBACCIO.   Me?
    MOSCA.   Yes, and my patron.
    CORBACCIO. This act shall disinherit him   75
                                    [indeed.
Here is the will.
    MOSCA.   'Tis well, sir.
    CORBACCIO.   Right and well:
Be you as careful now for me.   80
    [Enter VOLTORE behind.]
    MOSCA.   My life, sir,
Is not more tender'd;° I am only yours.
    CORBACCIO. How does he? Will he die shortly,
                                [think'st thou? 85
    MOSCA.   I fear

---

like Romans by suicide, as if honorably
like Grecians for pleasure
saffi police
boring being pierced (as punishment)
tender'd cared for

Nestor's the aged Homeric hero's

He'll outlast May.

CORBACCIO.　　　Today?

MOSCA.　　　No, last out May, sir.

CORBACCIO. Couldst thou not gi' him a dram?

5　MOSCA.　　　Oh, by no means, sir.

CORBACCIO. Nay, I'll not bid you.

VOLTORE [*coming forward*].　　　This is a

[knave, I see.

MOSCA [*aside*]. How! Signior Voltore! did he

10　　　　　　　　　　　　　　　[hear me?

VOLTORE.　　　Parasite!

MOSCA. Who's that?—Oh, sir, most timely

[welcome—

VOLTORE.　　　Scarce,

15　To the discovery of your tricks, I fear.

You are his, only? and mine also, are you not?

MOSCA. Who? I, sir!

VOLTORE.　　　You, sir. What device is this

About a will?

20　MOSCA.　　　A plot for you, sir.

VOLTORE.　　　　　　　Come,

Put not your foists° upon me; I shall scent 'em.

MOSCA. Did you not hear it?

VOLTORE.　　　Yes, I hear Corbaccio

25　Hath made your patron there his heir.

MOSCA.　　　　　　　'Tis true,

By my device, drawn to it by my plot,

With hope—

VOLTORE.　　　Your patron should

30　　　　　　　　　　　　　　[reciprocate?

And you have promis'd?

MOSCA.　　　　　　For your good I did, sir.

Nay, more, I told his son, brought, hid him

[here,

35　Where he might hear his father pass the deed;

Being persuaded to it by this thought, sir.

That the unnaturalness, first, of the act,

And then his father's oft disclaiming in him

(Which I did mean t' help on), would sure

40　　　　　　　　　　　　　　[enrage him

To do some violence upon his parent,

On which the law should take sufficient hold,

And you be stated in a double hope.

Truth be my comfort, and my conscience,

45　My only aim was to dig you a fortune

Out of these two rotten sepulchres—

VOLTORE. I cry thee mercy, Mosca.

Put ... foists　do not try your deceits

MOSCA.　　　Worth your patience,

And your great merit, sir. And see the change!

VOLTORE. Why, what success?　　　50

MOSCA.　　　Most hapless! You must help,

[sir.

Whilst we expected th' old raven, in comes

Corvino's wife, sent hither by her husband—

VOLTORE. What, with a present?　　　55

MOSCA.　　　No, sir, on visitation

(I'll tell you how anon); and, staying long,

The youth he grows impatient, rushes forth,

Seizeth the lady, wounds me, makes me swear

(Or he would murder her—that was his vow)　60

T' affirm my patron to have done her rape;

Which how unlike it is, you see! and hence,

With that pretext he's gone, t' accuse his father,

Defame my patron, defeat you—

VOLTORE.　　　Where's her husband?　　　65

Let him be sent for straight.

MOSCA.　　　Sir, I'll go fetch him.

VOLTORE. Bring him to the Scrutineo.°

MOSCA.　　　Sir, I will.

VOLTORE. This must be stopp'd.　　　70

MOSCA.　　　Oh, you do nobly, sir.

Alas, 'twas labor'd all, sir, for your good;

Nor was there want of counsel in the plot

But Fortune can, at any time, o'erthrow

The projects of a hundred learned clerks, sir.　75

CORBACCIO [*listening*]. What's that?

VOLTORE.　　　Wilt please you, sir, to go

[along?

[*Exit* CORBACCIO *followed by* VOLTORE.]

MOSCA. Patron, go in, and pray for our　　　80

[success.

VOLPONE. Need makes devotion; Heaven

[your labor bless!

[*Exeunt.*]

ACT IV

Scene i

[*A street.*]　　　85

[*Enter* SIR POLITIC WOULD-BE *and* PEREGRINE.]

POLITIC. I told you, sir, it was a plot; you see

What observation is. You mention'd° me

For some instructions; I will tell you, sir,

Scrutineo　Senate House

mention'd　applied to

(Since we are met here in this height of Venice)
Some few particulars I have set down,
Only for this meridian, fit to be known
Of your crude traveller; and they are these.
5   I will not touch, sir, at your phrase, or clothes,
For they are old.°
    PEREGRINE.   Sir, I have better.
    POLITIC.   Pardon,
I meant, as they are themes.
10   PEREGRINE.   Oh, sir, proceed;
I'll slander you no more of wit, good sir.
    POLITIC. First, for your garb,° it must be
                 [grave and serious,
Very reserv'd and lock'd; not tell a secret
15   On any terms, not to your father; scarce
A fable, but with caution, make sure choice
Both of your company and discourse; beware
You never speak a truth—
    PEREGRINE.   How!
20   POLITIC.   Not to strangers,
For those be they you must converse with most;
Others I would not know, sir, but at distance
So as I still might be a saver in° 'em—
You shall have tricks else pass'd upon you,
25   [hourly.
And then, for your religion, profess none,
But wonder at the diversity of all;
And, for your part, protest, were there no other
But simply the laws o' th' land, you could
30   [content you.
Nic. Machiavel and Monsieur Bodin,° both
Were of this mind. Then must you learn the use
And handling of your silver fork at meals,
The metal of your glass° (these are main
35   [matters
With your Italian); and to know the hour
When you must eat your melons and your figs.
    PEREGRINE. Is that a point of state too?
    POLITIC.   Here, it is;
40   For your Venetian, if he see a man
Preposterous in the least, he has him straight;
He has; he strips him. I'll acquaint you, sir,

I now have liv'd here, 'tis some fourteen
                 [months.
Within the first week of my landing here,   45
All took me for a citizen of Venice,
I knew the forms so well—
    PEREGRINE [aside].   And nothing else.
    POLITIC. I had read Contarene, took me a
                 [house, 50
Dealt with my Jews to furnish it with
                 [movables—°
Well, if I could but find one man, one man,
To mine own heart, whom I durst trust, I
                 [would— 55
    PEREGRINE. What? what, sir?
    POLITIC.   Make him rich; make him a
                 [fortune:
He should not think again. I would command it.
    PEREGRINE. As how?   60
    POLITIC.   With certain projects that I have,
Which I may not discover.
    PEREGRINE [aside].   If I had
But one to wager with, I would lay odds now,
He tells me instantly.   65
    POLITIC.   One is (and that
I care not greatly who knows) to serve the state
Of Venice with red herrings for three years,
And at a certain rate, from Rotterdam,
Where I have correspondence. There's a letter, 70
Sent me from one o' th' states,° and to that
                 [purpose;
He cannot write his name, but that's his mark.
    PEREGRINE. He is a chandler?°
    POLITIC.   No, a cheesemonger.   75
There are some other too with whom I treat
About the same negotiation;
And I will undertake it; for 'tis thus:
I'll do 't with ease; I have cast it all. Your hoy°
Carries but three men in her, and a boy;   80
And she shall make me three returns° a year:
So if there come but one of three, I save;°
If two, I can defalk.° But this is now,

movables household goods
states Dutchmen of high rank
chandler candlemaker (the paper being so greasy)
hoy small coastal vessel
returns round trips
I save I'm safe
defalk make a profit

old trite
garb demeanor
be . . . in play it safe with
Bodin a writer on statecraft, like **Contarene** (l. 49)
metal . . . glass fine distinctions in glassware

If my main project fail.
    PEREGRINE.   Then you have others?
    POLITIC. I should be loath to draw the subtle
                         [air
5 Of such a place without my thousand aims.
I'll not dissemble, sir: where'er I come,
I love to be considerative; and 'tis true,
I have at my free hours thought upon
Some certain goods unto the state of Venice,
10 Which I do call my cautions; and, sir, which
I mean, in hope of pension, to propound
To the Great Council, then unto the Forty,
So to the Ten.° My means are made already—
    PEREGRINE. By whom?
15   POLITIC.   Sir, one that though his place
                    [b'obscure
Yet he can sway, and they will hear him. He's
A *commandadore.*°
    PEREGRINE.   What, a common serjeant?
20   POLITIC. Sir, such as they are, put it in their
                    [mouths,
What they should say, sometimes; as well as
                    [greater.
I think I have my notes to show you—
25   [(*searching his pockets*)
    PEREGRINE.   Good, sir.
    POLITIC. But you shall swear unto me, on
                [your gentry,°
Not to anticipate—
30   PEREGRINE.   I, sir?
    POLITIC.   Nor reveal
A circumstance—my paper is not with me.
    PEREGRINE. O, but you can remember, sir.
    POLITIC.   My first is
35 Concerning tinder boxes. You must know,
No family is here without its box.
Now, sir, it being so portable a thing,
Put case that you or I were ill affected
Unto the state, sir; with it in our pockets,
40 Might not I go into the Arsenal,
Or you come out again, and none the wiser?
    PEREGRINE. Except yourself, sir.
    POLITIC.   Go to, then. I therefore

Great . . . Ten governing bodies of the Venetian Republic
commandadore sergeant-at-arms, a minor officer of the law courts
gentry honor as a gentleman

Advertise to the state, how fit it were
That none but such as were known patriots,   45
Sound lovers of their country, should be
                [suffer'd
T' enjoy them in their houses; and even those
Seal'd° at some office, and at such a bigness
As might not lurk in pockets.   50
    PEREGRINE.   Admirable!
    POLITIC. My next is, how t' inquire, and be
                [resolv'd
By present demonstration, whether a ship,
Newly arriv'd from Syria, or from   55
Any suspected part of all the Levant,
Be guilty of the plague; and where they use
To lie out forty, fifty days, sometimes,
About the Lazaretto,° for their trial,
I'll save that charge and loss unto the merchant, 60
And in an hour clear the doubt.
    PEREGRINE.   Indeed, sir?
    POLITIC. Or—I will lose my labor.
    PEREGRINE.   'My faith, that's much.
    POLITIC. Nay, sir, conceive me. 'Twill cost me 65
                [in onions,
Some thirty livres—
    PEREGRINE.   Which is one pound sterling.
    POLITIC. Beside my waterworks. For this I do,
                [sir: 70
First, I bring in your ship 'twixt two brick
                [walls—
But those the state shall venture.° On the one
I strain me a fair tarpaulin, and in that
I stick my onions, cut in halves; the other   75
Is full of loopholes, out at which I thrust
The noses of my bellows; and those bellows
I keep, with waterworks, in perpetual motion
(Which is the easi'st matter of a hundred).
Now, sir, your onion, which doth naturally   80
Attract th' infection, and your bellows blowing
The air upon him, will show, instantly,
By his chang'd color, if there be contagion;
Or else remain as fair as at the first.
Now 'tis known, 'tis nothing.   85
    PEREGRINE.   You are right, sir.
    POLITIC. I would I had my note.

Seal'd registered
About . . . Lazaretto in quarantine
venture invest in

PEREGRIN. 'Faith, so would I;
But you ha' done well for once, sir.
POLITIC.   Were I false,
Or would be made so, I could show you reasons
5 How I could sell this state now to the Turk,
Spite of their° galleys, or their—(*examining his*
[*papers*)
PEREGRINE.   Pray you, Sir Pol.
POLITIC. I have 'em not about me.
10 PEREGRINE.   That I fear'd.
They are there, sir?
POLITIC.   No, this is my diary,
Wherein I note my actions of the day.
PEREGRINE. 'Pray you let's see, sir.—What is
15   [here? "*Notandum*,°
A rat had gnawn my spur-leathers;
                    [notwithstanding,
I put on new, and did go forth; but first
I threw three beans over the threshold. *Item,*
20 I went and bought two toothpicks, whereof one
I burst immediately, in a discourse
With a Dutch merchant, 'bout *ragion' del*
[*stato.*°
From him I went and paid a *moccinigo*
25 For piecing my silk stockings; by the way
I cheapen'd° sprats; and at St. Mark's I
                    [urin'd."—
'Faith these are politic notes!
POLITIC.   Sir, I do slip
30 No action of my life, thus but I quote it.
PEREGRINE. Believe me, it is wise!
POLITIC.   Nay, sir, read forth.

Scene ii

[*Enter, at a distance,* LADY POLITIC WOULD-
BE, NANO, *and the two* WAITING WOMEN.]
35 LADY. Where should this loose knight be,
                [trow? Sure h' is hous'd.
NANO. Why, then he's fast.
LADY.   Ay, he plays both with me.
I pray you stay. This heat will do more harm
40 To my complexion than his heart is worth.
(I do not care to hinder, but to take him.)

How it comes off!
[*Rubs her cheeks.*]
WOMAN.   My master's yonder.
LADY.   Where?   45
WOMAN. With a young gentleman.
LADY.   That same's the party!
In man's apparel.—'Pray you, sir, jog° my
[knight.
I will be tender to his reputation,   50
However he demerit.
POLITIC.   My lady!
PEREGRINE.   Where?
POLITIC. 'Tis she indeed, sir; you shall know
                [her. She is, 55
Were she not mine, a lady of that merit,
For fashion and behavior, and for beauty,
I durst compare—
PEREGRINE.   It seems you are not jealous,
That dare commend her.   60
POLITIC.   Nay, and for
                [discourse—
PEREGRINE. Being your wife, she cannot miss
                [that.
POLITIC.   Madam,   65
Here is a gentleman, 'pray you use him fairly;
He seems a youth, but he is—
LADY.   None?
POLITIC.   Yes, one
Has put his face as soon into the world—   70
LADY. You mean, as early? But° today?
POLITIC.   How's this!
LADY. Why, in this habit,° sir; you apprehend
                [me.
Well, Master Would-be, this doth not become   75
                [you;
I had thought the odor, sir, of your good name
Had been more precious to you; that you would
                [not
Have done this dire massacre on your honor;   80
One of your gravity, and rank besides!
But knights, I see, care little for the oath
They make to ladies—chiefly their own ladies.
POLITIC. Now, by my spurs, the symbol of my
                [knighthood— 85

their   the Venetians'
Notandum   for the record
ragion' del stato   matters of state
cheapen'd   priced

jog   nudge
But   only
this habit   male attire

PEREGRINE [*aside*]. Lord, how his brain is
                [humbled° for an oath.
POLITIC. I reach you not.
LADY.   Right, sir: your polity
5 May bear it through thus.—[*To* PEREGRINE.]
               [Sir, a word with you.
I would be loath to contest publicly
With any gentlewoman, or to seem
Froward, or violent, as the courtier says;
10 It comes too near rusticity in a lady,
Which I would shun by all means; and however
I may deserve from Master Would-be, yet
'T have one fair gentlewoman thus be made
Th' unkind instrument to wrong another,
15 And one she knows not, ay, and to persever;
In my poor judgment, is not warranted
From being a solecism° in our sex,
If not in manners.
    PEREGRINE.   How is this!
20 POLITIC.   Sweet madam,
Come nearer to your aim.
    LADY.   Marry, and will, sir.
Since you provoke me with your impudence,
And laughter of your light land-siren here,
25 Your Sporus,° your hermaphrodite—
    PEREGRINE.   What's here?
Poetic fury and historic storms!
    POLITIC. The gentleman, believe it, is of worth
And of our nation.
30 LADY.   Ay, your Whitefriars nation?°
Come, I blush for you, Master Would-be, I;
And am asham'd you should ha' no more
                [forehead°
Than thus to be the patron, or St. George,°
35 To a lewd harlot, a base fricatrice,°
A female devil, in a male outside.
    POLITIC.   Nay,
An you be such a one! I must bid adieu

---

humbled brought low, i.e., to his heels
solecism impropriety
Sporus Roman eunuch, a notorious victim of the
  emperor Nero's perversions
Whitefriars nation criminals (Whitefriars being a district in London where lawbreakers were safe from
  arrest)
forehead self-respect
St. George the patron saint of England
fricatrice prostitute

To your delights. The case appears too liquid.°
    [*Exit.*]   40
    LADY. Ay, you may carry 't clear, with your
                [state-face!—
But for your carnival concupiscence,
Who here is fled for liberty of conscience,
From furious persecution of the marshal,   45
Her will I disc'ple.°
    PEREGRINE.   This is fine, i' faith!
And do you use° this often? Is this part
Of your wit's exercise, 'gainst you have
                [occasion? 50
Madam—
    LADY.   Go to, sir.
    PEREGRINE.   Do you hear me, lady?
Why, if your knight have set you to beg shirts,
Or to invite me home, you might have done it 55
A nearer way by far.
    LADY.   This cannot work you
Out of my snare.
    PEREGRINE.   Why, am I in it, then?
Indeed your husband told me you were fair, 60
And so you are; only your nose inclines,
That side that's next the sun, to the queen-
                [apple.°
    LADY. This cannot be endur'd by any
                [patience. 65

Scene iii

[*Enter* MOSCA.]
MOSCA. What's the matter, madam?
    LADY.   If the Senate
Right not my quest in this, I will protest 'em
To all the world no aristocracy.   70
    MOSCA. What is the injury, lady?
    LADY.   Why, the callet°
You told me of, here I have ta'en disguis'd.
    MOSCA. Who? this? what means your
               [Ladyship? The creature 75
I mention'd to you is apprehended now,
Before the Senate; you shall see her—
    LADY.   Where?

---

liquid transparent
disc'ple punish
use do
queen-apple red-cheeked apple
callet wench

Mosca. I'll bring you to her. This young
[gentleman,
I saw him land this morning at the port.
Lady. Is 't possible? How has my judgment
[wander'd!
5   Sir, I must, blushing, say to you, I have err'd;
And plead your pardon.
Peregrine.   What! more changes yet?
Lady. I hope you've not the malice to
10 [remember
A gentlewoman's passion. If you stay
In Venice here, please you to use me, sir—
Mosca. Will you go, madam?
Lady.   'Pray you, sir, use me; in faith,
15 The more you see me the more I shall conceive
You have forgot our quarrel.
   [Exeunt Lady Would-be, Mosca, Nano, and
Waiting Women.]
Peregrine.   This is rare!
20 Sir Politic Would-be? No, Sir Politic Bawd!
To bring me thus acquainted with his wife!
Well, wise Sir Pol, since you have practis'd thus
Upon my freshmanship, I'll try your salthead,°
What proof it is against a counterplot.
25   [Exit.]

Scene iv

[The Senate House.]
[Enter Voltore, Corbaccio, Corvino, and
Mosca.]
   Voltore. Well, now you know the carriage°
30 [of the business,
Your constancy is all that is requir'd
Unto the safety of it.
   [He stands aside.]
   Mosca.   Is the lie
35 Safely convey'd amongst us? Is that sure?
Knows every man his burden?°
   Corvino.   Yes.
   Mosca.   Then shrink not.
   Corvino. But knows the advocate° the truth?
40 Mosca.   Oh, sir,

By no means; I devis'd a formal tale,
That salv'd your reputation. But be valiant, sir.
   Corvino. I fear no one but him, that this his
[pleading
Should make him stand for a co-heir—   45
   Mosca.   Co-halter!
Hang him; we will but use his tongue, his noise,
As we do croaker's° here.
   Corvino.   Ay, what shall he do?
   Mosca. When we ha' done, you mean?   50
   Corvino.   Yes.
   Mosca.   Why, we'll think;
Sell him for mummia:° he's half dust already.—
[To Voltore.] Do you not smile, to see this
[buffalo,°   55
How he doth sport it with his head?—[Aside.]
[I should,
If all were well and past.—[To Corbaccio.] Sir,
[only you
Are he that shall enjoy the crop of all,   60
And these not know for whom they toil.
   Corbaccio.   Ay, peace.
   Mosca [to Corvino]. But you shall eat it.—
   [Aside.] Much!—[Then to Voltore again.]
[Worshipful sir,   65
Mercury° sit upon your thund'ring tongue,
Or the French Hercules,° and make your
[language
As conquering as his club, to beat along,
As with a tempest, flat, our adversaries;   70
But much more yours, sir.
   Voltore.   Here they come; ha' done.
   Mosca. I have another witness, if you need,
[sir,
I can produce.   75
   Voltore.   Who is it?
   Mosca.   Sir, I have her.

Scene v

[Enter four Avocatori, Bonario, Celia,
Notario, Commandadori, Saffi, and other
Officers of Justice.]   80

---

salthead seniority or "seasoned" experience, also
   connoting lechery
carriage setup
burden part
the advocate Voltore

croaker's Corbaccio's
mummia a drug made from mummies
buffalo cuckold (Corvino)
Mercury god of eloquence, perjury, and commerce
French Hercules Ogmius, a legendary spellbinder

1st Avocatore. The like of this the Senate
                    [never heard of.
2nd Avocatore. 'Twill come most strange to
                    [them when we report it.
5   4th Avocatore. The gentlewoman has been
                    [ever held
Of unreproved name.
    3rd Avocatore.   So, the young man.
    4th Avocatore. The more unnatural part
10   [that of his father.
    2nd Avocatore. More of the husband.
    1st Avocatore.   I not know to give
His act a name, it is so monstrous!
    4th Avocatore. But the impostor, he is a
15   [thing created
T' exceed example!
    1st Avocatore.   And all after-times!
    2nd Avocatore. I never heard a true
                    [voluptuary
20 Describ'd but him.
    3rd Avocatore.   Appear yet those were
                    [cited?
Notario. All but the old magnifico, Volpone.
1st Avocatore. Why is not he here?
25 Mosca.   Please your Fatherhoods.
Here is his advocate. Himself's so weak,
So feeble—
    4th Avocatore. What are you?
    Bonario.   His parasite,
30 His knave, his pander. I beseech the court
He may be forc'd to come, that your grave eyes
May bear strong witness of his strange
                    [impostures.
Voltore. Upon my faith and credit with your
35   [Virtues,
He is not able to endure the air.
    2nd Avocatore. Bring him, however.
    3rd Avocatore.   We will see him.
    4th Avocatore.   Fetch him.
40 Voltore. Your Fatherhoods' fit pleasures be
                    [obey'd;
[*Exeunt* Officers.]
But sure, the sight will rather move your pities
Than indignation. May it please the court,
45 In the meantime, he may be heard in me.
I know this place most void of prejudice,
And therefore crave it, since we have no reason
To fear our truth should hurt our cause.

3rd Avocatore.   Speak free.
Voltore. Then know, most honor'd fathers,   50
                    [I must now
Discover to your strangely abused ears,
The most prodigious and most frontless° piece
Of solid impudence and treachery
That ever vicious nature yet brought forth   55
To shame the state of Venice. This lewd
                    [woman,
That wants no artificial looks or tears
To help the visor she has now put on,
Hath long been known a close° adultress   60
To that lascivious youth there; not suspected,
I say, but known, and taken in the act
With him; and by this man, the easy husband,
Pardon'd; whose timeless° bounty makes him
                    [now 65
Stand here, the most unhappy, innocent person
That ever man's own goodness made accus'd.
For these, not knowing how to owe a gift
Of that dear grace, but with their shame, being
                    [plac'd 70
So above all powers of their gratitude,
Began to hate the benefit, and, in place
Of thanks, devise t' extirp° the memory
Of such an act. Wherein I pray your
                    [Fatherhoods 75
To observe the malice, yea, the rage of creatures
Discover'd in their evils; and what heart
Such take, ev'n from their crimes. But that anon
Will more appear. This gentleman, the father,
Hearing of this foul fact, with many others,   80
Which daily struck at his too tender ears,
And griev'd in nothing more than that he
                    [could not
Preserve himself a parent (his son's ills
Growing to that strange flood), at last decreed 85
To disinherit him.
    1st Avocatore.   These be strange turns!
    2nd Avocatore. The young man's fame was
                    [ever fair and honest.
    Voltore. So much more full of danger is his   90
                    [vice,

frontless shameless
close secret
timeless untimely
extirp extirpate

That can beguile so, under shade of virtue.
But, as I said, my honor'd sires, his father
Having this settled purpose, by what means
To him betray'd, we know not, and this day
5 Appointed for the deed; that parricide
I cannot style him better, by confederacy
Preparing this his paramour to be there,
Ent'red Volpone's house (who was the man,
Your Fatherhoods must understand, design'd
10 For the inheritance), there sought his father:—
But with what purpose sought he him, my
                                 [Lords?
I tremble to pronounce it, that a son
Unto a father, and to such a father,
15 Should have so foul, felonious intent—
It was to murder him; when, being prevented
By his more happy absence, what then did he?
Not check his wicked thoughts; no, now new
                                 [deeds
20 (Mischief doth ever end where it begins)—
An act of horror, fathers! He dragg'd forth
The aged gentleman that had there lain bedrid
Three years and more, out off his innocent
                                 [couch,
25 Naked upon the floor; there left him; wounded
His servant in the face, and with this strumpet,
The stale° to his forg'd practice, who was glad
To be so active,—I shall here desire
Your Fatherhoods to note but my collections,°
30 As most remarkable,—thought at once to stop
His father's ends, discredit his free choice
In the old gentleman,° redeem themselves,
By laying infamy upon this man,°
To whom, with blushing, they should owe their
35   [lives.
    1ST AVOCATORE. What proofs have you of
                                 [this?
    BONARIO.   Most honor'd fathers,
I humbly crave there be no credit given
40 To this man's mercenary tongue.
    2ND AVOCATORE.   Forbear.
    BONARIO. His soul moves in his fee.
    3RD AVOCATORE.   O, sir.

    BONARIO.   This fellow,
For six sols more would plead against his   45
                       [Maker.
    1ST AVOCATORE. You do forget yourself.
    VOLTORE.   Nay, nay, grave fathers,
Let him have scope! Can any man imagine
That he will spare his accuser, that would not   50
Have spar'd his parent?
    1ST AVOCATORE.   Well, produce your
                      [proofs.
    CELIA. I would I could forget I were a
                      [creature. 55
    VOLTORE. Signior Corbaccio.
    4TH AVOCATORE.   What is he?
    VOLTORE.   The father.
    2ND AVOCATORE. Has he had an oath?
    NOTARIO.   Yes.   60
    CORBACCIO.   What must I do now?
    NOTARIO. Your testimony's crav'd.
    CORBACCIO.   Speak to the knave?
I'll ha' my mouth first stopp'd with earth; my
                      [heart 65
Abhors his knowledge: I disclaim in him.
    1ST AVOCATORE. But for what cause?
    CORBACCIO.   The mere portent of nature.°
He is an utter stranger to my loins.
    BONARIO. Have they made° you to this!   70
    CORBACCIO.   I will not hear thee,
Monster of men, swine, goat, wolf, parricide;
Speak not, thou viper.
    BONARIO.   Sir, I will sit down,
And rather wish my innocence should suffer   75
Than I resist the authority of a father.
    VOLTORE. Signior Corvino.
    2ND AVOCATORE.   This is strange!
    1ST AVOCATORE.   Who's this?
    NOTARIO. The husband.   80
    4TH AVOCATORE.   Is he sworn?
    NOTARIO.   He is.
    3RD AVOCATORE.   Speak then.
    CORVINO. This woman, please your
                  [Fatherhoods, is a whore, 85
Of most hot exercise, more than a partridge,
Upon record—

---

stale decoy
collections conclusions, summary
gentleman Volpone
this man Corvino

The . . . nature the direct evidence of his unnatural
  behavior
made brought

1ST AVOCATORE.   No more.

CORVINO.   Neighs like a jennet.

NOTARIO. Preserve the honor of the court.

CORVINO.   I shall,

5   And modesty of your most reverend ears.
And yet I hope that I may say these eyes
Have seen her glu'd unto that piece of cedar,
That fine well-timber'd gallant; and that here°
The letters may be read, thorough the horn,°

10 That make the story perfect.

MOSCA [*aside to* CORVINO].   Excellent, sir!

CORVINO [*aside to* MOSCA]. There is no shame
                [in this now, is there?

MOSCA [*aside to* CORVINO].   None.

15 CORVINO. Or if I said, I hop'd that she were
                [onward
To her damnation, if there be a hell
Greater than whore and woman, a good
                [Catholic

20 May make the doubt.°

3RD AVOCATORE.   His grief hath made him
                [frantic.

1ST AVOCATORE. Remove him hence.

2ND AVOCATORE.   Look to the woman.

25 [*She swoons.*]

CORVINO.   Rare!
Prettily feign'd! again!

4TH AVOCATORE.   Stand from about her.

1ST AVOCATORE. Give her the air.

30 3RD AVOCATORE [*to* MOSCA].   What can
                [you say?

MOSCA.   My wound,
May 't please your Wisdoms, speaks for me,
                [receiv'd

35 In aid of my good patron, when he miss'd
His sought-for father, when that well-taught
                [dame
Had her cue giv'n her to cry out, "A rape!"

BONARIO. O most laid° impudence! Fathers—

40 3RD AVOCATORE.   Sir, be silent;

---

here on my forehead

horn of a cuckold; also the sheet of transparent horn
used to protect the page of a child's reader

Or . . . doubt or if I were to say I hoped that she
were going to hell, an orthodox Catholic might still
doubt whether there is a hell worse than being a
whore and woman

laid contrived

You had your hearing free, so must they theirs.

2ND AVOCATORE. I do begin to doubt th'
                [imposture here.

4TH AVOCATORE. This woman has too many
                [moods. 45

VOLTORE.   Grave fathers,
She is a creature of a most profess'd
And prostituted lewdness.

CORVINO.   Most impetuous!
Unsatisfied, grave fathers!   50

VOLTORE.   May her feignings
Not take your wisdoms. But this day she baited
A stranger, a grave knight, with her loose eyes
And more lascivious kisses. This man saw 'em
Together on the water, in a gondola.   55

MOSCA. Here is the lady herself, that saw
                ['em too,
Without; who then had in the open streets
Pursu'd them, but for saving her knight's
                [honor. 60

1ST AVOCATORE. Produce that lady.

2ND AVOCATORE.   Let her come.

[*Exit* MOSCA.]

4TH AVOCATORE.   These things,
They strike with wonder!   65

3RD AVOCATORE.   I am turn'd a stone!

Scene vi

[*Re-enter* MOSCA *with* LADY WOULD-BE.]

MOSCA. Be resolute, madam.

LADY.   Ay, this same is she.—
Out, thou chameleon harlot! now thine eyes   70
Vie tears with the hyena. Dar'st thou look
Upon my wronged face?—I cry your pardons.
I fear I have forgettingly transgress'd
Against the dignity of the court—

2ND AVOCATORE.   No, madam.   75

LADY. And been exorbitant—

2ND ADVOCATORE.   You have not, lady.

4TH AVOCATORE. These proofs are strong.

LADY.   Surely, I had no purpose
To scandalize your honors, or my sex's.   80

3RD AVOCATURE. We do believe it.

LADY.   Surely you may believe it.

2ND AVOCATORE. Madam, we do.

LADY.   Indeed you may; my breeding
Is not so coarse—   85

4TH AVOCATORE.   We know it.

LADY.   To offend
With pertinacy—
3RD AVOCATORE.   Lady—
LADY.   Such a presence;
5 No, surely.
1ST AVOCATORE.   We will think it.
LADY.   You may think it.
1ST AVOCATORE. Let her o'ercome—What
                              [witnesses have you,
10 To make good your report?
     BONARIO.   Our consciences.
     CELIA. And Heaven, that never fails the
                              [innocent.
     1ST AVOCATORE. These are no testimonies.
15   BONARIO.   Not in your courts,
Where multitude and clamor overcomes.
     1ST AVOCATORE. Nay, then you do wax
                              [insolent.
[VOLPONE *is brought in, as impotent.*]
20   VOLTORE.   Here, here,
The testimony comes that will convince,
And put to utter dumbness their bold tongues.
See here, grave fathers, here's the ravisher,
The rider on men's wives, the great impostor,
25 The grand voluptuary! Do you not think
These limbs should affect venery? or these eyes
Covet a concubine? Pray you mark these hands.
Are they not fit to stroke a lady's breasts?
Perhaps he doth dissemble!
30   BONARIO.   So he does.
     VOLTORE. Would you ha' him tortur'd?
     BONARIO.   I would have him prov'd.
     VOLTORE. Best try him then with goads, or
                              [burning irons;
35 Put him to the strappado; I have heard
The rack hath cur'd the gout; faith, give it him,
And help him of a malady; be courteous.
I'll undertake, before these honor'd fathers,
He shall have yet as many left diseases,
40 As she has known adulterers, or thou
                              [strumpets.
O, my most equal° hearers, if these deeds,
Acts of this bold and most exorbitant strain,
May pass with sufferance, what one citizen
45 But owes the forfeit of his life, yea, fame,
To him that dares traduce him? Which of you

equal equitable

Are safe, my honor'd fathers? I would ask,
With leave of your grave Fatherhoods, if their
                              [plot
Have any face or color like to truth?   50
Or if, unto the dullest nostril here,
It smell not rank, and most abhorred slander?
I crave your care of this good gentleman,
Whose life is much endanger'd by their fable;
And as for them, I will conclude with this: 55
That vicious persons, when they are hot, and
                              [flesh'd°
In impious acts, their constancy abounds:
Damn'd deeds are done with greatest
                              [confidence. 60
     1ST AVOCATORE. Take 'em to custody, and
                              [sever them.
     2ND AVOCATORE. 'Tis pity two such prodigies
                              [should live.
     1ST AVOCATORE. Let the old gentleman be   65
                              [return'd with care.
[*Exeunt* OFFICERS *with* VOLPONE.]
I am sorry our credulity wrong'd him.
     4TH AVOCATORE. These are two creatures!
     3RD AVOCATORE.   I have an earthquake in 70
                              [me!
     2ND AVOCATORE. Their shame, even in their
                              [cradles, fled their faces.
     4TH AVOCATORE. You have done a worthy
                              [service to the state, sir, 75
In their discovery.
     1ST AVOCATORE.   You shall hear, ere
                              [night,
What punishment the court decrees upon 'em.
[*Exeunt* AVOCATORI, NOTARIO, *and* OFFICERS 80
with BONARIO *and* CELIA.]
     VOLTORE. We thank your Fatherhoods.—
                              [How like you it?
     MOSCA.   Rare.
I'd ha' your tongue, sir, tipp'd with gold for   85
                              [this;
I'd ha' you be the heir to the whole city;
The earth I'd have want men ere you want
                              [living:
They are bound to erect your statue in St.   90
                              [Mark's.—
Signior Corvino, I would have you go

flesh'd plunged

And show yourself that you have conquer'd.

CORVINO.   Yes.

MOSCA. It was much better that you should
                            [profess

5 Yourself a cuckold thus, than that the other
Should have been prov'd.

CORVINO.   Nay, I consider'd that;
Now it is her fault.

MOSCA.   Then, it had been yours.

10 CORVINO. True.—[*Aside to* MOSCA.] I do
                      [doubt this advocate still.

MOSCA [*aside*].   I' faith,
You need not; I dare ease you of that care.

CORVINO [*aside*]. I trust thee, Mosca.

15 MOSCA [*aside*].   As your own soul, sir.
[*Exit* CORVINO.]

CORBACCIO.   Mosca!

MOSCA. Now for your business, sir.

CORBACCIO.   How? ha' you business?

20 MOSCA. Yes, yours, sir.

CORBACCIO.   O, none else?

MOSCA.   None else, not I.

CORBACCIO. Be careful then.

MOSCA.   Rest you with both your eyes,°
25   [sir.

CORBACCIO. Dispatch it.

MOSCA.   Instantly.

CORBACCIO.   And look that all,
Whatever, be put in, jewels, plate, monies,
30 Household stuff, bedding, curtains.

MOSCA.   Curtain-rings, sir;
Only, the advocate's fee must be deducted.

CORBACCIO. I'll pay him now; you'll be too
                      [prodigal.

35 MOSCA. Sir, I must tender it.

CORBACCIO.   Two *cecchines* is well.

MOSCA. No, six, sir.

CORBACCIO.   'Tis too much.

MOSCA.   He talk'd a great while;
40 You must consider that, sir.

CORBACCIO.   Well, there's three—

MOSCA. I'll give it him.

CORBACCIO.   Do so, and there's for thee.
[*Exit.*]

45 MOSCA [*aside*]. Bountiful bones! What horrid
                      [strange offence

Did he commit 'gainst nature, in his youth,
Worthy this age?—[*Aside to* VOLTORE.] You
                   [see, sir, how I work
Unto your ends; take you no notice.   50

VOLTORE.   No,
I'll leave you.

MOSCA [*aside*]. All is yours, the devil and all,
Good advocate.—Madam, I'll bring you home.

LADY. No, I'll go see your patron.   55

MOSCA.   That you shall not;
I'll tell you why. My purpose is to urge
My patron to reform his will, and for
The zeal you have shown today, whereas before
You were but third or fourth, you shall be now   60
Put in the first; which would appear as begg'd
If you were present. Therefore—

LADY.   You shall sway me.
[*Exeunt.*]

ACT V

Scene i

[*A room in* VOLPONE's *house.*]   65
[*Enter* VOLPONE.]

VOLPONE. Well, I am here, and all this brunt
                   [is past.
I ne'er was in dislike with my disguise
Till this fled moment: here 'twas good, in   70
                   [private;
But in the your public, *cave*,° whilst I breathe.
'Fore God, my left leg 'gan to have the cramp.
And I apprehended straight some power had
                   [struck me 75
With a dead palsy. Well, I must be merry,
And shake it off. A many of these fears
Would put me into some villainous disease,
Should they come thick upon me. I'll prevent
                   ['em. 80
Give me a bowl of lusty wine, to fright
This humor from my heart.—[*He drinks.*] Hum,
                   [hum, hum!—
'Tis almost gone already; I shall conquer.
Any device now of rare ingenious knavery,   85
That would possess me with a violent laughter,
Would make me up again!—[*Drinks again.*] So,
                   [so, so, so!—

Rest . . . eyes don't lose a wink of sleep

cave beware

This heat is life; 'tis blood by this time.—

[Mosca!

Scene ii

[*Enter* MOSCA.]

5 MOSCA. How now, sir? Does the day look

[clear again?

Are we recover'd, and wrought out of error,

Into our way, to see our path before us?

Is our trade free once more?

VOLPONE.   Exquisite Mosca!

10 MOSCA. Was it not carri'd learnedly?

VOLPONE.   And stoutly:

Good wits are greatest in extremities.

MOSCA. It were folly beyond thought to trust

Any grand act unto a cowardly spirit.

15 You are not taken with it enough, methinks.

VOLPONE. Oh, more than if I had enjoy'd the

[wench;

The pleasure of all womankind's not like it.

MOSCA. Why, now you speak, sir. We must

20   [here be fix'd;

Here we must rest;° this is our masterpiece;

We cannot think to go beyond this.

VOLPONE.   True,

Thou hast play'd thy prize, my precious Mosca.

25 MOSCA.   Nay, sir,

To gull the court—

VOLPONE.   And quite divert the torrent

Upon the innocent.

MOSCA.   Yes, and to make

30 So rare a music out of discords—

VOLPONE.   Right.

That yet to me's the strangest! how th' hast

[borne it!

That these, being so divided 'mongst

35   [themselves,

Should not scent somewhat, or in me or thee,

Or doubt their own side.

MOSCA.   True, they will not see' t.

Too much light blinds 'em, I think. Each of 'em

40 Is so possess'd and stuff'd with his own hopes

That anything unto the contrary,

Never so true, or never so apparent,

Never so palpable, they will resist it—

VOLPONE. Like a temptation of the Devil.

MOSCA.   Right, sir.   45

Merchants may talk of trade, and your great

[signiors

Of land that yields well; but if Italy

Have any glebe more fruitful than these

[fellows,   50

I am deceiv'd. Did not your advocate rare?°

VOLPONE. Oh—"My most honor'd fathers,

[my grave fathers,

Under correction of your Fatherhoods,

What face of truth is here? If these strange   55

[deeds

May pass, most honor'd fathers"—I had much

[ado

To forbear laughing.

MOSCA.   'T seem'd to me you sweat, sir.   60

VOLPONE. In troth, I did a little.

MOSCA.   But confess, sir,

Were you not daunted?

VOLPONE.   In good faith, I was

A little in a mist, but not dejected;   65

Never, but still myself.

MOSCA.   I think it, sir.

Now, so truth help me, I must needs say this,

[sir,

And out of conscience for your advocate,   70

He has taken pains, in faith, sir, and deserv'd

In my poor judgment, I speak it under favor,

Not to contrary you, sir, very richly—

Well—to be cozen'd.°

VOLPONE.   Troth, and I think so too,   75

By that I heard him in the latter end.

MOSCA. O, but before, sir: had you heard him

[first

Draw it to certain heads, then aggravate,

Then use his vehement figures°—I look'd still   80

When he would shift° a shirt; and doing this

Out of pure love, no hope of gain—

VOLPONE.   'Tis right.

I cannot answer him, Mosca, as I would,

Not yet; but for thy sake, at thy entreaty,   85

I will begin, ev'n now—to vex 'em all,

This very instant.

rest stop

rare excellently
cozen'd cheated
figures of speech and gesture
shift change (because of his violent exertions)

MOSCA.   Good, sir.
VOLPONE.   Call the dwarf
And eunuch forth.
MOSCA.   Castrone, Nano!
5   [*Enter* CASTRONE *and* NANO.]
NANO.   Here.
VOLPONE. Shall we have a jig now?
MOSCA.   What you please, sir.
VOLPONE.   Go,
10 Straight give out about the streets, you two,
That I am dead; do it with constancy,
Sadly, do you hear? Impute it to the grief
Of this late slander.
[*Exeunt* CASTRONE *and* NANO.]
15 MOSCA.   What do you mean, sir?
VOLPONE.   Oh,
I shall have instantly my Vulture, Crow,
Raven, come flying hither, on the news,
To peck for carrion, my she-wolf, and all,
20 Greedy, and full of expectation—
MOSCA. And then to have it ravish'd from their
                              [mouths?
VOLPONE. 'Tis true. I will ha' thee put on a
                              [gown,°
25 And take upon thee, as thou wert mine heir;
Show 'em a will. Open that chest, and reach
Forth one of those that has the blanks. I'll
                              [straight
Put in thy name.
30 MOSCA.   It will be rare, sir.
VOLPONE.   Ay,
When they e'en gape, and find themselves
                              [deluded—
MOSCA. Yes.
35 VOLPONE.   And thou use them scurvily.
                              [Dispatch;
Get on thy gown.
MOSCA.   But what, sir, if they ask
After the body?
40 VOLPONE.   Say it was corrupted.
MOSCA. I'll say it stunk, sir; and was fain
                              [t' have it
Coffin'd up instantly, and sent away.
VOLPONE. Anything; what thou wilt.—Hold,
45   [here's my will.
Get thee a cap, a count-book, pen and ink,

Papers afore thee; sit as thou wert taking
An inventory of parcels. I'll get up
Behind the curtain, on a stool, and harken;
Sometime peep over, see how they do look,   50
With what degrees their blood doth leave their
                              [faces!
O, 'twill afford me a rare meal of laughter.
MOSCA. Your advocate will turn stark dull
                              [upon it.   55
VOLPONE. It will take off his oratory's edge.
MOSCA. But your clarissimo,° old roundback,
                              [he
Will crump you° like a hog-louse, with the
                              [touch.   60
VOLPONE. And what Corvino?
MOSCA.   O, sir, look for him,
Tomorrow morning, with a rope and a dagger,
To visit all the streets; he must run mad.
My Lady too, that came into the court,   65
To bear false witness for your Worship—
VOLPONE.   Yes.
And kiss'd me 'fore the fathers, when my face
Flow'd all with oils—
MOSCA.   And sweat, sir. Why, your gold   70
Is such another med'cine, it dries up
All those offensive savors. It transforms
The most deformed, and restores 'em lovely,
As 'twere the strange poetical girdle.° Jove
Could not invent t' himself a shroud more   75
                              [subtle
To pass Acrisius'° guards. It is the thing
Makes all the world her grace, her youth, her
                              [beauty.
VOLPONE. I think she loves me.   80
MOSCA.   Who? the lady, sir?
She's jealous of you.
VOLPONE.   Dost thou say so?
[*Knocking within.*]
MOSCA.   Hark.   85
There's some already.
VOLPONE.   Look.
MOSCA.   It is the Vulture;

gown a gentleman's attire

clarissimo grandee (Corbaccio)
crump you crumple you up
girdle of Venus
Acrisius whose daughter, Danae, was seduced by
    Jove disguised in a shower of gold

He has the quickest scent.
VOLPONE.   I'll to my place,
Thou to thy posture.
    [*Goes behind the curtain.*]
5   MOSCA.   I am set.
    VOLPONE.   But, Mosca,
Play the artificer now; torture 'em rarely.

Scene iii

    [*Enter* VOLTORE.]
    VOLTORE. How now, my Mosca?
10   MOSCA [*writing*].   Turkey carpets, nine—
    VOLTORE. Taking an inventory! that is well.
    MOSCA. Two suits of bedding, tissue—
    VOLTORE.   Where's the will?
Let me read that the while.
15   [*Enter* SERVANTS *with* CORBACCIO *in a chair.*]
    CORBACCIO.   So, set me down,
And get you home.
    [*Exeunt* SERVANTS.]
    VOLTORE.   Is he come now, to trouble us?
20   MOSCA. Of cloth of gold, two more—
    CORBACCIO.   Is it done, Mosca?
    MOSCA. Of several velvets, eight—
    VOLTORE.   I like his care.
    CORBACCIO. Dost thou not hear?
25   [*Enter* CORVINO.]
    CORVINO.   Ha! is the hour come, Mosca?
    VOLPONE [*aside*]. Ay, now they muster.
    [*Peeps from behind a traverse.*°]
    CORVINO.   What does the advocate here?
30 Or this Corbaccio?
    CORBACCIO.   What do these here?
    [*Enter* LADY WOULD-BE.]
    LADY.   Mosca!
Is his thread° spun?
35   MOSCA.   Eight chests of linen—
    VOLPONE [*aside*].   Oh,
My fine Dame Would-be, too!
    CORVINO.   Mosca, the will,
That I may show it these, and rid 'em hence.
40   MOSCA. Six chests of diaper, four of damask
                                [—there.
    [*Gives the will.*]
    CORBACCIO. Is that the will?

MOSCA [*writing*].   Down-beds, and
                                [bolsters—   45
    VOLPONE [*aside*].   Rare!
Be busy still. Now they begin to flutter;
They never think of me. Look, see, see, see!
How their swift eyes run over the long deed,
Unto the name, and to the legacies,   50
What is bequeath'd them there—
    MOSCA.   Ten suits of hangings—
    VOLPONE [*aside*]. Ay, in their garters, Mosca.
                        [Now their hopes   55
Are at the gasp.
    VOLTORE.   Mosca the heir!
    CORBACCIO.   What's that?
    VOLPONE [*aside*]. My advocate is dumb; look
                        [to my merchant—°
He has heard of some strange storm; a ship is   60
                                [lost—
He faints. My Lady will swoon. Old glazen-
                                [eyes,
He hath not reach'd his despair yet.
    CORBACCIO.   All these   65
Are out of hope; I am, sure, the man.
    [*Takes the will.*]
    CORVINO.   But, Mosca—
    MOSCA. Two cabinets—
    CORVINO.   Is this in earnest?   70
    MOSCA.   One
Of ebony—
    CORVINO.   Or do you but delude me?
    MOSCA. The other, mother-of-pearl—I am
                        [very busy.   75
Good faith, it is a fortune thrown upon me—
Item, one salt° of agate—not my seeking.
    LADY. Do you hear, sir?
    MOSCA.   A perfum'd box—'pray you
                        [forbear;   80
You see I am troubled—made of an onyx—
    LADY.   How!
    MOSCA. Tomorrow or next day, I shall be at
                        [leisure
To talk with you all.   85
    CORVINO.   Is this my large hope's issue?
    LADY. Sir, I must have a fairer answer.
    MOSCA.   Madam!

---

traverse curtain
thread of life

merchant Corvino
salt salt-dish

Marry, and shall: 'pray you, fairly quit my
[house.
Nay, raise no tempest with your looks; but hark
[you,
5 Remember what your Ladyship off'red me
To put you in, an heir; go to; think on it.
And what you said e'en your best madams did
For maintentance, and why not you? Enough.
Go home, and use the poor Sir Pol, your knight,
10 [well,
For fear I tell some riddles; go, be melancholic.
    [*Exit* LADY WOULD-BE.]
    VOLPONE [*aside*]. Oh, my fine devil!
    CORVINO.   Mosca, pray you a word.
15 MOSCA. Lord! will not you take your dispatch
[hence yet?
Methinks, of all, you should have been th'
[example.
Why should you stay here? with what thought,
20 [what promise?
 Hear you; do not you know, I know you an ass,
And that you would most fain have been a
[wittol
If fortune would have let you? that you are
25 A declar'd cuckold, on good terms? This pearl,
You'll say, was yours? right; this diamond?
I'll not deny 't, but thank you. Much here else?
It may be so. Why, think that these good works
May help to hide your bad. I'll not betray you;
30 Although you be but extraordinary,°
And have it only in title, it sufficeth:
Go home; be melancholic too, or mad.
    [*Exit* CORVINO.]
    VOLPONE [*aside*]. Rare Mosca! how his
35 [villainy becomes him!
    VOLTORE [*aside*]. Certain he doth delude all
[these for me.
    CORBACCIO. Mosca the heir?
    VOLPONE [*aside*].   O, his four eyes have
40 [found it!
    CORBACCIO. I am cozen'd, cheated, by a
[parasite-slave;
Harlot, th' hast gull'd me.
    MOSCA.   Yes, sir. Stop your mouth,
45 Or I shall draw the only tooth is left.
Are not you he, that filthy covetous wretch,

but extraordinary a cuckold only in a special sense

With the three legs, that here, in hope of prey,
Have, any time this three year, snuff'd about,
With your most grov'ling nose, and would
[have hir'd 50
Me to the pois'ning of my patron, sir?
Are not you he that have today in court
Profess'd the disinheriting of your son?
Perjur'd yourself? Go home, and die, and stink;
If you but croak a syllable, all comes out: 55
Away, and call your porters! [*Exit* CORBACCIO.]
    [Go, go, stink.
    VOLPONE [*aside*]. Excellent varlet!°
    VOLTORE.   Now, my faithful Mosca,
I find thy constancy— 60
    MOSCA.   Sir!
    VOLTORE.   Sincere.
    MOSCA [*writing*].   A table
Of porphyry—I mar'l you'll be thus
[troublesome. 65
    VOLTORE. Nay, leave off now, they are gone.
    MOSCA.   Why, who are you?
What! who did send for you? Oh, cry you
[mercy,
Reverend sir! Good faith, I am griev'd for you, 70
That any chance of mine should thus defeat
Your (I must needs say) most deserving
[travails;
But I protest, sir, it was cast upon me,
And I could almost wish to be without it, 75
But that the will o' the' dead must be observ'd.
Marry, my joy is that you need it not;
You have a gift, sir, (thank your education)
Will never let you want, while there are men,
And malice, to breed causes.° Would I had 80
But half the like, for all my fortune, sir.
If I have any suits, as I do hope,
Things being so easy and direct, I shall not,
I will make bold with your obstreperous° aid
(Conceive me) for your fee, sir. In meantime, 85
You that have so much law, I know ha' the
[conscience
Not to be covetous of what is mine.
Good sir, I thank you for my plate; 'twill help
To set up a young man. Good faith, you look 90

varlet servant
causes law cases
obstreperous clamorous

As you were costive; best go home and purge,
           [sir.

[Exit VOLTORE.]

VOLPONE [coming from behind the curtain].

5 Bid him eat lettuce well. My witty mischief,
Let me embrace thee. O that I could now
Transform thee to a Venus!—Mosca, go,
Straight take my habit of clarissimo.°
And walk the streets; be seen, torment 'em

10   [more;
We must pursue, as well as plot. Who would
Have lost this feast?

    MOSCA.   I doubt° it will lose them.

    VOLPONE. O, my recovery shall recover all.

15 That I could now but think on some disguise
To meet 'em in, and ask 'em questions.
How I would vex 'em still at every turn!

    MOSCA. Sir, I can fit you.

    VOLPONE.   Canst thou?

20 MOSCA.   Yes, I know
One o' the commandadori, sir; so like you,
Him will I straight make drunk, and bring you
           [his habit.

    VOLPONE. A rare disguise, and answering thy
           [brain!

25 O, I will be a sharp disease unto 'em.

    MOSCA. Sir, you must look for curses—

    VOLPONE.   Till they burst;
The Fox fares ever best when he is curs'd.

30 [Exeunt.]

Scene iv

[A hall in SIR POLITIC's house.]

[Enter PEREGRINE disguised and three MER-
CATORI.]

    PEREGRINE. Am I enough disguis'd?

35 1ST MERCATORE.   I warrant you.

    PEREGRINE. All my ambition is to fright him
           [only.

    2ND MERCATORE. If you could ship him away,
           ['twere excellent.

40 3RD MERCATORE. To Zant, or to Aleppo!

    PEREGRINE.   Yes, and ha' his
Adventures put i' th' Book of Voyages,°

And his gull'd story regist'red for truth!
Well, gentlemen, when I am in awhile,
And that you think us warm in our discourse, 45
Know your approaches.

    1ST MERCATORE.   Trust it to our care.

[Exeunt MERCATORI.]

[Enter WAITING WOMAN.]

    PEREGRINE. Save you, fair lady! Is Sir Pol 50
           [within?

    WOMAN. I do not know, sir.

    PEREGRINE.   'Pray you say unto him
Here is a merchant, upon earnest business,
Desires to speak with him. 55

    WOMAN.   I will see, sir.

[Exit.]

    PEREGRINE.   'Pray you.
I see the family is all female here.

[Re-enter WAITING WOMAN.] 60

    WOMAN. He says, sir, he has weighty affairs
           [of state,
That now require him whole; some other time
You may possess him.

    PEREGRINE.   'Pray you say again, 65
If those require him whole, these will exact°
           [him,
Whereof I bring him tidings. [Exit WOMAN.]
           [What might be
His grave affair of state now! How to make 70
Bolognian sausages here in Venice, sparing
One o' th' ingredients?

[Re-enter WAITING WOMAN.]

    WOMAN.   Sir, he says he knows
By your word "tidings,"° that you are no 75
           [statesman,
And therefore wills you stay.

    PEREGRINE.   Sweet, 'pray you return him
I have not read so many proclamations,
And studied them for words, as he has done— 80
    But—here he deigns to come.

[Exit WOMAN.]

[Enter SIR POLITIC.]

    POLITIC.   Sir, I must crave
Your courteous pardon. There hath chanc'd 85
           [today

---

habit of clarissimo robes of state
doubt fear
Book of Voyages travel narratives, of which Richard
  Hakluyt's *Principal Navigations, Voyages and Dis-*
  coveries was the type

exact draw out; as opposed to *require*, which literally
  means *call back.* Peregrine is matching Sir Politic's
  Latinisms.
"tidings" (a plain English word)

Unkind disaster 'twixt my lady and me;
And I was penning my apology,
To give her satisfaction, as you came now.
    PEREGRINE. Sir, I am griev'd I bring you worse
5   [disaster.
The gentleman you met at th' port today,
That told you he was newly arriv'd—
    POLITIC.   Ay, was
A fugitive punk?°
10   PEREGRINE.   No, sir, a spy set on you;
And he has made relation to the Senate,
That you profess'd to him to have a plot
To sell the state of Venice to the Turk.
    POLITIC. O me!
15   PEREGRINE.   For which warrants are sign'd
                              [by this time,
To apprehend you, and to search your study
For papers—
    POLITIC.   Alas, sir, I have none, but notes
20 Drawn out of play-books—
    PEREGRINE.   All the better, sir.
    POLITIC. And some essays. What shall I do?
    PEREGRINE.   Sir, best
Convey yourself into a sugar-chest;
25 Or, if you could lie round, a frail were rare;°
And I could send you abroad.
    POLITIC.   Sir, I but talk'd so.
For discourse sake merely.
    [*They knock without.*]
30   PEREGRINE.   Hark! they are there.
    POLITIC. I am a wretch, a wretch!
    PEREGRINE.   What will you do, sir?
Have you ne'er a currant-butt° to leap into?
They'll put you to the rack; you must be
35   [sudden.
    POLITIC. Sir, I have an ingine—°
    3RD MERCATORE [*within*].   Sir Politic
                        [Would-be!
    2ND MERCATORE [*within*]. Where is he?
40   POLITIC.   That I've thought upon, before
                           [time.
    PEREGRINE. What is it?
    POLITIC.   I shall ne'er endure the
                      [torture.—

---

punk   prostitute
frail . . . rare   basket would be fine
currant-butt   wine cask
ingine   invention

Marry, it is, sir, of a tortoise shell,   45
Fitted for these extremities; 'pray you, sir, help
                               [me.
Here I have a place, sir, to put back my legs,
Please you to lay it on, sir [*lies down while*
PEREGRINE *places the shell upon him*], with this   50
                              [cap,
And my black gloves. I'll lie, sir, like a tortoise,
Till they are gone.
    PEREGRINE.   And call you this an ingine?
    POLITIC. Mine own device.—Good sir, bid my   55
                              [wife's women
To burn my papers.
    [*Exit* PEREGRINE.]
    [*The three* MERCATORI *rush in.*]
    1ST MERCATORE. Where's he hid?   60
    3RD MERCATORE.   We must,
And will, sure, find him.
    2ND MERCATORE.   Which is his study?
    [*Re-enter* PEREGRINE.]
    1ST MERCATORE.   What   65
Are you, sir?
    PEREGRINE.   I am a merchant, that came
                              [here
To look upon this tortoise.
    3RD MERCATORE.   How?   70
    1ST MERCATORE.   St. Mark!
What beast is this?
    PEREGRINE.   It is a fish.
    2ND MERCATORE.   Come out here!
    PEREGRINE. Nay, you may strike him, sir, and   75
                             [tread upon him;
He'll bear a cart.
    1ST MERCATORE.   What, to run over him?
    PEREGRINE.   Yes, sir.
    3RD MERCATORE. Let's jump upon him.   80
    2ND MERCATORE.   Can he not go?
    PEREGRINE.   He creeps, sir.
    1ST MERCATORE. Let's see him creep.
    PEREGRINE.   No, good sir, you will hurt
                            [him. 85
    2ND MERCATORE. Heart, I'll see him creep, or
                        [prick his guts.
    3RD MERCATORE. Come out here.
    PEREGRINE.   'Pray you, sir!—(*Aside to* SIR
                  [POLITIC.) Creep a little. 90
    1ST MERCATORE.   Forth.
    2ND MERCATORE. Yet further.
    PEREGRINE.   Good sir!—[*Aside.*] Creep!

2ND MERCATORE.   We'll see his legs.
[*They pull off the shell and discover him.*]
3RD MERCATORE. Gods so, he has garters!
1ST MERCATORE.   Ay, and gloves!
5   2ND MERCATORE.   Is this
Your fearful tortoise?
    PEREGRINE [*discovering himself*]. Now, Sir
                            [Pol, we are even;
For your next project I shall be prepar'd;
10   I am sorry for the funeral of your notes, sir.
    1ST MERCATORE. 'Twere a rare motion° to be
                            [seen in Fleet Street.
    2ND MERCATORE. Ay, i' the term.°
    1ST MERCATORE.   Or Smithfield,° in the
15   [fair.
    3RD MERCATORE. Methinks 'tis but a
                            [melancholic sight!
    PEREGRINE. Farewell, most politic tortoise.
[*Exeunt* PEREGRINE *and* MERCATORI.]
20   [*Re-enter* WAITING WOMAN.]
    POLITIC.   Where's my Lady?
Knows she of this?
    WOMAN.   I know not, sir.
    POLITIC.   Inquire.—
25   Oh, I shall be the fable of all feasts,
The freight of the gazetti,° ship-boys' tale;
And, which is worst, even talk for ordinaries.
    WOMAN. My Lady's come most melancholic
                            [home,
30   And says, sir, she will straight to sea, for
                            [physic.
    POLITIC. And I, to shun this place and clime
                            [for ever,
Creeping with house on back, and think it well
35   To shrink my poor head in my politic shell.
    [*Exeunt.*]

Scene v

[*A room in* VOLPONE'S *house.*]
[*Enter* VOLPONE *and* MOSCA, *the first in the
habit of a commandadore, the other of a claris-*
40   *simo.*]

VOLPONE. Am I then like him?
    MOSCA.   O, sir, you are he;
No man can sever you.
    VOLPONE.   Good.
    MOSCA.   But what am I?   45
    VOLPONE. 'Fore Heav'n, a brave clarissimo;
                            [thou becom'st it!
Pity thou wert not born one.
    MOSCA.   If I hold
My made one, 'twill be well.   50
    VOLPONE.   I'll go and see
What news first at the court.
    [*Exit.*]
    MOSCA.   Do so.—My Fox
Is out on his hole, and ere he shall re-enter,   55
I'll make him languish in his borrow'd case,°
Except he come to composition° with me.—
Androgyno, Castrone, Nano!
    [*Enter* ANDROGYNO, CASTRONE, *and* NANO.]
    ALL.   Here.   60
    MOSCA. Go, recreate yourselves abroad; go,
                            [sport.—
[*Exeunt all but* MOSCA.]
So, now I have the keys, and am possess'd.
Since he will needs be dead afore his time,   65
I'll bury him, or gain by him. I am his heir,
And so will keep me, till he share, at least.
To cozen him of all, were but a cheat
Well plac'd; no man would construe it a sin;
Let his sport pay for 't. This is call'd the Fox-   70
                            [trap.
    [*Exit.*]

Scene vi

[*A street.*]
[*Enter* CORBACCIO *and* CORVINO.]
    CORBACCIO. They say the court is set.   75
    CORVINO.   We must maintain
Our first tale good, for both our reputations.
    CORBACCIO. Why, mine's no tale, my son
                            [would there have kill'd me.
    CORVINO. That's true; I had forgot;—[*aside*]   80
                            [mine is, I am sure.—
But for your will, sir.
    CORBACCIO.   Ay, I'll come upon him

---

motion show
term when prisoners from the Fleet prison were led
  to trial
Smithfield London market, site of the great annual fair
The . . . gazetti grist for the gossip-sheets

case skin
composition terms

For that hereafter, now his patron's dead.
[*Enter* VOLPONE *disguised*.]
VOLPONE. Signior Corvino! and Corbaccio!
[sir,
5 Much joy unto you.
    CORVINO.   Of what?
    VOLPONE.   The sudden good
Dropp'd down upon you—
    CORBACCIO.   Where?
10   VOLPONE.   And none knows how—
From old Volpone, sir.
    CORBACCIO.   Out, errant knave!
VOLPONE. Let not your too much wealth, sir,
[make you furious.
15 CORBACCIO. Away, thou varlet.
    VOLPONE.   Why, sir?
    CORBACCIO.   Dost thou mock me?
VOLPONE. You mock the world, sir; did you
[not change wills?
20 CORBACCIO. Out, harlot.
    VOLPONE.   O! belike you are the man,
Signior Corvino? Faith, you carry it well;
You grow not mad withal; I love your spirit.
You are not overleaven'd with your fortune.
25 You should ha' some would swell now like a
[wine-vat,
With such an autumn.—Did he gi' you all, sir?
    CORVINO. Avoid, you rascal.
    VOLPONE.   Troth, your wife has shown
30 Herself a very woman; but you are well,
You need not care, you have a good estate,
To bear it out, sir, better by this chance—
Except Corbaccio have a share.
    CORBACCIO.   Hence, varlet.
35 VOLPONE. You will not be acknown, sir; why,
['tis wise.
Thus do all gamesters, at all games, dissemble:
No man will seem to win.
    [*Exeunt* CORVINO *and* CORBACCIO.]
40   Here comes my vulture,
Heaving his beak up i' the air, and snuffing.

Scene vii

[*Enter* VOLTORE.]
VOLTORE. Outstripp'd thus, by a parasite! a
[slave!
45 Would run on errands, and make legs for
[crumbs!

Well, what I'll do—
    VOLPONE.   The court stays for your
[Worship.
I e'en rejoice, sir, at your Worship's happiness, 50
And that it fell into so learned hands,
That understand the fingering—
    VOLTORE.   What do you mean?
VOLPONE. I mean to be a suitor to your
[Worship, 55
For the small tenement, out of reparations,
That at the end of your long row of houses,
By the Piscaria;° it was, in Volpone's time,
Your predecessor, ere he grew diseas'd,
A handsome, pretty, custom'd° bawdyhouse 60
As any was in Venice, none disprais'd;
But fell with him: his body and that house
Decay'd together.
    VOLTORE.   Come, sir, leave your prating.
    VOLPONE. Why, if your Worship give me but 65
[your hand
That I may ha' the refusal,° I have done.
'Tis a mere toy to you, sir, candle-rents;°
As your learn'd Worship knows—
    VOLTORE.   What do I know? 70
VOLPONE. Marry, no end of your wrath, sir;
[God decrease it!
VOLTORE. Mistaking knave! what, mock'st
[thou my misfortune?
[*Exit*.] 75
VOLPONE. His blessing on your heart, sir;
[would 'twere more!—
Now to my first again, at the next corner.
[*Exit*.]

Scene viii

[*Another corner of the street*.] 80
[*Enter* CORBACCIO *and* CORVINO, MOSCA *passant*.]
    CORBACCIO. See, in our habit! see the
[impudent varlet!
    CORVINO. That I could shoot mine eyes at 85
[him, like gun-stones.°

Piscaria fishmarket
custom'd well patronized
refusal option
candle-rents small change
gun-stones cannon balls

[*Enter* VOLPONE.]
VOLPONE. But is this true, sir, of the parasite?
CORBACCIO. Again, t' afflict us? monster!
VOLPONE.   In good faith, sir,
5 I am heartily griev'd, a beard of your grave
                              [length
Should be so overreach'd. I never brook'd
That parasite's hair; methought his nose should
                              [cozen:
10 There still was somewhat in his look, did
                              [promise
The bane of a clarissimo.
     CORBACCIO.   Knave—
     VOLPONE.   Methinks
15 Yet you, that are so traded i' the world,
A witty merchant, the fine bird, Corvino,
That have such moral emblems on your name,
Should not have sung° your shame, and
                              [dropp'd your cheese,
20 To let the Fox laugh at your emptiness.
     CORVINO. Sirrah, you think the privilege of
                              [the place,
And your red saucy cap, that seems to me
Nail'd to your jolt-head° with those two
25   [cecchines,°
Can warrant your abuses; come you hither;
You shall perceive, sir, I dare beat you;
                              [approach.
     VOLPONE. No haste, sir, I do know your valor
30   [well,
Since you durst publish what you are, sir.
     CORBACCIO.   Tarry,
I'd speak with you.
     VOLPONE.   Sir, sir, another time—
35   CORVINO. Nay, now.
     VOLPONE.   O God, sir! I were a wise man,
Would stand the fury of a distracted cuckold.
[MOSCA *walks by 'em.*]
     CORBACCIO. What, come again!
40   VOLPONE.   Upon 'em, Mosca; save me.
     CORBACCIO. The air's infected where he
                              [breathes.
     CORVINO.   Let's fly him.
[*Exeunt* CORVINO *and* CORBACCIO.]

VOLPONE. Excellent basilisk!° turn upon the 45
                              [Vulture.

Scene ix

[*Enter* VOLTORE.]
VOLTORE. Well, flesh-fly, it is summer with
                              [you now;
Your winter will come on.   50
     MOSCA.   Good advocate,
'Pray thee not rail, nor threaten out of place
                              [thus;
Thou 'lt make a solecism, as Madam says.
Get you a biggin more;° your brain breaks 55
                              [loose.
[*Exit.*]
VOLTORE. Well, sir.
     VOLPONE.   Would you ha' me beat the
                              [insolent slave? 60
Throw dirt upon his first good clothes?
     VOLTORE.   This same
Is doubtless some familiar!°
     VOLPONE.   Sir, the court,
In troth, stays for you. I am mad, a mule 65
That never read Justinian should get up
And ride an advocate. Had you no quirk
To avoid gullage, sir, by such a creature?
I hope you do but jest; he has not done 't;
This 's but confederacy to blind the rest.   70
You are the heir?
     VOLTORE.   A strange, officious,
Troublesome knave! Thou dost torment me.
     VOLPONE.   I know—
It cannot be, sir, that you should be cozen'd; 75
'Tis not within the wit of man to do it;
You are so wise, so prudent; and 'tis fit
That wealth and wisdom still should go
                              [together.
[*Exeunt.*]   80

Scene x

[*The Senate House.*]
[*Enter four* AVOCATORI, NOTARIO, BONARIO,
CELIA, CORBACCIO, CORVINO, COMMANDADORI,

---

sung like the crow whom the fox flattered in Aesop's
   fable
jolt-head blockhead   **cecchines** gold buttons

basilisk mythical serpent whose breath or look could
   kill
biggin more larger cap
familiar demon to tempt me

Saffi, *etc.*]

1st Avocatore. Are all the parties here?

Notario.   All but the advocate.

2nd Avocatore. And here he comes.

5 [*Enter* Voltore *and* Volpone.]

1st Avocatore.   Then bring 'em forth to
[sentence.

Voltore. O, my most honor'd fathers, let
[your mercy

10 Once win upon your justice, to forgive—
I am distracted—

Volpone [*aside*].   What will he do now?

Voltore.   Oh,
I know not which t' address myself to first;

15 Whether your Fatherhoods, or these
[innocents—

Corvino [*aside*]. Will he betray himself?

Voltore.   Whom equally
I have abus'd, out of most covetous ends—

20 Corvino. The man is mad!

Corbaccio.   What's that?

Corvino.   He is possess'd.°

Voltore. For which, now struck in
[conscience, here I prostrate

25 Myself at your offended feet, for pardon.

1st, 2nd Avocatori. Arise.

Celia.   O Heav'n, how just thou art!

Volpone.   I am caught
I' mine own noose—

30 Corvino [*to* Corbaccio]. Be constant, sir;
[naught now
Can help but impudence.°

1st Avocatore.   Speak forward.

Commandadore.   Silence!

35 Voltore. It is not passion in me, reverend
[fathers,
But only conscience, conscience, my good sires,
That makes me now tell truth. That parasite,
That knave, hath been the instrument of all.

40 1st Avocatore. Where is that knave? Fetch
[him.

Volpone.   I go.

[*Exit*.]

Corvino.   Grave fathers,

45 This man's distracted; he confess'd it now:

For, hoping to be old Volpone's heir,
Who now is dead—

3rd Avocatore.   How?

2nd Avocatore.   Is Volpone dead?

Corvino. Dead since, grave fathers.   50

Bonario.   O sure vengeance!

1st Avocatore.   Stay;
Then he was no deceiver?

Voltore.   Oh, no, none.
This parasite, grave fathers—   55

Corvino.   He does speak
Out of mere envy, 'cause the servant's made
The thing he gap'd for. Please your
[Fatherhoods,
This is the truth, though I'll not justify   60
The other, but he may be somedeal faulty.°

Voltore. Ay, to your hopes, as well as mine,
[Corvino;
But I'll use modesty.° Pleaseth your Wisdoms
To view these certain notes, and but confer°   65
[them;
As I hope favor, they shall speak clear truth.

Corvino. The Devil has ent'red him!

Bonario.   Or bides in you.

4th Avocatore. We have done ill, by a   70
[public officer
To send for him, if he be heir.

2nd Avocatore.   For whom?

4th Avocatore. Him that they call the
[parasite.   75

3rd Avocatore.   'Tis true,
He is a man of great estate, now left.

4th Avocatore. Go you, and learn his
[name, and say the court
Entreats his presence here, but to the clearing   80
Of some few doubts.

[*Exit* Notario.]

2nd Avocatore. This same's a labyrinth!

1st Avocatore. Stand you unto your first
[report?   85

Corvino.   My state,
My life, my fame—

Bonario.   Where is 't?

---

justify . . . faulty   guarantee that Mosca is not somewhat deceitful

modesty   moderation

confer   compare

possess'd   i.e., by a demon

impudence   sheer audacity

CORVINO.   Are at the stake.
1ST AVOCATORE. Is yours so too?
CORBACCIO.   The advocate's a knave,
And has a forked tongue—
5   2ND AVOCATORE.   Speak to the point.
CORBACCIO. So is the parasite too.
1ST AVOCATORE.   This is confusion.
VOLTORE. I do beseech your Fatherhoods,
                                      [read but those—
10   [*Giving them papers.*]
CORVINO. And credit nothing the false spirit
                                      [hath writ:
It cannot be but he's possess'd, grave fathers.
[*The scene closes.*]

Scene xi

15   [*A street.*]
[*Enter* VOLPONE.]
VOLPONE. To make a snare for mine own
                                      [neck, and run
My head into it, wilfully! with laughter!
20   When I had newly 'scap'd, was free and clear!
Out of mere wantonness! Oh, the dull devil
Was in this brain of mine when I devis'd it,
And Mosca gave it second; he must now
Help to sear up this vein, or we bleed dead.
25   [*Enter* NANO, ANDROGYNO, *and* CASTRONE.]
How now! Who let you loose? Whither go you
                                      [now?
What, to buy gingerbread, or to drown kitlings?
NANO. Sir, Master Mosca call'd us out of
30   [doors,
And bid us all go play, and took the keys.
ANDROGYNO. Yes.
VOLPONE. Did Master Mosca take the keys?
                                      [Why so!
35   I'm farther in. These are my fine conceits!°
I must be merry, with a mischief to me!
What a vile wretch was I, that could not bear
My fortune soberly? I must° ha' my crotchets,°
And my conundrums!—Well, go you, and seek
40   [him;
His meaning may be truer than my fear.
Bid him he straight come to me to the court;

conceits **fancy devices**
must had to
crotchets little eccentricities

Thither will I, and, if 't be possible,
Unscrew my advocate, upon new hopes.
When I provok'd him, then I lost myself.   45
[*Exeunt.*]

Scene xii

[*The Senate House.*]
[*AVOCATORI, etc., are discovered, as before.*]
1ST AVOCATORE. These things can ne'er be
                                      [reconcil'd. He here   50
[*Shows the papers.*]
Professeth that the gentleman was wrong'd,
And that the gentlewoman was brought thither,
Forc'd by her husband, and there left.
VOLTORE.   Most true.   55
CELIA. How ready is Heav'n to those that
                                      [pray!
1ST AVOCATORE.   But that
Volpone would have ravish'd her, he holds
Utterly false, knowing his impotence.   60
CORVINO. Grave fathers, he is possess'd;
                                      [again, I say,
Possess'd; nay, if there be possession,
And obsession, he has both.
3RD AVOCATORE.   Here comes our officer.   65
[*Enter* VOLPONE.]
VOLPONE. The parasite will straight be here,
                                      [grave fathers.
4TH AVOCATORE. You might invent some
                                      [other name, Sir Varlet.   70
3RD AVOCATORE. Did not the notary meet
                                      [him?
VOLPONE.   Not that I know.
4TH AVOCATORE. His coming will clear all.
2ND AVOCATORE.   Yet it is misty.   75
VOLTORE. May 't please your Fatherhoods—
VOLPONE [*whispers to the* ADVOCATE]. Sir, the
                                      [parasite
Will'd me to tell you that his master lives;
That you are still the man; your hopes the   80
                                      [same;
And this was only a jest—
VOLTORE.   How?
VOLPONE.   Sir, to try
If you were firm, and how you stood affected.   85
VOLTORE. Art sure he lives?
VOLPONE.   Do I live, sir?
VOLTORE.   O me!

I was too violent.
    VOLPONE.   Sir, you may redeem it.
They said you were possess'd; fall down, and
                    [seem so:
5 I'll help to make it good. [VOLTORE *falls.*] God
                    [bless the man!—
[*Aside to* VOLTORE.] Stop your wind hard, and
                  [swell.—See, see, see, see!
He vomits crooked pins!° His eyes are set,
10 Like a dead hare's hung in a poulter's shop!
His mouth's running away! Do you see,
                  [signior?
Now it is in his belly.
    CORVINO.   Ay, the devil!
15 VOLPONE. Now in his throat.
    CORVINO.   Ay, I perceive it plain.
VOLPONE. 'Twill out, 'twill out! stand clear.
                [See where it flies!
In shape of a blue toad, with a bat's wings!
20 Do not you see it, sir?
    CORBACCIO.   What? I think I do.
CORVINO. 'Tis too manifest.
    VOLPONE.   Look! he comes t' himself!
VOLTORE. Where am I?
25 VOLPONE.   Take good heart, the worst is
                [past, sir.
You're dispossess'd.
    1ST AVOCATORE. What accident is this?
    2ND AVOCATORE. Sudden and full of wonder!
30 3RD AVOCATORE.   If he were
Possess'd, as it appears, all this is nothing.
    CORVINO. He has been often subject to these
              [fits.
35 1ST AVOCATORE. Show him that writing:—do
              [you know it, sir?
VOLPONE [*aside to* VOLTORE]. Deny it, sir,
              [forswear it; know it not.
VOLTORE. Yes, I do know it well: it is my
              [hand;
40 But all that it contains is false.
    BONARIO.   O practice!
    2ND AVOCATORE. What maze is this!
    1ST AVOCATORE.   Is he not guilty then,
Whom you there name the parasite?
45 VOLTORE.   Grave fathers,
No more than his good patron, old Volpone.

crooked pins indicating demonic possession

4TH AVOCATORE. Why, he is dead.
    VOLTORE.   O no, my honor'd fathers.
He lives—
    1ST AVOCATORE.   How! lives? 50
VOLTORE.   Lives.
    2ND AVOCATORE.   This is subtler yet!
3RD AVOCATORE. You said he was dead!
    VOLTORE.   Never.
3RD AVOCATORE.   You said so! 55
CORVINO.   I heard so.
4TH AVOCATORE. Here comes the gentleman;
              [make him way.
[*Enter* MOSCA.]
3RD AVOCATORE.   A stool. 60
4TH AVOCATORE [*aside*]. A proper man! and,
              [Volpone dead,
A fit match for my daughter.
    3RD AVOCATORE.   Give him way.
VOLPONE [*aside to* MOSCA]. Mosca, I was 65
            [a'most lost: the advocate
Had betray'd all; but now it is recover'd;
All's on the hinge again—say I am living.
    MOSCA. What busy knave is this?—Most
            [reverend fathers, 70
I sooner had attended your grave pleasures,
But that my order for the funeral
Of my dear patron did require me—
    VOLPONE [*aside*].   Mosca!
MOSCA. Whom I intend to bury like a 75
            [gentleman.
VOLPONE [*aside*]. Ay, quick, and cozen me of
            [all.
2ND AVOCATORE.   Still stranger!
More intricate! 80
    1ST AVOCATORE.   And come about again!
4TH AVOCATORE [*aside*]. It is a match; my
            [daughter is bestow'd.
MOSCA [*aside to* VOLPONE]. Will you gi' me
            [half? 85
VOLPONE [*aside*].   First I'll be hanged.
MOSCA [*aside*]. I know
Your voice is good; cry not so loud.
    1ST AVOCATORE.   Demand
The advocate.—Sir, did not you affirm 90
Volpone was alive?
    VOLPONE.   Yes, and he is;
This gent'man told me so.—[*Aside to* MOSCA.]
            [Thou shalt have half.

MOSCA. Whose drunkard is this same? Speak,
               [some that know him;
I never saw his face.—[*Aside to* VOLPONE.] I
               [cannot now
5 Afford it you so cheap.
    VOLPONE [*aside*].   No?
    1ST AVOCATORE.   What say you?
    VOLTORE. The officer told me.
    VOLPONE.   I did, grave fathers,
10 And will maintain he lives, with mine own life,
And that this creature [*pointing to* MOSCA] told
             [me.—(*Aside.*) I was born
With all good stars my enemies.
    MOSCA.   Most grave fathers,
15 If such an insolence as this must pass
Upon me, I am silent; 'twas not this
For which you sent, I hope.
    2ND AVOCATORE.   Take him away.
    VOLPONE. Mosca!
20   3RD AVOCATORE. Let him be whipp'd.
    VOLPONE [*aside to* MOSCA].   Wilt thou
             [betray me?
Cozen me?
    3RD AVOCATORE.   And taught to bear
25   [himself
Toward a person of his rank.
    4TH AVOCATORE.   Away.
    MOSCA. I humbly thank your Fatherhoods.
    VOLPONE.   Soft, soft;—[*aside*] whipp'd!
30 And lose all that I have! If I confess,
It cannot be much more.
    4TH AVOCATORE.   Sir, are you married?
    VOLPONE. They'll be alli'd anon; I must be
             [resolute;
35 The Fox shall here uncase. (*He puts off his*
             [*disguise.*)
    MOSCA [*aside*].   Patron!
    VOLPONE.   Nay, now
My ruins shall not come alone; your match
40 I'll hinder sure; my substance shall not glue
             [you,
Nor screw you into a family.
    MOSCA [*aside*].   Why, patron!
    VOLPONE. I am Volpone, and this (*pointing*
45   [*to* MOSCA) is my knave;
This [*to* VOLTORE], his own knave; this (*to*
             [CORBACCIO), avarice's fool;
This [*to* CORVINO], a chimaera of wittol, fool,

             [and knave:
And, reverend fathers, since we all can hope   50
Naught but a sentence, let's not now despair it.
You hear me brief.
    CORVINO.   May it please your
             [Fatherhoods—
    COMMANDADORE.   Silence.   55
    1ST AVOCATORE. The knot is now undone, by
             [miracle!
    2ND AVOCATORE. Nothing can be more clear.
    3RD AVOCATORE.   Or can more prove
These innocent.   60
    1ST AVOCATORE.   Give 'em their liberty.
    BONARIO. Heaven could not long let such
             [gross crimes be hid.
    2ND AVOCATORE. If this be held the highway
             [to get riches, 65
May I be poor.
    3RD AVOCATORE. This 's not the gain, but
             [torment.
    1ST AVOCATORE. These possess wealth, as sick
             [men possess fevers, 70
Which trulier may be said to possess them.
    2ND AVOCATORE. Disrobe that parasite.
    CORVINO and MOSCA.   Most honor'd
             [fathers—
    1ST AVOCATORE. Can you plead aught to stay 75
             [the course of justice?
If you can, speak.
    CORVINO and VOLTORE. We beg favor.
    CELIA.   And mercy.
    1ST AVOCATORE. You hurt your innocence, 80
             [suing for the guilty.
Stand forth; and, first, the parasite. You appear
T' have been the chiefest minister, if not plotter,
In all these lewd impostures, and now, lastly,
Have with your impudence abus'd the court, 85
And habit of a gentleman of Venice,
Being a fellow of no birth or blood;
For which our sentence is, first, thou be
             [whipp'd;
Then live perpetual prisoner in our galleys. 90
    VOLPONE. I thank you for him.
    MOSCA.   Bane to thy wolfish nature!
    1ST AVOCATORE. Deliver him to the saffi.—
             [Thou, Volpone,
By blood and rank a gentleman, canst not fall 95
Under like censure; but our judgment on thee

Is that thy substance all be straight confiscate
To the hospital of the Incurabili.
And since the most was gotten by imposture,
By feigning lame, gout, palsy, and such
5   [diseases,
Thou art to lie in prison, cramp'd with irons,
Till thou be'st sick and lame indeed.—Remove
                                    [him.
    VOLPONE. This is called mortifying of a Fox.
10   1ST AVOCATORE. Thou, Voltore, to take away
                               [the scandal
Thou hast giv'n all worthy men of thy
                               [profession,
Art banish'd from their fellowship, and our
15   [state.—
Corbaccio!—Bring him near.—We here possess
Thy son of all thy state, and confine thee
To the monastery of San' Spirito;
Where, since thou knew'st not how to live well
20   [here,
Thou shalt be learn'd to die well.
    CORBACCIO   Ha! what said he?
    COMMANDADORE. You shall know anon, sir.
    1ST AVOCATORE.   Thou, Corvino, shalt
25 Be straight embark'd from thine own house,
                             [and row'd
Round about Venice, through the Grand Canal,
Wearing a cap, with fair long ass's ears,
Instead of horns; and so to mount, a paper
30 Pinn'd on thy breast, to the Berlina.°
    CORVINO.   Yes,
And mine eyes beat out with stinking fish,
Bruis'd fruit, and rotten eggs—'tis well. I am
                                [glad
35 I shall not see my shame yet.
    1ST AVOCATORE.   And to expiate
Thy wrongs done to thy wife, thou are to send
                                [her
Home to her father, with her dowry trebled;
40 And these are all your judgments.°
    ALL.   Honor'd fathers—
    1ST AVOCATORE. Which may not be revok'd.
                        [Now you begin,
When crimes are done and past, and to be
45   [punish'd,

To think what your crimes are.—Away with
                            [them!
Let all that see these vices thus rewarded,
Take heart, and love to study 'em. Mischiefs
                            [feed 50
Like beasts, till they be fat, and then they bleed.
    [*Exeunt.*]
                VOLPONE
The seasoning of a play is the applause.
Now, though the Fox be punish'd by the laws, 55
He yet doth hope, there is no suff'ring due,
For any fact which he hath done 'gainst you;
If there be, censure him; here he doubtful
                            [stands.
If not, fare jovially, and clap your hands. 60
    [*Exit.*]

Berlina pillory
judgments sentences

John Webster

1580?–1625?

The Duchess of Malfi

1613

The structure of *The Duchess of Malfi* is somewhat problematical, for Webster's attention is divided between the Duchess, who is the tragic protagonist and the principal focus of our admiration, and Daniel de Bosola, a partly choric figure, who stands at the center of the action and effectuates it while supplying also a running commentary on it. The play remains coherent in theme, nevertheless, for the malice and terror that Bosola and the Calabrian brothers unleash on the Duchess become part of a single fearful visitation that destroys first its chosen victims and at length its agents.

The three antagonists are clearly differentiated from one another even though they pose a single collective threat to the Duchess and her consort. The Duchess's elder brother, the Cardinal, is coldly diabolical, a true Machiavellian. It is he who first proposes that Bosola be retained in the Duchess's household as a spy; it is by his secret instigation that she is finally murdered. Her twin brother Ferdinand, being passionate rather than cold, demonic rather than diabolical, enters more openly into the schemes against her. An aristocratic pride —coupled, one supposes, with incestuous jealousy—compels him to oppose any marriage she might make with one of her subjects and to punish her when she does marry. Bosola (a type already familiar on the seventeenth-century stage) is a cynic and malcontent, preserving a critical detachment in desperate circumstances and amid competing claims. Presiding efficiently over the Duchess's persecution, he apparently experiences genuine compunction thereafter, but it is his nature to resist commitments of every sort.

It is impossible further to distinguish the purposes of the villains, because we seldom see them actually plotting. And indeed the violence and treachery that engulf the Duchess, being sudden, bizarre, and often wholly unaccountable, seem to emanate from some principle of malignity ulterior to its agents. A steady descant on corruption

JOHN WEBSTER

and disorder of every sort adds to the sense of universal evil at work: throughout, there are images of disease and decay, parasitism and predation, and general hopelessness. "Didst thou ever see a lark in a cage?" Bosola asks the Duchess in an oblique comment on her own condition. "Such is the soul in the body; this world is like her little turf of grass, and the Heaven o'er our heads, like her looking-glass, only gives us a miserable knowledge of the small compass of our prison."

Such, certainly, is the Duchess's situation after she is separated from her strangely passive consort and confined in her own palace. While Ferdinand lurks behind the scene, Bosola tests the limits of her psychic endurance—in a manner suggestive of the experiments of Nazi scientists on their helpless prisoners. "Who am I?" she asks him when he enters disguised as an old man. (He is, she must suppose, one of the madmen who have been released in the palace.) "Thou art a box of worm-seed," he answers. She presses her point: "Am I not thy duchess?" He refuses still to acknowledge her.

She shares, perceptibly, the pride and willfulness of her brother Ferdinand; she has been "fortified with a strange disdain" in her travail up to this point. But the threat to her ducal authority has now become a threat to her very sanity. When she asserts, "I am Duchess of Malfi still," she is affirming less her title than her own self-possession, which she retains even after the executioners enter. A sovereign still, she gives orders concerning her own strangulation: "Pull, and pull strongly," she tells the anonymous hooded figures, "for your able strength Must pull down Heaven upon me." After her death, Ferdinand enters; gazing on the sister he had sworn never to see again, he speaks the celebrated line, "Cover her face! Mine eyes dazzle: she died young." She becomes, in the poetic imagery, a single bright spot in the surrounding dark.

The antagonists are left in control of Malfi, their power seemingly impregnable, and Webster must devote the entire fifth act to disposing of them. This act succeeds (where it does not fail) because the fate of the surviving characters is independently interesting and because Webster's conception of what will inevitably happen when dissimulation has destroyed all human trust is both logically and poetically satisfying. The Duchess, haunting the consciences of Bosola and Ferdinand and showing her husband "a face folded in sorrow," remains a mildly importunate presence until the end.

This diffuse and richly textured play devolves in its later scenes into theatricality and never fully recovers from the too-early death of its protagonist. Yet Webster's vision of an unshakable poise is in the grand tradition of Elizabethan humanism and redeems his work from a measure of excess and disarray.

The Duchess
of Malfi

WEBSTER

CHARACTERS

FERDINAND   *Duke of Calabria*
THE CARDINAL   *his Brother*
ANTONIO BOLOGNA   *Steward of the household
  to the Duchess*
DELIO   *his Friend*
DANIEL DE BOSOLA   *Gentleman of the horse
  to the Duchess*
CASTRUCCIO
MARQUIS OF PESCARA
COUNT MALATESTE
RODERIGO
SILVIO
GRISOLAN
DOCTOR
Several Madmen, Pilgrims, Executioners,
  Officers, Attendants, etc.
DUCHESS OF MALFI
CARIOLA   *her Woman*
JULIA   *Castruccio's Wife, and the Cardinal's
  Mistress*
Old Lady, Ladies, and Children

SCENE. *Malfi, Rome, and Milan.*

ACT I

Scene i

[*The presence-chamber in the* DUCHESS'
palace at Malfi.]
[*Enter* ANTONIO *and* DELIO.]
5   DELIO. You are welcome to your country, dear
                                        [Antonio;
You have been long in France, and you return

A very formal Frenchman in your habit.
How do you like the French court?
     ANT. I admire it.   10
In seeking to reduce both state and people
To a fixed order, their judicious king
Begins at home, quits° first his royal palace
Of flattering sycophants, of dissolute
And infamous persons,—which he sweetly   15
                                        [terms
His master's masterpiece, the work of Heaven,
Considering duly that a prince's court
Is like a common fountain, whence should
                                        [flow 20
Pure silver drops in general,° but if't chance
Some cursed example poison't near the head,
Death and diseases through the whole land
                                        [spread.
And what is't makes this blessèd government   25
But a most provident council, who dare freely
Inform him the corruption of the times?
Though some o' the court hold it presumption
To instruct princes what they ought to do,
It is a noble duty to inform them   30
What they ought to foresee.—Here comes
                                        [Bosola,
The only court gall;° yet I observe his railing
Is not for simple love of piety.
Indeed, he rails at those things which he wants, 35
Would be as lecherous, covetous, or proud,
Bloody, or envious, as any man,
If he had means to be so.—Here's the cardinal.
     [*Enter the* CARDINAL *and* BOSOLA.]
     Bos. I do haunt you still.   40
     CARD. So.
     Bos. I have done you better service than to
be slighted thus. Miserable age, where only the
reward° of doing well is the doing of it!
     CARD. You enforce your merit too much.   45
     Bos. I fell into the galleys in your service;
where, for two years together, I wore two
towels instead of a shirt, with a knot on the
shoulder, after the fashion of a Roman mantle.
Slighted thus! I will thrive some way: black- 50

---

quits rids
in general for all
gall sore
only the reward the only reward

birds fatten best in hard weather; why not I in these dog days?°

CARD. Would you could become honest!

Bos. With all your divinity do but direct me
5 the way to it. I have known many travel far for it, and yet return as arrant knaves as they went forth, because they carried themselves always along with them. [*Exit* CARDINAL.] Are you gone? Some fellows, they say, are possessed
10 with the devil, but this great fellow were able to possess the greatest devil, and make him worse.

ANT. He hath denied thee some suit?

Bos. He and his brother are like plum-trees
15 that grow crooked over standing-pools; they are rich and o'er-laden with fruit, but none but crows, pies, and caterpillars feed on them. Could I be one of their flattering panders, I would hang on their ears like a horseleech, till
20 I were full, and then drop off. I pray, leave me. Who would rely upon these miserable dependencies, in expectation to be advanced tomorrow? What creature ever fed worse than hoping Tantalus?° Nor ever died any man more fear-
25 fully than he had hoped for a pardon. There are rewards for hawks and dogs when they have done us service; but for a soldier that hazards his limbs in a battle, nothing but a kind of geometry is his last supportation.

30 DELIO. Geometry?

Bos. Ay, to hang in a fair pair of slings, take his latter swing in the world upon an honorable pair of crutches, from hospital to hospital. Fare ye well, sir. And yet do not you scorn us; for
35 places in the court are but like beds in the hospital, where this man's head lies at that man's foot, and so lower and lower.

[*Exit.*]

DELIO. I knew this fellow seven years in the
[galleys
40 For a notorious murder; and 'twas thought The cardinal suborned it. He was released By the French general, Gaston de Foix,°

When he recovered Naples.

ANT. 'Tis great pity   45
He should be thus neglected. I have heard
He's very valiant. This foul melancholy
Will poison all his goodness; for, I'll tell you,
If too immoderate sleep be truly said
To be an inward rust unto the soul,   50
It then doth follow want of action
Breeds all black malcontents; and their close
[rearing,
Like moths in cloth, do hurt for want of
[wearing.° 55
DELIO. The presence 'gins° to fill: you
[promised me
To make me the partaker of the natures
Of some of your great courtiers.

ANT. The lord cardinal's,   60
And other strangers' that are now in court?
I shall.—Here comes the great Calabrian duke.

[*Enter* FERDINAND, CASTRUCCIO, SILVIO, ROD-
ERIGO, GRISOLAN, *and* ATTENDANTS.]

FERD. Who took the ring° oftenest?   65
SIL. Antonio Bologna, my lord.
FERD. Our sister duchess' great master of her household? Give him the jewel.—When shall we leave this sportive action, and fall to action indeed?   70
CAST. Methinks, my lord, you should not desire to go to war in person.
FERD. Now for some gravity:—Why, my lord?
CAST. It is fitting a soldier arise to be a prince,   75
but not necessary a prince descend to be a captain.
FERD. No?
CAST. No, my lord; he were far better do it by a deputy.   80
FERD. Why should he not as well sleep or eat by a deputy? This might take idle, offensive, and base office from him, whereas the other deprives him of honor.
CAST. Believe my experience: that realm is   85
never long in quiet where the ruler is a soldier.

---

dog days evil times
Tantalus from whom, in Hades, the fruit for which he reached forever receded
Gaston de Foix a brilliant military leader (1489–1512), who did not, however, assist in the recapture of Naples in 1501

and . . . wearing i.e., discontents, being reared in confinement, do the more harm, like moths in clothing that is not worn
presence 'gins presence-chamber begins
took the ring bore away a suspended ring on the point of his lance (a test of military horsemanship)

FERD. Thou toldest me thy wife could not endure fighting.

CAST. True, my lord.

FERD. And of a jest she broke° of a captain
5 she met full of wounds: I have forgot it.

CAST. She told him, my lord, he was a pitiful fellow, to lie, like the children of Ishmael, all in tents.°

FERD. Why, there's a wit were able to undo
10 all the surgeons o' the city; for although gallants should quarrel, and had drawn their weapons, and were ready to go to it, yet her persuasions would make them put up.

CAST. That she would, my lord.—How do
15 you like my Spanish gennet?°

ROD. He is all fire.

FERD. I am of Pliny's opinion, I think he was begot by the wind;° he runs as if he were ballasted with quicksilver.

20 SILVIO. True, my lord, he reels from the tilt° often.

ROD. GRIS. Ha, ha, ha!

FERD. Why do you laugh? Methinks you that are courtiers should be my touchwood, take fire
25 when I give fire; that is, laugh but when I laugh, were the subject never so witty.

CAST. True, my lord: I myself have heard a very good jest, and have scorned to seem to have so silly a wit as to understand it.

30 FERD. But I can laugh at your fool,° my lord.

CAST. He cannot speak, you know, but he makes faces? My lady cannot abide him.

FERD. No?

CAST. Nor endure to be in merry company;
35 for she says too much laughing and too much company fills her too full of the wrinkle.

FERD. I would, then, have a mathematical instrument made for her face, that she might not laugh out of compass.°—I shall shortly visit

you at Milan, Lord Silvio. 40

SILVIO. Your grace shall arrive most welcome.

FERD. You are a good horseman, Antonio: you have excellent riders in France. What do you think of good horsemanship?

ANT. Nobly, my lord: as out of the Grecian 45
horse° issued many famous princes, so out of brave horsemanship arise the first sparks of growing resolution, that raise the mind to noble action.

FERD. You have bespoke it worthily. 50

SILVIO. Your brother, the lord cardinal, and sister duchess.

[*Re-enter* CARDINAL, *with* DUCHESS, CARIOLA, *and* JULIA.]

CARD. Are the galleys come about? 55

GRIS. They are, my lord.

FERD. Here's the Lord Silvio is come to take his leave.

DELIO. Now, sir, your promise. What's that
[cardinal? 60
I mean his temper? They say he's a brave°
[fellow,
Will play his five thousand crowns at tennis,
[dance,
Court ladies, and one that hath fought single 65
[combats.

ANT. Some such flashes superficially hang on him for form; but observe his inward character: he is a melancholy churchman. The spring in his face is nothing but the engendering of 70 toads; where he is jealous of any man, he lays worse plots for them than ever was imposed on Hercules, for he strews in his way flatterers, panders, intelligencers, atheists, and a thousand such political monsters. He should have been 75 Pope; but instead of coming to it by the primitive decency of the church, he did bestow bribes so largely and so impudently as if he would have carried it away without Heaven's knowledge. Some good he hath done— 80

DELIO. You have given too much of him.
[What's his brother?

ANT. The duke there? A most perverse and
[turbulent nature.
What appears in him mirth is merely outside; 85

---

broke told
in tents in surgical dressings (a pun). The children of Abraham's son Ishmael (the Arabians) live in nomads' tents.
gennet a light fast horse
by the wind the Roman naturalist Pliny records that mares can be so impregnated
the tilt the impact of jousting
fool household jester
out of compass beyond measure

Grecian horse i.e., the Trojan horse
brave dashing

If he laugh heartily, it is to laugh
All honesty out of fashion.
    DELIO. Twins?
    ANT. In quality.
5 He speaks with others' tongues, and hears
                 [men's suits
With others' ears; will seem to sleep o' the
                 [bench
Only to entrap offenders in their answers;
10 Dooms men to death by information;°
Rewards by hearsay.
    DELIO. Then the law to him
Is like a foul black cobweb to a spider,—
He makes it his dwelling and a prison
15 To entangle those shall feed him.
    ANT. Most true:
He never pays debts unless they be shrewd
                 [turns,
And those he will confess that he doth owe.
20 Last, for his brother there, the cardinal,
They that do flatter him most say oracles
Hang at his lips; and verily I believe them,
For the devil speaks in them.
But for their sister, the right noble duchess,
25 You never fixed your eye on three fair medals
Cast in one figure,° of so different temper.
For her discourse, it is so full of rapture,
You only will begin then to be sorry
When she doth end her speech, and wish, in
30   [wonder,
She held it less vainglory to talk much,
Than your penance to hear her. Whilst she
                 [speaks,
She throws upon a man so sweet a look,
35 That it were able to raise one to a galliard°
That lay in a dead palsy, and to dote
On that sweet countenance; but in that look
There speaketh so divine a continence
As cuts off all lascivious and vain hope.
40 Her days are practiced in such noble virtue,
That sure her nights, nay, more, her very sleeps,
Are more in Heaven than other ladies' shrifts.
Let all sweet ladies break their flattering glasses,
And dress themselves in her.

DELIO. Fie, Antonio,   45
You play the wire-drawer with her
             [commendations.°
    ANT. I'll case the picture up: only thus much;
All her particular worth grows to this sum,—
She stains° the time past, lights the time to   50
             [come.
    CARI. You must attend my lady in the gallery,
Some half an hour hence.
    ANT. I shall.
    [Exeunt ANTONIO and DELIO.]   55
    FERD. Sister, I have a suit to you.
    DUCH. To me, sir?
    FERD. A gentleman here, Daniel de Bosola,
One that was in the galleys—
    DUCH. Yes, I know him.   60
    FERD. A worthy fellow he is: pray, let me
             [entreat for
The provisorship of your horse.°
    DUCH. Your knowledge of him
Commends him and prefers him.   65
    FERD. Call him hither.
    [Exit ATTENDANT.]
We are now upon parting. Good Lord Silvio,
Do us commend to all our noble friends
At the leaguer.°   70
    SILVIO. Sir, I shall.
    FERD. You are for Milan?
    SILVIO. I am.
    DUCH. Bring the caroches.° We'll bring you
             [down to the haven.   75
    [Exeunt DUCHESS, SILVIO, CASTRUCCIO, ROD-
ERIGO, GRISOLAN, CARIOLA, JULIA, and ATTEN-
DANTS.]
    CARD. Be sure you entertain that Bosola
For your intelligence. I would not be seen in't;   80
And therefore many times I have slighted him
When he did court our furtherance, as this
             [morning.
    FERD. Antonio, the great master of her
             [household,   85
Had been far fitter.

You . . . commendations   you attenuate her praises
stains   renders drab by comparison
provisorship . . . horse   i.e., the office of providing
  cavalry for the duchy
leaguer   camp
caroches   coaches

information   second-hand report
figure   mold
galliard   a lively dance

CARD. You are deceived in him.
His nature is too honest for such business.—
He comes; I'll leave you.
  [*Exit.*]
5 [*Re-enter* BOSOLA.]
  Bos. I was lured to you.
  FERD. My brother here, the cardinal, could
                                        [never
Abide you.
10   Bos. Never since he was in my debt.
    FERD. May be some oblique character in your
                                        [face
Made him suspect you.
    Bos. Doth he study physiognomy?
15 There's no more credit to be given to the face
Than to a sick man's urine, which some call
The physician's whore because she cozens him.
He did suspect me wrongfully.
    FERD. For that
20 You must give great men leave to take their
                                        [times.
Distrust doth cause us seldom be deceived:
You see the oft shaking of the cedar-tree
Fastens it more at root.
25   Bos. Yet, take heed;
For to suspect a friend unworthily
Instructs him the next way° to suspect you,
And prompts him to deceive you.
    FERD. There's gold.
30   Bos. So!
What follows? Never rained such showers as
                                        [these
Without thunderbolts i' the tail of them. Whose
                                [throat must I cut?
35 FERD. Your inclination to shed blood rides
                                        [post
Before my occasion to use you. I give you that
To live i' the court here, and observe the
                                        [duchess;
40 To note all the particulars of her havior,
What suitors do solicit her for marriage,
And whom she best affects.° She's a young
                                        [widow;
I would not have her marry again.
45   Bos. No, sir?

FERD. Do not you ask the reason; but be
                                [satisfied
I say I would not.
  Bos. It seems you would create me
One of your familiars.   50
    FERD. Familiar! What's that?
    Bos. Why, a very quaint invisible devil in
                                        [flesh,
An intelligencer.
    FERD. Such a kind of thriving thing   55
I would wish thee; and ere long thou mayest
                                        [arrive
At a higher place by't.
    Bos. Take your devils,
Which hell calls angels!° These cursed gifts   60
                                [would make
You a corrupter, me an impudent traitor;
And should I take these, they'd take me to hell.
    FERD. Sir, I'll take nothing from you that I
                                [have given. 65
There is a place that I procured for you
This morning, the provisorship o' the horse.
Have you heard on't?
    Bos. No.
    FERD. 'Tis yours. Is't not worth thanks?   70
    Bos. I would have you curse yourself now,
                                [that your bounty
(Which makes men truly noble) e'er should
                                        [make me
A villain. O, that to avoid ingratitude   75
For the good deed you have done me, I must do
All the ill man can invent! Thus the devil
Candies all sins o'er; and what Heaven terms
                                        [vile,
That names he complimental.   80
    FERD. Be yourself;
Keep your old garb of melancholy; 'twill
                                        [express
You envy those that stand above your reach,
Yet strive not to come near 'em. This will gain 85
Access to private lodgings, where yourself
May, like a politic dormouse—
    Bos. As I have seen some
Feed in a lord's dish, half asleep, not seeming
To listen to any talk; and yet these rogues   90

Instructs . . . way   is the readiest way of teaching him
affects   likes

angels   gold coins (having a design of St. Michael
  slaying a dragon)

Have cut his throat in a dream. What's my
[place?
The provisorship o' the horse? Say, then, my
[corruption
5 Grew out of horse-dung. I am your creature.
   FERD. Away!
   Bos. Let good men, for good deeds, covet
[good fame,
Since place and riches oft are bribes of shame.
10 Sometimes the devil doth preach.
   [Exit.]
   [Re-enter DUCHESS, CARDINAL, and CARIOLA.]
   CARD. We are to part from you, and your
[own discretion
15 Must now be your director.
   FERD. You are a widow:
You know already what man is; and therefore
Let not youth, high promotion, eloquence—
   CARD. No,
20 Nor any thing without the addition, honor,
Sway your high blood.
   FERD. Marry! they are most luxurious°
Will wed twice.
   CARD. O, fie!
25   FERD. Their livers are more spotted
Than Laban's sheep.°
   DUCH. Diamonds are of most value,
They say, that have passed through most
[jewellers' hands.
30   FERD. Whores by that rule are precious.
   DUCH. Will you hear me?
I'll never marry.
   CARD. So most widows say;
But commonly that motion° lasts no longer
35 Than the turning of an hourglass: the funeral
[sermon
And it end both together.
   FERD. Now hear me:
You live in a rank pasture here i' the court;
40 There is a kind of honey-dew that's deadly;
'Twill poison your fame; look to't. Be not
[cunning,

For they whose faces do belie their hearts
Are witches ere they arrive at twenty years;
Ay, and give the devil suck.   45
   DUCH. This is terrible good counsel.
   FERD. Hypocrisy is woven of a fine small
[thread,
Subtler than Vulcan's engine;° yet, believe't,
Your darkest actions, nay, your privat'st   50
[thoughts,
Will come to light.
   CARD. You may flatter yourself,
And take your own choice; privately be married
Under the eves of night—   55
   FERD. Think't the best voyage
That e'er you made; like the irregular crab,
Which, though't goes backward, thinks that it
[goes right
Because it goes its own way. But observe,   60
Such weddings may more properly be said
To be executed than celebrated.
   CARD. The marriage night
Is the entrance into some prison.
   FERD. And those joys,   65
Those lustful pleasures, are like heavy sleeps
Which do forerun man's mischief.
   CARD. Fare you well.
Wisdom begins at the end: remember it.
   [Exit.]   70
   DUCH. I think this speech between you both
[was studied,
It came so roundly off.
   FERD. You are my sister;
This was my father's poniard, do you see?   75
I'd be loath to see't look rusty, 'cause 'twas his.
I would have you give o'er these chargeable
[revels:°
A visor and a mask are whispering-rooms
That were never built for goodness—fare ye 80
[well—
And women like that part which, like the
[lamprey,
Hath never a bone in't.
   DUCH. Fie, sir!   85

---

luxurious sensually indulgent
Laban's sheep as described in Genesis 30:31–42. The
  liver (preceding line) was the supposed seat of the
  passions.
motion purpose

Vulcan's engine the net in which he trapped his wife
  Venus and her lover Mars
chargeable revels expensive festivities (which include
  masking)

FERD. Nay,
I mean the tongue; variety of courtship.
What cannot a neat knave with a smooth tale
Make a woman believe? Farewell, lusty widow.
5   [*Exit.*]
DUCH. Shall this move me? If all my royal
                        [kindred
Lay in my way unto this marriage,
I'd make them my low footsteps:° And even
10   [now,
Even in this hate, as men in some great battles,
By apprehending° danger, have achieved
Almost impossible actions (I have heard
                [soldiers say so),
15 So I through frights and threatenings will assay
This dangerous venture. Let old wives report
I winked° and chose a husband.—Cariola,
To thy known secrecy I have given up
More than my life—my fame.
20   CARI. Both shall be safe,
For I'll conceal this secret from the world
As warily as those that trade in poison
Keep poison from their children.
   DUCH. Thy protestation
25 Is ingenious° and hearty: I believe it.
Is Antonio come?
   CARI. He attends you.
   DUCH. Good, dear soul,
Leave me; but place thyself behind the arras,
30 Where thou mayst overhear us. Wish me good
                    [speed,
For I am going into a wilderness
Where I shall find nor path nor friendly clue
To be my guide.
35   [CARIOLA *goes behind the arras.*]
   [*Enter* ANTONIO.]
          I sent for you; sit down.
Take pen and ink, and write. Are you ready?
ANT. Yes.
40 DUCH. What did I say?
ANT. That I should write somewhat.
DUCH. O, I remember.
After these triumphs° and this large expense,

It's fit, like thrifty husbands,° we inquire
What's laid up for tomorrow.   45
   ANT. So please your beauteous excellence.
   DUCH. Beauteous!
Indeed, I thank you. I look young for your sake;
You have ta'en my cares upon you.
   ANT. I'll fetch your grace   50
The particulars of your revenue and expense.
   DUCH. O, you are
An upright treasurer, but you mistook;
For when I said I meant to make inquiry
What's laid up for tomorrow, I did mean   55
What's laid up yonder for me.
   ANT. Where?
   DUCH. In Heaven.
I am making my will (as 'tis fit princes should,
In perfect memory), and, I pray, sir, tell me,   60
Were not one better make it smiling, thus,
Than in deep groans and terrible ghastly looks,
As if the gifts we parted with procured
That violent distraction?
   ANT. O, much better.   65
   DUCH. If I had a husband now, this care were
                    [quit:
But I intend to make you overseer.°
What good deed shall we first remember? Say
   ANT. Begin with that first good deed began i'   70
                  [the world
After man's creation, the sacrament of
                  [marriage.
I'd have you first provide for a good husband;
Give him all.   75
   DUCH. All!
   ANT. Yes, your excellent self.
   DUCH. In a winding-sheet?°
   ANT. In a couple.
   DUCH. Saint Winifred, that were a strange   80
                  [will!
   ANT. 'Twere stranger if there were no will in
                  [you
To marry again.
   DUCH. What do you think of marriage?   85
   ANT. I take't, as those that deny purgatory,

---

low footsteps the first steps of a stair or ladder
apprehending seizing hold of
winked closed my eyes
ingenious ingenuous
triumphs festivities

husbands managers
overseer of the will
winding-sheet a shroud (because her husband is in the tomb). Antonio counters with a "couple" (of bed sheets).

It locally contains or Heaven or hell;
There's no third place in't.
    DUCH. How do you affect it?
    ANT. My banishment, feeding my
5   [melancholy,
Would often reason thus—
    DUCH. Pray, let's hear it.
    ANT. Say a man never marry, nor have
                  [children,
10 What takes that from him? Only the bare name
Of being a father, or the weak delight
To see the little wanton ride a-cock-horse
Upon a painted stick, or hear him chatter
Like a taught starling.
15   DUCH. Fie, fie, what's all this?
One of your eyes is bloodshot. Use my ring to't,
They say 'tis very sovereign.° 'Twas my
                  [wedding ring,
And I did vow never to part with it
20 But to my second husband.
    ANT. You have parted with it now.
    DUCH. Yes, to help your eyesight.
    ANT. You have made me stark blind.
    DUCH. How?
25   ANT. There is a saucy and ambitious devil
Is dancing in this circle.
    DUCH. Remove him.
    ANT. How?
    DUCH. There needs small conjuration when
30   [your finger
May do it: thus. Is it fit?
    [*She puts the ring upon his finger; he kneels.*]
    ANT. What said you?
    DUCH. Sir,
35 This goodly roof of yours is too low built;
I cannot stand upright in't nor discourse,
Without I raise it higher. Raise yourself;
Or, if you please, my hand to help you: so.
    [*Raises him.*]
40   ANT. Ambition, madam, is a great man's
                  [madness,
That is not kept in chains and close-pent rooms,
But in fair lightsome lodgings, and is girt
With the wild noise of prattling visitants,
45 Which makes it lunatic beyond all cure.
Conceive not I am so stupid but I aim

Whereto your favors tend: but he's a fool
That, being a-cold, would thrust his hands i' the
                  [fire
To warm them.   50
    DUCH. So, now the ground's broke,
You may discover what a wealthy mine
I make you lord of.
    ANT. O my unworthiness!
    DUCH. You were ill to sell° yourself.   55
This darkening of your worth is not like that
Which tradesman use i' the city; their false
                  [lights
Are to rid bad wares off. And I must tell you,
If you will know where breathes a complete   60
                  [man
(I speak it without flattery), turn your eyes,
And progress through yourself.
    ANT. Were there nor Heaven nor hell,
I should be honest. I have long served virtue,   65
And ne'er ta'en wages of her.
    DUCH. Now she pays° it.
The misery of us that are born great!
We are forced to woo, because none dare woo
                  [us;   70
And as a tyrant doubles with his words
And fearfully equivocates, so we
Are forced to express our violent passions
In riddles and in dreams, and leave the path
Of simple virtue, which was never made   75
To seem the thing it is not. Go, go brag
You have left me heartless; mine is in your
                  [bosom.
I hope 'twill multiply love there. You do
                  [tremble.   80
Make not your heart so dead a piece of flesh,
To fear more than to love me. Sir, be confident:
What is't distracts you? This is flesh and blood,
                  [sir;
'Tis not the figure cut in alabaster   85
Kneels at my husband's tomb. Awake, awake,
                  [man!
I do here put off all vain ceremony,
And only do appear to you a young widow
That claims you for her husband, and, like a   90
                  [widow,

were ill to sell are a poor salesman of
pays repays

---

sovereign curative

I use but half a blush in't.
    ANT. Truth speak for me;
I will remain the constant sanctuary
Of your good name.
5   DUCH. I thank you, gentle love;
And 'cause you shall not come to me in debt,
Being now my steward, here upon your lips
I sign your *Quietus est.*° This you should have
                [begged now.
10 I have seen children oft eat sweetmeats thus,
As fearful to devour them too soon.
    ANT. But for your brothers?
    DUCH. Do not think of them:
All discord without this circumference°
15 Is only to be pitied, and not feared.
Yet, should they know it, time will easily
Scatter the tempest.
    ANT. These words should be mine,
And all the parts you have spoke, if some part
20   [of it
Would not have savored flattery.
    DUCH. Kneel.
    [CARIOLA *comes from behind the arras.*]
    ANT. Ha!
25 DUCH. Be not amazed; this woman's of my
                  [counsel:
I have heard lawyers say, a contract in a
                  [chamber
Per verba de presenti° is absolute marriage.
30 [*She and* ANTONIO *kneel.*]
Bless, Heaven, this sacred gordian,° which let
                  [violence
Never untwine!
    ANT. And may our sweet affections, like the
35   [spheres,
Be still in motion!
    DUCH. Quickening, and make
The like soft music!
    ANT. That we may imitate the loving palms,
40 Best emblem of a peaceful marriage,
That never bore fruit, divided!

DUCH. What can the church force° more?
    ANT. That fortune may not know an accident,
Either of joy or sorrow, to divide
Our fixèd wishes!   45
    DUCH. How can the church build faster?°
We now are man and wife, and 'tis the church
That must echo this.—Maid, stand apart:
I now am blind.
    ANT. What's your conceit° in this?   50
    DUCH. I would have you lead your fortune°
                [by the hand
Unto your marriage bed.
(You speak in me this, for we now are one.)
We'll only lie, and talk together, and plot   55
To appease my humorous kindred; and if you
                [please,
Like the old tale in Alexander and Lodowick,°
Lay a naked sword between us, keep us chaste.
O, let me shroud my blushes in your bosom, 60
Since 'tis the treasury of all my secrets!
    [*Exeunt* DUCHESS *and* ANTONIO.]
    CARI. Whether the spirit of greatness or of
                [woman
Reign most in her, I know not; but it shows 65
A fearful madness. I owe her much of pity.
    [*Exit.*]

ACT II

Scene i

[*An apartment in the palace of the* DUCHESS.]
[*Enter* BOSOLA *and* CASTRUCCIO.]
    BOS. You say you would fain be taken for an 70
eminent courtier?°
    CAST. 'Tis the very main° of my ambition.
    BOS. Let me see. You have a reasonable good
face for't already, and your night-cap° expresses your ears sufficient largely. I would have 75

Quietus est acquittance from debt
without this circumference outside this circle (of
  her arms, which she throws around him)
Per . . . presenti by present acknowledgment (literally
  "by words in the present tense")
gordian knot. The Gordian knot of legend was cut
  by Alexander's sword.

force enforce
faster more firmly
conceit idea
your fortune your blind wife. Fortune is proverbially
  blind.
Lodowick Lodowick, having taken a wife in the name
  of his identical friend Alexander, interdicted consummation in the way described
courtier lawyer
main goal
night-cap lawyer's coif (slang)

you learn to twirl the strings of your band with
a good grace, and in a set speech, at the end of
every sentence, to hum three or four times, or
blow your nose till it smart again, to recover
5 your memory. When you come to be a president
in criminal causes, if you smile upon a prisoner,
hang him, but if you frown upon him and
threaten him, let him be sure to scape the gallows.

10   Cast. I would be a very merry president.

    Bos. Do not sup o' nights; 'twill beget you an
admirable wit.

    Cast. Rather it would make me have a good
stomach to quarrel; for they say, your roaring
15 boys° eat meat seldom, and that makes them so
valiant. But how shall I know whether the
people take me for an eminent fellow?

    Bos. I will teach a trick to know it. Give out
you lie a-dying, and if you hear the common
20 people curse you, be sure you are taken for one
of the prime night-caps.°

    [*Enter an* Old Lady.]
You come from painting now.

    Old Lady. From what?

25   Bos. Why, from your scurvy face-physic. To
behold thee not painted inclines somewhat near
a miracle. These in thy face here were deep ruts
and foul sloughs the last progress.° There was
a lady in France that, having had the small-pox,
30 flayed the skin off her face to make it more
level, and whereas before she looked like a nut-
meg-grater, after she resembled an abortive
hedgehog.

    Old Lady. Do you call this painting?

35   Bos. No, no, but you call it careening of an
old morphewed° lady, to make her disembogue
again.° There's rough-cast phrase to your plastic.°

    Old Lady. It seems you are well acquainted

with my closet. 40

    Bos. One would suspect it for a shop of
witchcraft, to find in it the fat of serpents,
spawn of snakes, Jew's spittle, and their young
children's ordure; and all these for the face.
I would sooner eat a dead pigeon taken from 45
the soles of the feet° of one sick of the plague
than kiss one of you fasting. Here are two of
you, whose sin of your youth is the very patrimony of the physician; makes him renew his
footcloth° with the spring, and change his high- 50
priced courtezan with the fall of the leaf. I do
wonder you do not loathe yourselves. Observe
my meditation now.

What thing is in this outward form of man
To be beloved? We account it ominous, 55
If nature do produce a colt, or lamb,
A fawn, or goat, in any limb resembling
A man, and fly from't as a prodigy.
Man stands amazed to see his deformity
In any other creature but himself. 60
But in our own flesh, though we bear diseases
Which have their true names only taken from
              [beasts,—
As the most ulcerous wolf° and swinish
              [measle,—° 65
Though we are eaten up of lice and worms,
And though continually we bear about us
A rotten and dead body, we delight
To hide it in rich tissue. All our fear,
Nay, all our terror, is lest our physician 70
Should put us in the ground to be made
              [sweet.—
Your wife's gone to Rome; you two couple, and
get you to the wells at Lucca° to recover your
aches. I have other work on foot. 75

    [*Exeunt* Castruccio *and* Old Lady.]
I observe our duchess
Is sick a-days, she pukes, her stomach seethes,
The fins° of her eyelids look most teeming blue,

---

roaring boys bullies
night-caps lawyers
the last progress i.e., the last time you passed over it
morphewed scurfy
careening . . . again ships were laid on their side (careened) to have their hulls scraped; they then put to sea (disembogued) again
rough-cast . . . to plastic rough plaster . . . for modeling

pigeon . . . from . . . the feet where it supposedly drew the noxious vapors from the head
footcloth trappings for his horse
wolf Latin *lupus* (wolf) is a name for an ulcer
measle a disease of swine, affecting the skin
wells at Lucca warm and curative springs
fins edges. They are blue like those of pregnant ("teeming") women.

She wanes i' the cheek, and waxes fat i' the
[flank,
And, contrary to our Italian fashion,
Wears a loose-bodied gown. There's somewhat
[in't.
5 I have a trick may chance discover it,
A pretty one: I have bought some apricocks,
The first our spring yields.
[*Enter* Antonio *and* Delio.]
10 Delio. And so long since married!
You amaze me.
    Ant. Let me seal your lips for ever:
For, did I think that any thing but the air
Could carry these words from you, I should
15 [wish
You had no breath at all.—Now, sir, in your
[contemplation?
You are studying to become a great wise fellow.
    Bos. O, sir, the opinion of wisdom is a foul
20 tetter that runs all over a man's body. If simplicity direct us to have no evil, it directs us to
a happy being, for the subtlest folly proceeds
from the subtlest wisdom. Let me be simply
honest.
25 Ant. I do understand your inside.
    Bos. Do you so?
    Ant. Because you would not seem to appear
[to the world
Puffed up with your preferment, you continue
30 This out-of-fashion melancholy. Leave it, leave
[it!
    Bos. Give me leave to be honest in any
phrase, in any compliment whatsoever. Shall I
confess myself to you? I look no higher than
35 I can reach. They are the gods that must ride on
winged horses. A lawyer's mule of a slow pace
will both suit my disposition and business; for,
mark me, when a man's mind rides faster than
his horse can gallop, they quickly both tire.
40 Ant. You would look up to Heaven, but I
[think
The devil, that rules i' the air,° stands in your
[light.
    Bos. O, sir, you are lord of the ascendant,°

chief man with the duchess; a duke was your 45
cousin-german removed. Say you are lineally
descended from King Pepin,° or he himself,
what of this? Search the heads of the greatest
rivers in the world, you shall find them but
bubbles of water. Some would think the souls 50
of princes were brought forth by some more
weighty cause than those of meaner persons.
They are deceived, there's the same hand to
them; the like passions sway them. The same
reason that makes a vicar to go to law for a 55
tithe-pig,° and undo his neighbors, makes them
spoil a whole province, and batter down goodly
cities with the cannon.
    [*Enter* Duchess *and* Ladies.]
    Duch. Your arm, Antonio. Do I not grow 60
[fat?
I am exceeding short-winded.—Bosola,
I would have you, sir, provide for me a litter,
Such a one as the Duchess of Florence rode in.
    Bos. The duchess used one when she was 65
[great with child.
    Duch. I think she did.—Come hither, mend
[my ruff.
Here, when? Thou art such a tedious lady, and
Thy breath smells of lemon-peels. Would thou 70
[hadst done!
Shall I swoon under thy fingers? I am
So troubled with the mother!°
    Bos. [*aside*]. I fear, too much.
    Duch. I have heard you say that the French 75
[courtiers
Wear their hats on 'fore the king.
    Ant. I have seen it.
    Duch. In the presence?
    Ant. Yes. 80
    Duch. Why should not we bring up that
[fashion?
'Tis ceremony more than duty that consists
In the removing of a piece of felt.
Be you the example to the rest o' the court, 85
Put on your hat first.
    Ant. You must pardon me:
I have seen, in colder countries than in France,

---

the air supposed haunt of evil spirits
lord . . . ascendant exerting a dominant influence
    (an astrological term)

King Pepin Charlemagne's father
tithe-pig the vicar's due as part of the church taxes
mother hysteria

Nobles stand bare to the prince; and the
                                [distinction
Methought showed reverently.
      Bos. I have a present for your grace.
  5   Duch. For me, sir?
      Bos. Apricocks, madam.
      Duch. O, sir, where are they?
I have heard of none to-year.°
      Bos. [aside]. Good! Her color rises.
 10   Duch. Indeed, I thank you; they are
                                [wondrous fair ones.
What an unskilful fellow is our gardener!
We shall have none this month.
      Bos. Will not your grace pare them?
 15   Duch. No: they taste of musk, methinks;
                                [indeed they do.
      Bos. I know not: yet I wish your grace had
                                [pared 'em.
      Duch. Why?
 20   Bos. I forgot to tell you, the knave gardener,
Only to raise his profit by them the sooner,
Did ripen them in horse dung.
      Duch. O, you jest—
You shall judge. Pray taste one.
 25   Ant. Indeed, madam,
I do not love the fruit.
      Duch. Sir, you are loath
To rob us of our dainties. 'Tis a delicate fruit;
They say they are restorative.
 30   Bos. 'Tis a pretty art,
This grafting.
      Duch. 'Tis so; a bettering of nature.
      Bos. To make a pippin grow upon a crab,°
A damson on a blackthorn.—[Aside.] How
 35   [greedily she eats them!
A whirlwind strike off these bawd farthingales!
For, but for that and the loose-bodied gown,
I should have discovered apparently
The young springal° cutting a caper in her
 40   [belly.
      Duch. I thank you, Bosola. They are right
                                [good ones,
If they do not make me sick.

to-year   this year
crab   crabapple stem
springal   stripling

      Ant. How now, madam!
      Duch. This green fruit and my stomach are   45
                                [not friends.
How they swell me!
      Bos. [aside]. Nay, you are too much swelled
                                [already.
      Duch. O, I am in an extreme cold sweat!   50
      Bos. I am very sorry.
      Duch. Lights to my chamber!—O good
                                [Antonio,
I fear I am undone!
      Delio. Lights there, lights!   55
      [Exeunt Duchess and Ladies. Exit, on the
other side, Bosola.]
      Ant. O my most trusty Delio, we are lost!
I fear she's fall'n in labor; and there's left
No time for her remove.   60
      Delio. Have you prepared
Those ladies to attend her? and procured
That politic safe conveyance for the midwife
Your duchess plotted?
      Ant. I have.   65
      Delio. Make use, then, of this forced
                                [occasion.
Give out that Bosola hath poisoned her
With these apricocks; that will give some color
For her keeping close.   70
      Ant. Fie, fie, the physicians
Will then flock to her.
      Delio. For that you may pretend
She'll use some prepared antidote of her own,
Lest the physicians should re-poison her.   75
      Ant. I am lost in amazement. I know not
                                [what to think on't.
      [Exeunt.]

Scene ii

[A hall in the same palace.]
[Enter Bosola.]   80
      Bos. So, so, there's no question but her tetch-
iness° and most vulturous eating of the apricocks are apparent signs of breeding.
      [Enter an Old Lady.]
Now?   85
      Old Lady. I am in haste, sir.

tetchiness   irritability

Bos. There was a young waiting-woman had a monstrous desire to see the glass-house°—

Old Lady. Nay, pray let me go.

Bos. And it was only to know what strange
5 instrument it was should swell up a glass to the fashion of a woman's belly.

Old Lady. I will hear no more of the glass-house. You are still abusing women?

Bos. Who, I? No; only, by the way now and
10 then, mention your frailties. The orange-tree bears ripe and green fruit and blossoms all together; and some of you give entertainment for pure love, but more for more precious reward. The lusty spring smells well, but droop-
15 ing autumn tastes well. If we have the golden showers that rained in the time of Jupiter the thunderer, you have the same Danäes° still, to hold up their laps to receive them. Didst thou never study the mathematics?

20 Old Lady. What's that, sir?

Bos. Why to know the trick how to make a many lines meet in one center. Go, go, give your foster daughters good counsel. Tell them, that the devil takes delight to hang at a wom-
25 an's girdle, like a false rusty watch, that she cannot discern how the time passes.

[*Exit* Old Lady.]

[*Enter* Antonio, Roderigo, *and* Grisolan.]

Ant. Shut up the court gates.

30 Rod. Why, sir? What's the danger?

Ant. Shut up the posterns presently, and
                                        [call
All the officers o' the court.

Gris. I shall instantly.

35 [*Exit*.]

Ant. Who keeps the key o' the park-gate?

Rod. Forobosco.

Ant. Let him bring't presently.

[*Re-enter* Grisolan *with* Servants.]

40 1st Serv. O, gentlemen o' the court, the foulest treason!

Bos. [*aside*]. If that these apricocks should be
                                [poisoned now,

Without my knowledge!

1st Serv. There was taken even now a Swit- 45
zer° in the duchess' bed chamber—

2nd Serv. A Switzer!

1st Serv. With a pistol in his great codpiece.°

Bos. Ha, ha, ha!

1st Serv. The codpiece was the case for't. 50

2nd Serv. There was a cunning traitor: who would have searched his codpiece?

1st Serv. True, if he had kept out of the ladies' chambers: and all the molds of his buttons were leaden bullets. 55

2nd Serv. O wicked cannibal! A fire-lock in's codpiece!

1st Serv. 'Twas a French plot, upon my life.

2nd Serv. To see what the devil can do!

Ant. All the officers here? 60

Servants. We are.

Ant. Gentlemen,
We have lost much plate you know; and but
                                [this evening
Jewels, to the value of four thousand ducats, 65
Are missing in the duchess' cabinet.
Are the gates shut?

Serv. Yes.

Ant. 'Tis the duchess' pleasure
Each officer be locked into his chamber 70
Till the sun-rising, and to send the keys
Of all their chests and of their outward doors
Into her bedchamber. She is very sick.

Rod. At her pleasure.

Ant. She entreats you take't not ill. The 75
                                [innocent
Shall be the more approved° by it.

Bos. Gentleman o' the wood-yard, where's
                                [your Switzer now?

1st Serv. By this hand, 'twas credibly re- 80
ported by one o' the black guard.°

[*Exeunt all except* Antonio *and* Delio.]

Delio. How fares it with the duchess?

Ant. She's exposed
Unto the worst of torture, pain and fear. 85

---

glass-house glassblowers' shop
Danäes Danäe, whom Jupiter visited in a golden shower, was a type of the mercenary woman

Switzer Swiss mercenary soldier
codpiece an appendage to tight-fitting breeches
approved vindicated
black guard kitchen servants

DELIO. Speak to her all happy comfort.
ANT. How I do play the fool with mine own
[danger!
You are this night, dear friend, to post to Rome.
5 My life lies in your service.
  DELIO. Do not doubt me.
  ANT. O, 'tis far from me. And yet fear
[presents me
Somewhat that looks like danger.
10 DELIO. Believe it,
'Tis but the shadow of your fear, no more.
How superstitiously we mind our evils!
The throwing down salt, or crossing of a hare,
Bleeding at nose, the stumbling of a horse,
15 Or singing of a cricket, are of power
To daunt whole man in us. Sir, fare you well!
I wish you all the joys of a blessed father.
And, for my faith, lay this unto your breast,—
Old friends, like old swords, still are trusted
20   [best.
  [Exit.]
  [Enter CARIOLA.]
  CARI. Sir, you are the happy father of a son.
Your wife commends him to you.
25 ANT. Blessèd comfort!—
For Heaven' sake tend her well. I'll presently
Go set a figure for's nativity.
  [Exeunt.]

Scene iii

[The court of the same palace.]
30 [Enter BOSOLA, with a dark lantern.]
  BOS. Sure I did hear a woman shriek. List, ha!
And the sound came, if I received it right,
From the duchess' lodgings. There's some
[stratagem
35 In the confining all our courtiers
To their several wards. I must have part of it;
My intelligence will freeze else. List, again!
It may be 'twas the melancholy bird,
Best friend of silence and of solitariness,
40 The owl, that screamed so.—Ha! Antonio!
  [Enter ANTONIO.]
  ANT. I heard some noise.—Who's there?
[What art thou? Speak.
  BOS. Antonio, put not your face nor body
45 To such a forced expression of fear.
I am Bosola, your friend.

ANT. Bosola!—
[Aside.] This mole does undermine me.—Heard
[you not
A noise even now?   50
  BOS. From whence?
  ANT. From the duchess' lodging.
  BOS. Not I. Did you?
  ANT. I did, or else I dreamed.
  BOS. Let's walk towards it.   55
  ANT. No: it may be 'twas
But the rising of the wind.
  BOS. Very likely.
Methinks 'tis very cold, and yet you sweat.
You look wildly.   60
  ANT. I have been setting a figure
For the duchess' jewels.
  BOS. Ah, and how falls your question?
Do you find it radical?°
  ANT. What's that to you?   65
'Tis rather to be questioned what design,
When all men were commanded to their
[lodgings,
Makes you a night-walker.
  BOS. In sooth, I'll tell you.   70
Now all the courts' asleep, I thought the devil
Had least to do here. I came to say my prayers.
And if it do offend you I do so,
You are a fine courtier.
  ANT. [aside]. This fellow will undo me.—   75
You gave the duchess apricocks today.
Pray Heaven they were not poisoned!
  BOS. Poisoned! A Spanish fig°
For the imputation.
  ANT. Traitors are ever confident   80
Till they are discovered. There were jewels
[stol'n too.
In my conceit, none are to be suspected
More than yourself.
  BOS. You are a false steward.   85
  ANT. Saucy slave, I'll pull thee up by the
[roots.
  BOS. May be the ruin will crush you to pieces.
  ANT. You are an impudent snake indeed, sir.
Are you scarce warm, and do you show your   90
[sting?

radical discoverable by astrology
Spanish fig an obscene gesture ("the finger")

You libel° well, sir.
 Bos. No, sir; copy it out,
And I will set my hand to't.
 Ant. [*aside*]. My nose bleeds.
5 One that were superstitious would count
This ominous, when it merely comes by chance.
Two letters, that are wrote here for my name,
Are drowned in blood!
Mere accident.—For you, sir, I'll take order
10 I' the morn you shall be safe:—[*Aside.*] 'Tis
       [that must color
Her lying-in.—Sir, this door you pass not.
I do not hold it fit that you come near
The duchess' lodgings, till you have quit°
15   [yourself.—
[*Aside.*] The great are like the base; nay, they
       [are the same,
When they seek shameful ways to avoid shame.
[*Exit.*]
20 Bos. Antonio hereabout did drop a paper.
Some of your help, false friend.°—O, here it is.
What's here? A child's nativity calculated!
      [(*Reads.*)
"The duchess was delivered of a son, 'tween
25 the hours twelve and one in the night, *Anno
Dom.* 1504,"—that's this year—"*decimo nono
Decembris*,"°—that's this night,—"taken according to the meridian of Malfi,"—that's our
duchess. Happy discovery!—"The lord of the
30 first house being combust in the ascendant,°
signifies short life; and Mars being in a human
sign, joined to the tail of the Dragon,° in the
eighth house, doth threaten a violent death.
Caetera non scrutantur."°
35 Why, now 'tis most apparent: this precise°

---

libel (1) slander, (2) write out a formal charge
quit acquitted
false friend addressed to his dark lantern
decimo nono Decembris December 19
The lord . . . ascendant the planet belonging to the sign of the Zodiac that is just rising above the horizon being close to the sun's path (hence "combust," burned up, deprived of influence)
Mars . . . Dragon Mars being in a sign with a human figure (like the Archer) and bearing a sinister relationship to the downward path of the moon (the Dragon's tail)
Caetera non scrutantur other things not examined
precise puritanical

       [fellow
Is the duchess' bawd.—I have it to my wish!
This is a parcel of intelligency
Our courtiers were cased up for. It needs must
       [follow 40
That I must be committed on pretence
Of poisoning her; which I'll endure, and laugh
       [at.
If one could find the father now! But that
Time will discover. Old Castruccio 45
I' the morning posts to Rome; by him I'll send
A letter that shall make her brothers' galls
O'erflow their livers. This was a thrifty way.
Though lust do mask in ne'er so strange
       [disguise, 50
She's oft found witty, but is never wise.
 [*Exit.*]

Scene iv

[*An apartment in the palace of the* Cardinal
at Rome.]
 [*Enter* Cardinal *and* Julia.] 55
 Card. Sit; thou art my best of wishes.
     [Prithee, tell me
What trick didst thou invent to come to Rome
Without thy husband.
 Julia. Why, my lord, I told him 60
I came to visit an old anchorite
Here for devotion.
 Card. Thou art a witty false one,—
I mean, to him.
 Julia. You have prevailed with me 65
Beyond my strongest thoughts. I would not now
Find you inconstant.
 Card. Do not put thyself
To such a voluntary torture, which proceeds
Out of your own guilt. 70
 Julia. How, my lord!
 Card. You fear
My constancy, because you have approved°
Those giddy and wild turnings in yourself.
 Julia. Did you e'er find them? 75
 Card. Sooth, generally for women,
A man might strive to make glass malleable
Ere he should make them fixèd.
 Julia. So, my lord.

---

approved experienced

CARD. We had need go borrow that fantastic
                                    [glass°
Invented by Galileo the Florentine
To view another spacious world i' the moon,
5 And look to find a constant woman there.
    JULIA. This is very well, my lord.
    CARD. Why do you weep?
Are tears your justification? The self-same tears
Will fall into your husband's bosom, lady,
10 With a loud protestation that you love him
Above the world. Come, I'll love you wisely,
That's jealously; since I am very certain
You cannot make me cuckold.
    JULIA. I'll go home
15 To my husband.
    CARD. You may thank me, lady,
I have taken you off your melancholy perch,
Bore you upon my fist, and showed you game,
And let you fly at it.—I pray thee, kiss me.—
20 When thou wast with thy husband, thou wast
                                    [watched
Like a tame elephant.—Still you are to thank
                                    [me.—
Thou hadst only kisses from him and high
25   [feeding;
But what delight was that? 'Twas just like one
That hath a little fingering on the lute,
Yet cannot tune it.—Still you are to thank me.
    JULIA. You told me of a piteous wound i' the
30   [heart
And a sick liver, when you wooed me first,
And spake like one in physic.°
    CARD. Who's that?—
    [Enter SERVANT.]
35 Rest firm; for my affection to thee,
Lightning moves slow to't.
    SERV. Madam, a gentleman
That's come post from Malfi desires to see you.
    CARD. Let him enter. I'll withdraw.
40 [Exit.]
    SERV. He says
Your husband, old Castruccio, is come to Rome,
Most pitifully tired with riding post.
    [Exit.]

[Enter DELIO.]   45
JULIA [aside]. Signior Delio! 'Tis one of my
                                    [old suitors.
DELIO. I was bold to come and see you.
JULIA. Sir, you are welcome.
DELIO. Do you lie here?   50
JULIA. Sure, your own experience
Will satisfy you no. Our Roman prelates
Do not keep lodging for ladies.
    DELIO. Very well.
I have brought you no commendations from   55
                                    [your husband,
For I know none by him.
    JULIA. I hear he's come to Rome.
DELIO. I never knew man and beast, of a
                                    [horse and a knight, 60
So weary of each other. If he had had a good
                                    [back,
He would have undertook to have borne his
                                    [horse,
His breech was so pitifully sore.   65
    JULIA. Your laughter
Is my pity.
    DELIO. Lady, I know not whether
You want money, but I have brought you
                                    [some. 70
    JULIA. From my husband?
DELIO. No, from mine own allowance.
JULIA. I must hear the condition ere I be
                                    [bound to take it.
DELIO. Look on't, 'tis gold. Hath it not a fine   75
                                    [color?
    JULIA. I have a bird more beautiful.
DELIO. Try the sound on't.
JULIA. A lute-string far exceeds it.
It hath no smell, like cassia or civet;   80
Nor is it physical, though some fond doctors
Persuade us seethe't in cullises.° I'll tell you,
This is a creature bred by—
    [Re-enter SERVANT.]
    SERV. Your husband's come,   85
Hath delivered a letter to the Duke of Calabria
That, to my thinking, hath put him out of his
                                    [wits.

    [Exit.]

---

glass the telescope
in physic under medical treatment. The liver (above)
    was the supposed seat of the passions.

Nor . . . cullises nor is it restorative, although some
    foolish doctors boil it in broths

JULIA. Sir, you hear.
Pray, let me know your business and your suit
As briefly as can be.
    DELIO. With good speed. I would wish you,
5 At such time as you are non-resident
With your husband, my mistress.
    JULIA. Sir, I'll go ask my husband if I shall,
And straight return your answer.
    [*Exit.*]
10   DELIO. Very fine!
Is this her wit, or honesty,° that speaks thus?
I heard one say the duke was highly moved
With a letter sent from Malfi. I do fear
Antonio is betrayed. How fearfully
15 Shows his ambition now! Unfortunate fortune!
They pass through whirlpools, and deep woes
                        [do shun,
Who the event weigh ere the action's done.
    [*Exit.*]

Scene v

20 [*Another apartment in the same palace.*]
[*Enter* CARDINAL, *and* FERDINAND *with a
letter.*]
    FERD. I have this night digged up a
                        [mandrake.°
25   CARD. Say you?
    FERD. And I am grown mad with't.
    CARD. What's the prodigy?
    FERD. Read there,—a sister damned! She's
                    [loose i' the hilts;°
30 Grown a notorious strumpet.
    CARD. Speak lower.
    FERD. Lower!
Rogues do not whisper't now, but seek to
                    [publish't
35 (As servants do the bounty of their lords)
Aloud, and with a covetous searching eye,
To mark who note them. O, confusion seize
                    [her!
She hath had most cunning bawds to serve her
40   [turn,
And more secure conveyances for lust

Than towns of garrison for service.
    CARD. Is't possible?
Can this be certain?
    FERD. Rhubarb, O, for rhubarb°   45
To purge this choler! Here's the cursèd day°
To prompt my memory; and here't shall stick
Till of her bleeding heart I make a sponge
To wipe it out.
    CARD. Why do you make yourself   50
So wild a tempest?
    FERD. Would I could be one,
That I might toss her palace 'bout her ears,
Root up her goodly forests, blast her meads,
And lay her general territory as waste   55
As she hath done her honors.
    CARD. Shall our blood,
The royal blood of Aragon and Castile,
Be thus attainted?
    FERD. Apply desperate physic!   60
We must not now use balsamum, but fire,
The smarting cupping-glass,° for that's the
                      [mean
To purge infected blood, such blood as hers.
There is a kind of pity in mine eye,—   65
I'll give it to my handkercher; and now 'tis here,
I'll bequeath this to her bastard.
    CARD. What to do?
    FERD. Why, to make soft lint for his mother's
                    [wounds, 70
When I have hewed her to pieces.
    CARD. Cursèd creature!
Unequal nature, to place women's hearts
So far upon the left side!
    FERD. Foolish men,   75
That e'er will trust their honor in a bark
Made of so slight weak bulrush as is woman,
Apt every minute to sink it!
    CARD. Thus ignorance, when it hath
                    [purchased honor, 80
It cannot wield it.
    FERD. Methinks I see her laughing—
Excellent hyena! Talk to me somewhat quickly,

---

honesty chastity
mandrake this plant was said, when dug up, to emit
  a shriek that drove men mad
loose i' the hilts immoral

rhubarb a purgative for yellow bile (choler), the
  source of anger
cursèd day the day named in Bosola's letter, to which
  Ferdinand points
cupping-glass to catch let blood

Or my imagination will carry me
To see her in the shameful act of sin.
   CARD. With whom?
   FERD. Haply with some strong-thighed
5   [bargeman,
Or one o' the woodyard that can quoit the
                  [sledge°
Or toss the bar, or else some lovely squire
That carries coals up to her privy lodgings.
10   CARD. You fly beyond your reason.
   FERD. Go to, mistress!
'Tis not your whore's milk that shall quench
                [my wildfire,
But your whore's blood.
15   CARD. How idly shows this rage, which
                [carries you,
As men conveyed by witches through the air,
On violent whirlwinds! This intemperate noise
Fitly resembles deaf men's shrill discourse,
20 Who talk aloud, thinking all other men
To have their imperfection.
   FERD. Have not you
My palsy?
   CARD. Yes, but I can be angry
25 Without this rupture. There is not in nature
A thing that makes man so deformed, so
                [beastly,
As doth intemperate anger. Chide yourself.
You have divers men who never yet expressed
30 Their strong desire of rest but by unrest,
By vexing of themselves. Come, put yourself
In tune.
   FERD. So I will only study to seem
The thing I am not. I could kill her now,
35 In you, or in myself; for I do think
It is some sin in us Heaven doth revenge
By her.
   CARD. Are you stark mad?
   FERD. I would have their bodies
40 Burnt in a coal-pit with the ventage stopped,
That their cursed smoke might not ascend to
                [Heaven;
Or dip the sheets they lie in in pitch or sulphur,
Wrap them in't, and then light them like a
45   [match;
Or else to boil their bastard to a cullis,

quoit the sledge throw the hammer

And give't his lecherous father to renew
The sin of his back.
   CARD. I'll leave you.
   FERD. Nay, I have done.   50
I am confident, had I been damned in hell,
And should have heard of this, it would have
                [put me
Into a cold sweat. In, in! I'll go sleep.
Till I know who leaps my sister, I'll not stir.   55
That known, I'll find scorpions to string my
                [whips,
And fix her in a general eclipse.
  [*Exeunt.*]

ACT III

Scene i

[*An apartment in the palace of the* DUCHESS.]   60
[*Enter* ANTONIO *and* DELIO.]
   ANT. Our noble friend, my most belovèd
                [Delio!
O, you have been a stranger long at court.
Came you along with the Lord Ferdinand?   65
   DELIO. I did, sir. And how fares your noble
                [duchess?
   ANT. Right fortunately well! She's an
                [excellent
Feeder of pedigrees; since you last saw her,   70
She hath had two children more, a son and
                [daughter.
   DELIO. Methinks 'twas yesterday. Let me but
                [wink
And not behold your face, which to mine eye   75
Is somewhat leaner, verily I should dream
It were within this half hour.
   ANT. You have not been in law, friend Delio,
Nor in prison, nor a suitor at the court,
Nor begged the reversion of some great man's   80
                [place,
Nor troubled with an old wife, which doth
                [make
Your time so insensibly hasten.
   DELIO. Pray, sir, tell me,   85
Hath not this news arrived yet to the ear
Of the lord cardinal?
   ANT. I fear it hath.
The Lord Ferdinand, that's newly come to court,
Doth bear himself right dangerously.   90

DELIO. Pray, why?
ANT. He is so quiet that he seems to sleep
The tempest out, as dormice do in winter.
Those houses that are haunted are most still
5 Till the devil be up.
DELIO. What say the common people?
ANT. The common rabble do directly say
She is a strumpet.
DELIO. And your graver heads
10 Which would be politic, what censure they?
ANT. They do observe I grow to infinite
[purchase,°
The left hand way, and all suppose the duchess
Would amend it, if she could. For, say they,
15 Great princes, though they grudge their officers
Should have such large and unconfinèd means
To get wealth under them, will not complain,
Lest thereby they should make them odious
Unto the people. For other obligation
20 Of love or marriage between her and me
They never dream of.
DELIO. The Lord Ferdinand
Is going to bed.
[*Enter* DUCHESS, FERDINAND, *and* ATTEN-
25 DANTS.]
FERD. I'll instantly to bed,
For I am weary.—I am to bespeak
A husband for you.
DUCH. For me, sir! Pray, who is't?
30 FERD. The great Count Malateste.
DUCH. Fie upon him!
A count? He's a mere stick of sugar candy;
You may look quite through him. When I
[choose
35 A husband, I will marry for your honor.
FERD. You shall do well in't.—How is't,
[worthy Antonio?
DUCH. But, sir, I am to have private
[conference with you
40 About a scandalous report is spread
Touching mine honor.
FERD. Let me be ever deaf to't.
One of Pasquil's paper bullets,° court-calumny,
A pestilent air, which princes' palaces

Are seldom purged of. Yet say that it were true, 45
I pour it in your bosom, my fixed love
Would strongly excuse, extenuate, nay, deny
Faults, were they apparent in you. Go, be safe
In your own innocency.
DUCH. [*aside*]. O blessed comfort! 50
This deadly air is purged.
[*Exeunt* DUCHESS, ANTONIO, DELIO, *and* AT-
TENDANTS.]
FERD. Her guilt treads on
Hot-burning colters.° 55
[*Enter* BOSOLA.]
Now, Bosola,
How thrives our intelligence?
BOS. Sir, uncertainly.
'Tis rumored she hath had three bastards, but 60
By whom we may go read i' the stars.
FERD. Why, some
Hold opinion all things are written there.
BOS. Yes, if we could find spectacles to read
[them. 65
I do suspect there hath been some sorcery
Used on the duchess.
FERD. Sorcery! To what purpose
BOS. To make her dote on some desertless
[fellow 70
She shames to acknowledge.
FERD. Can your faith give way
To think there's power in potions or in charms,
To make us love whether we will or no?
BOS. Most certainly. 75
FERD. Away! These are mere gulleries, horrid
[things,
Invented by some cheating mountebanks
To abuse us. Do you think that herbs or charms
Can force the will? Some trials have been made 80
In this foolish practice, but the ingredients
Were lenitive poisons, such as are of force
To make the patient mad; and straight the
[witch
Swears by equivocation they are in love. 85
The witchcraft lies in her rank blood. This
[night
I will force confession from her. You told me
You had got, within these two days, a false key
Into her bedchamber. 90

---

purchase property
Pasquil's . . . bullets lampoons, Pasquillo being a
  legendary master of insult

colters plowshares. This was an ordeal for chastity.

Bos. I have.
FERD. As I would wish.
Bos. What do you intend to do?
FERD. Can you guess?
5   Bos. No.
FERD. Do not ask, then.
He that can compass me, and know my drifts,
May say he hath put a girdle 'bout the world,
And sounded all her quicksands.
10   Bos. I do not
Think so.
FERD. What do you think, then, pray?
Bos. That you are
Your own chronicle too much, and grossly
15   Flatter yourself.
FERD. Give me thy hand; I thank thee.
I never gave pension but to flatterers,
Till I entertainèd thee. Farewell.
That friend a great man's ruin strongly checks,
20   Who rails into his belief all his defects.
[*Exeunt.*]

Scene ii

[*The bedchamber of the* DUCHESS.]
[*Enter* DUCHESS, ANTONIO, *and* CARIOLA.]
DUCH. Bring me the casket hither, and the
25   [glass.—
You get no lodging here tonight, my lord.
ANT. Indeed, I must persuade one.
DUCH. Very good!
I hope in time 'twill grow into a custom,
30   That noblemen shall come with cap and knee
To purchase a night's lodging of their wives.
ANT. I must lie here.
DUCH. Must! You are a lord of misrule.°
ANT. Indeed, my rule is only in the night.
35   DUCH. To what use will you put me?
ANT. We'll sleep together.
DUCH. Alas,
What pleasure can two lovers find in sleep!
CARI. My lord, I lie with her often, and I
40   [know
She'll much disquiet you.
ANT. See, you are complained of.

lord of misrule   one who presides over a night of
revelry and license

CARI. For she's the sprawling'st bedfellow.
ANT. I shall like her the better for that.
CARI. Sir, shall I ask you a question?   45
ANT. Ay, pray thee, Cariola.
CARI. Wherefore still, when you lie with my
                                            [lady,
Do you rise so early?
ANT. Laboring men   50
Count the clock oftenest, Cariola,
Are glad when their task's ended.
DUCH. I'll stop your mouth.
[*Kisses him.*]
ANT. Nay, that's but one; Venus had two soft   55
                                            [doves
To draw her chariot; I must have another—
[*She kisses him again.*]
When wilt thou marry, Cariola?
CARI. Never, my lord.   60
ANT. O, fie upon this single life! Forego it.
We read how Daphne, for her peevish flight,
Became a fruitless bay tree, Syrinx turned
To the pale empty reed, Anaxarete°
Was frozen into marble; whereas those   65
Which married, or proved kind unto their
                                            [friends,
Were by a gracious influence transhaped
Into the olive, pomegranate, mulberry,
Became flowers, precious stones, or eminent   70
                                            [stars.
CARI. This is a vain poetry. But I pray you
                                            [tell me,
If there were proposed me wisdom, riches, and
                                            [beauty, 75
In three several young men, which should I
                                            [choose?
ANT. 'Tis a hard question. This was Paris'
                                            [case,
And he was blind in't, and there was great   80
                                            [cause.
For how was't possible he could judge right,°

Anaxarete   petrified by Venus for her coldness to a
lover. Daphne and Syrinx suffered their transformations while fleeing Apollo and Pan, respectively.
The kindlier women (below) represent a jumble of
mythological associations.
judge right   in a beauty contest between Juno, Minerva, and Venus

Having three amorous goddesses in view,
And they stark naked? 'Twas a motion°
Were able to benight the apprehension
Of the severest counsellor of Europe.
5 Now I look on both your faces so well formed,
It puts me in mind of a question I would ask.
   CARI. What is't?
   ANT. I do wonder why hard-favored ladies,
For the most part, keep worse-favored
10   [waiting-women
To attend them, and cannot endure fair ones.
   DUCH. O, that's soon answered.
Did you ever in your life know an ill painter
Desire to have his dwelling next door to the
15   [shop
Of an excellent picture-maker? 'Twould
                            [disgrace
His face-making, and undo him. I prithee,
When were we so merry?—My hair tangles.
20   ANT. Pray thee, Cariola, let's steal forth the
                            [room,
And let her talk to herself. I have divers times
Served her the like, when she hath chafed
                         [extremely.
25 I love to see her angry. Softly, Cariola.
   [*Exeunt* ANTONIO *and* CARIOLA.]
   DUCH. Doth not the color of my hair 'gin to
                         [change?
When I wax gray, I shall have all the court
30 Powder their hair with arras,° to be like me.
You have cause to love me. I entered you into
                         [my heart
Before you would vouchsafe to call for the keys.
   [*Enter* FERDINAND *behind*.]
35 We shall one day have my brothers take you
                         [napping.
Methinks his presence, being now in court,
Should make you keep your own bed; but you'll
                         [say
40 Love mixed with fear is sweetest. I'll assure you,
You shall get no more children till my brothers
Consent to be your gossips.° Have you lost
                         [your tongue?

motion show
arras a white powder of orris root
gossips godparents to your children

'Tis welcome:
For know, whether I am doomed to live or die,   45
I can do both like a prince.
   FERD. Die, then, quickly!
   [*Giving her a poniard*.]
Virtue, where art thou hid? What hideous
                     [thing 50
Is it that doth eclipse thee?
   DUCH. Pray, sir, hear me.
   FERD. Or is it true thou art but a bare name,
And no essential thing?
   DUCH. Sir,—   55
   FERD. Do not speak.
   DUCH. No, sir:
I will plant my soul in mine ears, to hear you.
   FERD. O most imperfect light of human
                     [reason, 60
That mak'st us so unhappy to foresee
What we can least prevent! Pursue thy wishes,
And glory in them. There's in shame no
                     [comfort
But to be past all bounds and sense of shame.   65
   DUCH. I pray, sir, hear me: I am married.
   FERD. So!
   DUCH. Haply, not to your liking: but for
                     [that,
Alas, your shears do come untimely now   70
To clip the bird's wing that's already flown!
Will you see my husband?
   FERD. Yes, if I could change
Eyes with a basilisk.°
   DUCH. Sure, you came hither   75
By his confederacy.
   FERD. The howling of a wolf
Is music to thee, screech owl! Prithee, peace.—
Whate'er thou art that hast enjoyed my sister,
For I am sure thou hear'st me, for thine own   80
                     [sake
Let me not know thee. I came hither prepared
To work thy discovery; yet am now persuaded
It would beget such violent effects
As would damn us both. I would not for ten   85
                     [millions
I had beheld thee. Therefore use all means
I never may have knowledge of thy name.

basilisk mythical monster, the look of which killed

Enjoy thy lust still, and a wretched life,
On that condition.—And for thee, vile woman,
If thou do wish thy lecher may grow old
In thy embracements, I would have thee build
Such a room for him as our anchorites
To holier use inhabit. Let not the sun
Shine on him till he's dead. Let dogs and
                              [monkeys
Only converse with him, and such dumb things
To whom nature denies use to sound his name.
Do not keep a paraquito, lest she learn it;
If thou do love him, cut out thine own tongue,
Lest it bewray him.
    DUCH. Why might not I marry?
I have not gone about in this to create
Any new world or custom.
    FERD. Thou art undone;
And thou hast ta'en that massy sheet of lead
That hid thy husband's bones, and folded it
About my heart.
    DUCH. Mine bleeds for't.
    FERD. Thine! Thy heart!
What should I name't unless a hollow bullet
Filled with unquenchable wild-fire?
    DUCH. You are in this
Too strict; and were you not my princely
                              [brother,
I would say, too wilful. My reputation
Is safe.
    FERD. Dost thou know what reputation is?
I'll tell thee—to small purpose, since the
                              [instruction
Comes now too late.
Upon a time Reputation, Love, and Death
Would travel o'er the world, and it was
                              [concluded
That they should part and take three several
                              [ways.
Death told them they should find him in great
                              [battles,
Or cities plagued with plagues. Love gives them
                              [counsel
To inquire for him 'mongst unambitious
                              [shepherds,
Where dowries were not talked of, and
                              [sometimes
'Mongst quiet kindred that had nothing left

By their dead parents. "Stay," quoth
                              [Reputation,
"Do not forsake me; for it is my nature,
If once I part from any man I meet,
I am never found again." And so for you:
You have shook hands with Reputation,
And made him invisible. So, fare you well.
I will never see you more.
    DUCH. Why should only I,
Of all the other princes of the world,
Be cased up, like a holy relic? I have youth
And a little beauty.
    FERD. So you have some virgins
That are witches. I will never see thee more.
    [Exit.]
    [Re-enter ANTONIO with a pistol, and
CARIOLA.]
    DUCH. You saw this apparition?
    ANT. Yes, we are
Betrayed. How came he hither? I should turn
This to thee, for that.
    CARI. Pray, sir, do. And when
That you have cleft my heart, you shall read
                              [there
Mine innocence.
    DUCH. That gallery gave him entrance.
    ANT. I would this terrible thing would come
                              [again,
That, standing on my guard, I might relate
My warrantable love.—
    [She shows the poniard.]
                    Ha! what means this?
    DUCH. He left this with me.
    ANT. And it seems did wish
You would use it on yourself.
    DUCH. His action
Seemed to intend so much.
    ANT. This hath a handle to't,
As well as a point. Turn it towards him,
And so fasten the keen edge in his rank gall.
    [Knocking within.]
How now! Who knocks? More earthquakes?
    DUCH. I stand
As if a mine beneath my feet were ready
To be blown up.
    CARI. 'Tis Bosola.
    DUCH. Away!

O misery! Methinks unjust actions
Should wear these masks and curtains, and not
                                    [we.
You must instantly part hence. I have fashioned
5   [it already.
    [*Exit* ANTONIO.]
    [*Enter* BOSOLA.]
    Bos. The duke your brother is ta'en up in a
                                    [whirlwind;
10 Hath took horse, and 's rid post to Rome.
    DUCH. So late?
    Bos. He told me, as he mounted into the
                                    [saddle,
You were undone.
15 DUCH. Indeed, I am very near it.
    Bos. What's the matter?
    DUCH. Antonio, the master of our household,
Hath dealt so falsely with me in 's accounts.
My brother stood engaged with me° for money
20 Ta'en up of certain Neapolitan Jews,
And Antonio lets the bonds be forfeit.
    Bos. Strange!—[*Aside.*] This is cunning.
    DUCH. And hereupon
My brother's bills at Naples are protested
25 Against.°—Call up our officers.
    Bos. I shall.
    [*Exit.*]
    [*Re-enter* ANTONIO.]
    DUCH. The place that you must fly to is
30   [Ancona.
Hire a house there; I'll send after you
My treasure and my jewels. Our weak safety
Runs upon enginous wheels.° Short syllables
Must stand for periods. I must now accuse you
35 Of such a feignèd crime as Tasso calls
Magnanima menzogna, a noble lie,
'Cause it must shield our honors.—Hark! They
                                    [are coming.
    [*Re-enter* BOSOLA *and* OFFICERS.]
40 ANT. Will your grace hear me?
    DUCH. I have got well by you; you have
                                    [yielded me
A million of loss. I am like to inherit

The people's curses for your stewardship.
You had the trick in audit time to be sick,   45
Till I had signed your quietus; and that cured
                                    [you
Without help of a doctor.—Gentlemen,
I would have this man be an example to you all;
So shall you hold my favor. I pray, let him;°   50
For h'as done that, alas, you would not think
                                    [of,
And, because I intend to be rid of him,
I mean not to publish.—Use your fortune
                                    [elsewhere. 55
    ANT. I am strongly armed to brook my
                                    [overthrow,
As commonly men bear with a hard year.
I will not blame the cause on't; but do think
The necessity of my malevolent star   60
Procures this, not her humor. O, the inconstant
And rotten ground of service! You may see,
'Tis even like him, that in a winter night
Takes a long slumber o'er a dying fire,
A-loath to part from 't; yet parts thence as cold 65
As when he first sat down.
    DUCH. We do confiscate,
Towards the satisfying of your accounts,
All that you have.
    ANT. I am all yours; and 'tis very fit   70
All mine should be so.
    DUCH. So, sir, you have your pass.
    ANT. You may see, gentlemen, what 'tis to
                                    [serve
A prince with body and soul.   75
    [*Exit.*]
    Bos. Here's an example for extortion: what
moisture is drawn out of the sea, when foul
weather comes, pours down, and runs into the
sea again.   80
    DUCH. I would know what are your opinions
Of this Antonio.
    2ND OFF. He could not abide to see a pig's
head gaping. I thought your grace would find
him a Jew.°   85
    3RD OFF. I would you had been his officer, for
                                    [your own sake.

---

stood . . . me   was my security
protested Against   made subject to suit for recovery
runs . . . wheels   depends on intricate processes

let him   release him
a Jew   because he disliked the roasted pig's head

4TH OFF. You would have had more money.

1ST. OFF. He stopped his ears with black wool, and to those came to him for money said he was thick of hearing.

5 2ND OFF. Some said he was an hermaphrodite, for he could not abide a woman.

4TH OFF. How scurvy proud he would look when the treasury was full! Well, let him go.

1ST OFF. Yes, and the chippings of the but-
10 tery fly after him, to scour his gold chain.°

DUCH. Leave us.

[*Exeunt* OFFICERS.]

What do you think of these?

BOS. That these are rogues that in's
15   [prosperity,
But to have waited on his fortune, could have
                                  [wished
His dirty stirrup rivetted through their noses,
And followed after's mule, like a bear in a ring;
20 Would have prostituted their daughters to his
                                  [lust;
Made their first-born intelligencers; thought
                                  [none happy
But such as were born under his blest planet
25 And wore his livery. And do these lice drop off
                                  [now?
Well, never look to have the like again.
He hath left a sort° of flattering rogues behind
                                  [him;
30 Their doom must follow. Princes pay flatterers
In their own money: flatterers dissemble their
                                  [vices,
And they dissemble their lies. That's justice.
Alas, poor gentleman!
35 DUCH. Poor! He hath amply filled his coffers.

BOS. Sure, he was too honest. Pluto,° the god
                                  [of riches,
When he's sent by Jupiter to any man,
He goes limping, to signify that wealth
40 That comes on God's name comes slowly; but
                                  [when he's sent
On the devil's errand, he rides post and comes
                                  [in by scuttles.°

Let me show you what a most unvalued° jewel
You have in a wanton humor thrown away,   45
To bless the man shall find him. He was an
                                  [excellent
Courtier and most faithful; a soldier that
                                  [thought it
As beastly to know his own value too little   50
As devilish to acknowledge it too much.
Both his virtue and form deserved a far better
                                  [fortune.
His discourse rather delighted to judge itself
                                  [than show itself. 55
His breast was filled with all perfection,
And yet it seemed a private whispering room,
It made so little noise of't.

DUCH. But he was basely descended.

BOS. Will you make yourself a mercenary   60
                                  [herald,
Rather to examine men's pedigrees than
                                  [virtues?
You shall want him.°
For know an honest statesman to a prince   65
Is like a cedar planted by a spring;
The spring bathes the tree's root, the grateful
                                  [tree
Rewards it with his shadow. You have not done
                                  [so. 70
I would sooner swim to the Bermoothes° on
Two politicians' rotten bladders, tied
Together with an intelligencer's heart-string,
Than depend on so changeable a prince's
                                  [favor. 75
Fare thee well, Antonio! Since the malice of the
                                  [world
Would needs down with thee, it cannot be said
                                  [yet
That any ill happened unto thee, considering   80
                                  [thy fall
Was accompanied with virtue.

DUCH. O, you render me excellent music!

BOS. Say you?

DUCH. This good one that you speak of is my   85
                                  [husband.

BOS. Do I not dream! Can this ambitious age

gold chain   the badge of his office
sort   company
Pluto   Plutus
by scuttles   hurriedly

unvalued   invaluable
want him   feel his loss
Bermoothes   Bermudas

Have so much goodness in't as to prefer
A man merely for worth, without these shadows
Of wealth and painted honors? Possible?
    DUCH. I have had three children by him.
5   BOS. Fortunate lady!
For you have made your private nuptial bed
The humble and fair seminary° of peace.
No question but many an unbeneficed scholar
Shall pray for you for this deed, and rejoice
10 That some preferment in the world can yet
Arise from merit. The virgins of your land
That have no dowries shall hope your example
Will raise them to rich husbands. Should you
                    [want
15 Soldiers, 'twould make the very Turks and
                    [Moors
Turn Christians, and serve you for this act.
Last, the neglected poets of your time,
In honor of this trophy of a man,
20 Raised by that curious engine, your white hand,
Shall thank you, in your grave, for't; and make
                    [that
More reverend than all the cabinets°
Of living princes. For Antonio,
25 His fame shall likewise flow from many a pen,
When heralds shall want coats to sell to men.
    DUCH. As I taste comfort in this friendly
                    [speech,
So would I find concealment.
30   BOS. O, the secret of my prince,
Which I will wear on the inside of my heart!
    DUCH. You shall take charge of all my coin
                    [and jewels
And follow him; for he retires himself
35 To Ancona.
    BOS. So.
    DUCH. Whither, within few days,
I mean to follow thee.
    BOS. Let me think.
40 I would wish your grace to feign a pilgrimage
To our Lady of Loretto, scarce seven leagues
From fair Ancona; so may you depart
Your country with more honor, and your flight
Will seem a princely progress, retaining
45 Your usual train about you.

seminary seedbed
cabinets museums

    DUCH. Sir, your direction
Shall lead me by the hand.
    CARI. In my opinion,
She were better progress to the baths at Lucca,
Or go visit the Spa   50
In Germany;° for, if you will believe me,
I do not like this jesting with religion,
This feignèd pilgrimage.
    DUCH. Thou art a superstitious fool!
Prepare us instantly for our departure.   55
Past sorrows, let us moderately lament them;
For those to come, seek wisely to prevent them.
    [*Exeunt* DUCHESS *and* CARIOLA.]
    BOS. A politican is the devil's quilted anvil;
He fashions all sins on him, and the blows   60
Are never heard. He may work in a lady's
                    [chamber,
As here for proof. What rests but I reveal
All to my lord? O, this base quality°
Of intelligencer! Why, every quality i' the   65
                    [world
Prefers but gain or commendation.
Now for this act I am certain to be raised,
And men that paint weeds to the life are
                  [praised. 70
    [*Exit.*]

Scene iii

[*An apartment in the* CARDINAL's *palace at
Rome.*]
    [*Enter* CARDINAL, FERDINAND, MALATESTE,
PESCARA, DELIO, *and* SILVIO.]   75
    CARD. Must we turn soldier, then?
    MAL. The emperor,
Hearing your worth that way ere you attained
This reverend garment, joins you in commission
With the right fortunate soldier the Marquis of 80
                  [Pescara,
And the famous Lannoy.
    CARD. He that had the honor
Of taking the French king° prisoner?
    MAL. The same.   85
Here's a plot drawn for a new fortification

Germany i.e., where the "Dutch" live; in present
  Belgium
quality occupation
French king Francis I, captured at the battle of Pavia

At Naples.

FERD. This great Count Malateste, I perceive,
Hath got employment?

DELIO. No employment, my lord;
5 A marginal note in the muster-book, that he is
A voluntary° lord.

FERD. He's no soldier.

DELIO. He has worn gunpowder in's hollow
[tooth for the toothache.

10 SIL. He come to the leaguer° with a full intent
To eat fresh beef and garlic, means to stay
Till the scent be gone, and straight return to
[court.

DELIO. He hath read all the late service°
15 As the city chronicle relates it,
And keeps two pewterers going, only to
[express

Battles in model.°

SIL. Then he'll fight by the book.
20 DELIO. By the almanac, I think,
To choose good days and shun the critical.
That's his mistress' scarf.

SIL. Yes, he protests
He would do much for that taffeta.

25 DELIO. I think he would run away from a
[battle,

To save it from taking prisoner.

SIL. He is horribly afraid
Gunpowder will spoil the perfume on't.

30 DELIO. I saw a Dutchman break his pate once
For calling him pop-gun; he had his head
Have a bore in't like a musket.

SIL. I would he had made a touchhole to't.
He is indeed a guarded sumpter cloth,°
35 Only for the remove of the court.

[Enter BOSOLA.]

PES. Bosola arrived! What should be the
[business?

Some falling out amongst the cardinals.
40 These factions amongst great men, they are like
Foxes; when their heads are divided,

They carry fire in their tails,° and all the
[country
About them goes to wrack for't.

SIL. What's that Bosola? 45

DELIO. I knew him in Padua—a fantastical
scholar, like such who study to know how many
knots was in Hercules' club, of what color
Achilles' beard was, or whether Hector were
not troubled with the toothache. He hath stud- 50
ied himself half blear-eyed to know the true
symmetry of Caesar's nose by a shoeing-horn;
and this he did to gain the name of a speculative
man.

PES. Mark Prince Ferdinand. 55
A very salamander lives in's eye,
To mock the eager violence of fire.

SIL. That cardinal hath made more bad faces
with his oppression than ever Michael Angelo
made good ones. He lifts up's nose, like a foul 60
porpoise before a storm.

PES. The Lord Ferdinand laughs.

DELIO. Like a deadly cannon
That lightens ere it smokes.

PES. These are your true pangs of death, 65
The pangs of life, that struggle with great
[statesmen.

DELIO. In such a deformed silence witches
[whisper their charms.

CARD. Doth she make religion her riding 70
[hood
To keep her from the sun and tempest?

FERD. That, that damns her. Methinks her
[fault and beauty,
Blended together, show like leprosy: 75
The whiter the fouler. I make it a question
Whether her beggarly brats were ever
[christened.

CARD. I will instantly solicit the state of
[Ancona 80
To have them banished.

FERD. You are for Loretto?
I shall not be at your ceremony. Fare you
[well.—

---

voluntary volunteer
leaguer camp
service military news
model made of pewter; i.e., "tin soldiers"
guarded sumpter cloth ornamental horse cloth

fire . . . tails these incendiary foxes were used by
Samson to burn the Philistine grain fields (Judges
15:4)

Write to the Duke of Malfi, my young nephew
She had by her first husband, and acquaint him
With's mother's honesty.°
    Bos. I will.
5   Ferd. Antonio!
A slave that only smelled of ink and counters,
And never in's life looked like a gentleman,
But in the audit-time.—Go, go presently,
Draw me out an hundred and fifty of our horse,
10 And meet me at the fort-bridge.
    [*Exeunt.*]

Scene iv

[*The shrine of Our Lady of Loretto.*]
[*Enter* Two Pilgrims.]
    1st Pil. I have not seen a goodlier shrine than
15   [this;
Yet I have visited many.
    2nd Pil. The Cardinal of Aragon
Is this day to resign his cardinal's hat.
His sister duchess likewise is arrived
20 To pay her vow of pilgrimage. I expect
A noble ceremony.
    1st Pil. No question.—They come.
    [*Here the ceremony of the* Cardinal's *instal-*
ment, in the habit of a soldier, is performed by
25 *his delivering up his cross, hat, robes, and ring,*
at the shrine, and the investing of him with
sword, helmet, shield, and spurs; then Antonio,
the Duchess, *and their children, having pre-*
sented themselves at the shrine, are, by a form
30 *of banishment in dumb-show expressed to-*
wards them by the Cardinal *and the state of*
Ancona, banished: during all which ceremony,
this ditty is sung, to very solemn music, by
divers churchmen.]
35 Arms and honors deck thy story
To thy fame's eternal glory!
Adverse fortune ever fly thee;
No disastrous fate come nigh thee!
I alone will sing thy praises,
40 Whom to honor virtue raises;
And thy study, that divine is,
Bent to martial discipline is.

honesty chastity

Lay aside all those robes lie by thee;
Crown thy arts with arms, they'll beautify thee.
O worthy of worthiest name, adorned in this 45
    [manner,
Lead bravely thy forces on under war's warlike
    [banner!
O, mayst thou prove fortunate in all martial
    [courses! 50
Guide thou still by skill in arts and forces!
Victory attend thee nigh, whilst fame sings
    [loud thy powers;
Triumphant conquest crown thy head, and
    [blessings pour down showers! 55

    1st Pil. Here's a strange turn of state! Who
        [would have thought
So great a lady would have matched herself
Unto so mean a person? Yet the cardinal
Bears himself much too cruel. 60
    2nd Pil. They are banished.
    1st. Pil. But I would ask what power hath
        [this state
Of Ancona to determine of a free prince?
    2nd Pil. They are a free state, sir, and her 65
        [brother showed
How that the Pope, fore-hearing of her
        [looseness,
Hath seized into the protection of the church
The dukedom which she held as dowager. 70
    1st Pil. But by what justice?
    2nd Pil. Sure, I think by none,
Only her brother's instigation.
    1st Pil. What was it with such violence he
        [took 75
Off from her finger?
    2nd Pil. 'Twas her wedding ring,
Which he vowed shortly he would sacrifice
To his revenge.
    1st Pil. Alas, Antonio! 80
If that a man be thrust into a well,
No matter who sets hand to't, his own weight
Will bring him sooner to the bottom. Come,
    [let's hence.
Fortune makes this conclusion general, 85
All things do help the unhappy man to fall.
    [*Exeunt.*]

Scene v

[*Near Loretto.*]

[*Enter* DUCHESS, ANTONIO, CHILDREN, CARI-
OLA, *and* SERVANTS.]

    DUCH. Banished Ancona!

5   ANT. Yes, you see what power
Lightens in great men's breath.
    DUCH. Is all our train
Shrunk to this poor remainder?
    ANT. These poor men,
10 Which have got little in your service, vow
To take your fortune; but your wiser buntings,°
Now they are fledged, are gone.
    DUCH. They have done wisely.
This puts me in mind of death. Physicians thus,
15 With their hands full of money, use to give o'er
Their patients.
    ANT. Right the fashion of the world!
From decayed fortunes every flatterer shrinks;
Men cease to build where the foundation sinks.
20 DUCH. I had a very strange dream tonight.
    ANT. What was't?
    DUCH. Methought I wore my coronet of state,
And on a sudden all the diamonds
Were changed to pearls.
25 ANT. My interpretation
Is, you'll weep shortly, for to me the pearls
Do signify your tears.
    DUCH. The birds that live i' the field
On the wild benefit of nature live
30 Happier than we; for they may choose their
                            [mates,
And carol their sweet pleasures to the spring.
[*Enter* BOSOLA *with a letter.*]
    BOS. You are happily o'erta'en.
35 DUCH. From my brother?
    BOS. Yes, from the Lord Ferdinand your
                            [brother
All love and safety.
    DUCH. Thou dost blanch mischief,
40 Wouldst make it white. See, see, like to calm
                            [weather
At sea before a tempest, false hearts speak fair
To those they intend most mischief.

[*Reads.*]
    "Send Antonio to me; I want his head in a 45
business."
A politic equivocation!
He doth not want your counsel, but your head;
That is, he cannot sleep till you be dead.
And here's another pitfall that's strewed o'er 50
With roses. Mark it, 'tis a cunning one:
[*Reads.*]
    "I stand engaged for your husband for
several debts at Naples. Let not that trouble
him; I had rather have his heart than his 55
money:"—
And I believe so too.
    BOS. What do you believe?
    DUCH. That he so much distrusts my
                     [husband's love, 60
He will by no means believe his heart is with
                          [him
Until he sees it. The devil is not cunning enough
To circumvent us in riddles.
    BOS. Will you reject that noble and free 65
                        [league
Of amity and love which I present you?
    DUCH. Their league is like that of some politic
                       [kings,
Only to make themselves of strength and 70
                       [power
To be our after-ruin. Tell them so.
    BOS. And what from you?
    ANT. Thus tell him: I will not come.
    BOS. And what of this? 75
    ANT. My brothers have dispersed
Bloodhounds abroad; which till I hear are
                       [muzzled,
No truce, though hatched with ne'er such
                     [politic skill, 80
Is safe, that hangs upon our enemies' will.
I'll not come at them.
    BOS. This proclaims your breeding.
Every small thing draws a base mind to fear,
As the adamant° draws iron. Fare you well, sir; 85
You shall shortly hear from's.
[*Exit.*]
    DUCH. I suspect some ambush.
Therefore by all my love I do conjure you

---

buntings a kind of bird; buntings are (1) migratory
and (2) gregarious

adamant loadstone

To take your eldest son, and fly towards Milan.
Let us not venture all this poor remainder
In one unlucky bottom.°
    ANT. You counsel safely.
5 Best of my life, farewell, since we must part.
Heaven hath a hand in't; but no otherwise
Than as some curious artist° takes in sunder
A clock or watch, when it is out of frame,
To bring't in better order.
10   DUCH. I know not which is best,
To see you dead, or part with you.—Farewell,
                    [boy!
Thou art happy that thou hast not
                    [understanding
15 To know thy misery; for all our wit
And reading brings us to a truer sense
Of sorrow.—In the eternal church, sir,
I do hope we shall not part thus.
    ANT. O, be of comfort!
20 Make patience a noble fortitude,
And think not how unkindly we are used.
Man, like to cassia, is proved best being
                    [bruised.
    DUCH. Must I, like a slave-born Russian,
25 Account it praise to suffer tyranny?
And yet, O Heaven, thy heavy hand is in't!
I have seen my little boy oft scourge° his top,
And compared myself to't. Naught made me
                    [e'er
30 Go right but Heaven's scourge-stick.
    ANT. Do not weep.
Heaven fashioned us of nothing, and we strive
To bring ourselves to nothing.—Farewell,
                    [Cariola,
35 And thy sweet armful.—If I do never see thee
                    [more,
Be a good mother to your little ones,
And save them from the tiger. Fare you well.
    DUCH. Let me look upon you once more, for
40   [that speech
Came from a dying father. Your kiss is colder
Than that I have seen an holy anchorite
Give to a dead man's skull.
    ANT. My heart is turned to a heavy lump of

With which I sound my danger. Fare you well.   [lead, 45
    [*Exeunt* ANTONIO *and his* SON.]
    DUCH. My laurel is all withered.
    CARI. Look, madam, what a troop of armèd
                  [men 50
Make towards us!
    DUCH. O, they are very welcome.
When Fortune's wheel is overcharged with
                  [princes,
The weight makes it move swift. I would have 55
                  [my ruin
Be sudden.
    [*Re-enter* BOSOLA *visarded, with a* GUARD.]
          I am your adventure,° am I not?
    BOS. You are; you must see your husband no 60
                  [more.
    DUCH. What devil art thou that counterfeit'st
                  [Heaven's thunder?
    BOS. Is that terrible? I would have you tell me
                  [whether 65
Is that note worse that frights the silly birds
Out of the corn, or that which doth allure them
To the nets? You have harkened to the last too
                  [much.
    DUCH. O misery! Like to a rusty o'er-charged 70
                  [cannon,
Shall I never fly in pieces?—Come, to what
                  [prison?
    BOS. To none.
    DUCH. Whither, then? 75
    BOS. To your palace.
    DUCH. I have heard
That Charon's boat serves to convey all o'er
The dismal lake, but brings none back again.
    BOS. Your brothers mean you safety and pity. 80
    DUCH. Pity!
With such a pity men preserve alive
Pheasants and quails, when they are not fat
                  [enough
To be eaten. 85
    BOS. These are your children?
    DUCH. Yes.
    BOS. Can they prattle?
    DUCH. No;
But I intend, since they were born accursed, 90

---

bottom ship
curious artist skillful artisan
scourge activate with a whiplash

adventure quarry

Curses shall be their first language.
    Bos: Fie, madam!
Forget this base, low fellow,—
    Duch. Were I a man,
5 I'd beat that counterfeit face° into thy other.
    Bos. One of no birth.
    Duch. Say that he was born mean,
Man is most happy when's own actions
Be arguments and examples of his virtue.
10   Bos. A barren, beggarly virtue.
    Duch. I prithee, who is greatest? Can you
                        [tell?
Sad tales befit my woe. I'll tell you one.
A salmon, as she swam unto the sea,
15 Met with a dogfish, who encounters her
With this rough language: "Why art thou so
                        [bold
To mix thyself with our high state of floods,
Being no eminent courtier, but one
20 That for the calmest and fresh time o' the year
Dost live in shallow rivers, rank'st thyself
With silly smelts and shrimps? And darest thou
Pass by our dogship without reverence?"
"O!" quoth the salmon, "sister, be at peace.
25 Thank Jupiter we both have passed the net!
Our value never can be truly known,
Till in the fisher's basket we be shown.
I' the market then my price may be the higher,
Even when I am nearest to the cook and fire."
30 So to great men the moral may be stretchèd;
Men oft are valued high, when they're most
                       [wretched.—
But come, whither you please. I am armed
                      ['gainst misery;
35 Bent to all sways of the oppressor's will.
There's no deep valley but near some great hill.
    [Exeunt.]

ACT IV

Scene i

[An apartment in the Duchess' palace at
Malfi.]
40 [Enter Ferdinand and Bosola.]
    Ferd. How doth our sister duchess bear
                      [herself

counterfeit face his vizard

In her imprisonment?
    Bos. Nobly. I'll describe her.
She's sad as one long used to't, and she seems   45
Rather to welcome the end of misery
Than shun it; a behavior so noble
As gives a majesty to adversity.
You may discern the shape of loveliness
More perfect in her tears than in her smiles.   50
She will muse four hours together; and her
                        [silence,
Methinks, expresseth more than if she spake.
    Ferd. Her melancholy seems to be fortified
With a strange disdain.   55
    Bos. 'Tis so; and this restraint,
Like English mastiffs that grow fierce with
                        [tying,
Makes her too passionately apprehend
Those pleasures she's kept from.   60
    Ferd. Curse upon her!
I will no longer study in the book
Of another's heart. Inform her what I told you.
    [Exit.]
    [Enter Duchess.]   65
    Bos. All comfort to your grace!
    Duch. I will have none.
Pray thee, why dost thou wrap thy poisoned
                        [pills
In gold and sugar?   70
    Bos. Your elder brother, the Lord Ferdinand,
Is come to visit you, and sends you word,
'Cause once he rashly made a solemn vow
Never to see you more, he comes i' the night;
And prays you gently neither torch nor taper   75
Shine in your chamber. He will kiss your hand,
And reconcile himself, but for his vow
He dares not see you.
    Duch. At his pleasure.—
Take hence the lights.—He's come.   80
    [Enter Ferdinand.]
    Ferd. Where are you?
    Duch. Here, sir.
    Ferd. This darkness suits you well.
    Duch. I would ask you pardon.   85
    Ferd. You have it.
For I account it the honorabl'st revenge,
Where I may kill, to pardon.—Where are your
                      [cubs?
    Duch. Whom?   90

FERD. Call them your children,
For though our national law distinguish
                              [bastards
From true legitimate issue, compassionate
5   [nature
Makes them all equal.
    DUCH. Do you visit me for this?
You violate a sacrament o' the church
Shall make you howl in hell for't.
10   FERD. It had been well
Could you have lived thus always, for indeed,
You were too much i' the light.—But no more;
I come to seal my peace with you. Here's a hand
    [*Gives her a dead man's hand.*]
15 To which you have vowed much love. The ring
                              [upon't
You gave.
    DUCH. I affectionately kiss it.
    FERD. Pray, do, and bury the print of it in
20   [your heart.
I will leave this ring with you for a love-token,
And the hand as sure as the ring; and do not
                              [doubt
But you shall have the heart too. When you
25   [need a friend,
Send it to him that owned it; you shall see
Whether he can aid you.
    DUCH. You are very cold.
I fear you are not well after your travel.—
30 Ha! lights!—O, horrible!
    FERD. Let her have lights enough.
    [*Exit.*]
    DUCH. What witchcraft doth he practice, that
                              [he hath left
35 A dead man's hand here?
    [*Here is discovered, behind a curtain, the
    artificial figures of* ANTONIO *and his* CHILDREN,
    appearing as if they were dead.]
    BOS. Look you, here's the piece from which
40   ['twas ta'en.
He doth present you this sad spectacle,
That, now you know directly they are dead,
Hereafter you may wisely cease to grieve
For that which cannot be recoverèd.
45   DUCH. There is not between Heaven and
                              [earth one wish
I stay for after this. It wastes me more
Than were't my picture, fashioned out of wax,

Stuck with a magical needle, and then buried
In some foul dunghill. And yond's an excellent   50
                              [property
For a tyrant, which I would account mercy.
    BOS. What's that?
    DUCH. If they would bind me to that lifeless
                              [trunk,   55
And let me freeze to death.
    BOS. Come, you must live.
    DUCH. That's the greatest torture souls feel in
                              [hell,—
In hell, that they must live, and cannot die.   60
Portia,° I'll new kindle thy coals again,
And revive the rare and almost dead example
Of a loving wife.
    BOS. O, fie! despair? Remember
You are a Christian.   65
    DUCH. The church enjoins fasting.
I'll starve myself to death.
    BOS. Leave this vain sorrow.
Things being at the worst begin to mend. The
                              [bee   70
When he hath shot his sting into your hand,
May then play with your eyelid.
    DUCH. Good comfortable fellow,
Persuade a wretch that's broke upon the wheel
To have all his bones new set; entreat him live   75
To be executed again. Who must despatch me?
I account this world a tedious theater,
For I do play a part in't 'gainst my will.
    BOS. Come, be of comfort; I will save your
                              [life.   80
    DUCH. Indeed, I have not leisure to tend
So small a business.
    BOS. Now, by my life, I pity you.
    DUCH. Thou art a fool, then,
To waste thy pity on a thing so wretched   85
As cannot pity itself. I am full of daggers.
Puff, let me blow these vipers from me.
    [*Enter* SERVANT.]
What are you?
    SERV. One that wishes you long life.   90
    DUCH. I would thou wert hanged for the
                              [horrible curse
Thou hast given me. I shall shortly grow one

Portia upon her husband Brutus' death, Portia held
hot coals in her mouth until she suffocated

Of the miracles of pity. I'll go pray;—
No, I'll go curse.
   Bos. O, fie!
   Duch. I could curse the stars.
5   Bos. O, fearful!
   Duch. And those three smiling seasons of
                        [the year
Into a Russian winter; nay, the world
To its first chaos.
10   Bos. Look you, the stars shine still.
   Duch. O, but you must
Remember, my curse hath a great way to go.—
Plagues that make lanes through largest
                        [families
15 Consume them!—
   Bos. Fie, lady!
   Duch. Let them, like tyrants,
Never be remembered but for the ill they have
                        [done.
20 Let all the zealous prayers of mortified
Churchmen forget them!—
   Bos. O, uncharitable!
   Duch. Let Heaven a little while cease
                    [crowning martyrs
25 To punish them!—
Go, howl them this, and say I long to bleed:
It is some mercy when men kill with speed.
   [Exit.]
   [Re-enter FERDINAND.]
30 Ferd. Excellent, as I would wish; she's
                    [plagued in art.
These presentations are but framed in wax
By the curious master in that quality,
Vincentio Lauriola, and she takes them
35 For true substantial bodies.
   Bos. Why do you do this?
   Ferd. To bring her to despair.
   Bos. Faith, end here,
And go no farther in your cruelty.
40 Send her a penitential garment to put on
Next to her delicate skin, and furnish her
With beads and prayer books.
   Ferd. Damn her! That body of hers,
While that my blood ran pure in 't, was more
45   [worth
Than that which thou wouldst comfort, called
                     [a soul.
I will send her masques of common courtesans,

Have her meat served up by bawds and ruffians,
And, 'cause she'll needs be mad, I am resolved   50
To remove forth° the common hospital
All the mad-folk, and place them near her
                      [lodging.
There let them practice together, sing and
                      [dance, 55
And act their gambols to the full o' the moon.
If she can sleep the better for it, let her.
Your work is almost ended.
   Bos. Must I see her again?
   Ferd. Yes.   60
   Bos. Never.
   Ferd. You must.
   Bos. Never in mine own shape;
That's forfeited by my intelligence
And this last cruel lie. When you send me next, 65
The business shall be comfort.
   Ferd. Very likely!
Thy pity is nothing of kin to thee. Antonio
Lurks about Milan. Thou shalt shortly thither,
To feed a fire as great as my revenge,   70
Which never will slack till it have spent his
                      [fuel.
Intemperate agues make physicians cruel.
   [Exeunt.]

Scene ii

   [The same.]   75
   [Enter DUCHESS and CARIOLA.]
   Duch. What hideous noise was that?
   Cari. 'Tis the wild consort°
Of madmen, lady, which your tyrant brother
Hath placed about your lodging. This tyranny 80
I think, was never practised till this hour.
   Duch. Indeed, I thank him. Nothing but noise
                    [and folly
Can keep me in my right wits, whereas reason
And silence make me stark mad. Sit down; 85
Discourse to me some dismal tragedy.
   Cari. O, 'twill increase your melancholy.
   Duch. Thou art deceived.
To hear of greater grief would lessen mine.
This is a prison?   90
   Cari. Yes, but you shall live

forth out of
consort company

To shake this durance off.
    Duch. Thou art a fool.
The robin-redbreast and the nightingale
Never live long in cages.
5   Cari. Pray, dry your eyes.
What think you of, madam?
    Duch. Of nothing;
When I muse thus, I sleep.
    Cari. Like a madman, with your eyes open?
10   Duch. Dost thou think we shall know one
                    [another
In the other world?
    Cari. Yes, out of question.
    Duch. O, that it were possible we might
15 But hold some two days' conference with the
                    [dead!
From them I should learn somewhat, I am sure,
I never shall know here. I'll tell thee a miracle;
I am not mad yet, to my cause of sorrow.
20 The Heaven o'er my head seems made of
                    [molten brass,
The earth of flaming sulphur, yet I am not mad.
I am acquainted with sad misery
As the tanned galley-slave is with his oar.
25 Necessity makes me suffer constantly,
And custom makes it easy. Who do I look like
                    [now?
    Cari. Like to your picture in the gallery,
A deal of life in show, but none in practice.
30 Or rather like some reverend monument
Whose ruins are even pitied.
    Duch. Very proper;
And Fortune seems only to have her eyesight
To behold my tragedy.—How now!
35 What noise is that?
    [*Enter* Servant.]
    Serv. I am come to tell you
Your brother hath intended you some sport.
A great physician, when the Pope was sick
40 Of a deep melancholy, presented him
With several sorts of madmen, which wild
                    [object
Being full of change and sport, forced him to
                    [laugh,
45 And so the imposthume° broke. The self-same
                    [cure

imposthume abscess

The duke intends on you.
    Duch. Let them come in.
    Serv. There's a mad lawyer, and a secular
                    [priest; 50
A doctor that hath forfeited his wits
By jealousy; an astrologian
That in his works said such a day o' the month
Should be the day of doom, and, failing of't,
Ran mad; an English tailor crazed i' the brain 55
With the study of new fashions; a gentleman-
                    [usher
Quite beside himself with care to keep in mind
The number of his lady's salutations
Or "How do you" she employed him in each 60
                    [morning;
A farmer, too, an excellent knave in grain,°
Mad 'cause he was hindered transportation.°
And let one broker° that's mad loose to these,
You'd think the devil were among them. 65
    Duch. Sit, Cariola.—Let them loose when
                    [you please,
For I am chained to endure all your tyranny.
    [*Enter* Madmen.]
    [*Here this song is sung to a dismal kind of* 70
music by a Madman.]
O, let us howl some heavy note,
    Some deadly doggèd howl,
Sounding as from the threatening throat
    Of beasts and fatal fowl! 75
As ravens, screech owls, bulls, and bears,
    We'll bell and bawl our parts,
Till irksome noise have cloyed your ears
    And còrrosived your hearts.
At last, whenas our choir wants breath, 80
    Our bodies being blest,
We'll sing, like swans, to welcome death,
    And die in love and rest.

    1st Madman. Doomsday not come yet! I'll
draw it nearer by a perspective,° or make a 85
glass that shall set all the world on fire upon an
instant. I cannot sleep; my pillow is stuffed
with a litter of porcupines.

in grain a pun (1) ingrained, (2) trading in grain
hindered transportation prevented from exporting
broker pawnbroker
perspective telescope

2ND MADMAN. Hell is a mere glass-house, where the devils are continually blowing up women's souls on hollow irons, and the fire never goes out.

5 3RD MADMAN. I will lie with every woman in my parish the tenth night; I will tithe them over like haycocks.

4TH MADMAN. Shall my pothecary outgo me because I am a cuckold? I have found out his
10 roguery; he makes alum of his wife's urine, and sells it to puritans that have sore throats with overstraining.°

1ST MADMAN. I have skill in heraldry.

2ND MADMAN. Hast?

15 1ST MADMAN. You do give for your crest a woodcock's head with the brains picked out on't; you are a very ancient gentleman.

3RD MADMAN. Greek is turned Turk. We are only to be saved by the Helvetian translation.°

20 1ST MADMAN. Come on, sir, I will lay° the law to you.

2ND MADMAN. O, rather lay a corrosive. The law will eat to the bone.

3RD MADMAN. He that drinks but to satisfy
25 nature is damned.

4TH MADMAN. If I had my glass here, I would show a sight should make all the women here call me mad doctor.

1ST MADMAN. What's he? A rope-maker?

30 2ND MADMAN. No, no, no, a snuffling knave that, while he shows the tombs,° will have his hand in a wench's placket.

3RD MADMAN. Woe to the caroche° that brought home my wife from the masque at
35 three o'clock in the morning! It had a large featherbed in it.

4TH MADMAN. I have pared the devil's nails forty times, roasted them in raven's eggs, and cured agues with them.

40 3RD MADMAN. Get me three hundred milch-bats, to make possets to procure sleep.

4TH MADMAN. All the college may throw their caps at me. I have made a soap-boiler costive; it was my masterpiece.

[*Here a dance of* EIGHT MADMEN, *with music* 45 *answerable thereto; after which,* BOSOLA, *like an old man enters.*]

DUCH. Is he mad too?

SERV. Pray, question him. I'll leave you.

[*Exeunt* SERVANT *and* MADMEN.] 50

Bos. I am come to make thy tomb.

DUCH. Ha! My tomb?
Thou speak'st as if I lay upon my deathbed,
Gasping for breath. Dost thou perceive me
[sick? 55

Bos. Yes, and the more dangerously, since thy sickness is insensible.

DUCH. Thou art not mad, sure. Dost know
[me?

Bos. Yes. 60

DUCH. Who am I?

Bos. Thou art a box of worm-seed; at best but a salvatory of green mummy.° What's this flesh? A little crudded milk, fantastical puff-paste.° Our bodies are weaker than those 65 paper-prisons boys use to keep flies in; more contemptible, since ours is to preserve earth-worms. Didst thou ever see a lark in a cage? Such is the soul in the body; this world is like her little turf of grass, and the Heaven o'er our 70 heads, like her looking-glass, only gives us a miserable knowledge of the small compass of our prison.

DUCH. Am not I thy duchess?

Bos. Thou art some great woman, sure, for 75 riot begins to sit on thy forehead (clad in gray hairs) twenty years sooner than on a merry milkmaid's. Thou sleepest worse than if a mouse should be forced to take up her lodging in a cat's ear. A little infant that breeds its 80 teeth, should it lie with thee, would cry out, as if thou wert the more unquiet bedfellow.

DUCH. I am Duchess of Malfi still.

Bos. That makes thy sleeps so broken.
Glories, like glow-worms, afar off shine bright, 85

---

overstraining i.e., in the pulpit

Helvetian translation the Puritan-oriented Geneva Bible

lay interpret

shows the tombs moralizes on death. Puritans are again satirized.

caroche coach

salvatory . . . mummy ointment box of undried flesh (dry powered flesh was used in medicine)

puff-paste light pastry

But looked to near, have neither heat nor light.
DUCH. Thou art very plain.
Bos. My trade is to flatter the dead, not the
[living;
5   I am a tomb-maker.
DUCH. And thou comest to make my tomb?
Bos. Yes.
DUCH. Let me be a little merry.—Of what
stuff wilt thou make it?
10   Bos. Nay, resolve me first, of what fashion?
DUCH. Why, do we grow fanstastical in our
death-bed? Do we affect fashion in the grave?
Bos. Most ambitiously. Princes' images on
their tombs do not lie, as they were wont, seem-
15   ing to pray up to Heaven, but with their hands
under their cheeks,° as if they died of the
toothache. They are not carved with their eyes
fixed upon the stars; but as their minds were
wholly bent upon the world, the selfsame way
20   they seem to turn their faces.
DUCH. Let me know fully therefore the effect
Of this thy dismal preparation,
This talk fit for a charnel.
Bos. Now I shall.—
25   [*Enter* EXECUTIONERS, *with a coffin, cords, and
a bell.*]
Here is a present from your princely brothers;
And may it arrive welcome, for it brings
Last benefit, last sorrow.
30   DUCH. Let me see it.
I have so much obedience in my blood,
I wish it in their veins to do them good.
Bos. This is your last presence-chamber.
CARI. O my sweet lady!
35   DUCH. Peace! It affrights not me.
Bos. I am the common bellman,
That usually is sent to condemned persons
The night before they suffer.
DUCH. Even now thou said'st
40   Thou wast a tomb-maker.
Bos. 'Twas to bring you
By degrees to mortification. Listen.
Hark, now every thing is still—
The screech owl and the whistler shrill
45   Call upon our dame aloud,

---

under their cheeks i.e., they face sideways; a recent
(sixteenth-century) change in statuary fashion

And bid her quickly don her shroud!
Much you had of land and rent;
Your length in clay's now competent.
A long war disturbed your mind;
Here your perfect peace is signed.   50
Of what is't fools make such vain keeping?
Sin their conception, their birth weeping,
Their life a general mist of error,
Their death a hideous storm of terror.
Strew your hair with powders sweet,   55
Don clean linen, bathe your feet,
And (the foul fiend more to check)
A crucifix let bless your neck.
'Tis now full tide 'tween night and day;
End your groan, and come away.   60
CARI. Hence, villains, tyrants, murderers!
[Alas!
What will you do with my lady?—Call for help.
DUCH. To whom? To our next neighbors?
[They are mad-folks. 65
Bos. Remove that noise.
DUCH. Farewell, Cariola!
In my last will I have not much to give.
A many hungry guests have fed upon me;
Thine will be a poor reversion.   70
CARI. I will die with her,
DUCH. I pray thee, look thou giv'st my little
[boy
Some syrup for his cold, and let the girl
Say her prayers ere she sleep.   75
[CARIOLA *is forced out by the* EXECUTIONERS.]
Now what you please:
What death?
Bos. Strangling; here are your executioners.
DUCH. I forgive them.   80
The apoplexy, catarrh, or cough o' the lungs,
Would do as much as they do.
Bos. Doth not death fright you?
DUCH. Who would be afraid on't,
Knowing to meet such excellent company   85
In the other world?
Bos. Yet, methinks,
The manner of your death should much afflict
[you;
This cord should terrify you.   90
DUCH. Not a whit.
What would it pleasure me to have my throat
[cut

With diamonds? Or to be smotherèd
With cassia? Or to be shot to death with pearls?
I know death hath ten thousand several doors
For men to take their exits, and 'tis found
5 They go on such strange geometrical hinges,
You may open them both ways; any way, for
                                        [Heaven sake,
So I were out of your whispering. Tell my
                                        [brothers
10 That I perceive death, now I am well awake,
Best gift is they can give or I can take.
I would fain put off my last woman's fault,
I'd not be tedious to you.
        1ST EXECUT. We are ready.
15   DUCH. Dispose my breath how please you;
                                        [but my body
Bestow upon my women, will you?
        1ST EXECUT. Yes.
        DUCH. Pull, and pull strongly, for your able
20   [strength
Must pull down Heaven upon me.—
Yet stay; Heaven-gates are not so highly arched
As princes' palaces; they that enter there
Must go upon their knees [*kneels*].—Come,
25   [violent death,
Serve for mandragora to make me sleep!—
Go tell my brothers, when I am laid out,
They then may feed in quiet.
        [*The* EXECUTIONERS *strangle the* DUCHESS.]
30   BOS. Where's the waiting woman?
Fetch her. Some other strangle the children.
        [CARIOLA *is brought in by the* EXECUTIONERS.]
Look you, there sleeps your mistress.
        CARI. O, you are damned
35 Perpetually for this! My turn is next,
Is't not so ordered?
        BOS. Yes, and I am glad
You are so well prepared for't.
        CARI. You are deceived, sir,
40 I am not prepared for't, I will not die!
I will first come to my answer,° and know
How I have offended.
        BOS. Come, dispatch her.—
You kept her counsel; now you shall keep ours.
45   CARI. I will not die, I must not! I am
                                        [contracted
To a young gentleman.

my answer a formal hearing allowing for defense

1ST EXECUT. Here's your wedding ring.
        CARI. Let me but speak with the duke. I'll
                                        [discover 50
Treason to his person.
        BOS. Delays!—Throttle her.
        1ST EXECUT. She bites and scratches.
        CARI. If you kill me now,
I am damned. I have not been at confession   55
This two years.
        BOS. [*to* EXECUTIONERS]. When?
        CARI. I am quick with child.
        BOS. Why, then,
Your credit's saved.   60
        [*The* EXECUTIONERS *strangle* CARIOLA.]
                        Bear her into the next room;
Let this lie still.
        [*Exeunt the* EXECUTIONERS *with the body of*
CARIOLA.]   65
        [*Enter* FERDINAND.]
        FERD. Is she dead?
        BOS. She is what
You'd have her. But here begin your pity.
        [*Shows the* CHILDREN *strangled.*]   70
Alas, how have these offended?
        FERD. The death
Of young wolves is never to be pitied.
        BOS. Fix your eye here.
        FERD. Constantly.   75
        BOS. Do you not weep?
Other sins only speak; murder shrieks out.
The element of water moistens the earth,
But blood flies upwards and bedews the
                                        [heavens. 80
        FERD. Cover her face! Mine eyes dazzle: she
                                        [died young.
        BOS. I think not so; her infelicity
Seemed to have years too many.
        FERD. She and I were twins;   85
And should I die this instant, I had lived
Her time to a minute.
        BOS. It seems she was born first.
You have bloodily approved the ancient truth,
That kindred commonly do worse agree   90
Than remote strangers.
        FERD. Let me see her face
Again. Why didst not thou pity her? What
An excellent honest man mightst thou have
                                        [been, 95
If thou hadst born her to some sanctuary!

Or, bold in a good cause, opposed thyself,
With thy advancèd sword above thy head,
Between her innocence and my revenge!
I bade thee, when I was distracted of my wits,
5 Go kill my dearest friend, and thou hast done't.
For let me but examine well the cause:
What was the meanness of her match to me?
Only I must confess I had a hope,
Had she continued widow, to have gained
10 An infinite mass of treasure by her death.
And what was the main cause? Her marriage,
That drew a stream of gall quite through my
           [heart.
For thee, as we observe in tragedies
15 That a good actor many times is cursed
For playing a villain's part, I hate thee for't;
And, for my sake, say thou hast done much ill
           [well.
    Bos. Let me quicken your memory, for I
20   [perceive
You are falling into ingratitude. I challenge
The reward due to my service.
    Ferd. I'll tell thee
What I'll give thee.
25   Bos. Do.
    Ferd. I'll give thee a pardon
For this murder.
    Bos. Ha!
    Ferd. Yes, and 'tis
30 The largest bounty I can study to do thee.
By what authority didst thou execute
This bloody sentence?
    Bos. By yours.
    Ferd. Mine! Was I her judge?
35 Did any ceremonial form of law
Doom her to not-being? Did a còmplete jury
Deliver her conviction up i' the court?
Where shalt thou find this judgment registered,
Unless in hell? See, like a bloody fool,
40 Thou'st forfeited thy life, and thou shalt die
           [for't.
    Bos. The office of justice is perverted quite
When one thief hangs another. Who shall dare
To reveal this?
45   Ferd. O, I'll tell thee;
The wolf shall find her grave, and scrape it up,
Not to devour the corpse, but to discover
The horrid murder.
    Bos. You, not I, shall quake for't.

    Ferd. Leave me.   50
    Bos. I will first receive my pension.
    Ferd. You are a villain.
    Bos. When your ingratitude
Is judge, I am so.
    Ferd. O horror!   55
That not the fear of him which binds the devils
Can prescribe man obedience!—
Never look upon me more.
    Bos. Why, fare thee well.
Your brother and yourself are worthy men.   60
You have a pair of hearts are hollow graves,
Rotten, and rotting others; and your vengeance,
Like two chained bullets, still goes arm in arm.
You may be brothers; for treason, like the
           [plague, 65
Doth take much in a blood. I stand like one
That long hath ta'en a sweet and golden dream.
I am angry with myself, now that I wake.
    Ferd. Get thee into some unknown part o'
           [the world, 70
That I may never see thee.
    Bos. Let me know
Wherefore I should be thus neglected. Sir,
I served your tyranny, and rather strove
To satisfy yourself than all the world.   75
And though I loathed the evil, yet I loved
You that did counsel it; and rather sought
To appear a true servant than an honest man.
    Ferd. I'll go hunt the badger by owl-light.
'Tis a deed of darkness.   80
    [*Exit.*]
    Bos. He's much distracted. Off, my painted
           [honor!
While with vain hopes our faculties we tire,
We seem to sweat in ice and freeze in fire.   85
What would I do, were this to do again?
I would not change my peace of conscience
For all the wealth of Europe.—She stirs, here's
           [life!
Return, fair soul, from darkness, and lead mine 90
Out of this sensible hell! She's warm, she
           [breathes!
Upon thy pale lips I will melt my heart,
To store them with fresh color.—Who's there?
Some cordial drink!—Alas! I dare not call.   95
So pity would destroy pity.—Her eye opes,
And Heaven in it seems to ope, that late was
           [shut,

To take me up to mercy.
    Duch. Antonio!
    Bos. Yes, madam, he is living.
The dead bodies you saw were but feigned
5   [statues.
He's reconciled to your brothers; the Pope hath
                        [wrought
The atonement.
    Duch. Mercy!
10 [*Dies.*]
    Bos. O, she's gone again! There the cords of
                        [life broke.
O sacred innocence, that sweetly sleeps
On turtles'° feathers, whilst a guilty conscience
15 Is a black register wherein is writ
All our good deeds and bad—a perspective
That shows us hell! That we cannot be suffered
To do good when we have a mind to it!
This is manly sorrow!
20 These tears, I am very certain, never grew
In my mother's milk. My estate is sunk
Below the degree of fear. Where were
These penitent fountains while she was living?
O, they were frozen up! Here is a sight
25 As direful to my soul as is the sword
Unto a wretch hath slain his father. Come,
I'll bear thee hence,
And execute thy last will; that's deliver
Thy body to the reverend dispose
30 Of some good women. That the cruel tyrant
Shall not deny me. Then I'll post to Milan,
Where somewhat I will speedily enact
Worth my dejection.
    [*Exit.*]

ACT V

Scene i

35 [*A public place in Milan.*]
    [*Enter* Antonio *and* Delio.]
    Ant. What think you of my hope of
                        [reconcilement
To the Aragonian brethren?
40   Delio. I misdoubt it;
For though they have sent their letters of safe

                        [conduct
For your repair to Milan, they appear
But nets to entrap you. The Marquis of Pescara,
Under whom you hold certain land in cheat,°   45
Much 'gainst his noble nature hath been moved
To seize those lands, and some of his
                        [dependants
Are at this instant making it their suit
To be invested in your revenues.   50
I cannot think they mean well to your life
That do deprive you of your means of life,
Your living.
    Ant. You are still an heretic
To any safety I can shape myself.   55
    Delio. Here comes the marquis. I will make
                        [myself
Petitioner for some part of your land,
To know whither it is flying.
    Ant. I pray do.   60
    [*Enter* Pescara.]
    Delio. Sir, I have a suit to you.
    Pes. To me?
    Delio. An easy one.
There is the citadel of Saint Bennet,   65
With some demesnes of late in the possession
Of Antonio Bologna. Please you bestow them
                        [on me!
    Pes. You are my friend; but this is such a suit,
Nor fit for me to give, nor you to take.   70
    Delio. No, sir?
    Pes. I will give you ample reason for't
Soon in private. Here's the cardinal's mistress.
    [*Enter* Julia.]
    Julia. My lord, I am grown your poor   75
                        [petitioner,
And should be an ill beggar, had I not
A great man's letter here, the cardinal's,
To court you in my favor.
    [*Gives a letter.*]   80
    Pes. He entreats for you
The citadel of Saint Bennet, that belonged
To the banished Bologna.
    Julia. Yes.
    Pes. I could not have thought of a friend I   85
                        [could rather

---

turtles' turtledoves'   **cheat** escheat, subject to reverting to him

Pleasure with it. 'Tis yours.
    JULIA. Sir, I thank you.
And he shall know how doubly I am engaged
Both in your gift and speediness of giving,
5 Which makes your grant the greater.
    [*Exit.*]
    ANT. How they fortify
Themselves with my ruin!
    DELIO. Sir, I am
10 Little bound to you.
    PES. Why?
    DELIO. Because you denied this suit to me,
                         [and gave't
To such a creature.
15   PES. Do you know what it was?
It was Antonio's land—not forfeited
By course of law, but ravished from his throat
By the cardinal's entreaty. It were not fit
I should bestow so main a piece of wrong
20 Upon my friend. 'Tis a gratification
Only due to a strumpet, for it is injustice.
Shall I sprinkle the pure blood of innocents
To make those followers I call my friends
Look ruddier upon me? I am glad
25 This land, ta'en from the owner by such wrong,
Returns again unto so foul an use
As salary for his lust. Learn, good Delio,
To ask noble things of me, and you shall find
I'll be a noble giver.
30   DELIO. You instruct me well.
    ANT. Why, here's a man now would fright
                         [impudence
From sauciest beggars.
    PES. Prince Ferdinand's come to Milan,
35 Sick, as they give out, of an apoplexy,
But some say 'tis a frenzy. I am going
To visit him.
    [*Exit.*]
    ANT. 'Tis a noble old fellow.
40   DELIO. What course do you mean to take,
                         [Antonio?
    ANT. This night I mean to venture all my
                         [fortune,
Which is no more than a poor lingering life,
45 To the cardinal's worst of malice. I have got
Private access to his chamber, and intend
To visit him about the mid of night,

As once his brother did our noble duchess.
It may be that the sudden apprehension
Of danger,—for I'll go in mine own shape,— 50
When he shall see it fraught with love and duty,
May draw the poison out of him, and work
A friendly reconcilement. If it fail,
Yet it shall rid me of this infamous calling;
For better fall once than be ever falling. 55
    DELIO. I'll second you in all danger; and,
                         [howe'er,
My life keeps rank with yours.
    ANT. You are still my loved and best friend.
    [*Exeunt.*] 60

Scene ii

[*A gallery in the* CARDINAL'S *palace at Milan.*]
[*Enter* PESCARA *and* DOCTOR.]
    PES. Now, doctor, may I visit your patient?
    DOC. If't please your lordship; but he's 65
                         [instantly
To take the air here in the gallery
By my direction.
    PES. Pray thee, what's his disease?
    DOC. A very pestilent disease, my lord, 70
They call lycanthropia.
    PES. What's that?
I need a dictionary to't.
    DOC. I'll tell you.
In those that are possessed with't there 75
                         [o'erflows
Such melancholy humor they imagine
Themselves to be transformed into wolves,
Steal forth to churchyards in the dead of night,
And dig dead bodies up; as two nights since 80
One met the duke 'bout midnight in a lane
Behind Saint Mark's church, with the leg of a
                         [man
Upon his shoulder; and he howled fearfully,
Said he was a wolf, only the difference 85
Was, a wolf's skin was hairy on the outside,
His on the inside; bade them take their swords,
Rip up his flesh, and try. Straight I was sent for,
And, having ministered to him, found his grace
Very well recovered. 90
    PES. I am glad on't.
    DOC. Yet not without some fear

Of a relapse. If he grow to his fit again,
I'll go a nearer way to work with him
Than ever Paracelsus° dreamed of. If
They'll give me leave, I'll buffet his madness
                                    [out of him.
5   Stand aside; he comes.
        [*Enter* FERDINAND, CARDINAL, MALATESTE, *and*
    BOSOLA.]
        FERD. Leave me.
10 MAL. Why doth your lordship love this
                                    [solitariness?
    FERD. Eagles commonly fly alone; they are
    crows, daws, and starlings that flock together.
    Look! What's that follows me?
15 MAL. Nothing, my lord.
    FERD. Yes.
    MAL. 'Tis your shadow.
    FERD. Stay it; let it not haunt me.
    MAL. Impossible, if you move, and the sun
20   [shine.
    FERD. I will throttle it.
    [*Throws himself down on his shadow.*]
    MAL. O, my lord, you are angry with nothing.
    FERD. You are a fool. How is't possible I
25 should catch my shadow, unless I fall upon't?
    When I go to hell, I mean to carry a bribe; for,
    look you, good gifts evermore make way for the
    worst persons.
        PES. Rise, good my lord.
30 FERD. I am studying the art of patience.
        PES. 'Tis a noble virtue.
        FERD. To drive six snails before me from this
    town to Moscow; neither use goad nor whip
    to them, but let them take their own time.—
35 The patient'st man i' the world match me for
    an experiment!—And I'll crawl after like a
    sheep-biter.°
        CARD. Force him up.
        [*They raise him.*]
40 FERD. Use me well, you were best. What I
    have done, I have done. I'll confess nothing.
        DOC. Now let me come to him.—Are you
    mad, my lord? Are you out of your princely
    wits?

    FERD. What's he?   45
    PES. Your doctor.
    FERD. Let me have his beard sawed off, and
    his eyebrows filed more civil.
    DOC. I must do mad tricks with him, for
    that's the only way on't.—I have brought your 50
    grace a salamander's skin to keep you from
    sunburning.
        FERD. I have cruel sore eyes.
        DOC. The white of a cockatrix's egg is present
    remedy.   55
        FERD. Let it be a new laid one, you were
                                    [best.—
    Hide me from him! Physicians are like kings,—
    They brook no contradiction.
        DOC. Now he begins to fear me; now let   60
    me alone with him.
        CARD. How now! Put off your gown!
        DOC. Let me have some forty urinals filled
    with rose-water; he and I'll go pelt one another
    with them.—Now he begins to fear me.—Can   65
    you fetch a frisk, sir?—Let him go, let him go,
    upon my peril. I find by his eye he stands in awe
    of me. I'll make him as tame as a dormouse.
        FERD. Can you fetch your frisks, sir!—I will
    stamp him into a cullis,° flay off his skin, to   70
    cover one of the anatomies° this rogue hath set
    i' the cold yonder in Barber-Surgeons' Hall.—
    Hence, hence! You are all of you like beasts for
    sacrifice; there's nothing left of you but tongue
    and belly, flattery and lechery.   75
        [*Exit.*]
        PES. Doctor, he did not fear you thoroughly.
        DOC. True; I was somewhat too forward.
        BOS. Mercy upon me, what a fatal judgment
    Hath fall'n upon this Ferdinand!   80
        PES. Knows your grace
    What accident hath brought unto the prince
    This strange distraction?
        CARD. [*aside*]. I must feign somewhat.—
                                [Thus they say it grew. 85
    You have heard it rumored, for these many
                                    [years
    None of our family dies but there is seen

Paracelsus Swiss physician with twin penchants for
    magic and for empirical science
sheep-biter dog that stalks sheep

cullis stew
anatomies skeletons (for the study of barbers, who
    also performed surgical offices)

The shape of an old woman, which is given
By tradition to us to have been murdered
By her nephews for her riches. Such a figure
One night, as the prince sat up late at's book,
5 Appeared to him; when crying out for help,
The gentlemen of's chamber found his grace
All on a cold sweat, altered much in face
And language; since which apparition,
He hath grown worse and worse, and I much
10   [fear
He cannot live.
    Bos. Sir. I would speak with you.
    Pes. We'll leave your grace,
Wishing to the sick prince, our noble lord,
15 All health of mind and body.
        Card. You are most welcome.
    [*Exeunt* Pescara, Malateste, *and* Doctor.]
Are you come? So!—[*Aside.*] This fellow must
                                    [not know
20 By any means I had intelligence
In our duchess' death; for, though I counselled
                                        [it,
The full of all the engagement seemed to grow
From Ferdinand.—Now, sir, how fares our
25   [sister?
I do not think but sorrow makes her look
Like to an oft-dyed garment. She shall now
Taste comfort from me. Why do you look so
                                    [wildly?
30 O, the fortune of your master here the prince
Dejects you; but be you of happy comfort.
If you'll do one thing for me I'll entreat,
Though he had a cold tombstone o'er his bones,
I'd make you what you would be.
35   Bos. Any thing;
Give it me in a breath, and let me fly to't.
They that think long, small expedition win,
For musing much o' the end, cannot begin.
        [*Enter* Julia.]
40 Julia. Sir, will you come into supper?
    Card. I am busy; leave me.
    Julia [*aside*]. What an excellent shape hath
                                    [that fellow!
    [*Exit.*]
45   Card. 'Tis thus. Antonio lurks here in Milan.
Inquire him out, and kill him. While he lives,
Our sister cannot marry; and I have thought
Of an excellent match for her. Do this, and

                                [style me
Thy advancement.   50
    Bos. But by what means shall I find him out?
    Card. There is a gentleman called Delio
Here in the camp, that hath been long
                                [approved°
His loyal friend. Set eye upon that fellow.   55
Follow him to mass; may be Antonio,
Although he do account religion
But a school-name, for fashion of the world
May accompany him; or else go inquire out
Delio's confessor, and see if you can bribe   60
Him to reveal it. There are a thousand ways
A man might find to trace him; as to know
What fellows haunt the Jews for taking up
Great sums of money; for sure he's in want.
Or else to go to the picture-makers, and learn 65
Who bought her picture lately. Some of these
Haply may take.
    Bos. Well, I'll not freeze i' the business.
I would see that wretched thing, Antonio,
Above all sights i' the world.   70
    Card. Do, and be happy.
    [*Exit.*]
    Bos. This fellow doth breed basilisks in's
                                    [eyes,
He's nothing else but murder; yet he seems   75
Not to have notice of the duchess' death.
'Tis his cunning. I must follow his example.
There cannot be a surer way to trace
Than that of an old fox.
    [*Re-enter* Julia, *with a pistol.*]   80
Julia. So, sir, you are well met.
    Bos. How now!
Julia. Nay, the doors are fast enough:
Now, sir, I will make you confess your
                                [treachery. 85
    Bos. Treachery!
Julia. Yes, confess to me
Which of my women 'twas you hired to put
Love powder into my drink?
    Bos. Love powder?   90
Julia. Yes, when I was at Malfi.
Why should I fall in love with such a face else?
I have already suffered for thee so much pain,
The only remedy to do me good   95

approved known to be

Is to kill my longing.
   Bos. Sure, your pistol holds
Nothing but perfumes or kissing-comfits.°
Excellent lady!
5 You have a pretty way on't to discover
Your longing. Come, come, I'll disarm you,
And arm° you thus. Yet this is wondrous
                    [strange.
   Julia. Compare thy form and my eyes
10   [together,
You'll find my love no such great miracle.
Now you'll say
I am wanton. This nice° modesty in ladies
Is but a troublesome familiar
15 That haunts them.
   Bos. Know you me, I am a blunt soldier.
   Julia. The better!
Sure, there wants fire where there are no lively
                    [sparks
20 Of roughness.
   Bos. And I want compliment.
   Julia. Why, ignorance
In courtship cannot make you do amiss,
If you have a heart to do well.
25   Bos. You are very fair.
   Julia. Nay, if you lay beauty to my charge,
I must plead unguilty.
   Bos. Your bright eyes
Carry a quiver of darts in them sharper
30 Than sunbeams.
   Julia. You will mar me with commendation.
Put yourself to the charge of courting me,
Whereas now I woo you.
   Bos. [aside]. I have it, I will work upon this
35   [creature.—
Let us grow most amorously familiar.
If the great cardinal now should see me thus,
Would he not count me a villain?
   Julia. No; he might count me a wanton,
40 Not lay a scruple of offence on you.
For if I see and steal a diamond,
The fault is not i' the stone, but in me the thief
That purloins it. I am sudden with you.

kissing-comfits aromatic candies for the breath
arm embrace
nice punctilious

We that are great women of pleasure use to cut
                    [off 45
These uncertain wishes and unquiet longings,
And in an instant join the sweet delight
And the pretty excuse together. Had you been i'
                  [the street,
Under my chamber-window, even there   50
I should have courted you.
   Bos. O, you are an excellent lady!
   Julia. Bid me do somewhat for you presently
To express I love you.
   Bos. I will; and if you love me,   55
Fail not to effect it.
The cardinal is grown wondrous melancholy.
Demand the cause, let him not put you off
With feigned excuse; discover the main ground
                  [on't. 60
   Julia. Why would you know this?
   Bos. I have depended on him,
And I hear that he is fall'n in some disgrace
With the emperor. If he be, like the mice
That forsake falling houses, I would shift   65
To other dependence.
   Julia. You shall not need
Follow the wars. I'll be your maintenance.
   Bos. And I your loyal servant; but I cannot
Leave my calling.   70
   Julia. Not leave an ungrateful
General for the love of a sweet lady?
You are like some cannot sleep in featherbeds,
But must have blocks for their pillows.
   Bos. Will you do this?   75
   Julia. Cunningly.
   Bos. Tomorrow I'll expect the intelligence.
   Julia. Tomorrow! Get you into my cabinet;
You shall have it with you. Do not delay me,
No more than I do you. I am like one   80
That is condemned; I have my pardon
                [promised,
But I would see it sealed. Go, get you in.
You shall see me wind my tongue about his
                [heart 85
Like a skein of silk.
   [Exit Bosola.]
   [Re-enter Cardinal.]
   Card. Where are you?
   [Enter Servants.]   90

SERVANTS. Here.
CARD. Let none, upon your lives, have
                                    [conference
With the Prince Ferdinand, unless I know it.—
5 [*Aside.*] In this distraction he may reveal
The murder.
      [*Exeunt* SERVANTS.]
                    Yond's my lingering consumption.
I am weary of her, and by any means
10 Would be quit of.
      JULIA. How now, my lord! What ails you?
      CARD. Nothing.
      JULIA. O, you are much altered.
Come, I must be your secretary,° and remove
15 This lead from off your bosom. What's the
                                    [matter?
      CARD. I may not tell you.
      JULIA. Are you so far in love with sorrow
You cannot part with part of it? Or think you
20 I cannot love your grace when you are sad
As well as merry? Or do you suspect
I, that have been a secret to your heart
These many winters, cannot be the same
Unto your tongue?
25   CARD. Satisfy thy longing,—
The only way to make thee keep my counsel
Is, not to tell thee.
      JULIA. Tell your echo this,
Or flatterers, that like echoes still report
30 What they hear though most imperfect, and
                                    [not me.
For if that you be true unto yourself,
I'll know.
      CARD. Will you rack me?
35   JULIA. No, judgment shall
Draw it from you. It is an equal fault,
To tell one's secrets unto all or none.
      CARD. The first argues folly.
      JULIA. But the last tyranny.
40   CARD. Very well. Why, imagine I have
                                    [committed
Some secret deed which I desire the world
May never hear of.
      JULIA. Therefore may not I know it?
45 You have concealed for me as great a sin

secretary confidant

As adultery. Sir, never was occasion
For perfect trial of my constancy
Till now. Sir, I beseech you—
      CARD. You'll repent it.
      JULIA. Never.   50
      CARD. It hurries thee to ruin; I'll not tell thee.
Be well advised, and think what danger 'tis
To receive a prince's secrets. They that do,
Had need have their breasts hooped with
                                    [adamant 55
To contain them. I pray thee, yet be satisfied;
Examine thine own frailty; 'tis more easy
To tie knots than unloose them. 'Tis a secret
That, like a lingering poison, may chance lie
Spread in thy veins, and kill thee seven year   60
                                    [hence.
      JULIA. Now you dally with me.
      CARD. No more; thou shalt know it.
By my appointment the great Duchess of Malfi
And two of her young children, four nights   65
                                    [since,
Were strangled.
      JULIA. O Heaven, sir! What have you done!
      CARD. How now? How settles this? Think
                                    [you your bosom 70
Will be a grave dark and obscure enough
For such a secret?
      JULIA. You have undone yourself, sir.
      CARD. Why?
      JULIA. It lies not in me to conceal it.   75
      CARD. No?
Come, I will swear you to't upon this book.
      JULIA. Most religiously.
      CARD. Kiss it.
      [*She kisses the book.*]   80
Now you shall never utter it; thy curiosity
Hath undone thee. Thou'rt poisoned with that
                                    [book.
Because I knew thou couldst not keep my
                                    [counsel, 85
I have bound thee to't by death.
      [*Re-enter* BOSOLA.]
      Bos. For pity sake, hold!
      CARD. Ha, Bosola!
      JULIA. I forgive you   90
This equal piece of justice you have done;
For I betrayed your counsel to that fellow.

He overhead it; that was the cause I said
It lay not in me to conceal it.
    Bos. O foolish woman,
Couldst not thou have poisoned him?
5   Julia. 'Tis weakness,
Too much to think what should have been
                     [done. I go,
I know not whither.
    [Dies.]
10   Card. Wherefore com'st thou hither?
    Bos. That I might find a great man like
                     [yourself,
Not out of his wits as the Lord Ferdinand,
To remember my service.
15   Card. I'll have thee hewed in pieces.
    Bos. Make not yourself such a promise of
                     [that life
Which is not yours to dispose of.
    Card. Who placed thee here?
20   Bos. Her lust, as she intended.
    Card. Very well;
Now you know me for your fellow-murderer.
    Bos. And wherefore should you lay fair
                     [marble colors°
25   Upon your rotten purposes to me?
Unless you imitate some that do plot great
                     [treasons,
And when they have done, go hide themselves
                     [i' the graves
30   Of those were actors in't?
    Card. No more; there is
A fortune attends thee.
    Bos. Shall I go sue to Fortune any longer?
'Tis the fool's pilgrimage.
35   Card. I have honors in store for thee.
    Bos. There are many ways that conduct to
                     [seeming honor,
And some of them very dirty ones.
    Card. Throw to the devil
40   Thy melancholy. The fire burns well.
What need we keep a stirring of't, and make
A greater smother?° Thou wilt kill Antonio?
    Bos. Yes.
    Card. Take up that body.

marble colors as on wood painted to counterfeit
  marble
smother smoke

    Bos. I think I shall   45
Shortly grow the common bier for churchyards.
    Card. I will allow thee some dozen of
                     [attendants
To aid thee in the murder.
    Bos. O, by no means. Physicians that apply 50
horseleeches to any rank swelling use to cut off
their tails, that the blood may run through them
the faster. Let me have no train when I go to
shed blood, lest it make me have a greater
when I ride to the gallows.   55
    Card. Come to me after midnight, to help to
                     [remove
That body to her own lodging. I'll give out
She died o' the plague; 'twill breed the less
                     [inquiry 60
After her death.
    Bos. Where's Castruccio her husband?
    Card. He's rode to Naples, to take possession
Of Antonio's citadel.
    Bos. Believe me, you have done a very happy 65
                     [turn.
    Card. Fail not to come. There is the master
                     [key
Of our lodgings; and by that you may conceive
What trust I plant in you.   70
    Bos. You shall find me ready.
    [Exit Cardinal.]
O poor Antonio, though nothing be so needful
To thy estate as pity, yet I find
Nothing so dangerous; I must look to my   75
                     [footing.
In such slippery ice-pavements men had need
To be frost-nailed well, they may break their
                     [necks else;
The precedent's here afore me. How this man 80
Bears up in blood! Seems fearless! Why, 'tis
                     [well.
Security some men call the suburbs of hell,
Only a dead wall between. Well, good Antonio,
I'll seek thee out; and all my care shall be 85
To put thee into safety from the reach
Of these most cruel biters that have got
Some of thy blood already. It may be,
I'll join with thee in a most just revenge.
The weakest arm is strong enough that strikes 90
With the sword of justice. Still methinks the
                     [duchess

Haunts me. There, there!—'Tis nothing but my
[melancholy.
O Penitence, let me truly taste thy cup,
That throws men down only to raise them up!

5 [*Exit.*]

Scene iii

[*A fortification at Milan.*]
[*Enter* ANTONIO *and* DELIO.]
DELIO. Yond's the cardinal's window. This
[fortification
10 Grew from the ruins of an ancient abbey,
And to yond side o' the river lies a wall,
Piece of a cloister, which in my opinion
Gives the best echo that you ever heard
So hollow and so dismal, and withal
15 So plain in the distinction of our words,
That many have supposed it is a spirit
That answers.
ANT. I do love these ancient ruins.
We never tread upon them but we set
20 Our foot upon some reverend history.
And, questionless, here in this open court,
Which now lies naked to the injuries
Of stormy weather, some men lie interred
Loved the church so well, and gave so largely
25 [to't,
They thought it should have canopied their
[bones
Till doomsday; but all things have their end.
Churches and cities, which have diseases like
30 [to men,
Must have like death that we have.
ECHO. "Like death that we have."
DELIO. Now the echo hath caught you.
ANT. It groaned, methought, and gave
35 A very deadly accent.
ECHO. "Deadly accent."
DELIO. I told you 'twas a pretty one. You may
[make it
A huntsman, or a falconer, a musician,
40 Or a thing of sorrow.
ECHO. "A thing of sorrow."
ANT. Ay, sure, that suits it best.
ECHO. "That suits it best."
ANT. 'Tis very like my wife's voice.
45 ECHO. "Ay, wife's voice."
DELIO. Come, let us walk further from't.

I would not have you go to the cardinal's
[tonight.
Do not.
ECHO. "Do not." 50
DELIO. Wisdom doth not more moderate
[wasting sorrow
Than time. Take time for't; be mindful of thy
[safety.
ECHO. "Be mindful of thy safety." 55
ANT. Necessity compels me.
Make scrutiny throughout the passages
Of your own life, you'll find it impossible
To fly your fate.
ECHO. "O, fly your fate." 60
DELIO. Hark! The dead stones seem to have
[pity on you,
And give you good counsel.
ANT. Echo, I will not talk with thee,
For thou art a dead thing. 65
ECHO. "Thou art a dead thing."
ANT. My duchess is asleep now,
And her little ones, I hope sweetly. O Heaven,
Shall I never see her more?
ECHO. "Never see her more." 70
ANT. I marked not one repetition of the echo
But that; and on the sudden a clear light
Presented me a face folded in sorrow.
DELIO. Your fancy merely.
ANT. Come, I'll be out of this ague, 75
For to live thus is not indeed to live;
It is a mockery and abuse of life.
I will not henceforth save myself by halves;
Lose all, or nothing.
DELIO. Your own virtue save you! 80
I'll fetch your eldest son, and second you.
It may be that the sight of his° own blood
Spread in so sweet a figure may beget
The more compassion. However, fare you well!
Though in our miseries Fortune have a part, 85
Yet in our noble sufferings she hath none.
Contempt of pain, that we may call our own.
[*Exeunt.*]

Scene iv

[*An apartment in the* CARDINAL'S *palace.*]
[*Enter* CARDINAL, PESCARA, MALATESTE, ROD- 90

his i.e., the cardinal's

ERIGO, *and* GRISOLAN.]

CARD. You will not watch tonight by the sick
[prince;
His grace is very well recovered.

5　MAL. Good my lord, suffer us.

CARD. O, by no means;
The noise, and change of object in his eye,
Doth more distract him. I pray, all to bed;
And though you hear him in his violent fit,

10　Do not rise, I entreat you.

PES. So, sir; we shall not.

CARD. Nay, I must have you promise
Upon your honors, for I was enjoin'd to't
By himself; and he seemed to urge it sensibly.

15　PES. Let our honors bind this trifle.

CARD. Nor any of your followers.

MAL. Neither.

CARD. It may be, to make trial of your
[promise,

20　When he's aleep, myself will rise and feign
Some of his mad tricks, and cry out for help,
And feign myself in danger.

MAL. If your throat were cutting,
I'd not come at you, now I have protested

25　[against it.

CARD. Why, I thank you.

GRIS. 'Twas a foul storm tonight.

ROD. The Lord Ferdinand's chamber shook
[like an osier.

30　MAL. 'Twas nothing but pure kindness in the
[devil,
To rock his own child.

[*Exeunt all except the* CARDINAL.]

CARD. The reason why I would not suffer

35　[these
About my brother is, because at midnight
I may with better privacy convey
Julia's body to her own lodging. O, my
[conscience!

40　I would pray now, but the devil takes away my
[heart
For having any confidence in prayer.
About this hour I appointed Bosola
To fetch the body. When he hath served my

45　[turn,
He dies.

[*Exit.*]

[*Enter* BOSOLA.]

Bos. Ha! 'Twas the cardinal's voice. I heard
[him name　50
Bosola and my death. Listen; I hear one's
[footing.

[*Enter* FERDINAND.]

FERD. Strangling is a very quiet death.

Bos. [*aside*]. Nay, then, I see I must stand　55
[upon my guard.

FERD. What say you to that? Whisper softly;
do you agree to't? So; it must be done i' the
dark. The cardinal would not for a thousand
pounds the doctor should see it.　60

[*Exit.*]

Bos. My death is plotted; here the
[consequence of murder.
We value not desert nor Christian breath,
When we know black deeds must be cured with　65
[death.

[*Enter* ANTONIO *and* SERVANT.]

SERV. Here stay, sir, and be confident, I pray.
I'll fetch you a dark lantern.

[*Exit.*]　70

ANT. Could I take him at his prayers,
There were hope of pardon.

Bos. Fall right, my sword!—

[*Stabs him.*]

I'll not give thee so much leisure as to pray.　75

ANT. O, I am gone! Thou hast ended a long
[suit
In a minute.

Bos. What art thou?

ANT. A most wretched thing,　80
That only have this benefit in death,
To appear myself.°

[*Re-enter* SERVANT *with a lantern.*]

SERV. Where are you, sir?

ANT. Very near my home.—Bosola!　85

SERV. O, misfortune!

Bos. Smother thy pity, thou art dead else.—
[Antonio!
The man I would have saved 'bove mine own
[life!　90
We are merely the stars' tennis-balls, struck
[and bandied
Which way please them.—O good Antonio,

That . . . myself that have only your assistance in revealing myself as I die

I'll whisper one thing in thy dying ear
Shall make thy heart break quickly! Thy fair
        [duchess and two sweet children—
  Ant. Their very names
5 Kindle a little life in me.
  Bos. Are murdered.
  Ant. Some men have wished to die
At the hearing of sad things; I am glad
That I shall do't in sadness.° I would not now
10 Wish my wounds balmed nor healed, for I
        [have no use
To put my life to. In all our quest of greatness,
Like wanton boys, whose pastime is their care,
We follow after bubbles blown in the air.
15 Pleasure of life, what is't? Only the good hours
Of an ague; merely a preparative to rest,
To endure vexation. I do not ask
The process° of my death; only commend me
To Delio.
20   Bos. Break, heart!
  Ant. And let my son fly the courts of princes.
[*Dies.*]
  Bos. Thou seem'st to have loved Antonio?
  Serv. I brought him hither,
25 To have reconciled him to the cardinal.
  Bos. I do not ask thee that.
Take him up, if thou tender thine own life,
And bear him where the lady Julia
Was wont to lodge.—O, my fate moves swift!
30 I have this cardinal in the forge already;
Now I'll bring him to the hammer. O direful
        [misprision!°
I will not imitate things glorious,
No more than base; I'll be mine own example.—
35 On, on, and look thou represent, for silence,
The thing thou bear'st.
  [*Exeunt.*]

Scene v

[*Another apartment in the same.*]
[*Enter* Cardinal, *with a book.*]
40   Card. I am puzzled in a question about hell.
He says, in hell there's one material fire,
And yet it shall not burn all men alike.

Lay him by. How tedious is a guilty conscience!
When I look into the fishponds in my garden,
Methinks I see a thing armed with a rake,   45
That seems to strike at me.
  [*Enter* Bosola, *and* Servant *bearing* Anto-
nio's *body.*]
            Now, art thou come?
Thou look'st ghastly.   50
There sits in thy face some great determination
Mixed with some fear.
  Bos. Thus it lightens into action.
I am come to kill thee.
  Card. Ha!—Help! our guard!   55
  Bos. Thou art deceived;
They are out of thy howling.
  Card. Hold; and I will faithfully divide
Revenues with thee.
  Bos. Thy prayers and proffers   60
Are both unseasonable.
  Card. Raise the watch! We are betrayed!
  Bos. I have confined your flight.
I'll suffer your retreat to Julia's chamber,
But no further.   65
  Card. Help! We are betrayed!
  [*Enter, above,* Pescara, Malateste, Rod-
erigo, *and* Grisolan.]
  Mal. Listen.
  Card. My dukedom for rescue!   70
  Rod. Fie upon his counterfeiting!
  Mal. Why, 'tis not the cardinal.
  Rod. Yes, yes, 'tis he.
But I'll see him hanged ere I'll go down to him.
  Card. Here's a plot upon me; I am assaulted!   75
        [I am lost,
Unless some rescue.
  Gris. He doth this pretty well,
But it will not serve to laugh me out of mine
        [honor.   80
  Card. The sword's at my throat!
  Rod. You would not bawl so loud then.
  Mal. Come, come, let's go
To bed. He told us thus much aforehand.
  Pes. He wished you should not come at him;   85
        [but believe't,
The accent of the voice sounds not in jest.
I'll down to him, howsoever, and with engines
Force ope the doors.
  [*Exit above.*]   90

---

sadness sobriety
process attendant circumstances
misprision misapprehension

Rod. Let's follow him aloof,
And note how the cardinal will laugh at him.
[*Exeunt, above,* MALATESTE, RODERIGO, *and*
GRISOLAN.]
5 Bos. There's for you first,
'Cause you shall not unbarricade the door
To let in rescue.
[*Kills the* SERVANT.]
Card. What cause hast thou to pursue my
10   [life?
Bos. Look there.
Card. Antonio!
Bos. Slain by my hand unwittingly.
Pray, and be sudden. When thou killed'st thy
15   [sister,
Thou took'st from Justice her most equal
                                                      [balance,
And left her naught but her sword.
Card. O, mercy!
20 Bos. Now it seems thy greatness was only
                                                      [outward;
For thou fall'st faster of thyself than calamity
Can drive thee. I'll not waste longer time.
                                                      [There!
25 [*Stabs him.*]
Card. Thou hast hurt me.
Bos. Again!
[*Stabs him again.*]
Card. Shall I die like a leveret,
30 Without any resistance?—Help, help, help!
I am slain!
[*Enter* FERDINAND.]
Ferd. The alarum! Give me a fresh horse;
Rally the vanguard, or the day is lost.
35 Yield, yield! I give you the honor of arms,
Shake my sword over you. Will you yield?
Card. Help me; I am your brother!
Ferd. The devil!
My brother fight upon the adverse party!
40 [*He wounds the* CARDINAL, *and, in the scuffle,
gives* BOSOLA *his death wound.*]
There flies your ransom.
Card. O justice!
I suffer now for what hath former been.
45 Sorrow is held the eldest child of sin.
Ferd. Now you're brave fellows. Caesar's
fortune was harder than Pompey's; Caesar died
in the arms of prosperity, Pompey at the feet of

disgrace.° You both died in the field. The pain's
nothing. Pain many times is taken away with 50
the apprehension of greater, as the toothache
with the sight of the barber that comes to pull it
out. There's philosophy for you.
Bos. Now my revenge is perfect.—Sink, thou
                                          [main cause 55
[*Kills* FERDINAND.]
Of my undoing!—The last part of my life
Hath done me best service.
Ferd. Give me some wet hay; I am broken-
                                              [winded. 60
I do account this world but a dog kennel.
I will vault credit and affect high pleasures°
Beyond death.
Bos. He seems to come to himself,
Now he's so near the bottom.   65
Ferd. My sister, O my sister! There's the
                                          [cause on't.
Whether we fall by ambition, blood, or lust,
Like diamonds we are cut with our own dust.
[*Dies.*]   70
Card. Thou hast thy payment too.
Bos. Yes, I hold my weary soul in my teeth;
'Tis ready to part from me. I do glory
That thou, which stood'st like a huge pyramid
Begun upon a large and ample base,   75
Shalt end in a little point, a kind of nothing.
[*Enter below,* PESCARA, MALATESTE, ROD-
ERIGO, *and* GRISOLAN.]
Pes. How now, my lord!
Mal. O sad disaster!   80
Rod. How comes this?
Bos. Revenge for the Duchess of Malfi
                                          [murdered
By the Aragonian brethren; for Antonio
Slain by this hand; for lustful Julia   85
Poisoned by this man: and lastly for myself,
That was an actor in the main of all
Much 'gainst mine own good nature, yet i' the
                                          [end
Neglected.   90

Caesar . . . disgrace having defeated his competitor
Pompey (who was slain as he fled to Egypt), Julius
Caesar was assassinated in the Capitol while at the
height of his power
vault . . . pleasures exceed what is believable and
aspire to high pleasures

PES. How now, my lord!
CARD. Look to my brother.
He gave us these large wounds, as we were
[struggling
5 Here i' the rushes.° And now, I pray, let me
Be laid by and never thought of.
[*Dies.*]
PES. How fatally, it seems, he did withstand
His own rescue!
10 MAL. Thou wretched thing of blood
How came Antonio by his death?
Bos. In a mist; I know not how.
Such a mistake as I have often seen
In a play. O, I am gone!
15 We are only like dead walls or vaulted graves,
That, ruined, yield no echo. Fare you well.
It may be pain, but no harm, to me to die
In so good a quarrel. O, this gloomy world!
In what a shadow, or deep pit of darkness,
20 Doth womanish and fearful mankind live!
Let worthy minds ne'er stagger in distrust
To suffer death or shame for what is just.
Mine is another voyage.
[*Dies.*]
25 PES. The noble Delio, as I came to the palace,
Told me of Antonio's being here, and showed
[me
A pretty gentleman, his son and heir.
[*Enter* DELIO *and* ANTONIO'S SON.]
30 MAL. O sir, you come too late!
DELIO. I heard so, and
Was armed for't, ere I came. Let us make noble
[use
Of this great ruin; and join all our force
35 To establish this young hopeful gentleman
In's mother's right. These wretched eminent
[things
Leave no more fame behind 'em, than should
[one
40 Fall in a frost, and leave his print in snow;
As soon as the sun shines, it ever melts,
Both form and matter. I have ever thought
Nature doth nothing so great for great men
As when she's pleased to make them lords of
45 [truth.
Integrity of life is fame's best friend,

Which nobly, beyond death, shall crown the
[end.
[*Exeunt.*]

---

i' the rushes on the rush-strewn floor

Molière

(Jean Baptiste Poquelin)

1622–1673

The Miser

1668

Perhaps the most novel aspect of *The Miser*, if one compares it to either *Volpone* or Shakespeare's play treating of avarice, *The Merchant of Venice*, is its unruffled joy. The great Elizabethan plays show avarice corrupting its possessor and fearfully threatening the lives of his victims. There is a certain somberness, a quality of the deepest moral earnestness, underlying these plays, however gay they may appear in many scenes. In *The Miser*, however, vice creates no agonies and folly has no lasting sting. Harpagon, moreover, undergoes no morally revealing change. He is at the end as splendidly stupid, pinchpenny, and self-centered as he was at the beginning.

Such a difference reflects no difference in the judgment rendered. Molière, like Jonson and Shakespeare, sees avarice as dehumanising. It translates spirit into thing so that Volpone can lust for Celia somewhat as he lusts for Corvino's pearl, Shylock can put his daughter and his ducats into the same scale, and Harpagon can balance the treasure of filial happiness against the contents of his moneybox. Molière, however, is content to laugh at the avaricious as one might laugh at a monkey in the zoo. What a ludicrously unreasonable thing this miser is, he seems to say; how like a man, and yet how infinitely beneath him. And he invites the sensible members of his audience to share in his detached amusement.

It is this appeal to good sense that gives *The Miser* its distinctive qualities of plot, characterization, and device. The plot is elementary, a tissue of theatrical devices terminated by the miraculous reunion, in the nick of time, of a long separated family. Such a plot, conventional in its beginning and absurd in its ending, asks for no earnest contemplation. It is the staple of comic literature everywhere, meant only for delectation. The characters are similarly unreal. They are, in fact, stock types: the conventional lovers sentitious in dialogue; the two-dimensional miser as flat in delineation as his beloved coins; the clownish servant forever avoiding, forever getting a well-merited beating; and the busybody matchmaker contriving an endless series of engagements. They are as old-new as the props in the theater's basement and are hardly to be taken as flesh and blood. So also are the devices, which for all their multiplicity reduce to a kind of geometrical design—purpose against cross-purpose, the characters moving and speaking in the exaggerated and jerky style we associate now with vaudeville humor and early animated cartoons.

Molière develops his play in this manner because he assumes and invites us to assume a stable world with stable values. Such a world is safe in its virtue—vice cannot threaten it, secure in its wisdom—folly cannot subvert it. It can confront the absurdities of flesh and the aberrations of spirit with the humane enjoyment that comes from having mastered them. It can laugh at La Flèche's patching things up between Harpagon and Cleanth—without changing anything at all—or at Harpagon's seizing his own arm in the panic he experiences when the moneybox is stolen. It can smile at and with the absurd conclusion, for although true love does not always find a way and separated families are not always reunited, it recognizes in the miracle a myth of its own aspirations and in the wise, tolerant, and humane Anselm, not only a foil to Harpagon, but the gentle embodiment of its own values.

The Miser

MOLIÈRE

Translated by Lloyd Parks

CHARACTERS

HARPAGON   *father of Cleanth and Elise, and in love with Marianne*
CLEANTH   *Harpagon's son, and in love with Marianne*
ELISE   *Harpagon's daughter, and in love with Valère*
VALÈRE   *Anselm's son, and in love with Elise*
MARIANNE   *Anselm's daughter, and in love with Cleanth*
ANSELM   *father of Valère and Marianne*
FROSINE   *a woman of intrigue*
MASTER SIMON   *a broker*
MASTER JACQUES   *Harpagon's coachman and cook*
LA FLÈCHE   *Cleanth's valet*
DAME CLAUDE   *Harpagon's maid*
BRINDAVOINE   *Harpagon's lackey*
LA MERLUCHE   *Harpagon's lackey*
A COMMISSARY AND HIS CLERK

SCENE. *Paris, Harpagon's house.*

ACT I

[*Enter* VALÈRE *and* ELISE.]

VALÈRE. What is it, charming Elise? Are you melancholy? After all the obliging assurances you so kindly gave of faith in me? Alas! I see you sighing in the midst of my joy! Tell me, do you regret our engagement—to which my ardor

5

Reprinted by permission of Lloyd C. Parks. Mr. Parks wishes to express his gratitude to Eric Bentley for his help in this translation.

has perhaps constrained you?

ELISE. No, Valère, I could not regret what I have done for you. I feel myself drawn by powers far too sweet, and I lack strength to wish that things were not as they are. But to tell the truth, I fear to think of the consequences. I am afraid that I love you a little more than I ought.

VALÈRE. Ah! Elise, what can you have to fear from the kindness you have shown me?

ELISE. Alas! a hundred things: my father's wrath, reproaches from my family, the censure of the world—but most of all, Valère, a change in your heart and that criminal coldness with which those of your sex most often repay the over-ardent testimonies of innocent love.

VALÈRE. Oh! do not do me the wrong of judging me by others. Suspect me of anything, Elise, but not that I should fail in my duty to you. I love you too much for that, and I will love you as long as I live.

ELISE. Ah! that is the way you all talk. All men are alike in their speech; their actions alone reveal their differences.

VALÈRE. If our actions alone reveal what we are, then at least wait and judge my heart by mine; and do not invent crimes for me simply because unhappy apprehension has bred unjust fear. I beg you, do not kill me with mortal blows of outrageous suspicion. Give me time to convince you, by a thousand and one proofs, that my intentions are honorable.

ELISE. Alas! how easily we are persuaded by those we love! Yes, Valère, I think you have no room in your heart for deceit. I am convinced that you love me truly, and will always be faithful to me. I have no wish to doubt you; I am sad only because I fear I may be blamed by others.

VALÈRE. What is it that worries you?

ELISE. I would have nothing to fear if everyone saw you as I do. For in your very person I see enough to justify what I have done. My heart has all your merit for its defense, reinforced by that gratitude which Heaven has bade me owe you. Not an hour passes but I picture to myself the terrible catastrophe which brought us into one another's sight; your amazing generosity, which made you risk your life to preserve mine from the fury of the waves; the great pains you took, how tenderly you cared for me after lifting me from the water; and the assiduous homage of your ardent love, which neither time nor difficulty has discouraged; which causes you to neglect both family and fatherland; which detains you in this place, and makes you hide your rank for my sake; and which has reduced you to wearing my father's livery. All of this has certainly made a wonderful impression on me, and in my eyes is justification enough for the engagement I have consented to. But perhaps that is not enough to justify it to the world, nor am I sure that everyone feels as I do.

VALÈRE. For all that you have said, it is only through my love that I pretend to merit your esteem, and as for your scruples, a father like yours is justification enough for anything you might do. His excessive avarice and the austere manner in which he lives with his children might well authorize far stranger things than this. Pardon me, charming Elise, for talking this way in front of you, but you know there is no good to be said on that score. But, if, as I hope, I can finally find my parents again, it will not be hard to win him over. I am waiting impatiently for news of them, and I will go and inquire if it is much longer in coming.

ELISE. Oh! Valère, do not go away, I beg you. Think only of winning my father's confidence.

VALÈRE. You have seen how I go about it; you saw how artfully compliant I was obliged to be in order to introduce myself into his service—under what mask of sympathy and agreement I disguise my feelings to please him—what role I play to gain his affection. And I am making admirable progress. I have discovered that, to win men over, there is no better way than to trick yourself out in their inclinations, fall in with their maxims, burn incense to their faults, and applaud everything they do. One need have no fear of overdoing complaisance. No matter how obviously you play on their feelings, the shrewdest men are always the greatest dupes when it comes to flattery. There is nothing so impertinent or so ridiculous that you can't make them swallow it—if you season it well with praise. Sincerity, of course, suffers a little by this trade. But if you need certain men, you must adapt yourself to them. And, since there is no other way of winning them over, it is not the flatterers who are at fault, but those who wish to be flattered.

ELISE. Why don't you try to gain my brother's support too—in the event my maid should decide to tell our secret?

VALÈRE. I cannot manage both of them at the same time. The father's temperament and the son's are so opposed, it would be hard to accommodate the confidings of both at once. But you, for your part, could approach your brother, and avail yourself of his friendship to get him to act on our behalf. There he comes now. I'll withdraw. Use the occasion to sound him out, but don't disclose our affair unless you think the time is ripe.

[Exit.]

ELISE. I don't know if I will have the courage to confide in him.

[Enter CLEANTH.]

CLEANTH. I am very happy to find you alone, Elise. I have been burning to unburden a secret to you.

ELISE. Here I am, ready to listen, Cleanth. What do you wish to tell me?

CLEANTH. A thousand things, Elise—all bound up in three words: I'm in love.

ELISE. You are in love?

CLEANTH. I am in love. But before I say more, I know I am dependent on my father; that the name of son subjects me to his wishes; that we should not commit ourselves without the consent of those who brought us into the world; that Heaven has made them the masters of our troth; that we are enjoined not to pledge it except by their direction; that having never been affected by foolish passions, they are in a condition to be deceived much less often than we are, and can see more clearly what is best for us. I know that we ought to trust the light of their prudence rather than the blindness of our passion and that the extravagance of youth most often lures us toward the precipice of sorrow. I am telling all this to you, Elise, so that you won't take the trouble to tell it to me. For, to tell the truth, my love will not listen. So, please do not make objections.

ELISE. Are you engaged, Cleanth, to her whom you love?

CLEANTH. No, but I am resolved to be. And again I beg you not to offer any reasons to dissuade me.

ELISE. Am I such a stranger, Cleanth?

CLEANTH. No, Elise; but you are not in love. You do not know the violence that tender love does to our hearts. I mistrust your prudence.

ELISE. Alas! Cleanth, let us not talk of my prudence. There is no one who is not deficient in that at least once in a lifetime; and if I opened my heart to you, perhaps in your eyes I should seem far less prudent than you are.

CLEANTH. Ah! I wish to Heaven, that your heart, like mine . . .

ELISE. First of all, let us finish with your affair. Tell me, who is she, . . .

CLEANTH. A young lady who has lived but a short time in this neighborhood, and who seems to have been made to inspire love in all who see her. Nature never shaped anything more lovable. I felt transported the moment I saw her. Her name is Marianne and she lives under the protection of her mother—a good woman who is almost always ill, and whom her daughter holds in such loving regard, it is unbelievable. She waits on her, takes pity on her, and consoles her so tenderly that it touches your heart. She has the most charming way in the world of going about her business. A thousand graces shine through her every action. Such alluring sweetness, such engaging goodness, such adorable civility! such . . . Oh! Elise, if you could only see her!

ELISE. I see a great deal of her, Cleanth, through what you have told me. And to understand her, it is enough for me that you love her.

CLEANTH. I have discovered, in a roundabout way, that they are not very well provided for, and that even with frugal management, they can hardly stretch their income far enough to cover all their needs. Imagine, Elise, what a pleasure it would be to be able to raise the fortunes of the person one loves, adroitly to supply a little help for the modest needs of a virtuous

family. And think how unpleasant it must be for me to be powerless to taste that pleasure because of my father's stinginess, to be powerless to surprise this beautiful girl with some
5 proof of my love for her.

ELISE. Oh! Cleanth, I can easily conceive how exasperated you must feel.

CLEANTH. Ah! Elise, much more so than you can imagine. Really, have you ever seen any-
10 thing more cruel than the rigorous economy he imposes on us, than this queer stinginess under which we languish? What good will wealth do us, if it comes only when we are past the age when we can most enjoy it, if even to maintain
15 myself I am now obliged to go into debt on every side, and if I am reduced with you to seeking help from tradesmen to find the means to wear decent clothes? I really wanted to ask you to help me find out father's attitude toward my
20 present feelings. If I find him contrary, I am resolved to go away, in the company of that wonderful creature, to enjoy whatever fortune Providence may offer us. I am having somebody look everywhere for money to borrow for this
25 purpose; and, if your affairs are in the same state as mine, if Father insists on opposing our desires, we will both leave him, and free ourselves of this tyranny, to which his insupportable avarice has so long subjected us.

30 ELISE. It is only too true that he gives us more reason every day to regret our mother's death, and that . . .

CLEANTH. I can hear his voice. Let us go somewhere else to conclude our confidences. Later
35 we will join forces and assault his hard heart together.

[*Exeunt.*]

[*Enter* HARPAGON *and* LA FLÈCHE.]

HARPAGON. Get out of here at once, and don't
40 answer back! Go on, leave my house! You master-mind of crime! You born gallows bait!

FLÈCHE [*aside*]. I have never seen anything so wicked as this cursèd old man, and I believe, begging your pardon, he has a devil in his flesh.

45 HARPAGON. Are you muttering between your teeth?

FLÈCHE. Why chase me out of the house?

HARPAGON. As though you didn't know why!

Scoundrel! Go quickly before I beat you!

FLÈCHE. What have I done? 50

HARPAGON. You have done enough to make me want you to leave.

FLÈCHE. My master your son gave me orders to wait for him.

HARPAGON. Go and wait for him in the street, 55 not here in my house, standing there as stiff and straight as a post to watch what goes on and profit from everything. . . . I will not have someone continually spying on my business, a traitor whose cursèd eyes besiege all my ac- 60 tions, devour all I possess, and ferret about in every corner for something to steal.

FLÈCHE. How the deuce do you expect anyone to steal from you? Can you rob a man when he keeps everything under lock and key, and 65 stands guard day and night?

HARPAGON. I will lock up whatever I think should be locked up, and I will stand guard as I please. [*To audience.*] There, isn't that the talk of a spy who watches everything you do? I 70 tremble lest he suspect something about my money. [*To* LA FLÈCHE.] Are you the kind of man who would go about spreading the story that I have money hidden away?

FLÈCHE. *Do* you have money hidden away? 75

HARPAGON. No, you rascal, I didn't say that. [*Aside.*] I'm losing my temper. [*To* LA FLÈCHE.] I mean, would you go around spreading the story that I do have some—out of malice?

FLÈCHE. Hoho! what difference does it make 80 to us, if you have or have not? Things are always the same for us anyway.

HARPAGON. Ha! you play the reasoner! I'll teach you how to reason with your ears. [*Lifting his hand to give* LA FLÈCHE *a box on the ear.*] 85 One last time—get out of here!

FLÈCHE. All right, I'm going.

HARPAGON. Wait. You're not taking anything of mine with you?

FLÈCHE. What could I take of yours? 90

HARPAGON. Come here, so I can see. Show me your hands.

FLÈCHE. They they are.

HARPAGON [*sarcastically*]. Your other hands.

FLÈCHE. My other hands? 95

HARPAGON. Yes.

FLÈCHE [*good-humoredly*]. There they are.

HARPAGON [*pointing to* LA FLÈCHE'S *breeches*]. Have you put anything inside there?

FLÈCHE. See for yourself.

5 HARPAGON [*feeling the knees of* LA FLÈCHE'S *breeches*]. These breeches are just right for hiding stolen goods, and I wish somebody had been hanged for it. . . .

FLÈCHE. Ah! how well a man like that de-
10 serves what he fears, and what pleasure it would give me to steal from him.

HARPAGON. Eh?

FLÈCHE. What?

HARPAGON. What did you say about stealing?

15 FLÈCHE. I said that you are poking everywhere to see if I have stolen anything from you.

HARPAGON. That's what I intend to do.

FLÈCHE [*aside*]. A pox on avarice and the avaricious!

20 HARPAGON. How's that? What did you say?

FLÈCHE. What did I say?

HARPAGON. Yes. What did you say about avarice and the avaricious?

FLÈCHE. I said, a pox on avarice and the avari-
25 cious.

HARPAGON. Who are you talking about?

FLÈCHE. About avaricious men.

HARPAGON. And who are they, these avaricious men?

30 FLÈCHE. They are misers and villains.

HARPAGON. But who do you mean by that?

FLÈCHE. What are you so upset about?

HARPAGON. I am upset about what I ought to be upset about.

35 FLÈCHE. Do you think I mean you?

HARPAGON. I think what I think. But I want you to tell me who you were speaking to when you said that.

FLÈCHE. I . . . I was speaking to my beret.

40 HARPAGON. And I might well knock it off.

FLÈCHE. Would you stop me from cursing avaricious men?

HARPAGON. No, but I'll stop you from chatter-ing and being insolent. Keep quiet.

45 FLÈCHE. I haven't named anybody.

HARPAGON. I'll thrash you if you talk.

FLÈCHE. If your nose feels snotty, blow it.

HARPAGON. Will you be quiet?

FLÈCHE. Yes, in spite of myself.

HARPAGON. Ah! ah! 50

FLÈCHE [*showing him one of his waist-coat pockets*]. Look, here's another pocket. Are you satisfied?

HARPAGON. Come now, give it back to me without any more searching. 55

FLÈCHE. What?

HARPAGON. What you took from me.

FLÈCHE. I took nothing from you.

HARPAGON. Are you sure?

FLÈCHE. Positive. 60

HARPAGON. Goodbye! Go to the devil!

FLÈCHE. Well, I must say, I have been very handsomely dismissed!

HARPAGON. At least I have laid something to your conscience. 65

[*Exit* LA FLÈCHE.]

That rascal of a valet makes me uneasy, and I don't care to see the limping cur around here. [*Alone.*] It's certainly no small worry having a large sum of money in this house, and it's a 70 lucky man who has his fortune well invested, and can carry what he needs for expenses on his own person. It's no little problem to find, in an entire house, a safe hiding place for it. Because, to my way of thinking, your strong-boxes are 75 suspect; I'd never trust my money to one. In my opinion they are nothing but bait for thieves, they are what a thief always goes after first.

[*Enter* CLEANTH *and* ELISE *unnoticed.*] 80

Still, I don't know if it was wise to bury the ten thousand écus° I was paid yesterday in the gar-den. Ten thousand gold écus is a rather large sum to have about the house. [*Noticing* CLEANTH *and* ELISE.] Oh! Heavens! I must have 85 given myself away! I must have been carried away by anxiety— and I think I spoke out loud while I was reasoning with myself all alone here. . . . What's the matter?

CLEANTH. Nothing, Father. 90

HARPAGON. Have you been there very long?

écus the monetary units mentioned in the play had the following values: twelve **deniers** = one **sol**; twenty sols = one **franc**; three francs = one **écu**; ten francs = one **pistole**; twenty francs = one **gold louis**

ELISE. We have just come.

HARPAGON. You heard . . .

CLEANTH. What, Father?

HARPAGON. There . . .

5 ELISE. What?

HARPAGON. What I just said.

CLEANTH. No.

HARPAGON. Yes, you did, you did.

ELISE. I beg your pardon, but we didn't.

10 HARPAGON. I can plainly see you heard something. I was talking to myself about how hard it is to find money these days, and I said that anyone who happens to have ten thousand écus about the house is a very lucky man.

15 CLEANTH. We held back for fear of interrupting you.

HARPAGON. I am only too glad to let you know what I said. So you won't get it all wrong and think it is I who have the ten thousand écus.

20 CLEANTH. We don't concern ourselves with your affairs.

HARPAGON. Would to God I had that much money, ten thousand écus!

CLEANTH. I don't believe it.

25 HARPAGON. It would be a fine thing for me.

ELISE. These are matters . . .

HARPAGON. I could certainly use it.

CLEANTH. I think that . . .

HARPAGON. It would set me up very com-

30 fortably.

ELISE. You are . . .

HARPAGON. I wouldn't complain then, as I do now, about how hard the times are!

CLEANTH. My God, Father, you have no

35 room to complain: everyone knows you are well off.

HARPAGON. What! I am well off? Those who say so are liars. Nothing could be more untrue. And those who go around spreading such a

40 story are all villains.

ELISE. Don't be angry.

HARPAGON. It is very strange that my own children should betray me and become my enemies.

45 CLEANTH. Am I your enemy because I say you are well off?

HARPAGON. Yes. That kind of talk and your extravagant spending will one day cause some-body to come here and to cut my throat, under the impression that my clothes are lined with 50 money.

CLEANTH. What extravagant spending have I done?

HARPAGON. What? Is there anything more scandalous than the sumptuous clothes that you 55 parade all over the city? Yesterday I was criticizing your sister, but this is far worse. This cries out to Heaven for vengeance; and, taking you from head to foot, there is enough on you to buy a good piece of property. I have told 60 you twenty times, son, that your ways displease me very much. You are breaking your neck to look like a marquis, and in order to go about dressed as you are, I am sure you must be stealing from me. 65

CLEANTH. Ha! how could I steal from you?

HARPAGON. How should I know? Then where do you get the means to keep up your fashionable appearance?

CLEANTH. I, Father? Why, I gamble, and, 70 since I am very lucky, I put all the money I win on my back.

HARPAGON. That is very ill-advised. If you are lucky at cards you ought to profit by it, and invest your money at an honest interest, so 75 that one day you will find it has . . . I should like very much to know, not to mention the rest, what good are all those ribbons you are garnished with from head to foot, as if half a dozen laces° would not be enough to hold up 80 your breeches? Is it really necessary to spend your money on wigs, when you can wear the hair that grows on your head, which doesn't cost a sou? I'll wager your wigs and ribbons alone are worth at least twenty pistoles. And 85 twenty pistoles bring in eight francs, six sols, and eight deniers a year, even at eight per cent interest.

CLEANTH. You are quite right.

HARPAGON. Enough of that; let us talk about 90 something else. Eh? [*Aside, seeing* CLEANTH *and* ELISE *making signs to one another.*] I think they are signalling one another to pick my pockets.

---

laces ties lacing the breeches to the doublet. Men of fashion often ornamented their laces with ribbons.

[*To* CLEANTH *and* ELISE.] What do those signs mean?

ELISE. We were bargaining as to who should speak first, my brother or myself. Both of us have something to tell you.

HARPAGON. And I, too, have something to tell both of you.

CLEANTH. It is about marriage, Father, that we wish to speak with you.

HARPAGON. And it is marriage also that I want to discuss with you.

ELISE. Oh! Father!

HARPAGON. Why "Oh! Father!"? Is it the word, daughter, or the thing that frightens you?

CLEANTH. Marriage could be frightening in both respects, depending on how you mean it. And we are afraid that our inclinations might not agree with your choice.

HARPAGON. Have a little patience. Don't get alarmed. I know what is best for you both, and neither one of you will have reason to complain of anything I intend to do. Now, to begin at the beginning, tell me, have you ever seen a girl named Marianne, who lives not far from here?

CLEANTH. Yes, Father.

HARPAGON [*to* ELISE]. And you?

ELISE. I have heard of her.

HARPAGON. What do you think of this girl, Cleanth?

CLEANTH. An extremely charming person.

HARPAGON. Her physiognomy?

CLEANTH. Very honest and intelligent.

HARPAGON. Her air and manner?

CLEANTH. Exquisite, to be sure.

HARPAGON. Don't you think a girl like that is worth some consideration?

CLEANTH. Yes, Father.

HARPAGON. That she might be a very desirable match?

CLEANTH. Very desirable.

HARPAGON. That she looks very much as though she would make a good housewife?

CLEANTH. No doubt.

HARPAGON. And that a husband would be completely satisfied with her?

CLEANTH. Surely.

HARPAGON. There is one slight obstacle. I am afraid she may not have as much money as one might reasonably expect.

CLEANTH. Ah! Father, money is no consideration when it is a question of marrying an honest woman.

HARPAGON. Pardon me, if I disagree! But there is always this to be said: if a fortune does not measure up to one's expectations, one can always try to make it up some other way.

CLEANTH. Of course.

HARPAGON. Well—I am happy to find that you agree with me, because her maidenly conduct and sweet disposition have won my heart, and I am resolved to marry her. Provided she has some kind of property.

CLEANTH. Eh?

HARPAGON. What?

CLEANTH. You say you have resolved . . .

HARPAGON. To marry Marianne.

CLEANTH. Who? you, you?

HARPAGON. Yes. I, I, I! What do you mean by that?

CLEANTH. I feel dizzy all of a sudden. I think I'll go.

[*Exit* CLEANTH.]

HARPAGON. It will pass. Quick, go into the kitchen and drink a large glass of plain water. [*To* ELISE.] There's one of your lily-livered dandies—no more constitution than a chicken! Well, daughter, that's what I have decided for myself. As for your brother, I have a certain widow in mind that someone spoke to me about this very morning. And as for you, I am going to give you to Signor Anselm.

ELISE. To Signor Anselm?

HARPAGON. Yes. A man who is mature, prudent and wise, who is not over fifty, and who is famous for his great wealth.

ELISE. I would rather not get married at all, Father, if you please.

HARPAGON. And I, my little girl, my pet, would rather you did get married, if you please.

ELISE. I beg your pardon, Father.

HARPAGON. I beg your pardon, daughter.

ELISE. I am Signor Anselm's most humble servant, but, with your permission, I will not marry him.

HARPAGON. I am your very humble valet, but, with your permission, you shall marry him—this very evening.

ELISE. This very evening?

HARPAGON. This very evening.

ELISE. That shall never be, Father.

HARPAGON. That shall be, daughter.

ELISE. No.

5 HARPAGON. Yes.

ELISE. I tell you, no.

HARPAGON. I tell you, yes.

ELISE. You shall never force me to do such a thing.

10 HARPAGON. I shall force you to do such a thing.

ELISE. I would kill myself sooner than marry such a husband.

HARPAGON. You will not kill yourself, and

15 you shall marry him. Such audacity! Did you ever hear of a daughter talking to her father that way?

ELISE. Did you ever hear of a father marrying off his daughter that way?

20 HARPAGON. It is a match which will admit of no objection. And I will wager that everyone will approve my choice.

ELISE. And I will wager that no reasonable person could possibly approve it.

25 HARPAGON. Here is Valère. Would you be willing to let him be the judge of this matter for both of us?

ELISE. I'll consent to that.

HARPAGON. Will you abide by his decision?

30 ELISE. Yes. I will stand by whatever he says.

HARPAGON. It's settled then.

[*Enter* VALÈRE.]

Here, Valère. We have elected you to decide who is in the right, my daughter or myself.

35 VALÈRE. You, sir, there's no contradicting that.

HARPAGON. You know, of course, what we are talking about.

VALÈRE. No, but you couldn't be wrong; you

40 are reason itself.

HARPAGON. Tonight I want to give her a husband who is as rich as he is wise, and the hussy tells me to my face she will have no part of him. What do you say to that?

45 VALÈRE. What do I say to that?

HARPAGON. Yes.

VALÈRE. Hoho!

HARPAGON. What?

VALÈRE. I say that fundamentally I am of

your opinion; and that you couldn't possibly be 50
wrong; but on the other hand, she is not absolutely in the wrong either, and . . .

HARPAGON. How so! Signor Anselm is a considerable match. He is a gentleman: noble, cultured, poised, intelligent and very rich; and he 55
has no children left from his first marriage. Could she do better?

VALÈRE. True, but she might tell you that you are hurrying things somewhat, and that she ought to have a little time at least to find out 60
whether she can adapt her temperament to . . .

HARPAGON. This is an opportunity that must be grasped by the forelock. This match offers me an advantage which I would find in no other. He has agreed to take her without a 65
dowry and . . .

VALÈRE. Without a dowry?

HARPAGON. Yes.

VALÈRE. Ah! I have nothing more to say. You see, here is a reason that is entirely convincing; 70
one can only defer to it. . . .

HARPAGON. To me it represents a considerable saving.

VALÈRE. Certainly. There's no denying it. It's true your daughter may suggest to you that 75
marriage is a more important step than you are inclined to think; that it is a question of being happy or unhappy for the rest of one's life; and that a partnership which will last till death should never be entered on without great pre- 80
caution.

HARPAGON. Without a dowry!

VALÈRE. You are right. That decides everything, naturally. Though there are those who might tell you that in such matters you cer- 85
tainly ought to have some regard for your daughter's inclinations, and that the great difference in age, in temperament, and in sensibility would render such a marriage liable to very unhappy accidents. 90

HARPAGON. Without a dowry!

VALÈRE. Oh! there's no gainsaying that, as everyone knows. Who the deuce would argue the point? Not that there aren't many fathers who are more interested in their daughters' 95
happiness than in the money they give with them; who would never sacrifice them to their own interest; and who seek, above all else, to

insure that sweet conformity in marriage which is a continuous source of honor, tranquillity and joy, and which . . .

HARPAGON. Without a dowry!

5 VALÈRE. Very true. That closes every mouth. Without a dowry! An irrefutable argument!

HARPAGON. Wait! I think I hear a dog barking. [*Aside.*] Is someone trying to get at my money? [*To* VALÈRE.] Don't move; I'll be back 10 in a minute.

[*Exit* HARPAGON.]

ELISE. Are you joking, Valère, talking to him this way?

VALÈRE. I don't want to sour him. This way I 15 can better accomplish my own ends. Opposing his ideas to his face is a sure way to spoil everything. There are certain minds you have to take by the bias.° Some temperaments are inimical to any kind of resistance: they stiffen them- 20 selves against the truth, and always balk when they confront the straight road of reason. You can guide them where you want to take them only by leading them in a roundabout way. Pretend that you consent to what he wants; 25 you will be more certain to get your way in the end. . . .

ELISE. But this marriage, Valère?

VALÈRE. We'll break it on the bias.

ELISE. What can we contrive if it is to be con- 30 cluded tonight?

VALÈRE. You must ask them to delay it. Feign a sickness.

ELISE. But they will discover the pretense— if they call in the doctor.

35 VALÈRE. Are you joking? Do doctors know anything about sickness? Come now, with doctors you can have any sickness you please, and they will find reasons for your having it, and tell you where it comes from.

40 [*Enter* HARPAGON.]

HARPAGON [*aside*]. It was nothing, thank God!

VALÈRE. As a last resort we could run away and leave all this behind. And if your love, 45 Elise, is capable of firmness . . . [*seeing* HARPAGON]. Yes, a daughter should obey her father.

She should have no concern for what her husband is like; and, when such a powerful argument as *without a dowry* intervenes, she should be ready to accept whatever is given her. 50

HARPAGON. Good! That was well said, that!

VALÈRE. Sir, I beg pardon if I have been too forward, and for having made so bold as to talk to her this way.

HARPAGON. What do you mean? I am de- 55 lighted. And I want to give you absolute power over her. [*To* ELISE.] There's no good running away. [ELISE *moves to the end of the stage*.] I give him the same authority over you that God gave me, and I expect you to do everything he 60 tells you.

VALÈRE [*to* ELISE]. After that how can you resist my remonstrances! Sir, I will follow her and continue the lessons I have been giving her.

HARPAGON. Yes, you will oblige me. Truly . . . 65

VALÈRE. I think it is good to pull in the reins with her.

HARPAGON. That's right, you should. . . .

VALÈRE. Don't worry about a thing; I am sure I can manage this. 70

HARPAGON. Do, do as you like. I am going to take a little walk through the city. I'll be back shortly.

VALÈRE. Yes, money is the most precious thing in the world, and you ought to thank 75 God for the honest father He has given you. He knows what it takes to live. When someone offers to take a girl without a dowry, she ought not to look any further. Everything is included in *without a dowry*; it takes the place of beauty, 80 youth, birth, honor, intelligence and probity.

[*Exeunt* VALÈRE *and* ELISE.]

HARPAGON. Ah! bravo, bravo! Spoken like an oracle. Lucky the man with such a servant!

ACT II

[CLEANTH *is on stage. Enter* LA FLÈCHE.] 85

CLEANTH. Ah! you traitor! What new mischief have you been getting into? Didn't I give you orders? . . .

FLÈCHE. Yes, sir! I came here with every intention of waiting for you, but your father, the 90 most ungracious man in the world, chased me

by the bias by indirection

out of the house, in spite of myself, and I came close to getting a beating.

CLEANTH. How goes our business? Things are more pressing now than ever. Since I last saw
5 you, I have discovered that my own father is my rival.

FLÈCHE. Your father is in love?

CLEANTH. Yes; and I had all the trouble in the world to keep him from seeing how much this
10 news distressed me.

FLÈCHE. Him, dabbling in love? What the devil can he be thinking of? Does public opinion mean nothing to him? Was love made for men built like that?

15 CLEANTH. It must be for my sins that he has got this idea into his head.

FLÈCHE. For what reason do you keep your love a secret from him?

CLEANTH. So that he will be less suspicious.
20 So that he won't suspect my actions should it become necessary to try and prevent his marriage. What answer did they give you?

FLÈCHE. By Heaven, sir, those that have to borrow are in a very bad way! A man has to
25 put up with strange things when he is reduced, as you are, to putting himself into the hands of sharks.

CLEANTH. You couldn't get the money?

FLÈCHE. Not exactly. Our Master Simon, the
30 broker, who was recommended to us as an energetic, determined man, assures me he has left no stone unturned to serve you—and that your face alone has won his heart.

CLEANTH. Will I get the fifteen thousand
35 francs I asked for?

FLÈCHE. Yes, but there are some trifling conditions attached—which you must accept, if you expect anything to be done.

CLEANTH. Did he let you speak to the man
40 who is supposed to lend the money?

FLÈCHE. Oh, really, it is not so simple as all that. He took more pains to hide himself than you do yourself; it is all much more mysterious than you might think. They will by no means
45 tell his name, and they are going to bring you together today in a private house, so that he can learn from your own lips who your family is and what your expectations are. But I don't

have the slightest doubt that your father's name alone will make things easy for you. 50

CLEANTH. And especially the fact that our mother is dead, whose property no one can take from me.

FLÈCHE. Here are a few articles which he himself dictated to our go-between, to be shown 55
to you before any action will be taken.

"Supposing that the lender is satisfied with the collateral offered, and that the borrower has reached his majority and is from a family whose estate is large, solid, assured and free 60
from all encumbrance, a valid and precise contract will be drawn up in the presence of a notary, the most honest man available, who, for that reason, must be chosen by the lender, to whom it is of the utmost importance that the 65
contract be properly drawn up."

CLEANTH. I have no objection to that.

FLÈCHE. "The lender, in order not to burden his conscience with any scruples, intends to charge no more than six per cent interest." 70

CLEANTH. Six per cent interest? By Jove, an honest fellow indeed! There is no reason to complain about that.

FLÈCHE. Indeed not!

"But, since the said lender does not have the 75
sum required in his own house, and because, in order to oblige the borrower, he is forced to borrow himself at the rate of twenty per cent, it is only fair that the said, first borrower should pay this interest without prejudice to the 80
other, considering that it is only to oblige him that the said lender will borrow the sum requested."

CLEANTH. What the devil! What Jew, what Arab am I dealing with? That's more than 85
twenty-five per cent interest!

FLÈCHE. That's right. That's what I told him. You had better look into it yourself.

CLEANTH. What is there to look into? I need money. I will have to agree to anything. 90

FLÈCHE. That's what I told him.

CLEANTH. Is there something else?

FLÈCHE. Only a small item.

"Of the fifteen thousand francs that are requested, the lender can count on only twelve 95
thousand francs in cash. As for the remaining

thousand écus, the borrower must take them in furniture, clothing, and jewelry, a list of which follows this note, and which the said lender has, in all good faith, priced as moderately as he possibly can."

CLEANTH. What does he mean by that?

FLÈCHE. Listen to the list.

"First: one four-poster bed, with Hungarian point lace handsomely sewn on olive-colored cloth, with six chairs, and a counterpane of the same material; all in good condition and lined with changeable red and blue taffeta.

"In addition: one bedstead canopy of good, dry rose-colored serge, with silk fringes."

CLEANTH. What does he expect me to do with that?

FLÈCHE. Hold on.

"In addition: a set of tapestries; the subject of which is *The Amours of Gombaut and Macaea.*°

"In addition: one large walnut table, with twelve columns, or turned pillars, pulling out at either end, and fitted with half-a-dozen joint stools under it."

CLEANTH. My God! What good will that do me?

FLÈCHE. Be patient.

"In addition: three large muskets inlaid with mother-of-pearl, with three matching tripods.

"In addition: one brick furnace with two retorts and three recipients, very useful for anyone interested in distilling.

"In addition: a Bologna lute with all its strings, or few lacking.

"In addition: a troll-madam° table and a chess board, with a goose game restored from the Greeks; all very fine to pass away the time when one has nothing to do.

"In addition: a lizard skin, three feet long, and half-filled with straw—a very agreeable curiosity to hang from a bedroom ceiling.

"The total mentioned above, easily worth more than four thousand, five hundred francs, is reduced in price to one thousand écus by the moderation of the lender."

CLEANTH. May the plague choke him and his moderation, the traitor! Cut-throat that he is! Have you ever heard of such usury? Can't he be satisfied with the furious interest he demands, without making me take all the junk he has heaped up, for three thousand francs? I won't get more than two hundred écus for the lot! And yet I must resign myself and consent to whatever he wants. He is in a position to make me accept anything. The dog has me by the throat.

FLÈCHE. Sir, I see you taking the very same road, no offense intended, that Panurge° followed to his ruin: taking money in advance, buying dear and selling cheap, and eating your wheat in the blade.

CLEANTH. What would you have me do? You see what young men are reduced to by the cursèd avarice of their fathers! Is it any wonder, after this, that the sons should wish their fathers' death?

FLÈCHE. I must confess, the stinginess of yours would infuriate the calmest man in the world. I am not strongly inclined toward the gallows, thank God, and when I am with my colleagues, seeing them taking big chances for small gains, I always know when to pull my iron out of the fire, and when it is prudent to drop out of any adventure that smells ever so little of the gallows. But, to tell the truth, the way your father acts tempts me very much to steal from him. And I think, if I did rob him, I would be doing a good deed.

CLEANTH. Give me the note; I want to look it over again.

[*Enter* MASTER SIMON *and* HARPAGON.]

SIMON. Yes sir, he is a young man in need of money. The state of his affairs obliges him to find some, and he will agree to anything you prescribe.

HARPAGON. But are you convinced, Master Simon, that I will run no risk? Are you acquainted with the name, the fortune and the

---

The Amours . . . Macaea a popular rustic romance of the time

troll-madam game played with ivory balls rolled into numbered holes or compartments

Panurge the improvident rascal in Rabelais' *Gargantua and Pantagruel*

family of the party for whom you are speaking?

SIMON. No, I cannot give you any definite information about him; and it was only by chance that he was directed to me; but he himself will enlighten you about everything. And his man assures me that you will be satisfied when you meet him. All I can tell you is that his family is very rich, that his mother is already dead, and that he will guarantee, if you wish it, that his father will die before eight months are out.

HARPAGON. That is something, indeed. Charity, Master Simon, obliges us to make others happy when it is in our power to do so.

SIMON. To be sure.

FLÈCHE [*low to* CLEANTH]. What does this mean? Our Master Simon talking to your father!

CLEANTH [*low to* LA FLÈCHE]. Could they have told him who I am? or have you betrayed me?

SIMON [*noticing* CLEANTH *and* LA FLÈCHE]. Aha! you are in a hurry! Who told you this was the house? [*To* HARPAGON.] In any event, sir, it was not I who revealed your name and lodgings. But, in my opinion, no great harm has been done: they are discreet fellows, and now you can discuss your business together.

HARPAGON. What?

SIMON. This is the gentleman who wants to borrow the fifteen thousand francs, the one I was telling you about.

HARPAGON. What! you rascal! It is you who abandon yourself to such culpable extremities!

CLEANTH. What! Father, it is you who carry on this shameful business!

[*Exit* MASTER SIMON *and* LA FLÈCHE.]

HARPAGON. It is you who want to ruin yourself by such deplorable borrowing!

CLEANTH. It is you who seek to enrich yourself by this criminal usury!

HARPAGON. Do you dare, after that, to show your face to me?

CLEANTH. Do you dare, after that, to show your face to the world?

HARPAGON. Tell me, aren't you ashamed to descend to such debauchery, to hurl yourself into horrible expenditure, and shamefully to squander the wealth that your ancestors have amassed for you by the sweat of their brows?

CLEANTH. How can you help but blush for disgracing your class this way with this trade you practice, sacrificing your honor and reputation to your insatiable desire to pile écu on écu and outdoing, in point of interest, the most infamous subtleties ever invented by the most notorious usurers?

HARPAGON. Get out of my sight, scoundrel, get out of my sight!

CLEANTH. Who is the greater criminal in your opinion: the man who buys money because he needs it, or the man who steals money but has no use for it?

HARPAGON. Leave the room I tell you, and stop chafing my ears.

[*Exit* CLEANTH.]

I am not a bit sorry that this has happened; it is a warning to me to watch everything he does more closely than ever.

[*Enter* FROSINE.]

FROSINE. Sir . . .

HARPAGON. Wait a moment. I'll be back to talk with you. [*Aside.*] It's about time I take a peek at my money.

[*Exit.*]

[*Enter* LA FLÈCHE.]

FLÈCHE. The whole thing is very amusing. He must surely have a large store of supplies somewhere in the house, because we couldn't find a thing that's listed in the inventory he gave us.

FROSINE. Ah! it's you, my poor La Flèche! To what do we owe this meeting?

FLÈCHE. Aha! it's you, Frosine! What are *you* doing here?

FROSINE. What I do everywhere else: play the go-between in negotiations, make myself useful to others, and profit as much as I possibly can by whatever slight talent I may have. You know that in this world one is obliged to live by one's wits. And for women like myself Heaven has provided no other source of income than intrigue and persistency.

FLÈCHE. Do you have some business with the master of the house?

FROSINE. Yes, I am transacting some small business for him—for which I hope to be compensated.

FLÈCHE. By him? Ah! in faith, you'll have to be pretty sharp to get anything out of *him*; I warn you, money costs very dearly in this house.

5 FROSINE. There are certain services that are wonderfully effective.

FLÈCHE. I am your humble servant. But you don't know Signor Harpagon, yet. Signor Harpagon is of all humans the least human, the 10 hardest and tightest mortal of all mortals. No service can push his gratitude far enough to make him unclench his fists. Of praise, esteem, benevolent words and friendship as much as you like, but money?—nothing doing. There 15 is nothing more dry and withered than his favors and caresses, and "give" is a word for which he has such an aversion that he never says "I give," but "I lend, you good-day."

FROSINE. Mercy me! I know the art of milking 20 a man. I have the secret for bringing out his tenderness, for tickling his heart, for finding his soft spot.

FLÈCHE. Useless here! If money is involved, I defy you to touch the man in question. On that 25 score he is a Turk; and his turkery is the despair of all who know him; you could be dying, and he wouldn't turn a hair. In a word, he loves money more than reputation, honor or virtue, and the sight of anyone who expects to be paid 30 throws him into convulsions. It wounds him mortally. It pierces his heart. It tears out his entrails. And if. . . . He's coming back; I must be going.

[*Exit.*]

35 [*Enter* HARPAGON.]

HARPAGON [*aside*]. All is as it should be. [*To* FROSINE.] How now! What is it, Frosine?

FROSINE. Ah! Mercy me, how well you are looking! You are the very picture of health!

40 HARPAGON. Who? I?

FROSINE. Never have I seen your color so fresh and jovial.

HARPAGON. Really?

FROSINE. Never in your life were you as 45 young as you are now; I see men of twenty-five who are older than you.

HARPAGON. Nevertheless, Frosine, I'm a good sixty years old.

FROSINE. Well, what is that, sixty years old? A worry indeed! It's the bloom of life, that is. 50 And now you are entering on a man's prime season.

HARPAGON. That's true. However, twenty years less wouldn't do me any harm, as I see it.

FROSINE. Are you joking? You have no need 55 of them. You bid fair to live to be a hundred.

HARPAGON. Do you think so?

FROSINE. Of course. You show every indication. Hold still a bit. Oh, there it is! There it is! Between your two eyes!—a sign of long life! 60

HARPAGON. Do you know something about these things?

FROSINE. Certainly. Show me your hand. Ah! Mercy me, what a life line!

HARPAGON. How's that? 65

FROSINE. Don't you see how far that line goes?

HARPAGON. Well, yes. What does it mean?

FROSINE. By my faith, I said a hundred years, but you will pass the one hundred and twenty 70 mark.

HARPAGON. Is it possible?

FROSINE. You deserve a beating. I tell you, you will bury your children and your children's children. 75

HARPAGON. So much the better! How goes our little transaction?

FROSINE. Need you ask? Did anyone ever see me start anything I couldn't finish? I have an especially wonderful talent for marriages. There 80 aren't two people in the world that I couldn't find a way to couple in no time at all. If I had the notion, I believe I could marry the Grand Turk° to the Republic of Venice. But, to be sure, there wasn't any such great difficulty in- 85 volved in this affair. Since I have business at their house, I have already discussed you at length with both of them; and I told the mother what plans you had conceived for Marianne, on seeing her pass through the street and take the 90 air at her window.

Grand Turk the Sultan. Turkey and Venice were conventional instances of irreconcilable hostility.

HARPAGON. She answered . . .

FROSINE. She received the proposition with joy! And when I informed her that you are very desirous her daughter should be present to-
5 night at the signing of the marriage contract which is to take place here, she readily con-sented. And she has entrusted her daughter to me for the evening.

HARPAGON. I am obliged, Frosine, to give a
10 supper for Signor Anselm, and I would like her to attend this feast.

FROSINE. A good idea. After dinner, she is to pay your daughter a visit; from here she plans to go and see the fair; and afterwards she can
15 come back for supper.

HARPAGON. Fine! They can go together in my carriage. Which I will lend them.

FROSINE. That will suit her perfectly.

HARPAGON. But, Frosine, have you talked to
20 the mother about the money she can give her daughter? Did you tell her she ought to help a little, herself? That she should make some special effort? That she should bleed herself for an occasion like this? For, I tell you again,
25 no one marries a girl unless she brings some-thing in.

FROSINE. What! This is a girl who will bring you twelve thousand francs a year.

HARPAGON. Twelve thousand francs a year?
30 FROSINE. Yes. First of all: those who raised and nurtured her were very sparing on food. She is a girl used to living on salad, milk, cheese, and apples, and consequently doesn't require a richly set table, or fancy jellies or
35 barley syrup all the time, or all the other del-icacies that most women must have. And this is no trifling matter. It will make a difference of at least three thousand francs a year. Besides, she feels that true elegance lies in simplicity,
40 and she doesn't care for magnificent clothes, or rich jewelry, or sumptuous furniture—things which young ladies are usually so passionately addicted to. And that little item is worth more than four thousand francs a year. What's more,
45 she has a tremendous aversion to cards—a thing not common in women nowadays. I know of one in our neighborhood who, at thirties and

forties,° mind you, lost twenty thousand francs this year! But suppose we take only a quarter of that. Five thousand francs a year for cards,
50 and four thousand francs for clothes and jewelry, make nine thousand francs. And we will figure one thousand écus for food. Isn't that your twelve thousand francs a year—every sou of it?
55 HARPAGON. Yes, not bad: but this account has nothing real in it.

FROSINE. I beg your pardon. Is the great sobriety that she will bring to your marriage nothing real? Or her inheritence of a great love
60 of simplicity in dress? Or the acquisition of a great fund of hatred for cards?

HARPAGON. It is a mockery to try and make up a dowry out of the expenses that she won't put me to. I won't give a receipt for something
65 I don't receive. I must be able to touch some-thing.

FROSINE. Mercy me! you will touch enough. They spoke to me about a certain country where they have some property. You shall be the mas-
70 ter of it.

HARPAGON. That remains to be seen. But Frosine, there is something else that bothers me. The girl is young, as you can see, and young people usually like only their own kind, and
75 seek only their company. I am afraid that a man of my age might not be to her taste, and that this might cause some little disorder in my house, which would not suit me at all!

FROSINE. Ah! how little you know her! This
80 is another thing about her that I was going to mention. She has a frightful aversion to all young men, and feels no love except for the old.

HARPAGON. Her?

FROSINE. Yes, her. I wish you could hear her
85 on that subject. She can't so much as stand the sight of a young fellow; but she is in ecstasy, she tells me, when she can look at a handsome old man with a majestic beard. For her, the oldest are the most charming. And I warn you
90 not to go and make yourself look younger than

---

thirties and forties the card game *trente et quarante* or *rouge et noir*, distantly related to blackjack

you are. She likes a man to be sixty at the very least. It wasn't four months ago, that, all set to be married, she broke off the marriage on the spot because her lover let it be known he was only fifty-six years old—and didn't use spectacles to sign the contract.

HARPAGON. Just for that?

FROSINE. Yes. She says she simply couldn't be satisfied with a man of fifty-six, and above all, she is for the nose that wears spectacles.

HARPAGON. Really, this is something altogether new!

FROSINE. It goes much deeper than most people know. Like most young girls she has a few paintings and a few prints in her room, but what do you think the subjects are? Adonises? Cephaluses? Parises? or Apollos? No. They are handsome portraits of Saturn, of King Priam, of old Nestor, and good father Anchises° on his son's shoulders!

HARPAGON. That is admirable! I should never have suspected it. And I am very happy to learn she has that kind of disposition. In fact, had *I* been a woman, I wouldn't have liked young men at all.

FROSINE. I can well believe you. What are they but fancy drugs? And to love them, ha! They are nothing but handsome idiots, good-looking fops that make you envy their complexions. I'd really like to know what there is to them!

HARPAGON. As for me, I can't understand it. I don't know why some women are so fond of them.

FROSINE. They must be stark mad. To find youth amiable! Is there any common sense in it? Are they men, these young dandies? Can you become attached to one of those animals?

HARPAGON. That's what I have always said—with their effeminate, milk-fed voices, and their three little wisps of beard turned up like cat's whiskers, with their mouse-colored wigs, and their sloppy breeches, and their puffed-out stomachs!

FROSINE. They are well-built, indeed, compared with a person like you! [*To the audience.*] There's a man for you! There is someone who is a pleasure to look at! This is how a man should be made and dressed to inspire love.

HARPAGON. You like the way I look?

FROSINE. I should say! You are ravishing, you ought to have your portrait painted. Turn round a bit, if you please. You couldn't be better. Let me see you walk. [*To the audience.*] Here is a body that is trim, supple and tall as it ought to be. And not marked by any infirmity.

HARPAGON. None to speak of, thank God! [*Coughs.*] Except my catarrh that bothers me from time to time.

FROSINE. That is nothing. Your catarrh is not unbecoming to you. You cough gracefully.

HARPAGON. But tell me, hasn't Marianne seen me yet? Hasn't she noticed me at all, passing by her house?

FROSINE. No. But we have talked about you a great deal. I sketched a portrait of your person for her. And I did not fail to boast of your merits and the advantage it would be for her to a have a husband like you.

HARPAGON. You have done well. And I thank you.

FROSINE. I would like, sir, to ask a small favor of you. I have a lawsuit that I am on the point of losing for want of a little money; and you could easily assure my winning this suit if you would show me some little kindness. [HARPAGON *frowns.*] Ah! how well you will please her! What a marvellous impression your old-fashioned ruff will make! But she will be especially charmed by your breeches, attached to your doublet with laces; they'll make her go wild over you. A laced-up lover will seem to her a wonderful treat.

HARPAGON. Really, it delights me to hear you say it.

FROSINE. To tell the truth, sir, this suit is of the utmost importance to me. I am ruined if I lose it, and the least bit of help would set everything right for me. [HARPAGON *frowns.*] I wish you could have seen the rapture in her face when she heard me speak of you. Her eyes sparkled with joy as I recited your qualities. In short, I left her in a state of extreme impatience

---

Adonises . . . Anchises types of youthful beauty contrasted with types of elderly worth

to see this marriage entirely concluded.

HARPAGON. You have given me great pleasure, Frosine. And I must confess, I am under all the obligation in the world to you.

5 FROSINE. I beg you, sir, to give me the slight help I need. It will put me on my feet again. And I will be eternally indebted to you.

HARPAGON. Goodbye! I must get my mail ready.

10 FROSINE. I assure you, sir, you couldn't relieve me in a greater need.

HARPAGON. I will leave orders, so my coach will be ready to take you to the fair.

FROSINE. I would not importune you, were I 15 not forced to do so—out of necessity.

HARPAGON. And I'll see to it that supper is ready early so that you won't get sick.

FROSINE. Do not refuse me this favor, I beg of you.

20 HARPAGON. I am going. There, someone is calling me. I'll see you by and by.

[*Exit* HARPAGON.]

FROSINE. May the fever rack you! Cur! Villain! The devil take you! The miser was deaf 25 to all my attacks. Nevertheless I must not drop his suit: for in any case, there is the other party. I am sure of a good reward from them!

ACT III

[*On stage:* HARPAGON, CLEANTH, ELISE, VALÈRE, DAME CLAUDE, MASTER JACQUES, BRINDA-30 VOINE, *and* LA MERLUCHE.]

HARPAGON. Here, all of you come here. I want to give you orders for this evening, and assign everyone a job. Step forward, Dame Claude. Let's begin with you. Good, I see you 35 are already armed. I consign to you the task of cleaning up the house; and be especially careful not to rub the furniture too hard, or you'll wear it out. Furthermore, I assign you to see to the bottles during supper. And if any of 40 them are carried off, or if anything is broken, you will be responsible, and I'll deduct it from your wages.

JACQUES [*aside*]. A convenient punishment.

HARPAGON [*to* DAME CLAUDE]. Go. . . . [*Exit* 45 DAME CLAUDE.] You, Brindavoine, and you, La Merluche, are appointed to rinse the glasses, and to serve the wine—but only when someone is thirsty. And don't follow the example of those impudent lackeys who go and *incite* peo-50 ple to drink and put the notion in their heads when they aren't even thinking about it. Wait until they have asked you more than once, and remember always to bring a lot of water.

JACQUES [*aside*]. Yes, pure wine goes to the head. 55

MERLUCHE. Shall we take our canvas smocks off, sir?

HARPAGON. Yes, when you see the guests coming, and be careful not to spoil your clothes.

BRINDAVOINE. You know very well, sir, that 60 one side of my doublet is covered with a big spot of lamp-oil.

MERLUCHE. And I, sir, have a big hole in the back of my breeches, and I can be seen, begging your pardon . . . 65

HARPAGON. Peace! Keep that side discreetly turned toward the wall, and always show your front side to the world. And you, always hold your hat like this [*holds his hat over his chest*] when you serve. 70

[*Exeunt* LA MERLUCHE *and* BRINDAVOINE.]

And as for you, my daughter, keep an eye open when they clear away the table, and see to it that nothing goes to waste. That's a proper job for a young girl. But meanwhile, prepare your-75 self to receive my fiancée, who is coming to pay you a visit, and take you to the fair with her. Did you hear what I said?

ELISE. Yes, Father.

HARPAGON. And you, my son, the dandy 80 whose latest escapade I was so good as to forgive, don't you go getting any ideas either and make sour faces at her.

CLEANTH. I, Father? Sour faces? And for what reason? 85

HARPAGON. By God, we know the drift of children whose fathers remarry, and how they feel toward what is called a stepmother. But, if you would like me to forget your last prank, I especially recommend that you treat this per-90 son to some of your most cheerful looks and give her the best reception you possibly can.

CLEANTH. To tell you the truth, Father, I

cannot promise you to be very glad she is to become my stepmother. I should be lying if I told you I would. But as for receiving her well and showing her a pleasant face, I promise to

5 obey you punctually on that score.

HARPAGON. At least take care you do.

CLEANTH. You will see you will have no reason to complain.

HARPAGON. You will do wisely. [*Exeunt*

10 CLEANTH *and* ELISE.] Valère, help me with this. Oh, there you are, Master Jacques! Come here. I have saved you for the last.

JACQUES. Is it to your coachman, sir, or is it to your cook you wish to speak? For I am one and

15 the other.

HARPAGON. To the two of you.

JACQUES. But to which of us first?

HARPAGON. To the cook.

JACQUES. One moment then if you please.

20 [*Takes off his coachman's coat and appears dressed as a cook.*]

HARPAGON. What the deuce kind of ceremony is this?

JACQUES. You have only to speak.

25 HARPAGON. I have committed myself, Master Jacques, to give a supper tonight.

JACQUES [*aside*]. This is miraculous!

HARPAGON. Tell me now, will you give us a fine feast?

30 JACQUES. Yes, if you give me a good deal of money.

HARPAGON. What the devil! always money! It seems they have nothing else to say: money, money, money! That's the sword they keep by

35 their bed, money!

VALÈRE. I have never heard a more impertinent answer. How miraculous it is to be able to set out a fine feast when you have a lot of money! It is the easiest thing in the world to do,

40 and there is no man so poor in wit that he couldn't do as much. But it is a clever man who can talk about providing a fine feast for little money!

JACQUES. A fine feast for little money?

45 VALÈRE. Yes.

JACQUES. By my faith, Mr. Steward, you would oblige us if you would let us in on your secret—and if you will take my place as cook!

You meddle so much in this house already, you might as well be the factotum.   50

HARPAGON. Be quiet. What will we need?

JACQUES. There is your steward who will provide a fine feast at small cost.

HARPAGON. Ha! I want you to answer me.

JACQUES. How many will you be at table?   55

HARPAGON. We will be eight or ten. When there is enough for eight, there is plenty for ten.

VALÈRE. Naturally.

JACQUES. Very well, we will need four kinds   60
of soup and five other dishes. Soups, entrées . . .

HARPAGON. What the devil! That's enough to feed a whole city.

JACQUES. Roast . . .

HARPAGON [*putting his hand over* MASTER   65
JACQUES' *mouth*]. Ah! traitor, you are eating up all my money!

JACQUES. Side dishes . . .

HARPAGON [*putting his hand over* MASTER
JACQUES' *mouth again*]. More?   70

VALÈRE. Do you want to make everybody split open? Do you think our master invites people in order to *murder* them with food? Go and read the rules of health a while—and ask the doctors if there is anything more prejudicial   75
to man than excessive eating.

HARPAGON. He is right.

VALÈRE. Learn, Master Jacques, you and the like of you, that a table overloaded with food is a cut-throat; that if you want to prove yourself   80
a friend to those you invite, frugality should reign at the meals you serve; and that, according to the saying of the ancients, we should eat to live, and not live to eat.

HARPAGON. Oh! but that was well said! Come   85
here, I want to embrace you for that saying. It is the most beautiful sentence I have ever heard in my life. We should live to eat, and not eat to li. . . . No, that isn't it. How was it you said it?   90

VALÈRE. We should eat to live, and not live to eat.

HARPAGON. Yes, do you hear that? Who was the great man who said it?

VALÈRE. At the moment I can't recall his   95
name.

HARPAGON. Remember to write it down for me. I want to have it carved in gold letters above the mantelpiece in my dining room.

VALÈRE. I won't forget. And as for your sup-
5 per, you have only to leave it to me. I will order things to be done as they should be.

HARPAGON. Take care of it then.

JACQUES. So much the better; it will mean less trouble for me.

10 HARPAGON. We should have those things that people don't eat much of, that satisfy the appetite quickly: a nice mutton stew, rather fat, with some kind of meat-pie well garnished and chestnuts to go with it. Yes, that! And let there
15 be a lot of it.

VALÈRE. Leave everything to me.

HARPAGON. Now, Master Jacques, my coach must be cleaned up.

JACQUES. One moment. That was addressed
20 to the coachman. [*Exit, and reappears in his coachman's coat.*] You said . . . ?

HARPAGON. That you should clean up my coach, and have my horses ready to drive to the fair.

25 JACQUES. Your horses, sir? Faith, they are in no condition to walk. I won't say they are down on their litters. The poor beasts don't have any, so I'd be speaking very improperly. But you make them observe such strict fasts
30 that they are now no more than ideas or ghosts or appearances of horses.

HARPAGON. No wonder they are sick; they do nothing.

JACQUES. And because they do nothing, sir,
35 must they eat nothing? It would be much better for them, poor animals, to work a lot, and to eat accordingly. It breaks my heart to see them so weak, because, to tell the truth, I have so much affection for my horses, that when I see
40 them suffer, it's just as though it were myself. Every day I take food out of my own mouth to feed them; it is a very hard nature, sir, that feels no pity for the next one.

HARPAGON. It won't be much work for them
45 to go as far as the fair.

JACQUES. No, sir, I haven't the courage to drive them, and it would lie on my conscience if I hit them with the whip, in the condition they're in. How do you expect them to pull a carriage?—they can't even pull themselves. 50

VALÈRE. Sir, I will ask our neighbor Picard if he will be good enough to drive them. Besides, we shall need him here to help prepare the supper.

JACQUES. Very well! I'd still rather they died 55 under someone else's hands and not mine.

VALÈRE. Master Jacques is intent on cavilling.

JACQUES. Mister Steward is intent on seeming indispensable.

HARPAGON. Peace! 60

JACQUES. Sir, I can't stand flatterers, and I can see what he is doing. He continually restricts the bread, the wine, the wood, the salt, and the candles just to scratch your ear, to win your favor. It makes me angry. And it grieves me to 65 hear what people say about you every day. Because I feel a real affection for you, in spite of myself; and after my horses, you are the person I like most.

HARPAGON. Could I learn from you, Master 70 Jacques, what people say about me?

JACQUES. Yes, sir, if I could be sure it wouldn't make you angry.

HARPAGON. No, not in the least.

JACQUES. Pardon me, but I know very well 75 you'd fly into a rage.

HARPAGON. Not at all. On the contrary, it will give me great pleasure to learn what is said about me.

JACQUES. Sir, since it is your wish, I tell you 80 frankly: people everywhere are laughing at you. They taunt us with a thousand jokes about you on all sides, and they are never so happy as when tearing you to ribbons or making up countless stories about your stinginess. One 85 says that you have special almanacs printed, in which you have doubled the quarter-days° and vigils,° so you can take advantage of the fasts you impose on your household. Another says you always have a quarrel ready to pick 90 with your valets when it is time for holiday gifts, or when they are leaving, so you'll have

---

quarter-days at the four quarters of the year (March, June, Sept., Dec.) when debts fell due
vigils periods of fasting

a reason for not giving them anything. This one tells the story that you once tried to bring your neighbor's cat to court for eating up the remainder of a leg of mutton. Somebody else says that you yourself were caught coming to steal your horses' oats, and that in the dark your coachman, the one before me, gave you I don't know how many blows with his stick, which you didn't care to say anything about. Shall I go on? We can't go anywhere without hearing people pull you apart. You are the talk of the town, the laughing-stock of the world. And they never refer to you except by the name of miser, cut-throat, villain, or shark.

HARPAGON. You are a fool, a scoundrel, a rascal, an insolent knave! [*Beats him.*]

JACQUES. There! Didn't I say it would be that way? You wouldn't believe me. I warned you that you would get angry if I told you the truth.

HARPAGON. Then learn how to talk.

[*Exit* HARPAGON.]

VALÈRE. As far as I can see, Master Jacques, you are poorly paid for your frankness.

JACQUES. By God! Mister Upstart, playing the man of importance, it is none of your business. Save your laughs for your own beating when you get it, and don't come laughing at mine.

VALÈRE. Ah! good Master Jacques, please don't be angry.

JACQUES [*aside*]. He's backing down. I'll pretend to be tough, and if he is fool enough to be afraid of me, I'll give him a little thrashing. Did you know, Mister Comedian, that I myself never laugh?—and that if you get my temper up you are likely to be laughing out of the other side of your mouth?

VALÈRE. Gently now!

JACQUES. Why gently? What if I don't feel like being gentle?

VALÈRE. Please!

JACQUES. You are an impertinent fellow.

VALÈRE. Good Master Jacques!

JACQUES. There is no such a person as good Master Jacques. If I get a stick, I'll beat the importance out of you.

VALÈRE [*picking up the stick on the table*]. What did you say? a stick?

JACQUES. Oh! I wasn't talking about that one.

VALÈRE. Did you know, Mister Fool, that I am man enough to thrash you?

JACQUES. I don't doubt it.

VALÈRE. That you are, by any standard, nothing but a miserable cook?

JACQUES. I know very well.

VALÈRE. And that you don't know me yet?

JACQUES. I beg your pardon.

VALÈRE. You'll beat me, you say?

JACQUES. I was joking.

VALÈRE. And your joking is not to my taste. This will teach you that you're a scurvy joker. [*Beats him.*]

[*Exit* VALÈRE.]

JACQUES. A pox on sincerity! It's a wretched practice. Here and now I renounce it, and I will never tell the truth again. As for my master, I'll let that go—he has some right to beat me. But, as for this steward, I'll take my revenge if I can.

[*Enter* FROSINE *and* MARIANNE.]

FROSINE. Do you know, Master Jacques, if your master is at home?

JACQUES. Yes, he certainly is. I know it all too well!

FROSINE. Tell him, pray, that we are here.

[*Exit* MASTER JACQUES.]

MARIANNE. Ah! Frosine, I am in such a strange state! If I must tell what I feel: I am very much afraid of this interview.

FROSINE. But why? What is it that worries you?

MARIANNE. Alas! Need you ask? Can't you imagine the alarm of a person just about to see the rack she is to be tortured on?

FROSINE. I can plainly see that Harpagon is not the rack you would choose to embrace if you're thinking of an agreeable death. And I know by your expression that the dandy you were telling me about is somewhere in your thoughts.

MARIANNE. Yes, Frosine. That I do not wish to deny. The respectful visits he paid at our house have had, I must confess, some effect on my heart.

FROSINE. But have you learned *who* he is?

MARIANNE. No, I don't in the least know *who*

he is, but I do know he is fashioned in a way that inspires love and that, if the choice were left at my disposal, I would take him sooner than any other, and that he contributes not a
5 little to make me find the husband you would give me a horrible torment.

FROSINE. Mercy me! all those dandies are agreeable enough, and they play their parts very well, but most of them are poor as church-
10 mice. You would do much better to take an old husband who will leave you a lot of money. I will admit that the senses will not find full measure on the side which I am speaking for, and there are some slightly distasteful details to be
15 endured with such a husband—but it won't be for long. His death, believe me, will soon put you in a position to pick a more attractive one, who will make up for everything.

MARIANNE. Bless me, Frosine, it seems a very
20 strange business when, to be happy, one must hope or wait for the demise of someone. And death does not always lend itself to the plans we make.

FROSINE. Are you joking? You are marrying
25 him only on the understanding that he will soon leave you a widow. That ought to be one of the articles in the contract. It would be very impertinent in him not to die before three months are out.
30 [*Enter* HARPAGON.]
Speak of the devil . . .

MARIANNE. Ah! Frosine, what a face!

HARPAGON. Do not be offended, my beauty, if I come to you wearing spectacles. I know that
35 your charms are striking enough—are visible enough by themselves—that there is no need of glasses to perceive them. But after all, it is through glasses we observe the stars, and I maintain and guarantee that you are a star.
40 And what a star! The most beautiful star in the realm of stars. Frosine, she doesn't say a word, and she doesn't show, so it seems to me, that she is at all pleased to see me.

FROSINE. That is because she is still all sur-
45 prise. And then, the girls nowadays are always shy about showing straightway what is in their hearts.
[*Enter* ELISE.]

HARPAGON. You are right. [*To* MARIANNE.]
Here, darling beauty, is my daughter, who has 50 come to greet you.

MARIANNE. I acquit myself, madam, much too tardily of this visit.

ELISE. You have done that, madam, which I ought to have done. It was my place to antic- 55 ipate you.

HARPAGON. You see how tall she is; but weeds grow fast.

MARIANNE [*aside to* FROSINE]. Oh, what an unpleasant man! 60

HARPAGON. What does the beauty say?

FROSINE. That she thinks you are wonderful.

HARPAGON. You do me too much honor, adorable darling.

MARIANNE [*aside to* FROSINE]. Such an an- 65 imal!

HARPAGON. I am obliged for your sentiments.

MARIANNE. [*aside to* FROSINE]. I can't stand any more of this.
[*Enter* CLEANTH.] 70

HARPAGON. Here is my son, who also comes to pay you his respects.

MARIANNE [*aside to* FROSINE]. Ah! Frosine, what a coincidence! This is the very person I spoke to you about. 75

FROSINE. The adventure is fantastic.

HARPAGON. I see you are astonished to find that I have such big children; but I shall soon be rid of them both.

CLEANTH. Madam, to tell the truth, this is an 80 encounter which I by no means expected; and my father surprised me not a little when he told me a while ago of his intentions.

MARIANNE. I can say the same for myself. This is an unforeseen meeting, which has sur- 85 prised me as much as it has you. I too was not at all prepared for such an encounter.

CLEANTH. It is true that my father, madam, could not make a handsomer choice, and the honor of seeing you is a real joy for me; but 90 for all that, I will not assure you that I rejoice over the design you may have to become my stepmother. That compliment, I confess, is too much for me; it is a title, if you please, that I do not want for you. This speech may seem 95 brutal in the eyes of some, but I am sure you are a person who will take it in the right sense. You can easily imagine, madam, that this is a marriage which is bound to be somewhat repugnant to me; for you know what kind of man I am and how much it clashes with my interests. In short, you willl not be offended if I tell you, with my father's permission, that if things depended on me, these nuptials would never take place.

HARPAGON. Your compliment is very impertinent! What a nice confession to make to her!

MARIANNE. And I, in answer to you, have this to say: our feelings are quite mutual. If it is true that you would find it repugnant to have me for a stepmother, it would be no less so for me, I assure you, to have you for a stepson. Do not think, pray, that it is I who seek to be the source of your uneasiness. I should be very sorry to cause you any displeasure; and if I did not see myself forced to it by an absolute power, I give you my word, I would never consent to a marriage that pains you.

HARPAGON. She is right. A stupid compliment like that deserves a stupid answer. I beg pardon, my beauty, for my son's impertinence. He is a young ass who doesn't yet know the weight of his own words.

MARIANNE. I assure you that what he said has not offended me in the least. On the contrary, it has been a pleasure to hear him express his true sentiments. I like that kind of confession from him. If he had spoken in any other way, I would have far less esteem for him.

HARPAGON. It is very kind of you to forgive his faults this way. Time will make him wiser, and you will see that he will have a change of heart.

CLEANTH. No, Father, it is not capable of change; and I earnestly entreat madam to believe that.

HARPAGON. Just see how extravagant he is! He goes on more rashly than ever.

CLEANTH. Would you have me belie my heart?

HARPAGON. Again! Would you mind changing the subject?

CLEANTH. Very well, since you wish me to speak in a different manner ... Permit me, madam, to put myself in my father's place, to confess that I have never seen anything in the world as lovely as you; that I can conceive nothing to equal the happiness of pleasing you; and that the title of your husband is a glory, a felicity, that I would prefer to the destiny of the greatest prince on earth. Yes, madam, the happiness of possessing you, is, in my estimation, the fairest of all fortunes; it is the goal of my whole ambition. I would do anything to make such a conquest; and the most powerful obstacles ...

HARPAGON. Moderation, son, if you please.

CLEANTH. This is a compliment I am paying the lady, for you.

HARPAGON. By God! I have a tongue to express myself, and I have no need of a proxy the likes of you. Here, bring chairs.

FROSINE. No. It will be better for us to go directly to the fair. Then we'll be back early and have the whole time afterward to talk with you.

HARPAGON. Then tell them to hitch up the horses to the carriage. I beg you to excuse me, my beauty, for not having thought to give you a little refreshment before you start out.

CLEANTH. I have provided for that, Father. I had them bring a few plates of Chinese oranges, some lemons, and some preserves; which I sent for in your name.

HARPAGON [aside to VALÈRE]. Valère!

VALÈRE. He's out of his head.

CLEATH. Do you think, Father, that it isn't enough? Madam will please have the kindness to excuse it.

MARIANNE. It was not at all necessary.

CLEANTH. Have you ever, madam, seen more fire in a diamond than in this one you see on my father's finger? [Takes ring off HARPAGON's finger.]

MARIANNE. It is true that it shines quite brightly.

CLEANTH. You must see it from close up. [Puts ring on MARIANNE's hand.]

MARIANNE. It is very handsome, I must say, and it sparkles a great deal.

[Begins to take ring off her finger.]

CLEANTH. No, no, madam; it is on hands much too lovely. My father makes you a present of it.

HARPAGON. I?

CLEANTH. Isn't it true, Father, that you want the lady to keep it for love of you?

HARPAGON [*aside to* CLEANTH]. What is this?

5   CLEANTH. Foolish question. He makes a sign to me that I should make you accept it.

MARIANNE. I don't at all want . . .

CLEANTH. Are you joking? He has no intention of taking it back.

10   HARPAGON [*aside*]. I'm losing my temper.

MARIANNE. It would be . . .

CLEANTH. No, I tell you, you will offend him.

MARIANNE. Please . . .

CLEANTH. Out of the question.

15   HARPAGON [*aside*]. A pox . . .

CLEANTH. Your refusal is making him angry.

HARPAGON [*aside to* CLEANTH]. Ah! you traitor!

CLEANTH. You see he's getting desperate.

20   HARPAGON. You murderer, you!

CLEANTH. Father, it's not my fault. I am doing what I can to oblige her to keep it, but she is determined.

HARPAGON [*aside to* CLEANTH]. Scoundrel!

25   CLEANTH. You are the cause, madam, of my father's quarreling with me.

HARPAGON [*aside to* CLEANTH]. Knave!

CLEANTH. You will make him ill. Please, madam, do not resist any longer.

30   FROSINE. Mercy me! What a fuss! Keep the ring if the gentleman wants you to have it.

MARIANNE. So that you won't fly into a rage, I will keep it for the time being; and I will find another opportunity to return it.

35   [*Enter* BRINDAVOINE.]

BRINDAVOINE. Sir, there's a man here who wants to talk to you.

HARPAGON. Tell him I am busy, and to come back some other time.

40   BRINDAVOINE. He says he has money for you.

HARPAGON [*to* MARIANNE]. Please excuse me. I'll be back presently.

[*Enter* LA MERLUCHE *running; collides with* HARPAGON *and knocks him down.*]

45   MERLUCHE. Sir . . .

HARPAGON. Ah! I am dying!

CLEANTH. What is it, Father, are you hurt?

HARPAGON. The traitor must surely have been paid by my debtors to make me break my neck.

VALÈRE [*to* HARPAGON]. There's no harm   50 done.

MERLUCHE. I beg your pardon, sir, I thought I did right to come running.

HARPAGON. What are you here for, murderer?

MERLUCHE. To tell you that neither of your   55 horses has any shoes.

HARPAGON. Take them to the blacksmith, right away.

CLEANTH. While waiting for the horses to be shod, Father, I will do the honors of the house   60 for you, and conduct madam into the garden, where I shall have the refreshments served.

[*Exeunt* FROSINE, ELISE, MARIANNE, *and* CLEANTH.]

HARPAGON. Valère, keep an eye on all that;   65 and take care, pray, to save me as much as you can, so that we can send it back to the dealer.

VALÈRE. Rest assured.

[*Exit* VALÈRE.]

HARPAGON. Oh, impertinent son! You are   70 trying to ruin me!

ACT IV

[*Enter* CLEANTH, MARIANNE, ELISE, *and* FROSINE.]

CLEANTH. Let us go in again; we shall be much better off in here. There is no longer any-   75 one suspect around, and we can speak freely.

ELISE. Yes, madam, my brother has confided to me the love he bears you. I know what pain and frustration such obstacles can cause; and it is a most kindly sympathy, I assure you, that   80 provokes my interest in your adventure.

MARIANNE. It is a sweet consolation to see a person like you interested in oneself, and I implore you, madam, always to cherish your generous friendship for me—so capable of   85 softening the cruel blows of misfortune.

FROSINE. By my faith, you are unlucky people, both of you, for not having told me about your affair before all this happened. I could, no doubt, have warded off these troubles. I   90 wouldn't have brought matters to such a pass as this.

CLEANTH. What can you expect? It is my evil

destiny has willed it so. But, dear Marianne, what have you resolved to do?

MARIANNE. Alas! am I in a position to resolve anything? Dependent as I am, can I do more
5 than hope?

CLEANTH. Is there nothing in your heart to encourage me but barren hope? No benevolent pity? No helpful kindness? No lively affection at all?

10 MARIANNE. What can I tell you? Put yourself in my place, and see what I can do. Advise me. Order me. I put myself in your hands. And I believe you are too reasonable to demand more of me than is allowed by honor and decorum.

15 CLEANTH. Alas! to what am I reduced if you limit me to the pallid sentiments that rigorous honor and scrupulous decorum will allow?

MARIANNE. But what would you have me do? Even though I could ignore many of the niceties
20 which our sex is obliged to observe, I have too much consideration for my mother. She has reared me with extreme tenderness. I could never resolve to do anything that would cause her displeasure. Go and speak to her. Do every-
25 thing in your power to win her over. You may do and say whatever you please; I give you my permission. And if it is only a question of declaring in your favor, I readily consent to make a confession to her of all that I feel for
30 you.

CLEANTH. Frosine, my poor Frosine, would you help us?

FROSINE. By my faith, is there any need to ask? I will with all my heart. You know that by
35 nature I am human enough. Heaven didn't give me a heart of bronze, and I am only too eager to do little services for people when I see they love one another sincerely and honorably. What can we do about this?

40 CLEANTH. Think a little, I beg you.

MARIANNE. Show us a way.

ELISE. Invent something that will undo what you have done.

FROSINE. That is rather difficult. [To MARI-
45 ANNE.] As to your mother, she is not altogether unreasonable: perhaps you could win her over, and make her decide to transfer the gift she intends for the father to the son. [To CLEANTH.]

But the worst part of this is that your father
is—your father. 50

CLEANTH. That's understood.

FROSINE. I mean he will bear a grudge if she refuses him openly, and he will be in no humor afterward to give his consent to your marriage. It will be necessary, to do it well, that 55 the refusal come from himself. We must try by some means to make her distasteful to him.

CLEANTH. You are right.

FROSINE. Yes, I am right. I know it very well. That is what has to be done. But the deuce of it 60 is to find a way. Wait; if we had a woman, getting on in years, with my talent, and who could act well enough to counterfeit a lady of quality, with the help of a train made up in a hurry and some bizarre name of marchioness or 65 viscountess, who we could pretend comes from Brittany, I could be clever enough to convince him that she was a rich person who, besides her houses, had a hundred thousand écus in solid silver, that she was hopelessly in love 70 with him, and wanted to be his wife so badly that she would sign over all her property to him in a marriage contract. I don't in the least doubt that he would lend an ear to the proposition. For, in short, although he loves you very much, 75 he loves money a little more. And, once blinded by this illusion, once he has consented to what concerns you most, it will matter little after-ward if he is undeceived when he looks more closely into the estate of our marchioness. 80

CLEANTH. This is all very well thought out.

FROSINE. Leave it to me. I just thought of a friend of mine who is the very woman we want.

CLEANTH. Rest assured, Frosine, of my grati-tude if you succeed in this. But dear Marianne, 85 let us begin by persuading your mother; there is still much to be done to break off this marriage. For your part, I beseech you, make every effort you possibly can. Use all the power that her love for you gives you over her. Unfold your 90 eloquent graces without reserve—those all-powerful charms that Heaven has located in your eyes and lips. And forget none, please, of those tender expressions, or those soft en-treaties, or those touching caresses to which, I 95 am persuaded, no one could refuse anything.

[*Enter* HARPAGON.]

MARIANNE. I will do all in my power, and I won't forget a thing.

HARPAGON [*aside*]. Hey! what's this? My son kisses the hand of his future stepmother; and his future stepmother does not offer much resistance. Could there be more to this than meets the eye?

ELISE. Here is my father.

HARPAGON. The carriage is ready. You can leave when you please.

CLEANTH. Since you are not going, Father, I will drive them myself.

HARPAGON. No, stay. They can go just as well by themselves. I need you here.

[*Exeunt* FROSINE, ELISE, *and* MARIANNE.]

HARPAGON. Oh! by the way, apart from the question of her becoming your stepmother, what do you think of this person?

CLEANTH. What do I think of her?

HARPAGON. Yes—of her manner, her figure, her beauty, and her wit?

CLEANTH. So so.

HARPAGON. What do you mean?

CLEANTH. To tell you frankly, I did not find her what I thought her to be. She has the manner of an out-and-out coquette, her figure is rather awkward, her beauty is mediocre, and she has a very common kind of wit. But don't think, Father, that I am trying to set you against her. Because, stepmother for stepmother, I like this one as much as I would any other.

HARPAGON. Nevertheless you were telling her a while ago . . .

CLEANTH. I did say a few nice things to her in your name—but that was to please you.

HARPAGON. So then, you don't feel the slightest inclination for her?

CLEANTH. I? None at all.

HARPAGON. That's too bad, for it puts an end to an idea that came into my head. Seeing her here made me reflect on my age, and I thought to myself that people might find fault with me for marrying such a young girl. This consideration made me abandon my plans; but, since I have already asked her to marry and am bound by my word, I would have given her to you—if you had not shown such an aversion.

CLEANTH. To me?

HARPAGON. To you.

CLEANTH. In marriage?

HARPAGON. In marriage.

CLEANTH. Listen. It is true she is not much to my taste. But to make you happy, Father, I will resign myself to marrying her—since it is your wish.

HARPAGON. Mine? I am more reasonable than you think. I would not force your inclination.

CLEANTH. Pardon me, I will do myself this violence out of love for you.

HARPAGON. No, no. A marriage can never be happy where there is no affection.

CLEANTH. Affection is something, Father, that will come afterwards, perhaps. They say that love is often the fruit of marriage.

HARPAGON. No, the venture ought not to be risked on the man's side. There may be painful consequences to which I would not care to expose myself. If you had felt some inclination for her earlier, I would have had you marry her in my place. But since that is not the case, I will carry out my first plan, and marry her myself.

CLEANTH. Very well, Father, since this is the way things are, I am obliged to bare my heart to you: I must reveal our secret. The truth is that I have loved her since the first time I saw her out walking, that my intention up to a while ago was to ask you if I could have her for my wife, and that nothing has held me back but your declaration of your own sentiments and fear of displeasing you.

HARPAGON. Have you visited her?

CLEANTH. Yes, Father.

HARPAGON. Very often?

CLEANTH. Often enough—for the time I had.

HARPAGON. Were you well received?

CLEANTH. Very well. But they did not know who I was. That is why Marianne was so surprised a while ago.

HARPAGON. Did you declare your passion to her, and your intention of marrying her?

CLEANTH. Certainly, and I have even broached the subject a little to her mother.

HARPAGON. Did she give your proposal a hearing?

CLEANTH. Yes, a very civil one.

HARPAGON. And does her daughter return your love appreciably?

CLEANTH. If appearances are to be trusted, I
5 am persuaded, Father, that she feels some affection for me.

HARPAGON. I am happy to learn such a secret. It is exactly what I wanted to know. And now, son, do you know what you will have to do?
10 You will have to think, if you please, about getting over your love, about giving up your pursuit of this person whom I intend for myself, and about marrying, in a short time, the woman I have chosen for you!

15 CLEANTH. So, Father, you have tricked me! Very well! Since things have come to this pass, I declare to you that I will never cease loving Marianne, that I will go to any limit to dispute the conquest with you, and though you have
20 the mother's consent on your side, I will perhaps find others who will fight for me.

HARPAGON. What? You scoundrel! You have the audacity to stalk my game?

CLEANTH. It is you who are stalking mine: I
25 knew her first.

HARPAGON. Am I not your father? Don't you owe me your respect?

CLEANTH. These are not matters in which the children are obliged to defer to their fathers.
30 Love knows no master.

HARPAGON. I'll teach you to know me—by the mastery of a good stick.

CLEANTH. All your threats will do no good.

HARPAGON. Will you renounce Marianne?

35 CLEANTH. On no account.

HARPAGON. Bring me a stick, quickly.

[Enter MASTER JACQUES.]

JACQUES. Now, now, now! gentlemen, what is this? What can you be thinking of?

40 CLEANTH. I laugh at it all.

JACQUES. Ah! gently, sir.

HARPAGON. To talk with such impudence!

JACQUES. Oh! sir, please.

CLEANTH. I won't yield an inch.

45 JACQUES. Eh, what? to your father?

HARPAGON. Leave him to me.

[Menaces CLEANTH with his stick.]

JACQUES. Eh, what? to your son? Once more, leave off, for my sake.

HARPAGON. I want to make *you*, Master 50 Jacques, judge of this affair—to prove I am right.

JACQUES. I am willing. [To CLEANTH.] Go a little farther off.

HARPAGON. I am in love with a girl I want to 55 marry, and that scoundrel has the impudence to be in love with the same girl at the same time, and intends, despite my orders, to marry her.

JACQUES. Ah! he is in the wrong. 60

HARPAGON. Isn't it a shocking thing for a son to enter into competition with his father? Shouldn't he, out of respect, refrain from meddling where my affections are involved?

JACQUES. You are right. Let me talk to him. 65 Stay here.

[Goes to CLEANTH.]

CLEANTH. Yes, of course, since he has chosen you for judge, I'll not back out. It isn't important to me who it is, and I am too willing to 70 refer myself to you, Master Jacques, in this matter of our difference.

JACQUES. You do me great honor.

CLEANTH. I am very much taken with a young lady who returns all my interest, and who has 75 tenderly received the offer of my heart; and my father has taken it into his head to trouble our love by making her an offer of marriage.

JACQUES. He is in the wrong, surely.

CLEANTH. Isn't he ashamed, at his age, to 80 dream of marrying? Is it becoming in him to be amorous? Wouldn't he do better to leave that business to young fellows?

JACQUES. You are right; he is making a fool of himself. Let me say a few words to him. 85 [Returns to HARPAGON.] Well, your son is not so strange as you make him out to be; he has submitted to reason. He says he knows that he owes you respect, that he was carried away by the heat of the argument, and that he will not 90 refuse to submit to anything that pleases you, provided you intend to treat him better than you have done, and that you give him someone in marriage with whom he will have reason to be satisfied. 95

HARPAGON. Ah, tell him, Master Jacques, that with this provision, he may expect anything he *wants* from me; and that, Marianne excepted, he is at liberty to choose any girl he pleases.

JACQUES. Leave it to me. [*To* CLEANTH.] Well, your father is not as unreasonable as you make him out to be, and he admitted to me that it was only your rage that roused his temper, that he is angry only about the way you conducted yourself, and that he will be very much disposed to grant all your wishes provided you will go about it gently, and show him the deference, respect, and submission that a son owes his father.

CLEANTH. Ah! Master Jacques, you can assure him that if he grants me Marianne, he will see that I will always be the most submissive man in the world, and that I will never do anything except by his wish.

JACQUES [*going to* HARPAGON]. It's done. He consents to what you ask.

HARPAGON. It's the happiest conclusion in the world.

JACQUES [*going to* CLEANTH]. It's all decided. He is satisfied with your promises.

CLEANTH. Heaven be praised!

JACQUES [*in the middle of the stage*]. Gentlemen, you have only to talk together. Here you are in agreement now, and you were about to fall out because of a misunderstanding!

CLEANTH. My poor Master Jacques, I will be obliged to you for life.

JACQUES. It was nothing, sir.

HARPAGON. You have made me happy, Master Jacques, and you deserve a reward. [MASTER JACQUES *puts out his hand.*] Go—I shall remember it, I assure you.

JACQUES. I kiss your hand.

[*Exit* MASTER JACQUES.]

CLEANTH. I beg your pardon, Father, for showing my temper in that way.

HARPAGON. It was nothing.

CLEANTH. I assure you, it gives me all the concern in the world.

HARPAGON. As for myself, it gives me all the joy in the world to see you reasonable.

CLEANTH. How good of you to forget my fault so quickly!

HARPAGON. One easily forgets his child's faults when one sees him return to the path of duty.

CLEANTH. What! you harbor no resentment for all my extravagance?

HARPAGON. You oblige me not to by the submission and respect you show.

CLEANTH. And I, I promise you, Father, will bear the memory of your kindness to the grave.

HARPAGON. And I, I promise you that there is nothing you shall not have from me.

CLEANTH. Ah! Father, I have nothing more to ask: you gave me all when you gave me Marianne.

HARPAGON. What?

CLEANTH. I say, Father, that you have made me too happy. You gave me all when you agreed to give me Marianne.

HARPAGON. Who said anything about giving you Marianne?

CLEANTH. You, Father.

HARPAGON. I?

CLEANTH. Certainly.

HARPAGON. What! You are the one who promised to renounce her.

CLEANTH. I renounce her?

HARPAGON. Yes.

CLEANTH. Not in the least.

HARPAGON. You haven't abandoned your pretensions to her?

CLEANTH. On the contrary, I am more determined than ever.

HARPAGON. What! you rascal, again?

CLEANTH. Nothing can change my mind.

HARPAGON. Let me at you, traitor!

CLEANTH. Do whatever you please.

HARPAGON. I forbid you ever to see me again.

CLEANTH. It's all the same to me.

HARPAGON. I abandon you.

CLEANTH. Abandon me.

HARPAGON. I disown you as my son.

CLEANTH. So be it.

HARPAGON. I disinherit you.

CLEANTH. Anything you like.

HARPAGON. And I give you my curse.

CLEANTH. I have no need of your gifts.

[*Exit* HARPAGON.]

[*Enter* LA FLÈCHE.]

FLÈCHE. Ah! sir! I have found you just in time! Follow me quickly.

CLEANTH. What's the matter?

FLÈCHE. Follow me, I tell you—our troubles are over.

CLEANTH. What?

FLÈCHE [shows him the chest]. Here's your way out.

CLEANTH. How?

5 FLÈCHE. Your father's treasure. I dug it up!

CLEANTH. Where was it?

FLÈCHE. You shall know everything. Run. I hear him screaming.

[Exeunt LA FLÈCHE and CLEANTH.]

10 [Enter HARPAGON.]

HARPAGON. Stop thief! Stop thief! Stop assassin! Stop murderer! Justice, Divine Justice! I am ruined! I've been murdered! He cut my throat, he stole my money! Who can it be?

15 What's become of him? Where is he? Where is he hiding? What shall I do to find him? Where shall I run? Where shan't I run? Isn't that he there? Isn't this he here? Who's this? [Sees his own shadow and grabs his own arm.] Stop!

20 Give me back my money, you rogue . . . Ah! it is myself. My mind is unhinged, and I don't know where I am, who I am, or what I am doing. [Falls to his knees.] Alas! my poor money, my poor money, my dear friend, they have taken you

25 from me. And since they carried you off, I've lost my support, my consolation, my joy. Everything is at an end for me; I have no more to do in this world! I cannot live without you! It's finished. I can no more. [Lies down.] I am

30 dying. I am dead. I am buried! Isn't there anybody who would like to bring me back to life by returning my dear money or by telling me who took it? [Rising to his knees.] What did you say? It was nobody. [Stands.] Whoever

35 did the job must have watched very closely for his chance; for he chose exactly the time when I was talking to my treacherous son. [Takes his hat and cane.] I'll go out. I'll go and demand justice. I'll order them to torture everyone in

40 my house for a confession: the maids, the valets, my son, my daughter—and myself too! What a crowd of people! Everybody I cast my eyes on arouses my suspicion, and everything seems to be my thief. Eh! what are you talking

45 about there? About the man that robbed me? Why are you making that noise up there? Is my thief there? [Kneels and addresses the audience.] Please, if anyone has any information

about my thief, I beg you to tell me. Are you sure he isn't hidden there among you? They all 50 look at me and laugh. [Rises.] You will probably see that they all had a part in this robbery. Here, quick, commissaries, archers, provosts, judges, tortures, scaffolds, and executioners! I want to have everybody hanged. And 55 if I don't recover my money, I'll hang myself afterward!

ACT V

[On stage: HARPAGON, the COMMISSARY, and his CLERK.]

COMMISSARY. Leave me alone. I know my 60 business, thank God! I didn't start investigating robberies yesterday. I wish I had a sack of francs for every man I've sent to the gallows!

HARPAGON. All the magistrates are interested in taking this case in hand. What's more, if no 65 one sees to it that I recover my money, I shall demand justice from Justice herself!

COMMISSARY. We must follow the prescribed procedure. How much was it you said was in this moneybox? 70

HARPAGON. Ten thousand écus, to the sou.

COMMISSARY. Ten thousand écus?

HARPAGON. Ten thousand écus.

COMMISSARY. It was a considerable theft.

HARPAGON. No penalty would be too great 75 for the enormity of the crime. If it goes unpunished, nothing is too sacred to be safe.

COMMISSARY. In what coin was the sum?

HARPAGON. In good gold louis and solid pistoles. 80

COMMISSARY. Whom do you suspect of this theft?

HARPAGON. Everybody! I want you to arrest the whole city and the suburbs!

COMMISSARY. We musn't frighten anyone, 85 take my word for it. We must try and obtain some evidence quietly. Then afterward we can proceed more rigorously in recovering the deniers that were taken from you.

[Enter MASTER JACQUES from the kitchen.] 90

JACQUES. I'll be back in a little while. First I want you to cut his throat. Then I want you to singe his feet. Then I want you to put him in boiling water. Then I want you to hang him from the ceiling.

HARPAGON. Who? The man who robbed me?

5 JACQUES. I was talking about the suckling pig your steward just sent me. I want to dress him for you according to my fancy.

HARPAGON. That is not the question. You must talk to this gentleman about something else.

10 COMMISSARY. Don't be frightened. I am not a man who would cause you scandal. Everything will be done quietly.

JACQUES. Is the gentleman one of your supper guests?

15 COMMISSARY. Now, my dear friend, you must hide nothing from your master.

JACQUES. Faith, sir, I will show you all I know: I will treat you the best I possibly can.

HARPAGON. We aren't talking about that.

20 JACQUES. If I can't give you as fine a feast as I want to, it's the fault of a certain gentleman, a certain steward, who has clipped my wings with the scissors of his economy.

HARPAGON. Traitor! We are investigating

25 something more important than supper. I want you to give me information about the money that was stolen from me.

JACQUES. Did someone steal your money?

HARPAGON. Yes, you rascal! And I'll have you

30 hanged if you don't give it back.

COMMISSARY. For Heaven's sake, don't bully him! I can see by his face he's an honest man. Without making us send him to jail, he will tell you everything you want to know. Yes, my

35 friend, if you tell us what you know, no harm will come to you. You will be rewarded by your master, as you deserve to be. Just this morning someone took his money. Is it possible you don't have some information about this matter?

40 JACQUES [*aside*]. Exactly what I need to get my revenge on our steward! Ever since he came into this house he has been the favorite—only *his* advice is listened to. Then, too, the beating he gave me sticks in my craw.

45 HARPAGON. What are you mumbling about?

COMMISSARY. Leave him alone. He is preparing to give you satisfaction. I told you he is an honest man.

JACQUES. Sir, since you want me to tell you something about this business, I think it was a 50 certain gentleman, a certain steward, who did the job.

HARPAGON. Valère?

JACQUES. Yes.

HARPAGON. He? Who seemed to be so trust- 55 worthy?

JACQUES. Himself. I think he is the one who robbed you.

HARPAGON. On what grounds do you think so? 60

JACQUES. On what grounds?

HARPAGON. Yes.

JACQUES. I think so . . . on the grounds that . . . I think so.

COMMISSARY. But it is necessary that you tell 65 us what proof you have.

HARPAGON. Did you see him sneaking around the place where I kept my money?

JACQUES. Yes, certainly. Where did you keep your money? 70

HARPAGON. In the garden.

JACQUES. Exactly. I saw him sneaking through the garden. What was this money in?

HARPAGON. A moneybox.

JACQUES. That's it. I saw him with a money- 75 box.

HARPAGON. This moneybox . . . What did it look like? I'll soon see if it was mine.

JACQUES. What did it look like?

HARPAGON. Yes. 80

JACQUES. It looked like . . . it looked like a moneybox.

COMMISSARY. Of course. But describe it a little, so we can see . . .

JACQUES. It was a large moneybox. 85

HARPAGON. The one that was stolen from me was small.

JACQUES. Oh, yes—it was small if you want to look at it that way. I call it large on account of what it contained. 90

COMMISSARY. What color was it?

JACQUES. What color?

COMMISSARY. Yes.

JACQUES. It was the color of . . . yes, the color of it was . . . Can't you help me out a bit? 95

HARPAGON. Eh!

JACQUES. Wasn't it red?

HARPAGON. No, gray.

JACQUES. Oh! yes, grayish-red. That's what I meant to say.

5 HARPAGON. There isn't the slightest doubt. That is definitely it. Write, sir, write down his testimony. Heavens! who's to be trusted nowadays? You can't put your faith in anything! After this, I fear I am a man who might rob 10 himself.

JACQUES. Sir, he is coming back. At least don't go and tell him it was I who told you this.

[*Enter* VALÈRE.]

HARPAGON. Advance. Come. Confess the 15 darkest deed, the most horrible atrocity ever committed.

VALÈRE. What do you mean, sir?

HARPAGON. What! traitor, you do not even blush for your crime?

20 VALÈRE. What crime can you be talking of?

HARPAGON. What crime am I talking of? Infamous! As though you didn't know what I mean! It is useless for you to try and cover up. The deed has been discovered. Someone has just 25 told me all. Really! How could you abuse my kindness that way—insinuate yourself into my house to betray me—to play a trick of that kind on me!

VALÈRE. Sir, since someone has told you all, 30 I shall not try to find a way out. I deny nothing.

JACQUES [*aside*]. Hoho! Could I have guessed right without thinking?

VALÈRE. It was my intention to speak to you about it, and I wanted to wait for more favor- 35 able conditions to do so. But since things are the way they are, I beg you not to be angry. Be good enough to hear my reasons.

HARPAGON. And what wonderful reasons can you give me, infamous thief?

40 VALÈRE. Ah! sir, I have not deserved those names. It is true I am guilty of an offense against you. But, after all, my fault is pardonable.

HARPAGON. How, pardonable? A premed- 45 itated crime? An assassination of this sort?

VALÈRE. Please don't lose your temper. When you have heard me, you will see that the evil done is not so great as you make it out.

HARPAGON. The evil is not so great as I make it out! What? My blood! My entrails!—You 50 scoundrel!

VALÈRE. Your blood, sir, has not fallen into evil hands. I belong to a class which is not beneath it, and there is nothing in all this for which I cannot make full reparation. 55

HARPAGON. That is my intention precisely— that you shall make full restitution of what you have ravished from me.

VALÈRE. Your honor, sir, shall be fully satisfied. 60

HARPAGON. It has nothing to do with honor. But, tell me, what ever possessed you to do it?

VALÈRE. Alas! You are asking me?

HARPAGON. Yes, I really am.

VALÈRE. A god who is his own excuse for 65 everything he does: Love.

HARPAGON. Love?

VALÈRE. Yes.

HARPAGON. A beautiful love, a beautiful love indeed! Love of my gold louis. 70

VALÈRE. No, sir, it was not in the least your wealth that tempted me. That wasn't what dazzled me. And I swear I will make no claims whatsoever on your property, provided you let me keep what I have. 75

HARPAGON. I will do no such thing, by God! See how insolent he is! He wants to keep the proceeds of his theft.

VALÈRE. Do you call it a theft?

HARPAGON. Do I call it a theft! A treasure 80 like that!

VALÈRE. A treasure indeed! The most precious you have, without a doubt! But your giving me such a treasure would be no real loss to you. I ask you on bended knee to give this enchanting 85 treasure. If you want to do right you will grant my request.

HARPAGON. I will do nothing of the kind. What is he saying?

VALÈRE. We have promised to be faithful to 90 one another. We have vowed never to separate.

HARPAGON. Your vow is admirable. Your promise is amusing.

VALÈRE. We are engaged to an eternal union.

HARPAGON. I shall forbid the banns, I assure 95 you.

VALÈRE. Naught but death can part us.

HARPAGON. You are certainly bewitched by my money.

VALÈRE. I have told you, sir, it was not selfish
5 interest that drove me to do what I have done.
My heart was not impelled by the motives you
suspect. A nobler idea was my inspiration.

HARPAGON. You'll see: it is out of Christian
charity he wants to keep my money! But I'll set
10 all to rights. The law, you brazen scoundrel,
will make me amends for everything!

VALÈRE. You may proceed as you like in the
matter. I am ready to suffer any violence that
will please you. But at least believe, I beg, that
15 if any harm is done, I am the only one to accuse.
Your daughter is in no way to blame for any of
this.

HARPAGON. Certainly I believe that. It would
be very strange, indeed, if my daughter had a
20 part in this crime. But I want to get my treasure
back. I want you to confess where you have
carried it off to!

VALÈRE. I? Your treasure has not been carried off at all, but is here—at home.

25 HARPAGON [*aside*]. Oh, my dear moneybox!
[*To* VALÈRE.] My treasure has not left the
house?

VALÈRE. No, sir.

HARPAGON. Well. Tell me now, haven't you
30 even . . . tampered a bit?

VALÈRE. I, tamper? Ah! you do us both a great
wrong. The love that consumes me is wholly
pure and respectful.

HARPAGON [*aside*]. He's consumed with love
35 for my moneybox?

VALÈRE. I would have died rather than reveal
to your treasure a single offensive thought. It
would have been an insult to so much honor and
virtue.

40 HARPAGON [*aside.*]. My moneybox honorable
and virtuous?

VALÈRE. I limited my desires to the pleasure
of merely seeing. No criminal act has profaned
the passion that is inspired by those lovely
45 eyes.

HARPAGON [*aside*]. My moneybox's lovely
eyes? He talks like a lover discussing his mistress.

VALÈRE. Dame Claude, sir, knows the truth
of this adventure. She can bear witness . . .   50

HARPAGON. What! my maid is an accomplice
in this business?

VALÈRE. Yes, sir, she stood as a witness at our
engagement. But it was not until she had
learned how honorable were my intentions that   55
she helped me to persuade your daughter to
pledge her fidelity to me and accept my pledge
in return.

HARPAGON [*aside*]. Ha? Is his fear of the law
making his mind wander? [*To* VALÈRE.] Why   60
confuse us by bringing my daughter into this?

VALÈRE. I tell you, sir, I had all the trouble
in the world to persuade modesty to grant what
love desired.

HARPAGON. Whose modesty?   65

VALÈRE. Your daughter's. And it wasn't until
yesterday that she was able to make up her
mind and sign a mutual promise of marriage
with me.

HARPAGON. My daughter signed a promise of   70
marriage with you?

VALÈRE. Just as I, on my part, signed one with
her.

HARPAGON. O Heavens! Another disgrace!

JACQUES [*to the* COMMISSARY]. Write, sir,   75
write.

HARPAGON. Aggravation of misfortune! Excess of despair! Come, sir, do the duty of your
office. Draw me up an indictment against him
as a thief and an instigator.   80

VALÈRE. Those are names which do not belong to me. When it is known who I am . . .

[*Enter* ELISE, MARIANNE, *and* FROSINE.]

HARPAGON. Ah! profligate daughter! Unworthy of a father like me! This is how you put   85
into practice the lessons I gave you! You let
yourself become infatuated with an infamous
thief! You promise him your hand without my
consent! But you will be undone, both of you.
[*To* ELISE.] Four good, strong walls will answer 90
for your conduct. [*To* VALÈRE.] A good, tall
gallows will give me satisfaction for your
audacity.

VALÈRE. It is not your passion that will judge
the matter. I will at least be heard before I am   95
condemned.

HARPAGON. I was mistaken to say the gallows. You will be broken alive on the wheel.

ELISE. Ah! Father, be a little more human in your sentiments, I beseech you. Do not push things to the violent extreme of paternal power. Do not let yourself be carried away by the first impulse of passion. Give yourself time. Consider what you wish to do. Take pains. Look more closely at the person who has roused your wrath. He is not what your eyes have judged him to be. You will find it far less strange that I should have given myself to him when you learn that, were it not for him, you would have lost me long ago, and forever. Yes, Father, he is the man who saved me from the great peril, the peril you know I was so close to in the water—the man to whom you owe the life of the same daughter who ...

HARPAGON. All that is nothing. It would have been better for me had he let you drown and not do what he has done.

ELISE. Father, out of paternal love for me ...

HARPAGON. No, no! I won't hear another word. The law must do its duty.

JACQUES [aside]. You'll pay for the beating you gave me.

FROSINE [aside]. This is a queer mix-up.

[Enter ANSELM.]

ANSELM. What is it, Signor Harpagon? I see you are very much disturbed.

HARPAGON. Ah! Signor Anselm, you now behold the most unfortunate of men. Here is I don't know how much trouble and disorder to complicate the contract you came to sign! My money has been attacked! My honor has been attacked! And there stands a traitor, a profligate who has violated all that is most sacred to man —who has insinuated himself into my house under the name of servant in order to steal my money and seduce my daughter!

VALÈRE. Who cares about this money that you make so much noise about?

HARPAGON. Yes, they have made each other a promise of marriage. This outrage is your concern, Signor Anselm. You are the man who ought to take action against him. Have him prosecuted by the law! Revenge yourself for his insolence!

ANSELM. I have no intention of forcing myself on anybody or of making any claims to a heart that has already given itself to another. But of course I am ready to fight for your interests. As if the cause were my own.

HARPAGON. This gentleman here is an honest commissary, who assures me that he will neglect no part of his official duty. [To the COMMISSARY.] Indict him, sir, in due form! And make everything sound very criminal!

VALÈRE. I don't see what sort of crime you can make out of my passion for your daughter or what punishment you think I can be condemned to for our engagement. When it is known who I am ...

HARPAGON. I don't give a damn for all those tales. Nowadays the world is only too full of thieves of nobility, of impostors who take advantage of their insignificance and impudently bedeck themselves with the first illustrious name they take a fancy to.

VALÈRE. I'll have you know I am too honest to adorn myself with aught that is not mine. All Naples can testify to my birth.

ANSELM. Careful. Watch what you say. You run a greater risk here than you think. You have before you a man to whom all Naples is known and who can easily see through a trumped-up story.

VALÈRE. I am a man with nothing to fear. If you know Naples, you know who Don Thomas d'Alburcy was.

ANSELM. Of course I know who he was. Few people were better acquainted with him than I.

HARPAGON. I don't give a damn for Don Thomas or Don Smith.

ANSELM. Please, let him talk. We will see what he has to say about him.

VALÈRE. I have this to say: it was he who brought me into the world.

ANSELM. He?

VALÈRE. Yes.

ANSELM. Come now. You deceive yourself. Try some other story that might be more successful. Don't expect to save yourself by this imposture.

VALÈRE. Watch what you say. This is no imposture. I advance no claim that I cannot easily justify.

ANSELM. What! You dare to call yourself the son of Thomas d'Alburcy?

VALÈRE. I dare. And I am ready to defend that truth against no matter whom.

ANSELM. Fantastic audacity! Learn to your confusion that it was sixteen years ago, at the very least, that the man you speak of perished at sea with his wife and children while trying to save their lives from the cruel persecutions that accompanied the disorder at Naples and which precipitated the exile of more than one noble family.

VALÈRE. Yes, but learn to your own confusion, that his seven-year-old son, with a single servant, was saved from the shipwreck by a Spanish vessel—and that the son then saved now speaks to you. Learn that the captain of that vessel, touched by my misfortune, took a liking to me and brought me up as his own son —that arms have been my occupation since the time I was able to hold them—that I learned a short time ago that my father is not dead, as I had always thought—that while passing through this city in search of him an adventure planned by Heaven gave me a glimpse of charming Elise—that the sight of her made me a slave to her beauty—and that the violence of my love and her father's severity made me resolve to enter into his house and send another in search of my parents.

ANSELM. What proof do you have beyond your bare word that this is not a fable you have constructed on a foundation of truth?

VALÈRE. The Spanish captain, a ruby signet that belonged to my father, an agate bracelet that my mother placed upon my arm, and old Pedro, the servant who with me was saved from the shipwreck.

MARIANNE. Alas! I myself can answer for what you have said. You are not deceiving us. Your account has made clear to me that you are my brother!

VALÈRE. You, my sister?

MARIANNE. Yes. My heart was moved the moment you opened your mouth. Our mother, whom you will see again, has diverted me a thousand times with the misfortunes of our family. Heaven did not suffer us either to perish in that unhappy shipwreck—but our lives were saved only at the expense of our liberty. They were pirates who took us, my mother and me, off the wreckage of our vessel. After ten years of slavery, we regained our liberty through a happy accident, and returned to Naples. There we found that all our property had been sold and were not able to uncover any news of my father. We sailed for Genoa, where my mother went to gather up the sad remains of our dissipated family fortune. From there, fleeing the barbarous injustice of her kinsmen, she came to these parts, where she has lived scarcely more than a languishing life.

ANSELM. O Heaven—such are the signs of Thy power! How clearly Thou hast shown us that Thou alone canst work miracles! Embrace me, children both! Mingle your joy with that of your father!

VALÈRE. You are our father?

MARIANNE. Is it for you my mother has shed so many tears?

ANSELM. Yes, my daughter, yes, my son, I am Don Thomas d'Alburcy, whom Heaven saved from the waves with all the money he had with him—and who, believing for more than sixteen years you all were dead, was preparing, after long voyages, to seek the consolation of a new family through marriage with a good and gentle young lady. When I saw how much my life would be in danger should I return to Naples, I abandoned the idea forever. Having found a way to sell what I had there, I established my residence here. Under the name of Anselm I sought to leave behind the sorrows of the name which has caused me so many reverses.

HARPAGON. Is that your son?

ANSELM. Yes.

HARPAGON. I hold you responsible for the ten thousand écus he stole from me.

ANSELM. He? He stole from you?

HARPAGON. He himself.

VALÈRE. Who told you?

HARPAGON. Master Jacques.

VALÈRE. It is you that say so?

JACQUES. Look, I'm not saying a thing.

HARPAGON. Yes. This gentleman is the com-
5 missary who took down his testimony.

VALÈRE. Can you believe me capable of such
a villainous deed?

HARPAGON. Capable or not capable, I want my
money back.

10 [*Enter* CLEANTH *and* LA FLÈCHE.]

CLEANTH. Torment yourself no longer,
Father. Accuse no one. I have uncovered some
information about your affair, and I have come
to tell you that, if you will resign yourself to
15 letting me marry Marianne, your money will
be returned to you.

HARPAGON. Where is it?

CLEANTH. Don't worry. It's in a place that I
will answer for. Everything depends on me. It
20 only remains for you to tell me your decision.
You can choose whether to give me Marianne
or lose your moneybox.

HARPAGON. Nothing has been removed from
it?

25 CLEANTH. Nothing. Let us see if it is your
intention to subscribe to this marriage and join
your consent to that of her mother—who has
given her the liberty to choose between us two.

MARIANNE. But you do not realize that his
30 consent is not enough, or that Heaven, along
with my brother, whom you now behold [*points
to* VALÈRE] has restored my father to me. You
must win me from *him*.

ANSELM. Heaven, my children, did not restore
35 me to you in order that I should oppose your
desires. Signor Harpagon, you very well know
that the choice of a young lady falls to the son
and not to the father. Come now, don't make
people say what is too obvious to need expres-
40 sion. Give your consent to this double ceremony
as I have.

HARPAGON. Before I can make up my mind, I
must see my moneybox.

CLEANTH. You shall see it safe and sound.

45 HARPAGON. I have no money to give my
children for their marriages.

ANSELM. Oh well, I have some for both of
them. Don't let that bother you.

HARPAGON. You will commit yourself to stand
the cost of both these marriages?   50

ANSELM. Yes, I will commit myself. Are you
satisfied?

HARPAGON. Yes, provided that you have me a
suit made for the wedding.

ANSELM. Agreed. Come, let us indulge the   55
happiness which this joyous day bestows upon
us.

COMMISSARY. Hold, gentlemen! Hold on, one
moment, if you please! Who is going to pay for
all the writing I've done?   60

HARPAGON. We have no need of your writing.

COMMISSARY. No? But I, on the other hand,
can't pretend to have done it for nothing.

HARPAGON [*points to* MASTER JACQUES]. As
payment I give you this man. Take him and   65
hang him.

JACQUE:. Alas! what is a man supposed to
do? They beat me before for telling the truth.
Now they want to hang me for lying.

ANSELM. Signor Harpagon, you ought to par-   70
don him his trickery.

HARPAGON. You'll pay the commissary then.

ANSELM. So be it. Let us go at once and share
our joy with your mother.

HARPAGON. And I, to see my dear, dear   75
moneybox.

William Wycherley

1640–1715

The Country Wife

1675

The characters in *The Country Wife* appear to have stepped directly out of the fashionable drawing rooms of seventeenth-century London. More accurately, they have walked straight into a highly stylized stage-game governed by a few simple axioms: first, that a gentleman and a lady will freely copulate if left together in private—unless they are man and wife; second, that husbands exist to be cuckolded and their wives to be willingly seduced; third, that pretenders to respectability and virtue ("honor") are almost invariably hypocrites, fools, or villains. Such axioms hardly offer a steady and comprehensive view of social life, but neither are they altogether fictitious. Some readers have been so repelled by them as to regard this as "the most bestial" of all plays. Others have found it a superlative satire against marital jealousy, still others merely an audacious fantasy, and some an early prophecy of the revolution that would eventually overturn the old European aristocratic order itself. It is easy to exaggerate this last possibility, although sexual liberty—"free love"—has more than once been enlisted to "raise consciousness" in the wider cause of political liberty and equality.

What *The Country Wife* is is a first-class comedy directly in the tradition of Molière. This means that it is not in the ordinary sense realistic, that its moral perspectives are ironic, never absolute, and that the energy of the dialogue is both high and exquisitely controlled. But Wycherley's was a more skeptical intelligence than Molière's. He was, in seventeenth-century parlance, a "libertine" or freethinker, which is to say that he tended to regard social institutions and ethical ideals as justified only insofar as they serve the interests of pleasure and convenience; otherwise they are nuisances —or worse. In his view abstract principles all too readily serve tyranny, the outward tyranny of social repression as well as the inward tyranny of repressive conscience. Specifically, *The Country Wife,* like many other comedies of its kind and time, sees

279

matrimony as only a legal form of bondage and prostitution from which anyone in his or her right mind would seek escape, either deviously (by "hypocrisy") or openly, by defying convention. Violations of such bondage can be regarded, then, as striking a blow for personal liberty, especially if the defiance is enlightened.

In such a perspective of liberty, both Mr. Horner and Margery Pinchwife honor the promptings of natural impulse as primary. Both are in revolt—the one consciously, the other instinctively—against conventional inhibitions. Hence their unabashed search for sexual gratification may be read as a sincere impulse toward personal freedom. This is particularly true of Margery, who is not cynically motivated, whereas Horner is. Her virtue, in contrast to that of Lady Fidget and her friends—who also seek pleasure but uphold the tyranny of convention—is to see straight through the pretentions and try to evade them. Horner, not dissimilarly, is a necessary and benevolent predator in a society operating by the axioms already stated. His pretending impotence to gratify his appetite is only a mirror image of his "victims'" counterfeiting honor. His virtue is sophisticated wit, a lucid and clever intelligence unencumbered with principles. He and Margery Pinchwife naturally gravitate to each other from mutually attractive poles of sophistication and naiveté. A stage tradition established at the first performances is worth noting. Horner is to be played by an actor of magnetic charm and virility, Margery by an actress having a figure bewitchingly attractive in the silk stockings and tight *culottes* that she dons in her disguise as a youth. Their animal endowments are for Wycherley the badges of native worth.

If we grant Wycherley the rules of his game, he pays back with a series of richly comic entertainments, scenes increasingly risqué and absurd, as first one husband then another complacently or ignorantly yields his wife to Horner's ministrations. The climax, of course, is a near miss, as the all-too-honest Margery begins to blurt out the plain truth of Horner's proven potency. For an instant the whole fabric of deceit and polite tyranny seems ready to collapse, but the scene ends in a kind of seven-voice chorus ironically acquiescing in things as they are. Yet there is no disguising the fact that Horner is still sitting pretty and that Margery has set foot on the crooked path to freedom.

The vocal effects throughout the play are remarkable, for their cadenced emphasis and the execution of skillful variations on a single word and theme—virtuoso passages difficult to illustrate except in performance. Examples are the famous or infamous "china scene" in Act IV, the drinking party in Act V —building elaborate chords on the notes of "virtue" and "honor"—and, above all, the fifth act finale beginning with Alithea's "There's doctrine for all husbands, Mr. Harcourt."

To anyone who does not concede Wycherley's denial of principles higher than pleasure and convenience, he allows the possible exception of Harcourt and Alithea, who are neither ignorant, unfashionable, cynical, nor dishonest—just comparatively pallid and no source of inspiration to their author. The focal plane of his sympathies is not deep, but what it lacks in depth it makes good in sharpness of observation capable of making his audience wince. For he enrolls us in complicity, like it or not. To understand his notorious and recurrent double entendres is to acknowledge, no matter how uneasily, that we are capable of being his accomplices in ribald skepticism. Harcourt and Alithea are all very well as conciliating gestures toward decorum, but they do not prevent Horner and Margery from soliciting not so much our respect as an involuntary warmth of approval, however guilty or reluctant. Judged as moral or immoral, or neither, *The Country Wife* will not let its audience easily off the hook of a difficult moral choice.

The Country Wife

WYCHERLEY

CHARACTERS

MR. HORNER
MR. HARCOURT
MR. DORILANT
MR. PINCHWIFE
MR. SPARKISH
SIR JASPER FIDGET
MRS. MARGERY PINCHWIFE
MRS. ALITHEA
LADY FIDGET
MRS. DAINTY FIDGET
MRS. SQUEAMISH
OLD LADY SQUEAMISH
LUCY *Alithea's maid*
WAITERS, SERVANTS, AND ATTENDANTS
A BOY
A QUACK

SCENE. *London.*

ACT I

[HORNER's *lodging.*]

[*Enter* HORNER, *and* QUACK *following him at a distance.*]

HORNER [*aside*]. A quack is as fit for° a pimp
5 as a midwife for a bawd; they are still but in
their way both helpers of nature.—[*Aloud.*]
Well, my dear Doctor, hast thou done what I
desired?

QUACK. I have undone you for ever with the
10 women, and reported you throughout the whole
town as bad as an eunuch, with as much trouble
as if I had made you one in earnest.

HORNER. But have you told all the midwives

you know, the orange-wenches° at the playhouses, the city husbands, and old fumbling 15
keepers of this end of the town, for they'll be
the readiest to report it?

QUACK. I have told all the chambermaids,
waiting-women, tire-women, and old women
of my acquaintance; nay, and whispered it as a 20
secret to 'em, and to the whisperers of Whitehall;° so that you need not doubt 'twill spread,
and you will be as odious to the handsome
young women as—

HORNER. As the small-pox. Well— 25

QUACK. And to the married women of this
end of the town, as—

HORNER. As the great ones;° nay, as their
own husbands.

QUACK. And to the city dames, as aniseed 30
Robin,° of filthy and contemptible memory;
and they will frighten their children with your
name, especially their females.

HORNER. And cry, Horner's coming to carry
you away. I am only afraid 'twill not be be- 35
lieved. You told 'em 'twas by an English-French
disaster, and an English-French chirurgeon,°
who has given me at once not only a cure, but
an antidote for the future against that damned
malady, and that worse distemper, love, and all 40
other women's evils?

QUACK. Your late journey into France has
made it the more credible, and your being here
a fortnight before you appeared in public looks
as if you apprehended the shame, which I won- 45
der you do not. Well, I have been hired by
young gallants to belie 'em t'other way, but you
are the first would be thought a man unfit for
women.

HORNER. Dear Mr. Doctor, let vain rogues 50

---

orange-wenches girls who sold fruit in the theater.
Many were prostitutes.

Whitehall the royal palace, a center of rumor and
gossip

great ones venereal diseases

aniseed Robin a London street character supposed
to be a hermaphrodite. Why he was nicknamed
"aniseed" is not known.

English-French chirurgeon surgeon who treats venereal diseases (such as had presumably deprived
Horner of his potency)

for to be

be contented only to be thought abler men than they are; generally 'tis all the pleasure they have, but mine lies another way.

QUACK. You take, methinks, a very preposterous way to it, and as ridiculous as if we operators in physic should put forth bills° to disparage our medicaments, with hopes to gain customers.

HORNER. Doctor, there are quacks in love as well as physic, who get but the fewer and worse patients for their boasting; a good name is seldom got by giving it one's self; and women no more than honor are compassed by bragging. Come, come, Doctor, the wisest lawyer never discovers the merits of his cause till the trial; the wealthiest man conceals his riches, and the cunning gamester his play. Shy husbands and keepers, like old rooks, are not to be cheated but by a new unpractised trick: false friendship will pass now no more than false dice upon 'em; no, not in the city.

[Enter BOY.]

BOY. There are two ladies and a gentleman coming up.

[Exit.]

HORNER. A pox! some unbelieving sisters of my former acquaintance, who, I am afraid, expect their sense should be satisfied of the falsity of the report. No—this formal fool and women!

[Enter SIR JASPER FIDGET, LADY FIDGET, and MRS. DAINTY FIDGET.]

QUACK. His wife and sister.

SIR JASPER FIDGET. My coach breaking just now before your door, sir, I look upon as an occasional reprimand to me, sir, for not kissing your hands,° sir, since your coming out of France, sir; and so my disaster, sir, has been my good fortune, sir; and this is my wife and sister, sir.

HORNER. What then, sir?

SIR JASPER FIDGET. My lady, and sister, sir.— Wife, this is Master Horner.

LADY FIDGET. Master Horner, husband!

SIR JASPER FIDGET. My lady, my Lady Fidget, sir.

HORNER. So, sir.

SIR JASPER FIDGET. Won't you be acquainted with her, sir?—[Aside.] So, the report is true, I find, by his coldness or aversion to the sex; but I'll play the wag with him.—Pray salute my wife, my lady, sir.

HORNER. I will kiss no man's wife, sir, for him, sir; I have taken my eternal leave, sir, of the sex already, sir.

SIR JASPER FIDGET [aside]. Ha! ha! ha! I'll plague him yet.—Not know my wife, sir?

HORNER. I do know your wife, sir; she's a woman, sir, and consequently a monster, sir, a greater monster than a husband, sir.

SIR JASPER FIDGET. A husband! how, sir?

HORNER. So, sir; but I make no more cuckolds, sir. [Makes horns.]

SIR JASPER FIDGET. Ha! ha! ha! Mercury! Mercury!°

LADY FIDGET. Pray, Sir Jasper, let us be gone from this rude fellow.

MRS. DAINTY FIDGET. Who, by his breeding, would think he had ever been in France?

LADY FIDGET. Foh! he's but too much a French fellow, such as hate women of quality and virtue for their love to their husbands, Sir Jasper; a woman is hated by 'em as much for loving her husband as for loving their money. But pray, let's be gone.

HORNER. You do well, madam, for I have nothing that you came for; I have brought over not so much as a bawdy picture, new postures,° nor the second part of the Escole des Filles;° nor—

QUACK [apart to HORNER]. Hold, for shame sir! what d'ye mean? You'll ruin yourself for ever with the sex—

SIR JASPER FIDGET. Ha! ha! ha! he hates women perfectly, I find.

MRS. DAINTY FIDGET. What pity 'tis he should!

---

bills   handbills
kissing your hands   paying a formal visit

Mercury   Sir Jasper implies that an overdose of mercury, used in treating syphillis, rendered Horner impotent.
postures   depictions of postures for copulation
Escole des Filles   School for Whores, a pornographic book

LADY FIDGET. Ay, he's a base rude fellow for't. But affectation makes not a woman more odious to them than virtue.

HORNER. Because your virtue is your greatest
5 affectation, madam.

LADY FIDGET. How, you saucy fellow! would you wrong my honor?

HORNER. If I could.

LADY FIDGET. How d'ye mean, sir?

10 SIR JASPER FIDGET. Ha! ha! ha! no, he can't wrong your Ladyship's honor, upon my honor; he, poor man—hark you in your ear—a mere eunuch.

LADY FIDGET. O filthy French beast! foh! foh!
15 why do we stay? let's be gone. I can't endure the sight of him.

SIR JASPER FIDGET. Stay but till the chairs° come; they'll be here presently.

LADY FIDGET. No, no.

20 SIR JASPER FIDGET. Nor can I stay longer. 'Tis —let me see, a quarter and a half quarter of a minute past eleven. The council° will be sat; I must away. Business must be preferred always before love and ceremony with the wise, Mr.
25 Horner.

HORNER. And the impotent, Sir Jasper.

SIR JASPER FIDGET. Ay, ay, the impotent, Master Horner; ha! ha! ha!

LADY FIDGET. What, leave us with a filthy man
30 alone in his lodgings?

SIR JASPER FIDGET. He's an innocent man now, you know. Pray stay, I'll hasten the chairs to you.—Mr. Horner, your servant; I should be glad to see you at my house. Pray come and
35 dine with me, and play at cards with my wife after dinner; you are fit for women at that game yet, ha! ha!—[*Aside.*] 'Tis as much a husband's prudence to provide innocent diversion for a wife as to hinder her unlawful plea-
40 sures; and he had better employ her than let her employ herself.—Farewell.

HORNER. Your servant, Sir Jasper.

[*Exit* SIR JASPER.]

LADY FIDGET. I will not stay with him, foh!—

HORNER. Nay, madam, I beseech you stay, 45 if it be but to see I can be as civil to ladies yet as they would desire.

LADY FIDGET. No, no, foh! you cannot be civil to ladies.

MRS. DAINTY FIDGET. You as civil as ladies 50 would desire?

LADY FIDGET. No, no, no, foh! foh! foh!

[*Exeunt* LADY FIDGET *and* MRS. DAINTY FIDGET.]

QUACK. Now, I think I, or you yourself, 55 rather, have done your business with the women.

HORNER. Thou art an ass. Don't you see already, upon the report and my carriage,° this grave man of business leaves his wife in my 60 lodgings, invites me to his house and wife, who before would not be acquainted with me out of jealousy?

QUACK. Nay, by this means you may be the more acquainted with the husbands, but the 65 less with the wives.

HORNER. Let me alone; if I can but abuse the husbands, I'll soon disabuse the wives. Stay— I'll reckon you up the advantages I am like to have by my stratagem. First, I shall be rid of 70 all my old acquaintances, the most insatiable sorts of duns, that invade our lodgings in a morning; and next to the pleasure of making a new mistress is that of being rid of an old one, and of all old debts. Love, when it comes to be 75 so, is paid the most unwillingly.

QUACK. Well, you may be so rid of your old acquaintances; but how will you get any new ones?

HORNER. Doctor, thou wilt never make a good 80 chemist,° thou art so incredulous and impatient. Ask but all the young fellows of the town if they do not lose more time, like huntsmen, in starting the game, than in running it down. One knows not where to find 'em, who will or will 85 not. Women of quality are so civil you can hardly distinguish love from good breeding,

---

chairs sedan chairs, sent for because the carriage broke down
council the King's Privy Council, of which Sir Jasper is a member

carriage behavior (in avoiding the society of ladies)
a good chemist chemists, like alchemists before them, were expected to be men of exemplary virtue

and a man is often mistaken; but now I can be sure she that shows an aversion to me loves the sport, as those women that are gone, whom I warrant to be right. And then the next thing
5 is, your women of honor, as you call 'em, are only chary of their reputations, not their persons; and 'tis scandal they would avoid, not men. Now may I have, by the reputation of an eunuch, the privileges of one, and be seen in
10 a lady's chamber in a morning as early as her husband; kiss virgins before their parents or lovers; and may be, in short, the *passe-partout*° of the town. Now, Doctor.

QUACK. Nay, now you shall be the doctor,
15 and your process is so new that we do not know but it may succeed.

HORNER. Not so new neither; *probatum est,*° Doctor.

QUACK. Well, I wish you luck and many
20 patients, whilst I go to mine.

[*Exit.*]

[*Enter* HARCOURT *and* DORILANT.]

HARCOURT. Come, your appearance at the play yesterday has, I hope, hardened you for
25 the future against the women's contempt and the men's raillery; and now you'll abroad as you were wont.

HORNER. Did I not bear it bravely?

DORILANT. With a most theatrical impudence,
30 nay, more than the orange-wenches show there, or a drunken vizard-mask,° or a great-bellied° actress; nay, or the most impudent of creatures, an ill poet; or what is yet more impudent, a second-hand critic.

35 HORNER. But what say the ladies? have they no pity?

HARCOURT. What ladies? The vizard-masks, you know, never pity a man when all's gone, though in their service.

40 DORILANT. And for the women in the boxes, you'd never pity them when 'twas in your power.

HARCOURT. They say 'tis pity but all that deal with common women should be served so.

45 DORILANT. Nay, I dare swear they won't admit you to play at cards with them, go to plays with 'em, or do the little duties which other shadows of men are wont to do for 'em.

HORNER. Who do you call shadows of men?

50 DORILANT. Half-men.

HORNER. What, boys?

DORILANT. Ay, your old boys, old *beaux garçons,*° who, like superannuated stallions, are suffered to run, feed, and whinny with the
55 mares as long as they live, though they can do nothing else.

HORNER. Well, a pox on love and wenching! Women serve but to keep a man from better company. Though I can't enjoy them, I shall
60 you the more. Good fellowship and friendship are lasting, rational, and manly pleasures.

HARCOURT. For all that, give me some of those pleasures you call effeminate too; they help to relish one another.

65 HORNER. They disturb one another.

HARCOURT. No, mistresses are like books. If you pore upon them too much, they doze you, and make you unfit for company; but if used discreetly, you are the fitter for conversation
70 by 'em.

DORILANT. A mistress should be like a little country retreat near the town; not to dwell in constantly, but only for a night and away, to taste the town the better when a man returns.

75 HORNER. I tell you, 'tis as hard to be a good fellow, a good friend, and a lover of women, as 'tis to be a good fellow, a good friend, and a lover of money. You cannot follow both, then choose your side. Wine gives you liberty, love
80 takes it away.

DORILANT. Gad, he's in the right on't.

HORNER. Wine gives you joy; love, grief and tortures, besides the chirurgeon's. Wine makes us witty; love, only sots. Wine makes us sleep;
85 love breaks it.

DORILANT. By the world, he has reason, Harcourt.

HORNER. Wine makes—

---

passe-partout   master key
probatum est   "it has been put to the test," as previously in the classical comedy *The Eunuch* by the Roman dramatist Terence
vizard-mask   a fashionable prostitute
great-bellied   obviously pregnant

beaux garçons   dandies; men-about-town

DORILANT. Ay, wine makes us—makes us princes; love makes us beggars, poor rogues, egad—and wine—

HORNER. So, there's one converted.—No, no,
5 love and wine, oil and vinegar.

HARCOURT. I grant it; love will still be uppermost.

HORNER. Come, for my part, I will have only those glorious manly pleasures of being very
10 drunk and very slovenly.

[*Enter* BOY.]

BOY. Mr. Sparkish is below, sir.

[*Exit.*]

HARCOURT. What, my dear friend! a rogue
15 that is fond of me, only I think, for abusing him.

DORILANT. No, he can no more think the men laugh at him than that women jilt him, his opinion of himself is so good.

20 HORNER. Well, there's another pleasure by drinking I thought not of—I shall lose his acquaintance, because he cannot drink; and you know 'tis a very hard thing to be rid of him, for he's one of those nauseous offerers at wit,
25 who, like the worst fiddlers, run themselves into all companies.

HARCOURT. One that, by being in the company of men of sense, would pass for one.

HORNER. And may so to the short-sighted
30 world, as a false jewel amongst true ones is not discerned at a distance. His company is as troublesome to us as a cuckold's when you have a mind to his wife's.

HARCOURT. No, the rogue will not let us enjoy
35 one another, but ravishes our conversation, though he signifies no more to't than Sir Martin Mar-all's° gaping, and awkward thrumming upon the lute, does to his man's voice and music.

40 DORILANT. And to pass for a wit in town shows himself a fool every night to us, that are guilty of the plot.

HORNER. Such wits as he are, to a company of reasonable men, like rooks to the gamesters,

who only fill a room at the table, but are so far 45
from contributing to the play, that they only
serve to spoil the fancy of those that do.

DORILANT. Nay, they are used like rooks too,
snubbed, checked, and abused; yet the rogues
will hang on. 50

HORNER. A pox on 'em, and all that force
nature, and would be still what she forbids 'em!
Affectation is her greatest monster.

HARCOURT. Most men are the contraries to
that they would seem. Your bully, you see, is a 55
coward with a long sword; the little humbly
fawning physician, with his ebony cane, is he
that destroys men.

DORILANT. The usurer, a poor rogue, possessed of mouldy bonds and mortgages; and we 60
they call spendthrifts are only wealthy who
lay out his money upon daily new purchases of
pleasure.

HORNER. Ay, your arrantest cheat is your
trustee or executor, your jealous man, the 65
greatest cuckold, your churchman the greatest
atheist, and your noisy pert rogue of a wit, the
greatest fop, dullest ass, and worst company,
as you shall see; for here he comes.

[*Enter* SPARKISH.] 70

SPARKISH. How is't, sparks?° how is't? Well,
faith, Harry, I must rally thee a little, ha! ha!
ha! upon the report in town of thee, ha! ha!
ha! I can't hold i'faith; shall I speak?

HORNER. Yes; but you'll be so bitter then. 75

SPARKISH. Honest Dick and Frank here shall
answer for me, I will not be extreme bitter, by
the universe.

HARCOURT. We will be bound in ten-thousand-pound bond, he shall not be bitter at all. 80

DORILANT. Nor sharp, nor sweet.

HORNER. What, not downright insipid?

SPARKISH. Nay then, since you are so brisk,
and provoke me, take what follows. You must
know, I was discoursing and rallying with 85
some ladies yesterday, and they happened to
talk of the fine new signs in town.

HORNER. Very fine ladies, I believe.

SPARKISH. Said I, I know where the best new
sign is.—Where? says one of the ladies.—In 90

Martin Mar-all in a comedy by Dryden a character
who serenades his mistress in pantomime while his
servant actually makes the music

sparks witty gentlemen

Covent Garden, I replied.—Said another, In what street?—In Russell Street, answered I.—Lord, says another, I'm sure there was ne'er a fine new sign there yesterday.—Yes, but there
5 was, said I again, and it came out of France, and has been there a fortnight.

DORILANT. A pox! I can hear no more, prithee.

HORNER. No, hear him out; let him tune his crowd° a while.

10 HARCOURT. The worst music, the greatest preparation.

SPARKISH. Nay, faith, I'll make you laugh.—It cannot be, says a third lady.—Yes, yes, quoth I again.—Says a fourth lady—

15 HORNER. Look to't, we'll have no more ladies.

SPARKISH. No—then mark, mark, now. Said I to the fourth, Did you never see Mr. Horner? he lodges in Russell Street, and he's a sign° of a man, you know, since he came out of France;
20 ha! ha! ha!

HORNER. But the devil take me if thine be the sign of a jest.

SPARKISH. With that they all fell a-laughing, till they bepissed themselves. What, but it does
25 not move you, methinks? Well, I see one had as good go to law without a witness, as break a jest without a laugher on one's side.—Come, come, sparks, but where do we dine? I have left at Whitehall an earl to dine with you.

30 DORILANT. Why, I thought thou hadst loved a man with a title better than a suit with a French trimming to't.

HARCOURT. Go to him again.

SPARKISH. No, sir, a wit to me is the greatest
35 title in the world.

HORNER. But go dine with your earl, sir; he may be exceptious.° We are your friends, and will not take it ill to be left, I do assure you.

HARCOURT. Nay, faith, he shall go to him.

40 SPARKISH. Nay, pray, gentlemen.

DORILANT. We'll thrust you out, if you won't; what, disappoint anybody for us?

SPARKISH. Nay, dear gentlemen, hear me.

HORNER. No, no, sir, by no means; pray go, sir.   45

SPARKISH. Why, dear rogues—

DORILANT. No, no.

[*They all thrust him out of the room.*]

ALL. Ha! ha! ha!

[SPARKISH *returns.*]   50

SPARKISH. But, sparks, pray hear me. What, d'ye think I'll eat then with gay shallow fops and silent coxcombs? I think wit as necessary at dinner as a glass of good wine, and that's the reason I never have any stomach when I eat   55
alone.—Come, but where do we dine?

HORNER. Even where you will.

SPARKISH. At Chateline's?

DORILANT. Yes, if you will.

SPARKISH. Or at the Cock?   60

DORILANT. Yes, if you please.

SPARKISH. Or at the Dog and Partridge?

HORNER. Ay, if you have a mind to't; for we shall dine at neither.

SPARKISH. Pshaw! with your fooling we shall   65
lose the new play; and I would no more miss seeing a new play the first day, than I would miss sitting in the wits' row. Therefore I'll go fetch my mistress,° and away.

[*Exit.*]   70

[HORNER, HARCOURT, DORILANT *remain; enter* MR. PINCHWIFE.]

HORNER. Who have we here? Pinchwife?

PINCHWIFE. Gentlemen, your humble servant.

HORNER. Well, Jack, by thy long absence from   75
the town, the grumness of thy countenance, and the slovenliness of thy habit, I should give thee joy, should I not, of marriage?

PINCHWIFE [*aside*]. Death! does he know I'm married too? I thought to have concealed it from   80
him at least.—My long stay in the country will excuse my dress; and I have a suit of law that brings me up to town, that puts me out of humor. Besides, I must give Sparkish tomorrow five thousand pound to lie with my sister.   85

HORNER. Nay, you country gentlemen, rather than not purchase, will buy anything; and he is

---

crowd fiddle
sign mere representation
exceptious take exception to your breaking an engagement

mistress in the seventeenth century this term was a title of courtesy or endearment for a lady, either married or unmarried

a cracked title,° if we may quibble. Well, but am I to give thee joy? I heard thou wert married.

PINCHWIFE. What then?

HORNER. Why, the next thing that is to be
5 heard is, thou'rt a cuckold.

PINCHWIFE [*aside*]. Insupportable name!

HORNER. But I did not expect marriage from such a whoremaster as you, one that knew the town so much, and women so well.

10 PINCHWIFE. Why, I have married no London wife.

HORNER. Pshaw! that's all one. That grave circumspection in marrying a country wife is like refusing a deceitful pampered Smithfield
15 jade° to go and be cheated by a friend in the country.

PINCHWIFE [*aside*]. A pox on him and his simile!—At least we are a little surer of the breed there, know what her keeping has been,
20 whether foiled° or unsound.

HORNER. Come, come, I have known a clap gotten in Wales; and there are cousins, justices' clerks, and chaplains in the country, I won't say coachmen. But she's handsome and young?

25 PINCHWIFE [*aside*]. I'll answer as I should do. —No, no; she has no beauty but her youth, no attraction but her modesty; wholesome, home-ly, and huswifely; that's all.

DORILANT. He talks as like a grazier° as he
30 looks.

PINCHWIFE. She's too awkward, ill-favored, and silly to bring to town.

HARCOURT. Then methinks you should bring her to be taught breeding.

35 PINCHWIFE. To be taught! no, sir, I thank you. Good wives and private soldiers should be ignorant. [*Aside*.] I'll keep her from your in-structions, I warrant you.

HARCOURT [*aside*]. The rogue is as jealous as
40 if his wife were not ignorant.

HORNER. Why, if she be ill-favored, there will be less danger here for you than by leaving her in the country. We have such variety of dainties that we are seldom hungry.

DORILANT. But they have always coarse, con-
45 stant, swingeing° stomachs in the country.

HARCOURT. Foul feeders indeed!

DORILANT. And your hospitality is great there.

HARCOURT. Open house; every man's wel-
50 come.

PINCHWIFE. So, so, gentlemen.

HORNER. But prithee, why wouldst thou mar-ry her? If she be ugly, ill-bred, and silly, she must be rich then.

55 PINCHWIFE. As rich as if she brought me twenty thousand pound out of this town; for she'll be as sure not to spend her moderate por-tion as a London baggage would be to spend hers, let it be what it would: so 'tis all one.
60 Then, because she's ugly, she's the likelier to be my own; and being ill-bred, she'll hate conver-sation; and since silly and innocent, will not know the difference betwixt a man of one-and-twenty and one of forty.

65 HORNER. Nine—to my knowledge. But if she be silly, she'll expect as much from a man of forty-nine, as from him of one-and-twenty. But methinks wit is more necessary than beau-ty; and I think no young woman ugly, that has
70 it, and no handsome woman agreeable without it.

PINCHWIFE. 'Tis my maxim, he's a fool that marries; but he's a greater that does not marry a fool. What is wit in a wife good for, but to
75 make a man a cuckold?

HORNER. Yes, to keep it from his knowledge.

PINCHWIFE. A fool cannot contrive to make her husband a cuckold.

HORNER. No; but she'll club° with a man that
80 can and what is worse, if she cannot make her husband a cuckold, she'll make him jealous and pass for one; and then 'tis all one.

PINCHWIFE. Well, well, I'll take care for one. My wife shall make me no cuckold, though she
85 had your help, Mr. Horner. I understand the town, sir.

---

cracked title bad bargain
Smithfield jade a mare sold at a London horse market where cheating was common
foiled of a horse, lamed; of a woman, deflowered
grazier cattle herder
swingeing whopping
club associate

DORILANT [*aside*]. His help!

HARCOURT [*aside*]. He's come newly to town, it seems, and has not heard how things are with him.

5 HORNER. But tell me, has marriage cured thee of whoring, which it seldom does?

HARCOURT. 'Tis more than age can do.

HORNER. No, the word is, I'll marry and live honest; but a marriage vow is like a penitent 10 gamester's oath, and entering into bonds and penalties to stint himself to such a particular small sum at play for the future, which makes him but the more eager; and not being able to hold out, loses his money again, and his forfeit 15 to boot.

DORILANT. Ay, ay, a gamester will be a gamester whilst his money lasts, and a whoremaster whilst his vigor.

HARCOURT. Nay, I have known 'em, when 20 they are broke, and can lose no more, keep a-fumbling with the box in their hands to fool with only, and hinder other gamesters.

DORILANT. That had wherewithal to make lusty stakes.

25 PINCHWIFE. Well, gentlemen, you may laugh at me; but you shall never lie with my wife; I know the town.

HORNER. But prithee, was not the way you were in better? is not keeping° better than 30 marriage?

PINCHWIFE. A pox on't! the jades would jilt me, I could never keep a whore to myself.

HORNER. So, then, you only married to keep a whore to yourself. Well, but let me tell you, 35 women, as you say, are like soldiers, made constant and loyal by good pay, rather than by oaths and covenants. Therefore I'd advise my friends to keep rather than marry, since too I find, by your example, it does not serve one's 40 turn; for I saw you yesterday in the eighteen-penny place° with a pretty country wench.

PINCHWIFE [*aside*]. How the devil! did he see my wife then? I sat there that she might not be seen. But she shall never go to a play again.

45 HORNER. What! dost thou blush at nine-and-forty for having been seen with a wench?

DORILANT. No, faith, I warrant 'twas his wife, which he seated there out of sight; for he's a cunning rogue, and understands the town.

HARCOURT. He blushes. Then 'twas his wife; 50 for men are now more ashamed to be seen with them in public than with a wench.

PINCHWIFE [*aside*]. Hell and damnation! I'm undone, since Horner has seen her, and they know 'twas she. 55

HORNER. But prithee, was it thy wife? She was exceedingly pretty; I was in love with her at that distance.

PINCHWIFE. You are like never to be nearer to her. Your servant, gentlemen. [*Offers to go.*] 60

HORNER. Nay, prithee stay.

PINCHWIFE. I cannot; I will not.

HORNER. Come, you shall dine with us.

PINCHWIFE. I have dined already.

HORNER. Come, I know thou hast not. I'll 65 treat thee, dear rogue; thou shalt spend none of thy Hampshire money today.

PINCHWIFE [*aside*]. Treat me! So, he uses me already like his cuckold.

HORNER. Nay, you shall not go. 70

PINCHWIFE. I must; I have business at home. [*Exit.*]

HARCOURT. To beat his wife. He's as jealous of her as a Cheapside husband of a Covent Garden wife.° 75

HORNER. Why, 'tis as hard to find an old whoremaster without jealousy and the gout, as a young one without fear or the pox.

As gout in age from pox in youth proceeds, So wenching past, then jealousy succeeds, 80 The worst disease that love and wenching

[breeds.

[*Exeunt.*]

ACT II

[*A room in* PINCHWIFE'S *house.*]

[MRS. MARGERY PINCHWIFE *and* ALITHEA. 85 PINCHWIFE *peeping behind at the door.*]

MRS. PINCHWIFE. Pray, sister, where are the best fields and woods to walk in, in London?

---

keeping keeping a prostitute

eighteen-penny place cheap, inconspicuous seats in a theater

Cheapside . . . Covent Garden wife as a merchant who has married into a newly rich family

ALITHEA. A pretty question! Why, sister, Mulberry Garden and St. James's Park; and, for close walks, the New Exchange.

MRS. PINCHWIFE. Pray, sister, tell me why my
5 husband looks so grum here in town, and keeps me up so close, and will not let me go a-walking, nor let me wear my best gown yesterday.

ALITHEA. Oh, he's jealous, sister.

MRS. PINCHWIFE. Jealous! what's that?

10 ALITHEA. He's afraid you should love another man.

MRS. PINCHWIFE. How should he be afraid of my loving another man, when he will not let me see any but himself?

15 ALITHEA. Did he not carry you yesterday to a play?

MRS. PINCHWIFE. Ay; but we sat amongst ugly people. He would not let me come near the gentry, who sat under us, so that I could not
20 see 'em. He told me none but naughty women sat there, whom they toused and moused. But I would have ventured, for all that.

ALITHEA. But how did you like the play?

MRS. PINCHWIFE. Indeed I was a-weary of the
25 play, but I liked hugeously the actors. They are the goodliest, properest men, sister!

ALITHEA. Oh, but you must not like the actors, sister.

MRS. PINCHWIFE. Ay, how should I help it,
30 sister? Pray, sister, when my husband comes in, will you ask leave for me to go a-walking?

ALITHEA [*aside*]. A-walking! ha! ha! Lord, a country-gentlewoman's pleasure is the drudgery of a footpost;° and she requires as much
35 airing as her husband's horses.—But here comes your husband. I'll ask, though I'm sure he'll not grant it.

MRS. PINCHWIFE. He says he won't let me go abroad for fear of catching the pox.

40 ALITHEA. Fy! the small-pox you should say.

[*Enter* PINCHWIFE.]

MRS. PINCHWIFE. O my dear, dear bud,° welcome home! Why dost thou look so fropish?

Who has nangered° thee?

PINCHWIFE. You're a fool. 45

[MRS. PINCHWIFE *goes aside, and cries.*]

ALITHEA. Faith, so she is, for crying for no fault, poor tender creature!

PINCHWIFE. What, you would have her as impudent as yourself, as arrant a jillflirt,° a gad- 50
der, a magpie; and to say all, a mere notorious town-woman?

ALITHEA. Brother, you are my only censurer; and the honor of your family shall sooner suffer in your wife there than in me, though I take the 55 innocent liberty of the town.

PINCHWIFE. Hark you, mistress, do not talk so before my wife.—The innocent liberty of the town!

ALITHEA. Why, pray, who boasts of any in- 60 trigue with me? what lampoon has made my name notorious? what ill women frequent my lodgings? I keep no company with any women of scandalous reputations.

PINCHWIFE. No, you keep the men of scan- 65 dalous reputations company.

ALITHEA. Where? would you not have me civil? answer 'em in a box at the plays, in the drawing-room at Whitehall, in St. James's Park, Mulberry Garden, or— 70

PINCHWIFE. Hold, hold! Do not teach my wife where the men are to be found; I believe she's the worse for your town-documents° already. I bid you keep her in ignorance, as I do.

MRS. PINCHWIFE. Indeed, be not angry with 75 her, bud, she will tell me nothing of the town, though I ask her a thousand times a day.

PINCHWIFE. Then you are very inquisitive to know, I find?

MRS. PINCHWIFE. Not I indeed, dear; I hate 80 London. Our place-house in the country is worth a thousand of't; would I were there again!

PINCHWIFE. So you shall, I warrant. But were you not talking of plays and players when I 85 came in? [*To* ALITHEA.] You are her encourager in such discourses.

MRS. PINCHWIFE. No, indeed, dear; she chid

---

footpost someone who goes errands on foot, who cannot afford to ride
bud a rustic term of endearment; but also meaning a yearling calf that has not yet grown horns (hence with the usual allusion to a cuckold's horns)

fropish . . . nangered peevish, angered
jillflirt giddy girl
town-documents information about London social life

me just now for liking the playermen.

PINCHWIFE [*aside*]. Nay, if she be so innocent as to own to me her liking them, there is no hurt in't.—Come, my poor rogue, but thou lik'st none better than me?

MRS. PINCHWIFE. Yes, indeed, but I do. The playermen are finer folks.

PINCHWIFE. But you love none better than me?

MRS. PINCHWIFE. You are mine own dear bud, and I know you. I hate a stranger.

PINCHWIFE. Ay, my dear, you must love me only, and not be like the naughty town-women, who only hate their husbands, and love every man else; love plays, visits, fine coaches, fine clothes, fiddles, balls, treats, and so lead a wicked town-life.

MRS. PINCHWIFE. Nay, if to enjoy all these things be a town-life, London is not so bad a place, dear.

PINCHWIFE. How! if you love me, you must hate London.

ALITHEA [*aside*]. The fool has forbid me discovering to her the pleasures of the town, and he is now setting her agog upon them himself.

MRS. PINCHWIFE. But, husband, do the town-women love the playermen too?

PINCHWIFE. Yes, I warrant you.

MRS. PINCHWIFE. Ay, I warrant you.

PINCHWIFE. Why, you do not, I hope?

MRS. PINCHWIFE. No, no, bud. But why have we no playermen in the country?

PINCHWIFE. Ha!—Mrs. Minx, ask me no more to go to a play.

MRS. PINCHWIFE. Nay, why love? I did not care for going; but when you forbid me, you make me, as 'twere, desire it.

ALITHEA [*aside*]. So 'twill be in other things, I warrant.

MRS. PINCHWIFE. Pray let me go to a play, dear.

PINCHWIFE. Hold your peace, I wo' not.

MRS. PINCHWIFE. Why, love?

PINCHWIFE. Why, I'll tell you.

ALITHEA [*aside*]. Nay, if he'll tell her, she'll give him more cause to forbid her that place.

MRS. PINCHWIFE. Pray why, dear?

PINCHWIFE. First, you like the actors; and the gallants may like you.

MRS. PINCHWIFE. What, a homely country girl! No, bud, nobody will like me.

PINCHWIFE. I tell you yes, they may.

MRS. PINCHWIFE. No, no, you jest—I won't believe; I will go.

PINCHWIFE. I tell you then, that one of the lewdest fellows in town, who saw you there, told me he was in love with you.

MRS. PINCHWIFE. Indeed! who, who, pray who was't?

PINCHWIFE [*aside*]. I've gone too far, and slipped before I was aware; how overjoyed she is!

MRS. PINCHWIFE. Was it any Hampshire gallant, any of our neighbors? I promise you, I am beholden to him.

PINCHWIFE. I promise you, you lie; for he would but ruin you, as he has done hundreds. He has no other love for women but that; such as he look upon women, like basilisks,° but to destroy 'em.

MRS. PINCHWIFE. Ay, but if he loves me, why should he ruin me? answer me to that. Methinks he should not, I would do him no harm.

ALITHEA. Ha! ha! ha!

PINCHWIFE. 'Tis very well; but I'll keep him from doing you any harm, or me either. But here comes company; get you in, get you in.

MRS. PINCHWIFE. But, pray, husband, is he a pretty gentleman that loves me?

PINCHWIFE. In, baggage, in. [*Thrusts her in, shuts the door.*]

[*Enter* SPARKISH *and* HARCOURT.]

What, all the lewd libertines of the town brought to my lodging by this easy coxcomb! 'Sdeath, I'll not suffer it.

SPARKISH. Here, Harcourt, do you approve my choice?—Dear little rogue. I told you I'd bring you acquainted with all my friends, the wits and—[HARCOURT *salutes her.*]

PINCHWIFE. Ay, they shall know her, as well as you yourself will, I warrant you.

SPARKISH. This is one of those, my pretty rogue, that are to dance at your wedding to-

---

basilisks legendary reptiles whose very glance was fatal morrow; and him you must bid welcome ever, to what you and I have.

PINCHWIFE [*aside*]. Monstrous!

SPARKISH. Harcourt, how dost thou like her, faith? Nay, dear, do not look down; I should hate to have a wife of mine out of countenance at anything.

PINCHWIFE [*aside*]. Wonderful!

SPARKISH. Tell me, I say, Harcourt, how dost thou like her? Thou hast stared upon her enough to resolve me.

HARCOURT. So infinitely well, that I could wish I had a mistress too, that might differ from her in nothing but her love and engagement to you.

ALITHEA. Sir, Master Sparkish has often told me that his acquaintance were all wits and railleurs, and now I find it.

SPARKISH. No, by the universe, madam, he does not rally now; you may believe him, I do assure you, he is the honestest, worthiest, true-hearted gentleman—a man of such perfect honor, he would say nothing to a lady he does not mean.

PINCHWIFE [*aside*]. Praising another man to his mistress!

HARCOURT. Sir, you are so beyond expectation obliging, that—

SPARKISH. Nay, egad, I am sure you do admire her extremely; I see't in your eyes.—He does admire you, madam.—By the world, don't you?

HARCOURT. Yes, above the world, or the most glorious part of it, her whole sex; and till now I never thought I should have envied you or any man about to marry, but you have the best excuse for marriage I ever knew.

ALITHEA. Nay, now, sir, I'm satisfied you are of the society of the wits and railleurs, since you cannot spare your friend, even when he is but too civil to you; but the surest sign is, since you are an enemy to marriage, for that I hear you hate as much as business or bad wine.

HARCOURT. Truly, madam, I never was an enemy to marriage till now, because marriage was never an enemy to me before.

ALITHEA. But why, sir, is marriage an enemy to you now? Because it robs you of your friend here? for you look upon a friend married as one gone into a monastery, that is, dead to the world.

HARCOURT. 'Tis indeed, because you marry him; I see, madam, you can guess my meaning. I do confess heartily and openly I wish it were in my power to break the match; by Heavens I would.

SPARKISH. Poor Frank!

ALITHEA. Would you be so unkind to me?

HARCOURT. No, no, 'tis not because I would be unkind to you.

SPARKISH. Poor Frank! no gad, 'tis only his kindness to me.

PINCHWIFE [*aside*]. Great kindness to you indeed! Insensible fop, let a man make love to his wife to his face!

SPARKISH. Come, dear Frank, for all my wife there, that shall be, thou shalt enjoy me sometimes, dear rogue. By my honor, we men of wit condole for our deceased brother in marriage, as much as for one dead in earnest; I think that was prettily said of me, ha, Harcourt?—But come, Frank, be not melancholy for me.

HARCOURT. No, I assure you, I am not melancholy for you.

SPARKISH. Prithee, Frank, dost think my wife that shall be there, a fine person?

HARCOURT. I could gaze upon her till I became as blind as you are.

SPARKISH. How as I am? how?

HARCOURT. Because you are a lover, and true lovers are blind, struck blind.

SPARKISH. True, true; but by the world, she has wit too, as well as beauty. Go, go with her into a corner, and try if she has wit; talk to her anything; she's bashful before me.

HARCOURT. Indeed if a woman wants wit in a corner, she has it nowhere.

ALITHEA [*aside to* SPARKISH]. Sir, you dispose of me a little before your time—

SPARKISH. Nay, nay, madam, let me have an earnest of your obedience, or—go, go, madam— [HARCOURT *courts* ALITHEA *aside*].

PINCHWIFE. How, sir! if you are not concerned for the honor of a wife, I am for that of a sister; he shall not debauch her. Be a pander to your own wife! bring men to her! let 'em make love before your face! thrust 'em into a corner together, then leave 'em in private! is this your town wit and conduct?

SPARKISH. Ha! ha! ha! a silly wise rogue would make one laugh more than a stark fool, ha! ha! I shall burst. Nay, you shall not dis-5 turb 'em; I'll vex thee, by the world.

[*Struggles with* PINCHWIFE *to keep him from* HARCOURT *and* ALITHEA.]

ALITHEA. The writings are drawn, sir, settle-10 ments made; 'tis too late, sir, and past all re-vocation.

HARCOURT. Then so is my death.

ALITHEA. I would not be unjust to him.

HARCOURT. Then why to me so?

15 ALITHEA. I have no obligation to you.

HARCOURT. My love.

ALITHEA. I had his before.

HARCOURT. You never had it; he wants, you see, jealousy, the only infallible sign of it.

20 ALITHEA. Love proceeds from esteem; he can-not distrust my virtue; besides, he loves me, or he would not marry me.

HARCOURT. Marrying you is no more sign of his love than bribing your woman, that he may 25 marry you, is a sign of his generosity. Marriage is rather a sign of interest than love; and he that marries a fortune covets a mistress, not loves her. But if you take marriage for a sign of love, take it from me immediately.

30 ALITHEA. No, now you have put a scruple in my head; but in short, sir, to end our dispute, I must marry him; my reputation would suffer in the world else.

HARCOURT. No; if you do marry him, with 35 your pardon, madam, your reputation suffers in the world, and you would be thought in necessity for a cloak.

ALITHEA. Nay, now you are rude, sir.—Mr Sparkish, pray come hither, your friend here 40 is very troublesome, and very loving.

HARCOURT [*aside to* ALITHEA]. Hold! hold!—

PINCHWIFE. D'ye hear that?

SPARKISH. Why, d'ye think I'll seem to be jealous, like a country bumpkin?

45 PINCHWIFE. No, rather be a cuckold, like a credulous cit.

HARCOURT. Madam, you would not have been so little generous as to have told him.

ALITHEA. Yes, since you could be so little 50 generous as to wrong him.

HARCOURT. Wrong him! no man can do't, he's beneath an injury; a bubble,° a coward, a sense-less idiot, a wretch so contemptible to all the world but you, that—

ALITHEA. Hold, do not rail at him, for since he 55 is like to be my husband, I am resolved to like him; nay, I think I am obliged to tell him you are not his friend.—Master Sparkish, Master Sparkish!

SPARKISH. What, what?—Now, dear rogue, 60 has not she wit?

HARCOURT [*speaks surlily*]. Not as much as I thought, and hoped she had.

ALITHEA. Mr. Sparkish, do you bring people to rail at you? 65

HARCOURT. Madam—

SPARKISH. How! no; but if he does rail at me, 'tis but in jest, I warrant; what we wits do for one another, and never take any notice of it.

ALITHEA. He spoke so scurrilously of you, I 70 had no patience to hear him; besides, he has been making love to me.

HARCOURT [*aside*]. True, damned tell-tale woman!

SPARKISH. Pshaw! to show his parts—we wits 75 rail and make love often, but to show our parts; as we have no affections, so we have no malice, we—

ALITHEA. He said you were a wretch below an injury— 80

SPARKISH. Pshaw!

HARCOURT [*aside*]. Damned, senseless, im-pudent, virtuous jade! Well, since she won't let me have her, she'll do as good, she'll make me hate her. 85

ALITHEA. A common bubble—

SPARKISH. Pshaw!

ALITHEA. A coward—

SPARKISH. Pshaw, pshaw!

ALITHEA. A senseless, drivelling idiot— 90

SPARKISH. How! did he disparage my parts? Nay, then, my honor's concerned, I can't put up that, sir, by the world—brother, help me to kill him—[*aside*] I may draw now, since we

bubble nitwit

have the odds of him—'tis a good occasion, too, before my mistress—[*offers to draw*].

ALITHEA. Hold, hold!

SPARKISH. What, what?

5 ALITHEA [*aside*]. I must not let 'em kill the gentleman neither, for his kindness to me. I am so far from hating him, that I wish my gallant had his person and understanding. Nay, if my honor—

10 SPARKISH. I'll be thy death.

ALITHEA. Hold, hold! Indeed, to tell the truth, the gentleman said after all, that what he spoke was but out of friendship to you.

SPARKISH. How! say I am—I am a fool, that 15 is no wit, out of friendship to me?

ALITHEA. Yes, to try whether I was concerned enough for you; and made love to me only to be satisfied of my virtue, for your sake.

HARCOURT [*aside*]. Kind, however.°

20 SPARKISH. Nay, if it were so, my dear rogue, I ask thee pardon; but why would not you tell me so, faith?

HARCOURT. Because I did not think on't, faith.

SPARKISH. Come, Horner does not come; Har-25 court, let's be gone to the new play.—Come, madam.

ALITHEA. I will not go if you intend to leave me alone in the box and run into the pit,° as you use to do.

30 SPARKISH. Pshaw! I'll leave Harcourt with you in the box to entertain you, and that's as good; if I sat in the box, I should be thought no judge but of trimmings.°—Come away, Harcourt, lead her down.

35 [*Exeunt* SPARKISH, HARCOURT, *and* ALITHEA.]

PINCHWIFE. Well, go thy ways, for the flower of the true town fops, such as spend their estates before they come to 'em, and are cuck-olds before they're married. But let me go back 40 to my own freehold.—How!

[*Enter* LADY FIDGET, MRS. DAINTY FIDGET, *and* MRS. SQUEAMISH.]

Kind, however because Alithea has put Harcourt's conduct in a good light
pit where ladies of dubious character showed them-selves conspicuously
trimmings of ladies' dresses (rather than of the ladies themselves)

LADY FIDGET. Your servant, sir; where is your lady? We are come to wait upon her to the new play. 45

PINCHWIFE. New play!

LADY FIDGET. And my husband will wait upon you presently.

PINCHWIFE [*aside*]. Damn your civility.— Madam, by no means; I will not see Sir Jasper 50 here till I have waited upon him at home; nor shall my wife see you till she has waited upon your ladyship at your lodgings.

LADY FIDGET. Now we are here, sir?

PINCHWIFE. No, madam. 55

MRS. DAINTY FIDGET. Pray, let us see her.

MRS. SQUEAMISH. We will not stir till we see her.

PINCHWIFE [*aside*]. A pox on you all!—[*Goes to the door, and returns.*] She has locked the 60 door, and is gone abroad.

LADY FIDGET. No, you have locked the door, and she's within.

MRS. DAINTY FIDGET. They told us below she was here. 65

PINCHWIFE [*aside*]. Will nothing do?—Well, it must out then. To tell you the truth, ladies, which I was afraid to let you know before, lest it might endanger your lives, my wife has just now the small-pox come out upon her; do not 70 be frightened, but pray be gone, ladies; you shall not stay here in danger of your lives; pray get you gone, ladies.

LADY FIDGET. No, no, we have all had 'em.

MRS. SQUEAMISH. Alack, alack! 75

MRS. DAINTY FIDGET. Come, come, we must see how it goes with her; I understand the disease.

LADY FIDGET. Come!

PINCHWIFE [*aside*]. Well, there is no being too 80 hard for women at their own weapon, lying, therefore I'll quit the field.

[*Exit.*]

MRS. SQUEAMISH. Here's an example of jeal-ousy! 85

LADY FIDGET. Indeed, as the world goes, I wonder there are no more jealous, since wives are so neglected.

MRS. DAINTY FIDGET. Pshaw! as the world goes, to what end should they be jealous? 90

LADY FIDGET. Foh! 'tis a nasty world.

MRS. SQUEAMISH. That men of parts, great acquaintance, and quality, should take up with and spend themselves and fortunes in keeping little playhouse creatures, foh!

LADY FIDGET. Nay, that women of understanding, great acquaintance, and good quality, should fall a-keeping too of little creatures, foh!

MRS. SQUEAMISH. Why, 'tis the men of quality's fault; they never visit women of honor and reputation as they used to do; and have not so much as common civility for ladies of our rank, but use us with the same indifferency and ill-breeding as if we were all married to 'em.

LADY FIDGET. She says true; 'tis an arrant shame women of quality should be so slighted; methinks birth—birth should go for something; I have known men admired, courted, and followed for their titles only.

MRS. SQUEAMISH. Ay, one would think men of honor should not love, no more than marry, out of their own rank.

MRS. DAINTY FIDGET. Fy, fy, upon 'em! they are come to think cross breeding for themselves best, as well as for their dogs and horses.

LADY FIDGET. They are dogs and horses for't.

MRS. SQUEAMISH. One would think, if not for love, for vanity a little.

MRS. DAINTY FIDGET. Nay, they do satisfy their vanity upon us sometimes; and are kind to us in their report, tell all the world they lie with us.

LADY FIDGET. Damned rascals, that we should be only wronged by 'em! To report a man has had a person, when he has not had a person, is the greatest wrong in the whole world that can be done to a person.

MRS. SQUEAMISH. Well, 'tis an arrant shame noble persons should be so wronged and neglected.

LADY FIDGET. But still 'tis an arranter shame for a noble person to neglect her own honor, and defame her own noble person with little inconsiderable fellows, foh!

MRS. DAINTY FIDGET. I suppose the crime against our honor is the same with a man of quality as with another.

LADY FIDGET. How! no, sure, the man of quality is likest one's husband, and therefore the fault should be the less.

MRS. DAINTY FIDGET. But then the pleasure should be the less.

LADY FIDGET. Fy, fy, fy, for shame, sister! whither shall we ramble? Be continent in your discourse, or I shall hate you.

MRS. DAINTY FIDGET. Besides, an intrigue is so much the more notorious for the man's quality.

MRS. SQUEAMISH. 'Tis true, nobody takes notice of a private man,° and therefore with him 'tis more secret; and the crime's the less when 'tis not known.

LADY FIDGET. You say true; i' faith, I think you are in the right on't; 'tis not an injury to a husband till it be an injury to our honors; so that a woman of honor loses no honor with a private person; and to say truth—

MRS. DAINTY FIDGET [apart to MRS. SQUEAMISH]. So, the little fellow is grown a private person—with her—

LADY FIDGET. But still my dear, dear honor—

[Enter SIR JASPER, HORNER, and DORILANT.]

SIR JASPER FIDGET. Ay, my dear, dear of honor, thou hast still so much honor in thy mouth—

HORNER [aside]. That she has none elsewhere.

LADY FIDGET. Oh, what d'ye mean to bring in these upon us?

MRS. DAINTY FIDGET. Foh! these are as bad as wits.

MRS. SQUEAMISH. Foh!

LADY FIDGET. Let us leave the room.

SIR JASPER FIDGET. Stay, stay; faith, to tell you the naked truth—

LADY FIDGET. Fy, Sir Jasper! do not use that word naked.

SIR JASPER FIDGET. Well, well, in short I have business at Whitehall, and cannot go to the play with you, therefore would have you go—

LADY FIDGET. With those two to a play?

SIR JASPER FIDGET. No, not with t'other, but with Mr. Horner; there can be no more scandal

private man not a person in public life and the public eye

to go with him than with Mr. Tattle, or Master Limberham.°

LADY FIDGET. With that nasty fellow! no—no.

5 SIR JASPER FIDGET. Nay, prithee, dear, hear me. [*Whispers to* LADY FIDGET.]

HORNER. Ladies—

[HORNER, DORILANT *drawing near* MRS. SQUEAMISH *and* MRS. DAINTY FIDGET.]

10 MRS. DAINTY FIDGET. Stand off.

MRS. SQUEAMISH. Do not approach us.

MRS. DAINTY FIDGET. You herd with the wits, you are obscenity all over.

MRS. SQUEAMISH. And I would as soon look
15 upon a picture of Adam and Eve without fig-leaves as any of you, if I could help it; therefore keep off, and do not make us sick.

DORILANT. What a devil are these?

HORNER. Why, these are pretenders to honor,
20 as critics to wit, only by censuring others; and as every raw, peevish, out-of-humored, affected, dull, tea-drinking, arithmetical fop, sets up for a wit by railing at men of sense, so these for honor, by railing at the court, and ladies
25 of as great honor as quality.

SIR JASPER FIDGET. Come, Mr. Horner, I must desire you to go with these ladies to the play, sir.

HORNER. I, sir?

30 SIR JASPER FIDGET. Ay, ay, come, sir.

HORNER. I must beg your pardon, sir, and theirs; I will not be seen in women's company in public again for the world.

SIR JASPER FIDGET. Ha, ha, strange aversion!

35 MRS. SQUEAMISH. No, he's for women's company in private.

SIR JASPER FIDGET. He—poor man—he—ha! ha! ha!

MRS. DAINTY FIDGET. 'Tis a greater shame
40 amongst lewd fellows to be seen in virtuous women's company, than for the women to be seen with them.

HORNER. Indeed, madam, the time was I only hated virtuous women, but now I hate the

other too; I beg your pardon, ladies. 45

LADY FIDGET. You are very obliging, sir, because we would not be troubled with you.

SIR JASPER FIDGET. In sober sadness, he shall go.

DORILANT. Nay, if he wo' not, I am ready to 50 wait upon the ladies, and I think I am the fitter man.

SIR JASPER FIDGET. You, sir! no, I thank you for that. Master Horner is a privileged man amongst the virtuous ladies, 'twill be a great 55 while before you are so; he! he! he! he's my wife's gallant; he! he! he! No, pray withdraw, sir, for as I take it, the virtuous ladies have no business with you.

DORILANT. And I am sure he can have none 60 with them. 'Tis strange a man can't come amongst virtuous women now, but upon the same terms as men are admitted into the Great Turk's seraglio.° But heavens keep me from being an ombre° player with 'em!—But where 65 is Pinchwife?

[*Exit.*]

SIR JASPER FIDGET. Come, come, man; what, avoid the sweet society of womankind? that sweet, soft, gentle, tame, noble creature, 70 woman, made for man's companion—

HORNER. So is that soft, gentle, tame, and more noble creature a spaniel, and has all their tricks; can fawn, lie down, suffer beating, and fawn the more; barks at your friends when 75 they come to see you, makes your bed hard, gives you fleas, and the mange sometimes. And all the difference is, the spaniel's the more faithful animal, and fawns but upon one master.

SIR JASPER FIDGET. He! he! he! 80

MRS. SQUEAMISH. Oh, the rude beast!

MRS. DAINTY FIDGET. Insolent brute!

LADY FIDGET. Brute! stinking, mortified, rotten French wether,° to dare—

SIR JASPER FIDGET. Hold, an't please your 85 ladyship.—For shame, Master Horner! your

---

Tattle . . . Limberham by implication, silly old gentlemen who are capable only of bearing gossip or of "bending a leg" (a limber ham) in flattery

Great Turk's seraglio harem of the Sultan of Turkey. The only men permitted there as guards or servants were eunuchs.
ombre a fashionable card game
French wether a castrated ram; a eunuch

mother was a woman.—[*Aside.*] Now shall I never reconcile 'em.—[*Aside to* LADY FIDGET.] Hark you, madam, take my advice in your anger. You know you often want one to make
5 up your drolling pack of ombre players, and you may cheat him easily; for he's an ill gamester, and consequently loves play. Besides, you know you have but two old civil gentlemen° (with stinking breaths too) to wait upon you
10 abroad; take in the third into your service. The others are but crazy;° and a lady should have a supernumerary gentleman-usher° as a supernumerary coach-horse, lest sometimes you should be forced to stay at home.
15 LADY FIDGET. But are you sure he loves play and has money?

SIR JASPER FIDGET. He loves play as much as you, and has money as much as I.

LADY FIDGET. Then I am contented to make
20 him pay for his scurrility. [*Aside.*] Money makes up in a measure all other wants in men. Those whom we cannot make hold for gallants, we make fine.°

SIR JASPER FIDGET [*aside*]. So, so; now to mol-
25 lify, to wheedle him.—[*Aside to* HORNER.] Master Horner, will you never keep civil company? Methinks 'tis time now, since you are only fit for them. Come, come, man, you must e'en fall to visiting our wives, eating at our tables, drink-
30 ing tea with our virtuous relations after dinner, dealing cards to 'em, reading plays and gazettes to 'em, picking fleas out of their shocks° for 'em, collecting receipts, new songs, women, pages, and footmen for em.
35 HORNER. I hope they'll afford me better employment, sir.

SIR JASPER FIDGET. He! he! he! 'tis fit you know your work before you come into your place. And since you are unprovided of a lady
40 to flatter, and a good house to eat at, pray fre-

quent mine, and call my wife mistress, and she shall call you gallant, according to the custom.

HORNER. Who, I?

SIR JASPER FIDGET. Faith, thou shalt for my sake; come, for my sake only. 45

HORNER. For your sake—

SIR JASPER FIDGET [*to* LADY FIDGET]. Come, come, here's a gamester for you; let him be a little familiar sometimes; nay, what if a little rude? Gamesters may be rude with ladies, you 50 know.

LADY FIDGET. Yes; losing gamesters have a privilege with women.

HORNER. I always thought the contrary, that the winning gamester had most privilege with 55 women; for when you have lost your money to a man, you'll lose anything you have—all you have, they say—and he may use you as he pleases.

SIR JASPER FIDGET. He! he! he! well, win or 60 lose, you shall have your liberty with her.

LADY FIDGET. As he behaves himself, and for your sake I'll give him admittance and freedom.

HORNER. All sorts of freedom, madam?

SIR JASPER FIDGET. Ay, ay, ay, all sorts of 65 freedom thou canst take. And so go to her, begin thy new employment; wheedle her, jest with her, and be better acquainted one with another.

HORNER [*aside*]. I think I know her already; 70 therefore may venture with her my secret for hers. [HORNER *and* LADY FIDGET *whisper.*]

SIR JASPER FIDGET. Sister, cuz,° I have provided an innocent playfellow for you there.

MRS. DAINTY FIDGET. Who, he? 75

MRS. SQUEAMISH. There's a playfellow, indeed!

SIR JASPER FIDGET. Yes, sure. What, he is good enough to play at cards, blindman's-buff, or the fool with, sometimes! 80

MRS. SQUEAMISH. Foh! we'll have no such playfellows.

MRS. DAINTY FIDGET. No, sir; you shan't choose playfellows for us, we thank you.

SIR JASPER FIDGET. Nay, pray hear me. [*Whis-* 85 *pering to them.*]

---

civil gentlemen Mr. Tattle and Mr. Limberham, already mentioned
crazy ailing; shaky
gentleman-usher a servant to tend the door and perform small personal services, as Sir Jasper explains in a moment
fine pay
shocks lap dogs

cuz (or **coz**) *cousin*, a merely friendly endearment

LADY FIDGET. But, poor gentleman, could you be so generous, so truly a man of honor, as for the sakes of us women of honor, to cause yourself to be reported no man? No man! and to suffer yourself the greatest shame that could fall upon a man, that none might fall upon us women by your conversation? But, indeed, sir, as perfectly, perfectly the same man as before your going into France, sir? as perfectly, perfectly, sir?

HORNER. As perfectly, perfectly, madam. Nay, I scorn you should take my word; I desire to be tried only, madam.

LADY FIDGET. Well, that's spoken again like a man of honor: all men of honor desire to come to the test. But, indeed, generally you men report such things of yourselves, one does not know how or whom to believe; and it is come to that pass we dare not take your words no more than your tailor's, without some staid servant of yours be bound with you. But I have so strong a faith in your honor, dear, dear, noble sir, that I'd forfeit mine for yours, at any time, dear sir.

HORNER. No, madam, you should not need to forfeit it for me; I have given you security already to have you harmless, my late reputation being so well known in the world, madam.

LADY FIDGET. But if upon any future falling-out, or upon a suspicion of my taking the trust out of your hands to employ some other, you yourself should betray your trust, dear sir? I mean, if you'll give me leave to speak obscenely, you might tell, dear sir.

HORNER. If I did, nobody would believe me. The reputation of impotency is as hardly recovered again in the world as that of cowardice, dear madam.

LADY FIDGET. Nay, then, as one may say, you may do your worst, dear, dear sir.

SIR JASPER FIDGET. Come, is your ladyship reconciled to him yet? have you agreed on matters? For I must be gone to Whitehall.

LADY FIDGET. Why, indeed, Sir Jasper, Master Horner is a thousand, thousand times a better man than I thought him. Cousin Squeamish, sister Dainty, I can name him now. Truly, not long ago, you know, I thought his very name

obscenity; and I would as soon have lain with him as have named him.

SIR JASPER FIDGET. Very likely, poor madam.

MRS. DAINTY FIDGET. I believe it.

MRS. SQUEAMISH. No doubt on't.

SIR JASPER FIDGET. Well, well—that your ladyship is as virtuous as any she, I know, and him all the town knows—he! he! he! Therefore, now you like him, get you gone to your business together; go, go to your business, I say, pleasure; whilst I go to my pleasure, business.

LADY FIDGET. Come, then, dear gallant.

HORNER. Come away, my dearest mistress.

SIR JASPER FIDGET. So, so; why, 'tis as I'd have it.

[*Exit.*]

HORNER. And as I'd have it.

LADY FIDGET.
Who for his business from his wife will run,
Takes the best care to have her business
　　　　　　　　　　　　　　　　[done.

[*Exeunt omnes.*]

ACT III

Scene i

[*A room in* PINCHWIFE'S *house.*]

[*Enter* ALITHEA *and* MRS. PINCHWIFE.]

ALITHEA. Sister, what ails you? You are grown melancholy.

MRS. PINCHWIFE. Would it not make any one melancholy to see you go every day fluttering abroad, whilst I must stay at home like a poor lonely sullen bird in a cage?

ALITHEA. Ay, sister, but you came young, and just from the nest to your cage, so that I thought you liked it, and could be as cheerful in't as others that took their flight themselves early, and are hopping abroad in the open air.

MRS. PINCHWIFE. Nay, I confess I was quiet enough till my husband told me what pure° lives the London ladies live abroad, with their dancing, meetings, and junketings, and dressed every day in their best gowns; and I warrant you, play at nine-pins every day of the week, so they do.

pure flourishing

[*Enter* PINCHWIFE.]

PINCHWIFE. Come, what's here to do? You are putting the town-pleasures in her head, and setting her a-longing.

5 ALITHEA. Yes, after nine-pins. You suffer none to give her those longings you mean but yourself.

PINCHWIFE. I tell her of the vanities of the town like a confessor.

10 ALITHEA. A confessor! just such a confessor as he that, by forbidding a silly ostler to grease the horse's teeth,° taught him to do't.

PINCHWIFE. Come, Mistress Flippant, good precepts are lost when bad examples are still 15 before us; the liberty you take abroad makes her hanker after it, and out of humor at home. Poor wretch! she desired not to come to London; I would bring her.

ALITHEA. Very well.

20 PINCHWIFE. She has been this week in town, and never desired till this afternoon to go abroad.

ALITHEA. Was she not at a play yesterday?

PINCHWIFE. Yes, but she ne'er asked me; I 25 was myself the cause of her going.

ALITHEA. Then if she ask you again, you are the cause of her asking, and not my example.

PINCHWIFE. Well, tomorrow night I shall be rid of you; and the next day, before 'tis light, 30 she and I'll be rid of the town, and my dreadful apprehensions.—Come, be not melancholy; for thou shalt go into the country after to-morrow, dearest.

ALITHEA. Great comfort!

35 MRS. PINCHWIFE. Pish! what d'ye tell me of the country for?

PINCHWIFE. How's this! what, pish at the country?

MRS. PINCHWIFE. Let me alone; I am not well.

40 PINCHWIFE. Oh, if that be all—what ails my dearest?

MRS. PINCHWIFE. Truly, I don't know; but I have not been well since you told me there was a gallant at the play in love with me.

PINCHWIFE. Ha!— 45

ALITHEA. That's by my example too!

PINCHWIFE. Nay, if you are not well, but are so concerned because a lewd fellow chanced to lie, and say he liked you, you'll make me sick too. 50

MRS. PINCHWIFE. Of what sickness?

PINCHWIFE. Oh, of that which is worse than the plague, jealousy.

MRS. PINCHWIFE. Pish, you jeer! I'm sure there's no such disease in our receipt-book at 55 home.

PINCHWIFE. No, thou never met'st with it, poor innocent.—[*Aside.*] Well, if thou cuckold me, 'twill be my own fault—for cuckolds and bastards are generally makers of their own 60 fortune.

MRS. PINCHWIFE. Well, but pray, bud, let's go to a play tonight.

PINCHWIFE. 'Tis just done, she comes from it. But why are you so eager to see a play? 65

MRS. PINCHWIFE. Faith, dear, not that I care one pin for their talk there; but I like to look upon the playermen, and would see, if I could, the gallant you say loves me; that's all, dear bud. 70

PINCHWIFE. Is that all, dear bud?

ALITHEA. This proceeds from my example!

MRS. PINCHWIFE. But if the play be done, let's go abroad, however, dear bud.

PINCHWIFE. Come, have a little patience and 75 thou shalt go into the country on Friday.

MRS. PINCHWIFE. Therefore I would see first some sights to tell my neighbors of. Nay, I will go abroad, that's once.

ALITHEA. I'm the cause of this desire, too! 80

PINCHWIFE. But now I think on't, who, who was the cause of Horner's coming to my lodgings today? That was you.

ALITHEA. No, you, because you would not let him see your handsome wife out of your 85 lodging.

MRS. PINCHWIFE. Why, O Lord! did the gentleman come hither to see me indeed?

PINCHWIFE. No, no. You are not cause of that damned question too, Mistress Alithea?— 90 [*Aside.*] Well, she's in the right of it. He is in love with my wife—and comes after her—'tis

---

to grease ... teeth hence, to put the horse off his feed, a trick of dishonest hostlers to economize on provender

so—but I'll nip his love in the bud, lest he should follow us into the country, and break his chariot-wheel near our house, on purpose for an excuse to come to't. But I think I know the town.

MRS. PINCHWIFE. Come, pray, bud, let's go abroad before 'tis late; for I will go, that's flat and plain.

PINCHWIFE [*aside*]. So! the obstinacy already of a town-wife; and I must, whilst she's here, humor her like one.—Sister, how shall we do, that she may not be seen or known?

ALITHEA. Let her put on her mask.

PINCHWIFE. Pshaw! a mask makes people but the more inquisitive, and is as ridiculous a disguise as a stage-beard; her shape, stature, habit will be known. And if we should meet with Horner, he would be sure to take acquaintance with us, must wish her joy, kiss her, talk to her, leer upon her, and the devil and all. No, I'll not use her to a mask; 'tis dangerous, for masks have made more cuckolds than the best faces that ever were known.

ALITHEA. How will you do then?

MRS. PINCHWIFE. Nay, shall we go? The Exchange° will be shut, and I have a mind to see that.

PINCHWIFE. So—I have it—I'll dress her up in the suit we are to carry down to her brother, little Sir James; nay, I understand the town-tricks. Come, let's go dress her. A mask! no—a woman masked, like a covered dish, gives a man curiosity and appetite; when, it may be, uncovered, 'twould turn his stomach; no, no.

ALITHEA. Indeed your comparison is something a greasy one: but I had a gentle gallant used to say, "A beauty masked, like the sun in eclipse, gathers together more gazers than if it shined out."

[*Exeunt.*]

Scene ii

[*The scene changes to the New Exchange, with* CLASP, *a book-seller, in his stall.*]

[*Enter* HORNER, HARCOURT, *and* DORILANT.]

DORILANT. Engaged to women, and not sup with us!

HORNER. Ay, a pox on 'em all!

HARCOURT. You were much a more reasonable man in the morning, and had as noble resolutions against 'em as a widower of a week's liberty.

DORILANT. Did I ever think to see you keep company with women in vain?

HORNER. In vain! no—'tis since I can't love 'em, to be revenged on 'em.

HARCOURT. Now your sting is gone, you looked in the box amongst all those women like a drone in the hive; all upon you, shoved and ill-used by 'em all, and thrust from one side to t'other.

DORILANT. Yet he must be buzzing amongst 'em still, like other old beetle-headed liquorish° drones. Avoid 'em, and hate 'em, as they hate you.

HORNER. Because I do hate 'em, and would hate 'em yet more, I'll frequent 'em. You may see by marriage, nothing makes a man hate a woman more than her constant conversation. In short, I converse with 'em as you do with rich fools, to laugh at 'em and use 'em ill.

DORILANT. But I would no more sup with women unless I could lie with 'em than sup with a rich coxcomb unless I could cheat him.

HORNER. Yes, I have known thee sup with a fool for his drinking; if he could set out your hand° that way only, you were satisfied, and if he were a wine-swallowing mouth, 'twas enough.

HARCOURT. Yes, a man drinks often with a fool, as he tosses with a marker,° only to keep his hand in ure.° But do the ladies drink?

HORNER. Yes, sir; and I shall have the pleasure at least of laying 'em flat with a bottle, and bring as much scandal that way upon 'em as formerly t'other.

HARCOURT. Perhaps you may prove as weak

---

liquorish greedy; lecherous
set . . . hand provide free drinks
marker scorekeeper at dice; not one of the gamblers
in ure in practice

The Exchange an arcade of fashionable shops and stalls, fine for strolling, "window-shopping," and meeting acquaintances

a brother amongst 'em that way as t'other.

DORILANT. Foh! drinking with women is as unnatural as scolding with 'em. But 'tis a pleasure of decayed fornicators, and the basest way of quenching love.

HARCOURT. Nay, 'tis drowning love, instead of quenching it. But leave us for civil women too!

DORILANT. Ay, when he can't be the better for 'em. We hardly pardon a man that leaves his friend for a wench, and that's a pretty lawful call.

HORNER. Faith, I would not leave you for 'em, if they would not drink.

DORILANT. Who would disappoint his company at Lewis's° for a gossiping?

HARCOURT. Foh! Wine and women, good apart, together as nauseous as sack and sugar. But hark you, sir, before you go, a little of your advice; an old maimed general, when unfit for action, is fittest for counsel. I have other designs upon women than eating and drinking with them; I am in love with Sparkish's mistress, whom he is to marry tomorrow. Now how shall I get her?

[*Enter* SPARKISH, *looking about.*]

HORNER. Why, here comes one will help you to her.

HARCOURT. He! he, I tell you, is my rival, and will hinder my love.

HORNER. No; a foolish rival and a jealous husband assist their rival's designs, for they are sure to make their women hate them, which is the first step to their love for another man.

HARCOURT. But I cannot come near his mistress but in his company.

HORNER. Still the better for you; for fools are most easily cheated when they themselves are accessories, and he is to be bubbled° of his mistress as of his money, the common mistress, by keeping him company.

SPARKISH. Who is that that is to be bubbled? Faith, let me snack;° I han't met with a bubble since Christmas. 'Gad, I think bubbles are like their brother woodcocks,° go out with the cold weather.

HARCOURT [*apart to* HORNER]. A pox! he did not hear all, I hope.

SPARKISH. Come, you bubbling rogues you, where do we sup?—Oh, Harcourt, my mistress tells me you have been making fierce love to her all the play long: ha! ha! But I—

HARCOURT. I make love to her!

SPARKISH. Nay, I forgive thee, for I think I know thee, and I know her; but I am sure I know myself.

HARCOURT. Did she tell you so? I see all women are like these of the Exchange; who, to enhance the price of their commodities, report to their fond customers offers which were never made 'em.

HORNER. Ay, women are as apt to tell before the intrigue, as men after it, and so show themselves the vainer sex. But hast thou a mistress, Sparkish? 'Tis as hard for me to believe it as that thou ever hadst a bubble, as you bragged just now.

SPARKISH. Oh, your servant, sir; are you at your raillery, sir? But we were some of us beforehand with you today at the play. The wits were something bold with you, sir; did you not hear us laugh?

HORNER. Yes; but I thought you had gone to plays to laugh at the poet's wit, not at your own.

SPARKISH. Your servant, sir; no, I thank you. 'Gad, I go to a play as to a country treat; I carry my own wine to one, and my own wit to t'other, or else I'm sure I should not be merry at either. And the reason why we are so often louder than the players is because we think we speak more wit, and so become the poet's rivals in his audience; for to tell you the truth, we hate the silly rogues, nay, so much that we find fault even with their bawdy upon the stage, whilst we talk nothing else in the pit as loud.

HORNER. But why shouldst thou hate the silly

Lewis's unknown; presumably a tavern
bubbled swindled
snack have a share in it

woodcocks game birds in season in the fall; anyone readily deceived

poets? Thou hast too much wit to be one; and they, like whores, are only hated by each other; and thou dost scorn writing, I'm sure.

SPARKISH. Yes; I'd have you to know I scorn writing; but women, women, that make men do all foolish things, make 'em write songs too. Everybody does it. 'Tis even as common with lovers as playing with fans; and you can no more help rhyming to your Phyllis, than drinking to your Phyllis.

HARCOURT. Nay, poetry in love is no more to be avoided than jealousy.

DORILANT. But the poets damned your songs, did they?

SPARKISH. Damn the poets! they turned 'em into burlesque, as they call it. That burlesque is a hocus-pocus trick they have got, which, by the virtue of *Hictius doctius, topsy turvy*,° they make a wise and witty man in the world, a fool upon the stage, you know not how; and 'tis therefore I hate 'em too, for I know not but it may be my own case; for they'll put a man into a play for looking asquint. Their predecessors were contented to make serving-men only their stage-fools; but these rogues must have gentlemen with a pox to 'em, nay, knights; and, indeed, you shall hardly see a fool upon the stage but he's a knight. And to tell you the truth, they have kept me these six years from being a knight in earnest, for fear of being knighted in a play, and dubbed a fool.

DORILANT. Blame 'em not, they must follow their copy, the age.

HARCOURT. But why shouldst thou be afraid of being in a play, who expose yourself every day in the playhouses, and at public places?

HORNER. 'Tis but being on the stage, instead of standing on a bench in the pit.

DORILANT. Don't you give money to painters to draw you like? and are you afraid of your pictures at length in a playhouse, where all your mistresses may see you?

SPARKISH. A pox! painters don't draw the small-pox or pimples in one's face. Come, damn all your silly authors whatever, all books and booksellers, by the world, and all readers, courteous or uncourteous!

HARCOURT. But who comes here, Sparkish?

[*Enter* MR. PINCHWIFE *and his wife in man's clothes,* ALITHEA, LUCY *her maid.*]

SPARKISH. Oh, hide me! There's my mistress too. [SPARKISH *hides himself behind* HARCOURT.]

HARCOURT. She sees you.

SPARKISH. But I will not see her. 'Tis time to go to Whitehall, and I must not fail the drawing-room.

HARCOURT. Pray, first carry me, and reconcile me to her.

SPARKISH. Another time. Faith, the king will have supped.

HARCOURT. Not with the worse stomach for thy absence. Thou art one of those fools that think their attendance at the king's meals as necessary as his physicians', when you are more troublesome to him than his doctors or his dogs.

SPARKISH. Pshaw! I know my interest, sir. Prithee hide me.

HORNER. Your servant, Pinchwife.—What, he knows us not!

PINCHWIFE [*to his wife aside*]. Come along.

MRS. PINCHWIFE. Pray, have you any ballads? give me sixpenny worth.

CLASP. We have no ballads.

MRS. PINCHWIFE. Then give me "Covent Garden Drollery,"° and a play or two.—Oh, here's "Tarugo's Wiles," and "The Slighted Maiden"; I'll have them.

PINCHWIFE [*apart to her*]. No; plays are not for your reading. Come along; will you discover yourself?

HORNER. Who is that pretty youth with him, Sparkish?

SPARKISH. I believe his wife's brother, because he's something like her; but I never saw her but once.

HORNER. Extremely handsome; I have seen a face like it too. Let us follow 'em.

Hictius doctius, topsy turvy nonsense formulas for performing sleight-of-hand

"Covent Garden Drollery," etc. popular ballads and plays of the time

[*Exeunt* PINCHWIFE, MRS. PINCHWIFE, ALITHEA, LUCY, HORNER, DORILANT *following them.*]

HARCOURT. Come, Sparkish, your mistress saw you, and will be angry you go not to her.
5 Besides, I would fain be reconciled to her, which none but you can do, dear friend.

SPARKISH. Well, that's a better reason, dear friend. I would not go near her now for hers or my own sake; but I can deny you nothing;
10 for though I have known thee a great while, never go, if I do not love thee as well as a new acquaintance.

HARCOURT. I am obliged to you indeed, dear friend. I would be well with her, only to be
15 well with thee still; for these ties to wives usually dissolve all ties to friends. I would be contented she should enjoy you a-nights, but I would have you to myself a-days as I have had, dear friend.

20 SPARKISH. And thou shalt enjoy me a-days, dear, dear friend, never stir; and I'll be divorced from her, sooner than from thee. Come along.

HARCOURT [*aside*]. So, we are hard put to't,
25 when we make our rival our procurer; but neither she nor her brother would let me come near her now. When all's done, a rival is the best cloak to steal to a mistress under, without suspicion; and when we have once got to her
30 as we desire, we throw him off like other cloaks.

[*Exit* SPARKISH, *and* HARCOURT *following him.*]

[*Re-enter* PINCHWIFE, MRS. PINCHWIFE *in*
35 *man's clothes.*]

PINCHWIFE [*to* ALITHEA]. Sister, if you will not go, we must leave you.—[*Aside.*] The fool her gallant and she will muster up all the young saunterers of this place, and they will leave their
40 dear seamstresses° to follow us. What a swarm of cuckolds and cuckold-makers are here!— Come, let's be gone, Mistress Margery.

MRS. PINCHWIFE. Don't you believe that; I han't half my bellyfull of sights yet.

45 PINCHWIFE. Then walk this way.

MRS. PINCHWIFE. Lord, what a power of brave signs are here! stay—the Bull's-Head, the Ram's-Head, and the Stag's-Head, dear—

PINCHWIFE. Nay, if every husband's proper sign here were visible, they would be all alike. 50

MRS. PINCHWIFE. What d'ye mean by that, bud?

PINCHWIFE. 'Tis no matter—no matter, bud.

MRS. PINCHWIFE. Pray tell me: nay, I will know. 55

PINCHWIFE. They would be all Bulls',° Stags', and Rams'-heads.

[*Exeunt* MR. PINCHWIFE *and* MRS. PINCHWIFE.]

[*Re-enter* SPARKISH, HARCOURT, ALITHEA, LUCY, *at the other door.*] 60

SPARKISH. Come, dear madam, for my sake you shall be reconciled to him.

ALITHEA. For your sake I hate him.

HARCOURT. That's something too cruel, madam, to hate me for his sake. 65

SPARKISH. Ay indeed, madam, too, too cruel to me, to hate my friend for my sake.

ALITHEA. I hate him because he is your enemy; and you ought to hate him too, for making love to me, if you love me. 70

SPARKISH. That's a good one! I hate a man for loving you! If he did love you, 'tis but what he can't help; and 'tis your fault, not his, if he admires you; I hate a man for being of my opinion? I'll ne'er do't, by the world! 75

ALITHEA. Is it for your honor, or mine, to suffer a man to make love to me, who am to marry you tomorrow?

SPARKISH. Is it for your honor, or mine, to have me jealous? That he makes love to you, is 80 a sign you are handsome; and that I am not jealous, is a sign you are virtuous. That I think is for your honor.

ALITHEA. But 'tis your honor too I am concerned for. 85

HARCOURT. But why, dearest madam, will you be more concerned for his honor than he is himself? Let his honor alone, for my sake and his. He! he has no honor—

SPARKISH. How's that? 90

HARCOURT. But what my dear friend can guard himself.

SPARKISH. Oh ho—that's right again.

HARCOURT. Your care of his honor argues his

---

seamstresses dressmakers, often also prostitutes

Bulls', etc. with the usual allusion to cuckold's horns

neglect of it, which is no honor to my dear friend here. Therefore once more, let his honor go which way it will, dear madam.

SPARKISH. Ay, ay; were it for my honor to
5 marry a woman whose virtue I suspected, and could not trust her in a friend's hands?

ALITHEA. Are you not afraid to lose me?

HARCOURT. He afraid to lose you, madam! No, no—you may see how the most estimable
10 and most glorious creature in the world is valued by him. Will you not see it?

SPARKISH. Right, honest Frank, I have that noble value for her that I cannot be jealous of her.

15 ALITHEA. You mistake him. He means, you care not for me, nor who has me.

SPARKISH. Lord, madam, I see you are jealous. Will you wrest a poor man's meaning from his words?

20 ALITHEA. You astonish me, sir, with your want of jealousy.

SPARKISH. And you make me giddy, madam, with your jealousy and fears, and virtue and honor. 'Gad, I see virtue makes a woman as
25 troublesome as a little reading or learning.

ALITHEA. Monstrous!

LUCY [behind]. Well, to see what easy husbands these women of quality can meet with! A poor chambermaid can never have such lady-
30 like luck. Besides, he's thrown away upon her. She'll make no use of her fortune, her blessing, none to a gentleman, for a pure cuckold, for it requires good breeding to be a cuckold.

ALITHEA. I tell you then plainly, he pursues
35 me to marry me.

SPARKISH. Pshaw.

HARCOURT. Come, madam, you see you strive in vain to make him jealous of me. My dear friend is the kindest creature in the world to
40 me.

SPARKISH. Poor fellow.

HARCOURT. But his kindness only is not enough for me, without your favor, your good opinion, dear madam: 'tis that must perfect
45 my happiness. Good gentleman, he believes all I say; would you would do so. Jealous of me! I would not wrong him nor you for the world.

SPARKISH. Look you there. Hear him, hear him, and do not walk away so. [ALITHEA *walks* 50 *carelessly to and fro.*]

HARCOURT. I love you, madam, so—

SPARKISH. How's that? Nay, now you begin to go too far indeed.

HARCOURT. So much, I confess, I say, I love 55 you, that I would not have you miserable, and cast yourself away upon so unworthy and inconsiderable a thing as what you see here. [*Clapping his hand on his breast, points at* SPARKISH.] 60

SPARKISH. No, faith, I believe thou wouldst not; now his meaning is plain; but I knew before thou wouldst not wrong me, nor her.

HARCOURT. No, no, Heavens forbid the glory of her sex should fall so low, as into the em- 65 braces of such a contemptible wretch, the last of mankind—my dear friend here—I injure him! [*Embracing* SPARKISH.]

ALITHEA. Very well.

SPARKISH. No, no, dear friend, I knew it.— 70 Madam, you see he will rather wrong himself than me, in giving himself such names.

ALITHEA. Do you not understand him yet?

SPARKISH. Yes, how modestly he speaks of himself, poor fellow! 75

ALITHEA. Methinks he speaks impudently of yourself, since—before yourself too; insomuch that I can no longer suffer his scurrilous abusiveness to you, no more than his love to me. [*Offers to go.*] 80

SPARKISH. Nay, nay, madam, pray stay—his love to you! Lord, madam, has he not spoke yet plain enough?

ALITHEA. Yes, indeed, I should think so.

SPARKISH. Well then, by the world, a man 85 can't speak civilly to a woman now, but presently she says he makes love to her. Nay, madam, you shall stay, with your pardon, since you have not yet understood him, till he has made an *éclaircissement*° of his love to you, 90 that is, what kind of love it is. Answer to thy catechism, friend; do you love my mistress here?

HARCOURT. Yes, I wish she would not doubt it.

SPARKISH. But how do you love her? 95

HARCOURT. With all my soul.

éclaircissement disclosure (a faddish French word)

ALITHEA. I thank him, methinks he speaks plain enough now.

SPARKISH [to ALITHEA]. You are out still.—But with what kind of love, Harcourt?

5 HARCOURT. With the best and truest love in the world.

SPARKISH. Look you there then, that is with no matrimonial love, I'm sure.

ALITHEA. How's that? do you say matrimonial 10 love is not best?

SPARKISH. 'Gad, I went too far ere I was aware. But speak for thyself, Harcourt, you said you would not wrong me nor her.

HARCOURT. No, no, madam, e'en take him for 15 Heaven's sake—

SPARKISH. Look you there, madam.

HARCOURT. Who should in all justice be yours, he that loves you most. [Claps his hand on his breast.]

20 ALITHEA. Look you there, Mr. Sparkish, who's that?

SPARKISH. Who should it be?—Go on, Harcourt.

HARCOURT. Who loves you more than women 25 titles, or fortune fools. [Points at SPARKISH.]

SPARKISH. Look you there, he means me still, for he points at me.

ALITHEA. Ridiculous!

HARCOURT. Who can only match your faith 30 and constancy in love.

SPARKISH. Ay.

HARCOURT. Who knows, if it be possible, how to value so much beauty and virtue.

SPARKISH. Ay.

35 HARCOURT. Whose love can no more be equalled in the world, than that heavenly form of yours.

SPARKISH. No.

HARCOURT. Who could no more suffer a rival 40 than your absence, and yet could no more suspect your virtue than his own constancy in his love to you.

SPARKISH. No.

HARCOURT. Who, in fine, loves you better 45 than his eyes, that first made him love you.

SPARKISH. Ay—Nay, madam, faith, you shan't go till—

ALITHEA. Have a care, lest you make me stay too long.

SPARKISH. But till he has saluted you; that I 50 may be assured you are friends, after his honest advice and declaration. Come, pray, madam, be friends with him.

[Enter PINCHWIFE, MRS. PINCHWIFE.]

ALITHEA. You must pardon me, sir, that I 55 am not yet so obedient to you.

PINCHWIFE. What, invite your wife to kiss men? Monstrous! Are you not ashamed? I will never forgive you.

SPARKISH. Are you not ashamed that I should 60 have more confidence in the chastity of your family than you have? You must not teach me; I am a man of honor, sir, though I am frank and free; I am frank, sir—

PINCHWIFE. Very frank, sir, to share your 65 wife with your friends.

SPARKISH. He is an humble, menial friend, such as reconciles the differences of the marriage bed; you know man and wife do not always agree; I design him for that use, there- 70 fore would have him well with my wife.

PINCHWIFE. A menial friend!—you will get a great many menial friends, by showing your wife as you do.

SPARKISH. What then? It may be I have a 75 pleasure in't, as I have to show fine clothes at a playhouse the first day, and count money before poor rogues.

PINCHWIFE. He that shows his wife or money will be in danger of having them borrowed 80 sometimes.

SPARKISH. I love to be envied, and would not marry a wife that I alone could love; loving alone is as dull as eating alone. Is it not a frank age? and I am a frank person; and to tell you 85 the truth, it may be I love to have rivals in a wife; they make her seem to a man still but as a kept mistress; and so good night, for I must to Whitehall.—Madam, I hope you are now reconciled to my friend; and so I wish you a 90 good night, madam, and sleep if you can; for tomorrow you know I must visit you early with a canonical gentleman.° Good night, dear Harcourt.

canonical gentleman clergyman

[*Exit* SPARKISH.]

HARCOURT. Madam, I hope you will not refuse my visit tomorrow, if it should be earlier
with a canonical gentleman than Mr. Spar-
5 kish's.

PINCHWIFE. This gentlewoman is yet under
my care, therefore you must yet forbear your
freedom with her, sir. [*Coming between* ALI-
THEA *and* HARCOURT.]

10 HARCOURT. Must, sir?

PINCHWIFE. Yes, sir, she is my sister.

HARCOURT. 'Tis well she is, sir—for I must be
her servant, sir.—Madam—

PINCHWIFE. Come away, sister, we had been
15 gone if it had not been for you, and so avoided
these lewd rake-hells, who seem to haunt us.

[*Enter* HORNER, DORILANT.]

HORNER. How now, Pinchwife!

PINCHWIFE. Your servant.

20 HORNER. What! I see a little time in the country makes a man turn wild and unsociable, and
only fit to converse with his horses, dogs, and
his herds.

PINCHWIFE. I have business, sir, and must
25 mind it; your business is pleasure; therefore
you and I must go different ways.

HORNER. Well, you may go on, but this pretty
young gentleman—[*takes hold of* MRS. PINCH-
WIFE].

30 HARCOURT. The lady—

DORILANT. And the maid—

HORNER. Shall stay with us; for I suppose
their business is the same with ours, pleasure.

PINCHWIFE [*aside*]. 'Sdeath, he knows her,
35 she carries it so sillily! Yet if he does not, I
should be more silly to discover it first.

ALITHEA. Pray, let us go, sir.

PINCHWIFE. Come, come—

HORNER [*to* MRS. PINCHWIFE]. Had you not
40 rather stay with us?—Prithee, Pinchwife, who
is this pretty young gentleman?

PINCHWIFE. One to whom I'm a guardian.—
[*Aside*.] I wish I could keep her out of your
hands.

45 HORNER. Who is he? I never saw anything so
pretty in all my life.

PINCHWIFE. Pshaw! do not look upon him so
much, he's a poor bashful youth; you'll put

him out of countenance.—Come away, brother.
[*Offers to take her away*.]   50

HORNER. Oh, your brother!

PINCHWIFE. Yes, my wife's brother.—Come,
come, she'll stay supper for us.

HORNER. I thought so, for he is very like her
I saw you at the play with, whom I told you I   55
was in love with.

MRS. PINCHWIFE [*aside*]. O jeminy! is this he
that was in love with me? I am glad on't, I vow,
for he's a curious fine gentleman, and I love him
already, too.—[*To* PINCHWIFE.] Is this he, bud?   60

PINCHWIFE [*to his wife*]. Come away, come
away.

HORNER. Why, what haste are you in? Why
won't you let me walk with him?

PINCHWIFE. Because you'll debauch him: he's   65
yet young and innocent, and I would not have
him debauched for anything in the world.—
[*Aside*.] How she gazes on him! the devil!

HORNER. Harcourt, Dorilant, look you here,
this is the likeness of that dowdy he told us of,   70
his wife; did you ever see a lovelier creature?
The rogue has reason to be jealous of his wife,
since she is like him, for she would make all
that see her in love with her.

HARCOURT. And, as I remember now, she is   75
as like him here as can be.

DORILANT. She is indeed very pretty, if she be
like him.

HORNER. Very pretty? a very pretty condemnation!—she is a glorious creature, beau-   80
tiful beyond all things I ever beheld.

PINCHWIFE. So, so.

HARCOURT. More beautiful than a poet's first
mistress of imagination.

HORNER. Or another man's last mistress of   85
flesh and blood.

MRS. PINCHWIFE. Nay, now you jeer, sir;
pray don't jeer me.

PINCHWIFE. Come, come.—[*Aside*.] By Heavens, she'll discover herself!   90

HORNER. I speak of your sister, sir.

PINCHWIFE. Ay, but saying she was handsome, if like him, made him blush.—[*Aside*.] I
am upon a rack!

HORNER. Methinks he is so handsome he   95
should not be a man.

PINCHWIFE [*aside*]. Oh, there 'tis out! he has discovered her! I am not able to suffer any longer.—[*To his wife.*] Come, come away, I say.

5 HORNER. Nay, by your leave, sir, he shall not go yet. [*Aside to them.*] Harcourt, Dorilant, let us torment this jealous rogue a little.

HARCOURT. ⎫
DORILANT. ⎬ How?
⎭

10 HORNER. I'll show you.

PINCHWIFE. Come, pray let him go, I cannot stay fooling any longer; I tell you his sister stays supper for us.

HORNER. Does she? Come then, we'll all go 15 sup with her and thee.

PINCHWIFE. No, now I think on't, having stayed so long for us, I warrant she's gone to bed.—[*Aside.*] I wish she and I were well out of their hands.—Come, I must rise early tomor- 20 row, come.

HORNER. Well then, if she be gone to bed, I wish her and you a good night. But pray, young gentleman, present my humble service to her.

MRS. PINCHWIFE. Thank you heartily, sir.

25 PINCHWIFE [*aside*]. 'Sdeath she will discover herself yet in spite of me.—He is something more civil to you, for your kindness to his sis- ter, than I am, it seems.

HORNER. Tell her, dear sweet little gentle- 30 man, for all your brother there, that you have revived the love I had for her at first sight in the playhouse.

MRS. PINCHWIFE. But did you love her in- deed, and indeed?

35 PINCHWIFE [*aside*]. So, so.--Away, I say.

HORNER. Nay, stay.—Yes, indeed, and in- deed, pray do you tell her so, and give her this kiss from me. [*Kisses her.*]

PINCHWIFE [*aside*]. O Heavens! what do I 40 suffer? Now 'tis too plain he knows her, and yet—

HORNER. And this, and this—[*kisses her again*].

MRS. PINCHWIFE. What do you kiss me for? 45 I am no woman.

PINCHWIFE [*aside*]. So, there, 'tis out.—Come, I cannot, nor will stay any longer.

HORNER. Nay, they shall send your lady a kiss too. Here, Harcourt, Dorilant, will you not? [*They kiss her.*] 50

PINCHWIFE [*aside*]. How! do I suffer this? Was I not accusing another just now for this rascally patience, in permitting his wife to be kissed before his face? Ten thousand ulcers gnaw away their lips.—Come, come. 55

HORNER. Good night, dear little gentleman; madam, good night; farewell, Pinchwife.— [*Apart to* HARCOURT *and* DORILANT.] Did not I tell you I would raise his jealous gall?

[*Exeunt* HORNER, HARCOURT, *and* DORILANT.] 60

PINCHWIFE. So, they are gone at last; stay, let me see first if the coach be at this door.

[*Exit.*]

[HORNER. HARCOURT, DORILANT *return.*]

HORNER. What, not gone yet? Will you be 65 sure to do as I desired you, sweet sir?

MRS. PINCHWIFE. Sweet sir, but what will you give me then?

HORNER. Anything. Come away into the next walk. 70

[*Exit, haling away* MRS. PINCHWIFE.]

ALITHEA. Hold! hold! what d'ye do?

LUCY. Stay, stay, hold—

HARCOURT. Hold, madam, hold, let him pre- sent him—he'll come presently; nay, I will 75 never let you go till you answer my question. [ALITHEA, LUCY, *struggling with* HARCOURT *and* DORILANT.]

LUCY. For God's sake, sir, I must follow 'em.

DORILANT. No, I have something to present 80 you with too, you shan't follow them.

[PINCHWIFE *returns.*]

PINCHWIFE. Where?—how—what's become of?—gone!—whither?

LUCY. He's only gone with the gentleman, 85 who will give him something, an't please your worship.

PINCHWIFE. Something!—give him something, with a pox!—where are they?

ALITHEA. In the next walk only, brother. 90

PINCHWIFE. Only, only! where, where?

[*Exit* PINCHWIFE *and returns presently, then goes out again.*]

HARCOURT. What's the matter with him?

Why so much concerned? But, dearest madam—

ALITHEA. Pray let me go, sir; I have said and suffered enough already.

HARCOURT. Then you will not look upon, nor pity, my sufferings?

ALITHEA. To look upon 'em, when I cannot help 'em, were cruelty, not pity; therefore, I will never see you more.

HARCOURT. Let me then, madam, have my privilege of a banished lover, complaining or railing, and giving you but a farewell reason why, if you cannot condescend to marry me, you should not take that wretch, my rival.

ALITHEA. He only, not you, since my honor is engaged so far to him, can give me a reason why I should not marry him; but if he be true, and what I think him to me; I must be so to him. Your servant, sir.

HARCOURT. Have women only constancy when 'tis a vice, and, like Fortune, only true to fools?

DORILANT [*to* LUCY, *who struggles to get from him.*] Thou shalt not stir, thou robust creature; you see, I can deal with you, therefore you should stay the rather, and be kind.

[*Enter* PINCHWIFE.]

PINCHWIFE. Gone, gone, not to be found! quite gone! ten thousand plagues go with 'em! which way went they?

ALITHEA. But into t'other walk, brother.

LUCY. Their business will be done presently sure, an't please your worship; it can't be long in doing, I'm sure on't.

ALITHEA. Are they not there?

PINCHWIFE. No, you know where they are, you infamous wretch, eternal shame of your family, which you do not dishonor enough yourself, you think, but you must help her to do it too, thou legion of bawds!

ALITHEA. Good brother—

PINCHWIFE. Damned, damned sister!

ALITHEA. Look you here, she's coming.

[*Enter* MRS. PINCHWIFE *in man's clothes, running, with her hat under her arm, full of oranges and dried fruit,* HORNER *following.*]

MRS. PINCHWIFE. O dear bud, look you here what I have got, see!

PINCHWIFE [*aside, rubbing his forehead*]. And what I have got here too, which you can't see.

MRS. PINCHWIFE. The fine gentleman has given me better things yet.

PINCHWIFE. Has he so?—[*Aside.*] Out of breath and colored!°—I must hold yet.

HORNER. I have only given your little brother an orange, sir.

PINCHWIFE [*to* HORNER]. Thank you, sir.— [*Aside.*] You have only squeezed my orange, I suppose, and given it me again; yet I must have a city patience.—[*To his wife.*] Come, come away.

MRS. PINCHWIFE. Stay, till I have put up my fine things, bud.

[*Enter* SIR JASPER FIDGET.]

SIR JASPER FIDGET. O, Master Horner, come, come, the ladies stay for you; your mistress, my wife, wonders you make not more haste to her.

HORNER. I have stayed this half hour for you here, and 'tis your fault I am not now with your wife.

SIR JASPER FIDGET. But, pray, don't let her know so much; the truth on't is, I was advancing a certain project to his majesty— about—I'll tell you.

HORNER. No, let's go, and hear it at your house.—Good night, sweet little gentleman; one kiss more, you'll remember me now, I hope. [*Kisses her.*]

DORILANT. What, Sir Jasper, will you separate friends? He promised to sup with us, and if you take him to your house, you'll be in danger of our company too.

SIR JASPER FIDGET. Alas! gentlemen, my house is not fit for you; there are none but civil women there, which are not for your turn. He, you know, can bear with the society of civil women now, ha! ha! ha! besides, he's one of my family—he's—he! he! he!

DORILANT. What is he?

SIR JASPER FIDGET. Faith, my eunuch, since you'll have it; he! he! he!

colored blushing

[*Exeunt* SIR JASPER FIDGET *and* HORNER.]

DORILANT. I rather wish thou wert his or my cuckold. Harcourt, what a good cuckold is lost there for want of a man to make him one!
5 Thee and I cannot have Horner's privilege, who can make use of it.

HARCOURT. Ay, to poor Horner 'tis like coming to an estate at three-score, when a man can't be the better for't.

10 PINCHWIFE. Come.

MRS. PINCHWIFE. Presently, bud.

DORILANT. Come, let us go too.—[*To* ALITHEA.] Madam, your servant.—[*To* LUCY.] Good night, strapper.

15 HARCOURT. Madam, though you will not let me have a good day or night, I wish you one; but dare not name the other half of my wish.

ALITHEA. Good night, sir, for ever.

MRS. PINCHWIFE. I don't know where to put
20 this here, dear bud, you shall eat it; nay, you shall have part of the fine gentleman's good things, or treat, as you call it, when we come home.

PINCHWIFE. Indeed, I deserve it, since I fur-
25 nished the best part of it. [*Strikes away the orange.*]

The gallant treats presents, and gives the ball,

But 'tis the absent cuckold pays for all.

ACT IV

Scene i

30 [PINCHWIFE'S *house in the morning.*]

[*Enter* LUCY, ALITHEA *dressed in new clothes.*]

LUCY. Well, madam, now have I dressed you, and set you out with so many ornaments, and
35 spent upon you ounces of essence and pul-villio;° and all this for no other purpose but as people adorn and perfume a corpse for a stinking second-hand grave; such, or as bad, I think Master Sparkish's bed.

40 ALITHEA. Hold your peace.

LUCY. Nay, madam, I will ask you the reason why you should banish poor Master Harcourt for ever from your sight; how could you be so hard-hearted?

ALITHEA. 'Twas because I was not hard- 45 hearted.

LUCY. No, no; 'twas stark love and kindness, I warrant.

ALITHEA. It was so; I would see him no more because I love him. 50

LUCY. Hey day, a very pretty reason!

ALITHEA. You do not understand me.

LUCY. I wish you may yourself.

ALITHEA. I was engaged to marry, you see, another man, whom my justice will not suffer 55 me to deceive or injure.

LUCY. Can there be a greater cheat or wrong done to a man than to give him your person without your heart? I should make a con-science of it. 60

ALITHEA. I'll retrieve it for him after I am married a while.

LUCY. The woman that marries to love better will be as much mistaken as the wencher that marries to live better. No, 65 madam, marrying to increase love is like gaming to become rich; alas! you only lose what little stock you had before.

ALITHEA. I find by your rhetoric you have been bribed to betray me. 70

LUCY. Only by his merit, that has bribed your heart, you see, against your word and rigid honor. But what a devil is this honor! 'tis sure a disease in the head, like the megrim or falling-sickness,° that always hurries people 75 away to do themselves mischief. Men lose their lives by it; women, what's dearer to 'em, their love, the life of life.

ALITHEA. Come, pray talk you no more of honor, nor Master Harcourt; I wish the other 80 would come to secure my fidelity to him and his right in me.

LUCY. You will marry him then?

ALITHEA. Certainly; I have given him already my word, and will my hand too, to 85 make it good, when he comes.

LUCY. Well, I wish I may never stick pin more, if he be not an arrant natural to° t'other fine gentleman.

pulvillio scented powder

megrim or falling-sickness dizziness or epilepsy
natural to fool as compared with

ALITHEA. I own he wants the wit of Harcourt, which I will dispense withal for another want he has, which is want of jealousy, which men of wit seldom want.

5 LUCY. Lord, madam, what should you do with a fool to your husband? You intend to be honest, don't you? Then that husbandly virtue, credulity, is thrown away upon you.

ALITHEA. He only that could suspect my
10 virtue should have cause to do it; 'tis Sparkish's confidence in my truth that obliges me to be so faithful to him.

LUCY. You are not sure his opinion may last.

ALITHEA. I am satisfied 'tis impossible for
15 him to be jealous after the proofs I have had of him. Jealousy in a husband—Heaven defend me from it! it begets a thousand plagues to a poor woman, the loss of her honor, her quiet, and her—

20 LUCY. And her pleasure.

ALITHEA. What d'ye mean, impertinent?

LUCY. Liberty is a great pleasure, madam.

ALITHEA. I say, loss of her honor, her quiet, nay, her life sometimes; and what's as bad
25 almost, the loss of this town; that is, she is sent into the country, which is the last ill-usage of a husband to a wife, I think.

LUCY [*aside*]. Oh, does the wind lie there?— Then of necessity, madam, you think a man
30 must carry his wife into the country, if he be wise. The country is as terrible, I find, to our young English ladies, as a monastery to those abroad; and, on my virginity, I think they would rather marry a London jailer than a
35 high sheriff of a county, since neither can stir from his employment. Formerly women of wit married fools for a great estate, a fine seat,° or the like; but now 'tis for a pretty seat only in Lincoln's Inn Fields,° St. James's Fields, or the
40 Pall Mall.

[*Enter* SPARKISH, *and* HARCOURT, *dressed like a parson.*]

SPARKISH. Madam, your humble servant, a happy day to you, and to us all.

45 HARCOURT. Amen.

ALITHEA. Who have we here?

SPARKISH. My Chaplain, faith—O madam, poor Harcourt remembers his humble service to you; and, in obedience to your last commands, refrains coming into your sight.   50

ALITHEA. Is not that he?

SPARKISH. No, fy, no; but to show that he ne'er intended to hinder our match, has sent his brother here to join our hands. When I get me a wife, I must get her a chaplain, according   55 to the custom; this is his brother, and my chaplain.

ALITHEA. His brother!

LUCY. [*aside*]. And your chaplain, to preach in your pulpit then—   60

ALITHEA. His brother!

SPARKISH. Nay, I knew you would not believe it.—I told you, sir, she would take you for your brother Frank.

ALITHEA. Believe it!   65

LUCY [*aside*]. His brother! ha! ha! ha! He has a trick left still, it seems.

SPARKISH. Come, my dearest, pray let us go to church before the canonical hour° is past.

ALITHEA. For shame, you are abused still.   70

SPARKISH. By the world, 'tis strange now you are so incredulous.

ALITHEA. 'Tis strange you are so credulous.

SPARKISH. Dearest of my life, hear me. I tell you this is Ned Harcourt of Cambridge, by the   75 world; you see he has a sneaking college look. 'Tis true he's something like his brother Frank; and they differ from each other no more than in their age, for they were twins.

LUCY. Ha! ha! he!   80

ALITHEA. Your servant, sir; I cannot be so deceived, though you are. But come, let's hear, how do you know what you affirm so confidently?

SPARKISH. Why, I'll tell you all. Frank Har-   85 court coming to me this morning to wish me joy, and present his service to you, I asked him if he could help me to a parson. Whereupon he told me he had a brother in town who was in orders; and he went straight away, and sent   90 him, you see there, to me.

---

fine seat   well-situated country house
Lincoln's Inn Fields, etc.   fashionable places for promenades

canonical hour   noon. Weddings were required to be performed in the morning.

ALITHEA. Yes, Frank goes and puts on a black coat, then tells you he is Ned; that's all you have for't.

SPARKISH. Pshaw! pshaw! I tell you, by the
5 same token, the midwife put her garter about Frank's neck, to know 'em asunder, they were so like.

ALITHEA. Frank tells you this too?

SPARKISH. Ay, and Ned there too; nay, they
10 are both in a story.

ALITHEA. So, so; very foolish.

SPARKISH. Lord, if you won't believe one, you had best try him by your chambermaid there; for chambermaids must needs know
15 chaplains from other men, they are so used to 'em.

LUCY. Let's see; nay, I'll be sworn he has the canonical smirk, and the filthy clammy palm of a chaplain.

20 ALITHEA. Well, most reverend doctor, pray let us make an end of this fooling.

HARCOURT. With all my soul, divine heavenly creature, when you please.

ALITHEA. He speaks like a chaplain indeed.

25 SPARKISH. Why, was there not soul, divine, heavenly, in what he said?

ALITHEA. Once more, most impertinent black coat, cease your persecution, and let us have a conclusion of this ridiculous love.

30 HARCOURT [aside]. I had forgot; I must suit my style to my coat, or I wear it in vain.

ALITHEA. I have no more patience left; let us make once an end of this troublesome love, I say.

35 HARCOURT. So be it, seraphic lady, when your honor shall think it meet and convenient so to do.

SPARKISH. 'Gad, I'm sure none but a chaplain could speak so, I think.

40 ALITHEA. Let me tell you, sir, this dull trick will not serve your turn; though you delay our marriage, you shall not hinder it.

HARCOURT. Far be it from me, munificent patroness, to delay your marriage; I desire
45 nothing more than to marry you presently, which I might do, if you yourself would; for my noble, good-natured, and thrice generous patron here would not hinder it.

SPARKISH. No, poor man, not I, faith.

HARCOURT. And now, madam, let me tell 50 you plainly nobody else shall marry you. By Heavens! I'll die first, for I'm sure I should die after it.

LUCY. How his love has made him forget his function, as I have seen it in real parsons! 55

ALITHEA. That was spoken like a chaplain too? Now you understand him, I hope.

SPARKISH. Poor man, he takes it heinously to be refused; I can't blame him, 'tis putting an indignity upon him, not to be suffered; but 60 you'll pardon me, madam, it shan't be; he shall marry us; come away, pray, madam.

LUCY. Ha! ha! he! more ado! 'tis late.

ALITHEA. Invincible stupidity! I tell you, he would marry me as your rival, not as your 65 chaplain.

SPARKISH. Come, come, madam. [Pulling her away.]

LUCY. I pray, madam, do not refuse this reverend divine the honor and satisfaction of 70 marrying you; for I dare say he has set his heart upon't, good doctor.

ALITHEA. What can you hope or design by this?

HARCOURT [aside]. I could answer her, a 75 reprieve for a day only, often revokes a hasty doom. At worst, if she will not take mercy on me, and let me marry her, I have at least the lover's second pleasure, hindering my rival's enjoyment, though but for a time. 80

SPARKISH. Come, madam, t'is e'en twelve o'clock, and my mother charged me never to be married out of the canonical hours. Come, come; Lord, here's such a deal of modesty, I warrant, the first day. 85

LUCY. Yes, an't please your worship, married women show all their modesty the first day, because married men show all their love the first day.

[Exeunt SPARKISH, ALITHEA, HARCOURT, and 90 LUCY.]

Scene ii

[The scene changes to a bedchamber, where appear PINCHWIFE and MRS. PINCHWIFE.]

PINCHWIFE. Come, tell me, I say.

MRS. PINCHWIFE. Lord! han't I told it an hundred times over?

PINCHWIFE [*aside*]. I would try, if in the repetition of the ungrateful tale, I could find her altering it in the least circumstance; for if her story be false, she is so too.—Come, how was't, baggage?

MRS. PINCHWIFE. Lord, what pleasure you take to hear it, sure!

PINCHWIFE. No, you take more in telling it, I find; but speak, how was't?

MRS. PINCHWIFE. He carried me up into the house next to the Exchange.

PINCHWIFE. So, and you two were only in the room!

MRS. PINCHWIFE. Yes, for he sent away a youth that was there, for some dried fruits and China orange.

PINCHWIFE. Did he so? Damn him for it— and for—

MRS. PINCHWIFE. But presently came up the gentlewoman of the house.

PINCHWIFE. Oh, 'twas well she did; but what did he do whilst the fruit came?

MRS. PINCHWIFE. He kissed me an hundred times, and told me he fancied he kissed my fine sister, meaning me, you know, whom he said he loved with all his soul, and bid me be sure to tell her so, and to desire her to be at her window, by eleven of the clock this morning, and he would walk under at that time.

PINCHWIFE [*aside*]. And he was as good as his word, very punctual; a pox reward him for't.

MRS. PINCHWIFE. Well, and he said if you were not within, he would come up to her, meaning me, you know, bud, still.

PINCHWIFE [*aside*]. So—he knew her certainly; but for this confession, I am obliged to her simplicity.—But what, you stood very still when he kissed you?

MRS. PINCHWIFE. Yes, I warrant you; would you have had me discover myself?

PINCHWIFE. But you told me he did some beastliness to you, as you call it; what was't?

MRS. PINCHWIFE. Why, he put—

PINCHWIFE. What?

MRS. PINCHWIFE. Why, he put the tip of his tongue between my lips, and so mousled me— and I said, I'd bite it.

PINCHWIFE. An eternal canker seize it, for a dog!

MRS. PINCHWIFE. Nay, you need not be so angry with him neither, for to say truth, he has the sweetest breath I ever knew.

PINCHWIFE. The devil! you were satisfied with it then, and would do it again?

MRS. PINCHWIFE. Not unless he should force me.

PINCHWIFE. Force you, changeling!° I tell you, no woman can be forced.

MRS. PINCHWIFE. Yes, but she may sure, by such a one as he, for he's a proper, goodly, strong man; 'tis hard, let me tell you, to resist him.

PINCHWIFE. [*aside*]. So, 'tis plain she loves him, yet she has not love enough to make her conceal it from me; but the sight of him will increase her aversion for me and love for him, and that love instruct her how to deceive me and satisfy him, all idiot as she is. Love! 'twas he gave women first their craft, their art of deluding. Out of Nature's hands they came plain, open, silly, and fit for slaves, as she and Heaven intended 'em; but damned Love—well —I must strangle that little monster whilst I can deal with him.—Go fetch pen, ink, and paper out of the next room.

MRS. PINCHWIFE. Yes, bud.

PINCHWIFE. Why should women have more invention in love than men? It can only be because they have more desires, more soliciting passions, more lust, and more of the devil.

[MRS. PINCHWIFE *returns.*]
Come, minx, sit down and write.

MRS. PINCHWIFE. Ay, dear bud, but I can't do't very well.

PINCHWIFE. I wish you could not at all.

MRS. PINCHWIFE. But what should I write for?

PINCHWIFE. I'll have you write a letter to your lover.

MRS. PINCHWIFE. O Lord, to the fine gentleman a letter!

changeling idiot

PINCHWIFE. Yes, to the fine gentleman.

MRS. PINCHWIFE. Lord, you do but jeer; sure you jest.

PINCHWIFE. I am not so merry; come, write
5 as I bid you.

MRS. PINCHWIFE. What, do you think I am a fool?

PINCHWIFE [aside]. She's afraid I would not dictate any love to him, therefore she's un-
10 willing.—But you had best begin.

MRS. PINCHWIFE. Indeed, and indeed, but I won't, so I won't.

PINCHWIFE. Why?

MRS. PINCHWIFE. Because he's in town; you
15 may send for him if you will.

PINCHWIFE. Very well, you would have him brought to you; is it come to this? I say, take the pen and write, or you'll provoke me.

MRS. PINCHWIFE. Lord, what d'ye make a
20 fool of me for? Don't I know that letters are never writ but from the country to London, and from London into the country? Now he's in town, and I am in town too; therefore I can't write to him, you know.

25 PINCHWIFE [aside]. So, I am glad it is no worse; she is innocent enough yet.—Yes, you may, when your husband bids you, write letters to people that are in town.

MRS. PINCHWIFE. Oh, may I so? then I'm
30 satisfied.

PINCHWIFE. Come, begin [dictates]—"Sir"—

MRS. PINCHWIFE. Shan't I say, "Dear Sir"? You know one says always something more than bare "Sir."

35 PINCHWIFE. Write as I bid you, or I will write whore with this penknife in your face.

MRS. PINCHWIFE. Nay, good bud [she writes] —"Sir"—

PINCHWIFE. "Though I suffered last night
40 your nauseous, loathed kisses and embraces" —Write!

MRS. PINCHWIFE. Nay, why should I say so? You know I told you he had a sweet breath.

PINCHWIFE. Write!

45 MRS. PINCHWIFE. Let me but put out "loathed."

PINCHWIFE. Write, I say!

MRS. PINCHWIFE. Well then. [Writes.]

PINCHWIFE. Let's see, what have you writ?—
[Takes the paper and reads.] "Though I suf- 50
fered last night your kisses and embraces"—
Thou impudent creature! where is "nauseous"
and "loathed"?

MRS. PINCHWIFE. I can't abide to write such
filthy words. 55

PINCHWIFE. Once more write as I'd have you,
and question it not, or I will spoil thy writing
with this. I will stab out those eyes that cause
my mischief. [Holds up the penknife.]

MRS. PINCHWIFE. O Lord! I will. 60

PINCHWIFE. So—so—let's see now.—[Reads.]
"Though I suffered last night your nauseous,
loathed kisses and embraces"—go on—"yet I
would not have you presume that you shall
ever repeat them"—so—.[She writes.] 65

MRS. PINCHWIFE. I have writ it.

PINCHWIFE. On, then—"I then concealed
myself from your knowledge, to avoid your
insolencies."—[She writes.]

MRS. PINCHWIFE. So— 70

PINCHWIFE. "The same reason, now I am out
of your hands"—.[She writes.]

MRS. PINCHWIFE. So—

PINCHWIFE. "Makes me own to you my unfortunate, though innocent frolic, of being in 75
man's clothes"—.[She writes.]

MRS. PINCHWIFE. So—

PINCHWIFE. "That you may for evermore
cease to pursue her, who hates and detests you"
—.[She writes on.] 80

MRS. PINCHWIFE. So-h—[sighs].

PINCHWIFE. What, do you sigh?—"detests
you—as much as she loves her husband and
her honor."

MRS. PINCHWIFE. I vow, husband, he'll ne'er 85
believe I should write such a letter.

PINCHWIFE. What, he'd expect a kinder
from you? Come, now your name only.

MRS. PINCHWIFE. What, shan't I say "Your
most faithful humble servant till death"? 90

PINCHWIFE. No, tormenting fiend!—[Aside.]
Her style, I find, would be very soft.—Come,
wrap it up now, whilst I go fetch wax and a
candle; and write on the backside, "For Mr.
Horner." 95

[Exit PINCHWIFE.]

MRS. PINCHWIFE. "For Mr. Horner."—So, I am glad he has told me his name. Dear Mr. Horner! But why should I send thee such a letter that will vex thee, and make thee angry
5 with me?—Well, I will not send it.—Ay, but then my husband will kill me—for I see plainly he won't let me love Mr. Horner—but what care I for my husband? I won't, so I won't, send poor Mr. Horner such a letter.—
10 But then my husband—but oh, what if I writ at bottom my husband made me write it?— Ay, but then my husband would see't.—Can one have no shift?° Ah, a London woman would have had a hundred presently. Stay—
15 what if I should write a letter, and wrap it up like this, and write upon't too? Ay, but then my husband would see't—I don't know what to do.—But yet evads° I'll try, so I will—for I will not send this letter to poor Mr. Horner,
20 come what will on't.

"Dear, sweet Mr. Horner"—[*she writes and repeats what she hath writ*]—so—"my husband would have me send you a base, rude, unmannerly letter; but I won't"—so—"and
25 would have me forbid you loving me; but I won't"—so—"and would have me say to you, I hate you, poor Mr. Horner; but I won't tell a lie for him"—there—"for I'm sure if you and I were in the country at cards together"—
30 so—"I could not help treading on your toe under the table"—so—"or rubbing knees with you, and staring in your face, till you saw me" —very well—"and then looking down, and blushing for an hour together"—so—"but I
35 must make haste before my husband come; and now he has taught me to write letters, you shall have longer ones from me, who am, dear, dear, poor, dear Mr. Horner, your most humble friend, and servant to command till
40 death.—Margery Pinchwife."

Stay, I must give him a hint at bottom—so —now wrap it up just like t'other—so—now write "For Mr. Horner"—But oh now, what shall I do with it? for here comes my husband.
45 [*Enter* PINCHWIFE.]

PINCHWIFE [*aside*]. I have been detained by a sparkish coxcomb, who pretended a visit to me; but I fear 'twas to my wife.—What, have you done?
MRS. PINCHWIFE. Ay, ay, bud, just now. 50
PINCHWIFE. Let's see't; what d'ye tremble for? what, you would not have it go?
MRS. PINCHWIFE. Here.—[*Aside*.] No, I must not give him that; so I had been served if I had given him this. [*He opens and reads the* 55 *first letter.*]
PINCHWIFE. Come, where's the wax and seal?
MRS. PINCHWIFE [*aside*]. Lord, what shall I do now? Nay, then I have it.—Pray let me see't. Lord, you think me so arrant a fool I 60 cannot seal a letter; I will do't, so I will. [*Snatches the letter from him, changes it for the other, seals it, and delivers it to him.*]
PINCHWIFE. Nay, I believe you will learn that, and other things too, which I would not 65 have you.
MRS. PINCHWIFE. So, han't I done it curiously?°—[*Aside*.] I think I have; there's my letter going to Mr. Horner, since he'll needs have me send letters to folks. 70
PINCHWIFE. 'Tis very well; but I warrant you would not have it go now?
MRS. PINCHWIFE. Yes, indeed, but I would, bud, now.
PINCHWIFE. Well, you are a good girl then. 75 Come, let me lock you up in your chamber till I come back; and be sure you come not within three strides of the window when I am gone, for I have a spy in the street.—[*Exit* MRS. PINCHWIFE. PINCHWIFE *locks the door.*] At least, 80 'tis fit she think so. If we do not cheat women, they'll cheat us, and fraud may be justly used with secret enemies, of which a wife is the most dangerous; and he that has a handsome one to keep, and a frontier town, must provide 85 against treachery, rather than open force. Now I have secured all within, I'll deal with the foe without, with false intelligence. [*Holds up the letter.*]
[*Exit.*] 90

shift method of evasion
evads in faith

curiously nicely

Scene iii

[*The scene changes to* HORNER's *lodging.*]
[*Enter* QUACK *and* HORNER.]

QUACK. Well, sir, how fadges° the new design? Have you not the luck of all your brother projectors, to deceive only yourself at last?

HORNER. No, good domine° doctor, I deceive you, it seems, and others too; for the grave matrons, and old, rigid husbands think me as unfit for love as they are; but their wives, sisters, and daughters know, some of 'em, better things already.

QUACK. Already!

HORNER. Already, I say. Last night I was drunk with half-a-dozen of your civil persons, as you call 'em, and people of honor, and so was made free of their society and dressing-rooms for ever hereafter; and am already come to the privileges of sleeping upon their pallets, warming smocks, tying shoes and garters, and the like, doctor, already, already, doctor.

QUACK. You have made use of your time, sir.

HORNER. I tell thee, I am now no more interruption to 'em when they sing, or talk bawdy, than a little squab° French page who speaks no English.

QUACK. But do civil persons and women of honor drink, and sing bawdy songs?

HORNER. Oh, amongst friends, amongst friends. For your bigots in honor are just like those in religion; they fear the eye of the world more than the eye of Heaven, and think there is no virtue but railing at vice, and no sin but giving scandal. They rail at a poor little kept player, and keep themselves some young modest pulpit comedian° to be privy to their sins in their closets,° not to tell 'em of them in their chapels.

QUACK. Nay, the truth on't is, priests,

amongst the women now, have quite got the better of us lay-confessors, physicians.

HORNER. And they are rather their patients; but—

[*Enter* LADY FIDGET, *looking about her.*]
Now we talk of women of honor, here comes one. Step behind the screen there, and but observe if I have not particular privileges with the women of reputation already, doctor, already.

[QUACK *retires.*]

LADY FIDGET. Well, Horner, am not I a woman of honor? You see, I'm as good as my word.

HORNER. And you shall see, madam, I'll not be behindhand with you in honor; and I'll be as good as my word too, if you please but to withdraw into the next room.

LADY FIDGET. But first, my dear sir, you must promise to have a care of my dear honor.

HORNER. If you talk a word more of your honor, you'll make me incapable to wrong it. To talk of honor in the mysteries of love, is like talking of Heaven or the Diety in an operation of witchcraft just when you are employing the devil; it makes the charm impotent.

LADY FIDGET. Nay, fy! let us not be smutty. But you talk of mysteries and bewitching to me; I don't understand you.

HORNER. I tell you, madam, the word money in a mistress's mouth, at such a nick of time, is not a more disheartening sound to a younger brother, than that of honor to an eager lover like myself.

LADY FIDGET. But you can't blame a lady of my reputation to be chary.

HORNER. Chary! I have been chary of it already, by the report I have caused of myself.

LADY FIDGET. Ay, but if you should ever let other women know that dear secret, it would come out. Nay, you must have a great care of your conduct; for my acquaintance are so censorious (oh, 'tis a wicked, censorious world, Mr. Horner!), I say, are so censorious and detracting that perhaps they'll talk to the prejudice of my honor, though you should not let them know the dear secret.

fadges prospers
domine master
squab plump
comedian who cuts a ridiculous figure in a show of piety
in their closets in private

HORNER. Nay, madam, rather than they shall prejudice your honor, I'll prejudice theirs; and, to serve you, I'll lie with 'em all, make the secret their own, and then they'll keep it. I am a
5 Machiavel in love, madam.

LADY FIDGET. Oh, no, sir, not that way.

HORNER. Nay, the devil take me if censorious women are to be silenced any other way.

LADY FIDGET. A secret is better kept, I hope,
10 by a single person than a multitude; therefore pray do not trust anybody else with it, dear, dear Mr. Horner. [*Embracing him.*]

[*Enter* SIR JASPER FIDGET.]

SIR JASPER FIDGET. How now!

15 LADY FIDGET [*aside*]. Oh my husband!—prevented—and what's almost as bad, found with my arms about another man—that will appear too much—what shall I say?—Sir Jasper, come hither. I am trying if Mr. Horner
20 were ticklish, and he's as ticklish as can be. I love to torment the confounded toad; let you and I tickle him.

SIR JASPER FIDGET. No, your ladyship will tickle him better without me, I suppose. But is
25 this your buying china? I thought you had been at the china-house.

HORNER [*aside*]. China-house; that's my cue, I must take it.—A pox! can't you keep your impertinent wives at home? Some men are
30 troubled with the husbands, but I with the wives; but I'd have you to know, since I cannot be your journeyman by night, I will not be your drudge by day, to squire your wife about, and be your man of straw, or scarecrow only to pies
35 and jays,° that would be nibbling at your forbidden fruit; I shall be shortly the hackney° gentleman-usher of the town.

SIR JASPER FIDGET [*aside*]. He! he! he! poor fellow, he's in the right on't, faith. To squire
40 women about for other folks is as ungrateful an employment as to tell money for other folks. —He! he! he! be'n't angry, Horner.

LADY FIDGET. No, 'tis I have more reason to be angry, who am left by you to go abroad
45 indecently alone; or, what is more indecent, to

pin myself upon such ill-bred people of your acquaintance as this is.

SIR JASPER FIDGET. Nay, prithee, what has he done?

LADY FIDGET. Nay, he has done nothing. 50

SIR JASPER FIDGET. But what d'ye take ill, if he has done nothing?

LADY FIDGET. Ha! ha! ha! faith, I can't but laugh, however; why, d'ye think the unmannerly toad would come down to me to the 55 coach? I was fain to come up to fetch him, or go without him, which I was resolved not to do; for he knows china very well, and has himself very good, but will not let me see it lest I should beg some; but I will find it out, and have what 60 I came for yet.

[*Exit* LADY FIDGET, *followed by* HORNER *to the door.*]

HORNER [*apart to* LADY FIDGET]. Lock the door, madam. So, she has got into my chamber 65 and locked me out. Oh the impertinency of womankind! Well, Sir Jasper, plain-dealing is a jewel; if ever you suffer your wife to trouble me again here she shall carry you home a pair of horns, by my lord mayor she shall; though 70 I cannot furnish you myself, you are sure, yet I'll find a way.

SIR JASPER FIDGET. Ha! ha! he!—[*Aside.*] At my first coming in, and finding her arms about him, tickling him it seems, I was half jealous, 75 but now I see my folly.—He! he! he! poor Horner.

HORNER. Nay, though you laugh now, 'twill be my turn ere long. Oh, women, more impertinent, more cunning, and more mischievous 80 than their monkeys, and to me almost as ugly! —Now is she throwing my things about and rifling all I have; but I'll get in to her the back way, and so rifle her for it.

SIR JASPER FIDGET. Ha! ha! ha! poor angry 85 Horner.

HORNER. Stay here a little, I'll ferret her out to you presently, I warrant.

[*Exit at the other door.*]

[SIR JASPER *calls through the door to his wife;* 90 *she answers from within.*]

SIR JASPER FIDGET. Wife! my Lady Fidget! wife! he is coming in to you the back way.

pies and jays tattlers and dandies
the hackney commonest available

LADY FIDGET. Let him come and welcome, which way he will.

SIR JASPER FIDGET. He'll catch you, and use you roughly, and be too strong for you.

5 LADY FIDGET. Don't you trouble yourself, let him if he can.

QUACK [*behind*]. This indeed I could not have believed from him, nor any but my own eyes.

10 [*Enter* MRS. SQUEAMISH.]

MRS. SQUEAMISH. Where's this woman-hater, this toad, this ugly, greasy, dirty sloven?

SIR JASPER FIDGET [*aside*]. So, the women all will have him ugly; methinks he is a comely

15 person, but his wants make his form contemptible to 'em; and 'tis e'en as my wife said yesterday, talking of him, that a proper handsome eunuch was as ridiculous a thing as a gigantic coward.

20 MRS. SQUEAMISH. Sir Jasper, your servant. Where is the odious beast?

SIR JASPER FIDGET. He's within in his chamber, with my wife; she's playing the wag with him.

25 MRS. SQUEAMISH. Is she so? and he's a clownish beast, he'll give her no quarter, he'll play the wag with her again, let me tell you. Come, let's go help her.—What, the door's locked?

30 SIR JASPER FIDGET. Ay, my wife locked it.

MRS. SQUEAMISH. Did she so? Let us break it open then.

SIR JASPER FIDGET. No, no; he'll do her no hurt.

35 MRS. SQUEAMISH. No.—[*Aside*]. But is there no other way to get in to 'em? Whither goes this? I will disturb 'em.

[*Exit* MRS. SQUEAMISH *at another door.*]

[*Enter* OLD LADY SQUEAMISH.]

40 OLD LADY SQUEAMISH. Where is this harlotry, this impudent baggage, this rambling tomrigg?° O Sir Jasper, I'm glad to see you here; did you not see my vile grandchild come in hither just now?

45 SIR JASPER FIDGET. Yes.

OLD LADY SQUEAMISH. Ay, but where is she then? where is she? Lord, Sir Jasper, I have e'en

rattled myself to pieces in pursuit of her. But can you tell what she makes here? They say below, no woman lodges here. 50

SIR JASPER FIDGET. No.

OLD LADY SQUEAMISH. No! what does she here then? Say, if it be not a woman's lodging, what makes she here? But are you sure no woman lodges here? 55

SIR JASPER FIDGET. No, nor no man neither; this is Mr. Horner's lodging.

OLD LADY SQUEAMISH. Is it so, are you sure?

SIR JASPER FIDGET. Yes, yes.

OLD LADY SQUEAMISH. So; then there's no 60 hurt in't, I hope. But where is he?

SIR JASPER FIDGET. He's in the next room with my wife.

OLD LADY SQUEAMISH. Nay, if you trust him with your wife, I may with my Biddy. They say 65 he's a merry harmless man now, e'en as harmless a man as ever come out of Italy with a good voice,° and as pretty, harmless company for a lady as a snake without his teeth.

SIR JASPER FIDGET. Ay, ay, poor man. 70

[*Enter* MRS. SQUEAMISH.]

MRS. SQUEAMISH. I can't find 'em.—Oh, are you here, grandmother? I followed, you must know, my Lady Fidget hither; 'tis the prettiest lodging, and I have been staring on the prettiest 75 pictures—

[*Enter* LADY FIDGET *with a piece of china in her hand, and* HORNER *following.*]

LADY FIDGET. And I have been toiling and moiling for the prettiest piece of china, my dear. 80

HORNER. Nay, she has been too hard for me, do what I could.

MRS. SQUEAMISH. O Lord, I'll have some china too. Good Mr. Horner, don't think to give other people china, and me none; come in 85 with me too.

HORNER. Upon my honor, I have none left now.

MRS. SQUEAMISH. Nay, nay, I have known you deny your china before now, but you shan't 90 put me off so. Come.

HORNER. This lady had the last there.

LADY FIDGET. Yes, indeed, madam, to my certain knowledge, he has no more left.

___

tomrigg tomboy; immodest woman

with a good voice i.e., a male soprano, a eunuch

MRS. SQUEAMISH. Oh, but it may be he may have some you could not find.

LADY FIDGET. What, d'ye think if he had had any left, I would not have had it too? for we 5 women of quality never think we have china enough.

HORNER. Do not take it ill, I cannot make china for you all, but I will have a roll-waggon° for you too, another time.

10 MRS. SQUEAMISH. Thank you, dear toad.

LADY FIDGET [*to* HORNER *aside*]. What do you mean by that promise?

HORNER [*apart to* LADY FIDGET]. Alas, she has an innocent, literal understanding.

15 OLD LADY SQUEAMISH. Poor Mr. Horner! he has enough to do to please you all, I see.

HORNER. Ay, madam, you see how they use me.

OLD LADY SQUEAMISH. Poor gentleman, I pity 20 you.

HORNER. I thank you, madam. I could never find pity but from such reverend ladies as you are; the young ones will never spare a man.

MRS. SQUEAMISH. Come, come, beast, and go 25 dine with us; for we shall want a man at ombre after dinner.

HORNER. That's all their use of me, madam, you see.

MRS. SQUEAMISH. Come, sloven, I'll lead you, 30 to be sure of you. [*Pulls him by the cravat.*]

OLD LADY SQUEAMISH. Alas, poor man, how she tugs him! Kiss, kiss her; that's the way to make such women quiet.

HORNER. No, madam, that remedy is worse 35 than the torment; they know I dare suffer anything rather than do it.

OLD LADY SQUEAMISH. Prithee kiss her, and I'll give you her picture in little, that you admired so last night; prithee do.

40 HORNER. Well, nothing but that could bribe me. I love a woman only in effigy and good painting, as much as I hate them. I'll do't, for I could adore the devil well painted. [*Kisses* MRS. SQUEAMISH.]

45 MRS. SQUEAMISH. Foh, you filthy toad! nay, now I've done jesting.

OLD LADY SQUEAMISH. Ha! ha! ha! I told you so.

MRS. SQUEAMISH. Foh! a kiss of his—

SIR JASPER FIDGET. Has no more hurt in't than 50 one of my spaniel's.

MRS. SQUEAMISH. Nor no more good neither.

QUACK [*behind*]. I will now believe anything he tells me.

[*Enter* PINCHWIFE.] 55

LADY FIDGET. O Lord, here's a man! Sir Jasper, my mask, my mask! I would not be seen here for the world.

SIR JASPER FIDGET. What, not when I am with you? 60

LADY FIDGET. No, no, my honor—let's be gone.

MRS. SQUEAMISH. O grandmother, let us be gone; make haste, make haste, I know not how he may censure us. 65

LADY FIDGET. Be found in the lodging of anything like a man!—Away.

[*Exeunt* SIR JASPER FIDGET, LADY FIDGET, OLD LADY SQUEAMISH, MRS. SQUEAMISH.]

QUACK [*behind*]. What's here? another 70 cuckold? he looks like one, and none else sure have any business with him.

HORNER. Well, what brings my dear friend hither?

PINCHWIFE. Your impertinency. 75

HORNER. My impertinency!—Why, you gentlemen that have got handsome wives think you have a privilege of saying anything to your friends, and are as brutish as if you were our creditors. 80

PINCHWIFE. No, sir, I'll ne'er trust you any way.

HORNER. But why not, dear Jack? Why diffide° in me thou know'st so well?

PINCHWIFE. Because I do know you so well. 85

HORNER. Han't I been always thy friend, honest Jack, always ready to serve thee, in love or battle, before thou wert married, and am so still?

PINCHWIFE. I believe so; you would be my 90 second now, indeed.

HORNER. Well then, dear Jack, why so

---

roll-waggon a rare word; possibly, a small wheeled cart, as used for serving tea, and hence laden with china dishes

diffide not trust

unkind, so grum, so strange to me? Come, prithee, kiss me, dear rogue. Gad, I was always, I say, and am still as much thy servant as—

PINCHWIFE. As I am yours, sir. What, you
5 would send a kiss to my wife, is that it?

HORNER. So, there 'tis—a man can't show his friendship to a married man, but presently he talks of his wife to you. Prithee, let thy wife alone, and let thee and I be all one, as we were
10 wont. What, thou art as shy of my kindness as a Lombard Street alderman° of a courtier's civility at Locket's!°

PINCHWIFE. But you are overkind to me, as kind as if I were your cuckold already; yet I
15 must confess you ought to be kind and civil to me, since I am so kind, so civil to you, as to bring you this. Look you there, sir. [Delivers him a letter.]

HORNER. What is't?
20 PINCHWIFE. Only a love letter, sir.

HORNER. From whom?—how! this is from your wife—hum—and hum—[reads].

PINCHWIFE. Even from my wife, sir; am I not wondrous kind and civil to you now too?—
25 [Aside.] But you'll not think her so.

HORNER [aside]. Ha! is this a trick of his or hers?

PINCHWIFE. The gentleman's surprised I find. —What, you expected a kinder letter?
30 HORNER. No faith, not I, how could I?

PINCHWIFE. Yes, yes, I'm sure you did. A man so well made as you are must needs be disappointed if the women declare not their passion at first sight or opportunity.
35 HORNER [aside]. But what should this mean? Stay, the postscript.—[Reads aside.] "Be sure you love me, whatsoever my husband says to the contrary, and let him not see this, lest he should come home and pinch me, or kill my
40 squirrel."—It seems he knows not what the letter contains.

PINCHWIFE. Come, ne'er wonder at it so much.

HORNER. Faith, I can't help it.

as a **Lombard Street alderman** as a moneylender being flattered by stone-broke gentlemen looking for credit
Locket's a fashionable tavern

PINCHWIFE. Now, I think I have deserved 45 your infinite friendship and kindness, and have showed myself sufficiently an obliging kind friend and husband; am I not so, to bring a letter from my wife to her gallant?

HORNER. Ay, the devil take me, art thou, the 50 most obliging, kind friend and husband in the world, ha! ha!

PINCHWIFE. Well, you may be merry, sir; but in short I must tell you, sir, my honor will suffer no jesting. 55

HORNER. What dost thou mean?

PINCHWIFE. Does the letter want a comment? Then, know, sir, though I have been so civil a husband as to bring you a letter from my wife, to let you kiss and court her to my face, I will 60 not be a cuckold, sir, I will not.

HORNER. Thou art mad with jealousy. I never saw thy wife in my life but at the play yesterday, and I know not if it were she or no. I court her, kiss her! 65

PINCHWIFE. I will not be a cuckold, I say; there will be danger in making me a cuckold.

HORNER. Why, wert thou not well cured of thy last clap?

PINCHWIFE. I wear a sword. 70

HORNER. It should be taken from thee, lest thou shouldst do thyself a mischief with it; thou art mad, man.

PINCHWIFE. As mad as I am, and as merry as you are, I must have more reason from you ere 75 we part. I say again, though you kissed and courted last night my wife in man's clothes, as she confesses in her letter—

HORNER [aside]. Ha!

PINCHWIFE. Both she and I say you must not 80 design it again, for you have mistaken your woman, as you have done your man.

HORNER [aside]. Oh—I understand something now.—Was that thy wife? Why wouldst thou not tell me 'twas she? Faith, my freedom 85 with her was your fault, not mine.

PINCHWIFE [aside]. Faith, so 'twas.

HORNER. Fy! I'd never do't to a woman before her husband's face, sure.

PINCHWIFE. But I had rather you should do't 90 to my wife before my face, than behind my back; and that you shall never do.

HORNER. No—you will hinder me.

PINCHWIFE. If I would not hinder you, you see by her letter she would.

HORNER. Well, I must acquiesce then, and be contented with what she writes.

5 PINCHWIFE. I'll assure you 'twas voluntarily writ; I had no hand in't, you may believe me.

HORNER. I do believe thee, faith.

PINCHWIFE. And believe her too, for she's an innocent creature, has no dissembling in her;

10 and so fare you well, sir.

HORNER. Pray, however, present my humble service to her, and tell her I will obey her letter to a tittle, and fulfill her desires, be what they will, or with what difficulty soever I do't; and

15 you shall be no more jealous of me, I warrant her, and you.

PINCHWIFE. Well then, fare you well; and play with any man's honor but mine, kiss any man's wife but mine, and welcome.

20 [*Exit.*]

HORNER. Ha! ha! ha!—Doctor.

QUACK. It seems he has not heard the report of you, or does not believe it.

HORNER. Ha! ha!—now, doctor, what think

25 you?

QUACK. Pray let's see the letter—hum—[*reads the letter*]—"for—dear—love you—"

HORNER. I wonder how she could contrive it! What say'st thou to't? 'Tis an original.°

30 QUACK. So are your cuckolds, too, originals, for they are like no other common cuckolds, and I will henceforth believe it not impossible for you to cuckold the Grand Signior° amidst his guards of eunuchs, that I say.

35 HORNER. And I say for the letter, 'tis the first love letter that ever was without flames, darts, fates, destinies, lying and dissembling in't.

[*Enter* SPARKISH *pulling in* MR. PINCHWIFE.]

SPARKISH. Come back, you are a pretty

40 brother-in-law, neither go to church nor to dinner with your sister bride!

PINCHWIFE. My sister denies her marriage, and you see is gone away from you dissatisfied.

SPARKISH. Pshaw! upon a foolish scruple that

45 our parson was not in lawful orders, and did not say all the common prayer; but 'tis her

modesty only I believe. But let women be never so modest the first day, they'll be sure to come to themselves by night, and I shall have enough of her then. In the meantime, Harry Horner, 50 you must dine with me. I keep my wedding at my aunt's in the Piazza.°

HORNER. Thy wedding! What stale maid has lived to despair of a husband, or what young one of a gallant? 55

SPARKISH. Oh, your servant, sir—this gentleman's sister then,—no stale maid.

HORNER. I'm sorry for't.

PINCHWIFE [*aside*]. How comes he so concerned for her? 60

SPARKISH. You sorry for't? Why, do you know any ill by her?

HORNER. No, I know none but by thee; 'tis for her sake, not yours, and another man's sake that might have hoped, I thought. 65

SPARKISH. Another man! another man! What is his name?

HORNER. Nay, since 'tis past, he shall be nameless.—[*Aside.*] Poor Harcourt! I am sorry thou hast missed her. 70

PINCHWIFE [*aside*]. He seems to be much troubled at the match.

SPARKISH. Prithee, tell me—Nay, you shan't go, brother.

PINCHWIFE. I must of necessity, but I'll come 75 to you to dinner.

[*Exit.*]

SPARKISH. But, Harry, what, have I a rival in my wife already? But with all my heart, for he may be of use to me hereafter; for though my 80 hunger is now my sauce, and I can fall on heartily without, the time will come when a rival will be as good sauce for a married man to a wife, as an orange to veal.

HORNER. O thou damned rogue! thou hast set 85 my teeth on edge with thy orange.

SPARKISH. Then let's to dinner—there I was with you again. Come.

HORNER. But who dines with thee?

SPARKISH. My friends and relations, my 90 brother Pinchwife, you see, of your acquaintance.

HORNER. And his wife?

---

an original   most extraordinary
Grand Signior   the Sultan of Turkey

Piazza   The square of Covent Garden

SPARKISH. No, 'gad, he'll ne'er let her come amongst us good fellows; your stingy country coxcomb keeps his wife from his friends, as he does his little firkin of ale for his own drinking, and a gentleman can't get a smack on't; but his servants, when his back is turned, broach it at their pleasures, and dust it away, ha! ha! ha!—'Gad, I'm witty, I think, considering I was married today, by the world; but come—

HORNER. No, I will not dine with you, unless you can fetch her too.

SPARKISH. Pshaw! what pleasure canst thou have with women now, Harry?

HORNER. My eyes are not gone; I love a good prospect yet, and will not dine with you unless she does too; go fetch her, therefore, but do not tell her husband 'tis for my sake.

SPARKISH. Well, I'll go try what I can do; in the meantime, come away to my aunt's lodging; 'tis in the way to Pinchwife's.

HORNER. The poor woman has called for aid, and stretched forth her hand, doctor; I cannot but help her over the pale° out of the briars.

[*Exeunt* SPARKISH, HORNER, QUACK.]

Scene iv

[*The scene changes to* PINCHWIFE's *house.*]

[MRS. PINCHWIFE *alone, leaning on her elbow. A table, pen, ink, and paper.*]

MRS. PINCHWIFE. Well, 'tis e'en so, I have got the London disease they call love; I am sick of my husband, and for my gallant. I have heard this distemper called a fever, but methinks 'tis liker an ague; for when I think of my husband, I tremble, and am in a cold sweat, and have inclinations to vomit; but when I think of my gallant, dear Mr. Horner, my hot fit comes, and I am all in a fever indeed; and, as in other fevers, my own chamber is tedious to me, and I would fain be removed to his, and then methinks I should be well. Ah, poor Mr. Horner! Well, I cannot, will not stay here; therefore I'll make an end of my letter to him, which shall be a finer letter than my last, because I have studied it like anything. Oh, sick, sick! [*Takes the pen and writes.*]

pale fence

[*Enter* PINCHWIFE, *who, seeing her writing, steals softly behind her, and, looking over her shoulder, snatches the paper from her.*]

PINCHWIFE. What, writing more letters?

MRS. PINCHWIFE. O Lord, bud, why d'ye fright me so? [*She offers to run out; he stops her, and reads.*]

PINCHWIFE. How's this? nay, you shall not stir, madam;—"Dear, dear, dear Mr. Horner" —very well—I have taught you to write letters to good purpose—but let's see't. "First, I am to beg your pardon for my boldness in writing to you, which I'd have you to know I would not have done, had you not said first you loved me so extremely, which if you do, you will never suffer me to lie in the arms of another man whom I loathe, nauseate, and detest."—Now you can write these filthy words. But what follows?—"Therefore, I hope you will speedily find some way to free me from this unfortunate match, which was never, I assure you, of my choice, but I'm afraid 'tis already too far gone; however, if you love me, as I do you, you will try what you can do; but you must help me away before tomorrow, or else, alas! I shall be for ever out of your reach, for I can defer no longer our—our—"[*the letter concludes*] what is to follow "our"?—speak, what? Our journey into the country I suppose.—Oh woman, damned woman! and Love, damned Love, their old tempter! for this is one of his miracles; in a moment he can make those blind that could see, and those see that were blind, those dumb that could speak, and those prattle who were dumb before; nay, what is more than all, make these dough-baked, senseless, indocile animals, women, too hard for us, their politic lords and rulers, in a moment. But make an end of your letter, and then I'll make an end of you thus, and all my plagues together. [*Draws his sword.*]

MRS. PINCHWIFE. O Lord, O Lord, you are such a passionate man, bud!

[*Enter* SPARKISH.]

SPARKISH. How now, what's here to do?

PINCHWIFE. This fool here now!

SPARKISH. What, drawn upon your wife? You should never do that, but at night in the dark,

when you can't hurt her. This is my sister-in-
law, is it not? ay, faith, e'en our country Margery [*pulls aside her handkerchief*]; one may
know her. Come, she and you must go dine
5   with me; dinner's ready, come. But where's my
wife? Is she not come home yet? Where is she?

PINCHWIFE. Making you a cuckold; 'tis that
they all do, as soon as they can.

SPARKISH. What, the wedding-day? No, a
10   wife that designs to make a cully° of her husband will be sure to let him win the first stake
of love, by the world. But come, they stay
dinner for us; come, I'll lead down our Margery.

15   MRS. PINCHWIFE. No.—Sir, go, we'll follow
you.

SPARKISH. I will not wag without you.

PINCHWIFE [*aside*]. This coxcomb is a sensible
torment to me amidst the greatest in the world.

20   SPARKISH. Come, come, Madam Margery.

PINCHWIFE. No; I'll lead her my way: what,
would you treat your friends with mine, for
want of your own wife?—[*Leads her to the
other door, and locks her in and returns.*] I am
25   contented my rage should take breath—

SPARKISH [*aside*]. I told Horner this.

PINCHWIFE. Come now.

SPARKISH. Lord, how shy you are of your wife!
But let me tell you, brother, we men of wit have
30   amongst us a saying that cuckolding, like the
small-pox, comes with a fear; and you may
keep your wife as much as you will out of
danger of infection, but if her constitution
incline her to't, she'll have it sooner or later, by
35   the world, say they.

PINCHWIFE [*aside*]. What a thing is a cuckold,
that every fool can make him ridiculous!—
Well, sir—but let me advise you, now you are
come to be concerned, because you suspect the
40   danger, not to neglect the means to prevent it,
especially when the greatest share of the
malady will light upon your own head, for
Hows'e'er the kind wife's belly comes to
[swell,
45   The husband breeds for her, and first is ill.

cully dupe

ACT V

Scene i

[MR. PINCHWIFE's *house.*]
[*Enter* MR. PINCHWIFE *and* MRS. PINCHWIFE.
A table and candle.]

PINCHWIFE. Come, take the pen and make an
end of the letter, just as you intended; if you   50
are false in a tittle, I shall soon perceive it, and
punish you with this as you deserve.—[*Lays
his hand on his sword.*] Write what was to
follow—let's see—"You must make haste, and
help me away before tomorrow, or else I shall   55
be for ever out of your reach, for I can defer no
longer our"—what follows "our"?

MRS. PINCHWIFE. Must all out, then, bud?—
Look you there, then. [MRS. PINCHWIFE *takes
the pen and writes.*]   60

PINCHWIFE. Let's see—"For I can defer no
longer our—wedding—Your slighted Alithea."
—What's the meaning of this? My sister's
name to't? Speak, unriddle.

MRS. PINCHWIFE. Yes, indeed, bud.   65

PINCHWIFE. But why her name to't? Speak—
speak, I say.

MRS. PINCHWIFE. Ay, but you'll tell her then
again. If you would not tell her again—

PINCHWIFE. I will not—I am stunned, my   70
head turns round.—Speak.

MRS. PINCHWIFE. Won't you tell her, indeed,
and indeed?

PINCHWIFE. No; speak, I say.

MRS. PINCHWIFE. She'll be angry with me;   75
but I had rather she should be angry with me
than you, bud; and, to tell you the truth, 'twas
she made me write the letter, and taught me
what I should write.

PINCHWIFE [*aside*]. Ha! I thought the style   80
was somewhat better than her own.—But how
could she come to you to teach you, since I had
locked you up alone?

MRS. PINCHWIFE. Oh, through the keyhole,
bud.   85

PINCHWIFE. But why should she make you
write a letter for her to him, since she can write
herself?

MRS. PINCHWIFE. Why, she said because—for
I was unwilling to do it—   90

PINCHWIFE. Because what—because?

MRS. PINCHWIFE. Because, lest Mr. Horner should be cruel, and refuse her; or vain afterwards, and show the letter, she might disown it, the hand not being hers.

PINCHWIFE [aside]. How's this? Ha!—then I think I shall come to myself again. This changeling could not invent this lie, but if she could, why should she? she might think I should soon discover it.—Stay—now I think on't too, Horner said he was sorry she had married Sparkish; and her disowning her marriage to me makes me think she has evaded it for Horner's sake. Yet why should she take this course? But men in love are fools; women may well be so.—But hark you, madam, your sister went out in the morning, and I have not seen her within since.

MRS. PINCHWIFE. Alack-a-day, she has been crying all day above, it seems, in a corner.

PINCHWIFE. Where is she? Let me speak with her.

MRS. PINCHWIFE [aside]. O Lord, then he'll discover all!—Pray hold, bud; what, d'ye mean to discover me? She'll know I have told you then. Pray, bud, let me talk with her first.

PINCHWIFE. I must speak with her, to know whether Horner ever made her any promise, and whether she be married to Sparkish or no.

MRS. PINCHWIFE. Pray, dear bud, don't, till I have spoken with her, and told her that I have told you all; for she'll kill me else.

PINCHWIFE. Go then, and bid her come out to me.

MRS. PINCHWIFE. Yes, yes, bud.

PINCHWIFE. Let me see—

MRS. PINCHWIFE [aside]. I'll go, but she is not within to come to him. I have just got time to know of Lucy, her maid, who first set me on work, what lie I shall tell next; for I am e'en at my wit's end.

[Exit.]

PINCHWIFE. Well, I resolve it, Horner shall have her. I'd rather give him my sister than lend him my wife; and such an alliance will prevent his pretensions to my wife, sure. I'll make him of kin to her, and then he won't care for her.

[Mrs. PINCHWIFE returns.]

MRS. PINCHWIFE. O Lord, bud! I told you what anger you would make me with my sister.

PINCHWIFE. Won't she come hither?

MRS. PINCHWIFE. No, no. Alack-a-day, she's ashamed to look you in the face, and she says, if you go in to her, she'll run away downstairs, and shamefully go herself to Mr. Horner, who has promised her marriage, she says; and she will have no other, so she won't.

PINCHWIFE. Did he so?—promise her marriage!—then she shall have no other. Go tell her so; and if she will come and discourse with me a little concerning the means, I will about it immediately. Go.—[Exit Mrs. PINCHWIFE.] His estate is equal to Sparkish's, and his extraction as much better than his as his parts are; but my chief reason is I'd rather be akin to him by the name of brother-in-law than that of cuckold.

[Enter Mrs. PINCHWIFE.]

Well, what says she now?

MRS. PINCHWIFE. Why, she says she would only have you lead her to Horner's lodging; with whom she first will discourse the matter before she talks with you, which yet she cannot do; for alack, poor creature, she says she can't so much as look you in the face, therefore she'll come to you in a mask. And you must excuse her if she make you no answer to any question of yours, till you have brought her to Mr. Horner; and if you will not chide her, nor question her, she'll come out to you immediately.

PINCHWIFE. Let her come. I will not speak a word to her, nor require a word from her.

MRS. PINCHWIFE. Oh, I forgot; besides, she says she cannot look you in the face, though through a mask; therefore would desire you to put out the candle.

PINCHWIFE. I agree to all. Let her make haste. —There, 'tis out.—[Puts out the candle. Exit Mrs. PINCHWIFE.] My case is something better; I'd rather fight with Horner for not lying with my sister, than for lying with my wife; and of the two, I had rather find my sister too forward than my wife. I expected no other from her free education, as she calls it, and her passion for the town. Well, wife and sister are names which make us expect love and duty, pleasure and comfort; but we find 'em plagues and torments, and are equally, though differently, troublesome to their keeper, for we have as much ado to get people to lie with our sisters as to keep 'em from lying with our wives.

[*Enter* Mrs. Pinchwife *masked, and in hoods and scarfs, and a night-gown and petticoat*° *of* Alithea's, *in the dark.*]

What, are you come, sister? let us go then.— But first let me lock up my wife. Mrs. Margery, where are you?

Mrs. Pinchwife. Here, bud.

Pinchwife. Come hither, that I may lock you up; get you in.—[*Locks the door.*] Come, sister, where are you now?

[Mrs. Pinchwife *gives him her hand; but when he lets her go, she steals softly on the other side of him, and is led away by him for his sister,* Alithea.]

Scene ii

[*The scene changes to* Horner's *lodging.*]

[Quack, Horner.]

Quack. What, all alone? not so much as one of your cuckolds here, nor one of their wives! They use to take their turns with you, as if they were to watch you.

Horner. Yes, it often happens that a cuckold is but his wife's spy, and is more upon family duty when he is with her gallant abroad, hindering his pleasure, than when he is at home with her playing the gallant. But the hardest duty a married woman imposes upon a lover is keeping her husband company always.

Quack. And his fondness wearies you almost as soon as hers.

Horner. A pox! keeping a cuckold company, after you have had his wife, is as tiresome as the company of a country squire to a witty fellow of the town, when he has got all his money.

Quack. And as at first a man makes a friend of the husband to get the wife, so at last you are fain to fall out with the wife to be rid of the husband.

Horner. Ay, most cuckold-makers are true courtiers, when once a poor man has cracked his credit for 'em, they can't abide to come near him.

Quack. But at first, to draw him in, are so sweet, so kind, so dear! just as you are to Pinchwife. But what becomes of that intrigue with his wife?

Horner. A pox! he's as surly as an alderman that has been bit; and since he's so coy, his wife's kindness is in vain, for she's a silly innocent.

Quack. Did she not send you a letter by him?

Horner. Yes; but that's a riddle I have not yet solved. Allow the poor creature to be willing, she is silly too, and he keeps her up so close—

Quack. Yes, so close, that he makes her but the more willing, and adds but revenge to her love; which two, when met, seldom fail of satisfying each other one way or other.

Horner. What! here's the man we are talking of, I think.

[*Enter* Mr. Pinchwife, *leading in his wife masked, muffled, and in her sister's gown.*] Pshaw!

Quack. Bringing his wife to you is the next thing to bringing a love letter from her.

Horner. What means this?

Pinchwife. The last time, you know, sir, I brought you a letter; now, you see, a mistress; I think you'll say I am a civil man to you.

Horner. Ay, the devil take me, will I say thou art the civilest man I ever met with; and I have known some. I fancy I understand thee now better than I did the letter. But, hark thee, in thy ear—

Pinchwife. What?

Horner. Nothing but the usual question, man: is she sound, on thy word?

Pinchwife. What, you take her for a wench, and me for a pimp?

Horner. Pshaw! wench and pimp, paw° words; I know thou art an honest fellow, and

---

night-gown and petticoat loose cloak for evening wear and a fancy skirt

paw improper

hast a great acquaintance among the ladies, and perhaps hast made love for me, rather than let me make love to thy wife.

PINCHWIFE. Come, sir, in short, I am for no
5 fooling.

HORNER. Nor I neither; therefore prithee, let's see her face presently. Make her show, man; art thou sure I don't know her?

PINCHWIFE. I am sure you do know her.

10 HORNER. A pox! why dost thou bring her to me then?

PINCHWIFE. Because she's a relation of mine—

HORNER. Is she, faith, man? then thou art
15 still more civil and obliging, dear rogue.

PINCHWIFE. Who desired me to bring her to you.

HORNER. Then she is obliging, dear rogue.

PINCHWIFE. You'll make her welcome for my
20 sake, I hope.

HORNER. I hope she is handsome enough to make herself welcome. Prithee, let her unmask.

PINCHWIFE. Do you speak to her; she would never be ruled by me.

25 HORNER. Madam—[MRS. PINCHWIFE *whispers to* HORNER]. She says she must speak with me in private. Withdraw, prithee.

PINCHWIFE. [*aside*]. She's unwilling, it seems, I should know all her undecent conduct in this
30 business.—Well then, I'll leave you together, and hope when I am gone, you'll agree; if not, you and I shan't agree, sir.

HORNER. What means the fool? if she and I agree 'tis no matter what you and I do.
35 [*Whispers to* MRS. PINCHWIFE, *who makes signs with her hand for* PINCHWIFE *to be gone.*]

PINCHWIFE. In the meantime I'll fetch a parson, and find out Sparkish and disabuse him. You would have me fetch a parson, would
40 you not? Well then—now I think I am rid of her, and shall have no more trouble with her. Our sisters and daughters, like usurers' money, are safest when put out; but our wives, like their writings, never safe but in our closets
45 under lock and key.

[*Exit.*]

[*Enter* BOY.]

BOY. Sir Jasper Fidget, sir, is coming up.

[*Exit.*]

HORNER. Here's the trouble of a cuckold now 50 we are talking of. A pox on him! has he not enough to do to hinder his wife's sport, but he must other women's too?—Step in here, madam.

[*Exit* MRS. PINCHWIFE.] 55

[*Enter* SIR JASPER FIDGET.]

SIR JASPER FIDGET. My best and dearest friend.

HORNER [*aside to* QUACK]. The old style, doctor.—Well, be short, for I am busy. What 60 would your impertinent wife have now?

SIR JASPER FIDGET. Well guessed, i'faith; for I do come from her.

HORNER. To invite me to supper! Tell her, I can't come; go. 65

SIR JASPER FIDGET. Nay, now you are out, faith; for my lady, and the whole knot of the virtuous gang, as they call themselves, are resolved upon a frolic of coming to you tonight in masquerade, and are all dressed already. 70

HORNER. I shan't be at home.

SIR JASPER FIDGET [*aside*]. Lord, how churlish he is to women!—Nay, prithee don't disappoint 'em; they'll think 'tis my fault; prithee don't. I'll send in the banquet and the fiddles. But 75 make no noise on't; for the poor virtuous rogues would not have it known, for the world, that they go a-masquerading; and they would come to no man's ball but yours.

HORNER. Well, well—get you gone; and tell 80 'em, if they come, 'twill be at the peril of their honor and yours.

SIR JASPER FIDGET. He! he! he!—We'll trust you for that; farewell.

[*Exit.*] 85

HORNER.

Doctor, anon you too shall be my guest,
But now I'm going to a private feast.

[*Exeunt.*]

Scene iii

[*The scene changes to the piazza of Covent* 90 *Garden.*]

[SPARKISH, PINCHWIFE.]

SPARKISH [*with the letter in his hand*]. But who would have thought a woman could have been false to me? By the world, I could not have thought it.

PINCHWIFE. You were for giving and taking liberty; she has taken it only, sir, now you find
5 in that letter. You are a frank person, and so is she, you see there.

SPARKISH. Nay, if this be her hand—for I never saw it.

PINCHWIFE. 'Tis no matter whether that be
10 her hand or no; I am sure this hand, at her desire, led her to Mr. Horner, with whom I left her just now, to go fetch a parson to 'em at their desire too, to deprive you of her for ever; for it seems yours was but a mock marriage.

15 SPARKISH. Indeed, she would needs have it that 'twas Harcourt himself, in a parson's habit, that married us; but I'm sure he told me 'twas his brother Ned.

PINCHWIFE. Oh, there 'tis out; and you were
20 deceived, not she; for you are such a frank person. But I must be gone.—You'll find her at Mr. Horner's. Go, and believe your eyes.

[*Exit.*]

SPARKISH. Nay, I'll to her, and call her as
25 many crocodiles, sirens, harpies, and other heathenish names as a poet would do a mistress who had refused to hear his suit, nay more, his verses on her.—But stay, is not that she following a torch at t'other end of the
30 piazza? and from Horner's certainly—'tis so.

[*Enter* ALITHEA *following a torch, and* LUCY *behind.*]

You are well met, madam, though you don't think so. What, you have made a short visit to
35 Mr. Horner. But I suppose you'll return to him presently; by that time the parson can be with him.

ALITHEA. Mr. Horner and the parson, sir!

SPARKISH. Come, madam, no more dissem-
40 bling, no more jilting; for I am no more a frank person.

ALITHEA. How's this?

LUCY [*aside*]. So, 'twill work, I see.

SPARKISH. Could you find out no easy
45 country fool to abuse? none but me, a gentleman of wit and pleasure about the town? But it was your pride to be too hard for a man of parts, unworthy false woman! false as a friend

that lends a man money to lose; false as dice, who undo those that trust all they have to 'em. 50

LUCY [*aside*]. He has been a great bubble, by his similes, as they say.

ALITHEA. You have been too merry, sir, at your wedding-dinner, sure.

SPARKISH. What, d'ye mock me too? 55

ALITHEA. Or you have been deluded.

SPARKISH. By you.

ALITHEA. Let me understand you.

SPARKISH. Have you the confidence—I should call it something else, since you know your 60 guilt—to stand my just reproaches? You did not write an impudent letter to Mr. Horner? who I find now has clubbed with you in deluding me with his aversion for women, that I might not, forsooth, suspect him for my rival. 65

LUCY [*aside*]. D'ye think the gentleman can be jealous now, madam?

ALITHEA. I write a letter to Mr. Horner!

SPARKISH. Nay, madam, do not deny it. Your brother showed it me just now; and told me 70 likewise, he left you at Horner's lodging to fetch a parson to marry you to him, and I wish you joy, madam, joy, joy; and to him, too, much joy; and to myself more joy, for not marrying you. 75

ALITHEA [*aside*]. So, I find my brother would break off the match; and I can consent to't, since I see this gentleman can be made jealous. —O Lucy, by his rude usage and jealousy, he makes me almost afraid I am married to him. 80 Art thou sure 'twas Harcourt himself, and no parson, that married us?

SPARKISH. No, madam, I thank you. I suppose that was a contrivance too of Mr. Horner's and yours, to make Harcourt play the parson; but I 85 would as little as you have him one now, no, not for the world. For shall I tell you another truth? I never had any passion for you till now, for now I hate you. 'Tis true, I might have married your portion,° as other men of parts of the 90 town do sometimes; and so, your servant. And to show my unconcernedness, I'll come to your wedding, and resign you with as much joy as I would a stale wench to a new cully; nay, with

portion dowry

as much joy as I would after the first night, if I
had been married to you. There's for you; and
so your servant, servant.

[*Exit.*]

5 ALITHEA. How was I deceived in a man!

LUCY. You'll believe then a fool may be made
jealous now? For that easiness in him that
suffers him to be led by a wife, will likewise
permit him to be persuaded against her by
10 others.

ALITHEA. But marry Mr. Horner! my brother
does not intend it, sure; if I thought he did, I
would take thy advice, and Mr. Harcourt for
my husband. And now I wish that if there be
15 any overwise woman of the town, who, like
me, would marry a fool for fortune, liberty, or
title, first, that her husband may love play, and
be a cully to all the town but her, and suffer
none but Fortune to be mistress of his purse;
20 then, if for liberty, that he may send her into
the country under the conduct of some huswifely mother-in-law; and if for title, may the
world give 'em none but that of cuckold.

LUCY. And for her greater curse, madam,
25 may he not deserve it.

ALITHEA. Away, impertinent! Is not this my
old Lady Lanterlu's?

LUCY. Yes, madam.—[*Aside.*] And here I
hope we shall find Mr. Harcourt.

30 [*Exeunt.*]

Scene iv

[*The scene changes again to* HORNER'S
lodging. A table, banquet, and bottles.]

[*Enter* HORNER, LADY FIDGET, MRS. DAINTY
FIDGET, MRS. SQUEAMISH.]

35 HORNER. [*aside*]. A pox! they are come too
soon—before I have sent back my new mistress. All I have now to do is to lock her in, that
they may not see her.

LADY FIDGET. That we may be sure of our
40 welcome, we have brought our entertainment
with us, and are resolved to treat thee, dear
toad.

MRS. DAINTY FIDGET. And that we may be
merry to purpose, have left Sir Jasper and my
45 old Lady Squeamish quarreling at home at
backgammon.

MRS. SQUEAMISH. Therefore let us make use
of our time, lest they should chance to interrupt
us.

LADY FIDGET. Let us sit then. 50

HORNER. First, that you may be private, let
me lock this door and that, and I'll wait upon
you presently.

LADY FIDGET. No, sir, shut 'em only, and your
lips for ever; for we must trust you as much as 55
our women.

HORNER. You know all vanity's killed in me;
I have no occasion for talking.

LADY FIDGET. Now, ladies, supposing we had
drank each of us our two bottles, let us speak 60
the truth of our hearts.

MRS. DAINTY FIDGET *and* MRS. SQUEAMISH.
Agreed.

LADY FIDGET. By this brimmer,° for truth is
nowhere else to be found.—[*Aside to* HORNER.] 65
Not in thy heart, false man!

HORNER [*aside to* LADY FIDGET]. You have
found me a true man, I'm sure.

LADY FIDGET [*aside to* HORNER]. Not every
way.—But let us sit and be merry. [LADY 70
FIDGET *sings.*]

1

Why should our damned tyrants oblige us to
[live
On the pittance of pleasure which they only
[give? 75
We must not rejoice
With wine and with noise;
In vain we must wake in a dull bed alone,
Whilst to our warm rival, the bottle, they're
[gone. 80
Then lay aside charms,
And take up these arms.

2

'Tis wine only gives 'em their courage and
[wit;
Because we live sober, to men we submit. 85
If for beauties you'd pass,
Take a lick of the glass,

brimmer wine glass

'Twill mend your complexions, and when
[they are gone,
The best red we have is the red of the grape.
Then, sisters, lay't on,
5 And damn a good shape.

Mrs. Dainty Fidget. Dear brimmer! Well, in
token of our openness and plain-dealing, let us
throw our masks over our heads.
Horner. So, 'twill come to the glasses anon.
10 Mrs. Squeamish. Lovely brimmer! let me
enjoy him first.
Lady Fidget. No, I never part with a gallant
till I've tried him. Dear brimmer! that makest
our husbands short-sighted.
15 Mrs. Dainty Fidget. And our bashful gallants bold.
Mrs. Squeamish. And, for want of a gallant,
the butler lovely in our eyes.—Drink, eunuch.
Lady Fidget. Drink, thou representative of a
20 husband.—Damn a husband!
Mrs. Dainty Fidget. And, as it were a husband, an old keeper.°
Mrs. Squeamish. And an old grandmother.
Horner. And an English bawd, and a French
25 chirurgeon.
Lady Fidget. Ay, we have all reason to curse
'em.
Horner. For my sake, ladies?
Lady Fidget. No, for our own; for the first
30 spoils all young gallants' industry.
Mrs. Dainty Fidget. And the other's art
makes 'em bold only with common women.
Mrs. Squeamish. And rather run the hazard
of the vile distemper amongst them, than of a
35 denial amongst us.
Mrs. Dainty Fidget. The filthy toads choose
mistresses now as they do stuffs, for having
been fancied and worn by others.
Mrs. Squeamish. For being common and
40 cheap.
Lady Fidget. Whilst women of quality, like
the richest stuffs, lie untumbled, and unasked
for.
Horner. Ay, neat, and cheap, and new, often
45 they think best.

Mrs. Dainty Fidget. No, sir, the beasts will
be known by a mistress longer than by a suit.
Mrs. Squeamish. And 'tis not for cheapness
neither.
Lady Fidget. No; for the vain fops will take 50
up druggets° and embroider 'em. But I wonder
at the depraved appetites of witty men; they
use to be out of the common road, and hate
imitation. Pray tell me, beast, when you were a
man, why you rather chose to club with a 55
multitude in a common house for an entertainment than to be the only guest at a good table.
Horner. Why, faith, ceremony and expectation are unsufferable to those that are
sharp bent.° People always eat with the best 60
stomach at an ordinary,° where every man is
snatching for the best bit.
Lady Fidget. Though he get a cut over the
fingers.—But I have heard people eat most
heartily of another man's meat, that is, what 65
they do not pay for.
Horner. When they are sure of their welcome and freedom; for ceremony in love and
eating is as ridiculous as in fighting; falling on
briskly is all should be done on those occasions. 70
Lady Fidget. Well then, let me tell you, sir,
there is nowhere more freedom than in our
houses; and we take freedom from a young
person as a sign of good breeding; and a person
may be as free as he pleases with us, as frolic, 75
as gamesome, as wild as he will.
Horner. Han't I heard you all declaim
against wild men?
Lady Fidget. Yes; but for all that, we think
wildness in a man as desirable a quality as in a 80
duck or rabbit; a tame man! foh!
Horner. I know not, but your reputations
frightened me as much as your faces invited
me.
Lady Fidget. Our reputation! Lord, why 85
should you not think that we women made use
of our reputation, as you men of yours, only to
deceive the world with less suspicion? Our
virtue is like the statesman's religion, the

---

keeper of a prostitute

druggets course fabrics of mixed weave
sharp bent with a keen appetite
ordinary public eating house

Quaker's word, the gamester's oath, and the
great man's honor—but to cheat those that
trust us.

Mrs. Squeamish. And that demureness,
5 coyness, and modesty that you see in our faces
in the boxes at plays, is as much a sign of a kind
woman, as a vizard-mask in the pit.

Mrs. Dainty Fidget. For, I assure you,
women are least masked when they have the
10 velvet vizard on.

Lady Fidget. You would have found us
modest women in our denials only.

Mrs. Squeamish. Our bashfulness is only the
reflection of the men's.

15 Mrs. Dainty Fidget. We blush when they
are shamefaced.

Horner. I beg your pardon, ladies, I was
deceived in you devilishly. But why that mighty
pretense to honor?

20 Lady Fidget. We have told you; but sometimes 'twas for the same reason you men
pretend business often, to avoid ill company, to
enjoy the better and more privately those you
love.

25 Horner. But why would you ne'er give a
friend a wink then?

Lady Fidget. Faith, your reputation frightened us as much as ours did you, you were so
notoriously lewd.

30 Horner. And you so seemingly honest.

Lady Fidget. Was that all that deterred you?

Horner. And so expensive—you allow freedom, you say—

Lady Fidget. Ay, ay.

35 Horner. That I was afraid of losing my little
money, as well as my little time, both which
my other pleasures required.

Lady Fidget. Money! foh! you talk like a
little fellow now; do such as we expect money?

40 Horner. I beg your pardon, madam, I must
confess, I have heard that great ladies, like
great merchants, set but the higher prices upon
what they have, because they are not in necessity of taking the first offer.

45 Mrs. Dainty Fidget. Such as we make sale
of our hearts?

Mrs. Squeamish. We bribed for our love?
foh!

Horner. With your pardon, ladies, I know,
like great men in offices, you seem to exact 50
flattery and attendance only from your followers; but you have receivers° about you, and
such fees to pay a man is afraid to pass your
grants.° Besides, we must let you win at cards,
or we lose your hearts; and if you make an 55
assignation, 'tis at a goldsmith's, jeweller's, or
china-house, where for your honor you deposit
to him, he must pawn his to the punctual cit,°
and so paying for what you take up, pays for
what he takes up. 60

Mrs. Dainty Fidget. Would you not have us
assured of our gallants' love?

Mrs. Squeamish. For love is better known by
liberality than by jealousy.

Lady Fidget. For one may be dissembled, the 65
other not.—[Aside.] But my jealousy can be no
longer dissembled, and they are telling ripe.—
Come, here's to our gallants in waiting, whom
we must name, and I'll begin. This is my false
rogue. [Claps him on the back.] 70

Mrs. Squeamish. How!

Horner. So, all will out now.

Mrs. Squeamish [aside to Horner]. Did you
not tell me 'twas for my sake only you reported
yourself no man? 75

Mrs. Dainty Fidget [aside to Horner]. Oh,
wretch! did you not swear to me, 'twas for my
love and honor you passed for that thing you
do?

Horner. So, so. 80

Lady Fidget. Come, speak, ladies, this is my
false villain.

Mrs. Squeamish. And mine too.

Mrs. Dainty Fidget. And mine.

Horner. Well then, you are all three my false 85
rogues too, and there's an end on't.

Lady Fidget. Well then, there's no remedy;
sister sharers, let us not fall out, but have a care
of our honor. Though we get no presents, no
jewels of him, we are savers of our honor, the 90
jewel of most value and use, which shines yet
to the world unsuspected, though it be
counterfeit.

Horner. Nay, and is e'en as good as if it were

---

receivers servants to be bribed
pass your grants cross your threshold
punctual cit tradesman demanding prompt payment

true, provided the world think so; for honor, like beauty now, only depends on the opinion of others.

LADY FIDGET. Well, Harry Common, I hope
5 you can be true to three. Swear; but 'tis to no purpose to require your oath, for you are as often forsworn as you swear to new women.

HORNER. Come, faith, madam, let us e'en pardon one another; for all the difference I find
10 betwixt we men and you women, we forswear ourselves at the beginning of an amour; you as long as it lasts.

[*Enter* SIR JASPER FIDGET *and* OLD LADY SQUEAMISH.]

15 SIR JASPER FIDGET. Oh, my Lady Fidget, was this your cunning, to come to Mr. Horner without me? But you have been nowhere else, I hope.

LADY FIDGET. No, Sir Jasper.

20 OLD LADY SQUEAMISH. And you came straight hither, Biddy?

MRS. SQUEAMISH. Yes, indeed, lady grandmother.

SIR JASPER FIDGET. 'Tis well, 'tis well; I knew
25 when once they were thoroughly acquainted with poor Horner, they'd ne'er be from him. You may let her masquerade it with my wife and Horner, and I warrant her reputation safe.

[*Enter* BOY.]

30 BOY. O sir, here's the gentleman come, whom you bid me not suffer to come up without giving you notice, with a lady too, and other gentlemen.

HORNER. Do you all go in there, whilst I send
35 'em away; and, boy, do you desire 'em to stay below till I come, which shall be immediately.

[*Exeunt* SIR JASPER, OLD LADY SQUEAMISH, LADY FIDGET, MRS. DAINTY, MRS. SQUEAMISH.]

BOY. Yes, sir.

40 [*Exit.*]

[*Exit* HORNER *at the other door, and returns with* MRS. PINCHWIFE.]

HORNER. You would not take my advice, to be gone home before your husband came back;
45 he'll now discover all. Yet pray, my dearest, be persuaded to go home, and leave the rest to my management; I'll let you down the back way.

MRS. PINCHWIFE. I don't know the way home,

so I don't. 50

HORNER. My man shall wait upon you.

MRS. PINCHWIFE. No, don't you believe that I'll go at all; what, are you weary of me already?

HORNER. No, my life, 'tis that I may love you 55 long, 'tis to secure my love, and your reputation with your husband; he'll never receive you again else.

MRS. PINCHWIFE. What care I? d'ye think to frighten me with that? I don't intend to go to 60 him again; you shall be my husband now.

HORNER. I cannot be your husband, dearest, since you are married to him.

MRS. PINCHWIFE. Oh, would you make me believe that? Don't I see every day, at London 65 here, women leave their first husbands, and go and live with other men as their wives? Pish, pshaw! you'd make me angry, but that I love you so mainly.

HORNER. So, they are coming up.—In again, 70 in, I hear 'em.—[*Exit* MRS. PINCHWIFE.] Well, a silly mistress is like a weak place, soon got, soon lost, a man has scarce time for plunder; she betrays her husband first to her gallant, and then her gallant to her husband. 75

[*Enter* PINCHWIFE, ALITHEA, HARCOURT, SPARKISH, LUCY *and a* PARSON.]

PINCHWIFE. Come, madam, 'tis not the sudden change of your dress, the confidence of your asseverations, and your false witness there, 80 shall persuade me I did not bring you hither just now; here's my witness, who cannot deny it, since you must be confronted.—Mr. Horner, did not I bring this lady to you just now?

HORNER [*aside*]. Now must I wrong one 85 woman for another's sake—but that's no new thing with me, for in these cases I am still on the criminal's side against the innocent.

ALITHEA. Pray speak, sir.

HORNER [*aside*]. It must be so. I must be 90 impudent, and try my luck; impudence uses to be too hard for truth.

PINCHWIFE. What, are you studying an evasion or excuse for her! Speak, sir.

HORNER. No, faith, I am something backward 95 only to speak in women's affairs or disputes.

PINCHWIFE. She bids you speak.

ALITHEA. Ah, pray, sir, do, pray satisfy him.

HORNER. Then truly, you did bring that lady to me just now.

PINCHWIFE. Oh ho!

ALITHEA. How, sir?

5 HARCOURT. How, Horner?

ALITHEA. What mean you, sir? I always took you for a man of honor.

HORNER [aside]. Ay, so much a man of honor, that I must save my mistress, I thank you, come 10 what will on't.

SPARKISH. So, if I had had her, she'd have made me believe the moon had been made of a Christmas pie.

LUCY [aside]. Now could I speak, if I durst, 15 and solve the riddle, who am the author of it.

ALITHEA. O unfortunate woman! A combination against my honor! which most concerns me now, because you share in my disgrace, sir, and it is your censure, which I 20 must now suffer, that troubles me, not theirs.

HARCOURT. Madam, then have no trouble, you shall now see 'tis possible for me to love too, without being jealous; I will not only believe your innocence myself, but make all the 25 world believe it.—[Apart to HORNER.] Horner, I must now be concerned for this lady's honor.

HORNER. And I must be concerned for a lady's honor too.

HARCOURT. This lady has her honor, and I 30 will protect it.

HORNER. My lady has not her honor, but has given it me to keep, and I will preserve it.

HARCOURT. I understand you not.

HORNER. I would not have you.

35 MRS. PINCHWIFE [peeping in behind]. What's the matter with 'em all?

PINCHWIFE. Come, come, Mr. Horner, no more disputing; here's the parson, I brought him not in vain.

40 HARCOURT. No, sir, I'll employ him, if this lady please.

PINCHWIFE. How! what d'ye mean?

SPARKISH. Ay, what does he mean?

HORNER. Why, I have resigned your sister to 45 him; he has my consent.

PINCHWIFE. But he has not mine, sir; a woman's injured honor, no more than a man's, can be repaired or satisfied by any but him that first wronged it; and you shall marry her presently, or—[lays his hand on his sword]. 50

[Enter MRS. PINCHWIFE.]

MRS. PINCHWIFE [aside]. O Lord, they'll kill poor Mr. Horner! Besides, he shan't marry her whilst I stand by and look on; I'll not lose my second husband so. 55

PINCHWIFE. What do I see?

ALITHEA. My sister in my clothes!

SPARKISH. Ha!

MRS. PINCHWIFE [to MR. PINCHWIFE]. Nay, pray now don't quarrel about finding work for 60 the parson; he shall marry me to Mr. Horner; for now, I believe, you have enough of me.

HORNER [aside]. Damned, damned loving changeling!

MRS. PINCHWIFE. Pray, sister, pardon me for 65 telling so many lies of you.

HORNER. I suppose the riddle is plain now.

LUCY. No, that must be my work.—Good sir, hear me. [Kneels to MR. PINCHWIFE, who stands doggedly with his hat over his eyes.] 70

PINCHWIFE. I will never hear women again, but make 'em all silent thus—[offers to draw upon his wife].

HORNER. No, that must not be.

PINCHWIFE. You then shall go first, 'tis all one 75 to me. [Offers to draw on HORNER, stopped by HARCOURT.]

HARCOURT. Hold!

[Enter SIR JASPER FIDGET, LADY FIDGET, OLD LADY SQUEAMISH, MRS. DAINTY FIDGET, MRS. 80 SQUEAMISH.]

SIR JASPER FIDGET. What's the matter? what's the matter? pray, what's the matter, sir? I beseech you communicate, sir.

PINCHWIFE. Why, my wife has communicated, 85 sir, as your wife may have done too, sir, if she knows him, sir.

SIR JASPER FIDGET. Pshaw, with him! ha! ha! he!

PINCHWIFE. D'ye mock me, sir? A cuckold is 90 a kind of a wild beast; have a care, sir.

SIR JASPER FIDGET. No, sure, you mock me, sir. He cuckold you! it can't be, ha! ha! he! why, I'll tell you, sir—[offers to whisper].

PINCHWIFE. I tell you again, he has whored 95 my wife, and yours too, if he knows her, and all the women he comes near; 'tis not his dissembling, his hypocrisy, can wheedle me.

SIR JASPER FIDGET. How! does he dissemble? is he a hypocrite? Nay, then—how—wife—
sister, is he a hypocrite?

OLD LADY SQUEAMISH. A hypocrite! a dissembler! Speak, young harlotry, speak, how?

SIR JASPER FIDGET. Nay, then.—Oh my head too!—Oh thou libidinous lady!

OLD LADY SQUEAMISH. Oh thou harloting harlotry! hast thou done't then?

SIR JASPER FIDGET. Speak, good Horner, art thou a dissembler, a rogue? hast thou—

HORNER. Soh!

LUCY [*apart to* HORNER]. I'll fetch you off, and her too, if she will but hold her tongue.

HORNER [*apart to* LUCY]. Can'st thou? I'll give thee—

LUCY [*to* MR. PINCHWIFE]. Pray have but patience to hear me, sir, who am the unfortunate cause of all this confusion. Your wife is innocent, I only culpable; for I put her upon telling you all these lies concerning my mistress, in order to the breaking off the match between Mr. Sparkish and her, to make way for Mr. Harcourt.

SPARKISH. Did you so, eternal rotten tooth? Then, it seems, my mistress was not false to me, I was only deceived by you. Brother, that should have been, now man of conduct, who is a frank person now, to bring your wife to her lover, ha?

LUCY. I assure you, sir, she came not to Mr. Horner out of love, for she loves him no more—

MRS. PINCHWIFE. Hold, I told lies for you, but you shall tell none for me, for I do love Mr. Horner with all my soul, and nobody shall say me nay; pray, don't you go to make poor Mr. Horner believe to the contrary; 'tis spitefully done of you, I'm sure.

HORNER [*aside to* MRS. PINCHWIFE]. Peace, dear idiot.

MRS. PINCHWIFE. Nay, I will not peace.

PINCHWIFE. Not till I make you.

[*Enter* DORILANT, QUACK.]

DORILANT. Horner, your servant; I am the doctor's guest, he must excuse our intrusion.

QUACK. But what's the matter, gentlemen? for Heaven's sake, what's the matter?

HORNER. Oh, 'tis well you are come. 'Tis a censorious world we live in; you may have brought me a reprieve, or else I had died for a crime I never committed, and these innocent ladies had suffered with me; therefore, pray satisfy these worthy, honorable, jealous gentlemen—that—[*whispers*].

QUACK. Oh, I understand you; is that all?— Sir Jasper, by Heavens, and upon the word of a physician, sir—[*whispers to* SIR JASPER].

SIR JASPER FIDGET. Nay, I do believe you truly.—Pardon me, my virtuous lady, and dear of honor.

OLD LADY SQUEAMISH. What, then all's right again?

SIR JASPER FIDGET. Ay, ay, and now let us satisfy him too. [*They whisper with* MR. PINCHWIFE.]

PINCHWIFE. An eunuch! Pray, no fooling with me.

QUACK. I'll bring half the chirurgeons in town to swear it.

PINCHWIFE. They!—they'll swear a man that bled to death through his wounds died of an apoplexy.

QUACK. Pray, hear me, sir—why, all the town has heard the report of him.

PINCHWIFE. But does all the town believe it?

QUACK. Pray, inquire a little, and first of all these.

PINCHWIFE. I'm sure when I left the town, he was the lewdest fellow in't.

QUACK. I tell you, sir, he has been in France since; pray, ask but these ladies and gentlemen, your friend Mr. Dorilant. Gentlemen and ladies, han't you all heard the late sad report of poor Mr. Horner?

ALL THE LADIES. Ay, ay, ay.

DORILANT. Why, thou jealous fool, dost thou doubt it? he's an arrant French capon.

MRS. PINCHWIFE. 'Tis false, sir, you shall not disparage poor Mr. Horner, for to my certain knowledge—

LUCY. Oh, hold!

MRS. SQUEAMISH [*aside to* LUCY]. Stop her mouth!

LADY FIDGET [*to* PINCHWIFE]. Upon my honor, sir, 'tis as true—

MRS. DAINTY FIDGET. D'ye think we would have been seen in his company?

5 MRS. SQUEAMISH. Trust our unspotted reputations with him?

LADY FIDGET [*aside to* HORNER]. This you get, and we too, by trusting your secret to a fool.

HORNER. Peace, madam.—[*Aside to* QUACK.]
10 Well, doctor, is not this a good design, that carries a man on unsuspected, and brings him off safe?

PINCHWIFE [*aside*]. Well, if this were true— but my wife—

15 [DORILANT *whispers with* MRS. PINCHWIFE.]

ALITHEA. Come, brother, your wife is yet innocent, you see; but have a care of too strong an imagination, lest, like an over-concerned timorous gamester, by fancying an unlucky
20 cast, it should come. Women and fortune are truest still to those that trust 'em.

LUCY. And any wild thing grows but the more fierce and hungry for being kept up, and more dangerous to the keeper.

25 ALITHEA. There's doctrine for all husbands, Mr. Harcourt.

HARCOURT. I edify, madam, so much, that I am impatient till I am one.

DORILANT. And I edify so much by example,
30 I will never be one.

SPARKISH. And because I will not disparage my parts, I'll ne'er be one.

HORNER. And I, alas! can't be one.

PINCHWIFE. But I must be one—against my
35 will to a country wife, with a country murrain° to me!

MRS. PINCHWIFE [*aside*]. And I must be a country wife still too, I find; for I can't, like a city one, be rid of my musty husband, and do
40 what I list.

HORNER. Now, sir, I must pronounce your wife innocent, though I blush whilst I do it; and I am the only man by her now exposed to shame, which I will straight drown in wine, as
45 you shall your suspicion; and the ladies'

troubles we'll divert with a ballet.—Doctor, where are your maskers?

LUCY. Indeed, she's innocent, sir, I am her witness; and her end of coming out was but to see her sister's wedding; and what she has said 50
to your face of her love to Mr. Horner was but the usual innocent revenge on a husband's jealousy—was it not, madam, speak?

MRS. PINCHWIFE [*aside to* LUCY *and* HORNER]. Since you'll have me tell more lies.—Yes, 55
indeed, bud.

PINCHWIFE.
For my own sake fain I would all believe;
Cuckolds, like lovers, should themselves
[deceive. 60
But—[*sighs.*] his honor is least safe (too late
[I find)
Who trusts it with a foolish wife or friend.
[*A dance of cuckolds.*]
HORNER. 65
Vain fops but court and dress, and keep a
[pother,
To pass for women's men with one another;
But he who aims by woman to be prized,
First by the men, you see, must be despised. 70

---

murrain plague

Jean Racine

1639–1699

Phaedra

1677

Sobriety of plot design, rigorous intellectual clarity, and refinement of language—these are the acknowledged virtues of Racine, master of the French classical theater. Why, then, do they arouse in many modern readers and playgoers only perfunctory appreciation? Because Racine's real power lies in the philosophical anguish and the undeviating intellectual sincerity of which these virtues are only manifestations. Moreover, Racine is not readily understandable apart from the French language, French poetics, and the intellectual preoccupations of the court of Louis XIV. *Phaedra,* which Racine called "the clearest and most close-knit play I have written," is immediately related to those preoccupations, with the efforts of seventeenth-century European thought to preserve or salvage its classical and Christian heritage. Racine knew that he lived in a center of intellectual crisis. *Phaedra* is directly derived from the *Hippolytus* of Euripides, himself a philosophical skeptic, and, although remaining a period-piece in its way, it deals with some intellectual issues that still reverberate today.

Racine correctly renamed his version of the tragedy *Phaedra.* It is not an antiquarian piece of Greek theater revived. In the world of Euripides, sacred genealogies and invocations of the gods still seemed authentic. In Racine's world, the authenticity of all such invocations is in question. Even Theseus' all-too-instantly granted prayer that the god Neptune redeem an old pledge only serves to reveal "Neptune" as a mindless expression of infantile rage. The metaphors of destiny and of ethical value are, so to speak, within quotation marks, with the result that Phaedra comes to represent the human psyche facing the tortuous question of its identity, and so she is at the center of the play.

Phaedra is an audacious, although conditional, attempt to translate mythological and theological concepts into

JEAN RACINE

their psychological equivalents. The ideas at issue are those of fate and free will, the paradox of a soul that intuitively feels itself free yet is constrained or driven by irresistible forces. Growing out of Phaedra's intense passion for Hippolytus and her equally intense loathing of her passion, the tragic events are almost entirely internalized, almost exclusively psychic. Contrast Phaedra with Iocastê, the mother of Oedipus. Iocastê unknowingly commits the act of incest that Phaedra has only imagined. Iocastê is ruined, but she is not in her heart at fault. Whatever guilt she must accept is an imposition of the gods. Phaedra accepts her guilt as her own, with great anguish of spirit, and recognizes that her suffering is grounded in her very identity. Racine's Hippolytus, unlike Euripides', is mainly an accidental victim. His physical suffering, as narrated, is grotesque, but psychically he suffers little more than bewilderment and embarrassment. Phaedra, however, finds herself at the center of a labyrinth into which no rescuer can come.

What causes this suffering—self-conscious, involuntary, self-motivating, self-condemned? Some external imposition or internal compulsion? They can scarcely be differentiated, although they can be given different names. For Phaedra, in a moment of vision, the cause is "Venus":

C'est Vénus toute entière á sa proie attachée

Yet this "Venus"—"altogether devouring her prey"—is only another name for Phaedra's obsession, and the obsession itself is only a headless, primal drive violently at odds with the judgment of her conscious mind. Venus and her prey are one and the same. What had once been represented as fate or a divinity is here being converted into an aspect of the psyche itself.

A similar process of interpretation is discernible in Hippolytus' celebrated line characterizing Phaedra as "the daughter of Minos and of Pasiphaë." This line, defiant of poetic translation, explains Phaedra's plight as the result of a family curse descending through generations. In Racine this explanation is in question. What does such an explanation mean? To be the daughter of these parents is to be the incarnation of a father (Minos) so righteous in judgment that he will sentence Phaedra even from Hades, and equally of a mother (Pasiphaë) whose name is a synonym for sexual depravity. It means, in terms that might have seemed already outmoded to Racine, that man is at the mercy of divine justice and the prey of demonic forces, or, in terms more current, that man is divided at the intersection of reason and nature, or, in later conceptualizations, that the ego is compressed between the superego and the id, or that "existence precedes essence." These are formulaic abstractions.

Racine tends to treat abstractions, or at least parables—and in view of their implications for orthodox Christian doctrine, they are perilous ones. Although the play focuses on the confrontation of character with character, in scenes advancing with measured inevitability, it is as if behind each face there were another centuries-old countenance, anxiously contemplating human solitude in a world gradually losing faith in the reign of providence.

Racine had received a stern Catholic education in the theology of predestination, and after writing *Phaedra* he returned to a life of severe piety. It is scarcely accidental that in *Phaedra* he had boldly—and some thought amorally—called into thinly veiled question the viability of religious explanations for human motivation and the governance of states. Yet the great speeches of Phaedra, self-lacerating and luminously clear, are themselves the reverse of abstract. They express not so much speculation as the torments of a mind unable to consent to the conditions of its self-knowledge. Does any tragedy probe more deeply into sources of guilt and despair?

Phaedra

RACINE

Translated by John Cairncross

CHARACTERS

THESEUS   *son of Aegeus, King of Athens*
PHAEDRA   *wife of Theseus, daughter of Minos
    and Pasiphaë*
HIPPOLYTUS   *son of Theseus and Antiope,
    Queen of the Amazons*
ARICIA   *princess of the blood royal of Athens*
THERAMENES   *Hippolytus's governor*
OENONE   *Phaedra's nurse and confidante*
ISMENE   *Aricia's confidante*
PANOPE   *a woman of Phaedra's retinue*

SCENE. *Troezen, a town in the Peloponnesus.*

ACT I

Scene i

[HIPPOLYTUS, THERAMENES.]
HIPPOLYTUS. It is resolved, Theramenes. I go.
I will depart from Troezen's pleasant land.
5 Torn by uncertainty about the King,
I am ashamed of standing idly by.
For over half a year I have not heard
Of my dear father Theseus'° destiny

Nor even by what far sky he is concealed.
   THERAMENES. And where, my lord, would you   10
      [make search for him?
Already, to allay your proper fears,
I have scoured both the seas that Corinth joins;
I have sought news of Theseus on the shores
Of Acheron, the river of the dead;   15
Elis I searched, then sailed past Tenaros
On to the sea where Icarus came down.
What makes you hope that you may find his
      [trace
In some more favored region of the world?   20
Who knows indeed if it is his desire
To have the secret of his absence known?
And whether, as we tremble for his life,
He is not tasting all the joys of love,
And soon the outraged victim of his wiles. . . .   25
   HIPPOLYTUS. No more of this, Theramenes.
      [The King
Has seen the errors of his amorous youth.
He is above unworthy dalliance,
And, stronger than his old inconstancy,   30
Phaedra has in his heart long reigned alone.
But, to be brief, I must make search for him
Far from this city where I dare not stay.
   THERAMENES. Since when do you, my lord,
      [fear to frequent   35
These peaceful haunts you cherished as a boy,
Which I have seen you many a time prefer
To the loud pomp of Athens and the court?
What peril, or what trouble, drives you hence?
   HIPPOLYTUS. Those happy days are gone, and   40
      [all is changed,
Since to these shores the mighty gods have sent
The child of Minos° and Pasiphaë°.

Theseus one of the legendary Greek heroes, famed as hunter, traveler, seducer of women, companion of Hercules and Jason, conqueror of the Amazonian queen, Hippolyta, by whom he fathered Hippolytus. With the assistance of Ariadne he entered the labyrinth and slew the Minotaur; he brought Phaedra to Athens. He restored his father, Aegus, to the throne of Athens, from which he had been expelled

by descendants of Pallas and Erectheus, earlier kings. As the play opens, Theseus is absent on a legendary expedition that was to take him to Hades, in an attempt to rescue Proserpine from her abductor, the god Pluto. (In Act III, Scene v., Racine's Theseus gives a less mythical version of his journey.)

Minos legendary king of Crete, a son of Zeus (Jove) and father of Phaedra and of her sister Ariadne; after his death appointed one of the supreme judges in Hades

Pasiphaë his wife, a daughter of Helios, the sun. By copulating with a bull she conceived the Minotaur, half man and half bull, who was kept in a labyrinth. He yearly devoured seven youths and seven maidens surrendered by Athens as tributes to Minos.

From Phaedra and Other Plays, *translated by John Cairncross. Copyright* © *John Cairncross, 1963. Reprinted by permission of Penguin Books Ltd.*

THERAMENES. I understand. The cause of your
                                          [distress
Is known. The sight of Phaedra vexes you.
Theseus' new wife had scarcely seen you than
5 Your exile gave the measure of her power.
But now her hate that never let you be
Has vanished or is greatly on the wane.
Besides what perils threaten you from her—
A woman dying or who seeks to die?
10 Racked by a malady she will not name,
Tired of herself and of the light of day,
Phaedra has not the strength to do you ill.
    HIPPOLYTUS. I do not fear her vain hostility.
If I go hence, I flee, let me confess,
15 Another enemy . . . Aricia,
Last of a line that plotted Theseus' death.
    THERAMENES. What! Would you stoop to
                                    [persecute her too?
Though she is sprung of Pallas' cruel race,
20 She never joined in her false brothers' schemes.
Why hate her then if she is innocent?
    HIPPOLYTUS. I would not flee her if I hated
                                          [her.
    THERAMENES. My lord, may I explain your
25   [sudden flight?
Are you no more the man that once you were,
Relentless foe of all the laws of love
And of a yoke Theseus himself has borne?
Will Venus whom you haughtily disdained
30 Vindicate Theseus after all these years
By forcing you to worship with the throng
Of ordinary mortals at her shrine?
Are you in love?
    HIPPOLYTUS.   My friend, what have you
35   [said?
You who have known me since I first drew
                                          [breath,
You ask me shamefully to disavow
The feelings of a proud disdainful heart?
40 The Amazon, my mother, with her milk
Suckled me on that pride you wonder at.
And I myself, on reaching man's estate,
Approved my nature when I knew myself.
Serving me with unfeignéd loyalty,
45 You would relate my father's history.
You know how, as I hung upon your words,
My heart would glow at tales of his exploits

When you portrayed Theseus, that demi-god,
Consoling mortals for Alcides'° loss,
Monsters suppressed and brigands brought to   50
                                        [book—
Procrustes, Sciron, Sinis, Cercyon;
The giants' bones in Epidaurus strewn
And Crete red with the slaughtered Minotaur.
But, when you told me of less glorious deeds,   55
His word pledged and believed in countless
                                        [lands:
Helen in Sparta ravished from her home,
Salamis, scene of Periboea's tears;
Others whose very names he has forgot,   60
Too trusting spirits all deceived by him;
Wronged Ariadne crying to the winds;
Phaedra abducted, though for lawful ends;
You know how, loath to hear this sorry tale,
I often urged you quickly to conclude,   65
Happy could I have kept the shameful half
Of these adventures from posterity.
And am I to be vanquished in my turn?
And can the gods have humbled me so far?
In base defeat the more despicable   70
Since countless exploits plead on his behalf,
Whereas no monsters overcome by me
Have given me the right to err like him.
And, even if I were fated to succumb,
Should I have chosen to love Aricia?   75
Should not my wayward feelings have recalled
That she is barred from me eternally?
King Theseus frowns upon her and decrees
That she shall not prolong her brothers' line:
He fears this guilty stock will blossom forth, 80
And, to ensure her name shall end with her,
Condemns her to be single till she dies—
No marriage torch shall ever blaze for her.
Should I espouse her cause and brave his wrath?
Set an example to foolhardiness?   85
And, on a foolish passion launched, my
                                        [youth . . .
    THERAMENES. Ah! when your hour has once
                            [but struck, my lord,

Alcides Hercules. Theseus set out to rival Hercules'
famed "labors." Hippolytus here differentiates between his father's heroic feats and his amatory exploits, of which no Racinian hero could approve.

Heaven of our reasons takes but little heed.
Theseus opens your eyes despite yourself.
His hatred of Aricia has fanned
Your passion and has lent her added grace.
5   Besides, my lord, why fear a worthy love?
If it is sweet, will you not dare to taste?
Will you be always ruled by modesty?
Can you go wrong where Hercules has trod?
What hearts has Venus' power not subdued?
10 Where would you be yourself, who fight her
                                        [now,
If, combating her love, Antiope
Had never been consumed for Theseus?
However, what avails this haughty tone?
15 Confess it, all is changed; for some days past
You are less often seen, aloof and proud,
Speeding your chariot along the shore,
Or, skillful in the seagod Neptune's art,
Bending an untamed courser to the curb.
20 The woods less often to your cries resound;
Your eyes grow heavier with secret fire.
There is no doubt, you are consumed with love.
You perish from a malady you hide.
Has fair Aricia enraptured you?
25   HIPPOLYTUS. Theramenes, I go to seek the
                                        [King.
    THERAMENES. And will you see Phaedra
                                  [before you leave,
My lord?
30   HIPPOLYTUS.   I mean to. You may tell her
                                        [so.
See her I must, since duty so commands.
But what new burden weighs Oenone down?

Scene ii

[HIPPOLYTUS, OENONE, THERAMENES.]
35   OENONE. Alas, my lord, what cares can equal
                                        [mine?
The Queen is almost at her destined end.
In vain I watch over her night and day.
She's dying from a hidden malady;
40 Eternal discord reigns within her mind.
Her restless anguish tears her from her bed.
She longs to see the light, and yet, distraught
With pain, she bids me banish everyone . . .
But here she comes.
45   HIPPOLYTUS.   Enough. I'll take my leave

And will not show her my detested face.

Scene iii

[PHAEDRA, OENONE.]
    PHAEDRA. No further. Here, Oenone, let us
                                        [stay.
I faint, I fall; my strength abandons me.   50
My eyes are dazzled by the daylight's glare,
And my knees, trembling, give beneath my
                                        [weight.
Alas!
    OENONE.   May our tears move you,   55
                                  [mighty gods!
    PHAEDRA. How these vain jewels, these veils
                                  [weigh on me!
What meddling hand has sought to re-arrange
My hair, by braiding it across my brow?   60
All things contrive to grieve and thwart me, all.
    OENONE. How all her wishes war among
                                  [themselves!
Yourself, condemning your unlawful plans,
A moment past, bade us adorn your brow;   65
Yourself, summoning up your former strength,
Wished to come forth and see the light again.
Scarce have you seen it than you long to hide,
You hate the daylight you came forth to see.
    PHAEDRA. O shining founder° of an ill-   70
                                  [starred line,
You, whom my mother dared to boast her sire,
Who blush perhaps to see me thus distraught,
Sungod, for the last time, I look on you.
    OENONE. What? you will not give up this fell   75
                                  [desire?
And will you, always saying no to life,
Make mournful preparation for your death?
    PHAEDRA. Would I were seated in the forest's
                                  [shade!   80
When can I follow through the swirling dust
The lordly chariot's flight along the course?
    OENONE. What?
    PHAEDRA.   Madness! Where am I, what
                                  [have I said?   85
Whither have my desires, my reason strayed?
Lost, lost, the gods have carried it away.
Oenone, blushes sweep across my face;

founder Helios, father of Pasiphaë

My grievous shame stands all too clear
                              [revealed,
And tears despite me fill my aching eyes.
    OENONE. If you must blush, blush for your
5   [silence, for
It but inflames the fury of your ills.
Deaf to our wild entreaties, pitiless,
Will you allow yourself to perish thus?
What madness cuts you off in mid career?
10 What spell, what poison, has dried up the
                              [source?
Thrice have the shades of night darkened the
                              [skies
Since sleep last made its entry to your eyes,
15 And thrice the day has driven forth dim night
Since last your fainting lips took nourishment.
What dark temptation lures you to your doom?
What right have you to plot to end your life?
In this you wrong the gods from whom you
20   [spring,
You are unfaithful to your wedded lord;
Unfaithful also to your hapless sons,
Whom you would thrust beneath a heavy yoke.
Remember, that same day their mother dies,
25 Hope for the alien woman's son revives,
For that fierce enemy of you and yours,
That youth whose mother was an Amazon,
Hippolytus . . .
    PHAEDRA.   God!
30 OENONE.   *That* reproach struck home.
    PHAEDRA. Ah! wretched woman, what name
                              [crossed your lips?
    OENONE. Your anger now bursts forth, and
                              [rightly so.
35 I love to see you shudder at the name.
Live then. Let love and duty spur you on.
Live on. Do not allow a Scythian's son°
To lord it with his harsh and odious rule
Over the pride of Greece and of the gods.
40 Do not delay! for every moment kills.
Haste to replenish your enfeebled strength
While yet the fires of life, though all but spent,
Are burning and can still flame bright again.
    PHAEDRA. I have prolonged my guilty days

Scythian's son Hippolytus. As the son of an Amazon
he was regarded as an alien unfit to rule in Athens.

                              [too far. 45
    OENONE. What, are you harried by some keen
                              [remorse?
What crime could ever bring you to this pass?
Your hands were never stained with guiltless
                              [blood. 50
    PHAEDRA. Thanks be to Heaven, my hands
                              [have done no wrong.
Would God my heart were innocent as they!
    OENONE. What fearful project then have you
                              [conceived 55
Which strikes such terror deep into my heart?
    PHAEDRA. I have revealed enough. Spare me
                              [the rest.
I die, and my grim secret dies with me.
    OENONE. Keep silence then, inhuman one, 60
                              [and die;
But seek some other hand to close your eyes.
Although the candle of your life burns low,
I will go down before you to the dead.
Thither a thousand different roads converge, 65
My misery will choose the shortest one.
When have I ever failed you, cruel one?
Remember, you were born into my arms.
For you I have lost country, children, all.
Is this how you reward fidelity? 70
    PHAEDRA. What do you hope to gain by
                              [violence?
If I should speak, you would be thunderstruck.
    OENONE. And what, ye gods, could be more
                              [terrible 75
Than seeing you expire before my eyes?
    PHAEDRA. Even when you know my crime
                              [and cruel fate,
I yet will die, and die the guiltier.
    OENONE. By all the tears that I have shed for 80
                              [you,
And by your faltering knees I hold entwined,
Deliver me from dire uncertainty.
    PHAEDRA. You wish it. Rise.
    OENONE.   Speak. I await your words. 85
    PHAEDRA. What shall I say to her and where
                              [begin?
    OENONE. Wound me no longer by such vain
                              [affrights!
    PHAEDRA. Oh hate of Venus! Anger-laden 90
                              [doom!

Into what dark abyss love hurled my mother!
    OENONE. Ah, Queen, forget; and for all time
                    [to come
Eternal silence seal this memory.
5   PHAEDRA. Oh sister Ariadne, from what love
You died deserted on a barren shore!
    OENONE. What ails you, and what mortal
                    [agony
Drives you to fury against all your race?
10   PHAEDRA. Since Venus wills it, of this unblest
                    [line
I perish, I, the last and wretchedest.
    OENONE. You are in love?
    PHAEDRA.   Love's furies rage in me.
15   OENONE. For whom?
    PHAEDRA.   Prepare to hear the crowning
                    [woe.
I love . . . I tremble, shudder at the name;
I love . . .
20   [OENONE *leans forward.*]
    PHAEDRA.   You know that prince whom I
                    [myself
So long oppressed, son of the Amazon?
    OENONE. Hippolytus?
25   PHAEDRA.   *You* have pronounced his
                    [name.
    OENONE. Merciful heavens! My blood chills
                    [in my veins.
O grief! O crime! O lamentable race!
30   Ill-fated journey and thrice ill-starred coast!
Would we had never neared your dangerous
                    [shores!
    PHAEDRA. My malady goes further back. I
                    [scarce
35   Was bound by marriage to Aegeus' son;
My peace of mind, my happiness seemed sure—
Athens revealed to me my haughty foe.
As I beheld, I reddened, I turned pale.
A tempest raged in my distracted mind.
40   My eyes no longer saw. I could not speak.
I felt my body freezing, burning; knew
Venus was on me with her dreaded flames,
The fatal torments of a race she loathes.
By sleepless vows, I thought to ward her off.
45   I built a temple to her, rich and fair.
No hour went by but I made sacrifice,
Seeking my reason in the victims' flanks.

Weak remedies for love incurable!
In vain my hand burned incense on the shrine.
Even when my lips invoked the goddess' name,   50
I worshipped *him*. His image followed me.
Even on the altar's steps, my offerings
Were only to the god I dared not name.
I shunned him everywhere. O crowning woe!
I found him mirrored in his father's face!   55
Against myself at last I dared revolt.
I spurred my feelings on to harass him.
To banish my adoréd enemy,
I feigned a spite against this stepson, kept
Urging his exile, and my ceaseless cries   60
Wrested him from a father's loving arms.
I breathed more freely since I knew him gone.
The days flowed by, untroubled, innocent.
Faithful to Theseus, hiding my distress,
I nursed the issue of our ill-starred bed.   65
Ah vain precautions! Cruel destiny!
Brought by my lord himself to Troezen's
                    [shores,
I saw once more the foe I had expelled.
My open wound at once poured blood again.   70
The fire no longer slumbers in the veins.
All Venus' might has fastened on her prey.
I have a fitting horror for my crime;
I hate this passion and I loathe my life.
Dying, I could have kept my name unstained,   75
And my dark passion from the light of day;
Your tears, your pleas have forced me to
                    [confess,
And I will not regret what I have done,
If you, respecting the approach of death,   80
Will cease to vex me with reproaches, and
Your vain assistance will not try to fan
The last faint flicker still alight in me.

Scene iv

[PHAEDRA, OENONE, PANOPE.]
    PANOPE. Would I could hide from you the   85
                    [grievous news,
My lady, but I cannot hold it back.
Death has abducted your unconquered lord
And this mischance is known to all but you.
    OENONE. What, Panope?   90
    PANOPE.   The Queen in vain, alas!
Importunes heaven for Theseus' safe return,

For, from the vessels just arrived in port,
Hippolytus, his son, has learned his death.
    PHAEDRA. God!
    PANOPE.   Athens is divided in its choice
5 Of master. Some favor the prince, your son,
Others, forgetful of the State's decrees,°
Dare to support the foreign woman's son.
Rumor even has it that a bold intrigue
Wishes to give Aricia the throne.
10 I deemed it right to warn you of this threat.
Hippolytus is ready to set sail,
And in this turmoil it is to be feared
He may win fickle Athens to his cause.
    OENONE. Panope, cease! You may be sure the
15   [Queen
Will give due heed to this important news.

Scene v

[PHAEDRA, OENONE.]
    OENONE. Ah Queen, I had relinquished you
                     [to death
20 And thought to follow you down to the tomb.
I had no longer words to turn you back;
But this news bids you steer another course.
Now all is changed, and fortune smiles on you.
The King is dead, and you must take his place.
25 He leaves a son with whom your duty lies:
A slave without you; if you live, a king.
On whom in his misfortune can he lean?
If you are dead, no hand will dry his tears;
And his fond cries, borne upwards to the gods,
30 Will bring his forebears' anger down on you.
Live then, no longer tortured by reproach.
Your love becomes like any other love.
Theseus, in dying, has dissolved the bonds
Which made your love a crime to be abhorred.
35 You need no longer dread Hippolytus,
And you may see him and be guiltless still.
Perhaps, convinced of your hostility,
He is prepared to captain the revolt.
Quick, undeceive him; bend him to your will.
40 King of these fertile shores, Troezen is his.
But well he knows the laws assign your son
The soaring ramparts that Minerva° built.

---

decrees forbidding the throne to anyone not wholly
   of Greek parentage
Minerva or Athena, patron goddess of Athens

Both of you have a common enemy.
Join forces then against Aricia.
    PHAEDRA. Then be it so. Your counsels have   45
                     [prevailed.
I'll live, if I can be recalled to life,
And if the love I bear my son can still
In this grim hour revive my failing strength.

ACT II

Scene i

[ARICIA, ISMENE.]   50
    ARICIA. Hippolytus has asked to see me here?
Hippolytus wishes to say farewell?
Ismene, are you not mistaken?
    ISMENE.   No.
This is the first result of Theseus' death.   55
Make ready to receive from every side
Allegiances that Theseus filched from you.
Aricia is mistress of her fate,
And soon all Greece will bow the knee to her.
    ARICIA. This was no rumor then, Ismene.   60
                    [Now
My enemy, my tyrant is no more.
    ISMENE. Indeed. The gods no longer frown on
                    [you,
And Theseus wanders with your brothers'   65
                    [shades.
    ARICIA. By what adventure did he meet his
                    [end?
    ISMENE. The tales told of his death are past
                   [belief.   70
They say that in some amorous escapade
The waters closed over his faithless head.
The thousand tongues of rumor even assert
That with Pirithous he went down to Hell,
Beheld Cocytus and the somber shores,   75
Showed himself living to the shades below,
But that he could not, from the house of death,
Recross the river whence is no return.
    ARICIA. Can mortal man, before he breathes
                  [his last,   80
Descend into the kingdom of the dead?
What magic lured him to that dreaded shore?
    ISMENE. You alone doubt it. Theseus is no
                   [more.
Athens is stricken; Troezen knows the news,   85
And now pays tribute to Hippolytus.

Here in this palace, trembling for her son,
Phaedra takes counsel with her anxious friends.
    ARICIA. But will Hippolytus be kinder than
His father was to me, loosen my chains,
5 And pity my mishaps?
    ISMENE.   I think he will.
    ARICIA. Do you not know severe Hippolytus?
How can you hope that he will pity me,
Honoring in me alone a sex he spurns?
10 How constantly he has avoided us,
Haunting those places which he knows we
                     [shun!
    ISMENE. I know the tales of his unfeelingness;
But I have seen him in your presence, and
15 The legend of Hippolytus' reserve
Doubled my curiosity in him.
His aspect did not tally with his fame;
At the first glance from you he grew confused.
His eyes, seeking in vain to shun your gaze,
20 Brimming with languor, took their fill of you.
Although the name of lover wounds his pride,
He has a lover's eye, if not his tongue.
    ARICIA. How avidly, Ismene, does my heart,
Drink in these words, baseless though they
25   [may be!
Oh you who know me, can it be believed
That the sad plaything of a ruthless fate,
A heart that always fed on bitterness,
Should ever know the frenzied pangs of love?
30 Last of the issue of Earth's royal son,°
I only have escaped the scourge of war.
I lost, all in their springtime's flowering,
Six brothers, pride of an illustrious line.
The sword swept all away and drenched the
35   [earth,
Which drank, unwillingly, Erechtheus' blood.
You know that, since their death, a cruel law
Forbids all Greeks to seek me as their wife,
Since it was feared my offspring might one day
40 Kindle my brothers' ashes into life.
But you recall with what disdain I viewed
These moves of a suspicious conqueror,
For, as a lifelong enemy of love,
I rendered thanks to Theseus' tyranny,
45 Which merely helped to keep me fancy free.
My eyes had not yet lighted on his son.

royal son   Erectheus, the father of Aricia

Not that my eyes alone yield to the charm
Of his much vaunted grace, his handsomeness,
Bestowed by nature, but which he disdains,
And seems not even to realize he owns.   50
I love and prize in him far nobler gifts,
His father's virtues, not his weaknesses.
I love, let me confess, that manly pride,
Which never yet has bowed beneath love's
                   [yoke.   55
Phaedra in vain gloried in Theseus' sighs.
I am more proud, and spurn the easy prize
Of homage to a thousand others paid
And of a heart accessible to all.
But to bring an unbending spirit down,   60
To cause an aching where no feeling was,
To stun a conqueror with his defeat,
In vain revolt against a yoke he loves.
That rouses my ambition, my desire.
Even Hercules was easier to disarm.   65
Vanquished more often than Hippolytus,
He yielded a less glorious victory.
But, dear Ismene, what rash hopes are these?
For his resistance will be all too strong.
You yet may hear me, humble in my grief   70
Bewail the very pride I now admire.
Hippolytus in love? By what excess
Of fortune could I . . .
    ISMENE.   You yourself will hear.
Hither he comes.   75

Scene ii

[HIPPOLYTUS, ARICIA, ISMENE.]
    HIPPOLYTUS.   Princess, before I go
I deemed it right to let you know your fate.
My father is no more. My fears divined
The secret of his lengthy absence. Death,   80
Death only, ending his illustrious deeds,
Could hide him from the universe so long.
The gods at last deliver to the Fates
Alcides' friend, companion, and his heir.
I feel that, silencing your hate, even you   85
Hear in good part the honors due to him.
One hope alone tempers my mortal grief.
I can release you from a stern control,
Revoking laws whose harshness I deplore.
Yourself, your heart, do with them what you   90
                   [will;
And in this Troezen, now assigned to me

As my sage grandsire Pittheus'° heritage,
Which with a single voice proclaimed me king,
I leave you free as I am; nay, more free.
    ARICIA. Limit your boundless generosity.
5 By honoring me, despite adversity,
My lord, you place me, more than you believe,
Beneath those laws from which you set me free.
    HIPPOLYTUS. Athens, uncertain whom to
                    [choose as heir,
10 Talks of yourself, of me, and the Queen's son.
    ARICIA. Me?
    HIPPOLYTUS. I would not wish to deceive
                    [myself.
My claim appears to be annulled by law
15 Because my mother was an Amazon.
But, if my only rival for the throne
Were Phaedra's son, my stepbrother, I could
Protect my rights against the law's caprice.
If I do not assert my claim, it is
20 To hand, or rather to return, to you
A scepter given to your ancestors°
By that great mortal whom the earth begot.
Adoption placed it in Aegeus' hands.
Theseus, his son, defended and enlarged
25 The bounds of Athens, which proclaimed him
                    [king
And left your brothers in oblivion.
Athens recalls you now within her walls.
Too long has she deplored this endless feud;
30 Too long your noble kinsmen's blood has
                    [flown,
Drenching the very fields from which it sprang.
If Troezen falls to me, the lands of Crete
Offer a rich domain to Phaedra's son.
35 But Attica is yours. And I go hence
To unify our votes on your behalf.
    ARICIA. At all I hear, astounded and amazed,
I almost fear a dream deceives my ears.
Am I awake? Is it to be believed?
40 What god, my lord, inspired you with the
                    [thought?
How rightly is your glory spread abroad!
And how the truth surpasses your renown!
You in my favor will renounce your claim?

Pittheus grandfather of Theseus, who assigned his
    royal rights in Troezen to Hippolytus
ancestors Aricia's royal forebears

Surely it was enough to keep your heart   45
So long free from that hatred of my line,
That enmity . . .
    HIPPOLYTUS. *I* hate you, Princess? No.
However my aloofness be decried,
Do you believe a monster gave me birth?   50
What churlish breeding, what unbending hate
Would not have melted at the sight of you?
Could I resist the soft beguiling spell . . .
    ARICIA. What! My lord . . .
    HIPPOLYTUS.   No, I cannot now draw   55
                    [back!
Reason, I see, gives way to violence.
And, since I have begun to speak my mind,
Princess, I must go on: I must reveal
A secret that my heart cannot conceal.   60
Before you stands a pitiable prince,
Signal example of rash arrogance.
I who, in proud rebellion against love,
Have long mocked other captives' sufferings,
Who, pitying the shipwrecks of the weak,   65
Had thought to watch them always from the
                    [shore,
Am now, in bondage to the common law,
Cut from my moorings by a surging swell.
A single blow has quelled my recklessness: 70
My haughty spirit is at last in thrall.
For six long months ashamed and in despair,
Pierced by the shaft implanted in my side,
I battle with myself, with you, in vain.
Present I flee you; absent, you are near.   75
Deep in the woods, your image follows me.
The light of day, the shadows of the night,
Everything conjures up the charms I flee.
Each single thing delivers up my heart.
And, sole reward for all my fruitless care,   80
I seek but cannot find myself again,
Bow, chariot, javelins, all importune me;
The lessons Neptune taught me are forgot.
My idle steeds no longer know my voice,
And only to my cries the woods resound.   85
Perhaps the tale of so uncouth a love
Brings as you listen, blushes to your face.
What words with which to offer you a heart!
How strange a conquest for so fair a maid!
But you should prize the offering the more.   90
Remember that I speak an unknown tongue,
And do not scorn my clumsy gallantry,

Which, but for you, I never would have shown.

Scene iii

[HIPPOLYTUS, ARICIA, THERAMENES, ISMENE.]
THERAMENES. The Queen is coming, Prince.
                              [She looks for you.
5   HIPPOLYTUS. For me?
THERAMENES.   I do not know what she
                                   [intends.
You have been sent for by her messenger.
Before you leave, Phaedra would speak with
10   [you.
HIPPOLYTUS. What can I say? And what can
                              [she expect . . .
ARICIA. Consent at least, my lord, to hear
                              [her speak.
15 Although she was your bitter enemy,
You owe some shade of pity to her tears.
HIPPOLYTUS. Meanwhile you go. I leave, and
                              [am in doubt
Whether I have offended my beloved,
20 Or if my heart that I commit to you . . .
ARICIA. Go, Prince. Pursue your generous
                              [designs.
Make Athens' State pay homage to me. All
The gifts you offer to me I accept.
25 But Athens' empire, glorious though it be,
Is not your most endearing offering.

Scene iv

[HIPPOLYTUS, THERAMENES.]
HIPPOLYTUS. Are you all ready? But here
                              [comes the Queen.
30 Let everyone prepare with all dispatch
To sail. Go, give the signal; hasten back,
And free me from a tedious interview.

Scene v

[PHAEDRA, HIPPOLYTUS, OENONE.]
PHAEDRA [to OENONE *at the back of the*
35 *stage*]. He comes . . . My blood sweeps back into
                              [my heart.
Forgotten are the words I had prepared.
OENONE. Think of your son, who hopes in
                              [you alone.
40 PHAEDRA. They say that you are leaving us at
                              [once,
My lord. I come to join my tears to yours.

I come to tell you of a mother's fears.
My son is fatherless, and soon, too soon,
He must behold my death as well. Even now,   45
Numberless enemies beset his youth.
You, only you, can see to his defense.
But I am harried by remorse within.
I fear lest you refuse to hear his cries.
I tremble lest you visit on a son   50
Your righteous anger at a mother's crimes.
HIPPOLYTUS. How could I ever be so
                              [infamous?
PHAEDRA. If you should hate me, I would not
                              [complain,   55
For I appeared resolved to do you ill.
Deep in my inmost heart you could not read.
I drew upon myself your enmity,
And where I dwelt, I would not suffer you.
With unrelenting hate, I sought to be   60
Divided from you by a waste of seas.
I even ordained by an express decree
That in my presence none should speak your
                              [name.
But, if the punishment should fit the crime,   65
If hate alone could bring on me your hate,
Never did woman merit pity more
And less, my lord, deserve your enmity.
HIPPOLYTUS. A mother jealous of her
                              [children's rights 70
Rarely forgives another woman's son,
I realize; and from a second bed
Awkward suspicion all too often springs.
Another would have taken like offense,
And at her hands I might have suffered more.   75
PHAEDRA. Ah! My lord, heaven, I dare here
                              [attest,
Has quite dispensed me from the common rule.
Far other is the care that weighs on me.
HIPPOLYTUS. Lady, it is too early yet to   80
                              [grieve.
Who knows, your husband may be still alive.
Heaven may vouchsafe him to your tears again.
Protected by the seagod, not in vain
Will Theseus call on mighty Neptune's aid.   85
PHAEDRA. No mortal visits twice the house of
                              [death.
Since Theseus has beheld the somber shores,
In vain you hope a god will send him back,
And hungry Acheron holds fast his prey.   90

But no, he is not dead; he lives, in you.
Always I think I see my husband's face.
I see him, speak to him, and my fond heart . . .
My frenzied love bursts forth in spite of me.
5   HIPPOLYTUS. In this I see the wonder of your
                               [love.
Dead as he is, Theseus still lives for you.
Still does his memory inflame your heart.
   PHAEDRA. Yes, Prince, I pine, I am on fire for
10   [him.
I love King Theseus, not as once he was,
The fickle worshipper at countless shrines,
Dishonoring the couch of Hades' god;°
But constant, proud, and even a little shy;
15 Enchanting, young, the darling of all hearts,
Fair as the gods; or fair as you are now.
He had your eyes, your bearing, and your
                             [speech.
His face flushed with your noble modesty.
20 When towards my native Crete he cleft the
                             [waves,
Well might the hearts of Minos' daughters
                             [burn!
What were you doing then? Why without you
25 Did he assemble all the flower of Greece?
Why could you not, too young, alas, have fared
Forth with the ship that brought him to our
                             [shores?
You would have slain the monstrous Cretan
30   [bull
Despite the windings of his endless lair.
My sister would have armed you with the
                             [thread
To lead you through the dark entangled maze—
35 No. *I* would have forestalled her. For my love
Would instantly have fired me with the
                             [thought.
I, only I, would have revealed to you
The subtle windings of the labyrinth.
40 What care I would have lavished on your head!
A thread would not have reassured my fears.
Affronting danger side by side with you,
I would myself have wished to lead the way,
And Phaedra, with you in the labyrinth,
45 Would have returned with you or met her
                             [doom.

Hades' god Pluto

   HIPPOLYTUS. What do I hear? Have you
                         [forgotten that
King Theseus is my father, you his wife?
   PHAEDRA. What makes you think, my lord, I   50
                         [have forgot,
Or am no longer mindful of my name?
   HIPPOLYTUS. Forgive me. Blushing, I confess
                         [your words
Were innocent, and I misunderstood.   55
For very shame I cannot bear your gaze.
I go . . .
   PHAEDRA.   Ah, cruel, you have understood
Only too well. I have revealed enough.
Know Phaedra then, and all her wild desires.   60
I burn with love. Yet, even as I speak,
Do not imagine I feel innocent,
Nor think that my complacency has fed
The poison of the love that clouds my mind.
The hapless victim of heaven's vengeances,   65
I loathe myself more deeply than you do.
The gods are witness, they who in my breast
Have lit the fire fatal to all my line.
Those gods whose cruel glory it has been
To lead astray a feeble mortal's heart.   70
Yourself recall to mind the past, and how
I shunned you, cruel one, nay, drove you forth.
I strove to seem to you inhuman, vile;
The better to resist, I sought your hate.
But what availed my needless sufferings?   75
You hated me the more, I loved not less.
Even your misfortunes lent you added charms.
I pined, I drooped, in torments and in tears.
Your eyes alone could see that it is so,
If for a moment they could look at me.   80
Nay, this confession to you, ah! the shame,
Think you I made it of my own free will?
I meant to beg you, trembling, not to hate
My helpless children, whom I dared not fail.
My foolish heart, alas, too full of you,   85
Could talk to you of nothing but yourself.
Take vengeance. Punish me for loving you.
Come, prove yourself your father's worthy son,
And rid the world of a monstrosity.
I, Theseus' widow, dare to love his son!   90
This frightful monster must not now escape.
Here is my heart. Here must your blow strike
                           [home.
Impatient to atone for its offense,

I feel it strain to meet your mighty arm.
Strike. Or if it's unworthy of your blows,
Or such a death too mild for my deserts,
Or if you deem my blood too vile to stain
5 Your hand, lend me, if not your arm, your
                                    [sword.
Give me it!
    OENONE.   Ah! What are you doing? God!
Someone is coming. You must not be seen.
10 Come, let's go in, quick, to avoid disgrace.

Scene vi

[HIPPOLYTUS, THERAMENES.]
THERAMENES. Can that be Phaedra who was
                            [dragged away?
Why, my lord, why this sudden, sharp dismay?
15 I find you without sword, aghast and pale.
    HIPPOLYTUS. Flee, flee, Theramenes. I
                            [cannot speak,
Nor without horror look upon myself.
Phaedra. . . . No, mighty gods, let us consign
20 This shameful secret to oblivion.
    THERAMENES. If you will leave, the sails are
                            [all unfurled.
But Athens has already made her choice.
Her chieftains have consulted all the tribes.
25 Your brother° rules; and Phaedra wins the day.
    HIPPOLYTUS. Phaedra?
    THERAMENES.   A herald speaking Athens'
                            [will
Into her hands conveyed the reins of state.
30 Her son is king, my lord.
    HIPPOLYTUS.   Oh God, who knows
Her heart, is it her virtue you reward?
    THERAMENES. Meanwhile, vague rumors say
                            [the King still lives,
35 And even that in Epirus he was seen.
But I, who sought him there, my lord, I
                            [know . . .
    HIPPOLYTUS. No matter. Let us study every
                            [clue.
40 Have this new rumor traced back to its source.
But, if it does not then prove credible,
Let us depart and, at whatever cost,
Replace the scepter in more worthy hands.

---

brother half-brother, a son of Theseus and Phaedra

ACT III

Scene i

[PHAEDRA, OENONE.]
PHAEDRA. Ah, take away those royal honors.   45
                            [How
Can you importune me to show myself?
And why seek to beguile my grieving heart?
Rather conceal me. I have said too much.
My frantic passion has revealed itself.   50
I have said what should never have been heard.
God! how he listened to me. By what shifts
He long pretended not to understand.
How his whole being hankered to be gone.
And how his blushes added to my shame.   55
Why did you ever thwart my baneful plan?
Ah! when his sword was pointed at my breast,
Did he turn pale for me, or did he wrench
It from me? I had but to touch it once
To make it horrible for him, and for   60
The wretched sword to soil his cruel hands.
    OENONE. Thus your misfortunes breed self-
                            [pity, and
Only inflame a fire you ought to quench.
Daughter of Minos, should you not aspire   65
To seek your peace of mind in nobler cares?
Resort to flight from an ungrateful youth,
Reign, and assume the guidance of the State?
    PHAEDRA. *I* reign? *I* bring a State beneath my
                            [rule, 70
When reason reigns no longer over me;
When I have lost my self-dominion; when
Beneath a shameful sway I scarcely breathe;
When I am dying?
    OENONE.   Flee.   75
    PHAEDRA.   I cannot go.
    OENONE. You sent him into exile. Shun him
                            [now.
    PHAEDRA. Too late, too late. He knows my
                            [mad desires. 80
I have transgressed the bounds of modesty.
I to Hippolytus have bared my shame,
And hope, despite me, has seduced my heart,
You yourself, rallying my failing strength
When on my lips my soul was hovering,   85
By guileful counsels brought me back to life.
You gave me glimpses of a sinless love.
    OENONE. Alas! guilty or no of your mishaps,

What would I not have done to save your life?
But, if by insults you were ever stung,
Can you forget a haughty youth's disdain?
God! with what cruel, stern, unfeeling heart
5 He left you well-nigh prostrate at his feet!
How hateful was his virtuous haughtiness!
Why did not Phaedra see him with my eyes?
    PHAEDRA. He may discard this pride that
                          [angers you.
10 Bred in the forests, he is wild like them.
Hardened by rude upbringing, he perhaps
For the first time listens to words of love.
Perhaps his silence mirrors his surprise,
And our reproaches are too violent.
15   OENONE. An Amazon, forget not, gave him
                          [birth.
    PHAEDRA. Though a barbarian, yet did she
                          [love.
    OENONE. He hates all women with a deadly
20   [hate.
    PHAEDRA. No rival, then, will triumph over
                          [me.
In short, the time for good advice is past.
Serve my wild heart, Oenone, not my head.
25 If he is inaccessible to love,
Let us attack him at some weaker point.
He seemed attracted by an empire's rule.
He could not hide it; Athens beckoned him.
Thither his vessels' prows were headed, and
30 The white sails fluttered, streaming in the wind.
Oenone, play on his ambition. Go,
Dazzle him with the glitter of the crown.
Let him assume the sacred diadem.
Myself to bind it on is all I ask,
35 Yielding to him the power I cannot hold.
He will instruct my son how to command;
Perhaps he will be father to the boy.
Mother and son I will commit to him.
In short, try every means to win him round.
40 Your words will find a readier ear than mine.
Urge! Weep! Paint Phaedra at death's door.
You may assume a supplicating tone.
I will endorse it, whatsoe'er you do.
Go. Upon your success depends my fate.

Scene ii

45   PHAEDRA. O you who see the depths of this
                          [my shame,
Relentless Venus, is my fall complete?

Your cruelty could go no further. Now
You triumph. All your arrows have struck
                          [home. 50
O cruel goddess! if you seek new fame,
Attack a more rebellious enemy.
Frigid Hippolytus, flouting your wrath,
Has at your altars never bowed the knee.
Your name seems to offend his haughty ear. 55
Goddess, avenge yourself. Our cause is one.
Make him love . . . but Oenone, you are back.
Did he not listen? Does he loathe me still?

Scene iii

[PHAEDRA, OENONE.]
    OENONE. Your love is vain and you must stifle 60
                          [it,
O Queen, and summon up your former
                          [strength.
The King we thought was dead will soon be
                          [here; 65
Theseus is come; Theseus is on his way.
Headlong, the crowd rushes to welcome him.
I had gone out to seek Hippolytus
When, swelling to the heavens, a thousand
                          [cries . . . 70
    PHAEDRA. My husband lives. Oenone, say no
                          [more.
I have confessed a love that soils his name.
He is alive, and more I will not know.
    OENONE. What? 75
    PHAEDRA.   I foretold it but you would not
                          [hear.
Your tears prevailed over my keen remorse.
I died this morning worthy to be mourned;
I took your counsel and dishonored die. 80
    OENONE. You mean to die?
    PHAEDRA.   Great God, what have I done?
My husband and his son are on their way.
I will behold the witness of my guilt
Observe me as I dare approach the King, 85
My heart heavy with sighs he heard unmoved,
My eyes wet with the tears the wretch
                          [disdained.
Mindful of Theseus' honor, as he is,
Will he conceal from him my fierce desires? 90
Will he be false to father and to king,
Restrain the horror that he feels for me?
His silence would be vain, Oenone, for
I know my baseness, and do not belong

To those bold wretches who with brazen front
Can revel in their crimes unblushingly.
I know my transports and recall them all.
Even now I feel these very walls, these vaults,
5 Will soon give tongue and, with accusing voice,
Await my husband to reveal the truth.
Then, death, come free me from so many woes.
Is it so terrible to cease to live?
Death holds no terrors for the wretched. No.
10 I fear only the name I leave behind,
For my poor children what a heritage.
The blood of Jove° should make their spirit
[swell;
But, whatsoever pride that blood inspires,
15 A mother's crime lies heavy on her sons.
I tremble lest reports, alas, too true,
One day upbraid them with a mother's guilt.
I tremble lest, crushed by this odious weight,
Neither will ever dare hold up his head.
20 OENONE. Ah! do not doubt it. Pity both of
[them.
Never was fear more justified than yours.
But why expose them to such base affronts?
And why bear witness now against yourself?
25 That way lies ruin. Phaedra, they will say,
Fled from the dreaded aspect of her lord.
Hippolytus is fortunate indeed.
By laying down your life, you prove him right.
How can I answer your accuser's charge?
30 I will be all too easy to confound.
I will behold his hideous triumph as
He tells your shame to all who care to hear.
Ah! sooner let the flames of heaven fall.
But tell me truly do you love him still?
35 What do you feel for this audacious prince?
PHAEDRA. He is a fearful monster in my eyes.
OENONE. Then why concede him such a
[victory?
You fear him. Dare then to accuse him first
40 Of the offense he soon may charge you with.
Nothing is in his favor; all is yours—
His sword, left by good fortune in your hands,
Your present agitation, your past grief,
His father, turned against him by your cries,
45 And, last, his exile you yourself obtained.
PHAEDRA. Should I oppress and blacken

blood of Jove because Minos, Phaedra's father, was
  a son of Jove

[innocence?
OENONE. All I need is your silence to succeed.
Like you I tremble and I feel remorse.
Sooner would I affront a thousand deaths, 50
But, since without this remedy you die,
For me your life must come before all else.
Therefore I'll speak. Despite his wrath, the King
Will do naught to his son but banish him.
A father when he punishes is still 55
A father, and his judgment will be mild.
But, even if guiltless blood must still be shed,
What does your threatened honor not demand?
It is too precious to be compromised.
Its dictates, all of them, must be obeyed. 60
And, to safeguard your honor, everything,
Yes, even virtue, must be sacrificed.
But who comes here? Theseus!
PHAEDRA.   Hippolytus!
In his bold gaze my ruin is writ large. 65
Do as you will. My fate is in your hands.
My whirling mind has left me powerless.

Scene iv

[THESEUS, HIPPOLYTUS, PHAEDRA, OENONE,
THERAMENES.]
THESEUS. Fortune at last ceases to frown on 70
[me,
O Queen, and in your arms again . . .
PHAEDRA.   No more.
Do not profane your transports of delight.
No more do I deserve this tenderness. 75
You have been outraged. Jealous fortune's
[blows
During your absence have not spared your wife.
I am unworthy to approach you, and
Henceforth my only thought must be to hide. 80

Scene v

[THESEUS, HIPPOLYTUS, THERAMENES.]
THESEUS. Why this cold welcome to your
[father?
HIPPOLYTUS.   Sire,
Phaedra alone can solve this mystery. 85
But, if my ardent wish can move you still,
Allow me never to set eyes on her.
Suffer your trembling son to disappear
For ever from the place where Phaedra dwells.
THESEUS. You, my son, leave me? 90
HIPPOLYTUS.   Yes. It was not I

Who sought her. You, my lord, you brought
[her here.
For you, on leaving, brought Aricia
And your Queen, Phaedra, here to Troezen's
5   [shore.
You even committed them into my care.
But, since your safe return, why should I stay?
Long have I squandered in the woods of Greece
My manhood's skill on paltry enemies.
10 Should not I, fleeing shameful idleness,
Redden my javelins in more glorious blood?
Before you had attained my present years,
More than one tyrant, one ferocious beast,
Had felt the might of your unconquered arm;
15 Even then, you were the scourge of insolence.
You had cleared all the shores of both the seas.
The traveller now fares freely through the land.
Hercules, resting on his laurels' fame,
Already for his labors looked to you.
20 And I, a glorious father's unknown son,
Lag far behind even my mother's deeds.
Let me at least show you my mettle and,
If some fell monster has escaped your sword,
Place at your feet its honorable spoils.
25 Or let the memory of a glorious death,
Engraving in eternity my life,
Prove to the universe I was your son.
        THESEUS. What do I see? What horror spread
[around
30 Drives back from me, distraught, my family?
If I return, so feared, so undesired,
Oh heaven! why did you free me from my jail?
I had one friend° alone. He rashly tried
To seize the consort of Epirus' King.
35 I served his amorous plan reluctantly;
But fate in anger blinded both of us.
The tyrant took me by surprise unarmed.
I saw Pirithous, a woeful sight,
Thrown to fierce monsters by the barbarous
40   [king,
Who fed them on the blood of helpless men.
Myself in somber caverns he enchained

friend Pirithous, Theseus' friend and his companion
in many adventures. Legend reported that Pirithous
accompanied Theseus to Hades and was imprisoned
there by Pluto, although Theseus was rescued by
Hercules; again, Racine's Theseus gives a less mythical account of their misfortunes.

Beside the shadowy kingdom of the dead.
The gods at last relented towards me and
Allowed me to outwit my guardian.   45
I purged the world of a perfidious knave
And his own monsters battened on his flesh.
But when I joyfully prepared to meet
My dearest ones, all that the gods have spared,
Nay, when my soul, that is its own again,   50
Would feast itself upon so dear a sight,
Only with shudders am I welcomed home;
Everyone flees, rejecting my embrace.
Myself, filled with the horror I inspire,
Would I were prisoner in Epirus still.   55
Speak! Phaedra tells of outrage done to me.
Who played me false? Why am I unavenged?
Has Greece, so often guarded by my arm,
Afforded shelter to the criminal?
You do not answer. Is my son, my own   60
Dear son, in league, then, with my enemies?
Let us go in and end this grim suspense.
Let us discover criminal and crime,
And Phaedra tell us why she is distraught.

Scene vi

[HIPPOLYTUS, THERAMENES.]   65
HIPPOLYTUS. What meant these words that
[made my blood run cold?
Will Phaedra, still in her delirium,
Denounce herself, bring ruin on her head?
O God! What will the King say then? How love 70
Has spread its baleful poison through the
[house!
Myself, full of a passion he condemns,
As once he knew me, so he finds me still.
Gloomy forebodings terrify my soul.   75
But innocence has surely naught to fear.
Come, let me with some new and happier
Approach revive my father's tenderness,
And tell him of a love he may oppose
But which it is not in his power to change.   80

ACT IV

Scene i

[THESEUS, OENONE.]
THESEUS. What do I hear? A reckless libertine
Conceived this outrage on his father's name?
How harshly you pursue me, destiny.

I know not where I am, whither I go.
O son! O ill-rewarded tenderness!
Daring the scheme, detestable the thought.
To gain his lustful and nefarious ends,
5   The shameless villain had resort to force.
I recognized the sword he drew on her,
That sword I gave him for a nobler use.
Could all the ties of blood not hold him back?
Phaedra was slow in bringing him to book?
10   In keeping silent, Phaedra spared the knave?
    OENONE. Rather did Phaedra spare a father's
                      [tears.
Ashamed of a distracted lover's suit,
And of the vicious passion she had caused,
15   Phaedra, my lord, was dying and her hand
Was on the point of cutting short her days.
I saw her raise her arm, I ran to her.
I, only I, preserved her for your love,
And, pitying her distress and your alarm,
20   Reluctantly I lent her tears a voice.
    THESEUS. The criminal! He blanched despite
                      [himself.
As I drew near, I saw him start with fear.
I was astonished by his joyless mien;
25   His cold embraces froze my tenderness
But had this guilty love that eats him up
Already, even in Athens, shown itself?
    OENONE. My lord, recall how oft the Queen
                      [complained.
30   Infamous love gave rise to all her hate.
    THESEUS. And here in Troezen this flamed up
                      [again?
    OENONE. My lord, I have related all I know.
The grieving Queen too long remains alone;
35   Allow me to withdraw and go to her.

Scene ii

[THESEUS, HIPPOLYTUS.]
    THESEUS. Ah, it is he. Great gods! what eye
                      [would not
Be duped like mine by such nobility?
40   Must needs the brow of an adulterer
Be bright with virtue's sacred character?
And ought we not by fixed and certain signs
To see into perfidious mortals' hearts?
    HIPPOLYTUS. May I inquire of you what
45   [baleful cloud
Has overcast, my lord, your regal brow?

Will you not venture to confide in me?
    THESEUS. Villain! How dare you come before
                      [me now?
Monster, the thunderbolt too long has spared!   50
Last of the brigands whom I swept away!
After the frenzy of your wicked lust
Has driven you to assault your father's bed,
You dare to show your hateful face to me,
Here in this place full of your infamy,   55
And seek not out, under an unknown sky,
Countries to which your fame has never spread.
Flee, villain, flee. Brave not my hatred here
Nor tempt my anger that I scarce restrain.
I have my portion of eternal shame   60
To have begot so criminal a son,
Without his death, disgrace to my renown,
Soiling the glory of my labors past.
Flee, and if you desire not to be joined
To all the villains fallen by my hand,   65
Take care that never does the shining sun
Behold you in these palaces again.
Flee then, and never more return;
And of your hideous presence purge my realm.
And, Neptune, in time past if my strong hand   70
Of infamous assassins cleared your shores,
Remember that, to recompense my deeds,
You swore to grant the first of my desires.
In the long hardships of a cruel jail
I did not call on your immortal power;   75
With miser's care I put aside your aid,
Holding it in reserve for greater needs.
I call upon you now. Revenge my wrong.
I give this villain over to your wrath;
Drown in his blood his shameless foul desires.   80
Your favors will be measured by your rage.
    HIPPOLYTUS. Phaedra accuses me of sinful
                      [love?
So infinite a horror numbs my soul.
So many unforeseen and heavy blows   85
Rain down upon me that I cannot speak.
    THESEUS. Villain, you thought that Phaedra
                      [would conceal
In craven silence your vile insolence.
You should not, as you fled, have dropped the   90
                      [sword
That, in her hands, establishes your guilt.
Rather should you have crowned your perfidy
And at one stroke robbed her of speech and life.

HIPPOLYTUS. Rightly indignant at so black a
[lie,
I ought, my lord, to let the truth speak out,
But I will not resolve this mystery
5 Out of the deep respect that seals my lips.
And, if you will not deepen your distress,
Look at my life; remember who I am.
Some little crimes lead up to greater crimes.
Whoever goes beyond the bounds of law
10 Can in the end flout the most sacred rules.
No less than virtue, crime has its degrees,
And innocence has never yet been known
To swing at once to license's extreme.
A single day cannot change virtuous men
15 To craven and incestuous murderers.
Reared by a virtuous Amazon from birth,
I never have belied my mother's blood.
Pittheus, esteemed the wisest far of men,
Instructed me after I left her hands.
20 I do not seek to paint myself too fair;
But, if one virtue is my birthright, that
Is above all, my lord, as I have shown,
Hate of the crime that they accuse me of.
That is what I am famous for in Greece.
25 I carried virtue to the sternest lengths,
My obdurate austerity is known;
The daylight is not purer than my heart.
Yet I, they say, fired by unholy love . . .
THESEUS. Yes, by that very pride you stand
30 [condemned.
The reason why you were so cold is clear;
Phaedra alone entranced your lustful eyes.
And, by all other charms unmoved, your heart
Disdained to glow with innocent desire.
35 HIPPOLYTUS. No, father, for this may not be
[concealed,
I have not scorned to glow with virtuous love,
And at your feet confess my real offense.
I am in love; in love despite your ban.
40 Aricia is mistress of my heart
And Pallas' daughter has subdued your son.
I worship her and, flouting your command,
For her alone I pine, I am consumed.
THESEUS. You love her? God! The ruse is
45 [gross indeed!
You feign to err to justify yourself.
HIPPOLYTUS. For half a year I have been deep
[in love.

Trembling, I came to tell you so myself.
What! Can no word of mine unseal your eyes? 50
What fearful oath, to move you, must I swear?
May heaven and earth and everything that
[is . . .
THESEUS. Foulness goes hand in hand with
[perjury. 55
Cease! Spare me an importunate harangue,
If your false virtue has no other stay.
HIPPOLYTUS. To you I may seem false and full
[of guile.
Phaedra does justice to me in her heart. 60
THESEUS. Ah! how my wrath grows at your
[shamelessness.
HIPPOLYTUS. What time and what the place of
[banishment?
THESEUS. Were you beyond Alcides' pillars,° 65
[still
Would I believe your villainy too near.
HIPPOLYTUS. Crushed by the crime that you
[suspect me of,
If you desert me who will pity me? 70
THESEUS. Go seek out friends who in their
[viciousness
Applaud adultery and incest. These
Villains and ingrates, lawless, honorless,
Will shelter evildoers such as you. 75
HIPPOLYTUS. You harp on incest and adultery.
I will say naught; but Phaedra, as you know,
My lord, is of a mother, of a line,
Richer in all these horrors than my own.
THESEUS. What! are there no bounds to your 80
[frantic rage?
For the last time, begone from out my sight.
Go, libertine, before a father's wrath
Has you with ignominy torn from hence.

Scene iii

[THESEUS alone.] 85
THESEUS. Unhappy youth! Haste to your
[certain doom.
By the stream dreaded even of the gods
Neptune has given and will fulfil his word.
A god of vengeance follows hard on you. 90
I loved you and, in spite of your offense,
My heart is stirred for you forebodingly.

Alcides' pillars the Pillars of Hercules; i.e., Gibraltar

But you have forced me to pronounce your
            [doom.
Was ever wretched father outraged so?
O God who see my overwhelming grief,
5 How could I have begot so foul a child?

Scene iv

[PHAEDRA, THESEUS.]
PHAEDRA. My Lord, I come stricken with
            [terror, for
Your dreaded voice has reached me and I fear
10 Your menace may be given prompt effect.
If it is not too late, then spare your son.
Respect your flesh and blood, I beg of you,
And save me from the horror of his cries.
Do not lay up for me the endless grief
15 Of causing bloodshed by a father's hand.
    THESEUS. No, Queen, my hand has not bathed
            [in his blood,
But still the villain will not now escape.
Immortal hands are with his ruin charged.
20 This Neptune owes me. You will be avenged.
    PHAEDRA. This Neptune owes you. What?
            [Your anger calls . . .
    THESEUS. How! You already fear I may be
            [heard?
25 Rather unite your wishes with my own.
In all their heinousness depict his crimes;
Stir up my sluggish cold resentment, for
You do not know the measure of his crimes.
His fury showers affronts upon your name.
30 Your mouth, he says, speaks nothing but
            [deceit;
He swears Aricia has won his heart,
And that he loves her.
    PHAEDRA.   What!
35 THESEUS.   Those were his words.
But I am not the dupe of vain pretense.
Let us expect swift justice from the god.
I will myself to Neptune's altars go
To urge fulfilment of immortal oaths.

Scene v

40 [PHAEDRA *alone*.]
    PHAEDRA. He's gone. What tidings have
            [assailed my ears!
What smoldering fire awakens in my heart!
God! What a thunderbolt! What baleful news!

Flying with but one thought to aid his son, 45
I tore myself from pale Oenone's arms,
Yielding to the remorse that tortured me.
Who knows how far repentance would have
            [gone?
Perhaps I might even have accused myself? 50
Perhaps, had not my voice died in my throat,
The frightful truth would have escaped my lips.
Hippolytus can love but loves not me.
Aricia has won his heart, his troth.
Ah! when, inexorable to my pleas, 55
Hippolytus put on a front of steel,
I thought his heart for ever closed to love,
And against women all alike was armed.
Another none the less has conquered him.
She has found favor in his cruel eyes. 60
Perhaps he has a heart easy to move.
Alone of women me he cannot bear.
And I was hastening to his defense!

Scene vi

[PHAEDRA, OENONE.]
PHAEDRA. Oenone, do you know what I have 65
            [heard?
    OENONE. No, but I still am trembling, to be
            [frank.
As you rushed forth, I blanched at your intent.
I was afraid you would destroy yourself. 70
    PHAEDRA. Who would have thought it? There
            [was someone else.
    OENONE. What!
    PHAEDRA.   Yes. Hippolytus is deep in love.
This shy, invincible antagonist, 75
Whom my respect displeased, my tears
            [annoyed,
Whom I could never speak to unafraid,
Submissive, tamed, proclaims his own defeat.
Aricia is mistress of his heart. 80
    OENONE. Aricia?
    PHAEDRA.   Ah! unplumbed depths of woe!
For what new torments have I spared myself?
All I have suffered, jealous torments, fears,
Raging desire, the horror of remorse, 85
A cruel, harsh, intolerable slight,
Were a mere foretaste of my torments now.
They love each other. By what spell did they
Deceive me? How, where did they meet, since
            [when? 90

You knew. Why did you let me be misled?
Why did you keep from me their stealthy love?
Were they seen oft exchanging looks and
[words?
5   Deep in the forests were they wont to hide?
Alas! They had the utmost liberty.
Heaven smiled upon their innocent desires.
They followed where love led them, conscience
[free.
10   For them the dawn rose shining and serene.
And I, rejected by all living things,
I hid myself from day, I shunned the light;
Death was the only god I dared invoke.
I waited for the moment of my end,
15   Feeding on gall and drinking deep of tears.
Too closely watched, I did not even dare
Give myself up in freedom to my grief.
Trembling, this baleful pleasure I enjoyed
And, cloaking with a feignéd calm my woes,
20   Was often driven to forego my tears.
    OENONE. What good will their love do them?
[Never will
They meet again.
    PHAEDRA.   Their love will always live.
25   Even as I speak, ah cruel, deadly thought!
They flout the fury of my insane rage.
Despite this exile which will sever them
They swear a thousand oaths never to part.
No. No. Their happiness is gall to me.
30   Oenone, pity my wild jealousy.
Aricia must perish, and the King
Be stirred to wrath against her odious race.
No trifling retribution will suffice.
The sister has outdone her brothers' crime.
35   I will implore him in my jealous rage.
What am I doing? I have lost my mind!
I, jealous? and 'tis Theseus I implore!
My husband is alive and yet I pine.
For whom? Whose heart have I been coveting?
40   At every word my hair stands up on end.
Henceforth the measure of my crimes is full.
I reek with foulest incest and deceit.
My hands, that strain for murder and revenge,
Burn with desire to plunge in guiltless blood.
45   Wretch! and I live and can endure the gaze
Of the most sacred sun from which I spring.
My grandsire is the lord of all the gods;

My forebears fill the sky, the universe.
Where can I hide? In dark infernal night?
No, there my father holds the urn of doom.   50
Destiny placed it in his ruthless hands.
Minos judges in hell the trembling dead.
Ah! how his horror-stricken shade will start
To see before him his own daughter stand,
Forced to admit to such a host of sins   55
And some, perhaps, unknown even in hell!
What, father, will you say to that dread sight?
I see your hand slip from the fateful urn;
I see you searching for new punishments,
Yourself your own kin's executioner.   60
Forgive me. Venus' wrath has doomed your
[race.
Your daughter's frenzy shows that vengeance
[forth.
Alas, my sad heart never has enjoyed   65
The fruits of crimes whose dark shame follows
[me.
Dogged by misfortune to my dying breath,
I end upon the rack a life of pain.
    OENONE. Ah, Queen! dismiss these   70
[unbecoming fears,
And of your error take a different view.
You are in love. We cannot change our fate.
By destined magic you were swept along.
Is that so strange or so miraculous?   75
Has love then triumphed only over you?
Frailty is human and but natural.
Mortal, you must a mortal's lot endure.
This thraldom was imposed long, long ago.
The gods themselves that in Olympus dwell,   80
Who smite the evildoer with their bolt,
Have sometimes felt unlawful passions' fire.
    PHAEDRA. Great gods! What counsels dare
[you offer me?
Even to the last you seek to poison me.   85
Wretch! Thus it is that you have caused my
[doom.
You, when I fled from life, you called me back;
At your entreaties duty was forgot;
It was *you* made me see Hippolytus.   90
You meddling fool. Why did your impious lips,
Falsely accusing him, besmirch his life?
You may have killed him, if the gods have
[heard

A maddened father's sacrilegious wish.
I'll hear no more. Hence, loathsome monster,
[hence.
Go, leave me to my pitiable fate.
5 May the just heavens reward you fittingly,
And may your punishment forever fright
All who, as you have done, by base deceit,
Pander to ill-starred princes' weaknesses,
Urging them on to yield to their desires,
10 And dare to smooth the path of crime for them,
Vile flatterers, the most ill-fated boon
The anger of the gods can make to kings!
   Oenone. Ah God! to save her what have I
[not done,
15 But this is the reward I have deserved.

ACT V

Scene i

[Hippolytus, Aricia.]
   Aricia. What, in this peril you refuse to
[speak?
You leave a loving father undeceived?
20 Cruel one, can you, by my tears unmoved,
Consent without a sigh to part from me?
Go hence and leave me to my grieving heart.
But, if you go, at least preserve your life.
Defend your honor from a foul reproach
25 And force your father to revoke your doom.
There still is time. Wherefore, from what
[caprice,
Will you let Phaedra's slander hold the field?
Tell Theseus all.
30   Hippolytus.   Ah, what have I not said?
Should I make known the outrage to his bed
And by an all too frank relation bring
Over my father's brow a blush of shame?
This odious secret you alone have pierced.
35 My sole confidants are the gods and you.
Judge of my love, I have not hid from you
All I desired to hide even from myself.
But, since you have been sworn to secrecy,
Forget, if it be possible, my words.
40 And never may your pure unsullied lips
Recount the details of this horrid scene.
Let's trust the justice of the gods above.
Their interest lies in vindicating me.

Sooner or later Phaedra will be brought
To book and meet an ignominious doom.   45
That is the only boon I ask of you.
My anger takes all other liberties.
Reject the bondage under which you pine;
Dare to accompany me in my flight.
Tear yourself free from an unhallowed spot   50
Where virtue breathes a foul, polluted air.
Let us to cover our escape exploit
The wild confusion that my downfall spreads.
I can provide you with the means for flight.
The only guards controlling you are mine.   55
Mighty defenders will take up our cause.
Argos awaits us; Sparta summons us.
Let's bear our grievance to our new allies.
Phaedra must never profit from our fall
And drive us both from off my father's throne, 60
Making her son the heir to our estates.
Now is our chance. We must lay hands on it.
What holds you back? You seem to hesitate.
Only your interest thus emboldens me.
When I am ardent, why are you so cold?   65
Are you afraid to share an exile's lot?
   Aricia. Alas! How pleasant to be banished
[thus!
With what delight, linking my fate with yours,
By all the world forgotten I would live!   70
But, since we are not joined by that sweet bond,
Could I in honor flee from here with you?
I know that, even by the strictest code,
I may throw off your father's tutelage.
No bond of home or parents holds me back,   75
And flight from tyrants is permissible.
You love me, though, my lord, and my good
[name . . .
   Hippolytus. No. No. Your honor is too dear
[to me.   80
I come before you with a nobler plan.
Flee from my foes. Flee as my wedded wife.
Alone in exile, since heaven wills it so,
We need no man's consent to pledge our faith.
Not always torches blaze for Hymen's rites.   85
Not far from Troezen's gates, among these
[tombs,
My princely forebears' ancient burial place,
There stands a shrine dreaded of perjurers.
There mortals never swear an oath in vain.   90

Who breaks his word is punished instantly,
And men forsworn, afraid of certain death,
Are held in check by this most dreaded threat.
There, if you trust me, we will ratify
5 By solemn oath our everlasting love,
Taking to witness this old temple's god.
We'll pray him to be father to us both.
I'll call to witness the most sacred gods,
And chaste Diana, Juno the august,
10 And all the gods, witnesses of my love,
Will lend their blessing to my holy vows.
 ARICIA. The King is coming. Flee, make haste.
 [To cloak
My own departure, I will stay awhile.
15 Go now, but leave me someone I can trust
To lead my steps to the appointed place.

Scene ii

[THESEUS, ARICIA, ISMENE.]
 THESEUS. O God! lighten the darkness of my
 [mind.
20 Show me the truth that I am searching for.
 ARICIA. Make ready, dear Ismene, for our
 [flight.

Scene iii

[THESEUS, ARICIA.]
 THESEUS. Your color changes and you seem
25 [aghast,
Lady. What was the young prince doing here?
 ARICIA. My lord, he took eternal leave of me.
 THESEUS. You have subdued that proud
 [rebellious heart,
30 And his first raptures were inspired by you.
 ARICIA. My lord, I cannot well deny the truth.
Your unjust hatred is not shared by him.
He did not treat me like a criminal.
 THESEUS. I know. He swore eternal love to
35 [you.
Do not rely on that inconstant heart,
For he to others swore the selfsame oaths.
 ARICIA. He, Sire?
 THESEUS.   You ought to have restrained
40 [him. How
Could you endure to share his fickle heart?
 ARICIA. And how could you allow such
 [calumny
To tarnish the bright glory of his life?

Have you so little knowledge of his heart?   45
Can you not tell baseness from innocence?
Must from your eyes alone an odious cloud
Conceal his virtues which shine bright to all?
I cannot let him further be maligned.
Stop and repent of your assassin's prayer.   50
Fear, my lord, fear lest the unbending heavens
Hate you enough to grant you your desire.
Oft in their wrath they take our sacrifice.
Often their gifts are sent to scourge our sins.
 THESEUS. In vain you seek to cover his   55
 [offense.
Your passion blinds you to his faults. But I
Have faith in sure, trustworthy witnesses.
I have seen tears which surely were not feigned.
 ARICIA. Take care, my lord. Invincible, your   60
 [hands
Have freed the world from monsters
 [numberless;
But all are not destroyed. You still let live
One . . . But your son forbids me to proceed.   65
Knowing his wishes, I respect you still.
I would but grieve him if I dared to speak.
Following his restraint, I will withdraw
Rather than let the truth escape my lips.

Scene iv

[THESEUS alone.]   70
 THESEUS. What does she mean, and what do
 [these words hide,
Begun and broken off, begun again?
Is it their aim to trick me by a feint?
Are they in league to put me on the rack?   75
But I myself, despite my stern resolve,
What plaintive voice cries in my inmost heart?
A lurking burst of pity harrows me.
I'll have Oenone questioned once again;
I must have more light thrown upon the crime.   80
Guards, bring Oenone out to me alone.

Scene v

[THESEUS, PANOPE.]
 PANOPE. I do not know what the Queen
 [purposes,
But her distraction is a fearful sight.   85
Mortal despair cries from her haggard face,
And death has laid its paleness on her cheeks.
Oenone, driven out with shame, has plunged

Already into the unsounded sea.
We do not know what led her to this death;
The waves have closed for ever over her.
    THESEUS. What?
5   PANOPE.   This dark action did not calm
                       [the Queen.
Distraction grows in her storm-ridden heart.
Sometimes, to soothe her secret sufferings,
She takes her children, bathes them in her tears;
10 Then, suddenly, renouncing mother's love,
Shuddering with horror, will have none of
                       [them.
This way and that, she wanders aimlessly;
Wildly she looks at us, but knows us not.
15 She thrice has written, then has changed her
                       [mind,
And thrice torn up the letter she began.
See her, we beg you. We implore your help.
    THESEUS. Oenone's dead, and Phaedra seeks
20   [to die.
Call back my son, let him defend himself
And speak to me! I'll lend a willing ear.
[*Alone.*] Do not be overhasty with your gifts,
Neptune! I wish my prayer may not be heard.
25 Perhaps I have believed false witnesses,
Lifting too soon my cruel hand to you.
Ah! if you act, what will be my despair!

Scene vi

[THESEUS, THERAMENES.]
  THESEUS. What have you done with him,
30   [Theramenes?
I put him as a boy into your hands.
But why the tears that trickle down your
                       [cheeks?
What of my son?
35   THERAMENES. O tardy vain concern!
O unavailing love! Your son's no more.
    THESEUS. God!
    THERAMENES. I have seen the best of mortals
                       [die,
40 And the most innocent, I dare to add.
    THESEUS. Dead? When I open wide my arms
                     [to him,
The gods, impatient, hasten on his death?
What blow, what thunderbolt snatched him
45   [away?
    THERAMENES. Scarce were we issuing from

[Troezen's gates;
He drove his chariot; round about him ranged,
Copying his silence, were his cheerless guards.
Pensive, he followed the Mycenae road,   50
And let the reins hang loose upon his steeds.
These haughty steeds, that once upon a time,
Noble, high-spirited, obeyed his voice,
Now dull of eye and with dejected air
Seemed to conform to his despondent thoughts. 55
A ghastly cry from out the water's depths
That moment rent the quiet of the air.
From the earth's entrails then a fearful voice
Made answer with a groan to that dread cry.
Deep in our hearts the horror froze our blood. 60
The coursers' manes, on hearing, stood erect.
And now, there rose upon the liquid plain
A watery mountain seething furiously.
The surge drew near, dissolved and vomited
A raging monster from among the foam.   65
His forehead huge was armed with fearsome
                       [horns
And his whole body sheathed in yellow scales,
Half bull, half dragon, wild, impetuous.
His crupper curved in many a winding fold. 70
The shore quaked with his long-drawn
                     [bellowings.
The heavens beheld the monster, horror-struck;
It poisoned all the air; it rocked the earth.
The wave that brought it in recoiled aghast. 75
Everyone, throwing courage to the winds,
Took refuge in the temple near at hand.
Hippolytus alone, undaunted, stayed,
Reined in his steeds and seized his javelins,
Had at the monster and, with sure-flung dart, 80
Dealt him a gaping wound deep in his flank.
With rage and pain the monster, starting up,
Collapsed and, falling at the horses' feet,
Rolled over, opening wide his flaming jaws,
And covered them with smoke and blood and 85
                     [fire.
Carried away by terror, deaf, the steeds
No more responded to his curb or voice.
Their master spent his efforts all in vain.
They stained the bridle with their bloody foam. 90
In this wild tumult, it is even said,
A god appeared, goading their dusty flanks.
Over the rocks fear drove them headlong on;
The axle groaned and broke. Hippolytus

Saw his whole chariot shattered into bits.
He fell at last, entangled in the reins.
Forgive my grief. For me this picture spells
Eternal sorrow and perpetual tears.
5 I have beheld, my lord, your ill-starred son
Dragged by the horses that his hand had fed.
His voice that called them merely frightened
[them.
Onward they flew—his body one whole wound.
10 The plain resounded with our cries of woe.
At last they slackened their impetuous course.
They halted near the old ancestral tombs
Where all his royal forebears lie in state.
I and his guards hastened to him in tears.
15 The traces of his blood showed us the way.
The rocks were stained with it, the cruel thorns
Dripped with the bleeding remnants of his hair.
I saw him, called him; giving me his hand,
He opened, then that moment closed, his eyes.
20 "Heaven takes my life, though innocent," he
[cried.
"When I am dead, protect Aricia.
Friend, if my father ever learns the truth,
And pities the misfortunes of his son,
25 And would appease me in the life to come,
Tell him to show that princess clemency,
To give her back. . . ." And then he passed
[away,
And in my arms lay a disfigured corpse,
30 A tribute to the anger of the gods
That even his father would not recognize.
    THESEUS. My son, fond hope I have myself
[destroyed!
Inexorable, all too helpful gods!
35 What keen remorse will haunt me all my life!
    THERAMENES. Aricia then came upon the
[scene.
She came, my lord, fleeing your royal wrath,
Before the gods to pledge her faith to him.
40 As she drew near, she saw the reeking grass.
She saw, a grim sight for a lover's eyes,
Hippolytus, disfigured, deadly pale.
A while she tried to doubt her evil fate.
She sees the body of Hippolytus,
45 Yet still pursues the quest for her beloved.
But, in the end, only too sure 'tis he,
With one sad look, accusing heaven's spite,
Cold, moaning, and well nigh inanimate,

She falls, unconscious, at her sweetheart's feet.
Ismene, bending over her, in tears,   50
Summons her back to life, a life of pain.
And I have come, my lord, hating the world,
To tell you of Hippolytus' last wish
And to discharge the bitter embassy
Which he entrusted to me as he died.   55
But hither comes his deadly enemy.

Scene vii

[THESEUS, PHAEDRA, THERAMENES, PANOPE,
GUARDS.]
    THESEUS. Well, then, you triumph and my
[son's no more.   60
What grounds I have for fear! What cruel doubt
Gnaws at my heart, pleading his innocence!
But he is dead. Accept your victim. Joy
In his undoing, justified or no,
For I am willing to deceive myself.   65
Since you accuse him, I accept his guilt.
His death will make my tears flow fast enough
Without my seeking for enlightenment
Which could not ever bring him back to me
And might perhaps but sharpen my distress.   70
Let me flee, far from you and from these shores,
The bloody vision of my mangled son.
Stunned and pursued by this grim memory,
Would I were in another universe!
Everything seems to brand my wicked wrath.   75
My very name increases my despair.
Less known of mortals, I could hide myself.
I hate even the favors of the gods.
And now I must bewail their murderous gifts,
No longer tiring them with fruitless prayers. 80
Whatever they have done for me, their aid
Cannot give back what they have robbed me of.
    PHAEDRA. No, Theseus. No, I must at last
[speak out.
I must redress the wrong I did your son,   85
For he was innocent.
    THESEUS.   Wretch that I am!
If I condemned him, it was on your word.
Cruel one, do you hope to be forgiven . . .
    PHAEDRA. Each moment's precious. Listen.   90
[It was I,
Theseus, who on your virtuous, filial son
Made bold to cast a lewd, incestuous eye.
Heaven in my heart lit an ill-omened fire.

Detestable Oenone did the rest.
She feared your son, knowing my frenzy, might
Reveal a guilty passion he abhorred.
The wretch, exploiting my enfeebled state,
5   Rushed to denounce Hippolytus to you.
She has exacted justice on herself
And found beneath the waves too mild a death.
By now I would have perished by the sword,
But first I wished to clear my victim's name.
10   I wished, revealing my remorse to you,
To choose a slower road down to the dead.
I have instilled into my burning veins
A poison that Medea brought to Greece.
Already it has reached my heart and spread
15   A strange chill through my body. Even now
Only as through a cloud I see the bright
Heaven and the husband whom I still defile.
But death, robbing my eyes of light, will give
Back to the sun its tarnished purity.
20   PANOPE. Ah! she is dying.
         THESEUS.   Would the memory
Of her appalling misdeeds die with her!
Let us, now that my error's all too clear,
Go out and mourn over my ill-starred son.
25   Let us embrace my cherished son's remains
And expiate my mad atrocious wish,
Rendering him the honors he deserves,
And, to appease the anger of his shade,
Let his beloved, despite her brothers' crime,
30   Be as a daughter to me from this day.

William Congreve

1670–1729

The Way
of the World

1700

The Way of the World has, at least arguably,
the best-written dialogue to be found in
English comedy.

"Good Mirabell," urges Millamant, his
beloved, as she ponders their possible
marriage, "don't let us be familiar or fond,
nor kiss before folks, like my Lady Faddler
and Sir Francis; nor go to Hyde Park together
the first Sunday in a new chariot, to provoke
eyes and whispers; and then never be seen
there together again; as if we were proud of
one another the first week, and ashamed
of one another for ever after."

The precise word is *good* Mirabell (an
appeal to simple decency) rather than *dear*
or *sweet* or *beloved* Mirabell, for Millamant
is deathly afraid of what love without
decency can do. She knows that couples who
are "familiar or fond" or "kiss before folks"
(alliteration here adding piquancy to the
dialogue) and newlyweds self-conscious of
their beauty who ride through the park
together "to provoke eyes and whispers"
(a deft turn of phrase) will ignore each other
when the novelty of marriage wears off, as if
"proud of one another the first week, and
ashamed of one another for ever after" (a
tersely insightful observation).

This precision of style, recalling in some
ways the poetry of Congreve's contemporary,
Alexander Pope, tends to pass over the
heads of general audiences, but it has many
admirers. And it is at least partly available
to anyone willing to try to understand what
verbal elegance accomplishes in the context
of the play. For one thing, it is meant to be
a source of delight in itself: playgoers should
gasp with admiration at the verbal
gymnastics like spectators at a sporting
event or a ballet. The control of language
also has thematic implications: it harmonizes
with the rational self-control that men
must have to make their own destinies.

Mirabell and Millamant are two young
people deeply in love but quite aware that
marriage has many pitfalls. They are also
profoundly social beings accustomed to the
wit, the courtly ceremony, and the music

and art of privileged society, yet they perceive that their culture is weakened by folly and threatened by the cold and sometimes murderous predation beneath its superficial politesse. Being Congreve's creatures, this young couple wants to live in a world in which they have to surrender none of their values, to possess each other and their own souls while enriching their happiness with every worthwhile thing that society has to offer. The marriage is to be the good life, obtained through their intelligence and tact. Graces of speech and manner are at once an aspect of their ideal and a means of attaining it.

But Mirabell is not above employing craft as well as intelligence and tact in pursuing his ends. He has "used" Fainall in the past—involving Mrs. Fainall, albeit willingly, in a marital arrangement of truly staggering cynicism. And even though Mirabell's machinations are condoned (to him and to the other characters, it is "the way of the world"), there is some indication that Congreve does not wholly approve of them. If the world is so treacherous a place that one uses its deadly weapons almost as a matter of course, perhaps the only intelligent thing to do is to withdraw.

Congreve cannot expel such doubts. The action of the play—mirroring the way of the world as he saw it—is overcomplicated and darkened by hatreds and distresses that dim the happy union of the lovers. Yet the happy ending is more poignant for having been achieved in the midst of folly and corruption. It is a testament to the hopeful and fearful human need to establish a fostering and enduring love. The yearning of Mirabell and Millamant for a perfect marriage is the essence of love as Plato defined it: "the desire that good shall forever be present to us." The presence of melancholy and cynicism does not invalidate such a desire but rather makes it more urgent.

The Way of the World

CONGREVE

CHARACTERS°

Men

FAINALL   in love with Mrs. Marwood
MIRABELL   in love with Mrs. Millamant
WITWOUD }
PETULANT }   followers of Mrs. Millamant
SIR WILFULL WITWOUD   half brother to Witwoud, and nephew to Lady Wishfort
WAITWELL   servant to Mirabell

Women

LADY WISHFORT   enemy to Mirabell, for having falsely pretended love to her
MRS. MILLAMANT   a fine lady, niece to Lady Wishfort, and loves Mirabell
MRS. MARWOOD   friend to Mr. Fainall, and likes Mirabell
MRS. FAINALL   daughter to Lady Wishfort, and wife to Fainall, formerly friend to Mirabell
FOIBLE   woman to Lady Wishfort
MINCING   woman to Mrs. Millamant
BETTY   waitress at the chocolate house
PEG   under-servant to Lady Wishfort
DANCERS, FOOTMEN, and ATTENDANTS

SCENE. London.

Characters   the descriptive names are sometimes literal, sometimes suggestive. Suggestive names include Mirabell (from Latin mira—or its derivatives in other Romance languages—and French belle), admire the beautiful (woman); Millamant (French mille amants), lady of a thousand lovers; Fainall, feign all; Wishfort, wish for it; Marwood, would mar; Witwoud, would-be wit. Mrs. (an abbreviation for Mistress) denotes any young woman, married or unmarried.

ACT I

[*A chocolate house.*]

.   .   .

[MIRABELL *and* FAINALL *rising from cards,*
BETTY *waiting.*]

MIRA. You are a fortunate man, Mr. Fainall.

5 FAIN. Have we done?

MIRA. What you please. I'll play on to entertain you.

FAIN. No, I'll give you your revenge another
time, when you are not so indifferent; you are
10 thinking of something else now, and play too
negligently. The coldness of a losing gamester
lessens the pleasure of the winner. I'd no more
play with a man that slighted his ill fortune
than I'd make love to a woman who under-
15 valued the loss of her reputation.

MIRA. You have a taste extremely delicate,
and are for refining on your pleasures.

FAIN. Prithee, why so reserved? Something
has put you out of humor.

20 MIRA. Not at all. I happen to be grave today,
and you are gay; that's all.

FAIN. Confess, Millamant and you quarreled
last night after I left you; my fair cousin has
some humors that would tempt the patience of
25 a stoic. What, some coxcomb came in, and was
well received by her, while you were by?

MIRA. Witwoud and Petulant; and what was
worse, her aunt, your wife's mother, my evil
genius; or to sum up all in her own name, my
30 old Lady Wishfort came in.

FAIN. O, there it is then—she has a lasting
passion for you, and with reason. What, then
my wife was there?

MIRA. Yes, and Mrs. Marwood and three or
35 four more, whom I never saw before. Seeing
me, they all put on their grave faces, whispered
one another; then complained aloud of the
vapors,° and after fell into a profound silence.

FAIN. They had a mind to be rid of you.

40 MIRA. For which reason I resolved not to
stir. At last the good old lady broke through
her painful taciturnity, with an invective

against long visits. I would not have understood her, but Millamant joining in the argument, I rose and with a constrained smile told   45
her I thought nothing was so easy as to know
when a visit began to be troublesome. She
reddened and I withdrew, without expecting
her reply.

FAIN. You were to blame to resent what she   50
spoke only in compliance with her aunt.

MIRA. She is more mistress of herself than
to be under the necessity of such a resignation.

FAIN. What? though half her fortune depends upon her marrying with my lady's   55
approbation?

MIRA. I was then in such a humor that I
should have been better pleased if she had
been less discreet.

FAIN. Now I remember, I wonder not they   60
were weary of you: last night was one of their
cabal nights;° they have 'em three times a
week, and meet by turns, at one another's
apartments, where they come together like the
coroner's inquest, to sit upon the murdered   65
reputations of the week. You and I are excluded; and it was once proposed that all the
male sex should be excepted; but somebody
moved that to avoid scandal there might be one
man of the community; upon which Witwoud   70
and Petulant were enrolled members.

MIRA. And who may have been the
foundress of this sect? My Lady Wishfort, I
warrant, who publishes her detestation of
mankind, and full of the vigor of fifty-five,   75
declares for a friend and ratafia;° and let posterity shift for itself, she'll breed no more.

FAIN. The discovery of your sham addresses
to her, to conceal your love to her niece, has
provoked this separation. Had you dissembled   80
better, things might have continued in the
state of nature.

MIRA. I did as much as man could, with any
reasonable conscience: I proceeded to the very
last act of flattery with her, and was guilty of   85
a song in her commendation. Nay, I got a

vapors low spirits

cabal nights gossip sessions (suggesting meetings of
a conspiratorial society, or cabal)
ratafia fruit brandy

friend to put her into a lampoon and compliment her with the imputation of an affair with a young fellow, which I carried so far that I told her the malicious town took notice that
5 she was grown fat of a sudden; and when she lay in of a dropsy, persuaded her she was reported to be in labor. The devil's in't, if an old woman is to be flattered further, unless a man should endeavor downright personally to
10 debauch her; and that my virtue forbade me. But for the discovery of this amour, I am indebted to your friend, or your wife's friend, Mrs. Marwood.
FAIN. What should provoke her to be your
15 enemy, without she has made you advances which you have slighted? Women do not easily forgive omissions of that nature.
MIRA. She was always civil to me till of late. I confess I am not one of those coxcombs who
20 are apt to interpret a woman's good manners to her prejudice, and think that she who does not refuse 'em everything, can refuse 'em nothing.
FAIN. You are a gallant man, Mirabell; and
25 though you may have cruelty enough not to satisfy a lady's longing, you have too much generosity not to be tender of her honor. Yet you speak with an indifference which seems to be affected, and confess you are conscious of a
30 negligence.
MIRA. You pursue the argument with a distrust that seems to be unaffected, and confesses you are conscious of a concern for which the lady is more indebted to you than is your wife.
35 FAIN. Fie, fie, friend, if you grow censorious I must leave you.—I'll look upon the gamesters in the next room.
MIRA. Who are they?
FAIN. Petulant and Witwoud.—[To BETTY.]
40 Bring me some chocolate.
[Exit.]
MIRA. Betty, what says your clock?
BET. Turned of the last canonical hour,° sir.
MIRA. How pertinently the jade answers me!

canonical hour the morning hours, set aside for marriages by canon law

Ha? almost one a clock! [Looking on his 45 watch.]—O, y'are come—

. . .

[Enter a FOOTMAN.]
MIRA. Well, is the grand affair over? You have been something tedious.
FOOT. Sir, there's such coupling at Pancras° 50 that they stand behind one another, as 'twere in a country dance. Ours was the last couple to lead up; and no hopes appearing of dispatch, besides, the parson growing hoarse, we were afraid his lungs would have failed before it 55 came to our turn; so we drove around to Duke's Place, and there they were riveted in a trice.
MIRA. So, so, you are sure they are married?
FOOT. Married and bedded, sir. I am witness.
MIRA. Have you the certificate? 60
FOOT. Here it is, sir.
MIRA. Has the tailor brought Waitwell's clothes home, and the new liveries?
FOOT. Yes, sir.
MIRA. That's well. Do you go home again, 65 d'ye hear, and adjourn the consummation till farther order. Bid Waitwell shake his ears, and Dame Partlet° rustle up her feathers, and meet me at one a clock by Rosamond's Pond° that I may see her before she returns to her lady: and 70 as you tender your ears, be secret.

. . .

[Re-enter FAINALL.]
FAIN. Joy of your success, Mirabell; you look pleased.
MIRA. Aye, I have been engaged in a matter 75 of some sort of mirth, which is not yet ripe for discovery. I am glad this is not a cabal night. I wonder, Fainall, that you who are married, and of consequence should be discreet, will suffer your wife to be of such a party. 80
FAIN. Faith, I am not jealous. Besides, most

Pancras St. Pancras and St. James (in Duke's Place, named below) were churches in which marriages were performed without the delay of banns.
Dame Partlet Pertelote, favorite hen of Chaunticleer in Chaucer's Nun's Priest's Tale
Rosamond's Pond in St. James's Park

who are engaged are women and relations; and for the men, they are of a kind too contemptible to give scandal.

MIRA. I am of another opinion. The greater
5 the coxcomb, always the more the scandal: for a woman who is not a fool can have but one reason for associating with a man who is one.

FAIN. Are you jealous as often as you see Witwoud entertained by Millamant?

10 MIRA. Of her understanding I am, if not of her person.

FAIN. You do her wrong; for to give her her due, she has wit.

MIRA. She has beauty enough to make any
15 man think so; and complaisance enough not to contradict him who shall tell her so.

FAIN. For a passionate lover, methinks you are a man somewhat too discerning in the failings of your mistress.

20 MIRA. And for a discerning man, somewhat too passionate a lover; for I like her with all her faults, nay, like her for her faults. Her follies are so natural, or so artful, that they become her, and those affectations which in another
25 woman would be odious, serve but to make her more agreeable. I'll tell thee, Fainall, she once used me with that insolence that in revenge I took her to pieces; sifted her, and separated her failings; I studied 'em, and got 'em by rote. The
30 catalogue was so large that I was not without hopes, one day or other, to hate her heartily: to which end I so used myself to think of 'em that at length, contrary to my design and expectation, they gave me every hour less and
35 less disturbance, till in a few days it became habitual to me to remember 'em without being displeased. They are now grown as familiar to me as my own frailties, and in all probability in a little time longer I shall like 'em as well.

40 FAIN. Marry her, marry her; be half as well acquainted with her charms as you are with her defects, and my life on't, you are your own man again.

MIRA. Say you so?

45 FAIN. Aye, aye, I have experience; I have a wife, and so forth.

·   ·   ·

[*Enter* MESSENGER.]

MESS. Is one Squire Witwoud here?

BET. Yes. What's your business?

MESS. I have a letter for him, from his 50 brother Sir Wilfull, which I am charged to deliver into his own hands.

BET. He's in the next room, friend—that way.

[*Exit* MESSENGER.]

·   ·   ·

MIRA. What, is the chief of that noble family 55 in town, Sir Wilfull Witwoud?

FAIN. He is expected today. Do you know him?

MIRA. I have seen him. He promises to be an extraordinary person; I think you have the 60 honor to be related to him.

FAIN. Yes; he is half brother to this Witwoud by a former wife, who was sister to my Lady Wishfort, my wife's mother. If you marry Millamant, you must call cousins too. 65

MIRA. I had rather be his relation than his acquaintance.

FAIN. He comes to town in order to equip himself for travel.

MIRA. For travel! Why the man that I mean 70 is above forty.°

FAIN. No matter for that: 'tis for the honor of England that all Europe should know that we have blockheads of all ages.

MIRA. I wonder there is not an Act of 75 Parliament to save the credit of the nation, and prohibit the exportation of fools.

FAIN. By no means, 'tis better as 'tis; 'tis better to trade with a little loss than to be quite eaten up with being overstocked. 80

MIRA. Pray, are the follies of this knight-errant, and those of the squire his brother, anything related?

FAIN. Not at all. Witwoud grows by the knight, like a medlar grafted on a crab.° One 85 will melt in your mouth, and t'other set your

---

above forty a tour of the Continent normally taken after graduation from a university
medlar . . . crab lush eating apple grafted on a crab-apple stem

teeth on edge; one is all pulp, and the other all core.

MIRA. So one will be rotten before he be ripe, and the other will be rotten without ever being ripe at all.

FAIN. Sir Wilful is an odd mixture of bashfulness and obstinacy. But when he's drunk, he's as loving as the monster° in *The Tempest;* and much after the same manner. To give t'other his due, he has something of good nature, and does not always want wit.

MIRA. Not always; but as often as his memory fails him, and his commonplace of comparisons.° He is a fool with a good memory, and some few scraps of other folks' wit. He is one whose conversation can never be approved, yet it is now and then to be endured. He has indeed one good quality, he is not exceptious,° for he so passionately affects the reputation of understanding raillery that he will construe an affront into a jest; and call downright rudeness and ill language, satire and fire.

FAIN. If you have a mind to finish his picture, you have an opportunity to do it at full length. Behold the original.

.   .   .

[*Enter* WITWOUD.]

WIT. Afford me your compassion, my dears; pity me, Fainall, Mirabell, pity me.

MIRA. I do from my soul.

FAIN. Why, what's the matter?

WIT. No letters for me, Betty?

BET. Did not a messenger bring you one but now, sir?

WIT. Aye, but no other?

BET. No, sir.

WIT. That's hard, that's very hard. A messenger, a mule, a beast of burden, he has brought me a letter from the fool my brother, as heavy as a panegyric in a funeral sermon, or a copy of commendatory verses from one poet to another. And what's worse, 'tis as sure a forerunner of the author as an epistle dedicatory.

MIRA. A fool, and your brother, Witwoud?

WIT. Aye, aye, my half brother. My half brother he is, no nearer upon honor.

MIRA. Then 'tis possible he may be but half a fool.

WIT. Good, good, Mirabell, *le drôle!*° Good, good. Hang him, don't let's talk of him. Fainall, how does your lady? Gad. I say anything in the world to get this fellow out of my head. I beg pardon that I should ask a man of pleasure and the town a question at once so foreign and domestic. But I talk like an old maid at a marriage, I don't know what I say: but she's the best woman in the world.

FAIN. 'Tis well you don't know what you say, or else your commendation would go near to make me either vain or jealous.

WIT. No man in town lives well with a wife but Fainall. Your judgment, Mirabell?

MIRA. You had better step and ask his wife, if you would be credibly informed.

WIT. Mirabell.

MIRA. Aye.

WIT. My dear, I ask ten thousand pardons— Gad, I have forgot what I was going to say to you.

MIRA. I thank you heartily, heartily.

WIT. No, but prithee excuse me—my memory is such a memory.

MIRA. Have a care of such apologies, Witwoud—for I never knew a fool but he affected to complain, either of the spleen or his memory.

FAIN. What have you done with Petulant?

WIT. He's reckoning his money—my money it was. I have no luck today.

FAIN. You may allow him to win of you at play, for you are sure to be too hard for him at repartee. Since you monopolize the wit that is between you, the fortune must be his of course.

MIRA. I don't find that Petulant confesses the superiority of wit to be your talent, Witwoud.

WIT. Come, come, you are malicious now, and would breed debates. Petulant's my friend, and a very honest fellow, and a very pretty

---

the monster Caliban
commonplace of comparisons notebook of similes he has copied out
exceptious given to taking exception

le drôle! clever fellow!

fellow, and has a smattering—faith and troth a pretty deal of an odd sort of a small wit. Nay, I'll do him justice. I'm his friend, I won't wrong him. And if he had any judgment in the world, he would not be altogether contemptible. Come, come, don't detract from the merits of my friend.

FAIN. You don't take your friend to be over-nicely bred.

WIT. No, no, hang him, the rogue has no manners at all, that I must own—no more breeding than a bum-bailey,° that I grant you. 'Tis pity, faith; the fellow has fire and life.

MIRA. What, courage?

WIT. Hum, faith I don't know as to that—I can't say as to that.—Yes, faith, in a controversy he'll contradict anybody.

MIRA. Though 'twere a man whom he feared, or a woman whom he loved.

WIT. Well, well, he does not always think before he speaks. We have all our failings; you are too hard upon him, you are, faith. Let me excuse him—I can defend most of his faults, except one or two. One he has, that's the truth on't, if he were my brother, I could not acquit him. That indeed I could wish were otherwise.

MIRA. Aye marry, what's that, Witwoud?

WIT. O, pardon me! Expose the infirmities of my friend?—No, my dear, excuse me there.

FAIN. What! I warrant he's unsincere, or 'tis some such trifle.

WIT. No, no, what if he be? 'Tis no matter for that, his wit will excuse that. A wit should no more be sincere than a woman constant; one argues a decay of parts, as t'other of beauty.

MIRA. Maybe you think him too positive?

WIT. No, no, his being positive is an incentive to argument, and keeps up conversation.

FAIN. Too illiterate.°

WIT. That! that's his happiness. His want of learning gives him the more opportunities to show his natural parts.

MIRA. He wants words.

WIT. Aye; but I like him for that now; for

his want of words gives me the pleasure very often to explain his meaning.

FAIN. He's impudent.

WIT. No, that's not it.

MIRA. Vain.

WIT. No.

MIRA. What, he speaks unseasonable truths sometimes, because he has not wit enough to invent an evasion!

WIT. Truths! Ha, ha, ha! No, no, since you will have it—I mean, he never speaks truth at all—that's all. He will lie like a chambermaid, or a woman of quality's porter. Now that is a fault.

. . .

[*Enter* COACHMAN.]

COACH. Is Master Petulant here, mistress?

BET. Yes.

COACH. Three gentlewomen in a coach would speak with him.

FAIN. O brave Petulant, three!

BET. I'll tell him.

COACH. You must bring two dishes of chocolate and a glass of cinnamon water.

[*Exeunt* BETTY *and* COACHMAN.]

. . .

WIT. That should be for two fasting strumpets, and a bawd troubled with wind. Now you may know what the three are.

MIRA. You are free with your friend's acquaintance.

WIT. Aye, aye, friendship without freedom is as dull as love without enjoyment, or wine without toasting; but to tell you a secret, these are trulls whom he allows coach-hire, and something more by the week, to call on him once a day at public places.

MIRA. How?

WIT. You shall see he won't go to 'em because there's no more company here to take notice of him. Why this is nothing to what he used to do, before he found out this way, I have known him call for himself.—

FAIN. Call for himself? What dost thou mean?

WIT. Mean? Why he would slip you out of

bum-bailey arresting officer
illiterate ill-read

this chocolate house, just when you had been talking to him.—As soon as your back was turned—whip he was gone—then trip to his lodging, clap on a hood and scarf, and a mask,
5 slap into a hackney coach, and drive hither to the door again in a trice; where he would send in for himself—that I mean—call for himself, wait for himself; nay and what's more, not finding himself, sometimes leave a letter for
10 himself.

MIRA. I confess this is something extraordinary.—I believe he waits for himself now, he is so long a-coming. O, I ask his pardon.

· · ·

[*Enter* PETULANT *and* BETTY.]
15 BET. Sir, the coach stays.
[*Exit.*]
PET. Well, well; I come.—'Sbud,° a man had as good be a professed midwife, as a professed whoremaster, at this rate; to be knocked up and
20 raised at all hours, and in all places. Pox on 'em, I won't come.—D'ye hear, tell 'em I won't come. Let 'em snivel and cry their hearts out.

FAIN. You are very cruel, Petulant.

PET. All's one, let it pass—I have a humor to
25 be cruel.

MIRA. I hope they are not persons of condition that you use at this rate.

PET. Condition! Condition's a dried fig, if I am not in humor. By this hand, if they were
30 your—a—a—your what-d'ee-call-'ems themselves, they must wait or rub off,° if I want appetite.

MIRA. What-d'ee-call-'ems! What are they, Witwoud?
35 WIT. Empresses,° my dear.—By your what-d'ee-call-'ems he means sultana queens.

PET. Aye, Roxolanas.

MIRA. Cry you mercy.

FAIN. Witwoud says they are—
40 PET. What does he say th'are?

WIT. I? Fine ladies I say.

'**Sbud** a slang term (originally *God's body*, an oath on the body of Christ)
rub off leave
Empresses prostitutes (similar euphemisms follow)

PET. Pass on, Witwoud.—Hark'ee by this light his relations—two co-heiresses his cousins, and an old aunt, who loves caterwauling better than a conventicle.° 45

WIT. Ha, ha, ha! I had a mind to see how the rogue would come off.—Ha, ha, ha! Gad, I can't be angry with him, if he had said they were my mother and my sisters.

MIRA. No? 50

WIT. No; the rogue's wit and readiness of invention charm me, dear Petulant.

[*Re-enter* BETTY.]

BET. They are gone, sir, in great anger.

PET. Enough, let 'em trundle. Anger helps 55 complexion, saves paint.

FAIN. This continence is all dissembled; this is in order to have something to brag of the next time he makes court to Millamant, and swear he has abandoned the whole sex for her 60 sake.

MIRA. Have you not left off your impudent pretensions there yet? I shall cut your throat sometime or other, Petulant, about that business. 65

PET. Aye, aye, let that pass.—There are other throats to be cut.—

MIRA. Meaning mine, sir?

PET. Not I—I mean nobody.—I know nothing. But there are uncles and nephews in the 70 world—and they may be rivals.—What then? All's one for that—

MIRA. How! Hark'ee, Petulant, come hither —explain, or I shall call your interpreter.

PET. Explain? I know nothing.—Why, you 75 have an uncle, have you not, lately come to town, and lodges by my Lady Wishfort's?

MIRA. True.

PET. Why, that's enough.—You and he are not friends; and if he should marry and have a 80 child, you may be disinherited, ha?

MIRA. Where hast thou stumbled upon all this truth?

PET. All's one for that; why, then, say I know something. 85

MIRA. Come, thou art an honest fellow, Petulant, and shalt make love to my mistress,

conventicle meeting of religious dissenters

thou sha't, faith. What hast thou heard of my uncle?

PET. I, nothing, I. If throats are to be cut, let swords clash; snug's the word, I shrug and am silent.

MIRA. O raillery, raillery. Come, I know thou art in the women's secrets.—What, you're a cabalist. I know you stayed at Millamant's last night, after I went. Was there any mention made of my uncle or me? Tell me; if thou hadst but good nature equal to thy wit, Petulant, Tony Witwoud, who is now thy competitor in fame, would show as dim by thee as a dead whiting's eye by a pearl of Orient. He would no more be seen by° thee than Mercury is by the sun: come, I'm sure thou wo't tell me.

PET. If I do, will you grant me common sense then, for the future?

MIRA. Faith, I'll do what I can for thee, and I'll pray that Heaven may grant it thee in the meantime.

PET. Well, hark'ee.

[*They talk aside.*]

FAIN. Petulant and you both will find Mirabell as warm a rival as a lover.

WIT. Pshaw, pshaw, that she laughs at Petulant is plain. And for my part—but that it is almost a fashion to admire her, I should—hark'ee—to tell you a secret, but let it go no further—between friends, I shall never break my heart for her.

FAIN. How!

WIT. She's handsome; but she's a sort of an uncertain woman.

FAIN. I thought you had died for her.

WIT. Umh—no—

FAIN. She has wit.

WIT. 'Tis what she will hardly allow anybody else.—Now, demme, I should hate that, if she were as handsome as Cleopatra. Mirabell is not so sure of her as he thinks for.

FAIN. Why do you think so?

WIT. We stayed pretty late there last night, and heard something of an uncle to Mirabell, who is lately come to town, and is between him and the best part of his estate. Mirabell and he are at some distance, as my Lady Wishfort has been told; and you know she hates Mirabell, worse than a Quaker hates a parrot, or than a fishmonger hates a hard frost. Whether this uncle has seen Mrs. Millamant or not, I cannot say; but there were items of such a treaty being in embryo; and if it should come to life, poor Mirabell would be in some sort unfortunately fobbed° i' faith.

FAIN. 'Tis impossible Millamant should harken to it.

WIT. Faith, my dear, I can't tell; she's a woman and a kind of a humorist.°

MIRA. And this is the sum of what you could collect last night.

PET. The quintessence. Maybe Witwoud knows more, he stayed longer.—Besides they never mind him; they say anything before him.

MIRA. I thought you had been the greatest favorite.

PET. Aye, *tête à tête;*° but not in public, because I make remarks.

MIRA. You do?

PET. Aye, aye; pox, I'm malicious, man. Now he's soft, you know, they are not in awe of him. —The fellow's well bred, he's what you call a—what-d'ye-call-'em—a fine gentleman; but he's silly withal.

MIRA. I thank you, I know as much as my curiosity requires. Fainall, are you for the Mall?°

FAIN. Aye. I'll take a turn before dinner.

WIT. Aye, we'll all walk in the park; the ladies talked of being there.

MIRA. I thought you were obliged to watch for your brother Sir Wilfull's arrival.

WIT. No, no, he's come to his aunt's, my Lady Wishfort. Pox on him, I shall be troubled with him too. What shall I do with the fool?

PET. Beg him for his estate, that I may beg you afterwards, and so have but one trouble with you both.

WIT. O rare Petulant; thou art as quick as fire in a frosty morning; thou shalt to the Mall with us; and we'll be very severe.

seen by seen alongside
fobbed tricked
humorist whimsical person
tête à tête privately
the Mall a promenade in St. James's Park

PET. Enough, I'm in a humor to be severe.

MIRA. Are you? Pray then walk by your-selves.—Let not us be accessory to your putting the ladies out of countenance with your sense-
5 less ribaldry, which you roar out aloud as often as they pass by you; and when you have made a handsome woman blush, then you think you have been severe.

PET. What, what? Then let 'em either show
10 their innocence by not understanding what they hear, or else show their discretion by not hearing what they would not be thought to understand.

MIRA. But hast not thou then sense enough
15 to know that thou ought'st to be most ashamed thyself, when thou hast put another out by countenance?

PET. Not I, by this hand.—I always take blushing either for a sign of guilt, or ill breed-
20 ing.

MIRA. I confess you ought to think so. You are in the right, that you may plead the error of your judgment in defense of your practice.

Where modesty's ill manners, 'tis but fit
25   That impudence and malice pass for wit.

ACT II

[*St. James's Park.*]

.   .   .

[*Mrs. Fainall and Mrs. Marwood.*]

MRS. FAIN. Aye, aye, dear Marwood, if we will be happy, we must find the means in our-
30 selves, and among ourselves. Men are ever in extremes; either doting or averse. While they are lovers, if they have fire and sense, their jealousies are insupportable: and when they cease to love, (we ought to think at least) they
35 loathe. They look upon us with horror and dis-taste; they meet us like the ghosts of what we were, and as from such, fly from us.

MRS. MAR. True, 'tis an unhappy circum-stance of life that love should ever die before
40 us; and that the man so often should outlive the lover. But say what you will, 'tis better to be left than never to have been loved. To pass over

youth in dull indifference, to refuse the sweets of life because they once must leave us, is as preposterous as to wish to have been born old, 45 because we one day must be old. For my part, my youth may wear and waste, but it shall never rust in my possession.

MRS. FAIN. Then it seems you dissemble an aversion to mankind only in compliance to my 50 mother's humor.

MRS. MAR. Certainly. To be free, I have no taste of those insipid dry discourses with which our sex of force must entertain themselves apart from men. We may affect endearments to each 55 other, profess eternal friendships, and seem to dote like lovers; but 'tis not in our natures long to persevere. Love will resume his empire in our breasts, and every heart, or soon or late, receive and readmit him as its lawful tyrant. 60

MRS. FAIN. Bless me, how have I been de-ceived! Why, you profess a libertine.

MRS. MAR. You see my friendship by my freedom. Come, be as sincere, acknowledge that your sentiments agree with mine. 65

MRS. FAIN. Never.

MRS. MAR. You hate mankind?

MRS. FAIN. Heartily, inveterately.

MRS. MAR. Your husband?

MRS. FAIN. Most transcendently; aye, though 70 I say it, meritoriously.

MRS. MAR. Give me your hand upon it.

MRS. FAIN. There.

MRS. MAR. I join with you. What I have said 75 has been to try you.

MRS. FAIN. Is it possible? Dost thou hate those vipers, men?

MRS. MAR. I have done hating 'em, and am now come to despise 'em; the next thing I have to do is eternally to forget 'em. 80

MRS. FAIN. There spoke the spirit of an Amazon, a Penthesilea.°

MRS. MAR. And yet I am thinking sometimes to carry my aversion further.

MRS. FAIN. How? 85

MRS. MAR. Faith, by marrying. If I could but find one that loved me very well, and would be thoroughly sensible of ill usage, I think I should

Penthesilea   queen of the Amazons

do myself the violence of undergoing the ceremony.

MRS. FAIN. You would not make him a cuckold?

MRS. MAR. No; but I'd make him believe I did, and that's as bad.

MRS. FAIN. Why, had not you as good do it?

MRS. MAR. O, if he should ever discover it, he would then know the worst, and be out of his pain; but I would have him ever to continue upon the rack of fear and jealousy.

MRS. FAIN. Ingenious mischief! Would thou wert married to Mirabell.

MRS. MAR. Would I were.

MRS. FAIN. You change color.

MRS. MAR. Because I hate him.

MRS. FAIN. So do I; but I can hear him named. But what reason have you to hate him in particular?

MRS. MAR. I never loved him; he is and always was insufferably proud.

MRS. FAIN. By the reason you give for your aversion, one would think it dissembled; for you have laid a fault to his charge of which his enemies must acquit him.

MRS. MAR. O then it seems you are one of his favorable enemies. Methinks you look a little pale, and now you flush again.

MRS. FAIN. Do I? I think I am a little sick o' the sudden.

MRS. MAR. What ails you?

MRS. FAIN. My husband. Don't you see him? He turned short upon me unawares, and has almost overcome me.

. . .

[*Enter* FAINALL *and* MIRABELL.]

MRS. MAR. Ha, ha, ha! he comes opportunely for you.

MRS. FAIN. For you, for he has brought Mirabell with him.

FAIN. My dear.

MRS. FAIN. My soul.

FAIN. You don't look well today, child.

MRS. FAIN. D'ye think so?

MIRA. He is the only man that does, madam.

MRS. FAIN. The only man that would tell me so at least; and the only man from whom I could hear it without mortification.

FAIN. O my dear, I am satisfied of your tenderness; I know you cannot resent anything from me, especially what is an effect of my concern.

MRS. FAIN. Mr. Mirabell, my mother interrupted you in a pleasant relation last night. I would fain hear it out.

MIRA. The persons concerned in that affair have yet a tolerable reputation. I am afraid Mr. Fainall will be censorious.

MRS. FAIN. He has a humor more prevailing than his curiosity, and will willingly dispense with the hearing of one scandalous story to avoid giving an occasion to make another by being seen to walk with his wife. This way, Mr. Mirabell, and I dare promise you will oblige us both.

[*Exeunt* MRS. FAINALL *and* MIRABELL.]

. . .

FAIN. Excellent creature! Well, sure if I should live to be rid of my wife, I should be a miserable man.

MRS. MAR. Aye!

FAIN. For having only that one hope, the accomplishment of it of consequence must put an end to all my hopes; and what a wretch is he who must survive his hopes! Nothing remains when that day comes but to sit down and weep like Alexander, when he wanted other worlds to conquer.

MRS. MAR. Will you not follow 'em?

FAIN. Faith, I think not.

MRS. MAR. Pray let us; I have a reason.

FAIN. You are not jealous?

MRS. MAR. Of whom?

FAIN. Of Mirabell.

MRS. MAR. If I am, is it inconsistent with my love to you that I am tender of your honor?

FAIN. You would intimate then, as if there were a fellow-feeling between my wife and him.

MRS. MAR. I think she does not hate him to that degree she would be thought.

FAIN. But he, I fear, is too insensible.

MRS. MAR. It may be you are deceived.

FAIN. It may be so. I do now begin to apprehend it.

Mrs. Mar. What?

Fain. That I have been deceived, Madam, and you are false.

Mrs. Mar. That I am false! What mean you?

5 Fain. To let you know I see through all your little arts. Come, you both love him; and both have equally dissembled your aversion. Your mutual jealousies of one another have made you clash till you have both struck fire. I have seen
10 the warm confession reddening on your cheeks, and sparkling from your eyes.

Mrs. Mar. You do me wrong.

Fain. I do not. 'Twas for my ease to oversee° and willfully neglect the gross advances
15 made him by my wife; that by permitting her to be engaged I might continue unsuspected in my pleasures; and take you oftener to my arms in full security. But could you think, because the nodding husband would not wake, that e'er
20 the watchful lover slept?

Mrs. Mar. And wherewithal can you reproach me?

Fain. With infidelity, with loving another, with love of Mirabell.

25 Mrs. Mar. 'Tis false. I challenge you to show an instance that can confirm your groundless accusation. I hate him.

Fain. And wherefore do you hate him? He is insensible, and your resentment follows his
30 neglect. An instance! The injuries you have done him are a proof: your interposing in his love. What cause had you to make discoveries of his pretended passion? To undeceive the credulous aunt, and be the officious obstacle of
35 his match with Millamant?

Mrs. Mar. My obligations to my lady urged me. I had professed a friendship to her, and could not see her easy nature so abused by that dissembler.

40 Fain. What, was it conscience then? Professed a friendship! O the pious friendships of the female sex!

Mrs. Mar. More tender, more sincere, and more enduring than all the vain and empty
45 vows of men, whether professing love to us, or mutual faith to one another.

Fain. Ha, ha, ha! you are my wife's friend too.

Mrs. Mar. Shame and ingratitude! Do you reproach me? You, you upbraid me! Have I 50 been false to her, through strict fidelity to you, and sacrificed my friendship to keep my love inviolate? And have you the baseness to charge me with the guilt, unmindful of the merit! To you it should be meritorious that I have been 55 vicious: and do you reflect that guilt upon me, which should lie buried in your bosom?

Fain. You misinterpret my reproof. I meant but to remind you of the slight account you once could make of strictest ties, when set in 60 competition with your love to me.

Mrs. Mar. 'Tis false, you urged it with deliberate malice. 'Twas spoke in scorn, and I never will forgive it.

Fain. Your guilt, not your resentment, begets 65 your rage. If yet you loved, you could forgive a jealousy, but you are stung to find you are discovered.

Mrs. Mar. It shall be all discovered. You too shall be discovered; be sure you shall. I can but 70 be exposed.—If I do it myself, I shall prevent° your baseness.

Fain. Why, what will you do?

Mrs. Mar. Disclose it to your wife; own what has passed between us. 75

Fain. Frenzy!

Mrs. Mar. By all my wrongs I'll do't—I'll publish to the world the injuries you have done me, both in my fame° and fortune: with both I trusted you, you bankrupt in honor, as in- 80 digent of wealth.

Fain. Your fame I have preserved. Your fortune has been bestowed as the prodigality of your love would have it, in pleasures which we both have shared. Yet, had not you been false, 85 I had e'er this repaid it. 'Tis true. Had you permitted Mirabell with Millamant to have stolen their marriage, my lady had been incensed beyond all means of reconcilement. Millamant had forfeited the moiety° of her fortune, which 90

oversee overlook

prevent anticipate
fame reputation
moiety half

then would have descended to my wife. And wherefore did I marry, but to make lawful prize of a rich widow's wealth, and squander it on love and you?

5 Mrs. Mar. Deceit and frivolous pretense.

Fain. Death, am I not married? What's pretense? Am I not imprisoned, fettered? Have I not a wife? Nay, a wife that was a widow, a young widow, a handsome widow; and would

10 be again a widow, but that I have a heart of proof, and something of a constitution to bustle through the ways of wedlock and this world. Will you yet be reconciled to truth and me?

Mrs. Mar. Impossible. Truth and you are

15 inconsistent. I hate you, and shall forever.

Fain. For loving you?

Mrs. Mar. I loathe the name of love after such usage; and next to the guilt with which you would asperse me, I scorn you most. Fare-

20 well.

Fain. Nay, we must not part thus.

Mrs. Mar. Let me go.

Fain. Come, I'm sorry.

Mrs. Mar. I care not.—Let me go.—Break

25 my hands, do—I'd leave 'em to get loose.

Fain. I would not hurt you for the world. Have I no other hold to keep you here?

Mrs. Mar. Well, I have deserved it all.

Fain. You know I love you.

30 Mrs. Mar. Poor dissembling!—O that.—Well, it is not yet—

Fain. What? What is it not? What is it not yet? It is not yet too late—

Mrs. Mar. No, it is not yet too late—I have

35 that comfort.

Fain. It is, to love another.

Mrs. Mar. But not to loathe, detest, abhor mankind, myself, and the whole treacherous world.

40 Fain. Nay, this is extravagance. Come, I ask your pardon.—No tears.—I was to blame. I could not love you and be easy in my doubts. —Pray forbear.—I believe you; I'm convinced I've done you wrong; and any way, every way

45 will make amends. I'll hate my wife yet more, damn her, I'll part with her, rob her of all she's worth, and we'll retire somewhere, anywhere, to another world. I'll marry thee.—Be pacified.

—'Sdeath,° they come, hide your face, your tears.—You have a mask, wear it a moment. 50 This way, this way, be persuaded.

[*Exeunt.*]

. . .

[*Enter* Mirabell *and* Mrs. Fainall.]

Mrs. Fain. They are here yet.

Mira. They are turning into the other walk. 55

Mrs. Fain. While I only hated my husband, I could bear to see him, but since I have despised him, he's too offensive.

Mira. O, you should hate with prudence.

Mrs. Fain. Yes, for I have loved with in- 60 discretion.

Mira. You should have just so much disgust for your husband as may be sufficient to make you relish your lover.

Mrs. Fain. You have been the cause that I 65 have loved without bounds, and would you set limits to that aversion, of which you have been the occasion? Why did you make me marry this man?

Mira. Why do we daily commit disagreeable 70 and dangerous actions? To save that idol, reputation. If the familiarities of our loves had produced that consequence, of which you were apprehensive, where could you have fixed a father's name with credit, but on a husband? 75 I knew Fainall to be a man lavish of his morals, an interested and professing friend, a false and a designing lover; yet one whose wit and outward fair behavior have gained a reputation with the town, enough to make that woman 80 stand excused who has suffered herself to be won by his addresses. A better man ought not to have been sacrificed to the occasion; a worse had not answered to the purpose. When you are weary of him, you know your remedy. 85

Mrs. Fain. I ought to stand in some degree of credit with you, Mirabell.

Mira. In justice to you, I have made you privy to my whole design, and put it in your power to ruin or advance my fortune. 90

'Sdeath a slang term (originally *God's death*, an oath on the death of Christ)

MRS. FAIN. Whom have you instructed to represent your pretended uncle?

MIRA. Waitwell, my servant.

MRS. FAIN. He is an humble servant to Foible, my mother's woman, and may win her to your interest.

MIRA. Care is taken for that. She is won and worn by this time. They were married this morning.

MRS. FAIN. Who?

MIRA. Waitwell and Foible. I would not tempt my servant to betray me by trusting him too far. If your mother, in hopes to ruin me, should consent to marry my pretended uncle, he might, like Mosca in *The Fox*, stand upon terms;° so I made him sure beforehand.

MRS. FAIN. So, if my poor mother is caught in a contract, you will discover the imposture betimes, and release her by producing a certificate of her gallant's former marriage.

MIRA. Yes, upon condition that she consent to my marriage with her niece, and surrender the moiety of her fortune in her possession.

MRS. FAIN. She talked last night of endeavoring at a match between Millamant and your uncle.

MIRA. That was by Foible's direction, and my instruction, that she might seem to carry it more privately.

MRS. FAIN. Well, I have an opinion of your success, for I believe my lady will do anything to get an husband; and when she has this, which you have provided for her, I suppose she will submit to anything to get rid of him.

MIRA. Yes, I think the good lady would marry anything that resembled a man, though 'twere no more than what a butler could pinch out of a napkin.°

MRS. FAIN. Female frailty! We must all come to it, if we live to be old, and feel the craving of a false appetite when the true is decayed.

MIRA. An old woman's appetite is depraved like that of a girl—'tis the greensickness° of a second childhood; and like the faint offer of a latter spring, serves but to usher in the fall and withers in an affected bloom.

MRS. FAIN. Here's your mistress.

.   .   .

[*Enter* MRS. MILLAMANT, WITWOUD, MINCING.]

MIRA. Here she comes, i'faith, full sail, with her fan spread and streamers out, and a shoal of fools for tenders.—Ha, no, I cry her mercy!

MRS. FAIN. I see but one poor empty sculler, and he tows her woman after him.

MIRA. You seem to be unattended, madam. —You used to have the *beau monde*° throng after you; and a flock of gay fine perukes hovering round you.

WIT. Like moths about a candle—I had like to have lost my comparison for want of breath.

MILLA. O, I have denied myself airs today. I have walked as fast through the crowd—

WIT. As a favorite just disgraced, and with as few followers.

MILLA. Dear Mr. Witwoud, truce with your similitudes. For I am as sick of 'em—

WIT. As a physician of a good air—I cannot help it, madam, though 'tis against myself.

MILLA. Yet again! Mincing, stand between me and his wit.

WIT. Do, Mrs. Mincing, like a screen before a great fire. I confess I do blaze today, I am too bright.

MRS. FAIN. But dear Millamant, why were you so long?

MILLA. Long? Lord, have I not made violent haste? I have asked every living thing I met for you; I have inquired after you, as after a new fashion.

WIT. Madam, truce with your similitudes. No, you met her husband, and did not ask him for her.

MIRA. By your leave, Witwoud, that were like inquiring after an old fashion, to ask a husband for his wife.

WIT. Hum, a hit, a hit, a palpable hit, I confess it.

---

stand upon terms   set conditions (like Mosca in *Volpone* V.xii)

pinch out of a napkin   i.e., for a dinner-table novelty

greensickness   an anemia of adolescent girls

beau monde   fashionable world

Mrs. Fain. You were dressed before I came abroad.

Milla. Aye, that's true.—O, but then I had —Mincing, what had I? Why was I so long?

5 Minc. O mem, your la'ship stayed to peruse a packet of letters.

Milla. O, aye, letters—I had letters—I am persecuted with letters—I hate letters. Nobody knows how to write letters; and yet one has 10 'em, one does not know why. They serve one to pin up one's hair.

Wit. Is that the way? Pray, madam, do you pin up your hair with all your letters? I find I must keep copies.

15 Milla. Only with those in verse, Mr. Witwoud. I never pin up my hair with prose. I think I tried once, Mincing.

Minc. O mem, I shall never forget it.

Milla. Aye, poor Mincing tiffed° and tiffed 20 all the morning.

Minc. Till I had the cramp in my fingers, I'll vow, mem. And all to no purpose. But when your la'ship pins it up with poetry, it sits so pleasant the next day as anything, and is so 25 pure and so crips.°

Wit. Indeed, so crips?

Minc. You're such a critic, Mr. Witwoud. [*Exit* Mincing.]

Milla. Mirabell, did you take exceptions last 30 night? O, aye, and went away.—Now I think on't I'm angry.—No, now I think on't I'm pleased—for I believe I gave you some pain.

Mira. Does that please you?

Milla. Infinitely; I love to give pain.

35 Mira. You would affect a cruelty which is not in your nature; your true vanity is in the power of pleasing.

Milla. O, I ask your pardon for that. One's cruelty is one's power, and when one parts 40 with one's cruelty, one parts with one's power; and when one has parted with that, I fancy one's old and ugly.

Mira. Aye, aye, suffer your cruelty to ruin the object of your power, to destroy your 45 lover. And then how vain, how lost a thing

you'll be? Nay, 'tis true: you are no longer handsome when you've lost your lover; your beauty dies upon the instant: for beauty is the lover's gift; 'tis he bestows your charms— your glass is all a cheat. The ugly and the old, 50 whom the looking glass mortifies, yet after commendation can be flattered by it, and discover beauties in it: for that reflects our praises, rather than your face.

Milla. O, the vanity of these men! Fainall, 55 d'ye hear him? If they did not commend us, we were not handsome! Now you must know they could not commend one, if one was not handsome. Beauty the lover's gift! Lord, what is a lover, that it can give? Why, one makes lovers 60 as fast as one pleases, and they live as long as one pleases, and they die as soon as one pleases; and then, if one pleases, one makes more.

Wit. Very pretty. Why, you make no more of making of lovers, madam, than of making 65 so many card-matches.°

Milla. One no more owes one's beauty to a lover than one's wit to an echo. They can but reflect what we look and say; vain empty things if we are silent or unseen, and want a 70 being.

Mira. Yet, to those two vain empty things, you owe two of the greatest pleasures of your life.

Milla. How so? 75

Mira. To your lover you owe the pleasure of hearing yourselves praised; and to an echo the pleasure of hearing yourselves talk.

Wit. But I know a lady that loves talking so incessantly she won't give an echo fair play; 80 she has that everlasting rotation of tongue, that an echo must wait till she dies before it can catch her last words.

Milla. O, fiction; Fainall, let us leave these men. 85

Mira. [*aside to* Mrs. Fainall]. Draw off Witwoud.

Mrs. Fain. Immediately; I have a word or two for Mr. Witwoud.

[*Exeunt* Mrs. Fainall *and* Witwoud.] 90

. . .

---

tiffed arranged hair
crips substandard variant of *crisp*

card-matches strips of card dipped in sulfur

MIRA. I would beg a little private audience too.—You had the tyranny to deny me last night, though you knew I came to impart a secret to you that concerned my love.

5   MILLA. You saw I was engaged.

MIRA. Unkind. You had the leisure to entertain a herd of fools, things who visit you from their excessive idleness, bestowing on your easiness that time which is the encumbrance of 10 their lives. How can you find delight in such society? It is imposible they should admire you, they are not capable: or if they were, it should be to you as a mortification; for sure, to please a fool is some degree of folly.

15   MILLA. I please myself—besides, sometimes to converse with fools is for my health.

MIRA. Your health! Is there a worse disease than the conversation of fools?

MILLA. Yes, the vapors; fools are physic for 20 it, next to asafetida.°

MIRA. You are not in a course of fools?°

MILLA. Mirabell, if you persist in this offensive freedom, you'll displease me. I think I must resolve after all not to have you.—We shan't 25 agree.

MIRA. Not in our physic, it may be.

MILLA. And yet our distemper in all likelihood will be the same, for we shall be sick of one another. I shan't endure to be reprimanded 30 nor instructed; 'tis so dull to act always by advice, and so tedious to be told of one's faults. —I can't bear it. Well, I won't have you, Mirabell—I'm resolved—I think—you may go—ha, ha, ha! What would you give that you could 35 help loving me?

MIRA. I would give something that you did not know I could not help it.

MILLA. Come, don't look grave then. Well, what do you say to me?

40   MIRA. I say that a man may as soon make a friend by his wit, or a fortune by his honesty, as win a woman with plain-dealing and sincerity.

MILLA. Sententious Mirabell! prithee don't look with that violent and inflexible wise face, 45 like Solomon at the dividing of the child in an old tapestry hanging.°

MIRA. You are merry, madam, but I would persuade you for a moment to be serious.

MILLA. What, with that face? No, if you keep 50 your countenance, 'tis impossible I should hold mine. Well, after all, there is something very moving in a lovesick face. Ha, ha, ha!—Well I won't laugh, don't be peevish—heigho! Now I'll be melancholy, as melancholy as a watch- 55 light. Well, Mirabell, if ever you will win me, woo me now. Nay, if you are so tedious, fare you well; I see they are walking away.

MIRA. Can you not find in the variety of your disposition one moment— 60

MILLA. To hear you tell me Foible's married and your plot like to speed?—No.

MIRA. But how you came to know it—

MILLA. Unless by the help of the devil, you can't imagine; unless she should tell me herself. 65 Which of the two it may have been, I will leave you to consider; and when you have done thinking of that, think of me.

[Exit.]

⋆   ⋆   ⋆

MIRA. I have something more. Gone!—Think 70 of you! To think of a whirlwind, though 'twere in a whirlwind, were a case of more steady contemplation; a very tranquility of mind and mansion. A fellow that lives in a windmill has not a more whimsical dwelling than the heart 75 of a man that is lodged in a woman. There is no point of the compass to which they cannot turn, and by which they are not turned; and by one as well as another, for motion, not method, is their occupation. To know this, and yet con- 80 tinue to be in love, is to be made wise from the dictates of reason, and yet persevere to play the fool by the force of instinct. O, here come my pair of turtles°—what, billing so

---

asafetida a vile-smelling medicine
course of fools an implied analogy to "course of physic," a medical regimen

hanging the story of the Judgment of Solomon is found in I Kings iii.
turtles turtledoves

sweetly! Is not Valentine's Day over with you yet?

. . .

[*Enter* WAITWELL, FOIBLE.]

Sirrah Waitwell, why sure you think you
5 were married for your own recreation and not for my conveniency.

WAIT. Your pardon, sir. With submission, we have indeed been solacing in lawful delights, but still with an eye to business, sir. I have in-
10 structed her as well as I could. If she can take your directions as readily as my instructions, sir, your affairs are in a prosperous way.

MIRA. Give you joy, Mrs. Foible.

FOIB. O 'las, sir, I'm so ashamed—I'm afraid
15 my lady has been in a thousand inquietudes for me. But I protest, sir, I made as much haste as I could.

WAIT. That she did indeed, sir. It was my fault that she did not make more.
20 MIRA. That I believe.

FOIB. But I told my lady as you instructed me, sir. That I had a prospect of seeing Sir Rowland your uncle, and that I would put her ladyship's picture in my pocket to show him; which I'll
25 be sure to say has made him so enamored of her beauty that he burns with impatience to lie at her ladyship's feet and worship the original.

MIRA. Excellent Foible! Matrimony has made you eloquent in love.
30 WAIT. I think she has profited, sir. I think so.

FOIB. You have seen Madam Millamant, sir?

MIRA. Yes.

FOIB. I told her, sir, because I did not know that you might find an opportunity; she had so
35 much company last night.

MIRA. Your diligence will merit more. In the meantime—[*gives money*].

FOIB. O dear sir, your humble servant.

WAIT. Spouse.
40 MIRA. Stand off, sir, not a penny. Go on and prosper, Foible. The lease shall be made good and the farm stocked if we succeed.

FOIB. I don't question your generosity, sir. And you need not doubt of success. If you have
45 no more commands, sir, I'll be gone; I'm sure my lady is at her toilet, and can't dress till I come. O dear, I'm sure that [*looking out*] was Mrs. Marwood that went by in a mask; if she has seen me with you I'm sure she'll tell my lady. I'll make haste home and prevent her. 50 Your servant, sir. B'w'y,° Waitwell.

[*Exit.*]

. . .

WAIT. Sir Rowland, if you please. The jade's so pert upon her preferment she forgets her-self. 55

MIRA. Come, sir, will you endeavor to forget yourself—and transform into Sir Rowland.

WAIT. Why, sir, it will be impossible I should remember myself—married, knighted, and attended all in one day! 'Tis enough to make 60 any man forget himself. The difficulty will be how to recover my acquaintance and familiarity with my former self; and fall from my trans-formation to a reformation into Waitwell. Nay, I shan't be quite the same Waitwell neither— 65 for now I remember me, I'm married and can't be my own man again.

Aye, there's my grief; that's the sad change
[of life;
To lose my title, and yet keep my wife. 70
[*Exeunt.*]

ACT III

[*A room in* LADY WISHFORT'*s house.*]

. . .

[LADY WISHFORT *at her toilet,* PEG *waiting.*]
LADY. Merciful!° No news of Foible yet?
PEG. No, madam. 75

LADY. I have no more patience. If I have not fretted myself till I am pale again, there's no veracity in me. Fetch me the red—the red, do you hear, sweetheart? An arrant ash color, as I'm a person. Look you how this wench stirs! 80

B'w'y [God] b[e] w[ith] y[e]; i.e., good bye
Merciful! Merciful heaven!

Why dost thou not fetch me a little red? Didst thou not hear me, mopus?°

PEG. The red ratafia does your ladyship mean, or the cherry brandy?

5 LADY. Ratafia, fool. No, fool. Not the ratafia, fool. Grant me patience! I mean the Spanish paper,° idiot—complexion, darling. Paint, paint, paint, dost thou understand that, changeling, dangling thy hands like bobbins before 10 thee? Why dost thou not stir, puppet? Thou wooden thing upon wires!

PEG. Lord, madam, your ladyship is so impatient.—I cannot come at the paint, madam. Mrs. Foible has locked it up and carried the 15 key with her.

LADY. A pox take you both!—Fetch me the cherry brandy then.

[Exit PEG.]

.   .   .

I'm as pale and as faint, I look like Mrs. Qualm-20 sick, the curate's wife, that's always breeding. Wench, come, come, wench, what art thou doing? Sipping? Tasting? Save thee, dost thou not know the bottle?

.   .   .

[Re-enter PEG with a bottle and china cup.]
25 PEG. Madam, I was looking for a cup.

LADY. A cup, save thee, and what a cup hast thou brought! Dost thou take me for a fairy, to drink out of an acorn? Why didst thou not bring thy thimble? Hast thou ne'er a brass 30 thimble clinking in thy pocket with a bit of nutmeg? I warrant thee. Come, fill, fill.—So—again. [One knocks.] See who that is. Set down the bottle first. Here, here, under the table.— What, wouldst thou go with the bottle in thy 35 hand like a tapster? [Exit PEG.] As I'm a person, this wench has lived in an inn upon the road before she came to me, like Maritornes the Asturian in Don Quixote.° [Re-enter PEG.] No Foible yet?

PEG. No, madam, Mrs. Marwood.   40

LADY. O Marwood, let her come in. Come in, good Marwood.

.   .   .

[Enter MRS. MARWOOD.]
MRS. MAR. I'm surprised to find your ladyship in dishabille at this time of day.   45

LADY. Foible's a lost thing; has been abroad since morning, and never heard of since.

MRS. MAR. I saw her but now, as I came masked through the Park, in conference with Mirabell.   50

LADY. With Mirabell! You call my blood into my face, with mentioning that traitor. She durst not have the confidence. I sent her to negotiate an affair, in which if I'm detected I'm undone. If that wheedling villain has wrought 55 upon Foible to detect me, I'm ruined. O my dear friend, I'm a wretch of wretches if I'm detected.

MRS. MAR. O madam, you cannot suspect Mrs. Foible's integrity.

LADY. O, he carries poison in his tongue that 60 would corrupt integrity itself. If she has given him an opportunity, she has as good as put her integrity into his hands. Ah dear Marwood, what's integrity to an opportunity? Hark! I hear her—dear friend, retire into my closet, that 65 I may examine her with more freedom. You'll pardon me, dear friend, I can make bold with you. There are books over the chimney— Quarles and Prynne, and the Short View of the Stage, with Bunyan's works to entertain you.° 70 [To PEG.] Go, you thing, and send her in.

[Exit MRS. MARWOOD.]

.   .   .

[Enter FOIBLE.]
LADY. O Foible, where hast thou been? What hast thou been doing?   75

FOIB. Madam, I have seen the party.

---

mopus   stupid
Spanish paper   rouge
Don Quixote   *Don Quixote*, Part I, III.ii

entertain you   all her literature is religious or moralistic: Francis Quarles wrote *Divine Emblems*; John Bunyan, *Pilgrim's Progress*. William Prynne and (in *A Short View of the Immorality and Profaneness of the English Stage*) Congreve's detractor Jeremy Collier attacked playwrights and the stage.

LADY. But what hast thou done?

FOIB. Nay, 'tis your ladyship has done, and are to do; I have only promised. But a man so enamored—so transported! Well, if worshiping
5 of pictures be a sin—poor Sir Rowland, I say!

LADY. The miniature has been counted like— but hast thou not betrayed me, Foible? Hast thou not detected me to that faithless Mirabell? —What hadst thou to do with him in the Park?
10 Answer me, has he got nothing out of thee?

FOIB. [*aside*]. So, the devil has been before- hand with me. What shall I say?—Alas, mad- am, could I help it if I met that confident thing? Was I in fault? If you had heard how
15 he used me, and all upon your ladyship's ac- count, I'm sure you would not suspect my fidelity. Nay, if that had been the worst, I could have borne; but he had a fling at your ladyship too; and then I could not hold; but
20 i'faith I gave him his own.

LADY. Me? What did the filthy fellow say?

FOIB. O madam; 'tis a shame to say what he said—with his taunts and his fleers, tossing up his nose. Humh! (says he) What? you are
25 a-hatching some plot (says he) you are so early abroad, or catering° (says he), ferreting for some disbanded officer, I warrant—half pay is but thin subsistence (says he).—Well, what pension does your lady propose? Let me see
30 (says he) what, she must come down pretty deep now, she's superannuated (says he) and—

LADY. Ods my life, I'll have him—I'll have him murdered. I'll have him poisoned. Where does he eat? I'll marry a drawer to have him
35 poisoned in his wine. I'll send for Robin from Locket's°—immediately.

FOIB. Poison him? Poisoning's too good for him. Starve him, madam, starve him; marry Sir Rowland, and get him disinherited. O, you
40 would bless yourself, to hear what he said.

LADY. A villain!—superannuated!

FOIB. Humh! (says he) I hear you are laying

designs against me too (says he) and Mrs. Mil- lamant is to marry my uncle; (he does not suspect a word of your ladyship) but (says he) 45 I'll fit you for that, I warrant you (says he) I'll hamper you for that (says he) you and your old frippery too (says he). I'll handle you—

LADY. Audacious villain! handle me, would he durst—frippery? old frippery! Was there 50 ever such a foul-mouthed fellow? I'll be married tomorrow, I'll be contracted tonight.

FOIB. The sooner the better, madam.

LADY. Will Sir Rowland be here, say'st thou? When, Foible? 55

FOIB. Incontinently, madam. No new sheriff's wife expects the return of her husband after knighthood, with that impatience in which Sir Rowland burns for the dear hour of kissing your ladyship's hand after dinner. 60

LADY. Frippery! Superannuated frippery! I'll frippery the villain, I'll reduce him to frippery and rags. A tatterdemalion—I hope to see him hung with tatters, like a Long Lane penthouse,° or a gibbet-thief. A slander-mouthed railer—I 65 warrant the spend-thrift prodigal's in debt as much as the million lottery,° or the whole court upon a birthday.° I'll spoil his credit with his tailor. Yes, he shall have my niece with her fortune, he shall. 70

FOIB. He! I hope to see him lodge in Lud- gate first, and angle into Blackfriars for brass farthings with an old mitten.°

LADY. Aye, dear Foible; thank thee for that, dear Foible. He has put me out of all patience. 75 I shall never recompose my features to receive Sir Rowland with any economy of face. This wretch has fretted me that I am absolutely decayed. Look, Foible.

FOIB. Your ladyship has frowned a little too 80 rashly, indeed, madam. There are some cracks discernible in the white varnish.

---

catering pimping. The officers of disbanded regiments were likely prey.
Locket's a fashionable tavern where Robin was tap- ster or "drawer"

Long Lane penthouse stall in a street of old-clothes merchants
million lottery i.e., the arrears of a government lottery
birthday royal birthday, for which splendid new clothes were customarily bought
old mitten let down by inmates of the debtors' prison in the Blackfriars' district

LADY. Let me see the glass.—Cracks, say'st thou? Why I am arrantly flayed. I look like an old peeled wall. Thou must repair me, Foible, before Sir Rowland comes, or I shall never keep up to my picture.

FOIB. I warrant you, madam; a little art once made your picture like you and now a little of the same art must make you like your picture. Your picture must sit for you, madam.

LADY. But art thou sure Sir Rowland will not fail to come? Or will a' not fail when he does come? Will he be importunate, Foible, and push? For if he should not be importunate—I shall never break decorums.—I shall die with confusion, if I am forced to advance.—O no, I can never advance.—I shall swoon if he should expect advances. No, I hope Sir Rowland is better bred than to put a lady to the necessity of breaking her forms. I won't be too coy neither. I won't give him despair—but a little disdain is not amiss; a little scorn is alluring.

FOIB. A little scorn becomes your ladyship.

LADY. Yes, but tenderness becomes me best. —A sort of dyingness.—You see that picture has a sort of a—ha, Foible? A swimminess in the eyes. Yes, I'll look so. My niece affects it; but she wants features. Is Sir Rowland handsome? Let my toilet be removed—I'll dress above. I'll receive Sir Rowland here. Is he handsome? Don't answer me. I won't know: I'll be surprised. I'll be taken by surprise.

FOIB. By storm, madam. Sir Rowland's a brisk man.

LADY. Is he! O, then he'll importune, if he's a brisk man. I shall save decorums if Sir Rowland importunes. I have a mortal terror at the apprehension of offending against decorums. Nothing but importunity can surmount decorums. O, I'm glad he's a brisk man! Let my things be removed, good Foible.

[Exit.]

· · ·

[Enter MRS. FAINALL.]

MRS. FAIN. O Foible, I have been in a fright, lest I should come too late. That devil Marwood saw you in the park with Mirabell, and I'm afraid will discover it to my lady.

FOIB. Discover what, madam?

MRS. FAIN. Nay, nay, put not on that strange face. I am privy to the whole design and know Waitwell, to whom thou wert this morning married, is to personate Mirabell's uncle, and as such, winning my lady, to involve her in those difficulties from which Mirabell only must release her, by his making his conditions to have my cousin and her fortune left to her own disposal.

FOIB. O dear madam, I beg your pardon. It was not my confidence in your ladyship that was deficient, but I thought the former good correspondence between your ladyship and Mr. Mirabell might have hindered his communicating this secret.

MRS. FAIN. Dear Foible, forget that.

FOIB. O dear madam, Mr. Mirabell is such a sweet winning gentleman—but your ladyship is the pattern of generosity. Sweet lady, to be so good! Mr. Mirabell cannot choose but to be grateful. I find your ladyship has his heart still. Now, madam, I can safely tell your ladyship our success. Mrs. Marwood had told my lady; but I warrant I managed myself. I turned it all for the better. I told my lady that Mr. Mirabell railed at her. I laid horrid things to his charge, I'll vow; and my lady is so incensed that she'll be contracted to Sir Rowland tonight, she says—I warrant I worked her up, that he may have her for asking for, as they say of a Welsh maidenhead.

MRS. FAIN. O rare Foible!

FOIB. Madam, I beg your ladyship to acquaint Mr. Mirabell of his success. I would be seen as little as possible to speak to him—besides, I believe Madam Marwood watches me. She has a month's mind;° but I know Mr. Mirabell can't abide her.—[Calls.] John, remove my lady's toilet. Madam, your servant. My lady is so impatient, I fear she'll come for me if I stay.

MRS. FAIN. I'll go with you up the back stairs, lest I should meet her.

[Exeunt.]

· · ·

month's mind inclination

[*Enter* MRS. MARWOOD *from the closet.*]

MRS. MAR. Indeed, Mrs. Engine,° is it thus with you? Are you become a go-between of this importance? Yes, I shall watch you. Why, this wench is the *passe-partout*, a very master key to everybody's strongbox. My friend Fainall, have you carried it so swimmingly? I thought there was something in it; but it seems it's over with you. Your loathing is not from a want of appetite, then, but from a surfeit. Else you could never be so cool to fall from a principal to be an assistant; to procure for him! A pattern of generosity; that I confess. Well, Mr. Fainall, you have met with your match. O, man, man! Woman, woman! The devil's an ass: if I were a painter, I would draw him like an idiot, a driveler with a bib and bells. Man should have his head and horns, and woman the rest of him. Poor simple fiend! Madam Marwood has a month's mind, but he can't abide her.— 'Twere better for him you had not been his confessor in that affair without you could have kept his counsel closer. I shall not prove another pattern of generosity. He has not obliged me to that with those excesses of himself; and now I'll have none of him. Here comes the good lady, panting ripe, with a heart full of hope and a head full of care, like any chemist upon the day of projection.°

. . .

[*Enter* LADY WISHFORT.]

LADY. O dear Marwood, what shall I say for this rude forgetfulness? But my dear friend is all goodness.

MRS. MAR. No apologies, dear madam. I have been very well entertained.

LADY. As I'm a person I am in a very chaos to think I should so forget myself—but I have such an olio° of affairs really I know not what to do. [*Calls.*] Foible!—I expect my nephew Sir Wilfull every moment too.—Why, Foible!—He means to travel for improvement.

Mrs. Engine Mrs. Artifice
chemist . . . projection alchemist ready to complete his experiment
olio mixture

MRS. MAR. Methinks Sir Wilfull should rather think of marrying than traveling at his years. I hear he is turned of forty.

LADY. O, he's in less danger of being spoiled by his travels. I am against my nephew's marrying too young. It will be time enough when he comes back and has acquired discretion to choose for himself.

MRS. MAR. Methinks Mrs. Millamant and he would make a very fit match. He may travel afterwards. 'Tis a thing very usual with young gentlemen.

LADY. I promise you I have thought on't— and since 'tis your judgment, I'll think on't again. I assure you I will; I value your judgment extremely. On my word, I'll propose it.

. . .

[*Enter* FOIBLE.]

LADY. Come, come Foible—I had forgot my nephew will be here before dinner. I must make haste.

FOIB. Mr. Witwoud and Mr. Petulant are come to dine with your ladyship.

LADY. O dear, I can't appear till I am dressed. Dear Marwood, shall I be free with you again and beg you to entertain 'em? I'll make all imaginable haste. Dear friend, excuse me.

[*Exit.*]

. . .

[*Enter* MRS. MILLAMANT, MINCING.]

MILLA. Sure never anything was so unbred as that odious man.—Marwood, your servant.

MRS. MAR. You have a color. What's the matter?

MILLA. That horried fellow Petulant has provoked me into a flame—I have broke my fan. Mincing, lend me yours; is not all the powder out of my hair?

MRS. MAR. No. What has he done?

MILLA. Nay, he has done nothing; he has only talked. Nay, he has said nothing neither; but he has contradicted everything that has been said. For my part, I thought Witwoud and he would have quarreled.

MINC. I vow, mem, I thought once they would have fit.

MILLA. Well, 'tis a lamentable thing, I swear, that one has not the liberty of choosing one's acquaintance as one does one's clothes.

MRS. MAR. If we had that liberty, we should be as weary of one set of acquaintance, though never so good, as we are of one suit, though never so fine. A fool and a doily stuff° would now and then find days of grace, and be worn for variety.

MILLA. I could consent to wear 'em, if they would wear alike; but fools never wear out—they are such drap-de-Berry° things! Without one could give 'em to one's chambermaid after a day or two.

MRS. MAR. 'Twere better so indeed. Or what think you of the play house? A fine gay glossy fool should be given there, like a new masking habit after the masquerade is over, and we have done with the disguise. For a fool's visit is always a disguise, and never admitted by a woman of wit, but to blind her affair with a lover of sense. If you would but appear barefaced now and own Mirabell, you might as easily put off Petulant and Witwoud as your hood and scarf. And indeed 'tis time, for the town has found it: the secret is grown too big for the pretense: 'tis like Mrs. Primly's great belly; she may lace it down before, but it burnishes on her hips. Indeed, Millamant, you can no more conceal it than my Lady Strammel can her face, that goodly face, which in defiance of her Rhenish-wine tea will not be comprehended in a mask.

MILLA. I'll take my death, Marwood, you are more censorious than a decayed beauty, or a discarded toast.° Mincing, tell the men they may come up. My aunt is not dressing. Their folly is less provoking than your malice.

[*Exit* MINCING.]

. . .

MILLA. "The town has found it." What has it found? That Mirabell loves me is no more a secret than it is a secret that you discovered it to my aunt, or than the reason why you discovered it is a secret.

MRS. MAR. You are nettled.

MILLA. You're mistaken. Ridiculous!

MRS. MAR. Indeed, my dear, you'll tear another fan if you don't mitigate those violent airs.

MILLA. O silly! Ha, ha, ha! I could laugh immoderately. Poor Mirabell! His constancy to me has quite destroyed his complaisance for all the world beside. I swear, I never enjoined it him, to be so coy. If I had the vanity to think he would obey me, I would command him to show more gallantry. 'Tis hardly well bred to be so particular on one hand and so insensible on the other. But I despair to prevail, and so let him follow his own way. Ha, ha, ha! Pardon me, dear creature, I must laugh, ha, ha, ha! though I grant you 'tis a little barbarous, ha, ha, ha!

MRS. MAR. What pity 'tis, so much fine raillery, and delivered with so significant gesture, should be so unhappily directed to miscarry.

MILLA. Hah? Dear creature, I ask your pardon—I swear I did not mind you.

MRS. MAR. Mr. Mirabell and you both may think it a thing impossible, when I shall tell him by telling you—

MILLA. O dear, what? For it is the same thing, if I hear it.—Ha, ha, ha!

MRS. MAR. That I detest him, hate him, madam.

MILLA. O madam, why so do I—and yet the creature loves me, ha, ha, ha! How can one forbear laughing to think of it? I am a sibyl° if I am not amazed to think what he can see in me. I'll take my death, I think you are handsomer—and within a year or two as young. If you could but stay for me, I should overtake you.—But that cannot be. Well, that thought makes me melancholy. Now I'll be sad.

MRS. MAR. Your merry note may be changed sooner than you think.

MILLA. D'ye say so? Then I'm resolved I'll have a song to keep up my spirits.

. . .

---

doily stuff   cheap wool cloth
drap-de-Berry   long-wearing woolen cloth
discarded toast   lady no longer celebrated by toasts

sibyl   prophetess

[*Enter* MINCING.]

MINC. The gentlemen stay but to comb,° madam, and will wait on you.

MILLA. Desire Mrs. ——— that is in the next
5 room to sing the song I would have learnt yesterday. You shall hear it, madam—not that there's any great matter in it, but 'tis agreeable to my humor.

1

Love's but the frailty of the mind,
10 When 'tis not with ambition joined;
A sickly flame, which if not fed expires;
And feeding, wastes in self-consuming fires.

2

'Tis not to wound a wanton boy
Or amorous youth, that gives the joy;
15 But 'tis the glory to have pierced a swain,
For whom inferior beauties sighed in vain.

3

Then I alone the conquest prize,
When I insult a rival's eyes:
If there's delight in love, 'tis when I see
20 That heart which others bleed for, bleed for
[me.

.   .   .

[*Enter* PETULANT, WITWOUD.]

MILLA. Is your animosity composed, gentlemen?
25 WIT. Raillery, raillery, madam, we have no animosity. We hit off a little wit now and then, but no animosity. The falling out of wits is like the falling out of lovers. We agree in the main, like treble and bass. Ha, Petulant?
30 PET. Aye, in the main. But when I have a humor to contradict—

WIT. Aye, when he has a humor to contradict, then I contradict too. What, I know· my cue. Then we contradict one another like two
35 battledores;° for contradictions beget one another like Jews.

PET. If he says black's black—if I have a humor to say 'tis blue—let that pass.—All's one for that. If I have a humor to prove it, it must be granted.   40

WIT. Not positively must—but it may—it may.

PET. Yes, it positively must, upon proof positive.

WIT. Aye, upon proof positive it must; but   45
upon proof presumptive it only may. That's a logical distinction now, madam.

MRS. MAR. I perceive your debates are of importance and very learnedly handled.

PET. Importance is one thing, and learning's   50
another; but a debate's a debate, that I assert.

WIT. Petulant's an enemy to learning; he relies altogether on his parts.°

PET. No, I'm no enemy to learning; it hurts   55
not me.

MRS. MAR. That's a sign indeed it's no enemy to you.

PET. No, no, it's no enemy to anybody but them that have it.   60

MILLA. Well, an illiterate man's my aversion. I wonder at the impudence of any illiterate man, to offer to make love.

WIT. That I confess I wonder at too.

MILLA. Ah! to marry an ignorant that can   65
hardly read or write!

PET. Why should a man be any further from being married though he can't read than he is from being hanged? The ordinary's° paid for setting the Psalm, and the parish priest for   70
reading the ceremony. And for the rest which is to follow in both cases, a man may do it without book.—So all's one for that.

MILLA. D'ye hear the creature? Lord, here's company. I'll be gone.   75

[*Exeunt* MILLAMANT *and* MINCING.]

.   .   .

---

comb   comb their perukes
battledores   badminton rackets sending the shuttlecock back and forth

parts   innate abilities
ordinary   prison chaplain who reads a religious service before hangings (likened to the parish priest who reads marriage services)

[*Enter* SIR WILFULL WITWOUD *and* FOOTMAN.]

WIT. In the name of Bartlemew and his Fair,° what have we here?

MRS. MAR. 'Tis your brother, I fancy. Don't 5 you know him?

WIT. Not I.—Yes, I think it is he—I've almost forgot him; I have not seen him since the Revolution.°

FOOT. Sir, my lady's dressing. Here's com-10 pany; if you please to walk in, in the meantime.

SIR WIL. Dressing! What, it's but morning here, I warrant, with you in London; we should count it towards afternoon in our parts, down in Shropshire. Why, then belike my aunt han't 15 dined yet—ha, friend?

FOOT. Your aunt, Sir?

SIR. WIL. My aunt, sir, yes, my aunt, sir, and your lady, sir; your lady is my aunt, sir. Why, what, dost thou not know me, friend? Why, 20 then send somebody hither that does. How long hast thou lived with thy lady, fellow, ha?

FOOT. A week, sir; longer than anybody in the house, except my lady's woman.

SIR WIL. Why, then belike thou dost not 25 know thy lady, if thou see'st her, ha, friend?

FOOT. Why truly, sir, I cannot safely swear to her face in a morning, before she is dressed. 'Tis like I may give a shrewd guess at her by this time.

30 SIR WIL. Well, prithee try what thou canst do; if thou canst not guess, inquire her out, dost, hear, fellow? And tell her her nephew, Sir Wilfull Witwoud, is in the house.

FOOT. I shall, sir.

35 SIR WIL. Hold ye, hear me, friend; a word with you in your ear. Prithee who are these gallants?

FOOT. Really, sir, I can't tell; there come so many here, 'tis hard to know 'em all.

40 [*Exit.*]

. . .

SIR WIL. Oons,° this fellow knows less than a starling; I don't think a 'knows his own name.

MRS. MAR. Mr. Witwoud, your brother is not behind hand in forgetfulness—I fancy he has forgot you too. 45

WIT. I hope so.—The devil take him that remembers first, I say.

SIR WIL. Save you, gentleman and lady.

MRS. MAR. For shame, Mr. Witwoud; why don't you speak to him?—And you, sir. 50

WIT. Petulant, speak.

PET. And you, sir.

SIR WIL. [*salutes* MARWOOD]. No offense, I hope.

MRS. MAR. No sure, sir. 55

WIT. This is a vile dog, I see that already. No offense! Ha, ha, ha! To him; to him, Petulant, smoke him.°

PET. [*surveying him round*]. It seems as if you had come a journey, sir. Hem, hem. 60

SIR WIL. Very likely, sir, that it may seem so.

PET. No offense, I hope, sir.

WIT. Smoke the boots, the boots, Petulant, the boots. Ha, ha, ha!

SIR WIL. Maybe not, sir; thereafter as 'tis 65 meant, sir.

PET. Sir, I presume upon the information of your boots.

SIR WIL. Why, 'tis like you may, sir. If you are not satisfied with the information of my 70 boots, sir, if you will step to the stable, you may inquire further of my horse, sir.

PET. Your horse, sir! Your horse is an ass, sir!

SIR WIL. Do you speak by way of offense, 75 sir?

MRS. MAR. The gentleman's merry, that's all, sir.—[*Aside.*] 'Slife,° we shall have a quarrel betwixt an horse and an ass, before they find one another out. [*Aloud.*] You must not take 80 anything amiss from your friends, sir. You are among your friends, here, though it may be you don't know it.—If I am not mistaken, you are Sir Willful Witwoud.

SIR WIL. Right, lady; I am Sir Wilfull Wit-85 woud, so I write myself; no offense to anybody,

---

Fair St. Bartholomew's Fair, where freaks were exhibited

Revolution of 1688, when James II was deposed

Oons a slang term (originally *God's wounds*, an oath on the wounds of Christ)

smoke him deride him

'Slife a slang term (originally *God's life*)

I hope; and nephew to the Lady Wishfort of this mansion.

MRS. MAR. Don't you know this gentleman, sir?

5   SIR WIL. Hum! What, sure, 'tis not—yea by'r Lady, but 'tis—'sheart,° I know not whether 'tis or no.—Yea but 'tis, by the Wrekin.° Brother Antony! What, Tony, i'faith! What, dost thou not know me? By'r Lady, nor I thee, 10 thou art so becravated and so beperiwigged—'sheart, why dost not speak? Art thou o'erjoyed?

WIT. Odso, brother, is it you? Your servant, brother.

15   SIR WIL. Your servant! Why, yours, sir. Your servant again—'sheart, and your friend and servant to that—and a—[*puff*]—and a flapdragon° for your service, sir: and a hare's foot, and a hare's scut° for your service, sir; an you 20 be so cold and so courtly!

WIT. No offense, I hope, brother.

SIR WIL. 'Sheart, sir, but there is, and much offense. A pox, is this your Inns o' Court° breeding, not to know your friends and your 25 relations, your elders and your betters?

WIT. Why, Brother Wilfull of Salop,° you may be as short as a Shrewsbury cake,° if you please. But I tell you 'tis not modish to know relations in town. You think you're in the 30 country, where great lubberly brothers slabber and kiss one another when they meet, like a call of sergeants.°—'Tis not the fashion here; 'tis not indeed, dear brother.

SIR WIL. The fashion's a fool; and you're a 35 fop, dear brother. 'Sheart, I've suspected this—by'r Lady, I conjectured you were a fop, since you began to change the style of your letters and write in a scrap of paper gilt round the

edges, no bigger than a subpoena. I might expect this when you left off "Honored Brother" 40 and "hoping you are in good health," and so forth—to begin with a "Rat me, knight, I'm so sick of a last night's debauch"—'od's heart, and then tell a familiar tale of a cock and bull, and a whore and a bottle, and so conclude.—You 45 could write news before you were out of your time,° when you lived with honest Pumple-Nose, the attorney of Furnival's Inn.—You could entreat to be remembered then to your friends round the Wrekin. We could have ga- 50 zettes then, and Dawks's *Letter*, and the Weekly Bill,° till of late days.

PET. 'Slife, Witwoud, were you ever an attorney's clerk? Of the family of the Furnival's. Ha, ha, ha! 55

WIT. Aye, aye, but that was but for a while. Not long, not long; pshaw, I was not in my own power then. An orphan, and this fellow was my guardian; aye, aye, I was glad to consent to that man to come to London. He had 60 the disposal of me then. If I had not agreed to that, I might have been bound 'prentice to a felt-maker in Shrewsbury; this fellow would have bound me to a maker of felts.

SIR WIL. 'Sheart, and better than to be bound 65 to a maker of fops; where, I suppose, you have served your time; and now you may set up for yourself.

MRS. MAR. You intend to travel, sir, as I'm informed. 70

SIR WIL. Belike I may, madam. I may chance to sail upon the salt seas, if my mind hold.

PET. And the wind serve.

SIR WIL. Serve or not serve, I shan't ask license of you, sir; nor the weather-cock your 75 companion. I direct my discourse to the lady, sir. 'Tis like my aunt may have told you, madam.—Yes, I have settled my concerns, I may say now, and am minded to see foreign parts. If an' how that peace° holds, whereby, that is, 80 taxes abate.

'sheart   originally *God's heart*
Wrekin   a Shropshire mountain
flapdragon   raisin (i.e., a trifle)
scut   tail
Inns o' Court   societies that prepared law students for the bar
Salop   Shropshire
Shrewsbury cake   shortcake (deriving from Shrewsbury in Shropshire)
call of Sergeants   barristers admitted as a class (call) to a superior legal order or standing

your time   your apprenticeship to the attorney named
gazettes . . . Bill   i.e., newspapers, a weekly summary of the news, and the list of weekly deaths
peace   temporary peace with France

MRS. MAR. I thought you had designed for France at all adventures.

SIR WIL. I can't tell that; 'tis like I may and 'tis like I may not. I am somewhat dainty° in
5 making a resolution, because when I make it I keep it, I don't stand shill I, shall I, then; if I say't, I'll do't. But I have thoughts to tarry a small matter in town, to learn somewhat of your lingo first, before I cross the seas. I'd
10 gladly have a spice of your French as they say, whereby to hold discourse in foreign countries.

MRS. MAR. Here's an academy in town for that use.

SIR WIL. There is? 'Tis like there may.

15 MRS. MAR. No doubt you will return very much improved.

WIT. Yes, refined like a Dutch skipper from a whale-fishing.°

.   .   .

[*Enter* LADY WISHFORT *and* FAINALL.]
20 LADY. Nephew, you are welcome.

SIR WIL. Aunt, your servant.

FAIN. Sir Wilfull, your most faithful servant.

SIR WIL. Cousin Fainall, give me your hand.

LADY. Cousin Witwoud, your servant; Mr.
25 Petulant, your servant.—Nephew, you are welcome again. Will you drink anything after your journey, nephew, before you eat? Dinner's almost ready.

SIR WIL. I'm very well, I thank you, aunt.
30 However, I thank you for your courteous offer. 'Sheart, I was afraid you would have been in the fashion too, and have remembered to have forgot your relations. Here's your cousin Tony, belike, I mayn't call him brother for fear of
35 offense.

LADY. O, he's a railler, nephew—my cousin's a wit; and your great wits always rally their best friends to choose. When you have been abroad, nephew, you'll understand raillery bet-
40 ter.

[FAINALL *and* MRS. MARWOOD *talk apart.*]

SIR WIL. Why then let him hold his tongue in the meantime, and rail when that day comes.

.   .   .

[*Enter* MINCING.]

MINC. Mem, I come to acquaint your la'ship 45 that dinner is impatient.

SIR WIL. Impatient? Why then belike it won't stay till I pull off my boots. Sweetheart, can you help me to a pair of slippers?—My man's with his horses, I warrant. 50

LADY. Fie, fie, nephew, you would not pull off your boots here. Go down into the hall.— Dinner shall stay for you. My nephew's a little unbred; you'll pardon him, madam.—Gentlemen, will you walk? Marwood? 55

MRS. MAR. I'll follow you, madam—before Sir Wilfull is ready.

[*Exeunt,* MRS. MARWOOD *and* FAINALL *remaining.*]

.   .   .

FAIN. Why then Foible's a bawd, an arrant, 60 rank, match-making bawd. And I it seems am a husband, a rank husband; and my wife a very arrant, rank wife—all in the way of the world. 'Sdeath, to be a cuckold by anticipation, a cuckold in embryo! Sure I was born with budding 65 antlers like a young satyr, or a citizen's child.° 'Sdeath, to be outwitted, to be outjilted—outmatrimonied. If I had kept my speed like a stag, 'twere somewhat, but to crawl after, with my horns like a snail, and be outstripped by my 70 wife—'tis scurvy wedlock.

MRS. MAR. Then shake it off. You have often wished for an opportunity to part, and now you have it. But first prevent their plot.—The half of Millamant's fortune is too considerable 75 to be parted with to a foe, to Mirabell.

FAIN. Damn him, that had been mine—had you not made that fond discovery.°—That had been forfeited, had they been married. My wife

---

dainty cautious
whale-fishing i.e., retaining a persistent odor
always . . . choose i.e., always choose to rally (kid, josh) their best friends

citizen's child destined, as a member of the merchant class, to be cuckolded
fond discovery foolish revelation

had added luster to my horns. By that increase of fortune, I could have worn 'em tipped with gold, though my forehead had been furnished like a Deputy-Lieutenant's hall.°

5 MRS. MAR. They may prove a cap of maintenance° to you still, if you can away with your wife. And she's no worse than when you had her—I dare swear she had given up her game, before she was married.

10 FAIN. Hum! That may be—

MRS. MAR. You married her to keep you, and if you can contrive to have her keep you better than you expected, why should you not keep her longer than you intended?

15 FAIN. The means, the means.

MRS. MAR. Discover to my lady your wife's conduct; threaten to part with her. My lady loves her and will come to any composition to save her reputation. Take the opportunity of 20 breaking it, just upon the discovery of this imposture. My lady will be enraged beyond bounds and sacrifice niece and fortune and all at that conjuncture. And let me alone to keep her warm; if she should flag in her part, I will 25 not fail to prompt her.

FAIN. Faith, this has an appearance.

MRS. MAR. I'm sorry I hinted to my lady to endeavor a match between Millamant and Sir Wilfull. That may be an obstacle.

30 FAIN. O, for that matter leave me to manage him; I'll disable him for that; he will drink like a Dane; after dinner, I'll set his hand in.

MRS. MAR. Well, how do you stand affected towards your lady?

35 FAIN. Why, faith, I'm thinking of it. Let me see—I am married already; so that's over. My wife has played the jade with me—well, that's over too. I never loved her, or if I had, why that would have been over too by this time. Jealous 40 of her I cannot be, for I am certain; so there's an end of jealousy. Weary of her I am and shall be—no, there's no end of that; no, no, that were too much to hope. Thus far concerning my

repose. Now for my reputation. As to my own, I married not for it; so that's out of the ques- 45 tion. And as to my part in my wife's—why, she had parted with hers before; so bringing none to me, she can take none from me; 'tis against all rule of play that I should lose to one who has not wherewithal to stake. 50

MRS. MAR. Besides you forget, marriage is honorable.

FAIN. Hum! Faith, and that's well thought on; marriage is honorable, as you say; and if so, wherefore should cuckoldom be a discredit, 55 being derived from so honorable a root?

MRS. MAR. Nay, I know not; if the root be honorable, why not the branches?°

FAIN. So, so, why this point's clear. Well, how do we proceed? 60

MRS. MAR. I will contrive a letter which shall be delivered to my lady at the time when that rascal who is to act Sir Rowland is with her. It shall come as from an unknown hand—for the less I appear to know of the truth, the bet- 65 ter I can play the incendiary. Besides, I would not have Foible provoked if I could help it, because you know she knows some passages. Nay, I expect all will come out. But let the mine be sprung first, and then I care not if I am dis- 70 covered.

FAIN. If the worst come to the worst, I'll turn my wife to grass. I have already a deed of settlement of the best part of her estate; which I wheedled out of her; and that you shall par- 75 take at least.

MRS. MAR. I hope you are convinced that I hate Mirabell now: you'll be no more jealous?

FAIN. Jealous, no—by this kiss. Let husbands be jealous; but let the lover still believe: or if 80 he doubt; let it be only to endear his pleasure, and prepare the joy that follows, when he proves his mistress true. But let husbands' doubts convert to endless jealousy; or if they have belief, let it corrupt to superstition and 85 blind credulity. I am single, and will herd no more with 'em. True, I wear the badge, but I'll disown the order. And since I take my leave of

---

furnished ... hall i.e., with antlers
cap of maintenance in heraldry, a cap with points (hence fitting the horned head of the cuckold)

branches horns of the cuckold

'em, I care not if I leave 'em a common motto to their common crest.

All husbands must, or pain, or shame,
                [endure;
5 The wise too jealous are, fools too secure.

[*Exeunt.*]

ACT IV

[*Scene continues.*]

.   .   .

[LADY WISHFORT *and* FOIBLE.]
  LADY. Is Sir Rowland coming, say'st thou,
10 Foible? and are things in order?
  FOIB. Yes, madam. I have put wax lights in the sconces, and placed the footmen in a row in the hall, in their best liveries, with the coachman and postilion to fill up the equipage.
15 LADY. Have you pulvilled° the coachman and postilion, that they may not stink of the stable, when Sir Rowland comes by?
  FOIB. Yes, madam.
  LADY. And are the dancers and the music
20 ready, that he may be entertained in all points with correspondence to his passion?
  FOIB. All is ready, madam.
  LADY. And—well—and how do I look, Foible?
25 FOIB. Most killing well, madam.
  LADY. Well, and how shall I receive him? In what figure shall I give his heart the first impression? There is a great deal in the first impression. Shall I sit?—No, I won't sit—I'll
30 walk.—Aye, I'll walk from the door upon his entrance; and then turn full upon him.—No, that will be too sudden. I'll lie—aye, I'll lie down—I'll receive him in my little dressing-room, there's a couch.—Yes, yes, I'll give the
35 first impression on a couch.—I won't lie neither, but loll and lean upon one elbow; with one foot a little dangling off, jogging in a thoughtful way—yes—and then as soon as he appears, start, aye, start and be surprised, and rise to meet him in a pretty disorder—yes. O, 40 nothing is more alluring than a levee° from a couch in some confusion. It shows the foot to advantage and furnishes with blushes and recomposing airs beyond comparison. Hark! There's a coach. 45
  FOIB. 'Tis he, madam.
  LADY. O dear, has my nephew made his addresses to Millamant? I ordered him.
  FOIB. Sir Wilfull is set in to drinking, madam, in the parlor. 50
  LADY. 'Ods my life, I'll send him to her. Call her down, Foible; bring her hither. I'll send him as I go.—When they are together, then come to me, Foible, that I may not be too long alone with Sir Rowland. 55

[*Exit.*]

.   .   .

[*Enter* MRS. MILLAMANT *and* MRS. FAINALL.]
  FOIB. Madam, I stayed here to tell your ladyship that Mr. Mirabell has waited this half hour for an opportunity to talk with you. 60 Though my lady's orders were to leave you and Sir Wilfull together. Shall I tell Mr. Mirabell that you are at leisure.
  MILLA. No.—What would the dear man have? I am thoughtful and would amuse my- 65 self. Bid him come another time.

There never yet was woman made,
  Nor shall, but to be cursed.
[*Repeating and walking about.*]

That's hard! 70
  MRS. FAIN. You are very fond of Sir John Suckling today, Millamant, and the poets.
  MILLA. Heh? Aye, and filthy verses—so I am.
  FOIB. Sir Wilfull is coming, madam. Shall I send Mr. Mirabell away? 75
  MILLA. Aye, if you please, Foible, send him away—or send him hither, just as you will, dear Foible. I think I'll see him.—Shall I? Aye, let the wretch come.

---

pulvilled powdered

levee rising

Thyrsis, a youth of the inspiréd train.°
[*Repeating.*]

Dear Fainall, entertain Sir Wilfull. Thou hast
philosophy to undergo a fool, thou art married
5 and hast patience. I would confer with my own
thoughts.

Mrs. Fain. I am obliged to you that you
would make me your proxy in this affair, but
I have business of my own.

.   .   .

10 [*Enter* Sir Wilfull.]

O Sir Wilfull; you are come at the critical
instant. There's your mistress up to the ears in
love and contemplation. Pursue your point,
now or never.

15 Sir Wil. Yes; my aunt will have it so. I
would gladly have been encouraged with a
bottle or two, because I'm somewhat wary at
first, before I am acquainted; [*this while*
millamant *walks about repeating to herself*]
20 —but I hope, after a time, I shall break my
mind—that is upon further acquaintance. So
for the present, cousin, I'll take my leave. If so
be you'll be so kind to make my excuse, I'll
return to my company.—

25 Mrs. Fain. O fie, Sir Wilfull! What, you
must not be daunted!

Sir Wil. Daunted, no, that's not it; it is not
so much for that—for if so be that I set on't,
I'll do't. But only for the present, 'tis sufficient
30 till further acquaintance, that's all.—Your servant.

Mrs. Fain. Nay, I'll swear you shall never
lose so favorable an opportunity if I can help
it. I'll leave you together and lock the door.

35 [*Exit.*]

Sir Wil. Nay, nay, cousin—I have forgot my
gloves. What d'ye do? 'Sheart, a' has locked
the door indeed, I think.—Nay, cousin Fainall,
open the door.—Pshaw, what a vixen trick is
40 this? Nay, now a' has seen me too.—Cousin, I

made bold to pass through, as it were.—I think
this door's enchanted.—

Milla. [*repeating*].

I prithee spare me, gentle boy,
Press me no more for that slight toy.°   45

Sir Wil. Anan?° Cousin, your servant.

Milla.—"That foolish trifle of a heart"—Sir
Wilfull!

Sir Wil. Yes—your servant. No offense I
hope, cousin.   50

Milla. [*repeating*].

I swear it will not do its part,
Though thou dost thine, employ'st thy
[power and art.

[Natural, easy Suckling!   55

Sir Wil. Anan? Suckling? No such suckling
neither, cousin, nor stripling: I thank heaven
I'm no minor.

Milla. Ah rustic, ruder than Gothic.°

Sir Wil. Well, well, I shall understand your   60
lingo one of these days, cousin. In the meanwhile I must answer in plain English.

Milla. Have you any business with me, Sir
Wilfull?

Sir Wil. Not at present, cousin.—Yes, I made   65
bold to see, to come and know if that how you
were disposed to fetch a walk this evening, if
so be that I might not be troublesome, I would
have sought a walk with you.

Milla. A walk? What then?   70

Sir Wil. Nay nothing—only for the walk's
sake, that's all—

Milla. I nauseate walking; 'tis a country
diversion. I loathe the country and everything
that relates to it.   75

Sir Wil. Indeed! Hah! Look ye, look ye, you
do? Nay, 'tis like you may.—Here are choice
of pastimes here in town, as plays and the like;
that must be confessed indeed.—

Thyrsis . . . train from a poem by Edmund Waller
treating the flight of a nymph from her admiring
swain

I . . . toy from a song by Suckling
Anan? What now?
Gothic the Middle Ages

MILLA. Ah, *l'étourdi!*° I hate the town too.

SIR WIL. Dear heart, that's much.—Hah! that you should hate 'em both! Hah! 'tis like you may; there are some can't relish the town, and others can't away with the country—'tis like you may be one of those, cousin.

MILLA. Ha, ha, ha! Yes, 'tis like I may. You have nothing further to say to me?

SIR WIL. Not at present, cousin. 'Tis like when I have an opportunity to be more private, I may break my mind in some measure.—I conjecture you partly guess. However, that's as time shall try; but spare to speak and spare to speed, as they say.

MILLA. If it is of no great importance, Sir Wilfull, you will oblige me to leave me. I have just now a little business.

SIR WIL. Enough, enough, cousin. Yes, yes, all a case—when you're disposed, when you're disposed. Now's as well as another time; and another time as well as now. All's one for that. —Yes, yes, if your concerns call you, there's no haste; it will keep cold as they say.— Cousin, your servant. I think this door's locked.

MILLA. You may go this way, sir.

SIR WIL. Your servant—then with your leave I'll return to my company.

[*Exit.*]

MILLA. Aye, aye. Ha, ha, ha!

Like Phoebus sung the no less amorous
Boy.°

.   .   .

[*Enter* MIRABELL.]
MIRA.

Like Daphne she, as lovely and as coy.

Do you lock yourself up from me, to make my search more curious? Or is this pretty artifice contrived to signify that here the chase must end, and my pursuit be crowned, for you can fly no further? 40

MILLA. Vanity! No—I'll fly and be followed to the last moment. Though I am upon the very verge of matrimony, I expect you should solicit me as much as if I were wavering at the grate of a monastery,° with one foot over the 45 threshold. I'll be solicited to the very last, nay and afterwards.

MIRA. What, after the last?

MILLA. O, I should think I was poor and had nothing to bestow, if I were reduced to an in- 50 glorious ease, and freed from the agreeable fatigues of solicitation.

MIRA. But do not you know that when favors are conferred upon instant and tedious solicitation, that they diminish in their value 55 and that both the giver loses the grace, and the receiver lessens his pleasure?

MILLA. It may be in things of common ap- plication, but never sure in love. O, I hate a lover that can dare to think he draws a 60 moment's air, independent on the bounty of his mistress. There is not so impudent a thing in nature as the saucy look of an assured man, confident of success. The pedantic arrogance of a very husband has not so pragmatical° an 65 air. Ah! I'll never marry, unless I am first made sure of my will and pleasure.

MIRA. Would you have 'em both before mar- riage? Or will you be contented with the first now, and stay for the other till after grace? 70

MILLA. Ah, don't be impertinent.—My dear liberty, shall I leave thee? My faithful solitude, my darling contemplation, must I bid you then adieu? Ay-h adieu.—My morning thoughts, agreeable wakings, indolent slumbers, all ye 75 *douceurs, ye sommeils du matin,*° adieu.—I can't do't, 'tis more than impossible.—Posi- tively, Mirabell, I'll lie abed in a morning as long as I please.

MIRA. Then I'll get up in a morning as early 80 as I please.

MILLA. Ah, idle creature, get up when you

---

l'étourdi!   the giddy fellow!
like . . . Boy   from the Waller poem which she quoted above. Mirabell here caps her quotation.

grate of a monastery   door of a nunnery
pragmatical   self-assured
douceurs . . . matin   sweetnesses and morning slum- bers

will.—And d'ye hear? I won't be called names after I'm married; positively I won't be called names.

MIRA. Names!

MILLA. Aye, as wife, spouse, my dear, joy, jewel, love, sweetheart, and the rest of that nauseous cant, in which men and their wives are so fulsomely familiar—I shall never bear that.—Good Mirabell, don't let us be familiar or fond, nor kiss before folks, like my Lady Fadler° and Sir Francis; nor go to Hyde Park together the first Sunday in a new chariot, to provoke eyes and whispers; and then never be seen there together again, as if we were proud of one another the first week, and ashamed of one another ever after. Let us never visit together, nor go to a play together, but let us be very strange° and well bred; let us be as strange as if we had been married a great while, and as well bred as if we were not married at all.

MIRA. Have you any more conditions to offer? Hitherto your demands are pretty reasonable.

MILLA. Trifles—as liberty to pay and receive visits to and from whom I please; to write and receive letters, without interrogatories or wry faces on your part; to wear what I please; and choose conversation with regard only to my own taste; to have no obligation upon me to converse with wits that I don't like, because they are your acquaintance; or to be intimate with fools, because they may be your relations. Come to dinner when I please, dine in my dressing room when I'm out of humor, without giving a reason. To have my closet inviolate; to be sole empress of my tea table, which you must never presume to approach without first asking leave. And lastly, wherever I am, you shall always knock at the door before you come in. These articles subscribed, if I continue to endure you a little longer, I may by degrees dwindle into a wife.

MIRA. Your bill of fare is something advanced in this latter account. Well, have I liberty to offer conditions—that when you are dwindled into a wife, I may not be beyond measure enlarged into a husband?

MILLA. You have free leave, propose your utmost, speak and spare not.

MIRA. I thank you. *Imprimis*° then, I covenant that your acquaintance be general; that you admit no sworn confidante or intimate of your own sex; no she-friend to screen her affairs under your countenance and tempt you to make trial of a mutual secrecy. No decoy duck to wheedle you a fop-scrambling to the play in a mask—then bring you home in a pretended fright, when you think you shall be found out —and rail at me for missing the play, and disappointing the frolic which you had, to pick me up and prove my constancy.

MILLA. Detestable *imprimis*! I go to the play in a mask!

MIRA. *Item*, I article,° that you continue to like your own face as long as I shall; and while it passes current with me, that you endeavor not to new coin it. To which end, together with all vizards for the day, I prohibit all masks for the night, made of oiled-skins and I know not what—hog's bones, hare's gall, pig water, and the marrow of a roasted cat. In short, I forbid all commerce with the gentlewoman in whatd'ye-call-it court. *Item*, I shut my doors against all bawds with baskets, and pennyworths of muslin, china, fans, atlases,° etc. *Item*, when you shall be breeding—

MILLA. Ah! Name it not.

MIRA. Which may be presumed, with a blessing on our endeavors—

MILLA. Odious endeavors!

MIRA. I denounce against all strait lacing, squeezing for a shape, till you mold my boy's head like a sugar loaf; and instead of a manchild, make me father to a crooked billet. Lastly, to the dominion of the tea table I submit.—But with proviso that you exceed not in your province; but restrain yourself to native and simple tea-table drinks, as tea, chocolate,

---

Fadler fondler
strange reserved

Imprimis firstly (legal terminology)
article stipulate (another legal term)
atlases silks

and coffee. As likewise to genuine and authorized tea-table talk—such as mending of
fashions, spoiling reputations, railing at absent
friends, and so forth—but that on no account
5 you encroach upon the men's prerogative, and
presume to drink healths, or toast fellows; for
prevention of which, I banish all foreign
forces, all auxiliaries to the tea table, as orange
brandy, all aniseed, cinnamon, citron and
10 Barbados waters, together with ratafia and the
most noble spirit of clary.°—But for cowslip-
wine, poppy water, and all dormitives, those I
allow. These provisos admitted, in other things
I may prove a tractable and complying hus-
15 band.

MILLA. O, horrid provisos! filthy strong
waters! I toast fellows, odious men? I hate
your odious provisos.

MIRA. Then we're agreed. Shall I kiss your
20 hand upon the contract? And here comes
one to be a witness to the sealing of the deed.

.   .   .

[Enter MRS. FAINALL.]

MILLA. Fainall, what shall I do? Shall I have
him? I think I must have him.

25 MRS. FAIN. Aye, aye, take him, take him.
What should you do?

MILLA. Well then—I'll take my death I'm
in a horrid fright—Fainall, I shall never say it
—well—I think—I'll endure you.

30 MRS. FAIN. Fy, fy, have him, have him, and
tell him so in plain terms; for I am sure you
have a mind to him.

MILLA. Are you? I think I have—and the
horrid man looks as if he thought so too.—
35 Well, you ridiculous thing, you. I'll have you.—
I won't be kissed, nor I won't be thanked.
—Here, kiss my hand though.—So, hold your
tongue now, don't say a word.

MRS. FAIN. Mirabell, there's a necessity for
40 your obedience—you have neither time to talk
nor stay. My mother is coming; and in my
conscience if she should see you, would fall
into fits, and maybe not recover, time enough
to return to Sir Rowland; who, as Foible tells
45 me, is in a fair way to succeed. Therefore spare

your ecstasies for another occasion, and slip
down the back stairs, where Foible waits to
consult you.

MILLA. Aye, go, go. In the meantime I suppose you have said something to please me.   50

MIRA. I am all obedience.

[Exit.]

.   .   .

MRS. FAIN. Yonder Sir Wilfull's drunk, and
so noisy that my mother has been forced to
leave Sir Rowland to appease him; but he   55
answers her only with singing and drinking.
What they may have done by this time I know
not, but Petulant and he were upon quarreling
as I came by.

MILLA. Well, if Mirabell should not make a   60
good husband, I am a lost thing; for I find I
love him violently.

MRS. FAIN. So it seems, for you mind not
what's said to you.—If you doubt him, you
had best take up with Sir Wilfull.   65

MILLA. How can you name that superannuated lubber? foh!

.   .   .

[Enter WITWOUD from drinking.]

MRS. FAIN. So, is the fray made up, that
you have left 'em?   70

WIT. Left 'em? I could stay no longer—I
have laughed like ten christenings—I am tipsy
with laughing.—If I had stayed any longer, I
should have burst—I must have been let out
and pieced in the sides like an unsized camlet.°   75
—Yes, yes, the fray is composed; my lady
came in like a nolle prosequi° and stopped the
proceedings.

MILLA. What was the dispute?

WIT. That's the jest; there was no dispute.   80
They could neither of 'em speak for rage; and
so fell a-sputtering at one another like two
roasting apples.

.   .   .

[Enter PETULANT drunk.]

WIT. Now, Petulant? All's over, all's well?   85

orange brandy . . . clary a list of alcoholic drinks

unsized camlet unsized wool cloth
nolle prosequi a motion to withdraw a suit

Gad, my head begins to whim it about.—Why dost thou not speak? Thou art both as drunk and as mute as a fish.

Pet. Look you, Mrs. Millamant—if you can
5 love me, dear nymph—say it—and that's the conclusion—pass on, or pass off—that's all.

Wit. Thou hast uttered volumes, folios, in less than decimo sexto,° my dear Lacedemonian.° Sirrah Petulant, thou art an epit-
10 omizer of words.

Pet. Witwoud—you are an annihilator of sense.

Wit. Thou art a retailer of phrases, and dost deal in remnants of remnants, like a maker of
15 pincushions. Thou art in truth (metaphorically speaking) a speaker of shorthand.

Pet. Thou art (without a figure) just one-half of an ass, and Baldwin° yonder, thy half brother, is the rest.—A gemini° of asses split,
20 would make just four of you.

Wit. Thou dost bite, my dear mustard-seed; kiss me for that.

Pet. Stand off—I'll kiss no more males.—I have kissed your twin yonder in a humor of
25 reconciliation, till he—[*hiccup*]—rises upon my stomach like a radish.

Milla. Eh! filthy creature.—What was the quarrel?

Pet. There was no quarrel—there might
30 have been a quarrel.

Wit. If there had been words enow between 'em to have expressed provocation, they had gone together by the ears like a pair of castanets.

35 Pet. You were the quarrel.

Milla. Me!

Pet. If I have a humor to quarrel, I can make less matters conclude premises.—If you are not handsome, what then, if I have a humor to
40 prove it?—If I shall have my reward, say so; if not, fight for your face the next time yourself.—I'll go sleep.

Wit. Do, wrap thyself up like a woodlouse, and dream revenge—and hear me, if thou canst

learn to write by tomorrow morning, pen me a 45 challenge.—I'll carry it for thee.

Pet. Carry your mistress's monkey a spider°—go flea dogs, and read romances—I'll go to bed to my maid.
[*Exit.*] 50

Mrs. Fain. He's horridly drunk—how came you all in this pickle?

Wit. A plot, a plot, to get rid of the knight—your husband's advice; but he sneaked off.

. . .

[*Enter* Lady Wishfort, *and* Sir Wilfull 55 *drunk.*]

Lady. Out upon't, out upon't! At years of discretion, and comport yourself at this ranti-pole° rate!

Sir Wil. No offense, aunt. 60

Lady. Offense? As I'm a person, I'm ashamed of you.—Foh! how you stink of wine! D'ye think my niece will ever endure such a borachio!° you're an absolute borachio.

Sir. Wil. Borachio? 65

Lady. At a time when you should commence an amour, and put your best foot foremost—

Sir Wil. 'Sheart, an you grutch me your liquor, make a bill.—Give me more drink, and take my purse. [*Sings.*] 70

Prithee fill me the glass
'Till it laugh in my face,
With ale that is potent and mellow;
He that whines for a lass
Is an ignorant ass, 75
For a bumper has not its fellow.

But if you would have me marry my cousin—say the word and I'll do't—Wilfull will do't, that's the word—Wilfull will do't, that's my crest—my motto I have forgot. 80

Lady. My nephew's a little overtaken, cousin—but 'tis with drinking your health.—O' my word you are obliged to him—

Sir Wil. *In vino veritas,*° aunt.—If I drunk

---

folios . . . sexto folios are large books and decimo
  sextos are tiny ones
Lacedemonian Spartan, known for brevity of speech
Baldwin the ass in a medieval tale
gemini pair of twins

spider a supposed food of monkeys
rantipole boorish
borachio drunkard
In vino veritas in wine there is truth.

your health today, cousin—I am a borachio.
But if you have a mind to be married, say the
word, and send for the piper; Wilfull will do't.
If not, dust it away, and let's have t'other
5 round.—Tony, 'ods heart, where's Tony?—
Tony's an honest fellow, but he spits after a
bumper, and that's a fault.—[*Sings.*]

We'll drink and we'll never ha' done, boys,
Put the glass then around with the sun, boys,
10 Let Apollo's example invite us;
For he's drunk every night,
And that makes him so bright,
That he's able next morning to light us.

The sun's a good pimple,° an honest soaker, he
15 has a cellar at your Antipodes. If I travel, aunt,
I touch at your Antipodes.—Your Antipodes
are a good rascally sort of topsy-turvy fellows.
—If I had a bumper, I'd stand upon my head
and drink a health to 'em.—A match or no
20 match, cousin, with the hard name?—Aunt,
Wilfull will do't. If she has her maidenhead,
let her look to't; if she has not, let her keep her
own counsel in the meantime, and cry out at
the nine months' end.

25   MILLA. Your pardon, madam, I can stay no
longer—Sir Wilfull grows very powerful. Egh!
how he smells! I shall be overcome if I stay.
Come, cousin.
[*Exit with* MRS. FAINALL.]

.   .   .

30   LADY. Smells! he would poison a tallow-
chandler and his family. Beastly creature, I
know not what to do with him. Travel, quoth
a'; aye, travel, travel, get thee gone, get thee
but far enough, to the Saracens, or the Tartars,
35 or the Turks—for thou art not fit to live in a
Christian commonwealth, thou beastly pagan.
SIR WIL. Turks, no; no Turks, aunt. Your
Turks are infidels, and believe not in the grape.
Your Mahometan, your Mussulman is a dry
40 stinkard.—No offense, aunt. My map says that
your Turk is not so honest a man as your
Christian.—I cannot find by the map that your

pimple   drinking companion

Mufti° is orthodox—whereby it is a plain case,
that orthodox is a hard word, aunt, and—
[*hiccup*]—Greek for claret. [*Sings.*]   45

To drink is a Christian diversion,
Unknown to the Turk or the Persian:
Let Mahometan fools
Live by heathenish rules,
And be damned over tea cups and coffee.   50
But let British lads sing,
Crown a health to the king,
And a fig for your sultan and sophy.°

Ah, Tony!
[FOIBLE *whispers to* LADY WILFULL.]   55
LADY. Sir Rowland impatient? Good lack!
what shall I do with this beastly tumbrel?°—
Go lie down and sleep, you sot—or as I'm a
person, I'll have you bastinadoed with broomsticks. Call up the wenches with broomsticks.   60
SIR. WIL. Ahay? Wenches, where are the
wenches?
LADY. Dear cousin Witwoud, get him away,
and you will bind me to you inviolably. I have
an affair of moment that invades me with some   65
precipitation—you will oblige me to all
futurity.
WIT. Come, knight.—Pox on him, I don't
know what to say to him.—Will you go to a
cockmatch?   70
SIR WIL. With a wench, Tony? Is she a
shakebag,° sirrah? Let me bite your cheek for
that.
WIT. Horrible! He has a breath like a bag-
pipe.—Aye, aye, come, will you march, my   75
Salopian?°
SIR WIL. Lead on, little Tony—I'll follow
thee, my Anthony,° my Tantony. Sirrah, thou
shalt be my Tantony, and I'll be thy pig.

—And a fig for your sultan and sophy.   80
[*Exit singing with* WITWOUD.]

Mufti   Turkish religious dignitary
sophy   shah of Persia
tumbrel   heavy cart
shakebag   fighting cock
Salopian   native of Shropshire
Anthony   St. Anthony, patron saint of swineherds

LADY. This will never do. It will never make a match—at least before he has been abroad.

.   .   .

[*Enter,* WAITWELL *disguised as for* SIR ROW-LAND.]

5 LADY. Dear Sir Rowland, I am confounded with confusion at the retrospection of my own rudeness—I have more pardons to ask than the Pope distributes in the Year of Jubilee. But I hope where there is likely to be so near an 10 alliance, we may unbend the severity of decorum, and dispense with a little ceremony.

WAIT. My impatience, madam, is the effect of my transport—and till I have the possession of your adorable person, I am tantalized on the 15 rack; and do but hang, madam, on the tenter of expectation.

LADY. You have excess of gallantry, Sir Rowland; and press things to a conclusion, with a most prevailing vehemence. But a day or two 20 for decency of marriage.—

WAIT. For decency of funeral, madam. The delay will break my heart—or if that should fail, I shall be poisoned. My nephew will get an inkling of my designs, and poison me—and 25 I would willingly starve him before I die. I would gladly go out of the world with that satisfaction.—That would be some comfort to me, if I could but live so long as to be revenged on that unnatural viper.

30 LADY. Is he so unnatural, say you? Truly I would contribute much both to the saving of your life, and the accomplishment of your revenge.—Not that I respect° myself; though he has been a perfidious wretch to me.

35 WAIT. Perfidious to you!

LADY. O Sir Rowland, the hours that he has died away at my feet, the tears that he has shed, the oaths that he has sworn, the palpitations that he has felt, the trances and the 40 tremblings, the ardors and the ecstasies, the kneelings, and the risings, the heart-heavings and the hand-gripings, the pangs and the pathetic regards of his protesting eyes! O, no memory can register.

WAIT. What, my rival! Is the rebel my rival? 45 a' dies.

LADY. No, don't kill him at once, Sir Rowland; starve him gradually inch by inch.

WAIT. I'll do't. In three weeks he shall be barefoot; in a month out at knees with begging 50 an alms—he shall starve upward and upward, till he has nothing living but his head, and then go out in a stink like a candle's end upon a saveall.°

LADY. Well, Sir Rowland, you have the way. 55 —You are no novice in the labyrinth of love— you have the clue. But as I am a person, Sir Rowland, you must not attribute my yielding to any sinister appetite, or indigestion of widowhood; nor impute my complacency to 60 any lethargy of continence. I hope you do not think me prone to any iteration of nuptials.—

WAIT. Far be it from me—

LADY. If you do, I protest I must recede—or think that I have made a prostitution of de- 65 corums, but in the vehemence of compassion, and to save the life of a person of so much importance—

WAIT. I esteem it so—

LADY. Or else you wrong my condes- 70 cension—

WAIT. I do not, I do not—

LADY. Indeed you do.

WAIT. I do not, fair shrine of virtue.

LADY. If you think the least scruple of car- 75 nality was an ingredient—

WAIT. Dear madam, no. You are all camphor° and frankincense, all chastity and odor.

LADY. Or that— 80

.   .   .

[*Enter* FOIBLE.]

FOIB. Madam, the dancers are ready, and there's one with a letter, who must deliver it into your own hands.

LADY. Sir Rowland, will you give me leave? 85 Think favorably, judge candidly, and conclude

---

respect regard

saveall pan to catch drippings and let the candle burn entirely out

camphor a supposed antidote to desire

you have found a person who would suffer racks in honor's cause, dear Sir Rowland, and will wait on you incessantly.

[*Exit.*]

. . .

5 WAIT. Fie, fie!—What a slavery have I undergone! Spouse, hast thou any cordial? I want spirits.

FOIB. What a washy rogue art thou, to pant thus for a quarter of an hour's lying and swear-
10 ing to a fine lady?

WAIT. O, she is the antidote to desire. Spouse, thou wilt fare the worse for't. I shall have no appetite for iteration of nuptials this eight and forty hours. By this hand I'd rather
15 be a chairman in the dog days, than act Sir Rowland till this time tomorrow.

. . .

[*Enter* LADY WISHFORT *with a letter.*]

LADY. Call in the dancers.—Sir Rowland, we'll sit, if you please, and see the entertain-
20 ment.

[*Dance.*]

Now with your permission, Sir Rowland, I will peruse my letter.—I would open it in your presence, because I would not make you un-
25 easy. If it should make you uneasy, I would burn it—speak if it does—but you may see, the superscription is like a woman's hand.

FOIB. [*to him*]. By heaven! Mrs. Marwood's, I know it—my heart aches—get it from her.—
30 WAIT. A woman's hand? No, madam, that's no woman's hand, I see that already. That's somebody whose throat must be cut.

LADY. Nay, Sir Rowland, since you give me a proof of your passion by your jealousy, I
35 promise you I'll make a return, by a frank com-munication—you shall see it—we'll open it together—look you here.—[*Reads.*] *Madam, though unknown to you* (Look you there, 'tis from nobody that I know.)—*I have that honor*
40 *for your character, that I think myself obliged to let you know you are abused. He who pre-tends to be Sir Rowland is a cheat and a rascal.* —O Heavens! what's this?

FOIB. Unfortunate, all's ruined.

WAIT. How, how, let me see, let me see.— 45 [*Reads.*] *A rascal and disguised, and suborned for that imposture*—O villainy! O villainy!— *by the contrivance of*—

LADY. I shall faint, I shall die, oh!

FOIB. [*to him*]. Say, 'tis your nephew's hand. 50 —Quickly, his plot, swear, swear it.—

WAIT. Here's a villain! Madam, don't you perceive it, don't you see it?

LADY. Too well, too well. I have seen too much. 55

WAIT. I told you at first I knew the hand. A woman's hand? The rascal writes a sort of a large hand, your Roman hand—I saw there was a throat to be cut presently. If he were my son, as he is my nephew, I'd pistol him— 60

FOIB. O treachery! But are you sure, Sir Row-land, it is his writing?

WAIT. Sure? Am I here? Do I live? Do I love this pearl of India? I have twenty letters in my pocket from him in the same character. 65

LADY. How!

FOIB. O, what luck it is, Sir Rowland, that you were present at this juncture! This was the business that brought Mr. Mirabell disguised to Madam Millamant this afternoon. I thought 70 something was contriving, when he stole by me and would have hid his face.

LADY. How, how! I heard the villain was in the house indeed; and now I remember, my niece went away abruptly, when Sir Wilfull 75 was to have made his addresses.

FOIB. Then, then, madam, Mr. Mirabell waited for her in her chamber; but I would not tell your ladyship to discompose you when you were to receive Sir Rowland. 80

WAIT. Enough, his date is short.

FOIB. No, good Sir Rowland, don't incur the law.

WAIT. Law! I care not for law. I can but die, and 'tis in a good cause. My lady shall be 85 satisfied of my truth and innocence, though it cost me my life.

LADY. No, dear Sir Rowland, don't fight. If you should be killed I must never show my face—or be hanged. O, consider my reputation, 90

Sir Rowland—no, you shan't fight—I'll go and examine my niece; I'll make her confess. I conjure you, Sir Rowland, by all your love not to fight.

5 WAIT. I am charmed, madam, I obey. But some proof you must let me give you—I'll go for a black box, which contains the writings of my whole estate, and deliver that into your hands.

10 LADY. Aye, dear Sir Rowland, that will be some comfort. Bring the black box.

WAIT. And may I presume to bring a contract to be signed this night? May I hope so far?

LADY. Bring what you will; but come alive,
15 pray come alive. O, this is a happy discovery.

WAIT. Dead or alive I'll come—and married we will be in spite of treachery; aye, and get an heir that shall defeat the last remaining glimpse of hope in my abandoned nephew.
20 Come, my buxom widow:

E'er long you shall substantial proof receive
That I'm an errant knight—°

FOIB. [*aside*].

Or arrant knave.

ACT V

25 [*Scene continues.*]

.   .   .

[LADY WISHFORT *and* FOIBLE.]

LADY. Out of my house, out of my house, thou viper, thou serpent, that I have fostered! Thou bosom traitress, that I raised from
30 nothing!—Begone, begone, begone, go, go— that I took from washing of old gauze and weaving of dead hair,° with a bleak blue nose over a chafing dish of starved embers, and dining behind a traverse rag,° in a shop no
35 bigger than a bird cage—go, go, starve again,

do, do.

FOIB. Dear madam, I'll beg pardon on my knees.

LADY. Away, out, out, go set up for yourself again! Do, drive a trade, do, with your three- 40 pennyworth of small ware, flaunting upon a packthread, under a brandy-seller's bulk or against a dead wall by a ballad-monger. Go, hang out an old frisoneer-gorget,° with a yard of yellow colberteen° again; do; an old gnawed 45 mask, two rows of pins and a child's fiddle; a glass necklace with the beads broken, and a quilted nightcap with one ear. Go, go, drive a trade—these were your commodities, you treacherous trull, this was the merchandise you 50 dealt in when I took you into my house, placed you next myself, and made you governante° of my whole family. You have forgot this, have you, now you have feathered your nest?

FOIB. No, no, dear madam. Do but hear me, 55 have but a moment's patience—I'll confess all. Mr. Mirabell seduced me; I am not the first that he has wheedled with his dissembling tongue. Your ladyship's own wisdom has been deluded by him, then how should I, a poor 60 ignorant, defend myself? O madam, if you knew but what he promised me, and how he assured me your ladyship should come to no damage—or else the wealth of the Indies should not have bribed me to conspire against 65 so good, so sweet, so kind a lady as you have been to me.

LADY. No damage? What, to betray me, to marry me to a cast° servingman; to make me a receptacle, an hospital for a decayed pimp? 70 No damage? O, thou frontless° impudence, more than a big-bellied actress.

FOIB. Pray do but hear me, madam. He could not marry your ladyship, madam. No, indeed, his marriage was to have been void in law; for 75 he was married to me first, to secure your ladyship. He could not have bedded your ladyship;

errant knight   knight-errant, a chivalric hero
weaving . . . hair   i.e., making wigs
traverse rag   shabby curtain

frisoneer-gorget   wool neckpiece
colberteen   lace
governante   housekeeper
cast   discharged
frontless   brazen

for if he had consummated with your ladyship, he must have run the risk of the law, and been put upon his clergy.°—Yes, indeed, I inquired of the law in that case before I would meddle or make.

LADY. What, then I have been your property, have I? I have been convenient to you, it seems.—While you were catering for Mirabell, I have been broker for you? What, have you made a passive bawd of me?—This exceeds all precedent; I am brought to fine uses, to become a botcher of second-hand marriages between Abigails and Andrews!° I'll couple you. Yes, I'll baste you together, you and your philander.° I'll Duke's-Place you, as I'm a person. Your turtle is in custody already: you shall coo in the same cage, if there be constable or warrant in the parish.

[*Exit.*]

FOIB. O, that ever I was born! O, that I was ever married!—A bride, aye, I shall be a Bridewell-bride.° Oh!

. . .

[*Enter* MRS. FAINALL.]

MRS. FAIN. Poor Foible, what's the matter?

FOIB. O madam, my lady's gone for a constable. I shall be had to a justice, and put to Bridewell to beat hemp; poor Waitwell's gone to prison already.

MRS. FAIN. Have a good heart, Foible. Mirabell's gone to give security for him. This is all Marwood's and my husband's doing.

FOIB. Yes, yes, I know it, madam; she was in my lady's closet, and overheard all that you said to me before dinner. She sent the letter to my lady; and that missing effect, Mr. Fainall laid this plot to arrest Waitwell, when he pretended to go for the papers; and in the meantime Mrs. Marwood declared all to my lady.

put upon his clergy made to prove his literacy to secure trial before an ecclesiastical (rather than civil) court
botcher . . . Andrews repairer of old marriages between maids and valets
philander lover. They had been married at Duke's Place (see Act I).
Bridewell-bride i.e., in Bridewell, a women's prison

MRS. FAIN. Was there no mention made of me in the letter? My mother does not suspect my being in the confederacy? I fancy Marwood has not told her, though she has told my husband.

FOIB. Yes, madam; but my lady did not see that part. We stifled the letter before she read so far. Has that mischievous devil told Mr. Fainall of your ladyship then?

MRS. FAIN. Aye, all's out, my affair with Mirabell, everything discovered. This is the last day of our living together, that's my comfort.

FOIB. Indeed, madam, and so 'tis a comfort if you knew all. He has been even with your ladyship; which I could have told you long enough since, but I love to keep peace and quietness by my good will. I had rather bring friends together than set 'em at distance. But Mrs. Marwood and he are nearer related than ever their parents thought for!

MRS. FAIN. Say'st thou so, Foible? Canst thou prove this?

FOIB. I can take my oath of it, madam. So can Mrs. Mincing; we have had many a fair word from Madam Marwood, to conceal something that passed in our chamber one evening when you were at Hyde Park—and we were thought to have gone a-walking, but we went up unawares—though we were sworn to secrecy too; Madam Marwood took a book and swore us upon it, but it was but a book of poems.—So long as it was not a Bible-oath, we may break it with a safe conscience.

MRS. FAIN. This discovery is the most opportune thing I could wish. Now, Mincing?

. . .

[*Enter* MINCING.]

MINC. My lady would speak with Mrs. Foible, mem. Mr. Mirabell is with her; he has set your spouse at liberty, Mrs. Foible, and would have you hide yourself in my lady's closet, till my old lady's anger is abated. O, my old lady is in a perilous passion, at something Mr. Fainall has said; he swears, and my old lady cries. There's a fearful hurricane, I vow. He says, mem, how that he'll have my lady's fortune made over to him, or he'll be divorced.

MRS. FAIN. Does your lady or Mirabell know that?

MINC. Yes, mem, they have sent me to see
5 if Sir Wilfull be sober, and to bring him to them. My lady is resolved to have him, I think, rather than lose such a vast sum as six thousand pounds. O, come, Mrs. Foible, I hear my old lady.

10 MRS. FAIN. Foible, you must tell Mincing that she must prepare to vouch when I call her.

FOIB. Yes, yes, madam.

MINC. O yes, mem, I'll vouch anything for your ladyship's service, be what it will.

15 [*Exeunt* MINCING *and* FOIBLE.]

.   .   .

[*Enter* LADY WISHFORT *and* MRS. MARWOOD.]

LADY. O my dear friend, how can I enumerate the benefits that I have received from your goodness? To you I owe the timely discovery
20 of the false vows of Mirabell; to you I owe the detection of the impostor Sir Rowland. And now you are become an intercessor with my son-in-law, to save the honor of my house, and compound for the frailties of my daughter.
25 Well, friend, you are enough to reconcile me to the bad world, or else I would retire to deserts and solitudes; and feed harmless sheep by groves and purling streams. Dear Marwood, let us leave the world and retire by ourselves
30 and be shepherdesses.

MRS. MAR. Let us first dispatch the affair in hand, madam. We shall have leisure to think of retirement afterwards. Here is one who is concerned in the treaty.

35 LADY. O daughter, daughter, is it possible thou should'st be my child, bone of my bone, and flesh of my flesh, and as I may say, another me, and yet transgress the most minute particle of severe virtue? Is it possible
40 you should lean aside to iniquity, who have been cast in the direct mold of virtue? I have not only been a mold but a pattern for you, and a model for you, after you were brought into the world.

45 MRS. FAIN. I don't understand your ladyship.

LADY. Not understand? Why, have you not been naught?° Have you not been sophisticated?° Not understand? Here I am ruined to compound for your caprices and your cuckoldoms. I must pawn my plate and my jewels, 50 and ruin my niece, and all little enough—

MRS. FAIN. I am wronged and abused, and so are you. 'Tis a false accusation, as false as hell, as false as your friend there, aye, or your friend's friend, my false husband. 55

MRS. MAR. My friend, Mrs. Fainall? Your husband my friend, what do you mean?

MRS. FAIN. I know what I mean, madam, and so do you; and so shall the world at a time convenient. 60

MRS. MAR. I am sorry to see you so passionate, madam. More temper° would look more like innocence. But I have done. I am sorry my zeal to serve your ladyship and family should admit of misconstruction, or 65 make me liable to affront. You will pardon me, madam, if I meddle no more with an affair in which I am not personally concerned.

LADY. O dear friend, I am so ashamed that you should meet with such returns.—You 70 ought to ask pardon on your knees, ungrateful creature; she deserves more from you than all your life can accomplish.—O, don't leave me destitute in this perplexity! No, stick to me, my good genius. 75

MRS. FAIN. I tell you, madam, you're abused. —Stick to you? aye, like a leech, to suck your best blood.—She'll drop off when she's full. Madam, you shan't pawn a bodkin,° nor part with a brass counter, in composition for me. I 80 defy 'em all. Let 'em prove their aspersions; I know my own innocence, and dare stand a trial.

[*Exit.*]

.   .   .

LADY. Why, if she should be innocent, if she 85 should be wronged after all, ha? I don't know what to think—and I promise you, her education has been unexceptionable, I may say it;

naught naughty
sophisticated accomplished in wickedness
temper temperateness
bodkin hair- (or hat-) pin

for I chiefly made it my own care to initiate
her very infancy in the rudiments of virtue,
and to impress upon her tender years a young
odium and aversion to the very sight of men.
5 —Aye, friend, she would have shrieked if she
had but seen a man, till she was in her teens.
As I'm a person, 'tis true; she was never suffered to play with a male child, though but in
coats. Nay, her very babies° were of the
10 feminine gender. O, she never looked a man
in the face but her own father, or the chaplain,
and him we made a shift to put upon her for a
woman, by the help of his long garments and
his sleek face, till she was going in her fifteen.
15 Mrs. Mar. 'Twas much she should be deceived so long.
Lady. I warrant you, or she would never
have borne to have been catechized by him;
and have heard his long lectures against sing-
20 ing and dancing, and such debaucheries; and
going to filthy plays; and profane music-
meetings, where the lewd trebles squeek
nothing but bawdry, and the basses roar blasphemy. O, she would have swooned at the
25 sight or name of an obscene play-book—and
can I think after all this, that my daughter can
be naught? What, a whore? And thought it
excommunication to set her foot within the
door of a playhouse? O dear friend, I can't
30 believe it, no, no; as she says, let him prove it,
let him prove it.
Mrs. Mar. Prove it, madam? What, and
have your name prostituted in a public court;
yours and your daughter's reputation worried
35 at the bar by a pack of bawling lawyers? To be
ushered in with an Oyez° of scandal; and have
your case opened by an old fumbler lecher in
a quoif° like a man midwife, to bring your
daughter's infamy to light; to be a theme for
40 legal punsters, and quibblers by the statute; and
become a jest, against a rule of court, where
there is no precedent for a jest in any record;
not even in Doomsday Book;° to discompose

the gravity of the bench, and provoke naughty
interrogatories in more naughty law-Latin; 45
while the good judge, tickled with the proceeding, simpers under a gray beard, and
fidges off and on his cushion as if he had swallowed cantharides, or sate upon cowhage.°
Lady. O, 'tis very hard! 50
Mrs. Mar. And then to have my young
revelers of the Temple° take notes, like 'pren-
tices at a conventicle; and after talk it over
again in commons, or before drawers in an
eating house. 55
Lady. Worse and worse.
Mrs. Mar. Nay, this is nothing; if it would
end here 'twere well. But it must after this be
consigned by the shorthand writers to the
public press; and from thence be transferred 60
to the hands, nay into the throats and lungs of
hawkers, with voices more licentious than the
loud flounderman's;° and this you must hear
till you are stunned; nay, you must hear
nothing else for some days. 65
Lady. O, 'tis insupportable. No, no, dear
friend, make it up, make it up; aye, aye, I'll
compound. I'll give up all, myself and my all,
my niece and her all—anything, everything for
composition. 70
Mrs. Mar. Nay, madam, I advise nothing; I
only lay before you, as a friend, the inconven-
iencies which perhaps you have overseen. Here
comes Mr. Fainall. If he will be satisfied to
huddle up all in silence, I shall be glad. You 75
must think I would rather congratulate than
condole with you.

.   .   .

[Enter Fainall.]
Lady. Aye, aye, I do not doubt it, dear Marwood. No, no, I do not doubt it. 80
Fain. Well, madam; I have suffered myself
to be overcome by the importunity of this lady,
your friend, and am content you shall enjoy
your own proper estate during life; on con-

---

babies dolls
Oyez hear ye! (law French)
quoif lawyer's cap
Doomsday Book record book of William the Con-
    queror

swallowed . . . cowhage swallowed an aphrodisiac
    or sat on a plant with stinging hairs
revelers of the Temple law students
flounderman fish peddler

dition you oblige yourself never to marry, under such penalty as I think convenient.

LADY. Never to marry?

FAIN. No more Sir Rowlands—the next im-
5 posture may not be so timely detected.

MRS. MAR. That condition, I dare answer, my lady will consent to, without difficulty; she has already but too much experienced the per-fidiousness of men. Besides, madam, when we
10 retire to our pastoral solitude we shall bid adieu to all other thoughts.

LADY. Aye, that's true; but in case of neces-sity; as of health, or some such emergency—

FAIN. O, if you are prescribed marriage, you
15 shall be considered; I will only reserve to my-self the power to choose for you. If your physic be wholesome, it matters not who is your apothecary. Next, my wife shall settle on me the remainder of her fortune, not made over
20 already; and for her maintenance depend en-tirely on my discretion.

LADY. This is most inhumanly savage; ex-ceeding the barbarity of a Muscovite husband.

FAIN. I learned it from His Czarish Majesty's°
25 retinue, in a winter evening's conference over brandy and pepper, amongst other secrets of matrimony and policy, as they are at present practiced in the northern hemisphere. But this must be agreed unto, and that positively. Last-
30 ly, I will be endowed, in right of my wife, with that six thousand pound, which is the moiety of Mrs. Millamant's fortune in your possession; and which she has forfeited (as will appear by the last will and testament of your deceased
35 husband, Sir Jonathan Wishfort) by her dis-obedience in contracting herself against your consent or knowledge; and by refusing the offered match with Sir Wilfull Witwoud, which you, like a careful aunt, had provided for her.
40 LADY. My nephew was *non compos,*° and could not make his addresses.

FAIN. I come to make demands—I'll hear no objections.

LADY. You will grant me time to consider?

FAIN. Yes, while the instrument is drawing, 45
to which you must set your hand till more sufficient deeds can be perfected: which I will take care shall be done with all possible speed. In the meanwhile I will go for the said in-strument, and till my return you may balance 50 this matter in your own discretion.

[*Exit.*]

. . .

LADY. This insolence is beyond all precedent, all parallel; must I be subject to this merciless villain? 55

MRS. MAR. 'Tis severe indeed, madam, that you should smart for your daughter's wanton-ness.

LADY. 'Twas against my consent that she married this barbarian, but she would have 60 him, though her year° was not out.—Ah! her first husband, my son Languish, would not have carried it thus. Well, that was my choice, this is hers; she is matched now, with a witness—I shall be mad, dear friend. Is there no comfort 65 for me? Must I live to be confiscated at this rebel-rate?°—Here comes two more of my Egyptian plagues,° too.

. . .

[*Enter* MILLAMANT, SIR WILFULL.]

SIR WIL. Aunt, your servant. 70

LADY. Out, caterpillar, call not me aunt; I know thee not.

SIR WIL. I confess I have been a little in dis-guise, as they say.—'Sheart! and I'm sorry for't. What would you have? I hope I committed no 75 offense, aunt—and if I did, I am willing to make satisfaction; and what can a man say fairer? If I have broke anything I'll pay for't, and it cost a pound. And so let that content for what's past, and make no more words. For 80 what's to come, to pleasure you I'm willing to

---

Czarish Majesty Peter the Great, who visited London in 1698
non compos *non compos (mentis)*, not in possession of (mental faculties)

year of mourning
rebel-rate tax [rate], as were supporters of James II after the "Glorious" Revolution of 1688–89
Egyptian plagues plagues visited on Egypt through Moses, as described in Exodus vii–xii

marry my cousin. So, pray, let's all be friends. She and I are agreed upon the matter before a witness.

LADY. How's this, dear niece? Have I any
5 comfort? Can this be true?

MILLA. I am content to be a sacrifice to your repose, madam; and to convince you that I had no hand in the plot, as you were misinformed, I have laid my commands on Mirabell to come
10 in person, and be a witness that I give my hand to this flower of knighthood; and for the contract that passed between Mirabell and me, I have obliged him to make a resignation of it in your ladyship's presence.—He is without, and
15 waits your leave for admittance.

LADY. Well, I'll swear I am something revived at this testimony of your obedience; but I cannot admit that traitor—I fear I cannot fortify myself to support his appearance. He is as
20 terrible to me as a Gorgon; if I see him, I fear I shall turn to stone, petrify incessantly.

MILLA. If you disoblige him, he may resent your refusal, and insist upon the contract still. Then 'tis the last time he will be offensive to
25 you.

LADY. Are you sure it will be the last time?— If I were sure of that.—Shall I never see him again?

MILLA. Sir Willful, you and he are to travel
30 together, are you not?

SIR WIL. 'Sheart, the gentleman's a civil gentleman, aunt, let him come in; why, we are sworn brothers and fellow travelers. We are to be Pylades and Orestes°, he and I. He is to
35 be my interpreter in foreign parts. He has been overseas once already; and with proviso that I marry my cousin, will cross 'em once again, only to bear me company.—'Sheart, I'll call him in—an I set on't once, he shall come in; and
40 see who'll hinder him. [*Goes to the door and hems.*]

MRS. MAR. This is precious fooling, if it would pass; but I'll know the bottom of it.

LADY. O dear Marwood, you are not going?
45 MRS. MAR. Not far, madam; I'll return imme-

diately.

[*Exit.*]

. . .

[*Enter* MIRABELL.]

SIR WIL. [*aside*]. Look up, man, I'll stand by
50 you. 'Sbud an she do frown, she can't kill you —besides—hark'ee, she dare not frown desperately, because her face is none of her own. 'Sheart, an she should, her forehead would wrinkle like the coat of a cream cheese; but
55 mum for that, fellow traveler.

MIRA. If a deep sense of the many injuries I have offered to so good a lady, with a sincere remorse, and a hearty contrition, can but obtain the least glance of compassion, I am too
60 happy.—Ah madam, there was a time—but let it be forgotten—I confess I have deservedly forfeited the high place I once held of sighing at your feet. Nay kill me not by turning from me in disdain—I come not to plead for favor—
65 nay not for pardon. I am a suppliant only for pity—I am going where I never shall behold you more—

SIR WIL. [*aside*]. How, fellow traveler!— You shall go by yourself then.

70 MIRA. Let me be pitied first, and afterwards forgotten—I ask no more.

SIR WIL. By'r Lady a very reasonable request, and will cost you nothing, aunt.—Come, come, forgive and forget, aunt. Why you must,
75 an you are a Christian.

MIRA. Consider, madam, in reality you could not receive much prejudice; it was an innocent device, though I confess it had a face of guiltiness. It was at most an artifice which love con-
80 trived; and errors which love produces have ever been accounted venial. At least think it is punishment enough that I have lost what in my heart I hold most dear, that to your cruel indignation, I have offered up this beauty, and
85 with her my peace and quiet; nay, all my hopes of future comfort.

SIR WIL. An he does not move me, would I may never be o' the quorum.°—An it were not as good a deed as to drink, to give her to him
90 again, I would I might never take shipping.—

Orestes son and avenger of Agamemnon. His confidant Pylades is a legendary specimen of a loyal friend.

quorum of magistrates at court sessions

Aunt, if you don't forgive quickly I shall melt,
I can tell you that. My contract went no farther
than a little mouth glue,° and that's hardly dry.
—One doleful sigh more from my fellow trav-
5 eler and 'tis dissolved.

LADY. Well, nephew, upon your account.—
Ah, he has a false insinuating tongue!—Well,
sir, I will stifle my just resentment at my
nephew's request. I will endeavor what I can
10 to forget—but on proviso that you resign the
contract with my niece immediately.

MIRA. It is in writing and with papers of concern, but I have sent my servant for it and will
deliver it to you, with all acknowledgments
15 for your transcendent goodness.

LADY. [aside]. O, he has witchcraft in his eyes
and tongue! When I did not see him I could
have bribed a villain to his assassination; but
his appearance rakes the embers which have
20 so long lain smothered in my breast.—

. . .

[*Enter* FAINALL *and* MRS. MARWOOD.]

FAIN. Your date of deliberation, madam, is
expired. Here is the instrument; are you prepared to sign?
25 LADY. If I were prepared, I am not empowered. My niece exerts a lawful claim, having matched herself by my direction to Sir
Wilfull.

FAIN. That sham is too gross to pass on me—
30 though 'tis imposed on you, madam.

MILLA. Sir, I have given my consent.

MIRA. And, sir, I have resigned my pretensions.

SIR WIL. And, sir, I assert my right; and
35 will maintain it in defiance of you, sir, and of
your instrument. 'Sheart, an you talk of an
instrument, sir, I have an old fox° by my
thigh shall hack your instrument of ram vellum
to shreds, sir. It shall not be sufficient for a
40 *mittimus*° or a tailor's measure; therefore withdraw your instrument, sir, or by'r Lady I shall
draw mine.

LADY. Hold, nephew, hold.

MILLA. Good Sir Wilfull, respite your valor.

FAIN. Indeed? Are you provided of your 45
guard, with your single beefeater° there? But
I'm prepared for you; and insist upon my first
proposal. You shall submit your own estate to
my management and absolutely make over my
wife's to my sole use, as pursuant to the pur- 50
port and tenor of this other covenant. I suppose, madam, your consent is not requisite in
this case; nor, Mr. Mirabell, your resignation;
nor, Sir Wilfull, your right.—You may draw
your fox if you please, sir, and make a bear 55
garden flourish° somewhere else: for here it
will not avail. This, my Lady Wishfort, must
be subscribed, or your darling daughter's turned
adrift, like a leaky hulk to sink or swim, as she
and the current of this lewd town can agree. 60

LADY. Is there no means, no remedy, to stop
my ruin? Ungrateful wretch! Dost thou not
owe thy being, thy subsistence to my daughter's
fortune?

FAIN. I'll answer you when I have the rest of 65
it in my possession.

MIRA. But that you would not accept of a
remedy from my hands—I own I have not
deserved you should owe any obligation to me;
or else perhaps I could advise— 70

LADY. O, what? what? to save me and my
child from ruin, from want, I'll forgive all
that's past; nay, I'll consent to anything to
come, to be delivered from this tyranny.

MIRA. Aye, madam, but that is too late; my 75
reward is intercepted. You have disposed of her
who only could have made me a compensation
for all my services; but be it as it may, I am
resolved I'll serve you. You shall not be wronged in this savage manner. 80

LADY. How! Dear Mr. Mirabell, can you be so
generous at last? But it is not possible. Hark'ee,
I'll break my nephew's match, you shall have
my niece yet, and all her fortune, if you can but
save me from this imminent danger. 85

MIRA. Will you? I take you at your word. I
ask no more. I must have leave for two criminals to appear.

---

mouth glue verbal agreement
fox sword
mittimus verbal agreement

beefeater yeoman of the guard
bear garden flourish threatening gesture, as among
  the rowdy crowd at a bearbaiting

LADY. Aye, aye, anybody, anybody.
MIRA. Foible is one, and a penitent.

.   .   .

[*Enter* MRS. FAINALL, FOIBLE, MINCING.]
MRS. MAR. O, my shame! These corrupt
5 things are brought hither to expose me.
[MIRABELL *and* LADY *go to* MRS. FAINALL *and*
FOIBLE.]
FAIN. If it must all come out, why let 'em
know it, 'tis but *the way of the world*. That
10 shall not urge me to relinquish or abate one
tittle of my terms; no, I will insist the more.
FOIB. Yes indeed, madam, I'll take my Bible-
oath of it.
MINC. And so will I, mem.
15 LADY. O Marwood, Marwood, art thou false?
My friend deceive me? Hast thou been a wicked
accomplice with that profligate man?
MRS. MAR. Have you so much ingratitude and
injustice, to give credit against your friend
20 to the aspersions of two such mercenary trulls?
MINC. Mercenary, mem? I scorn your words.
'Tis true we found you and Mr. Fainall in the
blue garret; by the same token, you swore us to
secrecy upon Messalina's poems.° Mercenary?
25 No, if we would have been mercenary, we
should have held our tongues; you would have
bribed us sufficiently.
FAIN. Go, you are an insignificant thing!
Well, what are you the better for this? Is this
30 Mr. Mirabell's expedient? I'll be put off no
longer. You, thing that was a wife, shall smart
for this. I will not leave thee wherewithal to
hide thy shame: your body shall be naked as
your reputation.
35 MRS. FAIN. I despise you and defy your
malice! You have aspersed me wrongfully.—
I have proved your falsehood.—Go, you and
your treacherous—I will not name it, but starve
together—perish.
40 FAIN. Not while you are worth a groat, indeed, my dear. Madam, I'll be fooled no longer.
LADY. Ah, Mr. Mirabell, this is small comfort, the detection of this affair.

Messalina's poems mispronunciation of "Miscellany
poems." Messalina was the notoriously libidinous
wife of the Roman emperor Claudius I.

MIRA. O, in good time.—Your leave for the
other offender and penitent to appear, madam.   45

.   .   .

[*Enter* WAITWELL *with a box of writings*.]
LADY. O Sir Rowland! Well, rascal?
WAIT. What your ladyship pleases. I have
brought the black box at last, madam.
MIRA. Give it me. Madam, you remember   50
your promise.
LADY. Aye, dear sir.
MIRA. Where are the gentlemen?
WAIT. At hand, sir, rubbing their eyes, just
risen from sleep.   55
FAIN. 'Sdeath, what's this to me? I'll not
wait your private concerns.

.   .   .

[*Enter* PETULANT *and* WITWOUD.]
PET. How now? What's the matter? Who's
hand's out?   60
WIT. Heyday! What, are you all got together,
like players at the end of the last act?
MIRA. You may remember, gentlemen, I once
requested your hands as witnesses to a certain
parchment.   65
WIT. Aye, I do, my hand I remember—Petulant set his mark.
MIRA. You wrong him, his name is fairly
written, as shall appear. You do not remember,
gentlemen, anything of what that parchment   70
contained—[*undoing the box*].
WIT. No.
PET. Not I. I writ, I read nothing.
MIRA. Very well, now you shall know. Madam, your promise.   75
LADY. Aye, aye, sir, upon my honor.
MIRA. Mr. Fainall, it is now time you should
know that your lady, while she was at her own
disposal, and before you had by your insinuations wheedled her out of a pretended settle-   80
ment of the greatest part of her fortune—
FAIN. Sir! Pretended!
MIRA. Yes, sir. I say that this lady while a
widow, having, it seems, received some cautions
respecting your inconstancy and tyranny of   85
temper, which from her own partial opinion and
fondness of you she could never have suspected
—she did, I say, by the wholesome advice of

friends and of sages learned in the laws of this land, deliver this same as her act and deed to me in trust, and to the uses within mentioned. You may read if you please—[*holding out the* 5 *parchment*] though perhaps what is written on the back may serve your occasions.

FAIN. Very likely, sir. What's here? Damnation!—[*Reads.*] *A deed of conveyance of the whole estate real of Arabella Languish, widow,* 10 *in trust to Edward Mirabell.* Confusion!

MIRA. Even so, sir, 'tis *the way of the world,* sir; of the widows of the world. I suppose this deed may bear an elder date than what you have obtained from your lady?

15 FAIN. Perfidious fiend! Then thus I'll be revenged.

[*Offers to run at* MRS. FAINALL.]

SIR WIL. Hold, sir, now you may make your bear garden flourish somewhere else, sir.

20 FAIN. Mirabell, you shall hear of this, sir; be sure you shall. Let me pass, oaf.

[*Exit.*]

MRS. FAIN. Madam, you seem to stifle your resentment: you had better give it vent.

25 MRS. MAR. Yes, it shall have vent—and to your confusion, or I'll perish in the attempt.

[*Exit.*]

.   .   .

LADY. O daughter, daughter, 'tis plain thou hast inherited thy mother's prudence.

30 MRS. FAIN. Thank Mr. Mirabell, a cautious friend, to whose advice all is owing.

LADY. Well, Mr. Mirabell, you have kept your promise and I must perform mine. First I pardon for your sake Sir Rowland there and 35 Foible.—The next thing is to break the matter to my nephew—and how to do that—

MIRA. For that, madam, give yourself no trouble—let me have your consent. Sir Wilfull is my friend; he has had compassion upon 40 lovers, and generously engaged a volunteer in this action, for our service; and now designs to prosecute his travels.

SIR WIL. 'Sheart, aunt, I have no mind to marry. My cousin's a fine lady, and the gentle-45 man loves her, and she loves him, and they deserve one another. My resolution is to see foreign parts—I have set on't—and when I'm

set on't, I must do't. And if these two gentlemen would travel too, I think they may be spared. 50

PET. For my part, I say little—I think things are best off or on.

WIT. Igad, I understand nothing of the matter —I'm in a maze yet, like a dog in a dancing school. 55

LADY. Well, sir, take her, and with her all the joy I can give you.

MILLA. Why does not the man take me? Would you have me give myself to you over again? 60

MIRA. Aye, and over and over again. [*Kisses her hand.*] I would have you as often as possibly I can. Well, Heaven grant I love you not too well, that's all my fear.

SIR WIL. 'Sheart, you'll have time enough to 65 toy after you're married; or if you will toy now, let us have a dance in the meantime; that we who are not lovers may have some other employment besides looking on.

MIRA. With all my heart, dear Sir Wilfull. 70 What shall we do for music?

FOIB. O, sir, some that were provided for Sir Rowland's entertainment are yet within call.

[*A dance.*]

LADY. As I am a person I can hold out no 75 longer. I have wasted my spirits so today already, that I am ready to sink under the fatigue; and I cannot but have some fears upon me yet, that my son Fainall will pursue some desperate course. 80

MIRA. Madam, disquiet not yourself on that account; to my knowledge his circumstances are such, he must of force comply. For my part, I will contribute all that in me lies to a reunion. In the meantime, madam, [*to* MRS. FAINALL] let 85 me before these witnesses restore to you this deed of trust; it may be a means, well managed, to make you live easily together.

From hence let those be warned, who mean to [wed; 90
Lest mutual falsehood stain the bridal bed:
For each deceiver to his cost may find,
That marriage frauds too oft are paid in kind.

[*Exeunt omnes.*]

Richard Brinsley Sheridan

1751–1816

The Rivals

1775

The author of *The Rivals* was an ebullient young man of twenty-four, and one can argue that the only really apt comment on his play is pure and exuberant laughter. Unless there is laughter, at least, all comment is fruitless. When Mrs. Malaprop, with her customary misapplication of a word, writes, "Female punctuation forbids me to say more," or when Bob Acres' valet, to express admiration for his master's new clothes, says, "There a'nt a dog in the house but would bark," one is first of all amused; if he is not amused, there is no basis for discussing things further. But laughter is not likely to fail *The Rivals* now. It has brought merriment in both theater and study throughout its long history.

Sheridan's humor is of several kinds, and often of several kinds at once. The play can be sheerly witty; some of its quips—those of Captain Absolute's man Fag, for instance—could stand alone in collections of clever sayings. Sometimes it comments on prevailing mores and so moves toward "comedy of manners"; Lydia Languish and Faulkland, although differing from each other, are both parodies of fashionable sentimentality. And sometimes it puts personal eccentricities on display and so moves toward "comedy of humors"—a type already exemplified in this collection in parts of *Volpone* and *The Miser.* Inasmuch as Mrs. Malaprop has proved the most memorable person in the play, and inasmuch as she and her fellow eccentrics tend to upstage the hero and heroine in theatrical performances, humors comedy is perhaps the most vital of the three strains. But the real genius of the play lies in its simultaneous realization of more than one comic possibility. Sir Lucius O'Trigger, for example, intent on a duel, says to his puzzled adversary, "Pray, Sir, be easy: the quarrel is a very pretty quarrel as it stands—we should only spoil it by trying to explain it." The expression is at once so deft, and the penchant for bloodshed so extreme, that one cannot separate the wit from Sir Lucius's quarrelsome "humor."

Such a classification of things laughed at, however, if allowed to stand alone, would suggest fallaciously that comedy has no other task than to find matter for mirth. Comedy becomes disorderly and raucous unless it also satisfies our minds and consciences that it is provoking laughter at things that deserve ridicule. *The Rivals* is good comedy not only because it is lavish of humor but also because its sense of the absurd is both reasonable and moral. It quite frankly evaluates human relationships, especially between men and women, and postulates an ideal relationship based on a combination of good sense and genuine feeling. In their departures from this ideal, Sheridan's characters form that arabesque of follies at which we laugh.

Among the characters who err in their romantic relationships, Lydia Languish is deficient in both sense and feeling; until the last act she is more enamored of her own role as romantic lover than she is in love with Absolute. Faulkland, too, is more concerned with himself than with his affianced. Sir Lucius is fantastically willing to fight for a mistress; Bob Acres, ludicrously unwilling. And Mrs. Malaprop's weakness for Sir Lucius is mere wishful thinking, empty alike of reason and true passion.

In the midst of this company, Captain Absolute, although falling far short of personal perfection, represents the ideal, the "absolute" man. He is really in love. For the meltingly lovely Lydia he is willing to make extreme sacrifices. Yet he has not sacrificed his good sense to his sentiment. He does not love Lydia's faults. And he knows, as she does not, that, other things being equal, it is better to be young and in love on a substantial income than on a pitifully small one. It is this concept of the passionate yet reasonable man that gives the play its ethical center.

Without such an ethical center, *The Rivals* would fragment into a gallery of fantastics. Without its humor, it might embody the most admirable of lessons, but no audience would remain to admire.

The Rivals

SHERIDAN

CHARACTERS

CAPTAIN ABSOLUTE
LYDIA LANGUISH
SIR ANTHONY ABSOLUTE   *father of Captain Absolute*
MRS. MALAPROP   *aunt of Lydia Languish*
FAULKLAND
JULIA MELVILLE   *cousin of Lydia Languish*
BOB ACRES
SIR LUCIUS O'TRIGGER
FAG   *valet of Captain Absolute*
LUCY   *lady's maid of Lydia Languish*
DAVID   *valet of Bob Acres*
COACHMAN
MAID
BOY
SERVANTS

SCENE. *Bath.*°
TIME OF ACTION. *Within one day.*

ACT I

Scene i

[*A street in Bath.*]
[COACHMAN *crosses the stage.—Enter* FAG, *looking after him.*]   5
FAG. What!—Thomas! Sure, 'tis he?—What! —Thomas!—Thomas!

Bath a fashionable health and pleasure resort in southwest England. Places in Bath referred to include the **Pump Room,** where the fashionable assembled to drink the mineral waters; **Gyde's Porch,** an entranceway to some older ballrooms (?); the **North** and **South Parades,** or promenades; the **New Room(s),** ballroom(s) opened in 1771; **King's-Mead-Fields** in the outskirts of town; and **Spring Gardens,** a riverside picnic ground.

COACHMAN. Hey! Odd's life!°—Mr. Fag!—give us your hand, my old fellow-servant.

FAG. Excuse my glove, Thomas:—I'm dev'lish glad to see you, my lad: why, my prince
5 of charioteers, you look as hearty!—but who the deuce thought of seeing you in Bath!

COACHMAN. Sure, Master, Madam Julia, Harry, Mrs. Kate, and the postilion be all come!

FAG. Indeed!

10 COACHMAN. Aye! Master thought another fit of the gout was coming to make him a visit: so he'd a mind to gi't the slip, and whip! we were all off at an hour's warning.

FAG. Aye, aye! hasty in everything, or it
15 would not be Sir Anthony Absolute!

COACHMAN. But tell us, Mr. Fag, how does young master? Odd! Sir Anthony will stare to see the Captain here!

FAG. I do not serve Captain Absolute now.

20 COACHMAN. Why sure!

FAG. At present I am employed by Ensign Beverley.

COACHMAN. I doubt, Mr. Fag, you ha'n't changed for the better.

25 FAG. I have not changed, Thomas.

COACHMAN. No! why, didn't you say you had left young master?

FAG. No.—Well, honest Thomas, I must puzzle you no farther: briefly then—Captain
30 Absolute and Ensign Beverley are one and the same person.

COACHMAN. The devil they are!

FAG. So it is indeed, Thomas; and the *Ensign-*

half of my master being on guard at present—the *Captain* has nothing to do with me. 35

COACHMAN. So, so!—What, this is some freak, I warrant!—Do tell us, Mr. Fag, the meaning o't—you know I ha' trusted you.

FAG. You'll be secret, Thomas?

COACHMAN. As a coach-horse. 40

FAG. Why then the cause of all this is—LOVE —Love, Thomas, who (as you may get read to you) has been a masquerader ever since the days of Jupiter.

COACHMAN. Aye, aye;—I guessed there was 45 a lady in the case: but pray, why does your master pass only for *Ensign?* Now if he had shammed *General,* indeed—

FAG. Ah! Thomas, there lies the mystery o' the matter. Hark'ee, Thomas, my master is in 50 love with a lady of a very singular taste: a lady who likes him better as a *half-pay Ensign* than if she knew he was son and heir to Sir Anthony Absolute, a baronet of three thousand a year!

COACHMAN. That is an odd taste indeed!— 55 but has she got the stuff, Mr. Fag? is she rich, hey?

FAG. Rich!—why, I believe she owns half the stocks—Z——ds! Thomas, she could pay the national debt as easily as I could my washer- 60 woman! She has a lap-dog that eats out of gold —she feeds her parrot with small pearls—and all her thread-papers° are made of bank-notes!

COACHMAN. Bravo!—Faith!—Odd! I warrant she has a set of thousands° at least. But does 65 she draw kindly with the Captain?

FAG. As fond as pigeons.

COACHMAN. May one hear her name?

FAG. Miss Lydia Languish. But there is an old tough aunt in the way; though, by the bye, she 70 has never seen my master, for he got acquainted with Miss while on a visit in Gloucestershire.

COACHMAN. Well—I wish they were once harnessed together in matrimony.—But pray, Mr. Fag, what kind of a place is this Bath? I ha' 75 heard a deal of it—here's a mort o' merry-making, hey?

FAG. Pretty well, Thomas, pretty well—'tis

Odd's life the first of a number of minced oaths. These are profane expressions that have been mispronounced at some time in the past, either euphemistically or in the natural course of repetition, and that, as their origins have been forgotten, have passed into general slang. Modern examples are "Gosh!" "Darn!" "Goldern it!" "Golly Ned!" The less familiar minced oaths in *The Rivals,* together with the words they mince, include **Lud** Lord; **Odd** God; **Odd's life** God's life; **Odd rabbit it** (variant of "Odd rat it") God rot it; **Odd so** God's oath; **Oons** (variant of "Zounds") God's wounds, an oath on the wounds of Christ; **'Sdeath** God's death, an oath on the death of Christ; **Zooks** (variant of "Gadzooks") God's hooks, an oath on the nails of the cross; and **Zounds** God's wounds (see "Oons" above). Bob Acres' "referential oaths" put together the form "Odds" with terms from the context of his thought.

thread-papers papers on which thread is wound
set of thousands six-horse team worth thousands of pounds

a good lounge.° In the morning we go to the Pump-room (though neither my master nor I drink the waters); after breakfast we saunter on the Parades, or play a game at billiards; at night we dance: but d——n the place, I'm tired of it: their regular hours stupefy me—not a fiddle nor a card after eleven! However, Mr. Faulkland's gentleman and I keep it up a little in private parties—I'll introduce you there, Thomas: you'll like him much.

COACHMAN. Sure I know Mr. Du-Peigne—you know his master is to marry Madam Julia.

FAG. I had forgot.—But Thomas, you must polish a little—indeed you must. Here now—this wig! what the devil do you do with a *wig*, Thomas?—none of the London whips of any degree of *ton* wear *wigs* now.

COACHMAN. More's the pity! more's the pity, I say—Odd's life! when I heard how the lawyers and doctors had took to their own hair, I thought how 'twould go next:—Odd rabbit it! when the fashion had got foot on the Bar, I guessed 'twould mount to the Box!° But 'tis all out of character, believe me, Mr. Fag: and look'ee, I'll never gi' up mine—the lawyers and doctors may do as they will.

FAG. Well, Thomas, we'll not quarrel about that.

COACHMAN. Why, bless you, the gentlemen of the professions ben't all of a mind—for in our village now, tho'ff *Jack Gauge*, the *exciseman*, has ta'en to his carrots, there's little Dick, the farrier, swears he'll never forsake his *bob*, tho' all the college should appear with their own heads!°

FAG. Indeed! well said, Dick! But hold—mark! mark! Thomas.

COACHMAN. Zooks! 'tis the Captain!—Is that the lady with him?

FAG. No! no! that is Madam Lucy—my master's mistress's maid. They lodge at that

house—but I must after him to tell him the news.

COACHMAN. Odd! he's giving her money!—Well, Mr. Fag—

FAG. Good-bye, Thomas.—I have an appointment in Gyde's Porch this evening at eight; meet me there, and we'll make a little party.

[*Exeunt severally.*]

Scene ii

[*A dressing-room in* MRS. MALAPROP'S *lodgings.*]

[LYDIA *sitting on a sofa, with a book in her hand.* LUCY, *as just returned from a message.*]

LUCY. Indeed, Ma'am, I traversed half the town in search of it: I don't believe there's a circulating library in Bath I ha'n't been at.

LYDIA. And could not you get *The Reward of Constancy*?

LUCY. No, indeed, Ma'am.

LYDIA. Nor *The Fatal Connection*?

LUCY. No, indeed, Ma'am.

LYDIA. Nor *The Mistakes of the Heart*?

LUCY. Ma'am, as ill-luck would have it, Mr. Bull said Miss Sukey Saunter had just fetched it away.

LYDIA. Heigh-ho! Did you inquire for *The Delicate Distress*?

LUCY. Or *The Memoirs of Lady Woodford*? Yes, indeed, Ma'am. I asked everywhere for it; and I might have brought it from Mr. Frederick's, but Lady Slattern Lounger, who had just sent it home, had so soiled and dog's-eared it, it wa'n't fit for a Christian to read.

LYDIA. Heigh-ho!—Yes, I always know when Lady Slattern has been before me. She has a most observing thumb; and I believe cherishes her nails for the convenience of making marginal notes.—Well, child, what *have* you brought me?

LUCY. Oh! here, Ma'am. [*Taking books from under her cloak, and from her pockets.*] This is *The Gordian Knot*, and this *Peregrine Pickle*. Here are *The Tears of Sensibility* and *Humphry Clinker*. This is *The Memoirs of a Lady of Quality, written by herself*, and here the second volume of *The Sentimental Journey*.

LYDIA. Heigh-ho!—What are those books by the glass?

---

lounge place to spend leisure time

had got foot . . . Box i.e., had caught on among lawyers, I guessed it would then catch on among coachmen

has ta'en . . . heads has begun to wear his natural red hair, there's little Dick, the farrier, swears he'll never forsake his wig, though all his professional associates should appear wearing their own hair

Lucy. The great one is only *The Whole Duty of Man*—where I press a few blonds,° Ma'am.

Lydia. Very well—give me the *sal volatile*.

Lucy. Is it in a blue cover, Ma'am?

5 Lydia. My smelling bottle, you simpleton!

Lucy. Oh, the drops!—Here, Ma'am.

Lydia. Hold!—here's some one coming—quick! see who it is.

[*Exit* Lucy.]

10 Surely I heard my cousin Julia's voice!

[*Re-enter* Lucy.]

Lucy. Lud! Ma'am, here is Miss Melville.

Lydia. Is it possible!—

[*Enter* Julia.]

15 My dearest Julia, how delighted am I!—[*Embrace.*] How unexpected was this happiness!

Julia. True, Lydia—and our pleasure is the greater; but what has been the matter?—you were denied to me at first!

20 Lydia. Ah! Julia, I have a thousand things to tell you! But first inform me what has conjured you to Bath? Is Sir Anthony here?

Julia. He is—we are arrived within this hour, and I suppose he will be here to wait on 25 Mrs. Malaprop as soon as he is dressed.

Lydia. Then, before we are interrupted, let me impart to you some of my distress! I know your gentle nature will sympathize with me, though your prudence may condemn me! My 30 letters have informed you of my whole connexion with Beverley—but I have lost him, Julia! My aunt has discovered our intercourse by a note she intercepted, and has confined me ever since! Yet, would you believe it? she has 35 fallen absolutely in love with a tall Irish baronet she met one night since we have been here, at Lady Macshuffle's rout.°

Julia. You jest, Lydia!

Lydia. No, upon my word. She really carries 40 on a kind of correspondence with him, under a feigned name though, till she chooses to be known to him; but it is a *Delia* or a *Celia*, I assure you.

Julia. Then surely she is now more indulgent 45 to her niece.

Lydia. Quite the contrary. Since she has dis-covered her own frailty she is become more suspicious of mine. Then I must inform you of another plague! That odious Acres is to be in Bath to-day; so that I protest I shall be teased 50 out of all spirits!

Julia. Come, come, Lydia, hope the best. Sir Anthony shall use his interest with Mrs. Malaprop.

Lydia. But you have not heard the worst. 55 Unfortunately I had quarreled with my poor Beverley just before my aunt made the discovery, and I have not seen him since to make it up.

Julia. What was his offence? 60

Lydia. Nothing at all! But, I don't know how it was, as often as we had been together we had never had a quarrel! And, somehow, I was afraid he would never give me an opportunity. So last Thursday I wrote a letter to my-65 self to inform myself that Beverley was at that time paying his addresses to another woman. I signed it *your friend unknown*, showed it to Beverley, charged him with his falsehood, put myself in a violent passion, and vowed I'd 70 never see him more.

Julia. And you let him depart so, and have not seen him since?

Lydia. 'Twas the next day my aunt found the matter out. I intended only to have teased 75 him three days and a half, and now I've lost him forever!

Julia. If he is as deserving and sincere as you have represented him to me, he will never give you up so. Yet consider, Lydia, you tell me he 80 is but an ensign, and you have thirty thousand pounds!

Lydia. But you know I lose most of my fortune if I marry without my aunt's consent, till of age; and that is what I have determined 85 to do ever since I knew the penalty. Nor could I love the man who would wish to wait a day for the alternative.

Julia. Nay, this is caprice!

Lydia. What, does Julia tax me with caprice? 90 I thought her lover Faulkland had enured her to it.

Julia. I do not love even *his* faults.

Lydia. But a-propos—you have sent to him, I suppose?

blonds silk laces
rout evening party

JULIA. Not yet, upon my word, nor has he the least idea of my being in Bath. Sir Anthony's resolution was so sudden I could not inform him of it.

5 LYDIA. Well, Julia, you are your own mistress (though under the protection of Sir Anthony), yet have you for this long year been a slave to the caprice, the whim, the jealousy of this ungrateful Faulkland, who will ever delay assum-
10 ing the right of a husband, while you suffer him to be equally imperious as a lover.

JULIA. Nay, you are wrong entirely. We were contracted before my father's death. That, and some consequent embarrassments, have delayed
15 what I know to be my Faulkland's most ardent wish. He is too generous to trifle on such a point. And for his character, you wrong him there too. No, Lydia, he is too proud, too noble to be jealous: if he is captious, 'tis without
20 dissembling; if fretful, without rudeness. Unused to the fopperies of love, he is negligent of the little duties expected from a lover—but being unhackneyed in the passion, his affection is ardent and sincere; and as it engrosses his
25 whole soul, he expects every thought and emotion of his mistress to move in unison with his. Yet, though his pride calls for this full return, his humility makes him undervalue those qualities in him which would entitle him to it; and
30 not feeling why he should be loved to the degree he wishes, he still suspects that he is not loved enough. This temper, I must own, has cost me many unhappy hours; but I have learned to think myself his debtor for those im-
35 perfections which arise from the ardour of his attachment.

LYDIA. Well, I cannot blame you for defending him. But tell me candidly, Julia, had he never saved your life, do you think you should
40 have been attached to him as you are? Believe me, the rude blast that overset your boat was a prosperous gale of love to him.

JULIA. Gratitude may have strengthened my attachment to Mr. Faulkland, but I loved him
45 before he had preserved me; yet surely that alone were an obligation sufficient—

LYDIA. Obligation! Why, a water-spaniel would have done as much! Well, I should never think of giving my heart to a man because he could swim! 50

JULIA. Come, Lydia, you are too inconsiderate.

LYDIA. Nay, I do but jest.—What's here?

[Enter LUCY in a hurry.]

LUCY. O Ma'am, here is Sir Anthony Ab- 55 solute just come home with your aunt.

LYDIA. They'll not come here.—Lucy, do you watch.

[Exit LUCY.]

JULIA. Yet I must go. Sir Anthony does not 60 know I am here, and if we meet, he'll detain me, to show me the town. I'll take another opportunity of paying my respects to Mrs. Malaprop, when she shall treat me, as long as she chooses, with her select words so ingeniously 65 misapplied, without being mispronounced.

[Re-enter LUCY.]

LUCY. O lud! Ma'am, they are both coming upstairs.

LYDIA. Well, I'll not detain you, coz. Adieu, 70 my dear Julia. I'm sure you are in haste to send to Faulkland. There—through my room you'll find another stair-case.

JULIA. Adieu.—[Embrace.]

[Exit JULIA.] 75

LYDIA. Here, my dear Lucy, hide these books. Quick, quick! Fling Peregrine Pickle under the toilet—throw Roderick Random into the closet —put The Innocent Adultery into The Whole Duty of Man—thrust Lord Aimworth under 80 the sofa—cram Ovid behind the bolster—there —put The Man of Feeling into your pocket— so, so,—now lay Mrs. Chapone in sight, and leave Fordyce's Sermons open on the table.

LUCY. Oh burn it, Ma'am! the hair-dresser 85 has torn away as far as Proper Pride.

LYDIA. Never mind—open at Sobriety.— Fling me Lord Chesterfield's Letters.—Now for 'em.

[Enter MRS. MALAPROP, and SIR ANTHONY 90 ABSOLUTE.]

MRS. MALAPROP. There, Sir Anthony, there sits the deliberate simpleton who wants to disgrace her family, and lavish herself on a fellow not worth a shilling! 95

LYDIA. Madam, I thought you once—

MRS. MALAPROP. You thought, Miss! I don't know any business you have to think at all. Thought does not become a young woman. But the point we would request of you is, that you
5 will promise to forget this fellow—to illiterate him, I say, quite from your memory.

LYDIA. Ah! Madam! our memories are independent of our wills. It is not so easy to forget.

MRS. MALAPROP. But I say it is, Miss; there
10 is nothing on earth so easy as to *forget*, if a person chooses to set about it. I'm sure I have as much forgot your poor dear uncle as if he had never existed—and I thought it my duty so to do; and let me tell you, Lydia, these
15 violent memories don't become a young woman.

SIR ANTHONY. Why sure she won't pretend to remember what she's ordered not!—aye, this comes of her reading!

20 LYDIA. What crime, Madam, have I committed to be treated thus?

MRS. MALAPROP. Now don't attempt to extirpate yourself from the matter; you know I have proof controvertible of it. But tell me, will
25 you promise to do as you're bid? Will you take a husband of your friend's choosing?

LYDIA. Madam, I must tell you plainly, that had I no preference for anyone else, the choice you have made would be my aversion.

30 MRS. MALAPROP. What business have you, Miss, with *preference* and *aversion*? They don't become a young woman; and you ought to know, that as both always wear off, 'tis safest in matrimony to begin with a little
35 *aversion*. I am sure I hated your poor dear uncle before marriage as if he'd been a blackamoor—and yet, Miss, you are sensible what a wife I made!—and when it pleased heaven to release me from him, 'tis unknown what tears
40 I shed! But suppose we were going to give you another choice, will you promise us to give up this Beverley?

LYDIA. Could I belie my thoughts so far as to give that promise, my actions would cer-
45 tainly as far belie my words.

MRS. MALAPROP. Take yourself to your room. You are fit company for nothing but your own ill-humours.

LYDIA. Willingly, Ma'am—I cannot change for the worse. 50

[*Exit* LYDIA.]

MRS. MALAPROP. There's a little intricate hussy for you!

SIR ANTHONY. It is not to be wondered at, Ma'am—all this is the natural consequence of 55 teaching girls to read. Had I a thousand daughters, by heaven! I'd as soon have them taught the black art as their alphabet!

MRS. MALAPROP. Nay, nay, Sir Anthony, you are an absolute misanthropy. 60

SIR ANTHONY. In my way hither, Mrs. Malaprop, I observed your niece's maid coming forth from a circulating library! She had a book in each hand—they were half-bound volumes, with marble covers! From that 65 moment I guessed how full of duty I should see her mistress!

MRS. MALAPROP. Those are vile places, indeed!

SIR ANTHONY. Madam, a circulating library 70 in a town is as an evergreen tree of diabolical knowledge! It blossoms through the year! And depend on it, Mrs. Malaprop, that they who are so fond of handling the leaves, will long for the fruit at last. 75

MRS. MALAPROP. Fie, fie, Sir Anthony, you surely speak laconically!

SIR ANTHONY. Why, Mrs. Malaprop, in moderation, now, what would you have a woman know? 80

MRS. MALAPROP. Observe me, Sir Anthony. I would by no means wish a daughter of mine to be a progeny of learning; I don't think so much learning becomes a young woman; for instance—I would never let her meddle with 85 Greek, or Hebrew, or Algebra, or Simony, or Fluxions, or Paradoxes, or such inflammatory branches of learning—neither would it be necessary for her to handle any of your mathematical, astronomical, diabolical instruments; 90 —but, Sir Anthony, I would send her, at nine years old, to a boarding-school, in order to learn a little ingenuity and artifice. Then, Sir, she should have a supercilious knowledge in accounts—and as she grew up, I would have 95 her instructed in geometry, that she might know something of the contagious countries—but above all, Sir Anthony, she should be mistress of orthodoxy, that she might not misspell, and mispronounce words so shamefully as girls usually do; and likewise that she might reprehend the true meaning of what she is saying. This, Sir Anthony, is what I would have a woman know—and I don't think there is a superstitious article in it.

SIR ANTHONY. Well, well, Mrs. Malaprop, I will dispute the point no further with you; though I must confess that you are a truly moderate and polite arguer, for almost every third word you say is on my side of the question. But, Mrs. Malaprop, to the more important point in debate—you say you have no objection to my proposal.

MRS. MALAPROP. None, I assure you. I am under no positive engagement with Mr. Acres, and as Lydia is so obstinate against him, perhaps your son may have better success.

SIR ANTHONY. Well, Madam, I will write for the boy directly. He knows not a syllable of this yet, though I have for some time had the proposal in my head. He is at present with his regiment.

MRS. MALAPROP. We have never seen your son, Sir Anthony; but I hope no objection on his side.

SIR ANTHONY. Objection!—let him object if he dare! No, No, Mrs. Malaprop, Jack knows that the least demur puts me in a frenzy directly. My process was always very simple—in their young days, 'twas "Jack do this";—if he demurred—I knocked him down—and if he grumbled at that—I always sent him out of the room.

MRS. MALAPROP. Aye, and the properest way, o' my conscience!—nothing is so conciliating to young people as severity. Well, Sir Anthony, I shall give Mr. Acres his discharge, and prepare Lydia to receive your son's invocations; and I hope you will represent *her* to the Captain as an object not altogether illegible.

SIR ANTHONY. Madam, I will handle the subject prudently. Well, I must leave you—and let me beg you, Mrs. Malaprop, to enforce this matter roundly to the girl; take my advice—keep a tight hand; if she rejects this proposal—clap her under lock and key—and if you were just to let the servants forget to bring her dinner for three or four days, you can't conceive how she'd come about!

[*Exit* SIR ANTHONY.]

MRS. MALAPROP. Well, at any rate I shall be glad to get her from under my intuition. She has somehow discovered my partiality for Sir Lucius O'Trigger—sure, Lucy can't have betrayed me! No, the girl is such a simpleton, I should have made her confess it.—[*Calls.*] Lucy!—Lucy—Had she been one of your artificial ones, I should never have trusted her.

[*Enter* LUCY.]

LUCY. Did you call, Ma'am?

MRS. MALAPROP. Yes, girl. Did you see Sir Lucius while you was out?

LUCY. No, indeed, Ma'am, not a glimpse of him.

MRS. MALAPROP. You are sure, Lucy, that you never mentioned—

LUCY. O Gemini! I'd sooner cut my tongue out.

MRS. MALAPROP. Well, don't let your simplicity be imposed on.

LUCY. No, Ma'am.

MRS. MALAPROP. So, come to me presently, and I'll give you another letter to Sir Lucius; but mind, Lucy—if ever you betray what you are intrusted with (unless it be other people's secret to me) you forfeit my malevolence forever, and your being a simpleton shall be no excuse for your locality.

[*Exit* MRS. MALAPROP.]

LUCY. Ha! ha! ha!—So, my dear *simplicity,* let me give you a little respite—[*altering her manner*]—let girls in my station be as fond as they please of appearing expert, and knowing in their trusts—commend me to a mask of *silliness,* and a pair of sharp eyes for my own interest under it! Let me see to what account have I turned my *simplicity* lately—[*looks at a paper*]. For *abetting Miss Lydia Languish in a design of running away with an Ensign!—in money—sundry times—twelve pound twelve— gowns, five—hats, ruffles, caps, &c., &c.— numberless! From the said Ensign, within this last month, six guineas and a half.—About a*

quarter's pay!—Item, *from Mrs. Malaprop, for
betraying the young people to her*—when I
found matters were likely to be discovered—
two guineas, and a black paduasoy.—Item,
5 *from Mr. Acres, for carrying divers letters*—
which I never delivered—*two guineas, and a
pair of buckles.*—Item, *from Sir Lucius O'Trigger*—three crowns—*two gold pocket-pieces—
and a silver snuff-box!*—Well done, *simplicity!*
10 —Yet I was forced to make my Hibernian believe that he was corresponding, not with the
aunt, but with the *niece:* for, though not over-
rich, I found he had too much pride and
delicacy to sacrifice the feelings of a gentleman
15 to the necessities of his fortune.
   [*Exit.*]

ACT II

Scene i

[Captain Absolute's *lodgings.*]
[Captain Absolute *and* Fag.]
Fag. Sir, while I was there Sir Anthony came
20 in: I told him you had sent me to inquire after
his health, and to know if he was at leisure
to see you.
   Absolute. And what did he say on hearing I
was at Bath?
25 Fag. Sir, in my life I never saw an elderly
gentleman more astonished! He started back
two or three paces, rapped out a dozen inter-
jectoral oaths, and asked what the devil had
brought you here!
30 Absolute. Well, Sir, and what did you say?
   Fag. Oh, I lied, Sir— I forget the precise lie;
but you may depend on't, he got no truth from
me. Yet, with submission, for fear of blunders
in future, I should be glad to fix what *has*
35 brought us to Bath, in order that we may lie a
little consistently. Sir Anthony's servants were
curious, Sir, very curious indeed.
   Absolute. You have said nothing to them?
   Fag. Oh, not a word, Sir—not a word. Mr.
40 Thomas, indeed, the coachman (whom I take
to be the discreetest of whips)—
   Absolute. 'Sdeath!—you rascal! you have
not trusted him!
   Fag. Oh, *no,* Sir!—no—no—not a syllable,
45 upon my veracity! He was, indeed, a little in-

quisitive; but I was sly, Sir—devilish sly!—
My master (said I), honest Thomas (you know,
Sir, one says *honest* to one's inferiors), is come
to Bath to *recruit*—yes, Sir—I said, *to recruit*—
and whether for men, money, or constitution, 50
you know, Sir, is nothing to him, nor anyone
else.
   Absolute. Well—*recruit* will do—let it be
so—
   Fag. Oh, Sir, recruit will do surprisingly— 55
indeed, to give the thing an air, I told Thomas
that your Honour had already enlisted five
disbanded chairmen, seven minority waiters,
and thirteen billiard markers.°
   Absolute. You blockhead, never say more 60
than is necessary.
   Fag. I beg pardon, Sir—I beg pardon.—But
with submission, a lie is nothing unless one
supports it. Sir, whenever I draw on my invention for a good current lie, I always forge 65
indorsements, as well as the bill.
   Absolute. Well, take care you don't hurt
your credit by offering too much security. Is
Mr. Faulkland returned?
   Fag. He is above, Sir, changing his dress. 70
   Absolute. Can you tell whether he has been
informed of Sir Anthony's and Miss Melville's
arrival?
   Fag. I fancy not, Sir; he has seen no one
since he came in but his gentleman, who was 75
with him at Bristol.—I think, Sir, I hear Mr.
Faulkland coming down—
   Absolute. Go tell him I am here.
   Fag. Yes, Sir [*going*]. I beg pardon, Sir, but
should Sir Anthony call, you will do me the 80
favor to remember that we are *recruiting,* if you
please.
   Absolute. Well, well.
   Fag. And in tenderness to my character, if
your Honour could bring in the chairmen and 85
waiters, I shall esteem it as an obligation; for
though I never scruple a lie to serve my
master, yet it hurts one's conscience to be
found out.
   [*Exit.*] 90

***

five . . . markers five sedan chair bearers who have
been dismissed, seven unemployed waiters, and
thirteen men who chalk up scores in billiard rooms

ABSOLUTE. Now for my whimsical friend—if he does not know that his mistress is here, I'll tease him a little before I tell him—

[*Enter* FAULKLAND.]

5 Faulkland, you're welcome to Bath again; you are punctual in your return.

FAULKLAND. Yes; I had nothing to detain me when I had finished the business I went on. Well, what news since I left you? How stand 10 matters between you and Lydia?

ABSOLUTE. Faith, much as they were; I have not seen her since our quarrel; however, I expect to be recalled every hour.

FAULKLAND. Why don't you persuade her to 15 go off with you at once?

ABSOLUTE. What, and lose two-thirds of her fortune? You forget that, my friend. No, no, I could have brought her to that long ago.

FAULKLAND. Nay then, you trifle too long— 20 if you are sure of *her*, propose to the aunt *in your own character*, and write to Sir Anthony for his consent.

ABSOLUTE. Softly, softly, for though I am convinced my little Lydia would elope with me 25 as Ensign Beverley, yet am I by no means certain that she would take me with the impediment of our friend's consent, a regular humdrum wedding, and the reversion of° a good fortune on my side; no, no, I must pre- 30 pare her gradually for the discovery, and make myself necessary to her, before I risk it.— Well, but Faulkland, you'll dine with us to-day at the hotel?

FAULKLAND. Indeed, I cannot: I am not in 35 spirits to be of such a party.

ABSOLUTE. By heavens! I shall forswear your company. You are the most teasing, captious, incorrigible lover! Do love like a man!

FAULKLAND. I own I am unfit for company.

40 ABSOLUTE. Am not *I* a lover; aye, and a romantic one too? Yet do I carry everywhere with me such a confounded farrago of doubts, fears, hopes, wishes, and all the flimsy furniture of a country miss's brain!

45 FAULKLAND. Ah! Jack, your heart and soul are not, like mine, fixed immutably on one only

object. You throw for a large stake, but losing —you could stake, and throw again. But I have set my sum of happiness on this cast, and not to succeed were to be stripped of all. 50

ABSOLUTE. But, for heaven's sake! what grounds for apprehension can your whimsical brain conjure up at present?

FAULKLAND. What grounds for apprehension did you say? Heavens! are there not a thou- 55 sand! I fear for her spirits—her health—her life. My absence may fret her; her anxiety for my return, her fears for me, may oppress her gentle temper. And for her health—does not every hour bring me cause to be alarmed? If it 60 rains, some shower may even then have chilled her delicate frame! If the wind be keen, some rude blast may have affected her! The heat of noon, the dews of the evening, may endanger the life of her, for whom only I value mine. O! 65 Jack, when delicate and feeling souls are separated, there is not a feature in the sky, not a movement of the elements, not an aspiration of the breeze, but hints some cause for a lover's apprehension! 70

ABSOLUTE. Aye, but we may choose whether we will take the hint or not. So then, Faulkland, if you were convinced that Julia were well and in spirits, you would be entirely content?

FAULKLAND. I should be happy beyond 75 measure—I am anxious only for that.

ABSOLUTE. Then to cure your anxiety at once —Miss Melville is in perfect health, and is at this moment in Bath!

FAULKLAND. Nay, Jack—don't trifle with me. 80

ABSOLUTE. She is arrived here with my father within this hour.

FAULKLAND. Can you be serious?

ABSOLUTE. I thought you knew Sir Anthony better than to be surprised at a sudden whim 85 of this kind. Seriously then, it is as I tell you— upon my honour.

FAULKLAND. My dear friend!—Hollo, Du-Peigne! my hat—my dear Jack—now nothing on earth can give me a moment's uneasiness. 90

[*Enter* FAG.]

FAG. Sir, Mr. Acres just arrived is below.

ABSOLUTE. Stay, Faulkland, this Acres lives within a mile of Sir Anthony, and he shall tell

reversion of prospect of inheriting

you how your mistress has been ever since you left her.—Fag, show the gentleman up.

[*Exit* FAG.]

FAULKLAND. What, is he much acquainted in 5 the family?

ABSOLUTE. Oh, very intimate. I insist on your not going: besides, his character will divert you.

FAULKLAND. Well, I should like to ask him a 10 few questions.

ABSOLUTE. He is likewise a rival of mine— that is of my *other self's*, for he does not think his friend Captain Absolute ever saw the lady in question; and it is ridiculous enough to hear 15 him complain to me of *one Beverley*, a concealed skulking rival, who—

FAULKLAND. Hush! He's here.

[*Enter* ACRES.]

ACRES. Hah! my dear friend, noble captain, 20 and honest Jack, how dost thou? Just arrived, faith, as you see. Sir, your humble servant. Warm work on the roads, Jack!—Odds whips and wheels! I've travelled like a comet, with a tail of dust all the way as long as the Mall.°

25 ABSOLUTE. Ah! Bob, you are indeed an eccentric planet, but we know your attraction hither. Give me leave to introduce Mr. Faulkland to you; Mr. Faulkland, Mr. Acres.

ACRES. Sir, I am most heartily glad to see 30 you: Sir, I solicit your connexions.—Hey, Jack —what—this is Mr. Faulkland, who—?

ABSOLUTE. Aye, Bob, Miss Melville's Mr. Faulkland.

ACRES. Odd so! she and your father can be 35 but just arrived before me—I suppose you have seen them. Ah! Mr. Faulkland, you are indeed a happy man.

FAULKLAND. I have not seen Miss Melville yet, Sir. I hope she enjoyed full health and 40 spirits in Devonshire?

ACRES. Never knew her better in my life, Sir—never better. Odds blushes and blooms! she has been as healthy as the German Spa.°

the Mall the promenade in St. James's Park in London

the German spa the original health resort itself. Reference is to a long-established watering place in Belgium.

FAULKLAND. Indeed! I did hear that she had been a little indisposed. 45

ACRES. False, false, Sir—only said to vex you: quite the reverse, I assure you.

FAULKLAND. There, Jack, you see she has the advantage of me; I had almost fretted myself ill. 50

ABSOLUTE. Now are you angry with your mistress for not having been sick.

FAULKLAND. No, no, you misunderstand me: yet surely a little trifling indisposition is not an unnatural consequence of absence from 55 those we love. Now confess—isn't there something unkind in this violent, robust, unfeeling health?

ABSOLUTE. Oh, it was very unkind of her to be well in your absence, to be sure! 60

ACRES. Good apartments, Jack.

FAULKLAND. Well, Sir, but you were saying that Miss Melville has been so *exceedingly* well —what, then she has been merry and gay, I suppose? Always in spirits—hey? 65

ACRES. Merry! Odds crickets! she has been the belle and spirit of the company wherever she has been—so lively and entertaining! so full of wit and humour!

FAULKLAND. There, Jack, there! Oh, by my 70 soul! there is an innate levity in woman, that nothing can overcome. What! happy, and I away!

ABSOLUTE. Have done—how foolish this is! Just now you were only apprehensive for your 75 mistress's *spirits*.

FAULKLAND. Why, Jack, have I been the joy and spirit of the company?

ABSOLUTE. No, indeed, you have not.

FAULKLAND. Have I been lively and enter- 80 taining?

ABSOLUTE. Oh, upon my word, I acquit you.

FAULKLAND. Have I been full of wit and humour?

ABSOLUTE. No, faith; to do you justice, you 85 have been confoundedly stupid indeed.

ACRES. What's the matter with the gentleman?

ABSOLUTE. He is only expressing his great satisfaction at hearing that Julia has been so 90 well and happy—that's all—hey, Faulkland?

FAULKLAND. Oh! I am rejoiced to hear it—yes, yes, she has a *happy* disposition!

ACRES. That she has indeed. Then she is so accomplished—so sweet a voice—so expert at her harpsichord—such a mistress of flat and sharp, squallante, rumblante, and quiverante!° There was this time month—Odds minims and crotchets!° how she did chirrup at Mrs. Piano's concert!

FAUKLAND. There again, what say you to this? You see she has been all mirth and song—not a thought of me!

ABSOLUTE. Pho! man, is not music the food of love?

FAULKLAND. Well, well, it may be so.—Pray, Mr.—— what's his d——d name? Do you remember what songs Miss Melville sung?

ACRES. Not I, indeed.

ABSOLUTE. Stay now, they were some pretty, melancholy, purling-stream airs, I warrant; perhaps you may recollect; did she sing *"When absent from my soul's delight"*?

ACRES. No, that wa'nt it.

ABSOLUTE. Or *"Go, gentle gales"*?—*"Go, gentle gales!"* [*Sings.*]

ACRES. Oh no! nothing like it. Odds! now I recollect one of them—*"My heart's my own, my will is free."* [*Sings.*]

FAULKLAND. Fool! fool that I am! to fix all my happiness on such a trifler! 'Sdeath! to make herself the pipe° and ballad-monger of a circle! to soothe her light heart with catches and glees!° What can you say to this, Sir?

ABSOLUTE. Why, that I should be glad to hear my mistress had been so merry, *Sir.*

FAULKLAND. Nay, nay, nay—I am not sorry that she has been happy—no, no, I am glad of that—I would not have had her sad or sick—yet surely a sympathetic heart would have shown itself even in the choice of a song: she might have been temperately healthy, and, somehow, plaintively gay; but she has been dancing too, I doubt not!

ACRES. What does the gentleman say about dancing?

ABSOLUTE. He says the lady we speak of dances as well as she sings.

ACRES. Aye, truly, does she—there was at our last race-ball—

FAULKLAND. Hell and the devil! There! there! —I told you so! I told you so! Oh! she thrives in my absence! Dancing! But her whole feelings have been in opposition with mine! I have been anxious, silent, pensive, sedentary—my days have been hours of care, my nights of watchfulness. She has been all Health! Spirit! Laugh! Song! Dance! Oh! d——n'd, d——n'd levity!

ABSOLUTE. For heaven's sake! Faulkland, don't expose yourself so. Suppose she has danced, what then? Does not the ceremony of society often oblige—

FAULKLAND. Well, well, I'll contain myself. Perhaps, as you say, for form sake. What, Mr. Acres, you were praising Miss Melville's manner of dancing a *minuet*—hey?

ACRES. Oh I dare insure her for that—but what I was going to speak of was her *country dancing*. Odds swimmings! she has such an air with her!

FAULKLAND. Now disappointment on her! Defend this, Absolute, why don't you defend this? Country-dances! jigs, and reels! Am I to blame now? A minuet I could have forgiven—I should not have minded that—I say I should not have regarded a minuet—but *country-dances! Z——ds!* had she made one in a cotillion—I believe I could have forgiven even that—but to be monkey-led for a night! to run the gauntlet through a string of amorous palming puppies! to show paces like a managed filly! O Jack, there never can be but *one* man in the world whom a truly modest and delicate woman ought to pair with in a *country-dance;* and even then, the rest of the couples should be her great uncles and aunts!

ABSOLUTE. Aye, to be sure!—grandfathers and grandmothers!

FAULKLAND. If there be but one vicious mind in the Set, 'twill spread like a contagion—the action of their pulse beats to the lascivious movement of the jig—their quivering, warm-

---

squallante ... quiverante fictitious musical terms
minims and crotchets half-notes and quarter-notes
pipe piper
catches and glees humorous rounds and other part-songs

breathed sighs impregnate the very air—the atmosphere becomes electrical to love, and each amorous spark darts through every link of the chain! I must leave you—I own I am somewhat
5 flurried—and that confounded looby° has perceived it. [*Going.*]

ABSOLUTE. Nay, but stay, Faulkland, and thank Mr. Acres for his good news.

FAULKLAND. D——n his news!

10 [*Exit* FAULKLAND.]

ABSOLUTE. Ha! ha! ha! Poor Faulkland! Five minutes since—"nothing on earth could give him a moment's uneasiness!"

ACRES. The gentleman wa'n't angry at my
15 praising his mistress, was he?

ABSOLUTE. A little jealous, I believe, Bob.

ACRES. You don't say so? Ha! ha! jealous of me?—that's a good joke.

ABSOLUTE. There's nothing strange in that,
20 Bob: let me tell you, that sprightly grace and insinuating manner of yours will do some mischief among the girls here.

ACRES. Ah! you joke—ha! ha!—mischief— ha! ha! But you know I am not my own
25 property; my dear Lydia has forestalled me. She could never abide me in the country, because I used to dress so badly—but odds frogs and tambours!° I shan't take matters so here— now ancient madam has no voice in it. I'll make
30 my old clothes know who's master. I shall straightway cashier the hunting-frock, and render my leather breeches incapable. My hair has been in training some time.

ABSOLUTE. Indeed!

35 ACRES. Aye—and tho'ff the side-curls are a little restive, my hindpart takes to it very kindly.

ABSOLUTE. O, you'll polish, I doubt not.

ACRES. Absolutely, I propose so. Then if I
40 find out this Ensign Beverley, odds triggers and flints! I'll make him know the difference o't.

ABSOLUTE. Spoke like a man—but pray, Bob, I observe you have got an odd kind of a new method of swearing—

45 ACRES. Ha! ha! you've taken notice of it?

looby oaf
frogs and tambours ornamental loop fastenings and the embroidery on them

'Tis genteel, isn't it? I didn't invent it myself, though; but a commander in our militia—a great scholar, I assure you—says that there is no meaning in the common oaths, and that nothing but their antiquity makes them re- 50 spectable, because, he says, the ancients would never stick to an oath or two, but would say, by Jove! or by Bacchus! or by Mars! or by Venus! or by Pallas! according to the sentiment; so that to swear with propriety, says 55 my little major, the "oath should be an echo to the sense"; and this we call the *oath referential*, or *sentimental swearing*—ha! ha! ha! 'tis genteel, isn't it?

ABSOLUTE. Very genteel, and very new, in- 60 deed—and I dare say will supplant all other figures of imprecation.

ACRES. Aye, aye, the best terms will grow obsolete. Damns have had their day.

[*Enter* FAG.] 65

FAG. Sir, there is a gentleman below desires to see you. Shall I show him into the parlour?

ABSOLUTE. Aye—you may.

ACRES. Well, I must be gone—

ABSOLUTE. Stay; who is it, Fag? 70

FAG. Your father, Sir.

ABSOLUTE. You puppy, why didn't you show him up directly?

[*Exit* FAG.]

ACRES. You have business with Sir Anthony. 75 I expect a message from Mrs. Malaprop at my lodgings. I have sent also to my dear friend, Sir Lucius O'Trigger. Adieu, Jack! We must meet at night, when you shall give me a dozen bumpers to little Lydia. 80

ABSOLUTE. That I will, with all my heart.

[*Exit* ACRES.]

Now for a parental lecture. I hope he has heard nothing of the business that has brought me here. I wish the gout had held him fast in 85 Devonshire, with all my soul!

[*Enter* SIR ANTHONY.]

Sir, I am delighted to see you here; and looking so well! Your sudden arrival at Bath made me apprehensive for your health. 90

SIR ANTHONY. Very apprehensive, I dare say, Jack. What, you are recruiting here, hey?

ABSOLUTE. Yes, Sir, I am on duty.

SIR ANTHONY. Well, Jack, I am glad to see

you, though I did not expect it, for I was going to write to you on a little matter of business. Jack, I have been considering that I grow old and infirm, and shall probably not trouble 5 you long.

ABSOLUTE. Pardon me, Sir, I never saw you look more strong and hearty; and I pray frequently that you may continue so.

SIR ANTHONY. I hope your prayers may be 10 heard with all my heart. Well then, Jack, I have been considering that I am so strong and hearty, I may continue to plague you a long time. Now, Jack, I am sensible that the income of your commission, and what I have hitherto 15 allowed you, is but a small pittance for a lad of your spirit.

ABSOLUTE. Sir, you are very good.

SIR ANTHONY. And it is my wish, while yet I live, to have my boy make some figure in the 20 world. I have resolved, therefore, to fix you at once in a noble independence.

ABSOLUTE. Sir, your kindness overpowers me—such generosity makes the gratitude of reason more lively than the sensations even 25 of filial affection.

SIR ANTHONY. I am glad you are so sensible of my attention—and you shall be master of a large estate in a few weeks.

ABSOLUTE. Let my future life, Sir, speak my 30 gratitude: I cannot express the sense I have of your munificence. Yet, Sir, I presume you would not wish me to quit the army?

SIR ANTHONY. Oh, that shall be as your wife chooses.

35 ABSOLUTE. My wife, Sir!

SIR ANTHONY. Aye, aye—settle that between you—settle that between you.

ABSOLUTE. A *wife*, Sir, did you say?

SIR ANTHONY. Aye, a wife—why; did not I 40 mention her before?

ABSOLUTE. Not a word of her, Sir.

SIR ANTHONY. Odd so!—I mus'n't forget *her*, though. Yes, Jack, the independence I was talking of is by a marriage—the fortune is 45 saddled with a wife—but I suppose that makes no difference.

ABSOLUTE. Sir! Sir!—you amaze me!

SIR ANTHONY. Why, what the devil's the matter with the fool? Just now you were all gratitude and duty.

ABSOLUTE. I was, Sir—you talked to me of independence and a fortune, but not a word of a wife. 50

SIR ANTHONY. Why—what difference does that make? Odd's life, Sir! if you have the estate, you must take it with the live stock on it, as it stands.

ABSOLUTE. If my happiness is to be the price, 55 I must beg leave to decline the purchase. Pray, Sir, who is the lady?

SIR ANTHONY. What's that to you, Sir? Come, give me your promise to love, and to marry her directly. 60

ABSOLUTE. Sure, Sir, this is not very reasonable, to summon my affections for a lady I know nothing of!

SIR ANTHONY. I am sure, Sir, 'tis more unreasonable in you to *object* to a lady you know 65 nothing of.

ABSOLUTE. Then, Sir, I must tell you plainly that my inclinations are fixed on another— my heart is engaged to an angel.

SIR ANTHONY. Then pray let it send an 70 excuse. It is very sorry—but *business* prevents its waiting on her.

ABSOLUTE. But my vows are pledged to her.

SIR ANTHONY. Let her foreclose, Jack; let her foreclose; they are not worth redeeming: be- 75 sides, you have the angel's vows in exchange, I suppose; so there can be no loss there.

ABSOLUTE. You must excuse me, Sir, if I tell you, once for all, that in this point I cannot obey you. 80

SIR ANTHONY. Hark'ee, Jack: I have heard you for some time with patience—I have been cool—quite cool; but take care—you know I am compliance itself when I am not thwarted —no one more easily led when I have my own 85 way; but don't put me in a frenzy.

ABSOLUTE. Sir, I must repeat it—in this I cannot obey you.

SIR ANTHONY. Now, d——n me! if ever I call you *Jack* again while I live! 90

ABSOLUTE. Nay, Sir, but hear me.

SIR ANTHONY. Sir, I won't hear a word—not a word! not one word! so give me your promise by a nod—and I'll tell you what, Jack—I mean, you dog—if you don't, by—

ABSOLUTE. What, Sir, promise to link myself to some mass of ugliness! to—

5 SIR ANTHONY. Z—ds! Sirrah! the lady shall be as ugly as I choose: she shall have a hump on each shoulder; she shall be as crooked as the Crescent; her one eye shall roll like the Bull's in Cox's Museum°—she shall have a
10 skin like a mummy, and the beard of a Jew—she shall be all this, Sirrah!—yet I'll make you ogle her all day, and sit up all night to write sonnets on her beauty.

ABSOLUTE. This is reason and moderation
15 indeed!

SIR ANTHONY. None of your sneering, puppy! no grinning, jackanapes!

ABSOLUTE. Indeed, Sir, I never was in a worse humour for mirth in my life.

20 SIR ANTHONY. 'Tis false, Sir! I know you are laughing in your sleeve; I know you'll grin when I am gone, Sirrah!

ABSOLUTE. Sir, I hope I know my duty better.

SIR ANTHONY. None of your passion, Sir!
25 none of your violence! if you please. It won't do with me, I promise you.

ABSOLUTE. Indeed, Sir, I never was cooler in my life.

SIR ANTHONY. 'Tis a confounded lie!—I
30 know you are in a passion in your heart; I know you are, you hypocritical young dog! But it won't do.

ABSOLUTE. Nay, Sir, upon my word.

SIR ANTHONY. So you will fly out! Can't you
35 be cool, like me? What the devil good can *passion* do! *Passion* is of no service, you impudent, insolent, overbearing reprobate!—There you sneer again! don't provoke me! But you rely upon the mildness of my temper—you do, you
40 dog! you play upon the meekness of my disposition! Yet take care—the patience of a saint may be overcome at last!—but mark! I give you six hours and a half to consider of this: if you then agree, without any condition, to do
45 everything on earth that I choose, why—con-

found you! I may in time forgive you. If not, z—ds! don't enter the same hemisphere with me! don't dare to breathe the same air, or use the same light with me; but get an atmosphere and a sun of your own! I'll strip you of your 50 commission; I'll lodge a five-and-threepence in the hands of trustees,° and you shall live on the interest. I'll disown you, I'll disinherit you, I'll unget you! and—d—n me, if ever I call you Jack again! 55

[*Exit* SIR ANTHONY.]

[ABSOLUTE *solus*.]

ABSOLUTE. Mild, gentle, considerate Father—I kiss your hands. What a tender method of giving his opinion in these matters Sir Anthony 60 has! I dare not trust him with the truth. I wonder what old wealthy hag it is that he wants to bestow on me! Yet he married himself for love! and was in his youth a bold intriguer, and a gay companion! 65

[*Enter* FAG.]

FAG. Assuredly, Sir, our father is wrath to a degree; he comes downstairs eight or ten steps at a time—muttering, growling, and thumping the bannisters all the way: I, and the cook's 70 dog, stand bowing at the door—rap! he gives me a stroke on the head with his cane; bids me carry that to my master; then kicking the poor turnspit into the area,° d—ns us all for a puppy triumvirate! Upon my credit, Sir, were 75 I in your place, and found my father such very bad company, I should certainly drop his acquaintance.

ABSOLUTE. Cease your impertinence, Sir, at present. Did you come in for nothing more? 80 Stand out of the way!

[*Pushes him aside, and exit.*]

[FAG *solus*.]

FAG. Soh! Sir Anthony trims° my master. He is afraid to reply to his father—then vents his 85 spleen on poor Fag! When one is vexed by one person, to revenge one's self on another who happens to come in the way is the vilest

---

the Bull's . . . Museum a toy bull, a mechanical marvel of the time

lodge . . . trustees deposit five shillings and three-pence (a quarter-guinea) in the hands of executors
area sunken space before the basement door
trims abuses

injustice. Ah! it shows the worst temper—the basest—

[*Enter* ERRAND BOY.]

5 BOY. Mr. Fag! Mr. Fag! your master calls you.

FAG. Well, you little dirty puppy, you need not bawl so!—The meanest disposition! the—

BOY. Quick, quick, Mr. Fag!

FAG. *Quick, quick,* you impudent jackanapes! 10 am I to be commanded by you too? you little, impertinent, insolent, kitchen-bred—

[*Exit, kicking and beating him.*]

Scene ii

[*The North Parade.*]

[*Enter* LUCY.]

15 LUCY. So—I shall have another rival to add to my mistress's list—Captain Absolute. However, I shall not enter his name till my purse has received notice in form. Poor Acres is dismissed! Well, I have done him a last friendly 20 office in letting him know that Beverley was here before him. Sir Lucius is generally more punctual when he expects to hear from his *dear Dalia*, as he calls her: I wonder he's not here! I have a little scruple of conscience from 25 this deceit; though I should not be paid so well, if my hero knew that *Delia* was near fifty, and her own mistress.

[*Enter* SIR LUCIUS O'TRIGGER.]

SIR LUCIUS. Hah! my little embassadress— 30 upon my conscience, I have been looking for you; I have been on the South Parade this half-hour.

LUCY [*speaking simply*]. O Gemini! and I have been waiting for your worship here on 35 the North.

SIR LUCIUS. Faith!—maybe that was the reason we did not meet; and it is very comical, too, how you could go out and I not see you— for I was only taking a nap at the Parade 40 Coffee-house, and I chose the *window* on purpose that I might not miss you.

LUCY. My stars! Now I'd wager a sixpence I went by while you were asleep.

SIR LUCIUS. Sure enough it must have been 45 so—and I never dreamt it was so late, till I waked. Well, but my little girl, have you got nothing for me?

LUCY. Yes, but I have: I've got a letter for you in my pocket.

SIR LUCIUS. Oh faith! I guessed you weren't 50 come empty-handed—well—let me see what the dear creature says.

LUCY. There, Sir Lucius. [*Gives him a letter.*]

SIR LUCIUS [*reads*]. *Sir—there is often a sudden incentive impulse in love, that has a* 55 *greater induction than years of domestic combination: such was the commotion I felt at the first superfluous view of Sir Lucius O'Trigger.* —Very pretty, upon my word.—*Female punctuation forbids me to say more; yet let me add,* 60 *that it will give me joy infallible to find Sir Lucius worthy the last criterion of my affections.* DELIA. Upon my conscience! Lucy, your lady is a great mistress of language. Faith, she's quite the queen of the dictionary!—for 65 the devil a word dare refuse coming at her call—though one would think it was quite out of hearing.

LUCY. Aye, Sir, a lady of her experience—

SIR LUCIUS. Experience! what, at seventeen? 70

LUCY. O true, Sir—but then she reads so— my stars! how she will read off-hand!

SIR LUCIUS. Faith, she must be very deep read to write this way—though she is rather an arbitrary writer too—for here are a great 75 many poor words pressed into the service of this note, that would get their *habeas corpus* from any court in Christendom.

LUCY. Ah! Sir Lucius, if you were to hear how she talks of you! 80

SIR LUCIUS. Oh tell her I'll make her the best husband in the world, and Lady O'Trigger into the bargain! But we must get the old gentlewoman's consent—and do everything fairly.

LUCY. Nay, Sir Lucius, I thought you wa'n't 85 rich enough to be so nice!°

SIR LUCIUS. Upon my word, young woman, you have hit it: I am so poor that I can't afford to do a dirty action. If I did not want money I'd steal your mistress and her fortune with a 90 great deal of pleasure. However, my pretty girl [*gives her money*], here's a little something to buy you a ribband; and meet me in the evening, and I'll give you an answer to this. So,

nice scrupulous

hussy, take a kiss beforehand to put you in mind. [*Kisses her.*]

LUCY. O lud! Sir Lucius—I never seed such a gemman! My lady won't like you if you're so
5 impudent.

SIR LUCIUS. Faith she will, Lucy—That same —pho! what's the name of it?—*Modesty!*—is a quality in a lover more praised by the women than liked; so, if your mistress asks you
10 whether Sir Lucius ever gave you a kiss, tell her *fifty*—my dear.

LUCY. What, would you have me tell her a lie?

SIR LUCIUS. Ah, then, you baggage! I'll make
15 it a truth presently.

LUCY. For shame now; here is someone coming.

SIR LUCIUS. Oh faith, I'll quiet your conscience.
20 [*Sees* FAG.—*Exit, humming a tune.*]
[*Enter* FAG.]

FAG. So, so, Ma'am. I humbly beg pardon.

LUCY. O lud!—now, Mr. Fag, you flurry one so.
25 FAG. Come, come, Lucy, here's no one by— so a little less simplicity, with a grain or two more sincerity, if you please. You play false with us, Madam. I saw you give the baronet a letter. My master shall know this, and if he
30 don't call him out—I will.

LUCY. Ha! ha! ha! you gentlemen's gentlemen are so hasty. That letter was from Mrs. Malaprop, simpleton. She is taken with Sir Lucius's address.
35 FAG. How! what tastes some people have! Why, I suppose I have walked by her window an hundred times. But what says our young lady? Any message to my master?

LUCY. Sad news, Mr. Fag! A worse rival than
40 Acres! Sir Anthony Absolute has proposed his son.

FAG. What, Captain Absolute?

LUCY. Even so. I overheard it all.

FAG. Ha! ha! ha!—very good, faith. Good-
45 bye, Lucy, I must away with this news.

LUCY. Well—you may laugh, but it is true, I assure you. [*Going.*] But—Mr. Fag—tell your master not to be cast down by this.

FAG. Oh, he'll be so disconsolate!

LUCY. And charge him not to think of quar- 50 relling with young Absolute.

FAG. Never fear!—never fear!

LUCY. Be sure—bid him keep up his spirits.

FAG. We will—we will.
[*Exeunt severally.*] 55

ACT III

Scene i

[*The North Parade.*]
[*Enter* ABSOLUTE.]

ABSOLUTE. 'Tis just as Fag told me, indeed. Whimsical enough, faith! My father wants to *force* me to marry the very girl I am plotting 60 to run away with! He must not know of my connexion with her yet awhile. He has too summary a method of proceeding in these matters. However, I'll read my recantation instantly. My conversion is something sudden, 65 indeed, but I can assure him it is very *sincere.* —So, so—here he comes. He looks plaguy gruff. [*Steps aside.*]
[*Enter* SIR ANTHONY.]

SIR ANTHONY. No—I'll die sooner than for- 70 give him. *Die,* did I say? I'll live these fifty years to plague him. At our last meeting, his impudence had almost put me out of temper. An obstinate, passionate, self-willed boy! Who can he take after? This is my return for get- 75 ting him before all his brothers and sisters!— for putting him, at twelve years old, into a marching regiment, and allowing him fifty pounds a year, beside his pay ever since! But I have done with him; he's anybody's son for 80 me. I never will see him more—never—never —never—never!

ABSOLUTE. Now for a penitential face.

SIR ANTHONY. Fellow, get out of my way.

ABSOLUTE. Sir, you see a penitent before you. 85

SIR ANTHONY. I see an impudent scoundrel before me.

ABSOLUTE. A sincere penitent. I am come, Sir, to acknowledge my error, and to submit entirely to your will. 90

SIR ANTHONY. What's that?

ABSOLUTE. I have been revolving, and reflecting, and considering on your past goodness, and kindness, and condescension to me.

SIR ANTHONY. Well, Sir?

ABSOLUTE. I have been likewise weighing and balancing what you were pleased to mention concerning duty, and obedience, and authority.

5 SIR ANTHONY. Well, puppy?

ABSOLUTE. Why, then, Sir, the result of my reflections is—a resolution to sacrifice every inclination of my own to your satisfaction.

SIR ANTHONY. Why, now you talk sense—
10 absolute sense—I never heard anything more sensible in my life. Confound you, you shall be *Jack* again!

ABSOLUTE. I am happy in the appellation.

SIR ANTHONY. Why then, Jack, my dear Jack,
15 I will now inform you who the lady really is. Nothing but your passion and violence, you silly fellow, prevented my telling you at first. Prepare, Jack, for wonder and rapture! prepare! What think you of Miss Lydia Languish?

20 ABSOLUTE. Languish! What, the Languishes of Worcestershire?

SIR ANTHONY. Worcestershire! No. Did you never meet Mrs. Malaprop and her niece, Miss Languish, who came into our country just be-
25 fore you were last ordered to your regiment?

ABSOLUTE. Malaprop! Languish! I don't remember ever to have heard the names before. Yet, stay—I think I do recollect something.— *Languish! Languish!* She squints, don't she?
30 A little, red-haired girl?

SIR ANTHONY. Squints? A red-haired girl! Z——ds, no!

ABSOLUTE. Then I must have forgot; it can't be the same person.

35 SIR ANTHONY. Jack! Jack! what think you of blooming, love-breathing seventeen?

ABSOLUTE. As to that, Sir, I am quite indifferent. If I can please you in the matter, 'tis all I desire.

40 SIR ANTHONY. Nay, but Jack, such eyes! such eyes! so innocently wild! so bashfully irresolute! Not a glance but speaks and kindles some thought of love! Then, Jack, her cheeks! her cheeks, Jack! so deeply blushing at the in-
45 sinuations of her tell-tale eyes! Then, Jack, her lips!—O Jack, lips smiling at their own discretion; and if not smiling, more sweetly pouting, more lovely in sullenness!

ABSOLUTE. [*aside*]. That's she, indeed. Well done, old gentleman!

SIR ANTHONY. Then, Jack, her neck!—O Jack! Jack!

ABSOLUTE. And which is to be mine, Sir, the 50 niece or the aunt?

SIR ANTHONY. Why, you unfeeling, insensible puppy, I despise you! When I was of your age, such a description would have made me fly like a rocket! The *aunt*, indeed! Odd's life! 55 when I ran away with your mother, I would not have touched anything old or ugly to gain an empire.

ABSOLUTE. Not to please your father, Sir?

SIR ANTHONY. To please my father! Z——ds! 60 not to please—Oh, my father!—Odd so!—yes —yes!—if my father, indeed, had desired— that's quite another matter. Though he wa'n't the indulgent father that I am, Jack.

ABSOLUTE. I dare say not, Sir. 65

SIR ANTHONY. But, Jack, you are not sorry to find your mistress is so beautiful?

ABSOLUTE. Sir, I repeat it; if I please you in this affair, 'tis all I desire. Not that I think a woman the worse for being handsome; but, 70 Sir, if you please to recollect, you before hinted something about a hump or two, one eye, and a few more graces of that kind. Now, without being very nice, I own I should rather choose a wife of mine to have the usual number of 75 limbs, and a limited quantity of back: and though *one* eye may be very agreeable, yet as the prejudice has always run in favor of *two*, I would not wish to affect a singularity in that article. 80

SIR ANTHONY. What a phlegmatic sot it is! Why, Sirrah, you're an anchorite! a vile, insensible stock. You a soldier! you're a walking block, fit only to dust the company's regimentals on! Odd's life! I've a great mind to 85 marry the girl myself!

ABSOLUTE. I am entirely at your disposal, Sir; if you should think of addressing Miss Languish yourself, I suppose you would have me marry the *aunt*; or if you should change your 90 mind, and take the old lady—'tis the same to me—I'll marry the *niece*.

SIR ANTHONY. Upon my word, Jack, thou'rt

either a very great hypocrite, or—But come, I
know your indifference on such a subject must
be all a lie—I'm sure it must—come, now—
damn your demure face!—come, confess, Jack
5 —you have been lying—ha'n't you? you have
been playing the hypocrite, hey?—I'll never
forgive you if you ha'n't been lying and playing the hypocrite.

ABSOLUTE. I'm sorry, Sir, that the respect and
10 duty which I bear to you should be so mistaken.

SIR ANTHONY. Hang your respect and duty!
But come along with me, I'll write a note to
Mrs. Malaprop, and you shall visit the lady
15 directly. Her eyes shall be the Promethean
torch to you°—come along. I'll never forgive
you if you don't come back stark mad with
rapture and impatience. If you don't, egad, I'll
marry the girl myself!

20 [*Exeunt.*]

Scene ii

[JULIA's *dressing-room.*]
[FAULKLAND *solus.*]

FAULKLAND. They told me Julia would return
directly; I wonder she is not yet come! How
25 mean does this captious, unsatisfied temper
of mine appear to my cooler judgment! Yet I
know not that I indulge it in any other point:
but on this one subject, and to this one subject,
whom I think I love beyond my life, I am ever
30 ungenerously fretful, and madly capricious! I
am conscious of it—yet I cannot correct myself! What tender, honest joy sparkled in her
eyes when we met! How delicate was the
warmth of her expressions! I was ashamed to
35 appear less happy, though I had come resolved
to wear a face of coolness and upbraiding. Sir
Anthony's presence prevented my proposed
expostulations, yet I must be satisfied that she
has not been so *very* happy in my absence. She
40 is coming! Yes! I know the nimbleness of her
tread when she thinks her impatient Faulkland
counts the moments of her stay.

[*Enter* JULIA.]

be . . . you kindle a fire in you as Prometheus' torch,
lit on Olympus, first kindled fires on earth

JULIA. I had not hoped to see you again so
soon.   45

FAULKLAND. Could I, Julia, be contented with
my first welcome—restrained as we were by
the presence of a third person?

JULIA. O Faulkland, when your kindness can
make me thus happy, let me not think that I   50
discovered something of coldness in your first
salutation.

FAULKLAND. 'Twas but your fancy, Julia. I
was rejoiced to see you—to see you in such
health. Sure I had no cause for coldness?   55

JULIA. Nay then, I see you have taken something ill. You must not conceal from me what
it is.

FAULKLAND. Well then—shall I own to you—
that my joy at hearing of your health and ar- 60
rival here, by your neighbour Acres, was somewhat damped by his dwelling much on the high
spirits you had enjoyed in Devonshire—on
your mirth, your singing, dancing, and I know
not what! For such is my temper, Julia, that I   65
should regard every mirthful moment in your
absence as a treason to constancy. The mutual
tear that steals down the cheek of parting
lovers is a compact that no smile shall live
there till they meet again.   70

JULIA. Must I never cease to tax my Faulkland with this teasing minute caprice? Can the
idle reports of a silly boor weigh in your breast
against my tried affection?

FAULKLAND. They have no weight with me,   75
Julia: no, no—I am happy if you have been so
—yet only say that you did not sing with *mirth*
—say that you *thought* of Faulkland in the
dance.

JULIA. I never can be happy in your absence.   80
If I wear a countenance of content, it is to show
that my mind holds no doubt of my Faulkland's truth. If I seemed sad, it were to make
malice triumph, and say that I had fixed my
heart on one who left me to lament his roving, 85
and my own credulity. Believe me, Faulkland, I
mean not to upbraid you when I say that I have
often dressed sorrow in smiles, lest my friends
should guess whose unkindness had caused my
tears.   90

FAULKLAND. You were ever all goodness to

me. Oh, I am a brute when I but admit a doubt
of your true constancy!

JULIA. If ever, without such cause from you,
as I will not suppose possible, you find my
affections veering but a point, may I become
a proverbial scoff for levity and base ingratitude.

FAULKLAND. Ah! Julia, that last word is grat-
ing to me. I would I had no title to your *gratitude*! Search your heart, Julia; perhaps what
you have mistaken for love, is but the warm
effusion of a too thankful heart!

JULIA. For what quality must I love you?

FAULKLAND. For no quality! To regard me for
any quality of mind or understanding were
only to *esteem* me. And for person—I have
often wished myself deformed, to be convinced
that I owed no obligation *there* for any part of
your affection.

JULIA. Where Nature has bestowed a show of
nice attention in the features of a man, he
should laugh at it as misplaced. I have seen
men who in *this* vain article perhaps might
rank above you; but my heart has never asked
my eyes if it were so or not.

FAULKLAND. Now this is not well from *you*,
Julia. I despise person in a man. Yet if you
loved me as I wish, though I were an Æthiop,
you'd think none so fair.

JULIA. I see you are determined to be unkind.
The *contract* which my poor father bound us
in gives you more than a lover's privilege.

FAULKLAND. Again, Julia, you raise ideas that
feed and justify my doubts. I would not have
been more free—no—I am proud of my restraint. Yet—yet—perhaps your high respect
alone for this solemn compact has fettered
your inclinations, which else had made a wor-
thier choice. How shall I be sure, had you
remained unbound in thought and promise,
that I should still have been the object of your
persevering love?

JULIA. Then try me now. Let us be free as
strangers as to what is past: *my* heart will not
feel more liberty!

FAULKLAND. There now! so hasty, Julia! so
anxious to be free! If your love for me were

fixed and ardent, you would not loose your
hold, even though I wished it!

JULIA. Oh, you torture me to the heart! I
cannot bear it.

FAULKLAND. I do not mean to distress you. If
I loved you less I should never give you an
uneasy moment. But hear me. All my fretful
doubts arise from this: women are not used to
weigh, and separate the motives of their affections; the cold dictates of prudence, gratitude,
or filial duty, may sometimes be mistaken for
the pleadings of the heart. I would not boast—
yet let me say that I have neither age, person,
or character to found dislike on; my fortune
such as few ladies could be charged with *indiscretion* in the match. O Julia! when *Love* receives such countenance from *Prudence*, nice
minds will be suspicious of its birth.

JULIA. I know not whither your insinuations
would tend, but as they seem pressing to insult
me, I will spare you the regret of having done
so. I have given you no cause for this!

[*Exit in tears.*]

FAULKLAND. In tears! Stay, Julia: stay but for
a moment.—The door is fastened! Julia—my
soul—but for one moment. I hear her sobbing!
'Sdeath! what a brute am I to use her thus!
Yet stay!—Aye—she is coming now. How
little resolution there is in woman! How a few
soft words can turn them!—No, faith!—she is
not coming either! Why, Julia—my love—say
but that you forgive me—come but to tell me
that. Now, this is being *too* resentful.—Stay!
she *is* coming too—I thought she would—no
steadiness in anything! her going away must
have been a mere trick then. She sha'n't see
that I was hurt by it. I'll affect indifference.
[*Hums a tune: then listens.*]—No—Z——ds!
she's *not* coming!—nor don't intend it, I suppose. This is not *steadiness*, but *obstinacy*! Yet
I deserve it. What, after so long an absence to
quarrel with her tenderness!—'twas barbarous
and unmanly! I should be ashamed to see her
now. I'll wait till her just resentment is abated
—and when I distress her so again, may I lose
her forever, and be linked instead to some antique virago, whose gnawing passions, and

long-hoarded spleen shall make me curse my folly half the day, and all the night!

[*Exit.*]

Scene iii

[Mrs. Malaprop's *lodgings.*]

Mrs. Malaprop, *with a letter in her hand,* and Captain Absolute.]

Mrs. Malaprop. Your being Sir Anthony's son, Captain, would itself be a sufficient accommodation; but from the ingenuity of your appearance, I am convinced you deserve the character here given of you.

Absolute. Permit me to say, Madam, that as I never yet have had the pleasure of seeing Miss Languish, my principal inducement in this affair at present is the honour of being allied to Mrs. Malaprop; of whose intellectual accomplishments, elegant manners, and unaffected learning, no tongue is silent.

Mrs. Malaprop. Sir, you do me infinite honour! I beg, Captain, you'll be seated. [*Sit.*] Ah! few gentlemen now-a-days know how to value the ineffectual qualities in a woman! few think how a little knowledge becomes a gentlewoman! Men have no sense now but for the worthless flower of beauty!

Absolute. It is but too true, indeed, Ma'am. Yet I fear our ladies should share the blame—they think our admiration of *beauty* so great, that *knowledge* in *them* would be superfluous. Thus, like garden-trees, they seldom show fruit till time has robbed them of the more specious blossom. Few, like Mrs. Malaprop and the orange-tree, are rich in both at once!

Mrs. Malaprop. Sir—you overpower me with good-breeding. [*Aside.*] He is the very pineapple of politeness!—You are not ignorant, Captain, that this giddy girl has somehow contrived to fix her affections on a beggarly, strolling, eaves-dropping Ensign, whom none of us have seen, and nobody knows anything of.

Absolute. Oh, I have heard the silly affair before. I'm not at all prejudiced against her on *that* account.

Mrs. Malaprop. You are very good, and very considerate, Captain. I am sure I have done everything in my power since I exploded the affair! Long ago I laid my positive conjunctions on her never to think on the fellow again; I have since laid Sir Anthony's preposition before her; but, I'm sorry to say, she seems resolved to decline every particle that I enjoin her.

Absolute. It must be very distressing, indeed, Ma'am.

Mrs. Malaprop. Oh! it gives me the hydrostatics to such a degree! I thought she had persisted from corresponding with him; but behold this very day I have interceded another letter from the fellow! I believe I have it in my pocket.

Absolute [*aside*]. Oh the devil! my last note.

Mrs. Malaprop. Aye, here it is.

Absolute [*aside*]. Aye, my note, indeed! Oh the little traitress Lucy!

Mrs. Malaprop. There, perhaps you may know the writing. [*Gives him the letter.*]

Absolute. I think I have seen the hand before—yes, I certainly must have seen this hand before—

Mrs. Malaprop. Nay, but read it, Captain.

Absolute [*reads*]. "*My soul's idol, my adored Lydia!*"—Very tender, indeed!

Mrs. Malaprop. Tender! aye, and profane, too, o' my conscience!

Absolute. "*I am excessively alarmed at the intelligence you send me, the more so as my new rival*"—

Mrs. Malaprop. That's *you*, Sir.

Absolute. "*Has universally the character of being an accomplished gentleman, and a man of honour.*"—Well, that's handsome enough.

Mrs. Malaprop. Oh, the fellow had some design in writing so.

Absolute. That he had, I'll answer for him, Ma'am.

Mrs. Malaprop. But go on, Sir—you'll see presently.

Absolute. "*As for the old weather-beaten she-dragon who guards you*"—Who can he mean by that?

MRS. MALAPROP. Me! Sir—*me!*—he means *me!* There—what do you think now? But go on a little further.

ABSOLUTE. Impudent scoundrel!—*"it shall go hard but I will elude her vigilance, as I am told that the same ridiculous vanity which makes her dress up her coarse features, and deck her dull chat with hard words which she don't understand"*—

MRS. MALAPROP. There, Sir! an attack upon my language! What do you think of that?—an aspersion upon my parts of speech! Was ever such a brute! Sure if I reprehend anything in this world, it is the use of my oracular tongue, and a nice derangement of epitaphs!

ABSOLUTE. He deserves to be hanged and quartered! Let me see—*"same ridiculous vanity"*—

MRS. MALAPROP. You need not read it again, Sir.

ABSOLUTE. I beg pardon, Ma'am—*"does also lay her open to the grossest deceptions from flattery and pretended admiration"*—an impudent coxcomb!—*"so that I have a scheme to see you shortly with the old harridan's consent, and even to make her a go-between in our interviews."*—Was ever such assurance!

MRS. MALAPROP. Did you ever hear anything like it? He'll elude my vigilance, will he? Yes, yes! ha! ha! He's very likely to enter these doors! We'll try who can plot best!

ABSOLUTE. So we will, Ma'am—so we will. Ha! ha! ha! A conceited puppy, ha! ha! ha! Well, but Mrs. Malaprop, as the girl seems so infatuated by this fellow, suppose you were to wink at her corresponding with him for a little time—let her even plot an elopement with him—then do you connive at her escape—while *I,* just in the nick, will have the fellow laid by the heels, and fairly contrive to carry her off in his stead.

MRS. MALAPROP. I am delighted with the scheme; never was anything better perpetrated!

ABSOLUTE. But, pray, could not I see the lady for a few minutes now? I should like to try her temper a little.

MRS. MALAPROP. Why, I don't know—I doubt° she is not prepared for a visit of this kind. There is a decorum in these matters.

ABSOLUTE. O Lord! she won't mind *me*—only tell her Beverley—

MRS. MALAPROP. Sir!—

ABSOLUTE [*aside*]. Gently, good tongue.

MRS. MALAPROP. What did you say of Beverley?

ABSOLUTE. Oh, I was going to propose that you should tell her, by way of jest, that it was Beverley who was below—she'd come down fast enough then—ha! ha! ha!

MRS. MALAPROP. 'Twould be a trick she well deserves. Besides, you know the fellow tells her he'll get my consent to see her—ha! ha! Let him if he can, I say again. [*Calling.*] Lydia, come down here!—He'll make me a *go-between in their interviews!*—ha! ha! ha!—Come down, I say, Lydia!—I don't wonder at your laughing, ha! ha! ha!—his impudence is truly ridiculous.

ABSOLUTE. 'Tis very ridiculous, upon my soul, Ma'am, ha! ha! ha!

MRS. MALAPROP. The little hussy won't hear. Well, I'll go and tell her at once who it is. She shall know that Captain Absolute is come to wait on her. And I'll make her behave as becomes a young woman.

ABSOLUTE. As you please, Ma'am.

MRS. MALAPROP. For the present, Captain, your servant. Ah! you've not done laughing yet, I see—*elude my vigilance!*—yes, yes, ha! ha! ha!

[*Exit.*]

ABSOLUTE. Ha! ha! ha! one would think now that I might throw off all disguise at once, and seize my prize with security—but such is Lydia's caprice that to undeceive were probably to lose her. I'll see whether she knows me. [*Walks aside, and seems engaged in looking at the pictures.*]

[*Enter* LYDIA.]

LYDIA. What a scene am I now to go through! Surely nothing can be more dreadful than to be obliged to listen to the loathsome addresses of a stranger to one's heart. I have

doubt fear

heard of girls persecuted as I am, who have appealed in behalf of their favoured lover to the generosity of his rival: suppose I were to try it. There stands the hated rival—an officer,
5 too!—but oh, how unlike my Beverley! I wonder he don't begin. Truly he seems a very negligent wooer! Quite at his ease, upon my word! I'll speak first. [*Aloud.*] Mr. Absolute.

ABSOLUTE. Madam. [*Turns around.*]
10 LYDIA. O heavens! Beverley!

ABSOLUTE. Hush!—hush, my life! Softly! Be not surprised.

LYDIA. I am so astonished! and so terrified! and so overjoyed! For heaven's sake! how
15 came you here?

ABSOLUTE. Briefly—I have deceived your aunt. I was informed that my new rival was to visit here this evening, and contriving to have him kept away, have passed myself on
20 *her* for Captain Absolute.

LYDIA. Oh, charming! And she really takes you for young Absolute?

ABSOLUTE. Oh, she's convinced of it.

LYDIA. Ha! ha! ha! I can't forbear laughing
25 to think how her sagacity is overreached!

ABSOLUTE. But we trifle with our precious moments. Such another opportunity may not occur. Then let me now conjure my kind, my condescending angel, to fix the time when I
30 may rescue her from undeserved persecution, and with a licensed warmth plead for my reward.

LYDIA. Will you then, Beverley, consent to forfeit that portion of my paltry wealth? that
35 burden on the wings of love?

ABSOLUTE. Oh, come to me—rich only thus —in loveliness. Bring no portion to me but thy love—'twill be generous in you, Lydia—for well you know, it is the only dower your poor
40 Beverley can repay.

LYDIA. How persuasive are his words! How charming will poverty be with him!

ABSOLUTE. Ah! my soul, what a life will we then live! Love shall be our idol and support!
45 We will worship him with a monastic strictness; abjuring all worldly toys, to center every thought and action there. Proud of calamity, we will enjoy the wreck of wealth; while the surrounding gloom of adversity shall make the flame of our pure love show doubly bright. By 50 heavens! I would fling all goods of fortune from me with a prodigal hand to enjoy the scene where I might clasp my Lydia to my bosom, and say, the world affords no smile to me—but here. [*Embracing her.*]—[*Aside.*] If 55 she holds out now the devil is in it!

LYDIA [*aside*]. Now could I fly with him to the Antipodes! but my persecution is not yet come to a crisis.

[*Enter* MRS. MALAPROP, *listening.*] 60

MRS. MALAPROP [*aside*]. I am impatient to know how the little hussy deports herself.

ABSOLUTE. So pensive, Lydia!—is then your warmth abated?

MRS. MALAPROP [*aside*]. *Warmth abated!* 65 So! she has been in a passion, I suppose.

LYDIA. No—nor ever can while I have life.

MRS. MALAPROP [*aside*]. An ill-tempered little devil! She'll be *in a passion all her life—* will she? 70

LYDIA. Think not the idle threats of my ridiculous aunt can ever have any weight with me.

MRS. MALAPROP [*aside*]. Very dutiful, upon my word! 75

LYDIA. Let her choice be Captain Absolute, but Beverley is mine.

MRS. MALAPROP [*aside*]. I am astonished at her assurance!—to his face—this is to his face!

ABSOLUTE. Thus then let me enforce my suit. 80 [*Kneeling.*]

MRS. MALAPROP [*aside*]. Aye—poor young man! down on his knees entreating for pity! I can contain no longer.—[*Aloud.*] Why, thou vixen! I have overheard you. 85

ABSOLUTE [*aside*]. Oh, confound her vigilance!

MRS. MALAPROP. Captain Absolute—I know not how to apologize for her shocking rudeness. 90

ABSOLUTE [*aside*]. So—all's safe, I find.— [*Aloud.*] I have hopes, Madam, that time will bring the young lady—

MRS. MALAPROP. Oh, there's nothing to be hoped for from her! She's as headstrong as an 95 allegory on the banks of Nile.

LYDIA. Nay, Madam, what do you charge me with now?

MRS. MALAPROP. Why, thou unblushing rebel—didn't you tell this gentleman to his face that you loved another better?—didn't you say you never would be his?

LYDIA. No, Madam—I did not.

MRS. MALAPROP. Good heavens! what assurance! Lydia, Lydia, you ought to know that lying don't become a young woman! Didn't you boast that Beverley—that stroller Beverley—possessed your heart? Tell me that, I say.

LYDIA. 'Tis true, Ma'am, and none but Beverley—

MRS. MALAPROP. Hold—hold, Assurance! you shall not be so rude.

ABSOLUTE. Nay, pray Mrs. Malaprop, don't stop the young lady's speech: she's very welcome to talk thus—it does not hurt *me* in the least, I assure you.

MRS. MALAPROP. You are *too* good, Captain —*too* amiably patient—but come with me, Miss. Let us see you again soon, Captain. Remember what we have fixed.

ABSOLUTE. I shall, Ma'am.

MRS. MALAPROP. Come, take a graceful leave of the gentleman.

LYDIA. May every blessing wait on my Beverley, my loved Bev—

MRS. MALAPROP. Hussy! I'll choke the word in your throat!—come along—come along.

[*Exeunt severally,* ABSOLUTE *kissing his hand to* LYDIA—MRS. MALAPROP *stopping her from speaking.*]

Scene iv

[ACRES's *lodgings.*]

[ACRES *and* DAVID, ACRES *as just dressed.*]

ACRES. Indeed, David—do you think I become it so?

DAVID. You are quite another creature, believe me, master, by the Mass! an' we've any luck we shall see the Devon monkeyrony in all the print-shops° in Bath!

ACRES. Dress *does* make a difference, David.

DAVID. 'Tis all in all, I think. Difference! why, an' you were to go now to Clod-Hall, I am certain the old lady wouldn't know you: Master Butler wouldn't believe his own eyes, and Mrs. Pickle would cry, "Lard presarve me!"—our dairy-maid would come giggling to the door, and I warrant Dolly Tester, your Honour's favourite, would blush like my waistcoat. Oons! I'll hold a gallon, there a'n't a dog in the house but would bark, and I question whether *Phillis* would wag a hair of her tail!

ACRES. Aye, David, there's nothing like polishing.

DAVID. So I says of your Honour's boots; but the boy never heeds me!

ACRES. But, David, has Mr. De-la-Grace been here? I must rub up my balancing, and chasing, and boring.°

DAVID. I'll call again, Sir.

ACRES. Do—and see if there are any letters for me at the post office.

DAVID. I will. By the Mass, I can't help looking at your head! If I hadn't been by at the cooking, I wish I may die if I should have known the dish again myself!

[*Exit.*]

[ACRES *comes forward, practising a dancing step.*]

ACRES. Sink, slide—coupee! Confound the first inventor of cotillions! say I—they are as bad as algebra to us country gentlemen. I can walk a minuet easy enough when I'm forced! and I have been accounted a good stick in a country-dance. Odds jigs and tabours! I never valued your cross-over to couple—figure in—right and left—and I'd foot it with e'er a captain in the county! But these outlandish heathen allemandes and cotillions are quite beyond me! I shall never prosper at 'em, that's sure. Mine are true-born English legs—they don't understand their curst French lingo! their *pas* this, and *pas* that, and *pas* t'other! D——n me! my feet dont' like to be called paws! No,

---

an' . . . print-shops if we've any luck, we shall see pictures of you, the Devonshire dandy, in all the print-shops

balancing . . . boring anglicized French dancing terms. Acres continues to use such terms and to corrupt some of them.

'tis certain I have most anti-Gallican toes!

[*Enter* SERVANT.]

SERVANT. Here is Sir Lucius O'Trigger to wait on you, Sir.

5 ACRES. Show him in.

[*Enter* SIR LUCIUS.]

SIR LUCIUS. Mr. Acres, I am delighted to embrace you.

ACRES. My dear Sir Lucius, I kiss your

10 hands.

SIR LUCIUS. Pray, my friend, what has brought you so suddenly to Bath?

ACRES. Faith! I have followed Cupid's Jack-a-Lantern, and find myself in a quagmire at

15 last. In short, I have been very ill-used, Sir Lucius. I don't choose to mention names, but look on me as on a very ill-used gentleman.

SIR LUCIUS. Pray, what is the case? I ask no names.

20 ACRES. Mark me, Sir Lucius, I fall as deep as need be in love with a young lady—her friends take my part—I follow her to Bath—send word of my arrival, and receive answer that the lady is to be otherwise disposed of.

25 This, Sir Lucius, I call being ill-used.

SIR LUCIUS. Very ill, upon my conscience. Pray, can you divine the cause of it?

ACRES. Why, there's the matter: she has another lover, one Beverley, who, I am told, is

30 now in Bath. Odds slanders and lies! he must be at the bottom of it.

SIR LUCIUS. A rival in the case, is there? And you think he has supplanted you unfairly?

ACRES. Unfairly!—to be sure he has. He

35 never could have done it fairly.

SIR LUCIUS. Then sure you know what is to be done!

ACRES. Not I, upon my soul!

SIR LUCIUS. We wear no swords here, but

40 you understand me.

ACRES. What! fight him?

SIR LUCIUS. Aye, to be sure: what can I mean else?

ACRES. But he has given me no provocation.

45 SIR LUCIUS. Now, I think he has given you the greatest provocation in the world. Can a man commit a more heinous offence against another than to fall in love with the same woman? Oh, by my soul, it is the most unpardonable breach of friendship!

50 ACRES. Breach of friendship! Aye, aye; but I have no acquaintance with this man. I never saw him in my life.

SIR LUCIUS. That's no argument at all—he has the less right then to take such a liberty.

55 ACRES. 'Gad, that's true. I grow full of anger, Sir Lucius! I fire apace! Odds hilts and blades! I find a man may have a deal of valour in him and not know it! But couldn't I contrive to have a little right of my side?

60 SIR LUCIUS. What the devil signifies *right* when your *honour* is concerned? Do you think Achilles, or my little Alexander the Great ever inquired where the right lay? No, by my soul, they drew their broadswords, and left the lazy

65 sons of peace to settle the justice of it.

ACRES. Your words are a grenadier's march to my heart! I believe courage must be catching! I certainly do feel a kind of valour rising, as it were—a kind of courage, as I may say.

70 Odds flints, pans, and triggers! I'll challenge him directly.

SIR LUCIUS. Ah, my little friend! if we had Blunderbuss-Hall here—I could show you a range of ancestry, in the O'Trigger line, that

75 would furnish the New Room, every one of whom had killed his man! For though the mansion-house and dirty acres have slipped through my fingers, I thank heaven our honour, and the family-pictures, are as fresh

80 as ever.

ACRES. O Sir Lucius! I have had ancestors too! every man of 'em colonel or captain in the militia! Odds balls and barrels! say no more—I'm braced for it. The thunder of your words

85 has soured the milk of human kindness in my breast! Z——ds! as the man in the play says, "I could do such deeds!"

SIR LUCIUS. Come, come, there must be no passion at all in the case—these things should

90 always be done civilly.

ACRES. I must be in a passion, Sir Lucius—I must be in a rage. Dear Sir Lucius, let me be in a rage, if you love me. Come, here's pen and paper. [*Sits down to write*.] I would the ink

95 were red! Indite, I say, indite! How shall I

begin? Odds bullets and blades! I'll write a good bold hand, however.

SIR LUCIUS. Pray compose yourself.

ACRES. Come now, shall I begin with an oath? Do, Sir Lucius, let me begin with a damme.

SIR LUCIUS. Pho! pho! do the thing decently and like a Christian. Begin now—"*Sir*"—

ACRES. That's too civil by half.

SIR LUCIUS. "*To prevent the confusion that might arise*"—

ACRES. Well—

SIR LUCIUS. "*From our both addressing the same lady*"—

ACRES. Aye—there's the reason—"*same lady*"—Well—

SIR LUCIUS. "*I shall expect the honour of your company*"—

ACRES. Z——ds! I'm not asking him to dinner.

SIR LUCIUS. Pray be easy.

ACRES. Well then—"*honour of your company*"—

SIR LUCIUS. "*To settle our pretensions*"—

ACRES. Well—

SIR LUCIUS. Let me see—aye, King's-Mead-Fields will do—"*In King's-Mead-Fields.*"

ACRES. So that's done.—Well, I'll fold it up presently; my own crest—a hand and dagger shall be the seal.

SIR LUCIUS. You see now, this little explanation will put a stop at once to all confusion or misunderstanding that might arise between you.

ACRES. Aye, we fight to prevent any misunderstanding.

SIR LUCIUS. Now, I'll leave you to fix your own time. Take my advice, and you'll decide it this evening if you can; then let the worst come of it, 'twill be off your mind to-morrow.

ACRES. Very true.

SIR LUCIUS. So I shall see nothing more of you, unless it be by letter, till the evening. I would do myself the honour to carry your message; but, to tell you a secret, I believe I shall have just another affair on my own hands. There is a gay captain here who put a jest on me lately at the expense of my country, and I only want to fall in with the gentleman to call him out.

ACRES. By my valour, I should like to see you fight first! Odd's life! I should like to see you kill him, if it was only to get a little lesson.

SIR LUCIUS. I shall be very proud of instructing you. Well for the present—but remember now, when you meet your antagonist, do everything in a mild and agreeable manner. Let your courage be as keen, but at the same time as polished, as your sword.

[*Exeunt severally.*]

ACT IV

Scene i

[ACRES's *lodgings.*]

[ACRES *and* DAVID.]

DAVID. Then, by the Mass, Sir! I would do no such thing—ne'er a Sir Lucius O'Trigger in the kingdom should make me fight, when I wa'n't so minded. Oons! what will the old lady say when she hears o't!

ACRES. Ah! David, if you had heard Sir Lucius! Odds sparks and flames! he would have roused your valour.

DAVID. Not he, indeed. I hates such bloodthirsty cormorants. Look'ee, master, if you'd wanted a bout at boxing, quarterstaff, or shortstaff, I should never be the man to bid you cry off: but for your curst sharps and snaps,° I never knew any good come of 'em.

ACRES. But my honour, David, my honour! I must be very careful of my honour.

DAVID. Aye, by the Mass! and I would be very careful of it; and I think in return my *honour* couldn't do less than to be very careful of *me*.

ACRES. Odds blades! David, no gentleman will ever risk the loss of his honour!

DAVID. I say then, it would be but civil in *honour* never to risk the loss of a *gentleman*. Look'ee, master, this *honour* seems to me to be a marvellous false friend; aye, truly, a very courtier-like servant. Put the case, I was a

sharps and snaps   swords and pistols

gentleman (which, thank God, no one can say of me); well—my honour makes me quarrel with another gentleman of my acquaintance. So—we fight. (Pleasant enough that.) Boh!—I 5 kill him (the more's my luck). Now, pray who gets the profit of it? Why, my *honour*. But put the case that he kills me!—by the Mass! I go to the worms, and my honour whips over to my enemy!

10 ACRES. No, David—in that case—odds crowns and laurels!—your honour follows you to the grave.

DAVID. Now, that's just the place where I could make a shift to do without it.

15 ACRES. Z——ds, David, you're a coward! It doesn't become my valour to listen to you. What, shall I disgrace my ancestors? Think of that, David—think what it would be to disgrace my ancestors!

20 DAVID. Under favour, the surest way of not disgracing them is to keep as long as you can out of their company. Look'ee now, master, to go to them in such haste—with an ounce of lead in your brains—I should think might as 25 well be let alone. Our ancestors are very good kind of folks; but they are the last people I should choose to have a visiting acquaintance with.

ACRES. But David, now, you don't think 30 there is such very, very, *very* great danger, hey? Odds life! people often fight without any mischief done!

DAVID. By the Mass, I think 'tis ten to one against you! Oons! here to meet some lion-35 headed fellow, I warrant, with his d——n'd double-barrelled swords, and cut-and-thrust pistols! Lord bless us! it makes me tremble to think o't. Those be such desperate bloody-minded weapons! Well, I never could abide 40 'em! from a child I never could fancy 'em! I suppose there a'n't so merciless a beast in the world as your loaded pistol!

ACRES. Z——ds! I *won't* be afraid! Odds fire and fury! you sha'n't make me afraid! Here is 45 the challenge, and I have sent for my dear friend Jack Absolute to carry it for me.

DAVID. Aye, i' the name of mischief, let *him* be the messenger. For my part, I wouldn't lend

a hand to it for the best horse in your stable. By the Mass! it don't look like another letter! 50 It is, as I may say, a designing and malicious-looking letter! and I warrant smells of gun-powder, like a soldier's pouch! Oons! I wouldn't swear it mayn't go off!

ACRES. Out, you poltroon! You ha'n't the 55 valour of a grasshopper.

DAVID. Well, I say no more—'twill be sad news, to be sure, at Clod-Hall!—but I ha' done. How Phillis will howl when she hears of it! Aye, poor bitch, she little thinks what 60 shooting her master's going after! And I war-rant old Crop, who has carried your Honour, field and road, these ten years, will curse the hour he was born. [*Whimpering.*]

ACRES. It won't do, David—I am determined 65 to fight—so get along, you coward, while I'm in the mind.

[*Enter* SERVANT.]

SERVANT. Captain Absolute, Sir.

ACRES. Oh! show him up. 70

[*Exit* SERVANT.]

DAVID. Well, heaven send we be all alive this time to-morrow.

ACRES. What's that! Don't provoke me, David! 75

DAVID. Good-bye, master. [*Whimpering.*]

ACRES. Get along, you cowardly, dastardly, croaking raven.

[*Exit* DAVID.]

[*Enter* ABSOLUTE.] 80

ABSOLUTE. What's the matter, Bob?

ACRES. A vile, sheep-hearted blockhead! If I hadn't the valour of St. George and the dragon to boot—

ABSOLUTE. But what did you want with me, 85 Bob?

ACRES. Oh! There—[*gives him the chal-lenge*].

ABSOLUTE. "To Ensign Beverley." [*Aside.*] So—what's going on now? [*Aloud.*] Well, 90 what's this?

ACRES. A challenge!

ABSOLUTE. Indeed! Why, you won't fight him, will you, Bob?

ACRES. 'Egad, but I will, Jack. Sir Lucius has 95 wrought me to it. He has left me full of rage, and I'll fight this evening, that so much good passion mayn't be wasted.

ABSOLUTE. But what have I to do with this?

ACRES. Why, as I think you know something of this fellow, I want you to find him out for me, and give him this mortal defiance.

ABSOLUTE. Well, give it to me, and trust me he gets it.

ACRES. Thank you, my dear friend, my dear Jack; but it is giving you a great deal of trouble.

ABSOLUTE. Not in the least—I beg you won't mention it. No trouble in the world, I assure you.

ACRES. You are very kind. What it is to have a friend! You couldn't be my second—could you, Jack?

ABSOLUTE. Why no, Bob—not in *this* affair. It would not be quite so proper.

ACRES. Well then, I must get my friend Sir Lucius. I shall have your good wishes, however, Jack.

ABSOLUTE. Whenever he meets you, believe me.

[*Enter* SERVANT.]

SERVANT. Sir Anthony Absolute is below, inquiring for the Captain.

ABSOLUTE. I'll come instantly. Well, my little hero, success attend you. [*Going.*]

ACRES. Stay—stay, Jack. If Beverley should ask you what kind of a man your friend Acres is, do tell him I am a devil of a fellow—will you, Jack?

ABSOLUTE. To be sure I shall. I'll say you are a determined dog—hey, Bob?

ACRES. Aye, do, do—and if that frightens him, 'egad, perhaps he mayn't come. So tell him I generally kill a man a week—will you, Jack?

ABSOLUTE. I will, I will; I'll say you are called in the country "Fighting Bob!"

ACRES. Right, right—'tis all to prevent mischief; for I don't want to take his life if I clear my honour.

ABSOLUTE. No!—that's very kind of you.

ACRES. Why, you don't wish me to kill him —do you, Jack?

ABSOLUTE. No, upon my soul, I do not. But

a devil of a fellow, hey? [*Going.*]

ACRES. True, true—but stay—stay, Jack. You may add that you never saw me in such a rage before—a most devouring rage!

ABSOLUTE. I will, I will.

ACRES. Remember, Jack—a determined dog!

ABSOLUTE. Aye, aye, "Fighting Bob!"

[*Exeunt severally.*]

Scene ii

[MRS. MALAPROP's *lodgings*.]

[MRS. MALAPROP *and* LYDIA.]

MRS. MALAPROP. Why, thou perverse one! tell me what you can object to him? Isn't he a handsome man? tell me that. A genteel man? a pretty figure of a man?

LYDIA [*aside*]. She little thinks whom she is praising!—[*Aloud.*] So is Beverley, Ma'am.

MRS. MALAPROP. No caparisons, Miss, if you please! Caparisons don't become a young woman. No! Captain Absolute is indeed a fine gentleman!

LYDIA [*aside*]. Aye, the Captain Absolute *you* have seen.

MRS. MALAPROP. Then he's *so* well bred; *so* full of alacrity, and adulation! and has *so* much to say for himself—in such good language, too! His physiognomy so grammatical! Then his presence is so noble! I protest, when I saw him, I thought of what Hamlet says° in the play: "Hesperian curls!—the front of *Job* himself! An eye, like *March*, to threaten at command—a station, like Harry Mercury, new"—something about kissing on a hill— however, the similitude struck me directly.

LYDIA [*aside*]. How enraged she'll be presently when she discovers her mistake!

[*Enter* SERVANT.]

SERVANT. Sir Anthony and Captain Absolute are below, Ma'am.

MRS. MALAPROP. Show them up here.

[*Exit* SERVANT.]

---

what Hamlet says cf. Hamlet, III.iv, 56–59: "Hyperion's curls, the front of Jove himself, An eye like Mars, to threaten and command; A station like the herald Mercury New-lighted on a heaven-kissing hill."

Now, Lydia, I insist on your behaving as becomes a young woman. Show your good breeding at least, though you have forgot your duty.

LYDIA. Madam, I have told you my resolution; I shall not only give him no encouragement, but I won't even speak to, or look at him. [*Flings herself into a chair with her face from the door.*]

[*Enter* SIR ANTHONY *and* ABSOLUTE.]

SIR ANTHONY. Here we are, Mrs. Malaprop, come to mitigate the frowns of unrelenting beauty—and difficulty enough I had to bring this fellow. I don't know what's the matter; but if I hadn't held him by force, he'd have given me the slip.

MRS. MALAPROP. You have infinite trouble, Sir Anthony, in the affair. I am ashamed for the cause!—[*Aside to her.*] Lydia, Lydia, rise, I beseech you!—pay your respects!

SIR ANTHONY. I hope, Madam, that Miss Languish has reflected on the worth of this gentleman, and the regard due to her aunt's choice, and my alliance.—[*Aside to him.*] Now, Jack, speak to her!

ABSOLUTE [*aside*]. What the devil shall I do! —[*Aloud.*] You see, Sir, she won't even look at me whilst you are here. I knew she wouldn't! I told you so. Let me entreat you, Sir, to leave us together!

[ABSOLUTE *seems to expostulate with his father.*]

LYDIA [*aside*]. I wonder I ha'n't heard my aunt exclaim yet! Sure she can't have looked at him! Perhaps their regimentals are alike, and she is something blind.

SIR ANTHONY. I say, Sir, I won't stir a foot yet!

MRS. MALAPROP. I am sorry to say, Sir Anthony, that my affluence over my niece is very small.—[*Aside to her.*] Turn round, Lydia; I blush for you!

SIR ANTHONY. May I not flatter myself that Miss Languish will assign what cause of dislike she can have to my son! Why don't you begin, Jack?—[*Aside to him.*] Speak, you puppy—speak!

MRS. MALAPROP. It is impossible, Sir Anthony, she can have any. She will not *say* she

has.—[*Aside to her.*] Answer, hussy! why don't you answer?

SIR ANTHONY. Then, Madam, I trust that a childish and hasty predilection will be no bar to Jack's happiness.—[*Aside to him.*] Z——ds! Sirrah! why don't you speak?

LYDIA [*aside*]. I think my lover seems as little inclined to conversation as myself. How strangely blind my aunt must be!

ABSOLUTE. Hem! hem!—Madam—hem!— [ABSOLUTE *attempts to speak, then returns to* SIR ANTHONY.]—Faith! Sir, I am so confounded! and so—so—confused! I told you I should be so, Sir, I knew it. The—the—tremor of my passion entirely takes away my presence of mind.

SIR ANTHONY. But it don't take away your voice, fool, does it? Go up, and speak to her directly!

[ABSOLUTE *makes signs to* MRS. MALAPROP *to leave them together.*]

MRS. MALAPROP. Sir Anthony, shall we leave them together?—[*Aside to her.*] Ah! you stubborn little vixen!

SIR ANTHONY. Not yet, Ma'am, not yet!— [*Aside to him.*] What the devil are you at? Unlock your jaws, Sirrah, or—

[ABSOLUTE *draws near* LYDIA.]

ABSOLUTE [*aside*]. Now heaven send she may be too sullen to look round! I must disguise my voice.—[*Speaks in a low hoarse tone.*] Will not Miss Languish lend an ear to the mild accents of true love? Will not—

SIR ANTHONY. What the devil ails the fellow? Why don't you speak out?—not stand croaking like a frog in a quinsy!

ABSOLUTE. The—the—excess of my awe, and my—my—my modesty quite choke me!

SIR ANTHONY. Ah! your *modesty* again! I'll tell you what, Jack, if you don't speak out directly, and glibly, too, I shall be in such a rage! Mrs. Malaprop, I wish the lady would favour us with something more than a sidefront!

[MRS. MALAPROP *seems to chide* LYDIA.]

ABSOLUTE. So! All will out I see! [*Goes up to* LYDIA, *speaks softly.*] Be not surprised, my Lydia; suppress all surprise at present.

LYDIA [*aside*]. Heavens! 'tis Beverley's voice! Sure he can't have imposed on Sir Anthony, too!—[*Looks round by degrees, then starts up.*] Is this possible—my Beverley!—how can this be?—my Beverley?

ABSOLUTE [*aside*]. Ah! 'tis all over.

SIR ANTHONY. Beverley!—the devil!—Beverley! What can the girl mean? This is my son, Jack Absolute!

MRS. MALAPROP. For shame, hussy! for shame! your head runs so on that fellow that you have him always in your eyes! Beg Captain Absolute's pardon directly.

LYDIA. I see no Captain Absolute, but my loved Beverley!

SIR ANTHONY. Z——ds! the girl's mad!—her brain's turned by reading!

MRS. MALAPROP. O' my conscience, I believe so! What do you mean by Beverley, hussy? You saw Captain Absolute before to-day; there he is—your husband that shall be.

LYDIA. With all my soul, Ma'am. When I refuse my Beverley—

SIR ANTHONY. Oh! she's as mad as Bedlam! Or has this fellow been playing us a rogue's trick! Come here, Sirrah!—who the devil are you?

ABSOLUTE. Faith, Sir, I am not quite clear myself, but I'll endeavour to recollect.

SIR ANTHONY. Are you my son, or not? Answer for your mother, you dog, if you won't for me.

MRS. MALAPROP. Aye, Sir, who are you? Oh mercy! I begin to suspect!—

ABSOLUTE [*aside*]. Ye Powers of Impudence befriend me!—[*Aloud.*] Sir Anthony, most assuredly I am your wife's son; and that I sincerely believe myself to be *yours* also, I hope my duty has always shown.—Mrs. Malaprop, I am your most respectful admirer—and shall be proud to add *affectionate nephew*. —I need not tell my Lydia, that she sees her faithful Beverley, who, knowing the singular generosity of her temper, assumed that name, and a station which has proved a test of the most disinterested love, which he now hopes to enjoy in a more elevated character.

LYDIA [*sullenly*]. So!—there will be no elopement after all!

SIR ANTHONY. Upon my soul, Jack, thou art a very impudent fellow! to do you justice, I think I never saw a piece of more consummate assurance!

ABSOLUTE. Oh you flatter me, Sir—you compliment—'tis my *modesty* you know, Sir—my *modesty* that has stood in my way.

SIR ANTHONY. Well, I am glad you are not the dull, insensible varlet you pretended to be, however! I'm glad you have made a fool of your father, you dog—I am. So this was your *penitence*, your *duty*, and *obedience*! I thought it was d——d sudden! You *never heard their names before*, not you! *What!* The *Languishes of Worcestershire*, hey?—*if you could please me in the affair, 'twas all you desired!*—Ah! you dissembling villain! What!—[*pointing to* LYDIA] *she squints, don't she?—a little red-haired girl!*—hey? Why, you hypocritical young rascal! I wonder you a'n't ashamed to hold up your head!

ABSOLUTE. 'Tis with difficulty, Sir. I *am* confused—very much confused, as you must perceive.

MRS. MALAPROP. O lud! Sir Anthony!—a new light breaks in upon me! Hey! how! what! Captain, did *you* write the letters then? What! —am I to thank *you* for the elegant compilation of *"an old weather-beaten she-dragon"*— hey? O mercy! was it *you* that reflected on my *parts of speech*?

ABSOLUTE. Dear Sir! my modesty will be overpowered at last, if you don't assist me. I shall certainly not be able to stand it!

SIR ANTHONY. Come, come, Mrs. Malaprop, we must forget and forgive. Odd's life! matters have taken so clever a turn all of a sudden, that I could find in my heart to be so good-humoured! and so gallant!—hey! Mrs. Malaprop!

MRS. MALAPROP. Well, Sir Anthony, since *you* desire it, we will not anticipate the past; so mind, young people: our retrospection will now be all to the future.

SIR ANTHONY. Come, we must leave them together; Mrs. Malaprop, they long to fly into each other's arms. I warrant!—[*Aside.*] Jack—isn't the cheek as I said, hey?—and the eye, you rogue!—and the lip—hey? Come, Mrs.

Malaprop, we'll not disturb their tenderness—
theirs is the time of life for happiness!—
[*Sings.*] "Youth's the season made for joy"—
hey! Odd's life! I'm in such spirits, I don't
5 know what I couldn't do! Permit me, Ma'am.—
[*Gives his hand to* Mrs. Malaprop. *Sings.*]
Tol-de-rol!—'gad, I should like a little fooling
myself. Tol-de-rol! de-rol! [*Exit singing, and
handing* Mrs. Malaprop.]
10 [Lydia *sits sullenly in her chair.*]
Absolute [*aside*]. So much thought bodes
me no good.—[*Aloud.*] So grave, Lydia!
Lydia. Sir!
Absolute [*aside*]. So!—egad! I thought as
15 much! That d——d monosyllable has froze
me!—[*Aloud.*] What, Lydia, now that we are
as happy in our friends' consent, as in our
mutual vows—
Lydia [*peevishly*]. Friends' consent, indeed!
20 Absolute. Come, come, we must lay aside
some of our romance—a little *wealth* and comfort may be endured after all. And for your
fortune, the lawyers shall make such settle-
ments as—
25 Lydia. *Lawyers!* I *hate* lawyers!
Absolute. Nay then, we will not wait for
their lingering forms but instantly procure the
licence, and—
Lydia. The *licence!* I *hate* license!
30 Absolute. O my love! be not so unkind!
Thus let me intreat—[*kneeling*].
Lydia. Pshaw! what signifies kneeling when
you know I *must* have you?
Absolute [*rising*]. Nay, Madam, there shall
35 be no constraint upon your inclinations, I
promise you. If I have lost your heart, I resign
the rest.—[*Aside.*] 'Gad, I must try what a
little *spirit* will do.
Lydia [*rising*]. Then, Sir, let me tell you, the
40 interest you had there was acquired by a mean,
unmanly imposition, and deserves the punishment of fraud. What, you have been treating
me like a child!—humouring my romance! and
laughing, I suppose, at your success!
45 Absolute. You wrong me, Lydia, you wrong
me. Only hear—
Lydia. So, while *I* fondly imagined we were
deceiving my relations, and flattered myself
that I should outwit and incense them all—be-

hold! my hopes are to be crushed at once, by 50
my aunt's consent and approbation!—and *I*
am myself the only dupe at last! [*Walking
about in heat.*] But here, Sir, here is the picture
—Beverley's picture! [*taking a miniature from
her bosom*] which I have worn, night and day, 55
in spite of threats and entreaties! There, Sir
[*flings it to him*]—and be assured I throw the
original from my heart as easily.
Absolute. Nay, nay, Ma'am, we will not
differ as to that. Here [*taking out a picture*], 60
here is Miss Lydia Languish. What a difference! Aye, *there* is the heavenly assenting
smile that first gave soul and spirit to my
hopes!—those are the lips which sealed a vow,
as yet scarce dry in Cupid's calendar!—and 65
there, the half resentful blush that *would* have
checked the ardour of my thanks. Well, all
that's past—all over indeed! There, Madam, in
beauty, that copy is not equal to you, but in my
mind its merit over the original, in being still 70
the same, is such—that—I cannot find in my
heart to part with it. [*Puts it up again.*]
Lydia [*softening*]. 'Tis *your own* doing, Sir.
I—I—I suppose you are perfectly satisfied.
Absolute. Oh, most certainly. Sure now this 75
is much better than being in love! Ha! ha! ha!
—there's some spirit in *this!* What signifies
breaking some scores of solemn promises, half
an hundred vows, under one's hand, with the
marks of a dozen or two angels to witness!— 80
all that's of no consequence, you know. To be
sure, people will say that Miss didn't know her
own mind—but never mind that: or perhaps
they may be ill-natured enough to hint that the
gentleman grew tired of the lady and forsook 85
her—but don't let that fret you.
Lydia. There's no bearing his insolence.
[*Bursts into tears.*]
[*Enter* Mrs. Malaprop *and* Sir Anthony.]
Mrs. Malaprop [*entering*]. Come, we must 90
interrupt your billing and cooing a while.
Lydia. This is worse than your treachery
and deceit, you base ingrate! [*Sobbing.*]
Sir Anthony. What the devil's the matter
now! Z——ds! Mrs. Malaprop, this is the *odd- 95
est billing* and *cooing* I ever heard! But what
the deuce is the meaning of it? I'm quite
astonished!

ABSOLUTE. Ask the lady, Sir.

MRS. MALAPROP. Oh mercy! I'm quite anal-
ysed, for my part! Why, Lydia, what is the
reason of this?

5 LYDIA. Ask the *gentleman*, Ma'am.

SIR ANTHONY. Z——ds! I shall be in a
frenzy!—Why, Jack, you are not come out to
be anyone else, are you?

MRS. MALAPROP. Aye, Sir, there's no more
10 *trick*, is there? You are not like Cerberus, *three*
gentlemen at once, are you?

ABSOLUTE. You'll not let me speak. I say the
lady can account for this much better than I
can.

15 LYDIA. Ma'am, you once commanded me
never to think of Beverley again. There is the
man—I now obey you:—for, from this moment I renounce him forever.

[*Exit* LYDIA.]

20 MRS. MALAPROP. Oh mercy! and miracles!
what a turn here is! Why, sure, Captain, you
haven't behaved disrespectfully to my niece?

SIR ANTHONY. Ha! ha! ha!—ha! ha! ha!—
now I see it—ha! ha! ha!—now I see it—you
25 have been too lively, Jack.

ABSOLUTE. Nay, Sir, upon my word—

SIR ANTHONY. Come, no lying, Jack—I'm
sure 'twas so.

MRS. MALAPROP. O lud! Sir Anthony! Oh fie,
30 Captain!

ABSOLUTE. Upon my soul, Ma'am—

SIR ANTHONY. Come, no excuses, Jack; why,
your father, you rogue, was so before you: the
blood of the Absolutes was always impatient.
35 Ha! ha! ha! poor little Lydia!—why, you've
frightened her, you dog, you have.

ABSOLUTE. By all that's good, Sir—

SIR ANTHONY. Z——ds! say no more, I tell
you. Mrs. Malaprop shall make your peace.—
40 You must make his peace, Mrs. Malaprop; you
must tell her 'tis Jack's way—tell her 'tis all
our ways—it runs in the blood of our family!
Come, away, Jack—ha! ha! ha! Mrs. Malaprop
—a young villain! [*Pushes him out.*]

45 MRS. MALAPROP. Oh, Sir Anthony! Oh fie,
Captain!

[*Exeunt severally.*]

Scene iii

[*The North Parade.*]

[*Enter* SIR LUCIUS O'TRIGGER.]

SIR LUCIUS. I wonder where this Captain 50
Absolute hides himself. Upon my conscience!
these officers are always in one's way in love-
affairs. I remember I might have married Lady
Dorothy Carmine, if it had not been for a little
rogue of a major, who ran away with her before 55
she could get a sight of me! And I wonder too
what it is the ladies can see in them to be so
fond of them—unless it be a touch of the old
serpent in 'em, that makes the little creatures
be caught, like vipers, with a bit of red cloth.— 60
Hah!—isn't this the Captain coming?—faith it
is! There is a probability of succeeding about
that fellow that is mighty provoking! Who the
devil is he talking to? [*Steps aside.*]

[*Enter* CAPTAIN ABSOLUTE.] 65

ABSOLUTE. To what fine purpose I have been
plotting! A noble reward for all my schemes,
upon my soul! A little gypsy! I did not think
her romance could have made her so d——d
absurd either. 'Sdeath, I never was in a worse 70
humour in my life! I could cut my own throat,
or any other person's, with the greatest pleasure in the world!

SIR LUCIUS. Oh, faith! I'm in the luck of it—
I never could have found him in a sweeter tem- 75
per for my purpose—to be sure I'm just come
in the nick! Now to enter into conversation
with him, and so quarrel genteelly. [SIR LUCIUS
goes up to ABSOLUTE.]—With regard to that
matter, Captain, I must beg leave to differ in 80
opinion with you.

ABSOLUTE. Upon my word then, you must be
a very subtle disputant, because, Sir, I happened just then to be giving no opinion at all.

SIR LUCIUS. That's no reason. For give me 85
leave to tell you, a man may *think* an untruth
as well as *speak* one.

ABSOLUTE. Very true, Sir, but if a man never
utters his thoughts I should think they might
stand a chance of escaping controversy. 90

SIR LUCIUS. Then, Sir, you differ in opinion
with me, which amounts to the same thing.

ABSOLUTE. Hark'ee, Sir Lucius—if I had not before known you to be a gentleman, upon my soul, I should not have discovered it at this interview, for what you can drive at, unless 5 you mean to quarrel with me, I cannot conceive!

SIR LUCIUS. I humbly thank you, Sir, for the quickness of your apprehension. [*Bowing.*] You have named the very thing I would be at.

10 ABSOLUTE. Very well, Sir—I shall certainly not balk your inclinations—but I should be glad you would please to explain your motives.

SIR LUCIUS. Pray, Sir, be easy: the quarrel is a very pretty quarrel as it stands—we should 15 only spoil it by trying to explain it. However, your memory is very short or you could not have forgot an affront you passed on me within this week. So no more, but name your time and place.

20 ABSOLUTE. Well, Sir, since you are so bent on it, the sooner the better; let it be this evening —here, by the Spring-Gardens. We shall scarcely be interrupted.

SIR LUCIUS. Faith! that same interruption in 25 affairs of this nature shows very great ill-breeding. I don't know what's the reason, but in England, if a thing of this kind gets wind, people make such a pother that a gentleman can never fight in peace and quietness. How-30 ever, if it's the same to you, Captain, I should take it as a particular kindness if you'd let us meet in King's-Mead-Fields, as a little business will call me there about six o'clock, and I may dispatch both matters at once.

35 ABSOLUTE. 'Tis the same to me exactly. A little after six, then, we will discuss this matter more seriously.

SIR LUCIUS. If you please, Sir, there will be very pretty small-sword light, though it won't 40 do for a long shot. So that matter's settled! and my mind's at ease!

[*Exit* SIR LUCIUS.]

[*Enter* FAULKLAND, *meeting* ABSOLUTE.]

ABSOLUTE. Well met. I was going to look for 45 you. O Faulkland! all the daemons of spite and disappointment have conspired against me! I'm so vexed that if I had not the prospect of a resource in being knocked o' the head by and by, I should scarce have spirits to tell you the cause.   50

FAULKLAND. What can you mean? Has Lydia changed her mind? I should have thought her duty and inclination would now have pointed to the same object.

ABSOLUTE. Aye, just as the eyes do of a per- 55 son who squints: when her love-eye was fixed on me—t'other—her eye of duty, was finely obliqued:—but when duty bid her point that the same way—off t'other turned on a swivel, and secured its retreat with a frown!   60

FAULKLAND. But what's the resource you—

ABSOLUTE. Oh, to wind up the whole, a good-natured Irishman here has [*mimicking* SIR LUCIUS] begged leave to have the pleasure of cutting my throat, and I mean to indulge him 65 —that's all.

FAULKLAND. Prithee, be serious.

ABSOLUTE. 'Tis fact, upon my soul. Sir Lucius O'Trigger—you know him by sight—for some affront, which I am sure I never intended, has 70 obliged me to meet him this evening at six o'clock: 'tis on that account I wished to see you —you must go with me.

FAULKLAND. Nay, there must be some mistake, sure. Sir Lucius shall explain himself— 75 and I dare say matters may be accommodated. But this evening, did you say? I wish it had been any other time.

ABSOLUTE. Why? there will be light enough. There will (as Sir Lucius says) "be very pretty 80 small-sword light, though it won't do for a long shot." Confound his long shots!

FAULKLAND. But I am myself a good deal ruffled by a difference I have had with Julia. My vile tormenting temper has made me treat 85 her so cruelly that I shall not be myself till we are reconciled.

ABSOLUTE. By heavens, Faulkland, you don't deserve her.

[*Enter* SERVANT, *gives* FAULKLAND *a letter.*] 90

FAULKLAND. O Jack! this is from Julia. I dread to open it. I fear it may be to take a last leave—perhaps to bid me return her letters and restore—Oh! how I suffer for my folly!

ABSOLUTE. Here—let me see. [*Takes the letter and opens it.*] Aye, a final sentence indeed! —'tis all over with you, faith!

FAULKLAND. Nay, Jack—don't keep me in 5 suspense.

ABSOLUTE. Hear then.—"*As I am convinced that my dear* FAULKLAND'*s own reflections have already upbraided him for his last unkindness to me, I will not add a word on the subject. I* 10 *wish to speak with you as soon as possible.— Yours ever and truly,* JULIA."—There's stubbornness and resentment for you! [*Gives him the letter.*] Why, man, you don't seem one whit happier at this.

15 FAULKLAND. Oh, yes, I am—but—but—

ABSOLUTE. Confound your *buts*. You never hear anything that would make another man bless himself, but you immediately d——n it with a *but*.

20 FAULKLAND. Now, Jack, as you are my friend, own honestly—don't you think there is something forward, something indelicate, in this haste to forgive? Women should never sue for reconciliation: that should always come from 25 us. They should retain their coldness till *wooed* to kindness—and their *pardon*, like their *love*, should "not unsought be won."

ABSOLUTE. I have not patience to listen to you—thou'rt incorrigible!—so say no more on 30 the subject. I must go to settle a few matters. Let me see you before six—remember—at my lodgings. A poor industrious devil like me, who have toiled, and drudged, and plotted to gain my ends, and am at last disappointed by other 35 people's folly, may in pity be allowed to swear and grumble a little; but a captious sceptic in love, a slave to fretfulness and whim, who has no difficulties but of his own creating, is a subject more fit for ridicule than compassion!

40 [*Exit* ABSOLUTE.]

FAULKLAND. I feel his reproaches, yet I would not change this too exquisite nicety for the gross content with which *he* tramples on the thorns of love. His engaging me in this duel 45 has started an idea in my head, which I will instantly pursue. I'll use it as the touchstone of Julia's sincerity and disinterestedness. If her love prove pure and sterling ore, my name will rest on it with honour!—and once I've stamped it there, I lay aside my doubts forever—; but 50 if the dross of selfishness, the alloy of pride predominate, 'twill be best to leave her as a toy for some less cautious fool to sigh for.

[*Exit* FAULKLAND.]

ACT V

Scene i

[JULIA'*s dressing-room.*] 55

[JULIA *sola.*]

JULIA. How this message has alarmed me! What dreadful accident can he mean? why such charge to be alone? O Faulkland! how many unhappy moments, how many tears, 60 have you cost me!

[*Enter* FAULKLAND.]

JULIA. What means this?—why this caution, Faulkland?

FAULKLAND. Alas! Julia, I am come to take a 65 long farewell.

JULIA. Heavens! what do you mean?

FAULKLAND. You see before you a wretch whose life is forfeited. Nay, start not! the infirmity of my temper has drawn all this misery 70 on me. I left you fretful and passionate—an untoward accident drew me into a quarrel—the event is that I must fly this kingdom instantly. O Julia, had I been so fortunate as to have called you mine entirely before this mischance 75 had fallen on me, I should not so deeply dread my banishment!

JULIA. My soul is oppressed with sorrow at the nature of your misfortune: had these adverse circumstances arisen from a less fatal 80 cause, I should have felt strong comfort in the thought that I could now chase from your bosom every doubt of the warm sincerity of my love. My heart has long known no other guardian. I now entrust my person to your 85 honour—we will fly together. When safe from pursuit, my father's will may be fulfilled, and I receive a legal claim to be the partner of your sorrows, and tenderest comforter. Then on the bosom of your wedded Julia, you may lull your 90 keen regret to slumbering; while virtuous love, with a cherub's hand, shall smooth the brow of upbraiding thought, and pluck the thorn from compunction.

FAULKLAND. O Julia! I am bankrupt in gratitude! But the time is so pressing, it calls on
5 you for so hasty a resolution—would you not wish some hours to weigh the advantages you forego, and what little compensation poor Faulkland can make you beside his solitary love?

10 JULIA. I ask not a moment. No, Faulkland, I have loved you for yourself: and if I now, more than ever, prize the solemn engagement which so long has pledged us to each other, it is because it leaves no room for hard as-
15 persions on my fame, and puts the seal of duty to an act of love.—But let us not linger. Perhaps this delay—

FAULKLAND. 'Twill be better I should not venture out again till dark. Yet am I grieved to
20 think what numberless distresses will press heavy on your gentle disposition!

JULIA. Perhaps your fortune may be forfeited by this unhappy act. I know not whether 'tis so, but sure that alone can never make
25 us unhappy. The little I have will be sufficient to support us; and exile never should be splendid.

FAULKLAND. Aye, but in such an abject state of life, my wounded pride perhaps may in-
30 crease the natural fretfulness of my temper, till I become a rude, morose companion, beyond your patience to endure. Perhaps the recollection of a deed my conscience cannot justify may haunt me in such gloomy and
35 unsocial fits that I shall hate the tenderness that would relieve me, break from your arms, and quarrel with your fondness!

JULIA. If your thoughts should assume so unhappy a bent, you will the more want some
40 mild and affectionate spirit to watch over and console you, one who, by bearing *your* infirmities with gentleness and resignation, may teach you *so* to bear the evils of your fortune.

FAULKLAND. Julia, I have proved you to the
45 quick! and with this useless device I throw away all my doubts. How shall I plead to be forgiven this last unworthy effect of my restless, unsatisfied disposition?

JULIA. Has no such disaster happened as you related? 50

FAULKLAND. I am ashamed to own that it was all pretended; yet in pity, Julia, do not kill me with resenting a fault which never can be repeated, but sealing, this once, my pardon, let me to-morrow, in the face of 55 heaven, receive my future guide and monitress, and expiate my past folly by years of tender adoration.

JULIA. Hold, Faulkland! That you are free from a crime which I before feared to name, 60 heaven knows how sincerely I rejoice! These are tears of thankfulness for that! But that your cruel doubts should have urged you to an imposition that has wrung my heart, gives me now a pang more keen than I can express! 65

FAULKLAND. By heavens! Julia—

JULIA. Yet hear me. My father loved you, Faulkland! and you preserved the life that tender parent gave me; in his presence I pledged my hand—joyfully pledged it—where 70 before I had given my heart. When, soon after, I lost that parent, it seemed to me that Providence had, in Faulkland, shown me whither to transfer without a pause my grateful duty, as well as my affection: hence I have 75 been content to bear from you what pride and delicacy would have forbid me from another. I will not upbraid you by repeating how you have trifled with my sincerity.

FAULKLAND. I confess it all! yet hear— 80

JULIA. After such a year of trial, I might have flattered myself that I should not have been insulted with a new probation of my sincerity, as cruel as unnecessary! I now see it is not in your nature to be content or con- 85 fident in love. With this conviction, I never will be yours. While I had hopes that my persevering attention and unreproaching kindness might in time reform your temper, I should have been happy to have gained a 90 dearer influence over you; but I will not furnish you with a licensed power to keep alive an incorrigible fault, at the expense of one who never would contend with you.

FAULKLAND. Nay, but Julia, by my soul and 95 honour, if after this—

JULIA. But one word more. As my faith has once been given to you, I never will barter it with another. I shall pray for your happiness with the truest sincerity; and the dearest bles-
5 sing I can ask of heaven to send you will be to charm you from that unhappy temper which alone has prevented the performance of our solemn engagement. All I request of *you* is that you will yourself reflect upon this
10 infirmity, and when you number up the many true delights it has deprived you of, let it not be your *least* regret that it lost you the love of one, who would have followed you in beggary through the world!

15 [*Exit.*]

FAULKLAND. She's gone!—forever! There was an awful resolution in her manner, that riveted me to my place. O fool!—dolt!—barbarian! Curst as I am with more imperfections
20 than my fellow-wretches, kind Fortune sent a heaven-gifted cherub to my aid, and, like a ruffian, I have driven her from my side! I must now haste to my appointment. Well, my mind is tuned for such a scene. I shall wish
25 only to become a principal in it, and reverse the tale my cursed folly put me upon forging here. O love!—tormentor!—fiend! whose influence, like the moon's, acting on men of dull souls, makes idiots of them, but meeting
30 subtler spirits, betrays their course, and urges sensibility to madness!

[*Exit.*]

[*Enter* MAID *and* LYDIA.]

MAID. My mistress, Ma'am, I know, was
35 here just now—perhaps she is only in the next room.

[*Exit* MAID.]

LYDIA. Heigh-ho! Though he has used me so, this fellow runs strangely in my head. I
40 believe one lecture from my grave cousin will make me recall him.

[*Enter* JULIA.]

LYDIA. O Julia, I am come to you with such an appetite for consolation.—Lud! child,
45 what's the matter with you? You have been crying! I'll be hanged if that Faulkland has not been tormenting you!

JULIA. You mistake the cause of my uneasi-

ness. Something *has* flurried me a little. Nothing that you can guess at.—[*Aside.*] I would 50 not accuse Faulkland to a sister!

LYDIA. Ah! whatever vexations you may have, I can assure you mine surpass them.— You know who Beverley proves to be?

JULIA. I will now own to you, Lydia, that 55 Mr. Faulkland had before informed me of the whole affair. Had young Absolute been the person you took him for, I should not have accepted your confidence on the subject without a serious endeavour to counteract your 60 caprice.

LYDIA. So, then, I see I have been deceived by everyone! But I don't care—I'll never have him.

JULIA. Nay, Lydia— 65

LYDIA. Why, is it not provoking? when I thought we were coming to the prettiest distress imaginable, to find myself made a mere Smithfield bargain° of at last! There had I projected one of the most sentimental elopements! 70 so becoming a disguise! so amiable a ladder of ropes! Conscious moon—four horses—Scotch parson—with such surprise to Mrs. Malaprop, and such paragraphs in the newspapers! Oh, I shall die with disappointment! 75

JULIA. I don't wonder at it!

LYDIA. Now—sad reverse!—what have I to expect, but, after a deal of flimsy preparation, with a bishop's licence, and my aunt's blessing, to go simpering up to the altar; or perhaps be 80 cried three times in a country-church, and have an unmannerly fat clerk ask the consent of every butcher in the parish to join John Absolute and Lydia Languish, Spinster! Oh, that I should live to hear myself called Spinster! 85

JULIA. Melancholy, indeed!

LYDIA. How mortifying to remember the dear delicious shifts I used to be put to, to gain half a minute's conversation with this fellow! How often have I stole forth in the coldest 90 night in January, and found him in the garden, stuck like a dripping statue! There would he kneel to me in the snow, and sneeze and

Smithfield bargain article of trade. Smithfield was a London market

cough so pathetically! he shivering with cold, and I with apprehension! and while the freezing blast numbed our joints, how warmly would he press me to pity his flame, and glow with mutual ardour! Ah, Julia, that was something like being in love!

JULIA. If I were in spirits, Lydia, I should chide you only by laughing heartily at you: but it suits more the situation of my mind, at present, earnestly to entreat you not to let a man, who loves you with sincerity, suffer that unhappiness from your caprice, which I know too well caprice can inflict.

LYDIA. O lud! what has brought my aunt here?

[*Enter* MRS. MALAPROP, FAG, *and* DAVID.]

MRS. MALAPROP. So! so! here's fine work!—here's fine suicide, parricide, and simulation going on in the fields! and Sir Anthony not to be found to prevent the antistrophe!

JULIA. For heaven's sake, Madam, what's the meaning of this?

MRS. MALAPROP. That gentleman can tell you—'twas he enveloped the affair to me.

LYDIA [*to* FAG]. Do, Sir, will you, inform us.

FAG. Ma'am, I should hold myself very deficient in every requisite that forms the man of breeding if I delayed a moment to give all the information in my power to a lady so deeply interested in the affair as you are.

LYDIA. But quick! quick, Sir!

FAG. True, Ma'am, as you say, one should be quick in divulging matters of this nature; for should we be tedious, perhaps while we are flourishing on the subject, two or three lives may be lost!

LYDIA. O patience! Do, Ma'am, for heaven's sake! tell us what is the matter!

MRS. MALAPROP. Why, murder's the matter! slaughter's the matter! killing's the matter! But he can tell you the perpendiculars.

LYDIA. Then, prithee, Sir, be brief.

FAG. Why then, Ma'am—as to murder, I cannot take upon me to say—and as to slaughter, or manslaughter, that will be as the jury finds it.

LYDIA. But who, Sir—who are engaged in this?

FAG. Faith, Ma'am, one is a young gentleman whom I should be very sorry anything was to happen to—a very pretty behaved gentleman! We have lived much together, and always on terms.

LYDIA. But who is this? who! who! who!

FAG. My master, Ma'am, my master—I speak of my master.

LYDIA. Heavens! What, Captain Absolute!

MRS. MALAPROP. Oh, to be sure, you are frightened now!

JULIA. But who are with him, Sir?

FAG. As to the rest, Ma'am, this gentleman can inform you better than I.

JULIA [*to* DAVID]. Do speak, friend.

DAVID. Look'ee, my lady—by the Mass! there's mischief going on. Folks don't use to meet for amusement with fire-arms, fire-locks, fire-engines, fire-screens, fire-office,° and the devil knows what other crackers° beside! This, my lady, I say, has an angry favour.

JULIA. But who is there beside Captain Absolute, friend?

DAVID. My poor master—under favour, for mentioning him first. You know me, my lady —I am David, and my master, of course, is, or *was,* Squire Acres. Then comes Squire Faulkland.

JULIA. Do, Ma'am, let us instantly endeavour to prevent mischief.

MRS. MALAPROP. Oh fie—it would be very inelegant in us: we should only participate things.

DAVID. Ah! do, Mrs. Aunt, save a few lives. They are desperately given, believe me. Above all, there is that bloodthirsty Philistine, Sir Lucius O'Trigger.

MRS. MALAPROP. Sir Lucius O'Trigger! O mercy! have they drawn poor little dear Sir Lucius into the scrape? Why, how you stand, girl! you have no more feeling than one of the Derbyshire putrefactions!°

LYDIA. What are we to do, Madam?

---

fire-office office of a fire-insurance company
crackers explosives
putrefactions petrifactions, the rock formations for which Derbyshire is well known

MRS. MALAPROP. Why, fly with the utmost felicity, to be sure, to prevent mischief. Here, friend—you can show us the place?

FAG. If you please, Ma'am, I will conduct you.—David, do you look for Sir Anthony.

[*Exit* DAVID.]

MRS. MALAPROP. Come, girls!—this gentleman will exhort us.—Come, Sir, you're our envoy—lead the way, and we'll precede.

FAG. Not a step before the ladies for the world!

MRS. MALAPROP. You're sure you know the spot?

FAG. I think I can find it, Ma'am; and one good thing is we shall hear the report of the pistols as we draw near, so we can't well miss them; never fear, Ma'am, never fear.

[*Exeunt, he talking.*]

Scene ii

[*South Parade.*]

[*Enter* ABSOLUTE, *putting his sword under his greatcoat.*]

ABSOLUTE. A sword seen in the streets of Bath would raise as great an alarm as a mad dog. How provoking this is in Faulkland! never punctual! I shall be obliged to go without him at last. Oh, the devil! here's Sir Anthony! How shall I escape him? [*Muffles up his face, and takes a circle to go off.*]

[*Enter* SIR ANTHONY.]

SIR ANTHONY. How one may be deceived at a little distance! Only that I see he don't know me, I could have sworn that was Jack!—Hey! 'Gad's life! it is. Why, Jack!—what are you afraid of, hey!—Sure I'm right.—Why, Jack! —Jack Absolute! [*Goes up to him.*]

ABSOLUTE. Really, Sir, you have the advantage of me: I don't remember ever to have had the honour. My name is Saunderson, at your service.

SIR ANTHONY. Sir, I beg your pardon—I took you—hey!—why, z——ds! it is—stay—[*looks up to his face*]. So, so—your humble servant, Mr. Saunderson! Why, you scoundrel, what tricks are you after now?

ABSOLUTE. Oh! a joke, Sir, a joke! I came here on purpose to look for you, Sir.

SIR ANTHONY. You did! Well, I am glad you were so lucky. But what are you muffled up so for? What's this for?—hey?

ABSOLUTE. 'Tis cool, Sir; isn't it?—rather chilly, somehow. But I shall be late—I have a particular engagement.

SIR ANTHONY. Stay. Why, I thought you were looking for me? Pray, Jack, where is't you are going?

ABSOLUTE. Going, Sir!

SIR ANTHONY. Aye—where are you going?

ABSOLUTE. Where am I going?

SIR ANTHONY. You unmannerly puppy!

ABSOLUTE. I was going, Sir, to—to—to—to Lydia—Sir, to Lydia, to make matters up if I could; and I was looking for you, Sir, to—to—

SIR ANTHONY. To go with you, I suppose. Well, come along.

ABSOLUTE. Oh! z——ds! no, Sir, not for the world! I wished to meet with you, Sir—to—to —to—. You find it cool, I'm sure, Sir—you'd better not stay out.

SIR ANTHONY. Cool!—not at all. Well, Jack —and what will you say to Lydia?

ABSOLUTE. O, Sir, beg her pardon, humour her, promise and vow. But I detain you, Sir— consider the cold air on your gout.

SIR ANTHONY. Oh, not at all!—not at all! I'm in no hurry. Ah! Jack, you youngsters, when once you are wounded here—[*putting his hand to* ABSOLUTE's *breast*]. Hey! what the deuce have you got here?

ABSOLUTE. Nothing, Sir—nothing.

SIR ANTHONY. What's this? here's something d——d hard!

ABSOLUTE. Oh, trinkets, Sir! trinkets—a bauble for Lydia!

SIR ANTHONY. Nay, let me see your taste. [*Pulls his coat open, the sword falls.*] Trinkets! —a bauble for Lydia! Z——ds! Sirrah, you are not going to cut her throat, are you?

ABSOLUTE. Ha! ha! ha! I thought it would divert you, Sir; though I didn't mean to tell you till afterwards.

SIR ANTHONY. You didn't? Yes, this is a very diverting trinket, truly!

ABSOLUTE. Sir, I'll explain to you. You know, Sir, Lydia is romantic, dev'lish romantic, and very absurd of course. Now, Sir, I intend, if she refuses to forgive me, to unsheathe this sword and swear I'll fall upon its point, and expire at her feet!

SIR ANTHONY. Fall upon a fiddle-stick's end! Why, I suppose it is the very thing that would please her. Get along, you fool.

ABSOLUTE. Well, Sir, you shall hear of my success—you shall hear. "O Lydia!—forgive me, or this pointed steel"—says I.

SIR ANTHONY. "O, booby! stab away and welcome"—says she. Get along!—and d——n your trinkets!

[*Exit* ABSOLUTE.]

[*Enter* DAVID, *running.*]

DAVID. Stop him! Stop him! Murder! Thief! Fire! Stop fire! Stop fire! O! Sir Anthony— call! call! bid 'em stop! Murder! Fire!

SIR ANTHONY. Fire! Murder! Where?

DAVID. Oons! he's out of sight! and I'm out of breath, for my part! O, Sir Anthony, why didn't you stop him? why didn't you stop him?

SIR ANTHONY. Z——ds! the fellow's mad! Stop whom? Stop Jack?

DAVID. Aye, the Captain, Sir! there's murder and slaughter—

SIR ANTHONY. Murder!

DAVID. Aye, please you, Sir Anthony, there's all kinds of murder, all sorts of slaughter to be seen in the fields: there's fighting going on, Sir—bloody sword-and-gun fighting!

SIR ANTHONY. Who are going to fight, dunce?

DAVID. Everybody that I know of, Sir Anthony—everybody is going to fight; my poor master, Sir Lucius O'Trigger, your son, the Captain—

SIR ANTHONY. Oh, the dog! I see his tricks. —Do you know the place?

DAVID. King's-Mead-Fields.

SIR ANTHONY. You know the way?

DAVID. Not an inch; but I'll call the mayor— aldermen — constables—church-wardens—and beadles—we can't be too many to part them.

SIR ANTHONY. Come along—give me your shoulder! we'll get assistance as we go. The lying villain! Well, I shall be in such a frenzy! So—this was the history of his trinkets! I'll bauble him!

[*Exeunt.*]

Scene iii

[*King's-Mead-Fields.*]

[SIR LUCIUS *and* ACRES, *with pistols.*]

ACRES. By my valour! then, Sir Lucius, forty yards is a good distance. Odds levels and aims! I say it is a good distance.

SIR LUCIUS. Is it for muskets or small field-pieces? Upon my conscience, Mr. Acres, you must leave those things to me. Stay now—I'll show you. [*Measures paces along the stage.*] There now, that is a very pretty distance—a pretty gentleman's distance.

ACRES. Z——ds! we might as well fight in a sentry-box! I tell you, Sir Lucius, the farther he is off, the cooler I shall take my aim.

SIR LUCIUS. Faith! then I suppose you would aim at him best of all if he was out of sight!

ACRES. No, Sir Lucius, but I should think forty, or eight and thirty yards—

SIR LUCIUS. Pho! pho! nonsense! Three or four feet between the mouths of your pistols is as good as a mile.

ACRES. Odds bullets, no! By my valour! there is no merit in killing him so near: do, my dear Sir Lucius, let me bring him down at a long shot—a long shot, Sir Lucius, if you love me!

SIR LUCIUS. Well—the gentleman's friend and I must settle that. But tell me now, Mr. Acres, in case of an accident, is there any little will or commission I could execute for you?

ACRES. I am much obliged to you, Sir Lucius, but I don't understand—

SIR LUCIUS. Why, you may think there's no being shot at without a little risk, and if an unlucky bullet should carry a *quietus* with it —I say it will be no time then to be bothering you about family matters.

ACRES. A *quietus!*

SIR LUCIUS. For instance, now—if that should be the case—would you choose to be pickled and sent home? or would it be the same to you to lie here in the Abbey? I'm told there is very snug lying in the Abbey.

ACRES. Pickled! Snug lying in the Abbey! Odds tremors! Sir Lucius, don't talk so!

SIR LUCIUS. I suppose, Mr. Acres, you never were engaged in an affair of this kind before?

ACRES. No, Sir Lucius, never before.

SIR LUCIUS. Ah! that's a pity! there's nothing like being used to a thing. Pray now, how would you receive the gentleman's shot?

ACRES. Odds files! I've practiced that. There, Sir Lucius—there [*puts himself in an attitude*]—a side-front, hey? Odd! I'll make myself small enough: I'll stand edge-ways.

SIR LUCIUS. Now—you're quite out, for if you stand so when I take my aim—[*levelling at him*].

ACRES. Z——ds! Sir Lucius—are you sure it is not cocked?

SIR LUCIUS. Never fear.

ACRES. But—but—you don't know—it may go off of its own head!

SIR LUCIUS. Pho! be easy. Well, now if I hit you in the body, my bullet has a double chance, for if it misses a vital part on your right side, 'twill be very hard if it don't succeed on the left!

ACRES. A vital part!

SIR LUCIUS. But, there—fix yourself so. [*Placing him.*] Let him see the broad side of your full front—there—now a ball or two may pass clean through your body, and never do any harm at all.

ACRES. Clean through me! a ball or two clean through me!

SIR LUCIUS. Aye, may they; and it is much the genteelest attitude into the bargain.

ACRES. Look'ee! Sir Lucius—I'd just as lieve be shot in an awkward posture as a genteel one—so, by my valour! I will stand edge-ways.

SIR LUCIUS [*looking at his watch*]. Sure they don't mean to disappoint us. Hah? No, faith—I think I see them coming.

ACRES. Hey! what!—coming!—

SIR LUCIUS. Aye. Who are those yonder getting over the stile?

ACRES. There are two of them indeed! Well

—let them come—hey, Sir Lucius? We—we—we—we—won't run.

SIR LUCIUS. Run!

ACRES. No—I say—we *won't* run, by my valour!

SIR LUCIUS. What the devil's the matter with you?

ACRES. Nothing—nothing—my dear friend—my dear Sir Lucius—but—I—I—I don't feel quite so bold, somehow—as I did.

SIR LUCIUS. Oh fie! consider your honour.

ACRES. Aye—true—my honour. Do, Sir Lucius, edge in a word or two every now and then about my honour.

SIR LUCIUS [*looking*]. Well, here they're coming.

ACRES. Sir Lucius—if I wa'n't with you, I should almost think I was afraid. If my valour should leave me! Valour will come and go.

SIR LUCIUS. Then, pray, keep it fast while you have it.

ACRES. Sir Lucius—I doubt it is going—yes—my valour is certainly going! it is sneaking off! I feel it oozing out as it were at the palms of my hands!

SIR LUCIUS. Your honour—your honour. Here they are.

ACRES. Oh mercy! now that I were safe at Clod-Hall! or could be shot before I was aware!

[*Enter* FAULKLAND *and* ABSOLUTE.]

SIR LUCIUS. Gentlemen, your most obedient—hah!—what—Captain Absolute! So, I suppose, Sir, you are come here, just like myself—to do a kind office, first for your friend—then to proceed to business on your own account.

ACRES. What, Jack! my dear Jack! my dear friend!

ABSOLUTE. Hark'ee, Bob, Beverley's at hand.

SIR LUCIUS. Well, Mr. Acres, I don't blame your saluting the gentleman civilly. So, Mr. Beverley [*to* FAULKLAND], if you'll choose your weapons, the Captain and I will measure the ground.

FAULKLAND. *My* weapons, Sir!

ACRES. Odd's life! Sir Lucius, I'm not going to fight Mr. Faulkland; these are my particular friends.

SIR LUCIUS. What, Sir, did not you come here to fight Mr. Acres?

FAULKLAND. Not I, upon my word, Sir.

SIR LUCIUS. Well, now, that's mighty provoking! But I hope, Mr. Faulkland, as there are three of us come on purpose for the game, you won't be so cantankerous as to spoil the party by sitting out.

ABSOLUTE. Oh pray, Faulkland, fight to oblige Sir Lucius.

FAULKLAND. Nay, if Mr. Acres is so bent on the matter—

ACRES. No, no, Mr. Faulkland—I'll bear my disappointment like a Christian. Look'ee, Sir Lucius, there's no occasion at all for me to fight; and if it is the same to you, I'd as lieve let it alone.

SIR LUCIUS. Observe me, Mr. Acres—I must not be trifled with. You have certainly challenged somebody, and you came here to fight him. Now, if that gentleman is willing to represent him, I can't see, for my soul, why it isn't just the same thing.

ACRES. Why no, Sir Lucius—I tell you, 'tis one Beverley I've challenged—a fellow you see, that dare not show his face! If *he* were here, I'd make him give up his pretensions directly!

ABSOLUTE. Hold, Bob—let me set you right. There is no such man as Beverley in the case. The person who assumed that name is before you; and as his pretensions are the same in both characters, he is ready to support them in whatever way you please.

SIR LUCIUS. Well, this is lucky! Now you have an opportunity—

ACRES. What, quarrel with my dear friend Jack Absolute? Not if he were fifty Beverleys! Z——ds! Sir Lucius, you would not have me be so unnatural.

SIR LUCIUS. Upon my conscience, Mr. Acres, your valour has *oozed* away with a vengeance!

ACRES. Not in the least! Odds backs and abettors! I'll be your second with all my heart, and if you should get a *quietus*, you may command me entirely. I'll get you *snug lying* in the *Abbey here*; or *pickle* you, and send you over to Blunderbuss-Hall, or anything of the kind, with the greatest pleasure.

SIR LUCIUS. Pho! pho! you are little better than a coward.

ACRES. Mind, gentlemen, he calls me a *coward*; coward was the word, by my valour!

SIR LUCIUS. Well, Sir?

ACRES. Look'ee, Sir Lucius, 'tisn't that I mind the word coward—*coward* may be said in joke. But if you had called me a *poltroon*, odds daggers and balls!—

SIR LUCIUS. Well, Sir?

ACRES. —I should have thought you a very ill-bred man.

SIR LUCIUS. Pho! you are beneath my notice.

ABSOLUTE. Nay, Sir Lucius, you can't have a better second than my friend Acres. He is a most *determined dog*, called in the country, *Fighting Bob*. He generally *kills a man a week*; don't you, Bob?

ACRES. Aye—at home!

SIR LUCIUS. Well then, Captain, 'tis we must begin. So come out, my little counsellor [*draws his sword*], and ask the gentleman whether he will resign the lady without forcing you to proceed against him.

ABSOLUTE. Come on then, Sir [*draws*]; since you won't let it be an amicable suit, here's my reply.

[*Enter* SIR ANTHONY, DAVID, *and the Women*.]

DAVID. Knock 'em all down, sweet Sir Anthony; knock down my master in particular, and bind his hands over to their good behaviour!

SIR ANTHONY. Put up, Jack, put up, or I shall be in a frenzy. How came you in a duel, Sir?

ABSOLUTE. Faith, Sir, that gentleman can tell you better than I; 'twas he called on me, and you know, Sir, I serve his Majesty.

SIR ANTHONY. Here's a pretty fellow! I catch him going to cut a man's throat, and he tells me he serves his Majesty! Z——ds! Sirrah, then how durst you draw the King's sword against one of his subjects?

ABSOLUTE. Sir, I tell you! That gentleman called me out, without explaining his reasons.

SIR ANTHONY. Gad! Sir, how came you to call my son out, without explaining your reasons?

SIR LUCIUS. Your son, Sir, insulted me in a manner which my honour could not brook.

SIR ANTHONY. Z——ds! Jack, how durst you insult the gentleman in a manner which his honour could not brook?

MRS. MALAPROP. Come, come, let's have no honour before ladies. Captain Absolute, come here. How could you intimidate us so? Here's Lydia has been terrified to death for you.

ABSOLUTE. For fear I should be killed, or escape, Ma'am?

MRS. MALAPROP. Nay, no delusions to the past. Lydia is convinced; speak, child.

SIR LUCIUS. With your leave, Ma'am, I must put in a word here. I believe I could interpret the young lady's silence. Now mark—

LYDIA. What is it you mean, Sir?

SIR LUCIUS. Come, come, Delia, we must be serious now—this is no time for trifling.

LYDIA. 'Tis true, Sir; and your reproof bids me offer this gentleman my hand, and solicit the return of his affections.

ABSOLUTE. O! my little angel, say you so? Sir Lucius, I perceive there must be some mistake here. With regard to the affront which you affirm I have given you, I can only say that it could not have been intentional. And as you must be convinced that I should not fear to support a real injury, you shall now see that I am not ashamed to atone for an inadvertency. I ask your pardon. But for this lady, while honoured with her approbation, I will support my claim against any man whatever.

SIR ANTHONY. Well said, Jack! and I'll stand by you, my boy.

ACRES. Mind, I give up all my claim—I make no pretensions to anything in the world—and if I can't get a wife without fighting for her, by my valour! I'll live a bachelor.

SIR LUCIUS. Captain, give me your hand—an affront handsomely acknowledged becomes an obligation—and as for the lady, if she chooses to deny her own handwriting here—[takes out letters].

MRS. MALAPROP. Oh, he will dissolve my mystery! Sir Lucius, perhaps there's some mistake—perhaps, I can illuminate—

SIR LUCIUS. Pray, old gentlewoman, don't interfere where you have no business. Miss Languish, are you my Delia, or not?

LYDIA. Indeed, Sir Lucius, I am not.

[LYDIA and ABSOLUTE walk aside.]

MRS. MALAPROP. Sir Lucius O'Trigger, ungrateful as you are, I own the soft impeachment—pardon my blushes, I am Delia.

SIR LUCIUS. You Delia!—pho! pho! be easy.

MRS. MALAPROP. Why, thou barbarous Vandyke!—those letters are mine. When you are more sensible of my benignity, perhaps I may be brought to encourage your addresses.

SIR LUCIUS. Mrs. Malaprop, I am extremely sensible of your condescension; and whether you or Lucy have put this trick upon me, I am equally beholden to you. And to show you I'm not ungrateful—Captain Absolute! since you have taken that lady from me, I'll give you my Delia into the bargain.

ABSOLUTE. I am much obliged to you, Sir Lucius; but here's our friend, Fighting Bob, unprovided for.

SIR LUCIUS. Hah! little Valour—here, will you make your fourtune?

ACRES. Odds wrinkles! No. But give me your hand, Sir Lucius; forget and forgive; but if ever I give you a chance of *pickling* me again, say Bob Acres is a dunce, that's all.

SIR ANTHONY. Come, Mrs. Malaprop, don't be cast down—you are in your bloom yet.

MRS. MALAPROP. O Sir Anthony!—men are all barbarians—

[All retire but JULIA and FAULKLAND.]

JULIA [aside]. He seems dejected and unhappy—not sullen. There was some foundation, however, for the tale he told me. O woman! how true should be your judgment, when your resolution is so weak!

FAULKLAND. Julia! how can I sue for what I so little deserve? I dare not presume—yet Hope is the child of Penitence.

JULIA. Oh! Faulkland, you have not been more faulty in your unkind treatment of me than I am now in wanting inclination to resent it. As my heart honestly bids me place my weakness to the account of love, I should be ungenerous not to admit the same plea for yours.

FAULKLAND. Now I shall be blest indeed!

[SIR ANTHONY *comes forward.*]

SIR ANTHONY. What's going on here? So you have been quarrelling too, I warrant. Come,
5 Julia, I never interfered before; but let me have a hand in the matter at last. All the faults I have ever seen in my friend Faulkland seemed to proceed from what he calls the *delicacy* and *warmth* of his affection for you. There, marry
10 him directly, Julia; you'll find he'll mend surprisingly!

[*The rest come forward.*]

SIR LUCIUS. Come now, I hope there is no dissatisfied person but what is content; for as
15 I have been disappointed myself, it will be very hard if I have not the satisfaction of seeing other people succeed better—

ACRES. You are right, Sir Lucius. So, Jack, I wish you joy—Mr. Faulkland the same.—
20 Ladies,—come now, to show you I'm neither vexed nor angry, odds tabours and pipes! I'll order the fiddles in half an hour to the New Rooms, and I insist on your all meeting me there.
25 SIR ANTHONY. Gad! Sir, I like your spirit; and at night we single lads will drink a health to the young couples, and a husband to Mrs. Malaprop.

FAULKLAND. Our partners are stolen from us,
30 Jack—I hope to be congratulated by each other —*yours* for having checked in time the errors of an ill-directed imagination, which might have betrayed an innocent heart; and *mine*, for having, by her gentleness and candour,
35 reformed the unhappy temper of one who by it made wretched whom he loved most, and tortured the heart he ought to have adored.

ABSOLUTE. Well, Faulkland, we have both tasted the bitters, as well as the sweets, of love
40 —with this difference only, that *you* always prepared the bitter cup for yourself, while *I*—

LYDIA. Was always obliged to *me* for it, hey! Mr. Modesty?—But come, no more of that: our happiness is now as unalloyed as general.
45 JULIA. Then let us study to preserve it so; and while Hope pictures to us a flattering scene of future Bliss, let us deny its pencil those colors which are too bright to be lasting. When

Hearts deserving Happiness would unite their fortunes, Virtue would crown them with an 50 unfading garland of modest, hurtless flowers; but ill-judging Passion will force the gaudier Rose into the wreath, whose thorn offends them, when its leaves are dropt!

[*Exeunt omnes.*]   55

Henrik Ibsen

1828–1906

Hedda Gabler

1890

Ibsen has long been regarded as a special critic of Norwegian society in the 1870's and 1880's and hence as somewhat exclusively of his own time. Perhaps, however, the view of Ibsen as passé is now itself passé. He never was primarily a social critic, he was primarily dramatic craftsman and moralist. And his mature plays are still virtually unique in the firmness of their dramaturgy and of their moral conviction.

Hedda Gabler, the fruit of forty years of theatrical experience, represents his craftsmanship at its most assured. It is an almost perfectly artistic play—concentrated, coherent, symmetrical; and its structure is an almost perfect reflection of the nature of its leading character.

The central motive in the play is Hedda's desire to mold a human destiny. She conceives this destiny as a triumph of the Dionysian spirit, for she would know vicariously an abandon that she cannot know in her own person; and she selects a man as her deputy because, having rejected her own womanhood, she identifies herself with the dominant male role. The play rises naturally to crisis when she sends Lövborg out, so she imagines, to an evening of exultant revel. But the collapse of her venture is inherent in the spirit in which she conceived it. What she calls her "craving for life" is not a natural appetite; her will to dominate men incorporates also her will to destroy them; she has inevitably selected a weakling to do her living for her. When the third-act curtain rises on the gray weariness of the morning after, the play has turned as inevitably toward her catastrophe as before this it turned toward her illusory triumph. Her own character is a fate as unrelenting as any the Delphic Oracle could have pronounced. Hence the spare and classic structure of the play.

If *Hedda Gabler* is like the classic drama in its deft ordering of plot, it resembles it too in its multitude of ironies. But as its plot is spun not by divine agency but by human

449

character, so also its ironies are derived not from a metaphysical perspective but from an ethical one.

Enough of these ironies tend toward comedy to lighten the whole with a genuine if sometimes grim humor. There is, for example, Aunt Julia's utterly devoted, utterly damning admiration for a nephew whom "no one can beat" at "collecting and arranging things." There is Tesman's own perfectly daft accession of wonder when Hedda burns the manuscript ("I wonder, now, whether this sort of thing is usual in young wives? Eh?"). There is the descent from Hedda's breathless memory of "something beautiful, something fascinating—something daring" to the bathos of the thing remembered: the prurient girl, hiding behind an illustrated paper and listening to her young man talk about sex.

As these instances make clear, however, the disparities that such irony calls attention to are ethically revealing as well as sometimes amusing. Ibsen often invites a double perspective of this sort when he is most deeply earnest. When he wants to emphasize the difference between a superficial social view of people and a pro- foundly ethical view, he so orders his play that characters who are in sharp ethical contrast are placed in ironic juxtaposition.

Hedda herself is high fashion. She has style and wit, and a kind of verve. But from a moral perspective, the attributes for which she is so generally admired are inconsequential. To contrast with her, Ibsen introduces good people and right actions through the back and side doors, so to speak, in humble and almost ridiculous guise. Lovingkindness enters in the person of a garrulous maiden aunt bearing an old pair of embroidered morning slippers. Rectitude glimmers, goes out, then glimmers again in her dull and pedantic nephew. But the most exact foil to Hedda is the fragile young woman from the provinces, "dressed not quite in the latest fashion," who reveals little by little the fullness of womanly courage and passion. Through these lesser characters, Ibsen would show us that human goodness characteristically reveals itself in those whom complacency would overlook and pride disdain.

Hedda Gabler

IBSEN

*Translated by William Archer and
Sir Edmund Gosse*

CHARACTERS°

GEORGE TESMAN
HEDDA TESMAN   *his wife*
MISS JULIANA TESMAN   *his aunt*
MRS. ELVSTED
JUDGE BRACK
EILERT LÖVBORG
BERTA   *servant at the Tesman's*

SCENE. *Tesman's villa, in the west end of
Christiania.*

ACT I

[*A spacious, handsome and tastefully furnished drawing-room, decorated in dark colors.
5 In the back, a wide doorway with curtains
drawn back, leading into a smaller room dec-*

Characters: Judge Brack In Norway during the
1880's official position was a general determinant
of social standing, and official titles were in frequent
use. The titles that may prove obscure or misleading
in this translation are those of "Judge" Brack, an
assessor, or associate judge; "Secretary" Falk, a
cabinet minister; and "Sheriff" Elvsted, a district
magistrate. Tesman, as holder of a scholarship in
his field, has an officially conferred status though
he is called by no title.

From The Collected Works of Henrik Ibsen,
Volume X, *entirely revised and edited by William
Archer, copyright 1907 by Charles Scribner's Sons,
New York, 1935 by Frank Archer. Reprinted by
permission of the publishers.*

*orated in the same style as the drawing-room.
In the right-hand wall of the front room, a
folding door leading out to the hall. In the
opposite wall, on the left, a glass door, also* 10
*with curtains drawn back. Through the panes
can be seen part of a verandah outside, and
trees covered with autumn foliage. An oval
table, with a cover on it, and surrounded by
chairs, stands well forward. In front, by the* 15
*wall on the right, a wide stove of dark por-
celain, a high-backed arm-chair, a cushioned
foot-rest, and two foot-stools. A settee, with a
small round table in front of it, fills the upper
right-hand corner. In front, on the left, a little* 20
*way from the wall, a sofa. Farther back than
the glass door, a piano. On either side of the
doorway at the back a whatnot with terra-cotta
and majolica ornaments.—Against the back
wall of the inner room a sofa, with a table, and* 25
*one or two chairs. Over the sofa hangs the
portrait of a handsome elderly man in a General's uniform. Over the table a hanging lamp,
with an opal glass shade.—A number of bouquets are arranged about the drawing-room,* 30
*in vases and glasses. Others lie upon the tables.
The floors in both rooms are covered with thick
carpets.—Morning light. The sun shines in
through the glass door.*

MISS JULIANA TESMAN, *with her bonnet on* 35
*and carrying a parasol, comes in from the hall,
followed by* BERTA, *who carries a bouquet
wrapped in paper.* MISS TESMAN *is a comely
and pleasant-looking lady of about sixty-five.
She is nicely but simply dressed in a gray* 40
walking-costume. BERTA *is a middle-aged
woman of plain and rather countrified appearance.*]

MISS TESMAN [*stops close to the door, listens,
and says softly*]. Upon my word, I don't be- 45
lieve they are stirring yet!

BERTA [*also softly*]. I told you so, Miss. Remember how late the steamboat got in last
night. And then, when they got home!—good
Lord, what a lot the young mistress had to un- 50
pack before she could get to bed.

MISS TESMAN. Well, well—let them have
their sleep out. But let us see that they get a

good breath of the fresh morning air when
they do appear. [*She goes to the glass door and
throws it open.*]

5 BERTA [*beside the table, at a loss what to do
with the bouquet in her hand*]. I declare there
isn't a bit of room left. I think I'll put it down
here, Miss. [*She places it on the piano.*]

MISS TESMAN. So you've got a new mistress
10 now, my dear Berta. Heaven knows it was a
wrench to me to part with you.

BERTA [*on the point of weeping*]. And do
you think it wasn't hard for me too, Miss?
After all the blessed years I've been with you
and Miss Rina.

15 MISS TESMAN. We must make the best of it,
Berta. There was nothing else to be done.
George can't do without you, you see—he
absolutely can't. He has had you to look after
him ever since he was a little boy.

20 BERTA. Ah, but, Miss Julia, I can't help
thinking of Miss Rina lying helpless at home
there, poor thing. And with only that new girl,
too! She'll never learn to take proper care of an
invalid.

25 MISS TESMAN. Oh, I shall manage to train
her. And of course, you know, I shall take most
of it upon myself. You needn't be uneasy about
my poor sister, my dear Berta.

BERTA. Well, but there's another thing, Miss.
30 I'm so mortally afraid I shan't be able to suit
the young mistress.

MISS TESMAN. Oh, well—just at first there
may be one or two things—

BERTA. Most like she'll be terrible grand in
35 her ways.

MISS TESMAN. Well, you can't wonder at that
—General Gabler's daughter! Think of the sort
of life she was accustomed to in her father's
time. Don't you remember how we used to see
40 her riding down the road along with the General? In that long black habit—and with
feathers in her hat?

BERTA. Yes, indeed—I remember well
enough—! But good Lord, I should never have
45 dreamt in those days that she and Master
George would make a match of it.

MISS TESMAN. Nor I.—But, by-the-bye, Berta
—while I think of it: in future you mustn't

say Master George. You must say Dr. Tesman.

50 BERTA. Yes, the young mistress spoke of that
too—last night—the moment they set foot in
the house. Is it true, then, Miss?

MISS TESMAN. Yes, indeed it is. Only think,
Berta—some foreign university has made him
55 a doctor—while he has been abroad, you understand. I hadn't heard a word about it, until
he told me himself upon the pier.

BERTA. Well, well, he's clever enough for
anything, he is. But I didn't think he'd have
60 gone in for doctoring people too.

MISS TESMAN. No, no, it's not that sort of
doctor he is. [*Nods significantly.*] But let me
tell you, we may have to call him something
still grander before long.

65 BERTA. You don't say so! What can that be,
Miss?

MISS TESMAN [*smiling*]. H'm—wouldn't you
like to know! [*With emotion.*] Ah, dear, dear
—if my poor brother could only look up from
70 his grave now, and see what his little boy has
grown into! [*Looks around.*] But bless me,
Berta—why have you done this? Taken the
chintz covers off all the furniture?

BERTA. The mistress told me to. She can't
75 abide covers on the chairs, she says.

MISS TESMAN. Are they going to make this
their everyday sitting-room then?

BERTA. Yes, that's what I understood—from
the mistress. Master George—the doctor—he
80 said nothing.

[GEORGE TESMAN *comes from the right into
the inner room, humming to himself, and
carrying an unstrapped empty portmanteau.
He is a middle-sized, young-looking man of
85 thirty-three, rather stout, with a round, open,
cheerful face, fair hair and beard. He wears
spectacles, and is somewhat carelessly dressed
in comfortable indoor clothes.*]

MISS TESMAN. Good morning, good morning,
90 George.

TESMAN [*in the doorway between the
rooms*]. Aunt Julia! Dear Aunt Julia! [*Goes up
to her and shakes hands warmly.*] Come all
this way—so early! Eh?

95 MISS TESMAN. Why of course I had to come
and see how you were getting on.

TESMAN. In spite of your having had no proper night's rest?

MISS TESMAN. Oh, that makes no difference to me.

5 TESMAN. Well, I suppose you got home all right from the pier? Eh?

MISS TESMAN. Yes, quite safely, thank goodness. Judge Brack was good enough to see me right to my door.

10 TESMAN. We were so sorry we couldn't give you a seat in the carriage. But you saw what a pile of boxes Hedda had to bring with her.

MISS TESMAN. Yes, she had certainly plenty of boxes.

15 BERTA [*to* TESMAN]. Shall I go in and see if there's anything I can do for the mistress?

TESMAN. No thank you, Berta—you needn't. She said she would ring if she wanted anything.

20 BERTA [*going towards the right*]. Very well.

TESMAN. But look here—take this portmanteau with you.

BERTA [*taking it*]. I'll put it in the attic.

[*She goes out by the hall door.*]

25 TESMAN. Fancy, Auntie—I had the whole of that portmanteau chock full of copies of documents. You wouldn't believe how much I have picked up from all the archives I have been examining—curious old details that no 30 one has had any idea of—

MISS TESMAN. Yes, you don't seem to have wasted your time on your wedding trip, George.

TESMAN. No, that I haven't. But do take off 35 your bonnet, Auntie. Look here! Let me untie the strings—eh?

MISS TESMAN [*while he does so*]. Well, well —this is just as if you were still at home with us.

40 TESMAN [*with the bonnet in his hand, looks at it from all sides*]. Why, what a gorgeous bonnet you've been investing in!

MISS TESMAN. I bought it on Hedda's account.

45 TESMAN. On Hedda's account? Eh?

MISS TESMAN. Yes, so that Hedda needn't be ashamed of me if we happened to go out together.

TESMAN [*patting her cheek*]. You always think of everything, Aunt Julia. [*Lays the bon-* 50 *net on a chair beside the table.*] And now, look here—suppose we sit comfortably on the sofa and have a little chat, till Hedda comes.

[*They seat themselves. She places her parasol in the corner of the sofa.*] 55

MISS TESMAN [*takes both his hands and looks at him*]. What a delight it is to have you again, as large as life, before my very eyes, George! My George—my poor brother's own boy! 60

TESMAN. And it's a delight for me, too, to see you again, Aunt Julia! You, who have been father and mother in one to me.

MISS TESMAN. Oh, yes, I know you will always keep a place in your heart for your old 65 aunts.

TESMAN. And what about Aunt Rina? No improvement—eh?

MISS TESMAN. Oh, no—we can scarcely look for any improvement in her case, poor thing. 70 There she lies, helpless, as she has lain for all these years. But heaven grant I may not lose her yet awhile! For if I did, I don't know what I should make of my life, George—especially now that I haven't you to look after any more. 75

TESMAN [*patting her back*]. There, there, there—!

MISS TESMAN [*suddenly changing her tone*]. And to think that here you are a married man, George!—And that you should be the one to 80 carry off Hedda Gabler, the beautiful Hedda Gabler! Only think of it—she, that was so beset with admirers!

TESMAN [*hums a little and smiles complacently*]. Yes, I fancy I have several good 85 friends about town who would like to stand in my shoes—eh?

MISS TESMAN. And then this fine long wedding-tour you have had! More than five— nearly six months— 90

TESMAN. Well, for me it has been a sort of tour of research as well. I have had to do so much grubbing among old records—and to read no end of books too, Auntie.

MISS TESMAN. Oh, yes, I suppose so. [*More* 95 *confidentially, and lowering her voice a little.*]

But listen now, George—have you nothing—nothing special to tell me?

TESMAN. As to our journey?

MISS TESMAN. Yes.

5   TESMAN. No, I don't know of anything except what I have told you in my letters. I had a doctor's degree conferred on me—but that I told you yesterday.

MISS TESMAN. Yes, yes, you did. But what I
10 mean is—haven't you any—any—expectations—?

TESMAN. Expectations?

MISS TESMAN. Why, you know, George—I'm your old auntie!

15 TESMAN. Why, of course I have expectations.

MISS TESMAN. Ah!

TESMAN. I have every expectation of being a professor one of these days.

MISS TESMAN. Oh, yes, a professor—
20 TESMAN. Indeed, I may say I am certain of it. But my dear Auntie—you know all about that already!

MISS TESMAN [laughing to herself]. Yes, of course I do. You are quite right there. [Chang-
25 ing the subject.] But we were talking about your journey. It must have cost a great deal of money, George?

TESMAN. Well, you see—my handsome traveling-scholarship went a good way.

30 MISS TESMAN. But I can't understand how you can have made it go far enough for two.

TESMAN. No, that's not so easy to understand—eh?

MISS TESMAN. And especially traveling with
35 a lady—they tell me that makes it ever so much more expensive.

TESMAN. Yes, of course—it makes it a little more expensive. But Hedda had to have this trip, Auntie! She really had to. Nothing else
40 would have done.

MISS TESMAN. No, no, I suppose not. A wedding-tour seems to be quite indispensable nowadays.—But tell me now—have you gone thoroughly over the house yet?

45 TESMAN. Yes, you may be sure I have. I have been afoot ever since daylight.

MISS TESMAN. And what do you think of it all?

TESMAN. I'm delighted! Quite delighted!

Only I can't think what we are to do with the 50 two empty rooms between this inner parlor and Hedda's bedroom.

MISS TESMAN [laughing]. Oh, my dear George, I dare say you may find some use for them—in the course of time. 55

TESMAN. Why of course you are quite right, Aunt Julia! You mean as my library increases —eh?

MISS TESMAN. Yes, quite so, my dear boy. It was your library I was thinking of. 60

TESMAN. I am specially pleased on Hedda's account. Often and often, before we were engaged, she said that she would never care to live anywhere but in Secretary Falk's villa.

MISS TESMAN. Yes, it was lucky that this 65 very house should come into the market, just after you had started.

TESMAN. Yes, Aunt Julia, the luck was on our side, wasn't it—eh?

MISS TESMAN. But the expense, my dear 70 George! You will find it very expensive, all this.

TESMAN [looks at her, a little cast down]. Yes, I suppose I shall, Aunt!

MISS TESMAN. Oh, frightfully! 75

TESMAN. How much do you think? In round numbers?—Eh?

MISS TESMAN. Oh, I can't even guess until all the accounts come in.

TESMAN. Well, fortunately, Judge Brack has 80 secured the most favourable terms for me,—so he said in a letter to Hedda.

MISS TESSMAN. Yes, don't be uneasy, my dear boy.—Besides, I have given security for the furniture and all the carpets. 85

TESMAN. Security? You? My dear Aunt Julia —what sort of security could you give?

MISS TESMAN. I have given a mortgage on our annuity.

TESMAN [jumps up]. What! On your—and 90 Aunt Rina's annuity!

MISS TESMAN. Yes, I knew of no other plan, you see.

TESMAN [placing himself before her]. Have you gone out of your senses, Auntie! Your 95 annuity—it's all that you and Aunt Rina have to live upon.

MISS TESMAN. Well, well, don't get so excited about it. It's only a matter of form you know—Judge Brack assured me of that. It was he that was kind enough to arrange the whole affair for me. A mere matter of form, he said.

TESMAN. Yes, that may be all very well. But nevertheless—

MISS TESMAN. You will have your own salary to depend upon now. And, good heavens, even if we did have to pay up a little—! To eke things out a bit at the start—! Why, it would be nothing but a pleasure to us.

TESMAN. Oh, Auntie—will you never be tired of making sacrifices for me!

MISS TESMAN [*rises and lays her hands on his shoulders*]. Have I had any other happiness in this world except to smooth your way for you, my dear boy? You, who have had neither father nor mother to depend on. And now we have reached the goal, George! Things have looked black enough for us, sometimes; but, thank heaven, now you have nothing to fear.

TESMAN. Yes, it is really marvelous how everything has turned out for the best.

MISS TESMAN. And the people who opposed you—who wanted to bar the way for you—now you have them at your feet. They have fallen, George. Your most dangerous rival—his fall was the worst.—And now he has to lie on the bed he has made for himself—poor misguided creature.

TESMAN. Have you heard anything of Eilert? Since I went away, I mean.

MISS TESMAN. Only that he is said to have published a new book.

TESMAN. What! Eilert Lövborg! Recently—eh?

MISS TESMAN. Yes, so they say. Heaven knows whether it can be worth anything! Ah, when your new book appears—that will be another story, George! What is it to be about?

TESMAN. It will deal with the domestic industries of Brabant during the Middle Ages.

MISS TESMAN. Fancy—to be able to write on such a subject as that!

TESMAN. However, it may be some time before the book is ready. I have all these collections to arrange first, you see.

MISS TESMAN. Yes, collecting and arranging—no one can beat you at that. There you are

my poor brother's own son.

TESMAN. I am looking forward eagerly to setting to work at it; especially now that I have my own delightful home to work in.

MISS TESMAN. And, most of all, now that you have got the wife of your heart, my dear George.

TESMAN [*embracing her*]. Oh, yes, yes, Aunt Julia. Hedda—she is the best part of all! [*Looks towards the doorway.*] I believe I hear her coming—eh?

[HEDDA *enters from the left through the inner room. She is a woman of nine-and-twenty. Her face and figure show refinement and distinction. Her complexion is pale and opaque. Her steel-gray eyes express a cold, unruffled repose. Her hair is of an agreeable medium brown, but not particularly abundant. She is dressed in a tasteful, somewhat loose-fitting morning-gown.*]

MISS TESMAN [*going to meet* HEDDA]. Good morning, my dear Hedda! Good morning, and a hearty welcome.

HEDDA [*holds out her hand*]. Good morning, dear Miss Tesman! So early a call! This is kind of you.

MISS TESMAN [*with some embarrassment*]. Well—has the bride slept well in her new home?

HEDDA. Oh yes, thanks. Passably.

TESMAN [*laughing*]. Passably! Come, that's good, Hedda! You were sleeping like a stone when I got up.

HEDDA. Fortunately. Of course one has always to accustom one's self to new surroundings, Miss Tesman—little by little. [*Looking towards the left.*] Oh—there the servant has gone and opened the verandah door, and let in a whole flood of sunshine.

MISS TESMAN [*going towards the door*]. Well, then, we will shut it.

HEDDA. No, no, not that! Tesman, please draw the curtains. That will give a softer light.

TESMAN [*at the door*]. All right—all right. There now, Hedda, now you have both shade and fresh air.

HEDDA. Yes, fresh air we certainly must have, with all these stacks of flowers— But— won't you sit down, Miss Tesman?

MISS TESMAN. No, thank you. Now that I have seen that everything is all right here—thank heaven!—I must be getting home again. My sister is lying longing for me, poor thing.

5 TESMAN. Give her my very best love, Auntie; and say I shall look in and see her later in the day.

MISS TESMAN. Yes, yes, I'll be sure to tell her. But by-the-bye, George—[feeling in her 10 dress pocket]—I have almost forgotten—I have something for you here.

TESMAN. What is it, Auntie? Eh?

MISS TESMAN [produces a flat parcel wrapped in newspaper and hands it to him]. Look here, 15 my dear boy.

TESMAN [opening the parcel]. Well, I declare! Have you really saved them for me, Aunt Julia! Hedda, isn't this touching—eh?

HEDDA [beside the whatnot on the right]. 20 Well, what is it?

TESMAN. My old morning-shoes! My slippers.

HEDDA. Indeed. I remember you often spoke of them while we were abroad.

25 TESMAN. Yes, I missed them terribly. [Goes up to her.] Now you shall see them, Hedda!

HEDDA [going towards the stove]. Thanks, I really don't care about it.

TESMAN [following her]. Only think—ill as 30 she was, Aunt Rina embroidered these for me. Oh you can't think how many associations cling to them.

HEDDA [at the table]. Scarcely for me.

MISS TESMAN. Of course not for Hedda, 35 George.

TESMAN. Well, but now that she belongs to the family, I thought—

HEDDA [interrupting]. We shall never get on with this servant, Tesman.

40 MISS TESMAN. Not get on with Berta?

TESMAN. Why, dear, what puts that in your head? Eh?

HEDDA [pointing]. Look there! She has left her old bonnet lying about on a chair.

45 TESMAN [in consternation, drops the slippers on the floor]. Why, Hedda—

HEDDA. Just fancy, if any one should come in and see it.

TESMAN. But Hedda—that's Aunt Julia's bonnet. 50

HEDDA. Is it!

MISS TESMAN [taking up the bonnet]. Yes, indeed it's mine. And what's more, it's not old, Madame Hedda.

HEDDA. I really did not look closely at it, 55 Miss Tesman.

MISS TESMAN [trying on the bonnet]. Let me tell you it's the first time I have worn it—the very first time.

TESMAN. And a very nice bonnet it is too— 60 quite a beauty!

MISS TESMAN. Oh, it's no such great thing, George. [Looks around her.] My parasol—? Ah, here. [Takes it.] For this is mine too— [mutters]—not Berta's. 65

TESMAN. A new bonnet and a new parasol! Only think, Hedda!

HEDDA. Very handsome indeed.

TESMAN. Yes, isn't it? But Auntie, take a good look at Hedda before you go! See how 70 handsome she is!

MISS TESMAN. Oh, my dear boy, there's nothing new in that. Hedda was always lovely. [She nods and goes towards the right.]

TESMAN [following]. Yes, but have you 75 noticed what splendid condition she is in? How she has filled out on the journey?

HEDDA [crossing the room]. Oh, do be quiet—!

MISS TESMAN [who has stopped and turned]. 80 Filled out?

TESMAN. Of course you don't notice it so much now that she has that dress on. But I, who can see—

HEDDA [at the glass door, impatiently]. Oh, 85 you can't see anything.

TESMAN. It must be the mountain air in the Tyrol—

HEDDA [curtly, interrupting]. I am exactly as I was when I started. 90

TESMAN. So you insist; but I'm quite certain you are not. Don't you agree with me, Auntie?

MISS TESMAN [who has been gazing at her with folded hands]. Hedda is lovely—lovely— lovely. [Goes up to her, takes her head between 95 both hands, draws it downwards, and kisses *her hair*]. God bless and preserve Hedda Tesman—for George's sake.

HEDDA [*gently freeing herself*]. Oh—! Let me go.

5 MISS TESMAN [*in quiet emotion*]. I shall not let a day pass without coming to see you.

TESMAN. No you won't, will you, Auntie? Eh?

MISS TESMAN. Good-bye—good-bye!

10 [*She goes out by the hall door.* TESMAN *accompanies her. The door remains half open.* TESMAN *can be heard repeating his message to Aunt Rina and his thanks for the slippers.*

In the meantime, HEDDA *walks about the* 15 *room raising her arms and clenching her hands as if in desperation. Then she flings back the curtains from the glass door, and stands there looking out.*

Presently TESMAN *returns and closes the* 20 *door behind him.*]

TESMAN [*picks up the slippers from the floor*]. What are you looking at, Hedda?

HEDDA [*once more calm and mistress of herself*]. I am only looking at the leaves. They are 25 so yellow—so withered.

TESMAN [*wraps up the slippers and lays them on the table*]. Well you see, we are well into September now.

HEDDA [*again restless*]. Yes, to think of it! 30 —Already in—in September.

TESMAN. Don't you think Aunt Julia's manner was strange, dear? Almost solemn? Can you imagine what was the matter with her? Eh?

35 HEDDA. I scarcely know her, you see. Is she often like that?

TESMAN. No, not as she was today.

HEDDA [*leaving the glass door*]. Do you think she was annoyed about the bonnet?

40 TESMAN. Oh, scarcely at all. Perhaps a little, just at the moment—

HEDDA. But what an idea, to pitch her bonnet about in the drawing-room! No one does that sort of thing.

45 TESMAN. Well you may be sure Aunt Julia won't do it again.

HEDDA. In any case, I shall manage to make my peace with her.

TESMAN. Yes, my dear, good Hedda, if you only would. 50

HEDDA. When you call this afternoon, you might invite her to spend the evening here.

TESMAN. Yes, that I will. And there's one thing more you could do that would delight her heart. 55

HEDDA. What is it?

TESMAN. If you could only prevail on yourself to say *du*° to her. For my sake, Hedda? Eh?

HEDDA. No, no, Tesman—you really mustn't 60 ask that of me. I have told you so already. I shall try to call her "Aunt"; and you must be satisfied with that.

TESMAN. Well, well. Only I think now that you belong to the family, you— 65

HEDDA. H'm—I can't in the least see why— [*She goes up towards the middle doorway.*]

TESMAN [*after a pause*]. Is there anything the matter with you, Hedda? Eh?

HEDDA. I'm only looking at my old piano. It 70 doesn't go at all well with all the other things.

TESMAN. The first time I draw my salary, we'll see about exchanging it.

HEDDA. No, no—no exchanging. I don't want to part with it. Suppose we put it there 75 in the inner room, and then get another here in its place. When it's convenient, I mean.

TESMAN [*a little taken aback*]. Yes—of course we could do that.

HEDDA [*takes up the bouquet from the* 80 *piano*]. These flowers were not here last night when we arrived.

TESMAN. Aunt Julia must have brought them for you.

HEDDA [*examining the bouquet*]. A visiting- 85 card. [*Takes it out and reads.*] "Shall return later in the day." Can you guess whose card it is?

TESMAN. No. Whose? Eh?

HEDDA. The name is "Mrs. Elvsted." 90

---

du thou. Norwegian, like French and German, has a familiar second-person pronoun *du* ("thou") which is sharply distinguished from the formal or neutral *de* ("you"). The most significant occurrences of both pronouns are called attention to in footnotes.

TESMAN. Is it really? Sheriff Elvsted's wife? Miss Rysing that was.

HEDDA. Exactly. The girl with the irritating hair, that she was always showing off. An old 5 flame of yours, I've been told.

TESMAN [*laughing*]. Oh, that didn't last long; and it was before I knew you, Hedda. But fancy her being in town!

HEDDA. It's odd that she should call upon us. 10 I have scarcely seen her since we left school.

TESMAN. I haven't seen her either for— heaven knows how long. I wonder how she can endure to live in such an out-of-the-way hole —eh?

15 HEDDA [*after a moment's thought says suddenly*]. Tell me, Tesman—isn't it somewhere near there that he—that—Eilert Lövborg is living?

TESMAN. Yes, he is somewhere in that part 20 of the country.

[BERTA *enters by the hall door.*]

BERTA. That lady, ma'am, that brought some flowers a little while ago, is here again. [*Pointing.*] The flowers you have in your hand, 25 ma'am.

HEDDA. Ah, is she? Well, please show her in.

[BERTA *opens the door for* MRS. ELVSTED, *and goes out herself.—*MRS. ELVSTED *is a woman of fragile figure, with pretty, soft features. Her* 30 *eyes are light blue, large, round, and somewhat prominent, with a startled, inquiring expression. Her hair is remarkably light, almost flaxen, and unusually abundant and wavy. She is a couple of years younger than* HEDDA. *She* 35 *wears a dark visiting dress, tasteful, but not quite in the latest fashion.*]

HEDDA [*receives her warmly*]. How do you do, my dear Mrs. Elvsted? It's delightful to see you again.

40 MRS. ELVSTED [*nervously, struggling for self-control*]. Yes, it's a very long time since we met.

TESMAN [*gives her his hand*]. And we too— eh?

45 HEDDA. Thanks for your lovely flowers—

MRS. ELVSTED. Oh, not at all— I would have come straight here yesterday afternoon; but I heard that you were away—

TESMAN. Have you just come to town? Eh?

MRS. ELVSTED. I arrived yesterday, about 50 midday. Oh, I was quite in despair when I heard that you were not at home.

HEDDA. In despair! How so?

TESMAN. Why, my dear Mrs. Rysing—I mean Mrs. Elvsted— 55

HEDDA. I hope that you are not in any trouble?

MRS. ELVSTED. Yes, I am. And I don't know another living creature here that I can turn to.

HEDDA [*laying the bouquet on the table*]. 60 Come—let us sit here on the sofa—

MRS. ELVSTED. Oh, I am too restless to sit down.

HEDDA. Oh no, you're not. Come here. [*She draws* MRS. ELVSTED *down upon the sofa and* 65 *sits at her side.*]

TESMAN. Well? What is it, Mrs. Elvsted?

HEDDA. Has anything particular happened to you at home?

MRS. ELVSTED. Yes—and no. Oh—I am so 70 anxious you should not misunderstand me—

HEDDA. Then your best plan is to tell us the whole story, Mrs. Elvsted.

TESMAN. I suppose that's what you have come for—eh? 75

MRS. ELVSTED. Yes, yes—of course it is. Well then, I must tell you—if you don't already know—that Eilert Lövborg is in town, too.

HEDDA. Lövborg—!

TESMAN. What! Has Eilert Lövborg come 80 back? Fancy that, Hedda!

HEDDA. Well, well—I hear it.

MRS. ELVSTED. He has been here a week already. Just fancy—a whole week! In this terrible town, alone! With so many temptations 85 on all sides.

HEDDA. But my dear Mrs. Elvsted—how does he concern you so much?

MRS. ELVSTED [*looks at her with a startled air, and says rapidly*]. He was the children's 90 tutor.

HEDDA. Your children's?

MRS. ELVSTED. My husband's. I have none.

HEDDA. Your step-children's, then?

MRS. ELVSTED. Yes. 95

TESMAN [*somewhat hesitatingly*]. Then was

he—I don't know how to express it—was he
—regular enough in his habits to be fit for the
post? Eh?

MRS. ELVSTED. For the last two years his con-
5 duct has been irreproachable.

TESMAN. Has it indeed? Fancy that, Hedda!

HEDDA. I hear it.

MRS. ELVSTED. Perfectly irreproachable, I
assure you! In every respect. But all the same
10 —now that I know he is here—in this great
town—and with a large sum of money in his
hands—I can't help being in mortal fear for him.

TESMAN. Why did he not remain where he
was? With you and your husband? Eh?

15 MRS. ELVSTED. After his book was published
he was too restless and unsettled to remain
with us.

TESMAN. Yes, by-the-bye, Aunt Julia told me
he had published a new book.

20 MRS. ELVSTED. Yes, a big book, dealing with
the march of civilization—in broad outline, as
it were. It came out about a fortnight ago. And
since it has sold so well, and been so much
read—and made such a sensation—

25 TESMAN. Has it indeed? It must be something
he has had lying by since his better days.

MRS. ELVSTED. Long ago, you mean?

TESMAN. Yes.

MRS. ELVSTED. No, he has written it all since
30 he has been with us—within the last year.

TESMAN. Isn't that good news, Hedda? Think
of that.

MRS. ELVSTED. Ah, yes, if only it would last!

HEDDA. Have you seen him here in town?

35 MRS. ELVSTED. No, not yet. I have had the
greatest difficulty in finding out his address.
But this morning I discovered it at last.

HEDDA [*looks searchingly at her*]. Do you
know, it seems to me a little odd of your hus-
40 band—h'm—

MRS. ELVSTED [*starting nervously*]. Of my
husband! What?

HEDDA. That he should send you to town on
such an errand—that he does not come himself
45 and look after his friend.

MRS. ELVSTED. Oh, no, no—my husband has
no time. And besides, I—I had some shopping
to do.

HEDDA [*with a slight smile*]. Ah, that is a
different matter. 50

MRS. ELVSTED [*rising quickly and uneasily*].
And now I beg and implore you, Mr. Tesman
—receive Eilert Lövborg kindly if he comes to
you! And that he is sure to do. You see you
were such great friends in the old days. And 55
then you are interested in the same studies—
the same branch of science—so far as I can
understand.

TESMAN. We used to be, at any rate.

MRS. ELVSTED. That is why I beg so earnestly 60
that you—you too—will keep a sharp eye upon
him. Oh, you will promise me that, Mr. Tesman—won't you?

TESMAN. With the greatest of pleasure, Mrs.
Rysing— 65

HEDDA. Elvsted.

TESMAN. I assure you I shall do all I possibly
can for Eilert. You may rely upon me.

MRS. ELVSTED. Oh, how very, very kind of
you! [*Presses his hands.*] Thanks, thanks, 70
thanks! [*Frightened.*] You see, my husband is
very fond of him!

HEDDA [*rising*]. You ought to write to him,
Tesman. Perhaps he may not care to come to
you of his own accord. 75

TESMAN. Well, perhaps it would be the right
thing to do, Hedda? Eh?

HEDDA. And the sooner the better. Why not
at once?

MRS. ELVSTED [*imploringly*]. Oh, if you only 80
would!

TESMAN. I'll write this moment. Have you
his address, Mrs.—Mrs. Elvsted?

MRS. ELVSTED. Yes. [*Takes a slip of paper
from her pocket, and hands it to him.*] Here it is. 85

TESMAN. Good, good. Then I'll go in—
[*Looks about him.*] By-the-bye,—my slippers?
Oh, here. [*Takes the packet, and is about to
go.*]

HEDDA. Be sure you write him a cordial, 90
friendly letter. And a good long one too.

TESMAN. Yes, I will.

MRS. ELVSTED. But please, please don't say a
word to show that I have suggested it.

TESMAN. No, how could you think I would? 95
Eh?

[*He goes out to the right, through the inner room.*]

HEDDA [*goes up to* MRS. ELVSTED, *smiles, and says in a low voice*]. There. We have killed two birds with one stone.

MRS. ELVSTED. What do you mean?

HEDDA. Could you not see that I wanted him to go?

MRS. ELVSTED. Yes, to write the letter—

HEDDA. And that I might speak to you alone.

MRS. ELVSTED [*confused*]. About the same thing?

HEDDA. Precisely.

MRS. ELVSTED [*apprehensively*]. But there is nothing more, Mrs. Tesman! Absolutely nothing!

HEDDA. Oh, yes, but there is. There is a great deal more—I can see that. Sit here—and we'll have a cosy, confidential chat. [*She forces* MRS. ELVSTED *to sit in the easy-chair beside the stove, and seats herself on one of the foot-stools.*]

MRS. ELVSTED [*anxiously, looking at her watch*]. But, my dear Mrs. Tesman—I was really on the point of going.

HEDDA. Oh, you can't be in such a hurry.— Well? Now tell me something about your life at home.

MRS. ELVSTED. Oh, that is just what I care least to speak about.

HEDDA. But to me, dear—? Why, weren't we school-fellows?

MRS. ELVSTED. Yes, but you were in the class above me. Oh, how dreadfully afraid of you I was then!

HEDDA. Afraid of me?

MRS. ELVSTED. *Yes*, dreadfully. For when we met on the stairs you used always to pull my hair.

HEDDA. Did I, really?

MRS. ELVSTED. Yes, and once you said you would burn it off my head.

HEDDA. Oh, that was all nonsense, of course.

MRS. ELVSTED. Yes, but I was so silly in those days.—And since then, too—we have drifted so far—far apart from each other. Our circles have been so entirely different.

HEDDA. Well then, we must try to drift to-gether again. Now listen! At school we said *du* to each other; and we called each other by our Christian names—

MRS. ELVSTED. No, I am sure you must be mistaken.

HEDDA. No, not at all! I can remember quite distinctly. So now we are going to renew our old friendship. [*Draws the foot-stool closer to* MRS. ELVSTED.] There now! [*Kisses her cheek.*] You must say *du* to me and call me Hedda.

MRS. ELVSTED [*presses and pats her hands*]. Oh, how good and kind you are! I am not used to such kindness.

HEDDA. There, there, there! And I shall say *du* to you, as in the old days, and call you my dear Thora.

MRS. ELVSTED. My name is Thea.

HEDDA. Why, of course! I meant Thea. [*Looks at her compassionately.*] So you are not accustomed to goodness and kindness, Thea? Not in your own home?

MRS. ELVSTED. Oh, if I only had a home! But I haven't any; I have never had a home.

HEDDA [*looks at her for a moment*]. I almost suspected as much.

MRS. ELVSTED [*gazing helplessly before her*]. Yes—yes—yes.

HEDDA. I don't quite remember—was it not as housekeeper that you first went to Mr. Elvsted's?

MRS. ELVSTED. I really went as governess. But his wife—his late wife—was an invalid, —and rarely left her room. So I had to look after the housekeeping as well.

HEDDA. And then—at last—you became mistress of the house.

MRS. ELVSTED [*sadly*]. Yes, I did.

HEDDA. Let me see—about how long ago was that?

MRS. ELVSTED. My marriage?

HEDDA. Yes.

MRS ELVSTED. Five years ago.

HEDDA. To be sure; it must be that.

MRS. ELVSTED. Oh, those five years—! Or at all events the last two or three of them! Oh, if you could only imagine—

HEDDA [*giving her a little slap on the hand*]. *De*? Fie, Thea!

MRS. ELVSTED. Yes, yes, I will try— Well if
—you could only imagine and understand—

HEDDA [*lightly*]. Eilert Lövborg has been in
your neighborhood about three years, hasn't
5 he?

MRS. ELVSTED [*looks at her doubtfully*].
Eilert Lövborg? Yes—he has.

HEDDA. Had you known him before, in town
here?

10 MRS. ELVSTED. Scarcely at all. I mean—I
knew him by name of course.

HEDDA. But you saw a good deal of him in
the country?

MRS. ELVSTED. Yes, he came to us every day.
15 You see, he gave the children lessons; for in
the long run I couldn't manage it all myself.

HEDDA. No, that's clear.—And your husband—? I suppose he is often away from
home?

20 MRS. ELVSTED. Yes. Being Sheriff, you know,
he has to travel about a good deal in his district.

HEDDA [*leaning against the arm of the chair*].
Thea—my poor, sweet Thea—now you must
25 tell me everything—exactly as it stands.

MRS. ELVSTED. Well then, you must question
me.

HEDDA. What sort of a man is your husband,
Thea? I mean—you know—in everyday life.
30 Is he kind to you?

MRS. ELVSTED [*evasively*]. I am sure he
means well in everything.

HEDDA. I should think he must be altogether
too old for you. There is at least twenty years'
35 difference between you, is there not?

MRS. ELVSTED [*irritably*]. Yes, that is true,
too. Everything about him is repellent to me!
We have not a thought in common. We have
no single point of sympathy—he and I.

40 HEDDA. But is he not fond of you all the
same? In his own way?

MRS. ELVSTED. Oh, I really don't know. I
think he regards me simply as a useful property. And then it doesn't cost much to keep
45 me. I am not expensive.

HEDDA. That is stupid of you.

MRS. ELVSTED [*shakes her head*]. It cannot
be otherwise—not with him. I don't think he

really cares for any one but himself—and perhaps a little for the children. 50

HEDDA. And for Eilert Lövborg, Thea.

MRS. ELVSTED [*looking at her*]. For Eilert
Lövborg? What puts that into your head?

HEDDA. Well, my dear—I should say, when
he sends you after him all the way to town— 55
[*smiling almost imperceptibly*]. And besides,
you said so yourself, to Tesman.

MRS. ELVSTED [*with a little nervous twitch*].
Did I? Yes, I suppose I did. [*Vehemently, but
not loudly.*] No—I may just as well make a 60
clean breast of it at once! For it must all come
out in any case.

HEDDA. Why, my dear Thea—?

MRS. ELVSTED. Well, to make a long story
short: My husband did not know that I was 65
coming.

HEDDA. What! Your husband didn't know
it!

MRS. ELVSTED. No, of course not. For that
matter, he was away from home himself—he 70
was traveling. Oh, I could bear it no longer,
Hedda! I couldn't indeed—so utterly alone as
I should have been in future.

HEDDA. Well? And then?

MRS. ELVSTED. So I put together some of my 75
things—what I needed most—as quietly as
possible. And then I left the house.

HEDDA. Without a word?

MRS. ELVSTED. Yes—and took the train
straight to town. 80

HEDDA. Why, my dear, good Thea—to think
of you daring to do it!

MRS. ELVSTED [*rises and moves about the
room*]. What else could I possibly do?

HEDDA. But what do you think your husband 85
will say when you go home again?

MRS. ELVSTED [*at the table, looks at her*].
Back to him?

HEDDA. Of course.

MRS. ELVSTED. I shall never go back to him 90
again.

HEDDA [*rising and going towards her*]. Then
you have left your home—for good and all?

MRS. ELVSTED. Yes. There was nothing else
to be done. 95

HEDDA. But then—to take flight so openly.

MRS. ELVSTED. Oh, it's impossible to keep things of that sort secret.

HEDDA. But what do you think people will say of you, Thea?

5 MRS. ELVSTED. They may say what they like for aught I care. [Seats herself wearily and sadly on the sofa.] I have done nothing but what I had to do.

HEDDA [after a short silence]. And what are 10 your plans now? What do you think of doing?

MRS. ELVSTED. I don't know yet. I only know this, that I must live here, where Eilert Lövborg is—if I am to live at all.

HEDDA [takes a chair from the table, seats 15 herself beside her, and strokes her hands]. My dear Thea—how did this—this friendship—between you and Eilert Lövborg come about?

MRS. ELVSTED. Oh, it grew up gradually. I gained a sort of influence over him.

20 HEDDA. Indeed?

MRS. ELVSTED. He gave up his old habits. Not because I asked him to, for I never dared do that. But of course he saw how repulsive they were to me; and so he dropped them.

25 HEDDA [concealing an involuntary smile of scorn]. Then you have reclaimed him—as the saying goes—my little Thea.

MRS. ELVSTED. So he says himself, at any rate. And he, on his side, has made a real 30 human being of me—taught me to think, and to understand so many things.

HEDDA. Did he give you lessons too, then?

MRS. ELVSTED. No, not exactly lessons. But he talked to me—talked about such an infinity 35 of things. And then came the lovely, happy time when I began to share in his work—when he allowed me to help him!

HEDDA. Oh, he did, did he?

MRS. ELVSTED. Yes! He never wrote anything 40 without my assistance.

HEDDA. You were two good comrades, in fact?

MRS. ELVSTED [eagerly]. Comrades! Yes, fancy, Hedda—that is the very word he used! 45 —Oh, I ought to feel perfectly happy; and yet I cannot; for I don't know how long it will last.

HEDDA. Are you no surer of him than that?

MRS. ELVSTED [gloomily]. A woman's shadow stands between Eilert Lövborg and me.

HEDDA [looks at her anxiously]. Who can 50 that be?

MRS. ELVSTED. I don't know. Some one he knew in his—in his past. Some one he has never been able wholly to forget.

HEDDA. What has he told you—about this? 55

MRS. ELVSTED. He has only once—quite vaguely—alluded to it.

HEDDA. Well! And what did he say?

MRS. ELVSTED. He said that when they parted, she threatened to shoot him with a 60 pistol.

HEDDA [with cold composure]. Oh, nonsense! No one does that sort of thing here.

MRS. ELVSTED. No. And that is why I think it must have been that red-haired singing 65 woman whom he once—

HEDDA. Yes, very likely.

MRS. ELVSTED. For I remember they used to say of her that she carried loaded firearms.

HEDDA. Oh—then of course it must have 70 been she.

MRS. ELVSTED [wringing her hands]. And now just fancy, Hedda—I hear that this singing-woman—that she is in town again! Oh, I don't know what to do— 75

HEDDA [glancing towards the inner room]. Hush! Here comes Tesman. [Rises and whispers.] Thea—all this must remain between you and me.

MRS. ELVSTED [springing up]. Oh, yes, yes! 80 for heaven's sake—!

[GEORGE TESMAN, with a letter in his hand, comes from the right through the inner room.]

TESMAN. There now—the epistle is finished.

HEDDA. That's right. And now Mrs. Elvsted 85 is just going. Wait a moment—I'll go with you to the garden gate.

TESMAN. Do you think Berta could post the letter, Hedda dear?

HEDDA [takes it]. I will tell her to. 90

[BERTA enters from the hall.]

BERTA. Judge Brack wishes to know if Mrs. Tesman will receive him.

HEDDA. Yes, ask Judge Brack to come in. And look here—put this letter in the post. 95

BERTA [taking the letter]. Yes, ma'am.

[*She opens the door for* JUDGE BRACK *and goes out herself.* BRACK *is a man of forty-five; thick-set, but well-built and elastic in his movements. His face is roundish with an aristocratic profile. His hair is short, still almost black, and carefully dressed. His eyes are lively and sparkling. His eyebrows thick. His moustaches are also thick, with short-cut ends. He wears a well-cut walking-suit, a little too youthful for his age. He uses an eye-glass, which he now and then lets drop.*]

JUDGE BRACK [*with his hat in his hand, bowing*]. May one venture to call so early in the day?

HEDDA. Of course one may.

TESMAN [*presses his hand*]. You are welcome at any time. [*Introducing him.*] Judge Brack— Miss Rysing—

HEDDA. Oh—!

BRACK [*bowing*]. Ah—delighted—

HEDDA [*looks at him and laughs*]. It's nice to have a look at you by daylight, Judge!

BRACK. Do you find me—altered?

HEDDA. A little younger, I think.

BRACK. Thank you so much.

TESMAN. But what do you think of Hedda— eh? Doesn't she look flourishing? She has actually—

HEDDA. Oh, do leave me alone. You haven't thanked Judge Brack for all the trouble he has taken—

BRACK. Oh, nonsense—it was a pleasure to me—

HEDDA. Yes, you are a friend indeed. But here stands Thea all impatience to be off—so *au revoir*, Judge. I shall be back again presently. [*Mutual salutations.* MRS. ELVSTED *and* HEDDA *go out by the hall door.*]

BRACK. Well,—is your wife tolerably satisfied—

TESMAN. Yes, we can't thank you sufficiently. Of course she talks of a little re-arrangement here and there; and one or two things are still wanting. We shall have to buy some additional trifles.

BRACK. Indeed!

TESMAN. But we won't trouble you about these things. Hedda says she herself will look after what is wanting.—Shan't we sit down? Eh?

BRACK. Thanks, for a moment. [*Seats himself beside the table.*] There is something I wanted to speak to you about, my dear Tesman.

TESMAN. Indeed? Ah, I understand! [*Seating himself.*] I suppose it's the serious part of the frolic that is coming now. Eh?

BRACK. Oh, the money question is not so very pressing; though, for that matter, I wish we had gone a little more economically to work.

TESMAN. But that would never have done, you know! Think of Hedda, my dear fellow! You, who know her so well—. I couldn't possibly ask her to put up with a shabby style of living!

BRACK. No, no—that is just the difficulty.

TESMAN. And then—fortunately—it can't be long before I receive my appointment.

BRACK. Well, you see—such things are often apt to hang fire for a time.

TESMAN. Have you heard anything definite? Eh?

BRACK. Nothing exactly definite—[*interrupting himself*]. But, by-the-bye—I have one piece of news for you.

TESMAN. Well?

BRACK. Your old friend, Eilert Lövborg, has returned to town.

TESMAN. I know that already.

BRACK. Indeed! How did you learn it?

TESMAN. From that lady who went out with Hedda.

BRACK. Really? What was her name? I didn't quite catch it.

TESMAN. Mrs. Elvsted.

BRACK. Aha—Sheriff Elvsted's wife? Of course—he has been living up in their regions.

TESMAN. And fancy—I'm delighted to hear that he is quite a reformed character!

BRACK. So they say.

TESMAN. And then he has published a new book—eh?

BRACK. Yes, indeed he has.

TESMAN. And I hear it has made some sensation!

BRACK. Quite an unusual sensation.

TESMAN. Fancy—isn't that good news! A man of such extraordinary talents— I felt so grieved to think that he had gone irretrievably to ruin.

BRACK. That was what everybody thought.

TESMAN. But I cannot imagine what he will take to now! How in the world will he be able to make his living? Eh?

[*During the last words,* HEDDA *has entered by the hall door.*]

HEDDA [*to* BRACK, *laughing with a touch of scorn*]. Tesman is forever worrying about how people are to make their living.

TESMAN. Well, you see, dear—we were talking about poor Eilert Lövborg.

HEDDA [*glancing at him rapidly*]. Oh, indeed? [*Seats herself in the arm-chair beside the stove and asks indifferently.*] What is the matter with him?

TESMAN. Well—no doubt he has run through all his property long ago; and he can scarcely write a new book every year—eh? So I really can't see what is to become of him.

BRACK. Perhaps I can give you some information on that point.

TESMAN. Indeed!

BRACK. You must remember that his relations have a good deal of influence.

TESMAN. Oh, his relations, unfortunately have entirely washed their hands of him.

BRACK. At one time they called him the hope of the family.

TESMAN. At one time, yes! But he has put an end to all that.

HEDDA. Who knows? [*With a slight smile.*] I hear they have reclaimed him up at Sheriff Elvsted's—

BRACK. And then this book that he has published—

TESMAN. Well, well, I hope to goodness they may find something for him to do. I have just written to him. I asked him to come and see us this evening, Hedda dear.

BRACK. But, my dear fellow, you are booked for my bachelors' party this evening. You promised on the pier last night.

HEDDA. Had you forgotten, Tesman?

TESMAN. Yes, I had utterly forgotten.

BRACK. But it doesn't matter, for you may be sure he won't come.

TESMAN. What makes you think that? Eh?

BRACK [*with a little hesitation, rising and resting his hands on the back of his chair*]. My dear Tesman—and you too, Mrs. Tesman—I think I ought not to keep you in the dark about something that—that—

TESMAN. That concerns Eilert—?

BRACK. Both you and him.

TESMAN. Well, my dear Judge, out with it.

BRACK. You must be prepared to find your appointment deferred longer than you desired or expected.

TESMAN [*jumping up uneasily*]. Is there some hitch about it? Eh?

BRACK. The nomination may perhaps be made conditional on the result of a competition—

TESMAN. Competition! Think of that, Hedda!

HEDDA [*leans farther back in the chair*]. Aha—aha!

TESMAN. But who can my competitor be? Surely not—?

BRACK. Yes, precisely—Eilert Lövborg.

TESMAN [*clasping his hands*]. No, no—it's quite inconceivable! Quite impossible! Eh?

BRACK. H'm—that is what it may come to, all the same.

TESMAN. Well but, Judge Brack—it would show the most incredible lack of consideration for me. [*Gesticulates with his arms.*] For—just think—I'm a married man. We have been married on the strength of these prospects, Hedda and I; and run deep into debt; and borrowed money from Aunt Julia too. Good heavens, they had as good as promised me the appointment. Eh?

BRACK. Well, well, well—no doubt you will get it in the end; only after a contest.

HEDDA [*immovable in her arm-chair*]. Fancy, Tesman, there will be a sort of sporting interest in that.

TESMAN. Why, my dearest Hedda, how can you be so indifferent about it?

HEDDA [*as before*]. I am not at all indifferent. I am most eager to see who wins.

BRACK. In any case, Mrs. Tesman, it is best that you should know how matters stand. I mean—before you set about the little purchases I hear you are threatening.

5 HEDDA. This can make no difference.

BRACK. Indeed! Then I have no more to say. Good-bye! [*To* TESMAN.] I shall look in on my way back from my afternoon walk, and take you home with me.

10 TESMAN. Oh yes, yes—your news has quite upset me.

HEDDA [*reclining, holds out her hand*]. Good-bye, Judge; and be sure you call in the afternoon.

15 BRACK. Many thanks. Good-bye, good-bye!

TESMAN [*accompanying him to the door*]. Good-bye, my dear Judge! You must really excuse me—

[JUDGE BRACK *goes out by the hall door.*]

20 TESMAN [*crosses the room*]. Oh, Hedda— one should never rush into adventures. Eh?

HEDDA [*looks at him, smiling*]. Do you do that?

TESMAN. Yes, dear—there is no denying—it 25 was adventurous to go and marry and set up house upon mere expectations.

HEDDA. Perhaps you are right there.

TESMAN. Well—at all events, we have our delightful home, Hedda! Fancy, the home we 30 both dreamed of—the home we were in love with, I may almost say. Eh?

HEDDA [*rising slowly and wearily*]. It was part of our compact that we were to go into society—to keep open house.

35 TESMAN. Yes, if you only knew how I had been looking forward to it! Fancy—to see you as hostess—in a select circle? Eh? Well, well, well—for the present we shall have to get on without society, Hedda—only to invite Aunt 40 Julia now and then.—Oh, I intended you to lead such an utterly different life, dear—!

HEDDA. Of course I cannot have my man in livery just yet.

TESMAN. Oh no, unfortunately. It would be 45 out of the question for us to keep a footman, you know.

HEDDA. And the saddle-horse I was to have had—

TESMAN [*aghast*]. The saddle-horse!

HEDDA. —I suppose I must not think of that 50 now.

TESMAN. Good heavens, no!—that's as clear as daylight.

HEDDA [*goes up the room*]. Well, I shall have one thing at least to kill time with in the 55 meanwhile.

TESMAN [*beaming*]. Oh, thank heaven for that! What is it, Hedda? Eh?

HEDDA [*in the middle doorway, looks at him with covert scorn*]. My pistols, George. 60

TESMAN [*in alarm*]. Your pistols!

HEDDA [*with cold eyes*]. General Gabler's pistols.

[*She goes out through the inner room, to the left.*] 65

TESMAN [*rushes up to the middle doorway and calls after her*]. No, for heaven's sake, Hedda darling—don't touch those dangerous things! For my sake, Hedda! Eh?

ACT II

[*The room at the* TESMANS' *as in the first act,* 70 *except that the piano has been removed, and an elegant little writing-table with bookshelves put in its place. A smaller table stands near the sofa at the left. Most of the bouquets have been taken away.* MRS. ELVSTED'S *bouquet is* 75 *upon the large table in front.—It is afternoon.*

HEDDA, *dressed to receive callers, is alone in the room. She stands by the open glass door, loading a revolver. The fellow to it lies in an open pistol-case on the writing-table.*] 80

HEDDA [*looks down the garden, and calls*]. So you are here again, Judge!

BRACK [*is heard calling from a distance*]. As you see, Mrs. Tesman!

HEDDA [*raises the pistol and points*]. Now 85 I'll shoot you, Judge Brack!

BRACK [*calling unseen*]. No, no, no! Don't stand aiming at me!

HEDDA. This is what comes of sneaking in by the back way. [*She fires.*] 90

BRACK [*nearer*]. Are you out of your senses—!

HEDDA. Dear me—did I happen to hit you?

BRACK [*still outside*]. I wish you would let these pranks alone!

HEDDA. Come in then, Judge.

[JUDGE BRACK, *dressed as though for a men's party, enters by the glass door. He carries a light overcoat over his arm.*]

BRACK. What the deuce—haven't you tired of that sport, yet? What are you shooting at?

HEDDA. Oh, I am only firing in the air.

BRACK [*gently takes the pistol out of her hand*]. Allow me, madam! [*Looks at it.*] Ah—I know this pistol well! [*Looks around.*] Where is the case? Ah, here it is. [*Lays the pistol in it, and shuts it.*] Now we won't play at that game any more today.

HEDDA. Then what in heaven's name would you have me do with myself?

BRACK. Have you had no visitors?

HEDDA [*closing the glass door*]. Not one. I suppose all our set are still out of town.

BRACK. And is Tesman not at home either?

HEDDA [*at the writing-table, putting the pistol-case in a drawer which she shuts*]. No. He rushed off to his aunt's directly after lunch; he didn't expect you so early.

BRACK. H'm—how stupid of me not to have thought of that!

HEDDA [*turning her head to look at him*]. Why stupid?

BRACK. Because if I had thought of it I should have come a little—earlier.

HEDDA [*crossing the room*]. Then you would have found no one to receive you; for I have been in my room changing my dress ever since lunch.

BRACK. And is there no sort of little chink that we could hold a parley through?

HEDDA. You have forgotten to arrange one.

BRACK. That was another piece of stupidity.

HEDDA. Well, we must just settle down here —and wait. Tesman is not likely to be back for some time yet.

BRACK. Never mind; I shall not be impatient.

[HEDDA *seats herself in the corner of the sofa.* BRACK *lays his overcoat over the back of the nearest chair, and sits down, but keeps his hat in his hand. A short silence. They look at each other.*]

HEDDA. Well?

BRACK [*in the same tone*]. Well?

HEDDA. I spoke first.

BRACK [*bending a little forward*]. Come, let us have a cosy little chat, Mrs. Hedda.

HEDDA [*leaning further back in the sofa*]. Does it not seem like a whole eternity since our last talk? Of course I don't count those few words yesterday evening and this morning.

BRACK. You mean since our last confidential talk? Our last *tête-à-tête*?

HEDDA. Well, yes—since you put it so.

BRACK. Not a day has passed but I have wished that you were home again.

HEDDA. And I have done nothing but wish the same thing.

BRACK. You? Really, Mrs. Hedda? And I thought you had been enjoying your tour so much!

HEDDA. Oh, yes, you may be sure of that!

BRACK. But Tesman's letters spoke of nothing but happiness.

HEDDA. Oh, Tesman! You see, he thinks nothing so delightful as grubbing in libraries and making copies of old parchments, or whatever you call them.

BRACK [*with a spice of malice*]. Well, that is his vocation in life—or part of it at any rate.

HEDDA. Yes, of course; and no doubt when it's your vocation— But I! Oh, my dear Mr. Brack, how mortally bored I have been.

BRACK [*sympathetically*]. Do you really say so? In downright earnest?

HEDDA. Yes, you can surely understand it—! To go for six whole months without meeting a soul that knew anything of our circle, or could talk about the things we are interested in.

BRACK. Yes, yes—I too should feel that a deprivation.

HEDDA. And then, what I found most intolerable of all—

BRACK. Well?

HEDDA. —was being everlastingly in the company of—one and the same person—

BRACK [*with a nod of assent*]. Morning, noon, and night, yes—at all possible times and seasons.

HEDDA. I said "everlastingly."

BRACK. Just so. But I should have thought, with our excellent Tesman, one could—

HEDDA. Tesman is—a specialist, my dear Judge.

5 BRACK. Undeniably.

HEDDA. And specialists are not at all amusing to travel with. Not in the long run at any rate.

BRACK. Not even—the specialist one happens
10 to love?

HEDDA. Faugh—don't use that sickening word!

BRACK [*taken aback*]. What do you say, Mrs. Hedda?

15 HEDDA [*half laughing, half irritated*]. You should just try it! To hear of nothing but the history of civilization, morning, noon, and night—

BRACK. Everlastingly.

20 HEDDA. Yes, yes, yes! And then all this about the domestic industry of the middle ages—! That's the most disgusting part of it!

BRACK [*looks searchingly at her*]. But tell me —in that case, how am I to understand your
25 —? H'm—

HEDDA. My accepting George Tesman, you mean?

BRACK. Well, let us put it so.

HEDDA. Good heavens, do you see anything
30 so wonderful in that?

BRACK. Yes and no—Mrs. Hedda.

HEDDA. I had positively danced myself tired, my dear Judge. My day was done— [*With a slight shudder.*] Oh no—I won't say that; nor
35 think it either!

BRACK. You have assuredly no reason to.

HEDDA. Oh, reasons— [*Watching him closely.*] And George Tesman—after all, you must admit that he is correctness itself.

40 BRACK. His correctness and respectability are beyond all question.

HEDDA. And I don't see anything absolutely ridiculous about him.—Do you?

BRACK. Ridiculous? N—no—I shouldn't
45 exactly say so—

HEDDA. Well—and his powers of research, at all events, are untiring.—I see no reason why he should not one day come to the front, after all.

BRACK [*looks at her hesitatingly*]. I thought that you, like every one else, expected him to 50 attain the highest distinction.

HEDDA [*with an expression of fatigue*]. Yes, so I did.—And then, since he was bent, at all hazards, on being allowed to provide for me— I really don't know why I should not have 55 accepted his offer?

BRACK. No—if you look at it in that light—

HEDDA. It was more than my other adorers were prepared to do for me, my dear Judge.

BRACK [*laughing*]. Well, I can't answer for 60 all the rest; but as for myself, you know quite well that I have always entertained a—a certain respect for the marriage tie—for marriage as an institution, Mrs. Hedda.

HEDDA [*jestingly*]. Oh, I assure you I have 65 never cherished any hopes with respect to you.

BRACK. All I require is a pleasant and intimate interior, where I can make myself useful in every way, and am free to come and go as— a trusted friend— 70

HEDDA. Of the master of the house, do you mean?

BRACK [*bowing*]. Frankly—of the mistress first of all; but of course of the master, too, in the second place. Such a triangular friendship 75 —if I may call it so—is really a great convenience for all parties, let me tell you.

HEDDA. Yes, I have many a time longed for some one to make a third on our travels. Oh —those railway-carriage *tête-à-têtes*—! 80

BRACK. Fortunately your wedding journey is over now.

HEDDA [*shaking her head*]. Not by a long— long way. I have only arrived at a station on the line. 85

BRACK. Well, then the passengers jump out and move about a little, Mrs. Hedda.

HEDDA. I never jump out.

BRACK. Really?

HEDDA. No—because there is always some 90 one standing by to—

BRACK [*laughing*]. To look at your ankles, do you mean?

HEDDA. Precisely.

BRACK. Well but, dear me— 95

HEDDA [*with a gesture of repulsion*]. I won't

have it. I would rather keep my seat where I happen to be—and continue the *tête-à-tête*.

BRACK. But suppose a third person were to jump in and join the couple.

5 HEDDA. Ah—that is quite another matter!

BRACK. A trusted, sympathetic friend—

HEDDA. —with a fund of conversation on all sorts of lively topics—

BRACK. —and not the least bit of a specialist!

10 HEDDA [*with an audible sigh*]. Yes, that would be a relief indeed.

BRACK [*hears the front door open, and glances in that direction*]. The triangle is completed.

15 HEDDA [*half aloud*]. And on goes the train.

[GEORGE TESMAN, *in a gray walking-suit, with a soft felt hat, enters from the hall. He has a number of unbound books under his arm and in his pockets.*]

20 TESMAN [*goes up to the table beside the corner settee*]. Ouf—what a load for a warm day—all these books. [*Lays them on the table.*] I'm positively perspiring, Hedda. Hallo—are you there already, my dear Judge? Eh? Berta

25 didn't tell me.

BRACK [*rising*]. I came in through the garden.

HEDDA. What books have you got there?

TESMAN [*stands looking them through*].

30 Some new books on my special subjects—quite indispensable to me.

HEDDA. Your special subjects?

BRACK. Yes, books on his special subjects, Mrs. Tesman. [BRACK *and* HEDDA *exchange a*

35 *confidential smile.*]

HEDDA. Do you need still more books on your special subjects?

TESMAN. Yes, my dear Hedda, one can never have too many of them. Of course one must

40 keep up with all that is written and published.

HEDDA. Yes, I suppose one must.

TESMAN [*searching among his books*]. And look here—I have got hold of Eilert Lövborg's new book too. [*Offering it to her.*] Perhaps

45 you would like to glance through it, Hedda? Eh?

HEDDA. No, thank you. Or rather—afterwards perhaps.

TESMAN. I looked into it a little on the way home.   50

BRACK. Well, what do you think of it—as a specialist?

TESMAN. I think it shows quite remarkable soundness of judgment. He never wrote like that before. [*Putting the books together.*] Now 55 I shall take all these into my study. I'm longing to cut the leaves—! And then I must change my clothes. [*To* BRACK.] I suppose we needn't start just yet? Eh?

BRACK. Oh, dear no—there is not the 60 slightest hurry.

TESMAN. Well then, I will take my time. [*Is going with his books, but stops in the doorway and turns.*] By-the-bye, Hedda—Aunt Julia is not coming this evening.   65

HEDDA. Not coming? Is it that affair of the bonnet that keeps her away?

TESMAN. Oh, not at all. How could you think such a thing of Aunt Julia? Just fancy—! The fact is, Aunt Rina is very ill.   70

HEDDA. She always is.

TESMAN. Yes, but today she is much worse than usual, poor dear.

HEDDA. Oh, then it's only natural that her sister should remain with her. I must bear my 75 disappointment.

TESMAN. And you can't imagine, dear, how delighted Aunt Julia seemed to be—because you had come home looking so flourishing!

HEDDA [*half aloud, rising*]. Oh, those ever- 80 lasting aunts!

TESMAN. What?

HEDDA [*going to the glass door*]. Nothing.

TESMAN. Oh, all right.

[*He goes through the inner room, out to the 85 right.*]

BRACK. What bonnet were you talking about?

HEDDA. Oh, it was a little episode with Miss Tesman this morning. She had laid down her bonnet on the chair there—[*looks at him and 90 smiles*].—And I pretended to think it was the servant's.

BRACK [*shaking his head*]. Now my dear Mrs. Hedda, how could you do such a thing? To that excellent old lady, too!   95

HEDDA [*nervously crossing the room*]. Well,

you see—these impulses come over me all of a sudden; and I cannot resist them. [*Throws herself down in the easy-chair by the stove.*] Oh, I don't know how to explain it.

5 BRACK [*behind the easy-chair*]. You are not really happy—that is at the bottom of it.

HEDDA [*looking straight before her*]. I know of no reason why I should be—happy. Perhaps you can give me one?

10 BRACK. Well—amongst other things, because you have got exactly the home you had set your heart on.

HEDDA [*looks up at him and laughs*]. Do you too believe in that legend?

15 BRACK. Is there nothing in it, then?

HEDDA. Oh, yes, there is something in it.

BRACK. Well?

HEDDA. There is this in it, that I made use of Tesman to see me home from evening parties 20 last summer—

BRACK. I, unfortunately, had to go quite a different way.

HEDDA. That's true. I know you were going a different way last summer.

25 BRACK [*laughing*]. Oh fie, Mrs. Hedda! Well, then—you and Tesman—?

HEDDA. Well, we happened to pass here one evening; Tesman, poor fellow, was writhing in the agony of having to find conversation; so I 30 took pity on the learned man—

BRACK [*smiles doubtfully*]. You took pity? H'm—

HEDDA. Yes, I really did. And so—to help him out of his torment—I happened to say, in 35 pure thoughtlessness, that I should like to live in this villa.

BRACK. No more than that?

HEDDA. Not that evening.

BRACK. But afterwards?

40 HEDDA. Yes, my thoughtlessness had consequences, my dear Judge.

BRACK. Unfortunately that too often happens, Mrs. Hedda.

HEDDA. Thanks! So you see it was this en-45 thusiasm for Secretary Falk's villa that first constituted a bond of sympathy between George Tesman and me. From that came our engagement and our marriage, and our wedding

journey, and all the rest of it. Well, well, my dear Judge—as you make your bed so you 50 must lie, I could almost say.

BRACK. This is exquisite! And you really cared not a rap about it all the time?

HEDDA. No, heaven knows I didn't.

BRACK. But now? Now that we have made it 55 so homelike for you?

HEDDA. Uh—the rooms all seem to smell of lavender and dried rose-leaves.—But perhaps it's Aunt Julia that has brought that scent with her. 60

BRACK [*laughing*]. No, I think it must be a legacy from the late Mrs. Secretary Falk.

HEDDA. Yes, there is an odor of mortality about it. It reminds me of a bouquet—the day after the ball. [*Clasps her hands behind her* 65 *head, leans back in her chair and looks at him.*] Oh, my dear Judge—you cannot imagine how horribly I shall bore myself here.

BRACK. Why should not you, too, find some sort of vocation in life, Mrs. Hedda? 70

HEDDA. A vocation—that should attract me?

BRACK. If possible, of course.

HEDDA. Heaven knows what sort of a vocation that could be. I often wonder whether—[*breaking off*]. But that would never do either. 75

BRACK. Who can tell? Let me hear what it is.

HEDDA. Whether I might not get Tesman to go into politics, I mean.

BRACK [*laughing*]. Tesman? No, really now, political life is not the thing for him—not at all 80 in his line.

HEDDA. No, I daresay not.—But if I could get him into it all the same?

BRACK. Why—what satisfaction could you find in that? If he is not fitted for that sort of 85 thing, why should you want to drive him into it?

HEDDA. Because I am bored, I tell you! [*After a pause.*] So you think it quite out of the question that Tesman should ever get into the 90 ministry?

BRACK. H'm—you see, my dear Mrs. Hedda —to get into the ministry, he would have to be a tolerably rich man.

HEDDA [*rising impatiently*]. Yes, there we 95 have it! It is this genteel poverty I have

managed to drop into—! [*Crosses the room.*]
That is what makes life so pitiable! So utterly
ludicrous!—For that's what it is.

BRACK. Now *I* should say the fault lay else-
5 where.

HEDDA. Where, then?

BRACK. You have never gone through any
really stimulating experience.

HEDDA. Anything serious, you mean?

10 BRACK. Yes, you may call it so. But now you
may perhaps have one in store.

HEDDA [*tossing her head*]. Oh, you're thinking of the annoyances about this wretched pro-
fessorship! But that must be Tesman's own
15 affair. I assure you I shall not waste a thought
upon it.

BRACK. No, no. I daresay not. But suppose
now that what people call—in elegant language—a solemn responsibility were to come
20 upon you? [*Smiling.*] A new responsibility,
Mrs. Hedda?

HEDDA [*angrily*]. Be quiet! Nothing of that
sort will ever happen!

BRACK [*warily*]. We will speak of this again
25 a year hence—at the very outside.

HEDDA [*curtly*]. I have no turn for anything
of the sort, Judge Brack. No responsibilities
for me!

BRACK. Are you so unlike the generality of
30 women as to have no turn for duties which—?

HEDDA [*beside the glass door*]. Oh, be quiet,
I tell you!—I often think there is only one
thing in the world I have any turn for.

BRACK [*drawing near to her*]. And what is
35 that, if I may ask?

HEDDA [*stands looking out*]. Boring myself
to death. Now you know it. [*Turns, looks towards the inner room, and laughs.*] Yes, as I
thought! Here comes the Professor.

40 BRACK [*softly, in a tone of warning*]. Come,
come, come, Mrs. Hedda!

[GEORGE TESMAN, *dressed for the party, with
his gloves and hat in his hand, enters from the
right through the inner room.*]

45 TESMAN. Hedda, has no message come from
Eilert Lövborg? Eh?

HEDDA. No.

TESMAN. Then you'll see he'll be here presently.

BRACK. Do you really think he will come? 50

TESMAN. Yes, I am almost sure of it. For what
you were telling us this morning must have
been a mere floating rumor.

BRACK. You think so?

TESMAN. At any rate, Aunt Julia said she did 55
not believe for a moment that he would ever
stand in my way again. Fancy that!

BRACK. Well then, that's all right.

TESMAN [*placing his hat and gloves on a
chair on the right*]. Yes, but you must really 60
let me wait for him as long as possible.

BRACK. We have plenty of time yet. None of
my guests will arrive before seven or half-past.

TESMAN. Then meanwhile we can keep
Hedda company, and see what happens. Eh? 65

HEDDA [*placing BRACK's hat and overcoat
upon the corner settee*]. And at the worst Mr.
Lövborg can remain here with me.

BRACK [*offering to take his things*]. Oh,
allow me, Mrs. Tesman!—What do you mean 70
by "At the worst"?

HEDDA. If he won't go with you and Tesman.

TESMAN [*looks dubiously at her*]. But,
Hedda dear—do you think it would quite do 75
for him to remain with you? Eh? Remember,
Aunt Julia can't come.

HEDDA. No, but Mrs. Elvsted is coming. We
three can have a cup of tea together.

TESMAN. Oh, yes, that will be all right. 80

BRACK [*smiling*]. And that would perhaps be
the safest plan for him.

HEDDA. Why so?

BRACK. Well, you know, Mrs. Tesman, how
you used to gird at my little bachelor parties. 85
You declared they were adapted only for men
of the strictest principles.

HEDDA. But no doubt Mr. Lövborg's principles are strict enough now. A converted
sinner— 90

[BERTA *appears at the hall door.*]

BERTA. There's a gentleman asking if you
are at home, ma'am—

HEDDA. Well, show him in.

TESMAN [*softly*]. I'm sure it is he! Fancy 95
that!

[EILERT LÖVBORG *enters from the hall. He is
slim and lean; of the same age as TESMAN, but*

*looks older and somewhat worn-out. His hair
and beard are of a blackish brown, his face
long and pale, but with patches of color on the
cheek-bones. He is dressed in a well-cut black
visiting suit, quite new. He has dark gloves and
a silk hat. He stops near the door, and makes a
rapid bow, seeming somewhat embarrassed.*]

TESMAN [*goes up to him and shakes him
warmly by the hand*]. Well, my dear Eilert—
so at last we meet again!

EILERT LÖVBORG [*speaks in a subdued voice*].
Thanks for your letter, Tesman. [*Approaching
HEDDA.*] Will you too shake hands with me,
Mrs. Tesman?

HEDDA [*taking his hand*]. I am glad to see
you, Mr. Lövborg. [*With a motion of her
hand.*] I don't know whether you two gentlemen—?

LÖVBORG [*bowing slightly*]. Judge Brack, I
think.

BRACK [*doing likewise*]. Oh, yes,—in the old
days—

TESMAN [*to LÖVBORG, with his hands on his
shoulders*]. And now you must make yourself
entirely at home, Eilert! Mustn't he, Hedda?—
For I hear you are going to settle in town
again? Eh?

LÖVBORG. Yes, I am.

TESMAN. Quite right, quite right. Let me tell
you, I have got hold of your new book; but I
haven't had time to read it yet.

LÖVBORG. You may spare yourself the
trouble.

TESMAN. Why so?

LÖVBORG. Because there is very little in it.

TESMAN. Just fancy—how can you say so?

BRACK. But it has been very much praised, I
hear.

LÖVBORG. That was what I wanted; so I put
nothing into the book but what every one
would agree with.

BRACK. Very wise of you.

TESMAN. Well but, my dear Eilert—!

LÖVBORG. For now I mean to win myself a
position again—to make a fresh start.

TESMAN [*a little embarrassed*]. Ah, that is
what you wish to do? Eh?

LÖVBORG [*smiling, lays down his hat, and
draws a packet, wrapped in paper, from his
coat pocket*]. But when this one appears,
George Tesman, you will have to read it. For
this is the real book—the book I have put my
true self into.

TESMAN. Indeed? And what is it?

LÖVBORG. It is the continuation.

TESMAN. The continuation? Of what?

LÖVBORG. Of the book.

TESMAN. Of the new book?

LÖVBORG. Of course.

TESMAN. Why, my dear Eilert—does it not
come down to our own days?

LÖVBORG. Yes, it does; and this one deals
with the future.

TESMAN. With the future! But, good heavens,
we know nothing of the future!

LÖVBORG. No; but there is a thing or two to
be said about it all the same. [*Opens the
packet.*] Look here—

TESMAN. Why, that's not your handwriting.

LÖVBORG. I dictated it. [*Turning over the
pages.*] It falls into two sections. The first deals
with the civilizing forces of the future. And
here is the second—[*running through the pages
towards the end*]—forecasting the probable
line of development.

TESMAN. How odd now! I should never have
thought of writing anything of that sort.

HEDDA [*at the glass door, drumming on the
pane*]. H'm—I daresay not.

LÖVBORG [*replacing the manuscript in its
paper and laying the packet on the table*]. I
brought it, thinking I might read you a little of
it this evening.

TESMAN. That was very good of you, Eilert.
But this evening—? [*Looking at BRACK.*] I
don't quite see how we can manage it—

LÖVBORG. Well then, some other time. There
is no hurry.

BRACK. I must tell you, Mr. Lövborg—there
is a little gathering at my house this evening
—mainly in honor of Tesman, you know—

LÖVBORG [*looking for his hat*]. Oh—then I
won't detain you—

BRACK. No, but listen—will you not do me
the favor of joining us?

LÖVBORG [*curtly and decidedly*]. No, I can't
—thank you very much.

BRACK. Oh, nonsense—do! We shall be quite

a select little circle. And I assure you we shall have a "lively time," as Mrs. Hed—as Mrs. Tesman says.

LÖVBORG. I have no doubt of it. But never-
5 theless—

BRACK. And then you might bring your manuscript with you, and read it to Tesman at my house. I could give you a room to your-selves.

10 TESMAN. Yes, think of that, Eilert,—why shouldn't you? Eh?

HEDDA [interposing]. But, Tesman, if Mr. Lövborg would really rather not! I am sure Mr. Lövborg is much more inclined to remain here
15 and have supper with me.

LÖVBORG [looking at her]. With you, Mrs. Tesman?

HEDDA. And with Mrs. Elvsted.

LÖVBORG. Ah— [Lightly.] I saw her for a
20 moment this morning.

HEDDA. Did you? Well, she is coming this evening. So you see you are almost bound to remain, Mr. Lövborg, or she will have no one to see her home.

25 LÖVBORG. That's true. Many thanks, Mrs. Tesman—in that case I will remain.

HEDDA. Then I have one or two orders to give the servant—

[She goes to the hall door and rings. BERTA
30 enters. HEDDA talks to her in a whisper, and points towards the inner room. BERTA nods and goes out again.]

TESMAN [at the same time, to LÖVBORG]. Tell me, Eilert—is it this new subject—the future
35 —that you are going to lecture about?

LÖVBORG. Yes.

TESMAN. They told me at the bookseller's, that you are going to deliver a course of lec-tures this autumn.

40 LÖVBORG. That is my intention. I hope you won't take it ill, Tesman.

TESMAN. Oh no, not in the least! But—?

LÖVBORG. I can quite understand that it must be disagreeable to you.

45 TESMAN [cast down]. Oh, I can't expect you, out of consideration for me, to—

LÖVBORG. But I shall wait till you have re-ceived your appointment.

TESMAN. Will you wait? Yes, but—yes, but—are you not going to compete with me? Eh? 50

LÖVBORG. No; it is only the moral victory I care for.

TESMAN. Why, bless me—then Aunt Julia was right after all! Oh yes—I knew it! Hedda! Just fancy—Eilert Lövborg is not going to 55 stand in our way!

HEDDA [curtly]. Our way? Pray leave me out of the question.

[She goes up towards the inner room, where BERTA is placing a tray with decanters and 60 glasses on the table. HEDDA nods approval, and comes forward again. BERTA goes out.]

TESMAN [at the same time]. And you, Judge Brack—what do you say to this? Eh?

BRACK. Well, I say that a moral victory— 65 h'm—may be all very fine—

TESMAN. Yes, certainly. But all the same—

HEDDA [looking at TESMAN with a cold smile]. You stand there looking as if you were thunderstruck— 70

TESMAN. Yes—so I am—I almost think—

BRACK. Don't you see, Mrs. Tesman, a thunderstorm has just passed over?

HEDDA [pointing towards the inner room]. Will you not take a glass of cold punch, gentle- 75 men?

BRACK [looking at his watch]. A stirrup-cup? Yes, it wouldn't come amiss.

TESMAN. A capital idea, Hedda! Just the thing! Now that the weight has been taken off 80 my mind—

HEDDA. Will you not join them, Mr. Löv-borg?

LÖVBORG [with a gesture of refusal]. No, thank you. Nothing for me. 85

BRACK. Why, bless me—cold punch is surely not poison.

LÖVBORG. Perhaps not for every one.

HEDDA. I will keep Mr. Lövborg company in the meantime. 90

TESMAN. Yes, yes, Hedda dear, do.

[He and BRACK go into the inner room, seat themselves, drink punch, smoke cigarettes, and carry on a lively conversation during what follows. EILERT LÖVBORG remains beside the 95 stove. HEDDA goes to the writing-table.]

HEDDA [*raising her voice a little*]. Do you care to look at some photographs, Mr. Lövborg? You know Tesman and I made a tour in the Tyrol on our way home?

[*She takes up an album, and places it on the table beside the sofa, in the further corner of which she seats herself. EILERT LÖVBORG approaches, stops, and looks at her. Then he takes a chair and seats himself at her left, with his back towards the inner room.*]

HEDDA [*opening the album*]. Do you see this range of mountains, Mr. Lövborg? It's the Ortler group. Tesman has written the name underneath. Here it is: "The Ortler group near Meran."

LÖVBORG [*who has never taken his eyes off her, says softly and slowly*]. Hedda—Gabler!

HEDDA [*glancing hastily at him*]. Ah! Hush!

LÖVBORG [*repeats softly*]. Hedda Gabler!

HEDDA [*looking at the album*]. That was my name in the old days—when we two knew each other.

LÖVBORG. And I must teach myself never to say Hedda Gabler again—never, as long as I live.

HEDDA [*still turning over the pages*]. Yes, you must. And I think you ought to practice in time. The sooner the better, I should say.

LÖVBORG [*in a tone of indignation*]. Hedda Gabler married? And married to—George Tesman!

HEDDA. Yes—so the world goes.

LÖVBORG. Oh, Hedda, Hedda—how could you° throw yourself away!

HEDDA [*looks sharply at him*]. What? I can't allow this!

LÖVBORG. What do you mean? [*TESMAN comes into the room and goes towards the sofa.*]

HEDDA [*hears him coming and says in an indifferent tone*]. And this is a view from the Val d'Ampezzo, Mr. Lövborg. Just look at these peaks! [*Looks affectionately up at TESMAN.*] What's the name of these curious peaks, dear?

TESMAN. Let me see? Oh, those are the Dolomites.

HEDDA. Yes, that's it!—Those are the Dolomites, Mr. Lövborg.

TESMAN. Hedda dear,—I only wanted to ask whether I shouldn't bring you a little punch after all? For yourself at any rate—eh?

HEDDA. Yes, do, please; and perhaps a few biscuits.

TESMAN. No cigarettes?

HEDDA. No.

TESMAN. Very well.

[*He goes into the inner room and out to the right. BRACK sits in the inner room, and keeps an eye from time to time on HEDDA and LÖVBORG.*]

LÖVBORG [*softly, as before*]. Answer me, Hedda—how could you go and do this?

HEDDA [*apparently absorbed in the album*]. If you continue to say *du* to me I won't talk to you.

LÖVBORG. May I not say *du* when we are alone?

HEDDA. No. You may think it; but you mustn't say it.

LÖVBORG. Ah, I understand. It is an offense against George Tesman, whom you°—love.

HEDDA [*glances at him and smiles*]. Love? What an idea!

LÖVBORG. You don't love him then!

HEDDA. But I won't hear of any sort of unfaithfulness! Remember that.

LÖVBORG. Hedda—answer me one thing—

HEDDA. Hush!

[*TESMAN enters with a small tray from the inner room.*]

TESMAN. Here you are! Isn't this tempting? [*He puts the tray on the table.*]

HEDDA. Why do you bring it yourself?

TESMAN [*filling the glasses*]. Because I think it's such fun to wait upon you, Hedda.

HEDDA. But you have poured out two glasses. Mr. Lövborg said he wouldn't have any—

TESMAN. No, but Mrs. Elvsted will soon be here, won't she?

---

you *du*

you *de.* After this Lövborg reverts to the formal pronoun, which Hedda uses throughout.

HEDDA. Yes, by-the-bye—Mrs. Elvsted—

TESMAN. Had you forgotten her? Eh?

HEDDA. We were so absorbed in these photo-graphs. [*Shows him a picture.*] Do you remem-ber this little village?

TESMAN. Oh, it's that one just below the Brenner Pass. It was there we passed the night—

HEDDA. —and met that lively party of tourists.

TESMAN. Yes, that was the place. Fancy—if we could only have had you with us, Eilert! Eh? [*He returns to the inner room and sits beside* BRACK.]

LÖVBORG. Answer me this one thing, Hedda—

HEDDA. Well?

LÖVBORG. Was there no love in your friend-ship for me either? Not a spark—not a tinge of love in it?

HEDDA. I wonder if there was? To me it seems as though we were two good comrades —two thoroughly intimate friends. [*Smilingly.*] You especially were frankness itself.

LÖVBORG. It was you that made me so.

HEDDA. As I look back upon it all, I think there was really something beautiful, some-thing fascinating—something daring—in—in that secret intimacy—that comradeship which no living creature so much as dreamed of.

LÖVBORG. Yes, yes, Hedda! Was there not?— When I used to come to your father's in the afternoon—and the General sat over at the window reading his papers—with his back towards us—

HEDDA. And we two on the corner sofa—

LÖVBORG. Always with the same illustrated paper before us—

HEDDA. For want of an album, yes.

LÖVBORG. Yes, Hedda, and when I made my confessions to you—told you about myself, things that at that time no one else knew! There I would sit and tell you of my escapades —my days and nights of devilment. Oh, Hedda —what was the power in you that forced me to confess these things?

HEDDA. Do you think it was any power in me?

LÖVBORG. How else can I explain it? And all those—those roundabout questions you used to put to me—

HEDDA. Which you understood so particu-larly well—

LÖVBORG. How could you sit and question me like that? Question me quite frankly—

HEDDA. In roundabout terms, please observe.

LÖVBORG. Yes, but frankly nevertheless. Cross-question me about—all that sort of thing?

HEDDA. And how could you answer, Mr. Lövborg?

LÖVBORG. Yes, that is just what I can't under-stand—in looking back upon it. But tell me now, Hedda—was there not love at the bottom of our friendship? On your side, did you not feel as though you might purge my stains away if I made you my confessor? Was it not so?

HEDDA. No, not quite.

LÖVBORG. What was your motive, then?

HEDDA. Do you think it quite incomprehen-sible that a young girl—when it can be done—without any one knowing—

LÖVBORG. Well?

HEDDA. —should be glad to have a peep, now and then, into a world which—

LÖVBORG. Which—?

HEDDA. —which she is forbidden to know anything about?

LÖVBORG. So that was it?

HEDDA. Partly. Partly—I almost think.

LÖVBORG. Comradeship in the thirst for life. But why should not that, at any rate, have continued?

HEDDA. The fault was yours.

LÖVBORG. It was you that broke with me.

HEDDA. Yes, when our friendship threatened to develop into something more serious. Shame upon you, Eilert Lövborg! How could you think of wronging your—your frank comrade?

LÖVBORG [*clenching his hands*]. Oh, why did you not carry out your threat? Why did you not shoot me down?

HEDDA. Because I have such a dread of scan-dal.

LÖVBORG. Yes, Hedda, you are a coward at heart.

HEDDA. A terrible coward. [*Changing her*

tone.] But it was a lucky thing for you. And now you have found ample consolation at the Elvsteds'.

LÖVBORG. I know what Thea has confided to
5 you.

HEDDA. And perhaps you have confided to her something about us?

LÖVBORG. Not a word. She is too stupid to understand anything of that sort.

10 HEDDA. Stupid?

LÖVBORG. She is stupid about matters of that sort.

HEDDA. And I am cowardly. [*Bends over towards him, without looking him in the face,*
15 *and says more softly*—] But now I will confide something to you.

LÖVBORG [*eagerly*]. Well?

HEDDA. The fact that I dared not shoot you down—

20 LÖVBORG. Yes!

HEDDA. —that was not my most arrant cowardice—that evening.

LÖVBORG [*looks at her a moment, understands, and whispers passionately*]. Oh,
25 Hedda! Hedda Gabler! Now I begin to see a hidden reason beneath our comradeship! You° and I—! After all, then, it was your craving for life—

HEDDA [*softly, with a sharp glance*]. Take
30 care! Believe nothing of the sort!

[*Twilight has begun to fall. The hall door is opened from without by* BERTA.]

HEDDA [*closes the album with a bang and calls smilingly*]. Ah, at last! My darling Thea,
35 —come along!

[MRS. ELVSTED *enters from the hall. She is in evening dress. The door is closed behind her.*]

HEDDA [*on the sofa, stretches out her arms towards her*]. My sweet Thea—you can't think
40 how I have been longing for you!

[MRS. ELVSTED, *in passing, exchanges slight salutations with the gentlemen in the inner room, then goes up to the table and gives* HEDDA *her hands.* EILERT LÖVBORG *has risen.*
45 *He and* MRS. ELVSTED *greet each other with a silent nod.*]

MRS. ELVSTED. Ought I to go in and talk to your husband for a moment?

HEDDA. Oh, not at all. Leave those two alone. They will soon be going.   50

MRS. ELVSTED. Are they going out?

HEDDA. Yes, to a supper-party.

MRS. ELVSTED [*quickly, to* LÖVBORG]. Not you?

LÖVBORG. No.   55

HEDDA. Mr. Lövborg remains with us.

MRS. ELVSTED [*takes a chair and is about to seat herself at his side*]. Oh, how nice it is here!

HEDDA. No, thank you, my little Thea! Not 60
there! You'll be good enough to come over here to me. I will sit between you.

MRS. ELVSTED. Yes, just as you please.

[*She goes round the table and seats herself on the sofa on* HEDDA's *right.* LÖVBORG *re-seats* 65
himself on his chair.]

LÖVBORG [*after a short pause, to* HEDDA]. Is not she lovely to look at?

HEDDA [*lightly stroking her hair*]. Only to look at?   70

LÖVBORG. Yes. For we two—she and I—we are two real comrades. We have absolute faith in each other; so we can sit and talk with perfect frankness—

HEDDA. Not round about, Mr. Lövborg?   75

LÖVBORG. Well—

MRS. ELVSTED [*softly, clinging close to* HEDDA]. Oh, how happy I am, Hedda; for, only think, he says I have inspired him too.

HEDDA [*looks at her with a smile*]. Ah! Does 80
he say that, dear?

LÖVBORG. And then she is so brave, Mrs. Tesman!

MRS. ELVSTED. Good heavens—am I brave?

LÖVBORG. Exceedingly—where your comrade 85
is concerned.

HEDDA. Ah, yes—courage! If one only had that!

LÖVBORG. What then? What do you mean?

HEDDA. Then life would perhaps be liveable, 90
after all. [*With a sudden change of tone.*] But now, my dearest Thea, you really must have a glass of cold punch.

MRS. ELVSTED. No, thanks—I never take anything of that kind.   95

you *du*

HEDDA. Well then, you, Mr. Lövborg.

LÖVBORG. Nor I, thank you.

MRS. ELVSTED. No, he doesn't either.

HEDDA [looks fixedly at him]. But if I say you shall?

LÖVBORG. It would be no use.

HEDDA [laughing]. Then I, poor creature, have no sort of power over you?

LÖVBORG. Not in that respect.

HEDDA. But seriously, I think you ought to —for your own sake.

MRS. ELVSTED. Why, Helda—!

LÖVBORG. How so?

HEDDA. Or rather on account of other people.

LÖVBORG. Indeed?

HEDDA. Otherwise people might be apt to suspect that—in your heart of hearts—you did not feel quite secure—quite confident of yourself.

MRS. ELVSTED [softly]. Oh please, Hedda—

LÖVBORG. People may suspect what they like —for the present.

MRS. ELVSTED [joyfully]. Yes, let them!

HEDDA. I saw it plainly in Judge Brack's face a moment ago.

LÖVBORG. What did you see?

HEDDA. His contemptuous smile, when you dared not go with them into the inner room.

LÖVBORG. Dared not? Of course I preferred to stop here and talk to you.

MRS. ELVSTED. What could be more natural, Hedda?

HEDDA. But the Judge could not guess that. And I saw, too, the way he smiled and glanced at Tesman when you dared not accept his invitation to this wretched little supper-party of his.

LÖVBORG. Dared not! Do you say I dared not?

HEDDA. I don't say so. But that was how Judge Brack understood it.

LÖVBORG. Well, let him.

HEDDA. Then you are not going with them?

LÖVBORG. I will stay here with you and Thea.

MRS. ELVSTED. Yes, Hedda—how can you doubt that?

HEDDA [smiles and nods approvingly to LÖVBORG]. Firm as a rock! Faithful to your principles, now and forever! Ah, that is how a man should be! [Turns to MRS. ELVSTED and caresses her.] Well now, what did I tell you, when you came to us this morning in such a state of distraction—

LÖVBORG [surprised]. Distraction!

MRS. ELVSTED [terrified]. Hedda—oh Hedda—!

HEDDA. You can see for yourself; you haven't the slightest reason to be in such mortal terror —[interrupting herself]. There! Now we can all three enjoy ourselves!

LÖVBORG [who has given a start]. Ah—what is all this, Mrs. Tesman?

MRS. ELVSTED. Oh my God, Hedda! What are you saying? What are you doing?

HEDDA. Don't get excited! That horrid Judge Brack is sitting watching you.

LÖVBORG. So she was in mortal terror! On my account!

MRS. ELVSTED [softly and piteously]. Oh, Hedda—now you have ruined everything!

LÖVBORG [looks fixedly at her for a moment. His face is distorted]. So that was my comrade's frank confidence in me?

MRS. ELVSTED [imploringly]. Oh, my dearest friend—only let me tell you—

LÖVBORG [takes one of the glasses of punch, raises it to his lips, and says in a low, husky voice]. Your health, Thea!

[He empties the glass, puts it down, and takes the second.]

MRS. ELVSTED [softly]. Oh, Hedda, Hedda— how could you do this?

HEDDA. I do it? I? Are you crazy?

LÖVBORG. Here's your health, too, Mrs. Tesman. Thanks for the truth. Hurrah for the truth! [He empties the glass and is about to re-fill it.]

HEDDA [lays her hand on his arm]. Come, come—no more for the present. Remember you are going out to supper.

MRS. ELVSTED. No, no, no!

HEDDA. Hush! They are sitting watching you.

LÖVBORG [putting down the glass]. Now. Thea—tell me the truth—

MRS. ELVSTED. Yes.

LÖVBORG. Did your husband know that you had come after me?

MRS. ELVSTED [wringing her hands]. Oh, Hedda—do you hear what he is asking?

LÖVBORG. Was it arranged between you and him that you were to come to town and look after me? Perhaps it was the Sheriff himself that urged you to come? Aha, my dear—no
5 doubt he wanted my help in his office! Or was it at the card-table that he missed me?

MRS. ELVSTED [*softly, in agony*]. Oh, Lövborg, Lövborg—!

LÖVBORG [*seizes a glass and is on the point
10 of filling it*]. Here's a glass for the old Sheriff too!

HEDDA [*preventing him*]. No more just now. Remember, you have to read your manuscript to Tesman.

15 LÖVBORG [*calmly, putting down the glass*]. It was stupid of me all this, Thea—to take it in this way, I mean. Don't be angry with me, my dear, dear comrade. You shall see—both of you and the others—that if I was fallen
20 once—now I have risen again! Thanks to you, Thea.

MRS. ELVSTED [*radiant with joy*]. Oh, heaven be praised—!

[BRACK *has in the meantime looked at his
25 watch. He and* TESMAN *rise and come into the drawing-room.*]

BRACK [*takes his hat and overcoat*]. Well, Mrs. Tesman, our time has come.

HEDDA. I suppose it has.

30 LÖVBORG [*rising*]. Mine too, Judge Brack.

MRS. ELVSTED [*softly and imploringly*]. Oh, Lövborg, don't do it!

HEDDA [*pinching her arm*]. They can hear you!

35 MRS. ELVSTED [*with a suppressed shriek*]. Ow!

LÖVBORG [*to* BRACK]. You were good enough to invite me.

BRACK. Well, are you coming after all?

40 LÖVBORG. Yes, many thanks.

BRACK. I'm delighted—

LÖVBORG [*to* TESMAN, *putting the parcel of MS. in his pocket*]. I should like to show you one or two things before I send it to the prin-
45 ter's.

TESMAN. Fancy—that will be delightful. But, Hedda dear, how is Mrs. Elvsted to get home? Eh?

HEDDA. Oh, that can be managed somehow.

LÖVBORG [*looking towards the ladies*]. Mrs. 50 Elvsted? Of course, I'll come again and fetch her. [*Approaching.*] At ten or thereabouts, Mrs. Tesman? Will that do?

HEDDA. Certainly. That will do capitally.

TESMAN. Well, then, that's all right. But you 55 must not expect me so early, Hedda.

HEDDA. Oh, you may stop as long—as long as ever you please.

MRS. ELVSTED [*trying to conceal her anxiety*]. Well then, Mr. Lövborg—I shall remain here 60 until you come.

LÖVBORG [*with his hat in his hand*]. Pray do, Mrs. Elvsted.

BRACK. And now off goes the excursion train, gentlemen! I hope we shall have a lively time, 65 as a certain fair lady puts it.

HEDDA. Ah, if only the fair lady could be present unseen—!

BRACK. Why unseen?

HEDDA. In order to hear a little of your live- 70 liness at first hand, Judge Brack.

BRACK [*laughing*]. I should not advise the fair lady to try it.

TESMAN [*also laughing*]. Come, you're a nice one, Hedda! Fancy that! 75

BRACK. Well, good-bye, good-bye, ladies.

LÖVBORG [*bowing*]. About ten o'clock, then.

[BRACK, LÖVBORG, *and* TESMAN *go out by the hall door. At the same time* BERTA *enters from the inner room with a lighted lamp, which she* 80 *places on the dining-room table; she goes out by the way she came.*]

MRS. ELVSTED [*who has risen and is wandering restlessly about the room*]. Hedda—Hedda —what will come of all this? 85

HEDDA. At ten o'clock—he will be here. I can see him already—with vine-leaves° in his hair—flushed and fearless—

MRS. ELVSTED. Oh, I hope he may.

HEDDA. And then, you see—then he will 90 have regained control over himself. Then he will be a free man for all his days.

MRS. ELVSTED. Oh God!—if he would only come as you see him now!

HEDDA. He will come as I see him—so, and 95

vine-leaves the garland of Dionysus, symbol of divine intoxication

not otherwise! [*Rises and approaches* Thea.]
You may doubt him as long as you please;
I believe in him. And now we will try—

Mrs. Elvsted. You have some hidden motive
5 in this, Hedda!

Hedda. Yes, I have. I want for once in my
life to have power to mold a human destiny.

Mrs. Elvsted. Have you not the power?

Hedda. I have not—and have never had it.

10 Mrs. Elvsted. Not your husband's?

Hedda. Do you think that is worth the
trouble? Oh, if you could only understand how
poor I am. And fate has made you so rich!
[*Clasps her passionately in her arms.*] I think
15 I must burn your hair off, after all.

Mrs. Elvsted. Let me go! Let me go! I am
afraid of you, Hedda!

Berta [*in the middle doorway*]. Tea is laid
in the dining-room, ma'am.

20 Hedda. Very well. We are coming.

Mrs. Elvsted. No, no, no! I would rather go
home alone! At once.

Hedda. Nonsense! First you shall have a
cup of tea, you little stupid. And then—at ten
25 o'clock—Eilert Lövborg will be here—with
vine-leaves in his hair. [*She drags* Mrs. Elvsted
almost by force towards the middle doorway.]

ACT III

[*The room at the* Tesmans'. *The curtains are
drawn over the middle doorway, and also over
30 the glass door. The lamp, half turned down,
and with a shade over it, is burning on the
table. In the stove, the door of which stands
open, there has been a fire, which is now nearly
burnt out.*

35 Mrs. Elvsted, *wrapped in a large shawl, and
with her feet upon a foot-rest, sits close to the
stove, sunk back in the arm-chair.* Hedda, *fully
dressed, lies sleeping upon the sofa, with a
sofa-blanket over her.*]

40 Mrs. Elvsted [*after a pause, suddenly sits
up in her chair, and listens eagerly. Then she
sinks back again wearily, moaning to herself*].
Not yet!—Oh God—oh God—not yet!

[Berta *slips in by the hall door. She has a
letter in her hand.*] 45

Mrs. Elvsted [*turns and whispers eagerly*].
Well—has any one come?

Berta [*softly*]. Yes, a girl has brought this
letter.

Mrs. Elvsted [*quickly, holding out her* 50
hand]. A letter! Give it to me!

Berta. No, it's for Dr. Tesman, ma'am.

Mrs. Elvsted. Oh, indeed.

Berta. It was Miss Tesman's servant that
brought it. I'll lay it here on the table. 55

Mrs. Elvsted. Yes, do.

Berta [*laying down the letter*]. I think I had
better put out the lamp. It's smoking.

Mrs. Elvsted. Yes, put it out. It must soon
be daylight now. 60

Berta [*putting out the lamp*]. It is daylight
already, ma'am.

Mrs. Elvsted. Yes, broad day! And no one
come back yet—!

Berta. Lord bless you, ma'am! I guessed how 65
it would be.

Mrs. Elvsted. You guessed?

Berta. Yes, when I saw that a certain person
had come back to town—and that he went off
with them. For we've heard enough about that 70
gentleman before now.

Mrs. Elvsted. Don't speak so loud. You will
waken Mrs. Tesman.

Berta [*looks towards the sofa and sighs*].
No, no—let her sleep, poor thing. Shan't I put 75
some wood on the fire?

Mrs. Elvsted. Thanks, not for me.

Berta. Oh, very well. [*She goes softly out by
the hall door.*]

Hedda [*is awakened by the shutting of the* 80
door, and looks up]. What's that—?

Mrs. Elvsted. It was only the servant—

Hedda [*looking about her*]. Oh, we're
here—! Yes, now I remember. [*Sits erect upon
the sofa, stretches herself, and rubs her eyes.*] 85
What o'clock is it, Thea?

Mrs. Elvsted [*looks at her watch*]. It's past
seven.

Hedda. When did Tesman come home?

Mrs. Elvsted. He has not come. 90

HEDDA. Not come home yet?

MRS. ELVSTED [*rising*]. No one has come.

HEDDA. Think of our watching and waiting here till four in the morning—

5 MRS. ELVSTED [*wringing her hands*]. And how I watched and waited for him!

HEDDA [*yawns, and says with her hand before her mouth*]. Well, well—we might have spared ourselves the trouble.

10 MRS. ELVSTED. Did you get a little sleep?

HEDDA. Oh yes; I believe I have slept pretty well. Have you not?

MRS. ELVSTED. Not for a moment. I couldn't, Hedda!—not to save my life.

15 HEDDA [*rises and goes towards her*]. There, there, there! There's nothing to be so alarmed about. I understand quite well what has happened.

MRS. ELVSTED. Well, what do you think? 20 Won't you tell me?

HEDDA. Why, of course it has been a very late affair at Judge Brack's—

MRS. ELVSTED. Yes, yes, that is clear enough. But all the same—

25 HEDDA. And then, you see, Tesman hasn't cared to come home and ring us up in the middle of the night. [*Laughing.*] Perhaps he wasn't inclined to show himself either—immediately after a jollification.

30 MRS. ELVSTED. But in that case—where can he have gone?

HEDDA. Of course he has gone to his aunts' and slept there. They have his old room ready for him.

35 MRS. ELVSTED. No, he can't be with them; for a letter has just come for him from Miss Tesman. There it lies.

HEDDA. Indeed? [*Looks at the address.*] Why yes, it's addressed in Aunt Julia's own hand. 40 Well then, he has remained at Judge Brack's. And as for Eilert Lövborg—he is sitting, with vine-leaves in his hair, reading his manuscript.

MRS. ELVSTED. Oh Hedda, you are just saying things you don't believe a bit.

45 HEDDA. You really are a little blockhead, Thea.

MRS. ELVSTED. Oh yes, I suppose I am.

HEDDA. And how mortally tired you look.

MRS. ELVSTED. Yes, I am mortally tired.

HEDDA. Well then, you must do as I tell you. 50 You must go into my room and lie down for a little while.

MRS. ELVSTED. Oh no, no—I shouldn't be able to sleep.

HEDDA. I am sure you would. 55

MRS. ELVSTED. Well, but your husband is certain to come soon now; and then I want to know at once—

HEDDA. I shall take care to let you know when he comes. 60

MRS. ELVSTED. Do you promise me, Hedda?

HEDDA. Yes, rely upon me. Just you go in and have a sleep in the meantime.

MRS. ELVSTED. Thanks; then I'll try to. [*She goes off through the inner room.*] 65

[HEDDA *goes up to the glass door and draws back the curtains. The broad daylight streams into the room. Then she takes a little hand-glass from the writing-table, looks at herself in it, and arranges her hair. Next she goes to the* 70 *hall door and presses the bell-button.* BERTA *presently appears at the hall door.*]

BERTA. Did you want anything, ma'am?

HEDDA. Yes; you must put some more wood in the stove. I am shivering. 75

BERTA. Bless me—I'll make up the fire at once. [*She rakes the embers together and lays a piece of wood upon them; then stops and listens.*] That was a ring at the front door, ma'am. 80

HEDDA. Then go to the door. I will look after the fire.

BERTA. It'll soon burn up. [*She goes out by the hall door.*]

[HEDDA *kneels on the foot-rest and lays* 85 *some more pieces of wood in the stove. After a short pause,* GEORGE TESMAN *enters from the hall. He looks tired and rather serious. He steals on tiptoe towards the middle doorway and is about to slip through the curtains.*] 90

HEDDA [*at the stove, without looking up.*] Good morning.

TESMAN [*turns*]. Hedda! [*Approaching her.*] Good heavens—are you up so early? Eh?

HEDDA. Yes, I am up very early this morning.

TESMAN. And I never doubted you were still sound asleep! Fancy that, Hedda!

HEDDA. Don't speak so loud. Mrs. Elvsted is resting in my room.

TESMAN. Has Mrs. Elvsted been here all night?

HEDDA. Yes, since no one came to fetch her.

TESMAN. Ah, to be sure.

HEDDA [closes the door of the stove and rises]. Well, did you enjoy yourself at Judge Brack's?

TESMAN. Have you been anxious about me? Eh?

HEDDA. No, I should never think of being anxious. But I asked if you had enjoyed yourself.

TESMAN. Oh yes,—for once in a way. Especially the beginning of the evening; for then Eilert read me part of his book. We arrived more than an hour too early—fancy that! And Brack had all sorts of arrangements to make —so Eilert read to me.

HEDDA [seating herself by the table on the right]. Well? Tell me, then—

TESMAN [sitting on a foot-stool near the stove]. Oh Hedda, you can't conceive what a book that is going to be! I believe it is one of the most remarkable things that have ever been written. Fancy that!

HEDDA. Yes, yes; I don't care about that—

TESMAN. I must make a confession to you, Hedda. When he had finished reading—a horrid feeling came over me.

HEDDA. A horrid feeling?

TESMAN. I felt jealous of Eilert for having had it in him to write such a book. Only think, Hedda!

HEDDA. Yes, yes, I am thinking!

TESMAN. And then how pitiful to think that he—with all his gifts—should be irreclaimable after all.

HEDDA. I suppose you mean that he has more courage than the rest?

TESMAN. No, not at all—I mean that he is incapable of taking his pleasures in moderation.

HEDDA. And what came of it all—in the end?

TESMAN. Well, to tell the truth, I think it might best be described as an orgy, Hedda.

HEDDA. Had he vine-leaves in his hair?

TESMAN. Vine-leaves? No, I saw nothing of the sort. But he made a long, rambling speech in honor of the woman who had inspired him in his work—that was the phrase he used.

HEDDA. Did he name her?

TESMAN. No, he didn't; but I can't help thinking he meant Mrs. Elvsted. You may be sure he did.

HEDDA. Well—where did you part from him?

TESMAN. On the way to town. We broke up —the last of us at any rate—all together; and Brack came with us to get a breath of fresh air. And then, you see, we agreed to take Eilert home; for he had had far more than was good for him.

HEDDA. I daresay.

TESMAN. But now comes the strange part of it, Hedda; or, I should rather say, the melancholy part of it. I declare I am almost ashamed —on Eilert's account—to tell you—

HEDDA. Oh, go on—!

TESMAN. Well, as we were getting near town, you see, I happened to drop a little behind the others. Only for a minute or two—fancy that!

HEDDA. Yes, yes, yes, but—?

TESMAN. And then, as I hurried after them —what do you think I found by the wayside? Eh?

HEDDA. Oh, how should I know!

TESMAN. You mustn't speak of it to a soul, Hedda! Do you hear! Promise me, for Eilert's sake. [Draws a parcel, wrapped in paper, from his coat pocket.] Fancy, dear—I found this.

HEDDA. Is not that the parcel he had with him yesterday?

TESMAN. Yes, it is the whole of his precious, irreplaceable manuscript! And he had gone and lost it, and knew nothing about it. Only fancy, Hedda! So deplorably—

HEDDA. But why did you not give him back the parcel at once?

TESMAN. I didn't dare to—in the state he was then in—

HEDDA. Did you not tell any of the others that you had found it?

TESMAN. Oh, far from it! You can surely understand that, for Eilert's sake, I wouldn't do that.

HEDDA. So no one knows that Eilert Löv-borg's manuscript is in your possession?

TESMAN. No. And no one must know it.

HEDDA. Then what did you say to him after-wards?

TESMAN. I didn't talk to him again at all; for when we got in among the streets, he and two or three of the others gave us the slip and dis-appeared. Fancy that!

HEDDA. Indeed! They must have taken him home then.

TESMAN. Yes, so it would appear. And Brack, too, left us.

HEDDA. And what have you been doing with yourself since?

TESMAN. Well, I and some of the others went home with one of the party, a jolly fellow, and took our morning coffee with him; or perhaps I should rather call it our night coffee —eh? But now, when I have rested a little, and given Eilert, poor fellow, time to have his sleep out, I must take this back to him.

HEDDA [*holds out her hand for the packet*]. No—don't give it to him! Not in such a hurry, I mean. Let me read it first.

TESMAN. No, my dearest Hedda, I mustn't, I really mustn't.

HEDDA. You must not?

TESMAN. No—for you can imagine what a state of despair he will be in when he awakens and misses the manuscript. He has no copy of it, you must know! He told me so.

HEDDA [*looking searchingly at him*]. Can such a thing not be reproduced? Written over again?

TESMAN. No, I don't think that would be possible. For the inspiration, you see—

HEDDA. Yes, yes—I suppose it depends on that. [*Lightly.*] But, by-the-bye—here is a let-ter for you.

TESMAN. Fancy—!

HEDDA [*handing it to him*]. It came early this morning.

TESMAN. It's from Aunt Julia! What can it be? [*He lays the packet on the other foot-stool, opens the letter, runs his eye through it, and jumps up.*] Oh, Hedda—she says that poor Aunt Rina is dying!

HEDDA. Well, we were prepared for that.

TESMAN. And that if I want to see her again, I must make haste. I'll run in to them at once.

HEDDA [*suppressing a smile*]. Will you run?

TESMAN. Oh, dearest Hedda—if you could only make up your mind to come with me! Just think!

HEDDA [*rises and says wearily, repelling the idea*]. No, no, don't ask me. I will not look upon sickness and death. I loathe all sorts of ugliness.

TESMAN. Well, well, then—! [*Bustling around.*] My hat—My overcoat—? Oh, in the hall—I do hope I mayn't come too late, Hedda! Eh?

HEDDA. Oh, if you run—

[BERTA *appears at the hall door.*]

BERTA. Judge Brack is at the door, and wishes to know if he may come in.

TESMAN. At this time! No, I can't possibly see him.

HEDDA. But I can. [*To* BERTA.] Ask Judge Brack to come in.

[BERTA *goes out.*]

HEDDA [*quickly whispering*]. The parcel, Tesman! [*She snatches it up from the stool.*]

TESMAN. Yes, give it to me!

HEDDA. No, no, I will keep it till you come back.

[*She goes to the writing-table and places it in the book-case.* TESMAN *stands in a flurry of haste, and cannot get his gloves on.* JUDGE BRACK *enters from the hall.*]

HEDDA [*nodding to him*]. You are an early bird, I must say.

BRACK. Yes, don't you think so? [*To* TES-MAN.] Are you on the move, too?

TESMAN. Yes, I must rush off to my aunts'. Fancy—the invalid one is lying at death's door, poor creature.

BRACK. Dear me, is she indeed? Then on no account let me detain you. At such a critical moment—

TESMAN. Yes, I must really rush—Good-bye! Good-bye!

[*He hastens out by the hall door.*]

HEDDA [*approaching.*] You seem to have made a particularly lively night of it at your rooms, Judge Brack.

5 BRACK. I assure you I have not had my clothes off, Mrs. Hedda.

HEDDA. Not you, either?

BRACK. No, as you may see. But what has Tesman been telling you of the night's adven-
10 tures?

HEDDA. Oh, some tiresome story. Only that they went and had coffee somewhere or other.

BRACK. I have heard about that coffee-party already. Eilert Lövborg was not with them, I
15 fancy?

HEDDA. No, they had taken him home before that.

BRACK. Tesman, too?

HEDDA. No, but some of the others, he said.

20 BRACK [*smiling*]. George Tesman is really an ingenuous creature, Mrs. Hedda.

HEDDA. Yes, heaven knows he is. Then is there something behind all this?

BRACK. Yes, perhaps there may be.

25 HEDDA. Well then, sit down, my dear Judge, and tell your story in comfort.

[*She seats herself to the left of the table. BRACK sits near her, at the long side of the table.*]

30 HEDDA. Now then?

BRACK. I had special reasons for keeping track of my guests—or rather of some of my guests—last night.

HEDDA. Of Eilert Lövborg among the rest,
35 perhaps?

BRACK. Frankly, yes.

HEDDA. Now you make me really curious—

BRACK. Do you know where he and one or two of the others finished the night, Mrs.
40 Hedda?

HEDDA. If it is not quite unmentionable, tell me.

BRACK. Oh no, it's not at all unmentionable. Well, they put in an appearance at a particu-
45 larly animated soirée.

HEDDA. Of the lively kind?

BRACK. Of the very liveliest—

HEDDA. Tell me more of this, Judge Brack—

BRACK. Lövborg, as well as the others, had been invited in advance. I knew all about it. 50 But he had declined the invitation; for now, as you know, he has become a new man.

HEDDA. Up at the Elvsteds', yes. But he went after all, then?

BRACK. Well, you see, Mrs. Hedda—unhap- 55 pily the spirit moved him at my rooms last evening—

HEDDA. Yes, I hear he found inspiration.

BRACK. Pretty violent inspiration. Well, I fancy, that altered his purpose; for we men 60 folk are unfortunately not always so firm in our principles as we ought to be.

HEDDA. Oh, I am sure you are an exception, Judge Brack. But as to Lövborg—?

BRACK. To make a long story short—he 65 landed at last in Mademoiselle Diana's rooms.

HEDDA. Mademoiselle Diana's?

BRACK. It was Mademoiselle Diana that was giving the soirée, to a select circle of her admirers and her lady friends. 70

HEDDA. Is she a red-haired woman?

BRACK. Precisely.

HEDDA. A sort of a—singer?

BRACK. Oh yes—in her leisure moments. And moreover a mighty huntress—of men— 75 Mrs. Hedda. You have no doubt heard of her. Eilert Lövborg was one of her most enthusias-tic protectors—in the days of his glory.

HEDDA. And how did all this end?

BRACK. Far from amicably, it appears. After 80 a most tender meeting, they seem to have come to blows—

HEDDA. Lövborg and she?

BRACK. Yes. He accused her or her friends of having robbed him. He declared that his 85 pocket-book had disappeared—and other things as well. In short, he seems to have made a furious disturbance.

HEDDA. And what came of it all?

BRACK. It came to a general scrimmage, in 90 which the ladies as well as the gentlemen took part. Fortunately the police at last appeared on the scene.

HEDDA. The police too?

BRACK. Yes. I fancy it will prove a costly frolic for Eilert Lövborg, crazy being that he is.

HEDDA. How so?

5 BRACK. He seems to have made a violent resistance—to have hit one of the constables on the head and torn the coat off his back. So they had to march him off to the police-station with the rest.

10 HEDDA. How have you learnt all this?

BRACK. From the police themselves.

HEDDA [*gazing straight before her*]. So that is what happened. Then he had no vine-leaves in his hair.

15 BRACK. Vine-leaves, Mrs. Hedda?

HEDDA [*changing her tone*]. But tell me now, Judge—what is your real reason for tracking out Eilert Lövborg's movements so carefully?

BRACK. In the first place, it could not be en-
20 tirely indifferent to me if it should appear in the police-court that he came straight from my house.

HEDDA. Will the matter come into court, then?

25 BRACK. Of course. However, I should scarcely have troubled so much about that. But I thought that, as a friend of the family, it was my duty to supply you and Tesman with a full account of his nocturnal exploits.

30 HEDDA. Why so, Judge Brack?

BRACK. Why, because I have a shrewd suspicion that he intends to use you as a sort of blind.

HEDDA. Oh, how can you think such a
35 thing!

BRACK. Good heavens, Mrs. Hedda—we have eyes in our head. Mark my words! This Mrs. Elvsted will be in no hurry to leave town again.

40 HEDDA. Well, even if there should be anything between them, I suppose there are plenty of other places where they could meet.

BRACK. Not a single home. Henceforth, as before, every respectable house will be closed
45 against Eilert Lövborg.

HEDDA. And so ought mine to be, you mean?

BRACK. Yes. I confess it would be more than painful to me if this personage were to be made free of your house. How superfluous, how intrusive, he would be, if he were to force 50 his way into—

HEDDA. —into the triangle?

BRACK. Precisely. It would simply mean that I should find myself homeless.

HEDDA [*looks at him with a smile*]. So you 55 want to be the one cock in the basket—that is your aim.

BRACK [*nods slowly and lowers his voice*]. Yes, that is my aim. And for that I will fight— with every weapon I can command. 60

HEDDA [*her smile vanishing*]. I see you are a dangerous person—when it comes to the point.

BRACK. Do you think so?

HEDDA. I am beginning to think so. And I 65 am exceedingly glad to think—that you have no sort of hold over me.

BRACK [*laughing equivocally*]. Well, well, Mrs. Hedda—perhaps you are right there. If I had, who knows what I might be capable of? 70

HEDDA. Come, come now, Judge Brack. That sounds almost like a threat.

BRACK [*rising*]. Oh, not at all! The triangle, you know, ought, if possible, to be spontaneously constructed. 75

HEDDA. There I agree with you.

BRACK. Well, now I have said all I had to say; and I had better be getting back to town. Good-bye, Mrs. Hedda. [*He goes towards the glass door.*] 80

HEDDA [*rising*]. Are you going through the garden?

BRACK. Yes, it's a short cut for me.

HEDDA. And then it is the back way, too.

BRACK. Quite so. I have no objection to back 85 ways. They may be piquant enough at times.

HEDDA. When there is ball practice going on, you mean?

BRACK [*in the doorway, laughing to her*]. Oh, people don't shoot their tame poultry, I 90 fancy.

HEDDA [*also laughing*]. Oh no, when there is only one cock in the basket—

[*They exchange laughing nods of farewell.*

*He goes. She closes the door behind him.
HEDDA, who has become quite serious, stands
for a moment looking out. Presently she goes
and peeps through the curtain over the middle
5 doorway. Then she goes to the writing-table,
takes LÖVBORG's packet out of the book-case,
and is on the point of looking through its contents. BERTA is heard speaking loudly in the
hall. HEDDA turns and listens. Then she hastily
10 locks up the packet in the drawer, and lays the
key on the inkstand. EILERT LÖVBORG, with his
great coat on and his hat in his hand, tears
open the hall door. He looks somewhat confused and irritated.]*

15 LÖVBORG [*looking towards the hall*]. And I
tell you I must and will come in! There!

[*He closes the door, turns and sees HEDDA,
at once regains his self-control, and bows.*]

HEDDA [*at the writing-table*]. Well, Mr. Löv-
20 borg, this is rather a late hour to call for Thea.

LÖVBORG. You mean rather an early hour to
call on you. Pray pardon me.

HEDDA. How do you know that she is still
here?

25 LÖVBORG. They told me at her lodgings that
she had been out all night.

HEDDA [*going to the oval table*]. Did you
notice anything about the people of the house
when they said that?

30 LÖVBORG [*looks inquiringly at her*]. Notice
anything about them?

HEDDA. I mean, did they seem to think it
odd?

LÖVBORG [*suddenly understanding*]. Oh yes,
35 of course! I am dragging her down with me!
However, I didn't notice anything.—I suppose
Tesman is not up yet?

HEDDA. No—I think not—

LÖVBORG. When did he come home?

40 HEDDA. Very late.

LÖVBORG. Did he tell you anything?

HEDDA. Yes, I gathered that you had had an
exceedingly jolly evening at Judge Brack's.

LÖVBORG. Nothing more?

45 HEDDA. I don't think so. However, I was so
dreadfully sleepy—

[MRS. ELVSTED *enters through the curtains
of the middle doorway.*]

MRS. ELVSTED [*going towards him*]. Ah,
Lövborg! At last—! 50

LÖVBORG. Yes, at last. And too late!

MRS. ELVSTED [*looks anxiously at him*].
What is too late?

LÖVBORG. Everything is too late now. It is all
over with me. 55

MRS. ELVSTED. Oh no, no—don't say that!

LÖVBORG. You will say the same when you
hear—

MRS. ELVSTED. I won't hear anything!

HEDDA. Perhaps you would prefer to talk to 60
her alone! If so, I will leave you.

LÖVBORG. No, stay—you too. I beg you to
stay.

MRS. ELVSTED. Yes, but I won't hear anything, I tell you. 65

LÖVBORG. It is not last night's adventures
that I want to talk about.

MRS. ELVSTED. What is it then—?

LÖVBORG. I want to say that now our ways
must part. 70

MRS. ELVSTED. Part!

HEDDA [*involuntarily*]. I knew it!

LÖVBORG. You can be of no more service to
me, Thea.

MRS. ELVSTED. How can you stand there and 75
say that! No more service to you! Am I not to
help you now, as before? Are we not to go on
working together?

LÖVBORG. Henceforward I shall do no work.

MRS. ELVSTED [*despairingly*]. Then what am 80
I to do with my life?

LÖVBORG. You must try to live your life as if
you had never known me.

MRS. ELVSTED. But you know I cannot do
that! 85

LÖVBORG. Try if you cannot, Thea. You must
go home again—

MRS. ELVSTED [*in vehement protest*]. Never
in this world! Where you are, there will I be
also! I will not let myself be driven away like 90
this! I will remain here! I will be with you
when the book appears.

HEDDA [*half aloud, in suspense*]. Ah yes—
the book!

LÖVBORG [*looks at her*]. My book and 95
Thea's; for that is what it is.

MRS. ELVSTED. Yes, I feel that it is. And that is why I have a right to be with you when it appears! I will see with my own eyes how respect and honor pour in upon you afresh. And the happiness—the happiness—oh, I must share it with you!

LÖVBORG. Thea—our book will never appear.

HEDDA. Ah!

MRS. ELVSTED. Never appear!

LÖVBORG. Can never appear.

MRS. ELVSTED [*in agonized foreboding*]. Lövborg—what have you done with the manuscript?

HEDDA [*looks anxiously at him*]. Yes, the manuscript—?

MRS. ELVSTED. Where is it?

LÖVBORG. Oh Thea—don't ask me about it!

MRS. ELVSTED. Yes, yes, I will know. I demand to be told at once.

LÖVBORG. The manuscript—Well then—I have torn the manuscript into a thousand pieces.

MRS. ELVSTED [*shrieks*]. Oh no, no—!

HEDDA [*involuntarily*]. But that's not—

LÖVBORG [*looks at her*]. Not true, you think?

HEDDA [*collecting herself*]. Oh well, of course—since you say so. But it sounded so improbable—

LÖVBORG. It is true, all the same.

MRS. ELVSTED [*wringing her hands*]. Oh God—oh God, Hedda—torn his own work to pieces!

LÖVBORG. I have torn my own life to pieces. So why should I not tear my life-work too—?

MRS. ELVSTED. And you did this last night?

LÖVBORG. Yes, I tell you! Tore it into a thousand pieces and scattered them on the fiord—far out. There there is cool sea-water at any rate—let them drift upon it—drift with the current and the wind. And then presently they will sink—deeper and deeper—as I shall, Thea.

MRS. ELVSTED. Do you know, Lövborg, that what you have done with the book—I shall think of it to my dying day as though you had killed a little child.

LÖVBORG. Yes, you are right. It is a sort of child-murder.

MRS. ELVSTED. How could you, then—! Did not the child belong to me too?

HEDDA [*almost inaudibly*]. Ah, the child—

MRS. ELVSTED [*breathing heavily*]. It is all over then. Well, well, now I will go, Hedda.

HEDDA. But you are not going away from town?

MRS. ELVSTED. Oh, I don't know what I shall do. I see nothing but darkness before me. [*She goes out by the hall door.*]

HEDDA [*stands waiting for a moment*]. So you are not going to see her home, Mr. Lövborg?

LÖVBORG. I? Through the streets? Would you have people see her walking with me?

HEDDA. Of course I don't know what else may have happened last night. But is it so utterly irretrievable?

LÖVBORG. It will not end with last night—I know that perfectly well. And the thing is that now I have no taste for that sort of life either. I won't begin it anew. She has broken my courage and my power of braving life out.

HEDDA [*looking straight before her*]. So that pretty little fool has had her fingers in a man's destiny. [*Looks at him.*] But all the same, how could you treat her so heartlessly?

LÖVBORG. Oh, don't say that it was heartless!

HEDDA. To go and destroy what has filled her whole soul for months and years. You do not call that heartless!

LÖVBORG. To you I can tell the truth, Hedda.

HEDDA. The truth?

LÖVBORG. First promise me—give me your word—that what I now confide to you Thea shall never know.

HEDDA. I give you my word.

LÖVBORG. Good. Then let me tell you that what I said just now was untrue.

HEDDA. About the manuscript?

LÖVBORG. Yes. I have not torn it to pieces—nor thrown it into the fiord.

HEDDA. No, no—But—where is it then?

LÖVBORG. I have destroyed it none the less—utterly destroyed it, Hedda!

HEDDA. I don't understand.

LÖVBORG. Thea said that what I had done seemed to her like a child-murder.

HEDDA. Yes, so she said.

LÖVBORG. But to kill his child—that is not the worst thing a father can do to it.

HEDDA. Not the worst?

LÖVBORG. No. I wanted to spare Thea from hearing the worst.

HEDDA. Then what is the worst?

LÖVBORG. Suppose now, Hedda, that a man —in the small hours of the morning—came home to his child's mother after a night of riot and debauchery, and said: "Listen—I have been here and there—in this place and in that. And I have taken our child with me—to this place and to that. And I have lost the child— utterly lost it. The devil knows into what hands it may have fallen—who may have had their clutches on it."

HEDDA. Well—but when all is said and done, you know—that was only a book—

LÖVBORG. Thea's pure soul was in that book.

HEDDA. Yes, so I understand.

LÖVBORG. And you can understand, too, that for her and me together no future is possible.

HEDDA. What path do you mean to take then?

LÖVBORG. None. I will only try to make an end of it all—the sooner the better.

HEDDA [a step nearer to him]. Eilert Lövborg —listen to me. Will you not try to—to do it beautifully?

LÖVBORG. Beautifully? [Smiling.] With vine-leaves in my hair, as you used to dream in the old days—?

HEDDA. No, no. I have lost my faith in the vine-leaves. But beautifully, nevertheless! For once in a way!—Good-bye! You must go now —and do not come here any more.

LÖVBORG. Good-bye, Mrs. Tesman. And give George Tesman my love. [He is on the point of going.]

HEDDA. No, wait! I must give you a memento to take with you.

[She goes to the writing-table and opens the drawer and the pistol-case; then returns to LÖVBORG with one of the pistols.]

LÖVBORG [looks at her]. This? Is this the memento?

HEDDA [nodding slowly]. Do you recognize it? It was aimed at you once.

LÖVBORG. You should have used it then.

HEDDA. Take it—and do you use it now.

LÖVBORG [puts the pistol in his breast pocket]. Thanks!

HEDDA. And beautifully, Eilert Lövborg. Promise me that!

LÖVBORG. Good-bye, Hedda Gabler. [He goes out by the hall door.]

[HEDDA listens for a moment at the door. Then she goes up to the writing-table, takes out the packet of manuscript, peeps under the cover, draws a few of the sheets half out, and looks at them. Next she goes over and seats herself in the arm-chair beside the stove, with the packet in her lap. Presently she opens the stove door, and then the packet.]

HEDDA [throws one of the quires into the fire and whispers to herself]. Now I am burning your child, Thea!—Burning it, curly-locks! [Throwing one or two more quires into the stove.] Your child and Eilert Lövborg's. [Throws the rest in.] I am burning—I am burning your child.

ACT IV

[The same rooms at the TESMANS'. It is evening. The drawing-room is in darkness. The back room is lighted by the hanging lamp over the table. The curtains over the glass door are drawn close.

HEDDA, dressed in black, walks to and fro in the dark room. Then she goes into the back room and disappears for a moment to the left. She is heard to strike a few chords on the piano. Presently she comes in sight again, and returns to the drawing-room. BERTA enters from the right, through the inner room, with a lighted lamp, which she places on the table in front of the corner settee in the drawing-room. Her eyes are red with weeping, and she has black ribbons in her cap. She goes quietly and circumspectly out to the right. HEDDA goes up to the glass door, lifts the curtain a little aside, and looks out into the darkness. Shortly afterwards, MISS TESMAN, in mourning, with a bonnet and veil on, comes in from the hall. HEDDA goes towards her and holds out her hand.]

MISS TESMAN. Yes, Hedda, here I am, in mourning and forlorn; for now my poor sister has at last found peace.

HEDDA. I have heard the news already, as
5 you see. Tesman sent me a card.

MISS TESMAN. Yes, he promised me he would. But nevertheless I thought that to Hedda—here in the house of life—I ought myself to bring the tidings of death.

10 HEDDA. That was very kind of you.

MISS TESMAN. Ah, Rina ought not to have left us just now. This is not the time for Hedda's house to be a house of mourning.

HEDDA [*changing the subject*]. She died
15 quite peacefully, did she not, Miss Tesman?

MISS TESMAN. Oh, her end was so calm, so beautiful. And then she had the unspeakable happiness of seeing George once more—and bidding him good-bye.—Has he come home
20 yet?

HEDDA. No. He wrote that he might be detained. But won't you sit down?

MISS TESMAN. No thank you, my dear, dear Hedda. I should like to, but I have so much to
25 do. I must prepare my dear one for her rest as well as I can. She shall go to her grave looking her best.

HEDDA. Can I not help you in any way?

MISS TESMAN. Oh, you must not think of it!
30 Hedda Tesman must have no hand in such mournful work. Nor let her thoughts dwell on it either—not at this time.

HEDDA. One is not always mistress of one's thoughts—

35 MISS TESMAN [*continuing*]. Ah yes, it is the way of the world. At home we shall be sewing a shroud; and here there will soon be sewing too, I suppose—but of another sort, thank God!

40 [GEORGE TESMAN *enters by the hall door.*]

HEDDA. Ah, you have come at last!

TESMAN. You here, Aunt Julia? With Hedda? Fancy that!

MISS TESMAN. I was just going, my dear boy.
45 Well, have you done all you promised?

TESMAN. No; I'm really afraid I have forgotten half of it. I must come to you again tomorrow. Today my brain is all in a whirl. I can't keep my thoughts together.

MISS TESMAN. Why, my dear George, you 50 mustn't take it in this way.

TESMAN. Mustn't—? How do you mean?

MISS TESMAN. Even in your sorrow you must rejoice, as I do—rejoice that she is at rest.

TESMAN. Oh yes, yes—you are thinking of 55 Aunt Rina.

HEDDA. You will feel lonely now, Miss Tesman.

MISS TESMAN. Just at first, yes. But that will not last very long, I hope. I daresay I shall soon 60 find an occupant for poor Rina's little room.

TESMAN. Indeed? Who do you think will take it? Eh?

MISS TESMAN. Oh, there's always some poor invalid or other in want of nursing, unfor- 65 tunately.

HEDDA. Would you really take such a burden upon you again?

MISS TESMAN. A burden! Heaven forgive you, child—it has been no burden to me. 70

HEDDA. But suppose you had a total stranger on your hands—

MISS TESMAN. Oh, one soon makes friends with sick folk; and it's such an absolute necessity for me to have some one to live for. Well, 75 heaven be praised, there may soon be something in this house, too, to keep an old aunt busy.

HEDDA. Oh, don't trouble about anything here. 80

TESMAN. Yes, just fancy what a nice time we three might have together, if—?

HEDDA. If—?

TESMAN [*uneasily*]. Oh, nothing. It will all come right. Let us hope so—eh? 85

MISS TESMAN. Well, well, I daresay you two want to talk to each other. [*Smiling.*] And perhaps Hedda may have something to tell you too, George. Good-bye! I must go home to Rina. [*Turning at the door.*] How strange it is 90 to think that now Rina is with me and with my poor brother as well!

TESMAN. Yes, fancy that, Aunt Julia! Eh?

[MISS TESMAN *goes out by the hall door.*]

HEDDA [*follows* TESMAN *coldly and search- 95 ingly with her eyes*]. I almost believe your Aunt Rina's death affects you more than it does your Aunt Julia.

TESMAN. Oh, it's not that alone. It's Eilert I am so terribly uneasy about.

HEDDA [*quickly*]. Is there anything new about him?

5 TESMAN. I looked in at his rooms this afternoon, intending to tell him the manuscript was in safe keeping.

HEDDA. Well, did you not find him?

TESMAN. No. He wasn't at home. But after-
10 wards I met Mrs. Elvsted, and she told me he had been here early this morning.

HEDDA. Yes, directly after you had gone.

TESMAN. And he said that he had torn his manuscript to pieces—eh?

15 HEDDA. Yes, so he declared.

TESMAN. Why, good heavens, he must have been completely out of his mind! And I suppose you thought it best not to give it back to him, Hedda?

20 HEDDA. No, he did not get it.

TESMAN. But of course you told him that we had it?

HEDDA. No. [*Quickly.*] Did you tell Mrs. Elvsted?

25 TESMAN. No; I thought I had better not. But you ought to have told him. Fancy, if, in desperation, he should go and do himself some injury! Let me have the manuscript, Hedda! I will take it to him at once. Where is it?

30 HEDDA [*cold and immovable, leaning on the arm-chair*]. I have not got it.

TESMAN. Have not got it? What in the world do you mean?

HEDDA. I have burnt it—every line of it.

35 TESMAN [*with a violent movement of terror*]. Burnt! Burnt Eilert's manuscript!

HEDDA. Don't scream so. The servant might hear you.

TESMAN. Burnt! Why, good God—! No, no,
40 no! It's impossible!

HEDDA. It is so, nevertheless.

TESMAN. Do you know what you have done, Hedda? It's unlawful appropriation of lost property. Fancy that! Just ask Judge Brack,
45 and he'll tell you what it is.

HEDDA. I advise you not to speak of it—either to Judge Brack, or to any one else.

TESMAN. But how could you do anything so unheard-of? What put it into your head? What
possessed you? Answer me that—eh? 50

HEDDA [*suppressing an almost imperceptible smile*]. I did it for your sake, George.

TESMAN. For my sake!

HEDDA. This morning, when you told me about what he had read to you— 55

TESMAN. Yes, yes—what then?

HEDDA. You acknowledged that you envied his work.

TESMAN. Oh, of course I didn't mean that literally. 60

HEDDA. No matter—I could not bear the idea that any one should throw you into the shade.

TESMAN. [*in an outburst of mingled doubt and joy*]. Hedda! Oh, is this true? But—but—I never knew you to show your love like that 65 before. Fancy that!

HEDDA. Well, I may as well tell you that—just at this time—[*impatiently, breaking off*]. No, no; you can ask Aunt Julia. She will tell you, fast enough. 70

TESMAN. Oh, I almost think I understand you, Hedda! [*Clasps his hands together.*] Great heavens! do you really mean it! Eh?

HEDDA. Don't shout so. The servant might hear. 75

TESMAN [*laughing in irrepressible glee*]. The servant! Why, how absurd you are, Hedda. It's only my old Berta! Why, I'll tell Berta myself.

HEDDA [*clenching her hands together in desperation*]. Oh, it is killing me,—it is killing me, 80 all this!

TESMAN. What is, Hedda? Eh?

HEDDA [*coldly, controlling herself*]. All this —absurdity—George.

TESMAN. Absurdity! Do you see anything 85 absurd in my being overjoyed at the news! But after all perhaps I had better not say anything to Berta.

HEDDA. Oh—why not that too?

TESMAN. No, no, not yet! But I must cer- 90 tainly tell Aunt Julia. And then that you have begun to call me George too! Fancy that! Oh, Aunt Julia will be so happy—so happy.

HEDDA. When she hears that I have burnt Eilert Lövborg's manuscript—for your sake? 95

TESMAN. No, by-the-bye—that affair of the

manuscript—of course nobody must know about that. But that you love me° so much, Hedda—Aunt Julia must really share my joy in that! I wonder, now, whether this sort of thing is usual in young wives? Eh?

HEDDA. I think you had better ask Aunt Julia that question too.

TESMAN. I will indeed, some time or other. [*Looks uneasy and downcast again.*] And yet the manuscript—the manuscript! Good God! it is terrible to think what will become of poor Eilert now.

[MRS. ELVSTED, *dressed as in the first act, with hat and cloak, enters by the hall door.*]

MRS. ELVSTED [*greets them hurriedly, and says in evident agitation*]. Oh, dear Hedda, forgive my coming again.

HEDDA. What is the matter with you, Thea?

TESMAN. Something about Eilert Lövborg again—eh?

MRS. ELVSTED. Yes! I am dreadfully afraid some misfortune has happened to him.

HEDDA [*seizes her arm*]. Ah,—do you think so?

TESMAN. Why, good Lord—what makes you think that, Mrs. Elvsted?

MRS. ELVSTED. I heard them talking of him at my boarding-house—just as I came in. Oh, the most incredible rumors are afloat about him today.

TESMAN. Yes, fancy, so I heard too! And I can bear witness that he went straight home to bed last night. Fancy that!

HEDDA. Well, what did they say at the boarding-house?

MRS. ELVSTED. Oh, I couldn't make out anything clearly. Either they knew nothing definite, or else— They stopped talking when they saw me; and I did not dare to ask.

TESMAN [*moving about uneasily*]. We must hope—we must hope that you misunderstood them, Mrs. Elvsted.

MRS. ELVSTED. No, no; I am sure it was of him they were talking. And I heard something about the hospital or—

TESMAN. The hospital?

HEDDA. No—surely that cannot be!

MRS. ELVSTED. Oh, I was in such mortal terror! I went to his lodgings and asked for him there.

HEDDA. You could make up your mind to that, Thea!

MRS. ELVSTED. What else could I do? I really could bear the suspense no longer.

TESMAN. But you didn't find him either—eh?

MRS. ELVSTED. No. And the people knew nothing about him. He hadn't been home since yesterday afternoon, they said.

TESMAN. Yesterday! Fancy, how could they say that?

MRS. ELVSTED. Oh, I am sure something terrible must have happened to him.

TESMAN. Hedda dear—how would it be if I were to go and make inquiries—?

HEDDA. No, no—don't you mix yourself up in this affair.

[JUDGE BRACK, *with his hat in his hand, enters by the hall door, which* BERTA *opens, and closes behind him. He looks grave and bows in silence.*]

TESMAN. Oh, is that you, my dear Judge? Eh?

BRACK. Yes. It was imperative I should see you this evening.

TESMAN. I can see you have heard the news about Aunt Rina.

BRACK. Yes, that among other things.

TESMAN. Isn't it sad—eh?

BRACK. Well, my dear Tesman, that depends on how you look at it.

TESMAN [*looks doubtfully at him*]. Has anything else happened?

BRACK. Yes.

HEDDA [*in suspense*]. Anything sad, Judge Brack?

BRACK. That, too, depends on how you look at it, Mrs. Tesman.

MRS. ELVSTED [*unable to restrain her anxiety*]. Oh! it is something about Eilert Lövborg!

BRACK [*with a glance at her*]. What makes you think that, Madam? Perhaps you have already heard something—?

MRS. ELVSTED [*in confusion*]. No, nothing at all, but—

TESMAN. Oh, for heaven's sake, tell us!

---

love me "burn for me" in the Norwegian

BRACK [*shrugging his shoulders*]. Well, I regret to say Eilert Lövborg has been taken to the hospital. He is lying at the point of death.

MRS. ELVSTED [*shrieks*]. Oh God! Oh God—

TESMAN. To the hospital! And at the point of death.

HEDDA [*involuntarily*]. So soon then—

MRS. ELVSTED [*wailing*]. And we parted in anger, Hedda!

HEDDA [*whispers*]. Thea—Thea—be careful!

MRS. ELVSTED [*not heeding her*]. I must go to him! I must see him alive!

BRACK. It is useless, Madam. No one will be admitted.

MRS. ELVSTED. Oh, at least tell me what has happened to him? What is it?

TESMAN. You don't mean to say that he has himself— Eh?

HEDDA. Yes, I am sure he has.

TESMAN. Hedda, how can you—?

BRACK [*keeping his eyes fixed upon her*]. Unfortunately you have guessed quite correctly, Mrs. Tesman.

MRS. ELVSTED. Oh, how horrible!

TESMAN. Himself, then! Fancy that!

HEDDA. Shot himself!

BRACK. Rightly guessed again, Mrs. Tesman.

MRS. ELVSTED [*with an effort at self-control*]. When did it happen, Mr. Brack?

BRACK. This afternoon—between three and four.

TESMAN. But, good Lord, where did he do it? Eh?

BRACK [*with some hesitation*]. Where? Well—I suppose at his lodgings.

MRS. ELVSTED. No, that cannot be; for I was there between six and seven.

BRACK. Well, then, somewhere else. I don't know exactly. I only know that he was found—. He had shot himself—in the breast.

MRS. ELVSTED. Oh, how terrible! That he should die like that!

HEDDA [*to* BRACK]. Was it in the breast?

BRACK. Yes—as I told you.

HEDDA. Not in the temple?

BRACK. In the breast, Mrs. Tesman.

HEDDA. Well, well—the breast is a good place, too.

BRACK. How do you mean, Mrs. Tesman?

HEDDA [*evasively*]. Oh, nothing—nothing.

TESMAN. And the wound is dangerous, you say—eh?

BRACK. Absolutely mortal. The end has probably come by this time.

MRS. ELVSTED. Yes, yes, I feel it. The end! The end! Oh, Hedda—!

TESMAN. But tell me, how have you learnt all this?

BRACK [*curtly*]. Through one of the police. A man I had some business with.

HEDDA [*in a clear voice*]. At last a deed worth doing!

TESMAN [*terrified*]. Good heavens, Hedda! what are you saying?

HEDDA. I say there is beauty in this.

BRACK. H'm, Mrs. Tesman—

TESMAN. Beauty! Fancy that!

MRS. ELVSTED. Oh, Hedda, how can you talk of beauty in such an act!

HEDDA. Eilert Lövborg has himself made up his account with life. He has had the courage to do—the one right thing.

MRS. ELVSTED. No, you must never think that was how it happened! It must have been in delirium that he did it.

TESMAN. In despair!

HEDDA. That he did not. I am certain of that.

MRS. ELVSTED. Yes, yes! In delirium! Just as when he tore up our manuscript.

BRACK [*starting*]. The manuscript? Has he torn that up?

MRS. ELVSTED. Yes, last night.

TESMAN [*whispers softly*]. Oh, Hedda, we shall never get over this.

BRACK. H'm, very extraordinary.

TESMAN [*moving about the room*]. To think of Eilert going out of the world in this way! And not leaving behind him the book that would have immortalized his name—

MRS. ELVSTED. Oh, if only it could be put together again!

TESMAN. Yes, if it only could! I don't know what I would not give—

MRS. ELVSTED. Perhaps it can, Mr. Tesman.

TESMAN. What do you mean?

MRS. ELVSTED [*searches in the pocket of her dress*]. Look here. I have kept all the loose
5 notes he used to dictate from.

HEDDA [*a step forward*]. Ah—!

TESMAN. You have kept them, Mrs. Elvsted! Eh?

MRS. ELVSTED. Yes, I have them here. I put
10 them in my pocket when I left home. Here they still are—

TESMAN. Oh, do let me see them!

MRS. ELVSTED [*hands him a bundle of papers*]. But they are in such disorder—all mixed
15 up.

TESMAN. Fancy, if we could make something out of them, after all! Perhaps if we two put our heads together—

MRS. ELVSTED. Oh, yes, at least let us try—
20 TESMAN. We will manage it! We must! I will dedicate my life to this task.

HEDDA. You, George? Your life?

TESMAN. Yes, or rather all the time I can spare. My own collections must wait in the
25 meantime. Hedda—you understand, eh? I owe this to Eilert's memory.

HEDDA. Perhaps.

TESMAN. And so, my dear Mrs. Elvsted, we will give our whole minds to it. There is no
30 use in brooding over what can't be undone—eh? We must try to control our grief as much as possible, and—

MRS. ELVSTED. Yes, yes, Mr. Tesman, I will do the best I can.

35 TESMAN. Well then, come here. I can't rest until we have looked through the notes. Where shall we sit? Here? No, in there, in the back room. Excuse me, my dear Judge. Come with me, Mrs. Elvsted.

40 MRS. ELVSTED. Oh, if only it were possible!

[TESMAN *and* MRS. ELVSTED *go into the back room. She takes off her hat and cloak. They both sit at the table under the hanging lamp, and are soon deep in an eager examination of*
45 *the papers.* HEDDA *crosses to the stove and sits in the arm-chair. Presently* BRACK *goes up to her.*]

HEDDA [*in a low voice*]. Oh, what a sense of freedom it gives one, this act of Eilert Lövborg's.
50
BRACK. Freedom, Mrs. Hedda? Well, of course, it is a release for him—

HEDDA. I mean for me. It gives me a sense of freedom to know that a deed of deliberate courage is still possible in this world,—a deed 55 of spontaneous beauty.

BRACK [*smiling*]. H'm—my dear Mrs. Hedda—

HEDDA. Oh, I know what you are going to say. For you are a kind of a specialist too, like 60 —you know!

BRACK [*looking hard at her*]. Eilert Lövborg was more to you than perhaps you are willing to admit to yourself. Am I wrong?

HEDDA. I don't answer such questions. I only 65 know Eilert Lövborg has had the courage to live his life after his own fashion. And then—the last great act, with its beauty! Ah! that he should have the will and the strength to turn away from the banquet of life—so early. 70

BRACK. I am sorry, Mrs. Hedda,—but I fear I must dispel an amiable illusion.

HEDDA. Illusion?

BRACK. Which could not have lasted long in any case. 75

HEDDA. What do you mean?

BRACK. Eilert Lövborg did not shoot himself voluntarily.

HEDDA. Not voluntarily?

BRACK. No. The thing did not happen exactly 80 as I told it.

HEDDA [*in suspense*]. Have you concealed something? What is it?

BRACK. For poor Mrs. Elvsted's sake I idealized the facts a little. 85

HEDDA. What are the facts?

BRACK. First, that he is already dead.

HEDDA. At the hospital?

BRACK. Yes—without regaining consciousness. 90

HEDDA. What more have you concealed?

BRACK. This—the event did not happen at his lodgings.

HEDDA. Oh, that can make no difference.

BRACK. Perhaps it may. For I must tell you—Eilert Lövborg was found shot in—in Mademoiselle Diana's boudoir.

HEDDA [*makes a motion as if to rise, but sinks back again*]. That is impossible, Judge Brack! He cannot have been there again today.

BRACK. He was there this afternoon. He went there, he said, to demand the return of something which they had taken from him. Talked wildly about a lost child—

HEDDA. Ah—so that was why—

BRACK. I thought probably he meant his manuscript; but now I hear he destroyed that himself. So I suppose it must have been his pocket-book.

HEDDA. Yes, no doubt. And there—there he was found?

BRACK. Yes, there. With a pistol in his breast-pocket, discharged. The ball had lodged in a vital part.

HEDDA. In the breast—yes.

BRACK. No—in the bowels.

HEDDA [*looks up at him with an expression of loathing*]. That too! Oh, what curse is it that makes everything I touch turn ludicrous and mean?

BRACK. There is one point more, Mrs. Hedda—another disagreeable feature in the affair.

HEDDA. And what is that?

BRACK. The pistol he carried—

HEDDA [*breathless*]. Well? What of it?

BRACK. He must have stolen it.

HEDDA [*leaps up*]. Stolen it! That is not true! He did not steal it!

BRACK. No other explanation is possible. He must have stolen it— Hush!

[TESMAN *and* MRS. ELVSTED *have risen from the table in the back room, and come into the drawing-room.*]

TESMAN [*with the papers in both his hands*]. Hedda dear, it is almost impossible to see under that lamp. Think of that!

HEDDA. Yes, I am thinking.

TESMAN. Would you mind our sitting at your writing-table—eh?

HEDDA. If you like. [*Quickly.*] No, wait! Let me clear it first!

TESMAN. Oh, you needn't trouble, Hedda. There is plenty of room.

HEDDA. No, no; let me clear it, I say! I will take these things in and put them on the piano. There! [*She has drawn out an object, covered with sheet music, from under the book-case, places several other pieces of music upon it, and carries the whole into the inner room, to the left.* TESMAN *lays the scraps of paper on the writing-table, and moves the lamp there from the corner table.* HEDDA *returns.*]

HEDDA [*behind* MRS. ELVSTED'S *chair, gently ruffling her hair*]. Well, my sweet Thea,—how goes it with Eilert Lövborg's monument?

MRS. ELVSTED [*looks dispiritedly up at her*]. Oh, it will be terribly hard to put in order.

TESMAN. We must manage it. I am determined. And arranging other people's papers is just the work for me.

[HEDDA *goes over to the stove, and seats herself on one of the foot-stools.* BRACK *stands over her, leaning on the arm-chair.*]

HEDDA [*whispers*]. What did you say about the pistol?

BRACK [*softly*]. That he must have stolen it.

HEDDA. Why stolen it?

BRACK. Because every other explanation ought to be impossible, Mrs. Hedda.

HEDDA. Indeed?

BRACK [*glances at her*]. Of course Eilert Lövborg was here this morning. Was he not?

HEDDA. Yes.

BRACK. Were you alone with him?

HEDDA. Part of the time.

BRACK. Did you not leave the room whilst he was here?

HEDDA. No.

BRACK. Try to recollect. Were you not out of the room a moment?

HEDDA. Yes, perhaps just a moment—out in the hall.

BRACK. And where was your pistol-case during that time?

HEDDA. I had it locked up in—

BRACK. Well, Mrs. Hedda?

HEDDA. The case stood there on the writing-table.

BRACK. Have you looked since, to see whether both the pistols are there?

HEDDA. No.

BRACK. Well, you need not. I saw the pistol found in Lövborg's pocket, and I knew it at once as the one I had seen yesterday—and before, too.

HEDDA. Have you it with you?

BRACK. No; the police have it.

HEDDA. What will the police do with it?

BRACK. Search till they find the owner.

HEDDA. Do you think they will succeed?

BRACK [*bends over her and whispers*]. No, Hedda Gabler—not so long as I say nothing.

HEDDA [*looks frightened at him*]. And if you do not say nothing,—what then?

BRACK [*shrugs his shoulders*]. There is always the possibility that the pistol was stolen.

HEDDA [*firmly*]. Death rather than that.

BRACK [*smiling*]. People say such things—but they don't do them.

HEDDA [*without replying*]. And supposing the pistol was stolen, and the owner is discovered? What then?

BRACK. Well, Hedda—then comes the scandal.

HEDDA. The scandal!

BRACK. Yes, the scandal—of which you are mortally afraid. You will, of course, be brought before the court—both you and Mademoiselle Diana. She will have to explain how the thing happened—whether it was an accidental shot or murder. Did the pistol go off as he was trying to take it out of his pocket, to threaten her with? Or did she tear the pistol out of his hand, shoot him, and push it back into his pocket? That would be quite like her; for she is an able-bodied young person, this same Mademoiselle Diana.

HEDDA. But *I* have nothing to do with all this repulsive business.

BRACK. No. But you will have to answer the question: Why did you give Eilert Lövborg the pistol? And what conclusions will people draw from the fact that you did give it to him?

HEDDA [*lets her head sink*]. That is true. I did not think of that.

BRACK. Well, fortunately, there is no danger, so long as I say nothing.

HEDDA [*looks up at him*]. So I am in your power, Judge Brack. You have me at your beck and call, from this time forward.

BRACK [*whispers softly*]. Dearest Hedda—believe me—I shall not abuse my advantage.

HEDDA. I am in your power none the less. Subject to your will and your demands. A slave, a slave then! [*Rises impetuously.*] No, I cannot endure the thought of that! Never!

BRACK [*looks half-mockingly at her*]. People generally get used to the inevitable.

HEDDA [*returns his look*]. Yes, perhaps. [*She crosses to the writing-table. Suppressing an involuntary smile, she imitates* TESMAN'S *intonations.*] Well? Are you getting on, George? Eh?

TESMAN. Heaven knows, dear. In any case it will be the work of months.

HEDDA [*as before*]. Fancy that! [*Passes her hands softly through* MRS. ELVSTED'S *hair.*] Doesn't it seem strange to you, Thea? Here are you sitting with Tesman—just as you used to sit with Eilert Lövborg?

MRS. ELVSTED. Ah, if I could only inspire your husband in the same way.

HEDDA. Oh, that will come too—in time.

TESMAN. Yes, do you know, Hedda—I really think I begin to feel something of the sort. But won't you go and sit with Brack again?

HEDDA. Is there nothing I can do to help you two?

TESMAN. No, nothing in the world. [*Turning his head.*] I trust to you to keep Hedda company, my dear Brack.

BRACK [*with a glance at* HEDDA]. With the very greatest of pleasure.

HEDDA. Thanks. But I am tired this evening. I will go in and lie down a little on the sofa.

TESMAN. Yes, do dear—eh?

[HEDDA *goes into the back room and draws the curtains. A short pause. Suddenly she is heard playing a wild dance on the piano.*]

MRS. ELVSTED [*starts from her chair*]. Oh—what is that?

TESMAN [*runs to the doorway*]. Why, my

dearest Hedda—don't play dance music tonight! Just think of Aunt Rina! And of Eilert
too!

HEDDA [*puts her head out between the cur-*
5 *tains*]. And of Aunt Julia. And of all the rest
of them.—After this, I will be quiet. [*Closes the
curtains again.*]

TESMAN [*at the writing-table*]. It's not good
for her to see us at this distressing work. I'll
10 tell you what, Mrs. Elvsted,—you shall take
the empty room at Aunt Julia's, and then I will
come over in the evenings, and we can sit and
work there—eh?

HEDDA [*in the inner room*]. I hear what you
15 are saying, Tesman. But how am *I* to get
through the evenings out here?

TESMAN [*turning over the papers*]. Oh, I
daresay Judge Brack will be so kind as to look
in now and then, even though I am out.

20 BRACK [*in the arm-chair, calls out gaily*].
Every blessed evening, with all the pleasure in
life, Mrs. Tesman! We shall get on capitally
together, we two!

HEDDA [*speaking loud and clear*]. Yes, don't
25 you flatter yourself we will, Judge Brack? Now
that you are the one cock in the basket—

[*A shot is heard within.* TESMAN, MRS. ELV-
STED, *and* BRACK *leap to their feet.*]

TESMAN. Oh, now she is playing with those
30 pistols again.

[*He throws back the curtains and runs in,
followed by* MRS. ELVSTED. HEDDA *lies stretched
on the sofa, lifeless. Confusion and cries.*
BERTA *enters in alarm from the right.*]

35 TESMAN [*shrieks to* BRACK]. Shot herself!
Shot herself in the temple! Fancy that!

BRACK [*half-fainting in the arm-chair*]. Good
God!—people don't do such things.

Anton Chekhov

1860–1904

The Cherry Orchard

1904

There are ranges of significance in almost every detail of *The Cherry Orchard,* which give the playgoer a sense, sometimes rather mysterious, that a great many meaningful things are going on all the while and make the play delightful to read and reread closely. In Lyubov's first-act entrance, for example, we at once take in a number of significant impresssions, which, when dwelt on, we find to comprise all the major components of the play. In this scene Lyubov is preceded by the hobbling figure of the old house-servant Firs and followed by a chaotic assembly of family, friends, and servants. "Joyfully through her tears," she greets the room as her one-time nursery. "And here I am," she adds, "like a little child." But the other characters interrupt at once, one with an idle complaint about the train's not running on time, and another with a comment on the appetite of her pet dog. We perceive immediately that Lyubov's entrance is anticipated by a discordant happening and is shortly swallowed up in confusion. And if we dwell on the source of these impressions—Firs crossing the stage, Lyubov's reaction to the nursery, the idle interruptions—we see also a fuller metaphoric meaning: the order of things to which she would return is moribund now, although her feeling for it remains; and misrule or the absence of any intelligible rule has succeeded it.

In making every detail tell in this way, Chekhov inevitably states his major ideas over and over again. Their recurrence is not obtrusive, because they receive a different coloration every time they appear: as they are embodied in particular speeches they take on both the emotions and attitudes of the speaker and ours toward him. But they do recognizably recur, and we find them interacting with one another from the beginning of the play to the end. In other words, they are formal elements. Chekhov has used ideas somewhat as a composer uses melodic phrases. His play is a quasi-musical interweaving of memories of

495

a past order of things with the fact of present chaos.

The cherry orchard itself, a relic of the past order, is the most significant embodiment of idea in the work, and a simple catalogue of references to the orchard illustrates Chekhov's manner of developing and varying his themes. The first stage direction mentions the orchard: "The cherry trees are in flower." In Act I Lopahin says, "The cherry orchard must be cut down." And later in the act Lyubov exclaims, "Oh, my childhood, my innocence! . . . Oh, my orchard! . . . you are young again and full of happiness." Trofimov says in Act II that "Your orchard is a fearful thing . . . dreaming of centuries gone by and tortured by fearful visions. . . . We must first expiate our past." When Lopahin gains the estate in Act III he shouts, "Come, all of you, and look how Yermolay Lopahin will take his axe to the cherry orchard!" In Act IV Lyubov again addresses the orchard: "Oh, my orchard, my sweet beautiful orchard! my life, my youth, my happiness, good-bye!" And the last stage direction reads: "All is still again, and there is nothing heard but the strokes of the axe far away in the orchard."

Such is the form of *The Cherry Orchard* and such, in part, its meaning. It perhaps should be added that any discussion of the play, including this one, tends to take its tone too largely from the play's general import, which is sad and dark. Chekhov understands very well the over-all haplessness of the scene upon which he looks. But seeing the people in this scene clearly and steadily, he finds them in equal parts pitiful and absurd, and presents them with humor and compassion in delicate balance—so that the subtitle, *A Comedy in Four Acts,* is apt.

The Cherry Orchard

A Comedy in Four Acts

CHEKHOV

Translated by Constance Garnett

CHARACTERS°

MADAME RANEVSKY (LYUBOV ANDREYEVNA)
  the owner of the Cherry Orchard
ANYA *her daughter, aged* 17
VARYA *her adopted daughter, aged* 24
GAEV (LEONID ANDREYEVITCH) *brother of*
  Madame Ranevsky
LOPAHIN (YERMOLAY ALEXEYEVITCH)
  a merchant
TROFIMOV (PYOTR SERGEYEVITCH) *a student*
SEMYONOV-PISHTCHIK *a landowner*
CHARLOTTA IVANOVNA *a governess*
EPIHODOV (SEMYON PANTALEYEVITCH) *a clerk*
DUNYASHA *a maid*
FIRS *an old valet, aged* 87
YASHA *a young valet*
A VAGRANT
THE STATION MASTER

Characters: Russians have three names: a given name (Lyubov), a patronymic (Andreyevna = daughter of Andrey), and a surname (Ranevsky). In the Russia of Chekhov's day, decorum prescribed title and surname (Madame Ranevsky) for formal relationships; given name and patronymic (Lyubov Andreyevna) for relationships somewhat less formal; given name alone for familiarity; and a diminutive of the given name (Lyuba for Lyubov) to indicate affection or condescension.

Reprinted by permission of the publishers, Chatto and Windus Ltd., and Mr. David Garnett.

A Post-Office Clerk
Visitors, Servants

scene. *The estate of* Madame Ranevsky.

ACT I

[*A room, which has always been called the nursery. One of the doors leads into* Anya's *room. Dawn, sun rises during the scene. May, the cherry trees in flower, but it is cold in the garden° with the frost of early morning. Windows closed.*

Enter Dunyasha *with a candle and* Lopahin *with a book in his hand.*]

Lopahin. The train's in, thank God. What time is it?

Dunyasha. Nearly two o'clock. [*Puts out the candle.*] It's daylight already.

Lopahin. The train's late! Two hours, at least. [*Yawns and stretches.*] I'm a pretty one; what a fool I've been. Came here on purpose to meet them at the station and dropped asleep. . . . Dozed off as I sat in the chair. It's annoying. . . . You might have waked me.

Dunyasha. I thought you had gone. [*Listens.*] There, I do believe they're coming!

Lopahin [*listens*]. No, what with the luggage and one thing and another. [*A pause.*] Lyubov Andreyevna has been abroad five years; I don't know what she is like now. . . . She's a splendid woman. A good-natured, kindhearted woman. I remember when I was a lad of fifteen, my poor father—he used to keep a little shop here in the village in those days—gave me a punch in the face with his fist and made my nose bleed. We were in the yard here, I forget what we'd come about—he had had a drop. Lyubov Andreyevna—I can see her now—she was a slim young girl then—took me to wash my face, and then brought me into this very room, into the nursery. "Don't cry, little peasant," says she, "it will be well in time for your wedding day." . . . [*A pause.*] Little peasant. . . . My father was a peasant, it's true, but

---

garden orchard. The Russian word *sad*, which appears here and in the title, means both garden and orchard.

here am I in a white waistcoat and brown shoes, like a pig in a bun shop. Yes, I'm a rich man, but for all my money, come to think, a peasant I was, and a peasant I am. [*Turns over the pages of the book.*] I've been reading this book and I can't make head or tail of it. I fell asleep over it. [*A pause.*]

Dunyasha. The dogs have been awake all night, they feel that the mistress is coming.

Lopahin. Why, what's the matter with you, Dunyasha?

Dunyasha. My hands are all of a tremble. I feel as though I should faint.

Lopahin. You're a spoilt soft creature, Dunyasha. And dressed like a lady too, and your hair done up. That's not the thing. One must know one's place.

[*Enter* Epihodov *with a nosegay; he wears a pea-jacket and highly polished creaking top-boots; he drops the nosegay as he comes in.*]

Epihodov [*picking up the nosegay*]. Here! the gardener's sent this, says you're to put it in the dining-room. [*Gives* Dunyasha *the nosegay.*]

Lopahin. And bring me some kvass.

Dunyasha. I will.

[*Goes out.*]

Epihodov. It's chilly this morning, three degrees of frost, though the cherries are all in flower. I can't say much for our climate [*sighs*]. I can't. Our climate is not often propitious to the occasion. Yermolay Alexeyevitch, permit me to call your attention to the fact that I purchased myself a pair of boots the day before yesterday, and they creak, I venture to assure you, so that there's no tolerating them. What ought I to grease them with?

Lopahin. Oh, shut up! Don't bother me.

Epihodov. Every day some misfortune befalls me. I don't complain, I'm used to it, and I wear a smiling face.

[Dunyasha *comes in, hands* Lopahin *the kvass.*]

Epihodov. I am going. [*Stumbles against a chair, which falls over.*] There! [*As though triumphant.*] There you see now, excuse the expression, an accident like that among others . . . It's positively remarkable.

[*Goes out.*]

DUNYASHA. Do you know, Yermolay Alexeyevitch, I must confess, Epihodov has made me a proposal.

LOPAHIN. Ah!

DUNYASHA. I'm sure I don't know. . . . He's a harmless fellow, but sometimes when he begins talking, there's no making anything of it. It's all very fine and expressive, only there's no understanding it. I've a sort of liking for him too. He loves me to distraction. He's an unfortunate man; every day there's something. They tease him about it—two and twenty misfortunes they call him.

LOPAHIN [*listening*]. There! I do believe they're coming.

DUNYASHA. They are coming! What's the matter with me? . . . I'm cold all over.

LOPAHIN. They really are coming. Let's go and meet them. Will she know me? It's five years since I saw her.

DUNYASHA [*in a flutter*]. I shall drop this very minute. . . . Ah, I shall drop.

[*There is a sound of two carriages driving up to the house. LOPAHIN and DUNYASHA go out quickly. The stage is left empty. A noise is heard in the adjoining rooms. FIRS, who has driven to meet MADAME RANEVSKY, crosses the stage hurriedly leaning on a stick. He is wearing old-fashioned livery and a high hat. He says something to himself, but not a word can be distinguished. The noise behind the scene goes on increasing. A voice: "Come, let's go in here." Enter LYUBOV ANDREYEVNA, ANYA, and CHARLOTTA IVANOVNA with a pet dog on a chain, all in travelling dresses. VARYA in an out-door coat with a kerchief over her head, GAEV, SEMYONOV-PISHTCHIK, LOPAHIN, DUNYASHA with bag and parasol, servants with other articles. All walk across the room.*]

ANYA. Let's come in here. Do you remember what room this is, mamma?

LYUBOV [*joyfully, through her tears*]. The nursery!

VARYA. How cold it is, my hands are numb. [*To LYUBOV ANDREYEVNA.*] Your rooms, the white room and the lavender one, are just the same as ever, mamma.

LYUBOV. My nursery, dear delightful room. . . . I used to sleep here when I was little. . . . [*Cries.*] And here I am, like a little child. . . . [*Kisses her brother and VARYA, and then her brother again.*] Varya's just the same as ever, like a nun. And I knew Dunyasha. [*Kisses DUNYASHA.*]

GAEV. The train was two hours late. What do you think of that? Is that the way to do things?

CHARLOTTA [*to PISHTCHIK*]. My dog eats nuts, too.

PISHTCHIK [*wonderingly*]. Fancy that!

[*They all go out except ANYA and DUNYASHA.*]

DUNYASHA. We've been expecting you so long. [*Takes ANYA's hat and coat.*]

ANYA. I haven't slept for four nights on the journey. I feel dreadfully cold.

DUNYASHA. You set out in Lent, there was snow and frost, and now? My darling! [*Laughs and kisses her.*] I *have* missed you, my precious, my joy. I must tell you . . . I can't put it off a minute. . . .

ANYA [*wearily*]. What now?

DUNYASHA. Epihodov, the clerk, made me a proposal just after Easter.

ANYA. It's always the same thing with you. . . . [*Straightening her hair.*] I've lost all my hairpins. . . . [*She is staggering from exhaustion.*]

DUNYASHA. I don't know what to think, really. He does love me, he does love me so!

ANYA [*looking towards her door, tenderly*]. My own room, my windows just as though I had never gone away. I'm home! Tomorrow morning I shall get up and run into the garden. . . . Oh, if I could get to sleep! I haven't slept all the journey, I was so anxious and worried.

DUNYASHA. Pyotr Sergeyevitch came the day before yesterday.

ANYA [*joyfully*]. Petya!

DUNYASHA. He's asleep in the bath house, he has settled in there. I'm afraid of being in their way, says he. [*Glancing at her watch.*] I was to have waked him, but Varvara Mihalovna told me not to. Don't you wake him, says she.

[Enter VARYA *with a bunch of keys at her waist.*]

VARYA. Dunyasha, coffee and make haste. . . . Mamma's asking for coffee.

DUNYASHA. This very minute.

[*Goes out.*]

VARYA. Well, thank God, you've come. You're home again. [*Petting her.*] My little darling has come back! My precious beauty has come back again!

ANYA. I have had a time of it!

VARYA. I can fancy.

ANYA. We set off in Holy Week—it was so cold then, and all the way Charlotta would talk and show off her tricks. What did you want to burden me with Charlotta for?

VARYA. You couldn't have travelled all alone, darling. At seventeen!

ANYA. We got to Paris at last, it was cold there—snow. I speak French shockingly. Mamma lives on the fifth floor, I went up to her and there were a lot of French people, ladies, an old priest with a book. The place smelt of tobacco and so comfortless. I felt sorry, oh! so sorry for mamma all at once, I put my arms round her neck, and hugged her and wouldn't let her go. Mamma was as kind as she could be, and she cried. . . .

VARYA [*through her tears*]. Don't speak of it, don't speak of it!

ANYA. She had sold her villa at Mentone, she had nothing left, nothing. I hadn't a farthing left either, we only just had enough to get here. And mamma doesn't understand! When we had dinner at the stations, she always ordered the most expensive things and gave the waiters a whole rouble. Charlotta's just the same. Yasha too must have the same as we do; it's simply awful. You know Yasha is mamma's valet now, we brought him here with us.

VARYA. Yes, I've seen the young rascal.

ANYA. Well, tell me—have you paid the arrears on the mortgage?

VARYA. How could we get the money?

ANYA. Oh, dear! Oh, dear!

VARYA. In August the place will be sold.

ANYA. My goodness!

LOPAHIN [*peeps in at the door and moos like a cow*]. Moo! [*Disappears.*]

VARYA [*weeping*]. There, that's what I could do to him. [*Shakes her fist.*]

ANYA [*embracing* VARYA, *softly*]. Varya, has he made you an offer? [VARYA *shakes her head.*] Why, but he loves you. Why is it you don't come to an understanding? What are you waiting for?

VARYA. I believe that there never will be anything between us. He has a lot to do, he has no time for me . . . and takes no notice of me. Bless the man, it makes me miserable to see him. . . . Everyone's talking of our being married, everyone's congratulating me, and all the while there's really nothing in it; it's all like a dream! [*In another tone.*] You have a new brooch like a bee.

ANYA [*mournfully*]. Mamma bought it. [*Goes into her own room and in a light-hearted childish tone:*] And you know, in Paris I went up in a balloon!

VARYA. My darling's home again! My pretty is home again!

[DUNYASHA *returns with the coffee-pot and is making the coffee.*]

VARYA [*standing at the door*]. All day long, darling, as I go about looking after the house, I keep dreaming all the time. If only we could marry you to a rich man, then I should feel more at rest. Then I would go off by myself on a pilgrimage to Kiev, to Moscow . . . and so I would spend my life going from one place to another. . . . I would go on and on. . . . What bliss!

ANYA. The birds are singing in the garden. What time is it?

VARYA. It must be nearly three. It's time you were asleep, darling. [*Going into* ANYA's *room.*] What bliss!

[YASHA *enters with a rug and a travelling bag.*]

YASHA [*crosses the stage, mincingly*]. May one come in here, pray?

DUNYASHA. I shouldn't have known you, Yasha. How you have changed abroad.

YASHA. H'm! . . . And who are you?

DUNYASHA. When you went away, I was that

high. [*Shows distance from floor.*] Dunyasha, Fyodor's daughter. . . . You don't remember me!

YASHA. H'm! . . . You're a peach! [*Looks round and embraces her: she shrieks and drops a saucer. YASHA goes out hastily.*]

VARYA [*in the doorway, in a tone of vexation*]. What now?

DUNYASHA [*through her tears*]. I have broken a saucer.

VARYA. Well, that brings good luck.

ANYA [*coming out of her room*]. We ought to prepare mamma: Petya is here.

VARYA. I told them not to wake him.

ANYA [*dreamily*]. It's six years since father died. Then only a month later little brother Grisha was drowned in the river, such a pretty boy he was, only seven. It was more than mamma could bear, so she went away, went away without looking back. [*Shuddering.*] . . . How well I understand her, if only she knew! [*A pause.*] And Petya Trofimov was Grisha's tutor, he may remind her.

[*Enter FIRS: he is wearing a pea-jacket and a white waistcoat.*]

FIRS [*goes up to the coffee-pot, anxiously*]. The mistress will be served here. [*Puts on white gloves.*] Is the coffee ready? [*Sternly to DUNYASHA.*] Girl! Where's the cream?

DUNYASHA Ah, mercy on us!

[*Goes out quickly.*]

FIRS [*fussing round the coffee-pot*]. Ech! you good-for-nothing! [*Muttering to himself.*] Come back from Paris. And the old master used to go to Paris too . . . horses all the way. [*Laughs.*]

VARYA. What is it, Firs?

FIRS. What is your pleasure? [*Gleefully.*] My lady has come home! I have lived to see her again! Now I can die. [*Weeps with joy.*]

[*Enter LYUBOV ANDREYEVNA, GAEV, LOPAHIN, and SEMYONOV-PISHTCHIK; the latter is in a short-waisted full coat of fine cloth, and full trousers. GAEV, as he comes in, makes a gesture with his arms and his whole body, as though he were playing billiards.*]

LYUBOV. How does it go? Let me remember. Cannon off the red!

GAEV. That's it—in off the white! Why, once, sister, we used to sleep together in this very room, and now I'm fifty-one, strange as it seems.

LOPAHIN. Yes, time flies.

GAEV. What do you say?

LOPAHIN. Time, I say, flies.

GAEV. What a smell of patchouli!

ANYA. I'm going to bed. Good-night, mamma. [*Kisses her mother.*]

LYUBOV. My precious darling. [*Kisses her hands.*] Are you glad to be home? I can't believe it.

ANYA. Good-night, uncle.

GAEV [*kissing her face and hands*]. God bless you! How like you are to your mother! [*To his sister.*] At her age you were just the same, Lyuba.

[*ANYA shakes hands with LOPAHIN and PISHTCHIK, then goes out, shutting the door after her.*]

LYUBOV. She's quite worn out.

PISHTCHIK. Aye, it's a long journey, to be sure.

VARYA [*to LOPAHIN and PISHTCHIK*]. Well, gentlemen? It's three o'clock and time to say good-bye.

LYUBOV [*laughs*]. You're just the same as ever, Varya. [*Draws her to her and kisses her.*] I'll just drink my coffee and then we will all go and rest. [*FIRS puts a cushion under her feet.*] Thanks, friend. I am so fond of coffee, I drink it day and night. Thanks, dear old man. [*Kisses FIRS.*]

VARYA. I'll just see whether all the things have been brought in.

[*Goes out.*]

LYUBOV. Can it really be me sitting here? [*Laughs.*] I want to dance about and clap my hands. [*Covers her face with her hands.*] And I could drop asleep in a moment! God knows I love my country, I love it tenderly; I couldn't look out of the window in the train, I kept crying so. [*Through her tears.*] But I must drink my coffee, though. Thank you, Firs, thanks, dear old man. I'm so glad to find you still alive.

FIRS. The day before yesterday.

GAEV. He's rather deaf.

LOPAHIN. I have to set off for Harkov directly, at five o'clock. . . . It is annoying! I wanted to have a look at you, and a little talk.
5 . . . You are just as splendid as ever.

PISHTCHIK [*breathing heavily*]. Handsomer, indeed. . . . Dressed in Parisian style . . . completely bowled me over.

LOPAHIN. Your brother, Leonid Andreyevitch
10 here, is always saying that I'm a low-born knave, that I'm a money-grubber, but I don't care one straw for that. Let him talk. Only I do want you to believe in me as you used to. I do want your wonderful tender eyes to look at me
15 as they used to in the old days. Merciful God! My father was a serf of your father and of your grandfather, but you—you—did so much for me once, that I've forgotten all that; I love you as though you were my kin . . . more than
20 my kin.

LYUBOV. I can't sit still, I simply can't. . . . [*Jumps up and walks about in violent agitation.*] This happiness is too much for me. . . . You may laugh at me, I know I'm silly. . . . My
25 own bookcase. [*Kisses the bookcase.*] My little table.

GAEV. Nurse died while you were away.

LYUBOV [*sits down and drinks coffee*]. Yes, the Kingdom of Heaven be hers! You wrote me
30 of her death.

GAEV. And Anastasy is dead. Squinting Petruchka has left me and is in service now with the police captain in the town. [*Takes a box of caramels out of his pocket and sucks one.*]
35 PISHTCHIK. My daughter, Dashenka, wishes to be remembered to you.

LOPAHIN. I want to tell you something very pleasant and cheering. [*Glancing at his watch.*] I'm going directly . . . there's no time to say
40 much . . . well, I can say it in a couple of words. I needn't tell you your cherry orchard is to be sold to pay your debts; the 22nd of August is the date fixed for the sale; but don't you worry, dearest lady, you may sleep in peace, there is a
45 way of saving it. . . . This is what I propose. I beg your attention! Your estate is not twenty miles from the town, the railway runs close by it, and if the cherry orchard and the land

along the river bank were cut up into building plots and then let on lease for summer villas,
50 you would make an income of at least 25,000 roubles a year out of it.

GAEV. That's all rot, if you'll excuse me.

LYUBOV. I don't quite understand you, Yermolay Alexeyevitch.
55 LOPAHIN. You will get a rent of at least 25 roubles a year for a three-acre plot from summer visitors, and if you say the word now, I'll bet you what you like there won't be one square foot of ground vacant by the autumn,
60 all the plots will be taken up. I congratulate you; in fact, you are saved. It's a perfect situation with that deep river. Only, of course, it must be cleared—all the old buildings, for example, must be removed, this house too, which
65 is really good for nothing, and the old cherry orchard must be cut down.

LYUBOV. Cut down? My dear fellow, forgive me, but you don't know what you are talking about. If there is one thing interesting—re-
70 markable indeed—in the whole province, it's our cherry orchard.

LOPAHIN. The only thing remarkable about the orchard is that it's a very large one. There's a crop of cherries every alternate year, and
75 then there's nothing to be done with them, no one buys them.

GAEV. This orchard is mentioned in the "Encyclopaedia."

LOPAHIN [*glancing at his watch*]. If we don't
80 decide on something and don't take some steps, on the 22nd of August the cherry orchard and the whole estate too will be sold by auction. Make up your minds! There is no other way of saving it, I'll take my oath on
85 that. No, No!

FIRS. In the old days, forty or fifty years ago, they used to dry the cherries, soak them, pickle them, make jam too, and they used . . .

GAEV. Be quiet, Firs.
90 FIRS. And they used to send the preserved cherries to Moscow and to Harkov by the wagon-load. That brought the money in! And the preserved cherries in those days were soft and juicy, sweet and fragrant. . . . They knew
95 the way to do them then. . . .

LYUBOV. And where is the recipe now?

FIRS. It's forgotten. Nobody remembers it.

PISHTCHIK [to LYUBOV ANDREYEVNA]. What's it like in Paris? Did you eat frogs there?

5 LYUBOV. Oh, I ate crocodiles.

PISHTCHIK. Fancy that now!

LOPAHIN. There used to be only the gentlefolks and the peasants in the country, but now there are these summer visitors. All the towns, 10 even the small ones, are surrounded nowadays by these summer villas. And one may say for sure, that in another twenty years there'll be many more of these people and that they'll be everywhere. At present the summer visitor 15 only drinks tea in his verandah, but maybe he'll take to working his bit of land too, and then your cherry orchard would become happy, rich and prosperous. . . .

GAEV [indignant]. What rot!

20 [Enter VARYA and YASHA.]

VARYA. There are two telegrams for you, mamma. [Takes out keys and opens an old-fashioned bookcase with a loud crack.] Here they are.

25 LYUBOV. From Paris. [Tears the telegrams, without reading them.] I have done with Paris.

GAEV. Do you know, Lyuba, how old that bookcase is? Last week I pulled out the bottom 30 drawer and there I found the date branded on it. The bookcase was made just a hundred years ago. What do you say to that? We might have celebrated its jubilee. Though it's an inanimate object, still it is a book case.

35 PISHTCHIK [amazed]. A hundred years! Fancy that now.

GAEV. Yes. . . . It is a thing . . . [feeling the bookcase]. Dear, honored bookcase! Hail to thee who for more than a hundred years hast 40 served the pure ideals of good and justice; thy silent call to fruitful labor has never flagged in those hundred years, maintaining [in tears] in the generations of man, courage and faith in a brighter future and fostering in us ideals of 45 good and social consciousness [a pause].

LOPAHIN. Yes. . . .

LYUBOV. You are just the same as ever, Leonid.

GAEV [a little embarrassed]. Cannon off the

right into the pocket! 50

LOPAHIN [looking at his watch]. Well, it's time I was off.

YASHA [handing LYUBOV ANDREYEVNA medicine]. Perhaps you will take your pills now.

PISHTCHIK. You shouldn't take medicines, my 55 dear madam . . . they do no harm and no good. Give them here . . . honored lady. [Takes the pill-box, pours the pills into the hollow of his hand, blows on them, puts them in his mouth and drinks off some kvass.] There! 60

LYUBOV [in alarm]. Why, you must be out of your mind!

PISHTCHIK. I have taken all the pills.

LOPAHIN. What a glutton! [All laugh.]

FIRS. His honor stayed with us in Easter 65 week, ate a gallon and a half of cucumbers . . . [mutters].

LYUBOV. What is he saying?

VARYA. He has taken to muttering like that for the last three years. We are used to it. 70

YASHA. His declining years!

[CHARLOTTA IVANOVNA, a very thin, lanky figure in a white dress with a lorgnette in her belt, walks across the stage.]

LOPAHIN. I beg your pardon, Charlotta Ivan- 75 ovna, I have not had time to greet you. [Tries to kiss her hand.]

CHARLOTTA [pulling away her hand]. If I let you kiss my hand, you'll be wanting to kiss my elbow, and then my shoulder. 80

LOPAHIN. I've no luck today! [All laugh.] Charlotta Ivanovna, show us some tricks!

LYUBOV. Charlotta, do show us some tricks!

CHARLOTTA. I don't want to. I'm sleepy. [Goes out.] 85

LOPAHIN. In three weeks' time we shall meet again. [Kisses LYUBOV ANDREYEVNA's hand.] Good-bye till then—I must go. [To GAEV.] Good-bye. [Kisses PISHTCHIK.] Good-bye. [Gives his hand to VARYA, then to FIRS and 90 YASHA.] I don't want to go. [To LYUBOV ANDREYEVNA.] If you think over my plan for the villas and make up your mind, then let me know; I will lend you 50,000 roubles. Think of it seriously. 95

VARYA [angrily]. Well, do go, for goodness' sake.

LOPAHIN. I'm going, I'm going.

[*Goes out.*]

GAEV. Low-born knave! I beg pardon, though . . . Varya is going to marry him, he's Varya's fiancé.

VARYA. Don't talk nonsense, uncle.

LYUBOV. Well, Varya, I shall be delighted. He's a good man.

PISHTCHIK. He is, one must acknowledge, a most worthy man. And my Dashenka . . . says too that . . . she says . . . various things. [*Snores, but at once wakes up.*] But all the same, honored lady, could you oblige me . . . with a loan of 240 roubles . . . to pay the interest on my mortgage tomorrow?

VARYA [*dismayed*]. No, no.

LYUBOV. I really haven't any money.

PISHTCHIK. It will turn up. [*Laughs.*] I never lose hope. I thought everything was over, I was a ruined man, and lo and behold—the railway passed through my land and . . . they paid me for it. And something else will turn up again, if not today, then tomorrow . . . Dashenka'll win two hundred thousand . . . she's got a lottery ticket.

LYUBOV. Well, we've finished our coffee, we can go to bed.

FIRS [*brushes GAEV, reprovingly*]. You have got on the wrong trousers again! What am I to do with you?

VARYA [*softly*]. Anya's asleep. [*Softly opens the window.*] Now the sun's risen, it's not a bit cold. Look, mamma, what exquisite trees! My goodness! And the air! The starlings are singing!

GAEV [*opens another window*]. The orchard is all white. You've not forgotten it, Lyuba? That long avenue that runs straight, straight as an arrow, how it shines on a moonlight night. You remember? You've not forgotten?

LYUBOV [*looking out of the window into the garden*]. Oh, my childhood, my innocence! It was in this nursery I used to sleep, from here I looked out into the orchard, happiness waked with me every morning and in those days the orchard was just the same, nothing has changed. [*Laughs with delight.*] All, all white! Oh, my orchard! After the dark gloomy autumn, and the cold winter; you are young again, and full of happiness, the heavenly angels have never left you. . . . If I could cast off the burden that weighs on my heart, if I could forget the past!

GAEV. H'm! and the orchard will be sold to pay our debts; it seems strange. . . .

LYUBOV. See, our mother walking . . . all in white, down the avenue! [*Laughs with delight.*] It is she!

GAEV. Where?

VARYA. Oh, don't, mamma!

LYUBOV. There is no one. It was my fancy. On the right there, by the path to the arbor, there is a white tree bending like a woman. . . .

[*Enter TROFIMOV wearing a shabby student's uniform and spectacles.*]

LYUBOV. What a ravishing orchard! White masses of blossoms, blue sky. . . .

TROFIMOV. Lyubov Andreyevna! [*She looks round at him.*] I will just pay my respects to you and then leave you at once. [*Kisses her hand warmly.*] I was told to wait until morning, but I hadn't the patience to wait any longer. . . .

[*LYUBOV ANDREYEVNA looks at him in perplexity.*]

VARYA [*through her tears*]. This is Petya Trofimov.

TROFIMOV. Petya Trofimov, who was your Grisha's tutor. . . . Can I have changed so much?

[*LYUBOV ANDREYEVNA embraces him and weeps quietly.*]

GAEV [*in confusion*]. There, there, Lyuba.

VARYA [*crying*]. I told you, Petya, to wait till tomorrow.

LYUBOV. My Grisha . . . my boy . . . Grisha . . . my son!

VARYA. We can't help it, mamma, it is God's will.

TROFIMOV [*softly through his tears*]. There . . . there.

LYUBOV [*weeping quietly*]. My boy was lost . . . drowned. Why? Oh, why, dear Petya? [*More quietly.*] Anya is asleep in there, and I'm talking loudly . . . making this noise. . . . But, Petya? Why have you grown so ugly? Why do you look so old?

TROFIMOV. A peasant-woman in the train called me a mangy-looking gentleman.

LYUBOV. You were quite a boy then, a pretty little student, and now your hair's thin—and spectacles. Are you really a student still?

[*Goes towards the door.*]

TROFIMOV. I seem likely to be a perpetual student.

LYUBOV [*kisses her brother, then* VARYA]. Well, go to bed. . . . You are older too, Leonid.

PISHTCHIK [*follows her*]. I suppose it's time we were asleep. . . . Ugh! my gout. I'm staying the night! Lyubov Andreyevna, my dear soul, if you could . . . tomorrow morning . . . 240 roubles.

GAEV. That's always his story.

PISHTCHIK. 240 roubles . . . to pay the interest on my mortgage.

LYUBOV. My dear man, I have no money.

PISHTCHIK. I'll pay it back, my dear . . . a trifling sum.

LYUBOV. Oh, well, Leonid will give it you . . . You give him the money, Leonid.

GAEV. Me give it him! Let him wait till he gets it!

LYUBOV. It can't be helped, give it him. He needs it. He'll pay it back.

[LYUBOV ANDREYEVNA, TROFIMOV, PISHTCHIK, *and* FIRS *go out.* GAEV, VARYA, *and* YASHA *remain.*]

GAEV. Sister hasn't got out of the habit of flinging away her money. [*To* YASHA.] Get away, my good fellow, you smell of the henhouse.

YASHA [*with a grin*]. And you, Leonid Andreyevitch, are just the same as ever.

GAEV. What's that? [*To* VARYA.] What did he say?

VARYA [*to* YASHA]. Your mother has come from the village; she has been sitting in the servants' room since yesterday, waiting to see you.

YASHA. Oh, bother her!

VARYA. For shame!

YASHA. What's the hurry? She might just as well have come tomorrow.

[*Goes out.*]

VARYA. Mamma's just the same as ever, she hasn't changed a bit. If she had her own way, she'd give away everything.

GAEV. Yes. [*A pause.*] If a great many reme-dies are suggested for some disease, it means that the disease is incurable. I keep thinking and racking my brains; I have many schemes, a great many, and that really means none. If we could only come in for a legacy from somebody, or marry our Anya to a very rich man, or we might go to Yaroslavl and try our luck with our old aunt, the Countess. She's very, very rich, you know.

VARYA [*weeps*]. If God would help us.

GAEV. Don't blubber. Aunt's very rich, but she doesn't like us. First, sister married a lawyer instead of a nobleman. . . .

[ANYA *appears in the doorway.*]

GAEV. And then her conduct, one can't call it virtuous. She is good, and kind, and nice, and I love her, but, however one allows for extenuating circumstances, there's no denying that she's an immoral woman. One feels it in her slightest gesture.

VARYA [*in a whisper*]. Anya's in the doorway.

GAEV. What do you say? [*A pause.*] It's queer, there seems to be something wrong with my right eye. I don't see as well as I did. And on Thursday when I was in the district Court . . .

[*Enter* ANYA.]

VARYA. Why aren't you asleep, Anya?

ANYA. I can't get to sleep.

GAEV. My pet. [*Kisses* ANYA's *face and hands.*] My child. [*Weeps.*] You are not my niece, you are my angel, you are everything to me. Believe me, believe . . .

ANYA. I believe you, uncle. Everyone loves you and respects you . . . but, uncle dear, you must be silent . . . simply be silent. What were you saying just now about my mother, about your own sister? What made you say that?

GAEV. Yes, yes . . . [*puts his hand over his face*]. Really, that was awful! My God, save me! And today I made a speech to the bookcase . . . so stupid! And only when I had finished, I saw how stupid it was.

VARYA. It's true, uncle, you ought to keep quiet. Don't talk, that's all.

ANYA. If you could keep from talking, it would make things easier for you, too.

GAEV. I won't speak. [*Kisses* ANYA's *and*

VARYA's *hands.*] I'll be silent. Only this is about business. On Thursday I was in the district Court; well, there was a large party of us there and we began talking of one thing and another, and this and that, and do you know, I believe that it will be possible to raise a loan on an I.O.U. to pay the arrears on the mortgage.

VARYA. If the Lord would help us!

GAEV. I'm going on Tuesday; I'll talk of it again. [*To* VARYA.] Don't blubber. [*To* ANYA.] Your mamma will talk to Lopahin; of course, he won't refuse her. And as soon as you're rested you shall go to Yaroslavl to the Countess, your great-aunt. So we shall all set to work in three directions at once, and the business is done. We shall pay off arrears, I'm convinced of it. [*Puts a caramel in his mouth.*] I swear on my honor, I swear by anything you like, the estate shan't be sold. [*Excitedly.*] By my own happiness, I swear it! Here's my hand on it, call me the basest, vilest of men, if I let it come to an auction! Upon my soul I swear it!

ANYA [*her equanimity has returned, she is quite happy*]. How good you are, uncle, and how clever! [*Embraces her uncle.*] I'm at peace now! Quite at peace! I'm happy!

[*Enter* FIRS.]

FIRS [*reproachfully*]. Leonid Andreyevitch, have you no fear of God? When are you going to bed?

GAEV. Directly, directly. You can go, Firs. I'll . . . yes, I will undress myself. Come, children, bye-bye. We'll go into details tomorrow, but now go to bed. [*Kisses* ANYA *and* VARYA.] I'm a man of the 'eighties.° They run down that period, but still I can say I have had to suffer not a little for my convictions in my life. It's not for nothing that the peasant loves me. One must know the peasant! One must know how . . .

ANYA. At it again, uncle!

'eighties a period of political reaction in Russia. The 'sixties saw major political and social reforms; the 'seventies (l.65, p.507) saw those reforms undermined; the 'eighties saw a return to repressive oligarchy. Gaev thinks of his reactionary leanings as devotion to old-fashioned ideals.

VARYA. Uncle dear, you'd better be quiet!

FIRS [*angrily*]. Leonid Andreyevitch!

GAEV. I'm coming. I'm coming. Go to bed. Potted the shot—there's a shot for you! A beauty!

[*Goes out,* FIRS *hobbling after him.*]

ANYA. My mind's at rest now. I don't want to go to Yaroslavl, I don't like my great-aunt, but still my mind's at rest. Thanks to uncle. [*Sits down.*]

VARYA. We must go to bed. I'm going. Something unpleasant happened while you were away. In the old servants' quarters there are only the old servants, as you know—Efimyushka, Polya and Yevstigney—and Karp too. They began letting stray people in to spend the night—I said nothing. But all at once I heard they had been spreading a report that I gave them nothing but pease pudding to eat. Out of stinginess, you know. . . . And it was all Yevstigney's doing. . . . Very well, I said to myself. . . . If that's how it is, I thought, wait a bit. I sent for Yevstigney. . . . [*Yawns.*] He comes. . . . "How's this, Yevstigney," I said, "you could be such a fool as to? . . ." [*Looking at* ANYA.] Anitchka! [*A pause.*] She's asleep. [*Puts her arm round* ANYA.] Come to bed . . . come along! [*Leads her.*] My darling has fallen asleep! Come . . .

[*They go.*]

[*Far away beyond the orchard a shepherd plays on a pipe.* TROFIMOV *crosses the stage and, seeing* VARYA *and* ANYA, *stands still.*]

VARYA. Sh! asleep, asleep. Come, my own.

ANYA [*softly, half asleep*]. I'm so tired. Still those bells. Uncle . . . dear . . . mamma and uncle. . . .

VARYA. Come, my own, come along.

[*They go into* ANYA's *room.*]

TROFIMOV [*tenderly*]. My sunshine! My spring.

The Curtain Falls

ACT II

[*The open country. An old shrine, long abandoned and fallen out of the perpendicular; near it a well, large stones that have apparently once been tombstones, and an old garden seat.*

The road to GAEV's *house is seen. On one side rise dark poplars; and there the cherry orchard begins. In the distance a row of telegraph poles and far, far away on the horizon there is*
5 *faintly outlined a great town, only visible in very fine clear weather. It is near sunset.* CHARLOTTA, YASHA *and* DUNYASHA *are sitting on the seat.* EPIHODOV *is standing near, playing something mournful on a guitar. All sit*
10 *plunged in thought.* CHARLOTTA *wears an old forage cap; she has taken a gun from her shoulder and is tightening the buckle on the strap.*]

CHARLOTTA [*musingly*]. I haven't a real pass-
15 port of my own, and I don't know how old I am, and I always feel that I'm a young thing. When I was a little girl, my father and mother used to travel about to fairs and give perfor-mances—very good ones. And I used to dance
20 salto-mortale° and all sorts of things. And when papa and mamma died, a German lady took me and had me educated. And so I grew up and became a governess. But where I came from, and who I am, I don't know. . . . Who
25 my parents were, very likely they weren't married . . . I don't know. [*Takes a cucumber out of her pocket and eats.*] I know nothing at all. [*A pause.*] One wants to talk and has no one to talk to . . . I have nobody.

30 EPIHODOV [*plays on the guitar and sings*]. "What care I for the noisy world! What care I for friends or foes!" How agreeable it is to play on the mandolin!

DUNYASHA. That's a guitar, not a mandolin.
35 [*Looks in a hand-mirror and powders herself.*]

EPIHODOV. To a man mad with love, it's a mandolin. [*Sings.*] "Were her heart but aglow with love's mutual flame." [YASHA *joins in.*]

CHARLOTTA. How shockingly these people
40 sing! Foo! Like jackals!

DUNYASHA [*to* YASHA]. What happiness, though, to visit foreign lands.

YASHA. Ah, yes! I rather agree with you there. [*Yawns, then lights a cigar.*]

45 EPIHODOV. That's comprehensible. In foreign lands everything has long since reached full

complexion.

YASHA. That's so, of course.

EPIHODOV. I'm a cultivated man, I read remarkably books of all sorts, but I can never 50
make out the tendency I am myself precisely
inclined for, whether to live or to shoot myself,
speaking precisely, but nevertheless I always
carry a revolver. Here it is . . . [*shows revolver*]. 55

CHARLOTTA. I've had enough, and now I'm
going. [*Puts on the gun.*] Epihodov, you're a
very clever fellow, and a very terrible one too,
all the women must be wild about you. Br-r-r!
[*Goes.*] These clever fellows are all so stupid; 60
there's not a creature for me to speak to. . . .
Always alone, alone, nobody belonging to me
. . . and who I am, and why I'm on earth, I
don't know.

[*Walks away slowly.*] 65

EPIHODOV. Speaking precisely, not touching
upon other subjects, I'm bound to admit about
myself, that destiny behaves mercilessly to me,
as a storm to a little boat. If, let us suppose, I
am mistaken, then why did I wake up this 70
morning, to quote an example, and look round,
and there on my chest was a spider of fearful
magnitude . . . like this. [*Shows with both
hands.*] And then I take up a jug of kvass, to
quench my thirst, and in it there is something 75
in the highest degree unseemly of the nature of
a cockroach. [*A pause.*] Have you read
Buckle?° [*A pause.*] I am desirous of troubling
you, Dunyasha, with a couple of words.

DUNYASHA. Well, speak. 80

EPIHODOV. I should be desirous to speak with
you alone. [*Sighs.*]

DUNYASHA [*embarrassed*]. Well—only bring
me my mantle first. It's by the cupboard. It's
rather damp here. 85

EPIHODOV. Certainly. I will fetch it. Now I
know what I must do with my revolver.

[*Takes guitar and goes off playing on it.*]

YASHA. Two and twenty misfortunes! Between ourselves, he's a fool. [*Yawns.*] 90

DUNYASHA. God grant he doesn't shoot himself! [*A pause.*] I am so nervous, I'm always in

---

salto-mortale the "leap of death," a standing somer-
sault in which only the feet touch the ground

Buckle nineteenth-century English historian, highly
regarded in Russia as an advanced thinker

a flutter. I was a little girl when I was taken into our lady's house, and now I have quite grown out of peasant ways, and my hands are white, as white as a lady's. I'm such a delicate, sensitive creature, I'm afraid of everything. I'm so frightened. And if you deceive me, Yasha, I don't know what will become of my nerves.

YASHA [*kisses her*]. You're a peach! Of course a girl must never forget herself; what I dislike more than anything is a girl being flighty in her behavior.

DUNYASHA. I'm passionately in love with you, Yasha; you are a man of culture—you can give your opinion about anything. [*A pause.*]

YASHA [*yawns*]. Yes, that's so. My opinion is this: if a girl loves anyone, that means that she has no principles. [*A pause.*] It's pleasant smoking a cigar in the open air. [*Listens.*] Someone's coming this way . . . it's the gentle-folk. [DUNYASHA *embraces him impulsively.*] Go home, as though you had been to the river to bathe; go by that path, or else they'll meet you and suppose I have made an appointment with you here. That I can't endure.

DUNYASHA [*coughing softly*]. The cigar has made my head ache. . . .

[*Goes off.*]

[YASHA *remains sitting near the shrine. Enter* LYUBOV ANDREYEVNA, GAEV, *and* LOPAHIN.]

LOPAHIN. You must make up your mind once for all—there's no time to lose. It's quite a simple question, you know. Will you consent to letting the land for building or not? One word in answer: Yes or no? Only one word!

LYUBOV. Who is smoking such horrible cigars here? [*Sits down.*]

GAEV. Now the railway line has been brought near, it's made things very convenient. [*Sits down.*] Here we have been over and lunched in town. Cannon off the white! I should like to go home and have a game.

LYUBOV. You have plenty of time.

LOPAHIN. Only one word! [*Beseechingly.*] Give me an answer!

GAEV [*yawning*]. What do you say?

LYUBOV [*looks in her purse*]. I had quite a lot of money here yesterday, and there's scarcely any left today. My poor Varya feeds

us all on milk soup for the sake of economy; the old folks in the kitchen get nothing but pease pudding, while I waste my money in a senseless way. [*Drops purse, scattering gold pieces.*] There, they have all fallen out! [*Annoyed.*]

YASHA. Allow me, I'll soon pick them up. [*Collects the coins.*]

LYUBOV. Pray do, Yasha. And what did I go off to the town to lunch for? Your restaurant's a wretched place with its music and the table-cloth smelling of soap. . . . Why drink so much, Leonid? And eat so much? And talk so much? Today you talked a great deal again in the restaurant, and all so inappropriately. About the era of the 'seventies, about the decadents. And to whom? Talking to waiters about decadents!°

LOPAHIN. Yes.

GAEV [*waving his hand*]. I'm incorrigible; that's evident. [*Irritably to* YASHA.] Why is it you keep fidgeting about in front of us!

YASHA [*laughs*]. I can't help laughing when I hear your voice.

GAEV [*to his sister*]. Either I or he . . .

LYUBOV. Get along! Go away, Yasha.

YASHA [*gives* LYUBOV ANDREYEVNA *her purse*]. Directly. [*Hardly able to suppress his laughter.*] This minute . . .

[*Goes off.*]

LOPAHIN. Deriganov, the millionaire, means to buy your estate. They say he is coming to the sale himself.

LYUBOV. Where did you hear that?

LOPAHIN. That's what they say in town.

GAEV. Our aunt in Yaroslavl has promised to send help; but when, and how much she will send, we don't know.

LOPAHIN. How much will she send? A hundred thousand? Two hundred?

LYUBOV. Oh, well! . . . Ten or fifteen thousand, and we must be thankful to get that.

LOPAHIN. Forgive me, but such reckless people as you are—such queer, unbusiness-like people—I never met in my life. One tells you

decadents artists and thinkers of the 1890's whose pursuit of novelty in art and politics was widely stigmatized as corrupt

in plain Russian your estate is going to be sold, and you seem not to understand it.

LYUBOV. What are we to do? Tell us what to do.

LOPAHIN. I do tell you every day. Every day I say the same thing. You absolutely must let the cherry orchard and the land on building leases; and do it at once, as quick as may be—the auction's close upon us! Do understand! Once make up your mind to build villas, and you can raise as much money as you like, and then you are saved.

LYUBOV. Villas and summer visitors—forgive me saying so—it's so vulgar.

GAEV. There I perfectly agree with you.

LOPAHIN. I shall sob, or scream, or fall into a fit. I can't stand it! You drive me mad! [To GAEV.] You're an old woman!

GAEV. What do you say?

LOPAHIN. An old woman! [Gets up to go.]

LYUBOV [in dismay]. No, don't go! Do stay, my dear friend! Perhaps we shall think of something.

LOPAHIN. What is there to think of?

LYUBOV. Don't go, I entreat you! With you here it's more cheerful, anyway. [A pause.] I keep expecting something, as though the house were going to fall about our ears.

GAEV [in profound dejection]. Potted the white! It fails—a kiss.

LYUBOV. We have been great sinners. . . .

LOPAHIN. You have no sins to repent of.

GAEV [puts a caramel in his mouth]. They say I've eaten up my property in caramels. [Laughs.]

LYUBOV. Oh, my sins! I've always thrown my money away recklessly like a lunatic. I married a man who made nothing but debts. My husband died of champagne—he drank dreadfully. To my misery I loved another man, and immediately—it was my first punishment—the blow fell upon me, here, in the river . . . my boy was drowned and I went abroad—went away for ever, never to return, not to see that river again . . . I shut my eyes, and fled, distracted, and he after me . . . pitilessly, brutally. I bought a villa at Mentone, for he fell ill there, and for three years I had no rest day or night. His illness wore me out, my soul was dried up. And last year, when my villa was sold to pay my debts, I went to Paris and there he robbed me of everything and abandoned me for another woman; and I tried to poison myself. . . . So stupid, so shameful! . . . And suddenly I felt a yearning for Russia, for my country, for my little girl . . . [dries her tears]. Lord, Lord, be merciful! Forgive my sins! Do not chastise me more! [Takes a telegram out of her pocket.] I got this today from Paris. He implores forgiveness, entreats me to return. [Tears up the telegram.] I fancy there is music somewhere. [Listens.]

GAEV. That's our famous Jewish orchestra. You remember, four violins, a flute and a double bass.

LYUBOV. That still in existence? We ought to send for them one evening, and give a dance.

LOPAHIN [listens]. I can't hear. . . . [Hums softly.] "For money the Germans will turn a Russian into a Frenchman."° [Laughs.] I did see such a piece at the theatre yesterday! It was funny!

LYUBOV. And most likely there was nothing funny in it. You shouldn't look at plays, you should look at yourselves a little oftener. How grey your lives are! How much nonsense you talk.

LOPAHIN. That's true. One may say honestly, we live a fool's life. [Pause.] My father was a peasant, an idiot; he knew nothing and taught me nothing, only beat me when he was drunk, and always with his stick. In reality I am just such another blockhead and idiot. I've learnt nothing properly. I write a wretched hand. I write so that I feel ashamed before folks, like a pig.

LYUBOV. You ought to get married, my dear fellow.

LOPAHIN. Yes . . . that's true.

LYUBOV. You should marry our Varya, she's a good girl.

"For money the Germans . . . Frenchman" i.e. for money the Germans (numbers of whom had settled in Russia as "experts" in various fields) will turn the barbarian into a model of elegance

LOPAHIN. Yes.

LYUBOV. She's a good-natured girl, she's busy all day long, and what's more, she loves you. And you have liked her for ever so long.

5 LOPAHIN. Well? I'm not against it. . . . She's a good girl. [*Pause.*]

GAEV. I've been offered a place in the bank: 6,000 roubles a year. Did you know?

LYUBOV. You would never do for that! You 10 must stay as you are.

[*Enter* FIRS *with overcoat.*]

FIRS. Put it on, sir, it's damp.

GAEV [*putting it on*]. You bother me, old fellow.

15 FIRS. You can't go on like this. You went away in the morning without leaving word. [*Looks him over.*]

LYUBOV. You look older, Firs!

FIRS. What is your pleasure?

20 LOPAHIN. You look older, she said.

FIRS. I've had a long life. They were arranging my wedding before your papa was born. . . . [*Laughs.*] I was the head footman before the emancipation° came. I wouldn't con-
25 sent to be set free then; I stayed on with the old master. . . . [*A pause.*] I remember what rejoicings they made and didn't know themselves what they were rejoicing over.

LOPAHIN. Those were fine old times. There 30 was flogging anyway.

FIRS [*not hearing*]. To be sure! The peasants knew their place, and the masters knew theirs; but now they're all at sixes and sevens, there's no making it out.

35 GAEV. Hold your tongue, Firs. I must go to town tomorrow. I have been promised an introduction to a general, who might let us have a loan.

LOPAHIN. You won't bring that off. And you 40 won't pay your arrears, you may rest assured of that.

LYUBOV. That's all his nonsense. There is no such general.

[*Enter* TROFIMOV, ANYA, *and* VARYA.]

45 GAEV. Here come our girls.

ANYA. There's mamma on the seat.

the emancipation of the serfs in 1861

LYUBOV [*tenderly*]. Come here, come along. My darlings! [*Embraces* ANYA *and* VARYA.] If you only knew how I love you both. Sit beside me, there, like that. [*All sit down.*] 50

LOPAHIN. Our perpetual student is always with the young ladies.

TROFIMOV. That's not your business.

LOPAHIN. He'll soon be fifty, and he's still a student. 55

TROFIMOV. Drop your idiotic jokes.

LOPAHIN. Why are you so cross, you queer fish?

TROFIMOV. Oh, don't persist!

LOPAHIN [*laughs*]. Allow me to ask you 60 what's your idea of me?

TROFIMOV. I'll tell you my idea of you, Yermolay Alexeyevitch: you are a rich man, you'll soon be a millionaire. Well, just as in the economy of nature a wild beast is of use, who 65 devours everything that comes in his way, so you too have your use. [*All laugh.*]

VARYA. Better tell us something about the planets, Petya.

LYUBOV. No, let us go on with the conversa- 70 tion we had yesterday.

TROFIMOV. What was it about?

GAEV. About pride.

TROFIMOV. We had a long conversation yesterday, but we came to no conclusion. In 75 pride, in your sense of it, there is something mystical. Perhaps you are right from your point of view; but if one looks at it simply, without subtlety, what sort of pride can there be, what sense is there in it, if man in his 80 physiological formation is very imperfect, if in the immense majority of cases he is coarse, dull-witted, profoundly unhappy? One must give up glorification of self. One should work, and nothing else. 85

GAEV. One must die in any case.

TROFIMOV. Who knows? And what does it mean—dying? Perhaps man has a hundred senses, and only the five we know are lost at death, while the other ninety-five remain alive. 90

LYUBOV. How clever you are, Petya!

LOPAHIN [*ironically*]. Fearfully clever!

TROFIMOV. Humanity progresses, perfecting its powers. Everything that is beyond its ken now will one day become familiar and comprehensible; only we must work, we must with all our powers aid the seeker after truth. Here among us in Russia the workers are few in number as yet. The vast majority of the intellectual people I know, seek nothing, do nothing, are not fit as yet for work of any kind. They call themselves intellectual, but they treat their servants as inferiors, behave to the peasants as though they were animals, learn little, read nothing seriously, do practically nothing, only talk about science and know very little about art. They are all serious people, they all have severe faces, they all talk of weighty matters and air their theories, and yet the vast majority of us—ninety-nine per cent—live like savages, at the least thing fly to blows and abuse, eat piggishly, sleep in filth and stuffiness, bugs everywhere, stench and damp and moral impurity. And it's clear all our fine talk is only to divert our attention and other people's. Show me where to find the crèches° there's so much talk about, and the reading-rooms? They only exist in novels: in real life there are none of them. There is nothing but filth and vulgarity and Asiatic apathy. I fear and dislike very serious faces. I'm afraid of serious conversations. We should do better to be silent.

LOPAHIN. You know, I get up at five o'clock in the morning, and I work from morning to night; and I've money, my own and other people's, always passing through my hands, and I see what people are made of all round me. One has only to begin to do anything to see how few honest, decent people there are. Sometimes when I lie awake at night, I think: "Oh! Lord, thou hast given us immense forests, boundless plains, the widest horizons, and living here we ourselves ought really to be giants."

LYUBOV. You ask for giants! They are no good except in story-books; in real life they frighten us.

[EPIHODOV advances in the background, playing on the guitar.]

LYUBOV [dreamily]. There goes Epihodov.

ANYA [dreamily]. There goes Epihodov.

crèches day nurseries

GAEV. The sun has set, my friends.

TROFIMOV. Yes.

GAEV [not loudly, but, as it were, declaiming]. O nature, divine nature, thou art bright with eternal luster, beautiful and indifferent! Thou, whom we call mother, thou dost unite within thee life and death! Thou dost give life and dost destroy!

VARYA [in a tone of supplication]. Uncle!

ANYA. Uncle, you are at it again!

TROFIMOV. You'd much better be cannoning off the red!

GAEV. I'll hold my tongue, I will.

[All sit plunged in thought. Perfect stillness. The only thing audible is the muttering of FIRS. Suddenly there is a sound in the distance, as it were from the sky—the sound of a breaking harp-string, mournfully dying away.]

LYUBOV. What is that?

LOPAHIN. I don't know. Somewhere far away a bucket fallen and broken in the pits. But somewhere very far away.

GAEV. It might be a bird of some sort—such as a heron.

TROFIMOV. Or an owl.

LYUBOV [shudders]. I don't know why, but it's horrid. [A pause.]

FIRS. It was the same before the calamity—the owl hooted and the samovar hissed all the time.

GAEV. Before what calamity?

FIRS. Before the emancipation. [A pause.]

LYUBOV. Come, my friends, let us be going; evening is falling. [To ANYA.] There are tears in your eyes. What is it, darling? [Embraces her.]

ANYA. Nothing, mamma; it's nothing.

TROFIMOV. There is somebody coming.

[THE WAYFARER appears in a shabby white forage cap and an overcoat; he is slightly drunk.]

WAYFARER. Allow me to inquire, can I get to the station this way?

GAEV. Yes. Go along that road.

WAYFARER. I thank you most feelingly. [Coughing.] The weather is superb. [Declaims.] My brother, my suffering brother! . . . Come out to the Volga! Whose groan do you hear? . . .

[*To* VARYA.] Mademoiselle, vouchsafe a hungry Russian thirty kopeks.

[VARYA *utters a shriek of alarm.*]

LOPAHIN [*angrily*]. There's a right and a wrong way of doing everything!

LYUBOV [*hurriedly*]. Here, take this. [*Looks in her purse.*] I've no silver. No matter—here's gold for you.

WAYFARER. I thank you most feelingly!

[*Goes off.*]

[*Laughter.*]

VARYA [*frightened*]. I'm going home—I'm going. . . . Oh, mamma, the servants have nothing to eat, and you gave him gold!

LYUBOV. There's no doing anything with me. I'm so silly! When we get home, I'll give you all I possess. Yermolay Alexeyevitch, you will lend me some more . . . !

LOPAHIN. I will.

LYUBOV. Come, friends, it's time to be going. And Varya, we have made a match of it for you. I congratulate you.

VARYA [*through her tears*]. Mamma, that's not a joking matter.

LOPAHIN. "Ophelia, get thee to a nunnery!"

GAEV. My hands are trembling; it's a long while since I had a game of billiards.

LOPAHIN. "Ophelia! Nymph, in thy orisons be all my sins remember'd.'"

LYUBOV. Come, it will soon be supper-time.

VARYA. How he frightened me! My heart's simply throbbing.

LOPAHIN. Let me remind you, ladies and gentlemen: on the 22nd of August the cherry orchard will be sold. Think about that! Think about it!

[*All go off, except* TROFIMOV *and* ANYA.]

ANYA [*laughing*]. I'm grateful to the wayfarer! He frightened Varya and we are left alone.

TROFIMOV. Varya's afraid we shall fall in love with each other, and for days together she won't leave us. With her narrow brain she can't grasp that we are above love. To eliminate the petty and transitory which hinders us from being free and happy—that is the aim and meaning of our life. Forward! We go forward irresistibly towards the bright star that shines yonder in the distance. Forward! Do not lag behind, friends.

ANYA [*claps her hands*]. How well you speak! [*A pause.*] It is divine here today.

TROFIMOV. Yes, it's glorious weather.

ANYA. Somehow, Petya, you've made me so that I don't love the cherry orchard as I used to. I used to love it so dearly. I used to think that there was no spot on earth like our garden.

TROFIMOV. All Russia is our garden. The earth is great and beautiful—there are many beautiful places in it. [*A pause.*] Think only, Anya, your grandfather, and great-grandfather, and all your ancestors were slave-owners—the owners of living souls—and from every cherry in the orchard, from every leaf, from every trunk there are human creatures looking at you. Cannot you hear their voices? Oh, it is awful! Your orchard is a fearful thing, and when in the evening or at night one walks about the orchard, the old bark on the trees glimmers dimly in the dusk, and the old cherry trees seem to be dreaming of centuries gone by and tortured by fearful visions. Yes! We are at least two hundred years behind, we have really gained nothing yet, we have no definite attitude to the past, we do nothing but theorize or complain of depression or drink vodka. It is clear that to begin to live in the present we must first expiate our past, we must break with it; and we can expiate it only by suffering, by extraordinary unceasing labor. Understand that, Anya.

ANYA. The house we live in has long ceased to be our own, and I shall leave it, I give you my word.

TROFIMOV. If you have the house keys, fling them into the well and go away. Be free as the wind.

ANYA [*in ecstasy*]. How beautifully you said that!

TROFIMOV. Believe me, Anya, believe me! I am not thirty yet, I am young, I am still a student, but I have gone through so much already! As soon as winter comes, I am hungry, sick, careworn, poor as a beggar, and what ups and downs of fortune have I not known! And my soul was always, every minute, day and night,

full of inexplicable forebodings. I have a foreboding of happiness, Anya. I see glimpses of it
already.

ANYA [*pensively*]. The moon is rising.

5 [EPIHODOV *is heard playing still the same
mournful song on the guitar. The moon rises.
Somewhere near the poplars* VARYA *is looking
for* ANYA *and calling* "Anya! Where are you?"]

TROFIMOV. Yes, the moon is rising. [*A
10 pause.*] Here is happiness—here it comes! It is
coming nearer and nearer; already I can hear its
footsteps. And if we never see it—if we may
never know it—what does it matter? Others
will see it after us.

15 VARYA'S VOICE. Anya! Where are you?

TROFIMOV. That Varya again! [*Angrily.*] It's
revolting!

ANYA. Well, let's go down to the river. It's
lovely there.

20 TROFIMOV. Yes, let's go.

[*They go.*]

VARYA'S VOICE. Anya! Anya!

The Curtain Falls

ACT III

[*A drawing-room divided by an arch from a
larger drawing-room. A chandelier burning.*
25 *The Jewish orchestra, the same that was mentioned in Act II, is heard playing in the ante-
room. It is evening. In the larger drawing-room
they are dancing the grand chain. The voice of*
SEMYONOV-PISHTCHIK: "Promenade à une
30 paire!" *Then enter the drawing-room in couples
first* PISHTCHIK *and* CHARLOTTA IVANOVNA, *then*
TROFIMOV *and* LYUBOV ANDREYEVNA, *thirdly*
ANYA *with the* POST-OFFICE CLERK, *fourthly*
VARYA *with the* STATION MASTER, *and other*
35 *guests.* VARYA *is quietly weeping and wiping
away her tears as she dances. In the last couple
is* DUNYASHA. *They move across the drawing-
room.* PISHTCHIK *shouts:* "Grand rond, balan-
cez!" *and* "Les Cavaliers à genou et remerciez
40 vos dames." FIRS *in a swallow-tail coat brings
in seltzer water on a tray.* PISHTCHIK *and
TROFIMOV enter the drawing-room.*]

PISHTCHIK. I am a full-blooded man; I have
already had two strokes. Dancing's hard work

for me, but as they say, if you're in the pack, 45
you must bark with the rest. I'm as strong, I
may say, as a horse. My parent, who would
have his joke—may the Kingdom of Heaven
be his!—used to say about our origin that the
ancient stock of the Semyonov-Pishtchiks was 50
derived from the very horse that Caligula made
a member of the senate. [*Sits down.*] But I've
no money, that's where the mischief is. A hungry dog believes in nothing but meat. . . .
[*Snores, but at once wakes up.*] That's like 55
me . . . I can think of nothing but money.

TROFIMOV. There really is something horsy
about your appearance.

PISHTCHIK. Well . . . a horse is a fine beast . . .
a horse can be sold. 60

[*There is the sound of billiards being played
in an adjoining room.* VARYA *appears in the
arch leading to the larger drawing-room.*]

TROFIMOV [*teasing*]. Madame Lopahin!
Madame Lopahin! 65

VARYA [*angrily*]. Mangy-looking gentleman!

TROFIMOV. Yes, I am a mangy-looking
gentleman, and I'm proud of it!

VARYA [*pondering bitterly*]. Here we have
hired musicians and nothing to pay them! 70

[*Goes out.*]

TROFIMOV [*to* PISHTCHIK]. If the energy you
have wasted during your lifetime in trying to
find the money to pay your interest, had gone
to something else, you might in the end have 75
turned the world upside down.

PISHTCHIK. Nietzsche, the philosopher, a very
great and celebrated man . . . of enormous
intellect . . . says in his works, that one can
make° forged bank-notes. 80

TROFIMOV. Why, have you read Nietzsche?

PISHTCHIK. What next . . . Dashenka told me.
. . . And now I am in such a position, I might
just as well forge bank-notes. The day after
tomorrow I must pay 310 roubles—130 I have 85
procured. [*Feels in his pockets, in alarm.*] The
money's gone! I have lost my money! [*Through
his tears.*] Where's the money? [*Gleefully.*]
Why, here it is behind the lining. . . . It has
made me hot all over. 90

one can make it is ethical to make

[*Enter* LYUBOV ANDREYEVNA *and* CHARLOTTA IVANOVNA.]

LYUBOV [*hums the Lezginka*°]. Why is Leonid so long? What can he be doing in town? [*To* DUNYASHA.] Offer the musicians some tea.

TROFIMOV. The sale hasn't taken place, most likely.

LYUBOV. It's the wrong time to have the orchestra, and the wrong time to give a dance. Well, never mind. [*Sits down and hums softly.*]

CHARLOTTA [*gives* PISHTCHIK *a pack of cards*]. Here's a pack of cards. Think of any card you like.

PISHTCHIK. I've thought of one.

CHARLOTTA. Shuffle the pack now. That's right. Give it here, my dear Mr. Pishtchik. Ein, zwei, drei—now look, it's in your breast pocket.

PISHTCHIK [*taking a card out of his breast pocket*]. The eight of spades! Perfectly right! [*Wonderingly.*] Fancy that now!

CHARLOTTA [*holding pack of cards in her hands, to* TROFIMOV]. Tell me quickly which is the top card.

TROFIMOV. Well, the queen of spades.

CHARLOTTA. It is! [*To* PISHTCHIK.] Well, which card is uppermost?

PISHTCHIK. The ace of hearts.

CHARLOTTA. It is! [*Claps her hands, pack of cards disappears.*]

Ah! what lovely weather it is today!

[*A mysterious feminine voice which seems coming out of the floor answers her.* "Oh, yes, it's magnificent weather, madam."]

CHARLOTTA. You are my perfect ideal.

VOICE. And I greatly admire you too, madam.

STATION MASTER [*applauding*]. The lady ventriloquist—bravo!

PISHTCHIK [*wonderingly*]. Fancy that now! Most enchanting Charlotta Ivanovna, I'm simply in love with you.

CHARLOTTA. In love? [*Shrugging shoulders.*] What do you know of love, guter Mensch, aber schlechter Musikant.°

TROFIMOV [*pats* PISHTCHIK *on the shoulder*].

You dear old horse. . . . 45

CHARLOTTA. Attention, please! Another trick! [*Takes a travelling rug from the chair.*] Here's a very good rug; I want to sell it. [*Shaking it out.*] Doesn't anyone want to buy it?

PISHTCHIK [*wonderingly*]. Fancy that! 50

CHARLOTTA. Ein, zwei, drei! [*Quickly picks up rug she has dropped; behind the rug stands* ANYA; *she makes a curtsey, runs to her mother, embraces her and runs back into the larger drawing-room amidst general enthusiasm.*] 55

LYUBOV [*applauds*]. Bravo! Bravo!

CHARLOTTA. Now again! Ein, zwei, drei! [*Lifts up the rug; behind the rug stands* VARYA, *bowing.*]

PISHTCHIK [*wonderingly*]. Fancy that now! 60

CHARLOTTA. That's the end. [*Throws the rug at* PISHTCHIK, *makes a curtsey, runs into the larger drawing-room.*]

PISHTCHIK [*hurries after her*]. Mischievous creature! Fancy! 65

[*Goes out.*]

LYUBOV. And still Leonid doesn't come. I can't understand what he's doing in the town so long! Why, everything must be over by now. The estate is sold, or the sale has not taken 70 place. Why keep us so long in suspense?

VARYA [*trying to console her*]. Uncle's bought it. I feel sure of that.

TROFIMOV [*ironically*]. Oh, yes!

VARYA. Great-aunt sent him an authorization 75 to buy it in her name, and transfer the debt. She's doing it for Anya's sake, and I'm sure God will be merciful. Uncle will buy it.

LYUBOV. My aunt in Yaroslavl sent fifteen thousand to buy the estate in her name, she 80 doesn't trust us—but that's not enough even to pay the arrears. [*Hides her face in her hands.*] My fate is being sealed today, my fate . . .

TROFIMOV [*teasing* VARYA]. Madame Lopa- 85 hin.

VARYA [*angrily*]. Perpetual student! Twice already you've been sent down° from the University.

LYUBOV. Why are you angry, Varya? He's 90

---

the Lezginka a sprightly Caucasian dance tune
guter Mensch . . . Musikant "a good man but a bad musician"

sent down expelled

teasing you about Lopahin. Well, what of that? Marry Lopahin if you like, he's a good man, and interesting; if you don't want to, don't! Nobody compels you, darling.

5   VARYA. I must tell you plainly, mamma, I look at the matter seriously; he's a good man, I like him.

LYUBOV. Well, marry him. I can't see what you're waiting for.

10   VARYA. Mamma, I can't make him an offer myself. For the last two years, everyone's been talking to me about him. Everyone talks; but he says nothing or else makes a joke. I see what it means. He's growing rich, he's absorbed in

15 business, he has no thoughts for me. If I had money, were it ever so little, if I had only a hundred roubles, I'd throw everything up and go far away. I would go into a nunnery.

TROFIMOV. What bliss!

20   VARYA [to TROFIMOV]. A student ought to have sense! [In a soft tone with tears.] How ugly you've grown, Petya! How old you look! [To LYUBOV ANDREYEVNA, no longer crying.] But I can't do without work, mamma; I must

25 have something to do every minute.

[Enter YASHA.]

YASHA [hardly restraining his laughter]. Epihodov has broken a billiard cue!

[Goes out.]

30   VARYA. What is Epihodov doing here? Who gave him leave to play billiards? I can't make these people out.

[Goes out.]

LYUBOV. Don't tease her, Petya. You see she

35 has grief enough without that.

TROFIMOV. She is so very officious, meddling in what's not her business. All the summer she's given Anya and me no peace. She's afraid of a love affair between us. What's it to do with

40 her? Besides, I have given no grounds for it. Such triviality is not in my line. We are above love!

LYUBOV. And I suppose I am beneath love. [Very uneasily.] Why is it Leonid's not here?

45 If only I could know whether the estate is sold or not! It seems such an incredible calamity that I really don't know what to think. I am distracted . . . I shall scream in a minute . . . I shall do something stupid. Save me, Petya, tell me something, talk to me! 50

TROFIMOV. What does it matter whether the estate is sold today or not? That's all done with long ago. There's no turning back, the path is overgrown. Don't worry yourself, dear Lyubov Andreyevna. You mustn't deceive yourself; for 55 once in your life you must face the truth!

LYUBOV. What truth? You see where the truth lies, but I seem to have lost my sight, I see nothing. You settle every great problem so boldly, but tell me, my dear boy, isn't it be- 60 cause you're young—because you haven't yet understood one of your problems through suffering? You look forward boldly, and isn't it that you don't see and don't expect anything dreadful because life is still hidden from your 65 young eyes? You're bolder, more honest, deeper than we are, but think, be just a little magnanimous, have pity on me. I was born here, you know, my father and mother lived here, my grandfather lived here, I love this house. I 70 can't conceive of life without the cherry orchard, and if it really must be sold, then sell me with the orchard. [Embraces TROFIMOV, kisses him on the forehead.] My boy was drowned here. [Weeps.] Pity me, my dear kind 75 fellow.

TROFIMOV. You know I feel for you with all my heart.

LYUBOV. But that should have been said differently, so differently. [Takes out her 80 handkerchief, telegram falls on the floor.] My heart is so heavy today. It's so noisy here, my soul is quivering at every sound, I'm shuddering all over, but I can't go away; I'm afraid to be quiet and alone. Don't be hard on me, 85 Petya . . . I love you as though you were one of ourselves. I would gladly let you marry Anya—I swear I would—only, my dear boy, you must take your degree, you do nothing— you're simply tossed by fate from place to 90 place. That's so strange. It is, isn't it? And you must do something with your beard to make it grow somehow. [Laughs.] You look so funny!

TROFIMOV [picks up the telegram]. I've no wish to be a beauty. 95

LYUBOV. That's a telegram from Paris. I get

one every day. One yesterday and one today. That savage creature is ill again, he's in trouble again. He begs forgiveness, beseeches me to go, and really I ought to go to Paris to see him. You 5 look shocked, Petya. What am I to do, my dear boy, what am I to do? He is ill, he is alone and unhappy, and who'll look after him, who'll keep him from doing the wrong thing, who'll give him his medicine at the right time? And 10 why hide it or be silent? I love him, that's clear. I love him! I love him! He's a millstone about my neck, I'm going to the bottom with him, but I love that stone and can't live without it. [*Presses* Trofimov's *hand.*] Don't think ill of 15 me, Petya, don't tell me anything, don't tell me . . .

Trofimov [*through his tears*]. For God's sake forgive my frankness: why, he robbed you!

Lyubov. No! No! No! You mustn't speak like 20 that. [*Covers her ears.*]

Trofimov. He is a wretch! You're the only person that doesn't know it! He's a worthless creature! A despicable wretch!

Lyubov [*getting angry, but speaking with* 25 *restraint*]. You're twenty-six or twenty-seven years old, but you're still a schoolboy.

Trofimov. Possibly.

Lyubov. You should be a man at your age! You should understand what love means! And 30 you ought to be in love yourself. You ought to fall in love! [*Angrily.*] Yes, yes, and it's not purity in you, you're simply a prude, a comic fool, a freak.

Trofimov [*in horror*]. The things she's say- 35 ing!

Lyubov. I am above love! You're not above love, but simply as our Firs here says, "You are a good-for-nothing." At your age not to have a mistress!

40 Trofimov [*in horror*]. This is awful! The things she is saying! [*Goes rapidly into the larger drawing-room clutching his head.*] This is awful! I can't stand it! I'm going. [*Goes off, but at once returns.*] All is over between us!

45 [*Goes off into the ante-room.*]

Lyubov [*shouts after him*]. Petya! Wait a minute! You funny creature! I was joking! Petya!

[*There is a sound of somebody running quickly downstairs and suddenly falling with a* 50 *crash.* Anya *and* Varya *scream, but there is a sound of laughter at once.*]

Lyubov. What has happened?

[Anya *runs in.*]

Anya [*laughing*]. Petya's fallen downstairs! 55 [*Runs out.*]

Lyubov. What a queer fellow that Petya is!

[*The* Station Master *stands in the middle of the larger room and reads "The Magdalene,"° by Alexey Tolstoy. They listen to him,* 60 *but before he has recited many lines strains of a waltz are heard from the ante-room and the reading is broken off. All dance.* Trofimov, Anya, Varya, *and* Lyubov Andreyevna *come in from the ante-room.*] 65

Lyubov. Come, Petya—come, pure heart! I beg your pardon. Let's have a dance! [*Dances with* Petya.]

[Anya *and* Varya *dance.* Firs *comes in, puts his stick down near the side-door.* Yasha *also* 70 *comes into the drawing-room and looks on at the dancing.*]

Yasha. What is it, old man?

Firs. I don't feel well. In old days we used to have generals, barons and admirals dancing at 75 our balls, and now we send for the post-office clerk and the station master and even they're not overanxious to come. I am getting feeble. The old master, the grandfather, used to give sealing-wax for all complaints. I have been 80

The Magdalene a poem which celebrates Christ's sudden appearance at a banquet of dazzling magnificence. Its opening lines follow:

The crowd seethes—merrymaking, laughter,
The sound of lutes and clash of cymbals;
All around are greenness, flowers,
And between the columns at the entrance of the
[house
Sections of heavy brocade
Are raised in patterned ribbons.
The chambers are richly furnished,
Crystal and gold burn everywhere;
The courtyard is filled with drivers and horses.
Crowding at the huge banquet table
The noisy chorus of guests celebrates;
Their criss-cross conversation
Goes on, fusing with the music.

(Trans. Horace W. Dewey)

taking sealing-wax for twenty years or more. Perhaps that's what's kept me alive.

YASHA. You bore me, old man! [*Yawns.*] It's time you were done with.

5 FIRS. Ach, you're a good-for-nothing! [*Mutters.*]

[TROFIMOV *and* LYUBOV ANDREYEVNA *dance in larger room and then on to the stage.*]

LYUBOV. Merci. I'll sit down a little. [*Sits 10 down.*] I'm tired.

[*Enter* ANYA.]

ANYA [*excitedly*]. There's a man in the kitchen has been saying that the cherry orchard's been sold today.

15 LYUBOV. Sold to whom?

ANYA. He didn't say to whom. He's gone away.

[*She dances with* TROFIMOV, *and they go off into the larger room.*]

20 YASHA. There was an old man gossiping there, a stranger.

FIRS. Leonid Andreyevitch isn't here yet, he hasn't come back. He has his light overcoat on, *demi-saison*, he'll catch cold for sure. Ach! 25 Foolish young things!

LYUBOV. I feel as though I should die. Go, Yasha, find out to whom it has been sold.

YASHA. But he went away long ago, the old chap. [*Laughs.*]

30 LYUBOV [*with slight vexation*]. What are you laughing at? What are you pleased at?

YASHA. Epihodov is so funny. He's a silly fellow, two and twenty misfortunes.

LYUBOV. Firs, if the estate is sold, where will 35 you go?

FIRS. Where you bid me, there I'll go.

LYUBOV. Why do you look like that? Are you ill? You ought to be in bed.

FIRS. Yes. [*Ironically.*] Me go to bed and 40 who's to wait here? Who's to see to things without me? I'm the only one in all the house.

YASHA [*to* LYUBOV ANDREYEVNA]. Lyubov Andreyevna, permit me to make a request of you; if you go back to Paris again, be so kind 45 as to take me with you. It's positively impossible for me to stay here. [*Looking about him; in an undertone.*] There's no need to say it, you

see for yourself—an uncivilized country, the people have no morals, and then the dullness! The food in the kitchen's abominable, and then 50 Firs runs after one muttering all sorts of unsuitable words. Take me with you, please do!

[*Enter* PISHTCHIK.]

PISHTCHIK. Allow me to ask you for a waltz, my dear lady. [LYUBOV ANDREYEVNA *goes with* 55 *him.*] Enchanting lady, I really must borrow of you just 180 roubles [*dances*], only 180 roubles.

[*They pass into the larger room.*]

YASHA [*hums softly*]. "Knowest thou my 60 soul's emotion."

[*In the larger drawing-room, a figure in a gray top hat and in check trousers is gesticulating and jumping about. Shouts of "Bravo, Charlotta Ivanovna."*] 65

DUNYASHA [*she has stopped to powder herself*]. My young lady tells me to dance. There are plenty of gentlemen, and too few ladies, but dancing makes me giddy and makes my heart beat. Firs, the post-office clerk said something 70 to me just now that quite took my breath away.

[*Music becomes more subdued.*]

FIRS. What did he say to you?

DUNYASHA. He said I was like a flower.

YASHA [*yawns*]. What ignorance! 75

[*Goes out.*]

DUNYASHA. Like a flower. I am a girl of such delicate feelings, I am awfully fond of soft speeches.

FIRS. Your head's being turned. 80

[*Enter* EPIHODOV.]

EPIHODOV. You have no desire to see me, Dunyasha. I must be an insect. [*Sighs.*] Ah! life!

DUNYASHA. What is it you want? 85

EPIHODOV. Undoubtedly you may be right. [*Sighs.*] But of course, if one looks at it from that point of view, if I may so express myself, you have, excuse my plain speaking, reduced me to a complete state of mind. I know my 90 destiny. Every day some misfortune befalls me and I have long ago grown accustomed to it, so that I look upon my fate with a smile. You gave me your word, and though I . . .

DUNYASHA. Let us have a talk later, I entreat you, but now leave me in peace, for I am lost in reverie. [*Plays with her fan.*]

EPIHODOV. I have a misfortune every day, and if I may venture to express myself, I merely smile at it, I even laugh.

[VARYA *enters from the larger drawing-room.*]

VARYA. You still have not gone, Epihodov. What a disrespectful creature you are, really! [*To* DUNYASHA.] Go along, Dunyasha! [*To* EPIHODOV.] First you play billiards and break the cue, then you go wandering about the drawing-room like a visitor!

EPIHODOV. You really cannot, if I may so express myself, call me to account like this.

VARYA. I'm not calling you to account, I'm speaking to you: You do nothing but wander from place to place and don't do your work. We keep you as a counting-house clerk, but what use you are I can't say.

EPIHODOV [*offended*]. Whether I work or whether I walk, whether I eat or whether I play billiards, is a matter to be judged by persons of understanding and my elders.

VARYA. You dare to tell me that! [*Firing up.*] You dare! You mean to say I've no understanding. Begone from here! This minute!

EPIHODOV [*intimidated*]. I beg you to express yourself with delicacy.

VARYA [*beside herself with anger*]. This moment! get out! away! [*He goes towards the door, she following him.*] Two and twenty misfortunes! Take yourself off! Don't let me set eyes on you! [EPIHODOV *has gone out, behind the door his voice, "I shall lodge a complaint against you."*] What! You're coming back? [*Snatches up the stick* FIRS *has put down near the door.*] Come! Come! Come! I'll show you! What! you're coming? Then take that! [*She swings the stick, at the very moment that* LOPAHIN *comes in.*]

LOPAHIN. Very much obliged to you!

VARYA [*angrily and ironically*]. I beg your pardon!

LOPAHIN. Not at all! I humbly thank you for your kind reception!

VARYA. No need of thanks for it. [*Moves away, then looks round and asks softly:*] I haven't hurt you?

LOPAHIN. Oh, no! Not at all! There's an immense bump coming up, though!

VOICES FROM LARGER ROOM. Lopahin has come! Yermolay Alexeyevitch!

PISHTCHIK. What do I see and hear? [*Kisses* LOPAHIN.] There's a whiff of cognac about you, my dear soul, and we're making merry here too!

[*Enter* LYUBOV ANDREYEVNA.]

LYUBOV. Is it you, Yermolay Alexeyevitch? Why have you been so long? Where's Leonid?

LOPAHIN. Leonid Andreyevitch arrived with me. He is coming.

LYUBOV [*in agitation*]. Well! Well! Was there a sale? Speak!

LOPAHIN [*embarrassed, afraid of betraying his joy*]. The sale was over at four o'clock. We missed our train—had to wait till half-past nine. [*Sighing heavily.*] Ugh! I feel a little giddy.

[*Enter* GAEV. *In his right hand he has purchases, with his left hand he is wiping away his tears.*]

LYUBOV. Well, Leonid? What news? [*Impatiently, with tears.*] Make haste, for God's sake!

GAEV [*makes her no answer, simply waves his hand. To* FIRS, *weeping*]. Here, take them; there's anchovies, Kertch herrings. I have eaten nothing all day. What I have been through! [*Door into the billiard room is open. There is heard a knocking of balls and the voice of* YASHA *saying "Eighty-seven." * GAEV'S *expression changes, he leaves off weeping.*] I am fearfully tired. Firs, come and help me change my things.

[*Goes to his own room across the larger drawing-room.*]

PISHTCHIK. How about the sale? Tell us, do!

LYUBOV. Is the cherry orchard sold?

LOPAHIN. It is sold.

LYUBOV. Who has bought it?

LOPAHIN. I have bought it.

[*A pause.* LYUBOV *is crushed; she would fall*

down if she were not standing near a chair and table. VARYA *takes keys from her waistband, flings them on the floor in middle of drawing-room and goes out.*]

5   LOPAHIN. I have bought it! Wait a bit, ladies and gentlemen, pray. My head's a bit muddled, I can't speak. [*Laughs.*] We came to the auction. Deriganov was there already. Leonid Andreye-vitch only had 15,000 and Deriganov bid
10   30,000, besides the arrears, straight off. I saw how the land lay. I bid against him. I bid 40,000, he bid 45,000, I said 55, and so he went on, adding 5 thousands and I adding 10. Well ... So it ended. I bid 90, and it was knocked
15   down to me. Now the cherry orchard's mine! Mine! [*Chuckles.*] My God, the cherry or-chard's mine! Tell me that I'm drunk, that I'm out of my mind, that it's all a dream. [*Stamps with his feet.*] Don't laugh at me! If my father
20   and my grandfather could rise from their graves and see all that has happened! How their Yer-molay, ignorant, beaten Yermolay, who used to run about barefoot in winter, how that very Yermolay has bought the finest estate in the
25   world! I have bought the estate where my father and grandfather were slaves, where they weren't even admitted into the kitchen. I am asleep, I am dreaming! It is all fancy, it is the work of your imagination plunged in the dark-
30   ness of ignorance. [*Picks up keys, smiling fondly.*] She threw away the keys; she means to show she's not the housewife now. [*Jingles the keys.*] Well, no matter. [*The orchestra is heard tuning up.*] Hey, musicians! Play! I want
35   to hear you. Come, all of you, and look how Yermolay Lopahin will take the axe to the cherry orchard, how the trees will fall to the ground! We will build houses on it and our grandsons and great-grandsons will see a new
40   life springing up there. Music! Play up!

[*Music begins to play.* LYUBOV ANDREYEVNA *has sunk into a chair and is weeping bitterly.*]

LOPAHIN [*reproachfully*]. Why, why didn't you listen to me? My poor friend! Dear lady,
45   there's no turning back now. [*With tears.*] Oh, if all this could be over, oh, if our miserable disjointed life could somehow soon be changed!

PISHTCHIK [*takes him by the arm; in an undertone*]. She's weeping, let us go and leave her alone. Come.   50

[*Takes him by the arm and leads him into the larger drawing-room.*]

LOPAHIN. What's that? Musicians, play up! All must be as I wish it. [*With irony.*] Here comes the new master, the owner of the cherry   55
orchard! [*Accidentally tips over a little table, almost upsetting the candelabra.*] I can pay for everything!

[*Goes out with* PISHTCHIK. *No one remains on the stage or in the larger drawing-room except*   60
LYUBOV, *who sits huddled up, weeping bitterly. The music plays softly.* ANYA *and* TROFIMOV *come in quickly.* ANYA *goes up to her mother and falls on her knees before her.* TROFIMOV *stands at the entrance to the larger drawing-*   65
room.]

ANYA. Mamma! Mamma, you're crying, dear, kind, good mamma! My precious! I love you! I bless you! The cherry orchard is sold, it is gone, that's true, that's true! But don't weep,   70
mamma! Life is still before you, you have still your good, pure heart! Let us go, let us go, dar-ling, away from here! We will make a new gar-den, more splendid than this one; you will see it, you will understand. And joy, quiet, deep   75
joy, will sink into your soul like the sun at even-ing! And you will smile, mamma! Come, dar-ling, let us go!

The Curtain Falls

ACT IV

[SCENE: *Same as in Act I. There are neither curtains on the windows nor pictures on the*   80
walls: only a little furniture remains piled up in a corner as if for sale. There is a sense of desolation; near the outer door and in the back-ground of the scene are packed trunks, travel-ling bags, etc. On the left the door is open,   85
and from here the voices of VARYA *and* ANYA *are audible.* LOPAHIN *is standing waiting.* YASHA *is holding a tray with glasses full of champagne. In front of the stage* EPIHODOV *is tying up a box. In the background behind the scene a hum*   90

of talk from the peasants who have come to say goodbye. The voice of GAEV: "Thanks, brothers, thanks!"]

YASHA. The peasants have come to say good-bye. In my opinion, Yermolay Alexeyevitch, the peasants are good-natured, but they don't know much about things.

[*The hum of talk dies away. Enter across front of stage* LYUBOV ANDREYEVNA *and* GAEV. *She is not weeping, but is pale; her face is quivering—she cannot speak.*]

GAEV. You gave them your purse, Lyuba. That won't do—that won't do!

LYUBOV. I couldn't help it! I couldn't help it! [*Both go out.*]

LOPAHIN [*in the doorway, calls after them*]. You will take a glass at parting? Please do. I didn't think to bring any from the town, and at the station I could only get one bottle. Please take a glass. [*A pause.*] What? You don't care for any? [*Comes away from the door.*] If I'd known, I wouldn't have bought it. Well, and I'm not going to drink it. [YASHA *carefully sets the tray down on a chair.*] You have a glass, Yasha, anyway.

YASHA. Good luck to the travellers, and luck to those that stay behind! [*Drinks.*] This champagne isn't the real thing, I can assure you.

LOPAHIN. It cost eight roubles the bottle. [*A pause.*] It's devilish cold here.

YASHA. They haven't heated the stove today —it's all the same since we're going. [*Laughs.*]

LOPAHIN. What are you laughing for?

YASHA. For pleasure.

LOPAHIN. Though it's October, it's as still and sunny as though it were summer. It's just right for building! [*Looks at his watch; says in doorway:*] Take note, ladies and gentlemen, the train goes in forty-seven minutes: so you ought to start for the station in twenty minutes. You must hurry up!

[TROFIMOV *comes in from out of doors wearing a great-coat.*]

TROFIMOV. I think it must be time to start, the horses are ready. The devil only knows what's become of my goloshes; they're lost. [*In the doorway.*] Anya! My goloshes aren't here. I can't find them.

LOPAHIN. And I'm getting off to Harkov. I am going in the same train with you. I'm spending all the winter at Harkov. I've been wasting all my time gossiping with you and fretting with no work to do. I can't get on without work. I don't know what to do with my hands, they flap about so queerly, as if they didn't belong to me.

TROFIMOV. Well, we're just going away, and you will take up your profitable labors again.

LOPAHIN. Do take a glass.

TROFIMOV. No, thanks.

LOPAHIN. Then you're going to Moscow now?

TROFIMOV. Yes. I shall see them as far as the town, and tomorrow I shall go on to Moscow.

LOPAHIN. Yes, I daresay, the professors aren't giving any lectures, they're waiting for your arrival.

TROFIMOV. That's not your business.

LOPAHIN. How many years have you been at the University?

TROFIMOV. Do think of something newer than that—that's stale and flat. [*Hunts for goloshes.*] You know we shall most likely never see each other again, so let me give you one piece of advice at parting: don't wave your arms about—get out of the habit. And another thing, building villas, reckoning up that the summer visitors will in time become independent farmers—reckoning like that, that's not the thing to do either. After all, I am fond of you: you have fine delicate fingers like an artist, you've a fine delicate soul.

LOPAHIN [*embraces him*]. Good-bye, my dear fellow. Thanks for everything. Let me give you money for the journey, if you need it.

TROFIMOV. What for? I don't need it.

LOPAHIN. Why, you haven't got a halfpenny.

TROFIMOV. Yes, I have, thank you. I got some money for a translation. Here it is in my pocket. [*Anxiously.*] But where can my goloshes be!

VARYA [*from the next room*]. Take the nasty things! [*Flings a pair of goloshes onto the stage.*]

TROFIMOV. Why are you so cross, Varya? h'm! . . . but those aren't my goloshes.

LOPAHIN. I sowed three thousand acres with poppies in the spring, and now I have cleared forty thousand profit. And when my poppies were in flower, wasn't it a picture! So here, as I say, I made forty thousand, and I'm offering you a loan because I can afford to. Why turn up your nose? I am a peasant—I speak bluntly.

TROFIMOV. Your father was a peasant, mine was a chemist—and that proves absolutely nothing whatever. [LOPAHIN takes out his pocketbook.] Stop that—stop that. If you were to offer me two hundred thousand I wouldn't take it. I am an independent man, and everything that all of you, rich and poor alike, prize so highly and hold so dear, hasn't the slightest power over me—it's like so much fluff fluttering in the air. I can get on without you. I can pass by you. I am strong and proud. Humanity is advancing towards the highest truth, the highest happiness which is possible on earth, and I am in the front ranks.

LOPAHIN. Will you get there?

TROFIMOV. I shall get there. [A pause.] I shall get there, or I shall show others the way to get there.

[In the distance is heard the stroke of an axe on a tree.]

LOPAHIN. Good-bye, my dear fellow; it's time to be off. We turn up our noses at one another, but life is passing all the while. When I am working hard without resting, then my mind is more at ease, and it seems to me as though I too know what I exist for; but how many people there are in Russia, my dear boy, who exist, one doesn't know what for. Well, it doesn't matter. That's not what keeps things spinning. They tell me Leonid Andreyevitch has taken a situation. He is going to be a clerk at the bank—6,000 roubles a year. Only, of course, he won't stick to it—he's too lazy.

ANYA [in doorway]. Mamma begs you not to let them chop down the orchard until she's gone.

TROFIMOV. Yes, really, you might have the tact.

[Walks out across the front of the stage.]

LOPAHIN. I'll see to it! I'll see to it! Stupid fellows!

[Goes out after him.]

ANYA. Has Firs been taken to the hospital?

YASHA. I told them this morning. No doubt they have taken him.

ANYA [to EPIHODOV, who passes across the drawing-room]. Semyon Pantaleyevitch, inquire, please, if Firs has been taken to the hospital.

YASHA [in a tone of offense]. I told Yegor this morning—why ask a dozen times?

EPIHODOV. Firs is advanced in years. It's my conclusive opinion no treatment would do him good; it's time he was gathered to his fathers. And I can only envy him. [Puts a trunk down on a cardboard hat-box and crushes it.] There now, of course—I knew it would be so.

YASHA [jeeringly]. Two and twenty misfortunes!

VARYA [through the door]. Has Firs been taken to the hospital?

ANYA. Yes.

VARYA. Why wasn't the note for the doctor taken too?

ANYA. Oh, then, we must send it after them. [Goes out.]

VARYA [from the adjoining room]. Where's Yasha? Tell him his mother's come to say good-bye to him.

YASHA [waves his hand]. They put me out of all patience!

[DUNYASHA has all this time been busy about the luggage. Now, when YASHA is left alone, she goes up to him.]

DUNYASHA. You might just give me one look, Yasha. You're going away. You're leaving me. [Weeps and throws herself on his neck.]

YASHA. What are you crying for? [Drinks the champagne.] In six days I shall be in Paris again. Tomorrow we shall get into the express train and roll away in a flash. I can scarcely believe it! Vive la France! It doesn't suit me here—it's not the life for me; there's no doing anything. I have seen enough of the ignorance here. I have had enough of it. [Drinks champagne.] What are you crying for? Behave yourself properly, and then you won't cry.

DUNYASHA [*powders her face, looking in a pocket-mirror*]. Do send me a letter from Paris. You know how I loved you, Yasha—how I loved you! I am a tender creature, Yasha.

YASHA. Here they are coming!

[*Busies himself about the trunks, humming softly. Enter* LYUBOV ANDREYEVNA, GAEV, ANYA, *and* CHARLOTTA IVANOVNA.]

GAEV. We ought to be off. There's not much time now. [*Looking at* YASHA.] What a smell of herrings!

LYUBOV. In ten minutes we must get into the carriage. [*Casts a look about the room.*] Farewell, dear house, dear old home of our fathers! Winter will pass and spring will come, and then you will be no more; they will tear you down! How much those walls have seen! [*Kisses her daughter passionately.*] My treasure, how bright you look! Your eyes are sparkling like diamonds! Are you glad? Very glad?

ANYA. Very glad! A new life is beginning, mamma.

GAEV. Yes, really, everything is all right now. Before the cherry orchard was sold, we were all worried and wretched, but afterwards, when once the question was settled conclusively, irrevocably, we all felt calm and even cheerful. I am a bank clerk now—I am a financier—cannon off the red. And you, Lyuba, after all, you are looking better; there's no question of that.

LYUBOV. Yes. My nerves are better, that's true. [*Her hat and coat are handed to her.*] I'm sleeping well. Carry out my things, Yasha. It's time. [*To* ANYA.] My darling, we shall soon see each other again. I am going to Paris. I can live there on the money your Yaroslavl auntie sent us to buy the estate with—hurrah for auntie—but that money won't last long.

ANYA. You'll come back soon, mamma, won't you? I'll be working up for my examination in the high school, and when I have passed that, I shall set to work and be a help to you. We will read all sorts of things together, mamma, won't we? [*Kisses her mother's hands.*] We will read in the autumn evenings. We'll read lots of books, and a new wonderful world will open out before us. [*Dreamily.*]

Mamma, come soon.

LYUBOV. I shall come, my precious treasure. [*Embraces her.*]

[*Enter* LOPAHIN. CHARLOTTA *softly hums a song.*]

GAEV. Charlotta's happy; she's singing!

CHARLOTTA [*picks up a bundle like a swaddled baby*]. Bye, bye, my baby. [*A baby is heard crying: "Ooah! ooah!"*] Hush, hush, my pretty boy! [*Ooah! ooah!*] Poor little thing! [*Throws the bundle back.*] You must please find me a situation. I can't go on like this.

LOPAHIN. We'll find you one, Charlotta Ivanovna. Don't you worry yourself.

GAEV. Everyone's leaving us. Varya's going away. We have become of no use all at once.

CHARLOTTA. There's nowhere for me to be in the town. I must go away. [*Hums.*] What care I . . .

[*Enter* PISHTCHIK.]

LOPAHIN. The freak of nature!

PISHTCHIK [*gasping*]. Oh! . . . let me get my breath. . . . I'm worn out . . . my most honored . . . give me some water.

GAEV. Want some money, I suppose? Your humble servant! I'll go out of the way of temptation. [*Goes out.*]

PISHTCHIK. It's a long while since I have been to see you . . . dearest lady. [*To* LOPAHIN.] You are here . . . glad to see you . . . a man of immense intellect . . . take . . . here [*gives* LOPAHIN] 400 roubles. That leaves me owing 840.

LOPAHIN [*shrugging his shoulders in amazement*]. It's like a dream. Where did you get it?

PISHTCHIK. Wait a bit . . . I'm hot . . . a most extraordinary occurrence! Some Englishmen came along and found in my land some sort of white clay. [*To* LYUBOV ANDREYEVNA.] And 400 for you . . . most lovely . . . wonderful. [*Gives money.*] The rest later. [*Sips water.*] A young man in the train was telling me just now that a great philosopher advises jumping off a housetop. "Jump!" says he; "the whole gist of the problem lies in that." [*Wonderingly.*] Fancy that, now! Water, please!

LOPAHIN. What Englishmen?

PISHTCHIK. I have made over to them the rights to dig the clay for twenty-four years . . . and now, excuse me . . . I can't stay . . . I must be trotting on. I'm going to Znoikovo . . . to Kardamanovo. . . . I'm in debt all round. [*Sips.*] . . . To your very good health! . . . I'll come in on Thursday.

LYUBOV. We are just off to the town, and to-morrow I start for abroad.

PISHTCHIK. What! [*In agitation.*] Why to the town? Oh, I see the furniture . . . the boxes. No matter . . . [*through his tears*] . . . no matter . . . men of enormous intellect . . . these English-men. . . . Never mind . . . be happy. God will succor you . . . no matter . . . everything in this world must have an end. [*Kisses* LYUBOV ANDREYEVNA's *hand.*] If the rumor reaches you that my end has come, think of this . . . old horse, and say: "There once was such a man in the world . . . Semyonov-Pishtchik . . . the Kingdom of Heaven be his!" . . . most extra-ordinary weather . . . yes. [*Goes out in violent agitation, but at once returns and says in the doorway:*] Dashenka wishes to be remembered to you.

[*Goes out.*]

LYUBOV. Now we can start. I leave with two cares in my heart. The first is leaving Firs ill. [*Looking at her watch.*] We still have five minutes.

ANYA. Mamma, Firs has been taken to the hospital. Yasha sent him off this morning.

LYUBOV. My other anxiety is Varya. She is used to getting up early and working; and now, without work, she's like a fish out of water. She is thin and pale, and she's crying, poor dear! [*A pause.*] You are well aware, Yermolay Alexeyevitch, I dreamed of marrying her to you, and everything seemed to show that you would get married. [*Whispers to* ANYA *and motions to* CHARLOTTA *and both go out.*] She loves you—she suits you. And I don't know—I don't know why it is you seem, as it were, to avoid each other. I can't understand it!

LOPAHIN. I don't understand it myself, I con-fess. It's queer somehow, altogether. If there's still time, I'm ready now at once. Let's settle it straight off, and go ahead; but without you, I feel I shan't make her an offer.

LYUBOV. That's excellent. Why, a single moment's all that's necessary. I'll call her at once.

LOPAHIN. And there's champagne all ready too. [*Looking into the glasses.*] Empty! Some-one's emptied them already. [YASHA *coughs.*] I call that greedy.

LYUBOV [*eagerly*]. Capital! We will go out. Yasha, *allez!* I'll call her in. [*At the door.*] Varya, leave all that; come here. Come along!

[*Goes out with* YASHA.]

LOPAHIN [*looking at his watch*]. Yes.

[*A pause. Behind the door, smothered laughter and whispering, and, at last, enter* VARYA.]

VARYA [*looking a long while over the things*]. It is strange, I can't find it anywhere.

LOPAHIN. What are you looking for?

VARYA. I packed it myself, and I can't re-member. [*A pause.*]

LOPAHIN. Where are you going now, Varvara Mihailova?

VARYA. I? To the Ragulins. I have arranged to go to them to look after the house—as a housekeeper.

LOPAHIN. That's in Yashnovo? It'll be seventy miles away. [*A pause.*] So this is the end of life in this house!

VARYA [*looking among the things*]. Where is it? Perhaps I put it in the trunk. Yes, life in this house is over—there will be no more of it.

LOPAHIN. And I'm just off to Harkov—by this next train. I've a lot of business there. I'm leaving Epihodov here, and I've taken him on.

VARYA. Really!

LOPAHIN. This time last year we had snow already, if you remember; but now it's so fine and sunny. Though it's cold, to be sure—three degrees of frost.

VARYA. I haven't looked. [*A pause.*] And besides, our thermometer's broken. [*A pause.*]

[*Voice at the door from the yard:* "Yermolay Alexeyevitch!"]

LOPAHIN [*as though he had long been ex-pecting this summons*]. This minute!

[LOPAHIN *goes out quickly.* VARYA *sitting on the floor and laying her head on a bag full of*

clothes, sobs quietly. The door opens. LYUBOV
ANDREYEVNA *comes in cautiously.*]

LYUBOV. Well? [*A pause.*] We must be going.

VARYA [*has wiped her eyes and is no longer
crying*]. Yes, mamma, it's time to start. I shall
have time to get to the Ragulins today, if only
you're not late for the train.

LYUBOV [*in the doorway*]. Anya, put your
things on.

[*Enter* ANYA, *then* GAEV *and* CHARLOTTA
IVANOVNA. GAEV *has on a warm coat with a
hood. Servants and cabmen come in.* EPIHODOV
bustles about the luggage.]

LYUBOV. Now we can start on our travels.

ANYA [*joyfully*]. On our travels!

GAEV. My friends—my dear, my precious
friends! Leaving this house for ever, can I be
silent? Can I refrain from giving utterance at
leave-taking to those emotions which now flood
all my being?

ANYA [*supplicatingly*]. Uncle!

VARYA. Uncle, you mustn't!

GAEV [*dejectedly*]. Cannon and into the
pocket . . . I'll be quiet. . . .

[*Enter* TROFIMOV *and afterwards* LOPAHIN.]

TROFIMOV. Well, ladies and gentlemen, we
must start.

LOPAHIN. Epihodov, my coat!

LYUBOV. I'll stay just one minute. It seems
as though I have never seen before what the
walls, what the ceilings in this house were
like, and now I look at them with greediness,
with such tender love.

GAEV. I remember when I was six years old
sitting in that window on Trinity Day watching my father going to church.

LYUBOV. Have all the things been taken?

LOPAHIN. I think all. [*Putting on overcoat, to*
EPIHODOV.] You, Epihodov, mind you see everything is right.

EPIHODOV [*in a husky voice*]. Don't you
trouble, Yermolay Alexeyevitch.

LOPAHIN. Why, what's wrong with your
voice?

EPIHODOV. I've just had a drink of water, and
I choked over something.

YASHA [*contemptuously*]. The ignorance!

LYUBOV. We are going—and not a soul will
be left here.

LOPAHIN. Not till the spring.

VARYA [*pulls a parasol out of a bundle, as
though about to hit someone with it.* LOPAHIN
makes a gesture as though alarmed]. What is
it? I didn't mean anything.

TROFIMOV. Ladies and gentlemen, let us get
into the carriage. It's time. The train will be in
directly.

VARYA. Petya, here they are, your goloshes,
by that box. [*With tears.*] And what dirty old
things they are!

TROFIMOV [*putting on his goloshes*]. Let us
go, friends!

GAEV [*greatly agitated, afraid of weeping*].
The train—the station! Double baulk, ah!

LYUBOV. Let us go!

LOPAHIN. Are we all here? [*Locks the side-
door on left.*] The things are all here. We must
lock up. Let us go!

ANYA. Good-bye, home! Good-bye to the
old life!

TROFIMOV. Welcome to the new life!

[TROFIMOV *goes out with* ANYA. VARYA *looks
round the room and goes out slowly.* YASHA
and CHARLOTTA IVANOVNA, *with her dog, go
out.*]

LOPAHIN. Till the spring, then! Come, friends,
till we meet!

[*Goes out.*]

[LYUBOV ANDREYEVNA *and* GAEV *remain
alone. As though they had been waiting for
this, they throw themselves on each other's
necks, and break into subdued smothered sobbing, afraid of being overheard.*]

GAEV [*in despair*]. Sister, my sister!

LYUBOV. Oh, my orchard!—my sweet,
beautiful orchard! My life, my youth, my happiness, good-bye! good-bye!

VOICE OF ANYA [*calling gaily*]. Mamma!

VOICE OF TROFIMOV [*gaily, excitedly*]. Aa—
oo!

LYUBOV. One last look at the walls, at the
windows. My dear mother loved to walk about
this room.

GAEV. Sister, sister!

VOICE OF ANYA. Mamma!

VOICE OF TROFIMOV. Aa—oo!

LYUBOV. We are coming.

[*They go out.*]

[*The stage is empty. There is the sound of the doors being locked up, then of the carriages*
5 *driving away. There is silence. In the stillness there is the dull stroke of an axe in a tree, clanging with a mournful lonely sound. Footsteps are heard.* FIRS *appears in the doorway on the right. He is dressed as always—in a pea-*
10 *jacket and white waistcoat, with slippers on his feet. He is ill.*]

FIRS [*goes up to the doors, and tries the handles*]. Locked! They have gone. . . . [*Sits down on sofa.*] They have forgotten me. . . .
15 Never mind . . . I'll sit here a bit. . . . I'll be bound Leonid Andreyevitch hasn't put his fur coat on and has gone off in his thin overcoat. [*Sighs anxiously.*] I didn't see after him. . . . These young people . . . [*mutters something*
20 *that can't be distinguished*]. Life has slipped by as though I hadn't lived. [*Lies down.*] I'll lie down a bit. . . . There's no strength in you, nothing left you—all gone! Ech! I'm good for nothing. [*Lies motionless.*]
25   [*A sound is heard that seems to come from the sky, like a breaking harp-string, dying away mournfully. All is still again, and there is heard nothing but the strokes of the axe far away in the orchard.*]

The Curtain Falls

John Millington Synge

1871–1909

Riders to the Sea

1904

The story of *Riders to the Sea* is a mere moment in the lives of a few characters, but it holds within it the meaning of what they and millions like them have done and suffered. They have struggled for survival; they have gone down to defeat before the indifferent forces of wind and sea. Out of fatalism touched with faith and out of a supreme weariness, they resign themselves to defeat and in that resignation find release.

Synge captures this moment in the vivid dialect of the islanders. The images are sharp-edged and simple, held in the rise and fall of a speech as naturally cadenced as breathing. The rope is "on a nail by the white boards. I hung it up this morning, for the pig with the black feet was eating it." "There were two men . . . and they rowing round with poteen before the cocks crowed, and the oar of one of them caught the body, and they passing the black cliffs of the north." The images are held, too, in a larger, more complex rhythmic pattern. From start to finish the play is filled with its own echoes. We hear again and again of the pig, the boards, the pony until we begin to realize that such recurrence is itself an image of the lives portrayed—ever changing, ever the same. At the play's end Maurya lives over the deaths of her sons: "I was sitting here with Bartley, and he a baby, lying on my two knees, and I seen two women, and three women, and four women coming in, and they crossing themselves, and not saying a word . . . and there were men coming in after them, and they holding a thing in the half of a red sail." Then comes the stage direction: "She pauses again with her hand stretched out toward the door. It opens softly and old women begin to come in, crossing themselves." And later, "Then men carry in the body of Bartley, laid on a plank, with a bit of a sail over it." Present echoes past, past enters present in a moment that in the perfection of its presentation becomes an image of unchanging human experience.

Riders to the Sea

SYNGE

CHARACTERS

MAURYA   an old woman
BARTLEY   her son
CATHLEEN   her daughter
NORA   a younger daughter
MEN AND WOMEN

SCENE. *An Island off the West of Ireland.*

[*Cottage kitchen, with nets, oil-skins, spinning-wheel, some new boards standing by the wall, etc.* CATHLEEN, *a girl of about twenty,*
5 *finishes kneading cake, and puts it down in the pot-oven° by the fire; then wipes her hands, and begins to spin at the wheel.* NORA, *a young girl, puts her head in at the door.*]

NORA [*in a low voice*]. Where is she?
10 CATHLEEN. She's lying down, God help her, and may be sleeping, if she's able.

[NORA *comes in softly, and takes a bundle from under her shawl.*]

CATHLEEN [*spinning the wheel rapidly*]. What
15 is it you have?

NORA. The young priest is after bringing them. It's a shirt and a plain stocking were got off a drowned man in Donegal.

[CATHLEEN *stops her wheel with a sudden*
20 *movement, and leans out to listen.*]

NORA. We're to find out if it's Michael's they are, some time herself will be down looking by the sea.

CATHLEEN. How would they be Michael's,
25 Nora? How would he go the length of that way to the far north?

NORA. The young priest says he's known the like of it. "If it's Michael's they are," says he,

"you can tell herself he's got a clean burial by the grace of God, and if they're not his, let no 30
one say a word about them, for she'll be getting her death," says he, "with crying and lamenting."

[*The door which* NORA *half closed is blown open by a gust of wind.*] 35

CATHLEEN [*looking out anxiously*]. Did you ask him would he stop Bartley going this day with the horses to the Galway fair?

NORA. "I won't stop him," says he, "but let you not be afraid. Herself does be saying 40
prayers half through the night, and the Almighty God won't leave her destitute," says he, "with no son living."

CATHLEEN. Is the sea bad by the white rocks, Nora? 45

NORA. Middling bad, God help us. There's a great roaring in the west, and it's worse it'll be getting when the tide's turned to the wind. [*She goes over to the table with the bundle.*] Shall I open it now? 50

CATHLEEN. Maybe she'd wake up on us, and come in before we'd done. [*Coming to the table.*] It's a long time we'll be, and the two of us crying.

NORA [*goes to the inner door and listens*]. 55
She's moving about on the bed. She'll be coming in a minute.

CATHLEEN. Give me the ladder, and I'll put them up in the turf-loft, the way° she won't know of them at all, and maybe when the tide 60
turns she'll be going down to see would he be floating from the east.

[*They put the ladder against the gable of the chimney;* CATHLEEN *goes up a few steps and hides the bundle in the turf-loft.* MAURYA *comes* 65
from the inner room.]

MAURYA [*looking up at* CATHLEEN *and speaking querulously*]. Isn't it turf enough you have for this day and evening?

CATHLEEN. There's a cake baking at the fire 70
for a short space [*throwing down the turf*] and Bartley will want it when the tide turns if he goes to Connemara.

[NORA *picks up the turf and puts it round the pot-oven.*] 75

---

pot-oven heated iron plate covered by a pot

the way so that

MAURYA [*sitting down on a stool at the fire*]. He won't go this day with the wind rising from the south and west. He won't go this day, for the young priest will stop him surely.

5 NORA. He'll not stop him, mother, and I heard Eamon Simon and Stephen Pheety and Colum Shawn saying he would go.

MAURYA. Where is he itself?

NORA. He went down to see would there be 10 another boat sailing in the week, and I'm thinking it won't be long till he's here now, for the tide's turning at the green head,° and the hooker's tacking from the east.

CATHLEEN. I hear some one passing the big 15 stones.

NORA [*looking out*]. He's coming now, and he in a hurry.

BARTLEY [*comes in and looks round the room. Speaking sadly and quietly*]. Where is the bit 20 of new rope, Cathleen, was bought in Connemara?

CATHLEEN [*coming down*]. Give it to him, Nora; it's on a nail by the white boards. I hung it up this morning, for the pig with the black 25 feet was eating it.

NORA [*giving him a rope*]. Is that it, Bartley?

MAURYA. You'd do right to leave that rope, Bartley, hanging by the board. [BARTLEY *takes the rope*.] It will be wanting in this place, I'm 30 telling you, if Michael is washed up to-morrow morning, or the next morning, or any morning in the week, for it's a deep grave we'll make him by the grace of God.

BARTLEY [*beginning to work with the rope*]. 35 I've no halter the way I can ride down on the mare, and I must go now quickly. This is the one boat going for two weeks or beyond it, and the fair will be a good fair for horses I heard them saying below.

40 MAURYA. It's a hard thing they'll be saying below if the body is washed up and there's no man in it° to make the coffin, and I after giving a big price for the finest white boards you'd find in Connemara. [*She looks round at the* 45 *boards*.]

BARTLEY. How would it be washed up, and

we after looking each day for nine days, and a strong wind blowing a while back from the west and south?

50 MAURYA. If it wasn't found itself, that wind is raising the sea, and there was a star up against the moon, and it rising in the night. If it was a hundred horses, or a thousand horses you had itself, what is the price of a thousand horses against a son where there is one son 55 only?

BARTLEY [*working at the halter, to* CATHLEEN]. Let you go down each day, and see the sheep aren't jumping in on the rye, and if the jobber comes you can sell the pig with the black 60 feet if there is a good price going.

MAURYA. How would the like of her get a good price for a pig?

BARTLEY [*to* CATHLEEN]. If the west wind holds with the last bit of the moon let you and 65 Nora get up weed enough for another cock for the kelp.° It's hard set° we'll be from this day with no one in it but one man to work.

MAURYA. It's hard set we'll be surely the day you're drownd'd with the rest. What way 70 will I live and the girls with me, and I an old woman looking for the grave?

[BARTLEY *lays down the halter, takes off his old coat, and puts on a newer one of the same flannel*.] 75

BARTLEY [*to* NORA]. Is she coming to the pier?

NORA [*looking out*]. She's passing the green head and letting fall her sails.

BARTLEY [*getting his purse and tobacco*]. I'll 80 have half an hour to go down, and you'll see me coming again in two days, or in three days, or maybe in four if the wind is bad.

MAURYA [*turning round to the fire, and putting her shawl over her head*]. Isn't it a hard and 85 cruel man won't hear a word from an old woman, and she holding him from the sea?

CATHLEEN. It's the life of a young man to be going on the sea, and who would listen to an old woman with one thing and she saying it 90 over?

---

head headland, promontory
in it there

kelp ash of various seaweeds, used as a source for iodine. Bartley's request means: get seaweed enough to make another pile to be burned to ash.
set put to it

JOHN MILLINGTON SYNGE

BARTLEY [*taking the halter*]. I must go now quickly. I'll ride down on the red mare, and the gray pony'll run behind me. . . . The blessing of God on you.

5 [*He goes out.*]

MAURYA [*crying out as he is in the door*]. He's gone now, God spare us, and we'll not see him again. He's gone now, and when the black night is falling I'll have no son left in the 10 world.

CATHLEEN. Why wouldn't you give him your blessing and he looking round in the door? Isn't it sorrow enough is on every one in this house without your sending him out with an 15 unlucky word behind him, and a hard word in his ear?

[MAURYA *takes up the tongs and begins raking the fire aimlessly without looking round.*]

20 NORA [*turning towards her*]. You're taking away the turf from the cake.

CATHLEEN [*crying out*]. The Son of God forgive us, Nora, we're after forgetting his bit of bread.

25 [*She comes over to the fire.*]

NORA. And it's destroyed he'll be going till dark night, and he after eating nothing since the sun went up.

CATHLEEN [*turning the cake out of the oven*]. 30 It's destroyed he'll be, surely. There's no sense left on any person in a house where an old woman will be talking for ever.

[MAURYA *sways on her stool.*]

CATHLEEN [*cutting off some of the bread and* 35 *rolling it in a cloth; to* MAURYA]. Let you go down now to the spring well and give him this and he passing. You'll see him then and the dark word will be broken, and you can say "God speed you," the way he'll be easy in his 40 mind.

MAURYA [*taking the bread*]. Will I be in it as soon as himself?

CATHLEEN. If you go now quickly.

MAURYA [*standing up unsteadily*]. It's hard 45 set I am to walk.

CATHLEEN [*looking at her anxiously*]. Give her the stick, Nora, or maybe she'll slip on the big stones.

NORA. What stick?

CATHLEEN. The stick Michael brought from 50 Connemara.

MAURYA [*taking a stick* NORA *gives her*]. In the big world the old people do be leaving things after them for their sons and children, but in this place it is the young men do be 55 leaving things behind for them that do be old.

[*She goes out slowly.* NORA *goes over to the ladder.*]

CATHLEEN. Wait, Nora, maybe she'd turn back quickly. She's that sorry,° God help her, 60 you wouldn't know the thing she'd do.

NORA. Is she gone round by the bush?

CATHLEEN [*looking out*]. She's gone now. Throw it down quickly, for the Lord knows when she'll be out of it again. 65

NORA [*getting the bundle from the loft*]. The young priest said he'd be passing to-morrow, and we might go down and speak to him below if it's Michael's they are surely.

CATHLEEN [*taking the bundle*]. Did he say 70 what way they were found?

NORA [*coming down*]. "There were two men," says he, "and they rowing round with poteen before the cocks crowed, and the oar of one of them caught the body, and they pass- 75 ing the black cliffs of the north."

CATHLEEN [*trying to open the bundle*]. Give me a knife, Nora, the string's perished° with the salt water, and there's a black knot on it you wouldn't loosen in a week. 80

NORA [*giving her a knife*]. I've heard tell it was a long way to Donegal.

CATHLEEN [*cutting the string*]. It is surely. There was a man in here a while ago—the man sold us that knife—and he said if you set off 85 walking from the rocks beyond, it would be seven days you'd be in Donegal.

NORA. And what time would a man take, and he floating?

[CATHLEEN *opens the bundle and takes out* 90 *a bit of stocking. They look at them eagerly.*]

CATHLEEN [*in a low voice*]. The Lord spare

sorry wretched
perished stiffened

us, Nora! isn't it a queer hard thing to say if it's his they are surely?

NORA. I'll get his shirt off the hook the way we can put the one flannel on the other. [*She 5 looks through some clothes hanging in the corner*]. It's not with them, Cathleen, and where will it be?

CATHLEEN. I'm thinking Bartley put it on him in the morning, for his own shirt was 10 heavy with the salt in it. [*Pointing to the corner.*] There's a bit of a sleeve was of the same stuff. Give me that and it will do.

[NORA *brings it to her and they compare the flannel.*]

15 CATHLEEN. It's the same stuff, Nora; but if it is itself aren't there great rolls of it in the shops of Galway, and isn't it many another man may have a shirt of it as well as Michael himself?

NORA [*who has taken up the stocking and 20 counted the stitches, crying out*]. It's Michael, Cathleen, it's Michael; God spare his soul, and what will herself say when she hears this story, and Bartley on the sea?

CATHLEEN [*taking the stocking*]. It's a plain 25 stocking.

NORA. It's the second one of the third pair I knitted, and I put up three score stitches, and I dropped four of them.

CATHLEEN [*counts the stitches*]. It's that num-30 ber is in it. [*Crying out.*] Ah, Nora, isn't it a bitter thing to think of him floating that way to the far north, and no one to keen him but the black hags that do be flying on the sea?

NORA [*swinging herself round, and throw-35 ing out her arms on the clothes*]. And isn't it a pitiful thing when there is nothing left of a man who was a great rower and fisher, but a bit of an old shirt and a plain stocking?

CATHLEEN [*after an instant*]. Tell me is her-40 self coming, Nora? I hear a little sound on the path.

NORA [*looking out*]. She is, Cathleen. She's coming up to the door.

CATHLEEN. Put these things away before 45 she'll come in. Maybe it's easier she'll be after giving her blessing to Bartley, and we won't let on we've heard anything the time he's on the sea.

NORA [*helping* CATHLEEN *to close the bundle*]. We'll put them here in the corner. 50

[*They put them into a hole in the chimney corner.* CATHLEEN *goes back to the spinning-wheel.*]

NORA. Will she see it was crying I was?

CATHLEEN. Keep your back to the door the 55 way the light'll not be on you.

[NORA *sits down at the chimney corner, with her back to the door.* MAURYA *comes in very slowly, without looking at the girls, and goes over to her stool at the other side of the fire.* 60 *The cloth with the bread is still in her hand. The girls look at each other, and* NORA *points to the bundle of bread.*]

CATHLEEN [*after spinning for a moment*]. You didn't give him his bit of bread? 65

[MAURYA *begins to keen softly, without turning round.*]

CATHLEEN. Did you see him riding down?

[MAURYA *goes on keening.*]

CATHLEEN [*a little impatiently*]. God forgive 70 you; isn't it a better thing to raise your voice and tell what you seen, than to be making lamentation for a thing that's done? Did you see Bartley, I'm saying to you.

MAURYA [*with a weak voice*]. My heart's 75 broken from this day.

CATHLEEN [*as before*]. Did you see Bartley?

MAURYA. I seen the fearfulest thing.

CATHLEEN [*leaves her wheel and looks out*]. God forgive you; he's riding the mare now 80 over the green head, and the gray pony behind him.

MAURYA [*starts, so that her shawl falls back from her head and shows her white tossed hair. With a frightened voice.*] The gray pony be-85 hind him.

CATHLEEN [*coming to the fire*]. What is it ails you, at all?

MAURYA [*speaking very slowly*]. I've seen the fearfulest thing any person has seen, since 90 the day Bride Dara seen the dead man with the child in his arms.

CATHLEEN and NORA. Uah.

[*They crouch down in front of the old wom-an at the fire.*] 95

NORA. Tell us what it is you seen.

MAURYA. I went down to the spring well, and I stood there saying a prayer to myself. Then Bartley came along, and he riding on the red mare with the gray pony behind him. [*She puts up her hands, as if to hide something from her eyes.*] The Son of God spare us, Nora!

CATHLEEN. What is it you seen?

MAURYA. I seen Michael himself.

CATHLEEN [*speaking softly*]. You did not, mother; it wasn't Michael you seen, for his body is after being found in the far north, and he's got a clean burial by the grace of God.

MAURYA [*a little defiantly*]. I'm after seeing him this day, and he riding and galloping. Bartley came first on the red mare; and I tried to say "God speed you," but something choked the words in my throat. He went by quickly; and "the blessing of God on you," says he, and I could say nothing. I looked up then, and I crying, at the gray pony, and there was Michael upon it—with fine clothes on him, and new shoes on his feet.

CATHLEEN [*begins to keen*]. It's destroyed we are from this day. It's destroyed, surely.

NORA. Didn't the young priest say the Almighty God wouldn't leave her destitute with no son living?

MAURYA [*in a low voice, but clearly*]. It's little the like of him knows of the sea. . . . Bartley will be lost now, and let you call in Eamon and make me a good coffin out of the white boards, for I won't live after them. I've had a husband, and a husband's father, and six sons in this house—six fine men, though it was a hard birth I had with every one of them and they coming to the world—and some of them were found and some of them were not found, but they're gone now the lot of them. . . . There were Stephen, and Shawn, were lost in the great wind, and found after in the Bay of Gregory of the Golden Mouth, and carried up the two of them on the one plank, and in by that door.

[*She pauses for a moment, the girls start as if they heard something through the door that is half open behind them.*]

NORA [*in a whisper*]. Did you hear that, Cathleen? Did you hear a noise in the northeast?

CATHLEEN [*in a whisper*]. There's some one after crying out by the seashore.

MAURYA [*continues without hearing anything*]. There was Sheamus and his father, and his own father again, were lost in a dark night, and not a stick or sign was seen of them when the sun went up. There was Patch after was drowned out of a curragh that turned over. I was sitting here with Bartley, and he a baby, lying on my two knees, and I seen two women, and three women, and four women coming in, and they crossing themselves, and not saying a word. I looked out then, and there were men coming after them, and they holding a thing in the half of a red sail, and water dripping out of it—it was a dry day, Nora—and leaving a track to the door.

[*She pauses again with her hand stretched out towards the door. It opens softly and old women begin to come in, crossing themselves on the threshold, and kneeling down in front of the stage with red petticoats over their heads.*]

MAURYA [*half in a dream, to* CATHLEEN]. Is it Patch, or Michael, or what is it at all?

CATHLEEN. Michael is after being found in the far north, and when he is found there how could he be here in this place?

MAURYA. There does be a power of young men floating round in the sea, and what way would they know if it was Michael they had, or another man like him, for when a man is nine days in the sea, and the wind blowing, it's hard set his own mother would be to say what man was it.

CATHLEEN. It's Michael, God spare him, for they're after sending us a bit of his clothes from the far north.

[*She reaches out and hands* MAURYA *the clothes that belonged to Michael.* MAURYA *stands up slowly and takes them in her hands.* NORA *looks out.*]

NORA. They're carrying a thing among them and there's water dripping out of it and leaving a track by the big stones.

CATHLEEN [*in a whisper to the women who have come in*]. Is it Bartley it is?

ONE OF THE WOMEN. It is surely, God rest his soul.

[*Two younger women come in and pull out the table. Then men carry in the body of Bartley, laid on a plank, with a bit of a sail over it, and lay it on the table.*]

CATHLEEN [*to the women, as they are doing so*]. What way was he drowned?

ONE OF THE WOMEN. The gray pony knocked him into the sea, and he was washed out where there is a great surf on the white rocks.

[MAURYA *has gone over and knelt down at the head of the table. The women are keening softly and swaying themselves with a slow movement.* CATHLEEN *and* NORA *kneel at the other end of the table. The men kneel near the door.*]

MAURYA [*raising her head and speaking as if she did not see the people around her*]. They're all gone now, and there isn't anything more the sea can do to me. . . . I'll have no call now to be up crying and praying when the wind breaks from the south, and you can hear the surf is in the east, and the surf is in the west, making a great stir with the two noises, and they hitting one on the other. I'll have no call now to be going down and getting Holy Water in the dark nights after Samhain,° and I won't care what way the sea is when the other women will be keening. [*To* NORA.] Give me the Holy Water, Nora, there's a small sup still on the dresser.

[NORA *gives it to her.*]

MAURYA [*drops Michael's clothes across Bartley's feet, and sprinkles the Holy Water over him*]. It isn't that I haven't prayed for you, Bartley, to the Almighty God. It isn't that I haven't said prayers in the dark night till you wouldn't know what I'd be saying; but it's a great rest I'll have now, and it's time surely. It's a great rest I'll have now, and great sleeping in the long nights after Samhain, if it's only a bit of wet flour we do have to eat, and maybe a fish that would be stinking.

[*She kneels down again, crossing herself, and saying prayers under her breath.*]

CATHLEEN [*to an old man*]. Maybe yourself and Eamon would make a coffin when the sun rises. We have fine white boards herself bought, God help her, thinking Michael would be found, and I have a new cake you can eat while you'll be working.

THE OLD MAN [*looking at the boards*]. Are there nails with them?

CATHLEEN. There are not, Colum; we didn't think of the nails.

ANOTHER MAN. It's a great wonder she wouldn't think of the nails, and all the coffins she's seen made already.

CATHLEEN. It's getting old she is, and broken.

[MAURYA *stands up again very slowly and spreads out the pieces of Michael's clothes beside the body, sprinkling them with the last of the Holy Water.*]

NORA [*in a whisper to* CATHLEEN.] She's quiet now and easy; but the day Michael was drowned you could hear her crying out from this to the spring well. It's fonder she was of Michael, and would any one have thought that?

CATHLEEN [*slowly and clearly*]. An old woman will be soon tired with anything she will do, and isn't it nine days herself is after crying and keening, and making great sorrow in the house?

MAURYA [*puts the empty cup mouth downwards on the table, and lays her hands together on Bartley's feet*]. They're all together this time, and the end is come. May the Almighty God have mercy on Bartley's soul, and on Michael's soul, and on the souls of Sheamus and Patch, and Stephen and Shawn; [*bending her head*] and may He have mercy on my soul, Nora, and on the soul of every one is left living in the world.

[*She pauses, and the keen rises a little more loudly from the women, then sinks away.*]

MAURYA [*continuing*]. Michael has a clean burial in the far north, by the grace of the Almighty God. Bartley will have a fine coffin out of the white boards, and a deep grave surely. What more can we want than that? No man at all can be living for ever, and we must be satisfied.

[*She kneels down again and the curtain falls slowly.*]

Samhain November 1, the beginning of the Celtic winter half year.

August Strindberg

1849–1912

The Ghost Sonata

1907

Strindberg's Chamber Plays, of which *The Ghost Sonata* is the most celebrated example, were a twofold experiment. They were written to be performed in a small and intimate theater (as chamber music is written to be performed in a room rather than a concert hall), and they derive their formal organization as much from the recurrence and modulation of themes as from sequential plots. The intimate performance admits of furtive conversation and eavesdropping ("a world of intimations," Strindberg said, "where one expresses oneself in halftones and with a soft pedal"), and the musical form accommodates the variable turnings of a spectral and dreamlike imagination. Today, we observe, an enhanced intimacy of performance is still very often sought: *The Ghost Sonata* anticipates off-Broadway theater. And reactions against the "well-made play"—with its strong plot line implicitly affirming a rational and intelligible external world—are so abundant in contemporary drama that discontinuity of action seems on the verge of becoming the rule.

Strindberg is further anticipatory (he is specifically "surrealistic") in his literal and fantastic representations of metaphor. We say metaphorically, for example, that guilty memories can cease to be *visible* to the conscious mind. Taking the vehicle of that metaphor literally, Strindberg represents the old man Hummel as unable to *see* the milkmaid even when she stands before him ("Who on earth is he talking to?—I don't see anyone!"). Again, we say that a child suffering from emotional deprivation is in a manner *starved*. Strindberg, with his accustomed exaggeration, supplies the Colonel's household with a preternaturally voracious cook, who boils all nutriment from the food so that the daughter of the house visibly wastes away.

In this fanciful milieu events and images materialize on stage somewhat as they rise

533

to the top of the consciousness in dreams: they are at once disjointed and sharply delineated—laden with import yet resisting full explanation. Indeed, many particular circumstances in *The Ghost Sonata*—such as the meeting of the student and the young lady at Wagner's *Die Walküre*—seem plangent of meaning but actually signify either nothing at all or so many things that there is no choosing among them.

The play as a whole is nevertheless a work of art rather than a dream, and, despite some controlled vagaries, it focuses on a topic of abiding concern to Strindberg: namely, human parasitism. This theme is made concrete in images of the vampire and the leech—of vital energy sapped and nourishment drained off; or, alternatively, of slave-trading, kidnapping, and the theft of souls. The plot, simple in direction although complicated in its ramifications, turns on the reversal of a single power balance as the blackmailer Hummel is himself exposed and, having lost his domination, surrenders also his reason and his life. His ruling passion, the manipulation of persons, was apparently intertwined with the life force itself.

After Hummel's death, one thread of action remains to be unraveled: his daughter Adele has yet to receive the suitor he selected for her. She finds the young man sympathetic, but, having been sustained hitherto by illusion and subterfuge, she cannot endure his aggressive honesty; she withers, as her father had, before a recital of deceitfulness exposed.

This third scene, although extrinsic to the principal action, completes some carefully wrought thematic patterns. The active and masculine parasitism of Hummel has a passive and feminine counterpart. The student, whom Hummel had sought to hoodwink and chivvy, must survive also the poisonous attraction of the emaciated girl. All the elements entering into the close of the second scene recur at the close of the third. The theme of honesty dispelling a long-endured deceit is sounded. Death

impends for the person caught up in the deceit. The Colonel's manservant places a death screen before the victim. A *miserere* is pronounced. The harp sounds a prelude. And the student proclaims his own deliverance and the insight to which he has come:

> The harmless are happy.
> The guileless are good.

It is hard in an abstract description to keep these recurrences from appearing excessively studied. It is no doubt hazardous for a playwright to reproduce in drama the kind and degree of repetition that musical forms suggest to him. But Strindberg had powers of modulation equal to the task. The stark *miserere* for old Hummel, for example, pronounced by his hostile and desiccated former mistress ("It is over!—May god have mercy on his soul!"), yields to a tender petition for the strengthless girl, uttered by a young man who is by nature a healer and savior: "Child of this world of illusion and guilt and suffering and death . . . ! May the Lord of Heaven have mercy on you as you journey forth. . . ." With this petition, the last movement of Strindberg's sonata (to extend the metaphor of his title) comes to an end.

All subsequent history modifies a work of art in the consciousness, as T. S. Eliot once said. Strindberg's Chamber Plays, at one time occupying a kind of cul-de-sac, have now a well-defined place in the mainstream of dramatic literature. And the chief ornament of the group, *The Ghost Sonata*, having lost its taint of eccentricity, shines forth as genuinely original. If it continues to resist emulation, that is because such bold and resonant dramaturgy is hard to rival in any age.

The Ghost Sonata

STRINDBERG

Translated by Evert Sprinchorn

CHARACTERS°

THE OLD MAN   *Mr. Hummel*
THE STUDENT   *Arkenholz°*
THE MILKMAID   *an apparition*
THE SUPERINTENDENT'S WIFE
THE SUPERINTENDENT
THE DEAD MAN   *formerly a Consul*
THE WOMAN IN BLACK   *daughter of The Dead Man and The Superintendent's Wife*
THE COLONEL
THE MUMMY   *The Colonel's wife*
THE YOUNG LADY   *The Colonel's daughter, actually The Old Man's daughter*
BARON SKANSKORG   *engaged to The Woman in Black*

Characters the characters are involved in a skein of relationships so fantastic in its complication that a single list can hardly capture it. **The Woman in Black** is the illegitimate daughter of **The Superintendent's Wife** and the Consul (**The Dead Man**). Her fiancé, **Baron Skanskorg**, is divorcing another of the Consul's daughters to marry her. In addition, **The Colonel** once seduced Hummel's (**The Old Man**) former fiancée (**The Fiancée**); to even the score, Hummel seduced the Colonel's wife (**The Mummy**), who bore him a child, **The Young Lady.** The Mummy had, finally, a further affair with Baron Skanskorg.
Arkenholz the name (**Arkwood**) has Biblical resonances, perhaps especially of the saving vessel

From the book The Chamber Plays *by August Strindberg. The play "Ghost Sonata" was translated by Evert Sprinchorn. Copyright © 1972 by Evert Sprinchorn and Seabury Quinn, Jr. A Dutton Paperback. Published by E. P. Dutton & Co., Inc., and used with their permission.*

JOHANSSON   *Hummel's servant*
BENGTSSON   *The Colonel's manservant*
THE FIANCÉE   *Hummel's former fiancée, now a white-haired old woman*
THE COOK
BEGGARS
A HOUSEMAID

SCENE. *Stockholm.*

SCENE I

[*The first two floors of a facade of a new house on a city square. Only the corner of the house is visible, the ground floor terminating in a round room, the second floor in a balcony with a flagpole.*

When the curtains are drawn and the windows opened in the round room, one can see a white marble statue of a young woman surrounded by palms and bathed in sunlight. On the windowsill farthest to the left are pots of hyacinths°—blue, white, pink.

Hanging on the railing of the balcony on the second story are a blue silk bedspread and two white pillowcases. The windows to the left are covered with white sheets, signifying a death in the house. It is a bright Sunday morning.

A green park bench is downstage toward the left.

Downstage right is a drinking fountain, with a long-handled drinking cup hanging at its side. To the left a kiosk, plastered with advertisements. A telephone booth is also onstage.

The main entrance to the house is at the right. The stairs leading up from the sidewalk to the door are of marble and the railings are of mahogany and brass. On the sidewalk on both sides of the entryway are tubs with small laurels.

The corner of the house with the round room also faces a side street which runs upstage.

hyacinths these flowers, which will loom large in the third scene, suggest to Strindberg the sensuous but mindless appeal of a certain kind of woman. See translator's introduction to *The Chamber Plays*, p. xxii.

*On the first floor to the left of the entryway
is a window with a special mirror, quite common in Sweden around the turn of the century,
which enables those inside to view the passing
scene without sticking their heads out the
window.]*

AT RISE

*[The bells of several churches can be heard
ringing in the distance.*

*The double doors in the entryway are wide
open.* THE WOMAN IN BLACK *stands motionless
in the doorway.*

THE SUPERINTENDENT'S WIFE *is sweeping the
stairs and the sidewalk in front of the house.
Having finished that, she polishes the brass in
the entryway and then waters the laurels.*

Sitting in a wheelchair near the kiosk is THE
OLD MAN, *reading a newspaper. He has white
hair and beard and is wearing glasses.*

THE MILKMAID *comes in from around the
corner, carrying a wire basket filled with bottles. She is wearing a summer dress, with
brown shoes, black stockings, and white cap.
She takes off her cap and hangs it on the drinking fountain; wipes the sweat from her brow;
takes a drink from the cup; washes her hands;
arranges her hair, using the water in the fountain as a mirror.*

*The ringing of a steamship bell is heard, and
now and then the silence is broken by the
deep notes of the organs in the nearby
churches.*

After a few moments of silence, and after
THE MILKMAID *has finished arranging her hair,*
THE STUDENT *enters from the left. He is un-
shaven and looks as if he had not had any
sleep. He goes directly to the drinking fountain.*

Pause.]

THE STUDENT. Could I borrow the cup,
please?

[THE MILKMAID hugs the cup to herself.]
Aren't you through using it?

[THE MILKMAID stares at him in terror.]

THE OLD MAN *[to himself].* Who on earth is
he talking to?—I don't see anyone!—Is he
crazy? *[He continues to stare at them in
amazement.]*

THE STUDENT. What are you looking at?
Do I look so awful?—Well, I haven't slept a
wink all night, I suppose you think that I've
been out doing the town. . . .

[THE MILKMAID still stares at him in terror.]
Think I've been drinking, don't you?—Do I
smell like it?

[THE MILKMAID as before.]
I haven't had a chance to shave, I know that.
. . . Come on, let me have a drink of water.
After last night, I think I've earned it. *[Pause.]*
I guess I have to tell you the whole story. I've
spent the whole night bandaging wounds and
taking care of the injured people. You see, I
was there when the house collapsed last night.
. . . Well, that's it.

*[THE MILKMAID rinses the cup and offers
him a drink of water.]*
Thanks!

[THE MILKMAID does not move.]

THE STUDENT *[continues, slowly].* I wonder
if you would do me a big favor? *[Pause.]* The
thing is, my eyes are inflamed, as you can
see—but I've had my hands on wounds and
on corpses—so I don't want to risk using my
hands to wash my eyes. . . . I was wondering if
you would take this clean handkerchief, dip it
in that fresh water, and bathe my poor eyes
with it?—Would you do that?—Will you play
the Good Samaritan for me?

*[THE MILKMAID hesitates for a moment be-
fore doing as asked.]*
That's very kind of you. And here's something
for your trouble.—*[He has taken his wallet
out and is about to offer her some money.* THE
MILKMAID *makes a gesture of refusal.]* I'm
sorry. Forgive me. I'm still in a daze. . . .

THE OLD MAN *[to* THE STUDENT]. Forgive
my speaking to you, but I could not help hearing you say you were in on that terrible
accident yesterday evening. I was just sitting
here reading about it in the paper.

THE STUDENT. Is it already in the paper?

THE OLD MAN. The whole story! And

they've got a picture of you too. But they regret they were unable to obtain the name of the courageous young student. . . .

THE STUDENT [*looking at the paper*]. So that's me! What do you know!

THE OLD MAN. Who . . . who was that you were talking to just now?

THE STUDENT. Didn't you see?

[*Pause.*]

THE OLD MAN. I suppose I'm being nosey, but would you do me the honor of giving me your name?

THE STUDENT. Why do you want to know that? I don't care for publicity. First they praise you, then they blame you. Running people down has been built up into one of the fine arts. Besides, I'm not looking for any reward.

THE OLD MAN. Rich, I suppose?

THE STUDENT. Not at all! I haven't got a dime to my name.

THE OLD MAN. It's strange . . . but I can't help thinking that I've heard your voice before. . . . When I was a young man I had a friend who couldn't pronounce window, he always said winder. I've only met one person who said that, and that was him. The other is you, of course. Is it possible that you are related to Arkenholz, the wholesale dealer?

THE STUDENT. He was my father.

THE OLD MAN. Isn't fate strange? Then I have seen you when you were a child—under very difficult circumstances.

THE STUDENT. I suppose so. I understand I came into the world right in the middle of bankruptcy proceedings.

THE OLD MAN. Exactly!

THE STUDENT. May I ask what your name is?

THE OLD MAN. My name is Hummel.

THE STUDENT. Hummel? Then you're—Yes, I remember. . . .

THE OLD MAN. You've heard my name mentioned in your family?

THE STUDENT. Yes.

THE OLD MAN. And mentioned, perhaps, with a certain antipathy?

[THE STUDENT *remains silent.*]

I can well imagine! . . . No doubt you heard that I was the man who ruined your father? . . . Everyone who is ruined by stupid speculations comes to realize sooner or later that he was actually ruined by someone he couldn't fool. [*Pause.*] The truth of the matter is that your father fleeced me of seventeen thousand crowns, every cent I had saved up at the time.

THE STUDENT. It's remarkable how the same story can be told in two exactly opposite ways.

THE OLD MAN. Surely you don't think I'm being untruthful?

THE STUDENT. What do you think? My father didn't lie.

THE OLD MAN. That's true, a father never lies. . . . But I too am a father, and consequently . . .

THE STUDENT. What're you getting at?

THE OLD MAN. I saved your father from the worst possible misery, and he repaid me with all the terrible hatred of a man who feels obliged to be grateful. He taught his family to speak ill of me.

THE STUDENT. Maybe you made him ungrateful. The help you gave him was probably poisoned with unnecessary humiliations.

THE OLD MAN. My dear young man, all help is humiliating.

THE STUDENT. What do you want of me?

THE OLD MAN. Don't worry, I'm not asking for the money back. But if you would render me a few small services, I would consider myself well repaid. You see that I'm a cripple—some say it's my own fault—others blame my parents—personally I blame it all on life itself, with all its traps—in avoiding one you fall right into the next one. Anyway, I can't run up and down stairs—can't even pull bell cords. And so I ask you: help me!

THE STUDENT. What can I do?

THE OLD MAN. Well, first of all you might give my chair a push so that I can read the posters. I want to see what's playing tonight.

THE STUDENT [*pushing the wheelchair*]. Don't you have a man who takes care of you?

THE OLD MAN. Yes, but he's off on an errand. . . . Be right back. . . . You a medical student?

THE STUDENT. No, I'm studying languages. But I really don't know what I want to be.

THE OLD MAN. Aha!—How are you at mathematics?

5 THE STUDENT. Fairly good.

THE OLD MAN. Good! Good!—Would you possibly be interested in a job?

THE STUDENT. Sure, why not?

THE OLD MAN. Splendid! [*Reading the* 10 *posters.*] They're giving *Die Walküre* at the matinee. . . . That means that the Colonel will be there with his daughter. And since he always sits on the aisle in the sixth row, I'll put you next to him. . . . You go into that 15 telephone booth over there and order a ticket for seat number eighty-two in the sixth row.

THE STUDENT. You expect me to go to the opera in the middle of the day?

THE OLD MAN. That's right! Just you do as 20 I tell you and you won't regret it. I want to see you happy—rich and respected. Your debut last night as the courageous rescuer is the beginning of your fame. From now on your very name will be a great asset.

25 THE STUDENT [*going toward the telephone booth*]. I don't know what I'm getting into. It's crazy!

THE OLD MAN. Aren't you a gambler?

THE STUDENT. Yes, unfortunately. I always 30 lose.

THE OLD MAN. This will change your luck! —Go and telephone!

[*He picks up his newspaper and starts to read. In the meantime* THE LADY IN BLACK *has* 35 *come out on the sidewalk and is talking with* THE SUPERINTENDENT'S WIFE. THE OLD MAN *listens furtively, but the audience hears nothing.* THE STUDENT *returns.*] All set?

40 THE STUDENT. It's all taken care of.

THE OLD MAN. Take a look at that house.

THE STUDENT. I already have looked at it— very carefully. . . . I went by here yesterday, when the sun was glittering on the panes— 45 and dreaming of all the beauty and luxury there must be in that house, I said to my friend, "Imagine having an apartment there, four flights up, and a beautiful wife, and two

pretty kids, and twenty thousand crowns in dividends every year." 50

THE OLD MAN. Did you now? Did you say that? Well, well! I too am very fond of that house. . . .

THE STUDENT. Do you speculate in houses?

THE OLD MAN. Mmm—yes! But not in the 55 way you think. . . .

THE STUDENT. Do you know the people who live there?

THE OLD MAN. Every single one. At my age you know everyone, including their fathers 60 and their grandfathers—and you always find you're related to them somehow. I've just turned eighty. . . . But no one knows me, not really. . . . I take a great interest in human destinies. . . . 65

[*The curtains in the round room are drawn up.* THE COLONEL *is seen inside, dressed in civilian clothes. After having looked at the thermometer he moves away from the window and stands in front of the marble statue.*] 70 Look, there's the Colonel! You'll sit next to him this afternoon.

THE STUDENT. Is that him—the Colonel? I don't understand anything that's going on. It's like a fairy tale. 75

THE OLD MAN. My whole life, my dear young man, is like a book of fairy tales. But although the stories are different, one thread ties them all together and the same leitmotif recurs constantly. 80

THE STUDENT. Who is that marble statue in there?

THE OLD MAN. That's his wife, naturally. . . .

THE STUDENT. Was she so wonderful? Did he love her so much? 85

THE OLD MAN. Hmm yes . . . yes, of course. . . .

THE STUDENT. Well, tell me!

THE OLD MAN. Come now, you know we can't judge other people. . . . Suppose I were 90 to tell you that she left him, that he beat her, that she came back again and married him again, and that she is sitting in there right now like a mummy, worshiping her own statue, you would think I was crazy. 95

THE STUDENT. I can't understand it!

THE OLD MAN. That doesn't surprise me!—
And over there we have the hyacinth window.
That's where his daughter lives. She's out
horseback riding, but she'll be home soon. . . .

5 THE STUDENT. Who's the lady in black that's
talking to the caretaker?

THE OLD MAN. Well, that's a little complicated. But it's connected with the dead man
upstairs, there where you see the white sheets.

10 THE STUDENT. And who was he?

THE OLD MAN. A human being, like the rest
of us. The most conspicuous thing about him
was his vanity. . . . Now if you were a Sunday
child, you would soon see him come out of

15 that very door just to look at the consulate flag
at half-mast for himself. Yes, you see, he was a
consul. Liked nothing better than coronets and
lions, plumed hats and colored ribbons.

THE STUDENT. Sunday child, did you say? I

20 was actually born on a Sunday, so I'm told.

THE OLD MAN. Really! Are you—! I should
have guessed it. I could tell by the color of
your eyes. . . . But—then you can see . . . what
others can't see, haven't you noticed that?

25 THE STUDENT. I don't know what others see.
But sometimes—Well, there are some things
you don't talk about!

THE OLD MAN. I knew it, I knew it! But you
can talk to me about it. I understand—things

30 like that. . . .

THE STUDENT. Yesterday, for example. . . . I
was drawn to that little side street where the
house collapsed afterwards. . . . I walked down
the street and stopped in front of a house that

35 I had never seen before. . . . Then I noticed a
crack in the wall. I could hear the floor beams
snapping in two. I leaped forward and grabbed
up a child that was walking under the wall. . . .
The next moment the house collapsed. . . . I

40 escaped—but in my arms—where I thought I
had the child—there wasn't anything. . . .

THE OLD MAN. Remarkable. Remarkable. . . .
I always knew that. . . . But tell me something:
why were you making all those gestures just

45 now at the fountain? And why were you talking to yourself?

THE STUDENT. Didn't you see the milkmaid
I was talking to?

THE OLD MAN [*in horror*]. Milkmaid!?

THE STUDENT. Yes, of course. She handed me 50
the cup.

THE OLD MAN. Indeed? . . . so that's the way
it is? . . . Very well, I may not have second
sight, but I have other powers. . . .

[*A white-haired woman sits down at the* 55
window with the mirror.]

Look at the old lady in the window! Do you
see her? . . . Good, good! That was my fiancée
—once upon a time—sixty years ago. . . . I was
twenty. Don't be afraid, she doesn't recognize 60
me. We see each other every day, but it doesn't
mean a thing to me—although we once vowed
to love each other forever. Forever!

THE STUDENT. How foolish you were in those
days! Nowadays we don't tell girls things like 65
that.

THE OLD MAN. Forgive us, young man. We
didn't know any better! . . . But can you see
that that old woman was once young and
beautiful? 70

THE STUDENT. No, I can't . . . Well, maybe.
I like the way she turns her head to look at
things . . . I can't see her eyes.

[THE SUPERINTENDENT'S WIFE *comes out*
carrying a basket of spruce greens, which she 75
strews on the sidewalk, in accordance with
Swedish custom at funerals.]

THE OLD MAN. Aha, the wife of the superintendent! The lady in black is her daughter by
the dead man upstairs. That's why her husband 80
got the job as superintendent. . . . But the lady
in black has a lover—very aristocratic and
waiting to inherit a fortune. Right now he's in
the process of getting a divorce—from his
present wife, who is giving him a town house 85
just to get rid of him. The aristocratic lover
is the son-in-law of the dead man, and you see
his bed-clothes being aired on the balcony up
there.—Complicated, don't you think?

THE STUDENT. It's damned complicated! 90

THE OLD MAN. Yes, indeed it is, inside and
outside, although it all looks so simple.

THE STUDENT. But then who is the dead man?

THE OLD MAN. You just asked me and I told
you. If you could look around the corner where 95
the service entrance is, you'd see a pack of

poor people whom he used to help—when he felt like it.

THE STUDENT. Then I suppose he was a kind and charitable man?

5 THE OLD MAN. Oh, yes—sometimes.

THE STUDENT. Not always?

THE OLD MAN. No, that's how people are!—Listen, will you give me a little push over there in the sun? I'm so terribly cold. When you 10 never get to move around, the blood congeals. I'm going to die soon, I know that. But before I do there are a few things I want to take care of.—Feel my hand, just feel how cold I am.

THE STUDENT. My god! It's unbelievable! [He 15 tries to free his hand but THE OLD MAN holds on to it.]

THE OLD MAN. Don't leave me, I beg you—I'm tired, I'm lonely—but it hasn't always been this way, I tell you.—I have an infinitely long 20 life behind me—infinitely long—I've made people unhappy and people have made me unhappy, the one cancels out the other. But before I die I want to make you happy. . . . Our destinies are tangled together through your father 25 —and other things.

THE STUDENT. Let go, let go of my hand—you are drawing all my strength from me—you're freezing me to death—what do you want of me?

30 THE OLD MAN. Patience. You'll soon see and understand. . . . There she comes.—

THE STUDENT. The Colonel's daughter?

THE OLD MAN. Yes! His daughter! Just look at her!—Have you ever seen such a master- 35 piece?

THE STUDENT. She looks like the marble statue in there.

THE OLD MAN. She should. That's her mother!

40 THE STUDENT. Incredibly beautiful! "Can woman be so fair?" . . . "Und selig, wer das gute Schicksal hat, als Bräutigam sie heimzuführen!"

THE OLD MAN. Yes, indeed. "Happy the 45 man whose luck it is to bear her home to wedded bliss."—I see you appreciate her beauty. Not everyone recognizes it. . . . Well, then, it is ordained!

[THE YOUNG LADY enters from the left dressed in a riding habit, in the manner of a modern 50 English amazon, and, without taking notice of anyone, crosses slowly over to the door of the house. Before entering, she stops and says a few words to THE SUPERINTENDENT'S WIFE. THE STUDENT covers his eyes with his hands.] 55 Are you crying?

THE STUDENT. When I see how far beyond my reach my happiness is, what can I feel but despair?

THE OLD MAN. But I can open doors—and 60 hearts—if only I can find an arm to do my will. Serve me, and you shall be a lord of creation!

THE STUDENT. A devil's bargain? You want me to sell my soul? 65

THE OLD MAN. Sell nothing!—Don't you understand, all my life I have taken, taken! Now I crave to give, to give! But nobody will take what I have to offer. I'm a rich man, very rich—and without any heirs.—Oh, yes, I have 70 a good-for-nothing son who torments the life out of me. . . . You could become my son, become my heir while I'm still alive, enjoy life while I'm here to see it—at least from a distance. 75

THE STUDENT. What do you want me to do?

THE OLD MAN. First, go and hear Die Walküre!

THE STUDENT. That's already been taken care of. What else? 80

THE OLD MAN. This evening you shall be sitting in there—in the round room!

THE STUDENT. How do you expect me to get in?

THE OLD MAN. By way of Die Walküre! 85

THE STUDENT. Why did you pick me for your —your medium? Did you know me before?

THE OLD MAN. Of course, of course! I've had my eyes on you for a long time. . . . Ah! Look up there, on the balcony, where the maid 90 is raising the flag to half-mast for the Consul —and now she's turning over the bedclothes. . . . Do you see that blue quilt? It was made for two to sleep under, and now it covers only one. . . . 95

[THE YOUNG LADY, in a change of clothes,

appears at the window to water the hyacinths.]
There's my dear little girl. Look at her, just
look at her! . . . She's talking to the flowers
now. Isn't she just like a blue hyacinth herself?
5 She gives them water to drink, the purest
water, and they transform the water into color
and perfume.—Here comes the Colonel with a
newspaper. . . . Now he's pointing to your
picture! She's reading about your heroic deed.
10 —It's starting to cloud over. Suppose it starts
to rain? I'll be in a pretty mess if Johansson
doesn't come back soon.

[*It grows cloudy and dark.* THE OLD WOMAN
at the window mirror closes her window.]

15 I see my fiancée is closing up shop. . . . Seven-
ty-nine years. . . . That window mirror is the
only mirror she ever uses. That's because she
can't see herself in it, only the outside world
and from two directions at once. But the world
20 can see her. She doesn't realize that. . . . All
the same, not bad-looking for an old woman.

[*Now,* THE DEAD MAN, *wrapped in a winding
sheet, is seen coming out of the main door.*]

THE STUDENT. Oh my god, what—?

25 THE OLD MAN. What do you see?

THE STUDENT. Don't *you* see? Don't you see,
in the doorway, the dead man?

THE OLD MAN. No, I don't see anything.
But I'm not surprised. Tell me exactly what—

30 THE STUDENT. He's stepping out into the
street. . . . [*Pause.*] Now he's turning his head
and looking up at the flag.

THE OLD MAN. What did I tell you? Watch,
he will count every wreath and read every
35 calling card. I pity whoever is missing!

THE STUDENT. Now he's turning the corner.
. . .

THE OLD MAN. He's gone to count the poor
people at the service entrance. The poor add
40 such a nice touch to an obituary: "Received
the blessings of the populace!" Yes, but he
won't receive my blessing!—Just between us,
he was a big scoundrel.

THE STUDENT. But benevolent.

45 THE OLD MAN. A benevolent scoundrel.
Always thinking of his own magnificent
funeral. . . . When he could feel his end was
near, he embezzled fifty thousand crowns

from the state. . . . Now his daughter is running
around with another woman's husband and 50
wondering about the will. . . . The scoundrel
can hear every word we're saying. I hope he
gets an earful!—Here's Johansson.

[JOHANSSON *enters from the left.*]
Report! 55

[JOHANSSON *speaks to* THE OLD MAN, *but
the audience cannot hear what he says.*]
What do you mean, not at home? You're an
ass!—What about the telegram?—Not a word!
. . . go on, go on! . . . six o'clock this evening? 60
That's good!—An extra edition?—With all the
details about him? . . . Arkenholz, student . . .
born . . . his parents. . . . Splendid! . . . It's
beginning to rain, I think. . . . And what did he
say? . . . Really, really!—He didn't *want* to? 65
Well, he's going to have to!—Here comes the
Baron, or whatever he is!—Push me around
the corner, Johansson. I want to hear what
the poor people are saying.—And Arkenholz!
Don't go away. Do you understand?—Well, 70
come on, come on, what are you waiting for!

[JOHANSSON *pushes the wheelchair around
the corner.* THE STUDENT *has turned to look at*
THE YOUNG LADY *who is loosening the earth in
the hyacinth pots. Dressed in mourning,* BARON 75
SKANSKORG *enters and speaks to* THE LADY IN
BLACK, *who has been walking up and down
the sidewalk.*]

BARON SKANSKORG. What can we do about
it? We simply have to wait. 80

LADY IN BLACK [*intensely*]. But I can't wait,
don't you understand?

BARON SKANSKORG. Well, if that's the way
it is, you'll have to go to the country.

LADY IN BLACK. I don't want to do that! 85

BARON SKANSKORG. Come over here. Otherwise they'll hear what we're saying.

[*They move over toward the advertisement
column and continue their conversation unheard by the audience.* JOHANSSON *enters from* 90
the right.]

JOHANSSON [*to* THE STUDENT]. My master
asks you not to forget that other matter. . . .

THE STUDENT [*warily*]. Just a minute—I
want to know something first. Tell me, exactly 95
what is your employer's business?

JOHANSSON. What can I say? He's so many things, and he's been everything.

THE STUDENT. He's not crazy, is he?

JOHANSSON. What does it mean to be crazy?
5 All his life he's been looking for a Sunday child. That's what he says—but he might be making it up. . . .

THE STUDENT. What's he after? Money?

JOHANSSON. Power.—All day long he rides
10 around in his chariot like the great god Thor. . . . He keeps his eye on houses, tears them down, opens up streets, builds up city squares. But he also breaks into houses, sneaks in through the windows, ravages human lives,
15 kills his enemies, and forgives nothing and nobody. . . . Can you imagine that that little cripple was once a Don Juan. But no woman would ever stick with him.

THE STUDENT. Sounds inconsistent.

20 JOHANSSON. Oh, no. You see, he was so sly that he knew how to get the women to leave when he got bored with them. But that was a long time ago. Now he's more like a horse thief at a slave market. He steals people—in
25 more ways than one. . . . He literally stole me out of the hands of the law. I made a little mistake—that's all—and he was the only one who knew about it. But instead of putting me in jail, he made me his slave. I slave for him
30 just for my food—which isn't the best in the world.

THE STUDENT. What's he got up his sleeve? What's he want to do in this house?

JOHANSSON. I wouldn't want to say! I
35 wouldn't even know where to begin!

THE STUDENT. I think I'd better get out while the getting is good.

JOHANSSON. Look at the young lady! She's dropped her bracelet out of the window.

40 [*Her bracelet has fallen off* THE YOUNG LADY'*s arm and through the open window.* THE STUDENT *crosses over slowly, picks up the bracelet and hands it to* THE YOUNG LADY, *who thanks him stiffly.* THE STUDENT *goes back to*
45 JOHANSSON.]
I thought you said you were leaving. It isn't as easy as you think once *he* has slipped his net over your head. . . . And he's afraid of nothing between heaven and earth—yes, one thing—or rather one person. 50

THE STUDENT. I bet I know.

JOHANSSON. How can you know?

THE STUDENT. Just guessing! Could it be . . . he's afraid of a little Milkmaid?

JOHANSSON. He turns his head away when- 55 ever he sees a milk wagon. . . . Sometimes he talks in his sleep. He must have been in Hamburg once. . . .

THE STUDENT. Can I depend on him?

JOHANSSON. You can depend on him—to do 60 anything and everything!

THE STUDENT. What's he up to around the corner?

JOHANSSON. Eavesdropping on the poor. . . . Planting a word here and there, chipping away 65 at one stone at a time—until the whole house falls—metaphorically speaking. Oh yes, I've had an education. And I used to be a bookseller. . . . Are you leaving or staying?

THE STUDENT. I don't like to be ungrateful. 70 This man once saved my father, and all he's asking for now is a little favor in return.

JOHANSSON. What is that?

THE STUDENT. He wants me to go and see *Die Walküre.* 75

JOHANSSON. That's beyond me. . . . He's always got something up his sleeve. . . . Look at him, he's talking to the policeman. He's always in with the police. He makes use of them, gets them involved in his business, ties 80 them hand and foot with false promises of future possibilities. And all the while he's pumping them, pumping them.—Mark my words, before the night is over he'll be received in the round room. 85

THE STUDENT. What does he want in there? What's he got to do with the Colonel?

JOHANSSON. I'm not sure, but I've got my ideas. You'll be able to see for yourself when you go there! 90

THE STUDENT. I'll never get in there. . . .

JOHANSSON. That depends on you! Go to *Die Walküre.*

THE STUDENT. Is that the way?

JOHANSSON. If he said so, it is!—Look at him, just look at him! Riding his war chariot, drawn in triumph by the beggars, who don't get a cent for it, just a hint that something might come their way at his funeral!

[THE OLD MAN *enters standing in his wheelchair, drawn by one of the* BEGGARS, *and followed by the others.*]

THE OLD MAN. Let us hail the noble youth, who risked his own life to save so many in yesterday's accident! Hail Arkenholz!

[*The* BEGGARS *bare their heads but do not cheer.* THE YOUNG LADY, *standing in the window, waves her handkerchief.* THE COLONEL *looks at the scene from his window.* THE FIANCÉE *stands up at her window. The* HOUSEMAID *on the balcony raises the flag to the top.*] Hail the hero, my fellow citizens! I know indeed it is Sunday, but the ass in the pit and the ear in the field absolve us. And though I may not be a Sunday child, I can see into the future and I can heal the sick. I have even brought a drowned soul back to life. . . . That happened in Hamburg, yes, on a Sunday morning, just like this—

[THE MILKMAID *enters, seen only by* THE STUDENT *and* THE OLD MAN. *She stretches her arms above her head like a drowning person and stares fixedly at* THE OLD MAN. THE OLD MAN *sits down, and shrivels up in fear and terror.*] Get me out of here, Johansson! Quick—Arkenholz, don't you forget *Die Walküre!*

THE STUDENT. What is all this?

JOHANSSON. We shall see! We shall see!

SCENE II

[*In the round room. At the back of the stage a stove of white glazed porcelain, its mantel decorated with a mirror, a pendulum clock, and candelabra. At the right side of the stage a hallway can be seen and through it a view of a green room with mahogany furniture. At the left of the stage stands the statue in the shadow of the palm trees, and with a curtain which can be drawn to conceal it. In the rear wall to the left of the stove is the door to the hyacinth room, where* THE YOUNG LADY *is seen reading.* THE COLONEL's *back can be seen in the green room, where he is writing at his desk.*

THE COLONEL's *valet,* BENGTSSON, *wearing livery, enters from the hall, accompanied by* JOHANSSON, *who is dressed very formally as a waiter.*]

BENGTSSON. Now, Johansson, you'll have to wait on the table while I take care of the coats. Have you done this before?

JOHANSSON. During the day I push that war chariot, as you know, but in the evenings I work as a waiter at receptions. It's always been my dream to get into this house. . . . They're peculiar people, aren't they?

BENGTSSON. Well, yes, I think one might say that they're a little strange.

JOHANSON. Are we going to have a musicale this evening? Or what is the occasion?

BENGTSSON. Just the ordinary ghost supper, as we call it. They drink tea, without saying a word, or else the Colonel talks all by himself. And they champ their biscuits and crackers all at once and all in unison. They sound like a pack of rats in an attic.

JOHANSSON. Why do you call it the ghost supper?

BENGTSSON. They all look like ghosts. . . . This has been going on for twenty years—always the same people, always saying the same things. Or else keeping silent to avoid being embarrassed.

JOHANSSON. Where's the lady of the house? Isn't she around?

BENGTSSON. Oh, yes. But she's crazy. She keeps herself shut up in a closet because her eyes can't stand the light. She's sitting in there right now. [*He points to a wallpapered door.*°]

JOHANSSON. In there?

BENGTSSON. I told you they were a little peculiar.

---

wallpapered door doors were not infrequently so concealed in nineteenth-century Sweden. Hence this "is not one of the bizarre elements in the *Sonata*." [Translator's note.]

JOHANSSON. What on earth does she look like?

BENGTSSON. Like a mummy. Do you want to see her? [*He opens the papered door.*] There she sits!

JOHANSSON. Je-sus!

THE MUMMY [*babbling*]. Why do you open the door? Didn't I tell you to keep it closed?

BENGTSSON [*as if talking to a baby*]. Ta, ta, ta, ta, ta!—Is little chickadee going to be nice to me? Then little chickadee will get something good!—Pretty polly!

THE MUMMY [*like a parrot*]. Pretty polly! Are you there, Jacob? Jacob? Cluck, cluck!

BENGTSSON. She thinks she's a parrot—and maybe she is. [*To* THE MUMMY.] Come on, polly, whistle for us!

[THE MUMMY *whistles*.]

JOHANSSON. I thought I had seen everything, but this tops it all.

BENGTSSON. Well, when a house grows old, it turns moldy and rotten, and when people are together too much and torment each other too long, they go crazy. Take the lady in this house—shut up, polly!—this mummy has been sitting here for forty years—the same husband, same furniture, same relatives, same friends. . . . [*Closing the door on* THE MUMMY.] And imagine what's gone on in this house! Even I don't know the whole story. . . . Look at this statue. That's the lady of the house as a young girl!

JOHANSSON. Oh my god!—Is that the mummy?

BENGTSSON. Yes. It's enough to make one cry! But this lady—carried away by her imagination or something—has acquired certain of the peculiarities of the prating parrot. She can't stand cripples, for instance—or sick people. She can't even stand the sight of her own daughter because she's sick.

JOHANSSON. Is that young girl sick?

BENGTSSON. Yes. Didn't you know?

JOHANSSON. No. . . . What about the Colonel? Who is he?

BENGTSSON. Wait a while and you'll see!

JOHANSSON [*looking at the statue*]. It's terri-fying to realize that—How old is the lady now?

BENGTSSON. Who knows? But I've heard it said that when she was thirty-five she looked like she was nineteen.—And she convinced the Colonel that she was . . . here in this house. . . . Do you know what that black Japanese screen by the couch is for? It's called a death screen, and when somebody's going to die, it's placed around them, same as in a hospital.

JOHANSSON. What a horrible house. . . . That poor student thought that when he entered this house he would be entering paradise.

BENGTSSON. Which student? Oh, yes, of course! The one that's coming here tonight. The Colonel and his daughter met him at the opera and were captivated by him. . . . Hm. . . . But let me ask you a couple of questions. Who's your master? The financier in the wheel-chair?

JOHANSSON [*nodding*]. Yes, that's right.—Is he coming here too?

BENGTSSON. He's not invited.

JOHANSSON. Then he'll come uninvited—if necessary!

[THE OLD MAN *appears in the hallway, dressed in frock coat and high hat. He moves silently forward on his crutches, like a black spider, and eavesdrops on the servants.*]

BENGTSSON. I'll bet he's a real old mean one.

JOHANSSON. A perfect specimen!

BENGTSSON. He looks like the devil incarnate!

JOHANSSON. And he's a black magician, I tell you. He can go through locked doors—

THE OLD MAN [*coming forward and grab-bing* JOHANSSON *by the ear*]. Fool! Hold your tongue! [*To* BENGTSSON.] Announce me to the Colonel!

BENGTSSON. But we're expecting company here.

THE OLD MAN. I know you are! My visit is not unexpected—although undesired.

BENGTSSON. I see. What was the name? Mr. Hummel?

THE OLD MAN. That's right! Precisely!

[BENGTSSON *goes down the hall into the green room and closes the door.*]

[*To* JOHANSSON.] Disappear!

[JOHANSSON *hesitates.*]

Vanish!

[JOHANSSON *vanishes down the hall.* THE
5 OLD MAN *inspects the room. Stops in front of
the statue. Much amazed.*]

Amelia! . . . It is she! . . . Amelia! [*He roams
about the room fingering objects. Stops in front
of the mirror to adjust his wig. Returns to the
10 statue.*]

THE MUMMY [*from within the closet*]. Pretty
polly!

THE OLD MAN [*startled*]. What on earth!
Sounded like a parrot in the room. But I don't
15 see any.

THE MUMMY. You there, Jacob?

THE OLD MAN. Place is haunted.

THE MUMMY. Jacob!

THE OLD MAN. It's enough to frighten one!
20 . . . So that's the kind of secrets they've been
keeping in this house! [*With his back to the
closet he studies a portrait on the wall.*] There
he is!—The old Colonel himself!

THE MUMMY [*coming out of the closet, goes
25 up to* THE OLD MAN *from behind and gives his
wig a pull*]. Cluck, cluck. Cluck, cluck. Are
you dumb cluck—cluck?

THE OLD MAN [*frightened out of his skin*].
Oh my god in heaven!—Who are you?

30 THE MUMMY [*speaking in her normal voice*].
Is that you, Jacob?

THE OLD MAN. Yes. My name is Jacob.

THE MUMMY [*movingly*]. And my name is
Amelia!

35 THE OLD MAN. Oh no. . . . No, no. . . . Oh my
god! . . .

THE MUMMY. Yes, this is how I look!—And
that's how I did look once upon a time. Life
gives one a great education. Most of my life
40 I've spent in the closet, so that I won't have to
see—or be seen. . . . But you, Jacob, what are
you looking for here?

THE OLD MAN. My child! Our child!

THE MUMMY. She's sitting in there.

45 THE OLD MAN. Where?

THE MUMMY. In there, in the hyacinth room.

THE OLD MAN [*looking at* THE YOUNG
LADY]. Yes, there she is! [*Pause.*] And what
does her father think of her—I mean, the
Colonel—your husband?   50

THE MUMMY. I had a quarrel with him once,
and told him everything. . . .

THE OLD MAN. And? . . .

THE MUMMY. He didn't believe me. He said,
"That's what all women say when they want   55
to murder their husbands." . . . All the same
it was a terrible crime. His whole life has been
falsified, including his family tree. When I
look at his family record in the peerage, I say
to myself she's no better than a runaway   60
servant girl with a false birth certificate, and
girls like that are sent to the reformatory.

THE OLD MAN. A lot of people forge their
birth certificates. I seem to remember that even
you falsified the date of your birth.   65

THE MUMMY. It was my mother who put
me up to it. I'm not to blame for that! . . . And
furthermore, you played the biggest part in
our crime.

THE OLD MAN. Not true! Your husband   70
started it all when he stole my fiancée from
me! I was born unable to forgive until I have
punished. I've always looked upon it as an
imperative duty. And I still do!

THE MUMMY. What do you expect to find in 75
this house? What do you want here? And how
did you get in?—Does your business concern
my daughter? Keep your hands off her, I warn
you, or you'll die!

THE OLD MAN. I wish her nothing but the 80
best!

THE MUMMY. And you must have consideration for her father, too!

THE OLD MAN. Never!

THE MUMMY. Then you must die. In this   85
room. Behind that screen.

THE OLD MAN. Be that as it may. But I'm a
bulldog. I never let go.

THE MUMMY. You want to marry her to that
student. Why? He has nothing; he is nothing.   90

THE OLD MAN. He'll be a rich man, thanks
to me.

THE MUMMY. Are you one of the invited
guests tonight?

THE OLD MAN. No, but I've decided to invite myself to this ghost supper!

THE MUMMY. Do you know who'll be here?

THE OLD MAN. Not entirely.

5 THE MUMMY. The Baron—who lives upstairs, and whose father-in-law was buried this afternoon—

THE OLD MAN. Yes, the Baron—who is getting a divorce in order to marry the

10 daughter of the superintendent's wife. The Baron—who was once—your lover!

THE MUMMY. And then there'll be your former fiancée—whom my husband seduced. . . .

THE OLD MAN. A very select gathering. . . .

15 THE MUMMY. Oh god, why can't we die? If only we could die!

THE OLD MAN. Then why do you keep seeing each other?

THE MUMMY. Our crimes and our secrets and

20 our guilt bind us together! We have split up and gone our separate ways an infinite number of times. But we're always drawn back together again. . . .

THE OLD MAN. I believe the Colonel is

25 coming.

THE MUMMY. Then I'll go in to Adele. . . . [Pause.] Jacob, don't do anything foolish! Be considerate toward him. . . .

[A pause. She leaves.]

30 THE COLONEL [enters, cold and reserved]. Please sit down.

[THE OLD MAN takes his time seating himself. A pause. THE COLONEL stares at him.] Did you write this letter?

35 THE OLD MAN. I did.

THE COLONEL. And your name is Hummel?

THE OLD MAN. It is.

[Pause.]

THE COLONEL. Since it's clear that you have

40 bought up all my outstanding promissory notes, it follows that I'm completely at your mercy. Now what do you want?

THE OLD MAN. I want to be paid—in one way or another.

45 THE COLONEL. In what way?

THE OLD MAN. A very simple way. Don't let's talk about money. Allow me to come and go in your house—as a guest.

THE COLONEL. If that's all it takes to satisfy you— 50

THE OLD MAN. Thank you!

THE COLONEL. And what else?

THE OLD MAN. Dismiss Bengtsson!

THE COLONEL. Why? Bengtsson is my devoted servant. He's been with me during my whole 55 career. The army awarded him a medal for faithful service. Why should I dismiss him?

THE OLD MAN. I have no doubt he's a very fine man in your eyes. But he's not the man he seems to be! 60

THE COLONEL. Who is?

THE OLD MAN [taken aback]. True!—But Bengtsson must go!

THE COLONEL. Are you going to give orders in my house? 65

THE OLD MAN. Yes! Since I own everything that you can lay your eyes on—furniture, curtains, dinner service, linen . . . and other things. . . .

THE COLONEL. What other things? 70

THE OLD MAN. Everything. I own it all. Everything that you see here is mine!

THE COLONEL. I can't argue that. But my family honor, my coat of arms and my good name are things you cannot take from me! 75

THE OLD MAN. Yes, I can. They don't belong to you. [Pause.] You are not a nobleman.

THE COLONEL. I shall give you the opportunity of withdrawing those words!

THE OLD MAN [producing a piece of paper]. 80 If you will take the trouble to read this extract from the standard book of genealogy, you will see that the family whose name you have assumed has been extinct for over a century.

THE COLONEL [reading]. Of course I've heard 85 rumors like this before. But it was my father's name before it was mine. . . . [Reading on.] I can't deny it. You are quite right. . . . I am not a nobleman! Not even that. . . . Therefore I shall take this signet ring from off my hand 90 —Oh, but of course, excuse me: it belongs to you. There you are.

THE OLD MAN [putting the ring in his pocket]. Let us continue.—You are not a colonel either! 95

THE COLONEL. Am I not?

THE OLD MAN. No! You held a temporary commission as a colonel in the American Volunteers; but at the end of the Spanish-American War and the reorganization of the Army, all such titles were abolished.

THE COLONEL. Is that true?

THE OLD MAN [*reaching into his pocket*]. Do you want to see for yourself?

THE COLONEL. No, it won't be necessary. . . . Who are you? What gives you the right to sit there and strip me naked in this way?

THE OLD MAN. Patience, my good man! And as far as stripping is concerned—do you really want to know who you are?

THE COLONEL. Have you no decency?

THE OLD MAN. Take off that wig of yours and have a look at yourself in the mirror. And while you're at it, take out those false teeth and shave off that moustache and let Bengtsson unlace your metal corset, and then we shall see if a certain valet, Mr. *X*, won't recognize himself—a valet in a certain house who flirted with the maids in order to scrounge in the kitchen.

[THE COLONEL *reaches for the bell on the table.* THE OLD MAN *stops him, saying:*] I wouldn't touch that if I were you. If you call Bengtsson I'll order him arrested. . . . I believe your guests are arriving. Now let us be calm, and go on playing our old roles for a while longer.

THE COLONEL. Who are you? I've seen your eyes and heard your voice before.

THE OLD MAN. Never mind that. Be silent and do as you're told!

THE STUDENT [*enters and bows to* THE COLONEL]. How do you do, sir!

THE COLONEL. Welcome to my house, young man! Your heroism at that terrible accident has brought your name to everybody's lips. I deem it an honor to receive you in my house.

THE STUDENT. You're very kind, sir. It's a great honor for me, sir. I've never expected—well, my humble birth—and your illustrious name and your noble birth. . . .

THE COLONEL. Mr. Hummel, may I introduce Mr. Arkenholz, who is a student at the university. The ladies are in there, Mr. Arkenholz—

if you care to join them. I have a few more things I wanted to say to Mr. Hummel.

[THE COLONEL *shows* THE STUDENT *in to the hyacinth room where he remains visible to the audience, engaged in shy conversation with* THE YOUNG LADY.] An excellent young man—musical, sings, writes poetry. . . . If it weren't for his birth and social position I certainly wouldn't have anything against—my. . . .

THE OLD MAN. Against what?

THE COLONEL. Having my daughter—

THE OLD MAN. *Your* daughter! . . . Apropos of her, why does she always sit in that room?

THE COLONEL. She feels she has to sit in the hyacinth room whenever she's in the house. A peculiarity of hers. . . . Here comes Miss Beatrice von Holsteinkrona. Charming woman. Very active in the church and with an income that perfectly suits her position and circumstances. . . .

THE OLD MAN [*to himself*]. My fiancée!

[THE FIANCÉE *enters, white-haired and giving every appearance of being crazy.*]

THE COLONEL. Miss Holsteinkrona—Mr. Hummel.

[THE FIANCÉE *curtsies and takes a seat.* BARON SKANSKORG *enters next—dressed in mourning and with a strange look on his face—and sits down.*] Baron Skanskorg—

THE OLD MAN [*in an aside, without rising*]. A jewel thief, if ever I saw one. [*To The Colonel.*] Now let the mummy in, and the party can begin.

THE COLONEL [*in the doorway to the hyacinth room*]. Polly!

THE MUMMY [*enters*]. Cluck, cluck! Dumb-cluck!

THE COLONEL. Shall we invite the young people, too?

THE OLD MAN. No! Not the young people! They shall be spared.

[*They seat themselves in a circle. Silence.*]

THE COLONEL. Shall I ring for the tea?

THE OLD MAN. Why bother? No one cares for tea. Why play games?

[*Pause.*]

THE COLONEL. Then perhaps we should start a conversation?

THE OLD MAN [*slowly, deliberately and with frequent pauses*]. About the weather? Which we know. Ask each other how we're feeling? Which we also know. I prefer silence . . . in which one can hear thoughts and see the past. Silence cannot hide anything—which is more than you can say for words. I read the other day that the differences in languages originated among the primitive savages who sought to keep their secrets from the other tribes. Languages are therefore codes, and he who finds the key can understand all the languages of the world. But that doesn't mean that secrets cannot be discovered without a key. Especially in those cases where paternity must be proved. Legal proof is of course a different matter. Two false witnesses provide complete proof of whatever they agree to say. But in the kind of escapades I have in mind one doesn't take witnesses along. Nature herself has planted in man a blushing sense of shame, which seeks to hide what should be hidden. But we slip into certain situations without intending to, and chance confronts us with moments of revelation, when the deepest secrets are revealed, the mask is ripped from the imposter and the villain stands exposed. . . .

[*Pause. All look at each other in silence.*]
Extraordinary, how silent you all are! [*Long silence.*] Take this house, for example. In this estimable house, in this elegant home, where beauty, wealth, and culture are united. . . . [*Long silence.*] All of us sitting here, we know who we are, don't we? . . . I don't have to tell you. . . . And you know me although you pretend ignorance. . . . Sitting in that room is my daughter, yes mine, you know that too. . . . She had lost all desire to live, without knowing why. . . . She was withering away because of the air in this house, which reeks of crime, deception, and deceits of every kind. . . . That is why I had to find a friend for her, a friend from whose very presence she would apprehend the warmth and light radiated by a noble deed. . . . [*Long silence.*] That was my mission in this house. To pull up the weeds, to expose the crimes, to settle the accounts, so that these young people might make a new beginning in this home, which is my gift to them! [*Long silence.*] Listen to the ticking of the clock, like a deathwatch beetle in the wall! Listen to what it's saying: "time's-up, time's-up! . . ." When it strikes—in just a few moments—your time is up. Then you may go—not before. But the clock raises its arm before it strikes.

[*The clock can be heard preparing to strike the hour.*]
—Listen! It's warning you: "Clocks can strike!"—And I can strike too! [*He strikes the table with his crutch.*] Do you understand?

[*Silence.*]
THE MUMMY [*goes over to the clock and stops its pendulum. In her normal voice, speaking seriously*]. But I can stop time in its course. I can wipe out the past, and undo what is done. Not with bribes, not with threats—but through suffering and repentance. [*Approaching* THE OLD MAN.] We are poor miserable creatures, we know that. We have erred, we have transgressed, we, like all the rest. We are not what we seem to be. At bottom we are better than ourselves, since we abhor and detest our misdeeds. But when you, Jacob Hummel, with your false name, come here to sit in judgment over us, that proves that you are more contemptible than we! And you are not the one you seem to be! You are a slave trader, a stealer of souls! You once stole me with false promises. You murdered the Consul who was buried today, you strangled him with debts. You have stolen the student and shackled him with an imaginary debt of his father's, who never owed you a penny. . . .

[THE OLD MAN *has tried to rise and speak but has collapsed in his chair and shriveled up, and, like a dying insect, he shrivels up more and more during the following dialogue.*]
But there is one dark spot in your life, which I'm not sure about—although I have my suspicions. . . . I think that Bengtsson might help us. [*She rings the bell on the table.*]

THE OLD MAN. No! Not Bengtsson! Not him!

THE MUMMY. Then it is true? He does know! [*She rings again.*]

[*The little* MILKMAID *appears in the door to*

the hall, unseen by all except THE OLD MAN, *who shies in terror.* THE MILKMAID *disappears when* BENGTSSON *enters.*]
Bengtsson, do you know this man?

5 BENGTSSON. Yes, I know him and he knows me. Life has its ups and downs, as we all know, and I have been in his service, and once he was in mine. To be exact, he was a sponger in my kitchen for two whole years. Since he had to
10 be out of the house by three o'clock, dinner had to be ready at two, and those in the house had to eat the warmed-up food left by that ox. Even worse, he drank up the pure soup stock and the gravy, which then had to be diluted
15 with water. He sat there like a vampire, sucking all the marrow out of the house, and turned us all into skeletons. And he nearly succeeded in putting us into prison, when we accused the cook of being a thief. . . . Later I met this man
20 in Hamburg under another name. He had become a usurer or bloodsucker. And it was there that he was accused of having lured a young girl out onto the ice in order to drown her, for she was the only witness to a crime which he
25 was afraid would come to light. . . .

THE MUMMY [*passes her hand over* THE OLD MAN'*s face*]. That is the real you! Now empty your pockets of the notes and the will!

[JOHANSSON *appears in the door to the hall*
30 *and watches* THE OLD MAN *intently, knowing that his slavery is coming to an end.* THE OLD MAN *produces a bundle of papers which he throws on the table.*].

[THE MUMMY, *stroking* THE OLD MAN'*s back.*]
35 Pretty bird! Where's Jacob!

THE OLD MAN [*like a parrot*]. Jacob's here! [*Crows like a rooster.*]

THE MUMMY. Can clocks strike?

THE OLD MAN [*making clucking sounds*].
40 Clocks can strike! [*He imitates a cuckoo clock.*] Coo-coo! Coo-coo! Coo-coo! . . .

THE MUMMY [*opening the papered door to the closet*]. Now the clock has struck! Stand up, and enter the closet where I have sat for
45 twenty years, crying over our misdeeds. You'll find a rope in there, which can represent the one you strangled the Consul with, and with which you intended to strangle your bene-

factor. . . . Go in!

[THE OLD MAN *goes into the closet.* THE 50 MUMMY *closes the door.*]
Bengtsson! Put up the screen! The death screen!

[BENGTSSON *places the screen in front of the door.*] 55
It is over!—May god have mercy on his soul!

ALL. Amen!

[*Long silence.*]

[*In the hyacinth room* THE YOUNG LADY *can be seen sitting at a harp on which she accom-* 60 *panies* THE STUDENT. *After a prelude played by* THE YOUNG LADY, THE STUDENT *recites.*]

THE STUDENT.
I saw the sun
And from its blaze 65
There burst on me
The deepest truth:

Man reaps as he sows;
Blessed is he
Who sows the good. 70

For deeds done in anger
Kindness alone
Can make amends.

Bring cheer to those
Whom you have hurt, 75
And kindness reaps
Its own rewards.

The pure in heart
Have none to fear.
The harmless are happy. 80
The guileless are good.

SCENE III

[*A room decorated in a bizarre style, predominantly oriental. A profusion of hyacinths in all colors fills the room. On the porcelain tiled stove sits a large Buddha with a bulb of a* 85 *shalot* (Allium ascalonicum) *in its lap. The stem of the shalot rises from this bulb and bursts into a spherical cluster of white, starlike*

flowers. In the rear to the right a door leads to the round room. THE COLONEL *and* THE MUMMY *can be seen in there sitting motionless and silent. A part of the death screen is also visible.*
5 *To the left in the rear a door to the pantry and the kitchen.* THE STUDENT *and* THE YOUNG LADY *(Adele) are near a table, she seated at her harp, he standing beside her.*]

THE YOUNG LADY. Now you must sing a song
10 to my flowers!

THE STUDENT. Is this the flower of your soul?

THE YOUNG LADY. The one and only! Don't you love the hyacinth?

THE STUDENT. I love it above all other
15 flowers—its stem rising straight and slender, like a young maiden, from the round bulb, which floats on water and reaches its white rare roots down into clear, colorless nothingness. I love it for its colors: the snow-white,
20 innocent and pure—the golden yellow, sweet as honey—the shy pink, the ripe red—but above all the blue ones—blue as morning mist, deep-eyed blue, ever-faithful blue. I love them all—more than gold and pearls. Have loved
25 them ever since I was a child, have worshiped them because they possess all the virtues I lack . . . But still—

THE YOUNG LADY. What?

THE STUDENT. My love is not returned. These
30 beautiful blossoms hate and detest me.

THE YOUNG LADY. How?

THE STUDENT. Their fragrance—as strong and clear as the first winds of spring, sweeping down from the fields of melting snow—confuse
35 my senses—they deafen me, blind me, drive me out of my mind—impale me with their poisonous arrows that stab my heart and set my head afire! . . . Don't you know the legend of that flower? °
40 THE YOUNG LADY. No. Tell me.

THE STUDENT. First I must tell you what it means as a symbol. The bulb is the earth,

---

legend of that flower the exquisite youth Hyacinthus
was accidentally slain by his lover Apollo. The flower
that arose from his blood, the hyacinth, hence bears
on its leaves the letters *AI*, an exclamation of woe.

---

whether floating on water or buried deep in black humus. Here the stalk shoots up, straight as the axis of the world, and here at its upper 45 end are gathered together the six-pointed star flowers.

THE YOUNG LADY. Above the earth, the stars! How sublime! How did you know that? Where did you discover that? 50

THE STUDENT. I don't know. Let me think.— In your eyes! . . . So you see, it's an image of the whole cosmos. That's why Buddha sits there with the bulb of the earth in his lap, watching it constantly in order to see it shoot 55 up and burst forth and be transformed into a heaven. This poor earth shall become a heaven! That is what Buddha is waiting for!

THE YOUNG LADY. Of course! I see that now! —And don't the snowflakes have six points 60 like the hyacinth?

THE STUDENT. Exactly! Then snowflakes are falling stars—

THE YOUNG LADY. And the snowdrop is a snow-star—growing out of the snow. 65

THE STUDENT. And Sirius, the largest and most beautiful of all the stars in the firmament, golden-red Sirius is the narcissus with its golden-red chalice and its six white rays—

THE YOUNG LADY. Have you seen the shalot 70 burst into bloom?

THE STUDENT. Yes, of course I have! It hides its blossoms in a ball—a globe just like the celestial globe, strewn with white stars.

THE YOUNG LADY. How heavenly! Wonder- 75 ful! Whose idea was it?

THE STUDENT. Yours!

THE YOUNG LADY. Yours!

THE STUDENT. Ours. We have given birth to something together. We are wedded. . . . 80

THE YOUNG LADY. No, not yet. . . .

THE STUDENT. Why not? What else?

THE YOUNG LADY. Time—testing—patience.

THE STUDENT. Very well! Put me to the test! [*Pause.*] So silent? . . . Why do your parents 85 sit in there, silent, without saying a single word?

THE YOUNG LADY. Because they have nothing to say to each other, because they don't believe what the other says. My father explains it this way: He says, "What good does talking do, we can't fool each other anyway."

THE STUDENT. It makes me sick to hear things
5 like that. . . .

THE YOUNG LADY. The cook is coming this way. . . . Look at her, how big and fat she is. . . .

THE STUDENT. What does she want?

10 THE YOUNG LADY. She wants to ask me about dinner. I've been managing the house during my mother's illness.

THE STUDENT. What have we got to do with the kitchen?

15 THE YOUNG LADY. We have to eat, don't we? . . . Look at her, look at her. I can't bear to. . . .

THE STUDENT. Who is that bloated monster?

THE YOUNG LADY. She belongs to the Hummel family of vampires. She's eating us up. . . .

20 THE STUDENT. Why don't you fire her?

THE YOUNG LADY. She won't leave! We can't control her. We got her because of our sins. . . . Don't you see that we're wasting away, withering?

25 THE STUDENT. Don't you get enough food to eat?

THE YOUNG LADY. We get course after course, but all the strength is gone from the food. She boils the beef until there's nothing
30 left of it and serves us the sinews swimming in water while she herself drinks the stock. And when we have a roast, she cooks all the juice out of it and drinks it and eats the gravy. Everything she touches loses its flavor. It's as
35 if she sucked it up with her very eyes. We get the grounds when she has finished her coffee. She drinks the wine and fills up the bottles with water.

THE STUDENT. Get rid of her!

40 THE YOUNG LADY. We can't!

THE STUDENT. Why not?

THE YOUNG LADY. We don't know! She won't leave! No one can control her. . . . She has taken all our strength from us.

45 THE STUDENT. Let me get rid of her for you.

THE YOUNG LADY. Oh, no! I guess this is how it's supposed to be. . . . Here she is! She'll ask

me what we're having for dinner—I'll tell her this and that—she'll make objections—and finally we'll have what she says.   50

THE STUDENT. Then let her decide in the first place!

THE YOUNG LADY. She won't do that.

THE STUDENT. What a strange house! It's haunted, isn't it?   55

THE YOUNG LADY. Yes.—She's turning back now. She saw you!

THE COOK [*in the doorway*]. Hah, that ain't why! [*Grinning so that all her teeth show.*]

THE STUDENT. Get out!   60

THE COOK. When I feel like it I will! [*Pause.*] Now I feel like it!

[*She vanishes.*]

THE YOUNG LADY. Don't lose your temper. Learn to be patient. She's part of the trials   65
and tribulations we have to go through in this home. And we've got a housemaid, too! Whom we have to clean up after!

THE STUDENT. I can feel myself sinking into the earth!—*Cor in aethere!*°—Let's have   70
music!

THE YOUNG LADY. Wait!

THE STUDENT. No! Music now!

THE YOUNG LADY. Patience!—This room is called the testing room. It's beautiful to look   75
at, but it's full of imperfections.

THE STUDENT. I don't believe it. But if it's true we'll just have to ignore them. It's beautiful, but a little cold. Why don't you start the fire?   80

THE YOUNG LADY. Because it smokes up the room.

THE STUDENT. Can't you have the chimney cleaned?

THE YOUNG LADY. It doesn't help! . . . Do you   85
see that writing table?

THE STUDENT. What an extraordinarily handsome piece!

THE YOUNG LADY. But it wobbles. Every day I lay a piece of cork under that foot, but the   90
housemaid takes it away when she sweeps, and I have to cut a new piece. The penholder is

Cor in aethere   heart in air

covered with ink every morning, and so is the
inkstand, and I have to clean them up after her,
as regularly as the sun goes up. [*Pause.*] What
do you hate most to do?

5　THE STUDENT. To sort the week's wash!
[*Grimaces in disgust.*]

THE YOUNG LADY. That's what I have to do!
[*Grimacing in disgust.*]

THE STUDENT. What else?

10　THE YOUNG LADY. To be awakened in the
middle of the night, to have to get up and close
the banging window—which the housemaid
forgot to close.

THE STUDENT. Go on.

15　THE YOUNG LADY. To climb up on a ladder
and fix the damper on the stovepipe after the
maid broke off the cord.

THE STUDENT. Go on.

THE YOUNG LADY. To sweep up after her, to
20　dust after her, and to start the fire in the stove
after her—all she does is throw on some wood!
To adjust the damper, to dry the glasses, to set
the table *over* and *over* again, to pull the corks
out of the bottles, to open the windows and air
25　the rooms, to make and remake my bed, to
rinse the water bottle when it's green with
sediment, to buy matches and soap, which
we're always out of, to wipe the chimneys and
trim the wicks to keep the lamps from smoking
30　—and to keep the lamps from going out I have
to fill them myself when we have company. . . .

THE STUDENT. Let's have music!

THE YOUNG LADY. You have to wait!—First
comes the drudgery, the drudgery of keeping
35　oneself above the dirt of life.

THE STUDENT. But you're well off. You've got
two servants!

THE YOUNG LADY. Doesn't make any difference! Even if we had three! Living is such a
40　nuisance, and I get so tired at times. . . .
Imagine, if on top of it all one had a nursery
and a baby crib.

THE STUDENT. The dearest of joys!

THE YOUNG LADY. The dearest in more ways
45　than one. . . . Is life really worth so much
trouble?

THE STUDENT. I suppose that depends on the
reward you expect for all your troubles. . . .

There's nothing I wouldn't do to win your
hand.　50

THE YOUNG LADY. Don't say that! You can
never have me!

THE STUDENT. Why not?

THE YOUNG LADY. You mustn't ask.
[*Pause.*]　55

THE STUDENT. You dropped your bracelet out
of the window. . . .

THE YOUNG LADY. Because my hand has
grown so thin.

[*Pause.* THE COOK *appears with a Japanese*　60
bottle in her hand.]
She's the one who's eating me—and all the rest
of us.

THE STUDENT. What is she holding in her
hand?　65

THE YOUNG LADY. It's a bottle of coloring
matter. It's got letters on it that look like scorpions. It's filled with soya sauce—which takes
the place of gravy, which is transformed into
soup, which serves as stock for cooking cab-　70
bage in, which is used to make mock turtle
soup. . . .

THE STUDENT. Get out!

THE COOK. You suck the sap from us, and
we from you. We take the blood and give you　75
back water—with coloring added. This is the
coloring!—I'm leaving now, but that doesn't
mean I haven't stayed as long as I wanted to.
[*She leaves.*]

THE STUDENT. Why was Bengtsson given a　80
medal?

THE YOUNG LADY. Because of his great
merits.

THE STUDENT. Has he no faults?

THE YOUNG LADY. Yes, many great ones. But　85
you don't get medals for them.
[*They smile at each other.*]

THE STUDENT. You have a great many secrets
in this house.

THE YOUNG LADY. As in all houses. Permit us　90
to keep ours.
[*Pause.*]

THE STUDENT. Do you admire frankness?

THE YOUNG LADY. Yes, within moderation.

THE STUDENT. Sometimes there comes over　95
me a crazy desire to say everything I'm think-

ing. But I know the world would collapse completely if one were completely honest. [*Pause.*] I went to a funeral the other day. . . . In church. . . . Very solemn, very beautiful.

5 THE YOUNG LADY. Mr. Hummel's funeral?

THE STUDENT. Yes, my false benefactor's. At the head of the coffin stood an old friend of the deceased. He carried the mace. The priest impressed me especially, his dignified manner
10 and his moving words. I cried. We all cried. And afterwards we went to a restaurant. . . . And there I learned that the macebearer had been the lover of the dead man's son.

[THE YOUNG LADY *stares at him, trying to*
15 *understand him.*]

And that the dead man had borrowed money from his son's admirer. . . . [*Pause.*] The day after that, they arrested the priest for embezzling church funds! It's a pretty story, isn't
20 it?

[THE YOUNG LADY *turns her head away in disgust. Pause.*]

Do you know what I think of you now?

THE YOUNG LADY. You must not tell me or
25 I'll die!

THE STUDENT. But I must or I'll die!

THE YOUNG LADY. In an asylum they say whatever they feel like.

THE STUDENT. Exactly right! That's where my
30 father ended up—in a madhouse.

THE YOUNG LADY. Was he ill?

THE STUDENT. No, he was quite healthy. But he was crazy! It just came over him. Let me tell you how it happened. . . . Like all of us, he had
35 his circle of acquaintances, whom for convenience' sake he called his friends. Of course they were a pretty sorry bunch of good-for-nothings—like most people. But he had to have some acquaintances, he couldn't just sit alone.
40 Now one doesn't tell a person what one really thinks of him, not in ordinary conversation anyway—and my father didn't either. He knew how false they were. He saw through their deceitfulness right to the bottom of their souls.
45 But he was an intelligent man, brought up to behave properly, and so he was always polite. But one day he held a big party. It was in the evening, he was tired after a day's work, and

under the strain of forcing himself to hold his tongue half the time and of talking nonsense 50 with his guests the other half. . . .

[THE YOUNG LADY *shudders in fear.*]

Well, whatever the reason, at the dinner table he rapped for silence, raised his glass, and began to make a speech. . . . Then something 55 loosed the trigger, and in a long oration he stripped naked every single person there, one after another. Told them of all their deceits. And at the end, exhausted, he sat right down in the middle of the table and told them all to 60 go to hell!

[THE YOUNG LADY *moans.*]

I was there and heard it all, and I shall never forget what happened afterwards. . . . Father and Mother began to fight, the guests rushed 65 for the door—and my father was taken off to the madhouse where he died! [*Pause.*] If you keep silent too long, stagnant water begins to accumulate and things begin to rot. That's what's happening in this house. Something's 70 rotting here. And I thought it was paradise when I saw you come in here for the first time. . . . It was a Sunday morning, and I stood looking into these rooms. I saw a colonel who wasn't a colonel. I had a magnanimous bene- 75 factor who turned out to be a bandit and had to hang himself. I saw a mummy who wasn't one, and a maiden who—speaking of which, where can one find virginity? Where is beauty to be found? In nature, and my mind when it's 80 all dressed up in its Sunday clothes. Where do honor and faith exist? In fairy tales and children's games! Where can you find anything that fulfills its promise? Only in one's imagination! . . . Now your flowers have poisoned me, 85 and I have passed the poison back. I begged you to become my wife in my home. We played and we sang. We created poetry together. And then came the cook. . . . *Sursum corda!* Try just once again to pluck fire and brightness 90 from the golden harp! Please try! I beg you, I implore you on my knees! . . . Very well. Then I shall do it myself. [*He takes the harp but no sound comes from the strings.*] It is silent and deaf. Tell me, why are beautiful flowers so 95 poisonous, and the most beautiful the most

deadly? Why? The whole of creation, all of life, is cursed and damned. . . . Why would you not become my bride? Because you are sick, infected at the very core of life. . . . Now I can
5 feel that vampire in the kitchen beginning to suck the blood from me. She must be one of those lamias that suck the blood of suckling babes. It's always in the kitchen that the children are nipped in the bud. And if not there,
10 then in the bedroom. . . . There are poisons that seal the eyes and poisons that open them. I must have been born with the latter kind in my veins, because I cannot see what is ugly as beautiful and I cannot call what is evil good.
15 I cannot. They say that Christ harrowed hell. What they really meant was that he descended to earth, to this penal colony, to this madhouse and morgue of a world. And the inmates crucified Him when He tried to free them. But
20 the robber they let free. Robbers always win sympathy. . . . Woe! Woe to all of us! Saviour of the World, save us! We are perishing!

[THE YOUNG LADY has collapsed more and more during this speech. She is obviously
25 dying. She rings the bell. BENGTSSON enters.]

THE YOUNG LADY. Bring the screen. Quickly! I'm dying.

[BENGTSSON returns with the screen, opens it, and places it in front of THE YOUNG LADY.]

30 THE STUDENT. Your liberator is coming! Welcome, pale and gentle one. . . . And you, you beautiful, innocent, lost soul, who suffer for no fault of your own, sleep, sleep a dreamless sleep. And when you wake again . . . may you
35 be greeted by a sun that doesn't scorch, in a home without dust, by friends without faults, and by a love without flaw. . . . Buddha, wise and gentle Buddha, sitting there waiting for a heaven to grow out of the earth, grant us the
40 purity of will and the patience to endure our trials, that your hopes will not come to nought. [The harp strings begin to move and hum. Pure white light pours into the room.]

I saw the sun
45 And from its blaze
There burst on me
The deepest truth:

Man reaps as he sows;
Blessed is he
Who sows the good. 50

For deeds done in anger
Kindness alone
Can make amends.

Bring cheer to those
Whom you have hurt, 55
And kindness reaps
Its own rewards.

The pure in heart
Have none to fear
The harmless are happy. 60
The guileless are good.

[A moaning is heard from behind the screen.]
You poor little child! Child of this world of illusion and guilt and suffering and death— 65
this world of eternal change and disappointment and never-ending pain! May the Lord of Heaven have mercy on you as you journey forth. . . .

[The room vanishes. In the distance Boeck- 70
lin's The Island of the Dead appears.° Music—soft, pleasant, and melancholy—is heard coming from the island.]

Curtain

appears bearing, Strindberg proposes, the Apocalypse 21:4 as a legend: "And God shall wipe away all tears from their eyes; and there shall be no more death, neither sorrow, nor crying, neither shall there be any more pain: for the former things are passed away."

Luigi Pirandello

1867–1936

Six Characters in Search of an Author

1921

As Pirandello's title indicates, one should check his accustomed expectations with his coat before he enters the theater. The play is about *characters,* which are not the same as *actors,* although actors play them, and not the same as *people,* although they bleed when pricked, laugh when tickled, and die—after a fashion—when drowned or shot.

The ostensive topic of the play, then, is the theater. Its world is the boards, lights, and props; the actors, managers, and prompters; the books, plots, and characters. And its integrating motive is, as the critic Francis Fergusson says, " 'to take the stage'—with all that this suggestive phrase implies." In Fergusson's apt summary, "The real actors and the director want to take it for the realistic purposes—vain or (with the box-office in mind) venal—of their rehearsal. Each of the characters wants to take it for the rationalized myth which is, or would be, his very being."

As the characters vie with the actors for the stage, the play brilliantly exploits the paradoxes implicit in its central metaphor. The astonished spectator is asked to consider competing approximations of reality: the immutable world of the dramatist's creation, the ordered but conventionalized world of the theater, and the evanescent and disordered world of his own personal experience. Is he himself more significantly alive than the perennial if stereotypical roles of an acting company? Or than the intensely realized and proverbially immortal figments of the artistic imaginations? What is truth? the play demands. And, having teased us with its paradoxes, it leaves the question unanswered.

Except for the Manager, who keeps bumping into these paradoxes—now manfully seeking to surmount them, now impatiently brushing them aside—the acting troupe is thinly drawn. The actors are shallow, vain, and pedestrian in their responses. Yet they occupy the stage from first to last, along with the characters, and serve a multitude of functions. They support the Manager's skeptical and pragmatic opinion, urging him toward a popular and commonsense point of view. With him they provide moments of amusement, raising their noses at the characters, indulging in fits of jealousy, and themselves becoming, for splendid moments, the butt of the Father's and the Step-Daughter's laughter. More significantly, as they seek to render the drama before them banal and conventional, they both intensify its horror and lend it esthetic distance, setting it off for our own clearer vision.

The horror we experience derives immediately from the deeds and interrelations of the six characters: the stillbirth of the original marriage, the revolting intimacy of Father and Step-Daughter in the bordello, the emotional incapacitation of the Son, the agony of the Mother unable to commune with him, and the deaths of the little children by drowning and suicide. These are nevertheless only the stuff of melodrama. Our emotion goes deeper than that.

The characters are trapped by self-isolation. Whatever they say to one another, they are unable to escape from or mitigate the egocentricity that each brings to the common doom. The Father may express his sentiments for the Mother, but he cannot influence her feelings. The son may be told again and again how he is destroying Mother and children, but he cannot desist. Each is locked in the prison of himself—fulfilling thereby one theological and literary definition of damnation.

They are really not in this world but in a kind of hell. In the world of our personal experience, the shames and agonies yield little by little to the ministry of time. We simply forget. Or, by reliving our failures and embarrassments in dreams and memories and conversations, we wear them down. It is not so for these characters. For them there is no rest from pain, because they are *characters*. For them, to die is not to sleep, because they are immortal: death is only a point on the circumference of an endless circle; the final gunshot only presages recurrences of the same agony. Furthermore, the characters are forever self-conscious. In every moment until the end of time each will rationalize his dilemma, extenuate his faults, and struggle to shift from his shoulders the burden of shame. None will ever know where he really stands. For each of them—as also, ultimately, for the Manager and the actors— the quality and texture and even the actuality of his existence will always evade him. The only constants are that he will remain alone and that he will suffer.

Six Characters so blends its grimness, its banality, and its philosophical play that to focus on any one at the expense of the others is to miss the richness of Pirandello's evocation. But there is a question of how, ideally, one ought to respond to the ambivalence of this theater piece. Pirandello himself ultimately chose to stand apart from his characters rather than with them. More the contemplative spectator than the empathic witness, closer to Shaw than to Ibsen, he somewhat curiously subtitled his play "A *Comedy* in the Making" (italics added).

Six Characters in Search of an Author

A Comedy in the Making

PIRANDELLO

CHARACTERS OF THE COMEDY IN THE MAKING

THE FATHER
THE MOTHER
THE STEP-DAUGHTER
THE SON
THE BOY
THE CHILD
(*The last two do not speak*)
MADAME PACE

ACTORS OF THE COMPANY

THE MANAGER
LEADING LADY
LEADING MAN
SECOND LADY LEAD
L'INGÉNUE
JUVENILE LEAD
OTHER ACTORS AND ACTRESSES
PROPERTY MAN
PROMPTER
MACHINIST
MANAGER'S SECRETARY
DOOR-KEEPER

SCENE-SHIFTERS
STAGE HANDS

Daytime. The Stage of a Theatre

N.B. *The Comedy is without acts or scenes. The performance is interrupted once, without the curtain being lowered, when the manager and the chief characters withdraw to arrange the scenario. A second interruption of the action takes place when, by mistake, the stage hands let the curtain down.*

ACT I

[*The spectators will find the curtain raised and the stage as it usually is during the day time. It will be half dark, and empty, so that from the beginning the public may have the impression of an impromptu performance.*

Prompter's box and a small table and chair for the MANAGER.

Two other small tables and several chairs scattered about as during rehearsals.

The ACTORS *and* ACTRESSES *of the company enter from the back of the stage: first one, then another, then two together; nine or ten in all. They are about to rehearse a Pirandello play: "Mixing It Up". Some of the company move off towards their dressing rooms. The* PROMPTER *who has the "book" under his arm, is waiting for the* MANAGER *in order to begin the rehearsal.*

The ACTORS *and* ACTRESSES, *some standing, some sitting, chat and smoke. One perhaps reads a paper; another cons his part.*

Finally, the MANAGER *enters and goes to the table prepared for him. His* SECRETARY *brings him his mail, through which he glances. The* PROMPTER *takes his seat, turns on a light, and opens the "book."*]

THE MANAGER [*throwing a letter down on the table*]. I can't see. [*To* PROPERTY MAN.] Let's have a little light, please!

PROPERTY MAN. Yes sir, yes, at once. [*A light comes down on to the stage.*]

THE MANAGER [*clapping his hands*]. Come along! Come along! Second act of "Mixing It Up." [*Sits down.*]

[*The* Actors *and* Actresses *go from the front of the stage to the wings, all except the three who are to begin the rehearsal.*]

The Prompter [*reading the "book"*]. "Leo
5 Gala's house. A curious room serving as dining-room and study."

The Manager [*to* Property Man]. Fix up the old red room.

Property Man [*noting it down*]. Red set.
10 All right!

The Prompter [*continuing to read from the "book"*]. "Table already laid and writing desk with books and papers. Book-shelves. Exit rear to Leo's bedroom. Exit left to kitchen. Principal
15 exit to right."

The Manager [*energetically*]. Well, you understand: The principal exit over there; here, the kitchen. [*Turning to* Actor *who is to play the part of* Socrates.] You make your en-
20 trances and exits here. [*To* Property Man.] The baize doors at the rear, and curtains.

Property Man [*noting it down*]. Right!

Prompter [*reading as before*]. "When the curtain rises, Leo Gala, dressed in cook's cap
25 and apron is busy beating an egg in a cup. Philip, also dressed as a cook, is beating another egg. Guido Venanzi is seated and listening."

Leading Man [*to* Manager]. Excuse me,
30 but must I absolutely wear a cook's cap?

The Manager [*annoyed*]. I imagine so. It says so there anyway. [*Pointing to the "book."*]

Leading Man. But it's ridiculous!

35 The Manager [*jumping up in a rage*]. Ridiculous? Ridiculous? Is it my fault if France won't send us any more good comedies, and we are reduced to putting on Pirandello's works, where nobody understands anything,
40 and where the author plays the fool with us all? [*The* Actors *grin. The* Manager *goes to* Leading Man *and shouts.*] Yes sir, you put on the cook's cap and beat eggs. Do you suppose that with all this egg-beating business you are
45 on an ordinary stage? Get that out of your head. You represent the shell of the eggs you are beating! [*Laughter and comments among*

the Actors.] Silence! and listen to my explanations, please! [*To* Leading Man.] "The empty form of reason without the fullness of 50 instinct, which is blind."—You stand for reason, your wife is instinct. It's a mixing up of the parts, according to which you who act your own part become the puppet of yourself. Do you understand? 55

Leading Man. I'm hanged if I do.

The Manager. Neither do I. But let's get on with it. It's sure to be a glorious failure anyway. [*Confidentially.*] But I say, please face three-quarters. Otherwise, what with the 60 abstruseness of the dialogue, and the public that won't be able to hear you, the whole thing will go to hell. Come on! come on!

Prompter. Pardon sir, may I get into my box? There's a bit of a draft. 65

The Manager. Yes, yes, of course!

[*At this point, the* Door-keeper *has entered from the stage door and advances towards the* Manager's *table, taking off his braided cap. During this maneuver, the* Six Characters 70 *enter, and stop by the door at back of stage, so that when the* Door-keeper *is about to announce their coming to the* Manager, *they are already on the stage. A tenuous light surrounds them, almost as if irradiated by them* 75 *—the faint breath of their fantastic reality.*

This light will disappear when they come forward towards the actors. They preserve, however, something of the dream lightness in which they seem almost suspended; but this 80 *does not detract from the essential reality of their forms and expressions.*

He who is known as the Father *is a man of about 50: hair, reddish in color, thin at the temples; he is not bald, however; thick* 85 *moustaches, falling over his still fresh mouth, which often opens in an empty and uncertain smile. He is fattish, pale; with an especially wide forehead. He has blue, oval-shaped eyes, very clear and piercing. Wears light trousers* 90 *and a dark jacket. He is alternatively mellifluous and violent in his manner.*

The Mother *seems crushed and terrified as if by an intolerable weight of shame and* abasement. *She is dressed in modest black and wears a thick widow's veil of crêpe. When she lifts this, she reveals a wax-like face. She always keeps her eyes downcast.*

5 *The* STEP-DAUGHTER *is dashing, almost impudent, beautiful. She wears mourning too, but with great elegance. She shows contempt for the timid half-frightened manner of the wretched* BOY (14 *years old, and also dressed*
10 *in black); on the other hand, she displays a lively tenderness for her little sister, the* CHILD *(about four), who is dressed in white, with a black silk sash at the waist.*

The SON (22) *tall, severe in his attitude of*
15 *contempt for the* FATHER, *supercilious and indifferent to the* MOTHER. *He looks as if he had come on the stage against his will.*]

DOOR-KEEPER [*cap in hand*]. Excuse me, sir . . .
20 THE MANAGER [*rudely*]. Eh? What is it?

DOOR-KEEPER [*timidly*]. These people are asking for you, sir.

THE MANAGER [*furious*]. I am rehearsing, and you know perfectly well no one's allowed
25 to come in during rehearsals! [*Turning to the* CHARACTERS.] Who are you, please? What do you want?

THE FATHER [*coming forward a little, followed by the others who seem embarrassed*].
30 As a matter of fact . . . we have come here in search of an author . . .

THE MANAGER [*half angry, half amazed*]. An author? What author?

THE FATHER. Any author, sir.
35 THE MANAGER. But there's no author here. We are not rehearsing a new piece.

THE STEP-DAUGHTER [*vivaciously*]. So much the better, so much the better! We can be your new piece.
40 AN ACTOR [*coming forward from the others*]. Oh, do you hear that?

THE FATHER [*to* STEP-DAUGHTER]. Yes, but if the author isn't here . . . [*to* MANAGER] unless you would be willing . . .
45 THE MANAGER. You are trying to be funny.

THE FATHER. No, for Heaven's sake, what are you saying? We bring you a drama, sir.

THE STEP-DAUGHTER. We may be your fortune.

THE MANAGER. Will you oblige me by going 50 away? We haven't time to waste with mad people.

THE FATHER [*mellifluously*]. Oh sir, you know well that life is full of infinite absurdities, which, strangely enough, do not even need to 55 appear plausible, since they are true.

THE MANAGER. What the devil is he talking about?

THE FATHER. I say that to reverse the ordinary process may well be considered a 60 madness: that is, to create credible situations, in order that they may appear true. But permit me to observe that if this be madness, it is the sole *raison d'être* of your profession, gentlemen. [*The* ACTORS *look hurt and perplexed.*] 65

THE MANAGER [*getting up and looking at him*]. So our profession seems to you one worthy of madmen then?

THE FATHER. Well, to make seem true that which isn't true . . . without any need . . . for 70 a joke as it were. . . . Isn't that your mission, gentlemen: to give life to fantastic characters on the stage?

THE MANAGER [*interpreting the rising anger of the* COMPANY]. But I would beg you to 75 believe, my dear sir, that the profession of the comedian is a noble one. If today, as things go, the playwrights give us stupid comedies to play and puppets to represent instead of men, remember we are proud to have given life to 80 immortal works here on these very boards! [*The* ACTORS, *satisfied, applaud their* MANAGER.]

THE FATHER [*interrupting furiously*]. Exactly, perfectly, to living beings more alive than those who breathe and wear clothes: beings less 85 real perhaps, but truer! I agree with you entirely. [*The* ACTORS *look at one another in amazement.*]

THE MANAGER. But what do you mean? Before, you said . . . 90

THE FATHER. No, excuse me, I meant it for you, sir, who were crying out that you had no time to lose with madmen, while no one better than yourself knows that nature uses the instrument of human fantasy in order to pursue her creative purpose.

THE MANAGER. Very well,—but where does all this take us?

5 THE FATHER. Nowhere! It is merely to show you that one is born to life in many forms, in many shapes, as tree, or as stone, as water, as butterfly, or as woman. So one may also be born a character in a play.

10 THE MANAGER [*with feigned comic dismay*]. So you and these other friends of yours have been born characters?

THE FATHER. Exactly, and alive as you see! [MANAGER *and* ACTORS *burst out laughing.*]

15 THE FATHER [*hurt*]. I am sorry you laugh, because we carry in us a drama, as you can guess from this woman here veiled in black.

THE MANAGER [*losing patience at last and almost indignant*]. Oh, chuck it! Get away

20 please! Clear out of here! [*To* PROPERTY MAN.] For Heaven's sake, turn them out!

THE FATHER [*resisting*]. No, no, look here, we . . .

THE MANAGER [*roaring*]. We come here to

25 work, you know.

LEADING ACTOR. One cannot let oneself be made such a fool of.

THE FATHER [*determined, coming forward*]. I marvel at your incredulity, gentlemen. Are

30 you not accustomed to see the characters created by an author spring to life in yourselves and face each other? Just because there is no "book" [*pointing to the* PROMPTER's *box*] which contains us, you refuse to believe . . .

35 THE STEP-DAUGHTER [*advances towards* MANAGER, *smiling and coquettish*]. Believe me, we are really six most interesting characters, sir; side-tracked however.

THE FATHER. Yes, that is the word! [*To*

40 MANAGER *all at once.*] In the sense, that is, that the author who created us alive no longer wished, or was no longer able, materially to put us into a work of art. And this was a real crime, sir; because he who has had the luck

45 to be born a character can laugh even at death. He cannot die. The man, the writer, the instrument of the creation will die, but his creation does not die. And to live for ever, it does not need to have extraordinary gifts or to be able to work wonders. Who was Sancho Panza?

50 Who was Don Abbondio?° Yet they live eternally because—live germs as they were— they had the fortune to find a fecundating matrix, a fantasy which could raise and nourish them: make them live for ever!

55 THE MANAGER. That is quite all right. But what do you want here, all of you?

THE FATHER. We want to live.

THE MANAGER [*ironically*]. For Eternity?

THE FATHER. No, sir, only for a moment . . .

60 in you.

AN ACTOR. Just listen to him!

LEADING LADY. They want to live, in us . . . !

JUVENILE LEAD [*pointing to the* STEP-DAUGHTER]. I've no objection, as far as that one is

65 concerned!

THE FATHER. Look here! look here! The comedy has to be made. [*To the* MANAGER.] But if you and your actors are willing, we can soon concert it among ourselves.

70 THE MANAGER [*annoyed*]. But what do you want to concert? We don't go in for concerts here. Here we play dramas and comedies!

THE FATHER. Exactly! That is just why we have come to you.

75 THE MANAGER. And where is the "book"?

THE FATHER. It is in us! [*The* ACTORS *laugh.*] The drama is in us, and we are the drama. We are impatient to play it. Our inner passion drives us on to this.

80 THE STEP-DAUGHTER [*disdainful, alluring, treacherous, full of impudence*]. My passion, sir! Ah, if you only knew! My passion for him! [*Points to the* FATHER *and makes a pretense of embracing him. Then she breaks out*

85 *into a loud laugh.*]

THE FATHER [*angrily*]. Behave yourself! And please don't laugh in that fashion.

THE STEP-DAUGHTER. With your permission, gentlemen, I, who am a two months' orphan,

90 will show you how I can dance and sing.

Don Abbondio the parish priest in Manzoni's *The Betrothed (I Promessi Sposi,* 1825-1826)

[*Sings and then dances* Prenez garde à Tchou-Tchin-Tchou.°]

> Les chinois sont un peuple malin,
> De Shangaî à Pekin,
> 5   Ils ont mis des écriteaux partout:
> Prenez garde à Tchou-Tchin-Tchou.

ACTORS AND ACTRESSES. Bravo! Well done! Tip-top!

THE MANAGER. Silence! This isn't a café 10 concert, you know! [*Turning to the* FATHER *in consternation.*] Is she mad?

THE FATHER. Mad? No, she's worse than mad.

THE STEP-DAUGHTER [*to* MANAGER]. Worse? 15 Worse? Listen! Stage this drama for us at once! Then you will see that at a certain moment I . . . when this little darling here . . . [*takes the* CHILD *by the hand and leads her to the* MANAGER]. Isn't she a dear? [*Takes her up* 20 *and kisses her.*] Darling! Darling! [*Puts her down again and adds feelingly.*] Well, when God suddenly takes this dear little child away from that poor mother there; and this imbecile here [*seizing hold of the* BOY *roughly and push-* 25 *ing him forward*] does the stupidest things, like the fool he is, you will see me run away. Yes, gentlemen, I shall be off. But the moment hasn't arrived yet. After what has taken place between him and me [*indicates the* FATHER 30 *with a horrible wink*] I can't remain any longer in this society, to have to witness the anguish of this mother here for that fool . . . [*indicates the* SON]. Look at him! Look at him! See how indifferent, how frigid he is, because he is the 35 legitimate son. He despises me, despises him [*pointing to the* BOY], despises this baby here; because . . . we are bastards. [*Goes to the* MOTHER *and embraces her.*] And he doesn't

---

Prenez . . . Tchou-Tchin-Tchou "beware of Chu-Chin-Chow," a French version of "Chu-Chin-Chow," a lyric from the *Ziegfeld Follies of 1917* celebrating the current success on Broadway of the musical revue *Chu Chin Chow*, book by Oscar Asche, music by Frederic Norton. The first stanza of the French version follows: "The Chinese are a cunning folk, From Shanghai to Peking, They've put up posters everywhere: Beware of Chu-Chin Chow."

want to recognize her as his mother—she who is the common mother of us all. He looks 40 down upon her as if she were only the mother of us three bastards. Wretch! [*She says all this very rapidly, excitedly. At the word "bastards" she raises her voice, and almost spits out the final "Wretch!"*] 45

THE MOTHER [*to the* MANAGER, *in anguish*]. In the name of these two little children, I beg you . . . [*she grows faint and is about to fall*]. Oh God!

THE FATHER [*coming forward to support her* 50 *as do some of the* ACTORS]. Quick, a chair, a chair for this poor widow!

THE ACTORS. Is it true? Has she really fainted?

THE MANAGER. Quick, a chair! Here! 55 [*One of the* ACTORS *brings a chair, the* OTHERS *proffer assistance. The* MOTHER *tries to prevent the* FATHER *from lifting the veil which covers her face.*]

THE FATHER. Look at her! Look at her! 60

THE MOTHER. No, no; stop it please!

THE FATHER [*raising her veil*]. Let them see you!

THE MOTHER [*rising and covering her face with her hands, in desperation*]. I beg you, sir, 65 to prevent this man from carrying out his plan which is loathsome to me.

THE MANAGER [*dumbfounded*]. I don't understand at all. What is the situation? Is this lady your wife? [*To the* FATHER.] 70

THE FATHER. Yes, gentlemen: my wife!

THE MANAGER. But how can she be a widow if you are alive? [*The* ACTORS *find relief for their astonishment in a loud laugh.*]

THE FATHER. Don't laugh! Don't laugh like 75 that, for Heaven's sake. Her drama lies just here in this: she has had a lover, a man who ought to be here.

THE MOTHER [*with a cry*]. No! No!

THE STEP-DAUGHTER. Fortunately for her, he 80 is dead. Two months ago as I said. We are in mourning, as you see.

THE FATHER. He isn't here you see, not because he is dead. He isn't here—look at her a moment and you will understand—because 85 her drama isn't a drama of the love of two men for whom she was incapable of feeling anything except possibly a little gratitude—gratitude not for me but for the other. She isn't a 5 woman, she is a mother, and her drama—powerful sir, I assure you—lies, as a matter of fact, all in these four children she has had by two men.

THE MOTHER. I had them? Have you got the 10 courage to say that I wanted them? [*To the* COMPANY.] It was his doing. It was he who gave me that other man, who forced me to go away with him.

THE STEP-DAUGHTER. It isn't true.

15 THE MOTHER [*startled*]. Not true, isn't it?

THE STEP-DAUGHTER. No, it isn't true, it just isn't true.

THE MOTHER. And what can you know about it?

20 THE STEP-DAUGHTER. It isn't true. Don't believe it. [*To* MANAGER.] Do you know why she says so? For that fellow there. [*Indicates the* SON.] She tortures herself, destroys herself on account of the neglect of that son there; 25 and she wants him to believe that if she abandoned him when he was only two years old, it was because he [*indicates the* FATHER] made her do so.

THE MOTHER [*vigorously*]. He forced me to 30 it, and I call God to witness it. [*To the* MANAGER.] Ask him [*indicates* HUSBAND] if it isn't true. Let him speak. You [*to* DAUGHTER] are not in a position to know anything about it.

THE STEP-DAUGHTER. I know you lived in 35 peace and happiness with my father while he lived. Can you deny it?

THE MOTHER. No, I don't deny it . . .

THE STEP-DAUGHTER. He was always full of affection and kindness for you. [*To the* BOY, 40 *angrily*.] It's true, isn't it? Tell them! Why don't you speak, you little fool?

THE MOTHER. Leave the poor boy alone. Why do you want to make me appear ungrateful, daughter? I don't want to offend your father. 45 I have answered him that I didn't abandon my house and my son through any fault of mine, nor from any wilful passion.

THE FATHER. It is true. It was my doing.

LEADING MAN [*to the* COMPANY]. What a spectacle! 50

LEADING LADY. We are the audience this time.

JUVENILE LEAD. For once, in a way.

THE MANAGER [*beginning to get really interested*]. Let's hear them out. Listen!

THE SON. Oh yes, you're going to hear a 55 fine bit now. He will talk to you of the Demon of Experiment.

THE FATHER. You are a cynical imbecile. I've told you so already a hundred times. [*To the* MANAGER.] He tries to make fun of me on 60 account of this expression which I have found to excuse myself with.

THE SON [*with disgust*]. Yes, phrases! phrases!

THE FATHER. Phrases! Isn't everyone con- 65 soled when faced with a trouble or fact he doesn't understand, by a word, some simple word, which tells us nothing and yet calms us?

THE STEP-DAUGHTER. Even in the case of remorse. In fact, especially then. 70

THE FATHER. Remorse? No, that isn't true. I've done more than use words to quiet the remorse in me.

THE STEP-DAUGHTER. Yes, there was a bit of money too. Yes, yes, a bit of money. There 75 were the hundred lire he was about to offer me in payment, gentlemen . . .

[*Sensation of horror among the* ACTORS.]

THE SON [*to the* STEP-DAUGHTER]. This is vile. 80

THE STEP-DAUGHTER. Vile? There they were in a pale blue envelope on a little mahogany table in the back of Madame Pace's shop. You know Madame Pace—one of those ladies who attract poor girls of good family into their 85 ateliers, under the pretext of their selling *robes et manteaux.*°

THE SON. And he thinks he has bought the right to tyrannize over us all with those hundred lire he was going to pay; but which, 90 fortunately—note this, gentlemen—he had no chance of paying.

THE STEP-DAUGHTER. It was a near thing, though, you know! [*Laughs ironically*.]

robes et manteaux dresses and cloaks.

THE MOTHER [*protesting*]. Shame, my daughter, shame!

THE STEP-DAUGHTER. Shame indeed! This is my revenge! I am dying to live that scene . . .

5 The room . . . I see it . . . Here is the window with the mantles exposed, there the divan, the looking-glass, a screen, there in front of the window the little mahogany table with the blue envelope containing one hundred lire. I

10 see it. I see it. I could take hold of it . . . But you, gentlemen, you ought to turn your backs now: I am almost nude, you know. But I don't blush: I leave that to him. [*Indicating* FATHER.]

THE MANAGER. I don't understand this at all.

15 THE FATHER. Naturally enough. I would ask you, sir, to exercise your authority a little here, and let me speak before you believe all she is trying to blame me with. Let me explain.

THE STEP-DAUGHTER. Ah yes, explain it in

20 your own way.

THE FATHER. But don't you see that the whole trouble lies here. In words, words. Each one of us has within him a whole world of things, each man of us his own special world. And

25 how can we ever come to an understanding if I put in the words I utter the sense and value of things as I see them; while you who listen to me must inevitably translate them according to the conception of things each one of you

30 has within himself. We think we understand each other, but we never really do. Look here! This woman [*indicating the* MOTHER] takes all my pity for her as a specially ferocious form of cruelty.

35 THE MOTHER. But you drove me away.

THE FATHER. Do you hear her? I drove her away! She believes I really sent her away.

THE MOTHER. You know how to talk, and I don't; but, believe me, sir [*to* MANAGER], after

40 he had married me . . . who knows why? . . . I was a poor insignificant woman . . .

THE FATHER. But, good Heavens! it was just for your humility that I married you. I loved this simplicity in you. [*He stops when he sees*

45 *she makes signs to contradict him, opens his arms wide in sign of desperation, seeing how hopeless it is to make himself understood.*] You see she denies it. Her mental deafness,

believe me, is phenomenal, the limit: [*touches his forehead*] deaf, deaf, mentally deaf! She

50 has plenty of feeling. Oh yes, a good heart for the children; but the brain—deaf, to the point of desperation—!

THE STEP-DAUGHTER. Yes, but ask him how his intelligence has helped us.

55 THE FATHER. If we could see all the evil that may spring from good, what should we do? [*At this point the* LEADING LADY *who is biting her lips with rage at seeing the* LEADING MAN *flirting with the* STEP-DAUGHTER, *comes for-*

60 *ward and says to the* MANAGER:]

LEADING LADY. Excuse me, but are we going to rehearse today?

MANAGER. Of course, of course; but let's hear them out.

65 JUVENILE LEAD. This is something quite new.

L'INGÉNUE. Most interesting!

LEADING LADY. Yes, for the people who like that kind of thing. [*Casts a glance at* LEADING MAN.]

70 THE MANAGER [*to* FATHER]. You must please explain yourself quite clearly. [*Sits down.*]

THE FATHER. Very well then: listen! I had in my service a poor man, a clerk, a secretary of mine, full of devotion, who became friends

75 with her. [*Indicating the* MOTHER.] They understood one another, were kindred souls in fact, without, however, the least suspicion of any evil existing. They were incapable even of thinking of it.

80 THE STEP-DAUGHTER. So he thought of it—for them!

THE FATHER. That's not true. I meant to do good to them—and to myself, I confess, at the same time. Things had come to the point

85 that I could not say a word to either of them without their making a mute appeal, one to the other, with their eyes. I could see them silently asking each other how I was to be kept in countenance, how I was to be kept

90 quiet. And this, believe me, was just about enough of itself to keep me in a constant rage, to exasperate me beyond measure.

THE MANAGER. And why didn't you send him away then—this secretary of yours?

95 THE FATHER. Precisely what I did, sir. And

then I had to watch this poor woman drifting forlornly about the house like an animal without a master, like an animal one has taken in out of pity.

5 THE MOTHER. Ah yes . . . !

THE FATHER [*suddenly turning to the* MOTHER]. It's true about the son anyway, isn't it?

THE MOTHER. He took my son away from 10 me first of all.

THE FATHER. But not from cruelty. I did it so that he should grow up healthy and strong by living in the country.

THE STEP-DAUGHTER [*pointing to him iron-* 15 *ically*]. As one can see.

THE FATHER [*quickly*]. Is it my fault if he has grown up like this? I sent him to a wet nurse in the country, a peasant, as *she* did not seem to me strong enough, though she is of 20 humble origin. That was, anyway, the reason I married her. Unpleasant all this may be, but how can it be helped? My mistake possibly, but there we are! All my life I have had these confounded aspirations towards a certain moral 25 sanity. [*At this point the* STEP-DAUGHTER *bursts into a noisy laugh.*] Oh, stop it! Stop it! I can't stand it.

THE MANAGER. Yes, please stop it, for Heaven's sake.

30 THE STEP-DAUGHTER. But imagine moral sanity from him, if you please—the client of certain ateliers like that of Madame Pace!

THE FATHER. Fool! That is the proof that I am a man! This seeming contradiction, gentle-35 men, is the strongest proof that I stand here a live man before you. Why, it is just for this very incongruity in my nature that I have had to suffer what I have. I could not live by the side of that woman [*indicating the* MOTHER] 40 any longer; but not so much for the boredom she inspired me with as for the pity I felt for her.

THE MOTHER. And so he turned me out—

THE FATHER. —well provided for! Yes, I sent 45 her to that man, gentlemen . . . to let her go free of me.

THE MOTHER. And to free himself.

THE FATHER. Yes, I admit it. It was also a liberation for me. But great evil has come of it. I meant well when I did it; and I did it more 50 for her sake than mine. I swear it. [*Crosses his arms on his chest; then turns suddenly to the* MOTHER.] Did I ever lose sight of you until that other man carried you off to another town, like the angry fool he was? And on account 55 of my pure interest in you . . . my pure interest, I repeat, that had no base motive in it . . . I watched with the tenderest concern the new family that grew up around her. She can bear witness to this. [*Points to the* STEP-DAUGHTER.] 60

THE STEP-DAUGHTER. Oh yes, that's true enough. When I was a kiddie, so so high, you know, with plaits over my shoulders and knickers longer than my skirts, I used to see him waiting outside the school for me to come 65 out. He came to see how I was growing up.

THE FATHER. This is infamous, shameful!

THE STEP-DAUGHTER. No. Why?

THE FATHER. Infamous! infamous! [*Then excitedly to* MANAGER *explaining.*] After she 70 [*indicating* MOTHER] went away, my house seemed suddenly empty. She was my incubus, but she filled my house. I was like a dazed fly alone in the empty rooms. This boy here [*indicating the* SON] was educated away from 75 home, and when he came back, he seemed to me to be no more mine. With no mother to stand between him and me, he grew up entirely for himself, on his own, apart, with no tie of intellect or affection binding him to me. And 80 then—strange but true—I was driven, by curiosity at first and then by some tender sentiment, towards her family, which had come into being through my will. The thought of her began gradually to fill up the emptiness 85 I felt all around me. I wanted to know if she were happy in living out the simple daily duties of life. I wanted to think of her as fortunate and happy because far away from the complicated torments of my spirit. And so, 90 to have proof of this, I used to watch that child coming out of school.

THE STEP-DAUGHTER. Yes, yes. True. He used to follow me in the street and smiled at me, waved his hand, like this. I would look at him 95 with interest, wondering who he might be. I

told my mother, who guessed at once. [*The* Mother *agrees with a nod.*] Then she didn't want to send me to school for some days; and when I finally went back, there he was again
5 —looking so ridiculous—with a paper parcel in his hands. He came close to me, caressed me, and drew out a fine straw hat from the parcel, with a bouquet of flowers—all for me!

The Manager. A bit discursive this, you
10 know!

The Son [*contemptuously*]. Literature! Literature!

The Father. Literature indeed! This is life, this is passion!

15 The Manager. It may be, but it won't act.

The Father. I agree. This is only the part leading up. I don't suggest this should be staged. She [*pointing to the* Step-Daughter], as you see, is no longer the flapper with plaits
20 down her back—.

The Step-Daughter. —and the knickers showing below the skirt!

The Father. The drama is coming now, sir; something new, complex, most interesting.

25 The Step-Daughter. As soon as my father died . . .

The Father. —there was absolute misery for them. They came back here, unknown to me. Through her stupidity! [*Pointing to the*
30 Mother.] It is true she can barely write her own name; but she could anyhow have got her daughter to write to me that they were in need . . .

The Mother. And how was I to divine
35 all this sentiment in him?

The Father. That is exactly your mistake, never to have guessed any of my sentiments.

The Mother. After so many years apart, and all that had happened . . .

40 The Father. Was it my fault if that fellow carried you away? It happened quite suddenly; for after he had obtained some job or other, I could find no trace of them; and so, not unnaturally, my interest in them dwindled. But
45 the drama culminated unforeseen and violent on their return, when I was impelled by my miserable flesh that still lives. . . . Ah! what misery, what wretchedness is that of the man

who is alone and disdains debasing *liaisons*! Not old enough to do without women, and 50 not young enough to go and look for one without shame. Misery? It's worse than misery; it's a horror; for no woman can any longer give him love; and when a man feels this. . . . One ought to do without, you say? Yes, yes, 55 I know. Each of us when he appears before his fellows is clothed in a certain dignity. But every man knows what unconfessable things pass within the secrecy of his own heart. One gives way to the temptation, only to rise from 60 it again, afterwards, with a great eagerness to re-establish one's dignity, as if it were a tombstone to place on the grave of one's shame, and a monument to hide and sign the memory of our weaknesses. Everybody's in the same case. 65 Some folks haven't the courage to say certain things, that's all!

The Step-Daughter. All appear to have the courage to do them though.

The Father. Yes, but in secret. Therefore, 70 you want more courage to say these things. Let a man but speak these things out, and folks at once label him a cynic. But it isn't true. He is like all the others, better indeed, because he isn't afraid to reveal with the light 75 of the intelligence the red shame of human bestiality on which most men close their eyes so as not to see it.

Woman—for example, look at her case! She turns tantalizing inviting glances on you. You 80 seize her. No sooner does she feel herself in your grasp than she closes her eyes. It is the sign of her mission, the sign by which she says to man: "Blind yourself, for I am blind."

The Step-Daughter. Sometimes she can 85 close them no more: when she no longer feels the need of hiding her shame to herself, but dry-eyed and dispassionately, sees only that of the man who has blinded himself without love. Oh, all these intellectual complications 90 make me sick, disgust me—all this philosophy that uncovers the beast in man, and then seeks to save him, excuse him . . . I can't stand it, sir. When a man seeks to "simplify" life bestially, throwing aside every relic of human- 95 ity, every chaste aspiration, every pure feeling, all sense of ideality, duty, modesty, shame . . . then nothing is more revolting and nauseous than a certain kind of remorse—crocodiles' tears, that's what it is.

THE MANAGER. Let's come to the point. This is only discussion.

THE FATHER. Very good, sir! But a fact is like a sack which won't stand up when it is empty. In order that it may stand up, one has to put into it the reason and sentiment which have caused it to exist. I couldn't possibly know that after the death of that man, they had decided to return here, that they were in misery, and that she [pointing to the MOTHER] had gone to work as a modiste, and at a shop of the type of that of Madame Pace.

THE STEP-DAUGHTER. A real high-class modiste, you must know, gentlemen. In appearance, she works for the leaders of the best society; but she arranges matters so that these elegant ladies serve her purpose . . . without prejudice to other ladies who are . . . well . . . only so so.

THE MOTHER. You will believe me, gentlemen, that it never entered my mind that the old hag offered me work because she had her eye on my daughter.

THE STEP-DAUGHTER. Poor mamma! Do you know, sir, what that woman did when I brought her back the work my mother had finished? She would point out to me that I had torn one of my frocks, and she would give it back to my mother to mend. It was I who paid for it, always I; while this poor creature here believed she was sacrificing herself for me and these two children here, sitting up at night sewing Madame Pace's robes.

THE MANAGER. And one day you met there . . .

THE STEP-DAUGHTER. Him, him. Yes sir, an old client. There's a scene for you to play! Superb!

THE FATHER. She, the Mother arrived just then . . .

THE STEP-DAUGHTER [treacherously]. Almost in time!

THE FATHER [crying out]. No, in time! in time! Fortunately I recognized her . . . in time. And I took them back home with me to my house. You can imagine now her position and mine; she, as you see her; and I who cannot look her in the face.

THE STEP-DAUGHTER. Absurd! How can I possibly be expected—after that—to be a modest young miss, a fit person to go with his confounded aspirations for "a solid moral sanity"?

THE FATHER. For the drama lies all in this— in the conscience that I have, that each one of us has. We believe this conscience to be a single thing, but it is many-sided. There is one for this person, and another for that. Diverse consciences. So we have this illusion of being one person for all, of having a personality that is unique in all our acts. But it isn't true. We perceive this when, tragically perhaps, in something we do, we are as it were, suspended, caught up in the air on a kind of hook. Then we perceive that all of us was not in that act, and that it would be an atrocious injustice to judge us by that action alone, as if all our existence were summed up in that one deed. Now do you understand the perfidy of this girl? She surprised me in a place, where she ought not to have known me, just as I could not exist for her; and she now seeks to attach to me a reality such as I could never suppose I should have to assume for her in a shameful and fleeting moment of my life. I feel this above all else. And the drama, you will see, acquires a tremendous value from this point. Then there is the position of the others . . . his . . . [indicating the SON].

THE SON [shrugging his shoulders scornfully]. Leave me alone! I don't come into this.

THE FATHER. What? You don't come into this?

THE SON. I've got nothing to do with it, and don't want to have; because you know well enough I wasn't made to be mixed up in all this with the rest of you.

THE STEP-DAUGHTER. We are only vulgar folk! He is the fine gentleman. You may have noticed, Mr. Manager, that I fix him now and

again with a look of scorn while he lowers
his eyes—for he knows the evil he has done
me.

THE SON [*scarcely looking at her*]. I?

5   THE STEP-DAUGHTER. You! you! I owe my
life on the streets to you. Did you or did you
not deny us, with your behavior, I won't say
the intimacy of home, but even that mere
hospitality which makes guests feel at their
10 ease? We were intruders who had come to
disturb the kingdom of your legitimacy. I
should like to have you witness, Mr. Manager,
certain scenes between him and me. He says
I have tyrannized over everyone. But it was
15 just his behavior which made me insist on the
reason for which I had come into the house,—
this reason he calls "vile"—into his house,
with my mother who is his mother too. And
I came as mistress of the house.

20   THE SON. It's easy for them to put me always
in the wrong. But imagine, gentlemen, the
position of a son, whose fate it is to see arrive
one day at his home a young woman of
impudent bearing, a young woman who in-
25 quires for his father, with whom who knows
what business she has. This young man has
then to witness her return bolder than ever,
accompanied by that child there. He is obliged
to watch her treat his father in an equivocal
30 and confidential manner. She asks money of
him in a way that lets one suppose he must
give it her, *must*, do you understand, because
he has every obligation to do so.

THE FATHER. But I have, as a matter of fact,
35 this obligation. I owe it to your mother.

THE SON. How should I know? When had
I ever seen or heard of her? One day there
arrive with her [*indicating* STEP-DAUGHTER]
that lad and this baby here. I am told: "This
40 is *your* mother too, you know." I divine from
her manner [*indicating* STEP-DAUGHTER *again*]
why it is they have come home. I had rather not
say what I feel and think about it. I shouldn't
even care to confess to myself. No action can
45 therefore be hoped for from me in this affair.
Believe me, Mr. Manager, I am an "unrealized"
character, dramatically speaking; and I find

myself not at all at ease in their company.
Leave me out of it, I beg you.

THE FATHER. What? It is just because you   50
are so that . . .

THE SON. How do you know what I am like?
When did you ever bother your head about
me?

THE FATHER. I admit it. I admit it. But isn't   55
that a situation in itself? This aloofness of
yours which is so cruel to me and to your
mother, who returns home and sees you almost
for the first time grown up, who doesn't
recognize you but knows you are her son . . .   60
[*pointing out the* MOTHER *to the* MANAGER].
See, she's crying!

THE STEP-DAUGHTER [*angrily, stamping her
foot*]. Like a fool!

THE FATHER [*indicating* STEP-DAUGHTER]. She   65
can't stand him you know. [*Then referring
again to the* SON.] He says he doesn't come
into the affair, whereas he is really the hinge
of the whole action. Look at that lad who is
always clinging to his mother, frightened and   70
humiliated. It is on account of this fellow here.
Possibly his situation is the most painful of all.
He feels himself a stranger more than the
others. The poor little chap feels mortified,
humiliated at being brought into a home out   75
of charity as it were. [*In confidence.*] He is
the image of his father. Hardly talks at all.
Humble and quiet.

THE MANAGER. Oh, we'll cut him out. You've
no notion what a nuisance boys are on the   80
stage . . .

THE FATHER. He disappears soon, you know.
And the baby too. She is the first to vanish
from the scene. The drama consists finally in
this: when that mother re-enters my house,   85
her family—born outside of it, and shall we say
superimposed on the original—ends with the
death of the little girl, the tragedy of the boy
and the flight of the elder daughter. It cannot
go on, because it is foreign to its surroundings.   90
So after much torment, we three remain: I, the
mother, that son. Then, owing to the disap-
pearance of that extraneous family, we too
find ourselves strange to one another. We find

we are living in an atmosphere of mortal desolation which is the revenge, as he [*indicating* SON] scornfully said of the Demon of Experiment, that unfortunately hides in me.
5 Thus, sir, you see when faith is lacking, it becomes impossible to create certain states of happiness, for we lack the necessary humility. Vaingloriously, we try to substitute ourselves for this faith, creating thus for the rest of the
10 world a reality which we believe after their fashion, while, actually, it doesn't exist. For each one of us has his own reality to be respected before God, even when it is harmful to one's very self.
15 THE MANAGER. There is something in what you say. I assure you all this interests me very much. I begin to think there's the stuff for a drama in all this, and not a bad drama either.

THE STEP-DAUGHTER [*coming forward*].
20 When you've got a character like me.

THE FATHER [*shutting her up, all excited to learn the decision of the* MANAGER]. You be quiet!

THE MANAGER [*reflecting, heedless of inter-*
25 *ruption*]. It's new . . . hem . . . yes . . .

THE FATHER. Absolutely new!

THE MANAGER. You've got a nerve though, I must say, to come here and fling it at me like this . . .
30 THE FATHER. You will understand, sir, born as we are for the stage . . .

THE MANAGER. Are you amateur actors then?

THE FATHER. No. I say born for the stage, because . . .
35 THE MANAGER. Oh, nonsense. You're an old hand, you know.

THE FATHER. No sir, no. We act that rôle for which we have been cast, that rôle which we are given in life. And in my own case, passion
40 itself, as usually happens, becomes a trifle theatrical when it is exalted.

THE MANAGER. Well, well, that will do. But you see, without an author . . . I could give you the address of an author if you like . . .
45 THE FATHER. No, no. Look here! You must be the author.

THE MANAGER. I? What are you talking about?

THE FATHER. Yes, you, you! Why not?

THE MANAGER. Because I have never been 50 an author: that's why.

THE FATHER. Then why not turn author now? Everybody does it. You don't want any special qualities. Your task is made much easier by the fact that we are all here alive before you . . . 55

THE MANAGER. It won't do.

THE FATHER. What? When you see us live our drama . . .

THE MANAGER. Yes, that's all right. But you want someone to write it. 60

THE FATHER. No, no. Someone to take it down, possibly, while we play it, scene by scene! It will be enough to sketch it out at first, and then try it over.

THE MANAGER. Well . . . I am almost tempted. 65 It's a bit of an idea. One might have a shot at it.

THE FATHER. Of course. You'll see what scenes will come out of it. I can give you one, at once . . . 70

THE MANAGER. By Jove, it tempts me. I'd like to have a go at it. Let's try it out. Come with me to my office. [*Turning to the* ACTORS.] You are at liberty for a bit, but don't step out of the theatre for long. In a quarter of an 75 hour, twenty minutes, all back here again! [*To the* FATHER.] We'll see what can be done. Who knows if we don't get something really extraordinary out of it?

THE FATHER. There's no doubt about it. They 80 [*indicating the* CHARACTERS] had better come with us too, hadn't they?

THE MANAGER. Yes, yes. Come on! come on! [*Moves away and then turning to the* ACTORS.] Be punctual, please! [MANAGER *and the* SIX 85 CHARACTERS *cross the stage and go off. The other* ACTORS *remain, looking at one another in astonishment.*]

LEADING MAN. Is he serious? What the devil does he want to do? 90

JUVENILE LEAD. This is rank madness.

THIRD ACTOR. Does he expect to knock up a drama in five minutes?

JUVENILE LEAD. Like the improvisers!

LEADING LADY. If he thinks I'm going to take 95 part in a joke like this . . .

JUVENILE LEAD. I'm out of it anyway.

FOURTH ACTOR. I should like to know who they are. [*Alludes to* CHARACTERS.]

THIRD ACTOR. What do you suppose? Madmen or rascals!

JUVENILE LEAD. And he takes them seriously!

L'INGÉNUE. Vanity! He fancies himself as an author now.

LEADING MAN. It's absolutely unheard of. If the stage has come to this . . . well I'm . . .

FIFTH ACTOR. It's rather a joke.

THIRD ACTOR. Well, we'll see what's going to happen next.

[*Thus talking, the* ACTORS *leave the stage; some going out by the little door at the back; others retiring to their dressing-rooms.*

The curtain remains up.

The action of the play is suspended for twenty minutes.]

ACT II

[*The stage call-bells ring to warn the company that the play is about to begin again.*

The STEP-DAUGHTER *comes out of the* MANAGER's *office along with the* CHILD *and the* BOY. *As she comes out of the office, she cries:—*

Nonsense! nonsense! Do it yourselves! I'm not going to mix myself up in this mess. [*Turning to the* CHILD *and coming quickly with her on to the stage.*] Come on, Rosetta, let's run!

[*The* BOY *follows them slowly, remaining a little behind and seeming perplexed.*]

THE STEP-DAUGHTER [*stops, bends over the* CHILD *and takes the latter's face between her hands*]. My little darling! You're frightened, aren't you? You don't know where we are, do you? [*Pretending to reply to a question of the* CHILD.] What is the stage? It's a place, baby, you know, where people play at being serious, a place where they act comedies. We've got to act a comedy now, dead serious, you know; and you're in it also, little one. [*Embraces her, pressing the little head to her breast, and rocking the* CHILD *for a moment.*] Oh darling, darling, what a horrid comedy you've got to play! What a wretched part they've found for you! A garden . . . a fountain . . . look . . . just

suppose, kiddie, it's here. Where, you say? Why, right here in the middle. It's all pretense you know. That's the trouble, my pet: it's all make-believe here. It's better to imagine it though, because if they fix it up for you, it'll only be painted cardboard, painted cardboard for the rockery, the water, the plants. . . . Ah, but I think a baby like this one would sooner have a make-believe fountain than a real one, so she could play with it. What a joke it'll be for the others! But for you, alas! not quite such a joke: you who are real, baby dear, and really play by a real fountain that is big and green and beautiful, with ever so many bamboos around it that are reflected in the water, and a whole lot of little ducks swimming about. . . . No, Rosetta, no, your mother doesn't bother about you on account of that wretch of a son there. I'm in the devil of a temper, and as for that lad . . . [*seizes* BOY *by the arm to force him to take one of his hands out of his pockets*]. What have you got there? What are you hiding? [*Pulls his hand out of his pocket, looks into it and catches the glint of a revolver.*] Ah! where did you get this? [*The* BOY, *very pale in the face, looks at her, but does not answer.*] Idiot! If I'd been in your place, instead of killing myself, I'd have shot one of those two, or both of them: father and son.

[*The* FATHER *enters from the office, all excited from his work. The* MANAGER *follows him.*]

THE FATHER. Come on, come on dear! Come here for a minute! We've arranged everything. It's all fixed up.

THE MANAGER [*also excited*]. If you please, young lady, there are one or two points to settle still. Will you come along?

THE STEP-DAUGHTER [*following him towards the office*]. Ouff! what's the good, if you've arranged everything.

[*The* FATHER, MANAGER, *and* STEP-DAUGHTER *go back into the office again* (*off*) *for a moment. At the same time, the* SON *followed by the* MOTHER *comes out.*]

THE SON [*looking at the three entering office*]. Oh this is fine, fine! And to think I can't even get away!

[*The* MOTHER *attempts to look at him, but lowers her eyes immediately when he turns away from her. She then sits down. The* BOY *and the* CHILD *approach her. She casts a glance again at the* SON, *and speaks with humble tones, trying to draw him into conversation.*]

THE MOTHER. And isn't my punishment the worst of all? [*Then seeing from the* SON'S *manner that he will not bother himself about her.*] My God! Why are you so cruel? Isn't it enough for one person to support all this torment? Must you then insist on others seeing it also?

THE SON [*half to himself, meaning the* MOTHER *to hear, however*]. And they want to put it on the stage! If there was at least a reason for it! He thinks he has got at the meaning of it all. Just as if each one of us in every circumstance of life couldn't find his own explanation of it! [*Pauses.*] He complains he was discovered in a place where he ought not to have been seen, in a moment of his life which ought to have remained hidden and kept out of the reach of that convention which he has to maintain for other people. And what about my case? Haven't I had to reveal what no son ought ever to reveal: how father and mother live and are man and wife for themselves quite apart from that idea of father and mother which we give them? When this idea is revealed, our life is then linked at one point only to that man and that woman; and as such it should shame them, shouldn't it?

[*The* MOTHER *hides her face in her hands. From the dressing-rooms and the little door at the back of the stage the* ACTORS *and* STAGE MANAGER *return, followed by the* PROPERTY MAN, *and the* PROMPTER. *At the same moment, the* MANAGER *comes out of his office, accompanied by the* FATHER *and the* STEP-DAUGHTER.]

THE MANAGER. Come on, come on, ladies and gentlemen! Heh! you there, machinist!

MACHINIST. Yes sir?

THE MANAGER. Fix up the white parlor with the floral decorations. Two wings and a drop with a door will do. Hurry up!

[*The* MACHINIST *runs off at once to prepare the scene, and arranges it while the* MANAGER *talks with the* STAGE MANAGER, *the* PROPERTY MAN, *and the* PROMPTER *on matters of detail.*]

THE MANAGER [*to* PROPERTY MAN]. Just have a look, and see if there isn't a sofa or divan in the wardrobe . . .

PROPERTY MAN. There's the green one.

THE STEP-DAUGHTER. No no! Green won't do. It was yellow, ornamented with flowers—very large! and most comfortable!

PROPERTY MAN. There isn't one like that.

THE MANAGER. It doesn't matter. Use the one we've got.

THE STEP-DAUGHTER. Doesn't matter? It's most important!

THE MANAGER. We're only trying it now. Please don't interfere. [*To* PROPERTY MAN.] See if we've got a shop window—long and narrowish.

THE STEP-DAUGHTER. And the little table! The little mahogany table for the pale blue envelope!

PROPERTY MAN [*to* MANAGER]. There's that little gilt one.

THE MANAGER. That'll do fine.

THE FATHER. A mirror.

THE STEP-DAUGHTER. And the screen! We must have a screen. Otherwise how can I manage?

PROPERTY MAN. That's all right, Miss. We've got any amount of them.

THE MANAGER [*to the* STEP-DAUGHTER]. We want some clothes pegs too, don't we?

THE STEP-DAUGHTER. Yes, several, several!

THE MANAGER. See how many we've got and bring them all.

PROPERTY MAN. All right!

[*The* PROPERTY MAN *hurries off to obey his orders. While he is putting the things in their places, the* MANAGER *talks to the* PROMPTER *and then with the* CHARACTERS *and the* ACTORS.]

THE MANAGER [*to* PROMPTER]. Take your seat. Look here: this is the outline of the scenes, act by act. [*Hands him some sheets of paper.*] And now I'm going to ask you to do something out of the ordinary.

PROMPTER. Take it down in shorthand?

THE MANAGER [*pleasantly surprised*]. Exactly! Can you do shorthand?

PROMPTER. Yes, a little.

THE MANAGER. Good! [*Turning to a* STAGE HAND.] Go and get some paper from my office, plenty, as much as you can find.

5 [*The* STAGE HAND *goes off, and soon returns with a handful of paper which he gives to the* PROMPTER.]

THE MANAGER [*to* PROMPTER]. You follow the scenes as we play them, and try and get 10 the points down, at any rate the most important ones. [*Then addressing the* ACTORS.] Clear the stage, ladies and gentlemen! Come over here [*pointing to the left*] and listen attentively.

15 LEADING LADY. But, excuse me, we . . .

THE MANAGER [*guessing her thought*]. Don't worry! You won't have to improvise.

LEADING MAN. What have we to do then?

THE MANAGER. Nothing. For the moment 20 you just watch and listen. Everybody will get his part written out afterwards. At present we're going to try the thing as best we can. They're going to act now.

THE FATHER [*as if fallen from the clouds into* 25 *the confusion of the stage*]. We? What do you mean, if you please, by a rehearsal?

THE MANAGER. A rehearsal for them. [*Points to the* ACTORS.]

THE FATHER. But since we are the charac-30 ters . . .

THE MANAGER. All right: "characters" then, if you insist on calling yourselves such. But here, my dear sir, the characters don't act. Here the actors do the acting. The characters 35 are there, in the "book" [*pointing towards* PROMPTER'S *box*]—when there is a "book"!

THE FATHER. I won't contradict you; but excuse me, the actors aren't the characters. They want to be, they pretend to be, don't 40 they? Now if these gentlemen here are fortunate enough to have us alive before them . . .

THE MANAGER. Oh this is grand! You want to come before the public yourselves then?

THE FATHER. As we are . . .

45 THE MANAGER. I can assure you it would be a magnificent spectacle!

LEADING MAN. What's the use of us here anyway then?

THE MANAGER. You're not going to pretend that you can act? It makes me laugh! [*The* 50 ACTORS *laugh*.] There, you see, they are laughing at the notion. But, by the way, I must cast the parts. That won't be difficult. They cast themselves. [*To the* SECOND LADY LEAD.] You play the Mother. [*To the* FATHER.] We must 55 find her a name.

THE FATHER. Amalia, sir.

THE MANAGER. But that is the real name of your wife. We don't want to call her by her real name. 60

THE FATHER. Why ever not, if it is her name? . . . Still, perhaps, if that lady must . . . [*makes a slight motion of the hand to indicate the* SECOND LADY LEAD]. I see this woman here [*means the* MOTHER] as Amalia. But do as you 65 like. [*Gets more and more confused*.] I don't know what to say to you. Already, I begin to hear my own words ring false, as if they had another sound . . .

THE MANAGER. Don't you worry about it. 70 It'll be our job to find the right tones. And as for her name, if you want her Amalia, Amalia it shall be; and if you don't like it, we'll find another! For the moment though, we'll call the characters in this way: [*To* JUVENILE LEAD.] 75 You are the Son. [*To the* LEADING LADY.] You naturally are the Step-Daughter . . .

THE STEP-DAUGHTER [*excitedly*]. What? what? I, that woman there? [*Bursts out laughing*.] 80

THE MANAGER [*angry*]. What is there to laugh at?

LEADING LADY [*indignant*]. Nobody has ever dared to laugh at me. I insist on being treated with respect; otherwise I go away. 85

THE STEP-DAUGHTER. No, no, excuse me . . . I am not laughing at you . . .

THE MANAGER [*to* STEP-DAUGHTER]. You ought to feel honored to be played by . . .

LEADING LADY [*at once, contemptuously*]. 90 "That woman there" . . .

THE STEP-DAUGHTER. But I wasn't speaking of you, you know. I was speaking of myself—whom I can't see at all in you! That is all. I don't know . . . but . . . you . . . aren't in the 95 least like me . . .

THE FATHER. True. Here's the point. Look here, sir, our temperaments, our souls . . .

THE MANAGER. Temperament, soul, be hanged! Do you suppose the spirit of the piece is in you? Nothing of the kind!

THE FATHER. What, haven't we our own temperaments, our own souls?

THE MANAGER. Not at all. Your soul or whatever you like to call it takes shape here. The actors give body and form to it, voice and gesture. And my actors—I may tell you—have given expression to much more lofty material than this little drama of yours, which may or may not hold up on the stage. But if it does, the merit of it, believe me, will be due to my actors.

THE FATHER. I don't dare contradict you, sir; but, believe me, it is a terrible suffering for us who are as we are, with these bodies of ours, these features to see . . .

THE MANAGER [cutting him short and out of patience]. Good heavens! The make-up will remedy all that, man, the make-up . . .

THE FATHER. Maybe. But the voice, the gestures . . .

THE MANAGER. Now, look here! On the stage, you as yourself, cannot exist. The actor here acts you, and that's an end to it!

THE FATHER. I understand. And now I think I see why our author who conceived us as we are, all alive, didn't want to put us on the stage after all. I haven't the least desire to offend your actors. Far from it! But when I think that I am to be acted by . . . I don't know by whom . . .

LEADING MAN [on his dignity]. By me, if you've no objection!

THE FATHER [humbly, mellifluously]. Honored, I assure you, sir. [Bows.] Still, I must say that try as this gentleman may, with all his good will and wonderful art, to absorb me into himself . . .

LEADING MAN. Oh, chuck it! "Wonderful art!" Withdraw that, please!

THE FATHER. The performance he will give, even doing his best with make-up to look like me . . .

LEADING MAN. It will certainly be a bit difficult! [The ACTORS laugh.]

THE FATHER. Exactly! It will be difficult to act me as I really am. The effect will be rather —apart from the make-up—according as to how he supposes I am, as he senses me—if he does sense me—and not as I inside of myself feel myself to be. It seems to me then that account should be taken of this by everyone whose duty it may become to criticize us . . .

THE MANAGER. Heavens! The man's starting to think about the critics now! Let them say what they like. It's up to us to put on the play if we can. [Looking around.] Come on! come on! Is the stage set? [To the ACTORS and CHARACTERS.] Stand back—stand back! Let me see, and don't let's lose any more time! [To the STEP-DAUGHTER.] Is it all right as it is now?

THE STEP-DAUGHTER. Well, to tell the truth, I don't recognize the scene.

THE MANAGER. My dear lady, you can't possibly suppose that we can construct that shop of Madame Pace piece by piece here? [To the FATHER.] You said a white room with flowered wall paper, didn't you?

THE FATHER. Yes.

THE MANAGER. Well then. We've got the furniture right more or less. Bring that little table a bit further forward. [The STAGE HANDS obey the order. To PROPERTY MAN.] You go and find an envelope, if possible, a pale blue one; and give it to that gentleman. [Indicates FATHER.]

PROPERTY MAN. An ordinary envelope?

MANAGER AND FATHER. Yes, yes, an ordinary envelope.

PROPERTY MAN. At once, sir. [Exit.]

THE MANAGER. Ready, everyone! First scene —the Young Lady. [The LEADING LADY comes forward.] No, no, you must wait. I meant her [indicating the STEP-DAUGHTER]. You just watch—

THE STEP-DAUGHTER [adding at once]. How I shall play it, how I shall live it! . . .

LEADING LADY [offended]. I shall live it also, you may be sure, as soon as I begin!

THE MANAGER [*with his hands to his head*]. Ladies and gentlemen, if you please! No more useless discussions! Scene I: the young lady with Madame Pace: Oh! [*Looks around as if lost.*] And this Madame Pace, where is she?

THE FATHER. She isn't with us, sir.

THE MANAGER. Then what the devil's to be done?

THE FATHER. But she is alive too.

THE MANAGER. Yes, but where is she?

THE FATHER. One minute. Let me speak! [*Turning to the* ACTRESSES.] If these ladies would be so good as to give me their hats for a moment . . .

THE ACTRESSES [*half surprised, half laughing, in chorus*]. What?

Why?

Our hats?

What does he say?

THE MANAGER. What are you going to do with the ladies' hats? [*The* ACTORS *laugh.*]

THE FATHER. Oh nothing. I just want to put them on these pegs for a moment. And one of the ladies will be so kind as to take off her mantle . . .

THE ACTORS. Oh, what d'you think of that? Only the mantle?

He must be mad.

SOME ACTRESSES. But why?

Mantles as well?

THE FATHER. To hang them up here for a moment. Please be so kind, will you?

THE ACTRESSES [*taking off their hats, one or two also their cloaks, and going to hang them on the racks*]. After all, why not?

There you are!

This is really funny.

We've got to put them on show.

THE FATHER. Exactly; just like that, on show.

THE MANAGER. May we know why?

THE FATHER. I'll tell you. Who knows if, by arranging the stage for her, she does not come here herself, attracted by the very articles of her trade? [*Inviting the* ACTORS *to look towards the exit at back of stage.*] Look! Look!

[*The door at the back of stage opens and* MADAME PACE *enters and takes a few steps forward. She is a fat, oldish woman with puffy oxygenated hair. She is rouged and powdered, dressed with a comical elegance in black silk. Round her waist is a long silver chain from which hangs a pair of scissors. The* STEP-DAUGHTER *runs over to her at once amid the stupor of the* ACTORS.]

THE STEP-DAUGHTER [*turning towards her*]. There she is! There she is!

THE FATHER [*radiant*]. It's she! I said so, didn't I? There she is!

THE MANAGER [*conquering his surprise, and then becoming indignant*]. What sort of a trick is this?

LEADING MAN [*almost at the same time*]. What's going to happen next?

JUVENILE LEAD. Where does *she* come from?

L'INGÉNUE. They've been holding her in reserve, I guess.

LEADING LADY. A vulgar trick!

THE FATHER [*dominating the protests*]. Excuse me, all of you! Why are you so anxious to destroy in the name of a vulgar, commonplace sense of truth, this reality which comes to birth attracted and formed by the magic of the stage itself, which has indeed more right to live here than you, since it is much truer than you—if you don't mind my saying so? Which is the actress among you who is to play Madame Pace? Well, here is Madame Pace herself. And you will allow, I fancy, that the actress who acts her will be less true than this woman here, who is herself in person. You see my daughter recognized her and went over to her at once. Now you're going to witness the scene!

[*But the scene between the* STEP-DAUGHTER *and* MADAME PACE *has already begun despite the protest of the actors and the reply of the* FATHER. *It has begun quietly, naturally, in a manner impossible for the stage. So when the* ACTORS, *called to attention by the* FATHER, *turn round and see* MADAME PACE, *who has placed one hand under the* STEP-DAUGHTER's *chin to raise her head, they observe her at first with great attention, but hearing her speak in an unintelligible manner their interest begins to wane.*]

THE MANAGER. Well? well?

LEADING MAN. What does she say?

LEADING LADY. One can't hear a word.

JUVENILE LEAD. Louder! Louder please!

THE STEP-DAUGHTER [*leaving* MADAME PACE, *who smiles a Sphinx-like smile, and advancing towards the* ACTORS]. Louder? Louder? What are you talking about? These aren't matters which can be shouted at the top of one's voice. If I have spoken them out loud, it was to shame him and have my revenge. [*Indicates* FATHER.] But for Madame it's quite a different matter.

THE MANAGER. Indeed? indeed? But here, you know, people have got to make themselves heard, my dear. Even we who are on the stage can't hear you. What will it be when the public's in the theatre? And anyway, you can very well speak up now among yourselves, since we shan't be present to listen to you as we are now. You've got to pretend to be alone in a room at the back of a shop where no one can hear you.

[*The* STEP-DAUGHTER *coquettishly and with a touch of malice makes a sign of disagreement two or three times with her finger.*]

THE MANAGER. What do you mean by no?

THE STEP-DAUGHTER [*sotto voce, mysteriously*]. There's someone who will hear us if she [*indicating* MADAME PACE] speaks out loud.

THE MANAGER [*in consternation*]. What? Have you got someone else to spring on us now? [*The* ACTORS *burst out laughing.*]

THE FATHER. No, no sir. She is alluding to me. I've got to be here—there behind that door, in waiting; and Madame Pace knows it. In fact, if you will allow me, I'll go there at once, so I can be quite ready. [*Moves away.*]

THE MANAGER [*stopping him*]. No! Wait! wait! We must observe the conventions of the theatre. Before you are ready . . .

THE STEP-DAUGHTER [*interrupting him*]. No, get on with it at once! I'm just dying, I tell you, to act this scene. If he's ready, I'm more than ready.

THE MANAGER [*shouting*]. But, my dear young lady, first of all, we must have the scene between you and this lady . . . [*indicates* MADAME PACE]. Do you understand? . . .

THE STEP-DAUGHTER. Good Heavens! She's been telling me what you know already: that mamma's work is badly done again, that the material's ruined; and that if I want her to continue to help us in our misery I must be patient . . .

MADAME PACE [*coming forward with an air of great importance*]. Yes indeed, sir, I no wanta take advantage of her, I no wanta be hard . . .

[*Note.* MADAME PACE *is supposed to talk in a jargon half Italian, half English.*]

THE MANAGER [*alarmed*]. What? What? She talks like that? [*The* ACTORS *burst out laughing again.*]

THE STEP-DAUGHTER [*also laughing*]. Yes yes, that's the way she talks, half English, half Italian! Most comical it is!

MADAME PACE. Itta seem not verra polite gentlemen laugha atta me eef I trya best speaka English.

THE MANAGER. *Diamine!* Of course! Of course! Let her talk like that! Just what we want. Talk just like that, Madame, if you please! The effect will be certain. Exactly what was wanted to put a little comic relief into the crudity of the situation. Of course she talks like that! Magnificent!

THE STEP-DAUGHTER. Magnificent? Certainly! When certain suggestions are made to one in language of that kind, the effect is certain, since it seems almost a joke. One feels inclined to laugh when one hears her talk about an "old signore" "who wanta talka nicely with you." Nice old signore, eh, Madame?

MADAME PACE. Not so old my dear, not so old! And even if you no lika him, he won't make any scandal!

THE MOTHER [*jumping up amid the amazement and consternation of the* ACTORS *who had not been noticing her. They move to restrain her*]. You old devil! You murderess!

THE STEP-DAUGHTER [*running over to calm her* MOTHER]. Calm yourself, Mother, calm yourself! Please don't . . .

THE FATHER [*going to her also at the same time*]. Calm yourself! Don't get excited! Sit down now!

THE MOTHER. Well then, take that woman away out of my sight!

THE STEP-DAUGHTER [*to* MANAGER]. It is impossible for my mother to remain here.

THE FATHER [*to* MANAGER]. They can't be here together. And for this reason, you see: that woman there was not with us when we came . . . If they are on together, the whole thing is given away inevitably, as you see.

THE MANAGER. It doesn't matter. This is only a first rough sketch—just to get an idea of the various points of the scene, even confusedly . . . [*turning to the* MOTHER *and leading her to her chair*]. Come along, my dear lady, sit down now, and let's get on with the scene . . .

[*Meanwhile, the* STEP-DAUGHTER, *coming forward again, turns to* MADAME PACE.]

THE STEP-DAUGHTER. Come on, Madame, come on!

MADAME PACE [*offended*]. No, no, *grazie*. I not do anything witha your mother present.

THE STEP-DAUGHTER. Nonsense! Introduce this "old signore" who wants to talk nicely to me. [*Addressing the* COMPANY *imperiously.*] We've got to do this scene one way or another, haven't we? Come on! [*To* MADAME PACE.] You can go!

MADAME PACE. Ah yes! I go'way! I go'way! Certainly! [*Exits furious.*]

THE STEP-DAUGHTER [*to the* FATHER]. Now you make your entry. No, you needn't go over here. Come here. Let's suppose you've already come in. Like that, yes! I'm here with bowed head, modest like. Come on! Out with your voice! Say "Good morning, Miss" in that peculiar tone, that special tone . . .

THE MANAGER. Excuse me, but are you the Manager, or am I? [*To the* FATHER, *who looks undecided and perplexed.*] Get on with it, man! Go down there to the back of the stage. You needn't go off. Then come right forward here.

[*The* FATHER *does as he is told, looking troubled and perplexed at first. But as soon as he begins to move, the reality of the action affects him, and he begins to smile and to be more natural. The* ACTORS *watch intently.*]

THE MANAGER [*sotto voce, quickly to the* PROMPTER *in his box*]. Ready! ready? Get ready to write now.

THE FATHER [*coming forward and speaking in a different tone*]. Good afternoon, Miss!

THE STEP-DAUGHTER [*head bowed down slightly, with restrained disgust*]. Good afternoon!

THE FATHER [*looks under her hat which partly covers her face. Perceiving she is very young, he makes an exclamation, partly of surprise, partly of fear lest he compromise himself in a risky adventure*]. Ah . . . but . . . ah . . . I say . . . this is not the first time that you have come here, is it?

THE STEP-DAUGHTER [*modestly*]. No sir.

THE FATHER. You've been here before, eh? [*Then seeing her nod agreement.*] More than once? [*Waits for her to answer, looks under her hat, smiles, and then says.*] Well then, there's no need to be so shy, is there? May I take off your hat?

THE STEP-DAUGHTER [*anticipating him and with veiled disgust*]. No sir . . . I'll do it myself. [*Takes it off quickly.*]

[*The* MOTHER, *who watches the progress of the scene with the* SON *and the other two children who cling to her, is on thorns; and follows with varying expressions of sorrow, indignation, anxiety, and horror the words and actions of the other two. From time to time she hides her face in her hands and sobs.*]

THE MOTHER. Oh, my God, my God!

THE FATHER [*playing his part with a touch of gallantry*]. Give it to me! I'll put it down. [*Takes hat from her hands.*] But a dear little head like yours ought to have a smarter hat. Come and help me choose one from the stock, won't you?

L'INGÉNUE [*interrupting*]. I say . . . those are our hats you know.

THE MANAGER [*furious*]. Silence! silence! Don't try and be funny, if you please . . .we're playing the scene now I'd have you notice. [*To the* STEP-DAUGHTER.] Begin again, please!

THE STEP-DAUGHTER [*continuing*]. No thank you, sir.

5 THE FATHER. Oh, come now. Don't talk like that. You must take it. I shall be upset if you don't. There are some lovely little hats here; and then—Madame will be pleased. She expects it, anyway, you know.

10 THE STEP-DAUGHTER. No, no! I couldn't wear it!

THE FATHER. Oh, you're thinking about what they'd say at home if they saw you come in with a new hat? My dear girl, there's always 15 a way round these little matters, you know.

THE STEP-DAUGHTER [*all keyed up*]. No, it's not that. I couldn't wear it because I am . . . as you see . . . you might have noticed . . . [*showing her black dress*].

20 THE FATHER. . . . in mourning! Of course: I beg your pardon: I'm frightfully sorry . . .

THE STEP-DAUGHTER [*forcing herself to conquer her indignation and nausea*]. Stop! Stop! It's I who must thank you. There's no 25 need for you to feel mortified or specially sorry. Don't think any more of what I've said. [*Tries to smile.*] I must forget that I am dressed so . . .

THE MANAGER [*interrupting and turning to 30 the* PROMPTER]. Stop a minute! Stop! Don't write that down. Cut out that last bit. [*Then to the* FATHER *and* STEP-DAUGHTER.] Fine! it's going fine! [*To the* FATHER *only.*] And now you can go on as we arranged. [*To the* ACTORS.] 35 Pretty good that scene, where he offers her the hat, eh?

THE STEP-DAUGHTER. The best's coming now. Why can't we go on?

THE MANAGER. Have a little patience! [*To 40 the* ACTORS.] Of course, it must be treated rather lightly.

LEADING MAN. Still, with a bit of go in it!

LEADING LADY. Of course! It's easy enough! [*To* LEADING MAN.] Shall you and I try it now?

45 LEADING MAN. Why, yes! I'll prepare my entrance. [*Exit in order to make his entrance.*]

THE MANAGER [*to* LEADING LADY]. See here! The scene between you and Madame Pace is finished. I'll have it written out properly after. You remain here . . . oh, where are you going? 50

LEADING LADY. One minute. I want to put my hat on again. [*Goes over to hat-rack and puts her hat on her head.*]

THE MANAGER. Good! You stay here with your head bowed down a bit. 55

THE STEP-DAUGHTER. But she isn't dressed in black.

LEADING LADY. But I shall be, and much more effectively than you.

THE MANAGER [*to* STEP-DAUGHTER]. Be quiet 60 please, and watch! You'll be able to learn something. [*Clapping his hands.*] Come on! come on! Entrance, please!

[*The door at rear of stage opens, and the* LEADING MAN *enters with the lively manner* 65 *of an old gallant. The rendering of the scene by the* ACTORS *from the very first words is seen to be quite a different thing, though it has not in any way the air of a parody. Naturally, the* STEP-DAUGHTER *and the* FATHER, *not being able* 70 *to recognize themselves in the* LEADING LADY *and the* LEADING MAN, *who deliver their words in different tones and with a different psychology, express, sometimes with smiles, sometimes with gestures, the impression they* 75 *receive.*]

LEADING MAN. Good afternoon, Miss . . .

THE FATHER [*at once unable to contain himself*]. No! no!

[*The* STEP-DAUGHTER *noticing the way the* 80 LEADING MAN *enters, bursts out laughing.*]

THE MANAGER [*furious*]. Silence! And you please just stop that laughing. If we go on like this, we shall never finish.

THE STEP-DAUGHTER. Forgive me, sir, but it's 85 natural enough. This lady [*indicating* LEADING LADY] stands there still; but if she is supposed to be me, I can assure you that if I heard anyone say "Good afternoon" in that manner and in that tone, I should burst out laughing as I 90 did.

THE FATHER. Yes, yes, the manner, the tone . . .

THE MANAGER. Nonsense! Rubbish! Stand aside and let me see the action. 95

LEADING MAN. If I've got to represent an old

fellow who's coming into a house of an equivocal character . . .

THE MANAGER. Don't listen to them, for Heaven's sake! Do it again! It goes fine. [*Waiting for the* ACTORS *to begin again.*] Well?

LEADING MAN. Good afternoon, Miss.

LEADING LADY. Good afternoon.

LEADING MAN [*imitating the gesture of the* FATHER *when he looked under the hat, and then expressing quite clearly first satisfaction and then fear*]. Ah, but . . . I say . . . this is not the first time that you have come here, is it?

THE MANAGER. Good, but not quite so heavily. Like this. [*Acts himself.*] "This isn't the first time that you have come here" . . . [*To* LEADING LADY.] And you say: "No, sir."

LEADING LADY. No, sir.

LEADING MAN. You've been here before, more than once.

THE MANAGER. No, no, stop! Let her nod "yes" first. "You've been here before, eh?" [*The* LEADING LADY *lifts up her head slightly and closes her eyes as though in disgust. Then she inclines her head twice.*]

THE STEP-DAUGHTER [*unable to contain herself*]. Oh my God! [*Puts a hand to her mouth to prevent herself from laughing.*]

THE MANAGER [*turning round*]. What's the matter?

THE STEP-DAUGHTER. Nothing, nothing!

THE MANAGER [*to* LEADING MAN]. Go on!

LEADING MAN. You've been here before, eh? Well then, there's no need to be so shy, is there? May I take off your hat?

[*The* LEADING MAN *says this last speech in such a tone and with such gestures that the* STEP-DAUGHTER, *though she has her hand to her mouth, cannot keep from laughing.*]

LEADING LADY [*indignant*]. I'm not going to stop here to be made a fool of by that woman there.

LEADING MAN. Neither am I! I'm through with it!

THE MANAGER [*shouting to* STEP-DAUGHTER]. Silence! for once and all, I tell you!

THE STEP-DAUGHTER. Forgive me! forgive me!

THE MANAGER. You haven't any manners: that's what it is! You go too far.

THE FATHER [*endeavoring to intervene*]. Yes, it's true, but excuse her . . .

THE MANAGER. Excuse what? It's absolutely disgusting.

THE FATHER. Yes, sir, but believe me, it has such a strange effect when . . .

THE MANAGER. Strange? Why strange? Where is it strange?

THE FATHER. No sir; I admire your actors—this gentleman here, this lady; but they are certainly not us!

THE MANAGER. I should hope not. Evidently they cannot be you, if they are actors.

THE FATHER. Just so: actors! Both of them act our parts exceedingly well. But, believe me, it produces quite a different effect on us. They want to be us, but they aren't, all the same.

THE MANAGER. What is it then anyway?

THE FATHER. Something that is . . . that is theirs—and no longer ours . . .

THE MANAGER. But naturally, inevitably. I've told you so already.

THE FATHER. Yes, I understand . . . I understand . . .

THE MANAGER. Well then, let's have no more of it! [*Turning to the* ACTORS.] We'll have the rehearsals by ourselves, afterwards, in the ordinary way. I never could stand rehearsing with the author present. He's never satisfied! [*Turning to* FATHER *and* STEP-DAUGHTER.] Come on! Let's get on with it again; and try and see if you can't keep from laughing.

THE STEP-DAUGHTER. Oh, I shan't laugh any more. There's a nice little bit coming for me now: you'll see.

THE MANAGER. Well then: when she says "Don't think any more of what I've said. I must forget, etc.," you [*addressing the* FATHER] come in sharp with "I understand, I understand"; and then you ask her . . .

THE STEP-DAUGHTER [*interrupting*]. What?

THE MANAGER. Why she is in mourning.

THE STEP-DAUGHTER. Not at all! See here: when I told him that it was useless for me to be thinking about my wearing mourning, do you know how he answered me? "Ah well," he said, "then let's take off this little frock."

THE MANAGER. Great! Just what we want, to make a riot in the theatre!

THE STEP-DAUGHTER. But it's the truth!

THE MANAGER. What does that matter? Acting is our business here. Truth up to a certain point, but no further.

THE STEP-DAUGHTER. What do you want to do then?

THE MANAGER. You'll see, you'll see! Leave it to me.

THE STEP-DAUGHTER. No sir! What you want to do is to piece together a little romantic sentimental scene out of my disgust, out of all the reasons, each more cruel and viler than the other, why I am what I am. He is to ask me why I'm in mourning; and I'm to answer with tears in my eyes, that it is just two months since papa died. No sir, no! He's got to say to me; as he did say: "Well let's take off this little dress at once." And I; with my two months' mourning in my heart, went there behind that screen, and with these fingers tingling with shame . . .

THE MANAGER [running his hands through his hair]. For Heaven's sake! What are you saying?

THE STEP-DAUGHTER [crying out excitedly]. The truth! The truth!

THE MANAGER. It may be. I don't deny it, and I can understand all your horror; but you must surely see that you can't have this kind of thing on the stage. It won't go.

THE STEP-DAUGHTER. Not possible, eh? Very well! I'm much obliged to you—but I'm off!

THE MANAGER. Now be reasonable! Don't lose your temper!

THE STEP-DAUGHTER. I won't stop here! I won't! I can see you've fixed it all up with him in your office. All this talk about what is possible for the stage . . . I understand! He wants to get at his complicated "cerebral drama," to have his famous remorses and torments acted; but I want to act my part, my part!

THE MANAGER [annoyed, shaking his shoulders]. Ah! Just your part! But, if you will pardon me, there are other parts than yours: His [indicating the FATHER] and hers! [Indicating the MOTHER.] On the stage you can't have a character becoming too prominent and overshadowing all the others. The thing is to pack them all into a neat little framework and then act what is actable. I am aware of the fact that everyone has his own interior life which he wants very much to put forward. But the difficulty lies in this fact: to set out just so much as is necessary for the stage, taking the other characters into consideration, and at the same time hint at the unrevealed interior life of each. I am willing to admit, my dear young lady, that from your point of view it would be a fine idea if each character could tell the public all his troubles in a nice monologue or a regular one hour lecture. [Good humoredly.] You must restrain yourself, my dear, and in your own interest, too; because this fury of yours, this exaggerated disgust you show, may make a bad impression, you know. After you have confessed to me that there were others before him at Madame Pace's and more than once . . .

THE STEP-DAUGHTER [bowing her head, impressed]. It's true. But remember those others mean him for me all the same.

THE MANAGER [not understanding]. What? The others? What do you mean?

THE STEP-DAUGHTER. For one who has gone wrong, sir, he who was responsible for the first fault is responsible for all that follow. He is responsible for my faults, was, even before I was born. Look at him, and see if it isn't true!

THE MANAGER. Well, well! And does the weight of so much responsibility seem nothing to you? Give him a chance to act it, to get it over!

THE STEP-DAUGHTER. How? How can he act all his "noble remorses," all his "moral torments," if you want to spare him the horror of being discovered one day—after he had asked her what he did ask her—in the arms of her, that already fallen woman, that child, sir, that child he used to watch come out of school? [She is moved.]

[THE MOTHER at this point is overcome with emotion, and breaks out into a fit of crying. All are touched. A long pause.]

THE STEP-DAUGHTER [as soon as the MOTHER becomes a little quieter, adds resolutely and gravely]. At present, we are unknown to the public. Tomorrow, you will act us as you wish, treating us in your own manner. But do you really want to see drama, do you want to see it flash out as it really did?

THE MANAGER. Of course! That's just what I do want, so I can use as much of it as is possible.

THE STEP-DAUGHTER. Well then, ask that Mother there to leave us.

THE MOTHER [*changing her low plaint into a sharp cry*]. No! No! Don't permit it, sir, don't permit it!

THE MANAGER. But it's only to try it.

THE MOTHER. I can't bear it. I can't.

THE MANAGER. But since it has happened already . . . I don't understand!

THE MOTHER. It's taking place now. It happens all the time. My torment isn't a pretended one. I live and feel every minute of my torture. Those two children there—have you heard them speak? They can't speak any more. They cling to me to keep up my torment actual and vivid for me. But for themselves, they do not exist, they aren't any more. And she [*indicating the* STEP-DAUGHTER] has run away, she has left me, and is lost. If I now see her here before me, it is only to renew for me the tortures I have suffered for her too.

THE FATHER. The eternal moment! She [*indicating the* STEP-DAUGHTER] is here to catch me, fix me, and hold me eternally in the stocks for that one fleeting and shameful moment of my life. She can't give it up! And you sir, cannot either fairly spare me it.

THE MANAGER. I never said I didn't want to act it. It will form, as a matter of fact, the nucleus of the whole first act right up to her surprise. [*Indicates the* MOTHER.]

THE FATHER. Just so! This is my punishment: the passion in all of us that must culminate in her final cry.

THE STEP-DAUGHTER. I can hear it still in my ears. It's driven me mad, that cry!—You can put me on as you like; it doesn't matter. Fully dressed, if you like—provided I have at least the arm bare; because, standing like this [*she goes close to the* FATHER *and leans her head on his breast*] with my head so, and my arms round his neck, I saw a vein pulsing in my arm here; and then, as if that live vein had awakened disgust in me, I closed my eyes like this, and let my head sink on his breast. [*Turning to the* MOTHER.] Cry out mother! Cry out! [*Buries head in* FATHER's *breast, and with her shoulders raised as if to prevent her hearing the cry, adds in tones of intense emotion.*] Cry out as you did then!

THE MOTHER [*coming forward to separate them*]. No! My daughter, my daughter! [*And after having pulled her away from him.*] You brute! you brute! She is my daughter! Don't you see she's my daughter?

THE MANAGER [*walking backwards towards footlights*]. Fine! fine! Damned good! And then, of course—curtain!

THE FATHER [*going towards him excitedly*]. Yes, of course, because that's the way it really happened.

THE MANAGER [*convinced and pleased*]. Oh, yes, no doubt about it. Curtain here, curtain!

[*At the reiterated cry of the* MANAGER, *the* MACHINIST *lets the curtain down, leaving the* MANAGER *and the* FATHER *in front of it before the footlights.*]

THE MANAGER. The darned idiot! I said "curtain" to show the act should end there, and he goes and lets it down in earnest. [*To the* FATHER, *while he pulls the curtain back to go on to the stage again.*] Yes, yes, it's all right. Effect certain! That's the right ending. I'll guarantee the first act at any rate.

ACT III

[*When the curtain goes up again, it is seen that the* STAGE HANDS *have shifted the bit of scenery used in the last part, and have rigged up instead at the back of the stage a drop, with some trees, and one or two wings. A portion of a fountain basin is visible. The* MOTHER *is sitting on the right with the two children by her side. The* SON *is on the same side, but away from the others. He seems bored, angry, and full of shame. The* FATHER *and the* STEP-DAUGHTER *are also seated towards the right*

front. On the other side (left) are the ACTORS,
*much in the positions they occupied before the
curtain was lowered. Only the* MANAGER *is
standing up in the middle of the stage, with
his hand closed over his mouth in the act of
meditating.*]

THE MANAGER [*shaking his shoulders after
a brief pause*]. Ah yes: the second act! Leave
it to me, leave it all to me as we arranged, and
you'll see! It'll go fine!

THE STEP-DAUGHTER. Our entry into his
house [*indicates* FATHER] in spite of him . . .
[*indicates the* SON].

THE MANAGER [*out of patience*]. Leave it to
me, I tell you!

THE STEP-DAUGHTER. Do let it be clear, at any
rate, that it is in spite of my wishes.

THE MOTHER [*from her corner, shaking her
head*]. For all the good that's come of it . . .

THE STEP-DAUGHTER [*turning towards her
quickly*]. It doesn't matter. The more harm
done us, the more remorse for him.

THE MANAGER [*impatiently*]. I understand!
Good Heavens! I understand! I'm taking it into
account.

THE MOTHER [*supplicatingly*]. I beg you, sir,
to let it appear quite plain that for conscience'
sake I did try in every way . . .

THE STEP-DAUGHTER [*interrupting indignantly and continuing for the* MOTHER]. . . . to
pacify me, to dissuade me from spiting him.
[*To* MANAGER.] Do as she wants: satisfy her,
because it is true! I enjoy it immensely. Anyhow, as you can see, the meeker she is, the
more she tries to get at his heart, the more
distant and aloof does he become.

THE MANAGER. Are we going to begin this
second act or not?

THE STEP-DAUGHTER. I'm not going to talk
any more now. But I must tell you this: you
can't have the whole action take place in the
garden, as you suggest. It isn't possible!

THE MANAGER. Why not?

THE STEP-DAUGHTER. Because he [*indicates
the* SON *again*] is always shut up alone in his
room. And then there's all the part of that poor
dazed-looking boy there which takes place indoors.

THE MANAGER. Maybe! On the other hand,
you will understand—we can't change scenes
three or four times in one act.

THE LEADING MAN. They used to once.

THE MANAGER. Yes, when the public was up
to the level of that child there.

THE LEADING LADY. It makes the illusion
easier.

THE FATHER [*irritated*]. The illusion! For
Heaven's sake, don't say illusion. Please don't
use that word, which is particularly painful for
us.

THE MANAGER [*astounded*]. And why, if you
please?

THE FATHER. It's painful, cruel, really cruel;
and you ought to understand that.

THE MANAGER. But why? What ought we to
say then? The illusion, I tell you, sir, which
we've got to create for the audience . . .

THE LEADING MAN. With our acting.

THE MANAGER. The illusion of a reality.

THE FATHER. I understand; but you, perhaps,
do not understand us. Forgive me! You see . . .
here for you and your actors, the thing is only
—and rightly so . . . a kind of game . . .

THE LEADING LADY [*interrupting indignantly*]. A game! We're not children here, if
you please! We are serious actors.

THE FATHER. I don't deny it. What I mean is
the game, or play, of your art, which has to
give, as the gentleman says, a perfect illusion
of reality.

THE MANAGER. Precisely—!

THE FATHER. Now, if you consider the fact
that we [*indicates himself and the other five
CHARACTERS*], as we are, have no other reality
outside of this illusion . . .

THE MANAGER [*astonished, looking at his
ACTORS, who are also amazed*]. And what does
that mean?

THE FATHER [*after watching them for a
moment with a wan smile*]. As I say, sir, that
which is a game of art for you is our sole
reality. [*Brief pause. He goes a step or two
nearer the* MANAGER *and adds.*] But not only
for us, you know, by the way. Just you think
it over well. [*Looks him in the eyes.*] Can you
tell me who you are?

THE MANAGER [*perplexed, half smiling*]. What? Who am I? I am myself.

THE FATHER. And if I were to tell you that that isn't true, because you and I . . . ?

5 THE MANAGER. I should say you were mad—! [*The* ACTORS *laugh*.]

THE FATHER. You're quite right to laugh: because we are all making believe here. [*To* MANAGER.] And you can therefore object that

10 it's only for a joke that that gentleman there [*indicates the* LEADING MAN], who naturally is himself, has to be me, who am on the contrary myself—this thing you see here. You see I've caught you in a trap! [*The* ACTORS *laugh*.]

15 THE MANAGER [*annoyed*]. But we've had all this over once before. Do you want to begin again?

THE FATHER. No, no! That wasn't my meaning! In fact, I should like to request you

20 to abandon this game of art [*looking at the* LEADING LADY *as if anticipating her*] which you are accustomed to play here with your actors, and to ask you seriously once again: who are you?

25 THE MANAGER [*astonished and irritated, turning to his* ACTORS]. If this fellow here hasn't got a nerve! A man who calls himself a character comes and asks me who I am!

THE FATHER [*with dignity, but not offended*].

30 A character, sir, may always ask a man who he is. Because a character has really a life of his own, marked with his especial characteristics; for which reason he is always "somebody." But a man—I'm not speaking of you now—

35 may very well be "nobody."

THE MANAGER. Yes, but you are asking these questions of me, the boss, the manager! Do you understand?

THE FATHER. But only in order to know if

40 you, as you really are now, see yourself as you once were with all the illusions that were yours then, with all the things both inside and outside of you as they seemed to you—as they were then indeed for you. Well, sir, if you think of

45 all those illusions that mean nothing to you now, of all those things which don't even *seem* to you to exist any more, while once they *were* for you, don't you feel that—I won't say these

boards—but the very earth under your feet is sinking away from you when you reflect that 50 in the same way this *you* as you feel it today— all this present reality of yours—is fated to seem a mere illusion to you tomorrow?

THE MANAGER [*without having understood much, but astonished by the specious argu-* 55 *ment*]. Well, well! And where does all this take us anyway?

THE FATHER. Oh, nowhere! It's only to show you that if we [*indicating the* CHARACTERS] have no other reality beyond the illusion, you 60 too must not count overmuch on your reality as you feel it today, since, like that of yester-day, it may prove an illusion for you tomor-row.

THE MANAGER [*determining to make fun of* 65 *him*]. Ah, excellent! Then you'll be saying next that you, with this comedy of yours that you brought here to act, are truer and more real than I am.

THE FATHER [*with the greatest seriousness*]. 70 But of course; without doubt!

THE MANAGER. Ah, really?

THE FATHER. Why, I thought you'd under-stand that from the beginning.

THE MANAGER. More real than I? 75

THE FATHER. If your reality can change from one day to another . . .

THE MANAGER. But everyone knows it can change. It is always changing, the same as anyone else's. 80

THE FATHER [*with a cry*]. No, sir, not ours! Look here! That is the very difference! Our reality doesn't change: it can't change! It can't be other than what it is, because it is already fixed for ever. It's terrible. Ours is an immu- 85 table reality which should make you shudder when you approach us if you are really con-scious of the fact that your reality is a mere transitory and fleeting illusion, taking this form today and that tomorrow, according to 90 the conditions, according to your will, your sentiments, which in turn are controlled by an intellect that shows them to you today in one manner and tomorrow . . . who knows how? . . . Illusions of reality represented in this 95 fatuous comedy of life that never ends, nor can

ever end! Because if tomorrow it were to end
. . . then why, all would be finished.

THE MANAGER. Oh for God's sake, will you
at least finish with this philosophizing and let
us try and shape this comedy which you yourself have brought me here? You argue and
philosophize a bit too much, my dear sir. You
know you seem to me almost, almost . . .
[*stops and looks him over from head to foot*].
Ah, by the way, I think you introduced yourself to me as a—what shall . . . we say—a
"character," created by an author who did not
afterward care to make a drama of his own
creations.

THE FATHER. It is the simple truth, sir.

THE MANAGER. Nonsense! Cut that out,
please! None of us believes it, because it isn't a
thing, as you must recognize yourself, which
one can believe seriously. If you want to know,
it seems to me you are trying to imitate the
manner of a certain author whom I heartily
detest—I warn you—although I have unfortunately bound myself to put on one of his
works. As a matter of fact, I was just starting
to rehearse it, when you arrived. [*Turning to
the* ACTORS.] And this is what we've gained—
out of the frying-pan into the fire!

THE FATHER. I don't know to what author
you may be alluding, but believe me I feel
what I think; and I seem to be philosophizing
only for those who do not think what they
feel, because they blind themselves with their
own sentiment. I know that for many people
this self-blinding seems much more "human";
but the contrary is really true. For man never
reasons so much and becomes so introspective
as when he suffers; since he is anxious to get
at the cause of his sufferings, to learn who has
produced them, and whether it is just or unjust
that he should have to bear them. On the other
hand, when he is happy, he takes his happiness as it comes and doesn't analyze it, just as
if happiness were his right. The animals suffer
without reasoning about their sufferings. But
take the case of a man who suffers and begins
to reason about it. Oh no! it can't be allowed!
Let him suffer like an animal, and then—ah
yet, he is "human"!

THE MANAGER. Look here! Look here! You're
off again, philosophizing worse than ever.

THE FATHER. Because I suffer, sir! I'm not
philosophizing: I'm crying aloud the reason of
my sufferings.

THE MANAGER [*makes brusque movement
as he is taken with a new idea*]. I should like
to know if anyone has ever heard of a character who gets right out of his part and perorates
and speechifies as you do. Have you ever heard
of a case? I haven't.

THE FATHER. You have never met such a
case, sir, because authors, as a rule, hide the
labor of their creations. When the characters
are really alive before their author, the latter
does nothing but follow them in their action,
in their words, in the situations which they
suggest to him; and he has to will them the
way they will themselves—for there's trouble
if he doesn't. When a character is born, he
acquires at once such an independence, even
of his own author, that he can be imagined by
everybody even in many other situations
where the author never dreamed of placing
him; and so he acquires for himself a meaning
which the author never thought of giving him.

THE MANAGER. Yes, yes, I know this.

THE FATHER. What is there then to marvel at
in us? Imagine such a misfortune for characters
as I have described to you: to be born of an
author's fantasy, and be denied life by him;
and then answer me if these characters left
alive, and yet without life, weren't right in
doing what they did do and are doing now,
after they have attempted everything in their
power to persuade him to give them their stage
life. We've all tried him in turn, I, she [*indicating the* STEP-DAUGHTER] and she [*indicating the* MOTHER].

THE STEP-DAUGHTER. It's true. I too have
sought to tempt him, many, many times, when
he has been sitting at his writing table, feeling
a bit melancholy, at the twilight hour. He
would sit in his armchair too lazy to switch
on the light, and all the shadows that crept
into his room were full of our presence coming to tempt him. [*As if she saw herself still
there by the writing table, and was annoyed*

by the presence of the ACTORS.] Oh, if you would only go away, go away and leave us alone—mother here with that son of hers—I with that Child—that Boy there always alone

5 —and then I with him [*just hints at the* FATHER]—and then I alone, alone . . . in those shadows! [*Makes a sudden movement as if in the vision she has of herself illuminating those shadows she wanted to seize hold of herself.*]

10 Ah! my life! my life! Oh, what scenes we proposed to him—and I tempted him more than any of the others!

THE FATHER. Maybe. But perhaps it was your fault that he refused to give us life: because

15 you were too insistent, too troublesome.

THE STEP-DAUGHTER. . . . Nonsense! Didn't he make me so himself? [*Goes close to the* MANAGER *to tell him as if in confidence.*] In my opinion he abandoned us in a fit of de-

20 pression, of disgust for the ordinary theatre as the public knows it and likes it.

THE SON. Exactly what it was, sir; exactly that!

THE FATHER. Not at all! Don't believe it for

25 a minute. Listen to me! You'll be doing quite right to modify, as you suggest, the excesses both of this girl here, who wants to do too much, and of this young man, who won't do anything at all.

30 THE SON. No, nothing!

THE MANAGER. You too get over the mark occasionally, my dear sir, if I may say so.

THE FATHER. I? When? Where?

THE MANAGER. Always! Continuously! Then

35 there's this insistence of yours in trying to make us believe you are a character. And then too, you must really argue and philosophize less, you know, much less.

THE FATHER. Well, if you want to take away

40 from me the possibility of representing the torment of my spirit which never gives me peace, you will be suppressing me: that's all. Every true man, sir, who is a little above the level of the beasts and plants does not live for

45 the sake of living, without knowing how to live; but he lives so as to give a meaning and a value of his own to life. For me this is *everything*. I cannot give up this, just to represent

a mere fact as she [*indicating the* STEP-DAUGHTER] wants. It's all very well for her, 50 since her "vendetta" lies in the "fact." I'm not going to do it. It destroys my *raison d'être.*

THE MANAGER. Your *raison d'être!* Oh, we're going ahead fine! First she starts off, and then you jump in. At this rate, we'll never finish. 55

THE FATHER. Now, don't be offended! Have it your own way—provided, however, that within the limits of the parts you assign us each one's sacrifice isn't too great.

THE MANAGER. You've got to understand 60 that you can't go on arguing at your own pleasure. Drama is action, sir, action and not confounded philosophy.

THE FATHER. All right, I'll do just as much arguing and philosophizing as everybody does 65 when he is considering his own torments.

THE MANAGER. If the drama permits! But for Heaven's sake, man, let's get along and come to the scene.

THE STEP-DAUGHTER. It seems to me we've 70 got too much action with our coming into his house. [*Indicating* FATHER.] You said, before, you couldn't change the scene every five minutes.

THE MANAGER. Of course not. What we've 75 got to do is to combine and group up all the facts in one simultaneous, close-knit, action. We can't have it as you want, with your little brother wandering like a ghost from room to room, hiding behind doors and meditating a 80 project which—what did you say it did to him?

THE STEP-DAUGHTER. Consumes him, sir, wastes him away!

THE MANAGER. Well, it may be. And then at the same time, you want the little girl there to 85 be playing in the garden . . . one in the house, and the other in the garden: isn't that it?

THE STEP-DAUGHTER. Yes, in the sun, in the sun! That is my only pleasure: to see her happy and careless in the garden after the 90 misery and squalor of the horrible room where we all four slept together. And I had to sleep with her—I, do you understand?—with my vile contaminated body next to hers; with her folding me fast in her loving little arms. In the 95 garden, whenever she spied me, she would run to take me by the hand. She didn't care for the big flowers, only the little ones; and she loved to show me them and pet me.

THE MANAGER. Well then, we'll have it in the garden. Everything shall happen in the garden; and we'll group the other scenes there. [Calls a STAGE HAND.] Here, a backcloth with trees and something to do as a fountain basin. [Turning round to look at the back of the stage.] Ah, you've fixed it up. Good! [To STEP-DAUGHTER.] This is just to give an idea, of course. The Boy, instead of hiding behind the doors, will wander about here in the garden, hiding behind the trees. But it's going to be rather difficult to find a child to do that scene with you where she shows you the flowers. [Turning to the BOY.] Come forward a little, will you please? Let's try it now! Come along! come along! [Then seeing him come shyly forward, full of fear and looking lost.] It's a nice business, this lad here. What's the matter with him? We'll have to give him a word or two to say. [Goes close to him, puts a hand on his shoulders, and leads him behind one of the trees.] Come on! come on! Let me see you a little! Hide here . . . yes, like that. Try and show your head just a little as if you were looking for someone. . . . [Goes back to observe the effect, when the BOY at once goes through the action.] Excellent! fine! [Turning to STEP-DAUGHTER.] Suppose the little girl there were to surprise him as he looks round, and run over to him, so we could give him a word or two to say?

THE STEP-DAUGHTER. It's useless to hope he will speak, as long as that fellow there is here . . . [indicates the SON]. You must send him away first.

THE SON [jumping up]. Delighted! Delighted! I don't ask for anything better. [Begins to move away.]

THE MANAGER [at once stopping him]. No! No! Where are you going? Wait a bit!

[The MOTHER gets up alarmed and terrified at the thought that he is really about to go away. Instinctively she lifts her arms to prevent him, without, however, leaving her seat.]

THE SON [to MANAGER who stops him]. I've got nothing to do with this affair. Let me go please! Let me go!

THE MANAGER. What do you mean by saying you've got nothing to do with this?

THE STEP-DAUGHTER [calmly, with irony]. Don't bother to stop him: he won't go away.

THE FATHER. He has to act the terrible scene in the garden with his mother.

THE SON [suddenly resolute and with dignity]. I shall act nothing at all. I've said so from the very beginning. [To the MANAGER.] Let me go!

THE STEP-DAUGHTER [going over to the MANAGER]. Allow me? [Puts down the MANAGER's arm which is restraining the SON.] Well, go away then, if you want to! [The SON looks at her with contempt and hatred. She laughs and says.] You see, he can't, he can't go away! He is obliged to stay here, indissolubly bound to the chain. If I, who fly off when that happens which has to happen, because I can't bear him—if I am still here and support that face and expression of his, you can well imagine that he is unable to move. He has to remain here, has to stop with that nice father of his, and that mother whose only son he is. [Turning to the MOTHER.] Come on, mother, come along! [Turning to MANAGER to indicate her.] You see, she was getting up to keep him back. [To the MOTHER, beckoning her with her hand.] Come on! come on! [Then to MANAGER.] You can imagine how little she wants to show these actors of yours what she really feels; but so eager is she to get near him that. . . . There, you see? She is willing to act her part. [And in fact, the MOTHER approaches him; and as soon as the STEP-DAUGHTER has finished speaking, opens her arms to signify that she consents.]

THE SON [suddenly]. No! no! If I can't go away, then I'll stop here; but I repeat: I act nothing!

THE FATHER [to MANAGER excitedly]. You can force him, sir.

THE SON. Nobody can force me.

THE FATHER. I can.

THE STEP-DAUGHTER. Wait a minute, wait. . . . First of all, the baby has to go to the fountain . . . [*runs to take the* CHILD *and leads her to the fountain*].

THE MANAGER. Yes, yes of course; that's it. Both at the same time.

[*The* SECOND LADY LEAD *and the* JUVENILE LEAD *at this point separate themselves from the group of* ACTORS. *One watches the* MOTHER *attentively; the other moves about studying the movements and manner of the* SON *whom he will have to act.*]

THE SON [*to* MANAGER]. What do you mean by both at the same time? It isn't right. There was no scene between me and her. [*Indicates the* MOTHER.] Ask her how it was!

THE MOTHER. Yes, it's true. I had come into his room . . .

THE SON. Into my room, do you understand? Nothing to do with the garden.

THE MANAGER. It doesn't matter. Haven't I told you we've got to group the action?

THE SON [*observing the* JUVENILE LEAD *studying him*]. What do you want?

THE JUVENILE LEAD. Nothing! I was just looking at you.

THE SON [*turning towards the* SECOND LADY LEAD]. Ah! she's at it too: to re-act her part! [*Indicating the* MOTHER.]

THE MANAGER. Exactly! And it seems to me that you ought to be grateful to them for their interest.

THE SON. Yes, but haven't you yet perceived that it isn't possible to live in front of a mirror which not only freezes us with the image of ourselves, but throws our likeness back at us with a horrible grimace?

THE FATHER. That is true, absolutely true. You must see that.

THE MANAGER [*to* SECOND LADY LEAD *and* JUVENILE LEAD]. He's right! Move away from them!

THE SON. Do as you like. I'm out of this!

THE MANAGER. Be quiet, you, will you? And let me hear your mother! [*To* MOTHER.] You were saying you had entered . . .

THE MOTHER. Yes, into his room, because I couldn't stand it any longer. I went to empty my heart to him of all the anguish that tortures me . . . . But as soon as he saw me come in . . .

THE SON. Nothing happened! There was no scene. I went away, that's all! I don't care for scenes!

THE MOTHER. It's true, true. That's how it was.

THE MANAGER. Well now, we've got to do this bit between you and him. It's indispensable.

THE MOTHER. I'm ready . . . when you are ready. If you could only find a chance for me to tell him what I feel here in my heart.

THE FATHER [*going to* SON *in a great rage*]. You'll do this for your mother, for your mother, do you understand?

THE SON [*quite determined*]. I do nothing!

THE FATHER [*taking hold of him and shaking him*]. For God's sake, do as I tell you! Don't you hear your mother asking you for a favor? Haven't you even got the guts to be a son?

THE SON [*taking hold of the* FATHER]. No! No! And for God's sake stop it, or else . . . [*General agitation. The* MOTHER, *frightened, tries to separate them*].

THE MOTHER [*pleading*]. Please! Please!

THE FATHER [*not leaving hold of the* SON]. You've got to obey, do you hear?

THE SON [*almost crying from rage*]. What does it mean, this madness you've got? [*They separate.*] Have you no decency, that you insist on showing everyone our shame? I won't do it! I won't! And I stand for the will of our author in this. He didn't want to put us on the stage, after all!

THE MANAGER. Man alive! You came here . . .

THE SON [*indicating* FATHER]. *He* did! I didn't!

THE MANAGER. Aren't you here now?

THE SON. It was his wish, and he dragged us along with him. He's told you not only the things that did happen, but also things that have never happened at all.

THE MANAGER. Well, tell me then what did happen. You went out of your room without saying a word?

THE SON. Without a word, so as to avoid a scene!

THE MANAGER. And then what did you do?

THE SON. Nothing . . . walking in the garden . . . [*hesitates for a moment with expression of gloom*].

5   THE MANAGER [*coming closer to him, interested by his extraordinary reserve*]. Well, well . . . Walking in the garden . . .

THE SON [*exasperated*]. Why on earth do you insist? It's horrible! [*The* MOTHER *trembles,*
10   *sobs, and looks towards the fountain.*]

THE MANAGER [*slowly observing the glance and turning towards the* SON *with increasing apprehension*]. The baby?

THE SON. There in the fountain . . .

15   THE FATHER [*pointing with tender pity to the* MOTHER]. She was following him at the moment . . .

THE MANAGER [*to the* SON *anxiously*]. And then you . . .

20   THE SON. I ran over to her; I was jumping in to drag her out when I saw something that froze my blood . . . the boy standing stock still, with eyes like a madman's, watching his little drowned sister, in the fountain! [*The* STEP-
25   DAUGHTER *bends over the fountain to hide the* CHILD. *She sobs.*] Then . . . [*a revolver shot rings out behind the trees where the* BOY *is hidden*].

THE MOTHER [*with a cry of terror runs over*
30   *in that direction together with several of the* ACTORS *amid general confusion*]. My son! My son! [*Then amid the cries and exclamations one hears her voice.*] Help! Help!

THE MANAGER [*pushing the* ACTORS *aside*
35   *while they lift up the* BOY *and carry him off*]. Is he really wounded?

SOME ACTORS. He's dead! dead!

OTHER ACTORS. No, no, it's only make believe, it's only pretense!

THE FATHER [*with a terrible cry*]. Pretense?
40   Reality, sir, reality!

THE MANAGER. Pretense? Reality? To hell with it all! Never in my life has such a thing happened to me. I've lost a whole day over
45   these people, a whole day!

Curtain

George Bernard Shaw

1856–1950

Saint Joan

1923

Shaw called his play not *The Maid of Orleans,* nor *Joan of Arc,* but *Saint Joan,* with emphasis on the *Saint.* The term is to be understood in his sense, not the usual one. In a lengthy and argumentative preface he calls her "the first Protestant martyr," and this is paradoxical, because in Joan's lifetime (1412–1431) there were as yet no Protestant churches. Shaw means that his saint personifies the rights of private conscience. "What other judgment can I judge by but my own?" she exclaims at the critical moment of her trial, deeply shocking the judges who officially embody a contrary view. She was also, says Shaw, "one of the first apostles of Nationalism." Again, a paradox, because as yet there were no modern nation-states. In other words, Shaw's Joan exemplifies Shaw's theory of history: history is progressive, and progress comes through the often quite spontaneous and unself-conscious actions of men and women of genius. They are the agents of some vital force or spirit that guides the advance of civilization. Joan's sainthood is conferred on her by this spirit, in which Shaw believed as devoutly as a good Catholic believes in Providence.

Although Shaw at least pretends that his idea of sainthood is quite as Catholic as the Pope's, it would indeed be a trial of catholicity to suppose that religious truths can be so liberally rewritten. Clearly, Shaw does not believe in Heaven, even less in Hell, and his idea of Providence has less in common with Saint Paul than with Darwin. Shaw subtitles his play a "chronicle," and he does in fact incorporate some of the actual records of Joan's trial for heresy and witchcraft. But the chronicle is modernized to suit Shaw's theory. Her judges, in his view, are not scoundrels and bigots but merely prisoners of medieval ideas that are in process of being superseded by Joan's "Protestantism" and "Nationalism," ideas that Shaw is prepared to grant would be superseded in their turn. Nevertheless, for all the modernizing, these scenes from the life of Saint Joan—ranging from country to court, from court to battlefield, and onward to her martyrdom and her elevation to sainthood—are not at all unlike a traditional "saint's life," and they convey a consistent sense of the miraculous, from the homely miracle of the laying hens upward to the miraculous "radiance" that gathers on her head at the final moment. Even while he insists on an altogether human explanation for the miracles, Shaw does not cast away the emotions of surprise and joy.

In his preface Shaw also makes a large point of his pro-feminism in portraying Joan as a forerunner of the emancipated woman. This is perfectly just. Joan's short hair and masculine garb—even more, her bluff humor and down-to-earth good sense—are very much at odds with the delicacy of Victorian female types, very much at odds with the starchy piety of conventional feminine sainthood. Shaw's Joan shows no susceptibility to a romance of the heart. Still, in her wit and self-reliance she has more in common with Rosalind in *As You Like It* and Viola in *Twelfth Night* than with present-day liberationists. What Joan wins is the allegiance of men's hearts—an extremely old-fashioned achievement.

Shaw's play is not only a chronicle and a tract setting forth his own idea of history, it is also, properly speaking, a comedy, with more than a dash of melodrama in the scene describing Joan's martyrdom. It is a comedy not only because the situations are frequently funny and because it is populated with characters who say and do amusing things, both wittingly and not. It is comic also because whatever trace it has of tragic experience passes away in the renewed peacefulness and benignity of the conclusion. Hence, the epilogue, which has been unfavorably criticized, is appropriate even if not strictly necessary. It reasserts the geniality of the early scenes and the optimism of the postulates on which the play is based.

On some occasions Shaw himself was prepared to entertain the possibility that such postulates—all those witty but sometimes tedious debates over State and Church—are not the heart of the matter. A work of art, he felt, cannot fly except on the wings of its author's deeply held convictions, and (as he says in the preface to *Man and Superman*) "Effectiveness of assertion is the Alpha and Omega of style." Then he adds this significant sentence: "All the assertions get disproved sooner or later; and so we find the world full of a magnificent débris of artistic fossils, with the matter-of-fact credibility gone clean out of them, but the form still splendid." That "splendid form" in *Saint Joan* is to be perceived in the expert modulations of emotional tone, from scene to scene, and in the long crescendo of sympathy that climaxes with the reentrance of the Chaplain after Joan's death.

The esthetic achievement is even more evident in the evolution of Joan as a character, with her own speech and gesture, her own range of feeling, her individualistic style of thought, so that at length she stands forth as "real"—one of those persons whom we "know" through fiction or drama more convincingly than we might in real life. Shaw's Saint Joan may no more resemble the historical figure, now almost entirely obscured from us, than Shakespeare's immortal Cleopatra does the Egyptian queen of history. What is thus created through the dramatists' "splendid form" Shaw would have willingly pronounced a "miracle"—and this of a kind that he never presumed to explain.

Saint Joan

SHAW

CHARACTERS°
(In the order of their appearance)

ROBERT DE BAUDRICOURT *Commander of the
  Castle of Vaucouleurs*
STEWARD *de Baudricourt's servant*
JOAN *a country girl from Domrémy*
BERTRAND DE POULENGEY *a garrison officer*
LA TRÉMOUILLE *Lord Chamberlain to the King*
THE ARCHBISHOP OF RHEIMS *Councillor to
  the King*
GILLES DE RAIS ("BLUEBEARD") *a courtier*
LA HIRE *a military commander*
CHARLES VII (THE DAUPHIN) *King of France*
DUCHESS DE LA TRÉMOUILLE *wife of the Lord
  Chamberlain*
DUNOIS ("THE BASTARD") *Commander of the
  French army*
RICHARD DE BEAUCHAMP, EARL OF WARWICK
  Commander of the English forces
JOHN DE STOGUMBER *Warwick's chaplain*
CAUCHON *Bishop of Beauvais*
BROTHER JOHN LEMAITRE *The Inquisitor*
CANON JOHN D'ESTIVET ⎫
CANON DE COURCELLES ⎬ *Members of the
BROTHER MARTIN LADVENU ⎭ ecclesiastical court*

Characters Because Shaw took great care to introduce each character as the play progressed, he
pointedly omitted a preliminary list. Nevertheless, a
cast of characters is here provided for convenient
reference.

THE EXECUTIONER
AN ENGLISH SOLDIER
A CLERICAL GENTLEMAN FROM THE VATICAN

SCENE I

[*A fine spring morning on the river Meuse,
between Lorraine and Champagne, in the year
1429 A.D., in the castle of Vaucouleurs.*

CAPTAIN ROBERT DE BAUDRICOURT, *a military
squire, handsome and physically energetic, but* 5
*with no will of his own, is disguising that defect
in his usual fashion by storming terribly at his*
STEWARD, *a trodden worm, scanty of flesh,
scanty of hair, who might be any age from 18
to 55, being the sort of man whom age cannot* 10
wither because he has never bloomed.

*The two are in a sunny stone chamber on the
first floor of the castle. At a plain strong oak
table, seated in chair to match, the captain
presents his left profile. The* STEWARD *stands* 15
*facing him at the other side of the table, if so
deprecatory a stance as his can be called standing. The mullioned thirteenth-century window
is open behind him. Near it in the corner is a
turret with a narrow arched doorway leading* 20
*to a winding stair which descends to the court-
yard. There is a stout fourlegged stool under
the table, and a wooden chest under the
window.*]

ROBERT. No eggs! No eggs!! Thousand 25
thunders, man, what do you mean by no eggs?

STEWARD. Sir: it is not my fault. It is the
act of God.

ROBERT. Blasphemy. You tell me there are
no eggs; and you blame your Maker for it. 30

STEWARD. Sir: what can I do? I cannot lay
eggs.

ROBERT [*sarcastic*]. Ha! You jest about it.

STEWARD. No, sir, God knows. We all have
to go without eggs just as you have, sir. The 35
hens will not lay.

ROBERT. Indeed! [*Rising.*] Now listen to me,
you.

STEWARD [*humbly*]. Yes, sir.

ROBERT. What am I? 40

STEWARD. What are you, sir?

ROBERT [*coming at him*]. Yes: what am I?

Am I Robert, squire of Baudricourt and captain of this castle of Vaucouleurs; or am I a cowboy?

STEWARD. Oh, sir, you know you are a
5 greater man here than the king himself.

ROBERT. Precisely. And now, do you know what you are?

STEWARD. I am nobody, sir, except that I have the honor to be your steward.

10 ROBERT [*driving him to the wall, adjective by adjective*]. You have not only the honor of being my steward, but the privilege of being the worst, most incompetent, drivelling snivelling jibbering jabbering idiot of a steward in
15 France. [*He strides back to the table.*]

STEWARD [*cowering on the chest*]. Yes, sir: to a great man like you I must seem like that.

ROBERT [*turning*]. My fault, I suppose. Eh?

STEWARD [*coming to him deprecatingly*]. Oh,
20 sir: you always give my most innocent words such a turn!

ROBERT. I will give your neck a turn if you dare tell me, when I ask you how many eggs there are, that you cannot lay any.

25 STEWARD [*protesting*]. Oh sir, oh sir—

ROBERT. No: not oh sir, oh sir, but no sir, no sir. My three Barbary hens and the black are the best layers in Champagne. And you come and tell me that there are no eggs! Who
30 stole them? Tell me that, before I kick you out through the castle gate for a liar and a seller of my goods to thieves. The milk was short yesterday, too: do not forget that.

STEWARD [*desperate*]. I know, sir. I know
35 only too well. There is no milk: there are no eggs: tomorrow there will be nothing.

ROBERT. Nothing! You will steal the lot: eh?

STEWARD. No, sir: nobody will steal anything. But there is a spell on us: we are be-
40 witched.

ROBERT. That story is not good enough for me. Robert de Baudricourt burns witches and hangs thieves. Go. Bring me four dozen eggs and two gallons of milk here in this room be-
45 fore noon, or Heaven have mercy on your bones! I will teach you to make a fool of me. [*He resumes his seat with an air of finality.*]

STEWARD. Sir: I tell you there are no eggs. There will be none—not if you were to kill me for it—as long as The Maid is at the door. 50

ROBERT. The Maid! What maid? What are you talking about?

STEWARD. The girl from Lorraine, sir. From Domrémy.

ROBERT [*rising in fearful wrath*]. Thirty 55 thousand thunders! Fifty thousand devils! Do you mean to say that that girl, who had the impudence to ask to see me two days ago, and whom I told you to send back to her father with my orders that he was to give her a good 60 hiding, is here still?

STEWARD. I have told her to go, sir. She wont.

ROBERT. I did not tell you to tell her to go: I told you to throw her out. You have fifty men-at-arms and a dozen lumps of ablebodied 65 servants to carry out my orders. Are they afraid of her?

STEWARD. She is so positive, sir.

ROBERT [*seizing him by the scruff of the neck*]. Positive! Now see here. I am going to 70 throw you downstairs.

STEWARD. No, sir. Please.

ROBERT. Well, stop me by being positive. It's quite easy: any slut of a girl can do it.

STEWARD [*hanging limp in his hands*]. Sir, 75 sir: you cannot get rid of her by throwing me out. [ROBERT *has to let him drop. He squats on his knees on the floor, contemplating his master resignedly.*] You see, sir, you are much more positive than I am. But so is she. 80

ROBERT. I am stronger than you are, you fool.

STEWARD. No, sir: it isnt that: it's your strong character, sir. She is weaker than we are: she is only a slip of a girl; but we cannot make her go. 85

ROBERT. You parcel of curs: you are afraid of her.

STEWARD [*rising cautiously*]. No, sir: we are afraid of you; but she puts courage into us. She really doesnt seem to be afraid of any- 90 thing. Perhaps you could frighten her, sir.

ROBERT [*grimly*]. Perhaps. Where is she now?

STEWARD. Down in the courtyard, sir, talking

to the soldiers as usual. She is always talking
to the soldiers except when she is praying.

ROBERT. Praying! Ha! You believe she prays,
you idiot. I know the sort of girl that is always
5 talking to soldiers. She shall talk to me a bit.
[*He goes to the window and shouts fiercely
through it.*] Hallo, you there!

A GIRL'S VOICE [*bright, strong and rough*].
Is it me, sir?

10 ROBERT. Yes, you.

THE VOICE. Be you captain?

ROBERT. Yes, damn your impudence, I be
captain. Come up here. [*To the soldiers in the
yard.*] Shew her the way, you. And shove her
15 along quick. [*He leaves the window, and returns to his place at the table, where he sits
magisterially.*]

STEWARD [*whispering*]. She wants to go and
be a soldier herself. She wants you to give her
20 soldier's clothes. Armor, sir! And a sword!
Actually! [*He steals behind* ROBERT.]

[JOAN *appears in the turret doorway. She is
an ablebodied country girl of 17 or 18, respectably dressed in red, with an uncommon face:*
25 *eyes very wide apart and bulging as they often
do in very imaginative people, a long well-
shaped nose with wide nostrils, a short upper
lip, resolute but full-lipped mouth, and handsome fighting chin. She comes eagerly to the*
30 *table, delighted at having penetrated to*
BAUDRICOURT'S *presence at last, and full of
hope as to the result. His scowl does not check
or frighten her in the least. Her voice is
normally a hearty coaxing voice, very confi-*
35 *dent, very appealing, very hard to resist.*]

JOAN [*bobbing a curtsey*]. Good morning,
captain squire. Captain: you are to give me a
horse and armor and some soldiers, and send
me to the Dauphin. Those are your orders
40 from my Lord.

ROBERT [*outraged*]. Orders from your lord!
And who the devil may your lord be? Go back
to him, and tell him that I am neither duke
nor peer at his orders: I am squire of Bau-
45 dricourt; and I take no orders except from the
king.

JOAN [*reassuringly*]. Yes, squire: that is all

right. My Lord is the King of Heaven.

ROBERT. Why, the girl's mad. [*To the*
STEWARD.] Why didnt you tell me so, you 50
blockhead?

STEWARD. Sir: do not anger her: give her
what she wants.

JOAN [*impatient, but friendly*]. They all say
I am mad until I talk to them, squire. But you 55
see that it is the will of God that you are to
do what He has put into my mind.

ROBERT. It is the will of God that I shall
send you back to your father with orders to
put you under lock and key and thrash the 60
madness out of you. What have you to say
to that?

JOAN. You think you will, squire; but you
will find it all coming quite different. You said
you would not see me; but here I am. 65

STEWARD [*appealing*]. Yes, sir. You see, sir.

ROBERT. Hold your tongue, you.

STEWARD [*abjectly*]. Yes, sir.

ROBERT [*to* JOAN, *with a sour loss of confidence*]. So you are presuming on my seeing 70
you, are you?

JOAN [*sweetly*]. Yes, squire.

ROBERT [*feeling that he has lost ground,
brings down his two fists squarely on the table,
and inflates his chest imposingly to cure the 75
unwelcome and only too familiar sensation*].
Now listen to me. I am going to assert myself.

JOAN [*busily*]. Please do, squire. The horse
will cost sixteen francs. It is a good deal of
money; but I can save it on the armor. I can 80
find a soldier's armor that will fit me well
enough: I am very hardy; and I do not need
beautiful armor made to my measure like you
wear. I shall not want many soldiers: the
Dauphin will give me all I need to raise the 85
siege of Orleans.

ROBERT [*flabbergasted*]. To raise the siege
of Orleans!

JOAN [*simply*]. Yes, squire: that is what God
is sending me to do. Three men will be enough 90
for you to send with me if they are good men
and gentle to me. They have promised to come
with me. Polly and Jack and—

ROBERT. Polly!! You impudent baggage, do

you dare call squire Bertrand de Poulengey Polly to my face?

JOAN. His friends call him so, squire: I did not know he had any other name. Jack—

5 ROBERT. That is Monsieur John of Metz, I suppose?

JOAN. Yes, squire. Jack will come willingly: he is a very kind gentleman, and gives me money to give to the poor. I think John God- 10 save will come, and Dick the Archer, and their servants John of Honecourt and Julian. There will be no trouble for you, squire: I have arranged it all: you have only to give the order.

15 ROBERT [contemplating her in a stupor of amazement]. Well, I am damned!

JOAN [with unruffled sweetness]. No, squire: God is very merciful; and the blessed saints Catherine and Margaret, who speak to me 20 every day [he gapes], will intercede for you. You will go to paradise; and your name will be remembered for ever as my first helper.

RORERT [to the STEWARD, still much bothered, but changing his tone as he pursues a new 25 clue]. Is this true about Monsieur de Poul- engey?

STEWARD [eagerly]. Yes, sir, and about Monsieur de Metz too. They both want to go with her.

30 ROBERT [thoughtful]. Mf! [He goes to the window, and shouts into the courtyard.] Hallo! You there: send Monsieur de Poulengey to me, will you? [He turns to JOAN.] Get out; and wait in the yard.

35 JOAN [smiling brightly at him]. Right, squire. [She goes out.]

ROBERT [to the STEWARD]. Go with her, you, you dithering imbecile. Stay within call; and keep your eye on her. I shall have her up here 40 again.

STEWARD. Do so in God's name, sir. Think of those hens, the best layers in Champagne; and—

ROBERT. Think of my boot; and take your 45 backside out of reach of it.

[The STEWARD retreats hastily and finds him- self confronted in the doorway by BERTRAND DE POULENGEY, a lymphatic French gentleman- at-arms, aged 36 or thereabout, employed in the department of the provost-marshal, 50 dreamily absent-minded, seldom speaking un- less spoken to, and then slow and obstinate in reply: altogether in contrast to the self-assert- ive, loud-mouthed, superficially energetic, fundamentally will-less ROBERT. The STEWARD 55 makes way for him, and vanishes.]

[POULENGEY salutes, and stands awaiting orders.]

ROBERT [genially]. It isnt service, Polly. A friendly talk. Sit down. [He hooks the stool 60 from under the table with his instep.]

[POULENGEY relaxing, comes into the room; places the stool between the table and the window; and sits down ruminatively. ROBERT, half sitting on the end of the table, begins the 65 friendly talk.]

ROBERT. Now listen to me, Polly. I must talk to you like a father.

[POULENGEY looks up at him gravely for a moment, but says nothing.] 70

ROBERT. It's about this girl you are interested in. Now, I have seen her. I have talked to her. First, she's mad. That doesnt matter. Second, she's not a farm wench. She's a bourgeoise. That matters a good deal. I know her class 75 exactly. Her father came here last year to represent his village in a lawsuit: he is one of their notables. A farmer. Not a gentleman farmer: he makes money by it, and lives by it. Still, not a laborer. Not a mechanic. He 80 might have a cousin a lawyer, or in the Church. People of this sort may be of no account socially; but they can give a lot of bother to the authorities. That is to say, to me. Now no doubt it seems to you a very simple thing to 85 take this girl away, humbugging her into the belief that you are taking her to the Dauphin. But if you get her into trouble, you may get me into no end of a mess, as I am her father's lord, and responsible for her protection. So 90 friends or no friends, Polly, hands off her.

POULENGEY [with deliberate impressiveness]. I should as soon think of the Blessed Virgin herself in that way, as of this girl.

ROBERT [coming off the table]. But she says 95 you and Jack and Dick have offered to go with her. What for? You are not going to tell me that you take her crazy notion of going to the Dauphin seriously, are you?

POULENGEY [*slowly*]. There is something
5 about her. They are pretty foulmouthed and foulminded down there in the guardroom, some of them. But there hasnt been a word that has anything to do with her being a woman. They have stopped swearing before
10 her. There is something. Something. It may be worth trying.

ROBERT. Oh, come, Polly! pull yourself together. Commonsense was never your strong point; but this is a little too much. [*He retreats*
15 *disgustedly.*]

POULENGEY [*unmoved*]. What is the good of commonsense? If we had any commonsense we should join the Duke of Burgundy and the English king. They hold half the country, right
20 down to the Loire. They have Paris. They have this castle: you know very well that we had to surrender it to the Duke of Bedford, and that you are only holding it on parole. The Dauphin is in Chinon, like a rat in a corner,
25 except that he wont fight. We dont even know that he is the Dauphin: his mother says he isnt; and she ought to know. Think of that! the queen denying the legitimacy of her own son!

30 ROBERT. Well, she married her daughter to the English king. Can you blame the woman?

POULENGEY. I blame nobody. But thanks to her, the Dauphin is down and out; and we may as well face it. The English will take
35 Orleans: the Bastard will not be able to stop them.

ROBERT. He beat the English the year before last at Montargis. I was with him.

POULENGEY. No matter: his men are cowed
40 now; and he cant work miracles. And I tell you that nothing can save our side now but a miracle.

ROBERT. Miracles are all right, Polly. The only difficulty about them is that they dont
45 happen nowadays.

POULENGEY. I used to think so. I am not so sure now. [*Rising, and moving ruminatively towards the window.*] At all events this is not a time to leave any stone unturned. There is something about the girl. 50

ROBERT. Oh! You think the girl can work miracles, do you?

POULENGEY. I think the girl herself is a bit of a miracle. Anyhow, she is the last card left in our hand. Better play her than throw up 55 the game. [*He wanders to the turret.*]

ROBERT [*wavering*]. You really think that?

POULENGEY [*turning*]. Is there anything else left for us to think?

ROBERT [*going to him*]. Look here, Polly. If 60 you were in my place would you let a girl like that do you out of sixteen francs for a horse?

POULENGEY. I will pay for the horse.

ROBERT. You will!

POULENGEY. Yes: I will back my opinion. 65

ROBERT. You will really gamble on a forlorn hope to the tune of sixteen francs?

POULENGEY. It is not a gamble.

ROBERT. What else is it?

POULENGEY. It is a certainty. Her words and 70 her ardent faith in God have put fire into me.

ROBERT [*giving him up*]. Whew! You are as mad as she is.

POULENGEY [*obstinately*]. We want a few mad people now. See where the sane ones have 75 landed us!

ROBERT [*his irresoluteness now openly swamping his affected decisiveness*]. I shall feel like a precious fool. Still, if you feel sure—?

POULENGEY. I feel sure enough to take her to 80 Chinon—unless you stop me.

ROBERT. This is not fair. You are putting the responsibility on me.

POULENGEY. It is on you whichever way you decide. 85

ROBERT. Yes: thats just it. Which way am I to decide? You dont see how awkward this is for me. [*Snatching at a dilatory step with an unconscious hope that* JOAN *will make up his mind for him.*] Do you think I ought to have 90 another talk to her?

POULENGEY [*rising*]. Yes. [*He goes to the window and calls.*] Joan!

JOAN'S VOICE. Will he let us go, Polly?

POULENGEY. Come up. Come in. [*Turning to* 95 ROBERT.] Shall I leave you with her?

ROBERT. No: stay here; and back me up.

[POULENGEY *sits down on the chest.* ROBERT *goes back to his magisterial chair, but remains standing to inflate himself more imposingly.* JOAN *comes in, full of good news.*]

JOAN. Jack will go halves for the horse.

ROBERT. Well!! [*He sits, deflated.*]

POULENGEY [*gravely*]. Sit down, Joan.

JOAN [*checked a little, and looking to* ROBERT]. May I?

ROBERT. Do what you are told.

[JOAN *curtsies and sits down on the stool between them.* ROBERT *outfaces his perplexity with his most peremptory air.*]

ROBERT. What is your name?

JOAN [*chattily*]. They always call me Jenny in Lorraine. Here in France I am Joan. The soldiers call me The Maid.

ROBERT. What is your surname?

JOAN. Surname? What is that? My father sometimes calls himself d'Arc; but I know nothing about it. You met my father. He—

ROBERT. Yes, yes: I remember. You come from Domrémy in Lorraine, I think.

JOAN. Yes; but what does it matter? we all speak French.

ROBERT. Dont ask questions: answer them. How old are you?

JOAN. Seventeen: so they tell me. It might be nineteen. I dont remember.

ROBERT. What did you mean when you said that St Catherine and St Margaret talked to you every day?

JOAN. They do.

ROBERT. What are they like?

JOAN [*suddenly obstinate*]. I will tell you nothing about that: they have not given me leave.

ROBERT. But you actually see them; and they talk to you just as I am talking to you?

JOAN. No: it is quite different. I cannot tell you: you must not talk to me about my voices.

ROBERT. How do you mean? voices?

JOAN. I hear voices telling me what to do. They come from God.

ROBERT. They come from your imagination.

JOAN. Of course. That is how the messages of God come to us.

POULENGEY. Checkmate.

ROBERT. No fear! [*To* JOAN.] So God says you are to raise the siege of Orleans?

JOAN. And to crown the Dauphin in Rheims Cathedral.

ROBERT [*gasping*]. Crown the D———! Gosh!

JOAN. And to make the English leave France.

ROBERT [*sarcastic*]. Anything else?

JOAN [*charming*]. Not just at present, thank you, squire.

ROBERT. I suppose you think raising a siege is as easy as chasing a cow out of a meadow. You think soldiering is anybody's job?

JOAN. I do not think it can be very difficult if God is on your side, and you are willing to put your life in His hand. But many soldiers are very simple.

ROBERT [*grimly*]. Simple! Did you ever see English soldiers fighting?

JOAN. They are only men. God made them just like us; but He gave them their own country and their own language; and it is not His will that they should come into our country and try to speak our language.

ROBERT. Who has been putting such nonsense into your head? Dont you know that soldiers are subject to their feudal lord, and that it is nothing to them or to you whether he is the duke of Burgundy or the king of England or the king of France? What has their language to do with it?

JOAN. I do not understand that a bit. We are all subject to the King of Heaven; and He gave us our countries and our languages, and meant us to keep to them. If it were not so it would be murder to kill an Englishman in battle; and you, squire, would be in great danger of hell fire. You must not think about your duty to your feudal lord, but about your duty to God.

POULENGEY. It's no use, Robert: she can choke you like that every time.

ROBERT. Can she, by Saint Dennis! We shall see. [*To* JOAN.] We are not talking about God: we are talking about practical affairs. I ask you again, girl, have you ever seen English soldiers fighting? Have you ever seen them plundering, burning, turning the countryside into a desert? Have you heard no tales of their Black Prince who was blacker than the devil himself, or of the English king's father?

5 JOAN. You must not be afraid, Robert—

ROBERT. Damn you, I am not afraid. And who gave you leave to call me Robert?

JOAN. You were called so in church in the name of our Lord. All the other names are your 10 father's or your brother's or anybody's.

ROBERT. Tcha!

JOAN. Listen to me, squire. At Domrémy we had to fly to the next village to escape from the English soldiers. Three of them were left 15 behind, wounded. I came to know these three poor goddams quite well. They had not half my strength.

ROBERT. Do you know why they are called goddams?

20 JOAN. No. Everyone calls them goddams.

ROBERT. It is because they are always calling on their God to condemn their souls to perdition. That is what goddam means in their language. How do you like it?

25 JOAN. God will be merciful to them; and they will act like His good children when they go back to the country He made for them, and made them for. I have heard the tales of the Black Prince. The moment he touched the soil 30 of our country the devil entered into him and made him a black fiend. But at home, in the place made for him by God, he was good. It is always so. If I went into England against the will of God to conquer England, and tried to 35 live there and speak its language, the devil would enter into me; and when I was old I should shudder to remember the wickednesses I did.

ROBERT. Perhaps. But the more devil you 40 were the better you might fight. That is why the goddams will take Orleans. And you cannot stop them, nor ten thousand like you.

JOAN. One thousand like me can stop them. Ten like me can stop them with God on our side. 45 [*She rises impetuously, and goes at him, unable to sit quiet any longer.*] You do not understand, squire. Our soldiers are always beaten because they are fighting only to save their skins; and the shortest way to save your skin is to run away. Our knights are thinking 50 only of the money they will make in ransoms: it is not kill or be killed with them, but pay or be paid. But I will teach them all to fight that the will of God may be done in France; and then they will drive the poor goddams before 55 them like sheep. You and Polly will live to see the day when there will not be an English soldier on the soil of France; and there will be but one king there: not the feudal English king, but God's French one. 60

ROBERT [*to* POULENGEY]. This may be all rot, Polly; but the troops might swallow it, though nothing that we can say seems able to put any fight into them. Even the Dauphin might swallow it. And if she can put fight into him, 65 she can put it into anybody.

POULENGEY. I can see no harm in trying. Can you? And there is something about the girl—

ROBERT [*turning to* JOAN]. Now listen you to me; and [*desperately*] dont cut in before I 70 have time to think.

JOAN [*plumping down on the stool again, like an obedient schoolgirl*]. Yes, squire.

ROBERT. Your orders are, that you are to go to Chinon under the escort of this gentleman 75 and three of his friends.

JOAN [*radiant, clasping her hands*]. Oh, squire! Your head is all circled with light, like a saint's.

POULENGEY. How is she to get into the royal 80 presence?

ROBERT [*who has looked up for his halo rather apprehensively*]. I dont know: how did she get into my presence? If the Dauphin can keep her out he is a better man than I take 85 him for. [*Rising.*] I will send her to Chinon; and she can say I sent her. Then let come what may: I can do no more.

JOAN. And the dress? I may have a soldier's dress, maynt I, squire? 90

ROBERT. Have what you please. I wash my hands of it.

JOAN [*wildly excited by her success*]. Come, Polly. [*She dashes out.*]

ROBERT [*shaking* POULENGEY's *hand*]. Good- 95 bye, old man, I am taking a big chance. Few other men would have done it. But as you say, there is something about her.

POULENGEY. Yes: there is something about her. Goodbye. [*He goes out.*]

[ROBERT, *still very doubtful whether he has not been made a fool of by a crazy female, and a social inferior to boot, scratches his head and slowly comes back from the door.*]

[*The* STEWARD *runs in with a basket.*]

STEWARD. Sir, sir—

ROBERT. What now?

STEWARD. The hens are laying like mad, sir. Five dozen eggs!

ROBERT [*stiffens convulsively; crosses himself; and forms with his pale lips the words*]. Christ in heaven! [*Aloud but breathless.*] She did come from God.

SCENE II

[*Chinon, in Touraine. An end of the throne-room in the castle, curtained off to make an antechamber. The* ARCHBISHOP OF RHEIMS, *close on 50, a full-fed political prelate with nothing of the ecclesiastic about him except his imposing bearing, and the* LORD CHAMBERLAIN, MONSEIGNEUR DE LA TRÉMOUILLE, *a monstrous arrogant wineskin of a man, are waiting for the* DAUPHIN. *There is a door in the wall to the right of the two men. It is late in the afternoon on the 8th of March, 1429. The* ARCHBISHOP *stands with dignity whilst the* CHAMBERLAIN, *on his left, fumes about in the worst of tempers.*]

LA TRÉMOUILLE. What the devil does the Dauphin mean by keeping us waiting like this? I dont know how you have the patience to stand there like a stone idol.

THE ARCHBISHOP. You see, I am an archbishop; and an archbishop is a sort of idol. At any rate he has to learn to keep still and suffer fools patiently. Besides, my dear Lord Chamberlain, it is the Dauphin's royal privilege to keep you waiting, is it not?

LA TRÉMOUILLE. Dauphin be damned! saving your reverence. Do you know how much money he owes me?

THE ARCHBISHOP. Much more than he owes me, I have no doubt, because you are a much richer man. But I take it he owes you all you could afford to lend him. That is what he owes me.

LA TRÉMOUILLE. Twentyseven thousand: that was his last haul. A cool twentyseven thousand!

THE ARCHBISHOP. What becomes of it all? He never has a suit of clothes that I would throw to a curate.

LA TRÉMOUILLE. He dines on a chicken or a scrap of mutton. He borrows my last penny; and there is nothing to shew for it. [*A* PAGE *appears in the doorway.*] At last!

THE PAGE. No, my lord: it is not His Majesty. Monsieur de Rais is approaching.

LA TRÉMOUILLE. Young Bluebeard! Why announce him?

THE PAGE. Captain La Hire is with him. Something has happened, I think.

[GILLES DE RAIS, *a young man of 25, very smart and self-possessed, and sporting the extravagance of a little curled beard dyed blue at a clean-shaven court, comes in. He is determined to make himself agreeable, but lacks natural joyousness, and is not really pleasant. In fact when he defies the Church some eleven years later he is accused of trying to extract pleasure from horrible cruelties, and hanged. So far, however, there is no shadow of the gallows on him. He advances gaily to the* ARCHBISHOP. *The* PAGE *withdraws.*]

BLUEBEARD. Your faithful lamb, Archbishop. Good day, my lord. Do you know what has happened to La Hire?

LA TRÉMOUILLE. He has sworn himself into a fit, perhaps.

BLUEBEARD. No: just the opposite. Foul Mouthed Frank, the only man in Touraine who could beat him at swearing, was told by a soldier that he shouldnt use such language when he was at the point of death.

THE ARCHBISHOP. Nor at any other point. But was Foul Mouthed Frank on the point of death?

BLUEBEARD. Yes: he has just fallen into a well

and been drowned. La Hire is frightened out of his wits.

[CAPTAIN LA HIRE *comes in: a war dog with no court manners and pronounced camp ones.*]

5 BLUEBEARD. I have just been telling the Chamberlain and the Archbishop. The Archbishop says you are a lost man.

LA HIRE [*striding past* BLUEBEARD, *and planting himself between the* ARCHBISHOP *and* 10 LA TRÉMOUILLE]. This is nothing to joke about. It is worse than we thought. It was not a soldier, but an angel dressed as a soldier.

THE ARCHBISHOP
THE CHAMBERLAIN } [*exclaiming all together*]. An angel!
15 BLUEBEARD

LA HIRE. Yes, an angel. She has made her way from Champagne with half a dozen men through the thick of everything: Burgundians, Goddams, deserters, robbers, and Lord knows 20 who; and they never met a soul except the country folk. I know one of them: de Poulengey. He says she's an angel. If ever I utter an oath again may my soul be blasted to eternal damnation!

25 THE ARCHBISHOP. A very pious beginning, Captain.

[BLUEBEARD *and* LA TRÉMOUILLE *laugh at him. The* PAGE *returns.*]

THE PAGE. His Majesty.

30 [*They stand perfunctorily at court attention. The* DAUPHIN, *aged 26, really* KING CHARLES THE SEVENTH *since the death of his father, but as yet uncrowned, comes in through the curtains with a paper in his hands. He is a poor* 35 *creature physically; and the current fashion of shaving closely, and hiding every scrap of hair under the head-covering or headdress, both by women and men, makes the worst of his appearance. He has little narrow eyes, near* 40 *together, a long pendulous nose that droops over his thick short upper lip, and the expression of a young dog accustomed to be kicked, yet incorrigible and irrepressible. But he is neither vulgar nor stupid; and he has a cheeky* 45 *humor which enables him to hold his own in conversation. Just at present he is excited, like a child with a new toy. He comes to the* ARCH-

BISHOP'S *left hand.* BLUEBEARD *and* LA HIRE *retire towards the curtains.*]

CHARLES. Oh, Archbishop, do you know 50 what Robert de Baudricourt is sending me from Vaucouleurs?

THE ARCHBISHOP [*contemptuously*]. I am not interested in the newest toys.

CHARLES [*indignantly*]. It isnt a toy. [*Sulk-* 55 *ily.*] However, I can get on very well without your interest.

THE ARCHBISHOP. Your Highness is taking offence very unnecessarily.

CHARLES. Thank you. You are always ready 60 with a lecture, arnt you?

LA TRÉMOUILLE [*roughly*]. Enough grumbling. What have you got there?

CHARLES. What is that to you?

LA TRÉMOUILLE. It is my business to know 65 what is passing between you and the garrison at Vaucouleurs. [*He snatches the paper from the* DAUPHIN'S *hand, and begins reading it with some difficulty, following the words with his finger and spelling them out syllable by* 70 *syllable.*]

CHARLES [*mortified*]. You all think you can treat me as you please because I owe you money, and because I am no good at fighting. But I have the blood royal in my veins. 75

THE ARCHBISHOP. Even that has been questioned, your Highness. One hardly recognizes in you the grandson of Charles the Wise.

CHARLES. I want to hear no more of my 80 grandfather. He was so wise that he used up the whole family stock of wisdom for five generations, and left me the poor fool I am, bullied and insulted by all of you.

THE ARCHBISHOP. Control yourself, sir. These 85 outbursts of petulance are not seemly.

CHARLES. Another lecture! Thank you. What a pity it is that though you are an archbishop saints and angels dont come to see you!

THE ARCHBISHOP. What do you mean? 90

CHARLES. Aha! Ask that bully there [*pointing to* LA TRÉMOUILLE].

LA TRÉMOUILLE [*furious*]. Hold your tongue. Do you hear?

CHARLES. Oh, I hear. You neednt shout. The whole castle can hear. Why dont you go and shout at the English, and beat them for me?

LA TRÉMOUILLE [*raising his fist*]. You young—

CHARLES [*running behind the* ARCHBISHOP]. Dont you raise your hand to me. It's high treason.

LA HIRE. Steady, Duke! Steady!

THE ARCHBISHOP [*resolutely*]. Come, come! this will not do. My lord Chamberlain: please! please! we must keep some sort of order. [*To the* DAUPHIN.] And you, sir: if you cannot rule your kingdom, at least try to rule yourself.

CHARLES. Another lecture! Thank you.

LA TRÉMOUILLE [*handing the paper to the* ARCHBISHOP]. Here: read the accursed thing for me. He has sent the blood boiling into my head: I cant distinguish the letters.

CHARLES [*coming back and peering round* LA TRÉMOUILLE'S *left shoulder*]. I will read it for you if you like. I can read, you know.

LA TRÉMOUILLE [*with intense contempt, not at all stung by the taunt*]. Yes: reading is about all you are fit for. Can you make it out, Archbishop?

THE ARCHBISHOP. I should have expected more commonsense from De Baudricourt. He is sending some cracked country lass here—

CHARLES [*interrupting*]. No: he is sending a saint: an angel. And she is coming to me: to me, the king, and not to you, Archbishop, holy as you are. She knows the blood royal if you dont. [*He struts up to the curtains between* BLUEBEARD *and* LA HIRE.]

THE ARCHBISHOP. You cannot be allowed to see this crazy wench.

CHARLES [*turning*]. But I am the king; and I will.

LA TRÉMOUILLE [*brutally*]. Then she cannot be allowed to see you. Now!

CHARLES. I tell you I will. I am going to put my foot down—

BLUEBEARD [*laughing at him*]. Naughty! What would your wise grandfather say?

CHARLES. That just shews your ignorance, Bluebeard. My grandfather had a saint who used to float in the air when she was praying, and told him everything he wanted to know. My poor father had two saints, Marie de Maillé and the Gasque of Avignon. It is in our family; and I dont care what you say: I will have my saint too.

THE ARCHBISHOP. This creature is not a saint. She is not even a respectable woman. She does not wear women's clothes. She is dressed like a soldier, and rides round the country with soldiers. Do you suppose such a person can be admitted to your Highness's court?

LA HIRE. Stop. [*Going to the* ARCHBISHOP.] Did you say a girl in armor, like a soldier?

THE ARCHBISHOP. So De Baudricourt describes her.

LA HIRE. But by all the devils in hell—Oh, God forgive me, what am I saying?—by Our Lady and all the saints, this must be the angel that struck Foul Mouthed Frank dead for swearing.

CHARLES [*triumphantly*]. You see! A miracle!

LA HIRE. She may strike the lot of us dead if we cross her. For Heaven's sake, Archbishop, be careful what you are doing.

THE ARCHBISHOP [*severely*]. Rubbish! Nobody has been struck dead. A drunken blackguard who has been rebuked a hundred times for swearing has fallen into a well, and been drowned. A mere coincidence.

LA HIRE. I do not know what a coincidence is. I do know that the man is dead, and that she told him he was going to die.

THE ARCHBISHOP. We are all going to die, Captain.

LA HIRE [*crossing himself*]. I hope not. [*He backs out of the conversation.*]

BLUEBEARD. We can easily find out whether she is an angel or not. Let us arrange when she comes that I shall be the Dauphin, and see whether she will find me out.

CHARLES. Yes: I agree to that. If she cannot find the blood royal I will have nothing to do with her.

THE ARCHBISHOP. It is for the Church to make saints: let De Baudricourt mind his own business, and not dare usurp the function of his priest. I say the girl shall not be admitted.

BLUEBEARD. But, Archbishop—

THE ARCHBISHOP [*sternly*]. I speak in the Church's name. [*To the* DAUPHIN.] Do you dare say she shall?

CHARLES [*intimidated but sulky*]. Oh, if you make it an excommunication matter, I have nothing more to say, of course. But you havnt read the end of the letter. De Baudricourt says she will raise the siege of Orleans, and beat the English for us.

LA TRÉMOUILLE. Rot!

CHARLES. Well, will you save Orleans for us, with all your bullying?

LA TRÉMOUILLE [*savagely*]. Do not throw that in my face again: do you hear? I have done more fighting than you ever did or ever will. But I cannot be everywhere.

THE DAUPHIN. Well, thats something.

BLUEBEARD [*coming between the* ARCHBISHOP *and* CHARLES]. You have Jack Dunois at the head of your troops in Orleans: the brave Dunois, the handsome Dunois, the wonderful invincible Dunois, the darling of all the ladies, the beautiful bastard. Is it likely that the country lass can do what he cannot do?

CHARLES. Why doesnt he raise the siege, then?

LA HIRE. The wind is against him.

BLUEBEARD. How can the wind hurt him at Orleans? It is not on the Channel.

LA HIRE. It is on the river Loire; and the English hold the bridgehead. He must ship his men across the river and upstream, if he is to take them in the rear. Well, he cannot, because there is a devil of a wind blowing the other way. He is tired of paying the priests to pray for a west wind. What he needs is a miracle. You tell me that what the girl did to Foul Mouthed Frank was no miracle. No matter: it finished Frank. If she changes the wind for Dunois, that may not be a miracle either; but it may finish the English. What harm is there in trying?

THE ARCHBISHOP. [*who has read the end of the letter and become more thoughtful*]. It is true that De Baudricourt seems extraordinarily impressed.

LA HIRE. De Baudricourt is a blazing ass; but he is a soldier; and if he thinks she can beat the English, all the rest of the army will think so too.

LA TRÉMOUILLE [*to the* ARCHBISHOP, *who is hesitating*]. Oh, let them have their way. Dunois' men will give up the town in spite of him if somebody does not put some fresh spunk into them.

THE ARCHBISHOP. The Church must examine the girl before anything decisive is done about her. However, since his Highness desires it, let her attend the Court.

LA HIRE. I will find her and tell her. [*He goes out.*]

CHARLES. Come with me, Bluebeard; and let us arrange so that she will not know who I am. You will pretend to be me. [*He goes out through the curtains.*]

BLUEBEARD. Pretend to be that thing! Holy Michael! [*He follows the* DAUPHIN.]

LA TRÉMOUILLE. I wonder will she pick him out!

THE ARCHBISHOP. Of course she will.

LA TRÉMOUILLE. Why? How is she to know?

THE ARCHBISHOP. She will know what everybody in Chinon knows: that the Dauphin is the meanest-looking and worst-dressed figure in the Court, and that the man with the blue beard is Gilles de Rais.

LA TRÉMOUILLE. I never thought of that.

THE ARCHBISHOP. You are not so accustomed to miracles as I am. It is part of my profession.

LA TRÉMOUILLE [*puzzled and a little scandalized*]. But that would not be a miracle at all.

THE ARCHBISHOP [*calmly*]. Why not?

LA TRÉMOUILLE. Well, come! what is a miracle?

THE ARCHBISHOP. A miracle, my friend, is an event which creates faith. That is the purpose and nature of miracles. They may seem very wonderful to the people who witness them, and very simple to those who perform them. That does not matter: if they confirm or create faith they are true miracles.

LA TRÉMOUILLE. Even when they are frauds, do you mean?

THE ARCHBISHOP. Frauds deceive. An event which creates faith does not deceive: therefore it is not a fraud, but a miracle.

LA TRÉMOUILLE [*scratching his neck in his perplexity*]. Well, I suppose as you are an archbishop you must be right. It seems a bit fishy to me. But I am no churchman, and dont understand these matters.

THE ARCHBISHOP. You are not a churchman; but you are a diplomatist and a soldier. Could you make our citizens pay war taxes, or our soldiers sacrifice their lives, if they knew what is really happening instead of what seems to them to be happening?

LA TRÉMOUILLE. No, by Saint Dennis: the fat would be in the fire before sundown.

THE ARCHBISHOP. Would it not be quite easy to tell them the truth?

LA TRÉMOUILLE. Man alive, they wouldnt believe it.

THE ARCHBISHOP. Just so. Well, the Church has to rule men for the good of their souls as you have to rule them for the good of their bodies. To do that, the Church must do as you do: nourish their faith by poetry.

LA TRÉMOUILLE. Poetry! I should call it humbug.

THE ARCHBISHOP. You would be wrong, my friend. Parables are not lies because they describe events that have never happened. Miracles are not frauds because they are often —I do not say always—very simple and innocent contrivances by which the priest fortifies the faith of his flock. When this girl picks out the Dauphin among his courtiers, it will not be a miracle for me, because I shall know how it has been done, and my faith will not be increased. But as for the others, if they feel the thrill of the supernatural, and forget their sinful clay in a sudden sense of the glory of God, it will be a miracle and a blessed one. And you will find that the girl herself will be more affected than anyone else. She will forget how she really picked him out. So, perhaps, will you.

LA TRÉMOUILLE. Well, I wish I were clever enough to know how much of you is God's archbishop and how much the most artful fox in Touraine. Come on, or we shall be late for the fun; and I want to see it, miracle or no miracle.

THE ARCHBISHOP [*detaining him a moment*]. Do not think that I am a lover of crooked ways. There is a new spirit rising in men: we are at the dawning of a wider epoch. If I were a simple monk, and had not to rule men, I should seek peace for my spirit with Aristotle and Pythagoras rather than with the saints and their miracles.

LA TRÉMOUILLE. And who the deuce was Pythagoras?

THE ARCHBISHOP. A sage who held that the earth is round, and that it moves round the sun.

LA TRÉMOUILLE. What an utter fool! Couldnt he use his eyes?

[*They go out together through the curtains, which are presently withdrawn, revealing the full depth of the throne-room with the* COURT *assembled. On the right are two Chairs of State on a dais.* BLUEBEARD *is standing theatrically on the dais, playing the king, and, like the courtiers, enjoying the joke rather obviously. There is a curtained arch in the wall behind the dais; but the main door, guarded by* MEN-AT-ARMS, *is at the other side of the room; and a clear path across is kept and lined by the courtiers.* CHARLES *is in this path in the middle of the room.* LA HIRE *is on his right. The* ARCHBISHOP, *on his left, has taken his place by the dais:* LA TRÉMOUILLE *at the other side of it. The* DUCHESS DE LA TRÉMOUILLE, *pretending to be the Queen, sits in the Consort's chair, with a group of ladies in waiting close by, behind the* ARCHBISHOP.

The chatter of the COURTIERS *makes such a noise that nobody notices the appearance of the* PAGE *at the door.*]

THE PAGE. The Duke of—[*Nobody listens.*] The Duke of—[*The chatter continues. Indignant at his failure to command a hearing, he snatches the halberd of the nearest* MAN-AT-ARMS, *and thumps the floor with it. The chatter ceases; and everybody looks at him in silence.*] Attention! [*He restores the halberd to the* MAN-AT-ARMS.] The Duke of Vendôme presents Joan the Maid to his Majesty.

CHARLES [*putting his finger on his lip*]. Ssh! [*He hides behind the nearest courtier, peering out to see what happens.*]

BLUEBEARD [*majestically*]. Let her approach the throne.

[JOAN, *dressed as a soldier, with her hair bobbed and hanging thickly round her face, is led in by a bashful and speechless* NOBLEMAN, *from whom she detaches herself to stop and look round eagerly for the* DAUPHIN.]

THE DUCHESS [*to the nearest lady in waiting*]. My dear! Her hair!

[*All the ladies explode in uncontrollable laughter.*]

BLUEBEARD [*trying not to laugh, waving his hand in deprecation of their merriment*]. Ssh—ssh! Ladies! Ladies!!

JOAN [*not at all embarrassed*]. I wear it like this because I am a soldier. Where be Dauphin?

[*A titter runs through the* COURT *as she walks to the dais.*]

BLUEBEARD [*condescendingly*]. You are in the presence of the Dauphin.

[JOAN *looks at him sceptically for a moment, scanning him hard up and down to make sure. Dead silence, all watching her. Fun dawns in her face.*]

JOAN. Coom, Bluebeard! Thou canst not fool me. Where be Dauphin?

[*A roar of laughter breaks out as* GILLES, *with a gesture of surrender, joins in the laugh, and jumps down from the dais beside* LA TRÉMOUILLE. JOAN, *also on the broad grin, turns back, searching along the row of courtiers, and presently makes a dive, and drags out* CHARLES *by the arm.*]

JOAN [*releasing him and bobbing him a little curtsey*]. Gentle little Dauphin, I am sent to you to drive the English away from Orleans and from France, and to crown you king in the cathedral at Rheims, where all true kings of France are crowned.

CHARLES [*triumphant, to the* COURT]. You see, all of you: she knew the blood royal. Who dare say now that I am not my father's son? [*To* JOAN.] But if you want me to be crowned at Rheims you must talk to the Archbishop, not to me. There he is [*he is standing behind her*]!

JOAN [*turning quickly, overwhelmed with emotion*]. Oh, my lord! [*She falls on both knees before him, with bowed head, not daring to look up.*] My lord: I am only a poor country girl; and you are filled with the blessedness and glory of God Himself; but you will touch me with your hands, and give me your blessing, wont you?

BLUEBEARD [*whispering to* LA TRÉMOUILLE]. The old fox blushes.

LA TRÉMOUILLE. Another miracle!

THE ARCHBISHOP [*touched, putting his hand on her head*]. Child: you are in love with religion.

JOAN [*startled: looking up at him*]. Am I? I never thought of that. Is there any harm in it?

THE ARCHBISHOP. There is no harm in it, my child. But there is danger.

JOAN [*rising, with sunflush of reckless happiness irradiating her face*]. There is always danger, except in heaven. Oh, my lord, you have given me such strength, such courage. It must be a most wonderful thing to be Archbishop.

[*The* COURT *smiles broadly: even titters a little.*]

THE ARCHBISHOP [*drawing himself up sensitively*]. Gentlemen: your levity is rebuked by this maid's faith. I am, God help me, all unworthy; but your mirth is a deadly sin.

[*Their faces fall. Dead silence.*]

BLUEBEARD. My lord: we were laughing at her, not at you.

THE ARCHBISHOP. What? Not at my unworthiness but at her faith! Gilles de Rais: this maid prophesied that the blasphemer should be drowned in his sin—

JOAN [*distressed*]. No!

THE ARCHBISHOP [*silencing her by a gesture*]. I prophesy now that you will be hanged in yours if you do not learn when to laugh and when to pray.

BLUEBEARD. My lord: I stand rebuked. I am sorry: I can say no more. But if you prophesy that I shall be hanged, I shall never be able to resist temptation, because I shall always be telling myself that I may as well be hanged for a sheep as a lamb.

[*The* COURTIERS *take heart at this. There is more tittering.*]

JOAN [*scandalized*]. You are an idle fellow, Bluebeard; and you have great impudence to answer the Archbishop.

LA HIRE [*with a huge chuckle*]. Well said, lass! Well said!

JOAN [*impatiently to the* ARCHBISHOP]. Oh, my lord, will you send all these silly folks away so that I may speak to the Dauphin alone?

LA HIRE [*goodhumoredly*]. I can take a hint. [*He salutes; turns on his heel; and goes out.*]

THE ARCHBISHOP. Come, gentlemen. The Maid comes with God's blessing, and must be obeyed.

[*The* COURTIERS *withdraw, some through the arch, others at the opposite side. The* ARCHBISHOP *marches across to the door, followed by the* DUCHESS *and* LA TRÉMOUILLE. *As the* ARCHBISHOP *passes* JOAN, *she falls on her knees, and kisses the hem of his robe fervently. He shakes his head in instinctive remonstrance; gathers the robe from her; and goes out. She is left kneeling directly in the* DUCHESS's *way.*]

THE DUCHESS [*coldly*]. Will you allow me to pass, please?

JOAN [*hastily rising, and standing back*]. Beg pardon, maam, I am sure.

[*The* DUCHESS *passes on.* JOAN *stares after her; then whispers to the* DAUPHIN.]

JOAN. Be that Queen?

CHARLES. No. She thinks she is.

JOAN [*again staring after the* DUCHESS]. Oo-oo-oo-ooh! [*Her awestruck amazement at the figure cut by the magnificently dressed lady is not wholly complimentary.*]

LA TRÉMOUILLE [*very surly*]. I'll trouble your Highness not to gibe at my wife. [*He goes out. The others have already gone.*]

JOAN [*to the* DAUPHIN]. Who be old Gruff-and-Grum?

CHARLES. He is the Duke de la Trémouille.

JOAN. What be his job?

CHARLES. He pretends to command the army. And whenever I find a friend I can care for, he kills him.

JOAN. Why dost let him?

CHARLES [*petulantly moving to the throne side of the room to escape from her magnetic field*]. How can I prevent him? He bullies me. They all bully me.

JOAN. Art afraid?

CHARLES. Yes: I am afraid. It's no use preaching to me about it. It's all very well for these big men with their armor that is too heavy for me, and their swords that I can hardly lift, and their muscle and their shouting and their bad tempers. They like fighting: most of them are making fools of themselves all the time they are not fighting; but I am quiet and sensible; and I dont want to kill people: I only want to be left alone to enjoy myself in my own way. I never asked to be a king: it was pushed on me. So if you are going to say "Son of St Louis: gird on the sword of your ancestors, and lead us to victory" you may spare your breath to cool your porridge; for I cannot do it. I am not built that way; and there is an end of it.

JOAN [*trenchant and masterful*]. Blethers! We are all like that to begin with. I shall put courage into thee.

CHARLES. But I dont want to have courage put into me. I want to sleep in a comfortable bed, and not live in continual terror of being killed or wounded. Put courage into the others, and let them have their bellyful of fighting; but let me alone.

JOAN. It's no use, Charlie: thou must face what God puts on thee. If thou fail to make thyself king, thoult be a beggar: what else art fit for? Come! Let me see thee sitting on the throne. I have looked forward to that.

CHARLES. What is the good of sitting on the throne when the other fellows give all the orders? However! [*he sits enthroned, a piteous figure*] here is the king for you! Look your fill at the poor devil.

JOAN. Thourt not king yet, lad: thourt but Dauphin. Be not led away by them around thee. Dressing up dont fill empty noddle. I know the people: the real people that make thy bread for thee; and I tell thee they count no man king of France until the holy oil has been poured on his hair, and himself consecrated and crowned in Rheims Cathedral. And thou needs new clothes, Charlie. Why does not Queen look after thee properly?

CHARLES. We're too poor. She wants all the
5 money we can spare to put on her own back. Besides, I like to see her beautifully dressed; and I dont care what I wear myself: I should look ugly anyhow.

JOAN. There is some good in thee, Charlie;
10 but it is not yet a king's good.

CHARLES. We shall see. I am not such a fool as I look. I have my eyes open; and I can tell you that one good treaty is worth ten good fights. These fighting fellows lose all on the
15 treaties that they gain on the fights. If we can only have a treaty, the English are sure to have the worst of it, because they are better at fighting than at thinking.

JOAN. If the English win, it is they that will
20 make the treaty; and then God help poor France! Thou must fight, Charlie, whether thou will or no. I will go first to hearten thee. We must take our courage in both hands: aye, and pray for it with both hands too.

25 CHARLES [*descending from his throne and again crossing the room to escape from her dominating urgency*]. Oh do stop talking about God and praying. I cant bear people who are always praying. Isnt it bad enough to have
30 to do it at the proper times?

JOAN [*pitying him*]. Thou poor child, thou hast never prayed in thy life. I must teach thee from the beginning.

CHARLES. I am not a child: I am a grown man
35 and a father; and I will not be taught any more.

JOAN. Aye, you have a little son. He that will be Louis the Eleventh when you die. Would you not fight for him?

CHARLES. No: a horrid boy. He hates me.
40 He hates everybody, selfish little beast! I dont want to be bothered with children. I dont want to be a father; and I dont want to be a son: especially a son of St Louis. I dont want to be any of these fine things you all have your
45 heads full of: I want to be just what I am. Why cant you mind your own business, and let me mind mine?

JOAN [*again contemptuous*]. Minding your own business is like minding your own body: it's the shortest way to make yourself sick.
50 What is my business? Helping mother at home. What is thine? Petting lapdogs and sucking sugarsticks. I call that muck. I tell thee it is God's business we are here to do: not our own. I have a message to thee from God; and
55 thou must listen to it, though thy heart break with the terror of it.

CHARLES. I dont want a message; but can you tell me any secrets? Can you do any cures? Can you turn lead into gold, or anything of
60 that sort?

JOAN. I can turn thee into a king, in Rheims Cathedral; and that is a miracle that will take some doing, it seems.

CHARLES. If we go to Rheims, and have a
65 coronation, Anne will want new dresses. We cant afford them. I am all right as I am.

JOAN. As you are! And what is that? Less than my father's poorest shepherd. Thourt not lawful owner of thy own land of France till
70 thou be consecrated.

CHARLES. But I shall not be lawful owner of my own land anyhow. Will the consecration pay off my mortgages? I have pledged my last acre to the Archbishop and that fat bully. I
75 owe money even to Bluebeard.

JOAN [*earnestly*]. Charlie: I come from the land, and have gotten my strength working on the land; and I tell thee that the land is thine to rule righteously and keep God's peace in,
80 and not to pledge at the pawnshop as a drunken woman pledges her children's clothes. And I come from God to tell thee to kneel in the cathedral and solemnly give thy kingdom to Him for ever and ever, and become the greatest
85 king in the world as His steward and His bailiff, His soldier and His servant. The very clay of France will become holy: her soldiers will be the soldiers of God: the rebel dukes will be rebels against God: the English will fall on
90 their knees and beg thee let them return to their lawful homes in peace. Wilt be a poor little Judas, and betray me and Him that sent me?

CHARLES [*tempted at last*]. Oh, if I only dare!

JOAN. I shall dare, dare, and dare again, in God's name! Art for or against me?

5 CHARLES [*excited*]. I'll risk it. I warn you I shant be able to keep it up; but I'll risk it. You shall see. [*Running to the main door and shouting.*] Hallo! Come back, everybody. [*To* JOAN, *as he runs back to the arch opposite.*]

10 Mind you stand by and dont let me be bullied. [*Through the arch.*] Come along, will you: the whole Court. [*He sits down in the royal chair as they all hurry in to their former places, chattering and wondering.*] Now I'm in for it; but

15 no matter: here goes! [*To the* PAGE.] Call for silence, you little beast, will you?

THE PAGE [*snatching a halberd as before and thumping with it repeatedly*]. Silence for His Majesty the King. The King speaks. [*Peremp-

20 torily.*] Will you be silent there? [*Silence.*]

CHARLES [*rising*]. I have given the command of the army to The Maid. The Maid is to do as she likes with it. [*He descends from the dais.*]

25 [*General amazement.* LA HIRE, *delighted, slaps his steel thigh-piece with his gauntlet.*]

LA TRÉMOUILLE [*turning threateningly towards* CHARLES]. What is this? *I* command the army.

30 [JOAN *quickly puts her hand on* CHARLES'S *shoulder as he instinctively recoils.* CHARLES, *with a grotesque effort culminating in an extravagant gesture, snaps his fingers in the* CHAMBERLAIN'S *face.*]

35 JOAN. Thourt answered, old Gruff-and-Grum. [*Suddenly flashing out her sword as she divines that her moment has come.*] Who is for God and His Maid? Who is for Orleans with me?

40 LA HIRE [*carried away, drawing also*]. For God and His Maid! To Orleans!

ALL THE KNIGHTS [*following his lead with enthusiasm*]. To Orleans!

[JOAN, *radiant, falls on her knees in thanks-

45 giving to God. They all kneel, except the* ARCHBISHOP, *who gives his benediction with a sign, and* LA TRÉMOUILLE, *who collapses, cursing.*]

SCENE III

[*Orleans, May 29th, 1429.* DUNOIS, *aged 26,
is pacing up and down a patch of ground on* 50
*the south bank of the silver Loire, commanding
a long view of the river in both directions. He
has had his lance stuck up with a pennon,
which streams in a strong east wind. His shield
with its bend sinister° lies beside it. He has his* 55
*commander's baton in his hand. He is well
built, carrying his armor easily. His broad
brow and pointed chin give him an equilaterally
triangular face, already marked by active service and responsibility, with the expression of* 60
*a goodnatured and capable man who has no
affectations and no foolish illusions. His* PAGE
*is sitting on the ground, elbows on knees,
cheeks on fists, idly watching the water. It is
evening; and both man and boy are affected* 65
by the loveliness of the Loire.]

DUNOIS [*halting for a moment to glance up
at the streaming pennon and shake his head
wearily before he resumes his pacing*]. West
wind, west wind, west wind. Strumpet: stead-* 70
fast when you should be wanton, wanton when
you should be steadfast. West wind on the
silver Loire: what rhymes to Loire? [*He looks
again at the pennon, and shakes his fist at it.*]
Change, curse you, change, English harlot of 75
a wind, change. West, west, I tell you. [*With
a growl he resumes his march in silence, but
soon begins again.*] West wind, wanton wind,
wilful wind, womanish wind, false wind from
over the water, will you never blow again? 80

THE PAGE [*bounding to his feet*]. See! There! There she goes!

DUNOIS [*startled from his reverie: eagerly*]. Where? Who? The Maid?

THE PAGE. No: the kingfisher. Like blue 85
lightning. She went into that bush.

DUNOIS [*furiously disappointed*]. Is that all? You infernal young idiot: I have a mind to pitch you into the river.

THE PAGE [*not afraid, knowing his man*]. It 90

---

bend sinister a heraldic pattern denoting an illegitimate child, usually a descendant "on the left hand"
of royalty, as was true of Dunois

looked frightfully jolly, that flash of blue. Look! There goes the other!

DUNOIS [*running eagerly to the river brim*]. Where? Where?

5 THE PAGE [*pointing*]. Passing the reeds.

DUNOIS [*delighted*]. I see.

[*They follow the flight till the bird takes cover.*]

THE PAGE. You blew me up because you 10 were not in time to see them yesterday.

DUNOIS. You knew I was expecting The Maid when you set up your yelping. I will give you something to yelp for next time.

THE PAGE. Arnt they lovely? I wish I could 15 catch them.

DUNOIS. Let me catch you trying to trap them, and I will put you in the iron cage for a month to teach you what a cage feels like. You are an abominable boy.

20 THE PAGE [*laughs, and squats down as before*]!

DUNOIS [*pacing*]. Blue bird, blue bird, since I am friend to thee, change thou the wind for me. No: it does not rhyme. He who has sinned 25 for thee: thats better. No sense in it, though. [*He finds himself close to the* PAGE.] You abominable boy! [*He turns away from him.*] Mary in the blue snood, kingfisher color: will you grudge me a west wind?

30 A SENTRY'S VOICE WESTWARD. Halt! Who goes there?

JOAN'S VOICE. The Maid.

DUNOIS. Let her pass. Hither, Maid! To me!

[JOAN, *in splendid armor, rushes in in a* 35 *blazing rage. The wind drops; and the pennon flaps idly down the lance; but* DUNOIS *is too much occupied with* JOAN *to notice it.*]

JOAN [*bluntly*]. Be you Bastard of Orleans?

DUNOIS [*cool and stern, pointing to his* 40 *shield*]. You see the bend sinister. Are you Joan the Maid?

JOAN. Sure.

DUNOIS. Where are your troops?

JOAN. Miles behind. They have cheated me. 45 They have brought me to the wrong side of the river.

DUNOIS. I told them to.

JOAN. Why did you? The English are on the

other side!

DUNOIS. The English are on both sides.   50

JOAN. But Orleans is on the other side. We must fight the English there. How can we cross the river?

DUNOIS [*grimly*]. There is a bridge.

JOAN. In God's name, then, let us cross the   55 bridge, and fall on them.

DUNOIS. It seems simple; but it cannot be done.

JOAN. Who says so?

DUNOIS. I say so; and older and wiser heads   60 than mine are of the same opinion.

JOAN [*roundly*]. Then your older and wiser heads are fatheads: they have made a fool of you; and now they want to make a fool of me too, bringing me to the wrong side of the river.   65 Do you not know that I bring you better help than ever came to any general or any town?

DUNOIS [*smiling patiently*]. Your own?

JOAN. No: the help and counsel of the King of Heaven. Which is the way to the bridge?   70

DUNOIS. You are impatient, Maid.

JOAN. Is this a time for patience? Our enemy is at our gates; and here we stand doing nothing. Oh, why are you not fighting? Listen to me: I will deliver you from fear. I—   75

DUNOIS [*laughing heartily, and waving her off*]. No, no, my girl: if you delivered me from fear I should be a good knight for a story book, but a very bad commander of the army. Come! let me begin to make a soldier of you. [*He   80 takes her to the water's edge.*] Do you see those two forts at this end of the bridge? the big ones?

JOAN. Yes. Are they ours or the goddams'?

DUNOIS. Be quiet, and listen to me. If I   85 were in either of those forts with only ten men I could hold it against an army. The English have more than ten times ten goddams in those forts to hold them against us.

JOAN. They cannot hold them against God.   90 God did not give them the land under those forts: they stole it from Him. He gave it to us. I will take those forts.

DUNOIS. Single-handed?

JOAN. Our men will take them. I will lead   95 them.

DUNOIS. Not a man will follow you.

JOAN. I will not look back to see whether anyone is following me.

DUNOIS [*recognizing her mettle, and clapping* 5 *her heartily on the shoulder*]. Good. You have the makings of a soldier in you. You are in love with war.

JOAN [*startled*]. Oh! And the Archbishop said I was in love with religion.

10 DUNOIS. I, God forgive me, am a little in love with war myself, the ugly devil! I am like a man with two wives. Do you want to be like a woman with two husbands?

JOAN [*matter-of-fact*]. I will never take a 15 husband. A man in Toul took an action against me for breach of promise; but I never promised him. I am a soldier: I do not want to be thought of as a woman. I will not dress as a woman. I do not care for the things women 20 care for. They dream of lovers, and of money. I dream of leading a charge, and of placing the big guns. You soldiers do not know how to use the big guns: you think you can win battles with a great noise and smoke.

25 DUNOIS [*with a shrug*]. True. Half the time the artillery is more trouble than it is worth.

JOAN. Aye, lad; but you cannot fight stone walls with horses: you must have guns, and much bigger guns too.

30 DUNOIS [*grinning at her familiarity, and echoing it*]. Aye, lass; but a good heart and a stout ladder will get over the stoniest wall.

JOAN. I will be first up the ladder when we reach the fort, Bastard. I dare you to follow 35 me.

DUNOIS. You must not dare a staff officer, Joan: only company officers are allowed to indulge in displays of personal courage. Besides, you must know that I welcome you 40 as a saint, not as a soldier. I have daredevils enough at my call, if they could help me.

JOAN. I am not a daredevil: I am a servant of God. My sword is sacred: I found it behind the altar in the church of St Catherine, where 45 God hid it for me; and I may not strike a blow with it. My heart is full of courage, not of anger. I will lead; and your men will follow: that is all I can do. But I must do it: you shall not stop me.

DUNOIS. All in good time. Our men cannot 50 take those forts by a sally across the bridge. They must come by water, and take the English in the rear on this side.

JOAN [*her military sense asserting itself*]. Then make rafts and put big guns on them; 55 and let your men cross to us.

DUNOIS. The rafts are ready; and the men are embarked. But they must wait for God.

JOAN. What do you mean? God is waiting for them. 60

DUNOIS. Let Him send us a wind then. My boats are downstream: they cannot come up against both wind and current. We must wait until God changes the wind. Come: let me take you to the church. 65

JOAN. No. I love church; but the English will not yield to prayers: they understand nothing but hard knocks and slashes. I will not go to church until we have beaten them.

DUNOIS. You must: I have business for you 70 there.

JOAN. What business?

DUNOIS. To pray for a west wind. I have prayed; and I have given two silver candlesticks; but my prayers are not answered. Yours 75 may be: you are young and innocent.

JOAN. Oh yes: you are right. I will pray: I will tell St Catherine: she will make God give me a west wind. Quick: shew me the way to the church. 80

THE PAGE [*sneezes violently*]. At-cha!!!

JOAN. God bless you, child! Coom, Bastard.

[*They go out. The* PAGE *rises to follow. He picks up the shield, and is taking the spear as well when he notices the pennon, which is now* 85 *streaming eastward.*]

THE PAGE [*dropping the shield and calling excitedly after them*]. Seigneur! Seigneur! Mademoiselle!

DUNOIS [*running back*]. What is it? The 90 kingfisher? [*He looks eagerly for it up the river.*]

JOAN [*joining them*]. Oh, a kingfisher! Where?

THE PAGE. No: the wind, the wind, the wind [*pointing to the pennon*]: that is what made me sneeze.

DUNOIS [*looking at the pennon*]. The wind
5 has changed. [*He crosses himself.*] God has spoken. [*Kneeling and handing his baton to JOAN.*] You command the king's army. I am your soldier.

THE PAGE [*looking down the river*]. The
10 boats have put off. They are ripping upstream like anything.

DUNOIS [*rising*]. Now for the forts. You dared me to follow. Dare you lead?

JOAN [*bursting into tears and flinging her
15 arms round DUNOIS, kissing him on both cheeks*]. Dunois, dear comrade in arms, help me. My eyes are blinded with tears. Set my foot on the ladder, and say "Up, Joan."

DUNOIS [*dragging her out*]. Never mind the
20 tears: make for the flash of the guns.

JOAN [*in a blaze of courage*]. Ah!

DUNOIS [*dragging her along with him*]. For God and Saint Dennis!

THE PAGE [*shrilly*]. The Maid! The Maid!
25 God and The Maid! Hurray-ay-ay! [*He snatches up the shield and lance, and capers out after them, mad with excitement.*]

SCENE IV

[*A tent in the English camp. A bullnecked ENGLISH CHAPLAIN of 50 is sitting on a stool at
30 a table, hard at work writing. At the other side of the table an imposing NOBLEMAN, aged 46, is seated in a handsome chair turning over the leaves of an illuminated Book of Hours. The NOBLEMAN is enjoying himself: the CHAP-
35 LAIN is struggling with suppressed wrath. There is an unoccupied leather stool on the NOBLEMAN's left. The table is on his right.*]

THE NOBLEMAN. Now this is what I call workmanship. There is nothing on earth more
40 exquisite than a bonny book, with well-placed columns of rich black writing in beautiful borders, and illuminated pictures cunningly inset. But nowadays, instead of looking at books, people read them. A book might as well be one

of those orders for bacon and bran that you are 45 scribbling.

THE CHAPLAIN. I must say, my lord, you take our situation very coolly. Very coolly indeed.

THE NOBLEMAN [*supercilious*]. What is the matter? 50

THE CHAPLAIN. The matter, my lord, is that we English have been defeated.

THE NOBLEMAN. That happens, you know. It is only in history books and ballads that the enemy is always defeated. 55

THE CHAPLAIN. But we are being defeated over and over again. First, Orleans—

THE NOBLEMAN [*poohpoohing*]. Oh, Orleans!

THE CHAPLAIN. I know what you are going to say, my lord: that was a clear case of witchcraft 60 and sorcery. But we are still being defeated. Jargeau, Meung, Beaugency, just like Orleans. And now we have been butchered at Patay, and Sir John Talbot taken prisoner. [*He throws down his pen, almost in tears.*] I feel it, my lord: 65 I feel it very deeply. I cannot bear to see my countrymen defeated by a parcel of foreigners.

THE NOBLEMAN. Oh! you are an Englishman, are you?

THE CHAPLAIN. Certainly not, my lord: I am 70 a gentleman. Still, like your lordship, I was born in England; and it makes a difference.

THE NOBLEMAN. You are attached to the soil, eh?

THE CHAPLAIN. It pleases your lordship to be 75 satirical at my expense: your greatness privileges you to be so with impunity. But your lordship knows very well that I am not attached to the soil in a vulgar manner, like a serf. Still, I have a feeling about it; [*with growing agita-*80 *tion*] and I am not ashamed of it; and [*rising wildly*] by God, if this goes on any longer I will fling my cassock to the devil, and take arms myself, and strangle the accursed witch with my own hands. 85

THE NOBLEMAN [*laughing at him goodnaturedly*]. So you shall, chaplain: so you shall, if we can do nothing better. But not yet, not quite yet.

[*The CHAPLAIN resumes his seat very sulkily.*] 90

THE NOBLEMAN [*airily*]. I should not care

very much about the witch—you see, I have made my pilgrimage to the Holy Land; and the Heavenly Powers, for their own credit, can hardly allow me to be worsted by a village sorceress—but the Bastard of Orleans is a harder nut to crack; and as he has been to the Holy Land too, honors are easy between us as far as that goes.

THE CHAPLAIN. He is only a Frenchman, my lord.

THE NOBLEMAN. A Frenchman! Where did you pick up that expression? Are these Burgundians and Bretons and Picards and Gascons beginning to call themselves Frenchmen, just as our fellows are beginning to call themselves Englishmen? They actually talk of France and England as their countries. Theirs, if you please! What is to become of me and you if that way of thinking comes into fashion?

THE CHAPLAIN. Why, my lord? Can it hurt us?

THE NOBLEMAN. Men cannot serve two masters. If this cant of serving their country once takes hold of them, goodbye to the authority of their feudal lords, and goodbye to the authority of the Church. That is, goodbye to you and me.

THE CHAPLAIN. I hope I am a faithful servant of the Church; and there are only six cousins between me and the barony of Stogumber, which was created by the Conqueror. But is that any reason why I should stand by and see Englishmen beaten by a French bastard and a witch from Lousy Champagne?

THE NOBLEMAN. Easy, man, easy: we shall burn the witch and beat the bastard all in good time. Indeed I am waiting at present for the Bishop of Beauvais, to arrange the burning with him. He has been turned out of his diocese by her faction.

THE CHAPLAIN. You have first to catch her, my lord.

THE NOBLEMAN. Or buy her. I will offer a king's ransom.

THE CHAPLAIN. A king's ransom! For that slut!

THE NOBLEMAN. One has to leave a margin.

Some of Charles's people will sell her to the Burgundians; the Burgundians will sell her to us; and there will probably be three or four middlemen who will expect their little commissions.

THE CHAPLAIN. Monstrous. It is all those scoundrels of Jews: they get in every time money changes hands. I would not leave a Jew alive in Christendom if I had my way.

THE NOBLEMAN. Why not? The Jews generally give value. They make you pay; but they deliver the goods. In my experience the men who want something for nothing are invariably Christians.

[A PAGE appears.]

THE PAGE. The Right Reverend the Bishop of Beauvais: Monseigneur Cauchon.

[CAUCHON, aged about 60, comes in. The PAGE withdraws. The two Englishmen rise.]

THE NOBLEMAN [with effusive courtesy]. My dear Bishop, how good of you to come! Allow me to introduce myself: Richard de Beauchamp, Earl of Warwick, at your service.

CAUCHON. Your lordship's fame is well known to me.

WARWICK. This reverend cleric is Master John de Stogumber.

THE CHAPLAIN [glibly]. John Bowyer Spenser Neville de Stogumber, at your service, my lord: Bachelor of Theology, and Keeper of the Private Seal to His Eminence the Cardinal of Winchester.

WARWICK [to CAUCHON]. You call him the Cardinal of England, I believe. Our king's uncle.

CAUCHON. Messire John de Stogumber: I am always the very good friend of His Eminence. [He extends his hand to the CHAPLAIN, who kisses his ring.]

WARWICK. Do me the honor to be seated. [He gives CAUCHON his chair, placing it at the head of the table.]

[CAUCHON accepts the place of honor with a grave inclination. WARWICK fetches the leather stool carelessly, and sits in his former place. The CHAPLAIN goes back to his chair.

Though WARWICK has taken second place

in calculated deference to the BISHOP, *he assumes the lead in opening the proceedings as a matter of course. He is still cordial and expansive; but there is a new note in his voice*
5 *which means that he is coming to business.*]

WARWICK. Well, my Lord Bishop, you find us in one of our unlucky moments. Charles is to be crowned at Rheims, practically by the young woman from Lorraine; and—I must not deceive
10 you, nor flatter your hopes—we cannot prevent it. I suppose it will make a great difference to Charles's position.

CAUCHON. Undoubtedly. It is a masterstroke of The Maid's.

15 THE CHAPLAIN [*again agitated*]. We were not fairly beaten, my lord. No Englishman is ever fairly beaten.

[CAUCHON *raises his eyebrow slightly, then quickly composes his face.*]

20 WARWICK. Our friend here takes the view that the young woman is a sorceress. It would, I presume, be the duty of your reverend lordship to denounce her to the Inquisition, and have her burnt for that offence.

25 CAUCHON. If she were captured in my diocese: yes.

WARWICK [*feeling that they are getting on capitally*]. Just so. Now I suppose there can be no reasonable doubt that she is a sorceress.

30 THE CHAPLAIN. Not the least. An arrant witch.

WARWICK [*gently reproving the interruption*]. We are asking for the Bishop's opinion, Messire John.

35 CAUCHON. We shall have to consider not merely our own opinions here, but the opinions —the prejudices, if you like—of a French court.

WARWICK [*correcting*]. A Catholic court, my lord.

40 CAUCHON. Catholic courts are composed of mortal men, like other courts, however sacred their function and inspiration may be. And if the men are Frenchmen, as the modern fashion calls them, I am afraid the bare fact that an
45 English army has been defeated by a French one will not convince them that there is any sorcery in the matter.

THE CHAPLAIN. What! Not when the famous Sir John Talbot himself has been defeated and actually taken prisoner by a drab from the 50 ditches of Lorraine!

CAUCHON. Sir John Talbot, we all know, is a fierce and formidable soldier, Messire; but I have yet to learn that he is an able general. And though it pleases you to say that he has 55 been defeated by this girl, some of us may be disposed to give a little of the credit to Dunois.

THE CHAPLAIN [*contemptuously*]. The Bastard of Orleans!

CAUCHON. Let me remind— 60

WARWICK [*interposing*]. I know what you are going to say, my lord. Dunois defeated me at Montargis.

CAUCHON [*bowing*]. I take that as evidence that the Seigneur Dunois is a very able com- 65 mander indeed.

WARWICK. Your lordship is the flower of courtesy. I admit, on our side, that Talbot is a mere fighting animal, and that it probably served him right to be taken at Patay. 70

THE CHAPLAIN [*chafing*]. My lord: at Orleans this woman had her throat pierced by an English arrow, and was seen to cry like a child from the pain of it. It was a death wound; yet she fought all day; and when our men had 75 repulsed all her attacks like true Englishmen, she walked alone to the wall of our fort with a white banner in her hand; and our men were paralyzed, and could neither shoot nor strike whilst the French fell on them and drove 80 them on to the bridge, which immediately burst into flames and crumbled under them, letting them down into the river, where they were drowned in heaps. Was this your bastard's generalship? or were those flames the flames 85 of hell, conjured up by witchcraft?

WARWICK. You will forgive Messire John's vehemence, my lord; but he has put our case. Dunois is a great captain, we admit; but why could he do nothing until the witch came? 90

CAUCHON. I do not say that there were no supernatural powers on her side. But the names on that white banner were not the names of Satan and Beelzebub, but the blessed names of our Lord and His holy mother. And your commander who was drowned—Clahz-da I think you call him—

WARWICK. Glasdale. Sir William Glasdale.

5 CAUCHON. Glass-dell, thank you. He was no saint; and many of our people think that he was drowned for his blasphemies against The Maid.

WARWICK [*beginning to look very dubious*]. 10 Well, what are we to infer from all this, my lord? Has The Maid converted you?

CAUCHON. If she had, my lord, I should have known better than to have trusted myself here within your grasp.

15 WARWICK [*blandly deprecating*]. Oh! oh! My lord!

CAUCHON. If the devil is making use of this girl—and I believe he is—

WARWICK [*reassured*]. Ah! You hear, Mes-20 sire John? I knew your lordship would not fail us. Pardon my interruption. Proceed.

CAUCHON. If it be so, the devil has longer views than you give him credit for.

WARWICK. Indeed? In what way? Listen to 25 this, Messire John.

CAUCHON. If the devil wanted to damn a country girl, do you think so easy a task would cost him the winning of half a dozen battles? No, my lord: any trumpery imp could do that 30 much if the girl could be damned at all. The Prince of Darkness does not condescend to such cheap drudgery. When he strikes, he strikes at the Catholic Church, whose realm is the whole spiritual world. When he damns, he damns the 35 souls of the entire human race. Against that dreadful design The Church stands ever on guard. And it is as one of the instruments of that design that I see this girl. She is inspired, but diabolically inspired.

40 THE CHAPLAIN. I told you she was a witch.

CAUCHON [*fiercely*]. She is not a witch. She is a heretic.

THE CHAPLAIN. What difference does that make?

45 CAUCHON. You, a priest, ask me that! You English are strangely blunt in the mind. All these things that you call witchcraft are capable of a natural explanation. The woman's miracles would not impose on a rabbit: she does not claim them as miracles herself. What do her 50 victories prove but that she has a better head on her shoulders than your swearing Glass-dells and mad bull Talbots, and that the courage of faith, even though it be a false faith, will always outstay the courage of wrath? 55

THE CHAPLAIN [*hardly able to believe his ears*]. Does your lordship compare Sir John Talbot, three times Governor of Ireland, to a mad bull?!!!

WARWICK. It would not be seemly for you to 60 do so, Messire John, as you are still six removes from a barony. But as I am an earl, and Talbot is only a knight, I may make bold to accept the comparison. [*To the* BISHOP.] My lord: I wipe the slate as far as the witchcraft goes. None 65 the less, we must burn the woman.

CAUCHON. I cannot burn her. The Church cannot take life. And my first duty is to seek this girl's salvation.

WARWICK. No doubt. But you do burn people 70 occasionally.

CAUCHON. No. When The Church cuts off an obstinate heretic as a dead branch from the tree of life, the heretic is handed over to the secular arm. The Church has no part in what 75 the secular arm may see fit to do.

WARWICK. Precisely. And I shall be the secular arm in this case. Well, my lord, hand over your dead branch; and I will see that the fire is ready for it. If you will answer for The 80 Church's part, I will answer for the secular part.

CAUCHON [*with smouldering anger*]. I can answer for nothing. You great lords are too prone to treat The Church as a mere political convenience. 85

WARWICK [*smiling and propitiatory*]. Not in England, I assure you.

CAUCHON. In England more than anywhere else. No, my lord: the soul of this village girl is of equal value with yours or your king's 90 before the throne of God; and my first duty is to save it. I will not suffer your lordship to smile at me as if I were repeating a meaning-less form of words, and it were well understood between us that I should betray the girl to you. 95 I am no mere political bishop: my faith is to me

what your honor is to you; and if there be a
loophole through which this baptized child of
God can creep to her salvation, I shall guide
her to it.

5 THE CHAPLAIN [*rising in a fury*]. You are a
traitor.

CAUCHON [*springing up*]. You lie, priest.
[*Trembling with rage.*] If you dare do what this
woman has done—set your country above the
10 holy Catholic Church—you shall go to the fire
with her.

THE CHAPLAIN. My lord: I—I went too far.
I— [*He sits down with a submissive gesture.*]

WARWICK [*who has risen apprehensively*].
15 My lord: I apologize to you for the word used
by Messire John de Stogumber. It does not
mean in England what it does in France. In
your language traitor means betrayer: one who
is perfidious, treacherous, unfaithful, disloyal.
20 In our country it means simply one who is not
wholly devoted to our English interests.

CAUCHON. I am sorry: I did not understand.
[*He subsides into his chair with dignity.*]

WARWICK [*resuming his seat, much relieved*].
25 I must apologize on my own account if I have
seemed to take the burning of this poor girl
too lightly. When one has seen whole country-
sides burnt over and over again as mere items
in military routine, one has to grow a very thick
30 skin. Otherwise one might go mad: at all events,
I should. May I venture to assume that your
lordship also, having to see so many heretics
burned from time to time, is compelled to take
—shall I say a professional view of what would
35 otherwise be a very horrible incident?

CAUCHON. Yes: it is a painful duty: even, as
you say, a horrible one. But in comparison with
the horror of heresy it is less than nothing. I am
not thinking of this girl's body, which will suf-
40 fer for a few moments only, and which must in
any event die in some more or less painful manner, but of her soul, which may suffer to all
eternity.

WARWICK. Just so; and God grant that her
45 soul may be saved! But the practical problem
would seem to be how to save her soul without saving her body. For we must face it, my
lord: if this cult of The Maid goes on, our

cause is lost.

THE CHAPLAIN [*his voice broken like that of* 50
a man who has been crying]. May I speak, my
lord?

WARWICK. Really, Messire John, I had rather
you did not, unless you can keep your temper.

THE CHAPLAIN. It is only this. I speak under 55
correction; but The Maid is full of deceit: she
pretends to be devout. Her prayers and confessions are endless. How can she be accused
of heresy when she neglects no observance of
a faithful daughter of The Church? 60

CAUCHON [*flaming up*]. A faithful daughter
of The Church! The Pope himself at his
proudest dare not presume as this woman pre-
sumes. She acts as if she herself were The
Church. She brings the message of God to 65
Charles; and The Church must stand aside.
She will crown him in the cathedral of Rheims:
she, not The Church! She sends letters to the
king of England giving him God's command
through her to return to his island on pain of 70
God's vengeance, which she will execute. Let
me tell you that the writing of such letters
was the practice of the accursed Mahomet, the
anti-Christ. Has she ever in all her utterances
said one word of The Church? Never. It is 75
always God and herself.

WARWICK. What can you expect? A beggar
on horseback! Her head is turned.

CAUCHON. Who has turned it? The devil.
And for a mighty purpose. He is spreading 80
this heresy everywhere. The man Hus,° burnt
only thirteen years ago at Constance, infected
all Bohemia with it. A man named WcLeef,°
himself an anointed priest, spread the pestilence in England; and to your shame you let 85
him die in his bed. We have such people here
in France too: I know the breed. It is cancerous: if it be not cut out, stamped out, burnt

Hus John Huss (1369-1415), Czech religious reformer and national leader; tried for heresy and burned
at the stake

WcLeef John Wycliff (1328-1384), English religious
reformer and popular preacher, early translator of
the Bible into English; condemned for heresy but
not executed; influenced Huss and, later, Martin
Luther

out, it will not stop until it has brought the whole body of human society into sin and corruption, into waste and ruin. By it an Arab camel driver drove Christ and His Church out of Jerusalem, and ravaged his way west like a wild beast until at last there stood only the Pyrenees and God's mercy between France and damnation. Yet what did the camel driver do at the beginning more than this shepherd girl is doing? He had his voices from the angel Gabriel: she has her voices from St Catherine and St Margaret and the Blessed Michael. He declared himself the messenger of God, and wrote in God's name to the kings of the earth. Her letters to them are going forth daily. It is not the Mother of God now to whom we must look for intercession, but to Joan the Maid. What will the world be like when The Church's accumulated wisdom and knowledge and experience, its councils of learned, venerable pious men, are thrust into the kennel by every ignorant laborer or dairymaid whom the devil can puff up with the monstrous self-conceit of being directly inspired from heaven? It will be a world of blood, of fury, of devastation, of each man striving for his own hand: in the end a world wrecked back into barbarism. For now you have only Mahomet and his dupes, and the Maid and her dupes; but what will it be when every girl thinks herself a Joan and every man a Mahomet? I shudder to the very marrow of my bones when I think of it. I have fought it all my life; and I will fight it to the end. Let all this woman's sins be forgiven her except only this sin; for it is the sin against the Holy Ghost; and if she does not recant in the dust before the world, and submit herself to the last inch of her soul to her Church, to the fire she shall go if she once falls into my hand.

WARWICK [*unimpressed*]. You feel strongly about it, naturally.

CAUCHON. Do not you?

WARWICK. I am a soldier, not a churchman. As a pilgrim I saw something of the Mahometans. They were not so illbred as I had been led to believe. In some respects their conduct compared favorably with ours.

CAUCHON [*displeased*]. I have noticed this before. Men go to the East to convert the infidels. And the infidels pervert them. The Crusader comes back more than half a Saracen. Not to mention that all Englishmen are born heretics.

THE CHAPLAIN. Englishmen heretics!!! [*Appealing to* WARWICK.] My lord: must we endure this? His lordship is beside himself. How can what an Englishman believes be heresy? It is a contradiction in terms.

CAUCHON. I absolve you, Messire de Stogumber, on the ground of invincible ignorance. The thick air of your country does not breed theologians.

WARWICK. You would not say so if you heard us quarrelling about religion, my lord! I am sorry you think I must be either a heretic or a blockhead because, as a travelled man, I know that the followers of Mahomet profess great respect for our Lord, and are more ready to forgive St Peter for being a fisherman than your lordship is to forgive Mahomet for being a camel driver. But at least we can proceed in this matter without bigotry.

CAUCHON. When men call the zeal of the Christian Church bigotry I know what to think.

WARWICK. They are only east and west views of the same thing.

CAUCHON [*bitterly ironical*]. Only east and west! Only!!

WARWICK. Oh, my Lord Bishop, I am not gainsaying you. You will carry The Church with you; but you have to carry the nobles also. To my mind there is a stronger case against The Maid than the one you have so forcibly put. Frankly, I am not afraid of this girl becoming another Mahomet, and superseding The Church by a great heresy. I think you exaggerate that risk. But have you noticed that in these letters of hers, she proposes to all the kings of Europe, as she has already pressed on Charles, a transaction which would wreck the whole social structure of Christendom?

CAUCHON. Wreck The Church. I tell you so.

WARWICK [*whose patience is wearing out*]. My lord: pray get The Church out of your head for a moment; and remember that there are temporal institutions in the world as well as spiritual ones. I and my peers represent the feudal aristocracy as you represent The Church. We are the temporal power. Well, do you not see how this girl's idea strikes at us?

CAUCHON. How does her idea strike at you, except as it strikes at all of us, through The Church?

WARWICK. Her idea is that the kings should give their realms to God, and then reign as God's bailiffs.

CAUCHON [*not interested*]. Quite sound theologically, my lord. But the king will hardly care, provided he reign. It is an abstract idea: a mere form of words.

WARWICK. By no means. It is a cunning device to supersede the aristocracy, and make the king sole and absolute autocrat. Instead of the king being merely the first among his peers, he becomes their master. That we cannot suffer: we call no man master. Nominally we hold our lands and dignities from the king, because there must be a keystone to the arch of human society; but we hold our lands in our own hands, and defend them with our own swords and those of our own tenants. Now by The Maid's doctrine the king will take our lands—our lands!—and make them a present to God; and God will then vest them wholly in the king.

CAUCHON. Need you fear that? You are the makers of kings after all. York or Lancaster in England, Lancaster or Valois in France: they reign according to your pleasure.

WARWICK. Yes; but only as long as the people follow their feudal lords, and know the king only as a travelling show, owning nothing but the highway that belongs to everybody. If the people's thoughts and hearts were turned to the king, and their lords became only the king's servants in their eyes, the king could break us across his knee one by one; and then what should we be but liveried courtiers in his halls?

CAUCHON. Still you need not fear, my lord. Some men are born kings; and some are born statesmen. The two are seldom the same.

Where would the king find counsellors to plan and carry out such a policy for him?

WARWICK [*with a not too friendly smile*]. Perhaps in the Church, my lord.

[CAUCHON, *with an equally sour smile, shrugs his shoulders, and does not contradict him.*]

WARWICK. Strike down the barons; and the cardinals will have it all their own way.

CAUCHON [*conciliatory, dropping his polemical tone*]. My lord: we shall not defeat The Maid if we strive against one another. I know well that there is a Will to Power in the world. I know that while it lasts there will be a struggle between the Emperor and the Pope, between the dukes and the political cardinals, between the barons and the kings. The devil divides us and governs. I see you are no friend to The Church: you are an earl first and last, as I am a churchman first and last. But can we not sink our differences in the face of a common enemy? I see now that what is in your mind is not that this girl has never once mentioned The Church, and thinks only of God and herself, but that she has never once mentioned the peerage, and thinks only of the king and herself.

WARWICK. Quite so. These two ideas of hers are the same idea at bottom. It goes deep, my lord. It is the protest of the individual soul against the interference of priest or peer between the private man and his God. I should call it Protestantism if I had to find a name for it.

CAUCHON [*looking hard at him*]. You understand it wonderfully well, my lord. Scratch an Englishman, and find a Protestant.

WARWICK [*playing the pink of courtesy*]. I think you are not entirely void of sympathy with The Maid's secular heresy, my lord. I leave you to find a name for it.

CAUCHON. You mistake me, my lord. I have no sympathy with her political presumptions. But as a priest I have gained a knowledge of the minds of the common people; and there you will find yet another most dangerous idea. I can express it only by such phrases as France for the French, England for the English, Italy

for the Italians, Spain for the Spanish, and so forth. It is sometimes so narrow and bitter in country folk that it surprises me that this country girl can rise above the idea of her
5 village for its villagers. But she can. She does. When she threatens to drive the English from the soil of France she is undoubtedly thinking of the whole extent of country in which French is spoken. To her the French-speaking people
10 are what the Holy Scriptures describe as a nation. Call this side of her heresy Nationalism if you will: I can find you no better name for it. I can only tell you that it is essentially anti-Catholic and anti-Christian; for the Catholic
15 Church knows only one realm, and that is the realm of Christ's kingdom. Divide that kingdom into nations, and you dethrone Christ. Dethrone Christ, and who will stand between our throats and the sword? The world will
20 perish in a welter of war.

WARWICK. Well, if you will burn the Protestant, I will burn the Nationalist, though perhaps I shall not carry Messire John with me there. England for the English will appeal to
25 him.

THE CHAPLAIN. Certainly England for the English goes without saying: it is the simple law of nature. But this woman denies to England her legitimate conquests, given her by
30 God because of her peculiar fitness to rule over less civilized races for their own good. I do not understand what your lordships mean by Protestant and Nationalist: you are too learned and subtle for a poor clerk like myself.
35 But I know as a matter of plain commonsense that the woman is a rebel; and that is enough for me. She rebels against Nature by wearing man's clothes, and fighting. She rebels against The Church by usurping the divine authority
40 of the Pope. She rebels against God by her damnable league with Satan and his evil spirits against our army. And all these rebellions are only excuses for her great rebellion against England. That is not to be endured. Let her
45 perish. Let her burn. Let her not infect the whole flock. It is expedient that one woman die for the people.

WARWICK [rising]. My lord: we seem to be agreed.

CAUCHON [rising also, but in protest]. I will 50 not imperil my soul. I will uphold the justice of The Church. I will strive to the utmost for this woman's salvation.

WARWICK. I am sorry for the poor girl. I hate these severities. I will spare her if I can. 55

THE CHAPLAIN [implacably]. I would burn her with my own hands.

CAUCHON [blessing him]. Sancta simplicitas!°

SCENE V

[The ambulatory in the cathedral of Rheims, near the door of the vestry. A pillar bears one 60 of the stations of the cross. The organ is playing the people out of the nave after the coronation. JOAN is kneeling in prayer before the station. She is beautifully dressed, but still in male attire. The organ ceases as DUNOIS, also 65 splendidly arrayed, comes into the ambulatory from the vestry.]

DUNOIS. Come, Joan! you have had enough praying. After that fit of crying you will catch a chill if you stay here any longer. It is all 70 over: the cathedral is empty; and the streets are full. They are calling for The Maid. We have told them you are staying here alone to pray; but they want to see you again.

JOAN. No: let the king have all the glory. 75

DUNOIS. He only spoils the show, poor devil. No, Joan: you have crowned him; and you must go through with it.

JOAN [shakes her head reluctantly].

DUNOIS [raising her]. Come come! it will be 80 over in a couple of hours. It's better than the bridge at Orleans: eh?

JOAN. Oh, dear Dunois, how I wish it were the bridge at Orleans again! We lived at that bridge. 85

DUNOIS. Yes, faith, and died too: some of us.

Sancta simplicitas! Blessed simplicity! Huss was rumored so to have blessed an old woman even as she added fuel to the fire in which he was burned; Cauchon speaks sarcastically.

JOAN. Isnt it strange, Jack? I am such a coward: I am frightened beyond words before a battle; but it is so dull afterwards when there is no danger: oh, so dull! dull! dull!

5 DUNOIS. You must learn to be abstemious in war, just as you are in your food and drink, my little saint.

JOAN. Dear Jack: I think you like me as a soldier likes his comrade.

10 DUNOIS. You need it, poor innocent child of God. You have not many friends at court.

JOAN. Why do all these courtiers and knights and churchmen hate me? What have I done to them? I have asked nothing for myself except 15 that my village shall not be taxed; for we cannot afford war taxes. I have brought them luck and victory: I have set them right when they were doing all sorts of stupid things: I have crowned Charles and made him a real king; 20 and all the honors he is handing out have gone to them. Then why do they not love me?

DUNOIS [*rallying her*]. Sim-ple-ton! Do you expect stupid people to love you for shewing them up? Do blundering old military dug-outs° 25 love the successful young captains who supersede them? Do ambitious politicians love the climbers who take the front seats from them? Do archbishops enjoy being played off their own altars, even by saints? Why, I should be 30 jealous of you myself if I were ambitious enough.

JOAN. You are the pick of the basket here, Jack: the only friend I have among all these nobles. I'll wager your mother was from the 35 country. I will go back to the farm when I have taken Paris.

DUNOIS. I am not so sure that they will let you take Paris.

JOAN [*startled*]. What!

40 DUNOIS. I should have taken it myself before this if they had all been sound about it. Some of them would rather Paris took you, I think. So take care.

JOAN. Jack: the world is too wicked for me.

---

dug-outs retired officers recalled to military service in an emergency

---

If the goddams and the Burgundians do not 45 make an end of me, the French will. Only for my voices I should lose all heart. That is why I had to steal away to pray here alone after the coronation. I'll tell you something, Jack. It is in the bells I hear my voices. Not to-day, when 50 they all rang: that was nothing but jangling. But here in this corner, where the bells come down from heaven, and the echoes linger, or in the fields, where they come from a distance through the quiet of the countryside, my voices 55 are in them. [*The cathedral clock chimes the quarter.*] Hark! [*She becomes rapt.*] Do you hear? "Dear-child-of-God": just what you said. At the half-hour they will say "Be-brave-go-on." At the three-quarters they will say "I-am- 60 thy-Help." But it is at the hour, when the great bell goes after "God-will-save-France": it is then that St Margaret and St Catherine and sometimes even the blessed Michael will say things that I cannot tell beforehand. Then, oh 65 then—

DUNOIS [*interrupting her kindly but not sympathetically*]. Then, Joan, we shall hear whatever we fancy in the booming of the bell. You make me uneasy when you talk about 70 your voices: I should think you were a bit cracked if I hadnt noticed that you give me very sensible reasons for what you do, though I hear you telling others you are only obeying Madame Saint Catherine. 75

JOAN [*crossly*]. Well, I have to find reasons for you, because you do not believe in my voices. But the voices come first; and I find the reasons after: whatever you may choose to believe. 80

DUNOIS. Are you angry, Joan?

JOAN. Yes. [*Smiling.*] No: not with you. I wish you were one of the village babies.

DUNOIS. Why?

JOAN. I could nurse you for awhile. 85

DUNOIS. You are a bit of a woman after all.

JOAN. No: not a bit: I am a soldier and nothing else. Soldiers always nurse children when they get a chance.

DUNOIS. That is true. [*He laughs.*] 90

[KING CHARLES, *with* BLUEBEARD *on his left*

and LA HIRE *on his right, comes from the vestry, where he has been disrobing.* JOAN *shrinks away behind the pillar.* DUNOIS *is left between* CHARLES *and* LA HIRE.]

5 DUNOIS. Well, your Majesty is an anointed king at last. How do you like it?

CHARLES. I would not go through it again to be emperor of the sun and moon. The weight of those robes! I thought I should have dropped
10 when they loaded that crown on to me. And the famous holy oil they talked so much about was rancid: phew! The Archbishop must be nearly dead: his robes must have weighed a ton: they are stripping him still in the vestry.

15 DUNOIS [*drily*]. Your majesty should wear armor oftener. That would accustom you to heavy dressing.

CHARLES. Yes: the old jibe! Well, I am not going to wear armor: fighting is not my job.
20 Where is The Maid?

JOAN [*coming forward between* CHARLES *and* BLUEBEARD, *and falling on her knee*]. Sire: I have made you king: my work is done. I am going back to my father's farm.

25 CHARLES [*surprised, but relieved*]. Oh, are you? Well, that will be very nice.

[JOAN *rises, deeply discouraged.*]

CHARLES [*continuing heedlessly*]. A healthy life, you know.

30 DUNOIS. But a dull one.

BLUEBEARD. You will find the petticoats tripping you up after leaving them off for so long.

LA HIRE. You will miss the fighting. It's a bad habit, but a grand one, and the hardest of
35 all to break yourself of.

CHARLES [*anxiously*]. Still, we dont want you to stay if you would really rather go home.

JOAN [*bitterly*]. I know well that none of you will be sorry to see me go. [*She turns her
40 shoulder to* CHARLES *and walks past him to the more congenial neighborhood of* DUNOIS *and* LA HIRE.]

LA HIRE. Well, I shall be able to swear when I want to. But I shall miss you at times.

45 JOAN. La Hire: in spite of all your sins and swears we shall meet in heaven; for I love you as I love Pitou, my old sheep dog. Pitou could kill a wolf. You will kill the English wolves

until they go back to their country and become good dogs of God, will you not? 50

LA HIRE. You and I together: yes.

JOAN. No: I shall last only a year from the beginning.

ALL THE OTHERS. What!

JOAN. I know it somehow. 55

DUNOIS. Nonsense!

JOAN. Jack: do you think you will be able to drive them out?

DUNOIS [*with quiet conviction*]. Yes: I shall drive them out. They beat us because we 60 thought battles were tournaments and ransom markets. We played the fool while the goddams took war seriously. But I have learnt my lesson, and taken their measure. They have no roots here. I have beaten them before; and 65 I shall beat them again.

JOAN. You will not be cruel to them, Jack?

DUNOIS. The goddams will not yield to tender handling. We did not begin it.

JOAN [*suddenly*]. Jack: before I go home, let 70 us take Paris.

CHARLES [*terrified*]. Oh no no. We shall lose everything we have gained. Oh dont let us have any more fighting. We can make a very good treaty with the Duke of Burgundy. 75

JOAN. Treaty! [*She stamps with impatience.*]

CHARLES. Well, why not, now that I am crowned and anointed? Oh, that oil!

[*The* ARCHBISHOP *comes from the vestry, and joins the group between* CHARLES *and* BLUE- 80 BEARD.]

CHARLES. Archbishop: The Maid wants to start fighting again.

THE ARCHBISHOP. Have we ceased fighting, then? Are we at peace? 85

CHARLES. No: I suppose not; but let us be content with what we have done. Let us make a treaty. Our luck is too good to last; and now is our chance to stop before it turns.

JOAN. Luck! God has fought for us; and 90 you call it luck! And you would stop while there are still Englishmen on this holy earth of dear France!

THE ARCHBISHOP [*sternly*]. Maid: the king addressed himself to me, not to you. You forget 95 yourself. You very often forget yourself.

JOAN [*unabashed, and rather roughly*]. Then speak, you; and tell him that it is not God's will that he should take his hand from the plough.

5   THE ARCHBISHOP. If I am not so glib with the name of God as you are, it is because I interpret His will with the authority of The Church and of my sacred office. When you first came you respected it, and would not

10 have dared to speak as you are now speaking. You came clothed with the virtue of humility; and because God blessed your enterprises accordingly, you have stained yourself with the sin of pride. The old Greek tragedy is rising

15 among us. It is the chastisement of hubris.

  CHARLES. Yes: she thinks she knows better than everyone else.

  JOAN [*distressed, but naïvely incapable of seeing the effect she is producing*]. But I do

20 know better than any of you seem to. And I am not proud: I never speak unless I know I am right.

  BLUEBEARD } [*exclaiming* { Ha ha!
  CHARLES   } *together*]. { Just so.

25   THE ARCHBISHOP. How do you know you are right?

  JOAN. I always know. My voices—

  CHARLES. Oh, your voices, your voices. Why dont the voices come to me? I am king, not you.

30   JOAN. They do come to you; but you do not hear them. You have not sat in the field in the evening listening for them. When the angelus rings you cross yourself and have done with it; but if you prayed from your heart, and

35 listened to the thrilling of the bells in the air after they stop ringing, you would hear the voices as well as I do. [*Turning brusquely from him.*] But what voices do you need to tell you what the blacksmith can tell you: that you

40 must strike while the iron is hot? I tell you we must make a dash at Compiègne and relieve it as we relieved Orleans. Then Paris will open its gates; or if not, we will break through them. What is your crown worth without your

45 capital?

  LA HIRE. That is what I say too. We shall go through them like a red hot shot through a pound of butter. What do you say, Bastard?

  DUNOIS. If our cannon balls were all as hot as your head, and we had enough of them, we 50 should conquer the earth, no doubt. Pluck and impetuosity are good servants in war, but bad masters: they have delivered us into the hands of the English every time we have trusted to them. We never know when we are beaten: 55 that is our great fault.

  JOAN. You never know when you are victorious: that is a worse fault. I shall have to make you carry looking-glasses in battle to convince you that the English have not cut off 60 all your noses. You would have been besieged in Orleans still, you and your councils of war, if I had not made you attack. You should always attack; and if you only hold on long enough the enemy will stop first. You dont 65 know how to begin a battle; and you dont know how to use your cannons. And I do.

[*She squats down on the flags with crossed ankles, pouting.*]

  DUNOIS. I know what you think of us, 70 General Joan.

  JOAN. Never mind that, Jack. Tell them what you think of me.

  DUNOIS. I think that God was on your side; for I have not forgotten how the wind changed, 75 and how our hearts changed when you came; and by my faith I shall never deny that it was in your sign that we conquered. But I tell you as a soldier that God is no man's daily drudge, and no maid's either. If you are worthy of it 80 he will sometimes snatch you out of the jaws of death and set you on your feet again; but that is all: once on your feet you must fight with all your might and all your craft. For he has to be fair to your enemy too: dont forget 85 that. Well, he set us on our feet through you at Orleans; and the glory of it has carried us through a few good battles here to the coronation. But if we presume on it further, and trust to God to do the work we should do ourselves, 90 we shall be defeated; and serve us right!

  JOAN. But—

  DUNOIS. Sh! I have not finished. Do not think, any of you, that these victories of ours were won without generalship. King Charles: 95 you have said no word in your proclamations of my part in this campaign; and I make no complaint of that; for the people will run after The Maid and her miracles and not after the Bastard's hard work finding troops for her and 5 feeding them. But I know exactly how much God did for us through The Maid, and how much He left me to do by my own wits; and I tell you that your little hour of miracles is over, and that from this time on he who plays 10 the war game best will win—if the luck is on his side.

JOAN. Ah! if, if, if, if! If ifs and ans were pots and pans there'd be no need of tinkers. [Rising impetuously.] I tell you, Bastard, your 15 art of war is no use, because your knights are no good for real fighting. War is only a game to them, like tennis and all their other games: they make rules as to what is fair and what is not fair, and heap armor on themselves and on 20 their poor horses to keep out the arrows; and when they fall they cant get up, and have to wait for their squires to come and lift them to arrange about the ransom with the man that has poked them off their horse. Cant you see 25 that all the like of that is gone by and done with? What use is armor against gunpowder? And if it was, do you think men that are fighting for France and for God will stop to bargain about ransoms, as half your knights live by 30 doing? No: they will fight to win; and they will give up their lives out of their own hand into the hand of God when they go into battle, as I do. Common folks understand this. They cannot afford armor and cannot pay ransoms; 35 but they follow me half naked into the moat and up the ladder and over the wall. With them it is my life or thine, and God defend the right! You may shake your head, Jack; and Bluebeard may twirl his billygoat's beard 40 and cock his nose at me; but remember the day your knights and captains refused to follow me to attack the English at Orleans! You locked the gates to keep me in; and it was the townsfolk and the common people that fol- 45 lowed me, and forced the gate, and shewed you the way to fight in earnest.

BLUEBEARD [offended]. Not content with being Pope Joan, you must be Caesar and Alexander as well.

THE ARCHBISHOP. Pride will have a fall, Joan. 50

JOAN. Oh, never mind whether it is pride or not: is it true? is it commonsense?

LA HIRE. It is true. Half of us are afraid of having our handsome noses broken; and the other half are out for paying off their mort- 55 gages. Let her have her way, Dunois: she does not know everything; but she has got hold of the right end of the stick. Fighting is not what it was; and those who know least about it often make the best job of it. 60

DUNOIS. I know all that. I do not fight in the old way: I have learnt the lesson of Agincourt, of Poitiers and Crecy.° I know how many lives any move of mine will cost; and if the move is worth the cost I make it and pay the cost. 65 But Joan never counts the cost at all: she goes ahead and trusts to God: she thinks she has God in her pocket. Up to now she has had the numbers on her side; and she has won. But I know Joan; and I see that some day she will 70 go ahead when she has only ten men to do the work of a hundred. And then she will find that God is on the side of the big battalions. She will be taken by the enemy. And the lucky man that makes the capture will receive sixteen 75 thousand pounds from the Earl of Ouareek.°

JOAN [flattered]. Sixteen thousand pounds! Eh, laddie, have they offered that for me? There cannot be so much money in the world.

DUNOIS. There is, in England. And now tell 80 me, all of you, which of you will lift a finger to save Joan once the English have got her? I speak first, for the army. The day after she has been dragged from her horse by a goddam or a Burgundian, and he is not struck dead: the 85 day after she is locked in a dungeon, and the bars and bolts do not fly open at the touch of St Peter's angel: the day when the enemy finds

Agincourt, Poitiers, Crécy in the mid-fourteenth and early fifteenth centuries, battles in which the English defeated largely superior French forces and brought an end to old-fashioned chivalric tactics, which, Dunois says, were not sufficiently realistic
Ouareek French pronunciation of Warwick

out that she is as vulnerable as I am and not a bit more invincible, she will not be worth the life of a single soldier to us; and I will not risk that life, much as I cherish her as a
5 companion-in-arms.

JOAN. I dont blame you, Jack: you are right. I am not worth one soldier's life if God lets me be beaten; but France may think me worth my ransom after what God has done for her
10 through me.

CHARLES. I tell you I have no money; and this coronation, which is all your fault, has cost me the last farthing I can borrow.

JOAN. The Church is richer than you. I put
15 my trust in The Church.

THE ARCHBISHOP. Woman: they will drag you through the streets, and burn you as a witch.

JOAN [*running to him*]. Oh, my lord, do not say that. It is impossible. I a witch!
20 THE ARCHBISHOP. Peter Cauchon knows his business. The University of Paris has burnt a woman for saying that what you have done was well done, and according to God.

JOAN [*bewildered*]. But why? What sense is
25 there in it? What I have done is according to God. They could not burn a woman for speaking the truth.

THE ARCHBISHOP. They did.

JOAN. But you know that she was speaking
30 the truth. You would not let them burn me.

THE ARCHBISHOP. How could I prevent them?

JOAN. You would speak in the name of The Church. You are a great prince of The Church. I would go anywhere with your blessing to
35 protect me.

THE ARCHBISHOP. I have no blessing for you while you are proud and disobedient.

JOAN. Oh, why will you go on saying things like that? I am not proud and disobedient. I
40 am a poor girl, and so ignorant that I do not know A from B. How could I be proud? And how can you say that I am disobedient when I always obey my voices, because they come from God.
45 THE ARCHBISHOP. The voice of God on earth is the voice of the Church Militant; and all the voices that come to you are the echoes of your own wilfulness.

JOAN. It is not true.

THE ARCHBISHOP [*flushing angrily*]. You tell 50
the Archbishop in his cathedral that he lies; and yet you say you are not proud and disobedient.

JOAN. I never said you lied. It was you that as good as said my voices lied. When have 55
they ever lied? If you will not believe in them: even if they are only the echoes of my own commonsense, are they not always right? and are not your earthly counsels always wrong?

THE ARCHBISHOP [*indignantly*]. It is waste 60
of time admonishing you.

CHARLES. It always comes back to the same thing. She is right; and everyone else is wrong.

THE ARCHBISHOP. Take this as your last warning. If you perish through setting your 65
private judgment above the instructions of your spiritual directors, The Church disowns you, and leaves you to whatever fate your presumption may bring upon you. The Bastard has told you that if you persist in setting up 70
your military conceit above the counsels of your commanders—

DUNOIS [*interposing*]. To put it quite exactly, if you attempt to relieve the garrison in Compiègne without the same superiority in 75
numbers you had at Orleans—

THE ARCHBISHOP. The army will disown you, and will not rescue you. And His Majesty the King has told you that the throne has not the means of ransoming you. 80

CHARLES. Not a penny.

THE ARCHBISHOP. You stand alone: absolutely alone, trusting to your own conceit, your own ignorance, your own headstrong presumption, your own impiety in hiding all these sins under 85
the cloak of a trust in God. When you pass through these doors into the sunlight, the crowd will cheer you. They will bring you their little children and their invalids to heal: they will kiss your hands and feet, and do what 90
they can, poor simple souls, to turn your head, and madden you with the self-confidence that is leading you to your destruction. But you will be none the less alone: they cannot save you.

We and we only can stand between you and the stake at which our enemies have burnt that wretched woman in Paris.

JOAN [*her eyes skyward*]. I have better
5 friends and better counsel than yours.

THE ARCHBISHOP. I see that I am speaking in vain to a hardened heart. You reject our protection, and are determined to turn us all against you. In future, then, fend for yourself;
10 and if you fail, God have mercy on your soul.

DUNOIS. That is the truth, Joan. Heed it.

JOAN. Where would you all have been now if I had heeded that sort of truth? There is no help, no counsel, in any of you. Yes: I am
15 alone on earth: I have always been alone. My father told my brothers to drown me if I would not stay to mind his sheep while France was bleeding to death: France might perish if only our lambs were safe. I thought France would
20 have friends at the court of the king of France; and I find only wolves fighting for pieces of her poor torn body. I thought God would have friends everywhere, because He is the friend of everyone; and in my innocence I believed
25 that you who now cast me out would be like strong towers to keep harm from me. But I am wiser now; and nobody is any the worse for being wiser. Do not think you can frighten me by telling me that I am alone. France is
30 alone; and God is alone; and what is my loneliness before the loneliness of my country and my God? I see now that the loneliness of God is His strength: what would He be if He listened to your jealous little counsels? Well,
35 my loneliness shall be my strength too: it is better to be alone with God: His friendship will not fail me, nor His counsel, nor His love. In His strength I will dare, and dare, and dare, until I die. I will go out now to the common
40 people, and let the love in their eyes comfort me for the hate in yours. You will all be glad to see me burnt; but if I go through the fire I shall go through it to their hearts for ever and ever. And so, God, be with me!

45 [*She goes from them. They stare after her in glum silence for a moment. Then* GILLES DE RAIS *twirls his beard.*]

BLUEBEARD. You know, the woman is quite impossible. I dont dislike her, really; but what
50 are you to do with such a character?

DUNOIS. As God is my judge, if she fell into the Loire I would jump in in full armor to fish her out. But if she plays the fool at Compiègne, and gets caught, I must leave her to her doom.

55 LA HIRE. Then you had better chain me up; for I could follow her to hell when the spirit rises in her like that.

THE ARCHBISHOP. She disturbs my judgment too: there is a dangerous power in her out-
60 bursts. But the pit is open at her feet; and for good or evil we cannot turn her from it.

CHARLES. If only she would keep quiet, or go home!

[*They follow her dispiritedly.*]

SCENE VI

[*Rouen, 30th May 1431. A great stone hall
65 in the castle, arranged for a trial-at-law, but not a trial-by-jury, the court being the* BISHOP'*s court with the Inquisition participating: hence there are two raised chairs side by side for the* BISHOP *and the* INQUISITOR° *as judges. Rows of
70 chairs radiating from them at an obtuse angle are for the* CANONS, *the doctors of law and theology, and the* DOMINICAN MONKS, *who act as assessors. In the angle is a table for the scribes, with stools. There is also a heavy
75 rough wooden stool for the prisoner. All these are at the inner end of the hall. The further end is open to the courtyard through a row of arches. The court is shielded from the weather by screens and curtains.
80

Looking down the great hall from the middle of the inner end, the judicial chairs and scribes' table are to the right. The prisoner's stool is to the left. There are arched doors right and left. It is a fine sunshiny May morning.
85

WARWICK *comes in through the arched door-way on the judges' side, followed by his* PAGE.]

THE PAGE [*pertly*]. I suppose your lordship

Inquisitor a representative of the "Holy Office," charged directly by the papacy to inquire into heresy; an expert in theological questions and in court procedures

is aware that we have no business here. This is an ecclesiastical court; and we are only the secular arm.

WARWICK. I am aware of that fact. Will it please your impudence to find the Bishop of Beauvais for me, and give him a hint that he can have a word with me here before the trial, if he wishes?

THE PAGE [*going*]. Yes, my lord.

WARWICK. And mind you behave yourself. Do not address him as Pious Peter.

THE PAGE. No, my lord. I shall be kind to him, because, when The Maid is brought in, Pious Peter will have to pick a peck of pickled pepper.

[CAUCHON *enters through the same door with a* DOMINICAN MONK *and a* CANON, *the latter carrying a brief.*]

THE PAGE. The Right Reverend his lordship the Bishop of Beauvais. And two other reverend gentlemen.

WARWICK. Get out; and see that we are not interrupted.

THE PAGE. Right, my lord. [*He vanishes airily.*]

CAUCHON. I wish your lordship good-morrow.

WARWICK. Good-morrow to your lordship. Have I had the pleasure of meeting your friends before? I think not.

CAUCHON [*introducing the* MONK, *who is on his right*]. This, my lord, is Brother John Lemaître, of the order of St Dominic. He is acting as deputy for the Chief Inquisitor into the evil of heresy in France. Brother John: the Earl of Warwick.

WARWICK. Your Reverence is most welcome. We have no Inquisitor in England, unfortunately; though we miss him greatly, especially on occasions like the present.

[*The* INQUISITOR *smiles patiently, and bows. He is a mild elderly gentleman, but has evident reserves of authority and firmness.*]

CAUCHON [*introducing the* CANON, *who is on his left*]. This gentleman is Canon John D'Estivet, of the Chapter of Bayeux. He is acting as Promoter.

WARWICK. Promoter?

CAUCHON. Prosecutor, you would call him in civil law.

WARWICK. Ah! prosecutor. Quite, quite. I am very glad to make your acquaintance, Canon D'Estivet.

[D'ESTIVET *bows.* (*He is on the young side of middle age, well mannered, but vulpine beneath his veneer.*)]

WARWICK. May I ask what stage the proceedings have reached? It is now more than nine months since The Maid was captured at Compiègne by the Burgundians. It is fully four months since I bought her from the Burgundians for a very handsome sum, solely that she might be brought to justice. It is very nearly three months since I delivered her up to you, my Lord Bishop, as a person suspected of heresy. May I suggest that you are taking a rather unconscionable time to make up your minds about a very plain case? Is this trial never going to end?

THE INQUISITOR [*smiling*]. It has not yet begun, my lord.

WARWICK. Not yet begun! Why, you have been at it eleven weeks!

CAUCHON. We have not been idle, my lord. We have held fifteen examinations of The Maid: six public and nine private.

THE INQUISITOR [*always patiently smiling*]. You see, my lord, I have been present at only two of these examinations. They were proceedings of the Bishop's court solely, and not of the Holy Office. I have only just decided to associate myself—that is, to associate the Holy Inquisition—with the Bishop's court. I did not at first think that this was a case of heresy at all. I regarded it as a political case, and The Maid as a prisoner of war. But having now been present at two of the examinations, I must admit that this seems to be one of the gravest cases of heresy within my experience. Therefore everything is now in order; and we proceed to trial this morning. [*He moves towards the judicial chairs.*]

CAUCHON. This moment, if your lordship's convenience allows.

WARWICK [*graciously*]. Well, that is good news, gentlemen. I will not attempt to conceal from you that our patience was becoming strained.

CAUCHON. So I gathered from the threats of your soldiers to drown those of our people who favor The Maid.

WARWICK. Dear me! At all events their intentions were friendly to you, my lord.

CAUCHON [*sternly*]. I hope not. I am determined that the woman shall have a fair hearing. The justice of The Church is not a mockery, my lord.

THE INQUISITOR [*returning*]. Never has there been a fairer examination within my experience, my lord. The Maid needs no lawyers to take her part: she will be tried by her most faithful friends, all ardently desirous to save her soul from perdition.

D'ESTIVET. Sir: I am the Promoter; and it has been my painful duty to present the case against the girl; but believe me, I would throw up my case today and hasten to her defence if I did not know that men far my superiors in learning and piety, in eloquence and persuasiveness, have been sent to reason with her, to explain to her the danger she is running, and the ease with which she may avoid it. [*Suddenly bursting into forensic eloquence, to the disgust of* CAUCHON *and the* INQUISITOR, *who have listened to him so far with patronizing approval.*] Men have dared to say that we are acting from hate; but God is our witness that they lie. Have we tortured her? No. Have we ceased to exhort her; to implore her to have pity on herself; to come to the bosom of her Church as an erring but beloved child? Have we—

CAUCHON [*interrupting drily*]. Take care, Canon. All that you say is true; but if you make his lordship believe it I will not answer for your life, and hardly for my own.

WARWICK [*deprecating, but by no means denying*]. Oh, my lord, you are very hard on us poor English. But we certainly do not share your pious desire to save The Maid: in fact I tell you now plainly that her death is a political necessity which I regret but cannot help. If The Church lets her go—

CAUCHON [*with fierce and menacing pride*].

If The Church lets her go, woe to the man, were he the Emperor himself, who dares lay a finger on her! The Church is not subject to political necessity, my lord.

THE INQUISITOR [*interposing smoothly*]. You need have no anxiety about the result, my lord. You have an invincible ally in the matter: one who is far more determined than you that she shall burn.

WARWICK. And who is this very convenient partisan, may I ask?

THE INQUISITOR. The Maid herself. Unless you put a gag in her mouth you cannot prevent her from convicting herself ten times over every time she opens it.

D'ESTIVET. That is perfectly true, my lord. My hair bristles on my head when I hear so young a creature utter such blasphemies.

WARWICK. Well, by all means do your best for her if you are quite sure it will be of no avail. [*Looking hard at* CAUCHON.] I should be sorry to have to act without the blessing of The Church.

CAUCHON [*with a mixture of cynical admiration and contempt*]. And yet they say Englishmen are hypocrites! You play for your side, my lord, even at the peril of your soul. I cannot but admire such devotion; but I dare not go so far myself. I fear damnation.

WARWICK. If we feared anything we could never govern England, my lord. Shall I send your people in to you?

CAUCHON. Yes: it will be very good of your lordship to withdraw and allow the court to assemble.

[WARWICK *turns on his heel, and goes out through the courtyard.* CAUCHON *takes one of the judicial seats: and* D'ESTIVET *sits at the scribes' table, studying his brief.*]

CAUCHON [*casually, as he makes himself comfortable*]. What scoundrels these English nobles are!

THE INQUISITOR [*taking the other judicial chair on* CAUCHON'S *left*]. All secular power makes men scoundrels. They are not trained for the work; and they have not the Apostolic Succession. Our own nobles are just as bad.

[*The* BISHOP'S ASSESSORS *hurry into the hall,*

headed by CHAPLAIN DE STOGUMBER *and* CANON DE COURCELLES, *a young priest of* 30. *The scribes sit at the table, leaving a chair vacant opposite* D'ESTIVET. *Some of the* ASSESSORS take *their seats: others stand chatting, waiting for the proceedings to begin formally.* DE STOGUMBER, *aggrieved and obstinate, will not take his seat: neither will the* CANON, *who stands on his right.*]

CAUCHON. Good morning, Master de Stogumber. [*To the* INQUISITOR.] Chaplain to the Cardinal of England.

THE CHAPLAIN [*correcting him*]. Of Winchester, my lord. I have to make a protest, my lord.

CAUCHON. You make a great many.

THE CHAPLAIN. I am not without support, my lord. Here is Master de Courcelles, Canon of Paris, who associates himself with me in my protest.

CAUCHON. Well, what is the matter?

THE CHAPLAIN [*sulkily*]. Speak you, Master de Courcelles, since I do not seem to enjoy his lordship's confidence. [*He sits down in dudgeon next to* CAUCHON, *on his right.*]

COURCELLES. My lord: we have been at great pains to draw up an indictment of The Maid on sixtyfour counts. We are now told that they have been reduced, without consulting us.

THE INQUISITOR. Master de Courcelles: I am the culprit. I am overwhelmed with admiration for the zeal displayed in your sixtyfour counts; but in accusing a heretic, as in other things, enough is enough. Also you must remember that all the members of the court are not so subtle and profound as you, and that some of your very great learning might appear to them to be very great nonsense. Therefore I have thought it well to have your sixtyfour articles cut down to twelve—

COURCELLES [*thunderstruck*]. Twelve! ! !

THE INQUISITOR. Twelve will, believe me, be quite enough for your purpose.

THE CHAPLAIN. But some of the most important points have been reduced almost to nothing. For instance, The Maid has actually declared that the blessed saints Margaret and Catherine, and the holy Archangel Michael, spoke to her in French. That is a vital point.

THE INQUISITOR. You think, doubtless, that they should have spoken in Latin?

CAUCHON. No: he thinks they should have spoken in English.

THE CHAPLAIN. Naturally, my lord.

THE INQUISITOR. Well, as we are here agreed, I think, that these voices of The Maid are the voices of evil spirits tempting her to her damnation, it would not be very courteous to you, Master de Stogumber, or to the King of England, to assume that English is the devil's native language. So let it pass. The matter is not wholly omitted from the twelve articles. Pray take your places, gentlemen; and let us proceed to business.

[*All who have not taken their seats, do so.*]

THE CHAPLAIN. Well, I protest. That is all.

COURCELLES. I think it hard that all our work should go for nothing. It is only another example of the diabolical influence which this woman exercises over the court. [*He takes his chair, which is on the* CHAPLAIN's *right.*]

CAUCHON. Do you suggest that I am under diabolical influence?

COURCELLES. I suggest nothing, my lord. But it seems to me that there is a conspiracy here to hush up the fact that The Maid stole the Bishop of Senlis's horse.

CAUCHON [*keeping his temper with difficulty*]. This is not a police court. Are we to waste our time on such rubbish?

COURCELLES [*rising, shocked*]. My lord: do you call the Bishop's horse rubbish?

THE INQUISITOR [*blandly*]. Master de Courcelles: The Maid alleges that she paid handsomely for the Bishop's horse, and that if he did not get the money the fault was not hers. As that may be true, the point is one on which The Maid may well be acquitted.

COURCELLES. Yes, if it were an ordinary horse. But the Bishop's horse! how can she be acquitted for that? [*He sits down again, bewildered and discouraged.*]

THE INQUISITOR. I submit to you, with great respect, that if we persist in trying The Maid on trumpery issues on which we may have to declare her innocent, she may escape us on the great main issue of heresy, on which she seems so far to insist on her own guilt. I will ask you, therefore, to say nothing, when The Maid is brought before us, of these stealings of horses, and dancings round fairy trees with the village children, and prayings at haunted wells, and a dozen other things which you were diligently inquiring into until my arrival. There is not a village girl in France against whom you could not prove such things: they all dance round haunted trees, and pray at magic wells. Some of them would steal the Pope's horse if they got the chance. Heresy, gentlemen, heresy is the charge we have to try. The detection and suppression of heresy is my peculiar business: I am here as an inquisitor, not as an ordinary magistrate. Stick to the heresy, gentlemen; and leave the other matters alone.

CAUCHON. I may say that we have sent to the girl's village to make inquiries about her; and there is practically nothing serious against her.

THE CHAPLAIN [*rising and clamoring together*]. Nothing serious, my lord—What!
COURCELLES The fairy tree not—

CAUCHON [*out of patience*]. Be silent, gentlemen; or speak one at a time.

[COURCELLES *collapses into his chair intimidated.*]

THE CHAPLAIN [*sulkily resuming his seat*]. That is what The Maid said to us last Friday.

CAUCHON. I wish you had followed her counsel, sir. When I say nothing serious, I mean nothing that men of sufficiently large mind to conduct an inquiry like this would consider serious. I agree with my colleague the Inquisitor that it is on the count of heresy that we must proceed.

LADVENU [*a young but ascetically fine-drawn Dominican who is sitting next COURCELLES, on his right*]. But is there any great harm in the girl's heresy? Is it not merely her simplicity? Many saints have said as much as Joan.

THE INQUISITOR [*dropping his blandness and speaking very gravely*]. Brother Martin: if you had seen what I have seen of heresy, you would not think it a light thing even in its most apparently harmless and even lovable and pious origins. Heresy begins with people who are to all appearance better than their neighbors. A gentle and pious girl, or a young man who has obeyed the command of our Lord by giving all his riches to the poor, and putting on the garb of poverty, the life of austerity, and the rule of humility and charity, may be the founder of a heresy that will wreck both Church and Empire if not ruthlessly stamped out in time. The records of the holy Inquisition are full of histories we dare not give to the world, because they are beyond the belief of honest men and innocent women; yet they all began with saintly simpletons. I have seen this again and again. Mark what I say: the woman who quarrels with her clothes, and puts on the dress of a man, is like the man who throws off his fur gown and dresses like John the Baptist: they are followed, as surely as the night follows the day, by bands of wild women and men who refuse to wear any clothes at all. When maids will neither marry nor take regular vows, and men reject marriage and exalt their lusts into divine inspirations, then, as surely as the summer follows the spring, they begin with polygamy, and end by incest. Heresy at first seems innocent and even laudable; but it ends in such a monstrous horror of unnatural wickedness that the most tender-hearted among you, if you saw it at work as I have seen it, would clamor against the mercy of The Church in dealing with it. For two hundred years the Holy Office has striven with these diabolical madnesses; and it knows that they begin always by vain and ignorant persons setting up their own judgment against The Church, and taking it upon themselves to be the interpreters of God's will. You must not fall into the common error of mistaking these simpletons for liars and hypocrites. They believe honestly and sincerely that their diabolical inspiration is divine. Therefore you must be on your guard against your natural compassion. You are all, I hope, merciful men: how else could you have devoted your lives to the service of our gentle Savior? You are going to see before you a young girl, pious and chaste; for I must tell you, gentlemen, that the things said of her by

our English friends are supported by no evidence, whilst there is abundant testimony that
her excesses have been excesses of religion and
charity and not of worldliness and wantonness.
5 This girl is not one of those whose hard
features are the sign of hard hearts, and whose
brazen looks and lewd demeanor condemn
them before they are accused. The devilish
pride that has led her into her present peril has
10 left no mark on her countenance. Strange as
it may seem to you, it has even left no mark
on her character outside those special matters
in which she is proud; so that you will see a
diabolical pride and a natural humility seated
15 side by side in the selfsame soul. Therefore be
on your guard. God forbid that I should tell
you to harden your hearts; for her punishment
if we condemn her will be so cruel that we
should forfeit our own hope of divine mercy
20 were there one grain of malice against her in
our hearts. But if you hate cruelty—and if any
man here does not hate it I command him on
his soul's salvation to quit this holy court—
I say, if you hate cruelty, remember that noth-
25 ing is so cruel in its consequences as the
toleration of heresy. Remember also that no
court of law can be so cruel as the common
people are to those whom they suspect of
heresy. The heretic in the hands of the Holy
30 Office is safe from violence, is assured of a fair
trial, and cannot suffer death, even when guilty,
if repentance follows sin. Innumerable lives of
heretics have been saved because the Holy
Office has taken them out of the hands of the
35 people, and because the people have yielded
them up, knowing that the Holy Office would
deal with them. Before the Holy Inquisition
existed, and even now when its officers are not
within reach, the unfortunate wretch suspected
40 of heresy, perhaps quite ignorantly and un-
justly, is stoned, torn in pieces, drowned,
burned in his house with all his innocent
children, without a trial, unshriven, unburied
save as a dog is buried: all of them deeds hate-
45 ful to God and most cruel to man. Gentlemen:
I am compassionate by nature as well as by
my profession; and though the work I have
to do may seem cruel to those who do not know

how much more cruel it would be to leave it
undone, I would go to the stake myself sooner 50
than do it if I did not know its righteousness,
its necessity, its essential mercy. I ask you to
address yourself to this trial in that conviction.
Anger is a bad counsellor: cast out anger. Pity
is sometimes worse: cast out pity. But do not 55
cast out mercy. Remember only that justice
comes first. Have you anything to say, my
lord, before we proceed to trial?

CAUCHON. You have spoken for me, and
spoken better than I could. I do not see how 60
any sane man could disagree with a word that
has fallen from you. But this I will add. The
crude heresies of which you have told us are
horrible; but their horror is like that of the
black death: they rage for a while and then die 65
out, because sound and sensible men will not
under any incitement be reconciled to naked-
ness and incest and polygamy and the like. But
we are confronted today throughout Europe
with a heresy that is spreading among men not 70
weak in mind nor diseased in brain: nay, the
stronger the mind, the more obstinate the heretic. It is neither discredited by fantastic extremes nor corrupted by the common lusts of
the flesh; but it, too, sets up the private judg- 75
ment of the single erring mortal against the
considered wisdom and experience of The
Church. The mighty structure of Catholic
Christendom will never be shaken by naked
madmen or by the sins of Moab and Ammon. 80
But it may be betrayed from within, and
brought to barbarous ruin and desolation, by
this arch heresy which the English Commander
calls Protestantism.

THE ASSESSORS [*whispering*]. Protestantism! 85
What was that? What does the Bishop mean?
Is it a new heresy? The English Commander,
he said. Did you ever hear of Protestantism?
etc., etc.

CAUCHON [*continuing*]. And that reminds 90
me. What provision has the Earl of Warwick
made for the defence of the secular arm should
The Maid prove obdurate, and the people be
moved to pity her?

THE CHAPLAIN. Have no fear on that score, 95
my lord. The noble earl has eight hundred

men-at-arms at the gates. She will not slip through our English fingers even if the whole city be on her side.

CAUCHON [revolted]. Will you not add, God
5 grant that she repent and purge her sin?

THE CHAPLAIN. That does not seem to me to be consistent; but of course I agree with your lordship.

CAUCHON [giving him up with a shrug of
10 contempt]. The court sits.

THE INQUISITOR. Let the accused be brought in.

LADVENU [calling]. The accused. Let her be brought in.

15 [JOAN, chained by the ankles, is brought in through the arched door behind the prisoner's stool by a guard of ENGLISH SOLDIERS. With them is the EXECUTIONER and his ASSISTANTS. They lead her to the prisoner's stool, and place
20 themselves behind it after taking off her chain. She wears a page's black suit. Her long imprisonment and the strain of the examinations which have preceded the trial have left their mark on her; but her vitality still holds: she
25 confronts the court unabashed, without a trace of the awe which their formal solemnity seems to require for the complete success of its impressiveness.]

THE INQUISITOR [kindly]. Sit down, Joan.
30 [She sits on the prisoner's stool.] You look very pale today. Are you not well?

JOAN. Thank you kindly: I am well enough. But the Bishop sent me some carp; and it made me ill.

35 CAUCHON. I am sorry. I told them to see that it was fresh.

JOAN. You meant to be good to me, I know; but it is a fish that does not agree with me. The English thought you were trying to poison
40 me—

CAUCHON }
THE CHAPLAIN } [together]. { What!
{ No, my lord.

JOAN [continuing]. They are determined that I shall be burnt as a witch; and they sent their
45 doctor to cure me; but he was forbidden to bleed me because the silly people believe that a witch's witchery leaves her if she is bled; so

he only called me filthy names. Why do you leave me in the hands of the English? I should
50 be in the hands of The Church. And why must I be chained by the feet to a log of wood? Are you afraid I will fly away?

D'ESTIVET [harshly]. Woman: it is not for you to question the court: it is for us to
55 question you.

COURCELLES. When you were left unchained, did you not try to escape by jumping from a tower sixty feet high? If you cannot fly like a witch, how is it that you are still alive?

60 JOAN. I suppose because the tower was not so high then. It has grown higher every day since you began asking me questions about it.

D'ESTIVET. Why did you jump from the tower?

65 JOAN. How do you know that I jumped?

D'ESTIVET. You were found lying in the moat. Why did you leave the tower?

JOAN. Why would anybody leave a prison if they could get out?

70 D'ESTIVET. You tried to escape?

JOAN. Of course I did; and not for the first time either. If you leave the door of the cage open the bird will fly out.

D'ESTIVET [rising]. That is a confession of
75 heresy. I call the attention of the court to it.

JOAN. Heresy, he calls it! Am I a heretic because I try to escape from prison?

D'ESTIVET. Assuredly, if you are in the hands of The Church, and you wilfully take yourself
80 out of its hands, you are deserting The Church; and that is heresy.

JOAN. It is great nonsense. Nobody could be such a fool as to think that.

D'ESTIVET. You hear, my lord, how I am
85 reviled in the execution of my duty by this woman. [He sits down indignantly.]

CAUCHON. I have warned you before, Joan, that you are doing yourself no good by these pert answers.

90 JOAN. But you will not talk sense to me. I am reasonable if you will be reasonable.

THE INQUISITOR [interposing]. This is not yet in order. You forget, Master Promoter, that the proceedings have not been formally opened. The time for questions is after she has sworn on the Gospels to tell us the whole truth.

JOAN. You say this to me every time. I have said again and again that I will tell you all that
5 concerns this trial. But I cannot tell you the whole truth: God does not allow the whole truth to be told. You do not understand it when I tell it. It is an old saying that he who tells too much truth is sure to be hanged. I
10 am weary of this argument: we have been over it nine times already. I have sworn as much as I will swear; and I will swear no more.

COURCELLES. My lord: she should be put to the torture.

15 THE INQUISITOR. You hear, Joan? That is what happens to the obdurate. Think before you answer. Has she been shewn the instruments?

THE EXECUTIONER. They are ready, my lord.
20 She has seen them.

JOAN. If you tear me limb from limb until you separate my soul from my body you will get nothing out of me beyond what I have told you. What more is there to tell that you could
25 understand? Besides, I cannot bear to be hurt; and if you hurt me I will say anything you like to stop the pain. But I will take it all back afterwards; so what is the use of it?

LADVENU. There is much in that. We should
30 proceed mercifully.

COURCELLES. But the torture is customary.

THE INQUISITOR. It must not be applied wantonly. If the accused will confess voluntarily, then its use cannot be justified.

35 COURCELLES. But this is unusual and irregular. She refuses to take the oath.

LADVENU [*disgusted*]. Do you want to torture the girl for the mere pleasure of it?

COURCELLES [*bewildered*]. But it is not a
40 pleasure. It is the law. It is customary. It is always done.

THE INQUISITOR. That is not so, Master, except when the inquiries are carried on by people who do not know their legal business.

45 COURCELLES. But the woman is a heretic. I assure you it is always done.

CAUCHON [*decisively*]. It will not be done

today if it is not necessary. Let there be an end of this. I will not have it said that we proceeded on forced confessions. We have
50 sent our best preachers and doctors to this woman to exhort and implore her to save her soul and body from the fire: we shall not now send the executioner to thrust her into it.

COURCELLES. Your lordship is merciful, of
55 course. But it is a great responsibility to depart from the usual practice.

JOAN. Thou art a rare noodle, Master. Do what was done last time is thy rule, eh?

COURCELLES [*rising*]. Thou wanton: dost thou
60 dare call me noodle?

THE INQUISITOR. Patience, Master, patience: I fear you will soon be only too terribly avenged.

COURCELLES [*mutters*]. Noodle indeed! [*He
65 sits down, much discontented.*]

THE INQUISITOR. Meanwhile, let us not be moved by the rough side of a shepherd lass's tongue.

JOAN. Nay: I am no shepherd lass, though I
70 have helped with the sheep like anyone else. I will do a lady's work in the house—spin or weave—against any woman in Rouen.

THE INQUISITOR. This is not a time for vanity, Joan. You stand in great peril.

75 JOAN. I know it: have I not been punished for my vanity? If I had not worn my cloth of gold surcoat in battle like a fool, that Burgundian soldier would never have pulled me backwards off my horse; and I should not have
80 been here.

THE CHAPLAIN. If you are so clever at woman's work why do you not stay at home and do it?

JOAN. There are plenty of other women to do
85 it; but there is nobody to do my work.

CAUCHON. Come! we are wasting time on trifles. Joan: I am going to put a most solemn question to you. Take care how you answer; for your life and salvation are at stake on it.
90 Will you for all you have said and done, be it good or bad, accept the judgment of God's Church on earth? More especially as to the acts and words that are imputed to you in this trial

by the Promoter here, will you submit your case to the inspired interpretation of the Church Militant?

JOAN. I am a faithful child of The Church. I will obey The Church—

CAUCHON [*hopefully leaning forward*]. You will?

JOAN. —provided it does not command anything impossible.

[CAUCHON *sinks back in his chair with a heavy sigh. The* INQUISITOR *purses his lips and frowns.* LADVENU *shakes his head pitifully.*]

D'ESTIVET. She imputes to The Church the error and folly of commanding the impossible.

JOAN. If you command me to declare that all I have done and said, and all the visions and revelations I have had, were not from God, then that is impossible: I will not declare it for anything in the world. What God made me do I will never go back on; and what He has commanded or shall command I will not fail to do in spite of any man alive. That is what I mean by impossible. And in case The Church should bid me do anything contrary to the command I have from God, I will not consent to it, no matter what it may be.

THE ASSESSORS [*shocked and indignant*]. Oh! The Church contrary to God! What do you say now? Flat heresy. This is beyond everything, etc., etc.

D'ESTIVET [*throwing down his brief*]. My lord: do you need anything more than this?

CAUCHON. Woman: you have said enough to burn ten heretics. Will you not be warned? Will you not understand?

THE INQUISITOR. If the Church Militant tells you that your revelations and visions are sent by the devil to tempt you to your damnation, will you not believe that The Church is wiser than you?

JOAN. I believe that God is wiser than I; and it is His commands that I will do. All the things that you call my crimes have come to me by the command of God. I say that I have done them by the order of God: it is impossible for me to say anything else. If any Churchman says the contrary I shall not mind him: I shall mind God alone, whose command I always follow.

LADVENU [*pleading with her urgently*]. You do not know what you are saying, child. Do you want to kill yourself? Listen. Do you not believe that you are subject to the Church of God on earth?

JOAN. Yes. When have I ever denied it?

LADVENU. Good. That means, does it not, that you are subject to our Lord the Pope, to the cardinals, the archbishops, and the bishops for whom his lordship stands here today?

JOAN. God must be served first.

D'ESTIVET. Then your voices command you not to submit yourself to the Church Militant?

JOAN. My voices do not tell me to disobey The Church; but God must be served first.

CAUCHON. And you, and not The Church, are to be the judge?

JOAN. What other judgment can I judge by but my own?

THE ASSESSORS [*scandalized*]. Oh! [*They cannot find words.*]

CAUCHON. Out of your own mouth you have condemned yourself. We have striven for your salvation to the verge of sinning ourselves: we have opened the door to you again and again; and you have shut it in our faces and in the face of God. Dare you pretend, after what you have said, that you are in a state of grace?

JOAN. If I am not, may God bring me to it: if I am, may God keep me in it!

LADVENU. That is a very good reply, my lord.

COURCELLES. Were you in a state of grace when you stole the Bishop's horse?

CAUCHON [*rising in a fury*]. Oh, devil take the Bishop's horse and you too! We are here to try a case of heresy; and no sooner do we come to the root of the matter than we are thrown back by idiots who understand nothing but horses. [*Trembling with rage, he forces himself to sit down.*]

THE INQUISITOR. Gentlemen, gentlemen: in clinging to these small issues you are The Maid's best advocates. I am not surprised that his lordship has lost patience with you. What does the Promoter say? Does he press these trumpery matters?

D'ESTIVET. I am bound by my office to press everything; but when the woman confesses a heresy that must bring upon her the doom of

excommunication, of what consequence is it that she has been guilty also of offences which expose her to minor penances? I share the impatience of his lordship as to these minor
5 charges. Only, with great respect, I must emphasize the gravity of two very horrible and blasphemous crimes which she does not deny. First, she has intercourse with evil spirits, and is therefore a sorceress. Second, she wears
10 men's clothes, which is indecent, unnatural, and abominable; and in spite of our most earnest remonstrances and entreaties, she will not change them even to receive the sacrament.

JOAN. Is the blessed St Catherine an evil
15 spirit? Is St Margaret? Is Michael the Archangel?

COURCELLES. How do you know that the spirit which appears to you is an archangel? Does he not appear to you as a naked man?
20 JOAN. Do you think God cannot afford clothes for him?

[*The* ASSESSORS *cannot help smiling, especially as the joke is against* COURCELLES.]

LADVENU. Well answered, Joan.
25 THE INQUISITOR. It is, in effect, well answered. But no evil spirit would be so simple as to appear to a young girl in a guise that would scandalize her when he meant her to take him for a messenger from the Most High. Joan:
30 The Church instructs you that these apparitions are demons seeking your soul's perdition. Do you accept the instruction of The Church?

JOAN. I accept the messenger of God. How could any faithful believer in The Church
35 refuse him?

CAUCHON. Wretched woman: again I ask you, do you know what you are saying?

THE INQUISITOR. You wrestle in vain with the devil for her soul, my lord: she will not
40 be saved. Now as to this matter of the man's dress. For the last time, will you put off that impudent attire, and dress as becomes your sex?

JOAN. I will not.
45 D'ESTIVET [*pouncing*]. The sin of disobedience, my lord.

JOAN [*distressed*]. But my voices tell me I must dress as a soldier.

LADVENU. Joan, Joan: does not that prove to

you that the voices are the voices of evil spirits? 50 Can you suggest to us one good reason why an angel of God should give you such shameless advice?

JOAN. Why, yes: what can be plainer commonsense? I was a soldier living among 55 soldiers. I am a prisoner guarded by soldiers. If I were to dress as a woman they would think of me as a woman; and then what would become of me? If I dress as a soldier they think of me as a soldier, and I can live with them as 60 I do at home with my brothers. That is why St Catherine tells me I must not dress as a woman until she gives me leave.

COURCELLES. When will she give you leave?

JOAN. When you take me out of the hands 65 of the English soldiers. I have told you that I should be in the hands of The Church, and not left night and day with four soldiers of the Earl of Warwick. Do you want me to live with them in petticoats?
70
LADVENU. My lord: what she says is, God knows, very wrong and shocking; but there is a grain of worldly sense in it such as might impose on a simple village maiden.

JOAN. If we were as simple in the village as 75 you are in your courts and palaces, there would soon be no wheat to make bread for you.

CAUCHON. That is the thanks you get for trying to save her, Brother Martin.

LADVENU. Joan: we are all trying to save 80 you. His lordship is trying to save you. The Inquisitor could not be more just to you if you were his own daughter. But you are blinded by a terrible pride and self-sufficiency.

JOAN. Why do you say that? I have said 85 nothing wrong. I cannot understand.

THE INQUISITOR. The blessed St Athanasius has laid it down in his creed that those who cannot understand are damned. It is not enough to be simple. It is not enough even to be what 90 simple people call good. The simplicity of a darkened mind is no better than the simplicity of a beast.

JOAN. There is great wisdom in the simplicity of a beast, let me tell you; and sometimes great 95 foolishness in the wisdom of scholars.

LADVENU. We know that, Joan: we are not so foolish as you think us. Try to resist the temptation to make pert replies to us. Do you see that man who stands behind you [*he indicates the* EXECUTIONER]?

JOAN [*turning and looking at the man*]. Your torturer? But the Bishop said I was not to be tortured.

LADVENU. You are not to be tortured because you have confessed everything that is necessary to your condemnation. That man is not only the torturer: he is also the Executioner. Executioner: let The Maid hear your answers to my questions. Are you prepared for the burning of a heretic this day?

THE EXECUTIONER. Yes, Master.

LADVENU. Is the stake ready?

THE EXECUTIONER. It is. In the market-place. The English have built it too high for me to get near her and make the death easier. It will be a cruel death.

JOAN [*horrified*]. But you are not going to burn me now?

THE INQUISITOR. You realize it at last.

LADVENU. There are eight hundred English soldiers waiting to take you to the market-place the moment the sentence of excommunication has passed the lips of your judges. You are within a few short moments of that doom.

JOAN [*looking round desperately for rescue*]. Oh God!

LADVENU. Do not despair, Joan. The Church is merciful. You can save yourself.

JOAN [*hopefully*]. Yes: my voices promised me I should not be burnt. St Catherine bade me be bold.

CAUCHON. Woman: are you quite mad? Do you not yet see that your voices have deceived you?

JOAN. Oh no: that is impossible.

CAUCHON. Impossible! They have led you straight to your excommunication, and to the stake which is there waiting for you.

LADVENU [*pressing the point hard*]. Have they kept a single promise to you since you were taken at Compiègne? The devil has betrayed you. The Church holds out its arms to you.

JOAN [*despairing*]. Oh, it is true: it is true: my voices have deceived me. I have been mocked by devils: my faith is broken. I have dared and dared; but only a fool will walk into a fire: God, who gave me my commonsense, cannot will me to do that.

LADVENU. Now God be praised that He has saved you at the eleventh hour! [*He hurries to the vacant seat at the scribes' table, and snatches a sheet of paper, on which he sets to work writing eagerly.*]

CAUCHON. Amen!

JOAN. What must I do?

CAUCHON. You must sign a solemn recantation of your heresy.

JOAN. Sign? That means to write my name. I cannot write.

CAUCHON. You have signed many letters before.

JOAN. Yes; but someone held my hand and guided the pen. I can make my mark.

THE CHAPLAIN [*who has been listening with growing alarm and indignation*]. My lord: do you mean that you are going to allow this woman to escape us?

THE INQUISITOR. The law must take its course, Master de Stogumber. And you know the law.

THE CHAPLAIN [*rising, purple with fury*]. I know that there is no faith in a Frenchman. [*Tumult, which he shouts down.*] I know what my lord the Cardinal of Winchester will say when he hears of this. I know what the Earl of Warwick will do when he learns that you intend to betray him. There are eight hundred men at the gate who will see that this abominable witch is burnt in spite of your teeth.

THE ASSESSORS [*meanwhile*]. What is this? What did he say? He accuses us of treachery! This is past bearing. No faith in a Frenchman! Did you hear that? This is an intolerable fellow. Who is he? Is this what English Churchmen are like? He must be mad or drunk, etc., etc.

THE INQUISITOR [*rising*]. Silence, pray! Gentlemen: pray silence! Master Chaplain: bethink you a moment of your holy office: of what you are, and where you are. I direct you to sit down.

THE CHAPLAIN [*folding his arms doggedly,*

his face working convulsively]. I will NOT sit down.

CAUCHON. Master Inquisitor: this man has called me a traitor to my face before now.

5 THE CHAPLAIN. So you are a traitor. You are all traitors. You have been doing nothing but begging this damnable witch on your knees to recant all through this trial.

THE INQUISITOR [placidly resuming his seat].
10 If you will not sit, you must stand: that is all.

THE CHAPLAIN. I will NOT stand. [He flings himself back into his chair.]

LADVENU [rising with the paper in his hand]. My lord: here is the form of recantation for
15 The Maid to sign.

CAUCHON. Read it to her.

JOAN. Do not trouble. I will sign it.

THE INQUISITOR. Woman: you must know what you are putting your hand to. Read it to
20 her, Brother Martin. And let all be silent.

LADVENU [reading quietly]. "I, Joan, commonly called The Maid, a miserable sinner, do confess that I have most grievously sinned in the following articles. I have pretended to have
25 revelations from God and the angels and the blessed saints, and perversely rejected The Church's warnings that these were temptations by demons. I have blasphemed abominably by wearing an immodest dress, contrary to the
30 Holy Scripture and the canons of The Church. Also I have clipped my hair in the style of a man, and, against all the duties which have made my sex specially acceptable in heaven, have taken up the sword, even to the shedding
35 of human blood, inciting men to slay each other, invoking evil spirits to delude them, and stubbornly and most blasphemously imputing these sins to Almighty God. I confess to the sin of sedition, to the sin of idolatry, to the sin of
40 disobedience, to the sin of pride, and to the sin of heresy. All of which sins I now renounce and abjure and depart from, humbly thanking you Doctors and Masters who have brought me back to the truth and into the grace of our
45 Lord. And I will never return to my errors, but will remain in communion with our Holy Church and in obedience to our Holy Father the Pope of Rome. All this I swear by God

Almighty and the Holy Gospels, in witness whereto I sign my name to this recantation." 50

THE INQUISITOR. You understand this, Joan?

JOAN [listless]. It is plain enough, sir.

THE INQUISITOR. And it is true?

JOAN. It may be true. If it were not true, the fire would not be ready for me in the market- 55 place.

LADVENU [taking up his pen and a book, and going to her quickly lest she should compromise herself again]. Come, child: let me guide your hand. Take the pen. [She does so; and 60 they begin to write, using the book as a desk.] J.E.H.A.N.E. So. Now make your mark by yourself.

JOAN [makes her mark, and gives him back the pen, tormented by the rebellion of her soul 65 against her mind and body]. There!

LADVENU [replacing the pen on the table, and handing the recantation to CAUCHON with a reverence]. Praise be to God, my brothers, the lamb has returned to the flock; and the shep- 70 herd rejoices in her more than in ninety and nine just persons. [He returns to his seat.]

THE INQUISITOR [taking the paper from CAUCHON]. We declare thee by this act set free from the danger of excommunication in which thou 75 stoodest. [He throws the paper down to the table.]

JOAN. I thank you.

THE INQUISITOR. But because thou hast sinned most presumptuously against God and the Holy 80 Church, and that thou mayst repent thy errors in solitary contemplation, and be shielded from all temptation to return to them, we, for the good of thy soul, and for a penance that may wipe out thy sins and bring thee finally un- 85 spotted to the throne of grace, do condemn thee to eat the bread of sorrow and drink the water of affliction to the end of thy earthly days in perpetual imprisonment.

JOAN [rising in consternation and terrible 90 anger]. Perpetual imprisonment! Am I not then to be set free?

LADVENU [mildly shocked]. Set free, child, after such wickedness as yours! What are you dreaming of? 95

JOAN. Give me that writing. [She rushes to

the table; snatches up the paper; and tears it into fragments.] Light your fire: do you think I dread it as much as the life of a rat in a hole? My voices were right.

5 LADVENU. Joan! Joan!

JOAN. Yes: they told me you were fools [the word gives great offence], and that I was not to listen to your fine words nor trust to your charity. You promised me my life; but you lied 10 [indignant exclamations]. You think that life is nothing but not being stone dead. It is not the bread and water I fear: I can live on bread: when have I asked for more? It is no hardship to drink water if the water be clean. Bread has 15 no sorrow for me, and water no affliction. But to shut me from the light of the sky and the sight of the fields and flowers; to chain my feet so that I can never again ride with the soldiers nor climb the hills; to make me breathe 20 foul damp darkness, and keep from me everything that brings me back to the love of God when your wickedness and foolishness tempt me to hate Him: all this is worse than the furnace in the Bible that was heated seven 25 times. I could do without my warhorse; I could drag about in a skirt; I could let the banners and the trumpets and the knights and soldiers pass me and leave me behind as they leave the other women, if only I could still hear 30 the wind in the trees, the larks in the sunshine, the young lambs crying through the healthy frost, and the blessed blessed church bells that send my angel voices floating to me on the wind. But without these things I cannot live; 35 and by your wanting to take them away from me, or from any human creature, I know that your counsel is of the devil, and that mine is of God.

THE ASSESSORS [in great commotion]. Blas-40 phemy! blasphemy! She is possessed. She said our counsel was of the devil. And hers of God. Monstrous! The devil is in our midst, etc., etc.

D'ESTIVET [shouting above the din]. She is a relapsed heretic, obstinate, incorrigible, and 45 altogether unworthy of the mercy we have shewn her. I call for her excommunication.

THE CHAPLAIN [to the EXECUTIONER]. Light your fire, man. To the stake with her.

[The EXECUTIONER and his ASSISTANTS hurry out through the courtyard.] 50

LADVENU. You wicked girl: if your counsel were of God would He not deliver you?

JOAN. His ways are not your ways. He wills that I go through the fire to His bosom; for I am His child, and you are not fit that I should 55 live among you. That is my last word to you.

[The SOLDIERS seize her.]

CAUCHON [rising]. Not yet.

[They wait. There is a dead silence. CAUCHON turns to the INQUISITOR with an inquiring look. 60 The INQUISITOR nods affirmatively. They rise solemnly, and intone the sentence antiphonally.]

CAUCHON. We decree that thou art a relapsed heretic. 65

THE INQUISITOR. Cast out from the unity of the Church.

CAUCHON. Sundered from her body.

THE INQUISITOR. Infected with the leprosy of heresy. 70

CAUCHON. A member of Satan.

THE INQUISITOR. We declare that thou must be excommunicate.

CAUCHON. And now we do cast thee out, segregate thee, and abandon thee to the secular 75 power.

THE INQUISITOR. Admonishing the same secular power that it moderate its judgment of thee in respect of death and division of the limbs. [He resumes his seat.] 80

CAUCHON. And if any true sign of penitence appear in thee, to permit our Brother Martin to administer to thee the sacrament of penance.

THE CHAPLAIN. Into the fire with the witch. [He rushes at her, and helps the SOLDIERS to 85 push her out.]

[JOAN is taken away through the courtyard. The ASSESSORS rise in disorder, and follow the SOLDIERS, except LADVENU, who has hidden his face in his hands.] 90

CAUCHON [rising again in the act of sitting down]. No, no: this is irregular. The representative of the secular arm should be here to receive her from us.

THE INQUISITOR [also on his feet again]. That 95 man is an incorrigible fool.

CAUCHON. Brother Martin: see that everything is done in order.

LADVENU. My place is at her side, my lord. You must exercise your own authority. [*He hurries out.*]

CAUCHON. These English are impossible: they will thrust her straight into the fire. Look!

[*He points to the courtyard, in which the glow and flicker of fire can now be seen reddening the May daylight. Only the* BISHOP *and the* INQUISITOR *are left in the court.*]

CAUCHON [*turning to go*]. We must stop that.

THE INQUISITOR [*calmly*]. Yes; but not too fast, my lord.

CAUCHON [*halting*]. But there is not a moment to lose.

THE INQUISITOR. We have proceeded in perfect order. If the English choose to put themselves in the wrong, it is not our business to put them in the right. A flaw in the procedure may be useful later on: one never knows. And the sooner it is over, the better for that poor girl.

CAUCHON [*relaxing*]. That is true. But I suppose we must see this dreadful thing through.

THE INQUISITOR. One gets used to it. Habit is everything. I am accustomed to the fire: it is soon over. But it is a terrible thing to see a young and innocent creature crushed between these mighty forces, The Church and the Law.

CAUCHON. You call her innocent!

THE INQUISITOR. Oh, quite innocent. What does she know of The Church and the Law? She did not understand a word we were saying. It is the ignorant who suffer. Come, or we shall be late for the end.

CAUCHON [*going with him*]. I shall not be sorry if we are: I am not so accustomed as you.

[*They are going out when* WARWICK *comes in, meeting them.*]

WARWICK. Oh, I am intruding. I thought it was all over. [*He makes a feint of retiring.*]

CAUCHON. Do not go, my lord. It is all over.

THE INQUISITOR. The execution is not in our hands, my lord; but it is desirable that we should witness the end. So by your leave—
[*He bows, and goes out through the courtyard.*]

CAUCHON. There is some doubt whether your people have observed the forms of law, my lord.

WARWICK. I am told that there is some doubt whether your authority runs in this city, my lord. It is not in your diocese. However, if you will answer for that I will answer for the rest.

CAUCHON. It is to God that we both must answer. Good morning, my lord.

WARWICK. My lord: good morning.

[*They look at one another for a moment with unconcealed hostility. Then* CAUCHON *follows the* INQUISITOR *out.* WARWICK *looks round. Finding himself alone, he calls for attendance.*]

WARWICK. Hallo: some attendance here! [*Silence.*] Hallo, there! [*Silence.*] Hallo! Brian, you young blackguard, where are you? [*Silence.*] Guard! [*Silence.*] They have all gone to see the burning: even that child.

[*The silence is broken by someone frantically howling and sobbing.*]

WARWICK. What in the devil's name—?

[*The* CHAPLAIN *staggers in from the courtyard like a demented creature, his face streaming with tears, making the piteous sounds that* WARWICK *has heard. He stumbles to the prisoner's stool, and throws himself upon it with heartrending sobs.*]

WARWICK [*going to him and patting him on the shoulder*]. What is it, Master John? What is the matter?

THE CHAPLAIN [*clutching at his hands*]. My lord, my lord: for Christ's sake pray for my wretched guilty soul.

WARWICK [*soothing him*]. Yes, yes: of course I will. Calmly, gently—

THE CHAPLAIN [*blubbering miserably*]. I am not a bad man, my lord.

WARWICK. No, no: not at all.

THE CHAPLAIN. I meant no harm. I did not know what it would be like.

WARWICK [*hardening*]. Oh! You saw it, then?

THE CHAPLAIN. I did not know what I was doing. I am a hotheaded fool; and I shall be damned to all eternity for it.

WARWICK. Nonsense! Very distressing, no doubt; but it was not your doing.

THE CHAPLAIN [*lamentably*]. I let them do it.

If I had known, I would have torn her from their hands. You dont know: you havnt seen: it is so easy to talk when you dont know. You madden yourself with words: you damn your-
5 self because it feels grand to throw oil on the flaming hell of your own temper. But when it is brought home to you; when you see the thing you have done; when it is blinding your eyes, stifling your nostrils, tearing your heart,
10 then—then— [*Falling on his knees.*] O God, take away this sight from me; O Christ, deliver me from this fire that is consuming me! She cried to Thee in the midst of it: Jesus! Jesus! Jesus! She is in Thy bosom; and I am in hell
15 for evermore.

WARWICK [*summarily hauling him to his feet*]. Come come, man! you must pull yourself together. We shall have the whole town talking of this. [*He throws him not too gently into a*
20 *chair at the table.*] If you have not the nerve to see these things, why do you not do as I do, and stay away?

THE CHAPLAIN [*bewildered and submissive*]. She asked for a cross. A soldier gave her two
25 sticks tied together. Thank God he was an Englishman! I might have done it; but I did not: I am a coward, a mad dog, a fool. But he was an Englishman too.

WARWICK. The fool! they will burn him too
30 if the priests get hold of him.

THE CHAPLAIN [*shaken with a convulsion*]. Some of the people laughed at her. They would have laughed at Christ. They were French people, my lord: I know they were French.
35 WARWICK. Hush! someone is coming. Control yourself.

[LADVENU *comes back through the courtyard to* WARWICK's *right hand, carrying a bishop's cross which he has taken from a church. He is*
40 *very grave and composed.*]

WARWICK. I am informed that it is all over, Brother Martin.

LADVENU [*enigmatically*]. We do not know, my lord. It may have only just begun.
45 WARWICK. What does that mean, exactly?

LADVENU. I took this cross from the church for her that she might see it to the last: she had only two sticks that she put into her bosom. When the fire crept round us, and she saw that if I held the cross before her I should
50 be burnt myself, she warned me to get down and save myself. My lord: a girl who could think of another's danger in such a moment was not inspired by the devil. When I had to snatch the cross from her sight, she looked up
55 to heaven. And I do not believe that the heavens were empty. I firmly believe that her Savior appeared to her then in His tenderest glory. She called to Him and died. This is not the end for her, but the beginning.
60 WARWICK. I am afraid it will have a bad effect on the people.

LADVENU. It had, my lord, on some of them. I heard laughter. Forgive me for saying that I hope and believe it was English laughter.
65 THE CHAPLAIN [*rising frantically*]. No: it was not. There was only one Englishman there that disgraced his country; and that was the mad dog, de Stogumber. [*He rushes wildly out, shrieking.*] Let them torture him. Let them
70 burn him. I will go pray among her ashes. I am no better than Judas: I will hang myself.

WARWICK. Quick, Brother Martin: follow him: he will do himself some mischief. After him, quick.
75
[LADVENU *hurries out,* WARWICK *urging him. The* EXECUTIONER *comes in by the door behind the judges' chairs; and* WARWICK, *returning, finds himself face to face with him.*]

WARWICK. Well, fellow: who are you?
80 THE EXECUTIONER [*with dignity*]. I am not addressed as fellow, my lord. I am the Master Executioner of Rouen: it is a highly skilled mystery. I am come to tell your lordship that your orders have been obeyed.
85 WARWICK. I crave your pardon, Master Executioner; and I will see that you lose nothing by having no relics to sell. I have your word, have I, that nothing remains, not a bone, not a nail, not a hair?
90 THE EXECUTIONER. Her heart would not burn, my lord; but everything that was left is at the bottom of the river. You have heard the last of her.

WARWICK [*with a wry smile, thinking of what* LADVENU *said*]. The last of her? Hm! I wonder!

EPILOGUE

[*A restless fitfully windy night in June 1456, full of summer lightning after many days of heat.* KING CHARLES THE SEVENTH OF FRANCE, *formerly Joan's Dauphin, now Charles the Victorious, aged 51, is in bed in one of his royal chateaux. The bed, raised on a dais of two steps, is towards the side of the room so as to avoid blocking a tall lancet window in the middle. Its canopy bears the royal arms in embroidery. Except for the canopy and the huge down pillows there is nothing to distinguish it from a broad settee with bed-clothes and a valance. Thus its occupant is in full view from the foot.*

CHARLES *is not asleep: he is reading in bed, or rather looking at the pictures in Fouquet's Boccaccio with his knees doubled up to make a reading desk. Beside the bed on his left is a little table with a picture of the Virgin, lighted by candles of painted wax. The walls are hung from ceiling to floor with painted curtains which stir at times in the draughts. At first glance the prevailing yellow and red in these hanging pictures is somewhat flamelike when the folds breathe in the wind.*

The door is on CHARLES's *left, but in front of him close to the corner farthest from him. A large watchman's rattle, handsomely designed and gaily painted, is in the bed under his hand.*

CHARLES *turns a leaf. A distant clock strikes the half-hour softly.* CHARLES *shuts the book with a clap; throws it aside; snatches up the rattle; and whirls it energetically, making a deafening clatter.* LADVENU *enters, 25 years older, strange and stark in bearing, and still carrying the cross from Rouen.* CHARLES *evidently does not expect him; for he springs out of bed on the farther side from the door.*]

CHARLES. Who are you? Where is my gentleman of the bedchamber? What do you want?

LADVENU [*solemnly*]. I bring you glad tidings of great joy. Rejoice, O king; for the taint is removed from your blood, and the stain from your crown. Justice, long delayed, is at last triumphant.

CHARLES. What are you talking about? Who are you?

LADVENU. I am Brother Martin.

CHARLES. And who, saving your reverence, may Brother Martin be?

LADVENU. I held this cross when The Maid perished in the fire. Twenty-five years have passed since then: nearly ten thousand days. And on every one of those days I have prayed God to justify His daughter on earth as she is justified in heaven.

CHARLES [*reassured, sitting down on the foot of the bed*]. Oh, I remember now. I have heard of you. You have a bee in your bonnet about The Maid. Have you been at the inquiry?

LADVENU. I have given my testimony.

CHARLES. Is it over?

LADVENU. It is over.

CHARLES. Satisfactorily?

LADVENU. The ways of God are very strange.

CHARLES. How so?

LADVENU. At the trial which sent a saint to the stake as a heretic and a sorceress, the truth was told; the law was upheld; mercy was shewn beyond all custom; no wrong was done but the final and dreadful wrong of the lying sentence and the pitiless fire. At this inquiry from which I have just come, there was shameless perjury, courtly corruption, calumny of the dead who did their duty according to their lights, cowardly evasion of the issue, testimony made of idle tales that could not impose on a ploughboy. Yet out of this insult to justice, this defamation of The Church, this orgy of lying and foolishness, the truth is set in the noonday sun on the hilltop; the white robe of innocence is cleansed from the smirch of the burning faggots; the holy life is sanctified; the true heart that lived through the flame is consecrated; a great lie is silenced for ever; and a great wrong is set right before all men.

CHARLES. My friend: provided they can no longer say that I was crowned by a witch and a heretic, I shall not fuss about how the trick has been done. Joan would not have fussed about it if it came all right in the end: she was not that sort: I knew her. Is her rehabilitation complete? I made it pretty clear that there was to be no nonsense about it.

LADVENU. It is solemnly declared that her judges were full of corruption, cozenage, fraud, and malice. Four falsehoods.

CHARLES. Never mind the falsehoods: her judges are dead.

LADVENU. The sentence on her is broken, annulled, annihilated, set aside as non-existent, without value or effect.

CHARLES. Good. Nobody can challenge my consecration now, can they?

LADVENU. Not Charlemagne nor King David himself was more sacredly crowned.

CHARLES [rising]. Excellent. Think of what that means to me!

LADVENU. I think of what it means to her!

CHARLES. You cannot. None of us ever knew what anything meant to her. She was like nobody else; and she must take care of herself wherever she is; for I cannot take care of her; and neither can you, whatever you may think: you are not big enough. But I will tell you this about her. If you could bring her back to life, they would burn her again within six months, for all their present adoration of her. And you would hold up the cross, too, just the same. So [crossing himself] let her rest; and let you and I mind our own business, and not meddle with hers.

LADVENU. God forbid that I should have no share in her, nor she in me! [He turns and strides out as he came, saying:] Henceforth my path will not lie through palaces, nor my conversation be with kings.

CHARLES [following him towards the door, and shouting after him]. Much good may it do you, holy man! [He returns to the middle of the chamber, where he halts, and says quizzically to himself.] That was a funny chap. How did he get in? Where are my people? [He goes impatiently to the bed, and swings the rattle. A rush of wind through the open door sets the walls swaying agitatedly. The candles go out. He calls in the darkness.] Hallo! Someone come and shut the windows: everything is being blown all over the place. [A flash of summer lightning shews up the lancet window. A figure is seen in silhouette against it.] Who is there? Who is that? Help! Murder! [Thunder. He jumps into bed, and hides under the clothes.]

JOAN'S VOICE. Easy, Charlie, easy. What art making all that noise for? No one can hear thee. Thourt asleep. [She is dimly seen in a pallid greenish light by the bedside.]

CHARLES [peeping out]. Joan! Are you a ghost, Joan?

JOAN. Hardly even that, lad. Can a poor burnt-up lass have a ghost? I am but a dream that thourt dreaming. [The light increases: they become plainly visible as he sits up.] Thou looks older, lad.

CHARLES. I am older. Am I really asleep?

JOAN. Fallen asleep over thy silly book.

CHARLES. That's funny.

JOAN. Not so funny as that I am dead, is it?

CHARLES. Are you really dead?

JOAN. As dead as anybody ever is, laddie. I am out of the body.

CHARLES. Just fancy! Did it hurt much?

JOAN. Did what hurt much?

CHARLES. Being burnt.

JOAN. Oh, that! I cannot remember very well. I think it did at first; but then it all got mixed up; and I was not in my right mind until I was free of the body. But do not thou go handling fire and thinking it will not hurt thee. How hast been ever since?

CHARLES. Oh, not so bad. Do you know, I actually lead my army out and win battles? Down into the moat up to my waist in mud and blood. Up the ladders with the stones and hot pitch raining down. Like you.

JOAN. No! Did I make a man of thee after all, Charlie?

CHARLES. I am Charles the Victorious now. I had to be brave because you were. Agnes put a little pluck into me too.

JOAN. Agnes! Who was Agnes?

CHARLES. Agnes Sorel. A woman I fell in love with. I dream of her often. I never dreamed of you before.

JOAN. Is she dead, like me?

5 CHARLES. Yes. But she was not like you. She was very beautiful.

JOAN [*laughing heartily*]. Ha ha! I was no beauty: I was always a rough one: a regular soldier. I might almost as well have been a
10 man. Pity I wasn't: I should not have bothered you all so much then. But my head was in the skies; and the glory of God was upon me; and, man or woman, I should have bothered you as long as your noses were in the mud. Now tell
15 me what has happened since you wise men knew no better than to make a heap of cinders of me?

CHARLES. Your mother and brothers have sued the courts to have your case tried over
20 again. And the courts have declared that your judges were full of corruption and cozenage, fraud and malice.

JOAN. Not they. They were as honest a lot of poor fools as ever burned their betters.

25 CHARLES. The sentence on you is broken, annihilated, annulled: null, non-existent, without value or effect.

JOAN. I was burned, all the same. Can they unburn me?

30 CHARLES. If they could, they would think twice before they did it. But they have decreed that a beautiful cross be placed where the stake stood, for your perpetual memory and for your salvation.

35 JOAN. It is the memory and the salvation that sanctify the cross, not the cross that sanctifies the memory and the salvation. [*She turns away, forgetting him.*] I shall outlast that cross. I shall be remembered when men will
40 have forgotten where Rouen stood.

CHARLES. There you go with your self-conceit, the same as ever! I think you might say a word of thanks to me for having had justice done at last.

45 CAUCHON [*appearing at the window between them*]. Liar!

CHARLES. Thank you.

JOAN. Why, if it isnt Peter Cauchon! How are you, Peter? What luck have you had since you burned me? 50

CAUCHON. None. I arraign the justice of Man. It is not the justice of God.

JOAN. Still dreaming of justice, Peter? See what justice came to with me! But what has happened to thee? Art dead or alive? 55

CAUCHON. Dead. Dishonored. They pursued me beyond the grave. They excommunicated my dead body: they dug it up and flung it into the common sewer.

JOAN. Your dead body did not feel the spade 60 and the sewer as my live body felt the fire.

CAUCHON. But this thing that they have done against me hurts justice; destroys faith; saps the foundation of the Church. The solid earth sways like the treacherous sea beneath the feet 65 of men and spirits alike when the innocent are slain in the name of law, and their wrongs are undone by slandering the pure of heart.

JOAN. Well, well, Peter, I hope men will be the better for remembering me; and they 70 would not remember me so well if you had not burned me.

CAUCHON. They will be the worse for remembering me: they will see in me evil triumphing over good, falsehood over truth, 75 cruelty over mercy, hell over heaven. Their courage will rise as they think of you, only to faint as they think of me. Yet God is my witness I was just: I was merciful: I was faithful to my light: I could do no other than I did. 80

CHARLES [*scrambling out of the sheets and enthroning himself on the side of the bed*]. Yes: it is always you good men that do the big mischiefs. Look at me! I am not Charles the Good, nor Charles the Wise, nor Charles the 85 Bold. Joan's worshippers may even call me Charles the Coward because I did not pull her out of the fire. But I have done less harm than any of you. You people with your heads in the sky spend all your time trying to turn the 90 world upside down; but I take the world as it is, and say that top-side-up is right-side-up; and I keep my nose pretty close to the ground. And I ask you, what king of France has done better, or been a better fellow in his little way?

JOAN. Art really king of France, Charlie? Be the English gone?

DUNOIS [*coming through the tapestry on* JOAN's *left, the candles relighting themselves at the same moment, and illuminating his armour and surcoat cheerfully*]. I have kept my word: the English are gone.

JOAN. Praised be God! now is fair France a province in heaven. Tell me all about the fighting, Jack. Was it thou that led them? Wert thou God's captain to thy death?

DUNOIS. I am not dead. My body is very comfortably asleep in my bed at Chateaudun; but my spirit is called here by yours.

JOAN. And you fought them my way, Jack: eh? Not the old way, chaffering for ransoms; but The Maid's way: staking life against death, with the heart high and humble and void of malice, and nothing counting under God but France free and French. Was it my way, Jack?

DUNOIS. Faith, it was any way that would win. But the way that won was always your way. I give you best, lassie. I wrote a fine letter to set you right at the new trial. Perhaps I should never have let the priests burn you; but I was busy fighting; and it was The Church's business, not mine. There was no use in both of us being burned, was there?

CAUCHON. Ay! put the blame on the priests. But I, who am beyond praise and blame, tell you that the world is saved neither by its priests nor its soldiers, but by God and His Saints. The Church Militant sent this woman to the fire; but even as she burned, the flames whitened into the radiance of the Church Triumphant.

[*The clock strikes the third quarter. A rough male voice is heard trolling an improvised tune.*]

Rum tum trumpledum,
Bacon fat and rumpledum,

Old Saint mumpledum,
Pull his tail and stumpledum
    O my Ma—ry Ann!

[*A ruffianly* ENGLISH SOLDIER *comes through the curtains and marches between* DUNOIS *and* JOAN.]

DUNOIS. What villainous troubadour taught you that doggrel?

THE SOLDIER. No troubadour. We made it up ourselves as we marched. We were not gentlefolks and troubadours. Music straight out of the heart of the people, as you might say. Rum tum trumpledum, Bacon fat and rumpledum, Old Saint mumpledum, Pull his tail and stumpledum: that dont mean anything, you know; but it keeps you marching. Your servant, ladies and gentlemen. Who asked for a saint?

JOAN. Be you a saint?

THE SOLDIER. Yes, lady, straight from hell.

DUNOIS. A saint, and from hell!

THE SOLDIER. Yes, noble captain: I have a day off. Every year, you know. Thats my allowance for my one good action.

CAUCHON. Wretch! In all the years of your life did you do only one good action?

THE SOLDIER. I never thought about it: it came natural like. But they scored it up for me.

CHARLES. What was it?

THE SOLDIER. Why, the silliest thing you ever heard of. I—

JOAN [*interrupting him by strolling across to the bed, where she sits beside* CHARLES]. He tied two sticks together, and gave them to a poor lass that was going to be burned.

THE SOLDIER. Right. Who told you that?

JOAN. Never mind. Would you know her if you saw her again?

THE SOLDIER. Not I. There are so many girls! and they all expect you to remember them as if there was only one in the world. This one

must have been a prime sort; for I have a day off every year for her; and so, until twelve o'clock punctually, I am a saint, at your service, noble lords and lovely ladies.

5   CHARLES. And after twelve?

THE SOLDIER. After twelve, back to the only place fit for the likes of me.

JOAN [*rising*]. Back there! You! that gave the lass the cross!

10   THE SOLDIER [*excusing his unsoldierly conduct*]. Well, she asked for it; and they were going to burn her. She had as good a right to a cross as they had; and they had dozens of them. It was her funeral, not theirs. Where

15   was the harm in it?

JOAN. Man: I am not reproaching you. But I cannot bear to think of you in torment.

THE SOLDIER [*cheerfully*]. No great torment, lady. You see I was used to worse.

20   CHARLES. What! worse than hell?

THE SOLDIER. Fifteen years' service in the French wars. Hell was a treat after that.

[JOAN *throws up her arms, and takes refuge from despair of humanity before the picture of*

25   *the Virgin.*]

THE SOLDIER [*continuing*].—Suits me somehow. The day off was dull at first, like a wet Sunday. I dont mind it so much now. They tell me I can have as many as I like as soon as I

30   want them.

CHARLES. What is hell like?

THE SOLDIER. You wont find it so bad, sir. Jolly. Like as if you were always drunk without the trouble and expense of drinking. Tip

35   top company too: emperors and popes and kings and all sorts. They chip me about giving that young judy the cross; but I dont care: I stand up to them proper, and tell them that if she hadnt a better right to it than they, she'd

40   be where they are. That dumbfounds them, that does. All they can do is gnash their teeth, hell fashion; and I just laugh, and go off singing the old chanty: Rum tum trumple—Hullo! Who's that knocking at the door?

45   [*They listen. A long gentle knocking is heard.*]

CHARLES. Come in.

[*The door opens; and an old* PRIEST, *white-*

haired, bent, with a silly but benevolent smile, comes in and trots over to* JOAN.]   50

THE NEWCOMER. Excuse me, gentle lords and ladies. Do not let me disturb you. Only a poor old harmless English rector. Formerly chaplain to the cardinal: to my lord of Winchester. John de Stogumber, at your service. [*He looks at*   55 *them inquiringly.*] Did you say anything? I am a little deaf, unfortunately. Also a little— well, not always in my right mind, perhaps; but still, it is a small village with a few simple people. I suffice: I suffice: they love me there;   60 and I am able to do a little good. I am well connected, you see; and they indulge me.

JOAN. Poor old John! What brought thee to this state?

DE STOGUMBER. I tell my folks they must be   65 very careful. I say to them, "If you only saw what you think about you would think quite differently about it. It would give you a great shock. Oh, a great shock." And they all say "Yes, parson: we all know you are a kind man,   70 and would not harm a fly." That is a great comfort to me. For I am not cruel by nature, you know.

THE SOLDIER. Who said you were?

DE STOGUMBER. Well, you see, I did a very   75 cruel thing once because I did not know what cruelty was like. I had not seen it, you know. That is the great thing: you must see it. And then you are redeemed and saved.

CAUCHON. Were not the sufferings of our   80 Lord Christ enough for you?

DE STOGUMBER. No. Oh no: not at all. I had seen them in pictures, and read of them in books, and been greatly moved by them, as I thought. But it was no use: it was not our   85 Lord that redeemed me, but a young woman whom I saw actually burned to death. It was dreadful: oh, most dreadful. But it saved me. I have been a different man ever since, though a little astray in my wits sometimes.   90

CAUCHON. Must then a Christ perish in torment in every age to save those that have no imagination?

JOAN. Well, if I saved all those he would have been cruel to if he had not been cruel to   95 me, I was not burnt for nothing, was I?

DE STOGUMBER. Oh no; it was not you. My sight is bad: I cannot distinguish your features: but you are not she: Oh no: she was burned to a cinder: dead and gone, dead and
5 gone.

THE EXECUTIONER [*stepping from behind the bed curtains on* CHARLES'S *right, the bed being between them*]. She is more alive than you, old man. Her heart would not burn; and it would
10 not drown. I was a master at my craft: better than the master of Paris, better than the master of Toulouse; but I could not kill The Maid. She is up and alive everywhere.

THE EARL OF WARWICK [*sallying from the*
15 *bed curtains on the other side, and coming to* JOAN'S *left hand*]. Madam: my congratulations on your rehabilitation. I feel that I owe you an apology.

JOAN. Oh, please dont mention it.
20 WARWICK [*pleasantly*]. The burning was purely political. There was no personal feeling against you, I assure you.

JOAN. I bear no malice, my lord.

WARWICK. Just so. Very kind of you to meet
25 me in that way: a touch of true breeding. But I must insist on apologizing very amply. The truth is, these political necessities sometimes turn out to be political mistakes; and this one was a veritable howler; for your spirit con-
30 quered us, madam, in spite of our faggots. History will remember me for your sake, though the incidents of the connection were perhaps a little unfortunate.

JOAN. Ay, perhaps just a little, you funny
35 man.

WARWICK. Still, when they make you a saint, you will owe your halo to me, just as this lucky monarch owes his crown to you.

JOAN [*turning from him*]. I shall owe noth-
40 ing to any man: I owe everything to the spirit of God that was within me. But fancy me a saint! What would St Catherine and St Margaret say if the farm girl was cocked up beside them!

45 [*A clerical-looking* GENTLEMAN *in black frockcoat and trousers, and tall hat, in the fashion of the year* 1920, *suddenly appears before them in the corner on their right. They*

all stare at him. Then they burst into uncontrollable laughter.]
50 THE GENTLEMAN. Why this mirth, gentlemen?

WARWICK. I congratulate you on having invented a most extraordinarily comic dress.

THE GENTLEMAN. I do not understand. You
55 are all in fancy dress: I am properly dressed.

DUNOIS. All dress is fancy dress, is it not, except our natural skins?

THE GENTLEMAN. Pardon me: I am here on serious business, and cannot engage in friv-
60 olous discussions. [*He takes out a paper, and assumes a dry official manner.*] I am sent to announce to you that Joan of Arc, formerly known as The Maid, having been the subject of an inquiry instituted by the Bishop of
65 Orleans—

JOAN [*interrupting*]. Ah! They remember me still in Orleans.

THE GENTLEMAN [*emphatically to mark his indignation at the interruption*].—by the
70 Bishop of Orleans into the claim of the said Joan of Arc to be canonized as a saint—

JOAN [*again interrupting*]. But I never made any such claim.

THE GENTLEMAN [*as before*]. —The Church
75 has examined the claim exhaustively in the usual course, and, having admitted the said Joan successively to the ranks of Venerable and Blessed,—

JOAN [*chuckling*]. Me venerable!
80 THE GENTLEMAN. —has finally declared her to have been endowed with heroic virtues and favored with private revelations, and calls the said Venerable and Blessed Joan to the communion of the Church Triumphant as Saint
85 Joan.

JOAN [*rapt*]. Saint Joan!

THE GENTLEMAN. On every thirtieth day of May, being the anniversary of the death of the said most blessed daughter of God, there shall
90 in every Catholic church to the end of time be celebrated a special office in commemoration of her; and it shall be lawful to dedicate a special chapel to her, and to place her image on its altar in every such church. And it shall
95 be lawful and laudable for the faithful to kneel

and address their prayers through her to the Mercy Seat.

JOAN. Oh no. It is for the saint to kneel. [*She falls on her knees, still rapt.*]

5 THE GENTLEMAN [*putting up his paper, and retiring beside the* EXECUTIONER]. In Basilica Vaticana, the sixteenth day of May, nineteen hundred and twenty.

DUNOIS [*raising Joan*]. Half an hour to burn 10 you, dear Saint; and four centuries to find out the truth about you!

DE STOGUMBER. Sir: I was chaplain to the Cardinal of Winchester once. They always would call him the Cardinal of England. It 15 would be a great comfort to me and to my master to see a fair statue to The Maid in Winchester Cathedral. Will they put one there, do you think?

THE GENTLEMAN. As the building is tem-20 porarily in the hands of the Anglican heresy, I cannot answer for that.

[*A vision of the statue in Winchester Cathedral is seen through the window.*]

DE STOGUMBER. Oh look! look! that is Win-25 chester.

JOAN. Is that meant to be me? I was stiffer on my feet.

[*The vision fades.*]

THE GENTLEMAN. I have been requested by 30 the temporal authorities of France to mention that the multiplication of public statues to The Maid threatens to become an obstruction to traffic. I do so as a matter of courtesy to the said authorities, but must point out on behalf 35 of The Church that The Maid's horse is no greater obstruction to traffic than any other horse.

JOAN. Eh! I am glad they have not forgotten my horse.

40 [*A vision of the statue before Rheims Cathedral appears.*]

JOAN. Is that funny little thing me too?

CHARLES. That is Rheims Cathedral where you had me crowned. It must be you.

45 JOAN. Who has broken my sword? My sword was never broken. It is the sword of France.

DUNOIS. Never mind. Swords can be mended. Your soul is unbroken; and you are

the soul of France.

[*The vision fades. The* ARCHBISHOP *and the* 50 INQUISITOR *are now seen on the right and left of* CAUCHON.]

JOAN. My sword shall conquer yet: the sword that never struck a blow. Though men destroyed my body, yet in my soul I have seen 55 God.

CAUCHON [*kneeling to her*]. The girls in the field praise thee; for thou hast raised their eyes; and they see that there is nothing between them and heaven. 60

DUNOIS [*kneeling to her*]. The dying soldiers praise thee, because thou art a shield of glory between them and the judgment.

THE ARCHBISHOP [*kneeling to her*]. The princes of The Church praise thee, because 65 thou hast redeemed the faith their worldlinesses have dragged through the mire.

WARWICK [*kneeling to her*]. The cunning counsellors praise thee, because thou hast cut the knots in which they have tied their own 70 souls.

DE STOGUMBER [*kneeling to her*]. The foolish old men on their deathbeds praise thee, because their sins against thee are turned into blessings. 75

THE INQUISITOR [*kneeling to her*]. The judges in the blindness and bondage of the law praise thee, because thou hast vindicated the vision and the freedom of the living soul.

THE SOLDIER [*kneeling to her*]. The wicked 80 out of hell praise thee, because thou hast shewn them that the fire that is not quenched is a holy fire.

THE EXECUTIONER [*kneeling to her*]. The tormentors and executioners praise thee, because 85 thou hast shewn that their hands are guiltless of the death of the soul.

CHARLES [*kneeling to her*]. The unpretending praise thee, because thou hast taken upon thyself the heroic burdens that are too heavy 90 for them.

JOAN. Woe unto me when all men praise me! I bid you remember that I am a saint, and that saints can work miracles. And now tell me: shall I rise from the dead, and come back to 95 you a living woman?

[*A sudden darkness blots out the walls of the room as they all spring to their feet in consternation. Only the figures and the bed remain visible.*]

5 JOAN. What! Must I burn again? Are none of you ready to receive me?

CAUCHON. The heretic is always better dead. And mortal eyes cannot distinguish the saint from the heretic. Spare them. [*He goes out as* 10 *he came.*]

DUNOIS. Forgive us, Joan: we are not yet good enough for you. I shall go back to my bed. [*He also goes.*]

WARWICK. We sincerely regret our little 15 mistake; but political necessities, though occasionally erroneous, are still imperative; so if you will be good enough to excuse me— [*He steals discreetly away.*]

THE ARCHBISHOP. Your return would not 20 make me the man you once thought me. The utmost I can say is that though I dare not bless you, I hope I may one day enter into your blessedness. Meanwhile, however— [*He goes.*]

THE INQUISITOR. I who am of the dead, testi- 25 fied that day that you were innocent. But I do not see how The Inquisition could possibly be dispensed with under existing circumstances. Therefore— [*He goes.*]

DE STOGUMBER. Oh, do not come back: you 30 must not come back. I must die in peace. Give us peace in our time, O Lord! [*He goes.*]

THE GENTLEMAN. The possibility of your resurrection was not contemplated in the recent proceedings for your canonization. I must 35 return to Rome for fresh instructions. [*He bows formally, and withdraws.*]

THE EXECUTIONER. As a master in my profession I have to consider its interests. And, after all, my first duty is to my wife and chil- 40 dren. I must have time to think over this. [*He goes.*]

CHARLES. Poor old Joan! They have all run away from you except this blackguard who has to go back to hell at twelve o'clock. And 45 what can I do but follow Jack Dunois' example, and go back to bed too? [*He does so.*]

JOAN [*sadly*]. Goodnight, Charlie.

CHARLES [*mumbling in his pillows*]. Goo ni.

[*He sleeps. The darkness envelops the bed.*]

JOAN [*to the soldier*] And you, my one faith- 50 ful? What comfort have you for Saint Joan?

THE SOLDIER. Well, what do they all amount to, these kings and captains and bishops and lawyers and such like? They just leave you in the ditch to bleed to death; and the next thing 55 is, you meet them down there, for all the airs they give themselves. What I say is, you have as good a right to your notions as they have to theirs, and perhaps better. [*Settling himself for a lecture on the subject.*] You see, it's like 60 this. If— [*the first stroke of midnight is heard softly from a distant bell.*] Excuse me: a pressing appointment— [*He goes on tiptoe.*]

[*The last remaining rays of light gather into a white radiance descending on* JOAN. *The hour* 65 *continues to strike.*]

JOAN. O God that madest this beautiful earth, when will it be ready to receive Thy saints? How long, O Lord, how long?

The End

Sean O'Casey

1884–1964

Juno and the Paycock

1924

To an unusual degree *Juno and the Paycock* draws partly antagonistic dramatic elements together. At any given moment the distinctive focus of the play is located about midway between certain recognizable limits. The more obvious of these is matter-of-fact emphasis on details of Irish tenement life, personal misfortunes, and political strife. The other lies in the region of symbolism and is mainly discernible through a sad and often lyric undertone. Sometimes nostalgic, sometimes solemn, it gives the commonplace a touch of grandeur. Between these limits the play evokes an awareness of potential tragedy.

Rising and subsiding, but always developing, this awareness permits the fusion of otherwise conflicting moods. Thus, in the comic scenes between Joxer, the Captain, and Juno, the audience is led to perceive that their lives are fixed in social and personal misery that they cannot master and can hardly comprehend. This perception links what they say and do to a circumference of meaning that is felt rather than described.

How opposed moods shape the development of a scene and also clarify the focus of the entire play is impressively apparent in the second act. The jollification in honor of Captain Boyle's prospective inheritance contrasts ironically with the poverty of the setting and the growing foreboding that the prospects are empty. The comic spirit of the party, with its boasts and old songs, has an undertone of longing. It is suddenly broken by Johnny's scream that he has seen the ghost of the murdered Robbie Tancred. For a melodramatic instant the party feels the chill of supernatural fear. The celebrating resumes, again to be suspended by the entrance of Mrs. Tancred on her way to the funeral of her son. A last effort at comfortable cheer droops and perishes in the passing-by of the funeral and the distant murmur of the *Ave Maria*. Each contrasting development has its own integrity; at the same time the alternating moods bracket ever more narrowly the central area of awareness.

As O'Casey interweaves contrasting moods, he also merges different kinds of characterization. The effect is simultaneously to widen and particularize the tragic significance. Each of the main characters appears to some extent as both theatrical stereotype and distinct individual. Mary in her role of the ruined maiden is a somewhat melodramatic figure, and Joxer is identifiable as a "parasite" out of the old Roman comedy. Yet through vigorous touches of realism each character acquires a measure of individual pathos. Mary has read her Ibsen and reaches after a way of life less mean and ignorant than her environment allows; even Joxer keeps a wisp of dignity and a fleeting awareness of his own suffering.

In Juno, with her queen-goddess name and her cheerless personal destiny, the various modes and the central perception of the play are most fully defined. Under the aspect of comedy she is something of a Xanthippe, uselessly harrying her inadequate spouse. Under that of melodrama she is the long-suffering mother, hard-working and indestructible. In the realm of symbolism, which the play never wholly enters, she is a heroic and pathetic figure, a legendary queen of sorrows. But this symbolic undertone is subdued. Nothing vague is permitted. Yet mere uncompromising realism is lifted above itself, and well-worn stereotypes and reversals are renewed in vigor.

The two-pronged ending of the play epitomizes its method and its meaning. First comes the exit of Juno and Mary, without positive hope but without despair: "Sacred heart o' Jesus, take away our hearts o' stone, and give us hearts o' flesh!" As a curtain line, the sentiment would underscore the theme of suffering, but the tone is perhaps too poignant. "There is a pause," says the stage direction. Then Boyle and Joxer enter, "both of them very drunk." The maudlin stammering of the two cast-aways, as ignorant of their fate as they are helpless to alter it, is in counterpoint to Juno's words. The two endings partly fuse in an image of the old rivalry between creation and chaos.

Juno and the Paycock

O'CASEY

CHARACTERS°

"CAPTAIN" JACK BOYLE
JUNO BOYLE   *his wife*
JOHNNY BOYLE ⎫ *their children*
MARY BOYLE ⎬
"JOXER" DALY ⎭   *Residents in the Tenement*
MRS. MAISIE MADIGAN
"NEEDLE" NUGENT   *a tailor*
MRS. TANCRED
JERRY DEVINE
CHARLIE BENTHAM   *a school teacher*
AN IRREGULAR MOBILIZER
TWO IRREGULARS
A COAL-BLOCK VENDOR
A SEWING MACHINE MAN
TWO FURNITURE REMOVAL MEN
TWO NEIGHBOURS

SCENE. *The living apartment of a two-room tenancy of the Boyle family, in a tenement house in Dublin.*

A few days elapse between Acts I and II,
5 *and two months between Acts II and III.*

During Act III the curtain is lowered for a few minutes to denote the lapse of one hour. Period of the play, 1922.°

ACT I

[*The living room of a two-room tenancy occupied by the* BOYLE *family in a tenement* 10 *house in Dublin. Left, a door leading to another part of the house; left of door a window looking into the street; at back a dresser; farther to right at back, a window looking into the back of the house. Between the window and the* 15 *dresser is a picture of the Virgin; below the picture, on a bracket, is a crimson bowl in which a floating votive light is burning. Farther to the right is a small bed partly concealed by cretonne hangings strung on a twine. To the* 20 *right is the fireplace; near the fireplace is a door leading to the other room. Beside the fireplace is a box containing coal. On the mantelshelf is an alarm clock lying on its face. In a corner near the window looking into the back is a* 25 *galvanized bath. A table and some chairs. On the table are breakfast things for one. A teapot is on the hob and a frying-pan stands inside the fender. There are a few books on the dresser and one on the table. Leaning against the* 30 *dresser is a long-handled shovel—the kind invariably used by labourers when turning concrete or mixing mortar.* JOHNNY BOYLE *is sitting crouched beside the fire.* MARY *with her jumper off—it is lying on the back of a chair* 35 *—is arranging her hair before a tiny mirror perched on the table. Beside the mirror is stretched out the morning paper, which she looks at when she isn't gazing into the mirror. She is a well-made and good-looking girl of* 40

1922 a year in which the newly formed **Irish Free State,** made up of the southern and chiefly Catholic counties of Ireland, was torn by bitter dissension between **Staters,** who would accept the gains already won, and the **Die-hards and Republicans,** who insisted on full independence and a union including Northern Ireland, even at the price of renewed civil war. Although the Irish Republican Army was being replaced by an unarmed **Civic Guard,** some detachments of **Irregulars** were still agitating by terrorism for independence and union.

Characters: "Captain" Jack Boyle is the "paycock" (peacock), long a symbol of empty ostentation or exhibitionism.

Reprinted by permission of St. Martin's Press, Inc., Macmillan & Co., Ltd

twenty-two. Two forces are working in her mind—one, through the circumstances of her life, pulling her back; the other, through the influence of books she has read, pushing her
5 *forward. The opposing forces are apparent in her speech and her manners, both of which are degraded by her environment, and improved by her acquaintance—slight though it be— with literature. The time is early forenoon.]*

10 MARY [*looking at the paper*]. On a little bye-road, out beyant Finglas, he was found.

[*Mrs. BOYLE enters by door on right; she has been shopping and carries a small parcel in her hand. She is forty-five years of age, and twenty*
15 *years ago she must have been a pretty woman; but her face has now assumed that look which ultimately settles down upon the faces of the women of the working-class; a look of listless monotony and harassed anxiety, blending with*
20 *an expression of mechanical resistance. Were circumstances favourable, she would probably be a handsome, active and clever woman.]*

MRS. BOYLE. Isn't he come in yet?

MARY. No, mother.

25 MRS. BOYLE. Oh, he'll come in when he likes; struttin' about the town like a paycock with Joxer, I suppose. I hear all about Mrs. Tancred's son is in this mornin's paper.

MARY. The full details are in it this mornin';
30 seven wounds he had—one entherin' the neck, with an exit wound beneath the left shoulder-blade; another in the left breast penethratin' the heart, an' . . .

JOHNNY [*springing up from the fire*]. Oh,
35 quit that readin', for God's sake! Are yous losin' all your feelin's? It'll soon be that none of yous'll read anythin' that's not about butcherin'!

[*He goes quickly into the room on left.*]
40 MARY. He's gettin' very sensitive, all of a sudden!

MRS. BOYLE. I'll read it myself, Mary, by an' by, when I come home. Everybody's sayin' that he was a die-hard—thanks be to God that
45 Johnny had nothin' to do with him this long time. . . . [*Opening the parcel and taking out some sausages, which she places on a plate.*] Ah, then, if that father o' yours doesn't come

in soon for his breakfast, he may go without any; I'll not wait much longer for him. 50

MARY. Can't you let him get it himself when he comes in?

MRS. BOYLE. Yes, an' let him bring in Joxer Daly along with him? Ay, that's what he'd like, an' that's what he's waitin' for—till he 55 thinks I'm gone to work, an' then sail in with the boul'° Joxer, to burn all the coal an' dhrink all the tea in the place, to show them what a good Samaritan he is! But I'll stop here till he comes in, if I have to wait till tomorrow 60 mornin'.

VOICE OF JOHNNY INSIDE. Mother!

MRS. BOYLE. Yis?

VOICE OF JOHNNY. Bring us in a dhrink o' wather. 65

MRS. BOYLE. Bring in that fella a dhrink o' wather, for God's sake, Mary.

MARY. Isn't he big an' able enough to come out an' get it himself?

MRS. BOYLE. If you weren't well yourself 70 you'd like somebody to bring you in a dhrink o' wather. [*She brings in drink and returns.*]

MRS. BOYLE. Isn't it terrible to have to be waitin' this way! You'd think he was bringin twenty poun's a week into the house the way 75 he's goin' on. He wore out the Health Insurance long ago, he's afther wearin' out the unemployment dole, an', now, he's thryin' to wear out me! An' constantly singin', no less, when he ought always to be on his knees offerin' up a 80 Novena for a job!

MARY [*tying a ribbon fillet-wise around her head*]. I don't like this ribbon, ma; I think I'll wear the green—it looks betther than the blue.

MRS. BOYLE. Ah, wear whatever ribbon you 85 like, girl, only don't be botherin' me. I don't know what a girl on strike wants to be wearin' a ribbon round her head for or silk stockin's on her legs either; it's wearin' them things that make the employers think they're givin' yous 90 too much money.

MARY. The hour is past now when we'll ask the employers' permission to wear what we like.

boul' bold

MRS. BOYLE. I don't know why you wanted to walk out for Jennie Claffey; up to this you never had a good word for her.

MARY. What's the use of belongin' to a Trades Union if you won't stand up for your principles? Why did they sack her? It was a clear case of victimization. We couldn't let her walk the streets, could we?

MRS. BOYLE. No, of course yous couldn't— yous wanted to keep her company. Wan victim wasn't enough. When the employers sacrifice wan victim, the Trades Unions go wan betther be sacrificin' a hundred.

MARY. It doesn't matther what you say, ma —a principle's a principle.

MRS. BOYLE. Yis; an' when I go into oul' Murphy's tomorrow, an' he gets to know that, instead o' payin' all, I'm goin' to borry more, what'll he say when I tell him a principle's a principle? What'll we do if he refuses to give us any more on tick?

MARY. He daren't refuse—if he does, can't you tell him he's paid?

MRS. BOYLE. It's lookin' as if he was paid, whether he refuses or no.

[JOHNNY *appears at the door on left. He can be plainly seen now; he is a thin delicate fellow, something younger than* MARY. *He has evidently gone through a rough time. His face is pale and drawn; there is a tremulous look of indefinite fear in his eyes. The left sleeve of his coat is empty, and he walks with a slight halt.*]

JOHNNY. I was lyin' down: I thought yous were gone. Oul' Simon Mackay is thrampin' about like a horse over me head, an' I can't sleep with him—they're like thunder-claps in me brain! The curse o'—God forgive me for goin' to curse!

MRS. BOYLE. There, now; go back an' lie down agan, an' I'll bring you in a nice cup o' tay.

JOHNNY. Tay, tay, tay! You're always thinkin' o' tay. If a man was dyin', you'd thry to make him swally a cup o' tay!

[*He goes back.*]

MRS. BOYLE. I don't know what's goin' to be done with him. The bullet he got in the hip in Easter Week° was bad enough, but the bomb that shatthered his arm in the fight in O'Connell Street put the finishin' touch on him. I knew he was makin' a fool of himself. God knows I went down on me bended knees to him not to go agen the Free State.

MARY. He stuck to his principles, an', no matther how you may argue, ma, a principle's a principle.

VOICE OF JOHNNY. Is Mary goin' to stay here?

MARY. No, I'm not goin' to stay here; you can't expect me to be always at your beck an' call, can you?

VOICE OF JOHNNY. I won't stop here be meself!

MRS. BOYLE. Amn't I nicely handicapped with the whole o' yous! I don't know what any o' yous ud do without your ma. [*To* JOHNNY.] Your father'll be here in a minute, an' if you want anythin', he'll get it for you.

JOHNNY. I hate assin' him for anythin'. . . . He hates to be assed to stir. . . . Is the light lightin' before the picture o' the Virgin?

MRS. BOYLE. Yis, yis! The wan inside to St. Anthony isn't enough, but he must have another wan to the Virgin here!

[JERRY DEVINE *enters hastily. He is about twenty-five, well set, active and earnest. He is a type, becoming very common now in the Labour Movement, of a mind knowing enough to make the mass of his associates, who know less, a power, and too little to broaden that power for the benefit of all.* MARY *seizes her jumper and runs hastily into room left.*]

JERRY [*breathless*]. Where's the Captain, Mrs. Boyle, where's the Captain?

MRS. BOYLE. You may well ass a body that: he's wherever Joxer Daly is—dhrinkin' in some snug or another.

JERRY. Father Farrell is just afther stoppin' to tell me to run up an' get him to go to the new job that's goin' on in Rathmines; his cousin is foreman o' the job, an' Father Farrell was speakin' to him about poor Johnny an' his father bein' idle so long, an' the foreman told

Easter Week of April 1916, when bloody street-fighting broke out in Dublin

Father Farrell to send the Captain up an' he'd
give him a start—I wondher where I'd find
him?

MRS. BOYLE. You'll find he's ayther in Ryan's
or Foley's.

JERRY. I'll run round to Ryan's—I know it's
a great house o' Joxer's.

[*He rushes out.*]

MRS. BOYLE [*piteously*]. There now, he'll
miss that job, or I know for what! If he gets
win' o' the word, he'll not come back till
evenin', so that it'll be too late. There'll never
be any good got out o' him so long as he goes
with that shouldher-shruggin' Joxer. I killin'
meself workin', an' he sthruttin' about from
mornin' till night like a paycock!

[*The steps of two persons are heard coming
up a flight of stairs. They are the footsteps of
CAPTAIN BOYLE and JOXER. CAPTAIN BOYLE is
singing in a deep, sonorous, self-honouring
voice.*]

THE CAPTAIN. Sweet Spirit, hear me prayer!
Hear . . . oh . . . hear . . . me prayer . . . hear, oh,
hear . . . Oh, he . . . ar . . . oh, he . . . ar . . .
me . . . pray . . . er!

JOXER [*outside*]. Ah, that's a darlin' song, a
daaarlin' song!

MRS. BOYLE [*viciously*]. Sweet spirit hear his
prayer! Oh, then, I'll take me solemn affey-
davey, it's not for a job he's prayin'!

[*She sits down on the bed so that the cretonne hangings hide her from the view of those
entering. THE CAPTAIN comes slowly in. He is
a man of about sixty; stout, grey-haired and
stocky. His neck is short, and his head looks
like a stone ball that one sometimes sees on top
of a gate-post. His cheeks, reddish-purple, are
puffed out, as if he were always repressing an
almost irrepressible ejaculation. On his upper
lip is a crisp, tightly cropped moustache; he
carries himself with the upper part of his body
slightly thrown back, and his stomach slightly
thrust forward. His walk is a slow, consequential strut. His clothes are dingy, and he
wears a faded seaman's cap with a glazed
peak.*]

BOYLE [*to JOXER, who is still outside*]. Come

on, come on in, Joxer; she's gone out long ago,
man. If there's nothing else to be got, we'll
furrage out a cup o' tay, anyway. It's the only
bit I get in comfort when she's away. 'Tisn't
Juno should be her pet name at all, but Deirdre
of the Sorras,° for she's always grousin'.

[*JOXER steps cautiously into the room. He
may be younger than THE CAPTAIN but he looks
a lot older. His face is like a bundle of crinkled
paper; his eyes have a cunning twinkle; he is
spare and loosely built; he has a habit of
constantly shrugging his shoulders with a
peculiar twitching movement, meant to be
ingratiating. His face is invariably ornamented
with a grin.*]

JOXER. It's a terrible thing to be tied to a
woman that's always grousin'. I don't know
how you stick it—it ud put years on me. It's
a good job she has to be so often away, for
[*with a shrug*] when the cat's away, the mice
can play!

BOYLE [*with a commanding and complacent
gesture*]. Pull over to the fire, Joxer, an' we'll
have a cup o' tay in a minute.

JOXER. Ah, a cup o' tay's a darlin' thing, a
daaarlin' thing—the cup that cheers but
doesn't . . .

[*JOXER's rhapsody is cut short by the sight
of JUNO coming forward and confronting the
two cronies. Both are stupefied.*]

MRS. BOYLE [*with sweet irony—poking the
fire, and turning her head to glare at JOXER*].
Pull over to the fire, Joxer Daly, an' we'll have
a cup o' tay in a minute! Are you sure, now,
you wouldn't like an egg?

JOXER. I can't stop, Mrs. Boyle; I'm in a
desperate hurry, a desperate hurry.

MRS. BOYLE. Pull over to the fire, Joxer Daly;
people is always far more comfortabler here
than they are in their own place.

[*JOXER makes hastily for the door.*]

BOYLE [*stirs to follow him; thinks of something to relieve the situation—stops, and says
suddenly*]. Joxer!

JOXER [*at door ready to bolt*]. Yis?

Deirdre of the Sorras a tragic heroine of Irish legend

BOYLE. You know the foreman o' that job that's goin' on down in Killesther, don't you, Joxer?

JOXER [*puzzled*]. Foreman—Killesther? . . . .

BOYLE [*with a meaning look*]. He's a butty o' yours, isn't he?

JOXER [*the truth dawning on him*]. The foreman at Killesther—oh, yis, yis. He's an oul' butty o' mine—oh, he's a darlin' man, a daarlin' man.

BOYLE. Oh, then, it's a sure thing. It's a pity we didn't go down at breakfast first thing this mornin'—we might ha' been working now; but you didn't know it then.

JOXER [*with a shrug*]. It's betther late than never.

BOYLE. It's nearly time we got a start, anyhow; I'm fed up knockin' round, doin' nothin'. He promised you—gave you the straight tip?

JOXER. Yis. "Come down on the blow o' dinner," says he, "an' I'll start you, an' any friend you like to brin' with you." Ah, says I, you're a darlin' man, a daaarlin' man.

BOYLE. Well, it couldn't come at a better time—we're a long time waitin' for it.

JOXER Indeed we were; but it's a long lane that has no turnin'.

BOYLE. The blow up for dinner is at one— wait till I see what time it 'tis. [*He goes over to the mantelpiece, and gingerly lifts the clock.*]

MRS. BOYLE. Min' now, how you go on fiddlin' with that clock—you know the least little thing sets it asthray.

BOYLE. The job couldn't come at a better time; I'm feelin' in great fettle, Joxer. I'd hardly believe I ever had a pain in me legs, an' last week I was nearly crippled with them.

JOXER. That's betther and betther; ah, God never shut wan door but he opened another!

BOYLE. It's only eleven o'clock; we've lashins o' time. I'll slip on me oul' moleskins afther breakfast, an' we can saunter down at our ayse. [*Putting his hand on the shovel.*] I think, Joxer, we'd betther bring our shovels?

JOXER. Yis, Captain, yis; it's better to go fully prepared an' ready for all eventualities. You bring your long-tailed shovel, an' I'll bring me navvy.° We mighten' want them, an', then agen, we might: for want of a nail the shoe was lost, for want of a shoe the horse was lost, an' for want of a horse the man was lost—aw, that's a darlin' proverb, a daarlin' . . .

[*As JOXER is finishing his sentence, MRS. BOYLE approaches the door and JOXER retreats hurriedly. She shuts the door with a bang.*]

BOYLE [*suggestively*]. We won't be long pullin' ourselves together agen when I'm working for a few weeks.

[MRS. BOYLE *takes no notice.*]

BOYLE. The foreman on the job is an oul' butty o' Joxer's; I have an idea that I know him meself. [*Silence.*] . . . There's a button off the back o' me moleskin trousers. . . . If you leave out a needle an' thread I'll sew it on meself. . . . Thanks be to God, the pains in me legs is gone, anyhow!

MRS. BOYLE [*with a burst*]. Look here. Mr. Jacky Boyle, them yarns won't go down with Juno. I know you an' Joxer Daly of an oul' date, an', if you think you're able to come it over me with them fairy tales, you're in the wrong shop.

BOYLE. [*coughing subduedly to relieve the tenseness of the situation*]. U-u-u-ugh.

MRS. BOYLE. Butty o' Joxer's! Oh, you'll do a lot o' good as long as you continue to be a butty o' Joxer's!

BOYLE. U-u-u-ugh.

MRS. BOYLE. Shovel! Ah, then, me boyo, you'd do far more work with a knife an' fork than ever you'll do with a shovel! If there was e'er a genuine job goin' you'd be dh'other way about—not able to lift your arms with the pains in your legs! Your poor wife slavin' to keep the bit° in your mouth, an' you gallivantin' about all the day like a paycock!

BOYLE. It ud be betther for a man to be dead, betther for a man to be dead.

MRS. BOYLE [*ignoring the interruption*]. Everybody callin' you "Captain," an' you only wanst on the wather, in an oul' collier from

navvy pick or shovel
the bit a bite to eat

here to Liverpool, when anybody, to listen or look at you, ud take you for a second Christo For Columbus!

BOYLE. Are you never goin' to give us a rest?

MRS. BOYLE. Oh, you're never tired o' lookin' for a rest.

BOYLE. D'ye want to dhrive me out o' the house?

MRS. BOYLE. It ud be easier to dhrive you out o' the house than to dhrive you into a job. Here, sit down an' take your breakfast—it may be the last you'll get, for I don't know where the next is goin' to come from.

BOYLE. If I get this job we'll be all right.

MRS. BOYLE. Did ye see Jerry Devine?

BOYLE [testily]. No, I didn't see him.

MRS. BOYLE. No, but you seen Joxer. Well, he was here lookin' for you.

BOYLE. Well, let him look!

MRS. BOYLE. Oh, indeed, he may well look, for it ud be hard for him to see you, an' you stuck in Ryan's snug.

BOYLE. I wasn't in Ryan's snug—I don't go into Ryan's.

MRS. BOYLE. Oh, is there a mad dog there? Well, if you weren't in Ryan's you were in Foley's.

BOYLE. I'm telling you for the last three weeks I haven't tasted a dhrop of intoxicatin' liquor. I wasn't in ayther wan snug or dh'other—I could swear that on a prayer-book—I'm as innocent as the child unborn!

MRS. BOYLE. Well, if you'd been in for your breakfast you'd ha' seen him.

BOYLE [suspiciously]. What does he want me for?

MRS. BOYLE. He'll be back any minute an' then you'll soon know.

BOYLE. I'll dhrop out an' see if I can meet him.

MRS. BOYLE. You'll sit down an' take your breakfast, an' let me go to me work, for I'm an hour late already waitin' for you.

BOYLE. You needn't ha' waited, for I'll take no breakfast—I've a little spirit left in me still!

MRS. BOYLE. Are you goin' to have your breakfast—yes or no?

BOYLE [too proud to yield]. I'll have no breakfast—yous can keep your breakfast.

[Plaintively.] I'll knock out a bit somewhere, never fear.

MRS. BOYLE. Nobody's goin' to coax you—don't think that. [She vigorously replaces the pan and the sausages in the press.]

BOYLE. I've a little spirit left in me still.

[JERRY DEVINE enters hastily.]

JERRY. Oh, here you are at last! I've been searchin' for you everywhere. The foreman in Foley's told me you hadn't left the snug with Joxer ten minutes before I went in.

MRS. BOYLE. An' he swearin' on the holy prayer-book that he wasn't in no snug!

BOYLE [to JERRY]. What business is it o' yours whether I was in a snug or no? What do you want to be gallopin' about afther me for? Is a man not to be allowed to leave his house for a minute without havin' a pack o' spies, pimps an' informers cantherin' at his heels?

JERRY. Oh, you're takin' a wrong view of it, Mr. Boyle; I simply was anxious to do you a good turn. I have a message for you from Father Farrell: he says that if you go to the job that's on in Rathmines, an' ask for Foreman Mangan, you'll get a start.

BOYLE. That's all right, but I don't want the motions of me body to be watched the way an asthronomer ud watch a star. If you're folleyin' Mary aself, you've no pereeogative to be folleyin' me. [Suddenly catching his thigh.] U-ugh, I'm afther gettin' a terrible twinge in me right leg!

MRS. BOYLE. Oh, it won't be very long now till it travels into your left wan. It's miraculous that whenever he scents a job in front of him, his legs begin to fail him! Then, me bucko, if you lose this chance, you may go an' furrage for yourself!

JERRY. This job'll last for some time, too, Captain, an' as soon as the foundations are in, it'll be cushy enough.

BOYLE. Won't it be a climbin' job? How d'ye expect me to be able to go up a ladder with these legs? An', if I get up aself, how am I goin' to get down agen?

MRS. BOYLE [viciously]. Get wan o' the labourers to carry you down in a hod! You can't climb a laddher, but you can skip like a goat into a snug!

JERRY. I wouldn't let myself be let down that easy, Mr. Boyle; a little exercise, now, might do you all the good in the world.

BOYLE. It's a docthor you should have been, Devine—maybe you know more about the pains in me legs than meself that has them?

JERRY [*irritated*]. Oh, I know nothin' about the pains in your legs; I've brought the message that Father Farrell gave me, an' that's all I can do.

MRS. BOYLE. Here, sit down an' take your breakfast, an' go an' get ready; an' don't be actin' as if you couldn't pull a wing out of a dead bee.

BOYLE. I want no breakfast, I tell you; it ud choke me after all that's been said. I've a little spirit left in me still.

MRS. BOYLE. Well, let's see your spirit, then, an' go in at wanst an' put on your moleskin trousers!

BOYLE [*moving towards the door on left*]. It ud be betther for a man to be dead! U-ugh! There's another twinge in me other leg! Nobody but meself knows the sufferin' I'm goin' through with the pains in these legs o' mine! [*He goes into the room on left as* MARY *comes out with her hat in her hand.*]

MRS. BOYLE. I'll have to push off now, for I'm terrible late already, but I was determined to stay an' hunt that Joxer this time.

[*She goes off.*]

JERRY. Are you going out, Mary?

MARY. It looks like it when I'm putting on my hat, doesn't it?

JERRY. The bitther word agen, Mary.

MARY. You won't allow me to be friendly with you; if I thry, you deliberately misundherstand it.

JERRY. I didn't always misundherstand it; you were often delighted to have the arms of Jerry around you.

MARY. If you go on talkin' like this, Jerry Devine, you'll make me hate you!

JERRY. Well, let it be either a weddin' or a wake! Listen, Mary, I'm standin' for the Secretaryship of our Union. There's only one opposin' me; I'm popular with all the men, an' a good speaker—all are sayin' that I'll get elected.

MARY. Well?

JERRY. The job's worth three hundred an' fifty pounds a year, Mary. You an' I could live nice an' cosily on that; it would lift you out o' this place an' . . .

MARY. I haven't time to listen to you now —I have to go. [*She is going out when* JERRY *bars the way.*]

JERRY [*appealingly*]. Mary, what's come over you with me for the last few weeks? You hardly speak to me, an' then only a word with a face o' bitterness on it. Have you forgotten, Mary, all the happy evenin's that were as sweet as the scented hawthorn that sheltered the sides o' the road as we sauntered through the country?

MARY. That's all over now. When you get your new job, Jerry, you won't be long findin' a girl far betther than I am for your sweetheart.

JERRY. Never, never, Mary! No matther what happens you'll always be the same to me.

MARY. I must be off; please let me go, Jerry.

JERRY. I'll go a bit o' the way with you.

MARY. You needn't, thanks; I want to be by meself.

JERRY [*catching her arm*]. You're goin' to meet another fella; you've clicked with some one else, me lady!

MARY. That's no concern o' yours, Jerry Devine; let me go!

JERRY. I saw yous comin' out o' the Cornflower Dance Class, an' you hangin' on his arm—a thin, lanky strip of a Micky Dazzler, with a walkin' stick an' gloves!

VOICE OF JOHNNY [*loudly*]. What are you doin' there—pullin' about everything!

VOICE OF BOYLE [*loudly and viciously*]. I'm puttin' on me moleskin trousers!

MARY. You're hurtin' me arm! Let me go, or I'll scream, an' then you'll have the oul' fella out on top of us!

JERRY. Don't be so hard on a fella, Mary, don't be so hard.

BOYLE [*appearing at the door*]. What's the meanin' of all this hillabaloo?

MARY. Let me go, let me go!

BOYLE. D'ye hear me—what's all this hillabaloo about?

JERRY [*plaintively*]. Will you not give us one kind word, one kind word, Mary?

BOYLE. D'ye hear me talkin' to yous? What's all this hillabaloo for?

5 JERRY. Let me kiss your hand, your little, tiny, white hand!

BOYLE. Your little, tiny, white hand—are you takin' leave o' your senses, man?

[MARY *breaks away and rushes out.*]

10 BOYLE. This is nice goin's on in front of her father!

JERRY. Ah, dhry up, for God's sake!

[*He follows* MARY.]

BOYLE. Chiselurs° don't care a damn now
15 about their parents, they're bringin' their fathers' grey hairs down with sorra to the grave, an' laughin' at it, laughin' at it. Ah, I suppose it's just the same everywhere—the whole worl's in a state o' chassis!° [*He sits by*
20 *the fire.*] Breakfast! Well, they can keep their breakfast for me. Not if they went down on their bended knees would I take it—I'll show them I've a little spirit left in me still! [*He goes over to the press, takes out a plate and looks*
25 *at it.*] Sassige! Well, let her keep her sassige. [*He returns to the fire, takes up the teapot and gives it a gentle shake.*] The tay's wet right enough. [*A pause; he rises, goes to the press, takes out the sausage, puts it on the pan, and*
30 *puts both on the fire. He attends the sausage with a fork.*]

BOYLE [*singing*].
When the robins nest agen,
And the flowers are in bloom,
35 When the Springtime's sunny smile seems
        [to banish all sorrow an' gloom;
Then me bonny blue-ey'd lad, if me heart
        [be true till then—
He's promised he'll come back to me,
40 When the robins nest agen!

[*He lifts his head at the high note, and then drops his eyes to the pan.*]

BOYLE [*singing*].
When the . . .

Chiselurs children
chassis Boyle's way of saying *chaos*

[*Steps are heard approaching; he whips the* 45 *pan off the fire and puts it under the bed, then sits down at the fire. The door opens and a bearded man looking in says:*]
You don't happen to want a sewin' machine?

BOYLE [*furiously*]. No, I don't want e'er a 50 sewin' machine! [*He returns the pan to the fire, and commences to sing again.*]

BOYLE [*singing*].
When the robins nest agen,
And the flowers they are in bloom, 55
He's . . .

[*A thundering knock is heard at the street door.*]

BOYLE. There's a terrible tatheraraa—that's a stranger—that's nobody belongin' to the 60 house. [*Another loud knock.*]

JOXER [*sticking his head in at the door*]. Did ye hear them tatherarahs?

BOYLE. Well, Joxer, I'm not deaf.

JOHNNY [*appearing in his shirt and trousers* 65 *at the door on left; his face is anxious and his voice is tremulous*]. Who's that at the door; who's that at the door? Who gave that knock —d' yous hear me—are yous deaf or dhrunk or what? 70

BOYLE [*to* JOHNNY]. How the hell do I know who 'tis? Joxer, stick your head out o' the window an' see.

JOXER. An' mebbe get a bullet in the kisser? Ah, none o' them thricks for Joxer! It's betther 75 to be a coward than a corpse!

BOYLE [*looking cautiously out of the window*]. It's a fella in a thrench coat.

JOHNNY. Holy Mary, Mother o' God, I . . .

BOYLE. He's goin' away—he must ha' got 80 tired knockin'.

[JOHNNY *returns to the room on left.*]

BOYLE. Sit down an' have a cup o' tay, Joxer.

JOXER. I'm afraid the missus ud pop in on us agen before we'd know where we are. Some- 85 thin's tellin' me to go at wanst.

BOYLE. Don't be superstitious, man; we're Dublin men, an' not boyos that's only afther comin' up from the bog o' Allen—though if she did come in, right enough, we'd be caught 90 like rats in a thrap.

JOXER. An you know the sort she is—she wouldn't listen to reason—an' wanse bitten twice shy.

BOYLE [*going over to the window at back*]. If the worst came to the worst, you could dart out here, Joxer; it's only a dhrop of a few feet to the roof of the return room, an' the first minute she goes into dh'other room, I'll give you the bend, an' you can slip in an' away.

JOXER [*yielding to the temptation*]. Ah, I won't stop very long anyhow. [*Picking up a book from the table.*] Whose is the buk?

BOYLE. Aw, one o' Mary's; she's always readin' lately—nothin' but thrash, too. There's one I was lookin' at dh'other day: three stories, *The Doll's House, Ghosts,* an' *The Wild Duck* —buks only fit for chiselurs!

JOXER. Didja ever rade *Elizabeth, or Th' Exile o' Sibayria* . . . ah, it's a darlin' story, a daarlin' story!

BOYLE. You eat your sassige, an' never min' *Th' Exile o' Sibayria.*

[*Both sit down;* BOYLE *fills out tea, pours gravy on* JOXER'S *plate, and keeps the sausage for himself.*]

JOXER. What are you wearin' your moleskin trousers for?

BOYLE. I have to go to a job, Joxer. Just afther you'd gone, Devine kem runnin' in to tell us that Father Farrell said if I went down to the job that's goin' on in Rathmines I'd get a start.

JOXER. Be the holy, that's good news!

BOYLE. How is it good news? I wonder if you were in my condition, would you call it good news?

JOXER. I thought . . .

BOYLE. You thought! You think too sudden sometimes, Joxer. D'ye know, I'm hardly able to crawl with the pains in me legs!

JOXER. Yis, yis; I forgot the pains in your legs. I know you can do nothin' while they're at you.

BOYLE. You forgot; I don't think any of yous realize the state I'm in with the pains in me legs. What ud happen if I had to carry a bag o' cement?

JOXER. Ah, any man havin' the like of them pains id be down an' out, down an' out.

BOYLE. I wouldn't mind if he had said it to meself; but, no, oh no, he rushes in an' shouts it out in front o' Juno, an' you know what Juno is, Joxer. We all know Devine knows a little more than the rest of us, but he doesn't act as if he did; he's a good boy, sober, able to talk an' all that, but still . . .

JOXER. Oh, ay; able to argufy, but still . . .

BOYLE. If he's runnin' afther Mary, aself, he's not goin' to be runnin' after me. Captain Boyle's able to take care of himself. After all, I'm not gettin' brought up on Virol. I never heard him usin' a curse; I don't believe he was ever dhrunk in his life—sure he's not like a Christian at all!

JOXER. You're afther takin' the word out o' me mouth—afther all, a Christian's natural, but he's unnatural.

BOYLE. His oul' fella was just the same—a Wicklow man.

JOXER. A Wicklow man! That explains the whole thing. I've met many a Wicklow man in me time, but I never met wan that was any good.

BOYLE. "Father Farrell," says he, "sent me down to tell you." Father Farrell! . . . D'ye know, Joxer, I never like to be beholden to any o' the clergy.

JOXER. It's dangerous, right enough.

BOYLE. If they do anything for you, they'd want you to be livin' in the Chapel. . . . I'm goin' to tell you somethin', Joxer, that I wouldn't tell to anybody else—the clergy always had too much power over the people in this unfortunate country.

JOXER. You could sing that if you had an air to it!

BOYLE [*becoming enthusiastic*]. Didn't they prevent the people in '47° from seizin' the corn, an' they starvin'; didn't they down Parnell;° didn't they say that hell wasn't hot

---

'47 1847, a year of the potato famine

Parnell Charles Stewart Parnell (1847–1891), who led the fight in the British Parliament for Irish home rule. Upon being involved in a divorce scandal, he was opposed by many of his former supporters, including many of the Irish clergy.

enough nor eternity long enough to punish the
Fenians?° We don't forget, we don't forget
them things, Joxer. If they've taken everything
else from us, Joxer, they've left us our memory.

5 JOXER [*emotionally*]. For mem'ry's the only
friend that grief can call its own, that grief . . .
can . . . call . . . its own!

BOYLE. Father Farrell's beginnin' to take a
great intherest in Captain Boyle; because of

10 what Johnny did for his country, says he to
me wan day. It's a curious way to reward
Johnny be makin' his poor oul' father work.
But, that's what the clergy want, Joxer—work,
work, work for me an' you; havin' us mulin'

15 from mornin' till night, so that they may be in
bether fettle when they come hoppin' round
for their dues! Job! Well, let him give his job
to wan of his hymn-singin', prayer-spoutin',
craw-thumpin' Confraternity men!°

20 [*The voice of a* COAL-BLOCK VENDOR *is heard
chanting in the street.*]

VOICE OF COAL VENDOR. Blocks . . . coal-
blocks! Blocks . . . coal-blocks!

JOXER. God be with the young days when

25 you were steppin' the deck of a manly ship,
with the win' blowin' a hurricane through the
masts, an' the only sound you'd hear was,
"Port your helm!" an' the only answer, "Port
it is, sir!"

30 BOYLE. Them was days, Joxer, them was
days. Nothin' was too hot or too heavy for me
then. Sailin' from the Gulf o' Mexico to the
Antarctic Ocean. I seen things, I seen things,
Joxer, that no mortal man should speak about

35 that knows his Catechism. Ofen, an' ofen,
when I was fixed to the wheel with a marlin-
spike, an' the win's blowin' fierce an' the waves
lashin' an' lashin', till you'd think every minute
was goin' to be your last, an' it blowed, an'

40 blowed—blew is the right word, Joxer, but
blowed is what the sailors use. . . .

JOXER. Aw, it's a darlin' word, a daarlin'
word.

BOYLE. An', as it blowed an' blowed, I ofen
looked up at the sky an' assed meself the 45
question—what is the stars, what is the stars?

VOICE OF COAL VENDOR. Any blocks, coal-
blocks; blocks, coal-blocks!

JOXER. Ah, that's the question, that's the
question—what is the stars? 50

BOYLE. An' then, I'd have another look, an'
I'd ass meself—what is the moon?

JOXER. Ah, that's the question—what is the
moon, what is the moon?

[*Rapid steps are heard coming towards the* 55
door. BOYLE *makes desperate efforts to hide
everything;* JOXER *rushes to the window in a
frantic effort to get out;* BOYLE *begins to innocently lilt—"Oh, me darlin' Jennie, I will be
thrue to thee," when the door is opened, and* 60
the black face of the COAL VENDOR *appears.*]

THE COAL VENDOR. D'yes want any blocks?

BOYLE [*with a roar*]. No, we don't want any
blocks!

JOXER [*coming back with a sigh of relief*]. 65
That's afther puttin' the heart across me—I
could ha' sworn it was Juno. I'd bether be
goin', Captain; you couldn't tell the minute
Juno'd hop in on us.

BOYLE. Let her hop in; we may as well have 70
it out first as at last. I've made up me mind—
I'm not goin' to do only what she damn well
likes.

JOXER. Them sentiments does you credit,
Captain; I don't like to say anything as between 75
man an' wife, but I say as a butty, as a butty,
Captain, that you've stuck it too long, an' that
it's about time you showed a little spunk.
  How can a man die bether than facin'
                                [*fearful odds,* 80
For th' ashes of his fathers an' the temples
                                [*of his gods.*

BOYLE. She has her rights—there's no one
denyin' it, but haven't I me rights too?

JOXER. Of course you have—the sacred rights 85
o' man!

BOYLE. Today, Joxer, there's goin' to be
issued a proclamation be me, establishin' an
independent Republic, an' Juno'll have to take
an oath of allegiance. 90

JOXER. Be firm, be firm, Captain; the first few

minutes'll be the worst:—if you gently touch a nettle it'll sting you for your pains; grasp it like a lad of mettle, an't as soft as silk remains!

VOICE OF JUNO OUTSIDE. Can't stop, Mrs.
5 Madigan—I haven't a minute!

JOXER [*flying out of the window*]. Holy God, here she is!

BOYLE [*packing the things away with a rush in the press*]. I knew that fella ud stop till she
10 was in on top of us! [*He sits down by the fire.*]

[JUNO *enters hastily; she is flurried and excited.*]

JUNO. Oh, you're in—you must have been only afther comin' in?

15 BOYLE. No, I never went out.

JUNO. It's curious, then, you never heard the knockin'. [*She puts her coat and hat on bed.*]

BOYLE. Knockin'? Of course I heard the knockin'.

20 JUNO. An' why didn't you open the door, then? I suppose you were so busy with Joxer that you hadn't time.

BOYLE. I haven't seen Joxer since I seen him before. Joxer! What ud bring Joxer here?

25 JUNO. D'ye mean to tell me that the pair of yous wasn't collogin' together here when me back was turned?

BOYLE. What ud we be collogin' together about? I have somethin' else to think of besides
30 collogin' with Joxer. I can swear on all the holy prayer-books . . .

MRS. BOYLE. That you weren't in no snug! Go on in at wanst now, an' take off that moleskin trousers o' yours, an' put on a collar an'
35 tie to smarten yourself up a bit. There's a visitor comin' with Mary in a minute, an he has great news for you.

BOYLE. A job, I suppose; let us get wan first before we start lookin' for another.

40 MRS. BOYLE. That's the thing that's able to put the win' up you. Well, it's no job, but news that'll give you the chance o' your life.

BOYLE. What's all the mystery about?

MRS. BOYLE. G'win an' take off the moleskin
45 trousers when you're told!

[BOYLE *goes into room on left.* MRS. BOYLE *tidies up the room, puts the shovel under the bed, and goes to the press.*]

MRS. BOYLE. Oh, God bless us, looka the way everythin's thrun about! Oh, Joxer was
50 here, Joxer was here!

[MARY *enters with* CHARLIE BENTHAM; *he is a young man of twenty-five, tall, good-looking, with a very high opinion of himself generally. He is dressed in a brown coat, brown knee-
55 breeches, grey stockings, a brown sweater, with a deep blue tie; he carries gloves and a walking-stick.*]

MRS. BOYLE [*fussing round*]. Come in, Mr. Bentham; sit down, Mr. Bentham, in this chair;
60 it's more comfortabler than that, Mr. Bentham. Himself'll be here in a minute; he's just takin' off his trousers.

MARY. Mother!

BENTHAM. Please don't put yourself to any
65 trouble, Mrs. Boyle—I'm quite all right here, thank you.

MRS. BOYLE. An' to think of you knowin' Mary, an' she knowin' the news you had for us, an' wouldn't let on; but it's all the more
70 welcomer now, for we were on our last lap!

VOICE OF JOHNNY INSIDE. What are you kickin' up all the racket for?

BOYLE [*roughly*]. I'm takin' off me moleskin trousers!
75

JOHNNY. Can't you do it, then, without lettin' th' whole house know you're takin' off your trousers? What d'ye want puttin' them on an' takin' them off again?

BOYLE. Will you let me alone, will you let
80 me alone? Am I never goin' to be done thryin' to please th' whole o' yous?

MRS. BOYLE [*to* BENTHAM]. You must excuse th' state o' th' place, Mr. Bentham; th' minute I turn me back that man o' mine always makes
85 a litther o' th' place, a litther o' th' place.

BENTHAM. Don't worry, Mrs. Boyle; it's all right, I assure . . .

BOYLE [*inside*]. Where's me braces; where in th' name o' God did I leave me braces. . . . Ay,
90 did you see where I put me braces?

JOHNNY [*inside, calling out*]. Ma, will you come in here an' take da away ou' o' this or he'll dhrive me mad.

MRS. BOYLE [*going towards door*]. Dear,
95 dear, dear, that man'll be lookin' for somethin'

on th' day o' Judgement. [*Looking into room and calling to* BOYLE.] Look at your braces, man, hangin' round your neck!

BOYLE [*inside*]. Aw, Holy God!

5   MRS. BOYLE [*calling*]. Johnny, Johnny, come out here for a minute.

JOHNNY. Oh, leave Johnny alone, an' don't be annoyin' him!

MRS. BOYLE. Come on, Johnny, till I inthro-
10   duce you to Mr. Bentham. [*To* BENTHAM.] Me son, Mr. Bentham; he's afther goin' through the mill. He was only a chiselur of a Boy Scout in Easter Week, when he got hit in the hip; and his arm was blew off in the fight in O'Con-
15   nell Street. [JOHNNY *comes in.*] Here he is, Mr. Bentham; Mr. Bentham, Johnny. None can deny he done his bit for Irelan', if that's going to do him any good.

JOHNNY [*boastfully*]. I'd do it agen, ma, I'd
20   do it agen; for a principle's a principle.

MRS. BOYLE. Ah, you lost your best principle, me boy, when you lost your arm; them's the only sort o' principles that's any good to a workin' man.

25   JOHNNY. Ireland only half free'll never be at peace while she has a son left to pull a trigger.

MRS. BOYLE. To be sure, to be sure—no bread's a lot betther than half a loaf. [*Calling loudly in to* BOYLE.] Will you hurry up there?

30   [BOYLE *enters in his best trousers, which aren't too good, and looks very uncomfortable in his collar and tie.*]

MRS. BOYLE. This is me husband; Mr. Boyle, Mr. Bentham.

35   BENTHAM. Ah, very glad to know you, Mr. Boyle. How are you?

BOYLE. Ah, I'm not too well at all; I suffer terrible with pains in me legs. Juno can tell you there what . . .

40   MRS. BOYLE. You won't have many pains in your legs when you hear what Mr. Bentham has to tell you.

BENTHAM. Juno! What an interesting name! It reminds one of Homer's glorious story of
45   ancient gods and heroes.

BOYLE. Yis, doesn't it? You see, Juno was born an' christened in June; I met her in June; we were married in June, an' Johnny was born in June, so wan day I says to her, "You should

ha' been called Juno," an' the name stuck to   50
her ever since.

MRS. BOYLE. Here we can talk o' them things agen; let Mr. Bentham say what he has to say now.

BENTHAM. Well, Mr. Boyle, I suppose you'll   55
remember a Mr. Ellison of Santry—he's a relative of yours, I think.

BOYLE [*viciously*]. Is it that prognosticator an' procrastinator! Of course I remember him.

BENTHAM. Well, he's dead, Mr. Boyle . . .   60

BOYLE. Sorra many'll° go into mournin' for him.

MRS. BOYLE. Wait till you hear what Mr. Bentham has to say, an' then, maybe, you'll change your opinion.   65

BENTHAM. A week before he died he sent for me to write his will for him. He told me that there were two only that he wished to leave his property to; his second cousin Michael Finnegan of Santry, and John Boyle, his first   70
cousin of Dublin.

BOYLE [*excitedly*]. Me, is it me, me? . . . . . .

BENTHAM. You, Mr. Boyle; I'll read a copy of the will that I have here with me, which has been duly filed in the Court of Probate. [*He   75
takes a paper from his pocket and reads:*]

6th February, 1922.

This is the last Will and Testament of William Ellison, of Santry, in the County of Dublin. I hereby order and wish my property   80
to be sold and divided as follows:—

£20 to the St. Vincent De Paul Society.

£60 for Masses for the repose of my soul (5s. for Each Mass).

The rest of my property to be divided be-   85
tween my first and second cousins.

I hereby appoint Timothy Buckly, of Santry, and Hugh Brierly, of Coolock, to be my Executors.

(*Signed*)   WILLIAM ELLISON.   90
            HUGH BRIERLY.
            TIMOTHY BUCKLY.
            CHARLES BENTHAM, N.T.

BOYLE [*eagerly*]. An' how much'll be comin' out of it, Mr. Bentham?   95

BENTHAM. The Executors told me that half

Sorra many very few

of the property would be anything between £1500 and £2000.

MARY. A fortune, father, a fortune!

JOHNNY. We'll be able to get out o' this place now, an' go somewhere we're not known.

MRS. BOYLE. You won't have to trouble about a job for a while, Jack.

BOYLE [*fervently*]. I'll never doubt the goodness o' God agen.

BENTHAM. I congratulate you, Mr. Boyle. [*They shake hands.*]

BOYLE. An' now, Mr. Bentham, you'll have to have a wet.

BENTHAM. A wet?

BOYLE. A wet—a jar—a boul!

MRS. BOYLE. Jack, you're speakin' to Mr. Bentham, an' not to Joxer.

BOYLE [*solemnly*]. Juno . . . Mary . . . Johnny . . . we'll have to go into mournin' at wanst. . . . I never expected that poor Bill ud die so sudden. . . . Well, we all have to die some day . . . you, Juno, today . . . an' me, maybe, tomorrow. . . . It's sad, but it can't be helped. . . . Requiescat in pace . . . or, usin' our oul' tongue like St. Patrick or St. Briget, Guh sayeree jeea ayera!

MARY. Oh, father, that's not Rest in Peace; that's God save Ireland.

BOYLE. U-u-ugh, it's all the same—isn't it a prayer? . . . Juno, I'm done with Joxer; he's nothin' but a prognosticator an' a . . .

JOXER [*climbing angrily through the window and bounding into the room*]. You're done with Joxer, are you? Maybe you thought I'd stop on the roof all the night for you! Joxer out on the roof with the win' blowin' through him was nothin' to you an' your friend with the collar an' tie!

MRS. BOYLE. What in the name o' God brought you out on the roof; what were you doin' there?

JOXER [*ironically*]. I was dhreamin' I was standin' on the bridge of a ship, an' she sailin' the Antarctic Ocean, an' it blowed, an' blowed, an' I lookin' up at the sky an' sayin', what is the stars, what is the stars?

MRS. BOYLE [*opening the door and standing at it*]. Here, get ou' o' this, Joxer Daly; I was always thinkin' you had a slate off.

JOXER [*moving to the door*]. I have to laugh every time I look at the deep sea sailor; an' a row on a river ud make him sea-sick!

BOYLE. Get ou' o' this before I take the law into me own hands!

JOXER [*going out*]. Say aw rewaeawr,° but not good-bye. Lookin' for work, an' prayin' to God he won't get it!

[*He goes.*]

MRS. BOYLE. I'm tired tellin' you what Joxer was; maybe now you see yourself the kind he is.

BOYLE. He'll never blow the froth off a pint o' mine agen, that's a sure thing. Johnny . . . Mary . . . you're to keep yourselves to yourselves for the future. Juno, I'm done with Joxer. . . . I'm a new man from this out. . . . [*Clasping* JUNO's *hand, and singing emotionally.*]

Oh, me darlin' Juno, I will be thrue to thee;
Me own, me darlin' Juno, you're all the
[world to me.

The Curtain Falls

ACT II

[SCENE. *The same, but the furniture is more plentiful, and of a vulgar nature. A glaringly upholstered arm-chair and lounge; cheap pictures and photos everywhere. Every available spot is ornamented with huge vases filled with artificial flowers. Crossed festoons of coloured paper chains stretch from end to end of ceiling. On the table is an old attaché case. It is about six in the evening, and two days after Act I.* BOYLE, *in his shirt sleeves, is voluptuously stretched on the sofa; he is smoking a clay pipe. He is half asleep. A lamp is lighting on the table. After a few moments' pause the voice of* JOXER *is heard singing softly outside at the door—"Me pipe I'll smoke, as I dhrive me moke°—are you there, Mor . . . ee . . . ar . . . i . . . teee!"*]

BOYLE [*leaping up, takes a pen in his hand and busies himself with papers*]. Come along, Joxer, me son, come along.

aw rewaeawr *au revoir*
moke donkey

JOXER [*putting his head in*]. Are you be yourself?

BOYLE. Come on, come on; that doesn't matther; I'm masther now, an' I'm goin' to remain masther.

[JOXER *comes in.*]

JOXER. How d'ye feel now, as a man o' money?

BOYLE [*solemnly*]. It's a responsibility, Joxer, a great responsibility.

JOXER. I suppose 'tis now, though you wouldn't think it.

BOYLE. Joxer, han' me over that attackey case on the table there. [JOXER *hands the case.*] Ever since the Will was passed I've run hundhreds o' dockyments through me han's—I tell you, you have to keep your wits about you. [*He busies himself with papers.*]

JOXER. Well, I won't disturb you; I'll dhrop in when . . .

BOYLE [*hastily*]. It's all right, Joxer, this is the last one to be signed today. [*He signs a paper, puts it into the case, which he shuts with a snap, and sits back pompously in the chair.*] Now, Joxer, you want to see me; I'm at your service—what can I do for you, me man?

JOXER. I've just dhropped in with the £3:5s. that Mrs. Madigan riz on the blankets an' table for you, and she says you're to be in no hurry payin' it back.

BOYLE. She won't be long without it; I expect the first cheque for a couple o' hundhred any day. There's the five bob for yourself—go on, take it, man; it'll not be the last you'll get from the Captain. Now an' agen we have our differ, but we're there together all the time.

JOXER. Me for you, an' you for me, like the two Musketeers.

BOYLE. Father Farrell stopped me today an' tole me how glad he was I fell in for the money.

JOXER. He'll be stoppin' you ofen enough now; I suppose it was "Mr." Boyle with him?

BOYLE. He shuk me be the han'. . . .

JOXER [*ironically*]. I met with Napper Tandy, an' he shuk me be the han'!

BOYLE. You're seldom asthray, Joxer, but you're wrong shipped this time. What you're sayin' of Father Farrell is very near to blasfeemey. I don't like any one to talk disrespectful of Father Farrell.

JOXER. You're takin' me up wrong, Captain; I wouldn't let a word be said agen Father Farrell—the heart o' the rowl, that's what he is; I always said he was a darlin' man, a daarlin' man.

BOYLE. Comin' up the stairs who did I meet but that bummer, Nugent. "I seen you talkin' to Father Farrell," says he, with a grin on him. "He'll be folleyin' you," says he, "like a Guardian Angel from this out"—all the time the oul' grin on him, Joxer.

JOXER. I never seen him yet but he had that oul' grin on him!

BOYLE. "Mr. Nugent," says I, "Father Farrell is a man o' the people, an', as far as I know the History of me country, the priests was always in the van of the fight for Irelan's freedom."

JOXER [*fervently*].
Who was it led the van, Soggart Aroon?°
Since the fight first began, Soggart Aroon?

BOYLE. "Who are you tellin'?" says he. "Didn't they let down the Fenians, an' didn't they do in Parnell? An' now . . ." "You ought to be ashamed o' yourself," says I, interruptin' him, "not to know the History o' your country." An' I left him gawkin' where he was.

JOXER. Where ignorance 's bliss 'tis folly to be wise; I wondher did he ever read the Story o' Irelan'.

BOYLE. Be J. L. Sullivan? Don't you know he didn't?

JOXER. Ah, it's a darlin' buk, a daarlin' buk!

BOYLE. You'd betther be goin', now, Joxer, his Majesty, Bentham, 'll be here any minute, now.

JOXER. Be the way things is lookin', it'll be a match between him an' Mary. She's thrun over Jerry altogether. Well, I hope it will, for he's a darlin' man.

Soggart Aroon Gaelic for "priest beloved," a term referring to one of the leaders of an Irish rebellion in the eighteenth century

BOYLE. I'm glad you think so—I don't. [*Irritably.*] What's darlin' about him?

JOXER [*nonplussed*]. I only seen him twiced; if you want to know me, come an' live with me.

5 BOYLE. He's too ignified for me—to hear him talk you'd think he knew as much as a Boney's Oraculum.° He's given up his job as teacher, an' is goin' to become a solicitor in Dublin— he's been studyin' law. I suppose he thinks I'll
10 set him up, but he's wrong shipped. An' th' other fella—Jerry's as bad. The two o' them ud give you a pain in your face, listenin' to them; Jerry believin' in nothin', an' Bentham believin' in everythin'. One that says all is God an' no man;
15 an' th' other that says all is man an' no God!

JOXER. Well, I'll be off now.

BOYLE. Don't forget to dhrop down afther a while; we'll have a quiet jar, an' a song or two.

JOXER. Never fear.

20 BOYLE. An' tell Mrs. Madigan that I hope we'll have the pleasure of her organization at our little enthertainment.

JOXER. Righto; we'll come down together. [*He goes out.*]

25 [JOHNNY *comes from room on left, and sits down moodily at the fire.* BOYLE *looks at him for a few moments, and shakes his head. He fills his pipe.*]

VOICE OF JUNO AT THE DOOR. Open the door,
30 Jack; this thing has me nearly kilt with the weight.

[BOYLE *opens the door.* JUNO *enters carrying the box of a gramophone, followed by* MARY *carrying the horn, and some parcels.* JUNO
35 *leaves the box on the table and flops into a chair.*]

JUNO. Carryin' that from Henry Street was no joke.

BOYLE. U-u-ugh, that's a grand lookin'
40 insthrument—how much was it?

JUNO. Pound down, an' five to be paid at two shillin's a week.

BOYLE. That's reasonable enough.

JUNO. I'm afraid we're runnin' into too much debt; first the furniture, an' now this. 45

BOYLE. The whole lot won't be much out of £2000.

MARY. I don't know what you wanted a gramophone for—I know Charlie hates them; he says they're destructive of real music. 50

BOYLE. Desthructive of music—that fella ud give you a pain in your face. All a gramophone wants is to be properly played; it's thrue wondher is only felt when everythin's quiet— what a gramophone wants is dead silence! 55

MARY. But, father, Jerry says the same; afther all, you can only appreciate music when your ear is properly trained.

BOYLE. That's another fella ud give you a pain in your face. Properly thrained! I suppose 60 you couldn't appreciate football unless your fut was properly thrained.

MRS. BOYLE [*to* MARY]. Go on in ower that° an' dress, or Charlie 'll be in on you, an' tay nor nothin' 'll be ready. 65

[MARY *goes into room left.*]

MRS. BOYLE [*arranging table for tea*]. You didn't look at our new gramophone, Johnny?

JOHNNY. 'Tisn't gramophones I'm thinking of.

MRS. BOYLE. An' what is it you're thinkin' 70 of, allana?°

JOHNNY. Nothin', nothin', nothin'.

MRS. BOYLE. Sure, you must be thinkin' of somethin'; it's yourself that has yourself the way y'are; sleepin' wan night in me sisther's, 75 an' the nex' in your father's brother's—you'll get no rest goin' on that way.

JOHNNY. I can rest nowhere, nowhere, nowhere.

MRS. BOYLE. Sure, you're not thryin' to rest 80 anywhere.

JOHNNY. Let me alone, let me alone, let me alone, for God's sake.

[*A knock at street door.*]

MRS. BOYLE [*in a flutter*]. Here he is; here's 85 Mr. Bentham!

Boney's Oraculum Napoleon Bonaparte's *Oraculum*, or Book of Fate, or Lucky Dream Book, a widely popular compendium of occult lore that Napoleon ("Boney") was supposed to have used to read the future

ower that right away
allana dear one

BOYLE. Well, there's room for him; it's a pity there's not a brass band to play him in.

MRS. BOYLE. We'll han' the tay around, an' not be clusthered round the table, as if we
5 never seen nothin'.

[*Steps are heard approaching, and* JUNO, *opening the door, allows* BENTHAM *to enter.*]

JUNO. Give your hat an' stick to Jack, there . . . sit down, Mr. Bentham . . . no, not there
10 . . . in th' easy chair be the fire . . . there, that's bether. Mary'll be out to you in a minute.

BOYLE [*solemnly*]. I seen be the paper this mornin' that Consols° was down half per cent. That's serious, min' you, an' shows the whole
15 counthry's in a state o' chassis.

MRS. BOYLE. What's Consols, Jack?

BOYLE. Consols? Oh, Consols is—oh, there's no use tellin' women what Consols is—th' wouldn't undherstand.

20 BENTHAM. It's just as you were saying, Mr. Boyle . . .

[MARY *enters charmingly dressed.*]

BENTHAM. Oh, good evening, Mary; how pretty you're looking!

25 MARY [*archly*]. Am I?

BOYLE. We were just talkin' when you kem in, Mary, I was tellin' Mr. Bentham that the whole counthry's in a state o' chassis.

MARY [*to* BENTHAM]. Would you prefer the
30 green or the blue ribbon round me hair, Charlie?

MRS. BOYLE. Mary, your father's speakin'.

BOYLE [*rapidly*]. I was jus' tellin' Mr. Bentham that the whole counthry's in a state o'
35 chassis.

MARY. I'm sure you're frettin', da, whether it is or no.

MRS. BOYLE. With all our churches an' religions, the worl's not a bit the bether.

40 BOYLE [*with a commanding gesture*]. Tay!

[MARY *and* MRS. BOYLE *dispense the tea.*]

MRS. BOYLE. An' Irelan's takin' a leaf out o' the worl's buk; when we got the makin' of our own laws I thought we'd never stop to look
45 behind us, but instead of that we never stopped

to look before us! If the people ud folly up their religion betther there'd be a betther chance for us—what do you think, Mr. Bentham?

50 BENTHAM. I'm afraid I can't venture to express an opinion on that point, Mrs. Boyle; dogma has no attraction for me.

MRS. BOYLE. I forgot you didn't hold with us; what's this you said you were?

55 BENTHAM. A Theosophist, Mrs. Boyle.

MRS. BOYLE. An' what in the name o' God's a Theosophist?

BOYLE. A Theosophist, Juno, 's a—tell her, Mr. Bentham, tell her.

60 BENTHAM. It's hard to explain in a few words: Theosophy's founded on The Vedas, the religious books of the East. Its central theme is the existence of an all-pervading Spirit—the Life-Breath. Nothing really exists but this one
65 Universal Life-Breath. And whatever even seems to exist separately from this Life-Breath, doesn't really exist at all. It is all vital force in man, in all animals, and in all vegetation. This Life-Breath is called the Prawna.

70 MRS. BOYLE. The Prawna! What a comical name!

BOYLE. Prawna; yis, the Prawna. [*Blowing gently through his lips.*] That's the Prawna!

MRS. BOYLE. Whist, whist, Jack.

75 BENTHAM. The happiness of man depends upon his sympathy with this Spirit. Men who have reached a high state of excellence are called Yogi. Some men become Yogi in a short time, it may take others millions of years.

80 BOYLE. Yogi! I seen hundhreds of them in the streets o' San Francisco.

BENTHAM. It is said by these Yogi that if we practise certain mental exercises that we would have powers denied to others—for instance,
85 the faculty of seeing things that happen miles and miles away.

MRS. BOYLE. I wouldn't care to meddle with that sort o' belief; it's a very curious religion, altogether.

90 BOYLE. What's curious about it? Isn't all religions curious? If they weren't, you wouldn't get any one to believe them. But religions is passin' away—they've had their day like every-

thing else. Take the real Dublin people, f'rinstance: they know more about Charlie Chaplin an' Tommy Mix than they do about SS. Peter an' Paul!

5 MRS. BOYLE. You don't believe in ghosts, Mr. Bentham?

MARY. Don't you know he doesn't, mother?

BENTHAM. I don't know that, Mary. Scientists are beginning to think that what we call ghosts

10 are something seen by persons of a certain nature. They say that sensational actions, such as the killing of a person, demand great energy, and that that energy lingers in the place where the action occurred. People may live in the

15 place and see nothing, when some one may come along whose personality has some peculiar connection with the energy of the place, and, in a flash, the person sees the whole affair.

JOHNNY [*rising swiftly, pale and affected*].

20 What sort o' talk is this to be goin' on with? Is there nothin' betther to be talkin' about but the killin' o' people? My God, isn't it bad enough for these things to happen without talkin' about them!

25 [*He hurriedly goes into the room on left.*]

BENTHAM. Oh, I'm very sorry, Mrs. Boyle; I never thought . . .

MRS. BOYLE [*apologetically*]. Never mind, Mr. Bentham, he's very touchy.

30 [*A frightened scream is heard from* JOHNNY *inside.*]

MRS. BOYLE. Mother of God! What's that?

[*He rushes out again, his face pale, his lips twitching, his limbs trembling.*]

35 JOHNNY. Shut the door, shut the door, quick, for God's sake! Great God, have mercy on me! Blessed Mother o' God, shelter me, shelter your son!

MRS. BOYLE [*catching him in her arms*].

40 What's wrong with you? What ails you? Sit down, sit down, here, on the bed . . . there now . . . there now.

MARY. Johnny, Johnny, what ails you?

JOHNNY. I seen him, I seen him . . . kneelin'

45 in front o' the statue . . . merciful Jesus, have pity on me!

MRS. BOYLE [*to* BOYLE]. Get him a glass o' whisky . . . quick, man, an' don't stand gawkin'.

[BOYLE *gets the whisky.*]

JOHNNY. Sit here, sit here, mother . . . be- 50 tween me an' the door.

MRS. BOYLE. I'll sit beside you as long as you like, only tell me what was it came across you at all?

JOHNNY [*after taking some drink*]. I seen him. 55 . . . I seen Robbie Tancred kneelin' down before the statue . . . an' the red light shinin' on him . . . an' when I went in . . . he turned an' looked at me . . . an' I seen the woun's bleedin' in his breast. . . . Oh, why did he look at me like that 60 . . . it wasn't my fault that he was done in . . . Mother o' God, keep him away from me!

MRS. BOYLE. There, there, child, you've imagined it all. There was nothin' there at all —it was the red light you seen, an' the talk we 65 had put all the rest into your head. Here, dhrink more o' this—it'll do you good. . . . An', now, stretch yourself down on the bed for a little. [*To* BOYLE.] Go in, Jack, an' show him it was only in his own head it was. 70

BOYLE [*making no move*]. E-e-e-eh; it's all nonsense; it was only a shadda he saw.

MARY. Mother o' God, he made me heart lep!

BENTHAM. It was simply due to an overwrought imagination—we all get that way at 75 times.

MRS. BOYLE. There, dear, lie down in the bed, an' I'll put the quilt across you . . . e-e-e-eh, that's it . . . you'll be as right as the mail in a few minutes. 80

JOHNNY. Mother, go into the room an' see if the light's lightin' before the statue.

MRS. BOYLE [*to* BOYLE]. Jack, run in, an' see if the light's lightin' before the statue.

BOYLE [*to* MARY]. Mary, slip in an' see if the 85 light's lightin' before the statue.

[MARY *hesitates to go in.*]

BENTHAM. It's all right; Mary, I'll go.

[*He goes into the room; remains for a few moments, and returns.*] 90

BENTHAM. Everything's just as it was—the light burning bravely before the statue.

BOYLE. Of course; I knew it was all nonsense.

[*A knock at the door.*]

BOYLE [*going to open the door*]. E-e-e-eh. 95

[*He opens it, and* JOXER, *followed by* MRS.

MADIGAN, *enters.* MRS. MADIGAN *is a strong, dapper little woman of about forty-five; her face is almost always a wide-spread smile of complacency. She is a woman who, in a manner at least, can mourn with them that mourn, and rejoice with them that do rejoice. When she is feeling comfortable, she is inclined to be reminiscent; when others say anything, or following a statement made by herself, she has a habit of putting her head a little to one side, and nodding it rapidly several times in succession, like a bird pecking at a hard berry. Indeed, she has a good deal of the bird in her, but the bird instinct is by no means a melodious one. She is ignorant, vulgar and forward, but her heart is generous withal. For instance, she would help a neighbour's sick child; she would probably kill the child, but her intentions would be to cure it; she would be more at home helping a drayman to lift a fallen horse. She is dressed in a rather soiled grey dress and a vivid purple blouse; in her hair is a huge comb, ornamented with huge coloured beads. She enters with a gliding step, beaming smile and nodding head.* BOYLE *receives them effusively.*]

BOYLE. Come on in, Mrs. Madigan; come on in; I was afraid you weren't comin'. . . . [*Slyly.*] There's some people able to dhress, ay, Joxer?

JOXER. Fair as the blossoms that bloom in the May, an' sweet as the scent of the new mown hay. . . . Ah, well she may wear them.

MRS. MADIGAN [*looking at* MARY]. I know some as are as sweet as the blossoms in the May—oh, no names, no pack dhrill!°

BOYLE. An', now, I'll inthroduce the pair o' yous to Mary's intended: Mr. Bentham, this is Mrs. Madigan, an oul' back-parlour neighbour, that, if she could help it at all, ud never see a body shuk!

BENTHAM [*rising, and tentatively shaking the hand of* MRS. MADIGAN]. I'm sure, it's a great pleasure to know you, Mrs. Madigan.

MRS. MADIGAN. An' I'm goin' to tell you, Mr. Bentham, you're goin' to get as nice a bit o' skirt in Mary, there, as ever you seen in

your puff. Not like some of the dhressed up dolls that's knockin' about lookin' for men when it's a skelpin'° they want. I remember as well as I remember yestherday, the day she was born—of a Tuesday, the 25th o' June, in the year 1901, at thirty-three minutes past wan in the day be Foley's clock, the pub at the corner o' the street. A cowld day it was too, for the season o' the year, an' I remember sayin' to Joxer, there, who I met comin' up th' stairs, that the new arrival in Boyle's ud grow up a hardy chiselur if it lived, an' that she'd be somethin' one o' these days that nobody suspected, an' so signs on it, here she is today, goin' to be married to a young man lookin' as if he'd be fit to commensurate in any position in life it ud please God to call him!

BOYLE [*effusively*]. Sit down, Mrs. Madigan, sit down, me oul' sport. [*To* BENTHAM.] This is Joxer Daly, Past Chief Ranger of the Dear Little Shamrock Branch of the Irish National Foresters, an oul' front-top neighbour, that never despaired, even in the darkest days of Ireland's sorra.

JOXER. Nil desperandum, Captain, nil desperandum.

BOYLE. Sit down, Joxer, sit down. The two of us was often in a tight corner.

MRS. BOYLE. Ay, in Foley's snug!

JOXER. An' we kem out of it flyin', we kem out of it flyin', Captain.

BOYLE. An', now, for a dhrink—I know yous won't refuse an oul' friend.

MRS. MADIGAN [*to* JUNO]. Is Johnny not well, Mrs. . . .

MRS. BOYLE [*warningly*]. S-s-s-sh.

MRS. MADIGAN. Oh, the poor darlin'.

BOYLE. Well, Mrs. Madigan, is it tay or what?

MRS. MADIGAN. Well, speakin' for meself, I jus' had me tay a minute ago, an' I'm afraid to dhrink any more—I'm never the same when I dhrink too much tay. Thanks, all the same, Mr. Boyle.

BOYLE. Well, what about a bottle o' stout or a dhrop o' whisky?

MRS. MADIGAN. A bottle o' stout ud be a

---

pack dhrill formality

skelpin' spanking

little too heavy for me stummock afther me tay. . . . A-a-ah, I'll thry the ball o' malt.

[BOYLE *prepares the whisky.*]

MRS. MADIGAN. There's nothin' like a ball o'
5 malt occasional like—too much of it isn't good. [*To* BOYLE, *who is adding water.*] Ah, God, Johnny, don't put too much wather on it! [*She drinks.*] I suppose yous'll be lavin' this place.

10 BOYLE. I'm looking for a place near the sea; I'd like the place that you might say was me cradle, to be me grave as well. The sea is always callin' me.

JOXER. She is callin', callin', callin', in the
15 win', an' on the sea.

BOYLE. Another dhrop o' whisky, Mrs. Madigan?

MRS. MADIGAN. Well, now, it ud be hard to refuse seein' the suspicious times that's in it.°
20 BOYLE [*with a commanding gesture*]. Song! . . . Juno . . . Mary . . . "Home to Our Mount'-ins"!

MRS. MADIGAN [*enthusiastically*]. Hear, hear!

25 JOXER. Oh, tha's a darlin song, a daarlin' song!

MARY [*bashfully*]. Ah, no, da; I'm not in a singin' humour.

MRS. MADIGAN. Gawn with you, child, an'
30 you only goin' to be marrid; I remember as well as I remember yesterday,—it was on a lovely August evenin', exactly, accordin' to date, fifteen years ago, come the Tuesday folleyin' the nex' that's comin' on, when me own
35 man (the Lord be good to him) an' me was sittin' shy together in a doty° little nook on a counthry road, adjacent to The Stiles. "That'll scratch your lovely, little white neck," says he, ketchin' hould of a danglin' bramble branch,
40 holdin' clusters of the loveliest flowers you ever seen, an' breakin' it off, so that his arm fell, accidental like, roun' me waist, an' as I felt it tightenin', an' tightenin', an tightenin', I thought me buzzum was every minute goin'
45 to burst out into a roystherin' song about

that's in it   that we live in
doty   cosy

The little green leaves that were shakin'
                                       [on the threes,
The gallivantin' butterflies, an' buzzin'
                                       [o' the bees!
BOYLE. Ordher for the song!   50
JUNO. Come on, Mary—we'll do our best.

[JUNO *and* MARY *stand up, and choosing a suitable position, sing simply "Home to Our Mountains."*]

[*They bow to company, and return to their*   55
places.]

BOYLE [*emotionally, at the end of the song*]. Lull . . . me . . . to . . . rest!

JOXER [*clapping his hands*]. Bravo, bravo! Darlin' girulls, darlin' girulls!   60

MRS. MADIGAN. Juno, I never seen you in better form.

BENTHAM. Very nicely rendered indeed.

MRS. MADIGAN. A noble call, a noble call!

MRS. BOYLE. What about yourself, Mrs.   65
Madigan? [*After some coaxing,* MRS. MADIGAN *rises, and in a quavering voice sings the following verse.*]

If I were a blackbird I'd whistle and sing;
I'd follow the ship that my thrue love was in;   70
An' on the top riggin', I'd there build
                                       [me nest,
An' at night I would sleep on me Willie's
                                       [white breast!
[*Becoming husky, amid applause, she sits*   75
down.]

MRS. MADIGAN. Ah, me voice is too husky now, Juno; though I remember the time when Maisie Madigan could sign like a nightingale at matin' time. I remember as well as I remem-   80
ber yesterday, at a party given to celebrate the comin' of the first chiselur to Annie an' Benny Jimeson—who was the barber, yous may remember, in Henrietta Street, that, afther Easter Week, hung out a green, white an'   85
orange° pole, an', then, when the Tans° started their Jazz dancin', whipped it in agen, an'

green, white an' orange   the Irish national colors
Tans   or Black-and-Tans, the English troops that attempted to police Dublin and other parts of Ireland during the civil war. The reprisals with which the English countered Irish terrorism made the "Tans" both dreaded and detested.

stuck out a red, white an' blue° wan instead,
givin' as an excuse that a barber's pole was
strictly non-political—singin' "An You'll Remember Me," with the top notes quiverin' in
5 a dead hush of pethrified attention, folleyed
by a clappin' o' han's that shuk the tumblers
on the table, an' capped be Jimeson, the barber, sayin' that it was the best rendherin' of
"You'll Remember Me" he ever heard in his
10 natural!

BOYLE [peremptorily]. Ordher for Joxer's
song!

JOXER. Ah, no, I couldn't; don't ass me,
Captain.

15   BOYLE. Joxer's song, Joxer's song—give us
wan of your shut-eyed wans. [JOXER settles
himself in his chair; takes a drink; clears his
throat; solemnly closes his eyes, and begins to
sing in a very querulous voice.]

20   She is far from the lan' where her
                    [young hero sleeps,
An' lovers around her are sighing.
[He hesitates.]
An' lovers around her are sighin'
25   [. . . sighin' . . . sighin' . . .
[A pause.]
BOYLE [imitating JOXER].
And lovers around her are sighing!
What's the use of you thryin' to sing the song
30 if you don't know it?

MARY. Thry another one, Mr. Daly—maybe
you'd be more fortunate.

MRS. MADIGAN. Gawn, Joxer, thry another
wan.

35   JOXER [starting again].
I have heard the mavis singin' his love
                    [song to the morn;
I have seen the dew-dhrop clingin' to the
                    [rose jus' newly born;
40   but . . . but . . . [frantically] to the rose jus'
                    [newly born . . . newly born . . . born.
JOHNNY. Mother, put on the gramophone,
for God's sake, an' stop Joxer's bawlin'.

BOYLE [commandingly]. Gramophone! . . . I
45 hate to see fellas thryin' to do what they're not
able to do. [BOYLE arranges the gramophone,

red, white an' blue   the English colors

and is about to start it, when voices are heard
of persons descending the stairs.]

MRS. BOYLE [warningly]. Whisht, Jack, don't
put it on, don't put it on yet; this must be   50
poor Mrs. Tancred comin' down to go to the
hospital—I forgot all about them bringin' the
body to the church tonight. Open the door,
Mary, an' give them a bit o' light.

[MARY opens the door, and MRS. TANCRED—   55
a very old woman, obviously shaken by the
death of her son—appears, accompanied by
several NEIGHBOURS. The first few phrases are
spoken before they appear.]

FIRST NEIGHBOUR. It's a sad journey we're   60
goin' on, but God's good, an' the Republicans
won't be always down.

MRS. TANCRED. Ah, what good is that to me
now? Whether they're up or down—it won't
bring me darlin' boy from the grave.   65

MRS. BOYLE. Come in an' have a hot cup o'
tay, Mrs. Tancred, before you go.

MRS. TANCRED. Ah, I can take nothin' now,
Mrs. Boyle—I won't be long afther him.

FIRST NEIGHBOUR. Still an' all, he died a noble   70
death, an' we'll bury him like a king.

MRS. TANCRED. An' I'll go on livin' like a
pauper. Ah, what's the pains I suffered bringin'
him into the world to carry him to his cradle,
to the pains I'm sufferin' now, carryin' him out   75
o' the world to bring him to his grave!

MARY. It would be better for you not to go
at all, Mrs. Tancred, but to stay at home beside
the fire with some o' the neighbours.

MRS. TANCRED. I seen the first of him, an' I'll   80
see the last of him.

MRS. BOYLE. You'd want a shawl, Mrs. Tancred; it's a cowld night, an' the win's blowin'
sharp.

MRS. MADIGAN [rushing out]. I've a shawl   85
above.

MRS. TANCRED. Me home is gone, now; he
was me only child, an' to think that he was
lyin' for a whole night stretched out on the
side of a lonely counthry lane, with his head,   90
his darlin' head, that I ofen kissed an' fondled,
half hidden in the wather of a runnin' brook.
An' I'm told he was the leadher of the ambush
where me nex' door neighbour, Mrs. Mannin',

lost her Free State soldier son. An' now here's the two of us oul' women, standin' one on each side of a scales o' sorra, balanced be the bodies of our two dead darlin' sons. [MRS. MADIGAN *returns, and wraps a shawl around her.*] God bless you, Mrs. Madigan. . . . [*She moves slowly towards the door.*] Mother o' God, Mother o' God, have pity on the pair of us! . . . O Blessed Virgin, where were you when me darlin' son was riddled with bullets, when me darlin' son was riddled with bullets! . . . Sacred Heart of the Crucified Jesus, take away our hearts o' stone . . . an' give us hearts o' flesh! . . . Take away this murdherin' hate . . . an' give us Thine own eternal love!

[*They pass out of the room.*]

MRS. BOYLE [*explanatorily to* BENTHAM]. That was Mrs. Tancred of the two-pair back; her son was found, e'er yestherday, lyin' out beyant Finglas riddled with bullets. A die-hard he was, be all accounts. He was a nice quiet boy, but lattherly he went to hell, with his Republic first, an' Republic last an' Republic over all. He ofen took tay with us here, in the oul' days, an' Johnny, there, an' him used to be always together.

JOHNNY. Am I always to be havin' to tell you that he was no friend o' mine? I never cared for him, an' he could never stick me. It's not because he was Commandant of the Battalion that I was Quarther-Masther of, that we were friends.

MRS. BOYLE. He's gone, now—the Lord be good to him! God help his poor oul' creature of a mother, for no matther whose friend or enemy he was, he was her poor son.

BENTHAM. The whole thing is terrible, Mrs. Boyle; but the only way to deal with a mad dog is to destroy him.

MRS. BOYLE. An' to think of me forgettin' about him bein' brought to the church tonight, an' we singin' an' all, but it was well we hadn't the gramophone goin', anyhow.

BOYLE. Even if we had aself. We've nothin' to do with these things, one way or t'other. That's the Government's business, an' let them do what we're payin' them for doin'.

MRS. BOYLE. I'd like to know how a body's not to mind these things; look at the way they're afther leavin' the people in this very house. Hasn't the whole house, nearly, been massacreed? There's young Mrs. Dougherty's husband with his leg off; Mrs. Travers that had her son blew up be a mine in Inchegeela, in Co. Cork; Mrs. Mannin' that lost wan of her sons in an ambush a few weeks ago, an' now, poor Mrs. Tancred's only child gone West with his body made a collandher of. Sure, if it's not our business, I don't know whose business it is.

BOYLE. Here, there, that's enough about them things; they don't affect us, an' we needn't give a damn. If they want a wake, well, let them have a wake. When I was a sailor, I was always resigned to meet with a watery grave; an', if they want to be soldiers, well, there's no use o' them squealin' when they meet a soldier's fate.

JOXER. Let me like a soldier fall—me breast expandin' to th' ball!

MRS. BOYLE. In wan way, she deserves all she got; for lately, she let th' die-hards make an open house of th' place; an' for th' last couple of months, either when th' sun was risin', or when th' sun was settin', you had C.I.D. men° burstin' into your room, assin' you where were you born, where were you christened, where were you married, an' where would you be buried!

JOHNNY. For God's sake, let us have no more o' this talk.

MRS. MADIGAN. What about Mr. Boyle's song before we start th' gramophone?

MARY [*getting her hat, and putting it on*]. Mother, Charlie and I are goin' out for a little sthroll.

MRS. BOYLE. All right, darlin'.

BENTHAM [*going out with* MARY]. We won't be long away, Mrs. Boyle.

MRS. MADIGAN. Gwan, Captain, gwan.

BOYLE. E-e-e-e-eh, I'd want to have a few more jars in me, before I'd be in fettle for singin'.

C.I.D. men from the Criminal Investigation Department of Scotland Yard; later, Free State police agents on the trail of the die-hards

JOXER. Give us that poem you writ t'other day. [*To the rest.*] Aw, it's a darlin' poem, a daarlin' poem.

MRS. BOYLE. God bless us, is he startin' to write poetry!

BOYLE [*rising to his feet*]. E-e-e-e-eh. [*He recites in an emotional, consequential manner the following verses.*]

Shawn an' I were friends, sir, to me he was
[all in all.
His work was very heavy and his wages
[were very small.
None betther on th' beach as Docker, I'll
[go bail,
'Tis now I'm feelin' lonely, for today he
[lies in jail.
He was not what some call pious—seldom
[at church or prayer;
For the greatest scoundrels I know, sir, goes
[every Sunday there.
Fond of his pint—well, rather, but hated
[the Boss by creed
But never refused a copper to comfort a pal
[in need.

E-e-e-e-eh. [*He sits down.*]

MRS. MADIGAN. Grand, grand; you should folley that up, you should folley that up.

JOXER. It's a daarlin' poem!

BOYLE [*delightedly*]. E-e-e-e-eh.

JOHNNY. Are yous goin' to put on th' gramophone tonight, or are yous not?

MRS. BOYLE. Gwan, Jack, put on a record.

MRS. MADIGAN. Gwan, Captain, gwan.

BOYLE. Well, yous'll want to keep a dead silence.

[*He sets a record, starts the machine, and it begins to play "If you're Irish, come into the Parlour." As the tune is in full blare, the door is suddenly opened by a brisk, little bald-headed man, dressed circumspectly in a black suit; he glares fiercely at all in the room; he is "NEEDLE NUGENT," a tailor. He carries his hat in his hands.*]

NUGENT [*loudly, above the noise of the gramophone*]. Are yous goin' to have that thing bawlin' an' the funeral of Mrs. Tancred's son passin' the house? Have none of yous any respect for the Irish people's National regard for the dead?

[*BOYLE stops the gramophone.*]

MRS. BOYLE. Maybe, Needle Nugent, it's nearly time we had a little less respect for the dead, an' a little more regard for the livin'.

MRS. MADIGAN. We don't want you, Mr. Nugent, to teach us what we learned at our mother's knee. You don't look yourself as if you were dyin' of grief; if y'ass Maisie Madigan anything, I'd call you a real thrue die-hard an' live-soft Republican, attendin' Republican funerals in the day, an' stoppin' up half the night makin' suits for the Civic Guards!

[*Persons are heard running down to the street, some saying, "Here it is, here it is." NUGENT withdraws, and the rest, except JOHNNY, go to the window looking into the street, and look out. Sounds of a crowd coming nearer are heard; a portion are singing.*]

To Jesus' Heart all burning
With fervent love for men,
My heart with fondest yearning
Shall raise its joyful strain.
While ages course along,
Blest be with loudest song,
The Sacred Heart of Jesus
By every heart and tongue.

MRS. BOYLE. Here's the hearse, here's the hearse!

BOYLE. There's t'oul' mother walkin' behin' the coffin.

MRS. MADIGAN. You can hardly see the coffin with the wreaths.

JOXER. Oh, it's a darlin' funeral, a daarlin' funeral!

MRS. MADIGAN. We'd have a betther view from the street.

BOYLE. Yes—this place ud give you a crick in your neck.

[*They leave the room, and go down. JOHNNY sits moodily by the fire.*]

[*A young man enters; he looks at JOHNNY for a moment.*]

THE YOUNG MAN. Quarter-Master Boyle.

JOHNNY [*with a start*]. The Mobilizer!

THE YOUNG MAN. You're not at the funeral?

JOHNNY. I'm not well.

THE YOUNG MAN. I'm glad I've found you; you were stoppin' at your aunt's; I called there but you'd gone. I've to give you an ordher to attend a Battalion Staff meetin' the night afther tomorrow.

JOHNNY. Where?

5 THE YOUNG MAN. I don't know; you're to meet me at the Pillar at eight o'clock; then we're to go to a place I'll be told of tonight; there we'll meet a mothor that'll bring us to the meeting. They think you might be able to 10 know somethin' about them that gave the bend where Commandant Tancred was shelterin'.

JOHNNY. I'm not goin', then. I know nothing about Tancred.

THE YOUNG MAN [*at the door*]. You'd betther come for your own sake—remember your oath.

15 JOHNNY [*passionately*]. I won't go! Haven't I done enough for Ireland! I've lost me arm, an' me hip's desthroyed so that I'll never be able to walk right agen! Good God, haven't I done enough for Ireland?

20 THE YOUNG MAN. Boyle, no man can do enough for Ireland!

[*He goes.*]

[*Faintly in the distance the crowd is heard saying:*]

25 Hail, Mary, full of grace, the Lord is with [Thee;

Blessed art Thou amongst women, and [blessed, etc.

The Curtain Falls

ACT III

[SCENE. *The same as Act II. It is about half-* 30 *past six on a November evening; a bright fire is burning in the grate;* MARY, *dressed to go out, is sitting on a chair by the fire, leaning forward, her hands under her chin, her elbows on her knees. A look of dejection, mingled with* 35 *uncertain anxiety, is on her face. A lamp, turned low, is lighting on the table. The votive light under the picture of the Virgin gleams more redly than ever.* MRS BOYLE *is putting on her hat and coat. It is two months later.*]

40 MRS. BOYLE. An' has Bentham never even written to you since—not one line for the past month?

MARY [*tonelessly*]. Not even a line, mother.

MRS BOYLE. That's very curious. . . . What 45 came between the two of yous at all? To leave

you so sudden, an' yous so great together. . . . To go away t' England, an' not to even leave you his address. . . . The way he was always bringin' you to dances, I thought he was mad afther you. Are you sure you said nothin' to 50 him?

MARY. No, mother—at least nothing that could possibly explain his givin' me up.

MRS. BOYLE. You know you're a bit hasty at times, Mary, an' say things you shouldn't say. 55

MARY. I never said to him what I shouldn't say, I'm sure of that.

MRS. BOYLE. How are you sure of it?

MARY. Because I love him with all my heart and soul, mother. Why, I don't know; I often 60 thought to myself that he wasn't the man poor Jerry was, but I couldn't help loving him, all the same.

MRS. BOYLE. But you shouldn't be frettin' the way you are; when a woman loses a man, 65 she never knows what she's afther losin', to be sure, but, then, she never knows what she's afther gainin', either. You're not the one girl of a month ago—you look like one pinin' away. It's long ago I had a right to bring you to the 70 doctor, instead of waitin' till tonight.

MARY. There's no necessity, really, mother, to go to the doctor; nothing serious is wrong with me—I'm run down and disappointed, that's all. 75

MRS BOYLE. I'll not wait another minute; I don't like the look of you at all. . . . I'm afraid we made a mistake in throwin' over poor Jerry. . . . He'd have been betther for you than that Bentham. 80

MARY. Mother, the best man for a woman is the one for whom she has the most love, and Charlie had it all.

MRS. BOYLE. Well, there's one thing to be said for him—he couldn't have been thinkin' 85 of the money, or he wouldn't ha' left you. . . . It must ha' been somethin' else.

MARY [*wearily*]. I don't know . . . I don't know, mother . . . only I think . . .

MRS. BOYLE. What d'ye think? 90

MARY. I imagine . . . he thought . . . we weren't . . . good enough for him.

MRS. BOYLE. An' what was he himself, only a school teacher? Though I don't blame him

for fightin' shy of people like that Joxer fella an' that oul' Madigan wan—nice sort o' people for your father to inthroduce to a man like Mr. Bentham. You might have told me all about
5 this before now, Mary; I don't know why you like to hide everything from your mother; you knew Bentham, an' I'd ha' known nothin' about it if it hadn't bin for the Will; an' it was only today, afther long coaxin', that you let
10 out that he'd left you.

MARY. It would have been useless to tell you—you wouldn't understand.

MRS. BOYLE [*hurt*]. Maybe not. . . . Maybe I wouldn't understand. . . . Well, we'll be off
15 now. [*She goes over to the door left, and speaks to* BOYLE *inside.*]

MRS. BOYLE. We're goin' now to the doctor's. Are you goin' to get up this evenin'?

BOYLE [*from inside*]. The pain in me legs is
20 terrible! It's me should be poppin' off to the doctor instead o' Mary, the way I feel.

MRS BOYLE. Sorra mend you! A nice way you were in last night—carried in in a frog's march,° dead to the world. If that's the way
25 you'll go on when you get the money it'll be the grave for you, an asylum for me and the Poorhouse for Johnny.

BOYLE. I thought you were goin'?

MRS. BOYLE. That's what has you as you are
30 —you can't bear to be spoken to. Knowin' the way we are, up to our ears in debt, it's a wondher you wouldn't ha' got up to go to th' solicitor's an' see if we could ha' gettin' a little o' the money even.

35 BOYLE [*shouting*]. I can't be goin' up there night, noon an' mornin', can I? He can't give the money till he gets it, can he? I can't get blood out of a turnip, can I?

MRS. BOYLE. It's nearly two months since we
40 heard of the Will, an' the money seems as far off as ever. . . . I suppose you know we owe twenty poun's to oul' Murphy?

BOYLE. I've a faint recollection of you tellin' me that before.

45 MRS. BOYLE. Well, you'll go over to the shop yourself for the things in future—I'll face him no more.

BOYLE. I thought you said you were goin'?
MRS. BOYLE. I'm goin' now; come on, Mary.
BOYLE. Ey, Juno, ey! 50
MRS. BOYLE. Well, what d'ye want now?
BOYLE. Is there e'er a bottle o' stout left?
MRS. BOYLE. There's two o' them here still.

BOYLE. Show us in one o' them an' leave t'other there till I get up. An' throw us in the 55 paper that's on the table, an' the bottle o' Sloan's Liniment that's in th' drawer.

MRS. BOYLE [*getting the liniment and the stout*]. What paper is it you want—the Messenger? 60

BOYLE. *Messenger! The News o' the World!*

[MRS. BOYLE *brings in the things asked for and comes out again.*]

MRS. BOYLE [*at door*]. Mind the candle, now, an' don't burn the house over our heads. I left 65 t'other bottle o' stout on the table.

[*She puts bottle of stout on table. She goes out with* MARY. *A cork is heard popping inside. A pause; then outside the door is heard the voice of* JOXER *lilting softly:* "Me pipe I'll 70 smoke, as I dhrive me moke . . . are you . . . there . . . More . . . aar . . . i . . . tee!" *A gentle knock is heard and, after a pause, the door opens, and* JOXER, *followed by* NUGENT, *enters.*]

JOXER. Be God, they must all be out; I was 75 thinkin' there was somethin' up when he didn't answer the signal. We seen Juno an' Mary goin', but I didn't see him, an' it's very seldom he escapes me.

NUGENT. He's not goin' to escape me—he's 80 not goin' to be let go to the fair altogether.

JOXER. Sure, the house couldn't hould them lately; an' he goin' about like a mastherpiece of the Free State counthry; forgettin' their friends; forgettin' God—wouldn't even lift his 85 hat passin' a chapel! Sure they were bound to get a dhrop! An' you really think there's no money comin' to him afther all?

NUGENT. Not as much as a red rex,° man; I've been a bit anxious this long time over me 90 money, an' I went up to the solicitor's to find out all I could—ah, man, they were goin' to throw me down the stairs. They toul' me that the oul' cock himself had the stairs worn away

---

in a frog's march sprawled prone   **rex** cent

comin' up afther it, an' they black in the face tellin' him he'd get nothing'. Some way or another that the Will is writ he won't be entitled to get as much as a make!°

5 JOXER. Ah, I thought there was somethin' curious about the whole thing; I've bin havin' sthrange dreams for the last couple o' weeks. An' I notice that that Bentham fella doesn't be comin' here now—there must be somethin' on 10 the mat° there too. Anyhow, who, in the name o' God, ud leave anythin' to that oul' bummer? Sure it ud be unnatural. An' the way Juno an' him's been throwin' their weight about for the last few months! Ah him that goes a borrowin' 15 goes a sorrowin'!

NUGENT. Well, he's not goin' to throw his weight about in the suit I made for him much longer. I'm tellin' you seven poun's aren't to be found growin' on the bushes these days.

20 JOXER. An' there isn't hardly a neighbour in the whole street that hasn't lent him money on the strength of what he was goin' to get, but they're after backing the wrong horse. Wasn't it a mercy o' God that I'd nothin' to give 25 him! The softy I am, you know, I'd ha' lent him me last juice! I must have had somebody's good prayers. Ah, afther all, an honest man's the noblest work o' God! [BOYLE *coughs inside.*] Whisht, damn it, he must be inside in bed.

30 NUGENT. Inside o' bed or outside of it he's goin' to pay me for that suit, or give it back— he'll not climb up my back as easily as he thinks.

JOXER. Gwan in at wanst, man, an' get it off 35 him, an' don't be a fool.

NUGENT [*going to the door left, opening it and looking in*]. Ah, don't disturb yourself, Mr. Boyle; I hope you're not sick?

BOYLE. Th' oul' legs, Mr. Nugent, the oul' 40 legs.

NUGENT. I just called over to see if you could let me have anything off the suit?

BOYLE. E-e-e-eh, how much is this it is?

NUGENT. It's the same as it was at the start— 45 seven poun's.

BOYLE. I'm glad you kem, Mr. Nugent; I want a good heavy topcoat—Irish frieze, if you have it. How much would a top-coat like that be now?

NUGENT. About six poun's. 50

BOYLE. Six poun's—six an' seven, six an' seven is thirteen—that'll be thirteen poun's I'll owe you.

[JOXER *slips the bottle of stout that is on the table into his pocket.* NUGENT *rushes into the* 55 *room, and returns with the suit on his arm; he pauses at the door.*]

NUGENT. You'll owe me no thirteen poun's. Maybe you think you're bether able to owe it than pay it! 60

BOYLE [*frantically*]. Here, come back to hell ower that—where're you goin' with them clothes o' mine?

NUGENT. Where am I goin' with them clothes o' yours? Well, I like your damn cheek! 65

BOYLE. Here, what am I going to dhress meself in when I'm goin' out?

NUGENT. What do I care what you dhress yourself in? You can put yourself in a bolsther cover, if you like. 70

[*He goes towards the other door, followed by* JOXER.]

JOXER. What'll he dhress himself in! Gentleman Jack an' his frieze coat!

[*They go out.*] 75

BOYLE [*inside*]. Ey, Nugent, ey, Mr. Nugent, Mr. Nugent!

[*After a pause* BOYLE *enters hastily, buttoning the braces of his moleskin trousers; his coat and vest are on his arm; he throws these* 80 *on a chair and hurries to the door on right.*]

BOYLE. Ey, Mr. Nugent, Mr. Nugent!

JOXER [*meeting him at the door*]. What's up, what's wrong, Captain?

BOYLE. Nugent's been here an' took away 85 me suit—the only things I had to go out in!

JOXER. Tuk your suit—for God's sake! An' what were you doin' while he was takin' them?

BOYLE. I was in bed when he stole in like a thief in the night, an' before I knew even what 90 he was thinkin' of, he whipped them from the chair, an' was off like a redshank!°

---

make halfpenny
on the mat the matter

redshank backcountryman, proverbially fast and elusive

JOXER. An' what, in the name o' God, did he do that for?

BOYLE. What did he do it for? How the hell do I know what he done it for? Jealousy an' spite, I suppose.

JOXER. Did he not say what he done it for?

BOYLE. Amn't I afther tellin' you that he had them whipped up an' was gone before I could open me mouth?

JOXER. That was a very sudden thing to do; there mus' be somethin' behin' it. Did he hear anythin', I wondher?

BOYLE. Did he hear anythin'?—you talk very queer, Joxer—what could he hear?

JOXER. About you not gettin' the money, in some way or t'other?

BOYLE. An' what ud prevent me from gettin' th' money?

JOXER. That's jus' what I was thinkin'—what ud prevent you from gettin' the money—nothin', as far as I can see.

BOYLE [looking round for bottle of stout with an exclamation]. Aw, holy God!

JOXER. What's up, Jack?

BOYLE. He must have afther lifted the bottle o' stout that Juno left on the table!

JOXER [horrified]. Ah, no, ah, no! He wouldn't be afther doin' that, now.

BOYLE. An' who done it then? Juno left a bottle o' stout here, an' it's gone—it didn't walk, did it?

JOXER. Oh, that's shockin'; ah, man's inhumanity to man makes countless thousands mourn!

MRS. MADIGAN [appearing at the door]. I hope I'm not disturbin' you in any discussion on your forthcomin' legacy—if I may use the word—an' that you'll let me have a barny° for a minute or two with you, Mr. Boyle.

BOYLE. [uneasily]. To be sure, Mrs. Madigan —an oul' friends always welcome.

JOXER. Come in the evenin', come in th' mornin'; come when you're assed, or come without warnin', Mrs. Madigan.

BOYLE. Sit down, Mrs. Madigan.

barny   argument

MRS. MADIGAN [ominously]. Th' few words I have to say can be said standin'. Puttin' aside all formularies, I suppose you remember me lendin' you some time ago three poun's that I raised on blankets an' furniture in me uncle's?

BOYLE. I remember it well. I have it recorded in me book—three poun's five shillin's from Maisie Madigan, raised on articles pawned; an', item: fourpence, given to make up the price of a pint, on th' principle that no bird ever flew on wan wing; all to be repaid at par, when the ship comes home.

MRS. MADIGAN. Well, ever since I shoved in the blankets I've been perishing with th' cowld, an' I've decided, if I'll be too hot in th' nex' world aself, I'm not goin' to be too cowld in this wan; an' consequently, I want me three poun's, if you please.

BOYLE. This is a very sudden demand, Mrs. Madigan, an' can't be met; but I'm willin' to give you a receipt in full, in full.

MRS. MADIGAN. Come on, out with th' money, an' don't be jack-actin'.

BOYLE. You can't get blood out of a turnip, can you?

MRS. MADIGAN [rushing over and shaking him]. Gimme me money, y'oul' reprobate, or I'll shake the worth of it out of you!

BOYLE. Ey, houl' on, there; houl' on, there! You'll wait for your money now, me lassie!

MRS. MADIGAN [looking around the room and seeing the gramophone]. I'll wait for it, will I? Well, I'll not wait long; if I can't get th' cash, I'll get th' worth of it. [She catches up the gramophone.]

BOYLE. Ey, ey, there, where'r you goin' with that?

MRS. MADIGAN. I'm goin' to th' pawn to get me three quid five shillin's; I'll bring you th' ticket, an' then you can do what you like, me bucko.

BOYLE. You can't touch that, you can't touch that! It's not my property, an' it's not ped for yet!

MRS. MADIGAN. So much th' bETTher. It'll be an ayse to me conscience, for I'm takin' what

doesn't belong to you. You're not goin' to be
swankin' it like a paycock with Maisie Madigan's money—I'll pull some o' the gorgeous
feathers out o' your tail!

5 [*She goes off with the gramophone.*]

BOYLE. What's th' world comin' to at all?
I ass you, Joxer Daly, is there any morality
left anywhere?

JOXER. I wouldn't ha' believed it, only I seen
10 it with me own two eyes. I didn't think Maisie
Madigan was that sort of a woman; she has
either a sup taken, or she's heard somethin'.

BOYLE. Heard somethin'—about what, if it's
not any harm to ass you?

15 JOXER. She must ha' heard some rumour or
other that you weren't goin' to get th' money.

BOYLE. Who says I'm not goin' to get th'
money?

JOXER. Sure, I know—I was only sayin'.

20 BOYLE. Only sayin' what?

JOXER. Nothin'.

BOYLE. You were goin' to say somethin',
don't be a twisther.°

JOXER [*angrily*]. Who's a twisther?

25 BOYLE. Why don't you speak your mind,
then?

JOXER. You never twisted yourself—no, you
wouldn't know how!

BOYLE. Did you ever know me to twist; did
30 you ever know me to twist?

JOXER [*fiercely*]. Did you ever do anythin'
else! Sure, you can't believe a word that comes
out o' your mouth.

BOYLE. Here, get out, ower o' this; I always
35 knew you were a prognosticator an' a procrastinator!

JOXER [*going out as* JOHNNY *comes in*]. The
anchor's weighed, farewell, re . . . mem . . . ber
. . . me. Jacky Boyle, Esquire, infernal rogue
40 an' damned liar!

JOHNNY. Joxer an' you at it agen?—when are
you goin' to have a little respect for yourself,
an' not be always makin' a show of us all?

BOYLE. Are you goin' to lecture me now?

45 JOHNNY. Is mother back from the doctor yet,

twisther liar

with Mary?

[Mrs. BOYLE *enters; it is apparent from the
serious look on her face that something has
happened. She takes off her hat and coat without a word and puts them by. She then sits*
50 *down near the fire, and there is a few moments'
pause.*]

BOYLE. Well, what did the doctor say about
Mary?

MRS. BOYLE [*in an earnest manner and with*
55 *suppressed agitation*]. Sit down here, Jack; I've
something to say to you . . . about Mary.

BOYLE [*awed by her manner*]. About . . .
Mary?

MRS. BOYLE. Close that door there and sit
60 down here.

BOYLE [*closing the door*]. More throuble in
our native land, is it? [*He sits down.*] Well,
what is it?

MRS. BOYLE. It's about Mary.

65 BOYLE. Well, what about Mary—there's
nothin' wrong with her, is there?

MRS. BOYLE. I'm sorry to say there's a gradle
wrong with her.

BOYLE. A gradle wrong with her! [*Peevishly.*]
70 First Johnny an' now Mary; is the whole house
goin' to become an hospital! It's not consumption, is it?

MRS. BOYLE. No . . . it's not consumption . . .
it's worse.

75 JOHNNY. Worse! Well, we'll have to get her
into some place ower this, there's no one here
to mind her.

MRS. BOYLE. We'll all have to mind her now.
You might as well know now, Johnny, as an-
80 other time. [*To* BOYLE.] D'ye you know what
the doctor said to me about her, Jack?

BOYLE. How ud I know—I wasn't there,
was I?

MRS. BOYLE. He told me to get her married
85 at wanst.

BOYLE. Married at wanst! An' why did he
say the like o' that?

MRS. BOYLE. Because Mary's goin' to have a
baby in a short time.
90 BOYLE. Goin' to have a baby!—my God,
what'll Bentham say when he hears that?

MRS. BOYLE. Are you blind, man, that you can't see that it was Bentham that has done this wrong to her?

BOYLE [passionately]. Then he'll marry her, he'll have to marry her!

MRS. BOYLE. You know he's gone to England, an' God knows where he is now.

BOYLE. I'll folley him, I'll folley him, an' bring him back, an' make him do her justice. The scoundrel, I might ha' known what he was, with his yogees an' his prawna!

MRS. BOYLE. We'll have to keep it quiet till we see what we can do.

BOYLE. Oh, isn't this a nice thing to come on top o' me, an' the state I'm in! A pretty show I'll be to Joxer an' to that oul' wan, Madigan! Amn't I afther goin' through enough without havin' to go through this!

MRS. BOYLE. What you an' I'll have to go through'll be nothin to what poor Mary'll have to go through; for you an' me is middlin' old, an' most of our years is spent; but Mary'll have maybe forty years to face an' handle, an' every wan of them'll be tainted with a bitter memory.

BOYLE. Where is she? Where is she till I tell her off? I'm tellin' you when I'm done with her she'll be a sorry girl!

MRS. BOYLE. I left her in me sisther's till I came to speak to you. You'll say nothin' to her, Jack; ever since she left school she's earned her livin', an' your fatherly care never throubled the poor girl.

BOYLE. Gwan, take her part agen her father! But I'll let you see whether I'll say nothin' to her or no! Her an' her readin'! That's more o' th' blasted nonsense that has the house fallin' down on top of us! What did th' likes of her, born in a tenement house, want with readin'? Her readin's afther bringin' her to a nice pass —oh, it's madnin', madnin', madnin'!

MRS. BOYLE. When she comes back say nothin' to her, Jack, or she'll leave this place.

BOYLE. Leave this place! Ay, she'll leave this place, an' quick too!

MRS. BOYLE. If Mary goes, I'll go with her.

BOYLE. Well, go with her! Well, go, th' pair o' yous! I lived before I seen yous, an' I can live when yous are gone. Isn't this a nice thing to come rollin' in on top o' me afther all your prayin' to St. Anthony an' The Little Flower. An' she's a child o' Mary, too—I wonder what'll the nuns think of her now? An it'll be bellows'd all over th' disthrict before you could say Jack Robinson; an' whenever I'm seen they'll whisper, "That's th' father of Mary Boyle that had th' kid be th' swank she used to go with; d'ye know, d'ye know?" To be sure they'll know—more about it than I will meself!

JOHNNY. She should be dhriven out o' th' house she's brought disgrace on!

MRS. BOYLE. Hush, you, Johnny. We needn't let it be bellows'd all over the place; all we've got to do is to leave this place quietly an' go somewhere where we're not known, an' nobody'll be the wiser.

BOYLE. You're talkin' like a two-year-oul', woman. Where'll we get a place ou' o' this?— places aren't that easily got.

MRS. BOYLE. But, Jack, when we get the money . . .

BOYLE. Money—what money?

MRS. BOYLE. Why, oul' Ellison's money, of course.

BOYLE. There's no money comin' from oul' Ellison, or any one else. Since you heard of wan trouble, you might as well hear of another. There's no money comin' to us at all— the Will's a wash out!

MRS. BOYLE. What are you sayin', man—no money?

JOHNNY. How could it be a wash out?

BOYLE. The boyo that's afther doin' it to Mary done it to me as well. The thick made out the Will wrong; he said in th' Will, only first cousin an' second cousin, instead of mentionin' our names, an' now any one that thinks he's a first cousin or second cousin t'oul' Ellison can claim the money as well as me, an' they're springin' up in hundreds, an' comin' from America an' Australia, thinkin' to get their whack out of it, while all the time the lawyers is gobblin' it up, till there's not as much as ud buy a stockin' for your lovely daughter's baby!

MRS. BOYLE. I don't believe it, I don't believe it, I don't believe it!

JOHNNY. Why did you nothin' about this before?

5 MRS. BOYLE. You're not serious, Jack; you're not serious!

BOYLE. I'm tellin' you the scholar, Bentham, made a banjax° o' th' Will; instead o' sayin', "th' rest o' me property to be divided between 10 me first cousin, Jack Boyle, an' me second cousin, Mick Finnegan, o' Santhry," he writ down only, "me first an' second cousins," an' the world an' his wife are afther th' property now.

15 MRS. BOYLE. Now, I know why Bentham left poor Mary in th' lurch; I can see it all now—oh, is there not even a middlin' honest man left in th' world?

JOHNNY [to BOYLE]. An' you let us run into 20 debt, an' you borreyed money from everybody to fill yourself with beer! An' now, you tell us the whole thing's a wash out! Oh, if it's thrue, I'm done with you, for you're worse than me sisther Mary!

25 BOYLE. You hole your tongue, d'ye hear? I'll not take any lip from you. Go an' get Bentham if you want satisfaction for all that's afther happenin' us.

JOHNNY. I won't hole me tongue, I won't hole 30 me tongue! I'll tell you what I think of you, father an' all as you are . . . you . . .

MRS. BOYLE. Johnny, Johnny, Johnny, for God's sake, be quiet!

JOHNNY. I'll not be quiet, I'll not be quiet; 35 he's a nice father, isn't he? Is it any wondher Mary went asthray, when . . .

MRS. BOYLE. Johnny, Johnny, for my sake be quiet—for your mother's sake!

BOYLE. I'm goin' out now to have a few 40 dhrinks with th' last few makes I have, an' tell that lassie o' yours not to be here when I come back; for if I lay me eyes on her, I'll lay me han's on her, an' if I lay me han's on her, I won't be accountable for me actions!

45 JOHNNY. Take care somebody doesn't lay his

banjax hodgepodge

han's on you—y'oul' . . .

MRS. BOYLE. Johnny, Johnny!

BOYLE [at door, about to go out]. Oh, a nice son, an' a nicer daughter, I have. [Calling loudly upstairs.] Joxer, Joxer, are you there? 50

JOXER [from a distance]. I'm here, More . . . ee . . . aar . . . i . . . tee!

BOYLE. I'm goin' down to Foley's—are you comin'?

JOXER. Come with you? With that sweet call 55 me heart is stirred; I'm only waiting for the word, an' I'll be with you, like a bird!

[BOYLE and JOXER pass the door going out.]

JOHNNY [throwing himself on the bed]. I've a nice sisther, an' a nice father, there's no 60 bettin' on it. I wish to God a bullet or a bomb had whipped me ou' o' this long ago! Not one o' yous, not one o' yous, have any thought for me!

MRS. BOYLE [with passionate remonstrance]. 65 If you don't whisht, Johnny, you'll drive me mad. Who has kep' th' home together for the past few years—only me. An' who'll have to bear th' biggest part o' this throuble but me—but whinin' an' whingin' isn't going to do any 70 good.

JOHNNY. You're to blame yourself for a gradle of it—givin' him his own way in everything, an' never assin' to check him, no matther what he done. Why didn't you look 75 afther th' money? why . . .

[There is a knock at the door; MRS. BOYLE opens it; JOHNNY rises on his elbow to look and listen; two men enter.]

FIRST MAN. We've been sent up be th' 80 Manager of the Hibernian Furnishing Co., Mrs. Boyle, to take back the furniture that was got a while ago.

MRS. BOYLE. Yous'll touch nothin' here—how do I know who yous are? 85

FIRST MAN [showing a paper]. There's the ordher, ma'am. [Reading.] A chest o' drawers, a table, wan easy an' two ordinary chairs; wan mirror; wan chestherfield divan, an' a wardrobe an' two vases. [To his comrade.] Come 90 on, Bill, it's afther knockin' off time already.

JOHNNY. For God's sake, mother, run down

to Foley's an' bring father back, or we'll be left
without a stick.

[*The men carry out the table.*]

MRS. BOYLE. What good would it be? You
heard what he said before he went out.

JOHNNY. Can't you thry? He ought to be
here, an' the like of this goin' on.

[MRS. BOYLE *puts a shawl around her, as*
MARY *enters.*]

MARY. What's up, mother? I met men carryin' away the table, an' everybody's talking
about us not gettin' the money after all.

MRS. BOYLE. Everythin's gone wrong, Mary,
everythin'. We're not gettin' a penny out o'
the Will, not a penny—I'll tell you all when I
come back; I'm goin' for your father.

[*She runs out.*]

JOHNNY [*to* MARY, *who has sat down by the
fire*]. It's a wondher you're not ashamed to
show your face here, afther what has happened.

[JERRY *enters slowly; there is a look of
earnest hope on his face. He looks at* MARY
for a few moments.]

JERRY [*softly*]. Mary! [MARY *does not
answer.*] Mary, I want to speak to you for a
few moments, may I?

[MARY *remains silent;* JOHNNY *goes slowly
into room on left.*]

JERRY. Your mother has told me everything,
Mary, and I have come to you. . . . I have come
to tell you, Mary, that my love for you is
greater and deeper than ever. . . .

MARY [*with a sob*]. Oh, Jerry, Jerry, say no
more; all that is over now; anything like that
is impossible now!

JERRY. Impossible? Why do you talk like
that, Mary?

MARY. After all that has happened.

JERRY. What does it matter what has happened? We are young enough to be able to
forget all those things. [*He catches her hand.*]
Mary, Mary, I am pleading for your love. With
Labour, Mary, humanity is above everything;
we are the Leaders in the fight for a new life.
I want to forget Bentham, I want to forget that
you left me—even for a while.

MARY. Oh, Jerry, Jerry, you haven't the bitter word of scorn for me after all.

JERRY [*passionately*]. Scorn! I love you, love
you, Mary!

MARY [*rising, and looking him in the eyes*].
Even though . . .

JERRY. Even though you threw me over for
another man; even though you gave me many
a bitter word!

MARY. Yes, yes, I know; but you love me,
even though . . . even though . . . I'm . . . goin'
. . . goin' . . . . [*He looks at her questioningly,
and fear gathers in his eyes.*] Ah, I was
thinkin' so. . . . You don't know everything!

JERRY [*poignantly*]. Surely to God, Mary,
you don't mean that . . . that . . . that . . .

MARY. Now you know all, Jerry; now you
know all!

JERRY. My God, Mary, have you fallen as
low as that?

MARY. Yes, Jerry, as you say, I have fallen
as low as that.

JERRY. I didn't mean it that way, Mary . . .
it came on me so sudden, that I didn't mind
what I was sayin'. . . . I never expected this—
your mother never told me. . . . I'm sorry . . .
God knows, I'm sorry for you, Mary.

MARY. Let us say no more, Jerry; I don't
blame you for thinkin' it's terrible. . . . I suppose it is. . . . Everybody'll think the same. . . .
It's only as I expected—your humanity is just
as narrow as the humanity of the others.

JERRY. I'm sorry, all the same. . . . I shouldn't
have troubled you. . . . I wouldn't if I'd known
. . . if I can do anything for you . . . Mary . . .
I will.

[*He turns to go, and halts at the door.*]

MARY. Do you remember, Jerry, the verses
you read when you gave the lecture in the
Socialist Rooms some time ago, on Humanity's
Strife with Nature?

JERRY. The verses—no; I don't remember
them.

MARY. I do. They're runnin' in me head now—

An' we felt the power that fashion'd
All the lovely things we saw,
That created all the murmur
Of an everlasting law,
Was a hand of force an' beauty,
With an eagle's tearin' claw.

Then we saw our globe of beauty
Was an ugly thing as well,
A hymn divine whose chorus
Was an agonizin' yell;
5 Like the story of a demon,
That an angel had to tell.

Like a glowin' picture by a
Hand unsteady, brought to ruin;
Like her craters, if their deadness
10 Could give life unto the moon;
Like the agonizing horror
Of a violin out of tune.

[*There is a pause, and* DEVINE *goes slowly out.*]
15 JOHNNY [*returning*]. Is he gone?
MARY. Yes.
[*The two men re-enter.*]
FIRST MAN. We can't wait any longer for t'oul' fella—sorry, Miss, but we have to live
20 as well as th' nex' man.
[*They carry out some things.*]
JOHNNY. Oh, isn't this terrible! . . . I suppose you told him everything . . . couldn't you have waited for a few days . . . he'd have stopped
25 th' takin' of the things, if you'd kep' your mouth shut. Are you burnin' to tell every one of the shame you've brought on us?
MARY [*snatching up her hat and coat*]. Oh, this is unbearable!
30 [*She rushes out.*]
FIRST MAN [*re-entering*]. We'll take the chest o' drawers next—it's the heaviest.
[*The votive light flickers for a moment, and goes out.*]
35 JOHNNY [*in a cry of fear*]. Mother o' God, the light's afther goin' out!
FIRST MAN. You put the win' up me the way you bawled that time. The oil's all gone, that's all.
40 JOHNNY [*with an agonizing cry*]. Mother o' God, there's a shot I'm afther gettin'!
FIRST MAN. What's wrong with you, man? Is it a fit you're takin'?
JOHNNY. I'm afther feelin' a pain in me
45 breast, like the tearin' by of a bullet!
FIRST MAN. He's goin' mad—it's a wondher they'd leave a chap like that here be himself.

[*Two* IRREGULARS *enter swiftly; they carry revolvers; one goes over to* JOHNNY; *the other covers the two furniture men.*]
50 FIRST IRREGULAR [*to the men, quietly and incisively*]. Who are you—what are yous doin' here—quick!
FIRST MAN. Removin' furniture that's not paid for.
55 FIRST IRREGULAR. Get over to the other end of the room an' turn your faces to the wall—quick.
[*The two men turn their faces to the wall, with their hands up.*]
60 SECOND IRREGULAR [*to* JOHNNY]. Come on, Sean° Boyle, you're wanted; some of us have a word to say to you.
JOHNNY. I'm sick, I can't—what do you want with me?
65 SECOND IRREGULAR. Come on, come on; we've a distance to go, an' haven't much time—come on.
JOHNNY. I'm an oul' comrade—yous wouldn't shoot an oul' comrade.
70 SECOND IRREGULAR. Poor Tancred was an oul' comrade o' yours, but you didn't think o' that when you gave him away to the gang that sent him to his grave. But we've no time to waste; come on—here, Dermot, ketch his arm.
75 [*To* JOHNNY.] Have you your beads?°
JOHNNY. Me beads! Why do you ass me that, why do you ass me that?
SECOND IRREGULAR. Go on, go on, march!
JOHNNY. Are yous goin' to do in a comrade—
80 look at me arm, I lost it for Ireland.
SECOND IRREGULAR. Commandant Tancred lost his life for Ireland.
JOHNNY. Sacred Heart of Jesus, have mercy on me! Mother o' God, pray for me—be with
85 me now in the agonies o' death! . . . Hail, Mary, full o' grace . . . the Lord is . . . with Thee.
[*They drag out* JOHNNY BOYLE, *and the curtain falls. When it rises again the most of the furniture is gone.* MARY *and* MRS. BOYLE, *one*
90 *on each side, are sitting in a darkened room, by the fire; it is an hour later.*]

Sean John. The nationalistic Irregulars prefer the Gaelic form of the name.
beads Rosary

MRS. BOYLE. I'll not wait much longer . . . what did they bring him away in the mothor for? Nugent says he thinks they had guns . . . is me throubles never goin' to be over? . . . If anything ud happen to poor Johnny, I think I'd lose me mind . . . I'll go to the Police Station, surely they ought to be able to do somethin'.

[*Below is heard the sound of voices.*]

MRS. BOYLE. Whisht, is that something? Maybe, it's your father, though when I left him in Foley's he was hardly able to lift his head. Whisht!

[*A knock at the door, and the voice of* MRS. MADIGAN, *speaking very softly:* Mrs. Boyle, Mrs. Boyle. MRS. BOYLE *opens the door.*]

MRS. MADIGAN. Oh, Mrs. Boyle, God an' His Blessed Mother be with you this night!

MRS. BOYLE [*calmly*]. What is it, Mrs. Madigan? It's Johnny—something about Johnny.

MRS. MADIGAN. God send it's not. God send it's not Johnny!

MRS. BOYLE. Don't keep me waitin', Mrs. Madigan; I've gone through so much lately that I feel able for anything.

MRS. MADIGAN. Two polismen below wantin' you.

MRS. BOYLE. Wantin' me; an' why do they want me?

MRS. MADIGAN. Some poor fella's been found, an' they think it's, it's . . .

MRS. BOYLE. Johnny, Johnny!

MARY [*with her arms round her mother*]. Oh, mother, mother, me poor, darlin' mother.

MRS. BOYLE. Hush, hush, darlin'; you'll shortly have your own throuble to bear. [*To* MRS. MADIGAN.] An' why do the polis think it's Johnny, Mrs. Madigan?

MRS. MADIGAN. Because one o' the doctors knew him when he was attendin' with his poor arm.

MRS. BOYLE. Oh, it's thrue, then; it's Johnny, it's me son, me own son!

MARY. Oh, it's thrue, it's thrue what Jerry Devine says—there isn't a God, there isn't a God; if there was He wouldn't let these things happen!

MRS. BOYLE. Mary, Mary, you mustn't say them things. We'll want all the help we can get from God an' His Blessed Mother now! These things have nothin' to do with the Will o' God. Ah, what can God do agen the stupidity o' men!

MRS. MADIGAN. The polis want you to go with them to the hospital to see the poor body —they're waitin' below.

MRS. BOYLE. We'll go. Come, Mary, an' we'll never come back here agen. Let your father furrage for himself now; I've done all I could an' it was all no use—he'll be hopeless till the end of his days. I've got a little room in me sisther's where we'll stop till your throuble is over, an' then we'll work together for the sake of the baby.

MARY. My poor little child that'll have no father!

MRS. BOYLE. It'll have what's far betther— it'll have two mothers.

[*A rough voice shouting from below.*]

Are yous goin' to keep us waitin' for yous all night?

MRS. MADIGAN [*going to the door, and shouting down*]. Take your hour, there, take your hour! If yous are in such a hurry, skip off, then, for nobody wants you here—if they did yous wouldn't be found. For you're the same as yous were undher the British Government—never where yous are wanted! As far as I can see, the Polis as Polis, in this city, is Null an' Void!

MRS. BOYLE. We'll go, Mary, we'll go; you to see your poor dead brother, an' me to see me poor dead son!

MARY. I dhread it, mother, I dhread it!

MRS. BOYLE. I forgot, Mary, I forgot; your poor oul' selfish mother was only thinkin' of herself. No, no, you mustn't come—it wouldn't be good for you. You go on to me sisther's an' I'll face th' ordeal meself. Maybe I didn't feel sorry enough for Mrs. Tancred when her poor son was found as Johnny's been found now— because he was a Die-hard! Ah, why didn't I remember that then he wasn't a Die-hard or a Stater, but only a poor dead son! It's well I remember all that she said—an' it's my turn to say it now: What was the pain I suffered,

Johnny, bringin' you into the world to carry you to your cradle to the pains I'll suffer carryin' you out o' the world to bring you to your grave! Mother o' God, Mother o' God, have
5 pity on us all! Blessed Virgin, where were you when me darlin' son was riddled with bullets, when me darlin' son was riddled with bullets? Sacred Heart o' Jesus, take away our hearts o' stone, and give us hearts o' flesh! Take away
10 this murdherin' hate, an' give us Thine own eternal love!

[*They all go slowly out. There is a pause; then a sound of shuffling steps on the stairs outside. The door opens and* BOYLE *and* JOXER,
15 *both of them very drunk, enter.*]

BOYLE. I'm able to go no farther. . . . Two polis, ey . . . what were they doin' here, I wondher? . . . Up to no good, anyhow . . . an' Juno an' that lovely daughter o' mine with
20 them. [*Taking a sixpence from his pocket and looking at it.*] Wan single, solitary tanner left out of all I borreyed. . . . [*He lets it fall.*] The last o' the Mohicans. . . . The blinds is down, Joxer, the blinds is down!

25 JOXER [*walking unsteadily across the room, and anchoring at the bed*]. Put all . . . your throubles . . . in your oul' kit bag . . . an' smile . . . smile . . . smile!

BOYLE. The counthry'll have to steady itself
30 . . . it's goin' . . . to hell. . . . Where'r all . . . the chairs . . . gone to . . . steady itself, Joxer. . . . Chairs'll . . . have to . . . steady themselves. . . . No matther . . . what any one may . . . say . . . Irelan's sober . . . is Irelan' . . . free.

35 JOXER [*stretching himself on the bed*]. Chains . . . an' . . . slaveree . . . that's a darlin' motto . . . a daaarlin' . . . motto!

BOYLE. If th' worst comes . . . to th' worse . . . I can join a . . . flyin' . . . column.° . . . I done
40 . . . me bit . . . in Easther Week . . . had no business . . . to . . . be . . . there . . . but Captain Boyle's Captain Boyle!

JOXER. Breathes there a man with soul . . . so . . . de . . . ad . . . this . . . me . . . o . . . wn, me
45 nat . . . ive l . . . an'!

BOYLE [*subsiding into a sitting posture on the floor*]. Commandant Kelly died . . . in them . . . arms . . . Joxer. . . . Tell me Volunteer Butties . . . says he . . . that . . . I died for . . . Irelan'!

JOXER. D'jever rade Willie . . . Reilly . . . an' 50 his . . . own . . . Colleen . . . Bawn? It's a darlin' story, a daarlin' story!

BOYLE. I'm telling you . . . Joxer . . . th' whole worl's . . . in a terr . . . ible state o' . . . chassis!

The Curtain Falls

---

flyin' column   detachment of Irregulars

Eugene O'Neill

1888–1953

Desire Under the Elms

1924

O'Neill's play is not tragedy on the grand scale of *Oedipus, Hamlet,* or *Phaedra.* It is local tragedy, good—if the events were actually to occur—for a few inches of newspaper copy. The characters are lowly figures, significant only to themselves: a hardscrabble farmer, his hired hand of a son, his orphaned and impoverished wife. Their vocabularies are as meager as the soil of the farm, and their emotions, although powerful, are essentially primitive. If, like their tragic forebears, they engage the supernatural in their own consciousnesses, their gods and spirits lack objective reality. The hard Old Testament deity with whom Cabot communes is the projection of his own craggy nature. The spirit of Eben's mother, hovering like the elms over Eben and Abbie, is the expression of their own vulnerability and passion.

Like *Phaedra, Desire Under the Elms* concerns a father, son, and stepmother. However, whereas in Racine these characters profoundly revere the family union, in O'Neill they honor it not at all: for them the family is at best a cold, contractual relationship; at worst, it is a prison. Eben's incestuous passion, unlike Phaedra's, is self-endorsed, reciprocated, and consummated. It expresses oedipal hatred of the father and love of the mother—the morally uninhibited, psychologically unelaborated drives that energize the play's essentially external conflicts. These conflicts are reducible to the opposition between the desires of the father on the one hand and of the son and the stepmother on the other.

The desire over which the elms initially preside is lust for the land and the house. This is primarily the desire of Cabot, a hard old man, proud of his hardness and contemptuous of anything "soft." Cabot wishes either that his property could vanish with him at his death or that he could have a new son, a reincarnation of himself, to extend his possession into the future. His son Eben, whose mother had owned the farm, counters old Cabot's claim. Abbie, too,

EUGENE O'NEILL

taught by deprivation to value property, claims the house as her own: "It's purty—purty! I can't b'lieve it's r'ally mine."

Inevitably the elms come to preside over a second desire—the physical attraction of Eben and Abbie to each other. To this desire they yield in due course, after oscillating between attraction and antagonism. An inexorable conflict thence arises, for the child that is the product of their union is heir, in law, not to Abbie and Eben but to Abbie and Cabot. Old Cabot uses the fact against Eben: "The farm's her'n!" he cries. "An' the dust o' the road—that's your'n!" Considering himself betrayed, Eben pronounces a vengeance on Cabot, Abbie, and the child as well. "I wish he never was born. I wish he'd die this minit." And acting on this cue, Abbie precipitates the catastrophe that brings the play to its close.

Ideally the two desires—for fruitful land and for generative love—are united to provide identity, home, a way to flourish. But in *Desire Under the Elms* the two are irreconcilable alternatives. The curtain goes down with the father still cherishing his land, the stepmother cherishing her love, and the son—perhaps, in O'Neill's conception, doomed by an oedipal choice—aligned against his father and with his father's wife. For each, in the divisive scheme of the play, the basic desire is fulfilled, but the fulfillment entails isolation and death.

As critics, we may question the validity and depth of O'Neill's vision. To some it has seemed pessimistic if not cynical compared to the older, more heroic view of the American frontier. The house, the land, the overarching elms themselves are images from a nobler landscape. And the twisted and destructive passions here are inversions of the pioneer virtues of labor, self-discipline, and taciturn forebearance. In O'Neill the visions of Emerson, Thoreau, and Whitman seem blasted, although not utterly forgotten. To others O'Neill's vision has seemed both romantic and sentimental—Cabot, like Antaeus, gaining from the land a perennial vigor and apocalyptic grandeur, Eben and Abbie deriving from their passion, however infanticidal, a self-vindication at which reason demurs. But O'Neill's intensity and virtually unrivaled sense of theater make it hard for us, while reading or viewing his play, not to succumb. Whatever our objections, *Desire Under the Elms* retains a primal and compelling power.

Desire Under
the Elms

O'NEILL

CHARACTERS

EPHRAIM CABOT
SIMEON
PETER } *His sons*
EBEN
ABBIE PUTNAM

Young Girl, Two Farmers, The Fiddler, A
Sheriff, and other folk from the neighboring
farms.

The action of the entire play takes place in,
and immediately outside of, the Cabot farmhouse in New England, in the year 1850. The
south end of the house faces front to a stone
5 wall with a wooden gate at center opening on
a country road. The house is in good condition
but in need of paint. Its walls are a sickly
grayish, the green of the shutters faded. Two
enormous elms are on each side of the house.
10 They bend their trailing branches down over
the roof. They appear to protect and at the
same time subdue. There is a sinister maternity
in their aspect, a crushing, jealous absorption.
They have developed from the intimate con-
15 tact with the life of man in the house an appalling humaneness. They brood oppressively
over the house. They are like exhausted women
resting their sagging breasts and hands and
hair on its roof, and when it rains their tears
20 trickle down monotonously and rot on the
shingles.

There is a path running from the gate
around the right corner of the house to the
front door. A narrow porch is on this side. The
end wall facing us has two windows in its 25
upper story, two larger ones on the floor below. The two upper are those of the father's
bedroom and that of the brothers. On the left,
ground floor, is the kitchen—on the right, the
parlor, the shades of which are always drawn 30
down.

PART I

Scene i

[Exterior of the farmhouse. It is sunset of a
day at the beginning of summer in the year
1850. There is no wind and everything is still.
The sky above the roof is suffused with deep 35
colors, the green of the elms glows, but the
house is in shadows, seeming pale and washed
out by contrast.

A door opens and EBEN CABOT comes to the
end of the porch and stands looking down the 40
road to the right. He has a large bell in his
hand and this he swings mechanically, awaken-
ing a deafening clangor. Then he puts his
hands on his hips and stares up at the sky. He
sighs with a puzzled awe and blurts out with 45
halting appreciation.]

EBEN. God! Purty! [His eyes fall and he
stares about him frowningly. He is twenty-five,
tall and sinewy. His face is well-formed, good-
looking, but its expression is resentful and 50
defensive. His defiant, dark eyes remind one
of a wild animal's in captivity. Each day is a
cage in which he finds himself trapped but in-
wardly unsubdued. There is a fierce repressed
vitality about him. He has black hair, mus- 55
tache, a thin curly trace of beard. He is dressed
in rough farm clothes.

He spits on the ground with intense disgust,
turns and goes back into the house.

SIMEON and PETER come in from their work 60
in the fields. They are tall men, much older
than their half-brother [SIMEON is thirty-nine
and PETER thirty-seven], built on a squarer,
simpler model, fleshier in body, more bovine
and homelier in face, shrewder and more prac- 65

tical. *Their shoulders stoop a bit from years of
farm work. They clump heavily along in their
clumsy thick-soled boots caked with earth.
Their clothes, their faces, hands, bare arms*
5 *and throats are earth-stained. They smell of
earth. They stand together for a moment in
front of the house and, as if with the one impulse, stare dumbly at the sky, leaning on their
hoes. Their faces have a compressed, unre-*
10 *signed expression. As they look upward, this
softens.]*

SIMEON [*grudgingly*]. Purty.

PETER. Ay-eh.

SIMEON [*suddenly*]. Eighteen years ago.

15 PETER. What?

SIMEON. Jenn. My woman. She died.

PETER. I'd fergot.

SIMEON. I rec'lect—now an' agin. Makes it
lonesome. She'd hair long's a hoss' tail—and
20 yaller like gold!

PETER. Waal—she's gone. [*This with indifferent finality—then after a pause.*] They's
gold in the West, Sim.

SIMEON [*still under the influence of sunset—
25 vaguely*]. In the sky!

PETER. Waal—in a manner o' speakin'—
thar's the promise. [*Growing excited.*] Gold in
the sky—in the West—Golden Gate—Californi-a!—Golden West!—fields o' gold!

30 SIMEON [*excited in his turn*]. Fortunes layin'
just atop o' the ground waitin' t' be picked!
Solomon's mines, they says! [*For a moment
they continue looking up at the sky—then
their eyes drop.*]

35 PETER [*with sardonic bitterness*]. Here—it's
stones atop o' the ground—stones atop o'
stones—makin' stone walls—year atop o' year
—him 'n' yew 'n' me 'n' then Eben—makin'
stone walls fur him to fence us in!

40 SIMEON. We've wuked. Give our strength.
Give our years. Plowed 'em under in the
ground,—[*he stamps rebelliously*]—rottin'—
makin' soil for his crops! [*A pause.*] Waal—
the farm pays good for hereabouts.

45 PETER. If we plowed in Californi-a, they'd be
lumps o' gold in the furrow!

SIMEON. Californi-a's t'other side o' earth,
a'most. We got t' calc'late—

PETER [*after a pause*]. 'Twould be hard fur
me, too, to give up what we've 'arned here by 50
our sweat. [*A pause, EBEN sticks his head out
of the dining-room window, listening.*]

SIMEON. Ay-eh. [*A pause.*] Mebbe—he'll die
soon.

PETER [*doubtfully*]. Mebbe. 55

SIMEON. Mebbe—fur all we knows—he's
dead now.

PETER. Ye'd need proof.

SIMEON. He's been gone two months—with
no word. 60

PETER. Left us in the fields an evenin' like
this. Hitched up an' druv off into the West.
That's plum onnateral. He hain't never been
off this farm 'ceptin' t' the village in thirty year
or more, not since he married Eben's maw. [*A* 65
pause. Shrewdly.] I calc'late we might git him
declared crazy by the court.

SIMEON. He skinned 'em too slick. He got the
best o' all on 'em. They'd never b'lieve him
crazy. [*A pause.*] We got t' wait—till he's 70
under ground.

EBEN [*with a sardonic chuckle*]. Honor thy
father! [*They turn, startled, and stare at him.
He grins, then scowls.*] I pray he's died. [*They
stare at him. He continues matter-of-factly.*] 75
Supper's ready.

SIMEON *and* PETER [*together*]. Ay-eh.

EBEN [*gazing up at the sky*]. Sun's downin'
purty.

SIMEON *and* PETER [*together*]. Ay-eh. They's 80
gold in the West.

EBEN. Ay-eh. [*Pointing.*] Yonder atop o' the
hill pasture, ye mean?

SIMEON *and* PETER [*together*]. In Californi-a!

EBEN. Hunh? [*Stares at them indifferently for* 85
a second, then drawls.] Waal—supper's gittin'
cold. [*He turns back into kitchen.*]

SIMEON [*startled—smacks his lips*]. I air
hungry!

PETER [*sniffing*]. I smells bacon! 90

SIMEON [*with hungry appreciation*]. Bacon's
good!

PETER [*in same tone*]. Bacon's bacon! [*They
turn, shouldering each other, their bodies
bumping and rubbing together as they hurry* 95
clumsily to their food, like two friendly oxen

toward their evening meal. They disappear around the right corner of house and can be heard entering the door.]

Curtain

Scene ii

[*The color fades from the sky. Twilight be-*
5 *gins. The interior of the kitchen is now visible. A pine table is at center, a cook-stove in the right rear corner, four rough wooden chairs, a tallow candle on the table. In the middle of the*
10 *rear wall is fastened a big advertising poster with a ship in full sail and the word "California" in big letters. Kitchen utensils hang from nails. Everything is neat and in order but the atmosphere is of a men's camp kitchen rather than that of a home.*

15 *Places for three are laid.* EBEN *takes boiled potatoes and bacon from the stove and puts them on the table, also a loaf of bread and a crock of water.* SIMEON *and* PETER *shoulder in, slump down in their chairs without a word.*
20 EBEN *joins them. The three eat in silence for a moment, the two elder as naturally unrestrained as beasts of the field,* EBEN *picking at his food without appetite, glancing at them with a tolerant dislike.*]

25 SIMEON [*suddenly turns to* EBEN]. Looky here! Ye'd oughtn't t' said that, Eben.

PETER. 'Twa'n't righteous.

EBEN. What?

SIMEON. Ye prayed he'd died.

30 EBEN. Waal—don't yew pray it? [*A pause.*]

PETER. He's our Paw.

EBEN [*violently*]. Not mine!

SIMEON [*dryly*]. Ye'd not let no one else say that about yer Maw! Ha! [*He gives one abrupt*
35 *sardonic guffaw.* PETER *grins.*]

EBEN [*very pale*]. I meant—I hain't his'n—I hain't like him—he hain't me!

PETER [*dryly*]. Wait till ye've growed his age!

EBEN [*intensely*]. I'm Maw—every drop o'
40 blood! [*A pause. They stare at him with indifferent curiosity.*]

PETER [*reminiscently*]. She was good t' Sim 'n' me. A good step-maw's scurse.

SIMEON. She was good t' everyone.

45 EBEN [*greatly moved, gets to his feet and makes an awkward bow to each of them—stammering*]. I be thankful t' ye. I'm her—her heir. [*He sits down in confusion.*]

PETER [*after a pause—judicially*]. She was good even t' him.

50 EBEN [*fiercely*]. An' fur thanks he killed her!

SIMEON [*after a pause*]. No one never kills nobody. It's allus somethin'. That's the murderer.

55 EBEN. Didn't he slave Maw t' death?

PETER. He's slaved himself t' death. He's slaved Sim 'n' me 'n' yew t' death—on'y none o' us hain't died—yit.

60 SIMEON. It's somethin'—drivin' him—t' drive us!

EBEN [*vengefully*]. Waal—I hold him t' jedgment! [*Then scornfully.*] Somethin'! What's somethin'?

65 SIMEON. Dunno.

EBEN [*sardonically*]. What's drivin' yew to Californi-a, mebbe? [*They look at him in surprise.*] Oh, I've heerd ye! [*Then, after a pause.*] But ye'll never go t' the gold fields!

70 PETER [*assertively*]. Mebbe!

EBEN. Whar'll ye git the money?

PETER. We kin walk. It's an a'mighty ways—Californi-a—but if yew was t' put all the steps we've walked on this farm end t' end we'd be
75 in the moon!

EBEN. The Injuns skulp ye on the plains.

SIMEON [*with grim humor*]. We'll mebbe make 'em pay a hair fur a hair!

EBEN [*decisively*]. But t'aint that. Ye won't
80 never go because ye'll wait here fur yer share o' the farm, thinkin' allus he'll die soon.

SIMEON [*after a pause*]. We've a right.

PETER. Two-thirds belong t' us.

EBEN [*jumping to his feet*]. Ye've no right!
85 She wa'nt yewr Maw! It was her farm! Didn't he steal it from her? She's dead. It's my farm.

SIMEON [*sardonically*]. Tell that t' Paw—when he comes! I'll bet ye a dollar he'll laugh—fur once in his life. Ha! [*He laughs himself in one single mirthless bark.*]
90 PETER [*amused in turn, echoes his brother*]. Ha!

SIMEON [*after a pause*]. What've ye got held

agin us, Eben? Year arter year it's skulked in
yer eye—somethin'.

PETER. Ay-eh.

EBEN. Ay-eh. They's somethin'. [*Suddenly
exploding.*] Why didn't ye never stand between him 'n' my Maw when he was slavin'
her to her grave—t' pay her back fur the kindness she done t' yew? [*There is a long pause.
They stare at him in surprise.*]

SIMEON. Waal—the stock's got t' be watered.

PETER. 'R they was woodin' t' do.

SIMEON. 'R plowin'.

PETER. 'R hayin'.

SIMEON. 'R spreadin' manure.

PETER. 'R weedin'.

SIMEON. 'R prunin'.

PETER. 'R milkin'.

EBEN [*breaking in harshly*]. An' makin'
walls—stone atop o' stone—makin' walls till
yer heart's a stone ye heft up out o' the way o'
growth onto a stone wall t' wall in yer heart!

SIMEON [*matter-of-factly*]. We never had no
time t' meddle.

PETER [*to* EBEN]. Yew was fifteen afore yer
Maw died—an' big fur yer age. Why didn't ye
never do nothin'?

EBEN [*harshly*]. They was chores t' do,
wa'n't they? [*A pause—then slowly.*] It was
on'y arter she died I come to think o' it. Me
cookin'—doin' her work—that made me know
her, suffer her sufferin'—she'd come back t'
help—come back t' bile potatoes—come back
t' fry bacon—come back t' bake biscuits—
come back all cramped up t' shake the fire, an'
carry ashes, her eyes weepin' an' bloody with
smoke an' cinders same's they used t' be. She
still comes back—stands by the stove thar in
the evenin'—she can't find it nateral sleepin'
an' restin' in peace. She can't git used t' bein'
free—even in her grave.

SIMEON. She never complained none.

EBEN. She'd got too tired. She'd got too used
t' bein' too tired. That was what he done.
[*With vengeful passion.*] An' sooner'r later,
I'll meddle. I'll say the thin's I didn't say then t'
him! I'll yell 'em at the top o' my lungs. I'll see
t' it my Maw gits some rest an' sleep in her

grave! [*He sits down again, relapsing into a
brooding silence. They look at him with a
queer indifferent curiosity.*]

PETER [*after a pause*]. Whar in tarnation
d'ye s'pose he went, Sim?

SIMEON. Dunno. He druv off in the buggy,
all spick an' span, with the mare all breshed
an' shiny, druv off clackin' his tongue an' wav-
in' his whip. I remember it right well. I was
finishin' plowin', it was spring an' May an'
sunset, an' gold in the West, an' he druv off
into it. I yells "Whar ye goin', Paw?" an' he
hauls up by the stone wall a jiffy. His old
snake's eyes was glitterin' in the sun like he'd
been drinkin' a jugful an' he says with a mule's
grin: "Don't ye run away till I come back!"

PETER. Wonder if he knowed we was wantin'
fur Californi-a?

SIMEON. Mebbe. I didn't say nothin' and he
says, lookin' kinder queer an' sick: "I been
hearin' the hens cluckin' an' the roosters
crowin' all the durn day. I been listenin' t' the
cows lowin' an' everythin' else kickin' up till I
can't stand it no more. It's spring an' I'm feelin' damned," he says. "Damned like an old
bare hickory tree fit on'y fur burnin'," he says.
An' then I calc'late I must've looked a mite
hopeful, fur he adds real spry and vicious: "But
don't git no fool idee I'm dead. I've sworn t'
live a hundred an' I'll do it, if on'y t' spite yer
sinful greed! An' now I'm ridin' out t' learn
God's message t' me in the spring, like the
prophets done. An' yew git back t' yer plowin'," he says. An' he druv off singin' a hymn. I
thought he was drunk—'r I'd stopped him
goin'.

EBEN [*scornfully*]. No, ye wouldn't! Ye're
scared o' him. He's stronger—inside—than
both o' ye put together!

PETER [*sardonically*]. An' yew—be yew
Samson?

EBEN. I'm gittin' stronger. I kin feel it growin' in me—growin' an' growin'—till it'll bust
out—! [*He gets up and puts on his coat and a
hat. They watch him, gradually breaking into
grins.* EBEN *avoids their eyes sheepishly.*] I'm
goin' out for a spell—up the road.

PETER. T' the village?

SIMEON. T' see Minnie?

EBEN [*defiantly*]. Ay-eh!

PETER [*jeeringly*]. The Scarlet Woman!

5   SIMEON. Lust—that's what's growin' in ye!

EBEN. Waal—she's purty!

PETER. She's been purty fur twenty year!

SIMEON. A new coat o' paint'll make a heifer out of forty.

10   EBEN. She hain't forty!

PETER. If she hain't, she's teeterin' on the edge.

EBEN [*desperately*]. What d'yew know—

PETER. All they is . . . Sim knew her—an'

15   then me arter—

SIMEON. An' Paw kin tell yew somethin' too! He was fust!

EBEN. D'ye mean t' say he . . . ?

SIMEON [*with a grin*]. Ay-eh! We air his

20   heirs in everythin'!

EBEN [*intensely*]. That's more to it! That grows on it! It'll bust soon! [*Then violently.*] I'll go smash my fist in her face! [*He pulls open the door in rear violently.*]

25   SIMEON [*with a wink at* PETER—*drawlingly*]. Mebbe—but the night's wa'm—purty—by the time ye git thar mebbe ye'll kiss her instead!

PETER. Sart'n he will! [*They both roar with coarse laughter.* EBEN *rushes out and slams the*

30   *door—then the outside front door—comes around the corner of the house and stands still by the gate, staring up at the sky.*]

SIMEON [*looking after him*]. Like his Paw.

PETER. Dead spit an' image!

35   SIMEON. Dog'll eat dog!

PETER. Ay-eh. [*Pause. With yearning.*] Mebbe a year from now we'll be in Californi-a.

SIMEON. Ay-eh. [*A pause. Both yawn.*] Let's git t' bed. [*He blows out the candle. They go*

40   *out door in rear.* EBEN *stretches his arms up to the sky—rebelliously.*]

EBEN. Waal—thar's a star, an' somewhar's they's him, an' here's me, an' thar's Min up the road—in the same night. What if I does

45   kiss her? She's like t'night, she's soft 'n' wa'm, her eyes kin wink like a star, her mouth's wa'm, her arms're wa'm, she smells like a wa'm

plowed field, she's purty. . . . Ay-eh! By God A'mighty she's purty, an' I don't give a damn how many sins she's sinned afore mine or who 50 she's sinned 'em with, my sin's as purty as any one of 'em! [*He strides off down the road to the left.*]

Curtain

Scene iii

[*It is the pitch darkness just before dawn.* EBEN *comes in from the left and goes around to* 55 *the porch, feeling his way, chuckling bitterly and cursing half-aloud to himself.*]

EBEN. The cussed old miser! [*He can be heard going in the front door. There is a pause as he goes upstairs, then a loud knock on the* 60 *bedroom door of the brothers.*] Wake up!

SIMEON [*startledly*]. Who's thar?

EBEN [*pushing open the door and coming in, a lighted candle in his hand. The bedroom of the brothers is revealed. Its ceiling is the slop-* 65 *ing roof. They can stand upright only close to the center dividing wall of the upstairs.* SIMEON *and* PETER *are in a double bed, front.* EBEN'S *cot is to the rear.* EBEN *has a mixture of silly grin and vicious scowl on his face*]. I be! 70

PETER [*angrily*]. What in hell's-fire . . . ?

EBEN. I got news fur ye! Ha! [*He gives one abrupt sardonic guffaw.*]

SIMEON [*angrily*]. Couldn't ye hold it 'til we'd got our sleep? 75

EBEN. It's nigh sunup. [*Then explosively.*] He's gone an' married agen!

SIMEON *and* PETER [*explosively*]. Paw?

EBEN. Got himself hitched to a female 'bout thirty-five—an' purty, they says. . . . 80

SIMEON [*aghast*]. It's a durn lie!

PETER. Who says?

SIMEON. They been stringin' ye!

EBEN. Think I'm a dunce, do ye? The hull village says. The preacher from New Dover, 85 he brung the news—told it t' our preacher—New Dover, that's whar the old loon got himself hitched—that's whar the woman lived—

PETER [*no longer doubting—stunned*]. Waal . . . ! 90

SIMEON [*the same*]. Waal . . . !

EBEN [*sitting down on a bed—with vicious hatred*]. Ain't he a devil out o' hell? It's jest t' spite us—the damned old mule!

PETER [*after a pause*]. Everythin'll go t' her now.

SIMEON. Ay-eh. [*A pause—dully.*] Waal—if it's done—

PETER. It's done us. [*Pause—then persuasively.*] They's gold in the fields o' Californi-a, Sim. No good a-stayin' here now.

SIMEON. Jest what I was a-thinkin'. [*Then with decision.*] S'well fust's last! Let's light out and git this mornin'.

PETER. Suits me.

EBEN. Ye must like walkin'.

SIMEON [*sardonically*]. If ye'd grow wings on us we'd fly thar!

EBEN. Ye'd like ridin' better—on a boat, wouldn't ye? [*Fumbles in his pocket and takes out a crumpled sheet of foolscap.*] Waal, if ye sign this ye kin ride on a boat. I've had it writ out an' ready in case ye'd ever go. It says fur three hundred dollars t' each ye agree yewr shares o' the farm is sold t' me. [*They look suspiciously at the paper. A pause.*]

SIMEON [*wonderingly*]. But if he's hitched agen—

PETER. An' whar'd yew git that sum of money, anyways?

EBEN [*cunningly*]. I know whar it's hid. I been waitin'—Maw told me. She knew whar it lay fur years, but she was waitin'. . . . It's her'n—the money he hoarded from her farm an' hid from Maw. It's my money by rights now.

PETER. Whar's it hid?

EBEN [*cunningly*]. Whar yew won't never find it without me. Maw spied on him—'r she'd never knowed. [*A pause. They look at him suspiciously, and he at them.*] Waal, is it fa'r trade?

SIMEON. Dunno.

PETER. Dunno.

SIMEON [*looking at window*]. Sky's grayin'.

PETER. Ye better start the fire, Eben.

SIMEON. An' fix some vittles.

EBEN. Ay-eh. [*Then with a forced jocular heartiness.*] I'll git ye a good one. If ye're startin' t' hoof it t' Californi-a ye'll need somethin' that'll stick t' yer ribs. [*He turns to the door, adding meaningly.*] But ye kin ride on a boat if ye'll swap. [*He stops at the door and pauses. They stare at him.*]

SIMEON [*suspiciously*]. Whar was ye all night?

EBEN [*defiantly*]. Up t' Min's. [*Then slowly.*] Walkin' thar, fust I felt 's if I'd kiss her; then I got a-thinkin' o' what ye'd said o' him an' her an' I says, I'll bust her nose fur that! Then I got t' the village an' heerd the news an' I got madder'n hell an' run all the way t' Min's not knowin' what to do— [*He pauses—then sheepishly but more defiantly.*] Waal—when I seen her, I didn't hit her—nor I didn't kiss her nuther —I begun t' beller like a calf an' cuss at the same time, I was so durn mad—an' she got scared—an' I jest grabbed holt an' tuk her! [*Proudly.*] Yes, siree! I tuk her. She may've been his'n—an' yourn, too—but she's mine now!

SIMEON [*dryly*]. In love, air yew?

EBEN [*with lofty scorn*]. Love! I don't take no stock in sech slop!

PETER [*winking at* SIMEON]. Mebbe Eben's aimin' t' marry, too.

SIMEON. Min'd make a true faithful he'p-meet! [*They snicker.*]

EBEN. What do I care fur her—'ceptin' she's round an' wa'm? The p'int is she was his'n—an' now she b'longs t' me! [*He goes to the door —then turns—rebelliously.*] An' Min hain't sech a· bad un. They's worse'n Min in the world, I'll bet ye! Wait'll we see this cow the Old Man's hitched t'! She'll beat Min, I got a notion! [*He starts to go out.*]

SIMEON [*suddenly*]. Mebbe ye'll try t' make her your'n, too?

PETER. Ha! [*He gives a sardonic laugh of relish at this idea.*]

EBEN [*spitting with disgust*]. Her—here— sleepin' with him—stealin' my Maw's farm! I'd as soon pet a skunk 'r kiss a snake! [*He goes out. The two stare after him suspiciously. A pause. They listen to his steps receding.*]

PETER. He's startin' the fire.

SIMEON. I'd like t' ride t' Californi-a—but—

PETER. Min might o' put some scheme in his head.

SIMEON. Mebbe it's all a lie 'bout Paw marryin'. We'd best wait an' see the bride.

5 PETER. An' don't sign nothin' till we does!

SIMEON. Nor till we've tested it's good money! [*Then with a grin.*] But if Paw's hitched we'd be sellin' Eben somethin' we'd never git nohow!

10 PETER. We'll wait an' see. [*Then with sudden vindictive anger.*] An' till he comes, let's yew 'n' me not wuk a lick, let Eben tend to thin's if he's a mind t', let's us jest sleep an' eat an' drink likker an' let the hull damned farm go 15 t' blazes!

SIMEON [*excitedly*]. By God, we've 'arned a rest! We'll play rich fur a change. I hain't agoing to stir outa bed till breakfast's ready.

PETER. An' on the table!

20 SIMEON [*after a pause—thoughtfully*]. What d'ye calc'late she'll be like—our new Maw? Like Eben thinks?

PETER. More'n likely.

SIMEON [*vindictively*]. Waal—I hope she's a 25 she-devil that'll make him wish he was dead an' livin' in the pit o' hell fur comfort!

PETER [*fervently*]. Amen!

SIMEON [*imitating his father's voice*]. "I'm ridin' out t' learn God's message t' me in the 30 spring like the prophets done," he says. I'll bet right then an' thar he knew plumb well he was goin' whorin', the stinkin' old hypocrite!

Curtain

Scene iv

[*Same as Scene ii—shows the interior of the kitchen with a lighted candle on table. It is 35 gray dawn outside.* SIMEON *and* PETER *are just finishing their breakfast.* EBEN *sits before his plate of untouched food, brooding frowningly.*]

PETER [*glancing at him rather irritably*]. 40 Lookin' glum don't help none.

SIMEON [*sarcastically*]. Sorrowin' over his lust o' the flesh!

PETER [*with a grin*]. Was she yer fust?

EBEN [*angrily*]. None o' yer business. [*A 45 pause.*] I was thinkin' o' him. I got a notion

he's gittin' near—I kin feel him comin' on like yew kin feel malaria chill afore it takes ye.

PETER. It's too early yet.

SIMEON. Dunno. He'd like t' catch us nappin' —jest t' have somethin' t' hoss us 'round over. 50

PETER [*mechanically gets to his feet.* SIMEON *does the same*]. Waal—let's git t' wuk. [*They both plod mechanically toward the door before they realize. Then they stop short.*]

SIMEON [*grinning*]. Ye're a cussed fool, Pete 55 —and I be wuss! Let him see we hain't wukin'! We don't give a durn!

PETER [*as they go back to the table*]. Not a damned durn! It'll serve t' show him we're done with him. [*They sit down again.* EBEN 60 *stares from one to the other with surprise.*]

SIMEON [*grins at him*]. We're aimin' t' start bein' lilies o' the field.

PETER. Nary a toil 'r spin 'r lick o' wuk do we put in! 65

SIMEON. Ye're sole owner—till he comes— that's what ye wanted. Waal, ye got t' be sole hand, too.

PETER. The cows air bellerin'. Ye better hustle at the milkin'. 70

EBEN [*with excited joy*]. Ye mean ye'll sign the paper?

SIMEON [*dryly*]. Mebbe.

PETER. Mebbe.

SIMEON. We're considerin'. [*Peremptorily.*] 75 Ye better git t' wuk.

EBEN [*with queer excitement*]. It's Maw's farm agen! It's my farm! Them's my cows! I'll milk my durn fingers off fur cows o' mine! [*He goes out door in rear, they stare after him 80 indifferently.*]

SIMEON. Like his Paw.

PETER. Dead spit 'n' image!

SIMEON. Waal—let dog eat dog! [EBEN *comes out of front door and around the corner of the 85 house. The sky is beginning to grow flushed with sunrise.* EBEN *stops by the gate and stares around him with glowing, possessive eyes. He takes in the whole farm with his embracing glance of desire.*] 90

EBEN. It's purty! It's damned purty! It's mine! [*He suddenly throws his head back boldly and glares with hard, defiant eyes at the sky.*] Mine, d'ye hear? Mine! [*He turns and walks quickly off left, rear, toward the barn. The two brothers light their pipes.*]

SIMEON [*putting his muddy boots up on the table, tilting back his chair, and puffing defiantly*]. Waal—this air solid comfort—fur once.

PETER. Ay-eh. [*He follows suit. A pause. Unconsciously they both sigh.*]

SIMEON [*suddenly*]. He never was much o' a hand at milkin', Eben wa'n't.

PETER [*with a snort*]. His hands air like hoofs! [*A pause.*]

SIMEON. Reach down the jug thar! Let's take a swaller. I'm feelin' kind o' low.

PETER. Good idee! [*He does so—gets two glasses—they pour out drinks of whisky.*] Here's t' the gold in Californi-a!

SIMEON. An' luck t' find it! [*They drink—puff resolutely—sigh—take their feet down from the table.*]

PETER. Likker don't 'pear t' sot right.

SIMEON. We hain't used t' it this early. [*A pause. They become very restless.*]

PETER. Gittin' close in this kitchen.

SIMEON [*with immense relief*]. Let's git a breath o' air. [*They arise briskly and go out rear—appear around house and stop by the gate. They stare up at the sky with a numbed appreciation.*]

PETER. Purty!

SIMEON. Ay-eh. Gold's t' the East now.

PETER. Sun's startin' with us fur the Golden West.

SIMEON [*staring around the farm, his compressed face tightened, unable to conceal his emotion*]. Waal—it's our last mornin'—mebbe.

PETER [*the same*]. Ay-eh.

SIMEON [*stamps his foot on the earth and addresses it desperately*]. Waal—ye've thirty year o' me buried in ye—spread out over ye—blood an' bone an' sweat—rotted away—fertilizin' ye—richin' yer soul—prime manure, by God, that's what I been t' ye!

PETER. Ay-eh! An' me!

SIMEON. An' yew, Peter. [*He sighs—then spits.*] Waal—no use'n cryin' over spilt milk.

PETER. They's gold in the West—an' freedom, mebbe. We been slaves t' stone walls here.

SIMEON [*defiantly*]. We hain't nobody's slaves from this out—nor no thin's slaves nuther. [*A pause—restlessly.*] Speakin' o' milk, wonder how Eben's managin'?

PETER. I s'pose he's managin'.

SIMEON. Mebbe we'd ought t' help—this once.

PETER. Mebbe. The cows knows us.

SIMEON. An' likes us. They don't know him much.

PETER. An' the hosses, an' pigs, an' chickens. They don't know him much.

SIMEON. They knows us like brothers—an' likes us! [*Proudly.*] Hain't we raised 'em t' be fust-rate, number one prize stock?

PETER. We hain't—not no more.

SIMEON [*dully*]. I was fergettin'. [*Then resignedly.*] Waal, let's go help Eben a spell an' git waked up.

PETER. Suits me. [*They are starting off down left, rear, for the barn when* EBEN *appears from there hurrying toward them, his face excited.*]

EBEN [*breathlessly*]. Waal—thar they be! The old mule an' the bride! I seen 'em from the barn down below at the turnin'.

PETER. How could ye tell that far?

EBEN. Hain't I as far-sight as he's near-sight? Don't I know the mare 'n' buggy, an' two people settin' in it? Who else . . . ? An' I tell ye I kin feel 'em a-comin', too! [*He squirms as if he had the itch.*]

PETER [*beginning to be angry*]. Waal—let him do his own unhitchin'!

SIMEON [*angry in his turn*]. Let's hustle in an' git our bundles an' be a-goin' as he's a-comin'. I don't want never t' step inside the door agen arter he's back. [*They both start back around the corner of the house.* EBEN *follows them.*]

EBEN [*anxiously*]. Will ye sign it afore ye go?

PETER. Let's see the color o' the old skinflint's money an' we'll sign. [*They disappear left. The two brothers clump upstairs to get their bundles.* EBEN *appears in the kitchen, runs to window, peers out, comes back and pulls up*

a strip of flooring in under stove, takes out a
canvas bag and puts it on table, then sets the
floorboard back in place. The two brothers ap-
pear a moment after. They carry old carpet-
5 *bags.*]

EBEN [*puts his hand on bag guardingly*].
Have ye signed?

SIMEON [*shows paper in his hand*]. Ay-eh.
[*Greedily.*] Be that the money?

10 EBEN [*opens bag and pours out pile of*
twenty-dollar gold pieces]. Twenty-dollar
pieces—thirty of 'em. Count 'em. [PETER *does*
so, arranging them in stacks of five, biting one
or two to test them.]

15 PETER. Six hundred. [*He puts them in bag*
and puts it inside his shirt carefully.]

SIMEON [*handing paper to* EBEN]. Har ye be.

EBEN [*after a glance, folds it carefully and*
hides it under his shirt—gratefully]. Thank
20 yew.

PETER. Thank yew fur the ride.

SIMEON. We'll send ye a lump o' gold fur
Christmas. [*A pause.* EBEN *stares at them and*
they at him.]

25 PETER [*awkwardly*]. Waal—we're a-goin'.

SIMEON. Comin' out t' the yard?

EBEN. No. I'm waitin' in here a spell.
[*Another silence. The brothers edge awkwardly*
to door in rear—then turn and stand.]

30 SIMEON. Waal—good-by.

PETER. Good-by.

EBEN. Good-by. [*They go out. He sits down*
at the table, faces the stove and pulls out the
paper. He looks from it to the stove. His face,
35 *lighted up by the shaft of sunlight from the*
window, has an expression of trance. His lips
move. The two brothers come out to the gate.]

PETER [*looking off toward barn*]. Thar he be
—unhitchin'.

40 SIMEON [*with a chuckle*]. I'll bet ye he's
riled!

PETER. An' thar she be.

SIMEON. Let's wait 'n' see what our new Maw
looks like.

45 PETER [*with a grin*]. An' give him our part-
in' cuss!

SIMEON [*grinning*]. I feel like raisin' fun. I
feel light in my head an' feet.

PETER. Me, too. I feel like laffin' till I'd split
up the middle. 50

SIMEON. Reckon it's the likker?

PETER. No. My feet feel itchin' t' walk an'
walk—an' jump high over thin's—an'. . . .

SIMEON. Dance? [*A pause.*]

PETER [*puzzled*]. It's plumb onnateral. 55

SIMEON [*a light coming over his face*]. I
calc'late it's 'cause school's out. It's holiday.
Fur once we're free!

PETER [*dazedly*]. Free?

SIMEON. The halter's broke—the harness is 60
busted—the fence bars is down—the stone
walls air crumblin' an' tumblin'! We'll be
kickin' up an' tearin' away down the road!

PETER [*drawing a deep breath—oratorically*].
Anybody that wants this stinkin' old rock-pile 65
of a farm kin hev it. T'aint our'n, no sirree!

SIMEON [*takes the gate off its hinges and puts*
it under his arm]. We harby 'bolishes shet
gates, an' open gates, an' all gates, by thunder!

PETER. We'll take it with us fur luck an' let 70
'er sail free down some river.

SIMEON [*as a sound of voices comes from*
left, rear]. Har they comes! [*The two brothers*
congeal into two stiff, grim-visaged statues.
EPHRAIM CABOT *and* ABBIE PUTNAM *come in.* 75
CABOT *is seventy-five, tall and gaunt, with*
great, wiry, concentrated power, but stoop-
shouldered from toil. His face is as hard as if
it were hewn out of a boulder, yet there is a
weakness in it, a petty pride in its own nar- 80
row strength. His eyes are small, close to-
gether, and extremely near-sighted, blinking
continually in the effort to focus on objects,
their stare having a straining, ingrowing
quality. He is dressed in his dismal black Sun- 85
day suit. ABBIE *is thirty-five, buxom, full of*
vitality. Her round face is pretty but marred
by its rather gross sensuality. There is strength
and obstinacy in her jaw, a hard determination
in her eyes, and about her whole personality 90
the same unsettled, untamed, desperate quality
which is so apparent in EBEN.]

CABOT [*as they enter—a queer strangled*
emotion in his dry cracking voice]. Har we be
t' hum, Abbie. 95

ABBIE [*with lust for the word*]. Hum! [*Her*

eyes gloating on the house without seeming to see the two stiff figures at the gate.] It's purty— purty! I can't b'lieve it's r'ally mine.

CABOT [*sharply*]. Yewr'n? Mine! [*He stares at her penetratingly, she stares back. He adds relentingly.*] Our'n—mebbe! It was lonesome too long. I was growin' old in the spring. A hum's got t' hev a woman.

ABBIE [*her voice taking possession*]. A woman's got t' hev a hum!

CABOT [*nodding uncertainly*]. Ay-eh. [*Then irritably.*] Whar be they? Ain't thar nobody about—'r wukin'—'r nothin'?

ABBIE [*sees the brothers. She returns their stare of cold appraising contempt with interest —slowly*]. Thar's two men loafin' at the gate an' starin' at me like a couple o' strayed hogs.

CABOT [*straining his eyes*]. I kin see 'em— but I can't make out. . . .

SIMEON. It's Simeon.

PETER. It's Peter.

CABOT [*exploding*]. Why hain't ye wukin'?

SIMEON [*dryly*]. We're waitin' to welcome ye hum—yew an' the bride!

CABOT [*confusedly*]. Huh? Waal—this be yer new Maw, boys.

[*She stares at them and they at her.*]

SIMEON [*turns away and spits contemptuously*]. I see her!

PETER [*spits also*]. An' I see her!

ABBIE [*with the conqueror's conscious superiority*]. I'll go in an' look at *my* house. [*She goes slowly around to porch.*]

SIMEON [*with a snort*]. Her house!

PETER [*calls after her*]. Ye'll find Eben inside. Ye better not tell him it's *yewr* house.

ABBIE [*mouthing the name*]. Eben. [*Then quietly.*] I'll tell Eben.

CABOT [*with a contemptuous sneer*]. Ye needn't heed Eben. Eben's a dumb fool—like his Maw—soft an' simple!

SIMEON [*with his sardonic burst of laughter*]. Ha! Eben's a chip o' yew—spit 'n' image—hard 'n' bitter's a hickory tree! Dog'll eat dog. He'll eat ye yet, old man!

CABOT [*commandingly*]. Ye git t' wuk!

SIMEON [*as ABBIE disappears in house— winks at PETER and says tauntingly*]. So that

thar's our new Maw, be it? Whar in hell did ye dig her up? [*He and PETER laugh.*]

PETER. Ha! Ye'd better turn her in the pen with the other sows. [*They laugh uproariously, slapping their thighs.*]

CABOT [*so amazed at their effrontery that he stutters in confusion*]. Simeon! Peter! What's come over ye? Air ye drunk?

SIMEON. We're free, old man—free o' yew an' the hull damned farm! [*They grow more and more hilarious and excited.*]

PETER. An' we're startin' out fur the gold field o' Californi-a!

SIMEON. Ye kin take this place an' burn it!

PETER. An' bury it—fur all we cares!

SIMEON. We're free, old man! [*He cuts a caper.*]

PETER. Free! [*He gives a kick in the air.*]

SIMEON [*in a frenzy*]. Whoop!

PETER. Whoop! [*They do an absurd Indian war dance about the old man who is petrified between rage and the fear that they are insane.*]

SIMEON. We're free as Injuns! Lucky we don't skulp ye!

PETER. An' burn yer barn an' kill the stock!

SIMEON. An' rape yer new woman! Whoop! [*He and PETER stop their dance, holding their sides, rocking with wild laughter.*]

CABOT [*edging away*]. Lust fur gold—fur the sinful, easy gold o' Californi-a! It's made ye mad!

SIMEON [*tauntingly*]. Wouldn't yer like us to send ye back some sinful gold, ye old sinner?

PETER. They's gold besides what's in Californi-a! [*He retreats back beyond the vision of the old man and takes the bag of money and flaunts it in the air above his head, laughing.*]

SIMEON. And sinfuller, too!

PETER. We'll be voyagin' on the sea! Whoop! [*He leaps up and down.*]

SIMEON. Livin' free! Whoop! [*He leaps in turn.*]

CABOT [*suddenly roaring with rage*]. My cuss on ye!

SIMEON. Take our'n in trade fur it! Whoop!

CABOT. I'll hev ye both chained up in the asylum!

PETER. Ye old skinflint! Good-by!

SIMEON. Ye old blood sucker! Good-by!

CABOT. Go afore I . . . !

PETER. Whoop! [*He picks a stone from the road.* SIMEON *does the same.*]

SIMEON. Maw'll be in the parlor.

PETER. Ay-eh! One! Two!

CABOT [*frightened*]. What air ye . . . ?

PETER. Three! [*They both throw, the stones hitting the parlor window with a crash of glass, tearing the shade.*]

SIMEON. Whoop!

PETER. Whoop!

CABOT [*in a fury now, rushing toward them*]. If I kin lay hands on ye—I'll break yer bones fur ye! [*But they beat a capering retreat before him,* SIMEON *with the gate still under his arm.* CABOT *comes back, panting with impotent rage. Their voices as they go off take up the song of the gold-seekers to the old tune of* "Oh, Susannah!"]

"I jumped aboard the Liza ship,
And traveled on the sea.
And every time I thought of home
I wished it wasn't me!

Oh! Californi-a,
That's the land fur me!
I'm off to Californi-a!
With my wash bowl on my knee."

[*In the meantime, the window of the upper bedroom on right is raised and* ABBIE *sticks her head out. She looks down at* CABOT—*with a sigh of relief.*]

ABBIE. Waal—that's the last o' them two, hain't it? [*He doesn't answer. Then in possessive tones.*] This here's a nice bedroom, Ephraim. It's a r'al nice bed. Is it my room, Ephraim?

CABOT [*grimly—without looking up*]. Our'n! [*She cannot control a grimace of aversion and pulls back her head slowly and shuts the window. A sudden horrible thought seems to enter* CABOT'S *head.*] They been up to somethin'! Mebbe—mebbe they've pizened the stock—'r somethin'! [*He almost runs off down toward the barn. A moment later the kitchen door is slowly pushed open and* ABBIE *enters. For a moment she stands looking at* EBEN. *He does not notice her at first. Her eyes take him in*

penetratingly with a calculating appraisal of his strength as against hers. But under this her desire is dimly awakened by his youth and good looks. Suddenly he becomes conscious of her presence and looks up. Their eyes meet. He leaps to his feet, glowering at her speechlessly.*]

ABBIE [*in her most seductive tones which she uses all through this scene*]. Be you—Eben? I'm Abbie— [*She laughs.*] I mean, I'm yer new Maw.

EBEN [*viciously*]. No, damn ye!

ABBIE [*as if she hadn't heard—with a queer smile*]. Yer Paw's spoke a lot o' yew. . . .

EBEN. Ha!

ABBIE. Ye mustn't mind him. He's an old man. [*A long pause. They stare at each other.*] I don't want t' pretend playin' Maw t' ye, Eben. [*Admiringly.*] Ye're too big an' too strong fur that. I want t' be frens with ye. Mebbe with me fur a fren ye'd find ye'd like livin' here better. I kin make it easy fur ye with him, mebbe. [*With a scornful sense of power.*] I calc'late I kin git him t' do most anythin' fur me.

EBEN [*with bitter scorn*]. Ha! [*They stare again,* EBEN *obscurely moved, physically attracted to her—in forced stilted tones.*] Yew kin go t' the devil!

ABBIE [*calmly*]. If cussin' me does ye good, cuss all ye've a mind t'. I'm all prepared t' have ye agin me—at fust. I don't blame ye nuther. I'd feel the same at any stranger comin' t' take my Maw's place. [*He shudders. She is watching him carefully.*] Yew must've cared a lot fur yewr Maw, didn't ye? My Maw died afore I'd growed. I don't remember her none. [*A pause.*] But yew won't hate me long, Eben. I'm not the wust in the world—an' yew an' me've got a lot in common. I kin tell that by lookin' at ye. Waal—I've had a hard life, too—oceans o' trouble an' nuthin' but wuk fur reward. I was a orphan early an' had t' wuk fur others in other folks' hums. Then I married an' he turned out a drunken spreer an' so he had to wuk for others an' me too agen in other folks' hums, an' the baby died, an' my husband got sick an' died too, an' I was glad sayin' now I'm free fur once, on'y I diskivered right away all

I was free fur was t' wuk agen in other folks' hums, doin' other folks' wuk till I'd most give up hope o' ever doin' my own wuk in my own hum, an' then your Paw come. . . . [CABOT *appears returning from the barn. He comes to the gate and looks down the road the brothers have gone. A faint strain of their retreating voices is heard:* "Oh, Californi-a! That's the place for me." *He stands glowering, his fist clenched, his face grim with rage.*]

EBEN [*fighting against his growing attraction and sympathy—harshly*]. An' bought yew— like a harlot! [*She is stung and flushes angrily. She has been sincerely moved by the recital of her troubles. He adds furiously.*] An' the price he's payin' ye—this farm—was my Maw's, damn ye!—an' mine now!

ABBIE [*with a cool laugh of confidence*]. Yewr'n? We'll see 'bout that! [*Then strongly.*] Waal—what if I did need a hum? What else'd I marry an old man like him fur?

EBEN [*maliciously*]. I'll tell him ye said that!

ABBIE [*smiling*]. I'll say ye're lyin' a-purpose —an' he'll drive ye off the place!

EBEN. Ye devil!

ABBIE [*defying him*]. This be my farm—this be my hum—this be my kitchen—!

EBEN [*furiously, as if he were going to attack her.*] Shut up, damn ye!

ABBIE [*walks up to him—a queer coarse expression of desire in her face and body— slowly*]. An' upstairs—that be my bedroom— an' my bed! [*He stares into her eyes, terribly confused and torn. She adds softly.*] I hain't bad nor mean—'ceptin' fur an enemy—but I got t' fight fur what's due me out o' life, if I ever 'spect t' git it. [*Then putting her hand on his arm—seductively.*] Let's yew 'n' me be frens, Eben.

EBEN [*stupidly—as if hypnotized*]. Ay-eh. [*Then furiously flinging off her arm.*] No, ye durned old witch! I hate ye! [*He rushes out the door.*]

ABBIE [*looks after him smiling satisfiedly— then half to herself, mouthing the word*]. Eben's nice. [*She looks at the table, proudly.*] I'll wash up *my* dishes now. [EBEN *appears outside, slamming the door behind him. He comes around corner, stops on seeing his father, and stands staring at him with hate.*]

CABOT [*raising his arms to heaven in the fury he can no longer control*]. Lord God o' Hosts, smite the undutiful sons with Thy wust cuss!

EBEN [*breaking in violently*]. Yew 'n' yewr God! Allus cussin' folks—allus naggin' 'em!

CABOT [*oblivious to him—summoningly*]. God o' the old! God o' the lonesome!

EBEN [*mockingly*]. Naggin' His sheep t' sin! T' hell with yewr God! [CABOT *turns. He and* EBEN *glower at each other.*]

CABOT [*harshly*]. So it's yew. I might've knowed it. [*Shaking his finger threateningly at him.*] Blasphemin' fool! [*Then quickly.*] Why hain't ye t' wuk?

EBEN. Why hain't yew? They've went. I can't wuk it all alone.

CABOT [*contemptuously*]. Nor noways! I'm wuth ten o' ye yit, old's I be! Ye'll never be more'n half a man! [*Then, matter-of-factly.*] Waal—let's git t' the barn. [*They go. A last faint note of the* "Californi-a" *song is heard from the distance.* ABBIE *is washing her dishes.*]

Curtain

PART II

Scene i

[*The exterior of the farmhouse, as in Part I —a hot Sunday afternoon two months later.* ABBIE, *dressed in her best, is discovered sitting in a rocker at the end of the porch. She rocks listlessly, enervated by the heat, staring in front of her with bored, half-closed eyes.*

EBEN *sticks his head out of his bedroom window. He looks around furtively and tries to see —or hear—if anyone is on the porch, but although he has been careful to make no noise,* ABBIE *has sensed his movement. She stops rocking, her face grows animated and eager, she waits attentively.* EBEN *seems to feel her presence, he scowls back his thoughts of her and spits with exaggerated disdain—then with-*

draws back into the room. Abbie *waits, holding her breath as she listens with passionate eagerness for every sound within the house.*

Eben *comes out. Their eyes meet; his falter.*
5 *He is confused, he turns away and slams the door resentfully. At this gesture,* Abbie *laughs tantalizingly, amused but at the same time piqued and irritated. He scowls, strides off the porch to the path and starts to walk past her*
10 *to the road with a grand swagger of ignoring her existence. He is dressed in his store suit, spruced up, his face shines from soap and water.* Abbie *leans forward on her chair, her eyes hard and angry now, and, as he passes*
15 *her, gives a sneering, taunting chuckle.]*

Eben [*stung—turns on her furiously*]. What air yew cacklin' 'bout?

Abbie [*triumphant*]. Yew!

Eben. What about me?

20 Abbie. Ye look all slicked up like a prize bull.

Eben [*with a sneer*]. Waal—ye hain't so durned purty yerself, be ye? [*They stare into each other's eyes, his held by hers in spite of himself, hers glowingly possessive. Their phys-*
25 *ical attraction becomes a palpable force quivering in the hot air.*]

Abbie [*softly*]. Ye don't mean that, Eben. Ye may think ye mean it, mebbe, but ye don't. Ye can't. It's agin nature, Eben. Ye been
30 fightin' yer nature ever since the day I come —tryin' t' tell yerself I hain't purty t'ye. [*She laughs a low humid laugh without taking her eyes from his. A pause—her body squirms desirously—she murmurs languorously.*] Hain't
35 the sun strong an' hot? Ye kin feel it burnin' into the earth—Nature—makin' thin's grow —bigger 'n' bigger—burnin' inside ye—makin' ye want t' grow—into somethin' else—till ye're jined with it—an' it's your'n—but it
40 owns ye, too—an' makes ye grow bigger— like a tree—like them elums— [*She laughs again softly, holding his eyes. He takes a step toward her, compelled against his will.*] Nature'll beat ye, Eben. Ye might's well own
45 up t' it fust 's last.

Eben [*trying to break from her spell—confusedly*]. If Paw'd hear ye goin' on .... [*Re-*

sentfully.] But ye've made such a damned idjit out o' the old devil . . . ! [Abbie *laughs.*]

Abbie. Waal—hain't it easier fur yew with 50 him changed softer?

Eben [*defiantly*]. No. I'm fightin' him— fightin' yew—fightin' fur Maw's rights t' her hum! [*This breaks her spell for him. He glowers at her.*] An' I'm onto ye. Ye hain't 55 foolin' me a mite. Ye're aimin' t' swaller up everythin' an' make it your'n. Waal, you'll find I'm a heap sight bigger hunk nor yew kin chew! [*He turns from her with a sneer.*]

Abbie [*trying to regain her ascendancy—* 60 *seductively*]. Eben!

Eben. Leave me be! [*He starts to walk away.*]

Abbie [*more commandingly*]. Eben!

Eben [*stops resentfully*]. What d'ye want?

Abbie [*trying to conceal a growing excite-* 65 *ment*]. Whar air ye goin'?

Eben [*with malicious nonchalance*]. Oh—up the road a spell.

Abbie. T' the village?

Eben [*airily*]. Mebbe. 70

Abbie [*excitedly*]. T' see that Min, I s'pose?

Eben. Mebbe.

Abbie [*weakly*]. What d'ye want t' waste time on her fur?

Eben [*revenging himself now—grinning at* 75 *her*]. Ye can't beat Nature, didn't ye say? [*He laughs and again starts to walk away.*]

Abbie [*bursting out*]. An ugly old hake!

Eben [*with a tantalizing sneer*]. She's purtier'n yew be! 80

Abbie. That every wuthless drunk in the country has . . . .

Eben [*tauntingly*]. Mebbe—but she's better'n yew. She owns up fa'r 'n' squar' t' her doin's. 85

Abbie [*furiously*]. Don't ye dare compare . . . .

Eben. She don't go sneakin' an' stealin'— what's mine.

Abbie [*savagely seizing on his weak point*]. 90 Your'n? Yew mean—my farm?

Eben. I mean the farm yew sold yerself fur like any other old whore—my farm!

Abbie [*stung—fiercely*]. Ye'll never live t' see

the day when even a stinkin' weed on it 'll belong t' ye! [*Then in a scream.*] Git out o' my sight! Go on t' yer slut—disgracin' yer Paw' 'n' me! I'll git yer Paw t' horsewhip ye

5 off the place if I want t'! Ye're only livin' here 'cause I tolerate ye! Git along! I hate the sight o' ye! [*She stops panting and glaring at him.*]

EBEN [*returning her glance in kind*]. An' I hate the sight o' yew! [*He turns and strides*

10 *off up the road. She follows his retreating figure with concentrated hate. Old* CABOT *appears coming up from the barn. The hard, grim expression of his face has changed. He seems in some queer way softened, mellowed.*

15 *His eyes have taken on a strange, incongruous dreamy quality. Yet there is no hint of physical weakness about him—rather he looks more robust and younger.* ABBIE *sees him and turns away quickly with unconcealed aversion.*

20 *He comes slowly up to her.*]

CABOT [*mildly*]. War yew an' Eben quarrelin' agen?

ABBIE [*shortly*]. No.

CABOT. Ye was talkin' a'mighty loud. [*He*

25 *sits down on the edge of porch.*]

ABBIE [*snappishly*]. If ye heerd us they hain't no need askin' questions.

CABOT. I didn't hear what ye said.

ABBIE [*relieved*]. Waal—it wa'n't nothin' t'

30 speak on.

CABOT [*after a pause*]. Eben's queer.

ABBIE [*bitterly*]. He's the dead spit 'n' image o' yew!

CABOT [*queerly interested*]. D'ye think so,

35 Abbie? [*After a pause, ruminatingly.*] Me 'n' Eben's allus fit 'n' fit. I never could b'ar him now, he's so thunderin' soft—like his Maw.

ABBIE [*scornfully*]. Ay-eh! 'Bout as soft as yew be!

40 CABOT [*as if he hadn't heard*]. Mebbe I been too hard on him.

ABBIE [*jeeringly*]. Waal—ye're gittin' soft now—soft as slop! That's what Eben was sayin'.

45 CABOT [*his face instantly grim and ominous*]. Eben was sayin'? Waal, he'd best not do nothin' t' try me 'r he'll soon diskiver. . . . [*A pause. She keeps her face turned away. His*

gradually softens. He stares up at the sky.] Purty, hain't it? 50

ABBIE [*crossly*]. I don't see nothin' purty.

CABOT. The sky. Feels like a wa'm field up thar.

ABBIE [*sarcastically*]. Air yew aimin' t' buy up over the farm too? [*She snickers contemp-* 55 *tuously.*]

CABOT [*strangely*]. I'd like t' own my own place up thar. [*A pause.*] I'm gittin' old, Abbie. I'm gittin' ripe on the bough. [*A pause. She stares at him mystified. He goes on.*] It's allus 60 lonesome cold in the house—even when it's bilin' hot outside. Hain't yew noticed?

ABBIE. No.

CABOT. It's wa'm down t' the barn—nice smellin' an' warm—with the cows. [*A pause.*] 65 Cows is queer.

ABBIE. Like yew?

CABOT. Like Eben. [*A pause.*] I'm gittin' t' feel resigned t' Eben—jest as I got t' feel 'bout his Maw. I'm gittin' t' learn to b'ar his soft- 70 ness—jest like her'n. I calc'late I c'd a'most take t' him—if he wa'n't sech a dumb fool! [*A pause.*] I s'pose it's old age a-creepin' in my bones.

ABBIE [*indifferently*]. Waal—ye hain't dead 75 yet.

CABOT [*roused*]. No, I hain't, yew bet—not by a hell of a sight—I'm sound 'n' tough as hickory! [*Then moodily.*] But arter three score and ten the Lord warns ye t' prepare. [*A* 80 *pause.*] That's why Eben's come in my head. Now that his cussed sinful brothers is gone their path t' hell, they's no one left but Eben.

ABBIE [*resentfully*]. They's me, hain't they? [*Agitatedly.*] What's all this sudden likin' ye've 85 tuk to Eben? Why don't ye say nothin' 'bout me? Hain't I yer lawful wife?

CABOT [*simply*]. Ay-eh. Ye be. [*A pause— he stares at her desirously—his eyes grow avid—then with a sudden movement he seizes* 90 *her hands and squeezes them, declaiming in a queer camp-meeting preacher's tempo.*] Yew air my Rose o' Sharon! Behold, yew air fair; yer eyes air doves; yer lips air like scarlet; yer two breasts air like two fawns; yer navel be 95 like a round goblet; yer belly be like a heap o' wheat. . . . [*He covers her hand with kisses She does not seem to notice. She stares before her with hard angry eyes.*]

ABBIE [*jerking her hands away—harshly*].
5 So ye're plannin' t' leave the farm t' Eben, air ye?

CABOT [*dazedly*]. Leave . . . ? [*Then with resentful obstinacy.*] I hain't a-givin' it t' no one!

10 ABBIE [*remorselessly*]. Ye can't take it with ye.

CABOT [*thinks a moment—then reluctantly*]. No, I calc'late not. [*After a pause—with a strange passion.*] But if I could, I would, by
15 the Etarnal! 'R if I could, in my dyin' hour, I'd set it afire an' watch it burn—this house an' every ear o' corn an' every tree down t' the last blade o' hay! I'd sit an' know it was all a-dyin' with me an' no one else'd ever own
20 what was mine, what I'd made out o' nothin' with my own sweat 'n' blood! [*A pause—then he adds with a queer affection.*] 'Ceptin' the cows. Them I'd turn free.

ABBIE [*harshly*]. An' me?

25 CABOT [*with a queer smile*]. Ye'd be turned free, too.

ABBIE [*furiously*]. So that's the thanks I git fur marryin' ye—t' have ye change kind to Eben who hates ye, an' talk o' turnin' me out
30 in the road.

CABOT [*hastily*]. Abbie! Ye know I wa'n't. . . .

ABBIE [*vengefully*]. Just let me tell ye a thing or two 'bout Eben! Whar's he gone? T' see that
35 harlot, Min! I tried fur t' stop him. Disgracin' yew an' me—on the Sabbath, too!

CABOT [*rather guiltily*]. He's a sinner—nateral-born. It's lust eatin' his heart.

ABBIE [*enraged beyond endurance—wildly
40 vindictive*]. An' his lust fur me! Kin ye find excuses fur that?

CABOT [*stares at her—after a dead pause*]. Lust—fur yew?

ABBIE [*defiantly*]. He was tryin' t' make love
45 t' me—when ye heerd us quarrelin'.

CABOT [*stares at her—then a terrible expression of rage comes over his face—he springs to his feet shaking all over*]. By the A'mighty God—I'll end him!

50 ABBIE [*frightened now for* EBEN]. No! Don't ye!

CABOT [*violently*]. I'll git the shotgun an' blow his soft brains t' the top of them elums!

ABBIE [*throwing her arms around him*]. No,
55 Ephraim!

CABOT [*pushing her away violently*]. I will, by God!

ABBIE [*in a quieting tone*]. Listen, Ephraim. 'Twa'n't nothin' bad—on'y a boy's foolin'—
60 'twa'n't meant serious—jest jokin' an' teasin'. . . .

CABOT. Then why did ye say—lust?

ABBIE. It must hev sounded wusser'n I meant. An' I was mad at thinkin'—ye'd leave
65 him the farm.

CABOT [*quieter but still grim and cruel*]. Waal then, I'll horsewhip him off the place if that much'll content ye.

ABBIE [*reaching out and taking his hand*].
70 No. Don't think o' me! Ye mustn't drive him off. 'Tain't sensible. Who'll ye get to help ye on the farm? They's no one hereabouts.

CABOT [*considers this—then nodding his appreciation*]. Ye got a head on ye. [*Then irri-
75 tably.*] Waal, let him stay. [*He sits down on the edge of the porch. She sits beside him. He murmurs contemptuously.*] I oughtn't t' git riled so—at that 'ere fool calf. [*A pause.*] But har's the p'int. What son o' mine'll keep on
80 here t' the farm—when the Lord does call me? Simeon an' Peter air gone t' hell—an' Eben's follerin' 'em.

ABBIE. They's me.

CABOT. Ye're on'y a woman.

85 ABBIE. I'm yewr wife.

CABOT. That hain't me. A son is me—my blood—mine. Mine ought t' git mine. An' then it's still mine—even though I be six foot under. D'ye see?

90 ABBIE [*giving him a look of hatred*]. Ay-eh. I see. [*She becomes very thoughtful, her face growing shrewd, her eyes studying* CABOT *craftily.*]

CABOT. I'm gittin' old—ripe on the bough.
95 [*Then with a sudden forced reassurance.*] Not but what I hain't a hard nut t' crack even yet

—an' fur many a year t' come! By the Etarnal,
I kin break most o' the young fellers' backs at
any kind o' work any day o' the year!

ABBIE [*suddenly*]. Mebbe the Lord'll give *us*
5 a son.

CABOT [*turns and stares at her eagerly*]. Ye
mean—a son—t' me 'n' yew?

ABBIE [*with a cajoling smile*]. Ye're a strong
man yet, hain't ye? 'Tain't noways impossible,
10 be it? We know that. Why d'ye stare so? Hain't
ye never thought o' that afore? I been thinkin'
o' it all along. Ay-eh—an' I been prayin' it'd
happen, too.

CABOT [*his face growing full of joyous pride
15 and a sort of religious ecstasy*]. Ye been
prayin', Abbie?—fur a son?—t' us?

ABBIE. Ay-eh. [*With a grim resolution.*] I
want a son now.

CABOT [*excitedly clutching both of her
20 hands in his*]. It'd be the blessin' o' God, Abbie
—the blessin' o' God A'mighty on me—in my
old age—in my lonesomeness! They hain't
nothin' I wouldn't do fur ye then, Abbie. Ye'd
hev on'y t' ask it—anythin' ye'd a mind t'!

25 ABBIE [*interrupting*]. Would ye will the farm
t' me then—t' me an' it . . . ?

CABOT [*vehemently*]. I'd do anythin' ye
axed, I tell ye! I swar it! May I be everlastin'
damned t' hell if I wouldn't! [*He sinks to his
30 knees pulling her down with him. He trembles
all over with the fervor of his hopes.*] Pray t'
the Lord agen, Abbie. It's the Sabbath! I'll jine
ye! Two prayers air better nor one. "An' God
hearkened unto Rachel"! An' God hearkened
35 unto Abbie! Pray, Abbie! Pray fur him to
hearken! [*He bows his head, mumbling. She
pretends to do likewise but gives him a side
glance of scorn and triumph.*]

Curtain

Scene ii

[*About eight in the evening. The interior of
40 the two bedrooms on the top floor is shown.
EBEN is sitting on the side of his bed in the
room on the left. On account of the heat he has
taken off everything but his undershirt and
pants. His feet are bare. He faces front, brood-
45 ing moodily, his chin propped on his hands, a*

desperate expression on his face.

In the other room CABOT *and* ABBIE *are sitting side by side on the edge of their bed, an
old four-poster with feather mattress. He is in
his night shirt, she in her nightdress. He is still
50 in the queer, excited mood into which the
notion of a son has thrown him. Both rooms
are lighted dimly and flickeringly by tallow
candles.*]

CABOT. The farm needs a son.
55
ABBIE. I need a son.

CABOT. Ay-eh. Sometimes ye air the farm
an' sometimes the farm be yew. That's why I
clove t' ye in my lonesomeness. [*A pause. He
pounds his knee with his fist.*] Me an' the farm
60 has got t' beget a son!

ABBIE. Ye'd best go t' sleep. Ye're gittin'
thin's all mixed.

CABOT [*with an impatient gesture*]. No, I
hain't. My mind's clear's a well. Ye don't know
65 me, that's it. [*He stares hopelessly at the floor.*]

ABBIE [*indifferently*]. Mebbe. [*In the next
room* EBEN *gets up and paces up and down distractedly.* ABBIE *hears him. Her eyes fasten on
the intervening wall with concentrated atten-
70 tion.* EBEN *stops and stares. Their hot glances
seem to meet through the wall. Unconsciously
he stretches out his arms for her and she half
rises. Then aware, he mutters a curse at himself and flings himself face downward on the
75 bed, his clenched fists above his head, his face
buried in the pillow.* ABBIE *relaxes with a faint
sigh but her eyes remain fixed on the wall; she
listens with all her attention for some movement from* EBEN.]
80
CABOT [*suddenly raises his head and looks
at her—scornfully*]. Will ye ever know me—'r
will any man 'r woman? [*Shaking his head.*]
No. I calc'late 't wa'n't t' be. [*He turns away.
ABBIE looks at the wall. Then, evidently unable
85 to keep silent about his thoughts without looking at his wife, he puts out his hand and
clutches her knee. She starts violently, looks at
him, sees he is not watching her, concentrates
again on the wall and pays no attention to what
90 he says.*] Listen, Abbie. When I come here
fifty odd year ago—I was jest twenty an' the
strongest an' hardest ye ever seen—ten times

as strong an' fifty times as hard as Eben. Waal
—this place was nothin' but fields o' stones.
Folks laughed when I tuk it. They couldn't
know what I knowed. When ye kin make corn
5 sprout out o' stones, God's livin' in yew! They
wa'n't strong enuf fur that! They reckoned
God was easy. They laughed. They don't laugh
no more. Some died hereabouts. Some went
West an' died. They're all under ground—fur
10 follerin' arter an easy God. God hain't easy.
[*He shakes his head slowly.*] An' I growed
hard. Folks kept allus sayin' he's a hard man
like 'twas sinful t' be hard, so's at last I said
back at 'em: Waal then, by thunder, ye'll git
15 me hard an' see how ye like it! [*Then suddenly.*] But I give in t' weakness once. 'Twas
arter I'd been here two year. I got weak—des-
pairful—they was so many stones. They was
a party leavin', givin' up, goin' West. I jined
20 'em. We tracked on 'n' on. We come t' broad
medders, plains, whar the soil was black an'
rich as gold. Nary a stone. Easy. Ye'd on'y to
plow an' sow an' then set an' smoke yer pipe
an' watch thin's grow. I could o' been a rich
25 man—but somethin' in me fit me an' fit me—
the voice o' God sayin': "This hain't wuth
nothin' t' Me. Git ye back t' hum!" I got afeerd
o' that voice an' I lit out back t' hum here,
leavin' my claim an' crops t' whoever'd a mind
30 t' take 'em. Ay-eh. I actoolly give up what was
rightful mine! God's hard, not easy! God's in
the stones! Build my church on a rock—out o'
stones an' I'll be in them! That's what He
meant t' Peter! [*He sighs heavily—a pause.*]
35 Stones. I picked 'em up an' piled 'em into walls.
Ye kin read the years o' my life in them walls,
every day a hefted stone, climbin' over the hills
up and down, fencin' in the fields that was
mine, whar I'd made thin's grow out o' nothin'
40 —like the will o' God, like the servant o' His
hand. It wa'n't easy. It was hard an' He made
me hard fur it. [*He pauses.*] All the time I kept
gittin' lonesomer. I tuk a wife. She bore Simeon
an' Peter. She was a good woman. She wuked
45 hard. We was married twenty year. She never
knowed me. She helped but she never knowed
what she was helpin'. I was allus lonesome.
She died. After that it wa'n't so lonesome fur

a spell. [*A pause.*] I lost count o' the years. I
had no time t' fool away countin' 'em. Sim an'
50 Peter helped. The farm growed. It was all mine!
When I thought o' that I didn't feel lonesome.
[*A pause.*] But ye can't hitch yer mind t' one
thin' day an' night. I tuk another wife—Eben's
Maw. Her folks was contestin' me at law over
55 my deeds t' the farm—my farm! That's why
Eben keeps a-talkin' his fool talk o' this bein'
his Maw's farm. She bore Eben. She was purty
—but soft. She tried t' be hard. She couldn't.
She never knowed me nor nothin'. It was lone-
60 somer 'n hell with her. After a matter o' sixteen
odd years, she died. [*A pause.*] I lived with the
boys. They hated me 'cause I was hard. I hated
them 'cause they was soft. They coveted the
farm without knowin' what it meant. It made
65 me bitter 'n wormwood. It aged me—them
coveting what I'd made fur mine. Then this
spring the call come—the voice o' God cryin'
in my wilderness, in my lonesomeness—t' go
out an' seek an' find! [*Turning to her with
70 strange passion.*] I sought ye an' I found ye!
Yew air my Rose o' Sharon! Yer eyes air like.
. . . [*She has turned a blank face, resentful
eyes to his. He stares at her for a moment—
then harshly.*] Air ye any the wiser fur all I've
75 told ye?

ABBIE [*confusedly*]. Mebbe.

CABOT [*pushing her away from him angrily*].
Ye don't know nothin'—nor never will. If ye
don't hev a son t' redeem ye. . . . [*This is a tone
80 of cold threat.*]

ABBIE [*resentfully*]. I've prayed, hain't I?

CABOT [*bitterly*]. Pray agen—fur under-
standin'!

ABBIE [*a veiled threat in her tone*]. Ye'll have
85 a son out o' me, I promise ye.

CABOT. How kin ye promise?

ABBIE. I got second-sight mebbe. I kin foretell. [*She gives a queer smile.*]

CABOT. I believe ye have. Ye give me the
90 chills sometimes. [*He shivers.*] It's cold in this
house. It's oneasy. They's thin's pokin' about
in the dark—in the corner. [*He pulls on his
trousers, tucking in his night shirt, and pulls
on his boots.*]
95

ABBIE [*surprised*]. Whar air ye goin'?

CABOT [*queerly*]. Down whar it's restful—whar it's warm down t' the barn. [*Bitterly.*] I kin talk t' the cows. They know. They know the farm an' me. They'll give me peace. [*He turns to go out the door.*]

ABBIE [*a bit frightenedly*]. Air ye ailin' tonight, Ephraim?

CABOT. Growin'. Growin' ripe on the bough. [*He turns and goes, his boots clumping down the stairs. EBEN sits up with a start, listening. ABBIE is conscious of his movement and stares at the wall. CABOT comes out of the house around the corner and stands by the gate, blinking at the sky. He stretches up his hands in a tortured gesture.*] God A'mighty, call from the dark! [*He listens as if expecting an answer. Then his arms drop, he shakes his head and plods off toward the barn. EBEN and ABBIE stare at each other through the wall. EBEN sighs heavily and ABBIE echoes it. Both become terribly nervous, uneasy. Finally ABBIE gets up and listens, her ear to the wall. He acts as if he saw every move she was making, he becomes resolutely still. She seems driven into a decision—goes out the door in rear determinedly. His eyes follow her. Then as the door of his room is opened softly, he turns away, waits in an attitude of strained fixity. ABBIE stands for a second staring at him, her eyes burning with desire. Then with a little cry she runs over and throws her arms about his neck, she pulls his head back and covers his mouth with kisses. At first, he submits dumbly; then he puts his arms about her neck and returns her kisses, but finally, suddenly aware of his hatred, he hurls her away from him, springing to his feet. They stand speechless and breathless, panting like two animals.*]

ABBIE [*at last—painfully*]. Ye shouldn't, Eben—ye shouldn't—I'd make ye happy!

EBEN [*harshly*]. I don't want t' be happy—from yew!

ABBIE [*helplessly*]. Ye do, Eben! Ye do! Why d'ye lie?

EBEN [*viciously*]. I don't take t' ye, I tell ye! I hate the sight o' ye!

ABBIE [*with an uncertain troubled laugh*].

Waal, I kissed ye anyways—an' ye kissed back—yer lips was burnin'—ye can't lie 'bout that! [*Intensely.*] If ye don't care, why did ye kiss me back—why was yer lips burnin'?

EBEN [*wiping his mouth*]. It was like pizen on 'em. [*Then tauntingly.*] When I kissed ye back, mebbe I thought 'twas someone else.

ABBIE [*wildly*]. Min?

EBEN. Mebbe.

ABBIE [*torturedly*]. Did ye go t' see her? Did ye r'ally go? I thought ye mightn't. Is that why ye throwed me off jest now?

EBEN [*sneeringly*]. What if it be?

ABBIE [*raging*]. Then ye're a dog, Eben Cabot!

EBEN [*threateningly*]. Ye can't talk that way t' me!

ABBIE [*with a shrill laugh*]. Can't I? Did ye think I was in love with ye—a weak thin' like yew? Not much! I on'y wanted ye fur a purpose o' my own—an' I'll hev ye fur it yet 'cause I'm stronger'n yew be!

EBEN [*resentfully*]. I knowed well it was on'y part o' yer plan t' swaller everythin'!

ABBIE [*tauntingly*]. Mebbe!

EBEN [*furious*]. Git out o' my room!

ABBIE. This air my room an' ye're on'y hired help!

EBEN [*threateningly*]. Git out afore I murder ye!

ABBIE [*quite confident now*]. I hain't a mite afeerd. Ye want me, don't ye? Yes, ye do! An' yer Paw's son'll never kill what he wants! Look at yer eyes! They's lust fur me in 'em, burnin' 'em up! Look at yer lips now! They're tremblin' an' longin' t' kiss me, an' yer teeth t' bite! [*He is watching her now with a horrible fascination. She laughs a crazy triumphant laugh.*] I'm a-goin' t' make all o' this hum my hum! They's one room hain't mine yet, but it's a-goin t' be tonight. I'm a-goin' down now an' light up! [*She makes him a mocking bow.*] Won't ye come courtin' me in the best parlor, Mister Cabot?

EBEN [*staring at her—horribly confused—dully*]. Don't ye dare! It hain't been opened since Maw died an' was laid out thar! Don't ye . . . ! [*But her eyes are fixed on his so burningly that his will seems to wither before hers. He stands swaying toward her helplessly.*]

5   ABBIE [*holding his eyes and putting all her will into her words as she backs out the door*]. I'll expect ye afore long, Eben.

EBEN [*stares after her for a while, walking toward the door. A light appears in the parlor window. He murmurs*]. In the parlor? [*This
10   seems to arouse connotations for he comes back and puts on his white shirt, collar, half ties the tie mechanically, puts on coat, takes his hat, stands barefooted looking about him in bewilderment, mutters wonderingly.*] Maw!
15   Whar air yew? [*Then goes slowly toward the door in rear.*]

Curtain

Scene iii

[*A few minutes later. The interior of the parlor is shown. A grim, repressed room like a tomb in which the family has been interred
20   alive. ABBIE sits on the edge of the horsehair sofa. She has lighted all the candles and the room is revealed in all its preserved ugliness. A change has come over the woman. She looks awed and frightened now, ready to run
25   away.*

*The door is opened and EBEN appears. His face wears an expression of obsessed confusion. He stands staring at her, his arms hanging disjointedly from his shoulders, his feet
30   bare, his hat in his hand.*]

ABBIE [*after a pause—with a nervous, formal politeness*]. Won't ye set?

EBEN [*dully*]. Ay-eh. [*Mechanically he places his hat carefully on the floor near the door and
35   sits stiffly beside her on the edge of the sofa. A pause. They both remain rigid, looking straight ahead with eyes full of fear.*]

ABBIE. When I fust come in—in the dark—they seemed somethin' here.

40   EBEN [*simply*]. Maw.

ABBIE. I kin still feel—somethin'. . . .

EBEN. It's Maw.

ABBIE. At fust I was feered o' it. I wanted t' yell an' run. Now—since yew come—seems

like it's growin' soft an' kind t' me. [*Address-   45
ing the air—queerly.*] Thank yew.

EBEN. Maw allus loved me.

ABBIE. Mebbe it knows I love yew, too. Mebbe that makes it kind t' me.

EBEN [*dully*]. I dunno. I should think she'd   50
hate ye.

ABBIE [*with certainty*]. No. I kin feel it don't —not no more.

EBEN. Hate ye fur stealin' her place—here in her hum—settin' in her parlor whar she was   55
laid— [*He suddenly stops, staring stupidly before him.*]

ABBIE. What is it, Eben?

EBEN [*in a whisper*]. Seems like Maw didn't want me t' remind ye.   60

ABBIE [*excitedly*]. I knowed, Eben! It's kind t' me! It don't b'ar me no grudges fur what I never knowed an' couldn't help!

EBEN. Maw b'ars him a grudge.

ABBIE. Waal, so does all o' us.   65

EBEN. Ay-eh. [*With passion.*] I does, by God!

ABBIE [*taking one of his hands in hers and patting it*]. Thar! Don't git riled thinkin' o' him. Think o' yer Maw who's kind t' us. Tell   70
me about yer Maw, Eben.

EBEN. They hain't nothin' much. She was kind. She was good.

ABBIE [*putting one arm over his shoulder. He does not seem to notice—passionately*]. I'll   75
be kind and good t' ye!

EBEN. Sometimes she used t' sing fur me.

ABBIE. I'll sing fur ye!

EBEN. This was her hum. This was her farm.

ABBIE. This is my hum! This is my farm!   80

EBEN. He married her t' steal 'em. She was soft an' easy. He couldn't 'preciate her.

ABBIE. He can't 'preciate me!

EBEN. He murdered her with his hardness.

ABBIE. He's murderin' me!   85

EBEN. She died. [*A pause.*] Sometimes she used to sing fur me. [*He bursts into a fit of sobbing.*]

ABBIE [*both her arms around him—with wild passion.*] I'll sing fur ye! I'll die fur ye!   90
[*In spite of her overwhelming desire for him,*

there is a sincere maternal love in her manner and voice—a horribly frank mixture of lust and mother love.] Don't cry, Eben! I'll take yer Maw's place! I'll be everythin' she was t' ye!
5 Let me kiss ye, Eben! [*She pulls his head around. He makes a bewildered pretense of resistance. She is tender.*] Don't be afeered! I'll kiss ye pure, Eben—same 's if I was a Maw t' ye—an' ye kin kiss me back 's if yew was my
10 son—my boy—sayin' good-night t' me! Kiss me, Eben. [*They kiss in restrained fashion. Then suddenly wild passion overcomes her. She kisses him lustfully again and again and he flings his arms about her and returns her
15 kisses. Suddenly, as in the bedroom, he frees himself from her violently and springs to his feet. He is trembling all over, in a strange state of terror. ABBIE strains her arms toward him with fierce pleading.*] Don't ye leave me, Eben!
20 Can't ye see it hain't enuf—lovin' ye like a Maw—can't ye see it's got t' be that an' more —much more—a hundred times more—fur me t' be happy—fur yew t' be happy?

EBEN [*to the presence he feels in the room*].
25 Maw! Maw! What d'ye want? What air ye tellin' me?

ABBIE. She's tellin' ye t' love me. She knows I love ye an' I'll be good t' ye. Can't ye feel it? Don't ye know? She's tellin' ye t' love me,
30 Eben!

EBEN. Ay-eh. I feel—mebbe she—but—I can't figger out—why—when ye've stole her place —here in her hum—in the parlor whar she was—

35 ABBIE [*fiercely*]. She knows I love ye!

EBEN [*his face suddenly lighting up with a fierce, triumphant grin*]. I see it! I see why. It's her vengeance on him—so's she kin rest quiet in her grave!

40 ABBIE [*wildly*]. Vengeance o' God on the hull o' us! What d' we give a durn? I love ye, Eben! God knows I love ye! [*She stretches out her arms for him.*]

EBEN [*throws himself on his knees beside the
45 sofa and grabs her in his arms—releasing all his pent-up passion*]. An' I love yew, Abbie!— now I kin say it! I been dyin' fur want o' ye—

every hour since ye come! I love ye! [*Their lips meet in a fierce, bruising kiss.*]

Curtain

Scene iv

[*Exterior of the farmhouse. It is just dawn.
50 The front door at right is opened and EBEN comes out and walks around to the gate. He is dressed in his working clothes. He seems changed. His face wears a bold and confident expression, he is grinning to himself with
55 evident satisfaction. As he gets near the gate, the window of the parlor is heard opening and the shutters are flung back and ABBIE sticks her head out. Her hair tumbles over her shoulders in disarray, her face is flushed, she
60 looks at EBEN with tender, languorous eyes and calls softly.*]

ABBIE. Eben. [*As he turns—playfully.*] Jest one more kiss afore ye go. I'm goin' to miss ye fearful all day.
65

EBEN. An' me yew, ye kin bet! [*He goes to her. They kiss several times. He draws away, laughingly.*] Thar. That's enuf, hain't it? Ye won't hev none left fur next time.

ABBIE. I got a million o' 'em left fur yew!
70 [*Then a bit anxiously.*] D'ye r'ally love me, Eben?

EBEN [*emphatically*]. I like ye better'n any gal I ever knowed! That's gospel!

ABBIE. Likin' hain't lovin'.
75

EBEN. Waal then—I love ye. Now air yew satisfied?

ABBIE. Ay-eh, I be. [*She smiles at him adoringly.*]

EBEN. I better git t' the barn. The old critter's
80 liable t' suspicion an' come sneakin' up.

ABBIE [*with a confident laugh*]. Let him! I kin allus pull the wool over his eyes. I'm goin' t' leave the shutters open and let in the sun 'n' air. This room's been dead long enuf. Now it's
85 goin' t' be my room!

EBEN [*frowning*]. Ay-eh.

ABBIE [*hastily*]. I meant—our room.

EBEN. Ay-eh.

ABBIE. We made it our'n last night, didn't
90 we? We give it life—our lovin' did. [*A pause.*]

EBEN [*with a strange look*]. Maw's gone back t' her grave. She kin sleep now.

ABBIE. May she rest in peace! [*Then tenderly rebuking.*] Ye oughtn't t' talk o' sad
5 thin's—this mornin'.

EBEN. It jest come up in my mind o' itself.

ABBIE. Don't let it. [*He doesn't answer. She yawns.*] Waal, I'm a-goin' t' steal a wink o' sleep. I'll tell the Old Man I hain't feelin' pert.
10 Let him git his own vittles.

EBEN. I see him comin' from the barn. Ye better look smart an' git upstairs.

ABBIE. Ay-eh. Good-by. Don't ferget me. [*She throws him a kiss. He grins—then squares
15 his shoulders and awaits his father confidently. CABOT walks slowly up from the left, staring up at the sky with a vague face.*]

EBEN [*jovially*]. Mornin', Paw. Star-gazin' in daylight?
20 CABOT. Purty, hain't it?

EBEN [*looking around him possessively*]. It's a durned purty farm.

CABOT. I mean the sky.

EBEN [*grinning*]. How d'ye know? Them eyes
25 o' your'n can't see that fur. [*This tickles his humor and he slaps his thigh and laughs.*] Ho-ho! That's a good un!

CABOT [*grimly sarcastic*]. Ye're feelin' right chipper, hain't ye? Whar'd ye steal the likker?
30 EBEN [*good-naturedly*]. 'Tain't likker. Jest life. [*Suddenly holding out his hand—soberly.*] Yew 'n' me is quits. Let's shake hands.

CABOT [*suspiciously*]. What's come over ye?

EBEN. Then don't. Mebbe it's jest as well.
35 [*A moment's pause.*] What's come over me? [*Queerly.*] Didn't ye feel her passin'—goin' back t' her grave?

CABOT [*dully*]. Who?

EBEN. Maw. She kin rest now an' sleep con-
40 tent. She's quit with ye.

CABOT [*confusedly*]. I rested. I slept good—down with the cows. They know how t' sleep. They're teachin' me.

EBEN [*suddenly jovial again*]. Good fur the
45 cows! Waal—ye better git t' work.

CABOT [*grimly amused*]. Air ye bossin' me, ye calf?

EBEN [*beginning to laugh*]. Ay-eh! I'm bossin' yew! Ha-ha-ha! See how ye like it! Ha-ha-ha! I'm the prize rooster o' this roost. Ha- 50
ha-ha! [*He goes off toward the barn laughing.*]

CABOT [*looks after him with scornful pity*]. Soft-headed. Like his Maw. Dead spit 'n' image. No hope in him! [*He spits with contemptuous disgust.*] A born fool! [*Then mat- 55
ter-of-factly.*] Waal—I'm gittin' peckish. [*He goes toward door.*]

Curtain

PART III

Scene i

[*A night in late spring the following year. The kitchen and the two bedrooms upstairs are shown. The two bedrooms are dimly lighted 60
by a tallow candle in each. EBEN is sitting on the side of the bed in his room, his chin propped on his fists, his face a study of the struggle he is making to understand his conflicting emotions. The noisy laughter and music from 65
below where a kitchen dance is in progress annoy and distract him. He scowls at the floor.*

In the next room a cradle stands beside the double bed.

*In the kitchen all is festivity. The stove has 70
been taken down to give more room to the dancers. The chairs, with wooden benches added, have been pushed back against the walls. On these are seated, squeezed in tight against one another, farmers and their wives 75
and their young folks of both sexes from the neighboring farms. They are all chattering and laughing loudly. They evidently have some secret joke in common. There is no end of winking, of nudging, of meaning nods of the 80
head toward CABOT who, in a state of extreme hilarious excitement increased by the amount he has drunk, is standing near the rear door where there is a small keg of whisky and serving drinks to all the men. In the left corner, 85
front, dividing the attention with her husband, ABBIE is sitting in a rocking chair, a shawl wrapped about her shoulders. She is very pale, her face is thin and drawn, her eyes are fixed*

anxiously on the open door in rear as if waiting for someone.

The musician is tuning up his fiddle, seated in the far right corner. He is a lanky young
5 *fellow with a long, weak face. His pale eyes blink incessantly and he grins about him shyly with a greedy malice.]*

ABBIE [*suddenly turning to a young girl on her right*]. Whar's Eben?

10 YOUNG GIRL [*eyeing her scornfully*]. I dunno, Mrs. Cabot. I hain't seen Eben in ages. [*Meaningly.*] Seems like he's spent most o' his time t' hum since yew come.

ABBIE [*vaguely*]. I tuk his Maw's place.
15 YOUNG GIRL. Ay-eh. So I've heerd. [*She turns away to retail this bit of gossip to her mother sitting next to her. ABBIE turns to her left to a big stoutish middle-aged man whose flushed face and starting eyes show the amount*
20 *of "likker" he has consumed.*]

ABBIE. Ye hain't seen Eben, hev ye?

MAN. No, I hain't. [*Then he adds with a wink.*] If yew hain't, who would?

ABBIE. He's the best dancer in the county.
25 He'd ought t' come an' dance.

MAN [*with a wink*]. Mebbe he's doin' the dutiful an' walkin' the kid t' sleep. It's a boy, hain't it?

ABBIE [*nodding vaguely*]. Ay-eh—born two
30 weeks back—purty's a picter.

MAN. They all is—t' their Maws. [*Then in a whisper, with a nudge and a leer.*] Listen, Abbie—if ye ever git tired o' Eben, remember me! Don't fergit now! [*He looks at her un-*
35 *comprehending face for a second—then grunts disgustedly.*] Waal—guess I'll likker agin.[*He goes over and joins CABOT who is arguing noisily with an old farmer over cows. They all drink.*]
40 ABBIE [*this time appealing to nobody in particular*]. Wonder what Eben's a-doin'? [*Her remark is repeated down the line with many a guffaw and titter until it reaches the fiddler. He fastens his blinking eyes on ABBIE.*]
45 FIDDLER [*raising his voice*]. Bet I kin tell ye, Abbie, what Eben's doin'! He's down t' the church offerin' up prayers o' thanksgivin'. [*They all titter expectantly.*]

A MAN. What fur? [*Another titter.*]

FIDDLER. 'Cause unto him a— [*He hesitates* 50 *just long enough.*] brother is born! [*A roar of laughter. They all look from ABBIE to CABOT. She is oblivious, staring at the door. CABOT, although he hasn't heard the words, is irritated by the laughter and steps forward, glaring* 55 *about him. There is an immediate silence.*]

CABOT. What're ye all bleatin' about—like a flock o' goats? Why don't ye dance, damn ye? I axed ye here t' dance—t' eat, drink an' be merry—an' thar ye set cacklin' like a lot o' 60 wet hens with the pip! Ye've swilled my likker an' guzzled my vittles like hogs, hain't ye? Then dance fur me, can't ye? That's fa'r an' squar', hain't it? [*A grumble of resentment goes around but they are all evidently in too* 65 *much awe of him to express it openly.*]

FIDDLER [*slyly*]. We're waitin' fur Eben. [*A suppressed laugh.*]

CABOT [*with a fierce exultation*]. T' hell with Eben! Eben's done fur now! I got a new son! 70 [*His mood switching with drunken suddenness.*] But ye needn't t' laugh at Eben, none o' ye! He's my blood, if he be a dumb fool. He's better nor any o' yew! He kin do a day's work a'most up t' what I kin—an' that'd put any o' 75 yew pore critters t' shame!

FIDDLER. An' he kin do a good night's work too! [*A roar of laughter.*]

CABOT. Laugh, ye damn fools! Ye're right jist the same, Fiddler. He kin work day an' 80 night too, like I kin, if need be!

OLD FARMER [*from behind the keg where he is weaving drunkenly back and forth—with great simplicity*]. They hain't many t' touch ye, Ephraim—a son at seventy-six. That's a 85 hard man fur ye! I be on'y sixty-eight an' I couldn't do it. [*A roar of laughter in which CABOT joins uproariously.*]

CABOT [*slapping him on the back*]. I'm sorry fur ye, Hi. I'd never suspicion sech weakness 90 from a boy like yew!

OLD FARMER. An' I never reckoned yew had it in ye nuther, Ephraim. [*There is another laugh.*]

CABOT [*suddenly grim*]. I got a lot in me— 95 a hell of a lot—folks don't know on. [*Turning to THE FIDDLER.*] Fiddle 'er up, durn ye! Give 'em somethin' t' dance t'! What air ye, an orna-

ment? Hain't this a celebration? Then grease
yer elbow an' go it!

FIDDLER [*seizes a drink which the* OLD
FARMER *holds out to him and downs it*]. Here
5 goes! [*He starts to fiddle "Lady of the Lake."
Four young fellows and four girls form in two
lines and dance a square dance.* THE FIDDLER
*shouts directions for the different movements,
keeping his words in the rhythm of the music
10 and interspersing them with jocular personal
remarks to the dancers themselves. The people
seated along the walls stamp their feet and clap
their hands in unison.* CABOT *is especially active in this respect. Only* ABBIE *remains apa-
15 thetic, staring at the door as if she were alone
in a silent room.*]

FIDDLER. Swing your partner t' the right!
That's it, Jim! Give her a b'ar hug! Her Maw
hain't lookin'. [*Laughter.*] Change partners!
20 That suits ye, don't it, Essie, now ye got Reub
afore ye? Look at her redden up, will ye? Waal,
life is short an' so's love, as the feller says.
[*Laughter.*]

CABOT [*excitedly, stamping his foot*]. Go it,
25 boys! Go it, gals!

FIDDLER [*with a wink at the others*]. Ye're
the spryest seventy-six ever I sees, Ephraim!
Now if ye'd on'y good eyesight . . . ! [*Suppressed laughter. He gives* CABOT *no chance to
30 retort but roars.*] Promenade! Ye're walkin'
like a bride down the aisle, Sarah! Waal, while
they's life they's allus hope, I've heerd tell.
Swing your partner to the left! Gosh A'mighty,
look at Johnny Cook high-steppin'! They hain't
35 goin' t' be much strength left fur howin' in the
corn lot t'morrow. [*Laughter.*]

CABOT. Go it! Go it! [*Then suddenly, unable
to restrain himself any longer, he prances into
the midst of the dancers, scattering them, wav-
40 ing his arms about wildly.*] Ye're all hoofs!
Git out o' my road! Give me room! I'll show ye
dancin'. Ye're all too soft! [*He pushes them
roughly away. They crowd back toward the
walls, muttering, looking at him resentfully.*]
45 FIDDLER [*jeeringly*]. Go it, Ephraim! Go it!
[*He starts "Pop Goes the Weasel," increasing
the tempo with every verse until at the end he
is fiddling crazily as fast as he can go.*]

CABOT [*starts to dance, which he does very*

well and with tremendous vigor. Then he be- 50
gins to improvise, cuts incredibly grotesque
capers, leaping up and cracking his heels together, prancing around in a circle with body
bent in an Indian war dance, then suddenly
straightening up and kicking as high as he can 55
with both legs. He is like a monkey on a string.
And all the while he intersperses his antics
with shouts and derisive comments*]. Whoop!
Here's dancin' fur ye! Whoop! See that!
Seventy-six, if I'm a day! Hard as iron yet! 60
Beatin' the young 'uns like I allus done! Look
at me! I'd invite ye t' dance on my hundredth
birthday on'y ye'll all be dead by then. Ye're a
sickly generation! Yer hearts air pink, not red!
Yer veins is full o' mud an' water! I be the on'y 65
man in the county! Whoop! See that! I'm a
Injun! I've killed Injuns in the West afore ye
was born—an' skulped 'em too! They's a arrer
wound on my backside I c'd show ye! The hull
tribe chased me. I outrun 'em all—with the 70
arrer stuck in me! An' I tuk vengeance on 'em.
Ten eyes fur an eye, that was my motter!
Whoop! Look at me! I kin kick the ceilin' off
the room! Whoop!

FIDDLER [*stops playing—exhaustedly*]. God 75
A'mighty, I got enuf. Ye got the devil's
strength in ye.

CABOT [*delightedly*]. Did I beat yew, too?
Wa'al, ye played smart. Hev a swig. [*He pours
whisky for himself and* FIDDLER. *They* 80
drink. The others watch CABOT *silently with
cold, hostile eyes. There is a dead pause.*
THE FIDDLER *rests.* CABOT *leans against the
keg, panting, glaring around him confusedly.
In the room above,* EBEN *gets to his feet and* 85
*tiptoes out the door in rear, appearing a
moment later in the other bedroom. He moves
silently, even frightenedly, toward the cradle
and stands there looking down at the baby.
His face is as vague as his reactions are con-* 90
*fused, but there is a trace of tenderness, of
interested discovery. At the same moment that
he reaches the cradle,* ABBIE *seems to sense
something. She gets up weakly and goes to*
CABOT.] 95

ABBIE. I'm going up t' the baby.

CABOT [*with real solicitation*]. Air ye able
fur the stairs? D'ye want me t' help ye, Abbie?

ABBIE. No. I'm able. I'll be down agen soon.

CABOT. Don't ye get wore out! He needs ye, remember—our son does! [*He grins affectionately, patting her on the back. She shrinks* 5 *from his touch.*]

ABBIE [*dully*]. Don't—tech me. I'm goin'—up. [*She goes.* CABOT *looks after her. A whisper goes around the room.* CABOT *turns. It ceases. He wipes his forehead streaming with sweat.* 10 *He is breathing pantingly.*]

CABOT. I'm a-goin' out t' git fresh air. I'm feelin' a mite dizzy. Fiddle up thar! Dance, all o' ye! Here's likker fur them as wants it. Enjoy yerselves. I'll be back. [*He goes, closing the* 15 *door behind him.*]

FIDDLER [*sarcastically*]. Don't hurry none on our account! [*A suppressed laugh. He imitates* ABBIE.] Whar's Eben? [*More laughter.*]

A WOMAN [*loudly*]. What's happened in this 20 house is plain as the nose on yer face! [ABBIE *appears in the doorway upstairs and stands looking in surprise and adoration at* EBEN *who does not see her.*]

A MAN. Ssshh! He's li-ble t' be listenin' at 25 the door. That'd be like him. [*Their voices die to an intensive whispering. Their faces are concentrated on this gossip. A noise as of dead leaves in the wind comes from the room.* CABOT *has come out from the porch and stands* 30 *by the gate, leaning on it, staring at the sky blinkingly.* ABBIE *comes across the room silently.* EBEN *does not notice her until quite near.*]

EBEN [*starting*]. Abbie!

ABBIE. Ssshh! [*She throws her arms around* 35 *him. They kiss—then bend over the cradle together.*] Ain't he purty?—dead spit 'n' image o' yew!

EBEN [*pleased*]. Air he? I can't tell none.

ABBIE. E-zactly like!

40 EBEN [*frowningly*]. I don't like this. I don't like lettin' on what's mine's his'n. I been doin' that all my life. I'm gittin t' the end o' b'arin' it!

ABBIE [*putting her finger on his lips*]. We're 45 doin' the best we kin. We got t' wait. Somethin's bound t' happen. [*She puts her arms around him.*] I got t' go back.

EBEN. I'm going out. I can't b'ar it with the fiddle playin' an' the laughin'.

ABBIE. Don't git feelin' low. I love ye, Eben. 50 Kiss me. [*He kisses her. They remain in each other's arms.*]

CABOT [*at the gate, confusedly*]. Even the music can't drive it out—somethin'. Ye kin feel it droppin' off the elums, climbin' up the 55 roof, sneakin' down the chimney, pokin' in the corners! They's no peace in houses, they's no rest livin' with folks. Somethin's always livin' with ye. [*With a deep sigh.*] I'll go t' the barn an' rest a spell. [*He goes wearily toward the* 60 *barn.*]

FIDDLER [*tuning up*]. Let's celebrate the old skunk gittin' fooled! We kin have some fun now he's went. [*He starts to fiddle "Turkey in the Straw." There is real merriment now. The* 65 *young folks get up to dance.*]

Curtain

Scene ii

[*A half-hour later—Exterior—*EBEN *is standing by the gate looking up at the sky, an expression of dumb pain bewildered by itself on his face.* CABOT *appears, returning from the* 70 *barn, walking wearily, his eyes on the ground. He sees* EBEN *and his whole mood immediately changes. He becomes excited, a cruel, triumphant grin comes to his lips, he strides up and slaps* EBEN *on the back. From within comes the* 75 *whining of the fiddle and the noise of stamping feet and laughing voices.*]

CABOT. So har ye be!

EBEN [*startled, stares at him with hatred for a moment—then dully*]. Ay-eh. 80

CABOT [*surveying him jeeringly*]. Why hain't ye been in t' dance? They was all axin' fur ye.

EBEN. Let 'em ax!

CABOT. They's a hull passel o' purty gals.

EBEN. T' hell with 'em! 85

CABOT. Ye'd ought t' be marryin' one o' 'em soon.

EBEN. I hain't marryin' no one.

CABOT. Ye might 'arn a share o' a farm that way. 90

EBEN [*with a sneer*]. Like yew did, ye mean? I hain't that kind.

CABOT [*stung*]. Ye lie! 'Twas yer Maw's folks aimed t' steal my farm from me.

EBEN. Other folks don't say so. [*After a* 95

pause—defiantly.] An' I got a farm, anyways!

CABOT [*derisively*]. Whar?

EBEN [*stamps a foot on the ground*]. Har!

5 CABOT [*throws his head back and laughs coarsely*]. Ho-ho! Ye hev, hev ye? Waal, that's a good un!

EBEN [*controlling himself—grimly*]. Ye'll see!

10 CABOT [*stares at him suspiciously, trying to make him out—a pause—then with scornful confidence*]. Ay-eh. I'll see. So'll ye. It's ye that's blind—blind as a mole underground. [EBEN *suddenly laughs, one short sardonic bark: "Ha." A pause.* CABOT *peers at him with*

15 *renewed suspicion.*] Whar air ye hawin' 'bout? [EBEN *turns away without answering.* CABOT *grows angry.*] God A'mighty, yew air a dumb dunce! They's nothin' in that thick skull o' your'n but noise—like a empty keg it be!

20 [EBEN *doesn't seem to hear.* CABOT's *rage grows.*] Yewr farm! God A'mighty! If ye wa'n't a born donkey ye'd know ye'll never own stick nor stone on it, specially now arter him bein' born. It's his'n, I tell ye—his'n arter I die—but

25 I'll live a hundred jest t' fool ye all—an' he'll be growed then—yewr age a'most! [EBEN *laughs again his sardonic "Ha." This drives* CABOT *into a fury.*] Ha? Ye think ye kin git 'round that someways, do ye? Waal, it'll be

30 her'n, too—Abbie's—ye won't git 'round her —she knows yer tricks—she'll be too much fur ye—she wants the farm her'n—she was afeerd o' ye—she told me ye was sneakin' 'round tryin' t' make love t' her t' git her on

35 yer side . . . ye . . . ye mad fool, ye! [*He raises his clenched fists threateningly.*]

EBEN [*is confronting him choking with rage*]. Ye lie, ye old skunk! Abbie never said no sech thing!

40 CABOT [*suddenly triumphant when he sees how shaken* EBEN *is*]. She did. An' I says, I'll blow his brains t' the top o' them elums—an' she says no, that hain't sense, who'll ye git t'help ye on the farm in his place—an' then

45 she says yew'n me ought t' have a son—I know we kin, she says—an' I says, if we do, ye kin have anythin' I've got ye've a mind t'. An' she says, I wants Eben cut off so's this farm'll be mine when ye die! [*With terrible*

gloating.] An' that's what's happened, hain't 50 it? An' the farm's her'n! An' the dust o' the road—that's your'n! Ha! Now who's hawin'?

EBEN [*has been listening, petrified with grief and rage—suddenly laughs wildly and brokenly*]. Ha-ha-ha! So that's her sneakin' game— 55 all along!—like I suspicioned at fust—t' swaller it all—an' me, too . . . ! [*Madly.*] I'll murder her! [*He springs toward the porch but* CABOT *is quicker and gets in between.*]

CABOT. No, ye don't! 60

EBEN. Git out o' my road! [*He tries to throw* CABOT *aside. They grapple in what becomes immediately a murderous struggle. The old man's concentrated strength is too much for* EBEN. CABOT *gets one hand on his throat and* 65 *presses him back across the stone well. At the same moment,* ABBIE *comes out on the porch. With a stifled cry she runs toward them.*]

ABBIE. Eben! Ephraim! [*She tugs at the hand on* EBEN'S *throat.*] Let go, Ephraim! Ye're 70 chokin' him!

CABOT [*removes his hand and flings* EBEN *sideways full length on the grass, gasping and choking. With a cry,* ABBIE *kneels beside him, trying to take his head on her lap, but he* 75 *pushes her away.* CABOT *stands looking down with fierce triumph*]. Ye needn't t've fret, Abbie, I wa'n't aimin' t' kill him. He hain't wuth hangin' fur—not by a hell of a sight! [*More and more triumphantly.*] Seventy-six an' him 80 not thirty yit—an' look whar he be fur thinkin' his Paw was easy! No, by God, I hain't easy! An' him upstairs, I'll raise him t' be like me! [*He turns to leave them.*] I'm goin' in an' dance! —sing an' celebrate! [*He walks to the porch—* 85 *then turns with a great grin.*] I don't calc'late it's left in him, but if he gits pesky, Abbie, ye jest sing out. I'll come a-runnin' an' by the Etarnal, I'll put him across my knee an' birch him! Ha-ha-ha! [*He goes into the house laugh-* 90 *ing. A moment later his loud "whoop" is heard.*]

ABBIE [*tenderly*]. Eben. Air ye hurt? [*She tries to kiss him but he pushes her violently away and struggles to a sitting position.*] 95

EBEN [*gaspingly*]. T' hell—with ye!

ABBIE [*not believing her ears*]. It's me, Eben —Abbie—don't ye know me?

EBEN [*glowering at her with hatred*]. Ay-eh
—I know ye—now! [*He suddenly breaks down, sobbing weakly.*]

ABBIE [*fearfully*]. Eben—what's happened t' ye—why did ye look at me 's if ye hated me?

EBEN [*violently, between sobs and gasps*]. I do hate ye! Ye're a whore—a damn trickin' whore!

ABBIE [*shrinking back horrified*]. Eben! Ye don't know what ye're sayin'!

EBEN [*scrambling to his feet and following her—accusingly*]. Ye're nothin' but a stinkin' passel o' lies! Ye've been lyin' t' me every word ye spoke, day an' night, since we fust—done it. Ye've kept sayin' ye loved me. . . .

ABBIE [*frantically*]. I do love ye! [*She takes his hand but he flings hers away.*]

EBEN [*unheeding*]. Ye've made a fool o' me —a sick, dumb fool—a-purpose! Ye've been on'y playin' yer sneakin', stealin' game all along— gittin' me t' lie with ye so's ye'd hev a son he'd think was his'n, an' makin' him promise he'd give ye the farm and let me eat dust, if ye did git him a son! [*Staring at her with anguished, bewildered eyes.*] They must be a devil livin' in ye! T'ain't human t' be as bad as that be!

ABBIE [*stunned—dully*]. He told yew . . . ?

EBEN. Hain't it true? It hain't no good in yew lyin'.

ABBIE [*pleadingly*]. Eben, listen—ye must listen—it was long ago—afore we done nothin' —yew was scornin' me—goin' t' see Min— when I was lovin' ye—an' I said it t' him t' git vengeance on ye!

EBEN [*unheedingly. With tortured passion*]. I wish ye was dead! I wish I was dead along with ye afore this come! [*Ragingly.*] But I'll git my vengeance too! I'll pray Maw t' come back t' help me—t' put her cuss on yew an' him!

ABBIE [*brokenly*]. Don't ye, Eben! Don't ye! [*She throws herself on her knees before him, weeping.*] I didn't mean t' do bad t' ye! Fergive me, won't ye?

EBEN [*not seeming to hear her—fiercely*]. I'll git squar' with the old skunk—an' yew! I'll tell him the truth 'bout the son he's so proud o'! Then I'll leave ye here t' pizen each other —with Maw comin' out o' her grave at nights —an' I'll go t' the gold fields o' Californi-a whar Sim an' Peter be!

ABBIE [*terrified*]. Ye won't—leave me? Ye can't!

EBEN [*with fierce determination*]. I'm a-goin', I tell ye! I'll git rich thar an' come back an' fight him fur the farm he stole—an' I'll kick ye both out in the road—t' beg an' sleep in the woods—an' yer son along with ye—t' starve an' die! [*He is hysterical at the end.*]

ABBIE [*with a shudder—humbly*]. He's yewr son, too, Eben.

EBEN [*torturedly*]. I wish he never was born! I wish he'd die this minit! I wish I'd never sot eyes on him! It's him—yew havin' him—a-purpose t' steal—that's changed everythin'!

ABBIE [*gently*]. Did ye believe I loved ye— afore he come?

EBEN. Ay-eh—like a dumb ox!

ABBIE. An' ye don't believe no more?

EBEN. B'lieve a lyin' thief! Ha!

ABBIE [*shudders—then humbly*]. An' did ye r'ally love me afore?

EBEN [*brokenly*]. Ay-eh—an' ye was trickin' me!

ABBIE. An' ye don't love me now!

EBEN [*violently*]. I hate ye, I tell ye!

ABBIE. An' ye're truly goin' West—goin' t' leave me—all account o' him being born?

EBEN. I'm a-goin' in the mornin'—or may God strike me t' hell!

ABBIE [*after a pause—with a dreadful cold intensity—slowly*]. If that's what his comin 's done t' me—killin' yewr love—takin' yew away—my on'y joy—the on'y joy I ever knowed—like heaven t' me—purtier'n heaven —then I hate him, too, even if I be his Maw!

EBEN [*bitterly*]. Lies! Ye love him! He'll steal the farm fur ye! [*Brokenly.*] But t'ain't the farm so much—not no more—it's yew foolin' me—gittin' me t' love ye—lyin' yew loved me —jest t' git a son t' steal!

ABBIE [*distractedly*]. He won't steal! I'd kill him fust! I do love ye! I'll prove t' ye . . . !

EBEN [*harshly*]. T'ain't no use lyin' no more. I'm deaf t' ye! [*He turns away.*] I hain't seein' ye agen. Good-by!

ABBIE [*pale with anguish*]. Hain't ye even goin' t' kiss me—not once—arter all we loved?

EBEN [*in a hard voice*]. I hain't wantin' t' kiss ye never agen! I'm wantin' t' forgit I ever sot eyes on ye!

ABBIE. Eben!—ye mustn't—wait a spell—I want t' tell ye . . . .

EBEN. I'm a-goin' in t' git drunk. I'm a-goin' t' dance.

ABBIE [*clinging to his arm—with passionate earnestness*]. If I could make it—'s if he'd never come up between us—if I could prove t' ye I wa'n't schemin' t' steal from ye—so's everythin' could be jest the same with us, lovin' each other jest the same, kissin' an' happy the same's we've been happy afore he come—if I could do it—ye'd love me agen, wouldn't ye? Ye'd kiss me agen? Ye wouldn't never leave me, would ye?

EBEN [*moved*]. I calc'late not. [*Then shaking her hand off his arm—with a bitter smile.*] But ye hain't God, be ye?

ABBIE [*exultantly*]. Remember ye've promised! [*Then with strange intensity.*] Mebbe I kin take back one thin' God does!

EBEN [*peering at her*]. Ye're gittin' cracked, hain't ye? [*Then going towards door.*] I'm a-goin' t' dance.

ABBIE [*calls after him intensely*]. I'll prove t' ye! I'll prove I love ye better'n . . . . [*He goes in the door, not seeming to hear. She remains standing where she is, looking after him—then she finishes desperately.*] Better'n everythin' else in the world!

Curtain

Scene iii

[*Just before dawn in the morning—shows the kitchen and* CABOT's *bedroom. In the kitchen, by the light of a tallow candle on the table,* EBEN *is sitting, his chin propped on his hands, his drawn face blank and expressionless. His carpetbag is on the floor beside him. In the bedroom, dimly lighted by a small whale-oil lamp,* CABOT *lies asleep.* ABBIE *is bending over the cradle, listening, her face full of terror yet with an under-current of desperate triumph. Suddenly, she breaks down and sobs,*

appears about to throw herself on her knees beside the cradle; but the old man turns restlessly, groaning in his sleep, and she controls herself, and, shrinking away from the cradle with a gesture of horror, backs swiftly toward the door in rear and goes out. A moment later she comes into the kitchen and, running to EBEN, *flings her arms about his neck and kisses him wildly. He hardens himself, he remains unmoved and cold, he keeps his eyes straight ahead.*]

ABBIE [*hysterically*]. I done it, Eben! I told ye I'd do it! I've proved I love ye—better'n everythin'—so's ye can't never doubt me no more!

EBEN [*dully*]. Whatever ye done, it hain't no good now.

ABBIE [*wildly*]. Don't ye say that! Kiss me, Eben, won't ye? I need ye t' kiss me arter what I done! I need ye t' say ye love me!

EBEN [*kisses her without emotion—dully*]. That's fur goodby. I'm a-goin' soon.

ABBIE. No! No! Ye won't go—not now!

EBEN [*going on with his own thoughts*]. I been a-thinkin'—an' I hain't goin' t' tell Paw nothin'. I'll leave Maw t' take vengeance on ye. If I told him, the old skunk'd jest be stinkin' mean enuf to take it out on that baby. [*His voice showing emotion in spite of him.*] An' I don't want nothin' bad t' happen t' him. He hain't t' blame fur yew. [*He adds with a certain queer pride.*] An' he looks like me! An' by God, he's mine! An' some day I'll be a-comin' back an' . . . !

ABBIE [*too absorbed in her own thoughts to listen to him—pleadingly*]. They's no cause fur ye t' go now—they's no sense—it's all the same's it was—they's nothin' come b'tween us now—arter what I done!

EBEN [*something in her voice arouses him. He stares at her a bit frightenedly*]. Ye look mad, Abbie. What did ye do?

ABBIE. I—I killed him, Eben.

EBEN [*amazed*]. Ye killed him?

ABBIE [*dully*]. Ay-eh.

EBEN [*recovering from his astonishment—savagely*]. An' serves him right! But we got t' do somethin' quick t' make it look 's if the old

skunk'd killed himself when he was drunk.
We kin prove by 'em all how drunk he got.

ABBIE [*wildly*]. No! No! Not him! [*Laughing distractedly.*] But that's what I ought t'
5 done, hain't it? I oughter killed him instead!
Why didn't ye tell me?

EBEN [*appalled*]. Instead? What d'ye mean?

ABBIE. Not him.

EBEN [*his face grown ghastly*]. Not—not
10 that baby!

ABBIE [*dully*]. Ay-eh!

EBEN [*falls to his knees as if he'd been struck
—his voice trembling with horror*]. Oh, God
A'mighty! A'mighty God! Maw, whar was ye,
15 why didn't ye stop her?

ABBIE [*simply*]. She went back t' her grave
that night we fust done it, remember? I hain't
felt her about since. [*A pause.* EBEN *hides his
head in his hands, trembling all over as if he
20 had the ague. She goes on dully.*] I left the
piller over his little face. Then he killed himself. He stopped breathin'. [*She begins to weep
softly.*]

EBEN [*rage beginning to mingle with grief*].
25 He looked like me. He was mine, damn ye!

ABBIE [*slowly and brokenly*]. I didn't want
t' do it. I hated myself fur doin' it. I loved him.
He was so purty—dead spit 'n' image o' yew.
But I loved yew more—an' yew was goin'
30 away—far off whar I'd never see ye agen,
never kiss ye, never feel ye pressed agin me
agen—an' ye said ye hated me fur havin' him
—ye said ye hated him an' wished he was
dead—ye said if it hadn't been fur him comin'
35 it'd be the same's afore between us.

EBEN [*unable to endure this, springs to his
feet in a fury, threatening her, his twitching
fingers seeming to reach out for her throat*].
Ye lie! I never said—I never dreamed ye'd—
40 I'd cut off my head afore I'd hurt his finger!

ABBIE [*piteously, sinking on her knees*].
Eben, don't ye look at me like that—hatin' me
—not after what I done fur ye—fur us—so's
we could be happy agen—

45 EBEN [*furiously now*]. Shut up, or I'll kill ye!
I see yer game now—the same old sneakin'
trick—ye're aimin' t' blame me fur the murder
ye done!

ABBIE [*moaning—putting her hands over
her ears*]. Don't ye, Eben! Don't ye! [*She
50 grasps his legs.*]

EBEN [*his mood suddenly changing to horror,
shrinks away from her*]. Don't ye tech me!
Ye're pizen! How could ye—t' murder a pore
little critter— Ye must've swapped yer soul t'
55 hell! [*Suddenly raging.*] Ha! I kin see why ye
done it! Not the lies ye jest told—but 'cause ye
wanted t' steal agen—steal the last thin' ye'd
left me—my part o' him—no, the hull o' him—
ye saw he looked like me—ye knowed he was
60 all mine—an' ye couldn't b'ar it—I know ye!
Ye killed him fur bein' mine! [*All this has
driven him almost insane. He makes a rush
past her for the door—then turns—shaking
both fists at her, violently.*] But I'll take ven-
65 geance now! I'll git the Sheriff! I'll tell him
everythin'! Then I'll sing "I'm off to Californi-
a!" an' go—gold—Golden Gate—gold sun—
fields o' gold in the West! [*This last he half
shouts, half croons incoherently, suddenly
70 breaking off passionately.*] I'm a-goin' fur the
Sheriff t' come an' git ye! I want ye tuk away,
locked up from me! I can't stand t' luk at ye!
Murderer an' thief 'r not, ye still tempt me!
I'll give ye up t' the Sheriff. [*He turns and runs
75 out, around the corner of house, panting and
sobbing, and breaks into a swerving sprint
down the road.*]

ABBIE [*struggling to her feet, runs to the
door, calling after him*]. I love ye, Eben! I love
80 ye! [*She stops at the door weakly, swaying,
about to fall.*] I don't care what ye do—if ye'll
on'y love me agen— [*She falls limply to the
floor in a faint.*]

Curtain

Scene iv

[*About an hour later. Same as Scene iii.
85 Shows the kitchen and* CABOT'S *bedroom. It is
after dawn. The sky is brilliant with the sunrise. In the kitchen,* ABBIE *sits at the table, her
body limp and exhausted, her head bowed
down over her arms, her face hidden. Upstairs,
90 *CABOT *is still asleep but awakens with a start.
He looks toward the window and gives a snort
of surprise and irritation—throws back the*

covers and begins hurriedly pulling on his clothes. Without looking behind him, he begins talking to ABBIE *whom he supposes beside him.*]

5   CABOT. Thunder 'n' lightin', Abbie! I hain't slept this late in fifty year! Looks 's if the sun was full riz a'most. Must've been the dancin' an' likker. Must be gittin' old. I hope Eben's t' wuk. Ye might've tuk the trouble t' rouse
10 me, Abbie. [*He turns—sees no one there—surprised.*] Waal—whar air she? Gittin' vittles, I calc'late. [*He tiptoes to the cradle and peers down—proudly.*] Mornin', sonny. Purty's a picture! Sleepin' sound. He don't beller all
15 night like most o' 'em. [*He goes quietly out the door in rear—a few moments later enters kitchen—sees* ABBIE—*with satisfaction.*] So thar ye be. Ye got any vittles cooked?

  ABBIE. [*without moving*]. No.
20   CABOT [*coming to her, almost sympathetically*]. Ye feelin' sick?

  ABBIE. No.

  CABOT [*pats her on shoulder. She shudders*]. Ye'd best lie down a spell. [*Half jocularly.*]
25 Yer son'll be needin' ye soon. He'd ought t' wake up with a gnashin' appetite, the sound way he's sleepin'.

  ABBIE [*shudders—then in a dead voice*]. He hain't never goin' t' wake up.
30   CABOT [*jokingly*]. Takes after me this mornin'. I hain't slept so late in. . . .

  ABBIE. He's dead.

  CABOT [*stares at her—bewilderedly*]. What. . . .
35   ABBIE. I killed him.

  CABOT [*stepping back from her—aghast*]. Air ye drunk—'r crazy—'r . . . !

  ABBIE [*suddenly lifts her head and turns on him—wildly*]. I killed him, I tell ye! I smoth-
40 ered him. Go up an' see if ye don't b'lieve me! [CABOT *stares at her a second, then bolts out the rear door—can be heard bounding up the stairs—and rushes into the bedroom and over to the cradle.* ABBIE *has sunk back lifelessly*
45 *into her former position.* CABOT *puts his hand down on the body in the crib. An expression of fear and horror comes over his face.*]

  CABOT [*shrinking away—trembling*]. God

A'mighty! God A'mighty. [*He stumbles out the door—in a short while returns to the*
50 *kitchen—comes to* ABBIE, *the stunned expression still on his face—hoarsely.*] Why did ye do it? Why? [*As she doesn't answer, he grabs her violently by the shoulder and shakes her.*] I ax ye why ye done it! Ye'd better tell
55 me 'r . . . !

  ABBIE [*gives him a furious push which sends him staggering back and springs to her feet—with wild rage and hatred*]. Don't ye dare tech me! What right hev ye t' question me 'bout
60 him? He wa'n't yewr son! Think I'd have a son by yew? I'd die fust! I hate the sight o' ye an' allus did! It's yew I should've murdered, if I'd had good sense! I hate ye! I love Eben. I did from the fust. An' he was Eben's son—mine
65 an' Eben's—not your'n!

  CABOT [*stands looking at her dazedly—a pause—finding his words with an effort—dully*]. That was it—what I felt—pokin' round the corners—while ye lied—holdin' yerself from
70 me—sayin' ye'd a'ready conceived— [*He lapses into crushed silence—then with a strange emotion.*] He's dead, sart'n. I felt his heart. Pore little critter! [*He blinks back one tear, wiping his sleeve across his nose.*]
75

  ABBIE [*hysterically*]. Don't ye! Don't ye! [*She sobs unrestrainedly.*]

  CABOT [*with a concentrated effort that stiffens his body into a rigid line and hardens his face into a stony mask—through his teeth to*
80 *himself*]. I got t' be—like a stone—a rock o' jedgment! [*A pause. He gets complete control over himself—harshly.*] If he was Eben's, I be glad he air gone! An' mebbe I suspicioned it all along. I felt they was somethin' onnateral
85 —somewhars—the house got so lonesome— an' cold—drivin' me down t' the barn—t' the beasts o' the field. . . . Ay-eh. I must've suspicioned—somethin'. Ye didn't fool me—not altogether, leastways—I'm too old a bird—
90 growin' ripe on the bough. . . . [*He becomes aware he is wandering, straightens again, looks at* ABBIE *with a cruel grin.*] So ye'd like t' hev murdered me 'stead o' him, would ye? Waal, I'll live to a hundred! I'll live t' see ye hung!
95 I'll deliver ye up t' the jedgment o' God an'

the law! I'll git the Sheriff now. [*Starts for the door.*]

ABBE [*dully*]. Ye needn't. Eben's gone fur him.

CABOT [*amazed*]. Eben—gone fur the Sheriff?

ABBIE. Ay-eh.

CABOT. T' inform agen ye?

ABBIE. Ay-eh.

CABOT [*considers this—a pause—then in a hard voice*]. Waal, I'm thankful fur him savin' me the trouble. I'll git t' wuk. [*He goes to the door—then turns—in a voice full of strange emotion.*] He'd ought t' been my son, Abbie. Ye'd ought t' loved me. I'm a man. If ye'd loved me, I'd never told no Sheriff on ye no matter what ye did, if they was t' brile me alive!

ABBIE [*defensively*]. They's more to it nor yew know, makes him tell.

CABOT [*dryly*]. Fur yewr sake, I hope they be. [*He goes out—comes around to the gate—stares up at the sky. His control relaxes. For a moment he is old and weary. He murmurs despairingly.*] God A'mighty, I be lonesomer'n ever! [*He hears running footsteps from the left, immediately is himself again. EBEN runs in, panting exhaustedly, wild-eyed and mad looking. He lurches through the gate. CABOT grabs him by the shoulder. EBEN stares at him dumbly.*] Did ye tell the Sheriff?

EBEN [*nodding stupidly*]. Ay-eh.

CABOT [*gives him a push away that sends him sprawling—laughing with withering contempt*]. Good fur ye! A prime chip o' yer Maw ye be! [*He goes toward the barn, laughing harshly. EBEN scrambles to his feet. Suddenly CABOT turns—grimly threatening.*] Git off this farm when the Sheriff takes her—or, by God, he'll have t' come back an' git me fur murder, too! [*He stalks off. EBEN does not appear to have heard him. He runs to the door and comes into the kitchen. ABBIE looks up with a cry of anguished joy. EBEN stumbles over and throws himself on his knees beside her—sobbing brokenly.*]

EBEN. Fergive me!

ABBIE [*happily*]. Eben! [*She kisses him and pulls his head over against her breast.*]

EBEN. I love ye! Fergive me!

ABBIE [*ecstatically*]. I'd fergive ye all the sins in hell fur sayin' that! [*She kisses his head, pressing it to her with a fierce passion of possession.*]

EBEN [*brokenly*]. But I told the Sheriff. He's comin' fur ye!

ABBIE. I kin b'ar what happens t' me—now!

EBEN. I woke him up. I told him. He says, wait 'til I git dressed. I was waiting. I got to thinkin' o' yew. I got to thinkin' how I'd loved ye. It hurt like somethin' was bustin' in my chest an' head. I got t' cryin'. I knowed sudden I loved ye yet, an' allus would love ye!

ABBIE [*caressing his hair—tenderly*]. My boy, hain't ye?

EBEN. I begun t' run back. I cut across the fields an' through the woods. I thought ye might have time t' run away—with me—an' . . . .

ABBIE [*shaking her head*]. I got t' take my punishment—t' pay fur my sin.

EBEN. Then I want t' share it with ye.

ABBIE. Ye didn't do nothin'.

EBEN. I put it in yer head. I wisht he was dead! I as much as urged ye t' do it!

ABBIE. No. It was me alone!

EBEN. I'm as guilty as yew be! He was the child o' our sin.

ABBIE [*lifting her head as if defying God*]. I don't repent that sin! I hain't askin' God t' fergive that!

EBEN. Nor me—but it led up t' the other—an' the murder ye did, ye did 'count o' me—an' it's my murder, too, I'll tell the Sheriff—an' if ye deny it, I'll say we planned it t'gether —an' they'll all b'lieve me, fur they suspicion everythin' we've done, an' it'll seem likely an' true to 'em. An' it is true—way down. I did help ye—somehow.

ABBIE [*laying her head on his—sobbing*]. No! I don't want yew t' suffer!

EBEN. I got t' pay fur my part o' the sin! An' I'd suffer wust leavin' ye, goin' West, thinkin' o' ye day an' night, bein' out when yew was in— [*lowering his voice*] 'r bein' alive when yew was dead. [*A pause.*] I want t' share with ye, Abbie—prison 'r death 'r hell 'r anythin'! [*He looks into her eyes and forces a trembling* 5 *smile.*] If I'm sharin' with ye, I won't feel lonesome, leastways.

ABBIE [*weakly*]. Eben! I won't let ye! I can't let ye!

EBEN [*kissing her—tenderly*]. Ye can't he'p 10 yerself. I got ye beat fur once!

ABBIE [*forcing a smile—adoringly*]. I hain't beat—s'long's I got ye!

EBEN [*hears the sound of feet outside*]. Ssshh! Listen! They've come t' take us!

15 ABBIE. No, it's him. Don't give him no chance to fight ye, Eben. Don't say nothin'— no matter what he says. An' I won't neither. [*It is* CABOT. *He comes up from the barn in a great state of excitement and strides into the* 20 *house and then into the kitchen.* EBEN *is kneeling beside* ABBIE, *his arm around her, hers around him. They stare straight ahead.*]

CABOT [*stares at them, his face hard. A long pause—vindictively*]. Ye make a slick pair o' 25 murderin' turtle doves! Ye'd ought t' be both hung on the same limb an' left thar t' swing in the breeze an' rot—a warnin' t' old fools like me t' b'ar their lonesomeness alone—an' fur young fools like ye t' hobble their lust. [*A* 30 *pause. The excitement returns to his face, his eyes snap, he looks a bit crazy.*] I couldn't work today. I couldn't take no interest. T' hell with the farm! I'm leavin' it! I've turned the cows an' other stock loose! I've druv 'em into the 35 woods whar they kin be free! By freein' 'em, I'm freein' myself! I'm quittin' here today! I'll set fire t' house an' barn an' watch 'em burn, an' I'll leave yer Maw t' haunt the ashes, an' I'll will the fields back t' God, so that nothin' 40 human kin never touch 'em! I'll be a-goin' to Californi-a—t' jine Simeon an' Peter—true sons o' mine if they be dumb fools—an' the Cabots'll find Solomon's Mines t'gether! [*He suddenly cuts a mad caper.*] Whoop! What 45 was the song they sung? "Oh, Californi-a! That's the land fur me." [*He sings this—then gets on his knees by the floor-board under*

which the money was hid.] An' I'll sail thar on one o' the finest clippers I kin find! I've got the money! Pity ye didn't know whar this was hid- 50 den so's ye could steal. . . . [*He has pulled up the board. He stares—feels—stares again. A pause of dead silence. He slowly turns, slumping into a sitting position on the floor, his eyes like those of a dead fish, his face the sickly* 55 *green of an attack of nausea. He swallows painfully several times—forces a weak smile at last.*] So—ye did steal it!

EBEN [*emotionlessly*]. I swapped it t' Sim an' Peter fur their share o' the farm—t' pay their 60 passage t' Californi-a.

CABOT [*with one sardonic*] Ha! [*He begins to recover. Gets slowly to his feet—strangely.*] I calc'late God give it to 'em—not yew! God's hard, not easy! Mebbe they's easy gold in the 65 West but it hain't God's gold. It hain't fur me. I kin hear His voice warnin' me agen t' be hard an' stay on my farm. I kin see his hand usin' Eben t' steal t' keep me from weakness. I kin feel I be in the palm o' His hand, His fingers 70 guidin' me. [*A pause—then he mutters sadly.*] It's a-goin' t' be lonesomer now than ever it war afore—an' I'm gettin' old, Lord—ripe on the bough. . . . [*Then stiffening.*] Waal—what d'ye want? God's lonesome, hain't He? God's 75 hard an' lonesome! [*A pause. The* SHERIFF *with two men comes up the road from the left. They move cautiously to the door. The* SHERIFF *knocks on it with the butt of his pistol.*]

SHERIFF. Open in the name o' the law! [*They* 80 *start.*]

CABOT. They've come fur ye. [*He goes to the rear door.*] Come in, Jim! [*The three men enter.* CABOT *meets them in doorway.*] Jest a minit, Jim. I got 'em safe here. [*The Sheriff nods. He* 85 *and his companions remain in the doorway.*]

EBEN [*suddenly calls*]. I lied this mornin', Jim. I helped her to do it. Ye kin take me, too.

ABBIE [*brokenly*]. No!

CABOT. Take 'em both. [*He comes forward—* 90 *stares at* EBEN *with a trace of grudging admiration.*] Purty good—fur yew! Waal, I got t' round up the stock. Good-by.

EBEN. Good-by.

ABBIE. Good-by. [CABOT *turns and strides past the men—comes out and around the corner of the house, his shoulders squared, his face stony, and stalks grimly toward the barn.*
5 *In the meantime the Sheriff and men have come into the room.*]

SHERIFF [*embarrassedly*]. Waal—we'd best start.

ABBIE. Wait. [*Turns to* EBEN.] I love ye,
10 Eben.

EBEN. I love ye, Abbie. [*They kiss. The three men grin and shuffle embarrassedly.* EBEN *takes* ABBIE's *hand. They go out the door in rear, the men following, and come from the house,*
15 *walking hand in hand to the gate.* EBEN *stops there and points to the sunrise sky.*] Sun's a-rizin'. Purty, hain't it?

ABBIE. Ay-eh. [*They both stand for a moment looking up raptly in attitudes*
20 *strangely aloof and devout.*]

SHERIFF [*looking around at the farm enviously—to his companions*]. It's a jim-dandy farm, no denyin'. Wished I owned it!

Curtain

Federico García Lorca

1898–1936

The House of Bernarda Alba

1936

Lorca's matriarch stands consciously for social order, for the tradition that gives a community its foundation, and for the unwritten codes in which a society incorporates its values. Such codes govern the lives of men and women everywhere, restraining their anarchic impulses and guiding them toward reconciliation of personal and social needs. They regulate the parents' duties, the child's freedom, the attitudes held toward education, authority, and justice. Perhaps most significantly, they control the relations between the sexes, channeling into courtship, marriage, and the creation of the family an urge that might spend itself in promiscuity.

When Bernarda arranges Angustias' marriage, she obeys and enforces the code of her community as she does in rebuffing Martirio's suitor and in restraining Adela. Something, however, has gone wrong. The code no longer suits the needs that gave it being. It has turned hollow, external. "I don't pry into anyone's heart," says Bernarda, "but I want to put up a good front." A good front may well be the perversion of a good life, and Bernarda herself has turned pathologically rigid. With her husband's death she assumes a man's place and becomes governor of her family—but less governor than tyrant. No longer does she strive to accommodate her children's desires to the needs of society; she opposes the desires themselves. She hates the flesh for the rebellious will within it, hates her daughters for their hunger. "Hot coals in the place where she sinned!" she screams at the end of Act II, and in that cry her negation is proclaimed. She would literally burn out the source of life.

The home, which should be a miniature of a well-ordered society, turns under Bernarda's tyranny into a prison, its white walls gleaming down in ironic purity on the dying souls within. For eight years of unfelt mourning they will desperately embroider their hope-chest linens, tasting the truth of

713

FEDERICO GARCÍA LORCA

Amelia's conviction that "to be born a woman's the worst punishment." They will torment one another out of sisterly affection corroded to jealousy. Each in her own fashion will seize at any promise of redemption. Angustias, the power of love withering within her, reaches doubtfully toward a face that "seems to fade away." In the desperation of fantasy fulfillment, Martirio steals Pepe's picture. And Adela, who has "seen death under this roof" and who feels the fire of life, resolves to find freedom though she wear "the crown of thorns that belongs to the mistress of a married man."

What one finds in this prison, one finds in the village—in all the villages, Lorca implies, of Spain—for when the code becomes tyrannical, the inhibited will turns corrupt. Hence the prostitution to which Poncia's mother surrendered and the venomous hypocrisy with which Poncia inflames the prurience of the daughters. Hence the rape of Paca la Roseta, which the men discuss with superb impropriety at the funeral of Bernarda's husband. Every whisper sifting through the prison bars tells of flesh escaping into license or succumbing to mortification. Adelaida's "sweetheart doesn't let her go out even to the front doorstep. Before, she was gay. Now, not even powder on her face." And whether the flesh escapes or succumbs, the end is the denial of life. Act II ends with infanticide, Act III with suicide.

In the background the reapers sing their lyric of love, the stallion's hooves explode against his prison walls, and the mad grandmother croons her lullaby, "Little lamb, child of mine, Let's go to the shore of the sea . . . . Let's go to the palms at Bethlehem's gate." But maternal love is dead. The sea is far from the hot plains of the riverless village. And the gate of Bethlehem is farther yet. The Church, its representative, is indeed near, as its bells proclaim, but it seems not to enter in any redemptive way into the lives of the villagers.

The House of Bernarda Alba

A Drama About Women in the Villages of Spain

LORCA

Translated by James Graham-Lujan and Richard L. O'Connell

CHARACTERS

BERNARDA   *age 60*
MARIA JOSEFA   *Bernarda's mother, age 80*
ANGUSTIAS   *Bernarda's daughter, age 39*
MAGDALENA   *Bernarda's daughter, age 30*
AMELIA   *Bernarda's daughter, age 27*
MARTIRIO   *Bernarda's daughter, age 24*
ADELA   *Bernarda's daughter, age 20*
A MAID   *age 50*
LA PONCIA   *a maid, age 60*
PRUDENCIA   *age 50*
WOMEN IN MOURNING

The writer states that these Three Acts are

intended as a photographic document.

ACT I

[*A very white room in* BERNARDA ALBA'S *house. The walls are white. There are arched doorways with jute curtains tied back with tassels and ruffles. Wicker chairs. On the walls,*
5 *pictures of unlikely landscapes full of nymphs or legendary kings.*

It is summer. A great brooding silence fills the stage. It is empty when the curtain rises. Bells can be heard tolling outside.]

10 FIRST SERVANT [*entering*]. The tolling of those bells hits me right between the eyes.

PONCIA [*she enters, eating bread and sausage*]. More than two hours of mumbo jumbo. Priests are here from all the towns. The church
15 looks beautiful. At the first responsory for the dead, Magdalena fainted.

FIRST SERVANT. She's the one who's left most alone.

PONCIA. She's the only one who loved her
20 father. Ay! Thank God we're alone for a little. I came over to eat.

FIRST SERVANT. If Bernarda sees you . . . !

PONCIA. She's not eating today so she'd just as soon we'd all die of hunger! Domineering
25 old tyrant! But she'll be fooled! I opened the sausage crock.

FIRST SERVANT [*with an anxious sadness*]. Couldn't you give me some for my little girl, Poncia?

PONCIA. Go ahead! And take a fistful of 30 peas too. She won't know the difference today.

VOICE [*within*]. Bernarda!

PONCIA. There's the grandmother! Isn't she locked up tight?

FIRST SERVANT. Two turns of the key. 35

PONCIA. You'd better put the cross-bar up too. She's got the fingers of a lock-picker!

VOICE [*within*]. Bernarda!

PONCIA [*shouting*]. She's coming! [*To* THE SERVANT.] Clean everything up good. If Bernar- 40 da doesn't find things shining, she'll pull out the few hairs I have left.

SERVANT. What a woman!

PONCIA. Tyrant over everyone around her. She's perfectly capable of sitting on your heart 45 and watching you die for a whole year without turning off that cold little smile she wears on her wicked face. Scrub, scrub those dishes!

SERVANT. I've got blood on my hands from so much polishing of everything. 50

PONCIA. She's the cleanest, she's the decentest, she's the highest everything! A good rest her poor husband's earned!

[*The bells stop.*]

SERVANT. Did all the relatives come? 55

PONCIA. Just hers. His people hate her. They came to see him dead and make the sign of the cross over him; that's all.

SERVANT. Are there enough chairs?

PONCIA. More than enough. Let them sit on 60 the floor. When Bernarda's father died people stopped coming under his roof. She doesn't want them to see her in her "domain." Curse her!

SERVANT. She's been good to you.

PONCIA. Thirty years washing her sheets. 65 Thirty years eating her leftovers. Nights of watching when she had a cough. Whole days peeking through a crack in the shutters to spy on the neighbors and carry her the tale. Life without secrets one from the other. But in spite 70 of that—curse her! May the "pain of the piercing nail"° strike her in the eyes.

"pain of the piercing nail" translators' quotation marks seem designed to point out that Lorca's word for "nail" is the word commonly used for the nails of the cross

SERVANT. Poncia!

PONCIA. But I'm a good watchdog! I bark when I'm told and bite beggars' heels when she sics me on 'em. My sons work in her fields —both of them already married, but one of these days I'll have enough.

SERVANT. And then . . . ?

PONCIA. Then I'll lock myself up in a room with her and spit in her face—a whole year. "Bernarda, here's for this, that and the other!" Till I leave her—just like a lizard the boys have squashed. For that's what she is—she and her whole family! Not that I envy her her life. Five girls are left her, five ugly daughters—not counting Angustias the eldest, by her first husband, who has money—the rest of them, plenty of eyelets to embroider, plenty of linen petticoats, but bread and grapes when it comes to inheritance.°

SERVANT. Well, *I'd* like to have what they've got!

PONCIA. All we have is our hands and a hole in God's earth.

SERVANT. And that's the only earth they'll ever leave to us—to us who have nothing!

PONCIA [*at the cupboard*]. This glass has some specks.

SERVANT. Neither soap nor rag will take them off.

[*The bells toll.*]

PONCIA. The last prayer! I'm going over and listen. I certainly like the way our priest sings. In the Pater Noster his voice went up, and up —like a pitcher filling with water little by little. Of course, at the end his voice cracked, but it's glorious to hear it. No, there never was anybody like the old Sacristan—Tronchapinos. At my mother's Mass, may she rest in peace, he sang. The walls shook—and when he said "Amen," it was as if a wolf had come into the church. [*Imitating him.*] A-a-a-a-men! [*She starts coughing.*]

SERVANT. Watch out—you'll strain your windpipe!

PONCIA. I'd rather strain something else!

[*Goes out laughing.*]

daughters . . . inheritance i.e., of the five daughters only Angustias has a dowry

[THE SERVANT *scrubs. The bells toll.*]

SERVANT [*imitating the bells*]. Dong, dong, dong. Dong, dong, dong. May God forgive him!

BEGGAR WOMAN [*at the door, with a little girl*]. Blesséd be God!

SERVANT. Dong, dong, dong. I hope he waits many years for us! Dong, dong, dong.

BEGGAR [*loudly, a little annoyed*]. Blesséd be God!

SERVANT [*annoyed*]. Forever and ever!

BEGGAR. I came for the scraps.

[*The bells stop tolling.*]

SERVANT. You can go right out the way you came in. Today's scraps are for me.

BEGGAR. But you have somebody to take care of you—and my little girl and I are all alone!

SERVANT. Dogs are alone too, and they live.

BEGGAR. They always give them to me.

SERVANT. Get out of here! Who let you in anyway? You've already tracked up the place. [THE BEGGAR WOMAN *and* LITTLE GIRL *leave.* THE SERVANT *goes on scrubbing.*] Floors finished with oil, cupboards, pedestals, iron beds— but us servants, we can suffer in silence—and live in mud huts with a plate and a spoon. I hope someday not a one will be left to tell it. [*The bells sound again.*] Yes, yes—ring away. Let them put you in a coffin with gold inlay and brocade to carry it on—you're no less dead than I'll be, so take what's coming to you, Antonio María Benavides—stiff in your broadcloth suit and your high boots—take what's coming to you! You'll never again lift my skirts behind the corral door!

[*From the rear door, two by two, women in mourning with large shawls and black skirts and fans begin to enter. They come in slowly until the stage is full.*]

SERVANT [*breaking into a wail*]. Oh, Antonio María Benavides, now you'll never see these walls, nor break bread in this house again! I'm the one who loved you most of all your servants. [*Pulling her hair.*] *Must* I live on after you've gone? Must I go on living?

[*The women finish coming in, and* BERNARDA *and her five daughters enter.* BERNARDA *leans on a cane.*]

BERNARDA [*to* THE SERVANT]. Silence!

SERVANT [*weeping*]. Bernarda!

BERNARDA. Less shrieking and more work. You should have had all this cleaner for the wake. Get out. This isn't your place.

[THE SERVANT *goes off crying.*]

The poor are like animals—they seem to be made of different stuff.

FIRST WOMAN. The poor feel their sorrows too.

BERNARDA. But they forget them in front of a plateful of peas.

FIRST GIRL [*timidly*]. Eating is necessary for living.

BERNARDA. At your age one doesn't talk in front of older people.

WOMAN. Be quiet, child.

BERNARDA. I've never taken lessons from anyone. Sit down. Magdalena, don't cry. If you want to cry, get under your bed. Do you hear me?

SECOND WOMAN [*to* BERNARDA]. Have you started to work the fields?

BERNARDA. Yesterday.

THIRD WOMAN. The sun comes down like lead.

FIRST WOMAN. I haven't known heat like this for years.

[*Pause. They all fan themselves.*]

BERNARDA. Is the lemonade ready?

PONCIA. Yes, Bernarda.

[*She brings in a large tray full of little white jars which she distributes.*]

BERNARDA. Give the men some.

PONCIA. They're already drinking in the patio.

BERNARDA. Let them get out the way they came in. I don't want them walking through here.

A GIRL [*to* ANGUSTIAS]. Pepe el Romano was with the men during the service.

ANGUSTIAS. There he was.

BERNARDA. His mother was there. She saw his mother. Neither she nor I saw Pepe . . .

GIRL. I thought . . .

BERNARDA. The one who *was* there was Darajalí, the widower. Very close to your Aunt. We all of us saw him.

SECOND WOMAN [*aside, in a low voice*].

Wicked, worse than wicked woman!

THIRD WOMAN. A tongue like a knife!

BERNARDA. Women in church shouldn't look at any man but the priest—and him only because he wears skirts. To turn your head is to be looking for the warmth of corduroy.

FIRST WOMAN. Sanctimonious old snake!

PONCIA [*between her teeth*]. Itching for a man's warmth.

BERNARDA [*beating with her cane on the floor*]. Blesséd be God!°

ALL [*crossing themselves*]. Forever blesséd and praiséd.

BERNARDA. Rest in peace with holy company at your head.

ALL. Rest in peace!

BERNARDA. With the Angel Saint Michael, and his sword of justice.

ALL. Rest in peace!

BERNARDA. With the key that opens, and the hand that locks.

ALL. Rest in peace!

BERNARDA. With the most blesséd, and the little lights of the field.

ALL. Rest in peace!

BERNARDA. With our holy charity, and all souls on land and sea.

ALL. Rest in peace!

BERNARDA. Grant rest to your servant, Antonio María Benavides, and give him the crown of your blesséd glory.

ALL. Amen.

BERNARDA. [*She rises and chants.*] Requiem aeternam donat eis domine.

ALL [*standing and chanting in the Gregorian fashion*]. Et lux perpetua luce ab eis.°

[*They cross themselves.*]

FIRST WOMAN. May you have health to pray for his soul.

[*They start filing out.*]

THIRD WOMAN. You won't lack loaves of hot bread.

Blesséd be God! the following passage is a pastiche of ritual and folk phrases

Requiem . . . luce ab eis Bernarda and her visitors garble a refrain from the Offices for the Dead. The original means, "Grant them eternal rest, O Lord. And let the everlasting light shine upon them."

SECOND WOMAN. Nor a roof for your daughters.

[*They are all filing in front of* BERNARDA *and going out.* ANGUSTIAS *leaves by the door to the patio.*]

FOURTH WOMAN. May you go on enjoying your wedding wheat.

PONCIA. [*She enters, carrying a money bag.*] From the men—this bag of money for Masses.

BERNARDA. Thank them—and let them have a glass of brandy.

GIRL [*to* MAGDALENA]. Magdalena . . .

BERNARDA [*to* MAGDALENA, *who is starting to cry*]. Sh-h-h-h! [*She beats with her cane on the floor.*]

[*All the women have gone out.*]

BERNARDA [*to the women who have just left*]. Go back to your houses and criticize everything you've seen! I hope it'll be many years before you pass under the archway of my door again.

PONCIA. You've nothing to complain about. The whole town came.

BERNARDA. Yes, to fill my house with the sweat from their wraps and the poison of their tongues.

AMELIA. Mother, don't talk like that.

BERNARDA. What other way is there to talk about this cursèd village with no river—this village full of wells where you drink water always fearful it's been poisoned?

PONCIA. Look what they've done to the floor!

BERNARDA. As though a herd of goats had passed through. [PONCIA *cleans the floor.*] Adela, give me a fan.

ADELA. Take this one. [*She gives her a round fan with green and red flowers.*]

BERNARDA [*throwing the fan on the floor*]. Is that the fan to give to a widow? Give me a black one and learn to respect your father's memory.

MARTIRIO. Take mine.

BERNARDA. And you?

MARTIRIO. I'm not hot.

BERNARDA. Well, look for another, because you'll need it. For the eight years of mourning, not a breath of air will get in this house from the street. We'll act as if we'd sealed up doors and windows with bricks. That's what happened in my father's house—and in my grandfather's house. Meantime, you can all start embroidering your hope-chest linens. I have twenty bolts of linen in the chest from which to cut sheets and coverlets. Magdalena can embroider them.

MAGDALENA. It's all the same to me.

ADELA [*sourly*]. If you don't want to embroider them—they can go without. That way yours will look better.

MAGDALENA. Neither mine nor yours. I know I'm not going to marry. I'd rather carry sacks to the mill. Anything except sit here day after day in this dark room.

BERNARDA. That's what a woman is for.

MAGDALENA. Cursed be all women.

BERNARDA. In this house you'll do what I order. You can't run with the story to your father any more. Needle and thread for women. Whiplash and mules for men. That's the way it has to be for people who have certain obligations.

[ADELA *goes out.*]

VOICE. Bernarda! Let me out!

BERNARDA [*calling*]. Let her out now!

[THE FIRST SERVANT *enters.*]

FIRST SERVANT. I had a hard time holding her. In spite of her eighty years, your mother's strong as an oak.

BERNARDA. It runs in the family. My grandfather was the same way.

SERVANT. Several times during the wake I had to cover her mouth with an empty sack because she wanted to shout out to you to give her dishwater to drink at least, and some dog-meat, which is what she says you feed her.

MARTIRIO. She's mean!

BERNARDA [*to* SERVANT]. Let her get some fresh air in the patio.

SERVANT. She took her rings and the amethyst earrings out of the box, put them on, and told me she wants to get married.

[*The daughters laugh.*]

BERNARDA. Go with her and be careful she doesn't get near the well.

SERVANT. You don't need to be afraid she'll jump in.

BERNARDA. It's not that—but the neighbors can see her there from their windows.

5 [THE SERVANT *leaves*.]

MARTIRIO. We'll go change our clothes.

BERNARDA. Yes, but don't take the 'kerchiefs from your heads.

[ADELA *enters*.]

10 And Angustias?

ADELA [*meaningfully*]. I saw her looking out through the cracks of the back door. The men had just gone.

BERNARDA. And you, what were *you* doing

15 at the door?

ADELA. I went there to see if the hens had laid.

BERNARDA. But the men had already gone!

ADELA [*meaningfully*]. A group of them

20 were still standing outside.

BERNARDA [*furiously*]. Angustias! Angustias!

ANGUSTIAS [*entering*]. Did you want something?

BERNARDA. For what—and at whom—were

25 you looking?

ANGUSTIAS. Nobody.

BERNARDA. Is it decent for a woman of your class to be running after a man the day of her father's funeral? Answer me! Whom were you

30 looking at?

[*Pause*.]

ANGUSTIAS. I . . .

BERNARDA. Yes, you!

ANGUSTIAS. Nobody.

35 BERNARDA. Soft! Honeytongue! [*She strikes her*.]

PONCIA [*running to her*]. Bernarda, calm down! [*She holds her*. ANGUSTIAS *weeps*.]

BERNARDA. Get out of here, all of you!

40 [*They all go out*.]

PONCIA. She did it not realizing what she was doing—although it's bad, of course. It really disgusted me to see her sneak along to the patio. Then she stood at the window listening

45 to the men's talk which, as usual, was not the sort one should listen to.

BERNARDA. That's what they come to funerals for. [*With curiosity*.] What were they talking about?

PONCIA. They were talking about Paca la 50 Roseta. Last night they tied her husband up in a stall, stuck her on a horse behind the saddle, and carried her away to the depths of the olive grove.

BERNARDA. And what did she do? 55

PONCIA. She? She was just as happy—they say her breasts were exposed and Maximiliano held on to her as if he were playing a guitar. Terrible!

BERNARDA. And what happened? 60

PONCIA. What had to happen. They came back almost at daybreak. Paca la Roseta with her hair loose and a wreath of flowers on her head.

BERNARDA. She's the only bad woman we 65 have in the village.

PONCIA. Because she's not from here. She's from far away. And those who went with her are the sons of outsiders too. The men from here aren't up to a thing like that. 70

BERNARDA. No, but they like to see it, and talk about it, and suck their fingers over it.

PONCIA. They were saying a lot more things.

BERNARDA [*looking from side to side with a certain fear*]. What things? 75

PONCIA. I'm ashamed to talk about them.

BERNARDA. And my daughter heard them?

PONCIA. Of course!

BERNARDA. That one takes after her Aunts: white and mealy-mouthed and casting sheep's 80 eyes at any little barber's compliment. Oh, what one has to go through and put up with so people will be decent and not too wild!

PONCIA. It's just that your daughters are of an age when they ought to have husbands. 85 Mighty little trouble they give you. Angustias must be much more than thirty now.

BERNARDA. Exactly thirty-nine.

PONCIA. Imagine. And she's never had a beau . . . 90

BERNARDA [*furiously*]. None of them has ever had a beau and they've never needed one! They get along very well.

PONCIA. I didn't mean to offend you.

BERNARDA. For a hundred miles around there's no one good enough to come near them. The men in this town are not of their class. Do you want me to turn them over to the first shepherd?

PONCIA. You should have moved to another town.

BERNARDA. That's it. To sell them!

PONCIA. No, Bernarda, to change. . . . Of course, any place else, they'd be the poor ones.

BERNARDA. Hold your tormenting tongue!

PONCIA. One can't even talk to you. Do we, or do we not share secrets?

BERNARDA. We do not. You're a servant and I pay you. Nothing more.

PONCIA. But . . .

SERVANT [*entering*]. Don Arturo's here. He's come to see about dividing the inheritance.

BERNARDA. Let's go. [*To* THE SERVANT.] You start whitewashing the patio. [*To* LA PONCIA.] And you start putting all the dead man's clothes away in the chest.

PONCIA. We could give away some of the things.

BERNARDA. Nothing—not a button even! Not even the cloth we covered his face with.

[*She goes out slowly, leaning on her cane. At the door she turns to look at the two servants. They go out. She leaves.*]

[AMELIA *and* MARTIRIO *enter.*]

AMELIA. Did you take the medicine?

MARTIRIO. For all the good it'll do me.

AMELIA. But you took it?

MARTIRIO. I do things without any faith, but like clockwork.

AMELIA. Since the new doctor came you look livelier.

MARTIRIO. I feel the same.

AMELIA. Did you notice? Adelaida wasn't at the funeral.

MARTIRIO. I know. Her sweetheart doesn't let her go out even to the front doorstep. Before, she was gay. Now, not even powder on her face.

AMELIA. These days a girl doesn't know whether to have a beau or not.

MARTIRIO. It's all the same.

AMELIA. The whole trouble is all these wagging tongues that won't let us live. Adelaida has probably had a bad time.

MARTIRIO. She's afraid of our mother. Mother is the only one who knows the story of Adelaida's father and where he got his lands. Everytime she comes here, Mother twists the knife in the wound. Her father killed his first wife's husband in Cuba so he could marry her himself. Then he left her there and went off with another woman who already had one daughter, and then he took up with this other girl, Adelaida's mother, and married her after his second wife died insane.

AMELIA. But why isn't a man like that put in jail?

MARTIRIO. Because men help each other cover up things like that and no one's able to tell on them.

AMELIA. But Adelaida's not to blame for any of that.

MARTIRIO. No. But history repeats itself. I can see that everything is a terrible repetition. And she'll have the same fate as her mother and grandmother—both of them wife to the man who fathered her.

AMELIA. What an awful thing!

MARTIRIO. It's better never to look at a man. I've been afraid of them since I was a little girl. I'd see them in the yard, yoking the oxen and lifting grain sacks, shouting and stamping, and I was always afraid to grow up for fear one of them would suddenly take me in his arms. God has made me weak and ugly and has definitely put such things away from me.

AMELIA. Don't say that! Enrique Humanas was after you and he liked you.

MARTIRIO. That was just people's ideas! One time I stood in my nightgown at the window until daybreak because he let me know through his shepherd's little girl that he was going to come, and he didn't. It was all just talk. Then he married someone else who had more money than I.

AMELIA. And ugly as the devil.

MARTIRIO. What do men care about ugliness? All they care about is lands, yokes of oxen, and a submissive bitch who'll feed them.

AMELIA. Ay!

[MAGDALENA *enters.*]

MAGDALENA. What are you doing?

MARTIRIO. Just here.

5 AMELIA. And you?

MAGDALENA. I've been going through all the rooms. Just to walk a little, and look at Grandmother's needlepoint pictures—the little woolen dog, and the black man wrestling with the

10 lion—which we liked so much when we were children. Those were happier times. A wedding lasted ten days and evil tongues weren't in style. Today people are more refined. Brides wear white veils, just as in the cities, and we

15 drink bottled wine, but we rot inside because of what people might say.

MARTIRIO. Lord knows what went on then!

AMELIA [*to* MAGDALENA]. One of your shoelaces has come untied.

20 MAGDALENA. What of it?

AMELIA. You'll step on it and fall.

MAGDALENA. One less!

MARTIRIO. And Adela?

MAGDALENA. Ah! She put on the green dress

25 she made to wear for her birthday, went out to the yard, and began shouting: "Chickens! Chickens, look at me!" I had to laugh.

AMELIA. If Mother had only seen her!

MAGDALENA. Poor little thing! She's the

30 youngest one of us and still has her illusions. I'd give something to see her happy.

[*Pause.* ANGUSTIAS *crosses the stage, carrying some towels.*]

ANGUSTIAS. What time is it?

35 MAGDALENA. It must be twelve.

ANGUSTIAS. So late?

AMELIA. It's about to strike.

[ANGUSTIAS *goes out.*]

MAGDALENA [*meaningfully*]. Do you know

40 what? [*Pointing after* ANGUSTIAS.]

AMELIA. No.

MAGDALENA. Come on!

MARTIRIO. I don't know what you're talking about!

45 MAGDALENA. Both of you know it better than I do, always with your heads together, like two little sheep, but not letting anybody else in on it. I mean about Pepe el Romano!

MARTIRIO. Ah!

MAGDALENA [*mocking her*]. Ah! The whole 50 town's talking about it. Pepe el Romano is coming to marry Angustias. Last night he was walking around the house and I think he's going to send a declaration soon.

MARTIRIO. I'm glad. He's a good man. 55

AMELIA. Me too. Angustias is well off.

MAGDALENA. Neither one of you is glad.

MARTIRIO. Magdalena! What do you mean?

MAGDALENA. If he were coming because of Angustias' looks, for Angustias as a woman, 60 I'd be glad too, but he's coming for her money. Even though Angustias is our sister, we're her family here and we know she's old and sickly, and always has been the least attractive one of us! Because if she looked like a dressed-up 65 stick at twenty, what can she look like now, now that she's forty?

MARTIRIO. Don't talk like that. Luck comes to the one who least expects it.

AMELIA. But Magdalena's right after all! 70 Angustias has all her father's money; she's the only rich one in the house and that's why, now that Father's dead and the money will be divided, they're coming for her.

MAGDALENA. Pepe el Romano is twenty-five 75 years old and the best looking man around here. The natural thing would be for him to be after you, Amelia, or our Adela, who's twenty —not looking for the least likely one in this house, a woman who, like her father, talks 80 through her nose.

MARTIRIO. Maybe he likes that!

MAGDALENA. I've never been able to bear your hypocrisy.

MARTIRIO. Heavens! 85

[ADELA *enters.*]

MAGDALENA. Did the chickens see you?

ADELA. What did you want me to do?

AMELIA. If Mother sees you, she'll drag you by your hair! 90

ADELA. I had a lot of illusions about this dress. I'd planned to put it on the day we were going to eat watermelons at the well. There wouldn't have been another like it.

MARTIRIO. It's a lovely dress. 95

ADELA. And one that looks very good on

me. It's the best thing Magdalena's ever cut.

MAGDALENA. And the chickens, what did they say to you?

ADELA. They presented me with a few fleas that riddled my legs.

[*They laugh.*]

MARTIRIO. What you can do is dye it black.

MAGDALENA. The best thing you can do is give it to Angustias for her wedding with Pepe el Romano.

ADELA [*with hidden emotion*]. But Pepe el Romano . . .

AMELIA. Haven't you heard about it?

ADELA. No.

MAGDALENA. Well, now you know!

ADELA. But it can't be!

MAGDALENA. Money can do anything.

ADELA. Is that why she went out after the funeral and stood looking through the door? [*Pause.*] And that man would . . .

MAGDALENA. Would do anything.

[*Pause.*]

MARTIRIO. What are you thinking, Adela?

ADELA. I'm thinking that this mourning has caught me at the worst moment of my life for me to bear it.

MAGDALENA. You'll get used to it.

ADELA [*bursting out, crying with rage*]. I will not get used to it! I can't be locked up. I don't want my skin to look like yours. I don't want my skin's whiteness lost in these rooms. Tomorrow I'm going to put on my green dress and go walking in the streets. I want to go out!

[THE FIRST SERVANT *enters.*]

MAGDALENA [*in a tone of authority*]. Adela!

SERVANT. The poor thing! How she misses her father. . . .

[*She goes out.*]

MARTIRIO. Hush!

AMELIA. What happens to one will happen to all of us.

[ADELA *grows calm.*]

MAGDALENA. The servant almost heard you.

SERVANT [*entering*]. Pepe el Romano is coming along at the end of the street.

[AMELIA, MARTIRIO, and MAGDALENA *run hurriedly.*]

MAGDALENA. Let's go see him!

[*They leave rapidly.*]

SERVANT [*to* ADELA]. Aren't you going?

ADELA. It's nothing to me.

SERVANT. Since he has to turn the corner, you'll see him better from the window of your room.

[THE SERVANT *goes out.* ADELA *is left on the stage, standing doubtfully; after a moment, she also leaves rapidly, going toward her room.* BERNARDA *and* LA PONCIA *come in.*]

BERNARDA. Damned portions and shares.

PONCIA. What a lot of money is left to Angustias!

BERNARDA. Yes.

PONCIA. And for the others, considerably less.

BERNARDA. You've told me that three times now, when you know I don't want it mentioned! Considerably less; a lot less! Don't remind me any more.

[ANGUSTIAS *comes in, her face heavily made up.*]

Angustias!

ANGUSTIAS. Mother.

BERNARDA. Have you dared to powder your face? Have you dared to wash your face on the day of your father's death?

ANGUSTIAS. He wasn't my father. Mine died a long time ago. Have you forgotten that already?

BERNARDA. You owe more to this man, father of your sisters, than to your own. Thanks to him, your fortune is intact.

ANGUSTIAS. We'll have to see about that first!

BERNARDA. Even out of decency! Out of respect!

ANGUSTIAS. Let me go out, Mother!

BERNARDA. Let you go out? After I've taken that powder off your face, I will. Spineless! Painted hussy! Just like your Aunts! [*She removes the powder violently with her handkerchief.*] Now get out!

PONCIA. Bernarda, don't be so hateful!

BERNARDA. Even though my mother is crazy, I still have my five senses and I know what I'm doing.

[*They all enter.*]

MAGDALENA. What's going on here?

BERNARDA. Nothing's "going on here"!

MAGDALENA [*to* ANGUSTIAS]. If you're fight- ing over the inheritance, you're the richest one and can hang on to it all.

ANGUSTIAS. Keep your tongue in your pocket- 5 book!

BERNARDA [*beating on the floor*]. Don't fool yourselves into thinking you'll sway me. Until I go out of this house feet first I'll give the orders for myself and for you!

10 [*Voices are heard and* MARIA JOSEFA, BER- NARDA'S *mother, enters. She is very old and has decked out her head and breast with flowers.*]

MARIA JOSEFA. Bernarda, where is my man- tilla? Nothing, nothing of what I own will be 15 for any of you. Not my rings nor my black moiré dress. Because not a one of you is going to marry—not a one. Bernarda, give me my necklace of pearls.

BERNARDA [*to* THE SERVANT]. Why did you 20 let her get in here?

SERVANT [*trembling*]. She got away from me!

MARIA JOSEFA. I ran away because I want to marry—I want to get married to a beautiful manly man from the shore of the sea. Because 25 here the men run from women.

BERNARDA. Hush, hush, Mother!

MARIA JOSEFA. No, no—I won't hush. I don't want to see these single women, longing for marriage, turning their hearts to dust; and I 30 want to go to my home town. Bernarda, I want a man to get married to and be happy with!

BERNARDA. Lock her up!

MARIA JOSEFA. Let me go out, Bernarda!

35 [THE SERVANT *seizes* MARIA JOSEFA.]

BERNARDA. Help her, all of you!

[*They all grab the old woman.*]

MARIA JOSEFA. I want to get away from here! Bernarda! To get married by the shore of the 40 sea—by the shore of the sea!

Quick Curtain

ACT II

[*A white room in* BERNARDA'S *house. The doors on the left lead to the bedrooms.*]

BERNARDA'S *daughters are seated on low chairs, sewing.* MAGDALENA *is embroidering.*

LA PONCIA *is with them.*]

ANGUSTIAS. I've cut the third sheet. 45

MARTIRIO. That one goes to Amelia.

MAGDALENA. Angustias, shall I put Pepe's initials here too?

ANGUSTIAS [*dryly*]. No.

MAGDALENA [*calling*]. Adela, aren't you com- 50 ing?

AMELIA. She's probably stretched out on the bed.

PONCIA. Something's wrong with that one. 55 I find her restless, trembling, frightened—as if a lizard were between her breasts.

MARTIRIO. There's nothing, more or less, wrong with her than there is with all of us.

MAGDALENA. All of us except Angustias. 60

ANGUSTIAS. I feel fine, and anybody who doesn't like it can pop.

MAGDALENA. We all have to admit the nicest things about you are your figure and your tact.

ANGUSTIAS. Fortunately, I'll soon be out of 65 this hell.

MAGDALENA. Maybe you won't get out!

MARTIRIO. Stop this talk!

ANGUSTIAS. Besides, a good dowry is better than dark eyes in one's face! 70

MAGDALENA. All you say just goes in one ear and out the other.

AMELIA [*to* LA PONCIA]. Open the patio door and see if we can get a bit of a breeze.

[LA PONCIA *opens the door.*] 75

MARTIRIO. Last night I couldn't sleep because of the heat.

AMELIA. Neither could I.

MAGDALENA. I got up for a bit of air. There was a black storm cloud and a few drops even 80 fell.

PONCIA. It was one in the morning and the earth seemed to give off fire. I got up too. Angustias was still at the window with Pepe.

MAGDALENA [*with irony*]. That late? What 85 time did he leave?

ANGUSTIAS. Why do you ask, if you saw him?

AMELIA. He must have left about one-thirty.

ANGUSTIAS. Yes. How did you know?

AMELIA. I heard him cough and heard his 90 mare's hoofbeats.

PONCIA. But I heard him leave around four.

ANGUSTIAS. It must have been someone else!

PONCIA. No, I'm sure of it!

AMELIA. That's what it seemed to me, too.

MAGDALENA. That's very strange!

5 [Pause.]

PONCIA. Listen, Angustias, what did he say to you the first time he came by your window?

ANGUSTIAS. Nothing. What should he say? Just talked.

10 MARTIRIO. It's certainly strange that two people who never knew each other should suddenly meet at a window and be engaged.

ANGUSTIAS. Well, I didn't mind.

AMELIA. I'd have felt very strange about it.

15 ANGUSTIAS. No, because when a man comes to a window he knows, from all the busybodies who come and go and fetch and carry, that he's going to be told "yes."

MARTIRIO. All right, but he'd have to ask

20 you.

ANGUSTIAS. Of course!

AMELIA [inquisitively]. And how did he ask you?

ANGUSTIAS. Why, no way:—"You know I'm

25 after you. I need a good, well brought up woman, and that's you—if it's agreeable."

AMELIA. These things embarrass me!

ANGUSTIAS. They embarrass me too, but one has to go through it!

30 PONCIA. And did he say anything more?

ANGUSTIAS. Yes, he did all the talking.

MARTIRIO. And you?

ANGUSTIAS. I couldn't have said a word. My heart was almost coming out of my mouth. It

35 was the first time I'd ever been alone at night with a man.

MAGDALENA. And such a handsome man.

ANGUSTIAS. He's not bad looking.

PONCIA. Those things happen among people

40 who have an idea how to do things, who talk and say and move their hand. The first time my husband, Evaristo the Short-tailed, came to my window . . . Ha! Ha! Ha!

AMELIA. What happened?

45 PONCIA. It was very dark. I saw him coming along and as he went by he said, "Good evening," "Good evening," I said. Then we were both silent for more than half an hour. The sweat poured down my body. Then Evaristo got nearer and nearer as if he wanted to 50 squeeze in through the bars and said in a very low voice—"Come here and let me feel you!"

[They all laugh. AMELIA gets up, runs, and looks through the door.]

AMELIA. Ay, I thought Mother was coming! 55

MAGDALENA. What she'd have done to us!

[They go on laughing.]

AMELIA. Sh-h-h! She'll hear us.

PONCIA. Then he acted very decently. Instead of getting some other idea, he went to raising 60 birds, until he died. You aren't married but it's good for you to know, anyway, that two weeks after the wedding a man gives up the bed for the table, then the table for the tavern, and the woman who doesn't like it can just rot, weep- 65 ing in a corner.

AMELIA. You liked it.

PONCIA. I learned how to handle him!

MARTIRIO. Is it true that you sometimes hit him? 70

PONCIA. Yes, and once I almost poked out one of his eyes!

MAGDALENA. All women ought to be like that!

PONCIA. I'm one of your mother's school. 75 One time I don't know what he said to me, and then I killed all his birds—with the pestle!

[They laugh.]

MAGDALENA. Adela, child! Don't miss this.

AMELIA. Adela! 80

[Pause.]

MAGDALENA. I'll go see!

[She goes out.]

PONCIA. That child is sick!

MARTIRIO. Of course. She hardly sleeps! 85

PONCIA. What does she do, then?

MARTIRIO. How do I know what she does?

PONCIA. You probably know better than we do, since you sleep with just a wall between you. 90

ANGUSTIAS. Envy gnaws on people.

AMELIA. Don't exaggerate.

ANGUSTIAS. I can tell it in her eyes. She's getting the look of a crazy woman.

MARTIRIO. Don't talk about crazy women. This is one place you're not allowed to say that word.

[MAGDALENA *and* ADELA *enter*.]

MAGDALENA. Didn't you say she was asleep?

ADELA. My body aches.

MARTIRIO [*with a hidden meaning*]. Didn't you sleep well last night?

ADELA. Yes.

MARTIRIO. Then?

ADELA [*loudly*]. Leave me alone. Awake or asleep, it's no affair of yours. I'll do whatever I want to with my body.

MARTIRIO. I was just concerned about you!

ADELA. Concerned?—curious! Weren't you sewing? Well, continue! I wish I were invisible so I could pass through a room without being asked where I was going!

SERVANT [*entering*]. Bernarda is calling you. The man with the laces is here.

[*All but* ADELA *and* LA PONCIA *go out, and as* MARTIRIO *leaves, she looks fixedly at* ADELA.]

ADELA. Don't look at me like that! If you want, I'll give you my eyes, for they're younger, and my back to improve that hump you have, but look the other way when I go by.

PONCIA. Adela, she's your sister, and the one who most loves you besides!

ADELA. She follows me everywhere. Sometimes she looks in my room to see if I'm sleeping. She won't let me breathe, and always, "Too bad about that face!" "Too bad about that body! It's going to waste!" But I won't let that happen. My body will be for whomever I choose.

PONCIA [*insinuatingly, in a low voice*]. For Pepe el Romano, no?

ADELA [*frightened*]. What do you mean?

PONCIA. What I said, Adela!

ADELA. Shut up!

PONCIA [*loudly*]. Don't you think I've noticed?

ADELA. Lower your voice!

PONCIA. Then forget what you're thinking about!

ADELA. What do you know?

PONCIA. We old ones can see through walls. Where do you go when you get up at night?

ADELA. I wish you were blind!

PONCIA. But my head and hands are full of eyes, where something like this is concerned. I couldn't possibly guess your intentions. Why did you sit almost naked at your window, and with the light on and the window open, when Pepe passed by the second night he came to talk with your sister?

ADELA. That's not true!

PONCIA. Don't be a child! Leave your sister alone. And if you like Pepe el Romano, keep it to yourself. [ADELA *weeps*.] Besides, who says you can't marry him? Your sister Angustias is sickly. She'll die with her first child. Narrow waisted, old—and out of my experience I can tell you she'll die. Then Pepe will do what all widowers do in these parts: he'll marry the youngest and most beautiful, and that's you. Live on that hope, forget him, anything; but don't go against God's law.

ADELA. Hush!

PONCIA. I won't hush!

ADELA. Mind your own business. Snooper, traitor!

PONCIA. I'm going to stick to you like a shadow!

ADELA. Instead of cleaning the house and then going to bed and praying for the dead, you root around like an old sow about goings on between men and women—so you can drool over them.

PONCIA. I keep watch; so people won't spit when they pass our door.

ADELA. What a tremendous affection you've suddenly conceived for my sister.

PONCIA. I don't have any affection for any of you. I want to live in a decent house. I don't want to be dirtied in my old age!

ADELA. Save your advice. It's already too late. For I'd leap not over you, just a servant, but over my mother to put out this fire I feel in my legs and my mouth. What can you possibly say about me? That I lock myself in my room and will not open the door? That I don't sleep? I'm smarter than you! See if you can catch the hare with your hands.

PONCIA. Don't defy me, Adela, don't defy me! Because I can shout, light lamps, and make bells ring.

ADELA. Bring four thousand yellow flares and set them about the walls of the yard. No one can stop what has to happen.

PONCIA. You like him that much?

ADELA. That much! Looking in his eyes I seem to drink his blood in slowly.

PONCIA. I won't listen to you.

ADELA. Well, you'll have to! I've been afraid of you. But now I'm stronger than you!

[ANGUSTIAS enters.]

ANGUSTIAS. Always arguing!

PONCIA. Certainly. She insists that in all this heat I have to go bring her I don't know what from the store.

ANGUSTIAS. Did you buy me the bottle of perfume?

PONCIA. The most expensive one. And the face powder. I put them on the table in your room.

[ANGUSTIAS goes out.]

ADELA. And be quiet!

PONCIA. We'll see!

[MARTIRIO and AMELIA enter.]

MARTIRIO [to ADELA]. Did you see the laces?

AMELIA. Angustias', for her wedding sheets, are beautiful.

ADELA [to MARTIRIO, who is carrying some lace]. And these?

MARTIRIO. They're for me. For a nightgown.

ADELA [with sarcasm]. One needs a sense of humor around here!

MARTIRIO [meaningfully]. But only for me to look at. I don't have to exhibit myself before anybody.

PONCIA. No one ever sees us in our nightgowns.

MARTIRIO [meaningfully, looking at ADELA]. Sometimes they don't! But I love nice underwear. If I were rich, I'd have it made of Holland Cloth. It's one of the few tastes I've left.

PONCIA. These laces are beautiful for babies' caps and christening gowns. I could never afford them for my own. Now let's see if Angustias will use them for hers. Once she starts having children, they'll keep her running night and day.

MAGDALENA. I don't intend to sew a stitch on them.

AMELIA. And much less bring up some stranger's children. Look how our neighbors across the road are—making sacrifices for four brats.

PONCIA. They're better off than you. There at least they laugh and you can hear them fight.

MARTIRIO. Well, you go work for them, then.

PONCIA. No, fate has sent me to this nunnery!

[Tiny bells are heard distantly as though through several thicknesses of wall.]

MAGDALENA. It's the men going back to work.

PONCIA. It was three o'clock a minute ago.

MARTIRIO. With this sun!

ADELA [sitting down]. Ay! If only we could go out in the fields too!

MAGDALENA [sitting down]. Each class does what it has to!

MARTIRIO [sitting down]. That's it!

AMELIA [sitting down]. Ay!

PONCIA. There's no happiness like that in the fields right at this time of year. Yesterday morning the reapers arrived. Forty or fifty handsome young men.

MAGDALENA. Where are they from this year?

PONCIA. From far, far away. They came from the mountains! Happy! Like weathered trees! Shouting and throwing stones! Last night a woman who dresses in sequins and dances, with an accordion, arrived, and fifteen of them made a deal with her to take her to the olive grove. I saw them from far away. The one who talked with her was a boy with green eyes— tight knit as a sheaf of wheat.

AMELIA. Really?

ADELA. Are you sure?

PONCIA. Years ago another one of those women came here, and I myself gave my eldest son some money so he could go. Men need things like that.

ADELA. Everything's forgiven them.

AMELIA. To be born a woman's the worst possible punishment.

MAGDALENA. Even our eyes aren't our own.
[*A distant song is heard, coming nearer.*]
PONCIA. There they are. They have a beautiful song.

5 AMELIA. They're going out to reap now.
CHORUS.
The reapers have set out
Looking for ripe wheat;
They'll carry off the hearts
10 Of any girls they meet.
[*Tambourines and carrañacas° are heard.
Pause. They all listen in the silence cut by the
sun.*]
AMELIA. And they don't mind the sun!
15 MARTIRIO. They reap through flames.
ADELA. How I'd like to be a reaper so I could
come and go as I pleased. Then we could forget
what's eating us all.
MARTIRIO. What do you have to forget?
20 ADELA. Each one of us has something.
MARTIRIO [*intensely*]. Each one!
PONCIA. Quiet! Quiet!
CHORUS [*very distantly*].
Throw wide your doors and windows,
25 You girls who live in the town.
The reaper asks you for roses
With which to deck his crown.
PONCIA. What a song!
MARTIRIO [*with nostalgia*].
30 Throw wide your doors and windows,
You girls who live in the town.
ADELA [*passionately*].
The reaper asks you for roses
With which to deck his crown.
35 [*The song grows more distant.*]
PONCIA. Now they're turning the corner.
ADELA. Let's watch them from the window
of my room.
PONCIA. Be careful not to open the shutters
40 too much because they're likely to give them
a push to see who's looking.
[*The three leave.* MARTIRIO *is left sitting on
the low chair with her head between her
hands.*]
45 AMELIA [*drawing near her*]. What's wrong

carrañacas noise-makers(?)

with you?
MARTIRIO. The heat makes me feel ill.
AMELIA. And it's no more than that?
MARTIRIO. I was wishing it were November,
the rainy days, the frost—anything except this 50
unending summertime.
AMELIA. It'll pass and come again.
MARTIRIO. Naturally. [*Pause.*] What time
did you go to sleep last night?
AMELIA. I don't know. I sleep like a log. 55
Why?
MARTIRIO. Nothing. Only I thought I heard
someone in the yard.
AMELIA. Yes?
MARTIRIO. Very late. 60
AMELIA. And weren't you afraid?
MARTIRIO. No. I've heard it other nights.
AMELIA. We'd better watch out! Couldn't it
have been the shepherds?
MARTIRIO. The shepherds come at six. 65
AMELIA. Maybe a young, unbroken mule?
MARTIRIO [*to herself, with double meaning*].
That's it! That's it. An unbroken little mule.
AMELIA. We'll have to set a watch.
MARTIRIO. No. No. Don't say anything. It 70
may be I've just imagined it.
AMELIA. Maybe.
[*Pause.* AMELIA *starts to go.*]
MARTIRIO. Amelia!
AMELIA [*at the door*]. What? 75
[*Pause.*]
MARTIRIO. Nothing.
[*Pause.*]
AMELIA. Why did you call me?
[*Pause.*] 80
MARTIRIO. It just came out. I didn't mean to.
[*Pause.*]
AMELIA. Lie down for a little.
ANGUSTIAS. [*She bursts in furiously, in a
manner that makes a great contrast with pre-* 85
vious silence.] Where's that picture of Pepe I
had under my pillow? Which one of you has it?
MARTIRIO. No one.
AMELIA. You'd think he was a silver St.
Bartholomew. 90
ANGUSTIAS. Where's the picture?
[PONCIA, MAGDALENA, *and* ADELA *enter.*]

ADELA. What picture?

ANGUSTIAS. One of you has hidden it on me.

MAGDALENA. Do you have the effrontery to say that?

5 ANGUSTIAS. I had it in my room, and now it isn't there.

MARTIRIO. But couldn't it have jumped out into the yard at midnight? Pepe likes to walk around in the moonlight.

10 ANGUSTIAS. Don't joke with me! When he comes I'll tell him.

PONCIA. Don't do that! Because it'll turn up. [Looking at ADELA.]

ANGUSTIAS. I'd like to know which one of 15 you has it.

ADELA [looking at MARTIRIO]. Somebody has it! But not me!

MARTIRIO [with meaning]. Of course not you!

20 BERNARDA [entering, with her cane]. What scandal is this in my house in the heat's heavy silence? The neighbors must have their ears glued to the walls.

ANGUSTIAS. They've stolen my sweetheart's 25 picture!

BERNARDA [fiercely]. Who? Who?

ANGUSTIAS. They have!

BERNARDA. Which one of you? [Silence.] Answer me! [Silence.] [To LA PONCIA.] Search 30 their rooms! Look in their beds.° This comes of not tying you up with shorter leashes. But I'll teach you now! [To ANGUSTIAS.] Are you sure?

ANGUSTIAS. Yes.

35 BERNARDA. Did you look everywhere?

ANGUSTIAS. Yes, Mother.

[They all stand in an embarrassed silence.]

BERNARDA. At the end of my life—to make me drink the bitterest poison a mother knows. 40 [To PONCIA.] Did you find it?

PONCIA. Here it is.

BERNARDA. Where did you find it?

PONCIA. It was . . .

BERNARDA. Say it! Don't be afraid.

Look in their beds Poncia goes out, and reenters at l. 40

PONCIA [wonderingly]. Between the sheets 45 in Martirio's bed.

BERNARDA [to MARTIRIO]. Is that true?

MARTIRIO. It's true.

BERNARDA [advancing on her, beating her with her cane]. You'll come to a bad end yet, 50 you hypocrite! Trouble maker!

MARTIRIO [fiercely]. Don't hit me, Mother!

BERNARDA. All I want to!

MARTIRIO. If I let you! You hear me? Get back! 55

PONCIA. Don't be disrespectful to your mother!

ANGUSTIAS [holding BERNARDA]. Let her go, please!

BERNARDA. Not even tears in your eyes. 60

MARTIRIO. I'm not going to cry just to please you.

BERNARDA. Why did you take the picture?

MARTIRIO. Can't I play a joke on my sister? What else would I want it for? 65

ADELA [leaping forward, full of jealousy]. It wasn't a joke! You never like to play jokes. It was something else bursting in her breast— trying to come out. Admit it openly now.

MARTIRIO. Hush, and don't make me speak; 70 for if I should speak the walls would close together one against the other with shame.

ADELA. An evil tongue never stops inventing lies.

BERNARDA. Adela! 75

MAGDALENA. You're crazy.

AMELIA. And you stone us all with your evil suspicions.

MARTIRIO. But some others do things more wicked! 80

ADELA. Until all at once they stand forth stark naked and the river carries them along.

BERNARDA. Spiteful!

ANGUSTIAS. It's not my fault Pepe el Romano chose me! 85

ADELA. For your money.

ANGUSTIAS. Mother!

BERNARDA. Silence!

MARTIRIO. For your fields and your orchards.

MAGDALENA. That's only fair. 90

BERNARDA. Silence, I say! I saw the storm

coming but I didn't think it'd burst so soon. Oh, what an avalanche of hate you've thrown on my heart! But I'm not old yet—I have five chains for you, and this house my father built, so not even the weeds will know of my desolation. Out of here!

[*They go out.* BERNARDA *sits down desolately.* LA PONCIA *is standing close to the wall.* BERNARDA *recovers herself, and beats on the floor.*]

I'll have to let them feel the weight of my hand! Bernarda, remember your duty!

PONCIA. May I speak?

BERNARDA. Speak. I'm sorry you heard. A stranger is always out of place in a family.

PONCIA. What I've seen, I've seen.

BERNARDA. Angustias must get married right away.

PONCIA. Certainly. We'll have to get her away from here.

BERNARDA. Not her, him!

PONCIA. Of course. He's the one to get away from here. You've thought it all out.

BERNARDA. I'm not thinking. There are things that shouldn't and can't be thought out. I give orders.

PONCIA. And you think he'll be satisfied to go away?

BERNARDA [*rising*]. What are you imagining now?

PONCIA. He will, of course, marry Angustias.

BERNARDA. Speak up! I know you well enough to see that your knife's out for me.

PONCIA. I never knew a warning could be called murder.

BERNARDA. Have you some "warning" for me?

PONCIA. I'm not making any accusations, Bernarda. I'm only telling you to open your eyes and you'll see.

BERNARDA. See what?

PONCIA. You've always been smart, Bernarda. You've seen other people's sins a hundred miles away. Many times I've thought you could read minds. But, your children are your children, and now you're blind.

BERNARDA. Are you talking about Martirio?

PONCIA. Well, yes—about Martirio . . . [*With curiosity.*] I wonder why she hid the picture?

BERNARDA [*shielding her daughter*]. After all, she says it was a joke. What else could it be?

PONCIA [*scornfully*]. Do you believe that?

BERNARDA [*sternly*]. I don't merely believe it. It's so!

PONCIA. Enough of this. We're talking about your family. But if we were talking about your neighbor across the way, what would it be?

BERNARDA. Now you're beginning to pull the point of the knife out.

PONCIA [*always cruelly*]. No, Bernarda. Something very grave is happening here. I don't want to put the blame on your shoulders, but you've never given your daughters any freedom. Martirio is lovesick, I don't care what you say. Why didn't you let her marry Enrique Humanas? Why, on the very day he was coming to her window, did you send him a message not to come?

BERNARDA [*loudly*]. I'd do it a thousand times over! My blood won't mingle with the Humanas' while I live! His father was a shepherd.

PONCIA. And you see now what's happening to you with these airs!

BERNARDA. I have them because I can afford to. And you don't have them because you know where you came from!

PONCIA [*with hate*]. Don't remind me! I'm old now. I've always been grateful for your protection.

BERNARDA [*emboldened*]. You don't seem so!

PONCIA [*with hate, behind softness*]. Martirio will forget this.

BERNARDA. And if she doesn't—the worse for her. I don't believe this is that "very grave thing" that's happening here. Nothing's happening here. It's just that you wish it would! And if it should happen one day, you can be sure it won't go beyond these walls.

PONCIA. I'm not so sure of that! There are people in town who can also read hidden thoughts, from afar.

BERNARDA. How you'd like to see me and my daughters on our way to a whorehouse!

PONCIA. No one knows her own destiny!

BERNARDA. I know my destiny! And my daughters! The whorehouse was for a certain woman, already dead. . . .

5 PONCIA [*fiercely*]. Bernarda, respect the memory of my mother!

BERNARDA. Then don't plague me with your evil thoughts!

[*Pause.*]

10 PONCIA. I'd better stay out of everything.

BERNARDA. That's what you ought to do. Work and keep your mouth shut. The duty of all who work for a living.

PONCIA. But we can't do that. Don't you
15 think it'd be better for Pepe to marry Martirio or . . . yes! : . . Adela?

BERNARDA. No, I *don't* think so.

PONCIA [*with meaning*]. Adela! She's Romano's real sweetheart!

20 BERNARDA. Things are never the way we want them!

PONCIA. But it's hard work to turn them from their destined course. For Pepe to be with Angustias seems wrong to me—and to other
25 people—and even to the wind. Who knows if they'll get what they want?

BERNARDA. There you go again! Sneaking up on me—giving me bad dreams. But I won't listen to you, because if all you say should
30 come to pass—I'd scratch your face.

PONCIA. Frighten someone else with that.

BERNARDA. Fortunately, my daughters respect me and have never gone against my will!

PONCIA. That's right! But, as soon as they
35 break loose they'll fly to the rooftops!

BERNARDA. And I'll bring them down with stones!

PONCIA. Oh, yes! You were always the bravest one!

40 BERNARDA. I've always enjoyed a good fight!

PONCIA. But aren't people strange. You should see Angustias' enthusiasm for her lover, at her age! And he seems very smitten too. Yesterday my oldest son told me that when
45 he passed by with the oxen at four-thirty in the morning they were still talking.

BERNARDA. At four-thirty?

ANGUSTIAS [*entering*]. That's a lie!

PONCIA. That's what he told me.

BERNARDA [*to* ANGUSTIAS]. Speak up!   50

ANGUSTIAS. For more than a week Pepe has been leaving at one. May God strike me dead if I'm lying.

MARTIRIO [*entering*]. I heard him leave at four too.   55

BERNARDA. But did you see him with your eyes?

MARTIRIO. I didn't want to look out. Don't you talk now through the side window?

ANGUSTIAS. We talk through my bedroom   60 window.

[ADELA *appears at the door.*]

MARTIRIO. Then . . .

BERNARDA. What's going on here?

PONCIA. If you're not careful, you'll find out!   65 At least Pepe was at *one* of your windows— and at four in the morning too!

BERNARDA. Are you sure of that?

PONCIA. You can't be sure of anything in this life!   70

ADELA. Mother, don't listen to someone who wants us to lose everything we have.

BERNARDA. I know how to take care of myself! If the townspeople want to come bearing false witness against me, they'll run into a   75 stone wall! Don't any of you talk about this! Sometimes other people try to stir up a wave of filth to drown us.

MARTIRIO. I don't like to lie.

PONCIA. So there must be something.   80

BERNARDA. There won't be anything. I was born to have my eyes always open. Now I'll watch without closing them 'til I die.

ANGUSTIAS. I have the right to know.

BERNARDA. You don't have any right except   85 to obey. No one's going to fetch and carry for me. [*To* LA PONCIA.] And don't meddle in our affairs. No one will take a step without my knowing it.

SERVANT [*entering*]. There's a big crowd at   90 the top of the street, and all the neighbors are at their doors!

BERNARDA [*to* PONCIA]. Run see what's happening!

[*The girls are about to run out.*]   95 Where are you going? I always knew you for window-watching women and breakers of your mourning. All of you, to the patio!

[*They go out.* BERNARDA *leaves. Distant shouts are heard.* MARTIRIO *and* ADELA *enter and listen, not daring to step farther than the front door.*]

MARTIRIO. You can be thankful I didn't happen to open my mouth.

ADELA. I would have spoken too.

MARTIRIO. And what were you going to say? Wanting isn't doing!

ADELA. I do what I can and what happens to suit me. You've wanted to, but haven't been able.

MARTIRIO. You won't go on very long.

ADELA. I'll have everything!

MARTIRIO. I'll tear you out of his arms!

ADELA [*pleadingly*]. Martirio, let me be!

MARTIRIO. None of us will have him!

ADELA. He wants me for his house!

MARTIRIO. I saw how he embraced you!

ADELA. I didn't want him to. It's as if I were dragged by a rope.

MARTIRIO. I'll see you dead first!

[MAGDALENA *and* ANGUSTIAS *look in. The tumult is increasing.* THE SERVANT *enters with* BERNARDA. PONCIA *also enters from another door.*]

PONCIA. Bernarda!

BERNARDA. What's happening?

PONCIA. Librada's daughter, the unmarried one, had a child and no one knows whose it is!

ADELA. A child?

PONCIA. And to hide her shame she killed it and hid it under the rocks, but the dogs, with more heart than most Christians, dug it out and, as though directed by the hand of God, left it at her door. Now they want to kill her. They're dragging her through the streets— and down the paths and across the olive groves the men are coming, shouting so the fields shake.

BERNARDA. Yes, let them all come with olive whips and hoe handles—let them all come and kill her!

ADELA. No, not to kill her!

MARTIRIO. Yes—and let us go out too!

BERNARDA. And let whoever loses her de-

cency pay for it!

[*Outside a woman's shriek and a great clamor is heard.*]

ADELA. Let her escape! Don't you go out!

MARTIRIO [*looking at* ADELA]. Let her pay what she owes!

BERNARDA [*at the archway*]. Finish her before the guards come! Hot coals in the place where she sinned!

ADELA [*holding her belly*]. No! No!

BERNARDA. Kill her! Kill her!

Curtain

ACT III

[*Four white walls, lightly washed in blue, of the interior patio of* BERNARDA ALBA's *house. The doorways, illumined by the lights inside the rooms, give a tenuous glow to the stage.*

At the center there is a table with a shaded oil lamp about which BERNARDA *and her daughters are eating.* LA PONCIA *serves them.* PRUDENCIA *sits apart. When the curtain rises, there is a great silence interrupted only by the noise of plates and silverware.*]

PRUDENCIA. I'm going. I've made you a long visit. [*She rises.*]

BERNARDA. But wait, Prudencia. We never see one another.

PRUDENCIA. Have they sounded the last call to rosary?

PONCIA. Not yet.

[PRUDENCIA *sits down again.*]

BERNARDA. And your husband, how's he getting on?

PRUDENCIA. The same.

BERNARDA. We never see him either.

PRUDENCIA. You know how he is. Since he quarrelled with his brothers over the inheritance, he hasn't used the front door. He takes a ladder and climbs over the back wall.

BERNARDA. He's a real man! And your daughter?

PRUDENCIA. He's never forgiven her.

BERNARDA. He's right.

PRUDENCIA. I don't know what he told you. I suffer because of it.

BERNARDA. A daughter who's disobedient stops being a daughter and becomes an enemy.

PRUDENCIA. I let water run. The only consolation I've left is to take refuge in the church, but, since I'm losing my sight, I'll have to stop coming so the children won't make fun of me. [*A heavy blow is heard against the walls.*] What's that?

BERNARDA. The stallion. He's locked in the stall and he kicks against the wall of the house. [*Shouting.*] Tether him and take him out in the yard! [*In a lower voice.*] He must be too hot.

PRUDENCIA. Are you going to put the new mares to him?

BERNARDA. At daybreak.

PRUDENCIA. You've known how to increase your stock.

BERNARDA. By dint of money and struggling.

PONCIA [*interrupting*]. And she has the best herd in these parts. It's a shame that prices are low.

BERNARDA. Do you want a little cheese and honey?

PRUDENCIA. I have no appetite.

[*The blow is heard again.*]

PONCIA. My God!

PRUDENCIA. It quivered in my chest!

BERNARDA [*rising, furiously*]. Do I have to say things twice? Let him out to roll on the straw. [*Pause. Then, as though speaking to the stableman.*] Well, then lock the mares in the corral, but let him run free or he may kick down the walls. [*She returns to the table and sits again.*] Ay, what a life!

PRUDENCIA. You have to fight like a man.

BERNARDA. That's it.

[*ADELA gets up from the table.*]

Where are you going?

ADELA. For a drink of water.

BERNARDA [*raising her voice*]. Bring a pitcher of cool water. [*To ADELA.*] You can sit down.

[*ADELA sits down.*]

PRUDENCIA. And Angustias, when will she get married?

BERNARDA. They're coming to ask for her within three days.

PRUDENCIA. You must be happy.

ANGUSTIAS. Naturally!

AMELIA [*to MAGDALENA*]. You've spilled the salt!

MAGDALENA. You can't possibly have worse luck than you're having.

AMELIA. It always brings bad luck.

BERNARDA. That's enough!

PRUDENCIA [*to ANGUSTIAS*]. Has he given you the ring yet?

ANGUSTIAS. Look at it. [*She holds it out.*]

PRUDENCIA. It's beautiful. Three pearls. In my day, pearls signified tears.

ANGUSTIAS. But things have changed now.

ADELA. I don't think so. Things go on meaning the same. Engagement rings should be diamonds.

PONCIA. The most appropriate.

BERNARDA. With pearls or without them, things are as one proposes.

MARTIRIO. Or as God disposes.

PRUDENCIA. I've been told your furniture is beautiful.

BERNARDA. It cost sixteen thousand *reales*.

PONCIA [*interrupting*]. The best is the wardrobe with the mirror.

PRUDENCIA. I never saw a piece like that.

BERNARDA. We had chests.

PRUDENCIA. The important thing is that everything be for the best.

ADELA. And that you never know.

BERNARDA. There's no reason why it shouldn't be.

[*Bells are heard very distantly.*]

PRUDENCIA. The last call. [*To ANGUSTIAS.*] I'll be coming back to have you show me your clothes.

ANGUSTIAS. Whenever you like.

PRUDENCIA. Good evening—God bless you!

BERNARDA. Good-bye, Prudencia.

ALL FIVE DAUGHTERS [*at the same time*]. God go with you!

[*Pause. PRUDENCIA goes out.*]

BERNARDA. Well, we've eaten.

[*They rise.*]

ADELA. I'm going to walk as far as the gate to stretch my legs and get a bit of fresh air.

[*MAGDALENA sits down in a low chair and leans against the wall.*]

AMELIA. I'll go with you.

MARTIRIO. I too.

ADELA [*with contained hate*]. I'm not going to get lost!

AMELIA. One needs company at night.

[*They go out.* BERNARDA *sits down.* ANGUSTIAS *is clearing the table.*]

BERNARDA. I've told you once already! I want you to talk to your sister Martirio. What happened about the picture was a joke and you must forget it.

ANGUSTIAS. You know she doesn't like me.

BERNARDA. Each one knows what she thinks inside. I don't pry into anyone's heart, but I want to put up a good front and have family harmony. You understand?

ANGUSTIAS. Yes.

BERNARDA. Then that's settled.

MAGDALENA. [*She is almost asleep.*] Besides, you'll be gone in no time. [*She falls asleep.*]

ANGUSTIAS. Not soon enough for me.

BERNARDA. What time did you stop talking last night?

ANGUSTIAS. Twelve-thirty.

BERNARDA. What does Pepe talk about?

ANGUSTIAS. I find him absent-minded. He always talks to me as though he were thinking of something else. If I ask him what's the matter, he answers—"We men have our worries."

BERNARDA. You shouldn't ask him. And when you're married, even less. Speak if he speaks, and look at him when he looks at you. That way you'll get along.

ANGUSTIAS. But, Mother, I think he's hiding things from me.

BERNARDA. Don't try to find out. Don't ask him, and above all, never let him see you cry.

ANGUSTIAS. I should be happy, but I'm not.

BERNARDA. It's all the same.

ANGUSTIAS. Many nights I watch Pepe very closely through the window bars and he seems to fade away—as though he were hidden in a cloud of dust like those raised by the flocks.

BERNARDA. That's just because you're not strong.

ANGUSTIAS. I hope so!

BERNARDA. Is he coming tonight?

ANGUSTIAS. No, he went into town with his mother.

BERNARDA. Good, we'll get to bed early.

Magdalena!

ANGUSTIAS. She's asleep.

[ADELA, MARTIRIO, *and* AMELIA *enter.*]

AMELIA. What a dark night!

ADELA. You can't see two steps in front of you.

MARTIRIO. A good night for robbers, for anyone who needs to hide.

ADELA. The stallion was in the middle of the corral. White. Twice as large. Filling all the darkness.

AMELIA. It's true. It was frightening. Like a ghost.

ADELA. The sky has stars as big as fists.

MARTIRIO. This one stared at them till she almost cracked her neck.

ADELA. Don't you like them up there?

MARTIRIO. What goes on over the roof doesn't mean a thing to me. I have my hands full with what happens under it.

ADELA. Well, that's the way it goes with you!

BERNARDA. And it goes the same for you as for her.

ANGUSTIAS. Good night.

ADELA. Are you going to bed now?

ANGUSTIAS. Yes, Pepe isn't coming tonight. [*She goes out.*]

ADELA. Mother, why, when a star falls or lightning flashes, does one say:

Holy Barbara, blessed on high
May your name be in the sky
With holy water written high?

BERNARDA. The old people know many things we've forgotten.

AMELIA. I close my eyes so I won't see them.

ADELA. Not I. I like to see what's quiet and been quiet for years on end, running with fire.

MARTIRIO. But all that has nothing to do with us.

BERNARDA. And it's better not to think about it.

ADELA. What a beautiful night! I'd like to stay up till very late and enjoy the breeze from the fields.

BERNARDA. But we have to go to bed. Magdalena!

AMELIA. She's just dropped off.

BERNARDA. Magdalena!

MAGDALENA [*annoyed*]. Leave me alone!

BERNARDA. To bed!

MAGDALENA [*rising, in a bad humor*]. You don't give anyone a moment's peace!

[*She goes off grumbling.*]

5   AMELIA. Good night!

[*She goes out.*]

BERNARDA. You two get along, too.

MARTIRIO. How is it Angustias' sweetheart isn't coming tonight?

10   BERNARDA. He went on a trip.

MARTIRIO [*looking at* ADELA]. Ah!

ADELA. I'll see you in the morning!

[*She goes out.* MARTIRIO *drinks some water and goes out slowly, looking at the door to the* 15 yard. La PONCIA *enters.*]

PONCIA. Are you still here?

BERNARDA. Enjoying this quiet and not seeing anywhere the "very grave thing" that's happening here—according to you.

20   PONCIA. Bernarda, let's not go any further with this.

BERNARDA. In this house there's no question of a yes or a no. My watchfulness can take care of anything.

25   PONCIA. Nothing's happening outside. That's true, all right. Your daughters act and are as though stuck in a cupboard. But neither you nor anyone else can keep watch inside a person's heart.

30   BERNARDA. My daughters breathe calmly enough.

PONCIA. That's your business, since you're their mother. I have enough to do just with serving you.

35   BERNARDA. Yes, you've turned quiet now.

PONCIA. I keep my place—that's all.

BERNARDA. The trouble is you've nothing to talk about. If there were grass in this house, you'd make it your business to put the neigh-40 bors' sheep to pasture here.

PONCIA. I hide more than you think.

BERNARDA. Do your sons still see Pepe at four in the morning? Are they still repeating this house's evil litany?

45   PONCIA. They say nothing.

BERNARDA. Because they can't. Because there's nothing for them to sink their teeth in. And all because my eyes keep constant watch!

PONCIA. Bernarda! I don't want to talk about this because I'm afraid of what you'll do. But 50 don't you feel so safe.

BERNARDA. Very safe!

PONCIA. Who knows, lightning might strike suddenly. Who knows but what all of a sudden, in a rush of blood, your heart might stop. 55

BERNARDA. Nothing will happen here. I'm on guard now against all your suspicions.

PONCIA. All the better for you.

BERNARDA. Certainly, all the better!

SERVANT [*entering*]. I've just finished with 60 the dishes. Is there anything else, Bernarda?

BERNARDA [*rising*]. Nothing. I'm going to get some rest.

PONCIA. What time do you want me to call you? 65

BERNARDA. No time. Tonight I intend to sleep well.

[*She goes out.*]

PONCIA. When you're powerless against the sea, it's easier to turn your back on it and not 70 look at it.

SERVANT. She's so proud! She herself pulls the blindfold over her eyes.

PONCIA. I can do nothing. I tried to head things off, but now they frighten me too much. 75 You feel this silence?—in each room there's a thunderstorm—and the day it breaks, it'll sweep all of us along with it. But I've said what I had to say.

SERVANT. Bernarda thinks nothing can stand 80 against her, yet she doesn't know the strength a man has among women alone.

PONCIA. It's not all the fault of Pepe el Romano. It's true last year he was running after Adela; and she was crazy about him— 85 but she ought to keep her place and not lead him on. A man's a man.

SERVANT. And some there are who believe he didn't have to talk many times with Adela.

PONCIA. That's true. [*In a low voice.*] And 90 some other things.

SERVANT. I don't know what's going to happen here.

PONCIA. How I'd like to sail across the sea and leave this house, this battleground, behind! 95

SERVANT. Bernarda's hurrying the wedding and it's possible nothing will happen.

PONCIA. Things have gone much too far already. Adela is set° no matter what comes, and the rest of them watch without rest.

SERVANT. Martirio too . . . ?

PONCIA. That one's the worst. She's a pool of poison. She sees El Romano is not for her, and she'd sink the world if it were in her hand to do so.

SERVANT. How bad they all are!

PONCIA. They're women without men, that's all. And in such matters even blood is forgotten. Sh-h-h-h! [*She listens.*]

SERVANT. What's the matter?

PONCIA. [*She rises.*] The dogs are barking.

SERVANT. Someone must have passed by the back door.

[ADELA *enters wearing a white petticoat and corselet.*]

PONCIA. Aren't you in bed yet?

ADELA. I want a drink of water. [*She drinks from a glass on the table.*]

PONCIA. I imagined you were asleep.

ADELA. I got thirsty and woke up. Aren't you two going to get some rest?

SERVANT. Soon now.

[ADELA *goes out.*]

PONCIA. Let's go.

SERVANT. We've certainly earned some sleep. Bernarda doesn't let me rest the whole day.

PONCIA. Take the light.

SERVANT. The dogs are going mad.

PONCIA. They're not going to let us sleep.

[*They go out. The stage is left almost dark.* MARIA JOSEFA *enters with a lamb in her arms.*]

MARIA JOSEFA [*singing*].

Little lamb, child of mine,
Let's go to the shore of the sea,
The tiny ant will be at his doorway,
I'll nurse you and give you your bread.
Bernarda, old leopard-face,
And Magdalena, hyena-face,
Little lamb . . .
Rock, rock-a-bye,
Let's go to the palms at Bethlehem's gate.
[*She laughs.*]
Neither you nor I would want to sleep
The door will open by itself
And on the beach we'll go and hide

In a little coral cabin.
Bernarda, old leopard-face,
And Magdalena, hyena-face,
Little lamb . . .
Rock, rock-a-bye,
Let's go to the palms at Bethehem's gate.
[*She goes off singing.*]

[ADELA *enters. She looks about cautiously and disappears out the door leading to the corral.* MARTIRIO *enters by another door and stands in anguished watchfulness near the center of the stage. She also is in petticoats. She covers herself with a small black scarf.* MARIA JOSEFA *crosses before her.*]

MARTIRIO. Grandmother, where are you going?

MARIA JOSEFA. You are going to open the door for me? Who are you?

MARTIRIO. How did you get out here?

MARIA JOSEFA. I escaped. You, who are you?

MARTIRIO. Go back to bed.

MARIA JOSEFA. You're Martirio. Now I see you. Martirio, face of a martyr. And when are you going to have a baby? I've had this one.

MARTIRIO. Where did you get that lamb?

MARIA JOSEFA. I know it's a lamb. But can't a lamb be a baby? It's better to have a lamb than not to have anything. Old Bernarda, leopard-face, and Magdalena, hyena-face!

MARTIRIO. Don't shout.

MARIA JOSEFA. It's true. Everything's very dark. Just because I have white hair you think I can't have babies, but I can—babies and babies and babies. This baby will have white hair, and I'd have *this* baby, and another, and this *one* other; and with all of us with snow white hair we'll be like the waves—one, then another, and another. Then we'll all sit down and all of us will have white heads, and we'll be seafoam. Why isn't there any seafoam here? Nothing but mourning shrouds here.

MARTIRIO. Hush, hush.

MARIA JOSEFA. When my neighbor had a baby, I'd carry her some chocolate and later she'd bring me some, and so on—always and always and always. You'll have white hair, but your neighbors won't come. Now I have to go away, but I'm afraid the dogs will bite me. Won't you come with me as far as the

---

is set. i.e., has made up her mind

fields? I don't like fields. I like houses, but open houses, and the neighbor women asleep in their beds with their little tiny tots, and the men outside sitting in their chairs. Pepe el Romano is a giant. All of you love him. But he's going to devour you because you're grains of wheat. No, not grains of wheat. Frogs with no tongues!

MARTIRIO [*angrily*]. Come, off to bed with you. [*She pushes her.*]

MARIA JOSEFA. Yes, but then you'll open the door for me, won't you?

MARTIRIO. Of course.

MARIA JOSEFA [*weeping*].

Little lamb, child of mine,
Let's go to the shore of the sea,
The tiny ant will be at his doorway,
I'll nurse you and give you your bread.

[MARTIRIO *locks the door through which* MARIA JOSEFA *came out and goes to the yard door. There she hesitates, but goes two steps farther.*]

MARTIRIO [*in a low voice*]. Adela! [*Pause. She advances to the door. Then, calling.*] Adela!

[ADELA *enters. Her hair is disarranged.*]

ADELA. And what are you looking for me for?

MARTIRIO. Keep away from him.

ADELA. Who are you to tell me that?

MARTIRIO. That's no place for a decent woman.

ADELA. How you wish *you'd* been there!

MARTIRIO [*shouting*]. This is the moment for me to speak. This can't go on.

ADELA. This is just the beginning. I've had strength enough to push myself forward—the spirit and looks you lack. I've seen death under this roof, and gone out to look for what was mine, what belonged to me.

MARTIRIO. That soulless man came for another woman. You pushed yourself in front of him.

ADELA. He came for the money, but his eyes were always on me.

MARTIRIO. I won't allow you to snatch him away. He'll marry Angustias.

ADELA. You know better than I he doesn't love her.

MARTIRIO. I know.

ADELA. You know because you've seen— he loves me, me!

MARTIRIO [*desperately*]. Yes.

ADELA [*close before her*]. He loves me, *me!* He loves me, *me!*

MARTIRIO. Stick me with a knife if you like, but don't tell me that again.

ADELA. That's why you're trying to fix it so I won't go away with him. It makes no difference to you if he puts his arms around a woman he doesn't love. Nor does it to me. He could be a hundred years with Angustias, but for him to have his arms around me seems terrible to you—because you too love him! You love him!

MARTIRIO [*dramatically*]. Yes! Let me say it without hiding my head. Yes! My breast's bitter, bursting like a pomegranate. I love him!

ADELA [*impulsively, hugging her*]. Martirio, Martirio, I'm not to blame!

MARTIRIO. Don't put your arms around me! Don't try to smooth it over. My blood's no longer yours, and even though I try to think of you as a sister, I see you as just another woman. [*She pushes her away.*]

ADELA. There's no way out here. Whoever has to drown—let her drown. Pepe is mine. He'll carry me to the rushes along the river bank. . . .

MARTIRIO. He won't!

ADELA. I can't stand this horrible house after the taste of his mouth. I'll be what he wants me to be. Everybody in the village against me, burning me with their fiery fingers; pursued by those who claim they're decent, and I'll wear, before them all, the crown of thorns that belongs to the mistress of a married man.

MARTIRIO. Hush!

ADELA. Yes, yes. [*In a low voice.*] Let's go to bed. Let's let him marry Angustias. I don't care any more, but I'll go off alone to a little house where he'll come to see me whenever he wants, whenever he feels like it.

MARTIRIO. That'll never happen! Not while I have a drop of blood left in my body.

ADELA. Not just weak you, but a wild horse

I could force to his knees with just the strength of my little finger.

MARTIRIO. Don't raise that voice of yours to me. It irritates me. I have a heart full of a force so evil that, without my wanting to be, I'm drowned by it.

ADELA. You show us the way to love our sisters. God must have meant to leave me alone in the midst of darkness, because I can see you as I've never seen you before.

[*A whistle is heard and* ADELA *runs toward the door, but* MARTIRIO *gets in front of her.*]

MARTIRIO. Where are you going?

ADELA. Get away from that door!

MARTIRIO. Get by me if you can!

ADELA. Get away!

[*They struggle.*]

MARTIRIO [*shouts*]. Mother! Mother!

ADELA. Let me go!

[BERNARDA *enters. She wears petticoats and a black shawl.*]

BERNARDA. Quiet! Quiet! How poor I am without even a man to help me!

MARTIRIO [*pointing to* ADELA]. She was with him. Look at those skirts covered with straw!

BERNARDA [*going furiously toward* ADELA]. That's the bed of a bad woman!

ADELA [*facing her*]. There'll be an end to prison voices here!

[ADELA *snatches away her mother's cane and breaks it in two.*]

This is what I do with the tyrant's cane. Not another step. No one but Pepe commands me!

[MAGDALENA *enters.*]

MAGDALENA. Adela!

[LA PONCIA *and* ANGUSTIAS *enter.*]

ADELA. I'm his. [*To* ANGUSTIAS.] Know that —and go out in the yard and tell him. He'll be master in this house.

ANGUSTIAS. My God!

BERNARDA. The gun! Where's the gun?

[*She rushes out,* MARTIRIO *following.* AMELIA *enters and looks on frightened, leaning her head against the wall.*]

ADELA. No one can hold me back! [*She tries to go out.*]

ANGUSTIAS [*holding her*]. You're not getting out of here with your body's triumph! Thief!

Disgrace of this house!

MAGDALENA. Let her go where we'll never see her again!

[*A shot is heard.*]

BERNARDA [*entering*]. Just try looking for him now!

MARTIRIO [*entering*]. That does away with Pepe el Romano.

ADELA. Pepe! My God! Pepe!

[*She runs out.*]

PONCIA. Did you kill him?

MARTIRIO. No. He raced away on his mare!

BERNARDA. It was my fault. A woman can't aim.

MAGDALENA. Then, why did you say . . . ?

MARTIRIO. For her! I'd like to pour a river of blood over her head!

PONCIA. Curse you!

MAGDALENA. Devil!

BERNARDA. Although it's better this way!

[*A thud is heard.*]

Adela! Adela!

PONCIA [*at her door*]. Open this door!

BERNARDA. Open! Don't think the walls will hide your shame!

SERVANT [*entering*]. All the neighbors are up!

BERNARDA [*in a low voice, but like a roar*]. Open! Or I'll knock the door down! [*Pause. Everything is silent.*] Adela! [*She walks away from the door.*] A hammer!

[LA PONCIA *throws herself against the door. It opens and she goes in. As she enters, she screams and backs out.*]

What is it?

PONCIA. [*She puts her hand to her throat.*] May we never die like that!

[THE SISTERS *fall back.* THE SERVANT *crosses herself.* BERNARDA *screams and goes forward.*]

Don't go in!

BERNARDA. No, not I! Pepe, you're running now, alive, in the darkness, under the trees, but another day you'll fall. Cut her down! My daughter died a virgin. Take her to another room and dress her as though she were a virgin. No one will say anything about this! She died a virgin. Tell them, so that at dawn, the bells will ring twice.

MARTIRIO. A thousand times happy she, who had him.

BERNARDA. And I want no weeping. Death must be looked at face to face. Silence! [*To one daughter.*] Be still, I said! [*To another daughter.*] Tears when you're alone! We'll drown ourselves in a sea of mourning. She, the youngest daughter of Bernarda Alba, died a virgin. Did you hear me? Silence, silence, I said. Silence!

Curtain

Bertolt Brecht

1898–1956

The Good Woman of Setzuan

1943

Among the legends entering thematically into *The Good Woman of Setzuan* are those of humble folk who have entertained gods or angels (like Baucis and Philemon, the old Greek couple who offered hospitality to Zeus and Hermes in disguise), and those of cities or countries preserved by the presence in them of a remnant of righteous men ("And the Lord said, If I find in Sodom fifty righteous within the city, then I will spare all the place for their sakes." Genesis 18:26.). For Brecht is raising time-honored ethical questions. Where indeed are piety and virtue to be found? And how can they prove generally redemptive, or even survive, in the welter of human stupidity and selfishness?

Having set up these grand resonances, Brecht follows the personal and commercial fortunes of his heroine Shen Te, the Good Woman of the title, who receives as a reward for her hospitality to the gods a gift enabling her to set up a tobacco shop. Shen Te had earlier been selling herself for her livelihood: she is a version of the spiritually unsoiled prostitute, a minor stereotype of romantic literature. As she is by turns coldly efficient and freely charitable in managing her new business, her fortunes wax and wane with a stylized regularity—as in stories where good and bad fairies are alternately in the ascendant. Her sudden turnabouts, meanwhile, ring changes on the theme of the antithetical counterpart: of self and antiself, Dr. Jekyll and Mr. Hyde. Interwoven with her commercial vicissitudes, finally, are the changes of a simple and primal love story: Shen Te meets and falls in love with an aspiring airman—her fitting complement in his skyward yearnings although not in his conduct otherwise.

These conventional patterns—although giving the wry twist that is Brecht's trademark—affirm the simple and familiar quality of the action. And the dramaturgy consistently supports our impression that a fable or parable is unfolding rather than a chapter of "life." The setting is a fancifully

BERTOLT BRECHT

remote Chinese province. The players break the illusion by addressing the audience directly. And the characters are developed to the point where we experience quick starts of sympathy for them but no steady empathy; in Brecht's opinion, any "identification" with the persons of a drama produces a mindlessly emotional response. He had a didactic conception of his art— therein resembling G. B. Shaw, whose *Saint Joan* has both thematic and technical affinities with *The Good Woman.*

The message of this play is presented with clarity and animation. Brecht is aware, with realists of every age, that virtue can fail to procure instant and visible rewards. And he goes on to propose—as if in answer to the moralism that crime does not pay—that virtue does not pay either: it is exploited and in a manner punished. Leaving his heroine in anguish, her dilemma conspicuously unresolved, he twits his audience with a cynical proposition: "That virtue to which you so respectably subscribe is in itself ineffectual; to preserve what you hold dear, you must possess yourselves of the instruments of power and wield them unashamedly."

The stoic's answer to such apparent cynicism is that we are to follow virtue for its own sake, whatever the consequences. But this is too close to the view of Brecht's ridiculous and discredited gods. Not moral doctrine but human sympathy is the wellspring of his own Good Woman's goodness. "The charm of Miss Shen Te derives from the goodness of her heart." Kindly affections spring unbidden here and there throughout the play, deriving sometimes from physical attraction, sometimes from spontaneous impulses to succor and befriend. They spring, even, although without sustained energy, in the soiled and selfish soul of Shen Te's beloved Yang Sun. Brecht, who is unabashedly sardonic when he exhibits human baseness, is freely sentimental when he exhibits love

and good will. Surrendering neither his critical sense nor his good nature, he weaves a thematic whole that is at once bracing in its honesty and heartwarming in its benevolence.

Brecht, although a Marxist, evidently doubted that an ideal human condition could be programmed. He asserts his independence of any limiting orthodoxy, whether political or literary. He affirms (opposing the absurdists) that we can contemplate the unaccountable and arbitrary aspects of life without surrendering our own minds to irrationality. In contrast to the existentialists—those, at least, who are most preoccupied with human solitude—he presents a balanced view of men as social beings. And in contrast to all dramatists both bourgeois and proletarian who would see in the failure of humble protagonists the stuff of tragedy, Brecht delightfully and delightedly descants on the perennial comic theme: "What fools these mortals be!"

There has hardly been in the modern theater a saner or more engaging playwright than Bertolt Brecht.

The Good Woman of Setzuan

BRECHT

Translated by Eric Bentley

CHARACTERS

WONG, *a water seller*
THREE GODS
SHEN TE, *a prostitute, later a shopkeeper*
MRS. SHIN, *former owner of Shen Te's shop*
A FAMILY OF EIGHT (*husband, wife, brother, sister-in-law, grandfather, nephew, niece, boy*)
AN UNEMPLOYED MAN
A CARPENTER
MRS. MI TZU, *Shen Te's landlady*
YANG SUN, *an unemployed pilot, later a factory manager*
AN OLD WHORE
A POLICEMAN
AN OLD MAN
AN OLD WOMAN, *his wife*
MR. SHU FU, *a barber*
MRS. YANG, *mother of Yang Sun*
GENTLEMEN, VOICES, CHILDREN (3), etc.

PROLOGUE

[*At the gates of the half-westernized city of*

Bertolt Brecht, "The Good Woman of Setzuan" *from* Parables for the Theater: Two plays by Bertolt Brecht, *translated by Eric Bentley. University of Minnesota Press, Minneapolis. Copyright 1948 by Eric Bentley.*

Setzuan.° Evening. WONG *the Water Seller introduces himself to the audience.*]

WONG. I sell water here in the city of Setzuan. It isn't easy. When water is scarce, I 5 have long distances to go in search of it, and when it is plentiful, I have no income. But in our part of the world there is nothing unusual about poverty. Many people think only the gods can save the situation. And I hear from 10 a cattle merchant—who travels a lot—that some of the highest gods are on their way here at this very moment. Informed sources have it that heaven is quite disturbed at all the complaining. I've been coming out here to 15 the city gates for three days now to bid these gods welcome. I want to be the first to greet them. What about those fellows over there? No, no, they *work*. And that one there has ink on his fingers, he's no god, he must be a 20 clerk from the cement factory. *Those* two are another story. They look as though they'd like to beat you. But gods don't need to beat you, do they? [*Enter* THREE GODS.] What about those three? Old-fashioned clothes— 25 dust on their feet—they *must* be gods! [*He throws himself at their feet.*] Do with me what you will, illustrious ones!

FIRST GOD [*with an ear trumpet*]. Ah! [*He is pleased.*] So we were expected? 30

WONG [*giving them water*]. Oh, yes. And I *knew* you'd come.

FIRST GOD. We need somewhere to stay the night. You know of a place?

WONG. The whole town is at your service, 35 illustrious ones! What sort of a place would you like?

[*The* GODS *eye each other.*]

FIRST GOD. Just try the first house you come to, my son. 40

WONG. That would be Mr. Fo's place.

FIRST GOD. Mr. Fo.

city of Setzuan there is no such city, of course, although there is a Chinese province usually spelled Szechwan. The locale is "half-Westernized" to divorce it from national particularity.

WONG. One moment! [*He knocks at the first house.*]

VOICE FROM MR. FO'S. No!

[WONG *returns a little nervously.*]

5 WONG. It's too bad. Mr. Fo isn't in. And his servants don't dare do a thing without his consent. He'll have a fit when he finds out who they turned away, won't he?

FIRST GOD [*smiling*]. He will, won't he?

10 WONG. One moment! The next house is Mr. Cheng's. Won't he be thrilled?

FIRST GOD. Mr. Cheng.

[WONG *knocks.*]

VOICE FROM MR. CHENG'S. Keep your gods.

15 We have our own troubles!

WONG [*back with the* GODS]. Mr. Cheng is very sorry, but he has a houseful of relations. I think some of them are a bad lot, and naturally, he wouldn't like you to see them.

20 THIRD GOD. Are we so terrible?

WONG. Well, only with bad people, of course. Everyone knows the province of Kwan is always having floods.

SECOND GOD. Really? How's *that*?

25 WONG. Why, because they're so irreligious.

SECOND GOD. Rubbish. It's because they neglected the dam.

FIRST GOD [*to* SECOND]. Sh! [*To* WONG.] You're still in hopes, aren't you, my son?

30 WONG. Certainly. All Setzuan is competing for the honor! What happened up to now is pure coincidence. I'll be back. [*He walks away, but then stands undecided.*]

SECOND GOD. What did I tell you?

35 THIRD GOD. It *could* be pure coincidence.

SECOND GOD. The same coincidence in Shun, Kwan, and Setzuan? People just aren't religious any more, let's face the fact. Our mission has failed!

40 FIRST GOD. Oh come, we might run into a good person any minute.

THIRD GOD. How did the resolution read? [*Unrolling a scroll and reading from it.*] "The world can stay as it is if enough people are

45 found living lives worthy of human beings." Good people, that is. Well, what about this Water Seller himself? *He's* good, or I'm very much mistaken.

SECOND GOD. You're very much mistaken. When he gave us a drink, I had the impression 50 there was something odd about the cup. Well, look! [*He shows the cup to the* FIRST GOD.]

FIRST GOD. A false bottom!

SECOND GOD. The man is a swindler.

FIRST GOD. Very well, count *him* out. That's 55 one man among millions. And as a matter of fact, we only need one on *our* side. These atheists are saying, "The world must be changed because no one can *be* good and *stay* good." No one, eh? I say: let us find one—just 60 one—and we have those fellows where we want them!

THIRD GOD [*to* WONG]. Water Seller, is it so hard to find a place to stay?

WONG. Nothing could be easier. It's just me. 65 I don't go about it right.

THIRD GOD. Really? [*He returns to the others. A* GENTLEMAN *passes by.*]

WONG. Oh dear, they're catching on. [*He accosts the* GENTLEMAN.] Excuse the intrusion, 70 dear sir, but three gods have just turned up. Three of the very highest. They need a place for the night. Seize this rare opportunity—to have real gods as your guests!

GENTLEMAN [*laughing*]. A new way of find- 75 ing free rooms for a gang of crooks.

[*Exit* GENTLEMAN.]

WONG [*shouting at him*]. Godless rascal! Have you no religion, gentlemen of Setzuan? [*Pause.*] Patience, illustrious ones! [*Pause.*] 80 There's only one person left. Shen Te, the prostitute. She *can't* say no. [*Calls up to a window.*] Shen Te!

[SHEN TE *opens the shutters and looks out.*]

WONG. They're here, and nobody wants 85 them. Will you take them?

SHEN TE. Oh, no, Wong, I'm expecting a gentleman.

WONG. Can't you forget about him for to-night? 90

SHEN TE. The rent has to be paid by tomorrow or I'll be out on the street.

WONG. This is no time for calculation, Shen Te.

SHEN TE. Stomachs rumble even on the 95 Emperor's birthday, Wong.

Wong. Setzuan is one big dung hill!

Shen Te. Oh, very well! I'll hide till my gentleman has come and gone. Then I'll take them. [*She disappears.*]

5   Wong. They mustn't see her gentleman or they'll know what she is.

First God [*who hasn't heard any of this*]. I think it's hopeless.

[*They approach* Wong.]

10   Wong [*jumping, as he finds them behind him*]. A room has been found, illustrious ones! [*He wipes sweat off his brow.*]

Second God. Oh, good.

Third God. Let's see it.

15   Wong [*nervously*]. Just a minute. It has to be tidied up a bit.

Third God. Then we'll sit down here and wait.

Wong [*still more nervous*]. No, no! [*Hold-*
20 *ing himself back.*] Too much traffic, you know.

Third God [*with a smile*]. Of course, if you *want* us to move.

[*They retire a little. They sit on a doorstep.* Wong *sits on the ground.*]

25   Wong [*after a deep breath*]. You'll be staying with a single girl—the finest human being in Setzuan!

Third God. That's nice.

Wong [*to the audience*]. They gave me such
30 a look when I picked up my cup just now.

Third God. You're worn out, Wong.

Wong. A little, maybe.

First God. Do people here have a hard time of it?

35   Wong. The good ones do.

First God. What about yourself?

Wong. You mean I'm not good. That's true. And I don't have an easy time either!

[*During this dialogue, a* Gentleman *has*
40 *turned up in front of* Shen Te's *house, and has whistled several times. Each time* Wong *has given a start.*]

Third God [*to* Wong, *softly*]. Psst! I think he's gone now.

45   Wong [*confused and surprised*]. Ye-e-es.

[*The* Gentleman *has left now, and* Shen Te *has come down to the street.*]

Shen Te [*softly*]. Wong!

[*Getting no answer, she goes off down the street.* Wong *arrives just too late, forgetting*
50 *his carrying pole.*]

Wong [*softly*]. Shen Te! Shen Te! [*To himself.*] So she's gone off to earn the rent. Oh dear, I can't go to the gods *again* with no room to offer them. Having failed in the service of
55 the gods, I shall run to my den in the sewer pipe down by the river and hide from their sight!

[*He rushes off.* Shen Te *returns, looking for him, but finding the gods. She stops in con-*
60 *fusion.*]

Shen Te. You are the illustrious ones? My name is Shen Te. It would please me very much if my simple room could be of use to you.

Third God. Where is the Water Seller, Miss
65 . . . Shen Te?

Shen Te. I missed him, somehow.

First God. Oh, he probably thought you weren't coming, and was afraid of telling us.

Third God [*picking up the carrying pole*].
70 We'll leave this with you. He'll be needing it.

[*Led by* Shen Te, *they go into the house. It grows dark, then light. Dawn. Again escorted by* Shen Te, *who leads them through the half-*
75 *light with a little lamp, the* Gods *take their leave.*]

First God. Thank you, thank you, dear Shen Te, for your elegant hospitality! We shall not forget! And give our thanks to the Water Seller
80 —he showed us a good human being.

Shen Te. Oh, I'm not good. Let me tell you something: when Wong asked me to put you up, I hesitated.

First God. It's all right to hesitate if you
85 then go ahead! And in giving us that room you did much more than you knew. You proved that good people still exist, a point that has been disputed of late—even in heaven. Farewell!

Second God. Farewell!
90   Third God. Farewell!

Shen Te. Stop, illustrious ones! I'm not sure you're right. I'd like to be good, it's true, but there's the rent to pay. And that's not all: I sell myself for a living. Even so I can't make
95 ends meet, there's too much competition. I'd

like to honor my father and mother and speak nothing but the truth and not covet my neighbor's house. I should love to stay with one man. But how? How is it done? Even breaking only a *few* of your commandments, I can hardly manage.

FIRST GOD [*clearing his throat*]. These thoughts are but, um, the misgivings of an unusually good woman!

THIRD GOD. Goodbye, Shen Te! Give our regards to the Water Seller!

SECOND GOD. And above all: be good! Farewell!

FIRST GOD. Farewell!

THIRD GOD. Farewell!

[*They start to wave goodbye.*]

SHEN TE. But everything is so expensive, I don't feel sure I can do it!

SECOND GOD. That's not in our sphere. We never meddle with economics.

THIRD GOD. One moment.

[*They stop.*]

Isn't it true she might do better if she had more money?

SECOND GOD. Come, come! How could we ever account for it Up Above?

FIRST GOD. Oh, there are ways.

[*They put their heads together and confer in dumb show. To* SHEN TE, *with embarrassment.*] As you say you can't pay your rent, well, um, we're not paupers, so of course we *insist* on paying for our room. [*Awkwardly thrusting money into her hands.*] There! [*Quickly.*] But don't tell anyone! The incident is open to misinterpretation.

SECOND GOD. It certainly is!

FIRST GOD [*defensively*]. But there's no law against it! It was never decreed that a god mustn't pay hotel bills!

[*The* GODS *leave.*]

SCENE I

[*A small tobacco shop. The shop is not as yet completely furnished and hasn't started doing business.*]

SHEN TE [*to the audience*]. It's three days since the gods left. When they said they wanted to pay for the room, I looked down at my hand, and there was more than a thousand silver dollars! I bought a tobacco shop with the money, and moved in yesterday. I don't own the building, of course, but I can pay the rent, and I hope to do a lot of good here. Beginning with Mrs. Shin, who's just coming across the square with her pot. She had the shop before me, and yesterday she dropped in to ask for rice for her children.

[*Enter* MRS. SHIN. *Both women bow.*]

How do you do, Mrs. Shin.

MRS. SHIN. How do you do, Miss Shen Te. You like your new home?

SHEN TE. Indeed, yes. Did your children have a good night?

MRS. SHIN. In that hovel? The youngest is coughing already.

SHEN TE. Oh, dear!

MRS. SHIN. You're going to learn a thing or two in these slums.

SHEN TE. Slums? That's not what you said when you sold me the shop!

MRS. SHIN. Now don't start nagging! Robbing me and my innocent children of their home and then calling it a slum! That's the limit! [*She weeps.*]

SHEN TE [*tactfully*]. I'll get your rice.

MRS. SHIN. And a little cash while you're at it.

SHEN TE. I'm afraid I haven't sold anything yet.

MRS. SHIN [*screeching*]. I've got to have it. Strip the clothes from my back and then cut my throat, will you? I know what I'll do: I'll leave my children on your doorstep! [*She snatches the pot out of* SHEN TE's *hands.*]

SHEN TE. Please don't be angry. You'll spill the rice.

[*Enter an elderly* HUSBAND *and* WIFE *with their shabbily-dressed* NEPHEW.]

WIFE. Shen Te, dear! You've come into money, they tell me. And we haven't a roof over our heads! A tobacco shop. We had one too. But it's gone. Could we spend the night here, do you think?

NEPHEW [*appraising the shop*]. Not bad!

WIFE. He's our nephew. We're inseparable!

MRS. SHIN. And who are these . . . ladies and gentlemen?

SHEN TE. They put me up when I first came in from the country. [*To the audience.*] Of course, when my small purse was empty, they put me out on the street, and they may be afraid I'll do the same to them. [*To the new-comers, kindly.*] Come in, and welcome, though I've only one little room for you—it's behind the shop.

HUSBAND. That'll do. Don't worry.

WIFE [*bringing* SHEN TE *some tea*]. We'll stay over here, so we won't be in your way. Did you make it a tobacco shop in memory of your first real home? We can certainly give you a hint or two! That's one reason we came.

MRS. SHIN [*to* SHEN TE]. Very nice! As long as you have a few customers too!

HUSBAND. Sh! A customer!

[*Enter an* UNEMPLOYED MAN, *in rags*.]

UNEMPLOYED MAN. Excuse me. I'm unemployed.

[MRS. SHIN *laughs.*]

SHEN TE. Can I help you?

UNEMPLOYED MAN. Have you any damaged cigarettes? I thought there might be some damage when you're unpacking.

WIFE. What nerve, begging for tobacco! [*Rhetorically.*] Why don't they ask for bread?

UNEMPLOYED MAN. Bread is expensive. One cigarette butt and I'll be a new man.

SHEN TE [*giving him cigarettes*]. That's very important—to be a new man. You'll be my first customer and bring me luck.

[*The* UNEMPLOYED MAN *quickly lights a cigarette, inhales, and goes off, coughing.*]

WIFE. Was that right, Shen Te, dear?

MRS. SHIN. If this is the opening of a shop, you can hold the closing at the end of the week.

HUSBAND. I bet he had money on him.

SHEN TE. Oh, no, he said he hadn't!

NEPHEW. How d'you know he wasn't lying?

SHEN TE [*angrily*]. How do you know he was?

WIFE [*wagging her head*]. You're too good, Shen Te, dear. If you're going to keep this shop, you'll have to learn to say No.

HUSBAND. Tell them the place isn't yours to dispose of. Belongs to . . . some relative who insists on all accounts being strictly in order . . .

MRS. SHIN. That's right! What do you think you are—a philanthropist?

SHEN TE [*laughing*]. Very well, suppose I ask you for my rice back, Mrs. Shin?

WIFE [*combatively, at* MRS. SHIN]. So that's her rice?

[*Enter the* CARPENTER, *a small man.*]

MRS. SHIN [*who, at the sight of him, starts to hurry away*]. See you tomorrow, Miss Shen Te! [*Exit* MRS. SHIN.]

CARPENTER. Mrs. Shin, it's you I want!

WIFE [*to* SHEN TE]. Has she some claim on you?

SHEN TE. She's hungry. That's a claim.

CARPENTER. Are you the new tenant? And filling up the shelves already? Well, they're not yours, till they're paid for, ma'am. I'm the carpenter, so I should know.

SHEN TE. I took the shop "furnishings included."

CARPENTER. You're in league with that Mrs. Shin, of course. All right: I demand my hundred silver dollars.

SHEN TE. I'm afraid I haven't got a hundred silver dollars.

CARPENTER. Then you'll find it. Or I'll have you arrested.

WIFE [*whispering to* SHEN TE]. That relative: make it a cousin.

SHEN TE. Can't it wait till next month?

CARPENTER. No!

SHEN TE. Be a little patient, Mr. Carpenter, I can't settle all claims at once.

CARPENTER. Who's patient with me? [*He grabs a shelf from the wall.*] Pay up—or I take the shelves back!

WIFE. Shen Te! Dear! Why don't you let your . . . cousin settle this affair? [*To* CARPENTER.] Put your claim in writing. Shen Te's cousin will see you get paid.

CARPENTER [*derisively*]. Cousin, eh?

HUSBAND. Cousin, yes.

CARPENTER. I know these cousins!

NEPHEW. Don't be silly. He's a personal
5 friend of mine.

HUSBAND. What a man! Sharp as a razor!

CARPENTER. All right. I'll put my claim in
writing. [*Puts shelf on floor, sits on it, writes
out bill.*]

10 WIFE [*to SHEN TE*]. He'd tear the dress off
your back to get his shelves. Never recognize a
claim! That's my motto.

SHEN TE. He's done a job, and wants something in return. It's shameful that I can't give
15 it to him. What will the gods say?

HUSBAND. You did your bit when you took
us in.

[*Enter the BROTHER, limping, and the SISTER-
IN-LAW, pregnant.*]

20 BROTHER [*to HUSBAND and WIFE*]. So this is
where you're hiding out! There's family feeling
for you! Leaving us on the corner!

WIFE [*embarrassed, to SHEN TE*]. It's my
brother and his wife. [*To them.*] Now stop
25 grumbling, and sit quietly in that corner. [*To
SHEN TE.*] It can't be helped. She's in her fifth
month.

SHEN TE. Oh yes. Welcome!

WIFE [*to the couple*]. Say thank you.

30 [*They mutter something.*]

The cups are here. [*To SHEN TE.*] Lucky you
bought this shop when you did!

SHEN TE [*laughing and bringing tea*]. Lucky
indeed!

35 [*Enter MRS. MI TZU, the landlady.*]

MRS. MI TZU. Miss Shen Te? I am Mrs. Mi
Tzu, your landlady. I hope our relationship
will be a happy one? I like to think I give my
tenants modern, personalized service. Here is
40 your lease. [*To the others, as SHEN TE reads
the lease.*] There's nothing like the opening of
a little shop, is there? A moment of true
beauty! [*She is looking around.*] Not very
much on the shelves, of course. But everything
45 in the gods' good time! Where are your
references, Miss Shen Te?

SHEN TE. Do I *have* to have references?

MRS. MI TZU. After all, I haven't a notion
who you are!

HUSBAND. Oh, *we'd* be glad to vouch for 50
Miss Shen Te! We'd go through fire for her!

MRS. MI TZU. And who may *you* be?

HUSBAND [*stammering*]. Ma Fu, tobacco
dealer.

MRS. MI TZU. Where is your shop, Mr. . . . 55
Ma Fu?

HUSBAND. Well, um, I haven't a shop—I've
just sold it.

MRS. MI TZU. I see. [*To SHEN TE.*] Is there
no one else that knows you? 60

WIFE [*whispering to SHEN TE*]. Your cousin!
Your cousin!

MRS. MI TZU. This is a respectable house,
Miss Shen Te. I never sign a lease without
certain assurances. 65

SHEN TE [*slowly, her eyes downcast*]. I have
. . . a cousin.

MRS. MI TZU. On the square? Let's go over
and see him. What does he do?

SHEN TE [*as before*]. He lives . . . in another 70
city.

WIFE [*prompting*]. Didn't you say he was in
Shung?

SHEN TE. That's right. Shung.

HUSBAND [*prompting*]. I had his name on the 75
tip of my tongue. Mr. . . .

SHEN TE [*with an effort*]. Mr. . . . Shui . . .
Ta.

HUSBAND. That's it! Tall, skinny fellow!

SHEN TE. Shui Ta! 80

NEPHEW [*to CARPENTER*]. *You* were in touch
with him, weren't you? About the shelves?

CARPENTER [*surlily*]. Give him this bill. [*He
hands it over.*] I'll be back in the morning.

[*Exit CARPENTER.*] 85

NEPHEW [*calling after him, but with his eyes
on MRS. MI TZU*]. Don't worry! Mr. Shui Ta
pays on the nail!

MRS. MI TZU [*looking closely at SHEN TE*].
I'll be happy to make his acquaintance, Miss 90
Shen Te. [*Exit MRS. MI TZU.*]

[*Pause.*]

WIFE. By tomorrow morning she'll know
more about you than you do yourself.

SISTER-IN-LAW [*to* NEPHEW]. This thing isn't built to last.

[*Enter* GRANDFATHER.]

WIFE. It's Grandfather! [*To* SHEN TE.] Such a good old soul!

[*The* BOY *enters.*]

BOY [*over his shoulder*]. Here they are!

WIFE. And the boy, how he's grown! But he always could eat enough for ten.

[*Enter the* NIECE.]

WIFE [*to* SHEN TE]. Our little niece from the country. There are more of us now than in your time. The less we had, the more there were of us; the more there were of us, the less we had. Give me the key. We must protect ourselves from unwanted guests. [*She takes the key and locks the door.*] Just make yourself at home. I'll light the little lamp.

NEPHEW [*a big joke*]. I hope her cousin doesn't drop in tonight! The strict Mr. Shui Ta!

[SISTER-IN-LAW *laughs.*]

BROTHER [*reaching for a cigarette*]. One cigarette more or less . . .

HUSBAND. One cigarette more or less.

[*They pile into the cigarettes. The* BROTHER *hands a jug of wine round.*]

NEPHEW. Mr. Shui Ta'll pay for it!

GRANDFATHER [*gravely, to* SHEN TE]. How do you do?

[SHEN TE, *a little taken aback by the belatedness of the greeting, bows. She has the* CARPENTER's *bill in one hand, the landlady's lease in the other.*]

WIFE. How about a bit of a song? To keep Shen Te's spirits up?

NEPHEW. Good idea. Grandfather: you start!

Song of the Smoke

GRANDFATHER.

I used to think (before old age beset me)
    That brains could fill the pantry of the
                    [poor.
But where did all my cerebration get me?
    I'm just as hungry as I was before.
        So what's the use?

    See the smoke float free
    Into ever colder coldness!
      It's the same with me.

HUSBAND.

The straight and narrow path leads to
                    [disaster
And so the crooked path I tried to tread.
That got me to disaster even faster.
    (They say we shall be happy when we're
                    [dead.)
      So what's the use, etc.

NIECE.

You older people, full of expectation,
    At any moment now you'll walk the
                    [plank!
The future's for the younger generation!
    Yes, even if that future is a blank.
      So what's the use, etc.

NEPHEW [*to the* BROTHER]. Where'd you get that wine?

SISTER-IN-LAW [*answering for the* BROTHER]. He pawned the sack of tobacco.

HUSBAND [*stepping in*]. What? That tobacco was all we had to fall back on! You pig!

BROTHER. *You'd* call a man a pig because your wife was frigid! Did you refuse to drink it?

[*They fight. The shelves fall over.*]

SHEN TE [*imploringly*]. Oh, don't! Don't break everything! Take it, take it all, but don't destroy a gift from the gods!

WIFE [*disparagingly*]. This shop isn't big enough. I should never have mentioned it to Uncle and the others. When *they* arrive, it's going to be disgustingly overcrowded.

SISTER-IN-LAW. And did you hear our gracious hostess? She cools off quick!

[*Voices outside. Knocking at the door.*]

UNCLE'S VOICE. Open the door!

WIFE. Uncle? Is that you, Uncle?

UNCLE'S VOICE. Certainly, it's me. Auntie says to tell you she'll have the children here in ten minutes.

WIFE [*to* SHEN TE]. I'll have to let him in.

SHEN TE [*who scarcely hears her*].
The little lifeboat is swiftly sent down

Too many men too greedily
Hold on to it as they drown.

SCENE IA

[WONG's *den in a sewer pipe*.]

WONG [*crouching there*]. All quiet! It's four
5 days now since I left the city. The gods passed
this way on the second day. I heard their steps
on the bridge over there. They must be a long
way off by this time, so I'm safe.

[*Breathing a sigh of relief, he curls up and*
10 *goes to sleep. In his dream the pipe becomes*
transparent, and the GODS *appear*.]

[*Raising an arm, as if in self-defense*.] I
know, I know, illustrious ones! I found no one
to give you a room—not in all Setzuan! There,
15 it's out. Please continue on your way!

FIRST GOD [*mildly*]. But you did find someone. Someone who took us in for the night,
watched over us in our sleep, and in the early
morning lighted us down to the street with a
20 lamp.

WONG. It was . . . Shen Te, that took you in?

THIRD GOD. Who else?

WONG. And I ran away! "She isn't coming,"
I thought, "she just can't afford it."

25 GODS [*singing*].
O you feeble, well-intentioned, and yet
[feeble chap!
Where there's need the fellow thinks there
[is no goodness!
When there's danger he thinks courage
30 [starts to ebb away!
Some people only see the seamy side!
What hasty judgment! What premature
[desperation!

35 WONG. I'm *very* ashamed, illustrious ones.

FIRST GOD. Do us a favor, Water Seller. Go
back to Setzuan. Find Shen Te, and give us a
report on her. We hear that she's come into a
little money. Show interest in her goodness—
40 for no one can be good for long if goodness is
not in demand. Meanwhile we shall continue
the search, and find other good people. After
which, the idle chatter about the impossibility
of goodness will stop!

45 [*The* GODS *vanish*.]

SCENE II

[*A knocking*.]

WIFE. Shen Te! Someone at the door. Where
is she anyway?

NEPHEW. She must be getting the breakfast.
Mr. Shui Ta will pay for it. 50

[*The* WIFE *laughs and shuffles to the door.*
Enter MR. SHUI TA *and the* CARPENTER.]

WIFE. Who is it?

SHUI TA. I am Miss Shen Te's cousin.

WIFE. What? 55

SHUI TA. My name is Shui Ta.

WIFE. Her cousin?

NEPHEW. Her cousin?

NIECE. But that was a joke. She hasn't got a
cousin. 60

HUSBAND. So early in the morning?

BROTHER. What's all the noise?

SISTER-IN-LAW. This fellow says he's her
cousin.

BROTHER. Tell him to prove it. 65

NEPHEW. Right. If you're Shen Te's cousin,
prove it by getting the breakfast.

SHUI TA [*whose regime begins as he puts*
out the lamp to save oil. Loudly, to all present,
asleep or awake]. Would you all please get 70
dressed! Customers will be coming! I wish to
open my shop!

HUSBAND. *Your* shop? Doesn't it belong to
our good friend Shen Te?

[SHUI TA *shakes his head*.] 75

SISTER-IN-LAW. So we've been cheated.
Where *is* the little liar?

SHUI TA. Miss Shen Te has been delayed.
She wishes me to tell you there will be nothing
she can do—now I am here. 80

WIFE [*bowled over*]. I thought she was *good*!

NEPHEW. Do you have to believe *him*?

HUSBAND. *I* don't.

NEPHEW. Then do something.

HUSBAND. Certainly! I'll send out a search 85
party at once. You, you, you, and you, go out
and look for Shen Te.

[*As the* GRANDFATHER *rises and makes for*
the door.]

Not you, Grandfather, you and I will hold 90
the fort.

SHUI TA. You won't find Miss Shen Te. She has suspended her hospitable activity for an unlimited period. There are too many of you. She asked me to say: this is a tobacco shop, not a gold mine.

HUSBAND. Shen Te never said a thing like that. Boy, food! There's a bakery on the corner. Stuff your shirt full when they're not looking!

SISTER-IN-LAW. Don't overlook the raspberry tarts.

HUSBAND. And don't let the policeman see you.

[*The* BOY *leaves.*]

SHUI TA. Don't you depend on this shop now? Then why give it a bad name, by stealing from the bakery?

NEPHEW. Don't listen to him. Let's find Shen Te. She'll give him a piece of her mind.

SISTER-IN-LAW. Don't forget to leave us some breakfast.

[BROTHER, SISTER-IN-LAW, *and* NEPHEW *leave.*]

SHUI TA [*to the* CARPENTER]. You see, Mr. Carpenter, nothing has changed since the poet, eleven hundred years ago, penned these lines:

A governor was asked what was needed
To save the freezing people in the city.
He replied:
"A blanket ten thousand feet long
To cover the city and all its suburbs."

[*He starts to tidy up the shop.*]

CARPENTER. Your cousin owes me money. I've got witnesses. For the shelves.

SHUI TA. Yes, I have your bill. [*He takes it out of his pocket.*] Isn't a hundred silver dollars rather a lot?

CARPENTER. No deductions! I have a wife and children.

SHUI TA. How many children?

CARPENTER. Three.

SHUI TA. I'll make you an offer. Twenty silver dollars.

[*The* HUSBAND *laughs.*]

CARPENTER. You're crazy. Those shelves are real walnut.

SHUI TA. Very well. Take them away.

CARPENTER. What?

SHUI TA. They cost too much. Please take them away.

WIFE. Not bad! [*And she, too, is laughing.*]

CARPENTER [*a little bewildered*]. Call Shen Te, someone! [*To* SHUI TA.] She's *good!*

SHUI TA. Certainly. She's ruined.

CARPENTER [*provoked into taking some of the shelves*]. All right, you can keep your tobacco on the floor.

SHUI TA [*to the* HUSBAND]. Help him with the shelves.

HUSBAND [*grins and carries one shelf over to the door where the* CARPENTER *now is*]. Goodbye, shelves!

CARPENTER [*to the* HUSBAND]. You dog! You want my family to starve?

SHUI TA. I repeat my offer. I have no desire to keep my tobacco on the floor. Twenty silver dollars.

CARPENTER [*with desperate aggressiveness*]. One hundred!

[SHUI TA *shows indifference, looks through the window. The* HUSBAND *picks up several shelves.*]

[*To* HUSBAND.] You needn't smash them against the doorpost, you idiot! [*To* SHUI TA.] These shelves were made to measure. They're no use anywhere else!

SHUI TA. Precisely.

[*The* WIFE *squeals with pleasure.*]

CARPENTER [*giving up, sullenly*]. Take the shelves. Pay what you want to pay.

SHUI TA [*smoothly*]. Twenty silver dollars.

[*He places two large coins on the table. The* CARPENTER *picks them up.*]

HUSBAND [*brings the shelves back in*]. And quite enough too!

CARPENTER [*slinking off*]. Quite enough to get drunk on.

HUSBAND [*happily*]. Well, we got rid of *him!*

WIFE [*weeping with fun, gives a rendition of the dialogue just spoken*]. "Real walnut," says he. "Very well, take them away," says his lordship. "I have children," says he. "Twenty silver dollars," says his lordship. "They're no use anywhere else," says he. "Precisely," said his lordship! [*She dissolves into shrieks of merriment.*]

SHUI TA. And now: go!

HUSBAND. What's that?

SHUI TA. You're thieves, parasites. I'm giving you this chance. Go!

HUSBAND [*summoning all his ancestral dignity*]. That sort deserves no answer. Besides, one should never shout on an empty stomach.

WIFE. Where's that boy?

SHUI TA. Exactly. The boy. I want no stolen goods in this shop. [*Very loudly.*] I strongly advise you to leave! [*But they remain seated, noses in the air. Quietly.*] As you wish.

[SHUI TA *goes to the door. A* POLICEMAN *appears.* SHUI TA *bows.*]

I am addressing the officer in charge of this precinct?

POLICEMAN. That's right, Mr., um . . . what was the name, sir?

SHUI TA. Mr. Shui Ta.

POLICEMAN. Yes, of course, sir.

[*They exchange a smile.*]

SHUI TA. Nice weather we're having.

POLICEMAN. A little on the warm side, sir.

SHUI TA. Oh, a little on the warm side.

HUSBAND [*whispering to the* WIFE]. If he keeps it up till the boy's back, we're done for. [*Tries to signal* SHUI TA.]

SHUI TA [*ignoring the signal*]. Weather, of course, is one thing indoors, another out on the dusty street!

POLICEMAN. Oh, quite another, sir!

WIFE [*to the* HUSBAND]. It's all right as long as he's standing in the doorway—the boy will see him.

SHUI TA. Step inside for a moment! It's quite cool indoors. My cousin and I have just opened the place. And we attach the greatest importance to being on good terms with the, um, authorities.

POLICEMAN [*entering*]. Thank you, Mr. SHUI TA. It *is* cool!

HUSBAND [*whispering to the* WIFE]. And now the boy *won't* see him.

SHUI TA [*showing* HUSBAND *and* WIFE *to the* POLICEMAN]. Visitors, I think my cousin knows them. They were just leaving.

HUSBAND [*defeated*]. Ye-e-es, we were . . . just leaving.

SHUI TA. I'll tell my cousin you couldn't wait.

[*Noise from the street. Shouts of "Stop, thief!"*]

POLICEMAN. What's that?

[*The* BOY *is in the doorway with cakes and buns and rolls spilling out of his shirt. The* WIFE *signals desperately to him to leave. He gets the idea.*]

No, you don't! [*He grabs the* BOY *by the collar.*] Where's all this from?

BOY [*vaguely pointing*]. Down the street.

POLICEMAN [*grimly*]. So that's it. [*Prepares to arrest the* BOY.]

WIFE [*stepping in*]. And *we* knew nothing about it. [*To the* BOY.] Nasty little thief!

POLICEMAN [*dryly*]. Can you clarify the situation, Mr. Shui Ta?

[SHUI TA *is silent.*]

POLICEMAN [*who understands silence*]. Aha. You're all coming with me—to the station.

SHUI TA. I can hardly say how sorry I am that *my* establishment . . .

WIFE. Oh, he saw the boy leave not ten minutes ago!

SHUI TA. And to conceal the theft asked a policeman in?

POLICEMAN. Don't listen to her, Mr. Shui Ta, I'll be happy to relieve you of their presence one and all! [*To all three.*] Out! [*He drives them before him.*]

GRANDFATHER [*leaving last. Gravely*]. Good morning!

POLICEMAN. Good morning!

[SHUI TA, *left alone, continues to tidy up.* MRS. MI TZU *breezes in.*]

MRS. MI TZU. *You're* her cousin, are you? Then have the goodness to explain what all this means—police dragging people from a respectable house! By what right does your Miss Shen Te turn my property into a house of assignation?—Well, as you see, I know all!

SHUI TA. Yes. My cousin has the worst possible reputation: that of being poor.

MRS. MI TZU. No sentimental rubbish, Mr. Shui Ta. Your cousin was a common . . .

SHUI TA. Pauper. Let's use the uglier word.

MRS. MI TZU. I'm speaking of her conduct, not her earnings. But there must have *been* earnings, or how did she buy all this? Several elderly gentlemen took care of it, I suppose. I repeat: this is a respectable house! I have tenants who prefer not to live under the same roof with such a person.

SHUI TA [*quietly*]. How much do you want?

MRS. MI TZU [*he is ahead of her now*]. I beg your pardon.

SHUI TA. To reassure yourself. To reassure your tenants. How much will it cost?

MRS. MI TZU. You're a cool customer.

SHUI TA [*picking up the lease*]. The rent is high. [*He reads on.*] I assume it's payable by the month?

MRS. MI TZU. Not in her case.

SHUI TA [*looking up*]. What?

MRS. MI TZU. Six months' rent payable in advance. Two hundred silver dollars.

SHUI TA. Six . . . ! Sheer usury! And where am I to find it?

MRS. MI TZU. You should have thought of that before.

SHUI TA. Have you no heart, Mrs. Mi Tzu? It's true Shen Te acted foolishly, being kind to all those people, but she'll improve with time. I'll see to it she does. She'll work her fingers to the bone to pay her rent, and all the time be as quiet as a mouse, as humble as a fly.

MRS. MI TZU. Her social background . . .

SHUI TA. Out of the depths! She came out of the depths! And before she'll go back there, she'll work, sacrifice, shrink from nothing. . . . Such a tenant is worth her weight in gold, Mrs. Mi Tzu.

MRS. MI TZU. It's silver we were talking about, Mr. Shui Ta. Two hundred silver dollars or . . .

[*Enter the* POLICEMAN.]

POLICEMAN. Am I intruding, Mr. Shui Ta?

MRS. MI TZU. This tobacco shop is well-known to the police, I see.

POLICEMAN. Mr. Shui Ta has done us a service, Mrs. Mi Tzu. I am here to present our official felicitations!

MRS. MI TZU. That means less than nothing to me, sir. Mr. Shui Ta, all I can say is: I hope your cousin will find my terms acceptable. Good day, gentlemen. [*Exit.*]

SHUI TA. Good day, ma'am.

[*Pause.*]

POLICEMAN. Mrs. Mi Tzu a bit of a stumbling block, sir?

SHUI TA. She wants six months' rent in advance.

POLICEMAN. And you haven't got it, eh?

[SHUI TA *is silent.*]

But surely you can get it, sir? A man like you?

SHUI TA. What about a woman like Shen Te?

POLICEMAN. You're not staying, sir?

SHUI TA. No, and I won't be back. Do you smoke?

POLICEMAN [*taking two cigars, and placing them both in his pocket*]. Thank you, sir—I see your point. Miss Shen Te—let's mince no words—Miss Shen Te lived by selling herself. "What else could she have done?" you ask. "How else was she to pay the rent?" True. But the fact remains, Mr. Shui Ta, it is not respectable. Why not? A very deep question. But, in the first place, love—love isn't bought and sold like cigars, Mr. Shui Ta. In the second place, it isn't respectable to go waltzing off with someone that's paying his way, so to speak—it must be for love! Thirdly and lastly, as the proverb has it: not for a handful of rice but for love! [*Pause. He is thinking hard.*] "Well," you may say, "and what good is all this wisdom if the milk's already spilt?" Miss Shen Te is what she is. Is *where* she is. We have to face the fact that if she doesn't get hold of six months' rent pronto, she'll be back on the streets. The question then as I see it—everything in this world is a matter of opinion—the question as I see it is: *how* is she to get hold of this rent? How? Mr. Shui Ta: I don't know. [*Pause.*] I take that back, sir. It's just come to me. A husband. We must find her a husband!

[*Enter a little* OLD WOMAN.]

OLD WOMAN. A good cheap cigar for my

husband, we'll have been married forty years tomorrow and we're having a little celebration.

SHUI TA. Forty years? And you still want to celebrate?

5 OLD WOMAN. As much as we can afford to. We have the carpet shop across the square. We'll be good neighbors, I hope?

SHUI TA. I hope so too.

POLICEMAN [who keeps making discoveries].
10 Mr. Shui Ta, you know what we need? We need capital. And how do we acquire capital? We get married.

SHUI TA [to OLD WOMAN]. I'm afraid I've been pestering this gentleman with my per-
15 sonal worries.

POLICEMAN [lyrically]. We can't pay six months' rent, so what do we do? We marry money.

SHUI TA. That might not be easy.

20 POLICEMAN. Oh, I don't know. She's a good match. Has a nice, growing business. [To the OLD WOMAN.] What do you think?

OLD WOMAN [undecided]. Well—

POLICEMAN. Should she put an ad in the
25 paper?

OLD WOMAN [not eager to commit herself]. Well, if she agrees—

POLICEMAN. I'll write it for her. You lend us a hand, and we write an ad for you! [He
30 chuckles away to himself, takes out his note-book, wets the stump of a pencil between his lips, and writes away.]

SHUI TA [slowly]. Not a bad idea.

POLICEMAN. "What . . . respectable . . . man
35 . . . with small capital . . . widower . . . not excluded . . . desires . . . marriage . . . into flourishing . . . tobacco shop?" And now let's add: "am . . . pretty . . . " No! . . . "Prepossessing appearance."

40 SHUI TA. If you don't think that's an exaggeration?

OLD WOMAN. Oh, not a bit. I've seen her.

[The POLICEMAN tears the page out of his notebook, and hands it over to SHUI TA.]

45 SHUI TA [with horror in his voice]. How much luck we need to keep our heads above water! How many ideas! How many friends! [To the POLICEMAN.] Thank you, sir. I think I see my way clear.

SCENE III

[Evening in the municipal park. Noise of a 50 plane overhead. YANG SUN, a young man in rags, is following the plane with his eyes: one can tell that the machine is describing a curve above the park. YANG SUN then takes a rope out of his pocket, looking anxiously about him 55 as he does so. He moves toward a large willow. Enter TWO PROSTITUTES, one old, the other the NIECE whom we have already met.]

NIECE. Hello. Coming with me?

YANG SUN [taken aback]. If you'd like to buy 60 me a dinner.

OLD WHORE. Buy you a dinner! [To the NIECE.] Oh, we know him—it's the unem-ployed pilot. Waste no time on him!

NIECE. But he's the only man left in the park. 65 And it's going to rain.

OLD WHORE. Oh, how do you know?

[And they pass by. YANG SUN again looks about him, again takes his rope, and this time throws it round a branch of the willow tree. 70 Again he is interrupted. It is the TWO PROSTI-TUTES returning—and in such a hurry they don't notice him.]

NIECE. It's going to pour!

[Enter SHEN TE.] 75

OLD WHORE. There's that gorgon Shen Te! That drove your family out into the cold!

NIECE. It wasn't her. It was that cousin of hers. She offered to pay for the cakes. I've nothing against her. 80

OLD WHORE. I have, though. [So that SHEN TE can hear.] Now where could the little lady be off to? She may be rich now but that won't stop her snatching our young men, will it?

SHEN TE. I'm going to the tearoom by the pond. 85

NIECE. Is it true what they say? You're marrying a widower—with three children?

SHEN TE. Yes. I'm just going to see him.

YANG SUN [his patience at breaking point]. Move on there! This is a park, not a whore- 90 house!

OLD WHORE. Shut your mouth!

[But the TWO PROSTITUTES leave.]

YANG SUN. Even in the farthest corner of the park, even when it's raining, you can't get rid 95 of them! [He spits.]

SHEN TE [*overhearing this*]. And what right have you to scold them? [*But at this point she sees the rope.*] Oh!

YANG SUN. Well, what are you staring at?

5 SHEN TE. That rope. What is it for?

YANG SUN. Think! Think! I haven't a penny. Even if I had, I wouldn't spend it on you. I'd buy a drink of water.

[*The rain starts.*]

10 SHEN TE [*still looking at the rope*]. What is the rope for? You mustn't!

YANG SUN. What's it to you? Clear out!

SHEN TE [*irrelevantly*]. It's raining.

YANG SUN. Well, don't try to come under 15 this tree.

SHEN TE. Oh, no. [*She stays in the rain.*]

YANG SUN. Now go away. [*Pause.*] For one thing, I don't like your looks, you're bow-legged.

20 SHEN TE [*indignantly*]. That's not true!

YANG SUN. Well, don't show 'em to me. Look, it's raining. You better come under this tree.

[*Slowly, she takes shelter under the tree.*]

25 SHEN TE. Why did you want to do it?

YANG SUN. You really want to know? [*Pause.*] To get rid of you! [*Pause.*] You know what a flyer is?

SHEN TE. Oh yes, I've met a lot of pilots. At 30 the tearoom.

YANG SUN. You call *them* flyers? Think they know what a machine *is*? Just 'cause they have leather helmets? They gave the airfield director a bribe, that's the way *those* fellows got up in 35 the air! Try one of them out sometime. "Go up to two thousand feet," tell him, "then let it fall, then pick it up again with a flick of the wrist at the last moment." Know what he'll say to that? "It's not in my contract." Then again, 40 there's the landing problem. It's like landing on your own backside. It's no different, planes are human. Those fools don't understand. [*Pause.*] And I'm the biggest fool for reading the book on flying in the Peking school and 45 skipping the page where it says: "we've got enough flyers and we don't need you." I'm a mail pilot and no mail. You understand that?

SHEN TE [*shyly*]. Yes. I do.

YANG SUN. No, you don't. You'd never

understand that. 50

SHEN TE. When we were little we had a crane with a broken wing. He made friends with us and was very good-natured about our jokes. He would strut along behind us and call out to stop us going too fast for him. But every 55 spring and autumn when the cranes flew over the villages in great swarms, he got quite restless. [*Pause.*] I understood that. [*She bursts out crying.*]

YANG SUN. Don't! 60

SHEN TE [*quieting down*]. No.

YANG SUN. It's bad for the complexion.

SHEN TE [*sniffing*]. I've stopped.

[*She dries her tears on her big sleeve. Leaning against the tree, but not looking at her, he* 65 *reaches for her face.*]

YANG SUN. You can't even wipe your own face. [*He is wiping it for her with his handkerchief. Pause.*]

SHEN TE [*still sobbing*]. I don't know *any-* 70 *thing!*

YANG SUN. You interrupted me! What for?

SHEN TE. It's such a rainy day. You only wanted to do . . . *that* because it's such a rainy day. 75

[*To the audience.*]

In our country
The evenings should never be somber
High bridges over rivers
The gray hour between night and morning 80
And the long, long winter:
Such things are dangerous
For, with all the misery,
A very little is enough
And men throw away an unbearable life. 85

[*Pause.*]

YANG SUN. Talk about yourself for a change.

SHEN TE. What about me? I have a shop.

YANG SUN [*incredulous*]. You have a shop, do you? Never thought of walking the streets? 90

SHEN TE. I *did* walk the streets. Now I have a shop.

YANG SUN [*ironically*]. A gift of the gods, I suppose!

SHEN TE. How did you know? 95

YANG SUN [*even more ironical*]. One fine evening the gods turned up saying: here's some money!

SHEN TE [*quickly*]. One fine morning.

YANG SUN [*fed up*]. This isn't much of an entertainment.

[*Pause.*]

5 SHEN TE. I can play the zither a little. [*Pause.*] And I can mimic men. [*Pause.*] I got the shop, so the first thing I did was to give my zither away. I can be as stupid as a fish now, I said to myself, and it won't matter.

10 I'm rich now, I said
I walk alone, I sleep alone
For a whole year, I said
I'll have nothing to do with a man.

YANG SUN. And now you're marrying one!

15 The one at the tearoom by the pond?

[SHEN TE *is silent.*]

YANG SUN. What do you know about love?

SHEN TE. Everything.

YANG SUN. Nothing. [*Pause.*] Or d'you just

20 mean you enjoyed it?

SHEN TE. No.

YANG SUN [*again without turning to look at her, he strokes her cheek with his hand*]. You like that?

25 SHEN TE. Yes.

YANG SUN [*breaking off*]. You're easily satisfied, I must say. [*Pause.*] What a town!

SHEN TE. You have no friends?

YANG SUN [*defensively*]. Yes, I have!

30 [*Change of tone.*] But they don't want to hear I'm still unemployed. "What?" they ask. "Is there still water in the sea?" You have friends?

SHEN TE [*hesitating*]. Just a . . . cousin.

YANG SUN. Watch him carefully.

35 SHEN TE. He only came once. Then he went away. He won't be back.

[YANG SUN *is looking away.*]

But to be without hope, they say, is to be without goodness!

40 [*Pause.*]

YANG SUN. Go on talking. A voice is a voice.

SHEN TE. Once, when I was a little girl, I fell, with a load of brushwood. An old man picked me up. He gave me a penny too. Isn't

45 it funny how people who don't have very much like to give some of it away? They must like to show what they can do, and how could they show it better than by being kind? Being wicked is just like being clumsy. When we

sing a song, or build a machine, or plant some 50 rice, we're being kind. You're kind.

YANG SUN. You make it sound easy.

SHEN TE. Oh, no. [*Little pause.*] Oh! A drop of rain!

YANG SUN. Where'd you feel it? 55

SHEN TE. Between the eyes.

YANG SUN. Near the right eye? Or the left?

SHEN TE. Near the left eye.

YANG SUN. Oh, good. [*He is getting sleepy.*]

So you're through with men, eh? 60

SHEN TE [*with a smile*]. But I'm not bow-legged.

YANG SUN. Perhaps not.

SHEN TE. Definitely not.

[*Pause.*] 65

YANG SUN [*leaning wearily against the willow*]. I haven't had a drop to drink all day, I haven't eaten anything for *two* days. I couldn't love you if I tried.

[*Pause.*] 70

SHEN TE. I like it in the rain.

[Enter WONG *the Water Seller, singing.*]

The Song of the Water Seller in the Rain

"Buy my water," I am yelling
And my fury restraining
For no water I'm selling 75
'Cause it's raining, 'cause it's raining!
    I keep yelling: "Buy my water!"
    But no one's buying
    Athirst and dying
    And drinking and paying! 80
    Buy water!
    Buy water, you dogs!

Nice to dream of lovely weather!
Think of all the consternation
Were there no precipitation 85
Half a dozen years together!
Can't you hear them shrieking: "Water!"
Pretending they adore me!
They all would go down on their knees
    [before me! 90

Down on your knees!
Go down on your knees, you dogs!

What are lawns and hedges thinking?
What are fields and forests saying?

"At the cloud's breast we are drinking!
And we've no idea who's paying!"
         I keep yelling: "Buy my water!"
         But no one's buying
5   Athirst and dying
         And drinking and paying!
         Buy water!
         Buy water, you dogs!

[*The rain has stopped now.* SHEN TE *sees*
10 WONG *and runs toward him.*]
    SHEN TE. Wong! You're back! Your carrying
pole's at the shop.
    WONG. Oh, thank you, Shen Te. And how
is life treating *you*?
15 SHEN TE. I've just met a brave and clever
man. And I want to buy him a cup of your
water.
    WONG [*bitterly*]. Throw back your head and
open your mouth and you'll have all the water
20 you need—
    SHEN TE [*tenderly*].
         I want *your* water, Wong
         The water that has tired you so
         The water that you carried all this
25   [way
         The water that is hard to sell because
                              it's been raining
         I need it for the young man over there
                              [—he's a flyer!
30 A flyer is a bold man:
         Braving the storms
         In company with the clouds
         He crosses the heavens
         And brings to friends in far-away
35   [lands
         The friendly mail!
    [*She pays* WONG, *and runs over to* YANG
SUN *with the cup. But* YANG SUN *is fast asleep.*]
    [*Calling to* WONG, *with a laugh.*] He's fallen
40 asleep! Despair and rain and I have worn him
out!

SCENE IIIA

[WONG'S *den. The sewer pipe is transparent,
and the* GODS *again appear to* WONG *in a
dream.*]
45 WONG [*radiant*]. I've seen her, illustrious

ones! And she hasn't changed!
    FIRST GOD. That's good to hear.
    WONG. She loves someone.
    FIRST GOD. Let's hope the experience gives
her the strength to stay good!   50
    WONG. It does. She's doing good deeds all
the time.
    FIRST GOD. Ah? What sort? What sort of
good deeds, Wong?
    WONG. Well, she has a kind word for every- 55
body.
    FIRST GOD [*eagerly*]. And then?
    WONG. Hardly anyone leaves her shop with-
out tobacco in his pocket—even if he can't pay
for it.   60
    FIRST GOD. Not bad at all. Next?
    WONG. She's putting up a family of eight.
    FIRST GOD [*gleefully, to the* SECOND GOD].
Eight! [*To* WONG.] And that's not all, of
course!   65
    WONG. She bought a cup of water from me
even though it was raining.
    FIRST GOD. Yes, yes, yes, all these smaller
good deeds!
    WONG. Even they run into money. A little 70
tobacco shop doesn't make so much.
    FIRST GOD [*sententiously*]. A prudent gar-
dener works miracles on the smallest plot.
    WONG. She hands out rice every morning.
That eats up half her earnings.   75
    FIRST GOD [*a little disappointed*]. Well, as a
beginning . . .
    WONG. They call her the Angel of the Slums
—whatever the Carpenter may say!
    FIRST GOD. What's this? A carpenter speaks 80
ill of her?
    WONG. Oh, he only says her shelves weren't
paid for in full.
    SECOND GOD [*who has a bad cold and can't
pronounce his n's and m's*]. What's this? Not 85
paying a carpenter? Why was that?
    WONG. I suppose she didn't have the money.
    SECOND GOD [*severely*]. One pays what one
owes, that's in our book of rules! First the
letter of the law, then the spirit!   90
    WONG. But it wasn't Shen Te, illustrious
ones, it was her cousin. She called *him* in to help.
    SECOND GOD. Then her cousin must never
darken her threshold again!

WONG. Very well, illustrious ones! But in fairness to Shen Te, let me say that her cousin is a businessman.

FIRST GOD. Perhaps we should inquire what is customary? I find business quite unintelligible. But everybody's doing it. Business! Did the Seven Good Kings do business? Did Kung the Just sell fish?

SECOND GOD. In any case, such a thing must not occur again!

[The GODS start to leave.]

THIRD GOD. Forgive us for taking this tone with you. Wong, we haven't been getting enough sleep. The rich recommended us to the poor, and the poor tell us they haven't enough room.

SECOND GOD. Feeble, feeble, the best of them!

FIRST GOD. No great deeds! No heroic daring!

THIRD GOD. On such a *small* scale!

SECOND GOD. Sincere, yes, but what is actually *achieved*?

[One can no longer hear them.]

WONG [calling after them]. I've thought of something, illustrious ones: Perhaps you shouldn't ask—too—much—all—at—once!

SCENE IV

[The square in front of SHEN TE's tobacco shop. Beside SHEN TE's place, two other shops are seen: the carpet shop and a barber's. Morning. Outside SHEN TE's the GRANDFATHER, the SISTER-IN-LAW, the UNEMPLOYED MAN, and MRS. SHIN stand waiting.]

SISTER-IN-LAW. She's been out all night again.

MRS. SHIN. No sooner did we get rid of that crazy cousin of hers than Shen Te herself starts carrying on! Maybe she does give us an ounce of rice now and then, but can you depend on her? Can you depend on her?

[Loud voices from the Barber's.]

VOICE OF SHU FU. What are you doing in my shop? Get out—at once!

VOICE OF WONG. But sir. They all let me sell . . .

[WONG comes staggering out of the barber's shop pursued by MR. SHU FU, the barber, a fat man carrying a heavy curling iron.]

SHU FU. Get out, I said! Pestering my customers with your slimy old water! Get out! Take your cup!

[He holds out the cup. WONG reaches out for it. MR. SHU FU strikes his hand with the curling iron, which is hot. WONG howls.]

You had it coming, my man!

[Puffing, he returns to his shop. The UNEMPLOYED MAN picks up the cup and gives it to WONG.]

UNEMPLOYED MAN. You can report that to the police.

WONG. My hand! It's smashed up!

UNEMPLOYED MAN. Any bones broken?

WONG. I can't move my fingers.

UNEMPLOYED MAN. Sit down. I'll put some water on it.

[WONG sits.]

MRS. SHIN. The water won't cost you anything.

SISTER-IN-LAW. You might have got a bandage from Miss Shen Te till she took to staying out all night. It's a scandal.

MRS. SHIN [despondently]. If you ask me, she's forgotten we ever existed!

[Enter SHEN TE down the street, with a dish of rice.]

SHEN TE [to the audience]. How wonderful to see Setzuan in the early morning! I always used to stay in bed with my dirty blanket over my head afraid to wake up. This morning I saw the newspapers being delivered by little boys, the streets being washed by strong men, and fresh vegetables coming in from the country on ox carts. It's a long walk from where Yang Sun lives, but I feel lighter at every step. They say you walk on air when you're in love, but it's even better walking on the rough earth, on the hard cement. In the early morning, the old city looks like a great rubbish heap. Nice, though—with all its little lights. And the sky, so pink, so transparent, before the dust comes and muddies it! What a lot you miss if you never see your city rising from its slumbers like an honest old craftsman pumping his lungs full of air and reaching for his tools, as the poet says! [Cheerfully, to her

waiting guests.] Good morning, everyone, here's your rice! [*Distributing the rice, she comes upon* WONG.] Good morning, Wong, I'm quite lightheaded today. On my way over,
5 I looked at myself in all the shop windows. I'd love to be beautiful.

[*She slips into the carpet shop.* MR. SHU FU *has just emerged from his shop.*]

SHU FU [*to the audience*]. It surprises me
10 how beautiful Miss Shen Te is looking today! I never gave her a passing thought before. But now I've been gazing upon her comely form for exactly three minutes! I begin to suspect I am in love with her. She is overpoweringly
15 attractive! [*Crossly, to* WONG.] Be off with you, rascal!

[*He returns to his shop.* SHEN TE *comes back out of the carpet shop with the* OLD MAN *its proprietor and his wife—whom we have al-*
20 *ready met—the* OLD WOMAN. SHEN TE *is wearing a shawl. The* OLD MAN *is holding up a looking glass for her.*]

OLD WOMAN. Isn't it lovely? We'll give you a reduction because there's a little hole in it.
25 SHEN TE [*looking at another shawl on the* OLD WOMAN'S *arm*]. The other one's nice too.

OLD WOMAN [*smiling*]. Too bad there's no hole in that!

SHEN TE. That's right. My shop doesn't make
30 very much.

OLD WOMAN. And your good deeds eat it all up! Be more careful, my dear . . .

SHEN TE [*trying on the shawl with the hole*]. Just now, I'm light-headed! Does the color
35 suit me?

OLD WOMAN. You'd better ask a man.

SHEN TE [*to the* OLD MAN]. Does the color suit me?

OLD MAN. You'd better ask your young
40 friend.

SHEN TE. I'd like to have your opinion.

OLD MAN. It suits you, very well. But wear it this way: the dull side out.

[SHEN TE *pays up.*]
45 OLD WOMAN. If you decide you don't like it, you can exchange it. [*She pulls* SHEN TE *to one side.*] Has he got money?

SHEN TE [*with a laugh*]. Yang Sun? Oh, no.

OLD WOMAN. Then how're you going to pay

your rent? 50
SHEN TE. I'd forgotten about that.

OLD WOMAN. And next Monday is the first of the month! Miss Shen Te, I've got something to say to you. After we [*indicating her husband*] got to know you, we had our doubts 55 about that marriage ad. We thought it would be better if you'd let *us* help you. Out of our savings. We reckon we could lend you two hundred silver dollars. We don't need anything in writing—you could pledge us your tobacco 60 stock.

SHEN TE. You're prepared to lend money to a person like me?

OLD WOMAN. It's folks like you that need it. We'd think twice about lending anything to 65 your cousin.

OLD MAN [*coming up*]. All settled, my dear?

SHEN TE. I wish the gods could have heard what your wife was just saying, Mr. Ma. They're looking for good people who're happy 70 —and helping me makes you happy because you know it was love that got me into difficulties!

[*The old couple smile knowingly at each other.*] 75

OLD MAN. And here's the money, Miss Shen Te.

[*He hands her an envelope.* SHEN TE *takes it. She bows. They bow back. They return to their shop.*] 80

SHEN TE [*holding up her envelope*]. Look, Wong, here's six months' rent! Don't you believe in miracles now? And how do you like my new shawl?

WONG. For the young fellow I saw you with 85 in the park?

[SHEN TE *nods.*]

MRS. SHIN. Never mind all that. It's time you took a look at his hand!

SHEN TE. Have you hurt your hand? 90
MRS. SHIN. That barber smashed it with his hot curling iron. Right in front of our eyes.

SHEN TE [*shocked at herself*]. And I never noticed! We must get you to a doctor this minute or who knows what will happen? 95

UNEMPLOYED MAN. It's not a doctor he should see, it's a judge. He can ask for compensation. The barber's filthy rich.

WONG. You think I have a chance?

MRS. SHIN [*with relish*]. If it's really good and smashed. But is it?

WONG. I think so. It's very swollen. Could I get a pension?

MRS. SHIN. You'd need a witness.

WONG. Well, you all saw it. You could all testify.

[*He looks round. The* UNEMPLOYED MAN, *the* GRANDFATHER, *and the* SISTER-IN-LAW *are all sitting against the wall of the shop eating rice. Their concentration on eating is complete.*]

SHEN TE [*to* MRS. SHIN]. You saw it yourself.

MRS. SHIN. I want nothin' to do with the police. It's against my principles.

SHEN TE [*to* SISTER-IN-LAW]. What about you?

SISTER-IN-LAW. Me? I wasn't looking.

SHEN TE [*to the* GRANDFATHER, *coaxingly*]. Grandfather, *you'll* testify, won't you?

SISTER-IN-LAW. And a lot of good that will do. He's simple-minded.

SHEN TE [*to the* UNEMPLOYED MAN]. You seem to be the only witness left.

UNEMPLOYED MAN. My testimony would only hurt him. I've been picked up twice for begging.

SHEN TE. Your brother is assaulted, and you shut your eyes?

He is hit, cries out in pain, and you are
[silent?

The beast prowls, chooses and seizes his
[victim, and you say:

"Because we showed no displeasure, he has
[spared us."

If no one present will be a witness, I will.
I'll say *I* saw it.

MRS. SHIN [*solemnly*]. The name for that is perjury.

WONG. I don't know if I can accept that. Though maybe I'll have to. [*Looking at his hand.*] Is it swollen enough, do you think? The swelling's not going down?

UNEMPLOYED MAN. No, no, the swelling's holding up well.

WONG. Yes. It's *more* swollen if anything.

Maybe my wrist is broken after all. I'd better see a judge at once.

[*Holding his hand very carefully, and fixing his eyes on it, he runs off.* MRS. SHIN *goes quickly into the barber's shop.*]

UNEMPLOYED MAN [*seeing her*]. She is getting on the right side of Mr. Shu Fu.

SISTER-IN-LAW. You and I can't change the world, Shen Te.

SHEN TE. Go away! Go away all of you!

[*The* UNEMPLOYED MAN, *the* SISTER-IN-LAW, *and the* GRANDFATHER *stalk off, eating and sulking.*]

[*To the audience.*]
They've stopped answering
They stay put
They do as they're told
They don't care
Nothing can make them look up
But the smell of food.

[*Enter* MRS. YANG, YANG SUN'S *mother, out of breath.*]

MRS. YANG. Miss Shen Te. My son has told me everything. I am Mrs. Yang, Sun's mother. Just think. He's got an offer. Of a job as a pilot. A letter has just come. From the director of the airfield in Peking!

SHEN TE. So he can fly again? Isn't that wonderful!

MRS. YANG [*less breathlessly all the time*]. They won't give him the job for nothing. They want five hundred silver dollars.

SHEN TE. We can't let money stand in his way, Mrs. Yang!

MRS. YANG. If only you could help him out!

SHEN TE. I have the shop. I can try! [*She embraces* MRS. YANG.] I happen to have two hundred with me now. Take it. [*She gives her the old couple's money.*] It was a loan but they said I could repay it with my tobacco stock.

MRS. YANG. And they were calling Sun the Dead Pilot of Setzuan! A friend in need!

SHEN TE. We must find another three hundred.

MRS. YANG. How?

SHEN TE. Let me think. [*Slowly.*] I know someone who can help. I didn't want to call

on his services again, he's hard and cunning.
But a flyer must fly. And I'll make this the
last time.

[*Distant sound of a plane.*]

5   Mrs. Yang. If the man you mentioned can
do it. . . . Oh, look, there's the morning mail
plane, heading for Peking!

  Shen Te. The pilot can see us, let's wave!

[*They wave. The noise of the engine is*
10 *louder.*]

  Mrs. Yang. You know that pilot up there?

  Shen Te. Wave, Mrs. Yang! I know the pilot
who *will* be up there. He gave up hope. But
he'll do it now. One man to raise himself above
15 the misery, above us all.

[*To the audience.*]

Yang Sun, my lover:
Braving the storms
In company with the clouds
20 Crossing the heavens
And bringing to friends in far-away lands
The friendly mail!

SCENE IVA

[*In front of the inner curtain. Enter* Shen Te,
carrying Shui Ta's *mask. She sings.*]

The Song of Defenselessness

25   In our country
A useful man needs luck
Only if he finds strong backers can he prove
        [himself useful
The good can't defend themselves and
30 Even the gods are defenseless.

Oh, why don't the gods have their own
        [ammunition
And launch against badness their own
        [expedition
35 Enthroning the good and preventing sedition
And bringing the world to a peaceful
        [condition?

Oh, why don't the gods do the buying and
        [selling
40 Injustice forbidding, starvation dispelling

Give bread to each city and joy to each
        [dwelling?
Oh, why don't the gods do the buying and
        [selling?

[*She puts on* Shui Ta's *mask and sings in* 45
his voice.]

You can only help one of your luckless
        [brothers
By trampling down a dozen others

Why is it the gods do not feel indignation 50
And come down in fury to end exploitation
Defeat all defeat and forbid desperation
Refusing to tolerate such toleration?

Why is it?

SCENE V

[Shen Te's *tobacco shop. Behind the counter,* 55
Mr. Shui Ta, *reading the paper.* Mrs. Shin *is*
cleaning up. She talks and he takes no notice.]

  Mrs. Shin. And when certain rumors get
about, what *happens* to a little place like this?
It goes to pot. *I* know. So, if you want my ad- 60
vice, Mr. Shui Ta, find out just what exactly
has been going on between Miss Shen Te and
that Yang Sun from Yellow Street. And remember: a certain interest in Miss Shen Te
has been expressed by the barber next door, a 65
man with twelve houses and only one wife,
who, for that matter, is likely to drop off at
any time. A certain interest has been expressed. [*She relishes the phrase.*] He was even
inquiring about her means and, if *that* doesn't 70
prove a man is getting serious, what would?
[*Still getting no response, she leaves with her*
bucket.]

  Yang Sun's Voice. Is that Miss Shen Te's
tobacco shop? 75

  Mrs. Shin's Voice. Yes, it is, but it's Mr.
Shui Ta who's here today.

[Shui Ta *runs to the looking glass with the*
short, light steps of Shen Te, *and is just about*
to start primping, when he realizes his mistake, 80

and turns away, with a short laugh. Enter
YANG SUN. MRS. SHIN *enters behind him and*
slips into the back room to eavesdrop.]

YANG SUN. I am Yang Sun.

5 [SHUI TA *bows.*]

Is Miss Shen Te in?

SHUI TA. No.

YANG SUN. I guess you know our relationship? [*He is inspecting the stock.*] Quite a
10 place! And I thought she was just talking big.
I'll be flying again, all right. [*He takes a cigar,*
solicits and receives a light from SHUI TA.] You
think we can squeeze the other three hundred
out of the tobacco stock?

15 SHUI TA. May I ask if it is your intention to
sell at once?

YANG SUN. It was decent of her to come out
with the two hundred but they aren't much use
with the other three hundred still missing.

20 SHUI TA. Shen Te was overhasty promising
so much. She might have to sell the shop itself
to raise it. Haste, they say, is the wind that
blows the house down.

YANG SUN. Oh, she isn't a girl to keep a man
25 waiting. For one thing or the other, if you take
my meaning.

SHUI TA. I take your meaning.

YANG SUN [*leering*]. Uh, huh.

SHUI TA. Would you explain what the five
30 hundred silver dollars are for?

YANG SUN. Trying to sound me out? Very
well. The director of the Peking airfield is a
friend of mine from flying school. I give him
five hundred: he gets me the job.

35 SHUI TA. The price is high.

YANG SUN. Not as these things go. He'll
have to fire one of the present pilots—for
negligence. Only the man he has in mind isn't
negligent. Not easy, you understand. You
40 needn't mention that part of it to Shen Te.

SHUI TA [*looking intently at* YANG SUN].
Mr. Yang Sun, you are asking my cousin to
give up her possessions, leave her friends, and
place her entire fate in your hands. I presume
45 you intend to marry her?

YANG SUN. I'd be prepared to.

[*Slight pause.*]

SHUI TA. Those two hundred silver dollars
would pay the rent here for six months. If you
were Shen Te wouldn't you be tempted to con- 50
tinue in business?

YANG SUN. What? Can you imagine Yang
Sun the Flyer behind a counter? [*In an oily*
voice.] "A strong cigar or a mild one, worthy
sir?" Not in this century! 55

SHUI TA. My cousin wishes to follow the
promptings of her heart, and, from her own
point of view, she may even have what is
called the right to love. Accordingly, she has
commissioned me to help you to this post. 60
There is nothing here that I am not empowered
to turn immediately into cash. Mrs. Mi Tzu,
the landlady, will advise me about the sale.

[*Enter* MRS. MI TZU.]

MRS. MI TZU. Good morning, Mr. Shui Ta, 65
you wish to see me about the rent? As you
know it falls due the day after tomorrow.

SHUI TA. Circumstances have changed, Mrs.
Mi Tzu: my cousin is getting married. Her
future husband here, Mr. Yang Sun, will be 70
taking her to Peking. I am interested in selling
the tobacco stock.

MRS MI TZU. How much are you asking, Mr.
Shui Ta?

YANG SUN. Three hundred sil— 75

SHUI TA. Five hundred silver dollars.

MRS. MI TZU. How much did she pay for it,
Mr. Shui Ta?

SHUI TA. A thousand. And very little has
been sold. 80

MRS. MI TZU. She was robbed. But I'll make
you a special offer if you'll promise to be out
by the day after tomorrow. Three hundred
silver dollars.

YANG SUN [*shrugging*]. Take it, man, take it. 85

SHUI TA. It is not enough.

YANG SUN. Why not? Why not? Certainly,
it's enough.

SHUI TA. Five hundred silver dollars.

YANG SUN. But why? We only need three! 90

SHUI TA [*to* MRS. MI TZU]. Excuse me.
[*Takes* YANG SUN *on one side.*] The tobacco
stock is pledged to the old couple who gave
my cousin the two hundred.

YANG SUN. Is it in writing? 95

SHUI TA. No.

YANG SUN [*to* MRS. MI TZU]. Three hundred will do.

MRS. MI TZU. Of course, I need an assurance that Miss Shen Te is not in debt.

5 YANG SUN. Mr. Shui Ta?

SHUI TA. She is not in debt.

YANG SUN. When can you let us have the money?

10 MRS. MI TZU. The day after tomorrow. And remember: I'm doing this because I have a soft spot in my heart for young lovers! [*Exit.*]

YANG SUN [*calling after her*]. Boxes, jars and sacks—three hundred for the lot and the pain's over! [*To* SHUI TA.] Where else can we raise

15 money by the day after tomorrow?

SHUI TA. Nowhere. Haven't you enough for the trip and the first few weeks?

YANG SUN. Oh, certainly.

SHUI TA. How much, exactly?

20 YANG SUN. Oh, I'll dig it up, if I have to steal it.

SHUI TA. I see.

YANG SUN. Well, don't fall off the roof. I'll get to Peking somehow.

25 SHUI TA. Two people can't travel for nothing.

YANG SUN [*not giving* SHUI TA *a chance to answer*]. I'm leaving *her* behind. No millstones round *my* neck!

30 SHUI TA. Oh.

YANG SUN. Don't look at me like that!

SHUI TA. How precisely is my cousin to live?

YANG SUN. Oh, you'll think of something.

SHUI TA. A small request, Mr. Yang Sun.

35 Leave the two hundred silver dollars here until you can show me two tickets for Peking.

YANG SUN. You learn to mind your own business, Mr. Shui Ta.

SHUI TA. I'm afraid Miss Shen Te may not

40 wish to sell the shop when she discovers that . . .

YANG SUN. You don't know women. She'll want to. Even then.

SHUI TA [*a slight outburst*]. She is a human

45 being, sir! And not devoid of common sense!

YANG SUN. Shen Te is a woman: she *is* devoid of common sense. I only have to lay my hand on her shoulder, and church bells ring.

SHUI TA [*with difficulty*]. Mr. Yang Sun!

50 YANG SUN. Mr. Shui Whatever-it-is!

SHUI TA. My cousin is devoted to you . . . because . . .

YANG SUN. Because I have my hands on her breasts. Give me a cigar. [*He takes one for

55 himself, stuffs a few more in his pocket, then changes his mind and takes the whole box.*] Tell her I'll marry her, then bring me the three hundred. Or let her bring it. One or the other. [*Exit.*]

60 MRS. SHIN [*sticking her head out of the back room*]. Well, he has your cousin under his thumb, and doesn't care if all Yellow Street knows it!

SHUI TA [*crying out*]. I've lost my shop!

65 And he doesn't love me! [*He runs berserk through the room, repeating these lines incoherently. Then stops suddenly, and addresses* MRS. SHIN.] Mrs. Shin, you grew up in the gutter, like me. Are we lacking in hard-

70 ness? I doubt it. If you steal a penny from me, I'll take you by the throat till you spit it out! You'd do the same to me. The times are bad, this city is hell, but we're like ants, we keep coming, up and up the walls, however smooth!

75 Till bad luck comes. Being in love, for instance. *One* weakness is enough, and love is the deadliest.

MRS. SHIN [*emerging from the back room*]. You should have a little talk with Mr. Shu Fu

80 the Barber. He's a real gentleman and just the thing for your cousin. [*She runs off.*]

SHUI TA.

A caress becomes a stranglehold

A sigh of love turns to a cry of fear

85 Why are there vultures circling in the air?

A girl is going to meet her lover.

[SHUI TA *sits down and* MR. SHU FU *enters with* MRS SHIN.]

Mr. Shu Fu?

SHU FU. Mr. Shui Ta.

90 [*They both bow.*]

SHUI TA. I am told that you have expressed a certain interest in my cousin Shen Te. Let me set aside all propriety and confess: she is

95 at this moment in grave danger.

SHU FU. Oh, dear!

SHUI TA. She has lost her shop, Mr. Shu Fu.

SHU FU. The charm of Miss Shen Te, Mr. Shui Ta, derives from the goodness, not of her shop, but of her heart. Men call her the Angel of the Slums.

SHUI TA. Yet her goodness has cost her two hundred silver dollars in a single day: we must put a stop to it.

SHU FU. Permit me to differ, Mr. Shui Ta. Let us rather, open wide the gates to such goodness! Every morning, with pleasure tinged by affection, I watch her charitable ministrations. For they are hungry, and she giveth them to eat! Four of them, to be precise. Why only four? I ask. Why not four hundred? I hear she has been seeking shelter for the homeless. What about my humble cabins behind the cattle run? They are at her disposal. And so forth. And so on. Mr. Shui Ta, do you think Miss Shen Te could be persuaded to listen to certain ideas of mine? Ideas like these?

SHUI TA. Mr. Shu Fu, she would be honored.

[Enter WONG and the POLICEMAN. MR. SHU FU turns abruptly away and studies the shelves.]

WONG. Is Miss Shen Te here?

SHUI TA. No.

WONG. I am Wong the Water Seller. You are Mr. Shui Ta?

SHUI TA. I am.

WONG. I am a friend of Shen Te's.

SHUI TA. An intimate friend, I hear.

WONG [to the POLICEMAN]. You see? [To SHUI TA.] It's because of my hand.

POLICEMAN. He hurt his hand, sir, that's a fact.

SHUI TA [quickly]. You need a sling, I see. [He takes a shawl from the back room, and throws it to WONG.]

WONG. But that's her new shawl!

SHUI TA. She has no more use for it.

WONG. But she bought it to please someone!

SHUI TA. It happens to be no longer necessary.

WONG [making the sling]. She is my only witness.

POLICEMAN. Mr. Shui Ta, your cousin is supposed to have seen the Barber hit the Water Seller with a curling iron.

SHUI TA. I'm afraid my cousin was not present at the time.

WONG. But she was, sir! Just ask her! Isn't she in?

SHUI TA [gravely]. Mr. Wong, my cousin has her own troubles. You wouldn't wish her to add to them by committing perjury?

WONG. But it was she that told me to go to the judge!

SHUI TA. Was the judge supposed to heal your hand?

[MR. SHU FU turns quickly around. SHUI TA bows to SHU FU, and vice versa.]

WONG [taking the sling off, and putting it back]. I see how it is.

POLICEMAN. Well, I'll be on my way. [To WONG.] And you be careful. If Mr. Shu Fu wasn't a man who tempers justice with mercy, as the saying is, you'd be in jail for libel. Be off with you!

[Exit WONG, followed by POLICEMAN.]

SHUI TA. Profound apologies, Mr. Shu Fu.

SHU FU. Not at all, Mr. Shui Ta. [Pointing to the shawl.] The episode is over?

SHUI TA. It may take her time to recover. There are some fresh wounds.

SHU FU. We shall be discreet. Delicate. A short vacation could be arranged . . .

SHUI TA. First, of course, you and she would have to talk things over.

SHU FU. At a small supper in a small, but high-class, restaurant.

SHUI TA. I'll go and find her. [Exit into back room.]

MRS. SHIN [sticking her head in again]. Time for congratulations, Mr. Shu Fu?

SHU FU. Ah, Mrs. Shin! Please inform Miss Shen Te's guests they may take shelter in the cabins behind the cattle run!

[MRS. SHIN nods, grinning.]

[To the audience.] Well? What do you think of me, ladies and gentlemen? What could a man do more? Could he be less selfish? More farsighted? A small supper in a small but . . . Does that bring rather vulgar and clumsy thoughts into your mind? Ts, ts, ts. Nothing of the sort will occur. She won't even be

touched. Not even accidentally while passing
the salt. An exchange of ideas only. Over the
flowers on the table—white chrysanthemums,
by the way [*he writes down a note of this*]—
yes, over the white chrysanthemums, two
young souls will . . . shall I say "find each
other"? We shall NOT exploit the misfortune
of others. Understanding? Yes. An offer of
assistance? Certainly. But quietly. Almost inaudibly. Perhaps with a single glance. A glance
that could also—mean more.

MRS. SHIN [*coming forward*]. Everything
under control, Mr. Shu Fu?

SHU FU. Oh, Mrs. Shin, what do you know
about this worthless rascal Yang Sun?

MRS. SHIN. Why, he's the most worthless
rascal . . .

SHU FU. Is he really? You're sure? [*As she
opens her mouth.*] From now on, he doesn't
exist! Can't be found anywhere!

[*Enter YANG SUN.*]

YANG SUN. What's been going on here?

MRS. SHIN. Shall I call Mr. Shui Ta, Mr. Shu
Fu? He wouldn't want strangers in here!

SHU FU. Mr. Shui Ta is in conference with
Miss Shen Te. Not to be disturbed!

YANG SUN. Shen Te here? I didn't see her
come in. What kind of conference?

SHU FU [*not letting him enter the back
room*]. Patience, dear sir! And if by chance I
have an inkling who you are, pray take note
that Miss Shen Te and I are about to announce
our engagement.

YANG SUN. What?

MRS. SHIN. You didn't expect that, did you?

[*YANG SUN is trying to push past the barber
into the back room when SHEN TE comes out.*]

SHU FU. My dear Shen Te, ten thousand
apologies! Perhaps you . . .

YANG SUN. What is it, Shen Te? Have you
gone crazy?

SHEN TE [*breathless*]. My cousin and Mr.
Shu Fu have come to an understanding. They
wish me to hear Mr. Shu Fu's plans for helping
the poor.

YANG SUN. Your cousin wants to part us.

SHEN TE. Yes.

YANG SUN. And you've agreed to it?

SHEN TE. Yes.

YANG SUN. They told you I was bad.

[*SHEN TE is silent.*]

And suppose I am. Does that make me need
you less? I'm low. Shen Te, I have no money,
I don't do the right thing but at least I put up
a fight! [*He is near her now, and speaks in an
undertone.*] Have you no eyes? Look at him.
Have you forgotten already?

SHEN TE. No.

YANG SUN. How it was raining?

SHEN TE. No.

YANG SUN. How you cut me down from the
willow tree? Bought me water? Promised me
money to fly with?

SHEN TE [*shakily*]. Yang Sun, what do you
want?

YANG SUN. I want you to come with me.

SHEN TE [*in a small voice*]. Forgive me, Mr.
Shu Fu, I want to go with Mr. Yang Sun.

YANG SUN. We're lovers you know. Give me
the key to the shop.

[*SHEN TE takes the key from around her
neck. YANG SUN puts it on the counter. To
MRS. SHIN.*]

Leave it under the mat when you're through.
Let's go, Shen Te.

SHU FU. But this is rape! Mr. Shui Ta!!

YANG SUN [*to SHEN TE*]. Tell him not to
shout.

SHEN TE. Please don't shout for my cousin,
Mr. Shu Fu. He doesn't agree with me, I know,
but he's wrong. [*To the audience.*]

I want to go with the man I love
I don't want to count the cost
I don't want to consider if it's wise
I don't want to know if he loves me
I want to go with the man I love.

YANG SUN. That's the spirit.

[*And the couple leave.*]

SCENE VA

[*In front of the inner curtain. SHEN TE in
her wedding clothes, on the way to her wedding.*]

SHEN TE. Something terrible has happened.
As I left the shop with Yang Sun, I found the

old carpet dealer's wife waiting in the street, trembling all over. She told me her husband has taken to his bed—sick with all the worry and excitement over the two hundred silver
5 dollars they lent me. She said it would be best if I gave it back now. Of course, I had to say I would. She said she couldn't quite trust my cousin Shui Ta or even my fiancé Yang Sun. There were tears in her eyes. With my emo-
10 tions in an uproar, I threw myself into Yang Sun's arms, I couldn't resist him. The things he'd said to Shui Ta had taught Shen Te nothing. Sinking into his arms, I said to my-self:
15   To let no one perish, not even oneself
      To fill everyone with happiness, even oneself
      Is so good
How could I have forgotten those two old people? Yang Sun swept me away like a small
20 hurricane. But he's not a bad man, and he loves me. He'd rather work in the cement factory than owe his flying to a crime. Though, of course, flying *is* a great passion with Sun. Now, on the way to my wedding, I waver be-
25 tween fear and joy.

SCENE VI

[*The "private dining room" on the upper floor of a cheap restaurant in a poor section of town. With* SHEN TE: *the* GRANDFATHER, *the* SISTER-IN-LAW, *the* NIECE, MRS. SHIN, *the* UN-
30 EMPLOYED MAN. *In a corner, alone, a* PRIEST. *A* WAITER *pouring wine. Downstage,* YANG SUN *talking to his mother. He wears a dinner jacket.*]

YANG SUN. Bad news, Mamma. She came
35 right out and told me she can't sell the shop for me. Some idiot is bringing a claim because he lent her the two hundred she gave you.

MRS. YANG. What did *you* say? Of course, you can't marry her now.

40   YANG SUN. It's no use saying anything to *her*. I've sent for her cousin, Mr. Shui Ta. He said there was nothing in writing.

MRS. YANG. Good idea. I'll go out and look for him. Keep an eye on things.

[*Exit* MRS. YANG. SHEN TE *has been pouring* 45 *wine.*]

SHEN TE [*to the audience, pitcher in hand*]. I wasn't mistaken in him. He's bearing up well. Though it must have been an awful blow— giving up flying. I do love him so. [*Calling* 50 *across the room to him.*] Sun, you haven't drunk a toast with the bride!

YANG SUN. What do we drink to?

SHEN TE. Why, to the future!

YANG SUN. When the bridegroom's dinner 55 jacket won't be a hired one!

SHEN TE. But when the bride's dress will still get rained on sometimes!

YANG SUN. To everything we ever wished for! 60

SHEN TE. May all our dreams come true!

[*They drink.*]

YANG SUN [*with loud conviviality*]. And now, friends, before the wedding gets under way, I have to ask the bride a few questions. 65 I've no idea what kind of a wife she'll make, and it worries me. [*Wheeling on* SHEN TE.] For example. Can you make five cups of tea with three tea leaves?

SHEN TE. No. 70

YANG SUN. So I won't be getting very much tea. Can you sleep on a straw mattress the size of that book? [*He points to the large volume the* PRIEST *is reading.*]

SHEN TE. The two of us? 75

YANG SUN. The one of you.

SHEN TE. In that case, no.

YANG SUN. What a wife! I'm shocked!

[*While the audience is laughing, his mother returns. With a shrug of her shoulders, she* 80 *tells* YANG SUN *the expected guest hasn't ar-rived. The* PRIEST *shuts the book with a bang, and makes for the door.*]

MRS. YANG. Where are *you* off to? It's only a matter of minutes. 85

PRIEST [*watch in hand*]. Time goes on, Mrs. Yang, and I've another wedding to attend to. Also a funeral.

MRS. YANG [*irately*]. D'you think we planned it this way? I was hoping to manage with 90 one pitcher of wine, and we've run through two already. [*Points to empty pitcher. Loudly.*] My dear Shen Te, I don't know where your cousin can be keeping himself!

SHEN TE. My cousin?

5 MRS. YANG. Certainly. I'm old fashioned enough to think such a close relative should attend the wedding.

SHEN TE. Oh, Sun, is it the three hundred silver dollars?

10 YANG SUN [*not looking her in the eye*]. Are you deaf? Mother says she's old fashioned. And I say I'm considerate. We'll wait another fifteen minutes.

HUSBAND. Another fifteen minutes.

15 MRS. YANG [*addressing the company*]. Now you all know, don't you, that my son is getting a job as a mail pilot?

SISTER-IN-LAW. In Peking, too, isn't it?

MRS. YANG. In Peking, too! The two of us

20 are moving to Peking!

SHEN TE. Sun, tell your mother Peking is out of the question now.

YANG SUN. Your cousin'll tell her. If he agrees. I don't agree.

25 SHEN TE [*amazed, and dismayed*]. Sun!

YANG SUN. I hate this godforsaken Setzuan. What people! Know what they look like when I half close my eyes? Horses! Whinnying, fretting, stamping, screwing their necks up!

30 [*Loudly.*] And what is it the thunder says? They are su-per-flu-ous! [*He hammers out the syllables.*] They've run their last race! They can go trample themselves to death! [*Pause.*] I've got to get out of here.

35 SHEN TE. But I've promised the money to the old couple.

YANG SUN. And since you always do the wrong thing, it's lucky your cousin's coming. Have another drink.

40 SHEN TE [*quietly*]. My cousin can't be coming.

YANG SUN. How d'you mean?

SHEN TE. My cousin can't be where I am.

YANG SUN. Quite a conundrum!

45 SHEN TE [*desperately*]. Sun, I'm the one that loves you. Not my cousin. He was thinking of the job in Peking when he promised you the old couple's money—

YANG SUN. Right. And that's why he's bringing the three hundred silver dollars. Here 50 —to my wedding.

SHEN TE. He is not bringing the three hundred silver dollars.

YANG SUN. Huh? What makes you think that? 55

SHEN TE [*looking into his eyes*]. He says you only bought one ticket to Peking.

[*Short pause.*]

YANG SUN. That was yesterday. [*He pulls two tickets part way out of his inside pocket,* 60 *making her look under his coat.*] Two tickets. I don't want Mother to know. She'll get left behind. I sold her furniture to buy these tickets, so you see . . .

SHEN TE. But what's to become of the old 65 couple?

YANG SUN. What's to become of me? Have another drink. Or do you believe in moderation? If I drink, I fly again. And if you drink, you may learn to understand me. 70

SHEN TE. You want to fly. But I can't help you.

YANG SUN. "Here's a plane, my darling— but it's only got one wing!"

[*The WAITER enters.*] 75

WAITER. Mrs. Yang! Mrs. Yang!

MRS. YANG. Yes?

WAITER. Another pitcher of wine, ma'am?

MRS. YANG. We have enough, thanks. Drinking makes me sweat. 80

WAITER. Would you mind paying, ma'am?

MRS. YANG [*to everyone*]. Just be patient a few moments longer, everyone, Mr. Shui Ta is on his way over! [*To the WAITER.*] Don't be a spoilsport. 85

WAITER. I can't let you leave till you've paid your bill, ma'am.

MRS. YANG. But they know me here!

WAITER. That's just it.

PRIEST [*ponderously getting up*]. I humbly 90 take my leave. [*And he does.*]

MRS. YANG [*to the others, desperately*]. Stay where you are, everybody! The priest says he'll be back in two minutes!

YANG SUN. It's no good, Mamma. Ladies and gentlemen, Mr. Shui Ta still hasn't arrived and the priest has gone home. We won't detain you any longer.

[*They are leaving now.*]

GRANDFATHER [*in the doorway, having forgotten to put his glass down*]. To the bride! [*He drinks, puts down the glass, and follows the others.*]

[*Pause.*]

SHEN TE. Shall I go too?

YANG SUN. You? Aren't you the bride? Isn't this your wedding? [*He drags her across the room, tearing her wedding dress.*] If we can wait, you can wait. Mother calls me her falcon. She wants to see me in the clouds. But I think it may be St. Nevercome's Day before she'll go to the door and see my plane thunder by. [*Pause. He pretends the guests are still present.*] Why such a lull in the conversation, ladies and gentlemen? Don't you like it here? The ceremony is only slightly postponed—because an important guest is expected at any moment. Also because the bride doesn't know what love is. While we're waiting, the bridegroom will sing a little song. [*He does so.*]

The Song of St. Nevercome's Day

On a certain day, as is generally known,
One and all will be shouting: Hooray,
[hooray!
For the beggar maid's son has a solid-gold
[throne
And the day is St. Nevercome's Day
On St. Nevercome's, Nevercome's,
[Nevercome's Day
He'll sit on his solid-gold throne

Oh, hooray, hooray! That day goodness
[will pay!
That day badness will cost you your head!
And merit and money will smile and be
[funny
While exchanging salt and bread
On St. Nevercome's, Nevercome's,
[Nevercome's Day
While exchanging salt and bread

And the grass, oh, the grass will look down
[at the sky
And the pebbles will roll up the stream
And all men will be good without batting
[an eye
They will make of our earth a dream
On St. Nevercome's, Nevercome's,
[Nevercome's Day
They will make of our earth a dream

And as for me, that's the day I shall be
A flyer and one of the best
Unemployed man, you will have work to do
Washerwoman, you'll get your rest
On St. Nevercome's, Nevercome's,
[Nevercome's Day
Washerwoman, you'll get your rest.

MRS. YANG. It looks like he's not coming.
[*The three of them sit looking at the door.*]

SCENE VIA

[WONG's *den. The sewer pipe is again transparent and again the* GODS *appear to* WONG *in a dream.*]

WONG. I'm so glad you've come, illustrious ones. It's Shen Te. She's in great trouble from following the rule about loving thy neighbor. Perhaps she's *too* good for this world!

FIRST GOD. Nonsense! You are eaten up by lice and doubts!

WONG. Forgive me, illustrious one, I only meant you might design to intervene.

FIRST GOD. Out of the question! My colleague here intervened in some squabble or other only yesterday. [*He points to the* THIRD GOD *who has a black eye.*] The results are before us!

WONG. She had to call on her cousin again. But not even he could help. I'm afraid the shop is done for.

THIRD GOD [*a little concerned*]. Perhaps we should help after all?

FIRST GOD. The gods help those that help themselves.

WONG. What if we *can't* help ourselves, illustrious ones?

[*Slight pause.*]

SECOND GOD. Try, anyway! Suffering ennobles!

FIRST GOD. Our faith in Shen Te is unshaken!

THIRD GOD. We certainly haven't found any *other* good people. You can see where we spend our nights from the straw on our clothes.

WONG. You might help her find her way by—

FIRST GOD. The good man finds his own way here below!

SECOND GOD. The good woman too.

FIRST GOD. The heavier the burden, the greater her strength!

THIRD GOD. We're only onlookers, you know.

FIRST GOD. And everything will be all right in the end, O ye of little faith!

[*They are gradually disappearing through these last lines.*]

SCENE VII

[*The yard behind* SHEN TE's *shop. A few articles of furniture on a cart.* SHEN TE *and* MRS. SHIN *are taking the washing off the line.*]

MRS. SHIN. If you ask me, you should fight tooth and nail to keep the shop.

SHEN TE. How can I? I have to sell the tobacco to pay back the two hundred silver dollars today.

MRS. SHIN. No husband, no tobacco, no house and home! What are you going to live on?

SHEN TE. I can work. I can sort tobacco.

MRS. SHIN. Hey, look, Mr. Shui Ta's trousers! He must have left here stark naked!

SHEN TE. Oh, he may have another pair, Mrs. Shin.

MRS. SHIN. But if he's gone for good as you say, why has he left his pants behind?

SHEN TE. Maybe he's thrown them away.

MRS. SHIN. Can I take them?

SHEN TE. Oh, no.

[*Enter* MR. SHU FU, *running.*]

SHU FU. Not a word! Total silence! I know all. You have sacrificed your own love and happiness so as not to hurt a dear old couple who had put their trust in you! Not in vain does this district—for all its malevolent tongues!—call you the Angel of the Slums! That young man couldn't rise to your level, so you left him. And now, when I see you closing up the little shop, that veritable haven of rest for the multitude, well, I cannot, I cannot let it pass. Morning after morning I have stood watching in the doorway not unmoved—while you graciously handed out rice to the wretched. Is that never to happen again? Is the good woman of Setzuan to disappear? If only you would allow *me* to assist you! Now don't say anything! No assurances, no exclamations of gratitude! [*He has taken out his check book.*] Here! A blank check. [*He places it on the cart.*] Just my signature. Fill it out as you wish. Any sum in the world. I herewith retire from the scene, quietly, unobtrusively, making no claims, on tiptoe, full of veneration, absolutely selflessly . . . [*He has gone.*]

MRS. SHIN. Well! You're saved. There's always some idiot of a man . . . Now hurry! Put down a thousand silver dollars and let me fly to the bank before he comes to his senses.

SHEN TE. I can pay you for the washing without any check.

MRS. SHIN. What? You're not going to cash it just because you might have to marry him? Are you crazy? Men like him *want* to be led by the nose! Are you still thinking of that flyer? All Yellow Street knows how he treated you!

SHEN TE.

When I heard his cunning laugh, I was
                       [afraid
But when I saw the holes in his shoes, I loved
                       [him dearly.

MRS. SHIN. Defending that good for nothing after all that's happened!

SHEN TE [*staggering as she holds some of the washing*]. Oh!

MRS. SHIN [*taking the washing from her,*

dryly]. So you feel dizzy when you stretch and bend? There couldn't be a little visitor on the way? If that's it, you can forget Mr. Shu Fu's blank check: it wasn't meant for a christening present!

[*She goes to the back with a basket. SHEN TE's eyes follow MRS. SHIN for a moment. Then she looks down at her own body, feels her stomach, and a great joy comes into her eyes.*]

SHEN TE. O joy! A new human being is on the way. The world awaits him. In the cities the people say: he's got to be reckoned with, this new human being! [*She imagines a little boy to be present, and introduces him to the audience.*]

This is my son, the well-known flyer!
Say: Welcome
To the conqueror of unknown mountains
                    [and unreachable regions
Who brings us our mail across the
                    [impassable deserts!

[*She leads him up and down by the hand.*] Take a look at the world, my son. That's a tree. Tree, yes. Say: "Hello, tree!" And bow. Like this. [*She bows.*] Now you know each other. And, look, here comes the Water Seller. He's a friend, give him your hand. A cup of fresh water for my little son, please. Yes, it *is* a warm day. [*Handing the cup.*] Oh dear, a policeman, we'll have to make a circle round *him*. Perhaps we can pick a few cherries over there in the rich Mr. Pung's garden. But we mustn't be seen. You want cherries? Just like children with fathers. No, no, you can't go straight at them like that. Don't pull. We must learn to be reasonable. Well, have it your own way. [*She has let him make for the cherries.*] Can you reach? Where to put them? Your mouth is the best place. [*She tries one herself.*] Mmm, they're good. But the policeman, we must run! [*They run.*] Yes, back to the street. Calm now, so no one will notice us. [*Walking the street with her child, she sings.*]

Once a plum—'twas in Japan—
Made a conquest of a man
But the man's turn soon did come
For he gobbled up the plum

[*Enter WONG, with a CHILD by the hand. He coughs.*]

SHEN TE. Wong!

WONG. It's about the Carpenter, Shen Te. He's lost his shop, and he's been drinking. His children are on the streets. This is one. Can you help?

SHEN TE [*to the child*]. Come here, little man. [*Takes him down to the footlights. To the audience.*]

You there! A man is asking you for shelter!
A man of tomorrow says: what about today?
His friend the conqueror, whom you know,
Is his advocate!

[*To WONG.*] He can live in Mr. Shu Fu's cabin. I may have to go there myself. I'm going to have a baby. That's a secret—don't tell Yang Sun—we'd only be in his way. Can you find the Carpenter for me?

WONG. I knew you'd think of something. [*To the CHILD.*] Goodbye, son, I'm going for your father.

SHEN TE. What about your hand, Wong? I wanted to help, but my cousin . . .

WONG. Oh, I can get along with one hand, don't worry. [*He shows how he can handle his pole with his left hand alone.*]

SHEN TE. But your right hand! Look, take this cart, sell everything that's on it, and go to the doctor with the money . . .

WONG. She's still good. But first I'll bring the Carpenter. I'll pick up the cart when I get back. [*Exit WONG.*]

SHEN TE [*to the CHILD*]. Sit down over here, son, till your father comes.

[*The CHILD sits crosslegged on the ground. Enter the HUSBAND and WIFE, each dragging a large, full sack.*]

WIFE [*furtively*]. You're alone, Shen Te, dear?

[*SHEN TE nods. The WIFE beckons to the NEPHEW offstage. He comes on with another sack.*]

Your cousin's away?
[*SHEN TE nods.*]
He's not coming back?
SHEN TE. No. I'm giving up the shop.

WIFE. That's why we're here. We want to know if we can leave these things in your new home. Will you do us this favor?

SHEN TE. Why, yes, I'd be glad to.

5 HUSBAND [*cryptically*]. And if anyone asks about them, say they're yours.

SHEN TE. Would anyone ask?

WIFE [*with a glance back at her* HUSBAND]. Oh, someone might. The police, for instance.
10 They don't seem to like us. Where can we put it?

SHEN TE. Well, I'd rather not get in any more trouble . . . .

WIFE. Listen to her! The good woman of
15 Setzuan!

[SHEN TE *is silent.*]

HUSBAND. There's enough tobacco in those sacks to give us a new start in life. We could have our own tobacco factory!

20 SHEN TE [*slowly*]. You'll have to put them in the back room.

[*The sacks are taken offstage, while the* CHILD *is left alone. Shyly glancing about him, he goes to the garbage can, starts playing with*
25 *the contents, and eating some of the scraps. The others return.*]

WIFE. We're counting on you, Shen Te!

SHEN TE. Yes. [*She sees the* CHILD *and is shocked.*]

30 HUSBAND. We'll see you in Mr. Shu Fu's cabins.

NEPHEW. The day after tomorrow.

SHEN TE. Yes. Now, go. Go! I'm not feeling well.

35 [*Exeunt all three, virtually pushed off.*]
He is eating the refuse in the garbage can! Only look at his little gray mouth!
[*Pause. Music.*]
As this is the world *my* son will enter
40 I will study to defend him.
To be good to you, my son,
I shall be a tigress to all others
If I have to.
And I shall have to.

45 [*She starts to go.*] One more time, then. I hope really the last.

[*Exit* SHEN TE, *taking* SHUI TA'S *trousers.*

MRS. SHIN *enters and watches her with marked interest. Enter the* SISTER-IN-LAW *and the* GRANDFATHER.]

50 SISTER-IN-LAW. So it's true, the shop has closed down. And the furniture's in the back yard. It's the end of the road!

MRS. SHIN [*pompously*]. The fruit of high living, selfishness, and sensuality! Down the
55 primrose path to Mr. Shu Fu's cabins—with you!

SISTER-IN-LAW. Cabins? Rat holes! He gave them to us because his soap supplies only went mouldy there!

60 [*Enter the* UNEMPLOYED MAN.]

UNEMPLOYED MAN. Shen Te is moving?

SISTER-IN-LAW. Yes. She was sneaking away.

MRS. SHIN. She's ashamed of herself, and no wonder!

65 UNEMPLOYED MAN. Tell her to call Mr. Shui Ta or she's done for this time!

SISTER-IN-LAW. Tell her to call Mr. Shui Ta or *we're* done for this time!

[*Enter* WONG *and* CARPENTER, *the latter with*
70 *a* CHILD *on each hand.*]

CARPENTER. So we'll have a roof over our heads for a change!

MRS. SHIN. Roof? Whose roof?

CARPENTER. Mr. Shu Fu's cabins. And we
75 have little Feng to thank for it. [FENG, *we find, is the name of the child already there; his* FATHER *now takes him. To the other two.*] Bow to your little brother, you two! [*The* CARPENTER *and the two new arrivals bow to* FENG.]
80 [*Enter* SHUI TA.]

UNEMPLOYED MAN. Sst! Mr. Shui Ta!

[*Pause.*]

SHUI TA. And what is this crowd here for, may I ask?

85 WONG. How do you do, Mr. Shui Ta? This is the Carpenter. Miss Shen Te promised him space in Mr. Shu Fu's cabins.

SHUI TA. That will not be possible.

CARPENTER. We can't go there after all?

90 SHUI TA. All the space is needed for other purposes.

SISTER-IN-LAW. You mean we have to get out? But we've got nowhere to go.

SHUI TA. Miss Shen Te finds it possible to provide employment. If the proposition interests you, you may stay in the cabins.

SISTER-IN-LAW [*with distaste*]. You mean *work*? Work for Miss Shen Te?

SHUI TA. Making tobacco, yes. There are three bales here already. Would you like to get them?

SISTER-IN-LAW [*trying to bluster*]. We have our own tobacco! We were in the tobacco business before you were born!

SHUI TA [*to the* CARPENTER *and the* UNEMPLOYED MAN]. You *don't* have your own tobacco. What about you?

[*The* CARPENTER *and the* UNEMPLOYED MAN *get the point, and go for the sacks. Enter* MRS. MI TZU.]

MRS. MI TZU. Mr. Shui Ta? I've brought you your three hundred silver dollars.

SHUI TA. I'll sign your lease instead. I've decided not to sell.

MRS. MI TZU. What? You don't need the money for that flyer?

SHUI TA. No.

MRS. MI TZU. And you can pay six months' rent?

SHUI TA [*takes the barber's blank check from the cart and fills it out*]. Here is a check for ten thousand silver dollars. On Mr. Shu Fu's account. Look! [*He shows her the signature on the check.*] Your six months' rent will be in your hands by seven this evening. And now, if you'll excuse me.

MRS. MI TZU. So it's Mr. Shu Fu now. The flyer has been given his walking papers. These modern girls! In my day they'd have said she was flighty. That poor, deserted Mr. Yang Sun!

[*Exit* MRS. MI TZU. *The* CARPENTER *and the* UNEMPLOYED MAN *drag the three sacks back on the stage.*]

CARPENTER [*to* SHUI TA]. I don't know why I'm doing this for you.

SHUI TA. Perhaps your children want to eat, Mr. Carpenter.

SISTER-IN-LAW [*catching sight of the sacks*]. Was my brother-in-law here?

MRS. SHIN. Yes, he was.

SISTER-IN-LAW. I thought as much. I know those sacks! That's our tobacco!

SHUI TA. Really? I thought it came from my back room? Shall we consult the police on the point?

SISTER-IN-LAW [*defeated*]. No.

SHUI TA. Perhaps you will show me the way to Mr. Shu Fu's cabins?

[SHUI TA *goes off, followed by the* CARPENTER *and his two older children, the* SISTER-IN-LAW, *the* GRANDFATHER, *and the* UNEMPLOYED MAN. *Each of the last three drags a sack. Enter* OLD MAN *and* OLD WOMAN.]

MRS. SHIN. A pair of pants—missing from the clothes line one minute—and next minute on the honorable backside of Mr. Shui Ta!

OLD WOMAN. We thought Miss Shen Te was here.

MRS. SHIN [*preoccupied*]. Well, she's not.

OLD MAN. There was something she was going to give us.

WONG. She was going to help me too. [*Looking at his hand.*] It'll be too late soon. But she'll be back. This cousin has never stayed long.

MRS. SHIN [*approaching a conclusion*]. No, he hasn't, has he?

SCENE VIIA

[*The sewer pipe.* WONG *asleep. In his dream, he tells the* GODS *his fears. The* GODS *seem tired from all their travels. They stop for a moment and look over their shoulders at the Water Seller.*]

WONG. Illustrious ones, I've been having a bad dream. Our beloved Shen Te was in great distress in the rushes down by the rivers—the spot where the bodies of suicides are washed up. She kept staggering and holding her head down as if she was carrying something and it was dragging her down into the mud. When I called out to her, she said she had to take your Book of Rules to the other side, and not get it wet, or the ink would all come off. You had talked to her about the virtues, you know, the time she gave you shelter in Setzuan.

THIRD GOD. Well, but what do you suggest, my dear Wong?

WONG. Maybe a little relaxation of the rules, Benevolent One, in view of the bad times.

THIRD GOD. As for instance?

WONG. Well, um, good-will, for instance, might do instead of love?

THIRD GOD. I'm afraid that would create new problems.

5 WONG. Or, instead of justice, good sportsmanship?

THIRD GOD. That would only mean more work.

WONG. Instead of honor, outward propriety?

10 THIRD GOD. Still more work! No, no! The rules will have to stand, my dear Wong!

[*Wearily shaking their heads, all three journey on.*]

SCENE VIII

[SHUI TA's *tobacco factory in* SHU FU's
15 *cabins. Huddled together behind bars, several families, mostly women and children. Among these people the* SISTER-IN-LAW, *the* GRANDFATHER, *the* CARPENTER, *and his three children. Enter* MRS. YANG *followed by* YANG SUN.]

20 MRS. YANG [*to the audience*]. There's something I just *have* to tell you: strength and wisdom are wonderful things. The strong and wise Mr. Shui Ta has transformed my son from a dissipated good-for-nothing into a model
25 citizen. As you may have heard, Mr. Shui Ta opened a small tobacco factory near the cattle runs. It flourished. Three months ago—I shall never forget it—I asked for an appointment, and Mr. Shui Ta agreed to see us—me and my
30 son. I can see him now as he came through the door to meet us . . .

[*Enter* SHUI TA, *from a door.*]

SHUI TA. What can I do for you, Mrs. Yang?

MRS. YANG. This morning the police came
35 to the house. We find you've brought an action for breach of promise of marriage. In the name of Shen Te. You also claim that Sun came by two hundred silver dollars by improper means.

SHUI TA. That is correct.

40 MRS. YANG. Mr. Shui Ta, the money's all gone. When the Peking job didn't materialize, he ran through it all in three days. I know he's a good-for-nothing. He sold my furniture. He was moving to Peking without me. Miss Shen
45 Te thought highly of him at one time.

SHUI TA. What do *you* say, Mr. Yang Sun?

YANG SUN. The money's gone.

SHUI TA [*to* MRS. YANG]. Mrs. Yang, in consideration of my cousin's incomprehensible weakness for your son, I am prepared to give 50 him another chance. He can have a job—here. The two hundred silver dollars will be taken out of his wages.

YANG SUN. So it's the factory or jail?

SHUI TA. Take your choice. 55

YANG SUN. May I speak with Shen Te?

SHUI TA. You may not.

[*Pause.*]

YANG SUN [*sullenly*]. Show me where to go.

MRS. YANG. Mr. Shui Ta, you are kindness 60 itself: the gods will reward you! [*To* YANG SUN.] And honest work will make a man of you, my boy.

[YANG SUN *follows* SHUI TA *into the factory.* MRS. YANG *comes down again to the foot-* 65 *lights.*]

Actually, honest work didn't agree with him— at first. And he got no opportunity to distinguish himself till—in the third week—when the wages were being paid. . . . 70

[SHUI TA *has a bag of money. Standing next to his foreman—the former* UNEMPLOYED MAN —*he counts out the wages. It is* YANG SUN's *turn.*]

UNEMPLOYED MAN [*reading*]. Carpenter, six 75 silver dollars. Yang Sun, six silver dollars.

YANG SUN [*quietly*]. Excuse me, sir. I don't think it can be more than five. May I see? [*He takes the foreman's list.*] It says six working days. But that's a mistake, sir. I took a day off 80 for court business. And I won't take what I haven't earned, however miserable the pay is!

UNEMPLOYED MAN. Yang Sun. Five silver dollars. [*To* SHUI TA.] A rare case, Mr. Shui Ta!

SHUI TA. How is it the book says six when 85 it should say five?

UNEMPLOYED MAN. I must've made a mistake, Mr. Shui Ta. [*With a look at* YANG SUN.] It won't happen again.

SHUI TA [*taking* YANG SUN *aside*]. You don't 90 hold back, do you? You give your all to the firm. You're even honest. Do the foreman's mistakes always favor the workers?

YANG SUN. He does have . . . friends.

SHUI TA. Thank you. May I offer you any little recompense?

YANG SUN. Give me a trial period of one week, and I'll prove my intelligence is worth
5 more to you than my strength.

MRS. YANG SUN [*still down at the footlights*]. Fighting words, fighting words! That evening, I said to Sun: "If you're a flyer, then fly, my falcon! Rise in the world!" And he got
10 to be foreman. Yes, in Mr. Shui Ta's tobacco factory, he worked real miracles.

[*We see* YANG SUN *with his legs apart standing behind the workers who are handing along a basket of raw tobacco above their heads.*]
15 YANG SUN. Faster! Faster! You, there, d'you think you can just stand around now you're not foreman any more? It'll be your job to lead us in song. Sing!

[UNEMPLOYED MAN *starts singing. The others*
20 *join in the refrain.*]

Song of the Eighth Elephant

Chang had seven elephants—all much the
[same—
But then there was Little Brother
The seven, they were wild, Little Brother,
[he was tame
25 And to guard them Chang chose Little
[Brother

Run faster!
Mr. Chang has a forest park
Which must be cleared before tonight
30 And already it's growing dark!

When the seven elephants cleared that
[forest park
Mr. Chang rode high on Little Brother
35 While the seven toiled and moiled till dark
On his big behind sat Little Brother
Dig faster!
Mr. Chang has a forest park
Which must be cleared before tonight
40 And already it's growing dark!

And the seven elephants worked many an
[hour
Till none of them could work another
Old Chang, he looked sour, on the seven,
45 [he did glower

But gave a pound of rice to Little Brother
What was that?
Mr. Chang has a forest park
Which must be cleared before tonight
And already it's growing dark! 50

And the seven elephants hadn't any tusks
The one that had the tusks was Little
[Brother!
Seven are no match for one, if the one has
[a gun! 55
How old Chang did laugh at Little
[Brother!

Keep on digging!
Mr. Chang has a forest park
Which must be cleared before tonight 60
And already it's growing dark!

[*Smoking a cigar,* SHUI TA *strolls by.* YANG SUN, *laughing, has joined in the refrain of the third stanza and speeded up the tempo of the last stanza by clapping his hands.*] 65

MRS. YANG. And that's why I say: strength and wisdom are wonderful things. It took the strong and wise Mr. Shui Ta to bring out the best in Yang Sun. A real superior man is like a bell. If you ring it, it rings, and if you don't, 70 it don't, as the saying is.

SCENE IX

[SHEN TE'S *shop, now an office with club chairs and fine carpets. It is raining.* SHUI TA, *now fat, is just dismissing the* OLD MAN *and* OLD WOMAN. MRS. SHIN, *in obviously new* 75 *clothes, looks on, smirking.*]

SHUI TA. No! I can NOT tell you when we expect her back.

OLD WOMAN. The two hundred silver dollars came today. In an envelope. There was no 80 letter, but it must be from Shen Te. We want to write and thank her. May we have her address?

SHUI TA. I'm afraid I haven't got it.

OLD MAN [*pulling* OLD WOMAN'S *sleeve*]. 85 Let's be going.

OLD WOMAN. She's got to come back some time! [*They move off, uncertainly, worried.* SHUI TA *bows.*]

MRS. SHIN. They lost the carpet shop because they couldn't pay their taxes. The money arrived too late.

SHUI TA. They could have come to me.

MRS. SHIN. People don't like coming to you.

SHUI TA [*sits suddenly, one hand to his head*]. I'm dizzy.

MRS. SHIN. After all, you *are* in your seventh month. But old Mrs. Shin will be there in your hour of trial! [*She cackles feebly.*]

SHUI TA [*in a satisfied voice*]. Can I count on that?

MRS. SHIN. We all have our price, and mine won't be too high for the great Mr. Shui Ta! [*She opens* SHUI TA's *collar.*].

SHUI TA. It's for the child's sake. All of this.

MRS. SHIN. "All for the child," of course.

SHUI TA. I'm so fat. People must notice.

MRS. SHIN. Oh no, they think it's 'cause you're rich.

SHUI TA [*more feelingly*]. What will happen to the child?

MRS. SHIN. You ask that nine times a day. Why, it'll have the best that money can buy!

SHUI TA. He must never see Shui Ta.

MRS. SHIN. Oh, no. Always Shen Te.

SHUI TA. What about the neighbors? There are rumors, aren't there?

MRS. SHIN. As long as Mr. Shu Fu doesn't find out, there's nothing to worry about. Drink this.

[*Enter* YANG SUN *in a smart business suit, and carrying a businessman's brief case.* SHUI TA *is more or less in* MRS. SHIN's *arms.*]

YANG SUN [*surprised*]. I seem to be in the way.

SHUI TA [*ignoring this, rises with an effort*]. Till tomorrow, Mrs. Shin.

[MRS. SHIN *leaves with a smile, putting her new gloves on.*]

YANG SUN. Gloves now! She couldn't be fleecing you? And since when did *you* have a private life? [*Taking a paper from the brief case.*] You haven't been at your best lately, and things are getting out of hand. The police want to close us down. They say that at the most they can only permit twice the lawful number of workers.

SHUI TA [*evasively*]. The cabins are quite good enough.

YANG SUN. For the workers maybe, not for the tobacco. They're too damp. We must take over some of Mrs. Mi Tzu's buildings.

SHUI TA. Her price is double what I can pay.

YANG SUN. Not unconditionally. If she has me to stroke her knees she'll come down.

SHUI TA. I'll never agree to that.

YANG SUN. What's wrong? Is it the rain? You get so irritable whenever it rains.

SHUI TA. Never! I will never . . .

YANG SUN. Mrs. Mi Tzu'll be here in five minutes. *You* fix it. And Shu Fu will be with her. . . . What's all that noise?

[*During the above dialogue,* WONG *is heard off stage calling:* "The good Shen Te, where is she? Which of you has seen Shen Te, good people? Where is Shen Te?" *A knock. Enter* WONG.]

WONG. Mr. Shui Ta, I've come to ask when Miss Shen Te will be back, it's six months now . . . There are rumors. People say something's happened to her.

SHUI TA. I'm busy. Come back next week.

WONG [*excited*]. In the morning there was always rice on her doorstep—for the needy. It's been there again lately!

SHUI TA. And what do people conclude from this?

WONG. That Shen Te is still in Setzuan! She's been . . . [*He breaks off.*]

SHUI TA. She's been what? Mr. Wong, if you're Shen Te's friend, talk a little less about her, that's my advice to you.

WONG. I don't want your advice! Before she disappeared, Miss Shen Te told me something very important—she's pregnant!

YANG SUN. What? What was that?

SHUI TA [*quickly*]. The man is lying.

WONG. A good woman isn't so easily forgotten, Mr. Shui Ta.

[*He leaves.* SHUI TA *goes quickly into the back room.*]

YANG SUN [*to the audience*]. Shen Te pregnant? So that's why. Her cousin sent her away, so I wouldn't get wind of it. I have a son, a Yang appears on the scene, and what happens? Mother and child vanish into thin air! That scoundrel, that unspeakable . . . [*The sound of sobbing is heard from the back room.*] What was that? Someone sobbing? Who was it? Mr. Shui Ta the Tobacco King doesn't weep his heart out. And where does the rice come from that's on the doorstep in the morning?

[SHUI TA *returns. He goes to the door and looks out into the rain.*]

Where is she?

SHUI TA. Sh! It's nine o'clock. But the rain's so heavy, you can't hear a thing.

YANG SUN. What do you want to hear?

SHUI TA. The mail plane.

YANG SUN. What?

SHUI TA. I've been told *you* wanted to fly at one time. Is that all forgotten?

YANG SUN. Flying mail is night work. I prefer the daytime. And the firm is very dear to me—after all it belongs to my ex-fiancée, even if she's not around. And she's not, is she?

SHUI TA. What do you mean by that?

YANG SUN. Oh, well, let's say I haven't altogether—lost interest.

SHUI TA. My cousin might like to know that.

YANG SUN. I might not be indifferent—if I found she was being kept under lock and key.

SHUI TA. By whom?

YANG SUN. By you.

SHUI TA. What could you do about it?

YANG SUN. I could submit for discussion— my position in the firm.

SHUI TA. You are now my Manager. In return for a more appropriate position, you might agree to drop the enquiry into your ex-fiancée's whereabouts?

YANG SUN. I might.

SHUI TA. What position *would* be more appropriate?

YANG SUN. The one at the top.

SHUI TA. My own? [*Silence.*] And if I preferred to throw you out on your neck?

YANG SUN. I'd come back on my feet. With suitable escort.

SHUI TA. The police?

YANG SUN. The police.

SHUI TA. And when the police found no one?

YANG SUN. I might ask them not to overlook the back room. [*Ending the pretense.*] In short,

Mr. Shui Ta, my interest in this young woman has not been officially terminated. I should like to see more of her. [*Into* SHUI TA's *face.*] Besides, she's pregnant and needs a friend. [*He moves to the door.*] I shall talk about it with the Water Seller. [*Exit.*]

[SHUI TA *is rigid for a moment, then he quickly goes into the back room. He returns with* SHEN TE's *belongings: underwear, etc. He takes a long look at the shawl of the previous scene. He then wraps the things in a bundle which, upon hearing a noise, he hides under the table. Enter* MRS. MI TZU *and* MR. SHU FU. *They put away their umbrellas and galoshes.*]

MRS. MI TZU. I thought your manager was here, Mr. Shui Ta. He combines charm with business in a way that can only be to the advantage of all of us.

SHU FU. You sent for us, Mr. Shui Ta?

SHUI TA. The factory is in trouble.

SHU FU. It always is.

SHUI TA. The police are threatening to close us down unless I can show that the extension of our facilities is imminent.

SHU FU. Mr. Shui Ta, I'm sick and tired of your constantly expanding projects. I place cabins at your cousin's disposal; you make a factory of them. I hand your cousin a check; you present it. Your cousin disappears and you find the cabins too small and talk of yet more . . .

SHUI TA. Mr. Shu Fu, I'm authorized to inform you that Miss Shen Te's return is now imminent.

SHU FU. Imminent? It's becoming his favorite word.

MRS. MI TZU. Yes, what does it mean?

SHUI TA. Mrs. Mi Tzu, I can pay you exactly half what you asked for your buildings. Are you ready to inform the police that I am taking them over?

MRS. MI TZU. Certainly, if I can take over your manager.

SHU FU. What?

MRS. MI TZU. He's so efficient.

SHUI TA. I'm afraid I need Mr. Yang Sun.

MRS. MI TZU. So do I.

SHUI TA. He will call on you tomorrow.

SHU FU. So much the better. With Shen Te likely to turn up at any moment, the presence of that young man is hardly in good taste.

5 SHUI TA. So we have reached a settlement. In what was once the good Shen Te's little shop we are laying the foundations for the great Mr. Shui Ta's twelve magnificent super tobacco markets. You will bear in mind that though

10 they call me the Tobacco King of Setzuan, it is my cousin's interests that have been served . . .

VOICES [*off*]. The police, the police! Going to the tobacco shop! Something must have happened! [*Etc.*]

15 [*Enter* YANG SUN, WONG, *and the* POLICEMAN.]

POLICEMAN. Quiet there, quiet, quiet! [*They quiet down.*] I'm sorry, Mr. Shui Ta, but there's a report that you've been depriving Miss Shen

20 Te of her freedom. Not that I believe all I hear, but the whole city's in an uproar.

SHUI TA. That's a lie.

POLICEMAN. Mr. Yang Sun has testified that he heard someone sobbing in the back room.

25 SHU FU. Mrs. Mi Tzu and myself will testify that no one here has been sobbing.

MRS. MI TZU. We have been quietly smoking our cigars.

POLICEMAN. Mr. Shui Ta, I'm afraid I shall

30 have to take a look at that room. [*He does so. The room is empty.*] No one there, of course, sir.

YANG SUN. But I heard sobbing. What's that? [*He finds the clothes.*]

35 WONG. Those are Shen Te's things. [*To crowd.*] Shen Te's clothes are here!

VOICES [*Off. In sequence*]. Shen Te's clothes! They've been found under the table! Body of murdered girl still missing! Tobacco King sus-

40 pected!

POLICEMAN. Mr. Shui Ta, unless you can tell us where the girl is, I'll have to ask you to come along.

SHUI TA. I do not know.

45 POLICEMAN. I can't say how sorry I am, Mr. Shui Ta. [*He shows him the door.*]

SHUI TA. Everything will be cleared up in no time. There are still judges in Setzuan.

YANG SUN. I heard sobbing!

SCENE IXA

[WONG's *den. For the last time, the* GODS 50 *appear to the Water Seller in his dream. They have changed and show signs of a long journey, extreme fatigue, and plenty of mishaps. The* FIRST *no longer has a hat; the* THIRD *has lost a leg; all* THREE *are barefoot.*] 55

WONG. Illustrious ones, at last you're here. Shen Te's been gone for months and today her cousin's been arrested. They think he murdered her to get the shop. But I had a dream and in this dream Shen Te said her cousin was keep- 60 ing her prisoner. You must find her for us, illustrious ones!

FIRST GOD. We've found very few good people anywhere, and even they didn't keep it up. Shen Te is still the only one that stayed 65 good.

SECOND GOD. If she *has* stayed good.

WONG. Certainly she has. But she's vanished.

FIRST GOD. That's the last straw. All is lost! 70

SECOND GOD. A little moderation, dear colleague!

FIRST GOD [*plaintively*]. What's the good of moderation now? If she can't be found, we'll have to resign! The world is a terrible place! 75 Nothing but misery, vulgarity, and waste! Even the countryside isn't what it used to be. The trees are getting their heads chopped off by telephone wires, and there's such a noise from all the gunfire, and I can't stand those 80 heavy clouds of smoke, and—

THIRD GOD. The place is absolutely unlivable! Good intentions bring people to the brink of the abyss, and good deeds push them over the edge. I'm afraid our book of rules is 85 destined for the scrap heap—

SECOND GOD. It's people! They're a worthless lot!

THIRD GOD. The world is too cold!

SECOND GOD. It's people! They are too weak! 90

FIRST GOD. Dignity, dear colleagues, dignity! Never despair! As for this world, didn't we agree that we only have to find one human being who can stand the place? Well, we found her. True, we lost her again. We must find her again, that's all! And at once!

[*They disappear.*]

SCENE X

[*Courtroom. Groups:* SHU FU *and* MRS. MI TZU; YANG SUN *and* MRS. YANG; WONG, *the* CARPENTER, *the* GRANDFATHER, *the* NIECE, *the* OLD MAN, *the* OLD WOMAN; MRS. SHIN, *the* POLICEMAN; *the* UNEMPLOYED MAN, *the* SISTER-IN-LAW.]

OLD MAN. So much power isn't good for one man.

UNEMPLOYED MAN. And he's going to open twelve super tobacco markets!

WIFE. One of the judges is a friend of Mr. Shu Fu's.

SISTER-IN-LAW. Another one accepted a present from Mr. Shui Ta only last night. A great fat goose.

OLD WOMAN [*to* WONG]. And Shen Te is nowhere to be found.

WONG. Only the gods will ever know the truth.

POLICEMAN. Order in the court! My lords the judges!

[*Enter the* THREE GODS *in judges' robes. We overhear their conversation as they pass along the footlights to their bench.*]

THIRD GOD. We'll never get away with it, our certificates were so badly forged.

SECOND GOD. My predecessor's "sudden indigestion" will certainly cause comment.

FIRST GOD. But he *had* just eaten a whole goose.

UNEMPLOYED MAN. Look at that! *New* judges!

WONG. New judges. And what good ones!

[*The* THIRD GOD *hears this, and turns to smile at* WONG. *The* GODS *sit. The* FIRST GOD *beats on the bench with his gavel. The* POLICEMAN *brings in* SHUI TA *who walks with lordly steps. He is whistled at.*]

POLICEMAN [*to* SHUI TA]. Be prepared for a surprise. The judges have been changed.

[SHUI TA *turns quickly round, looks at them, and staggers.*]

NIECE. What's the matter now?

WIFE. The great Tobacco King nearly fainted.

HUSBAND. Yes, as soon as he saw the new judges.

WONG. Does *he* know who they are?

[SHUI TA *picks himself up, and the proceedings open.*]

FIRST GOD. Defendant Shui Ta, you are accused of doing away with your cousin Shen Te in order to take possession of her business. Do you plead guilty or not guilty?

SHUI TA. Not guilty, my lord.

FIRST GOD [*thumbing through the documents of the case*]. The first witness is the Policeman. I shall ask him to tell us something of the respective reputations of Miss Shen Te and Mr. Shui Ta.

POLICEMAN. Miss Shen Te was a young lady who aimed to please, my lord. She liked to live and let live, as the saying goes. Mr. Shui Ta, on the other hand, is a man of principle. Though the generosity of Miss Shen Te forced him at times to abandon half measures, unlike the girl, he was always on the side of the law, my lord. One time, he even unmasked a gang of thieves to whom his too trustful cousin had given shelter. The evidence, in short, my lord, proves that Mr. Shui Ta was *incapable* of the crime of which he stands accused!

FIRST GOD. I see. And are there others who could testify along, shall we say, the same lines?

[SHU FU *rises.*]

POLICEMAN [*whispering to* GODS]. Mr. Shu Fu—a very important person.

FIRST GOD [*inviting him to speak*]. Mr. Shu Fu!

SHU FU. Mr. Shui Ta is a businessman, my lord. Need I say more?

FIRST GOD. Yes.

SHU FU. Very well, I will. He is Vice President of the Council of Commerce and is about to be elected a Justice of the Peace. [*He returns to his seat.*]

WONG. Elected! *He gave him the job!*

[*With a gesture the* FIRST GOD *asks who* MRS. MI TZU *is.*]

POLICEMAN. Another very important person. Mrs. Mi Tzu.

FIRST GOD [*inviting her to speak*]. Mrs. Mi Tzu!

MRS. MI TZU. My lord, as Chairman of the Committee on Social Work, I wish to call attention to just a couple of eloquent facts: Mr. Shui Ta not only has erected a model factory with model housing in our city, he is a regular contributor to our home for the disabled. [*She returns to her seat.*]

POLICEMAN [*whispering*]. And she's a great friend of the judge that ate the goose!

FIRST GOD [*to the* POLICEMAN]. Oh, thank you. What next? [*To the Court, genially.*] Oh, yes. We should find out if any of the evidence is less favorable to the Defendant.

[WONG, *the* CARPENTER, *the* OLD MAN, *the* OLD WOMAN, *the* UNEMPLOYED MAN, *the* SISTER-IN-LAW, *and the* NIECE *come forward.*]

POLICEMAN [*whispering*]. Just the riff raff, my lord.

FIRST GOD [*addressing the "riff raff"*]. Well, um, riff raff—do you know anything of the Defendant, Mr. Shui Ta?

WONG. Too much, my lord.

UNEMPLOYED MAN. What don't we know, my lord?

CARPENTER. He ruined us.

SISTER-IN-LAW. He's a cheat.

NIECE. Liar.

WIFE. Thief.

BOY. Blackmailer.

BROTHER. Murderer.

FIRST GOD. Thank you. We should now let the Defendant state his point of view.

SHUI TA. I only came on the scene when Shen Te was in danger of losing what I had understood was a gift from the gods. Because I did the filthy jobs which someone had to do, they hate me. My activities were held down to the minimum, my lord.

SISTER-IN-LAW. He had us arrested!

SHUI TA. Certainly. You stole from the bakery!

SISTER-IN-LAW. Such concern for the bakery! You didn't want the shop for yourself, I suppose!

SHUI TA. I didn't want the shop overrun with parasites.

SISTER-IN-LAW. We had nowhere else to go.

SHUI TA. There were too many of you.

WONG. What about this old couple. Were *they* parasites?

OLD MAN. We lost our shop because of you!

OLD WOMAN. And we gave your cousin money!

SHUI TA. My cousin's fiancé was a flyer. The money had to go to *him*.

WONG. Did you care whether he flew or not? Did you care whether she married him or not? You wanted her to marry someone else! [*He points at* SHU FU.]

SHUI TA. The flyer unexpectedly turned out to be a scoundrel.

YANG SUN [*jumping up*]. Which was the reason you made him your Manager?

SHUI TA. Later on he improved.

WONG. And when he improved, you sold him to her? [*He points out* MRS. MI TZU.]

SHUI TA. She wouldn't let me have her premises unless she had him to stroke her knees!

MRS. MI TZU. What? The man's a pathological liar. [*To him.*] Don't mention my property to me as long as you live! Murderer! [*She rustles off, in high dudgeon.*]

YANG SUN [*pushing in*]. My lord, I wish to speak for the Defendant.

SISTER-IN-LAW. Naturally. He's your employer.

UNEMPLOYED MAN. And the worst slave driver in the country.

MRS. YANG. That's a lie! My lord, Mr. Shui Ta is a great man. He . . .

YANG SUN. He's this and he's that, but he is not a murderer, my lord. Just fifteen minutes before his arrest I heard Shen Te's voice in his own back room.

FIRST GOD. Oh? Tell us more!

YANG SUN. I heard sobbing, my lord!

FIRST GOD. But lots of women sob, we've been finding.

YANG SUN. Could I fail to recognize her voice?

5 SHU FU. No, you made her sob so often yourself, young man!

YANG SUN. Yes. But I also made her happy. Till he [*pointing at* SHUI TA] decided to sell her to you!

10 SHUI TA. Because you didn't love her.

WONG. Oh, no: it was for the money, my lord!

SHUI TA. And what was the money for, my lord? For the poor! And for Shen Te so she 15 could go on being good!

WONG. For the poor? That he sent to his sweatshops? And why didn't you let Shen Te be good when you signed the big check?

SHUI TA. For the child's sake, my lord.

20 CARPENTER. What about *my* children? What did he do about them?

[SHUI TA *is silent.*]

WONG. The shop was to be a fountain of goodness. That was the gods' idea. You came 25 and spoiled it!

SHUI TA. If I hadn't, it would have run dry!

MRS. SHIN. There's a lot in that, my lord.

WONG. What have you done with the good Shen Te, bad man? She *was* good, my lords, 30 she was, I swear it! [*He raises his hand in an oath.*]

THIRD GOD. What's happened to your hand, Water Seller?

WONG [*pointing to* SHUI TA]. It's all his 35 fault, my lord, *she* was going to send me to a doctor— [*To* SHUI TA.] You were her worst enemy!

SHUI TA. I was her only friend!

WONG. Where is she then? Tell us where 40 your good friend is!

[*The excitement of this exchange has run through the whole crowd.*]

ALL. Yes, where is she? Where is Shen Te? [*Etc.*]

45 SHUI TA. Shen Te had to go.

WONG. Where? Where to?

SHUI TA. I cannot tell you! I cannot tell you!

ALL. Why? Why did she have to go away? [*Etc.*]

WONG [*into the din with the first words, but* 50 *talking on beyond the others*]. Why not, why not? Why did she have to go away?

SHUI TA [*shouting*]. Because you'd all have torn her to shreds, that's why! My lords, I have a request. Clear the court! When only the 55 judges remain, I will make a confession.

ALL [*except* WONG, *who is silent, struck by the new turn of events*]. So he's guilty? He's confessing! [*Etc.*]

FIRST GOD [*using the gavel*]. Clear the 60 court!

POLICEMAN. Clear the court!

WONG. Mr. Shui Ta has met his match this time.

MRS. SHIN [*with a gesture toward the* 65 *judges*]. You're in for a little surprise.

[*The court is cleared. Silence.*]

SHUI TA. Illustrious ones!

[*The* GODS *look at each other, not quite believing their ears.*] 70

SHUI TA. Yes, I recognize you!

SECOND GOD [*taking matters in hand, sternly*]. What have you done with our good woman of Setzuan?

SHUI TA. I have a terrible confession to 75 make: I am she! [*He takes off his mask, and tears away his clothes.* SHEN TE *stands there.*]

SECOND GOD. Shen Te!

SHEN TE. Shen Te, yes. Shui Ta *and* Shen Te. Both. 80

Your injunction
To be good and yet to live
Was a thunderbolt:
It has torn me in two
I can't tell how it was 85
But to be good to others
And myself at the same time
I could not do it
Your world is not an easy one, illustrious
[ones! 90
When we extend our hand to a beggar, he
[tears it off for us
When we help the lost, we are lost ourselves.
And so

Since not to eat is to die
Who can long refuse to be bad?
As I lay prostrate beneath the weight of
                              [good intentions
5   Ruin stared me in the face
It was when I was unjust that I ate good
                              [meat
And hobnobbed with the mighty
Why?
10   Why are bad deeds rewarded?
Good ones punished?
I enjoy giving
I truly wished to be the Angel of the Slums
But washed by a foster-mother in the water
15   [of the gutter
I developed a sharp eye
The time came when pity was a thorn in my
                              [side
And, later, when kind words turned to ashes
20   [in my mouth
And anger took over
I became a wolf
Find me guilty, then, illustrious ones,
But know:
25   All that I have done I did
To help my neighbor
To love my lover
And to keep my little one from want
For your great, godly deeds, I was too poor,
30   [too small.
[*Pause.*]
FIRST GOD [*shocked*]. Don't go on making
yourself miserable, Shen Te! We're overjoyed
to have found you!
35   SHEN TE. I'm telling you I'm the bad man
who committed all those crimes!
FIRST GOD [*using—or failing to use—his
ear trumpet*]. The good woman who did all
those good deeds?
40   SHEN TE. Yes, but the bad man too!
FIRST GOD [*as if something had dawned*].
Unfortunate coincidences! Heartless neighbors!
THIRD GOD [*shouting in his ear*]. But how is
45   she to continue?
FIRST GOD. Continue? Well, she's a strong,
healthy girl . . .

SECOND GOD. You didn't hear what she
said!
FIRST GOD. I heard every word! She is con-   50
fused, that's all! [*He begins to bluster.*] And
what about this book of rules—we can't re-
nounce our rules, can we? [*More quietly.*]
Should the world be changed? How? By whom?
The world should *not* be changed! [*At a sign*   55
from him, the lights turn pink, and music
plays.]
And now the hour of parting is at hand.
Dost thou behold, Shen Te, yon fleecy
                              [cloud?   60
It is our chariot. At a sign from me
'Twill come and take us back to whence
                              [we came
Above the azure vault and silver stars . . .
SHEN TE. No! Don't go, illustrious ones!   65
FIRST GOD.
Our cloud has landed now in yonder field
From whence it will transport us back to
                              [heaven.
Farewell, Shen Te, let not thy courage fail   70
                              [thee . . .
[*Exeunt* GODS.]
SHEN TE. What about the old couple?
They've lost their shop! What about the Water
Seller and his hand? And I've got to defend   75
myself against the barber, because I don't love
him! And against Sun, because I do love him!
How? How?
[SHEN TE's *eyes follow the* GODS *as they are*
imagined to step into a cloud which rises and   80
moves forward over the orchestra and up be-
yond the balcony.]
FIRST GOD [*from on high*]. We have faith in
you, Shen Te!
SHEN TE. There'll be a child. And he'll have   85
to be fed. I can't stay here. Where shall I go?
FIRST GOD. Continue to be good, good
woman of Setzuan!
SHEN TE. I need my bad cousin!
FIRST GOD. But not very often!   90
SHEN TE. Once a week at least!
FIRST GOD. Once a month will be quite
enough!
SHEN TE [*shrieking*]. No, no! Help!

[*But the cloud continues to recede as the* GODS *sing.*]

Valedictory Hymn

What rapture, oh, it is to know
    A good thing when you see it
5   And having seen a good thing, oh,
    What rapture 'tis to flee it

Be good, sweet maid of Setzuan
    Let Shui Ta be clever
Departing, we forget the man
10   Remember your endeavor

Because through all the length of days
    Her goodness faileth never
Sing hallelujah! May Shen Te's
    Good name live on forever!

15   SHEN TE. Help!

Jean Giraudoux

1882–1944

The Madwoman of Chaillot

1945

To call *The Madwoman of Chaillot* a fantasy is an excellent way to recognize its playfully grotesque characterization and its casual dramatic structure. It is also an excellent way to discount the play as merely fantastic and charmingly trivial, which it is not. This "fantasy," set in "the Spring of next year," was written in Nazi-occupied Paris, and the cheerful consignment of the pointedly non-Germanic villains to a bottomless pit may be taken as a warning to collaborationists, a salute to the French underground resistance movement, and a fervent assurance of eventual liberation. But Giraudoux, who did not live to see his play produced, gave it a wider and more permanent significance.

Like George Orwell's much grimmer fantasy, *1984, The Madwoman of Chaillot* is an indelible metaphor of our society. The threat posed in the first act remains real. It is nothing short of the dehumanization of humanity. "I tell you, sir," says the President of International Substrate of Paris, Inc., "the only safeguard of order and discipline in the modern world is a standardized worker with interchangeable parts." "What would you rather have in garden," the Prospector demands, "—an almond tree or an oil well?" To the exploiters and the power-seekers the question is purely rhetorical. But the question persists and is not to be evaded by dividing the world into two camps—"ours," virtuous and free, and "theirs," vicious and enslaved. It is posed no less acutely by the glowing faith that happiness comes packaged in the latest appliance than by the promotion of totalitarian five-year plans.

Giraudoux would rather have the almond tree, and with it the vagabonds, the young lovers, and the madwomen of Paris— humanity with all its vagaries. One measure of his integrity is that he does not treat "the evil ones" as other than human beings, even when they are turning themselves and others into automatons. The President and the Prospector at their most detestable still have imagination and cynical good humor. It is because they remain at least partly human that their self-betrayal can be judged as an unforgivable betrayal.

In opposing them the mad countess is a model of sanity and benevolence. The riffraff are her steadfast allies, as are all people who innately revere life even when it is silly or humiliating. "To be alive," says the Madwoman, "is to be fortunate." And on that principle she and her companions undertake to save the world. Because "the greedy are stupid," the preparations for exterminating them leave time for the diverting conversations with which civilized people may properly occupy themselves. Giraudoux implies, however, that it is love rather more than conversation that makes civilization worth saving. The young lovers are, quite simply, what civilization is all about. Yet the amiable and happy people themselves cannot save it. It takes someone like the countess, who has suffered and has sympathy and is "mad" enough to try.

The irresistible upsurge of happiness in the final moments of the play is surely unparalleled in modern drama. When the Deaf-Mute speaks, he both echoes and fulfills the words of prophecy: "Then the eyes of the blind shall be opened, and the ears of the deaf unstopped. Then shall the lame man leap as an hart, and the tongue of the dumb sing." Even after the world has been liberated, not everything, of course, can come true. The Countess cannot retrieve the romance of her youth. The passing moment must be cherished as it passes. The revels now are ended, and the routine of living must continue. Has the liberation itself been only a blissful fantasy? The answer is that civilization has been enabled to remain human and redeemable. Very possibly it is a perennial function of the drama, through all the modes of tragedy and comedy, to keep it so.

The Madwoman of Chaillot

GIRAUDOUX

Translated by Maurice Valency

CHARACTERS

THE WAITER
THE LITTLE MAN
THE PROSPECTOR
THE PRESIDENT
THE BARON
THERESE
THE STREET SINGER
THE FLOWER GIRL
THE RAGPICKER
PAULETTE
THE DEAF-MUTE
IRMA
THE SHOELACE PEDDLER
THE BROKER
THE STREET JUGGLER
DR. JADIN
COUNTESS AURELIA   *Madwoman of Chaillot*
THE DOORMAN
THE POLICEMAN
PIERRE
THE SERGEANT
THE SEWER MAN
MME. CONSTANCE   *Madwoman of Passy*
MLLE. GABRIELLE   *Madwoman of St. Sulpice*
MME. JOSEPHINE   *Madwoman of La Concorde*

THE PRESIDENTS
THE PROSPECTORS
THE PRESS AGENTS
THE LADIES
THE ADOLPHE BERTAUTS

SCENE. *Paris.*

ACT I

[SCENE. *The café terrace at* CHEZ FRANCIS, *on the Place de l'Alma in Paris. The Alma is in the stately quarter of Paris known as Chaillot, between the Champs Elysées and the Seine,*
5 *across the river from the Eiffel Tower.*

Chez Francis has several rows of tables set out under its awning, and, as it is lunch time, a good many of them are occupied. At a table, downstage, a somewhat obvious BLONDE *with*
10 *ravishing legs is sipping a vermouth-cassis and trying hard to engage the attention of the* PROSPECTOR, *who sits at an adjacent table taking little sips of water and rolling them over his tongue with the air of a connoisseur. Down-*
15 *stage right, in front of the tables on the side-walk, is the usual Paris bench, a stout and uncomfortable affair provided by the municipality for the benefit of those who prefer to sit without drinking. A* POLICEMAN *lounges about,*
20 *keeping the peace without unnecessary exertion.*

TIME. *It is a little before noon in the Spring of next year.*]

[AT RISE. THE PRESIDENT *and* THE BARON *enter*
25 *with importance, and are ushered to a front table by* THE WAITER.]

THE PRESIDENT. Baron, sit down. This is a historic occasion. It must be properly celebrated. The waiter is going to bring out my
30 special port.

THE BARON. Splendid.

THE PRESIDENT [*offers his cigar case*]. Cigar? My private brand.

THE BARON. Thank you. You know, this all
35 gives me the feeling of one of those enchanted mornings in the *Arabian Nights* when thieves foregather in the market place. Thieves—pashas . . .

[*He sniffs the cigar judiciously, and begins lighting it.*] 40

THE PRESIDENT [*chuckles*]. Tell me about yourself.

THE BARON. Well, where shall I begin?

[THE STREET SINGER *enters. He takes off a battered black felt with a flourish and begins* 45 *singing an ancient mazurka.*]

STREET SINGER [*sings*].
Do you hear, Mademoiselle,
Those musicians of hell!

THE PRESIDENT. Waiter! Get rid of that man. 50

WAITER. He is singing *La Belle Polonaise.*

THE PRESIDENT. I didn't ask for the program. I asked you to get rid of him. [THE WAITER *doesn't budge.* THE SINGER *goes by himself.*] As you were saying, Baron . . . ? 55

THE BARON. Well, until I was fifty . . . [THE FLOWER GIRL *enters through the café door, center*] my life was relatively uncomplicated. It consisted of selling off one by one the various estates left me by my father. Three years ago, 60 I parted with my last farm. Two years ago, I lost my last mistress. And now—all that is left me is . . .

THE FLOWER GIRL [*to* THE BARON]. Violets, sir? 65

THE PRESIDENT. Run along.

[THE FLOWER GIRL *moves on.*]

THE BARON [*staring after her*]. So that, in short, all I have left now is my name.

THE PRESIDENT. Your name is precisely the 70 name we need on our board of directors.

THE BARON [*with an inclination of his head*]. Very flattering.

THE PRESIDENT. You will understand when I tell you that mine has been a very different 75 experience. I came up from the bottom. My mother spent most of her life bent over a wash-tub in order to send me to school. I'm eternally grateful to her, of course, but I must confess that I no longer remember her face. It was no 80 doubt beautiful—but when I try to recall it, I see only the part she invariably showed me —her rear.

THE BARON. Very touching.

THE PRESIDENT. When I was thrown out of 85 school for the fifth and last time, I decided to

find out for myself what makes the world go round. I ran errands for an editor, a movie star, a financier. . . . I began to understand a little what life is. Then, one day, in the sub-
5 way, I saw a face. . . . My rise in life dates from that day.

THE BARON. Really?

THE PRESIDENT. One look at that face, and I knew. One look at mine, and he knew. And
10 so I made my first thousand—passing a boxful of counterfeit notes. A year later, I saw another such face. It got me a nice berth in the narcotics business. Since then, all I do is to look out for such faces. And now here I am—president of
15 eleven corporations, director of fifty-two companies, and, beginning today, chairman of the board of the international combine in which you have been so good as to accept a post. [THE RAGPICKER passes, sees something under
20 THE PRESIDENT's table, and stoops to pick it up.] Looking for something?

THE RAGPICKER. Did you drop this?

THE PRESIDENT. I never drop anything.

THE RAGPICKER. Then this hundred-franc
25 note isn't yours?

THE PRESIDENT. Give it here.

[THE RAGPICKER gives him the note, and goes out.]

THE BARON. Are you sure it's yours?
30 THE PRESIDENT. All hundred-franc notes, Baron, are mine.

THE BARON. Mr. President, there's something I've been wanting to ask you. What exactly is the purpose of our new company? Or is that
35 an indiscreet question . . . ?

THE PRESIDENT. Indiscreet? Not a bit. Merely unusual. As far as I know, you're the first member of a board of directors ever to ask such a question.
40 THE BARON. Do we plan to exploit a commodity? A utility?

THE PRESIDENT. My dear sir, I haven't the faintest idea.

THE BARON. But if you don't know—who
45 does?

THE PRESIDENT. Nobody. And at the moment, it's becoming just a trifle embarrassing. Yes, my dear Baron, since we are now close business associates, I must confess that for the time being we're in a little trouble.
50

THE BARON. I was afraid of that. The stock issue isn't going well?

THE PRESIDENT. No, no—on the contrary. The stock issue is going beautifully. Yesterday morning at ten o'clock we offered 500,000
55 shares to the general public. By 10:05 they were all snapped up at par. By 10:20, when the police finally arrived, our offices were a shambles. . . . Windows smashed—doors torn off their hinges—you never saw anything so
60 beautiful in your life! And this morning our stock is being quoted over the counter at 124 with no sellers, and the orders are still pouring in.

THE BARON. But in that case—what is the
65 trouble?

THE PRESIDENT. The trouble is we have a tremendous capital, and not the slightest idea of what to do with it.

THE BARON. You mean all those people are
70 fighting to buy stock in a company that has no object?

THE PRESIDENT. My dear Baron, do you imagine that when a subscriber buys a share of stock, he has any idea of getting behind a
75 counter or digging a ditch? A stock certificate is not a tool, like a shovel, or a commodity, like a pound of cheese. What we sell a customer is not a share in a business, but a view of the Elysian Fields. A financier is a creative artist.
80 Our function is to stimulate the imagination. We are poets!

THE BARON. But in order to stimulate the imagination, don't you need some field of activity?
85

THE PRESIDENT. Not at all. What you need for that is a name. A name that will stir the pulse like a trumpet call, set the brain awhirl like a movie star, inspire reverence like a cathedral. *United General International Con-*
90 *solidated!* Of course that's been used. That's what a corporation needs.

THE BARON. And do we have such a name?

THE PRESIDENT. So far we have only a blank space. In that blank space a name must be
95 printed. This name must be a masterpiece. And

if I seem a little nervous today, it's because—
somehow—I've racked my brains, but it hasn't
come to me. Oho! Look at that! Just like the
answer to a prayer . . . ! [THE BARON *turns and*
5 *stares in the direction of* THE PROSPECTOR.] You
see? There's one. And what a beauty!

THE BARON. You mean that girl?

THE PRESIDENT. No, no, not the girl. That
face. You see . . . ? The one that's drinking
10 water.

THE BARON. You call that a face? That's a
tombstone.

THE PRESIDENT. It's a milestone. It's a sign-
post. But is it pointing the way to steel, or
15 wheat, or phosphates? That's what we have
to find out. Ah! He sees me. He understands.
He will be over.

THE BARON. And when he comes . . . ?

THE PRESIDENT. He will tell me what to do.

20 THE BARON. You mean business is done this
way? You mean, you would trust a stranger
with a matter of this importance?

THE PRESIDENT. Baron, I trust neither my
wife, nor my daughter, nor my closest friend.
25 My confidential secretary has no idea where I
live. But a face like that I would trust with my
inmost secrets. Though we have never laid
eyes on each other before, that man and I
know each other to the depths of our souls.
30 He's no stranger—he's my brother, he's myself. You'll see. He'll be over in a minute. [THE
DEAF-MUTE *enters and passes slowly among
the tables, placing a small envelope before each
customer. He comes to* THE PRESIDENT's *table.*]
35 What is this anyway? A conspiracy? We don't
want your envelopes. Take them away. [THE
DEAF-MUTE *makes a short but pointed speech
in sign language.*] Waiter, what the devil's he
saying?

40 WAITER. Only Irma understands him.

THE PRESIDENT. Irma? Who's Irma?

WAITER [*calls*]. Irma! It's the waitress inside,
sir. Irma!

[IRMA *comes out. She is twenty. She has the
45 face and figure of an angel.*]

IRMA. Yes?

WAITER. These gentlemen would . . .

THE PRESIDENT. Tell this fellow to get out of

here, for God's sake! [THE DEAF-MUTE *makes
another manual oration.*] What's he trying to 50
say, anyway?

IRMA. He says it's an exceptionally beautiful
morning, sir . . .

THE PRESIDENT. Who asked him?

IRMA. But, he says, it was nicer before the 55
gentleman stuck his face in it.

THE PRESIDENT. Call the manager!

[IRMA *shrugs. She goes back into the restaurant.* THE DEAF-MUTE *walks off, left. Meanwhile a* SHOELACE PEDDLER *has arrived.*] 60

PEDDLER. Shoelaces? Postcards?

THE BARON. I think I could use a shoelace.

THE PRESIDENT. No, no . . .

PEDDLER. Black? Tan?

THE BARON [*showing his shoes*]. What 65
would you recommend?

PEDDLER. Anybody's guess.

THE BARON. Well, give me one of each.

THE PRESIDENT [*putting a hand on* THE
BARON's *arm*]. Baron, although I am your chair- 70
man, I have no authority over your personal
life—none, that is, except to fix the amount
of your director's fees, and eventually to assign
a motor car for your use. Therefore, I am asking you, as a personal favor to me, not to 75
purchase anything from this fellow.

THE BARON. How can I resist so gracious a
request? [THE PEDDLER *shrugs, and passes on.*]
But I really don't understand. . . . What difference would it make? 80

THE PRESIDENT. Look here, Baron. Now that
you're with us, you must understand that between this irresponsible riffraff and us there
is an impenetrable barrier. *We* have no deal-
ings whatever with *them.* 85

THE BARON. But without us, the poor devil
will starve.

THE PRESIDENT. No, he won't. He expects
nothing from us. He has a clientele of his own.
He sells shoelaces exclusively to those who 90
have no shoes. Just as the necktie peddler sells
only to those who wear no shirts. And that's
why these street hawkers can afford to be insolent, disrespectful and independent. They
don't need us. They have a world of their own. 95
Ah! My broker. Splendid. He's beaming.

[THE BROKER *walks up and grasps* THE PRESI- DENT'S *hand with enthusiasm.*]

BROKER. Mr. President! My heartiest con- gratulations! What a day! What a day!

[THE STREET JUGGLER *appears, right. He re- moves his coat, folds it carefully, and puts it on the bench. Then he opens a suitcase, from which he extracts a number of colored clubs.*]

THE PRESIDENT [*presenting* THE BROKER]. Baron Tommard, of our Board of Directors. My broker. [THE BROKER *bows. So does* THE JUGGLER. THE BROKER *sits down and signals for a drink.* THE JUGGLER *prepares to juggle.*] What's happened?

BROKER. Listen to this. Ten o'clock this morn- ing. The market opens. [*As he speaks,* THE JUGGLER *provides a visual counterpart to* THE BROKER'S *lines, his clubs rising and falling in rhythm to* THE BROKER'S *words.*] Half million shares issued at par, par value a hundred, quoted on the curb at 124 and we start buying at 126, 127, 129—and it's going up—up—up— [THE JUGGLER'S *clubs rise higher and higher.*]— 132—133—138—141—141—141—141 . . .

THE BARON. May I ask . . . ?

THE PRESIDENT. No, no—any explanation would only confuse you.

BROKER. Ten forty-five we start selling short on rumors of a Communist plot, market bearish. . . . 141—138—133—132—and it's down— down—down—102—and we start buying back at 93. Eleven o'clock, rumors denied—95—98 —101—106—124—141—and by 11:30 we've got it all back—net profit three and a half mil- lion francs.

THE PRESIDENT. Classical. Pure. [THE JUGGLER *bows again. A* LITTLE MAN *leans over from a near-by table, listening intently, and trembling with excitement.*] And how many shares do we reserve to each member of the board?

BROKER. Fifty, as agreed.

THE PRESIDENT. Bit stingy, don't you think?

BROKER. All right—three thousand.

THE PRESIDENT. That's a little better. [*To* THE BARON.] You get the idea?

THE BARON. I'm beginning to get it.

BROKER. And now we come to the exciting part . . . [THE JUGGLER *prepares to juggle with balls of fire.*] Listen carefully: With 35 percent of our funded capital under Section 32 I buy 50,000 United at 36 which I immediately re- convert into 32,000 National Amalgamated two's preferred which I set up as collateral on 150,000 General Consols which I deposit against a credit of fifteen billion to buy Eastern Hen- nequin which I immediately turn into Argen- tine wheat realizing 136 percent of the original investment which naturally accrues as capital gain and not as corporate income thus saving twelve millions in taxes, and at once convert the 25 percent cotton reserve into lignite, and as our people swing into action in London and New York, I beat up the price on greige goods from 26 to 92—114—203—306—[THE JUGGLER *by now is juggling his fireballs in the sky. The balls no longer return to his hands*]—404 . . .

[THE LITTLE MAN *can stand no more. He rushes over and dumps a sackful of money on the table.*]

LITTLE MAN. Here—take it—please, take it!

BROKER [*frigidly*]. Who is this man? What is this money?

LITTLE MAN. It's my life's savings. Every cent. I put it all in your hands.

BROKER. Can't you see we're busy?

LITTLE MAN. But I beg you. . . . It's my only chance. . . . Please don't turn me away.

BROKER. Oh, all right. [*He sweeps the money into his pocket.*] Well?

LITTLE MAN. I thought—perhaps you'd give me a little receipt. . . .

THE PRESIDENT. My dear man, people like us don't give receipts for money. We take them.

LITTLE MAN. Oh, pardon. Of course. I was confused. Here it is. [*Scribbles a receipt.*] Thank you—thank you—thank you.

[*He rushes off joyfully.* THE STREET SINGER *reappears.*]

STREET SINGER [*sings*].
Do you hear, Mademoiselle,
Those musicians of hell!

THE PRESIDENT. What, again? Why does he keep repeating those two lines like a parrot?

WAITER. What else can he do? He doesn't know any more and the song's been out of print for years.

THE BARON. Couldn't he sing a song he knows?

WAITER. He likes this one. He hopes if he keeps singing the beginning someone will turn
5 up to teach him the end.

THE PRESIDENT. Tell him to move on. We don't know the song.

[THE PROFESSOR *strolls by, swinging his cane. He overhears.*]
10 PROFESSOR [*stops and addresses* THE PRESIDENT *politely*]. Nor do I, my dear sir. Nor do I. And yet, I'm in exactly the same predicament. I remember just two lines of my favorite song, as a child. A mazurka also, in case you're
15 interested. . . .

THE PRESIDENT. I'm not.

PROFESSOR. Why is it, I wonder, that one always forgets the words of a mazurka? I suppose they just get lost in that damnable rhy-
20 thm. All I remember is: [*He sings.*]

From England to Spain
I have drunk, it was bliss . . .

STREET SINGER [*walks over, and picks up the tune*].
25 Red wine and champagne
And many a kiss.

PROFESSOR. Oh, God! It all comes back to me . . . ! [*He sings.*]

Red lips and white hands I have known
30 Where the nightingales dwell. . . .

THE PRESIDENT [*holding his hands to his ears*]. Please—please . . .

STREET SINGER.
And to each one I've whispered, "My own,"
35 And to each one I've murmured: "Farewell."

THE PRESIDENT. Farewell. Farewell.

STREET SINGER, PROFESSOR [*duo*].
But there's one I shall never forget. . . .

THE PRESIDENT. This isn't a café. It's a circus!
40 [*The two go off, still singing: "There is one that's engraved in my heart." THE PROSPECTOR gets up slowly and walks toward THE PRESIDENT's table. He looks down without a word. There is a tense silence.*]
45 PROSPECTOR. Well?

THE PRESIDENT. I need a name.

PROSPECTOR [*nods, with complete comprehension*]. I need fifty thousand.

THE PRESIDENT. For a corporation.

PROSPECTOR. For a woman. 50

THE PRESIDENT. Immediately.

PROSPECTOR. Before evening.

THE PRESIDENT. Something . . .

PROSPECTOR. Unusual?

THE PRESIDENT. Something . . . 55

PROSPECTOR. Provocative?

THE PRESIDENT. Something . . .

PROSPECTOR. Practical.

THE PRESIDENT. Yes.

PROSPECTOR. Fifty thousand. Cash. 60

THE PRESIDENT. I'm listening.

PROSPECTOR. *International Substrate of Paris, Inc.*

THE PRESIDENT [*snaps his fingers*]. That's it! [*To* THE BROKER.] Pay him off. [THE BROKER 65 *pays with* THE LITTLE MAN's *money*.] Now— what does it mean?

PROSPECTOR. It means what it says. I'm a prospector.

THE PRESIDENT [*rises*]. A prospector! Allow 70 me to shake your hand. Baron, you are in the presence of one of nature's noblemen. Shake his hand. This is Baron Tommard. [*They shake hands.*] It is this man, my dear Baron, who smells out in the bowels of the earth those 75 deposits of metal or liquid on which can be founded the only social unit of which our age is capable—the corporation. Sit down, please. [*They all sit.*] And now that we have a name . . . 80

PROSPECTOR. You need a property.

THE PRESIDENT. Precisely.

PROSPECTOR. I have one.

THE PRESIDENT. A claim?

PROSPECTOR. Terrific. 85

THE PRESIDENT. Foreign?

PROSPECTOR. French.

THE BARON. In Indo-China?

BROKER. Morocco?

THE PRESIDENT. In France? 90

PROSPECTOR [*matter of fact*]. In Paris.

THE PRESIDENT. In Paris? You've been prospecting in Paris?

THE BARON. For women, no doubt.

THE PRESIDENT. For art? 95

BROKER. For gold?

PROSPECTOR. Oil.

BROKER. He's crazy.

THE PRESIDENT. Sh! He's inspired.

PROSPECTOR. You think I'm crazy. Well, they
5 thought Columbus was crazy.

THE BARON. Oil in Paris?

BROKER. But how is it possible?

PROSPECTOR. It's not only possible. It's
certain.

10 THE PRESIDENT. Tell us.

PROSPECTOR. You don't know, my dear sir,
what treasures Paris conceals. Paris is the least
prospected place in the world. We've gone
over the rest of the planet with a fine-tooth
15 comb. But has anyone ever thought of looking
for oil in Paris? Nobody. Before me, that is.

THE PRESIDENT. Genius!

PROSPECTOR. No. Just a practical man. I use
my head.

20 THE BARON. But why has nobody ever
thought of this before?

PROSPECTOR. The treasures of the earth, my
dear sir, are not easy to find nor to get at.
They are invariably guarded by dragons.
25 Doubtless there is some reason for this. For
once we've dug out and consumed the internal
ballast of the planet, the chances are it will
shoot off on some irresponsible tangent and
smash itself up in the sky. Well, that's the risk
30 we take. Anyway, that's not my business. A
prospector has enough to worry about.

THE BARON. I know—snakes—tarantulas—
fleas . . .

PROSPECTOR. Worse than that, sir. Civiliza-
35 tion.

THE PRESIDENT. Does that annoy you?

PROSPECTOR. Civilization gets in our way all
the time. In the first place, it covers the earth
with cities and towns which are damned
40 awkward to dig up when you want to see
what's underneath. It's not only the real-estate
people—you can always do business with
them—it's human sentimentality. How do you
do business with that?

45 THE PRESIDENT. I see what you mean.

PROSPECTOR. They say that where we pass,
nothing ever grows again. What of it? Is a
park any better than a coal mine? What's a

mountain got that a slag pile hasn't? What
would you rather have in your garden—an al- 50
mond tree or an oil well?

THE PRESIDENT. Well . . .

PROSPECTOR. Exactly. But what's the use of
arguing with these fools? Imagine the choicest
place you ever saw for an excavation, and 55
what do they put there? A playground for
children! Civilization!

THE PRESIDENT. Just show us the point where
you want to start digging. We'll do the rest.
Even if it's in the middle of the Louvre. Where's 60
the oil?

PROSPECTOR. Perhaps you think it's easy to
make an accurate fix in an area like Paris where
everything conspires to put you off the scent?
Women—perfume—flowers—history. You can 65
talk all you like about geology, but an oil
deposit, gentlemen, has to be smelled out. I
have a good nose. I go further. I have a phenomenal nose. But the minute I get the right
whiff—the minute I'm on the scent—a fra- 70
grance rises from what I take to be the spiritual
deposits of the past—and I'm completely at
sea. Now take this very point, for example,
this very spot.

THE BARON. You mean—right here in Chail- 75
lot?

PROSPECTOR. Right under here.

THE PRESIDENT. Good heavens!

[He looks under his chair.]

PROSPECTOR. It's taken me months to locate 80
the spot.

THE BARON. But what in the world makes
you think . . . ?

PROSPECTOR. Do you know this place, Baron?

THE BARON. Well, I've been sitting here for 85
thirty years.

PROSPECTOR. Did you ever taste the water?

THE BARON. The water? Good God, no!

PROSPECTOR. It's plain to see that you are no
prospector! A prospector, Baron, is addicted to 90
water as a drunkard to wine. Water, gentlemen, is the one substance from which the earth
can conceal nothing. It sucks out its innermost
secrets and brings them to our very lips. Well
—beginning at Notre Dame, where I first 95
caught the scent of oil three months ago, I

worked my way across Paris, glassful by glassful, sampling the water, until at last I came to
this café. And here—just two days ago—I took
a sip. My heart began to thump. Was it pos-
5 sible that I was deceived? I took another, a
third, a fourth, a fifth. I was trembling like a
leaf. But there was no mistake. Each time that
I drank, my taste-buds thrilled to the most
exquisite flavor known to a prospector—the
10 flavor of—[*with utmost lyricism*] Petroleum!

THE PRESIDENT. Waiter! Some water and four
glasses. Hurry. This round, gentlemen, is on
me. And as a toast—I shall propose International Substrate of Paris, Incorporated. [THE
15 WAITER *brings a decanter and the glasses.* THE
PRESIDENT *pours out the water amid profound
silence. They taste it with the air of connois-
seurs savoring something that has never before
passed human lips. Then they look at each
20 other doubtfully.* THE PROSPECTOR *pours himself a second glass and drinks it off.*] Well . . .

BROKER. Ye-es . . .

THE BARON. Mm . . .

PROSPECTOR. Get it?

25 THE BARON. Tastes queer.

PROSPECTOR. That's it. To the unpracticed
palate it tastes queer. But to the taste-buds of
the expert—ah!

THE BARON. Still, there's one thing I don't
30 quite understand . . .

PROSPECTOR. Yes?

THE BARON. This café doesn't have its own
well, does it?

PROSPECTOR. Of course not. This is Paris
35 water.

BROKER. Then why should it taste different
here than anywhere else?

PROSPECTOR. Because, my dear sir, the pipes
that carry this water pass deep through the
40 earth, and the earth just here is soaked with
oil, and this oil permeates the pores of the iron
and flavors the water it carries. Ever so little,
yes—but quite enough to betray its presence
to the sensitive tongue of the specialist.

45 THE BARON. I see.

PROSPECTOR. I don't say everyone is capable
of tasting it. No. But I—I can detect the presence of oil in water that has passed within

fifteen miles of a deposit. Under special circumstances, twenty. 50

THE PRESIDENT. Phenomenal!

PROSPECTOR. And so here I am with the
greatest discovery of the age on my hands—
but the blasted authorities won't let me drill
a single well unless I show them the oil! Now 55
how can I show them the oil unless they let me
dig? Completely stymied! Eh?

THE PRESIDENT. What? A man like you?

PROSPECTOR. That's what they think. That's
what they want. Have you noticed the strange 60
glamor of the women this morning? And the
quality of the sunshine? And this extraordinary
convocation of vagabonds buzzing about pro-
tectively like bees around a hive? Do you know
why it is? Because they know. It's a plot to 65
distract us, to turn us from our purpose. Well,
let them try. I know there's oil here. And I'm
going to dig it up, even if I . . . [*he smiles*].
Shall I tell you my little plan?

THE PRESIDENT. By all means. 70

PROSPECTOR. Well. . . . For heaven's sake,
what's that?

[*At this point,* THE MADWOMAN *enters. She
is dressed in the grand fashion of 1885, a taffeta skirt with an immense train—which she 75
has gathered up by means of a clothespin—
ancient button shoes, and a hat in the style of
Marie Antoinette. She wears a lorgnette on a
chain, and an enormous cameo pin at her
throat. In her hand she carries a small basket. 80
She walks in with great dignity, extracts a dinner bell from the bosom of her dress, and rings
it sharply.* IRMA *appears.*]

COUNTESS. Are my bones ready, Irma?

IRMA. There won't be much today, Countess. 85
We had broilers. Can you wait? While the
gentleman inside finishes eating?

COUNTESS. And my gizzard?

IRMA. I'll try to get it away from him.

COUNTESS. If he eats my gizzard, save me 90
the giblets. They will do for the tomcat that
lives under the bridge. He likes a few giblets
now and again.

IRMA. Yes, Countess.

[IRMA *goes back into the café.* THE COUNTESS 95
takes a few steps and stops in front of THE

PRESIDENT's *table. She examines him with undisguised disapproval.*]

THE PRESIDENT. Waiter. Ask that woman to move on.

WAITER. Sorry, sir. This is her café.

THE PRESIDENT. Is she the manager of the café?

WAITER. She's the Madwoman of Chaillot.

THE PRESIDENT. A Madwoman? She's mad?

WAITER. Who says she's mad?

THE PRESIDENT. You just said so yourself.

WAITER. Look, sir. You asked me who she was. And I told you. What's mad about her? She's the Madwoman of Chaillot.

THE PRESIDENT. Call a policeman.

[THE COUNTESS *whistles through her fingers. At once,* THE DOORMAN *runs out of the café. He has three scarves in his hands.*]

COUNTESS. Have you found it? My feather boa?

DOORMAN. Not yet, Countess. Three scarves. But no boa.

COUNTESS. It's five years since I lost it. Surely you've had time to find it.

DOORMAN. Take one of these, Countess. Nobody's claimed them.

COUNTESS. A boa like that doesn't vanish, you know. A feather boa nine feet long!

DOORMAN. How about this blue one?

COUNTESS. With my pink ruffle and my green veil? You're joking! Let me see the yellow. [*She tries it on.*] How does it look?

DOORMAN. Terrific.

[*With a magnificent gesture, she flings the scarf about her, upsetting* THE PRESIDENT's *glass and drenching his trousers with water. She stalks off without a glance at him.*]

THE PRESIDENT. Waiter! I'm making a complaint.

WAITER. Against whom?

THE PRESIDENT. Against her! Against you! The whole gang of you! That singer! That shoelace peddler! That female lunatic! Or whatever you call her!

THE BARON. Calm yourself, Mr. President. . . .

THE PRESIDENT. I'll do nothing of the sort! Baron, the first thing we have to do is to get rid of these people! Good heavens, look at them! Every size, shape, color and period of history imaginable. It's utter anarchy! I tell you, sir, the only safeguard of order and discipline in the modern world is a standardized worker with interchangeable parts. That would solve the entire problem of management. Here, the manager. . . . And there—one composite drudge grunting and sweating all over the world. Just we two. Ah, how beautiful! How easy on the eyes! How restful for the conscience!

THE BARON. Yes, yes—of course.

THE PRESIDENT. Order. Symmetry. Balance. But instead of that, what? Here in Chaillot, the very citadel of management, these insolent phantoms of the past come to beard us with their raffish individualism—with the right of the voiceless to sing, of the dumb to make speech, of trousers to have no seats and bosoms to have dinner bells!

THE BARON. But, after all, do these people matter?

THE PRESIDENT. My dear sir, wherever the poor are happy, and the servants are proud, and the mad are respected, our power is at an end. Look at that. That waiter! That madwoman! That flower girl! Do I get that sort of service? And suppose that I—president of twelve corporations and ten times a millionaire—were to stick a gladiolus in my buttonhole and start yelling— [*He tinkles his spoon in a glass violently, yelling.*] Are my bones ready, Irma?

THE BARON [*reprovingly*]. Mr. President . . .

[*People at the adjoining tables turn and stare with raised eyebrows.* THE WAITER *starts to come over.*]

THE PRESIDENT. You see? Now.

PROSPECTOR. We were discussing my plan.

THE PRESIDENT. Ah yes, your plan. [*He glances in the direction of* THE MADWOMAN's *table.*] Careful—she's looking at us.

PROSPECTOR. Do you know what a bomb is?

THE PRESIDENT. I'm told they explode.

PROSPECTOR. Exactly. You see that white building across the river. Do you happen to know what that is?

THE PRESIDENT. I do not.

PROSPECTOR. That's the office of the City

Architect. That man has stubbornly refused to give me a permit to drill for oil anywhere within the limits of the city of Paris. I've tried everything with him—influence, bribes, threats. He says I'm crazy. And now . . .

THE PRESIDENT. Oh, my God! What is this one trying to sell us? [*A little old man enters left, and doffs his hat politely. He is somewhat ostentatiously respectable—gloved, pomaded, and carefully dressed, with a white handkerchief peeping out of his breast pocket.*]

DR. JADIN. Nothing but health, sir. Or rather the health of the feet. But remember—as the foot goes, so goes the man. May I present myself . . . ? Dr. Gaspard Jadin, French Navy, retired. Former specialist in the extraction of ticks and chiggers. At present specializing in the extraction of bunions and corns. In case of sudden emergency, Martial ·the waiter will furnish my home address. My office is here, second row, third table, week days, twelve to five. Thank you very much.

[*He sits at his table.*]

WAITER. Your vermouth, Doctor?

DR. JADIN. My vermouth. My vermouths. How are your gallstones today, Martial?

WAITER. Fine. Fine. They rattle like anything.

DR. JADIN. Splendid. [*He spies* THE COUNTESS.] Good morning, Countess. How's the floating kidney? Still afloat? [*She nods graciously.*] Splendid. Splendid. So long as it floats, it can't sink.

THE PRESIDENT. This is impossible! Let's go somewhere else.

PROSPECTOR. No. It's nearly noon.

THE PRESIDENT. Yes. It is. Five to twelve.

PROSPECTOR. In five minutes' time you're going to see that City Architect blown up, building and all—boom!

BROKER. Are you serious?

PROSPECTOR. That imbecile has no one to blame but himself. Yesterday noon, he got my ultimatum—he's had twenty-four hours to think it over. No permit? All right. Within two minutes my agent is going to drop a little package in his coal bin. And three minutes after that, precisely at noon . . .

THE BARON. You prospectors certainly use modern methods.

PROSPECTOR. The method may be modern. But the idea is old. To get at the treasure, it has always been necessary to slay the dragon. I guarantee that after this, the City Architect will be more reasonable. The new one, I mean.

THE PRESIDENT. Don't you think we're sitting a little close for comfort?

PROSPECTOR. Oh no, no. Don't worry. And, above all, don't stare. We may be watched. [*A clock strikes.*] Why, that's noon. Something's wrong! Good God! What's this? [*A* POLICEMAN *staggers in bearing a lifeless body on his shoulders in the manner prescribed as "The Fireman's Lift."*] It's Pierre! My agent! [*He walks over with affected nonchalance.*] I say, Officer, what's that you've got?

POLICEMAN. Drowned man.

[*He puts him down on the bench.*]

WAITER. He's not drowned. His clothes are dry. He's been slugged.

POLICEMAN. Slugged is also correct. He was just jumping off the bridge when I came along and pulled him back. I slugged him, naturally, so he wouldn't drag me under. Life Saving Manual Rule 5: "In cases where there is danger of being dragged under, it is necessary to render the subject unconscious by means of a sharp blow." He's had that.

[*He loosens the clothes and begins applying artificial respiration.*]

PROSPECTOR. The stupid idiot! What the devil did he do with the bomb? That's what comes of employing amateurs!

THE PRESIDENT. You don't think he'll give you away?

PROSPECTOR. Don't worry. [*He walks over to the policeman.*] Say, what do you think you're doing?

POLICEMAN. Lifesaving. Artificial respiration. First aid to the drowning.

PROSPECTOR. But he's not drowning.

POLICEMAN. But he thinks he is.

PROSPECTOR. You'll never bring him round that way, my friend. That's meant for people who drown in water. It's not good at all for those who drown without water.

POLICEMAN. What am I supposed to do? I've just been sworn in. It's my first day on the beat. I can't afford to get in trouble. I've got to go by the book.

PROSPECTOR. Perfectly simple. Take him back to the bridge where you found him and throw him in. Then you can save his life and you'll get a medal. This way, you'll get fined for slugging an innocent man.

POLICEMAN. What do you mean, innocent? He was just going to jump when I grabbed him.

PROSPECTOR. Have you any proof of that?

POLICEMAN. Well, I saw him.

PROSPECTOR. Written proof? Witnesses?

POLICEMAN. No, but . . .

PROSPECTOR. Then don't waste time arguing. You're in trouble. Quick—before anybody notices—throw him in and dive after him. It's the only way out.

POLICEMAN. But I don't swim.

THE PRESIDENT. You'll learn how on the way down. Before you were born, did you know how to breathe?

POLICEMAN [convinced]. All right. Here we go.

[He starts lifting the body.]

DR. JADIN. One moment, please. I don't like to interfere, but it's my professional duty to point out that medical science has definitely established the fact of intra-uterine respiration. Consequently, this policeman, even before he was born, knew not only how to breathe but also how to cough, hiccup and belch.

THE PRESIDENT. Suppose he did—how does it concern you?

DR. JADIN. On the other hand, medical science has never established the fact of intra-uterine swimming or diving. Under the circumstances, we are forced to the opinion, Officer, that if you dive in you will probably drown.

POLICEMAN. You think so?

PROSPECTOR. Who asked you for an opinion?

THE PRESIDENT. Pay no attention to that quack, Officer.

DR. JADIN. Quack, sir?

PROSPECTOR. This is not a medical matter. It's a legal problem. The officer has made a grave error. He's new. We're trying to help him.

BROKER. He's probably afraid of the water.

POLICEMAN. Nothing of the sort. Officially, I'm afraid of nothing. But I always follow doctor's orders.

DR. JADIN. You see, Officer, when a child is born . . .

PROSPECTOR. Now, what does he care about when a child is born? He's got a dying man on his hands. . . . Officer, if you want my advice . . .

POLICEMAN. It so happens, I care a lot about when a child is born. It's part of my duty to aid and assist any woman in childbirth or labor.

THE PRESIDENT. Can you imagine!

POLICEMAN. Is it true, Doctor, what they say, that when you have twins, the first born is considered to be the youngest?

DR. JADIN. Quite correct. And what's more, if the twins happen to be born at midnight on December 31st, the older is a whole year younger. He does his military service a year later. That's why you have to keep your eyes open. And that's the reason why a queen always gives birth before witnesses. . . .

POLICEMAN. God! The things a policeman is supposed to know! Doctor, what does it mean if, when I get up in the morning sometimes . . .

PROSPECTOR [nudging THE PRESIDENT meaningfully]. The old woman . . .

BROKER. Come on, Baron.

THE PRESIDENT. I think we'd better all run along.

PROSPECTOR. Leave him to me.

THE PRESIDENT. I'll see you later.

[THE PRESIDENT steals off with THE BROKER and THE BARON.]

POLICEMAN [still in conference with DR. JADIN]. But what's really worrying me, Doctor, is this—don't you think it's a bit risky for a man to marry after forty-five?

[THE BROKER runs in breathlessly.]

BROKER. Officer! Officer!

POLICEMAN. What's the trouble?

BROKER. Quick! Two women are calling for help—on the sidewalk—Avenue Wilson!

POLICEMAN. Two women at once? Standing up or lying down?

BROKER. You'd better go and see. Quick!

PROSPECTOR. You'd better take the Doctor with you.

POLICEMAN. Come along, Doctor, come along. . . . [*Pointing to* PIERRE.] Tell him to wait till I get back. Come along, Doctor.

[*He runs out,* THE DOCTOR *following.* THE PROSPECTOR *moves over toward* PIERRE, *but* IRMA *crosses in front of him and takes the boy's hand.*]

IRMA. How beautiful he is! Is he dead, Martial?

WAITER [*handing her a pocket mirror*]. Hold this mirror to his mouth. If it clouds over . . .

IRMA. It clouds over.

WAITER. He's alive.

[*He holds out his hand for the mirror.*]

IRMA. Just a sec— [*She rubs it clean and looks at herself intently. Before handing it back, she fixes her hair and applies her lipstick. Meanwhile* THE PROSPECTOR *tries to get around the other side, but* THE COUNTESS' *eagle eye drives him off. He shrugs his shoulders and exits with* THE BARON.] Oh, look—he's opened his eyes!

[PIERRE *opens his eyes, stares intently at* IRMA *and closes them again with the expression of a man who is among the angels.*]

PIERRE [*murmurs*]. Oh! How beautiful!

VOICE [*from within the café*]. Irma!

IRMA. Coming. Coming.

[*She goes in, not without a certain reluctance.* THE COUNTESS *at once takes her place on the bench, and also the young man's hand.* PIERRE *sits up suddenly, and finds himself staring, not at* IRMA, *but into the very peculiar face of* THE COUNTESS. *His expression changes.*]

COUNTESS. You're looking at my iris? Isn't it beautiful?

PIERRE. Very.

[*He drops back, exhausted.*]

COUNTESS. The Sergeant was good enough to say it becomes me. But I no longer trust his taste. Yesterday, the flower girl gave me a lily, and he said it didn't suit me.

PIERRE [*weakly*]. It's beautiful.

COUNTESS. He'll be very happy to know that you agree with him. He's really quite sensitive. [*She calls.*] Sergeant!

PIERRE. No, please—don't call the police.

COUNTESS. But I must. I think I hurt his feelings.

PIERRE. Let me go, Madame.

COUNTESS. No, no. Stay where you are. Sergeant!

[PIERRE *struggles weakly to get up.*]

PIERRE. Please let me go.

COUNTESS. I'll do nothing of the sort. When you let someone go, you never see him again. I let Charlotte Mazumet go. I never saw her again.

PIERRE. Oh, my head.

COUNTESS. I let Adolphe Bertaut go. And I was holding him. And I never saw him again.

PIERRE. Oh, God!

COUNTESS. Except once. Thirty years later. In the market. He had changed a great deal— he didn't know me. He sneaked a melon from right under my nose, the only good one of the year. Ah, here we are. Sergeant!

[*The* POLICE SERGEANT *comes in with importance.*]

SERGEANT. I'm in a hurry, Countess.

COUNTESS. With regard to the iris. This young man agrees with you. He says it suits me.

SERGEANT [*going*]. There's a man drowning in the Seine.

COUNTESS. He's not drowning in the Seine. He's drowning here. Because I'm holding him tight—as I should have held Adolphe Bertaut. But if I let him go, I'm sure he will go and drown in the Seine. He's a lot better looking than Adolphe Bertaut, wouldn't you say?

[PIERRE *sighs deeply.*]

SERGEANT. How would I know?

COUNTESS. I've shown you his photograph. The one with the bicycle.

SERGEANT. Oh, yes. The one with the harelip.

COUNTESS. I've told you a hundred times! Adolphe Bertaut had no harelip. That was a scratch in the negative. [THE SERGEANT *takes out his notebook and pencil.*] What are you doing?

SERGEANT. I am taking down the drowned man's name, given name and date of birth.

COUNTESS. You think that's going to stop him from jumping in the river? Don't be silly, Sergeant. Put that book away and try to console him.

SERGEANT. I should try and console him?

COUNTESS. When people want to die, it is your job as a guardian of the state to speak out in praise of life. Not mine.

SERGEANT. I should speak out in praise of life?

COUNTESS. I assume you have some motive for interfering with people's attempts to kill each other, and rob each other, and run each other over? If you believe that life has some value, tell him what it is. Go on.

SERGEANT. Well, all right. Now look, young man . . .

COUNTESS. His name is Roderick.

PIERRE. My name is not Roderick.

COUNTESS. Yes, it is. It's noon. At noon all men become Roderick.

SERGEANT. Except Adolphe Bertaut.

COUNTESS. In the days of Adolphe Bertaut, we were forced to change the men when we got tired of their names. Nowadays, we're more practical—each hour on the hour all names are automatically changed. The men remain the same. But you're not here to discuss Adolphe Bertaut, Sergeant. You're here to convince the young man that life is worth living.

PIERRE. It isn't.

SERGEANT. Quiet. Now then—what was the idea of jumping off the bridge, anyway?

COUNTESS. The idea was to land in the river. Roderick doesn't seem to be at all confused about that.

SERGEANT. Now how can I convince anybody that life is worth living if you keep interrupting all the time?

COUNTESS. I'll be quiet.

SERGEANT. First of all, Mr. Roderick, you have to realize that suicide is a crime against the state. And why is it a crime against the state? Because every time anybody commits suicide, that means one soldier less for the army, one taxpayer less for the . . .

COUNTESS. Sergeant, isn't there something about life that you really enjoy?

SERGEANT. That I enjoy?

COUNTESS. Well, surely, in all these years, you must have found something worth living for. Some secret pleasure, or passion. Don't blush. Tell him about it.

SERGEANT. Who's blushing? Well, naturally, yes—I have my passions—like everybody else. The fact is, since you ask me—I love—to play —casino. And if the gentleman would like to join me, by and by when I go off duty, we can sit down to a nice little game in the back room with a nice cold glass of beer. If he wants to kill an hour, that is.

COUNTESS. He doesn't want to kill an hour. He wants to kill himself. Well? Is that all the police force has to offer by way of earthly bliss?

SERGEANT. Huh? You mean— [*He jerks a thumb in the direction of the pretty* BLONDE, *who has just been joined by a* BRUNETTE *of the same stamp.*] Paulette?

[*The young man groans.*]

COUNTESS. You're not earning your salary, Sergeant. I defy anybody to stop dying on your account.

SERGEANT. Go ahead, if you can do any better. But you won't find it easy.

COUNTESS. Oh, this is not a desperate case at all. A young man who has just fallen in love with someone who has fallen in love with him!

PIERRE. She hasn't. How could she?

COUNTESS. Oh, yes, she has. She was holding your hand, just as I'm holding it, when all of a sudden. . . . Did you ever know Marshal Canrobert's niece?

SERGEANT. How could he know Marshal Canrobert's niece?

COUNTESS. Lots of people knew her—when she was alive. [PIERRE *begins to struggle energetically.*] No, no, Roderick—stop—stop!

SERGEANT. You see? You won't do any better than I did.

COUNTESS. No? Let's bet. I'll bet my iris against one of your gold buttons. Right?—

Roderick, I know very well why you tried to drown yourself in the river.

PIERRE. You don't at all.

COUNTESS. It's because that Prospector want-
5 ed you to commit a horrible crime.

PIERRE. How did you know that?

COUNTESS. He stole my boa, and now he wants you to kill me.

PIERRE. Not exactly.

10 COUNTESS. It wouldn't be the first time they've tried it. But I'm not so easy to get rid of, my boy, oh, no. . . . Because . . .

[THE DOORMAN *rides in on his bicycle. He winks at* THE SERGEANT, *who has now seated*
15 *himself while* THE WAITER *serves him a beer.*]

DOORMAN. Take it easy, Sergeant.

SERGEANT. I'm busy saving a drowning man.

COUNTESS. They can't kill me because—I have no desire to die.

20 PIERRE. You're fortunate.

COUNTESS. To be alive is to be fortunate, Roderick. Of course, in the morning, when you first awake, it does not always seem so very gay. When you take your hair out of the
25 drawer, and your teeth out of the glass, you are apt to feel a little out of place in this world. Especially if you've just been dreaming that you're a little girl on a pony looking for straw-berries in the woods. But all you need to feel
30 the call of life once more is a letter in your mail giving you your schedule for the day— your mending, your shopping, that letter to your grandmother that you never seem to get around to. And so, when you've washed your
35 face in rose-water, and powdered it—not with this awful rice-powder they sell nowadays, which does nothing for the skin, but with a cake of pure white starch—and put on your pins, your rings, your brooches, bracelets, ear-
40 rings and pearls—in short, when you are dressed for your morning coffee—and have had a good look at yourself—not in the glass, naturally—it lies—but in the side of the brass gong that once belonged to Admiral Courbet
45 —then, Roderick, then you're armed, you're strong, you're ready—you can begin again.

[PIERRE *is listening now intently. There are tears in his eyes.*]

PIERRE. Oh, Madame . . . ! Oh, Madame . . . !

COUNTESS. After that, everything is pure de- 50
light. First the morning paper. Not, of course, these current sheets full of lies and vulgarity. I always read the *Gaulois*, the issue of March 22, 1903. It's by far the best. It has some delightful scandal, some excellent fashion 55
notes, and, of course, the last-minute bulletin on the death of Leonide Leblanc. She used to live next door, poor woman, and when I learn of her death every morning, it gives me quite a shock. I'd gladly lend you my copy, but it's 60
in tatters.

SERGEANT. Couldn't we find him a copy in some library?

COUNTESS. I doubt it. And so, when you've taken your fruit salts—not in water, naturally 65
—no matter what they say, it's water that gives you gas—but with a bit of spiced cake— then in sunlight or rain, Chaillot calls. It is time to dress for your morning walk. This takes much longer, of course—without a maid, 70
impossible to do it under an hour, what with your corset, corset-cover and drawers all of which lace or button in the back. I asked Madame Lanvin, a while ago, to fit the drawers with zippers. She was quite charming, but she 75
declined. She thought it would spoil the style.

[THE DEAF-MUTE *comes in.*]

WAITER. I know a place where they put zip-pers on anything.

[THE RAGPICKER *enters.*] 80

COUNTESS. I think Lanvin knows best. But I really manage very well, Martial. What I do now is, I lace them up in front, then twist them around to the back. It's quite simple, really. Then you choose a lorgnette, and then the 85
usual fruitless search for the feather boa that the Prospector stole—I know it was he: he didn't dare look me in the eye—and then all you need is a rubber band to slip around your parasol—I lost the catch the day I struck the 90
cat that was stalking the pigeon—it was worth it—ah, that day I earned my wages!

THE RAGPICKER. Countess, if you can use it, I found a nice umbrella catch the other day with a cat's eye in it. 95

COUNTESS. Thank you, Ragpicker. They say these eyes sometimes come to life and fill with tears. I'd be afraid . . .

PIERRE. Go on, Madame, go on . . .

COUNTESS. Ah! So life is beginning to interest you, is it? You see how beautiful it is?

PIERRE. What a fool I've been!

5 COUNTESS. Then, Roderick, I begin my rounds. I have my cats to feed, my dogs to pet, my plants to water. I have to see what the evil ones are up to in the district—those who hate people, those who hate plants, those who hate
10 animals. I watch them sneaking off in the morning to put on their disguises—to the baths, to the beauty parlors, to the barbers. But they can't deceive me. And when they come out again with blonde hair and false whiskers,
15 to pull up my flowers and poison my dogs, I'm there, and I'm ready. All you have to do to break their power is to cut across their path from the left. That isn't always easy. Vice moves swiftly. But I have a good long stride
20 and I generally manage. . . . Right, my friends? [THE WAITER and THE RAGPICKER nod their heads with evident approval.] Yes, the flowers have been marvelous this year. And the butcher's dog on the Rue Bizet, in spite of that
25 wretch that tried to poison him, is friskier than ever. . . .

SERGEANT. That dog had better look out. He has no license.

COUNTESS. He doesn't seem to feel the need
30 of one.

THE RAGPICKER. The Duchess de la Rochefoucauld's whippet is getting awfully thin. . . .

COUNTESS. What can I do? She bought that dog full grown from a kennel where they didn't
35 know his right name. A dog without his right name is bound to get thin.

THE RAGPICKER. I've got a friend who knows a lot about dogs—an Arab . . .

COUNTESS. Ask him to call on the Duchess.
40 She receives. Thursdays, five to seven. You see, then, Roderick. That's life. Does it appeal to you now?

PIERRE. It seems marvelous.

COUNTESS. Ah! Sergeant. My button. [THE
45 SERGEANT gives her his button and goes off. At this point THE PROSPECTOR enters.] That's only the morning. Wait till I tell you about the afternoon!

PROSPECTOR. All right, Pierre. Come along
50 now.

PIERRE. I'm perfectly all right here.

PROSPECTOR. I said, come along now.

PIERRE [to THE COUNTESS]. I'd better go, Madame.

COUNTESS. No. 55

PIERRE. It's no use. Please let go my hand.

PROSPECTOR. Madame, will you oblige me by letting my friend go?

COUNTESS. I will not oblige you in any way.

PROSPECTOR. All right. Then I'll oblige you 60
. . . !

[He tries to push her away. She catches up a soda water siphon and squirts it in his face.]

PIERRE. Countess . . .

COUNTESS. Stay where you are. This man 65
isn't going to take you away. In the first place, I shall need you in a few minutes to take me home. I'm all alone here and I'm very easily frightened.

[THE PROSPECTOR makes a second attempt to 70
drag PIERRE away. THE COUNTESS cracks him over the skull with the siphon. They join battle. THE COUNTESS whistles. THE DOORMAN comes, then the other VAGABONDS, and lastly the POLICE SERGEANT.] 75

PROSPECTOR. Officer! Arrest this woman!

SERGEANT. What's the trouble here?

PROSPECTOR. She refuses to let this man go.

SERGEANT. Why should she?

PROSPECTOR. It's against the law for a woman 80
to detain a man on the street.

IRMA. Suppose it's her son whom she's found again after twenty years?

THE RAGPICKER [gallantly]. Or her long-lost brother? The Countess is not so old. 85

PROSPECTOR. Officer, this is a clear case of disorderly conduct.

[THE DEAF-MUTE interrupts with frantic signals.]

COUNTESS. Irma, what is the Deaf-Mute say- 90
ing?

IRMA [interpreting]. The young man is in danger of his life. He mustn't go with him.

PROSPECTOR. What does he know?

IRMA. He knows everything.

PROSPECTOR. Officer, I'll have to take your number.

COUNTESS. Take his number. It's 2133. It adds up to nine. It will bring you luck.

SERGEANT. Countess, between ourselves, what are you holding him for, anyway?

COUNTESS. I'm holding him because it's very pleasant to hold him. I've never really held anybody before, and I'm making the most of it. And because so long as *I* hold him, he's free.

PROSPECTOR. Pierre, I'm giving you fair warning. . . .

COUNTESS. And I'm holding him because Irma wants me to hold him. Because if I let him go, it will break her heart.

IRMA. Oh, Countess!

SERGEANT [*to* THE PROSPECTOR]. All right, you—move on. Nobody's holding you. You're blocking traffic. Move on.

PROSPECTOR [*menacingly*]. I have your number. [*And murderously, to* PIERRE.] You'll regret this, Pierre.

[*Exit* PROSPECTOR.]

PIERRE. Thank you, Countess.

COUNTESS. They're blackmailing you, are they? [PIERRE *nods.*] What have you done? Murdered somebody?

PIERRE. No.

COUNTESS. Stolen something?

PIERRE. No.

COUNTESS. What then?

PIERRE. I forged a signature.

COUNTESS. Whose signature?

PIERRE. My father's. To a note.

COUNTESS. And this man has the paper, I suppose?

PIERRE. He promised to tear it up, if I did what he wanted. But I couldn't do it.

COUNTESS. But the man is mad! Does he really want to destroy the whole neighborhood?

PIERRE. He wants to destroy the whole city.

COUNTESS [*laughs*]. Fantastic.

PIERRE. It's not funny, Countess. He can do it. He's mad, but he's powerful, and he has friends. Their machines are already drawn up

and waiting. In three months' time you may see the city covered by a forest of derricks and drills.

COUNTESS. But what are they looking for? Have they lost something?

PIERRE. They're looking for oil. They're convinced that Paris is sitting on a lake of oil.

COUNTESS. Suppose it is. What harm does it do?

PIERRE. They want to bring the oil to the surface, Countess.

COUNTESS [*laughs*]. How silly! Is that a reason to destroy a city? What do they want with this oil?

PIERRE. They want to make war, Countess.

COUNTESS. Oh, dear, let's forget about these horrible men. The world is beautiful. It's happy. That's how God made it. No man can change it.

WAITER. Ah, Countess, if you only knew . . .

COUNTESS. If I only knew what?

WAITER. Shall we tell her now? Shall we tell her?

COUNTESS. What are you hiding from me?

THE RAGPICKER. Nothing, Countess. It's you who are hiding.

WAITER. You tell her. You've been a pitchman. You can talk.

ALL. Tell her. Tell her. Tell her.

COUNTESS. You're frightening me, my friends. Go on. I'm listening.

THE RAGPICKER. Countess, there was a time when old clothes were as good as new—in fact, they were better. Because when people wore clothes, they gave something to them. You may not believe it, but right this minute, the highest-priced shops in Paris are selling clothes that were thrown away thirty years ago. They're selling them for new. That's how good they were.

COUNTESS. Well?

THE RAGPICKER. Countess, there was a time when garbage was a pleasure. A garbage can was not what it is now. If it smelled a little strange, it was because it was a little confused —there was everything there—sardines, cologne, iodine, roses. An amateur might jump

to a wrong conclusion. But to a professional—
it was the smell of God's plenty.

COUNTESS. Well?

THE RAGPICKER. Countess, the world has
5 changed.

COUNTESS. Nonsense. How could it change?
People are the same, I hope.

THE RAGPICKER. No, Countess. The people
are not the same. The people are different.
10 There's been an invasion. An infiltration. From
another planet. The world is not beautiful any
more. It's not happy.

COUNTESS. Not happy? Is that true? Why
didn't you tell me this before?

15 THE RAGPICKER. Because you live in a dream,
Countess. And we don't like to disturb you.

COUNTESS. But how could it have happened?

THE RAGPICKER. Countess, there was a time
when you could walk around Paris, and all the
20 people you met were just like yourself. A little
cleaner, maybe, or dirtier, perhaps, or angry,
or smiling—but you knew them. They were
you. Well, Countess, twenty years ago, one
day, on the street, I saw a face in the crowd.
25 A face, you might say, without a face. The
eyes—empty. The expression—not human.
Not a human face. It saw me staring, and when
it looked back at me with its gelatine eyes, I
shuddered. Because I knew that to make room
30 for this one, one of us must have left the earth.
A while after, I saw another. And another.
And since then, I've seen hundreds come in—
yes—thousands.

COUNTESS. Describe them to me.

35 THE RAGPICKER. You've seen them yourself,
Countess. Their clothes don't wrinkle. Their
hats don't come off. When they talk, they don't
look at you. They don't perspire.

COUNTESS. Have they wives? Have they
40 children?

THE RAGPICKER. They buy the models out of
shop windows, furs and all. They animate
them by a secret process. Then they marry
them. Naturally, they don't have children.

45 COUNTESS. What work do they do?

THE RAGPICKER. They don't do any work.
Whenever they meet, they whisper, and then
they pass each other thousand-franc notes.

You see them standing on the corner by the
Stock Exchange. You see them at auctions—in 50
the back. They never raise a finger—they just
stand there. In theater lobbies, by the box
office—they never go inside. They don't do
anything, but wherever you see them, things
are not the same. I remember well the time 55
when a cabbage could sell itself just by being
a cabbage. Nowadays it's no good being a
cabbage—unless you have an agent and pay
him a commission. Nothing is free any more
to sell itself or give itself away. These days, 60
Countess, every cabbage has its pimp.

COUNTESS. I can't believe that.

THE RAGPICKER. Countess, little by little, the
pimps have taken over the world. They don't
do anything, they don't make anything—they 65
just stand there and take their cut. It makes a
difference. Look at the shopkeepers. Do you
ever see one smiling at a customer any more?
Certainly not. Their smiles are strictly for the
pimps. The butcher has to smile at the meat- 70
pimp, the florist at the rose-pimp, the grocer at
the fresh-fruit-and-vegetable pimp. It's all
organized down to the slightest detail. A pimp
for bird-seed. A pimp for fish-food. That's why
the cost of living keeps going up all the time. 75
You buy a glass of beer—it costs twice as much
as it used to. Why? 10 percent for the glass-
pimp, 10 percent for the beer-pimp, 20 percent
for the glass-of-beer-pimp—that's where our
money goes. Personally, I prefer the old- 80
fashioned type. Some of those men at least
were loved by the women they sold. But what
feelings can a pimp arouse in a leg of lamb?
Pardon my language, Irma.

COUNTESS. It's all right. She doesn't under- 85
stand it.

THE RAGPICKER. So now you know, Countess,
why the world is no longer happy. We are the
last of the free people of the earth. You saw
them looking us over today. Tomorrow, the 90
street-singer will start paying the song-pimp,
and the garbage-pimp will be after me. I tell
you, Countess, we're finished. It's the end of
free enterprise in this world!

COUNTESS. Is this true, Roderick? 95

PIERRE. I'm afraid it's true.

COUNTESS. Did you know about this, Irma?

IRMA. All I know is the Doorman says that faith is dead.

DOORMAN. I've stopped taking bets over the
5 phone.

JUGGLER. The very air is different, Countess. You can't trust it any more. If I throw my torches up too high, they go out.

THE RAGPICKER. The sky-pimp puts them out.

10 FLOWER GIRL. My flowers don't last over night now. They wilt.

JUGGLER. Have you noticed, the pigeons don't fly any more?

THE RAGPICKER. They can't afford to. They
15 walk.

COUNTESS. They're a lot of fools and so are you! You should have told me at once! How can you bear to live in a world where there is unhappiness? Where a man is not his own
20 master? Are you cowards? All we have to do is to get rid of these men.

PIERRE. How can we get rid of them? They're too strong.

[THE SERGEANT *walks up again.*]

25 COUNTESS [*smiling*]. The Sergeant will help us.

SERGEANT. Who? Me?

IRMA. There are a great many of them, Countess. The Deaf-Mute knows them all.
30 They employed him once, years ago, because he was deaf. [THE DEAF-MUTE *wigwags a short speech.*] They fired him because he wasn't blind. [*Another flash of sign language.*] They're all connected like the parts of a machine.

35 COUNTESS. So much the better. We shall drive the whole machine into a ditch.

SERGEANT. It's not that easy, Countess. You never catch these birds napping. They change before your very eyes. I remember when I
40 was in the detectives. . . . You catch a president, pfft! He turns into a trustee. You catch him as trustee, and pfft! he's not a trustee—he's an honorary vice-chairman. You catch a Senator dead to rights: he becomes Minister of
45 Justice. You get after the Minister of Justice—he is Chief of Police. And there you are—no longer in the detectives.

PIERRE. He's right, Countess. They have all

the power. And all the money. And they're greedy for more.

50 COUNTESS. They're greedy? Ah, then, my friends, they're lost. If they're greedy, they're stupid. If they're greedy—don't worry, I know exactly what to do. Roderick, by tonight you will be an honest man. And, Juggler, your
55 torches will stay lit. And your beer will flow freely again, Martial. And the world will be saved. Let's get to work.

THE RAGPICKER. What are you going to do?

COUNTESS. Have you any kerosene in the
60 house, Irma?

IRMA. Yes. Would you like some?

COUNTESS. I want just a little. In a dirty bottle. With a little mud. And some mange-cure, if you have it. [*To* THE DEAF-MUTE.] Deaf-
65 Mute! Take a letter. [IRMA *interprets in sign language. To* THE SINGER.] Singer, go and find Madame Constance.

[IRMA *and* THE WAITER *go into the café.*]

SINGER. Yes, Countess.

70 COUNTESS. Ask her to be at my house by two o'clock. I'll be waiting for her in the cellar. You may tell her we have to discuss the future of humanity. That's sure to bring her.

SINGER. Yes, Countess.

75 COUNTESS. And ask her to bring Mademoiselle Gabrielle and Madame Josephine with her. Do you know how to get in to speak to Madame Constance? You ring twice, and then meow three times like a cat. Do you know how
80 to meow?

SINGER. I'm better at barking.

COUNTESS. Better practice meowing on the way. Incidentally, I think Madame Constance knows all the verses of your mazurka. Remind
85 me to ask her.

SINGER. Yes, Countess.

[*Exit.*]

[IRMA *comes in. She is shaking the oily concoction in a little perfume vial, which she now
90 hands* THE COUNTESS.]

IRMA. Here you are, Countess.

COUNTESS. Thanks, Irma. [*She assumes a presidential manner.*] Deaf-Mute! Ready?

[IRMA *interprets in sign language.* THE
95 WAITER *has brought out a portfolio of letter*

paper and placed it on a table. THE DEAF-MUTE
sits down before it, and prepares to write.]

IRMA [*speaking for* THE DEAF-MUTE]. I'm
ready.

5 COUNTESS. My dear Mr.— What's his name?

[IRMA *wigwags the question to* THE DEAF-
MUTE, *who answers in the same manner. It is
all done so deftly that it is as if* THE DEAF-
MUTE *were actually speaking.*]

10 IRMA. They are all called Mr. President.

COUNTESS. My dear Mr. President: I have
personally verified the existence of a spontaneous outcrop of oil in the cellar of Number
21 Rue de Chaillot, which is at present occupied
15 by a dignified person of unstable mentality.
[THE COUNTESS *grins knowingly.*] This explains
why, fortunately for us, the discovery has so
long been kept secret. If you should wish to
verify the existence of this outcrop for your-
20 self, you may call at the above address at three
P.M. today. I am herewith enclosing a sample
so that you may judge the quality and con-
sistency of the crude. Yours very truly. Roderick, can you sign the Prospector's name?

25 PIERRE. You wish me to?

COUNTESS. One forgery wipes out the other.

[PIERRE *signs the letter.* THE DEAF-MUTE
types the address on an envelope.]

IRMA. Who is to deliver this?

30 COUNTESS. The Doorman, of course. On his
bicycle. And as soon as you have delivered it,
run over to the Prospector's office. Leave word
that the President expects to see him at my
house at three.

35 DOORMAN. Yes, Countess.

COUNTESS. I shall leave you now. I have many
pressing things to do. Among others, I must
press my red gown.

THE RAGPICKER. But this only takes care of
40 two of them, Countess.

COUNTESS. Didn't the Deaf-Mute say they
are all connected like the works of a machine?

IRMA. Yes.

COUNTESS. Then, if one comes, the rest will
45 follow. And we shall have them all. My boa,
please.

DOORMAN. The one that's stolen, Countess?

COUNTESS. Naturally. The one the Prospector

stole.

DOORMAN. It hasn't turned up yet, Countess. 50
But someone has left an ermine collar.

COUNTESS. Real ermine?

DOORMAN. Looks like it.

COUNTESS. Ermine and iris were made for
each other. Let me see it. 55

DOORMAN. Yes, Countess.

[*Exit* DOORMAN.]

COUNTESS. Roderick, you shall escort me.
You still look pale. I have some old Chartreuse
at home. I always take a glass each year. Last 60
year I forgot. You shall have it.

PIERRE. If there is anything I can do, Countess . . . ?

COUNTESS. There is a great deal you can do.
There are all the things that need to be done 65
in a room that no man has been in for twenty
years. You can untwist the cord on the blind
and let in a little sunshine for a change. You
can take the mirror off the wardrobe door, and
deliver me once and for all from the old harpy 70
that lives in the mirror. You can let the mouse
out of the trap. I'm tired of feeding it. [*To her
friends.*] Each man to his post. See you later,
my friends. [THE DOORMAN *puts the ermine
collar around her shoulders.*] Thank you, my 75
boy. It's rabbit. [*One o'clock strikes.*] Your
arm, Valentine.

PIERRE. Valentine?

COUNTESS. It's just struck one. At one, all
men become Valentine. 80

PIERRE [*he offers his arm*]. Permit me.

COUNTESS. Or Valentino. It's obviously far
from the same, isn't it, Irma? But they have
that much choice.

[*She sweeps out majestically with* PIERRE. 85
The others disperse. All but IRMA.]

IRMA [*clearing off the table*]. I hate ugliness.
I love beauty. I hate meanness. I adore kindness. It may not seem so grand to some to be
a waitress in Paris. I love it. A waitress meets 90
all sorts of people. She observes life. I hate to
be alone. I love people. But I have never said
I love you to a man. Men try to make me say
it. They put their arms around me—I pretend
I don't see it. They pinch me—I pretend I don't 95
feel it. They kiss me—I pretend I don't know

it. They take me out in the evening and make me drink—but I'm careful, I never say it. If they don't like it, they can leave me alone. Because when I say I love you to Him, He will know just by looking in my eyes that many have held me and pinched me and kissed me, but I have never said I love you to anyone in the world before. Never. No. [*Looking off in the direction in which* PIERRE *has gone, she whispers softly:*] I love you.

VOICE [*from within the café*]. Irma!

IRMA. Coming.

[*Exit.*]

Curtain

ACT II

[SCENE. *The cellar of* THE COUNTESS' *house. An ancient vault set deep in the ground, with walls of solid masonry, part brick and part great ashlars, mossy and sweating. A staircase of medieval pattern is built into the thickness of the wall, and leads up to the street level from a landing halfway down. In the corners of the cellar are piled casks, packing cases, bird-cages, and other odds and ends—the accumulation of centuries—the whole effect utterly fantastic.*

In the center of the vast underground room, some furniture has been arranged to give an impression of a sitting-room of the 1890's. There is a venerable chaise-longue piled with cushions that once were gay, three armchairs, a table with an oil lamp and a bowl of flowers, a shaggy rug. It is two P.M., *the same day.*]

[AT RISE. THE COUNTESS *is sitting over a bit of mending, in one of the armchairs.* IRMA *appears on the landing and calls down.*]

IRMA. Countess! The Sewer Man is here.

COUNTESS. Thank goodness, Irma. Send him down. [THE SEWER MAN *enters. He carries his hip-boots in his hand.*] How do you do, Mr. Sewer Man? [THE SEWER MAN *bows.*] But why do you have your boots in your hand instead of on your feet?

SEWER MAN. Etiquette, Countess. Etiquette.

COUNTESS. How very American! I'm told that Americans nowadays apologize for their gloves if they happen to take one's hand. As if the

skin of a human were nicer to touch than the skin of a sheep! And particularly if they have sweaty hands . . . !

SEWER MAN. My feet never sweat, Countess.

COUNTESS. How very nice! But please don't stand on ceremony here. Put your boots on. Put them on.

SEWER MAN [*complying*]. Thanks very much, Countess.

COUNTESS [*while he draws on his boots*]. I'm sure you must have a very poor opinion of the upper world, from what you see of it. The way people throw their filth into your territory is absolutely scandalous! I burn all my refuse, and I scatter the ashes. All I ever throw in the drain is flowers. Did you happen to see a lily float by this morning? Mine. But perhaps you didn't notice?

SEWER MAN. We notice a lot more down there, Countess, than you might think. You'd be surprised the things we notice. There's lots of things come along that were obviously intended for us—little gifts you might call them—sometimes a brand-new shaving brush —sometimes, *The Brothers Karamazov.* . . . Thanks for the lily, Countess. A very sweet thought.

COUNTESS. Tomorrow you shall have this iris. But now, let's come to the point. I have two questions to ask you.

SEWER MAN. Yes, Countess?

COUNTESS. First—and this has nothing to do with our problem—it's just something that has been troubling me. . . . Tell me, is it true that the sewer men of Paris have a king?

SEWER MAN. Oh, now, Countess, that's another of those fairy tales out of the Sunday supplements. It just seems those writers can't keep their minds off the sewers! It fascinates them. They keep thinking of us moving around in our underground canals like gondoliers in Venice, and it sends them into a fever of romance! The things they say about us! They say we have a race of girls down there who never see the light of day! It's completely fantastic! The girls naturally come out—every Christmas and Easter. And orgies by torchlight with gondolas and guitars! With troops of rats

that dance as they follow the piper. What nonsense! The rats are not allowed to dance. No, no, no. Of course we have no king. Down in the sewers, you'll find nothing but good
5 Republicans.

COUNTESS. And no queen?

SEWER MAN. No. We may run a beauty contest down there once in a while. Or crown a mermaid Queen of the May. But no queen
10 what you'd call a queen. And, as for these swimming races they talk so much about . . . possibly once in a while—in the summer—in the dog days . . .

COUNTESS. I believe you. I believe you. And
15 now tell me. Do you remember that night I found you here in my cellar—looking very pale and strange—you were half-dead as a matter of fact—and I gave you some brandy . . .

SEWER MAN. Yes, Countess.
20 COUNTESS. That night you promised if ever I should need it—you would tell me the secret of this room.

SEWER MAN. The secret of the moving stone?

COUNTESS. I need it now.
25 SEWER MAN. Only the King of the Sewer Men knows this secret.

COUNTESS. I'm sure of it. I know most secrets, of course. As a matter of fact, I have three magic words that will open any door that
30 words can open. I have tried them all—in various tones of voice. They don't seem to work. And this is a matter of life and death.

SEWER MAN. Look, Countess.

[He locates a brick in the masonry, and
35 pushes it. A huge block of stone slowly pivots and uncovers a trap from which a circular staircase winds into the bowels of the earth.]

COUNTESS. Good heavens! Where do those stairs lead?
40 SEWER MAN. Nowhere.

COUNTESS. But they must go somewhere.

SEWER MAN. They just go down.

COUNTESS. Let's go and see.

SEWER MAN. No, Countess. Never again.
45 That time you found me, I had a pretty close shave. I kept going down and around, and down and around for an hour, a year—I don't

know. There's no end to it, Countess. Once you start you can't stop. . . . Your head begins to turn—you're lost. No—once you start down, 50 there's no coming up.

COUNTESS. You came up.

SEWER MAN. I—I am a special case. Besides, I had my tools, my ropes. And I stopped in time. 55

COUNTESS. You could have screamed—shouted.

SEWER MAN. You could fire off a cannon.

COUNTESS. Who could have built a thing like this? 60

SEWER MAN. Paris is old, you know. Paris is very old.

COUNTESS. You don't suppose, by any chance, there is oil down there?

SEWER MAN. There's only death down there. 65

COUNTESS. I should have preferred a little oil too—or a vein of gold—or emeralds. You're quite sure there is nothing?

SEWER MAN. Not even rats.

COUNTESS. How does one lower this stone? 70

SEWER MAN. Simple. To open, you press here. And to close it, you push there. [He presses the brick. The stone descends.] Now there's two of us in the world that knows it.

COUNTESS. I won't remember long. Is it all 75 right if I repeat my magic words while I press it?

SEWER MAN. It's bound to help.

[IRMA enters.]

IRMA. Countess, Madame Constance and 80 Mademoiselle Gabrielle are here.

COUNTESS. Show them down, Irma. Thank you very much, Mr. Sewer Man.

SEWER MAN. Like that story about the steam laundry that's supposed to be running day and 85 night in my sewer . . . I can assure you . . .

COUNTESS [edging him toward the door]. Thank you very much.

SEWER MAN. Pure imagination! They never work nights. 90

[He goes off, bowing graciously.]

[CONSTANCE, the Madwoman of Passy, and GABRIELLE, the Madwoman of St. Sulpice, come down daintily. CONSTANCE is all in white. She *wears an enormous hat graced with ostrich plumes, and a lavender veil. GABRIELLE is costumed with the affected simplicity of the 1880's. She is atrociously made up in a remorseless parody of blushing innocence, and she minces down the stairs with macabre coyness.*]

CONSTANCE. Aurelia! Don't tell us they've found your feather boa?

GABRIELLE. You don't mean Adolphe Bertaut has proposed at last! I knew he would.

COUNTESS. How are you, Constance? [*She shouts.*] How are you, Gabrielle?

GABRIELLE. You needn't shout today, my dear. It's Wednesday. Wednesdays, I hear perfectly.

CONSTANCE. It's Thursday.

GABRIELLE. Oh, dear. Well, never mind. I'm going to make an exception just this once.

CONSTANCE [*to an imaginary dog who has stopped on the landing*]. Come along, Dickie. Come along. And stop barking. What a racket you're making! Come on, darling—we've come to see the longest boa and the handsomest man in Paris. Come on.

COUNTESS. Constance, it's not a question of my boa today. Nor of poor Adolphe. It's a question of the future of the human race.

CONSTANCE. You think it has a future?

COUNTESS. Please don't make silly jokes. Sit down and listen to me. Today we must make a decision which may alter the fate of the world.

CONSTANCE. Couldn't we do it tomorrow? I want to wash my slippers. Now, Dickie— please!

COUNTESS. We haven't a moment to waste. Where is Josephine? Well, we'd best have our tea, and the moment Josephine comes . . .

GABRIELLE. Josephine is sitting on her bench in front of the palace waiting for President Wilson to come out. She says she's sorry, but she positively must see him today.

CONSTANCE. Dickie!

COUNTESS. What a pity! [*She gets the tea things from the side table, pours tea and serves cake and honey.*] I wish she were here to help us. She has a first-class brain.

CONSTANCE. Go ahead, dear. We're listening. [*To* DICKIE.] What is it, Dickie? You want to sit in Aunt Aurelia's lap. All right, darling. Go on. Jump, Dickie.

COUNTESS. Constance, we love you, as you know. And we love Dickie. But this is a serious matter. So let's stop being childish for once.

CONSTANCE. And what does that mean, if you please?

COUNTESS. It means Dickie. You know perfectly well that we love him and fuss over him just as if he were still alive. He's a sacred memory and we wouldn't hurt his feelings for the world. But please don't plump him in my lap when I'm settling the future of mankind. His basket is in the corner—he knows where it is, and he can just go and sit in it.

CONSTANCE. So you're against Dickie too! You too!

COUNTESS. Constance! I'm not in the least against Dickie! I adore Dickie. But you know as well as I that Dickie is only a convention with us. It's a beautiful convention—but it doesn't have to bark all the time. Besides, it's you that spoil him. The time you went to visit your niece and left him with me, we got on marvelously together. He didn't bark, he didn't tear things, he didn't even eat. But when you're with him, one can pay attention to nothing else. I'm not going to take Dickie in my lap at a solemn moment like this, no, not for anything in the world. And that's that!

GABRIELLE [*very sweetly*]. Constance, dear, I don't mind taking him in my lap. He loves to sit in my lap, don't you, darling?

CONSTANCE. Kindly stop putting on angelic airs, Gabrielle. I know you very well. You're much too sweet to be sincere. There's plenty of times that I make believe that Dickie is here, when really I've left him home, and you cuddle and pet him just the same.

GABRIELLE. I adore animals.

CONSTANCE. If you adore animals, you shouldn't pet them when they're not there. It's a form of hypocrisy.

COUNTESS. Now, Constance, Gabrielle has as much right as you . . .

CONSTANCE. Gabrielle has no right to do what she does. Do you know what she does? She invites *people* to come to tea with us. *People* whom we know nothing about. *People* who exist only in her imagination.

COUNTESS. You think that's not an existence?

GABRIELLE. I don't invite them at all. They come by themselves. What can I do?

CONSTANCE. You might introduce us.

COUNTESS. If you think they're only imaginary, there's no point in your meeting them, is there?

CONSTANCE. Of course they're imaginary. But who likes to have imaginary people staring at one? Especially strangers.

GABRIELLE. Oh, they're really very nice. . . .

CONSTANCE. Tell me just one thing, Gabrielle —are they here now?

COUNTESS. Am I to be allowed to speak? Or is this going to be the same as the argument about inoculating Josephine's cat, when we didn't get to the subject at all!

CONSTANCE. Never! Never! Never! I'll never give my consent to that. [*To* DICKIE.] I'd never do a thing like that to you, Dickie sweet. . . . Oh, no! Oh, no!

[*She begins to weep softly.*]

COUNTESS. Good heavens! Now we have her in tears. What an impossible creature! With the fate of humanity hanging in the balance! All right, all right, stop crying. I'll take him in my lap. Come, Dickie, Dickie.

CONSTANCE. No. He won't go now. Oh, how can you be so cruel? Don't you suppose I know about Dickie? Don't you think I'd rather have him here alive and woolly and frisking around the way he used to? You have your Adolphe, Gabrielle has her birds. But I have only Dickie. Do you think I'd be so silly about him if it wasn't that it's only by pretending that he's here all the time that I get him to come sometimes, really? Next time I won't bring him!

COUNTESS. Now let's not get ourselves worked up over nothing. Come here, Dickie. . . . Irma is going to take you for a nice walk. [*She rings her bell.*] Irma!

[IRMA *appears on the landing.*]

CONSTANCE. No. He doesn't want to go. Besides, I didn't bring him today. So there!

COUNTESS. Very well, then, Irma, make sure the door is locked.

IRMA. Yes, Countess.

[IRMA *exits.*]

CONSTANCE. What do you mean? Why locked? Who's coming?

COUNTESS. If you'd let me get a word in, you'd know by now. A terrible thing has happened. This morning, this very morning, exactly at noon . . .

CONSTANCE [*thrilled*]. Oh, how exciting!

COUNTESS. Be quiet. This morning, exactly at noon, thanks to a young man who'd drowned himself in the Seine. . . . Oh, yes, while I think of it—do you know a mazurka called *La Belle Polonaise?*

CONSTANCE. Yes, Aurelia.

COUNTESS. Could you sing it now? This very minute?

CONSTANCE. Yes, Aurelia.

COUNTESS. All of it?

CONSTANCE. Yes, Aurelia. But who's interrupting now, Aurelia?

COUNTESS. You're right. Well, this morning, exactly at noon, I discovered a horrible plot. There is a group of men who intend to tear down the whole city!

CONSTANCE. Is that all?

GABRIELLE. But I don't understand, Aurelia. Why should men want to tear down the city? It was they themselves who put it up.

COUNTESS. You are so innocent, my poor Gabrielle. There are people in the world who want to destroy everything. They have the fever of destruction. Even when they pretend that they're building, it is only in order to destroy. When they put up a new building, they quietly knock down two old ones. They build cities so that they can destroy the countryside. They destroy space with telephones and time with airplanes. Humanity is now dedicated to the task of universal destruction. I am speaking, of course, primarily of the male sex.

GABRIELLE [*shocked*]. Oh . . . !

CONSTANCE. Aurelia! Must you talk sex in front of Gabrielle?

COUNTESS. There are *two* sexes.

CONSTANCE. Gabrielle is a virgin, Aurelia!

COUNTESS. Oh, she can't be as innocent as all that. She keeps canaries.

5 GABRIELLE. I think you're being very cruel about men, Aurelia. Men are big and beautiful, and as loyal as dogs. I preferred not to marry, it's true. But I hear excellent reports from friends who have had an opportunity to 10 observe them closely.

COUNTESS. My poor darling! You are still living in a dream. But one day, you will wake up as I have, and then you will see what is happening in the world! The tide has turned, 15 my dear. Men are changing back into beasts. They know it. They no longer try to hide it. There was once such a thing as manners. I remember a time when the hungriest was the one who took the longest to pick up his fork. 20 The one with the broadest grin was the one who needed most to go to the . . . It was such fun to keep them grinning like that for hours. But now they no longer pretend. Just look at them—snuffling their soup like pigs, tearing 25 their meat like tigers, crunching their lettuce like crocodiles! A man doesn't take your hand nowadays. He gives you his paw.

CONSTANCE. Would that trouble you so much if they turned into animals? Personally, I think 30 it's a good idea.

GABRIELLE. Oh, I'd love to see them like that. They'd be sweet.

CONSTANCE. It might be the salvation of the human race.

35 COUNTESS [*to* CONSTANCE]. You'd make a fine rabbit, wouldn't you?

CONSTANCE. I?

COUNTESS. Naturally. You don't think it's only the men who are changing? You change 40 along with them. Husbands and wives together. We're all one race, you know.

CONSTANCE. You think so? And why would my poor husband have to be a rabbit if he were alive?

45 COUNTESS. Remember his front teeth? When he nibbled his celery?

CONSTANCE. I'm happy to say, I remember absolutely nothing about him. All I remember on that subject is the time that Father Lacordaire tried to kiss me in the park. 50

COUNTESS. Yes, yes, of course.

CONSTANCE. And what does that mean, if you please, "Yes, yes, of course?"

COUNTESS. Constance, just this once, look us in the eye and tell us truly—did that really 55 happen or did you read about it in a book?

CONSTANCE. Now I'm being insulted!

COUNTESS. We promise you faithfully that we'll believe it all over again afterwards, won't we, Gabrielle? But tell us the truth this once. 60

CONSTANCE. How dare you question my memories? Suppose I said your pearls were false!

COUNTESS. They were.

CONSTANCE. I'm not asking what they were. I'm asking what they are. Are they false or 65 are they real?

COUNTESS. Everyone knows that little by little, as one wears pearls, they become real.

CONSTANCE. And isn't it exactly the same with memories? 70

COUNTESS. Now do not let us waste time. I must go on.

CONSTANCE. I think Gabrielle is perfectly right about men. There are still plenty who haven't changed a bit. There's an old Senator 75 who bows to Gabrielle every day when he passes her in front of the palace. And he takes off his hat each time.

GABRIELLE. That's perfectly true, Aurelia. He's always pushing an empty baby carriage, 80 and he always stops and bows.

COUNTESS. Don't be taken in, Gabrielle. It's all make-believe. And all we can expect from these make-believe men is itself make-believe. They give us facepowder made of stones, sau- 85 sages made of sawdust, shirts made of glass, stockings made of milk. It's all a vulgar pretense. And if that is the case, imagine what passes, these days, for virtue, sincerity, generosity and love! I warn you, Gabrielle, don't 90 let this Senator with the empty baby carriage pull the wool over your eyes.

GABRIELLE. He's really the soul of courtesy. He seems very correct.

COUNTESS. Those are the worst. Gabrielle, 95 beware! He'll make you put on black riding boots, while he dances the can-can around you, singing God knows what filth at the top of his voice. The very thought makes one's blood run cold!

5 GABRIELLE. You think that's what he has in mind?

COUNTESS. Of course. Men have lost all sense of decency. They are all equally disgusting. Just look at them in the evening, sitting at 10 their tables in the café, working away in unison with their tooth-picks, hour after hour, digging up roast beef, veal, onion . . .

CONSTANCE. They don't harm anyone that way.

15 COUNTESS. Then why do you barricade your door, and make your friends meow before you let them come up? Incidentally, we must make an interesting sight, Gabrielle and I, yowling together on your doorstep like a couple of tom-20 cats!

CONSTANCE. There's no need at all for you to yowl together. One would be quite enough. And you know perfectly well why I have to do it. It's because there are murderers.

25 COUNTESS. I don't quite see what prevents murderers from meowing like anybody else. But why are there murderers?

CONSTANCE. Why? Because there are thieves.

COUNTESS. And why are there thieves? Why 30 is there almost nothing but thieves?

CONSTANCE. Because they worship money. Because money is king.

COUNTESS. Ah—now we've come to it. Because we live in the reign of the Golden Calf. 35 Did you realize that, Gabrielle? Men now publicly worship the Golden Calf!

GABRIELLE. How awful! Have the authorities been notified?

COUNTESS. The authorities do it themselves, 40 Gabrielle.

GABRIELLE. Oh! Has anyone talked to the bishop?

COUNTESS. Nowadays only money talks to the bishop. And so you see why I asked you 45 to come here today. The world has gone out of its mind. Unless we do something, humanity is doomed! Constance, have you any suggestions?

CONSTANCE. I know what I always do in a case like this. . . . 50

COUNTESS. You write to the Prime Minister.

CONSTANCE. He always does what I tell him.

COUNTESS. Does he ever answer your letters?

CONSTANCE. He knows I prefer him not to. It might excite gossip. Besides, I don't always 55 write. Sometimes I wire. The time I told him about the Archbishop's frigidaire, it was by wire. And they sent a new one the very next day.

COUNTESS. There was probably a commission 60 in it for someone. And what do you suggest, Gabrielle?

CONSTANCE. Now, how can she tell you until she's consulted her voices?

GABRIELLE. I could go right home and consult 65 them, and we could meet again after dinner.

COUNTESS. There's no time for that. Besides, your voices are not real voices.

GABRIELLE [furious]. How dare you say a thing like that? 70

COUNTESS. Where do your voices come from? Still from your sewing-machine?

GABRIELLE. Not at all. They've passed into my hot-water bottle. And it's much nicer that way. They don't chatter any more. They gurgle. 75 But they haven't been a bit nice to me lately. Last night they kept telling me to let my canaries out. "Let them out. Let them out. Let them out."

CONSTANCE. Did you? 80

GABRIELLE. I opened the cage. They wouldn't go.

COUNTESS. I don't call that *voices*. Objects talk—everyone knows that. It's the principle of the phonograph. But to ask a hot-water 85 bottle for advice is silly. What does a hot-water bottle know? No, all we have to consult here is our own judgment.

CONSTANCE. Very well then, tell us what you have decided. Since you're asking our opinion, 90 you've doubtless made up your mind.

COUNTESS. Yes, I've thought the whole thing out. All I really needed to discover was the source of the infection. Today I found it.

CONSTANCE. Where? 95

COUNTESS. You'll see soon enough. I've baited

a trap. In just a few minutes, the rats will be here.

GABRIELLE [*in alarm*]. Rats!

COUNTESS. Don't be alarmed. They're still in
5 human form.

GABRIELLE. Heavens! What are you going to do with them?

COUNTESS. That's just the question. Suppose I get these wicked men all here at once—in my
10 cellar—have I the right to exterminate them?

GABRIELLE. To kill them?

[COUNTESS *nods*.]

CONSTANCE. That's not a question for us. You'll have to ask Father Bridet.

15 COUNTESS. I have asked him. Yes. One day, in confession, I told him frankly that I had a secret desire to destroy all wicked people. He said: "By all means, my child. And when you're ready to go into action, I'll lend you the jaw-
20 bone of an ass."

CONSTANCE. That's just talk. You get him to put that in writing.

GABRIELLE. What's your scheme, Aurelia?

COUNTESS. That's a secret.

25 CONSTANCE. It's not so easy to kill them. Let's say you had a tank full of vitriol all ready for them. You could never get them to walk into it. There's nothing so stubborn as a man when you want him to do something.

30 COUNTESS. Leave that to me.

CONSTANCE. But if they're killed, they're bound to be missed, and then we'll be fined. They fine you for every little thing these days.

COUNTESS. They won't be missed.

35 GABRIELLE. I wish Josephine were here. Her sister's husband was a lawyer. She knows all about these things.

COUNTESS. Do you miss a cold when it's gone? Or the germs that caused it? When the
40 world feels well again, do you think it will regret its illness? No, it will stretch itself joy-fully, and it will smile—that's all.

CONSTANCE. Just a moment! Gabrielle, are they here now? Yes or no?

45 COUNTESS. What's the matter with you now?

CONSTANCE. I'm simply asking Gabrielle if her friends are in the room or not. I have a right to know.

GABRIELLE. I'm not allowed to say.

CONSTANCE. I know very well they are. I'm 50 sure of it. Otherwise you wouldn't be making faces.

COUNTESS. May I ask what difference it makes to you if her friends are in the room?

CONSTANCE. Just this: If they're here, I'm 55 not going to say another word! I'm certainly not going to commit myself in a matter involv-ing the death sentence in the presence of third parties, whether they exist or not.

GABRIELLE. That's not being very nice to my 60 guests, is it?

COUNTESS. Constance, you must be mad! Or are you so stupid as to think that just because we're alone, there's nobody with us? Do you consider us so boring or repulsive that of all 65 the millions of beings, imaginary or otherwise, who are prowling about in space, there's not one who might possibly enjoy spending a little time with us? On the contrary, my dear—my house is full of guests always. They know that 70 here they have a place in the universe where they can come when they're lonely and be sure of a welcome. For my part, I'm delighted to have them.

GABRIELLE. Thank you, Aurelia. 75

CONSTANCE. You know perfectly well, Aure-lia . . .

COUNTESS. I know perfectly well that at this moment the whole universe is listening to us— and that every word we say echoes to the re- 80 motest star. To pretend otherwise is the sheerest hypocrisy.

CONSTANCE. Then why do you insult me in front of everybody? I'm not mean. I'm shy. I feel timid about giving an opinion in front 85 of such a crowd. Furthermore, if you think I'm so bad and so stupid, why did you invite me, in the first place?

COUNTESS. I'll tell you. And I'll tell you why, disagreeable as you are, I always give you the 90 biggest piece of cake and my best honey. It's because when you come there's always some-one with you—and I don't mean Dickie—I mean someone who resembles you like a sister, only she's young and lovely, and she sits 95 modestly to one side and smiles at me tenderly all the time you're bickering and quarreling, and never says a word. That's the Constance to whom I give the cake that you gobble, and it's because of her that you're here today, and

5 it's her vote that I'm asking you to cast in this crucial moment. And not yours, which is of no importance whatever.

CONSTANCE. I'm leaving.

COUNTESS. Be so good as to sit down. I can't

10 let her go yet.

CONSTANCE [crossing toward the stairs]. No. This is too much. I'm taking her with me.

[IRMA enters.]

IRMA. Madame Josephine.

15 COUNTESS. Thank heaven!

GABRIELLE. We're saved.

[JOSEPHINE, the Madwoman of La Concorde, sweeps in majestically in a get-up somewhere between the regal and the priestly.]

20 JOSEPHINE. My dear friends, today once again, I waited for President Wilson—but he didn't come out.

COUNTESS. You'll have to wait quite a while longer before he does. He's been dead since

25 1924.

JOSEPHINE. I have plenty of time.

COUNTESS. In anyone else, Josephine, these extravagances might seem a little childish. But a person of your judgment doubtless has her

30 reasons for wanting to talk to a man to whom no one would listen when he was alive. We have a legal problem for you. Suppose you had all the world's criminals here in this room. And suppose you had a way of getting rid of them

35 forever. Would you have the right to do it?

JOSEPHINE. Why not?

COUNTESS. Exactly my point.

GABRIELLE. But, Josephine, so many people!

JOSEPHINE. De minimis non curat lex!° The

40 more there are, the more legal it is. It's impersonal. It's even military. It's the cardinal principle of battle—you get all your enemies in one place, and you kill them all together at one time. Because if you had to track them down

45 one by one in their houses and offices, you'd

De . . . lex "the law does not concern itself with trifles"

get tired, and sooner or later you'd stop. I believe your idea is very practical, Aurelia. I can't imagine why we never thought of it before.

GABRIELLE. Well, if you think it's all right 50 to do it . . .

JOSEPHINE. By all means. Your criminals have had a fair trial, I suppose?

COUNTESS. Trial?

JOSEPHINE. Certainly. You can't kill anybody 55 without a trial. That's elementary. "No man shall be deprived of his life, liberty and property without due process of law."

COUNTESS. They deprive us of ours.

JOSEPHINE. That's not the point. You're not 60 accused of anything. Every accused—man, woman or child—has the right to defend himself at the bar of justice. Even animals. Before the Deluge, you will recall, the Lord permitted Noah to speak in defense of his fellow mortals. 65 He evidently stuttered. You know the result. On the other hand, Captain Dreyfus was not only innocent—he was defended by a marvelous orator. The result was precisely the same. So you see, in having a trial, you run no risk 70 whatever.

COUNTESS. But if I give them the slightest cause for suspicion—I'll lose them.

JOSEPHINE. There's a simple procedure prescribed in such cases. You can summon the 75 defendants by calling them three times—mentally, if you like. If they don't appear, the court may designate an attorney who will represent them. This attorney can then argue their case to the court, in absentia, and a judgment can 80 then be rendered, in contumacio.

COUNTESS. But I don't know any attorneys. And we have only ten minutes.

GABRIELLE. Hurry, Josephine, hurry!

JOSEPHINE. In case of emergency, it is per- 85 missible for the court to order the first passerby to act as attorney for the defense. A defense is like a baptism. Absolutely indispensable, but you don't have to know anything to do it. Ask Irma to get you somebody. Anybody. 90

COUNTESS. The Deaf-Mute?

JOSEPHINE. Well—that's getting it down a bit fine. That might be questionable on appeal.

COUNTESS [*calls*]. Irma! What about the Police Sergeant?

JOSEPHINE. He won't do. He's under oath to the state.

[IRMA *appears*.]

IRMA. Yes, Countess?

COUNTESS. Who's out there, Irma?

IRMA. All our friends, Countess. There's the Ragpicker and . . .

COUNTESS. Send down the Ragpicker.

CONSTANCE. Do you think it's wise to have all those millionaires represented by a ragpicker?

JOSEPHINE. It's a first-rate choice. Criminals are always represented by their opposites. Murderers, by someone who obviously wouldn't hurt a fly. Rapists, by a member of the League for Decency. Experience shows it's the only way to get an acquittal.

COUNTESS. But we must not have an acquittal. That would mean the end of the world!

JOSEPHINE. Justice is justice, my dear.

[THE RAGPICKER *comes down, with a stately air. Behind him, on the landing, appear the other* VAGABONDS.]

THE RAGPICKER. Greetings, Countess. Greetings, ladies. My most sincere compliments.

COUNTESS. Has Irma told you . . . ?

THE RAGPICKER. She said something about a trial.

COUNTESS. You have been appointed attorney for the defense.

THE RAGPICKER. Terribly flattered, I'm sure.

COUNTESS. You realize, don't you, how much depends on the outcome of this trial?

JOSEPHINE. Do you know the defendants well enough to undertake the case?

THE RAGPICKER. I know them to the bottom of their souls. I go through their garbage every day.

CONSTANCE. And what do you find there?

THE RAGPICKER. Mostly flowers.

GABRIELLE. It's true, you know, the rich are always surrounded with flowers.

CONSTANCE. How beautiful!

COUNTESS. Are you trying to prejudice the court?

THE RAGPICKER. Oh no, Countess, no.

COUNTESS. We want a completely impartial defense.

THE RAGPICKER. Of course, Countess, of course. Permit me to make a suggestion.

COUNTESS. Will you preside, Josephine?

THE RAGPICKER. Instead of speaking as attorney, suppose you let me speak directly as defendant. It will be more convincing, and I can get into it more.

JOSEPHINE. Excellent idea. Motion granted.

COUNTESS. We don't want you to be too convincing, remember.

THE RAGPICKER. Impartial, Countess, impartial.

JOSEPHINE. Well? Have you prepared your case?

THE RAGPICKER. How rich am I?

JOSEPHINE. Millions. Billions.

THE RAGPICKER. How did I get them? Theft? Murder? Embezzlement?

COUNTESS. Most likely.

THE RAGPICKER. Do I have a wife? A mistress?

COUNTESS. Everything.

THE RAGPICKER. All right. I'm ready.

GABRIELLE. Will you have some tea?

THE RAGPICKER. Is that good?

CONSTANCE. Very good for the voice. The Russians drink nothing but tea. And they talk like anything.

THE RAGPICKER. All right. Tea.

JOSEPHINE [*to* THE VAGABONDS]. Come in. Come in. All of you. You may take places. The trial is public. [THE VAGABONDS *dispose themselves on the steps and elsewhere.*] Your bell, if you please, Aurelia.

COUNTESS. But what if I should need to ring for Irma?

JOSEPHINE. Irma will sit here, next to me. If you need her, she can ring for herself. [*To the* POLICE SERGEANT *and the* POLICEMAN.] Conduct the accused to the bar. [*The officers conduct* THE RAGPICKER *to a bar improvised with a rocking chair and a packing case marked* FRAGILE. THE RAGPICKER *mounts the box. She rings the bell.*] The court is now in session. [*All sit.*] Counsel for the defense, you may take the oath.

THE RAGPICKER. I swear to tell the truth, the

whole truth, and nothing but the truth, so help me God.

JOSEPHINE. Nonsense! You're not a witness. You're an attorney. It's your duty to lie, con-
5 ceal and distort everything, and slander every-body.

THE RAGPICKER. All right. I swear to lie, con-ceal and distort everything, and slander every-body.

10 [JOSEPHINE *rings stridently.*]

JOSEPHINE. Quiet! Begin.

THE RAGPICKER. May it please the honorable, august and elegant Court . . .

JOSEPHINE. Flattery will get you nowhere.
15 That will do. The defense has been heard. Cross-examination.

COUNTESS. Mr. President . . .

THE RAGPICKER [*bowing with dignity*]. Madame.

20 COUNTESS. Do you know what you are charg-ed with?

THE RAGPICKER. I can't for the life of me 'imagine. My life is an open book. My ways are known to all. I am a pillar of the church
25 and the sole support of the Opera. My hands are spotless.

COUNTESS. What an atrocious lie! Just look at them!

CONSTANCE. You don't have to insult the
30 man. He's only lying to please you.

COUNTESS. Be quiet, Constance! You don't get the idea at all. [*To* THE RAGPICKER.] You are charged with the crime of worshipping money.

35 THE RAGPICKER. Worshipping money? Me?

JOSEPHINE. Do you plead guilty or not guilty? Which is it?

THE RAGPICKER. Why, Your Honor . . .

JOSEPHINE. Yes or no?

40 THE RAGPICKER. Yes or no? No! I don't wor-ship money, Countess. Heavens, no! Money worships me. It adores me. It won't let me alone. It's damned embarrassing, I can tell you.

JOSEPHINE. Kindly watch your language.

45 COUNTESS. Defendant, tell the Court how you came by your money.

THE RAGPICKER. The first time money came to me, I was a mere boy, a little golden-haired child in the bosom of my dear family. It came
50 to me suddenly in the guise of a gold brick which, in my innocence, I picked out of a gar-bage can one day while playing. I was hor-rified, as you can imagine. I immediately tried to get rid of it by swapping it for a little run-
55 down one-track railroad which, to my cons-ternation, at once sold itself for a hundred times its value. In a desperate effort to get rid of this money, I began to buy things. I bought the Northern Refineries, the Galeries Lafayette,
60 and the Schneider-Creusot Munition Works. And now I'm stuck with them. It's a horrible fate—but I'm resigned to it. I don't ask for your sympathy, I don't ask for your pity— all I ask for is a little common human under-
65 standing. . . .

[*He begins to cry.*]

COUNTESS. I object. This wretch is trying to play on the emotions of the Court.

JOSEPHINE. The Court has no emotions.

70 THE RAGPICKER. Everyone knows that the poor have no one but themselves to blame for their poverty. It's only just that they should suffer the consequences. But how is it the fault of the rich if they're rich?

75 COUNTESS. Dry your tears. You're deceiving nobody. If, as you say, you're ashamed of your money, why is it you hold onto it with such a death-grip?

THE RAGPICKER. Me?

80 STREET PEDDLER. You never part with a franc!

JUGGLER. You wouldn't even give the poor Deaf-Mute a sou!

THE RAGPICKER. Me, hold onto money? What slander! What injustice! What a thing to say
85 to me in the presence of this honorable, august and elegant Court! I spend all my time trying to spend my money. If I have tan shoes, I buy black ones. If I have a bicycle, I buy a motor car. If I have a wife, I buy . . .

90 JOSEPHINE [*rings*]. Order!

THE RAGPICKER. I dispatch a plane to Java for a bouquet of flowers. I send a steamer to Egypt for a basket of figs. I send a special representative to New York to fetch me an ice-
95 cream cone. And if it's not just exactly right, back it goes. But no matter what I do, I can't

get rid of my money! If I play a hundred to one shot, the horse comes in by twenty lengths. If I throw a diamond in the Seine, it turns up in the trout they serve me for lunch. Ten
5 diamonds—ten trout. Well, now, do you suppose I can get rid of forty millions by giving a sou to a deaf-mute? Is it even worth the effort?

CONSTANCE. He's right.

10 THE RAGPICKER. Ah! You see, my dear? At last, there is somebody who understands me! Somebody who is not only beautiful, but extraordinarily sensitive and intelligent.

COUNTESS. I object!

15 JOSEPHINE. Overruled!

THE RAGPICKER. I should be delighted to send you some flowers, Miss—directly I'm acquitted. What flowers do you prefer?

CONSTANCE. Roses.

20 THE RAGPICKER. You shall have a bale every morning for the next five years. Money means nothing to me.

CONSTANCE. And amaryllis.

THE RAGPICKER. I'll make a note of the name.
25 [*In his best lyrical style.*] The lady understands, ladies and gentlemen. The lady is no fool. She's been around and she knows what's what. If I gave the Deaf-Mute a franc, twenty francs, twenty million francs—I still wouldn't make
30 a dent in the forty times a thousand million francs that I'm afflicted with! Right, little lady?

CONSTANCE. Right.

JOSEPHINE. Proceed.

THE RAGPICKER. Like on the Stock Exchange.
35 If *you* buy a stock, it sinks at once like a plummet. But if *I* buy a stock, it turns around and soars like an eagle. If I buy it at 33 . . .

PEDDLER. It goes up to a thousand.

THE RAGPICKER. It goes to twenty thousand!
40 That's how I bought my twelve chateaux, my twenty villas, my 234 farms. That's how I endow the Opera and keep my twelve ballerinas.

FLOWER GIRL. I hope every one of them
45 deceives you every moment of the day!

THE RAGPICKER. How can they deceive me? Suppose they try to deceive me with the male chorus, the general director, the assistant elec-

trician or the English horn—I own them all, body and soul. It would be like deceiving me 50 with my big toe.

CONSTANCE. Don't listen, Gabrielle.

GABRIELLE. Listen to what?

THE RAGPICKER. No. I am incapable of jealousy. I have all the women—or I can have 55 them, which is the same thing. I get the thin ones with caviar—the fat ones with pearls . . .

COUNTESS. So you think there are no women with morals?

THE RAGPICKER. I mix morals with mink— 60 delicious combination. I drip pearls into protests. I adorn resistance with rubies. My touch is jeweled; my smile, a motor car. What woman can withstand me? I lift my little finger—and do they fall?—Like leaves in autumn—like 65 tin cans from a second-story window.

CONSTANCE. That's going a little too far!

COUNTESS. You see where money leads.

THE RAGPICKER. Of course. When you have no money, nobody trusts you, nobody believes 70 you, nobody likes you. Because to have money is to be virtuous, honest, beautiful and witty. And to be without is to be ugly and boring and stupid and useless.

COUNTESS. One last question. Suppose you 75 find this oil you're looking for. What do you propose to do with it?

THE RAGPICKER. I propose to make war! I propose to conquer the world!

COUNTESS. You have heard the defense, such 80 as it is. I demand a verdict of guilty.

THE RAGPICKER. What are you talking about? Guilty? I? I am never guilty!

JOSEPHINE. I order you to keep quiet.

THE RAGPICKER. I am never quiet! 85

JOSEPHINE. Quiet, in the name of the law!

THE RAGPICKER. I am the law. When I speak, that is the law. When I present my backside, it is etiquette to smile and to apply the lips respectfully. It is more than etiquette—it is a 90 cherished national privilege, guaranteed by the Constitution.

JOSEPHINE. That's contempt of court. The trial is over.

COUNTESS. And the verdict? 95

ALL. Guilty.

JOSEPHINE. Guilty as charged.

COUNTESS. Then I have full authority to carry out the sentence?

ALL. Yes!

COUNTESS. I can do what I like with them?

ALL. Yes!

COUNTESS. I have the right to exterminate them?

ALL. Yes!

JOSEPHINE. Court adjourned!

COUNTESS [to THE RAGPICKER]. Congratulations, Ragpicker. A marvelous defense. Absolutely impartial.

THE RAGPICKER. Had I known a little before, I could have done better. I could have prepared a little speech, like the time I used to sell the Miracle Spot Remover. . . .

JOSEPHINE. No need for that. You did very well, extempore. The likeness was striking and the style reminiscent of Clemenceau. I predict a brilliant future for you. Good-bye, Aurelia. I'll take our little Gabrielle home.

CONSTANCE. I'm going to walk along the river. [To DICKIE.] Oh! So here you are. And your ear all bloody! Dickie! Have you been fighting again? Oh, dear . . . !

COUNTESS [to THE RAGPICKER]. See that she gets home all right, won't you? She loses everything on the way. And in the queerest places. Her prayer book in the butcher shop. And her corset in church.

THE RAGPICKER [bowing and offering his arm]. Permit me, Madame.

STREET SINGER. Oh, Countess—my mazurka. Remember?

COUNTESS. Oh, yes, Constance, wait a moment. [To THE SINGER.] Well? Begin.

SINGER [sings].

Do you hear, Mademoiselle,
Those musicians of hell?

CONSTANCE. Why, of course, it's *La Belle Polonaise.* . . .

[She sings.]

From Poland to France
Comes this marvelous dance,
So gracious,
Audacious,
Will you foot it, perchance?

SINGER. I'm saved!

JOSEPHINE [reappearing at the head of the stairs].

Now my arm I entwine
Round these contours divine,
So pure, so impassioned,
Which Cupid has fashioned. . . .

GABRIELLE [reappearing also, she sings a quartet with the others].

Come, let's dance the mazurka, that
[devilish measure,
'Tis a joy that's reserved to the gods for
[their pleasure—
Let's gallop, let's hop,
With never a stop,
My blonde Polish miss,
Let our heads spin and turn
As the dance-floor we
[spurn—
There was never such
[pleasure as this!

[They all exit, dancing.]

IRMA. It's time for your afternoon nap.

COUNTESS. But suppose they come, Irma!

IRMA. I'll watch out for them.

COUNTESS. Thank you, Irma. I *am* tired. [She smiles.] Did you ever see a trial end more happily in your life?

IRMA. Lie down and close your eyes a moment.

[THE COUNTESS stretches out on the chaise-longue and shuts her eyes. IRMA tiptoes out. In a moment, PIERRE comes down softly, the feather boa in his hands. He stands over the chaise-longue, looking tenderly down at the sleeping woman, then kneels beside her and takes her hand.]

COUNTESS [without opening her eyes]. Is it you, Adolphe Bertaut?

PIERRE. It's only Pierre.

COUNTESS. Don't lie to me, Adolphe Bertaut. These are your hands. Why do you complicate things always? Say that it's you.

PIERRE. Yes. It is I.

COUNTESS. Would it cost you so much to call me Aurelia?

PIERRE. It's I, Aurelia.

COUNTESS. Why did you leave me, Adolphe

Bertaut? Was she so very lovely, this Georgette of yours?

PIERRE. No. You are a thousand times lovelier.

COUNTESS. But she was clever.

PIERRE. She was stupid.

COUNTESS. It was her soul, then, that drew you? When you looked into her eyes, you saw a vision of heaven, perhaps?

PIERRE. I saw nothing.

COUNTESS. That's how it is with men. They love you because you are beautiful and clever and soulful—and at the first opportunity they leave you for someone who is plain and dull and soulless. But why does it have to be like that, Adolphe Bertaut? Why?

PIERRE. Why, Aurelia?

COUNTESS. I know very well she wasn't rich. Because when I saw you that time at the grocer's, and you snatched the only good melon from right under my nose, your cuffs, my poor friend, were badly frayed. . . .

PIERRE. Yes. She was poor.

COUNTESS. "Was" poor? Is she dead then? If it's because she's dead that you've come back to me—then no. Go away. I will not take their leavings from the dead. I refuse to inherit you. . . .

PIERRE. She's quite well.

COUNTESS. Your hands are still the same, Adolphe Bertaut. Your touch is young and firm. Because it's the only part of you that has stayed with me. The rest of you is pretty far gone, I'm afraid. I can see why you'd rather not come near me when my eyes are open. It's thoughtful of you.

PIERRE. Yes. I've aged.

COUNTESS. Not I. I am young because I haven't had to live down my youth, like you. I have it with me still, as fresh and beautiful as ever. But when you walk now in the park at Colombes with Georgette, I'm sure . . .

PIERRE. There is no longer a park at Colombes.

COUNTESS. Is there a park still at St. Cloud? Is there a park at Versailles? I've never gone back to see. But I think, if they could move, those trees would have walked away in disgust the day you went there with Georgette. . . .

PIERRE. They did. Not many are left.

COUNTESS. You take her also, I suppose, to hear *Denise*?

PIERRE. No one hears *Denise* any more.

COUNTESS. It was on the way home from *Denise*, Adolphe Bertaut, that I first took your arm. Because it was windy and it was late. I have never set foot in that street again. I go the other way round. It's not easy, in the winter, when there's ice. One is quite apt to fall. I often do.

PIERRE. Oh, my darling—forgive me.

COUNTESS. No, never. I will never forgive you. It was very bad taste to take her to the very places where we'd been together.

PIERRE. All the same, I swear, Aurelia . . .

COUNTESS. Don't swear. I know what you did. You gave her the same flowers. You bought her the same chocolates. But has she any left? No. I have all your flowers still. I have twelve chocolates. No, I will never forgive you as long as I live.

PIERRE. I always loved you, Aurelia.

COUNTESS. You "loved" me? Then you too are dead, Adolphe Bertaut?

PIERRE. No. I love you. I shall always love you, Aurelia.

COUNTESS. Yes. I know. That much I've always known. I knew it the moment you went away, Adolphe, and I knew that nothing could ever change it. Georgette is in his arms now—yes. But he loves me. Tonight he's taken Georgette to hear *Denise*—yes. But he loves me. . . . I know it. You never loved her. Do you think I believed for one moment that absurd story about her running off with the osteopath? Of course not. Since you didn't love her, obviously she stayed with you. And, after that, when she came back, and I heard about her going off with the surveyor—I knew that couldn't be true, either. You'll never get rid of her, Adolphe Bertaut—never. Because you don't love her.

PIERRE. I need your pity, Aurelia. I need your love. Don't forget me. . . .

COUNTESS. Farewell, Adolphe Bertaut. Farewell. Let go my hand, and give it to little Pierre.

[PIERRE *lets go her hand, and after a moment takes it again.* THE COUNTESS *opens her eyes.*] Pierre? Ah, it's you. Has he gone?

PIERRE. Yes, Countess.

5 COUNTESS. I didn't hear him go. Oh, he knows how to make a quick exit, that one. [*She sees the boa.*] Good heavens! Wherever did you find it?

PIERRE. In the wardrobe, Countess. When I
10 took off the mirror.

COUNTESS. Was there a purple felt shopping bag with it?

PIERRE. Yes, Countess.

COUNTESS. And a little child's sewing box?

15 PIERRE. No, Countess.

COUNTESS. Oh, they're frightened now. They're trembling for their lives. You see what they're up to? They're quietly putting back all the things they have stolen. I never open
20 that wardrobe, of course, on account of the old woman in the mirror. But I have sharp eyes. I don't need to open it to see what's in it. Up to this morning, that wardrobe was empty. And now—you see? But, dear me, how stupid
25 they are! The one thing I really miss is my little sewing box. It's something they stole from me when I was a child. They haven't put it back? You're quite sure?

PIERRE. What was it like?

30 COUNTESS. Green cardboard with paper lace and gold stamping. I got it for Christmas when I was seven. They stole it the very next day. I cried my eyes out every time I thought of it —until I was eight.

35 PIERRE. It's not there, Countess.

COUNTESS. The thimble was gilt. I swore I'd never use any other. Look at my poor fingers. . . .

PIERRE. They've kept the thimble too.

40 COUNTESS. Splendid! Then I'm under no obligation to be merciful. Put the boa around my neck, Pierre. I want them to see me wearing it. They'll think it's a real boa.

[IRMA *runs in excitedly.*]

45 IRMA. Here they come, Countess! You were right—it's a procession. The street is full of limousines and taxis!

COUNTESS. I will receive them. [*As* PIERRE *hesitates to leave her.*] Don't worry. There's nothing to be frightened of. [PIERRE *goes out.*] 50 Irma, did you remember to stir the kerosene into the water?

IRMA. Yes, Countess. Here it is.

COUNTESS [*looking critically at the bottle*]. You might as well pour in what's left of the 55 tea. [IRMA *shakes up the liquid.*] Don't forget, I'm supposed to be deaf. I want to hear what they're thinking.

IRMA. Yes, Countess.

COUNTESS [*putting the finishing touches to* 60 *her make-up*]. I don't have to be merciful— but, after all, I do want to be just. . . .

[IRMA *goes up to the landing and exits. As soon as she is done,* THE COUNTESS *presses the brick, and the trap door opens. There is a con-* 65 *fused sound of auto horns in the street above, and the noise of an approaching crowd.*]

IRMA [*offstage*]. Yes, Mr. President. Come in, Mr. President. You're expected, Mr. President. This way, Mr. President. [THE PRESIDENTS 70 *come down, led by* THE PRESIDENT. *They all look alike, are dressed alike, and all have long cigars.*] The Countess is quite deaf, gentlemen. You'll have to shout. [*She announces.*] The presidents of the boards of directors! 75

THE PRESIDENT. I had a premonition, Madame, when I saw you this morning, that we should meet again. [THE COUNTESS *smiles vaguely. He continues, a tone louder.*] I want to thank you for your trust. You may place 80 yourself in our hands, with complete confidence.

SECOND PRESIDENT. Louder. The old trot can't hear you.

THE PRESIDENT. I have a letter here, Madame, 85 in which . . .

SECOND PRESIDENT. Louder. Louder.

THIRD PRESIDENT [*shouting*]. Is it true that you've located . . . ? [THE COUNTESS *stares at him blankly. He shouts at the top of his voice.*] 90 Oil? [THE COUNTESS *nods with a smile, and points down.* THE PRESIDENT *produces a legal paper and a fountain pen.*] Sign here.

COUNTESS. What is it? I haven't my glasses.

THE PRESIDENT. Your contract. 95

[*He offers the pen.*]

COUNTESS. Thank you.

SECOND PRESIDENT [*normal voice*]. What is it?

THIRD PRESIDENT. Waiver of all rights. [*He takes it back signed.*] Thank you. [*He hands it to* THE SECOND PRESIDENT.] Witness. [THE SECOND PRESIDENT *witnesses it.* THE PRESIDENT *passes it on to* THE THIRD PRESIDENT.] Notarize. [*The paper is notarized.* THE PRESIDENT *turns to* THE COUNTESS *and shouts.*] My congratulations. And now, Madame— [*He produces a gold brick wrapped in tissue paper.*] If you'll show us the well, this package is yours.

COUNTESS. What is it?

THE PRESIDENT. Pure gold. Twenty-four karat. For you.

COUNTESS. Thank you very much. [*She takes it.*] It's heavy.

SECOND PRESIDENT. Are you going to give her that?

THE PRESIDENT. Don't worry. We'll pick it up again on the way out. [*He shouts at* THE COUNTESS, *pointing at the trap door.*] Is this the way?

COUNTESS. That's the way.

[THE SECOND PRESIDENT *tries to slip in first.* THE PRESIDENT *pulls him back.*]

THE PRESIDENT. Just a minute, Mr. President. After me, if you don't mind. And watch those cigars. It's oil, you know.

[*But as he is about to descend,* THE COUNTESS *steps forward.*]

COUNTESS. Just one moment . . .

THE PRESIDENT. Yes?

COUNTESS. Did any of you happen to bring along a little sewing box?

THE PRESIDENT. Sewing box? [*He pulls back another impatient* PRESIDENT.] Take it easy.

COUNTESS. Or a little gold thimble?

THE PRESIDENT. Not me.

THE PRESIDENTS. Not us.

COUNTESS. What a pity!

THE PRESIDENT. Can we go down now?

COUNTESS. Yes. You may go down now. Watch your step!

[*They hurry down eagerly. When they have quite disappeared,* IRMA *appears on the landing and announces the next echelon.*]

IRMA. Countess, the Prospectors.

COUNTESS. Heavens! Are there more than one?

IRMA. There's a whole delegation.

COUNTESS. Send them down.

[THE PROSPECTOR *comes in, following his nose.*]

IRMA. Come in, please.

THE PROSPECTOR [*sniffing the air like a bloodhound*]. I smell something. . . . Who's that?

IRMA. The Countess. She is very deaf.

THE PROSPECTOR. Good.

[THE PROSPECTORS *also look alike. Sharp clothes, Western hats and long noses. They crowd down the stairs after* THE PROSPECTOR, *sniffing in unison.* THE PROSPECTOR *is especially talented. He casts about on the scent until it leads him to the decanter on the table. He pours himself a glass, drinks it off, and belches with much satisfaction. The others join him at once, and follow his example. They all belch in unison.*]

THE PROSPECTORS. Oil?

THE PROSPECTOR. Oil!

COUNTESS. Oil.

THE PROSPECTOR. Traces? Puddles?

COUNTESS. Pools. Gushers.

SECOND PROSPECTOR. Characteristic odor? [*He sniffs.*]

THE PROSPECTOR. Chanel Number 5. Nectar! Undoubtedly—the finest—rarest! [*He drinks.*] Sixty gravity crude: straight gasoline! [*To* THE COUNTESS.] How found? By blast? Drill?

COUNTESS. By finger.

THE PROSPECTOR [*whipping out a document*]. Sign here, please.

COUNTESS. What is it?

THE PROSPECTOR. Agreement for dividing the profits . . .

[THE COUNTESS *signs.*]

SECOND PROSPECTOR [*to* FIRST PROSPECTOR]. What is it?

THE PROSPECTOR [*pocketing the paper*]. Application to enter a lunatic asylum. Down there?

COUNTESS. Down there.

[THE PROSPECTORS *go down, sniffing.* IRMA *enters.*]

IRMA. The gentlemen of the press are here.

COUNTESS. The rest of the machine! Show them in.

IRMA. The Public Relations Counsellors! [*They enter, all shapes and sizes, all in blue pin-striped suits and black homburg hats.*] The Countess is very deaf, gentlemen. You'll have to shout!

FIRST PRESS AGENT. You don't say— Delighted to make the acquaintance of so charming and beautiful a lady . . .

SECOND PRESS AGENT. Louder. She can't hear you.

FIRST PRESS AGENT. What a face! [*Shouts.*] Madame, we are the press. You know our power. We fix all values. We set all standards. Your entire future depends on us.

COUNTESS. How do you do?

FIRST PRESS AGENT. What will we charge the old trull? The usual thirty?

SECOND PRESS AGENT. Forty.

THIRD PRESS AGENT. Sixty.

FIRST PRESS AGENT. All right—seventy-five. [*He fills in a form and offers it to* THE COUNTESS.] Sign here, Countess. This contract really gives you a break.

COUNTESS. That is the entrance.

FIRST PRESS AGENT. Entrance to what?

COUNTESS. The oil well.

FIRST PRESS AGENT. Oh, we don't need to see that, Madame.

COUNTESS. Don't need to see it?

FIRST PRESS AGENT. No, no—we don't have to see it to write about it. We can imagine it. An oil well is an oil well. "That's oil we know on earth, and oil we need to know."

[*He bows.*]

COUNTESS. But if you don't see it, how can you be sure the oil is there?

FIRST PRESS AGENT. If it's there, well and good. If it's not, by the time we get through, it will be. You underestimate the creative aspect of our profession, Madame. [THE COUNTESS *shakes her head, handing back the papers.*] I warn you, if you insist on rubbing our noses in this oil, it will cost you 10 percent extra.

COUNTESS. It's worth it.

[*She signs. They cross toward the trap door.*]

SECOND PRESS AGENT [*descending*]. You see, Madame, we of the press can refuse a lady nothing.

THIRD PRESS AGENT. Especially, such a lady.

[THIRD PRESS AGENT *starts going down.*]

SECOND PRESS AGENT [*going down; gallantly*]. It's plain to see, Madame, that even fountains of oil have their nymphs. . . . I can use that somewhere. That's copy!

[THE PRESS AGENTS *go down. As he disappears,* THE FIRST PRESS AGENT *steals the gold brick and blows a kiss gallantly to* THE COUNTESS, *who blows one back.*]

[*There is a high-pitched chatter offstage, and* IRMA *comes in, trying hard to hold back* THREE WOMEN *who pay no attention to her whatever. These* WOMEN *are tall, slender, and as soulless as if they were molded of wax. They march down the steps, erect and abstracted like animated window models, but chattering incessantly.*]

IRMA. But, ladies, please—you have no business here—you are not expected. [*To* THE COUNTESS] There are some strange ladies coming. . . .

COUNTESS. Show them in, Irma. [*The* WOMEN *come down, without taking the slightest interest in their surroundings.*] Who are you?

FIRST WOMAN. Madame, we are the most powerful pressure group in the world.

SECOND WOMAN. We are the ultimate dynamic.

THIRD WOMAN. The mainspring of all combinations.

FIRST WOMAN. Nothing succeeds without our assistance. Is that the well, Madame?

COUNTESS. That is the well.

FIRST WOMAN. Put out your cigarettes, girls. We don't want any explosions. Not with my brand-new eyelashes.

[*They go down, still chattering.* THE COUNTESS *crosses to the wall to close the trap. As she does so, there is a commotion on the landing.*]

IRMA. Countess . . .

[*A* MAN *rushes in breathlessly.*]

MAN. Just a minute! Just a minute!

[*He rushes for the trap door.*]

COUNTESS. Wait! Who are you?

MAN. I'm in a hurry. Excuse me. It's my only chance!

[*He rushes down.*]

COUNTESS. But . . . [*But he is gone. She shrugs her shoulders, and presses the brick. The trap closes. She rings the bell for* IRMA.] My gold brick! Why, they've stolen my gold brick! [*She moves toward the trap. It is now closed.*] Well, let them take their god with them.

[IRMA *enters and sees with astonishment that the stage is empty of all but* THE COUNTESS. *Little by little, the scene is suffused with light, faint at first, but increasing as if the very walls were glowing with the quiet radiance of universal joy. Only around the closed trap a shadow lingers.*]

IRMA. But what's happened? They've gone! They've vanished!

COUNTESS. They've evaporated, Irma. They were wicked. Wickedness evaporates.

[PIERRE *enters. He is followed by* THE VAGABONDS, *all of them. The new radiance of the world is now very perceptible. It glows from their faces.*]

PIERRE. Oh, Countess . . . !

WAITER. Countess, everything's changed. Now you can breathe again. Now you can see.

PIERRE. The air is pure. The sky is clear!

IRMA. Life is beautiful again.

THE RAGPICKER [*rushes in*]. Countess—the pigeons! The pigeons are flying!

FLOWER GIRL. They don't have to walk any more.

THE RAGPICKER. They're flying. . . . The air is like crystal. And young grass is sprouting on the pavements.

COUNTESS. Is it possible?

IRMA [*interpreting for* THE DEAF-MUTE]. Now, Juggler, you can throw your fireballs up as high as you please—they won't go out.

SERGEANT. On the street, utter strangers are shaking hands, they don't know why, and offering each other almond bars!

COUNTESS. Oh, my friends . . .

WAITER. Countess, we thank you. . . .

[*They go on talking with happy and animated gestures, but we no longer hear them, for their words blend into a strain of unearthly music which seems to thrill from the uttermost confines of the universe. And out of this music comes a voice.*]

FIRST VOICE. Countess . . .

[*Only* THE COUNTESS *hears it. She turns from the group of* VAGABONDS *in wonder.*]

SECOND VOICE. Countess . . .

THIRD VOICE. Countess . . .

[*As she looks up in rapture,* THE FIRST VOICE *speaks again.*]

FIRST VOICE. Countess, we thank you. We are the friends of animals.

SECOND VOICE. We are the friends of people.

THIRD VOICE. We are the friends of friendship.

FIRST VOICE. You have freed us!

SECOND VOICE. From now on, there will be no hungry cats. . . .

THIRD VOICE. And we shall tell the Duchess her dog's right name!

[THE VOICES *fade off. And now another group of voices is heard.*]

FIRST VOICE. Countess, we thank you. We are the friends of flowers.

SECOND VOICE. From now on, every plant in Paris will be watered. . . .

THIRD VOICE. And the sewers will be fragrant with jasmine!

[*These voices, too, are silent. For an instant, the stage is vibrant with music. Then* THE DEAF-MUTE *speaks, and his voice is the most beautiful of all.*]

DEAF-MUTE. Sadness flies on the wings of the morning, and out of the heart of darkness comes the light.

[*Suddenly a group of figures detaches itself from the shadows. These are exactly similar in face and figure and in dress. They are shabby in the fashion of 1900 and their cuffs are badly frayed. Each bears in his hand a ripe melon.*]

FIRST ADOLPHE BERTAUT. Countess, we thank you. We too, are freed at last. We are the Adolphe Bertauts of the world.

SECOND ADOLPHE BERTAUT. We are no longer timid.

THIRD ADOLPHE BERTAUT. We are no longer weak.

FIRST ADOLPHE BERTAUT. From this day on,

we shall hold fast to what we love. For your sake, henceforth, we shall be handsome, and our cuffs forever immaculate and new. Countess, we bring you this melon and with it our hearts . . . ! [*They all kneel.*] Will you do us the honor to be our wife?

COUNTESS [*sadly*]. Too late! Too late! [*She waves them aside. They take up their melons sadly and vanish. The voices of* THE VAGA-BONDS *are heard again, and the music dies.*] Too late! Too late!

PIERRE. Too late, Countess?

IRMA. Too late for what?

COUNTESS. I say that it's too late for them. On the twenty-fourth of May, 1881, the most beautiful Easter in the memory of man, it was not too late. And on the fifth of September, 1887, the day they caught the trout and broiled it on the open fire by the brook at Villeneuve, it was not too late. And it was even not too late for them on the twenty-first of August, 1897, the day the Czar visited Paris with his guard. But they did nothing and they said nothing, and now—kiss each other, you two, this very instant!

IRMA. You mean . . . ?

PIERRE. You mean . . . ?

IRMA. But, Countess . . .

COUNTESS. It's three hours since you've met and known and loved each other. Kiss each other quickly. [PIERRE *hesitates.*] Look at him. He hesitates. He trembles. Happiness frightens him. . . . How like a man! Oh, Irma, kiss him, kiss him! If two people who love each other let a single instant wedge itself between them, it grows—it becomes a month, a year, a century; it becomes too late. Kiss him, Irma, kiss him while there is time, or in a moment his hair will be white and there will be another madwoman in Paris! Oh, make her kiss him, all of you! [*They kiss.*] Bravo! Oh, if only you'd had the courage to do that thirty years ago, how different I would be today! Dear Deaf-Mute, be still—your words dazzle our eyes! And Irma is too busy to translate for you. [*They kiss once more.*] Well, there we are. The world is saved. And you see how simple it all was? Nothing is ever so wrong in this world that a sensible woman can't set it right in the course of an afternoon. Only, the next time, don't wait until things begin to look black. The minute you notice anything, tell me at once.

THE RAGPICKER. We will, Countess. We will.

COUNTESS [*puts on her hat. Her tone becomes businesslike*]. Irma. My bones. My gizzard.

IRMA. I have them ready, Countess.

COUNTESS. Good. [*She puts the bones into her basket and starts for the stairs.*] Well, let's get on to more important things. Four o'clock. My poor cats must be starved. What a bore for them if humanity had to be saved every afternoon. They don't think much of it, as it is.

Curtain

Arthur Miller

1915–

Death of a Salesman

1949

"New York and Boston of today," the settings that Arthur Miller specifies, do not in fact comprise the whole imaginative territory of *Death of a Salesman*. It includes, as well, memories of a former era, the 1920's and 1930's, the period of the great "Boom" and the succeeding Great Depression that overwhelms Willy Loman, the Salesman, during the last days of his life. The times and places are totally American and middle class, scenes of inflated hopes and later of deflated dreams. For Willy, America was "full of beautiful towns and fine, upstanding people," a land of "success" symbolized by such "self-made" tycoons as Thomas Edison and B. F. Goodrich, who thrived in a time of almost unchecked capitalist expansion and officially proclaimed "prosperity" ("In 1928 I had a big year").

As a salesman, Willy is a superb symbol for an era of contradictions. He is specifically a "road man," one of the now-diminished tribe of "drummers" who peddled their wares and spread the gospel of success and profits up and down the land. Equipped with sample cases and ribald anecdotes, full of glad-handing, back-thumping, first-name-dropping optimism ("the sky's the limit"), their existence was at once gregarious and oddly solitary. Their livelihood was hazardous, subject to the vagaries of sales-commission earnings, their confident air of bluff heartiness often contrasting with the regular loneliness of cheap hotels and the pinching anxiety stemming from unrelieved competitiveness, called "playing the game," the rules of which the salesman was powerless to set or alter or even to criticize, at least out loud. His world was staunchly and narrowly masculine, much wanting in human kindness, not altogether ungenerous, but suspicious of love. This world, depicted in *Death of a Salesman,* is an indictment out of American Marxism of the 1930's. "You end up," Willy confesses, "more dead than alive." Where *Desire Under the Elms* would demolish the American

ARTHUR MILLER

agrarian pastoral, *Death of a Salesman* undermines the idyll of "suburbia."

Yet *Death of a Salesman* is not only a social tract. It is, explicitly, the tragedy of a man who has some noble traits, no matter how inarticulately expressed. As his wife Linda insists, "Attention, attention must be finally paid to such a person." In this aging nobody there are rudiments of promethean restlessness. In his struggle to define his aspirations, he searches far less for riches than for love. His life oscillates between confidence and despair: "personality always wins the day"; "I'm always in a race with the junkyard." His final yearning for a meaningful death recapitulates and reassesses his life.

As theater, the play is in the modernist tradition, deriving much in theme and technique from Chekhov and O'Neill. It is a chronicle and an elegy, although with elements of bleak satire. It is also, formally, a tragedy that centers accurately on Willy Loman. All other characters have their being essentially in relation to his and are the persons in a dream that he tries to relive and reinterpret. All the characters address the question of Willy's destiny.

The setting of the play is an interpenetration of times and of levels of Willy's consciousness. In the present, the last days of his life, the physical boundaries are observed; in scenes from the past the boundaries soften and are passed through as if by magic. This past is not merely recollected, it is reenacted in Willy's last agitated striving to understand a father whom he scarcely knew and sons whom he involuntarily betrayed.

In the final scenes the play reaches a mythic dimension emphasized by intermingling of symbolic times and places. Willy, "the son of a great and very wild-hearted man," tries again to plant seeds in the ruined garden, and his brother Ben, now more than ever a potent figure of mystery, reappears to promise a final success that will redeem the failures of a life of tawdry dreams and stunted affections. "It's dark there," Ben warns, speaking of the death toward which he beckons, "but full of diamonds." That is a last deception, consonant with the unfulfillment of the past, but Willy accepts it as inviting to a heroism not altogether discredited by the lure of romantic illusions. Although Willy's death, like the conditions of his life as a salesman, "came with the territory," that territory is not so much America of the 1930's as the realm of unrealized aspirations. He dies, by choice, the death appointed and makes it, no less truly than an Othello or an Antony, his own.

Death of a Salesman

Certain Private Conversations
in Two Acts and a Requiem

MILLER

CHARACTERS

WILLY LOMAN
LINDA
BIFF
HAPPY
BERNARD
THE WOMAN
LETTA
CHARLEY
UNCLE BEN
HOWARD WAGNER
JENNY
STANLEY
MISS FORSYTHE
WAITER

SCENE. *The action takes place in Willy Lo-man's house and yard and in various places he visits in the New York and Boston of today.*

ACT I

[*A melody is heard, played upon a flute. It is small and fine, telling of grass and trees and the horizon. The curtain rises.*

Before us is the SALESMAN'S *house. We are aware of towering, angular shapes behind it, surrounding it on all sides. Only the blue light of the sky falls upon the house and forestage; the surrounding area shows an angry glow of orange. As more light appears we see a solid vault of apartment houses around the small, fragile-seeming home. An air of the dream clings to the place, a dream rising out of reality. The kitchen at center seems actual enough, for there is a kitchen table with three chairs, and a refrigerator. But no other fixtures are seen. At the back of the kitchen there is a draped entrance, which leads to the living-room. To the right of the kitchen, on a level raised two feet, is a bedroom furnished only with a brass bedstead and a straight chair. On a shelf over the bed a silver athletic trophy stands. A window opens on to the apartment house at the side.*

Behind the kitchen, on a level raised six and a half feet, is the boys' bedroom, at present barely visible. Two beds are dimly seen, and at the back of the room a dormer window. (This bedroom is above the unseen living-room.) At the left a stairway curves up to it from the kitchen.

The entire setting is wholly or, in some places, partially transparent. The roof-line of the house is one-dimensional; under and over it we see the apartment buildings. Before the house lies an apron, curving beyond the fore-stage into the orchestra. This forward area serves as the back yard as well as the locale of all Willy's imaginings and of his city scenes. Whenever the action is in the present the ac-tors observe the imaginary wall-lines, entering the house only through its door at the left. But in the scenes of the past these boundaries are broken, and characters enter or leave a room by stepping "through" a wall on to the forestage.]

[*From the right,* WILLY LOMAN, *the Sales-man, enters, carrying two large sample cases. The flute plays on. He hears but is not aware of it. He is past sixty years of age, dressed quietly. Even as he crosses the stage to the doorway of the house, his exhaustion is ap-parent. He unlocks the door, comes into the kitchen, and thankfully lets his burden down, feeling the soreness of his palms. A word-sigh*

escapes his lips—it might be "Oh, boy, oh, boy." He closes the door, then carries his cases out into the living-room, through the draped kitchen doorway. LINDA, *his wife, has stirred*
5 *in her bed at the right. She gets out and puts on a robe, listening. Most often jovial, she has developed an iron repression of her exceptions to* WILLY's *behavior—she more than loves him, she admires him, as though his mercurial*
10 *nature, his temper, his massive dreams and little cruelties, served her only as sharp reminders of the turbulent longings within him, longings which she shares but lacks the temperament to utter and follow to their end.*]

15 LINDA [*hearing* WILLY *outside the bedroom, calls with some trepidation*]. Willy!

WILLY. It's all right. I came back.

LINDA. Why? What happened? [*Slight pause.*] Did something happen, Willy?

20 WILLY. No, nothing happened.

LINDA. You didn't smash the car, did you?

WILLY [*with casual irritation*]. I said nothing happened. Didn't you hear me?

LINDA. Don't you feel well?

25 WILLY. I'm tired to the death. [*The flute has faded away. He sits on the bed beside her, a little numb.*] I couldn't make it. I just couldn't make it, Linda.

LINDA [*very carefully, delicately*]. Where
30 were you all day? You look terrible.

WILLY. I got as far as a little above Yonkers. I stopped for a cup of coffee. Maybe it was the coffee.

LINDA. What?

35 WILLY [*after a pause*]. I suddenly couldn't drive any more. The car kept going off on to the shoulder, y'know?

LINDA [*helpfully*]. Oh. Maybe it was the steering again. I don't think Angelo knows the
40 Studebaker.

WILLY. No, it's me. Suddenly I realize I'm goin' sixty miles an hour and I don't remember the last five minutes. I'm—I can't seem to—keep my mind to it.

45 LINDA. Maybe it's your glasses. You never went for your new glasses.

WILLY. No, I see everything. I came back ten miles an hour. It took me nearly four hours from Yonkers.

50 LINDA [*resigned*]. Well, you'll just have to take a rest, Willy, you can't continue this way.

WILLY. I just got back from Florida.

LINDA. But you didn't rest your mind. Your mind is over-active, and the mind is what
55 counts, dear.

WILLY. I'll start out in the morning. Maybe I'll feel better in the morning. [*She is taking off his shoes.*] These goddam arch supports are killing me.

60 LINDA. Take an aspirin. Should I get you an aspirin? It'll soothe you.

WILLY [*with wonder*]. I was driving along, you understand? And I was fine. I was even observing the scenery. You can imagine, me
65 looking at scenery, on the road every week of my life. But it's so beautiful up there, Linda, the trees are so thick, and the sun is warm. I opened the windshield and just let the warm air bathe over me. And then all of a sudden I'm
70 goin' off the road! I'm tellin' ya, I absolutely forgot I was driving. If I'd've gone the other way over the white line I might've killed somebody. So I went on again—and five minutes later I'm dreamin' again, and I nearly
75 —[*He presses two fingers against his eyes.*] I have such thoughts, I have such strange thoughts.

LINDA. Willy, dear. Talk to them again. There's no reason why you can't work in New
80 York.

WILLY. They don't need me in New York. I'm the New England man. I'm vital in New England.

LINDA. But you're sixty years old. They can't
85 expect you to keep travelling every week.

WILLY. I'll have to send a wire to Portland. I'm supposed to see Brown and Morrison tomorrow morning at ten o'clock to show the line. Goddammit, I could sell them! [*He starts
90 putting on his jacket.*]

LINDA [*taking the jacket from him*]. Why don't you go down to the place tomorrow and tell Howard you've simply got to work in New York? You're too accommodating, dear.

95 WILLY. If old man Wagner was alive I'd a been in charge of New York now! That man

was a prince, he was a masterful man. But that boy of his, that Howard, he don't appreciate. When I went north the first time, the Wagner Company didn't know where New England was!

LINDA. Why don't you tell those things to Howard, dear?

WILLY [*encouraged*]. I will, I definitely will. Is there any cheese?

LINDA. I'll make you a sandwich.

WILLY. No, go to sleep. I'll take some milk. I'll be up right away. The boys in?

LINDA. They're sleeping. Happy took Biff on a date tonight.

WILLY [*interested*]. That so?

LINDA. It was so nice to see them shaving together, one behind the other, in the bathroom. And going out together. You notice? The whole house smells of shaving lotion.

WILLY. Figure it out. Work a lifetime to pay off a house. You finally ·own it, and there's nobody to live in it.

LINDA. Well, dear, life is a casting off. It's always that way.

WILLY. No, no, some people—some people accomplish something. Did Biff say anything after I went this morning?

LINDA. You shouldn't have criticized him, Willy, especially after he just got off the train. You mustn't lose your temper with him.

WILLY. When the hell did I lose my temper? I simply asked him if he was making any money. Is that a criticism?

LINDA. But, dear, how could he make any money?

WILLY [*worried and angered*]. There's such an undercurrent in him. He became a moody man. Did he apologize when I left this morning?

LINDA. He was crestfallen, Willy. You know how he admires you. I think if he finds himself, then you'll both be happier and not fight any more.

WILLY. How can he find himself on a farm? Is that a life? A farmhand? In the beginning, when he was young, I thought, well, a young man, it's good for him to tramp around, take a lot of different jobs. But it's more than ten years now and he has yet to make thirty-five dollars a week!

LINDA. He's finding himself, Willy.

WILLY. Not finding yourself at the age of thirty-four is a disgrace!

LINDA. Shh!

WILLY. The trouble is he's lazy, goddammit!

LINDA. Willy, please!

WILLY. Biff is a lazy bum!

LINDA. They're sleeping. Get something to eat. Go on down.

WILLY. Why did he come home? I would like to know what brought him home.

LINDA. I don't know. I think he's still lost, Willy. I think he's very lost.

WILLY. Biff Loman is lost. In the greatest country in the world a young man with such —personal attractiveness, gets lost. And such a hard worker. There's one thing about Biff— he's not lazy.

LINDA. Never.

WILLY [*with pity and resolve*]. I'll see him in the morning; I'll have a nice talk with him. I'll get him a job selling. He could be big in no time. My God! Remember how they used to follow him around in high school? When he smiled at one of them their faces lit up. When he walked down the street. . . . [*He loses himself in reminiscences.*]

LINDA [*trying to bring him out of it*]. Willy, dear, I got a new kind of American-type cheese today. It's whipped.

WILLY. Why do you get American when I like Swiss?

LINDA. I just thought you'd like a change—

WILLY. I don't want a change! I want Swiss cheese. Why am I always being contradicted?

LINDA [*with a covering laugh*]. I thought it would be a surprise.

WILLY. Why don't you open a window in here, for God's sake?

LINDA [*with infinite patience*]. They're all open, dear.

WILLY. The way they boxed us in here. Bricks and windows, windows and bricks.

LINDA. We should've bought the land next door.

WILLY. The street is lined with cars. There's

not a breath of fresh air in the neighborhood. The grass don't grow any more, you can't raise a carrot in the backyard. They should've had a law against apartment houses. Remem-
5 ber those two beautiful elm trees out there? When I and Biff hung the swing between them?

LINDA. Yeah, like being a million miles from the city.

10 WILLY. They should've arrested the builder for cutting those down. They massacred the neighborhood. [*Lost.*] More and more I think of those days, Linda. This time of year it was lilac and wistaria. And then the peonies would
15 come out, and the daffodils. What a fragrance in this room!

LINDA. Well, after all, people had to move somewhere.

WILLY. No, there's more people now.

20 LINDA. I don't think there's more people, I think—

WILLY. There's more people! That's what's ruining this country! Population is getting out of control. The competition is maddening!
25 Smell the stink from that apartment house! And another one on the other side. . . . How can they whip cheese?

[*On* WILLY'S *last line,* BIFF *and* HAPPY *raise themselves up in their beds, listening.*]

30 LINDA. Go down, try it. And be quiet.

WILLY [*turning to* LINDA, *guiltily*]. You're not worried about me, are you, sweetheart?

BIFF. What's the matter?

HAPPY. Listen!

35 LINDA. You've got too much on the ball to worry about.

WILLY. You're my foundation and my support, Linda.

LINDA. Just try to relax, dear. You make
40 mountains out of molehills.

WILLY. I won't fight with him any more. If he wants to go back to Texas, let him go.

LINDA. He'll find his way.

WILLY. Sure. Certain men just don't get
45 started till later in life. Like Thomas Edison, I think. Or B. F. Goodrich. One of them was deaf. [*He starts for the bedroom doorway.*] I'll put my money on Biff.

LINDA. And Willy—if it's warm Sunday we'll drive in the country. And we'll open the wind- 50 shield, and take lunch.

WILLY. No, the windshields don't open on the new cars.

LINDA. But you opened it today.

WILLY. Me? I didn't. [*He stops.*] Now isn't 55 that peculiar! Isn't that remarkable—[*He breaks off in amazement and fright as the flute is heard distantly.*]

LINDA. What, darling?

WILLY. That is the most remarkable thing. 60

LINDA. What, dear?

WILLY. I was thinking of the Chevvy. [*Slight pause.*] Nineteen twenty-eight . . . when I had that red Chevvy—[*Breaks off.*] That funny? I coulda sworn I was driving that Chevvy today. 65

LINDA. Well, that's nothing. Something must've reminded you.

WILLY. Remarkable. Ts. Remember those days? The way Biff used to simonize that car? The dealer refused to believe there was eighty 70 thousand miles on it. [*He shakes his head.*] Heh! [*To* LINDA.] Close your eyes, I'll be right up. [*He walks out of the bedroom.*]

HAPPY [*to* BIFF]. Jesus, maybe he smashed up the car again! 75

LINDA [*calling after* WILLY]. Be careful on the stairs, dear! The cheese is on the middle shelf! [*She turns, goes over to the bed, takes his jacket, and goes out of the bedroom.*]

[*Light has risen on the boys' room. Unseen,* 80 WILLY *is heard talking to himself, "Eighty thousand miles," and a little laugh.* BIFF *gets out of bed, comes downstage a bit, and stands attentively.* BIFF *is two years older than his brother* HAPPY, *well built, but in these days* 85 *bears a worn air and seems less self-assured. He has succeeded less, and his dreams are stronger and less acceptable than* HAPPY'S. HAPPY *is tall, powerfully made. Sexuality is like a visible color on him, or a scent that many* 90 *women have discovered. He, like his brother, is lost, but in a different way, for he has never allowed himself to turn his face toward defeat and is thus more confused and hard-skinned, although seemingly more content.*] 95

HAPPY [*getting out of bed*]. He's going to

get his license taken away if he keeps that up. I'm getting nervous about him, y'know, Biff?

BIFF. His eyes are going.

5 HAPPY. No, I've driven with him. He sees all right. He just doesn't keep his mind on it. I drove into the city with him last week. He stops at a green light and then it turns red and he goes. [*He laughs.*]

BIFF. Maybe he's color-blind.

10 HAPPY: Pop? Why, he's got the finest eye for color in the business. You know that.

BIFF [*sitting down on his bed*]. I'm going to sleep.

HAPPY. You're not still sour on Dad, are 15 you, Biff?

BIFF. He's all right, I guess.

WILLY [*underneath them in the living-room*]. Yes, sir, eighty thousand miles—eighty-two thousand!

20 BIFF. You smoking?

HAPPY [*holding out a pack of cigarettes*]. Want one?

BIFF [*taking a cigarette*]. I can never sleep when I smell it.

25 WILLY. What a simonizing job, heh!

HAPPY [*with deep sentiment*]. Funny, Biff, y'know? Us sleeping in here again? The old beds. [*He pats his bed affectionately.*] All the talk that went across those two beds, huh? 30 Our whole lives.

BIFF. Yeah. Lotta dreams and plans.

HAPPY [*with a deep and masculine laugh*]. About five hundred women would like to know what was said in this room.

35 [*They share a soft laugh.*]

BIFF. Remember that big Betsy something— what the hell was her name—over on Bushwick Avenue?

HAPPY [*combing his hair*]. With the collie 40 dog!

BIFF. That's the one. I got you in there, remember?

HAPPY. Yeah, that was my first time—I think. Boy, there was a pig! [*They laugh, al-* 45 *most crudely.*] You taught me everything I know about women. Don't forget that.

BIFF. I bet you forgot how bashful you used to be. Especially with girls.

HAPPY. Oh, I still am, Biff.

BIFF. Oh, go on. 50

HAPPY. I just control it, that's all. I think I got less bashful and you got more so. What happened, Biff? Where's the old humor, the old confidence? [*He shakes* BIFF's *knee.* BIFF *gets up and moves restlessly about the room.*] 55 What's the matter?

BIFF. Why does Dad mock me all the time?

HAPPY. He's not mocking you, he—

BIFF. Everything I say there's a twist of mockery on his face. I can't get near him. 60

HAPPY. He just wants you to make good, that's all. I wanted to talk to you about Dad for a long time, Biff. Something's—happening to him. He—talks to himself.

BIFF. I noticed that this morning. But he 65 always mumbled.

HAPPY. But not so noticeable. It got so embarrassing I sent him to Florida. And you know something? Most of the time he's talking to you. 70

BIFF. What's he say about me?

HAPPY. I can't make it out.

BIFF. What's he say about me?

HAPPY. I think the fact that you're not settled, that you're still kind of up in the air . . . 75

BIFF. There's one or two other things depressing him, Happy.

HAPPY. What do you mean?

BIFF. Never mind. Just don't lay it all to me.

HAPPY. But I think if you got started—I 80 mean—is there any future for you out there?

BIFF. I tell ya, Hap, I don't know what the future is. I don't know—what I'm supposed to want.

HAPPY. What do you mean? 85

BIFF. Well, I spent six or seven years after high school trying to work myself up. Shipping clerk, salesman, business of one kind or another. And it's a measly manner of existence. To get on that subway on the hot 90 mornings in summer. To devote your whole life to keeping stock, or making phone calls, or selling or buying. To suffer fifty weeks of the year for the sake of a two-week vacation, when all you really desire is to be outdoors, 95 with your shirt off. And always to have to get ahead of the next fella. And still—that's how you build a future.

HAPPY. Well, you really enjoy it on a farm? Are you content out there?

BIFF [with rising agitation]. Hap, I've had twenty or thirty different kinds of job since I left home before the war, and it always turns out the same. I just realized it lately. In Nebraska when I herded cattle, and the Dakotas, and Arizona, and now in Texas. It's why I came home now, I guess, because I realized it. This farm I work on, it's spring there now, see? And they've got about fifteen new colts. There's nothing more inspiring or—beautiful than the sight of a mare and a new colt. And it's cool there now, see? Texas is cool now, and it's spring. And whenever spring comes to where I am, I suddenly get the feeling, my God, I'm not gettin' anywhere. What the hell am I doing, playing around with horses, twenty-eight dollars a week! I'm thirty-four years old, I oughta be makin' my future. That's when I come running home. And now, I get here, and I don't know what to do with myself. [After a pause.] I've always made a point of not wasting my life, and everytime I come back here I know that all I've done is to waste my life.

HAPPY. You're a poet, you know that, Biff? You're a—you're an idealist!

BIFF. No, I'm mixed up very bad. Maybe I oughta get married. Maybe I oughta get stuck into something. Maybe that's my trouble. I'm like a boy. I'm not married, I'm not in business, I just—I'm like a boy. Are you content, Hap? You're a success, aren't you? Are you content?

HAPPY. Hell, no!

BIFF. Why? You're making money, aren't you?

HAPPY [moving about with energy, expressiveness]. All I can do now is wait for the merchandise manager to die. And suppose I get to be merchandise manager? He's a good friend of mine, and he just built a terrific estate on Long Island. And he lived there about two months and sold it, and now he's building another one. He can't enjoy it once it's finished. And I know that's just what I would do. I don't know what the hell I'm workin' for. Sometimes I sit in my apartment—all alone. And I think of the rent I'm paying. And it's crazy. But then, it's what I always wanted. My own apartment, a car, and plenty of women. And still, goddammit, I'm lonely.

BIFF [with enthusiasm]. Listen, why don't you come out West with me?

HAPPY. You and I, heh?

BIFF. Sure, maybe we could buy a ranch. Raise cattle, use our muscles. Men built like we are should be working out in the open.

HAPPY [avidly]. The Loman Brothers, heh?

BIFF [with vast affection]. Sure, we'd be known all over the counties!

HAPPY [enthralled]. That's what I dream about, Biff. Sometimes I want to just rip my clothes off in the middle of the store and outbox that goddam merchandise manager. I mean I can outbox, outrun, and outlift anybody in that store, and I have to take orders from those common, petty sons-of-bitches till I can't stand it any more.

BIFF. I'm tellin' you, kid, if you were with me I'd be happy out there.

HAPPY [enthused]. See, Biff, everybody around me is so false that I'm constantly lowering my ideals . . .

BIFF. Baby, together we'd stand up for one another, we'd have someone to trust.

HAPPY. If I were around you—

BIFF. Hap, the trouble is we weren't brought up to grub for money. I don't know how to do it.

HAPPY. Neither can I!

BIFF. Then let's go!

HAPPY. The only thing is—what can you make out there?

BIFF. But look at your friend. Builds an estate and then hasn't the peace of mind to live in it.

HAPPY. Yeah, but when he walks into the store the waves part in front of him. That's fifty-two thousand dollars a year coming through the revolving door, and I got more in my pinky finger than he's got in his head.

BIFF. Yeah, but you just said—

HAPPY. I gotta show some of those pompous,

self-important executives over there that Hap Loman can make the grade. I want to walk into the store the way he walks in. Then I'll go with you, Biff. We'll be together yet, I 5 swear. But take those two we had tonight. Now weren't they gorgeous creatures?

BIFF. Yeah, yeah, most gorgeous I've had in years.

HAPPY. I get that any time I want, Biff. 10 Whenever I feel disgusted. The only trouble is, it gets like bowling or something. I just keep knockin' them over and it doesn't mean anything. You still run around a lot?

BIFF. Naa. I'd like to find a girl—steady, 15 somebody with substance.

HAPPY. That's what I long for.

BIFF. Go on! You'd never come home.

HAPPY. I would! Somebody with character, with resistance! Like Mom, y'know? You're 20 gonna call me a bastard when I tell you this. That girl Charlotte I was with tonight is engaged to be married in five weeks. [*He tries on his new hat.*]

BIFF. No kiddin'!

25 HAPPY. Sure, the guy's in line for the vice-presidency of the store. I don't know what gets into me, maybe I just have an over-developed sense of competition or something, but I went and ruined her, and furthermore I 30 can't get rid of her. And he's the third executive I've done that to. Isn't that a crummy characteristic? And to top it all, I go to their weddings! [*Indignantly, but laughing.*] Like I'm not supposed to take bribes. Manufacturers 35 offer me a hundred-dollar bill now and then to throw an order their way. You know how honest I am, but it's like this girl, see. I hate myself for it. Because I don't want the girl, and, still, I take it and—I love it!

40 BIFF. Let's go to sleep.

HAPPY. I guess we didn't settle anything, heh?

BIFF. I just got one idea that I think I'm going to try.

HAPPY. What's that?

45 BIFF. Remember Bill Oliver?

HAPPY. Sure, Oliver is very big now. You want to work for him again?

BIFF. No, but when I quit he said something to me. He put his arm on my shoulder, and he said, "Biff, if you ever need anything, come to 50 me."

HAPPY. I remember that. That sounds good.

BIFF. I think I'll go to see him. If I could get ten thousand or even seven or eight thousand dollars I could buy a beautiful ranch. 55

HAPPY. I bet he'd back you. 'Cause he thought highly of you, Biff. I mean, they all do. You're well liked, Biff. That's why I say to come back here, and we both have the apartment. And I'm tellin' you, Biff, any babe you 60 want . . .

BIFF. No, with a ranch I could do the work I like and still be something. I just wonder though. I wonder if Oliver still thinks I stole that carton of basketballs. 65

HAPPY. Oh, he probably forgot that long ago. It's almost ten years. You're too sensitive. Anyway, he didn't really fire you.

BIFF. Well, I think he was going to. I think that's why I quit. I was never sure whether he 70 knew or not. I know he thought the world of me, though. I was the only one he'd let lock up the place.

WILLY [*below*]. You gonna wash the engine, Biff? 75

HAPPY. Shh!

[BIFF *looks at* HAPPY, *who is gazing down, listening.* WILLY *is mumbling in the parlor.*]

HAPPY. You hear that?

[*They listen.* WILLY *laughs warmly.*] 80

BIFF [*growing angry*]. Doesn't he know Mom can hear that?

WILLY. Don't get your sweater dirty, Biff!

[*A look of pain crosses* BIFF's *face.*]

HAPPY. Isn't that terrible? Don't leave again, 85 will you? You'll find a job here. You gotta stick around. I don't know what to do about him, it's getting embarrassing.

WILLY. What a simonizing job!

BIFF. Mom's hearing that! 90

WILLY. No kiddin', Biff, you got a date? Wonderful!

HAPPY. Go on to sleep. But talk to him in the morning, will you?

BIFF [*reluctantly getting into bed*]. With her 95 in the house. Brother!

HAPPY [*getting into bed*]. I wish you'd have a good talk with him.

[*The light on their room begins to fade.*]

BIFF [*to himself in bed*]. That selfish, stupid . . .

HAPPY. Sh . . . Sleep, Biff.

[*Their light is out. Well before they have finished speaking, WILLY's form is dimly seen below in the darkened kitchen. He opens the refrigerator, searches in there, and takes out a bottle of milk. The apartment houses are fading out, and the entire house and surroundings become covered with leaves. Music insinuates itself as the leaves appear.*]

WILLY. Just wanna be careful with those girls, Biff, that's all. Don't make any promises. No promises of any kind. Because a girl, y'know, they always believe what you tell 'em, and you're very young, Biff, you're too young to be talking seriously to girls.

[*Light rises on the kitchen. WILLY, talking, shuts the refrigerator door and comes downstage to the kitchen table. He pours milk into a glass. He is totally immersed in himself, smiling faintly.*]

WILLY. Too young entirely, Biff. You want to watch your schooling first. Then when you're all set, there'll be plenty of girls for a boy like you. [*He smiles broadly at a kitchen chair.*] That so? The girls pay for you? [*He laughs.*] Boy, you must really be makin' a hit.

[*WILLY is gradually addressing—physically —a point off-stage, speaking through the wall of the kitchen, and his voice has been rising in volume to that of a normal conversation.*]

WILLY. I been wondering why you polish the car so careful. Ha! Don't leave the hubcaps, boys. Get the chamois to the hubcaps. Happy, use newspaper on the windows, it's the easiest thing. Show him how to do it, Biff! You see, Happy? Pad it up, use it like a pad. That's it, that's it, good work. You're doin' all right, Hap. [*He pauses, then nods in approbation for a few seconds, then looks upward.*] Biff, first thing we gotta do when we get time is clip that big branch over the house. Afraid it's gonna fall in a storm and hit the roof. Tell you what. We get a rope and sling her around, and then we climb up there with a couple of saws and take her down. Soon as you finish the car, boys, I wanna see ya. I got a surprise for you, boys.

BIFF [*offstage*]. Whatta ya got, Dad?

WILLY. No, you finish first. Never leave a job till you're finished—remember that. [*Looking toward the "big trees."*] Biff, up in Albany I saw a beautiful hammock. I think I'll buy it next trip, and we'll hang it right between those two elms. Wouldn't that be something? Just swingin' there under those branches. Boy, that would be . . .

[*YOUNG BIFF and YOUNG HAPPY appear from the direction WILLY was addressing. HAPPY carries rags and a pail of water. BIFF, wearing a sweater with a block "S," carries a football.*]

BIFF [*pointing in the direction of the car offstage*]. How's that, Pop, professional?

WILLY. Terrific. Terrific job, boys. Good work, Biff.

HAPPY. Where's the surprise, Pop?

WILLY. In the back seat of the car.

HAPPY. Boy! [*He runs off.*]

BIFF. What is it, Dad? Tell me, what'd you buy?

WILLY [*laughing, cuffs him*]. Never mind, something I want you to have.

BIFF [*turns and starts off*]. What is it, Hap?

HAPPY [*offstage*]. It's a punching bag!

BIFF. Oh, Pop!

WILLY. It's got Gene Tunney's signature on it!

[*HAPPY runs onstage with a punching bag.*]

BIFF. Gee, how'd you know we wanted a punching bag?

WILLY. Well, it's the finest thing for the timing.

HAPPY [*lies down on his back and pedals with his feet*]. I'm losing weight, you notice, Pop?

WILLY [*to HAPPY*]. Jumping rope is good too.

BIFF. Did you see the new football I got?

WILLY [*examining the ball*]. Where'd you get a new ball?

BIFF. The coach told me to practice my passing.

WILLY. That so? And he gave you the ball, heh?

BIFF. Well, I borrowed it from the locker room. [*He laughs confidentially.*]

WILLY [*laughing with him at the theft*]. I want you to return that.

5 HAPPY. I told you he wouldn't like it!

BIFF [*angrily*]. Well, I'm bringing it back!

WILLY [*stopping the incipient argument, to* HAPPY]. Sure, he's gotta practice with a regulation ball, doesn't he? [*To* BIFF.] Coach'll 10 probably congratulate you on your initiative!

BIFF. Oh, he keeps congratulating my initiative all the time, Pop.

WILLY. That's because he likes you. If somebody else took that ball there'd be an uproar. 15 So what's the report, boys, what's the report?

BIFF. Where'd you go this time, Dad? Gee we were lonesome for you.

WILLY [*pleased, puts an arm around each boy and they come down to the apron*]. Lone- 20 some, heh?

BIFF. Missed you every minute.

WILLY. Don't say? Tell you a secret, boys. Don't breathe it to a soul. Someday I'll have my own business, and I'll never have to leave 25 home any more.

HAPPY. Like Uncle Charley, heh?

WILLY. Bigger than Uncle Charley! Because Charley is not—liked. He's liked, but he's not —well liked.

30 BIFF. Where'd you go this time, Dad?

WILLY. Well, I got on the road, and I went north to Providence. Met the Mayor.

BIFF. The Mayor of Providence!

WILLY. He was sitting in the hotel lobby.

35 BIFF. What'd he say?

WILLY. He said, "Morning!" And I said, "You got a fine city here, Mayor." And then he had coffee with me. And then I went to Waterbury. Waterbury is a fine city. Big clock 40 city, the famous Waterbury clock. Sold a nice bill there. And then Boston—Boston is the cradle of the Revolution. A fine city. And a couple of other towns in Mass., and on to Portland and Bangor and straight home!

45 BIFF. Gee, I'd love to go with you sometime, Dad.

WILLY. Soon as summer comes.

HAPPY. Promise?

WILLY. You and Hap and I, and I'll show you all the towns. America is full of beautiful 50 towns and fine, upstanding people. And they know me, boys, they know me up and down New England. The finest people. And when I bring you fellas up, there'll be open sesame for all of us, 'cause one thing, boys: I have friends. 55 I can park my car in any street in New England, and the cops protect it like their own. This summer, heh?

BIFF and HAPPY [*together*]. Yeah! You bet!

WILLY. We'll take our bathing-suits. 60

HAPPY. We'll carry your bags, Pop!

WILLY. Oh, won't that be something! Me comin' into the Boston stores with you boys carryin' my bags. What a sensation!

[BIFF *is prancing around, practicing passing* 65 *the ball.*]

WILLY. You nervous, Biff, about the game?

BIFF. Not if you're gonna be there.

WILLY. What do they say about you in school, now that they made you captain? 70

HAPPY. There's a crowd of girls behind him every time the classes change.

BIFF [*taking* WILLY'S *hand*]. This Saturday, Pop, this Saturday—just for you, I'm going to break through for a touchdown. 75

HAPPY. You're supposed to pass.

BIFF. I'm takin' one play for Pop. You watch me, Pop, and when I take off my helmet, that means I'm breakin' out. Then watch me crash through that line! 80

WILLY [*kisses* BIFF]. Oh, wait'll I tell this in Boston!

[BERNARD *enters in knickers. He is younger than* BIFF, *earnest and loyal, a worried boy.*]

BERNARD. Biff, where are you? You're sup- 85 posed to study with me today.

WILLY. Hey, looka Bernard. What're you lookin' so anemic about, Bernard?

BERNARD. He's gotta study, Uncle Willy. He's got Regents next week. 90

HAPPY [*tauntingly, spinning* BERNARD *around*]. Let's box, Bernard!

BERNARD. Biff! [*He gets away from* HAPPY.] Listen, Biff, I heard Mr. Birnbaum say that if you don't start studyin' math he's gonna flunk 95 you, and you won't graduate. I heard him!

WILLY. You better study with him, Biff. Go ahead now.

BERNARD. I heard him!

BIFF. Oh, Pop, you didn't see my sneakers! [*He holds up a foot for* WILLY *to look at.*]

WILLY. Hey, that's a beautiful job of printing!

BERNARD [*wiping his glasses*]. Just because he printed University of Virginia on his sneakers doesn't mean they've got to graduate him, Uncle Willy!

WILLY [*angrily*]. What're you talking about? With scholarships to three universities they're gonna flunk him?

BERNARD. But I heard Mr. Birnbaum say—

WILLY. Don't be a pest, Bernard! [*To his boys.*] What an anemic!

BERNARD. Okay, I'm waiting for you in my house, Biff.

[BERNARD *goes off. The* LOMANS *laugh.*]

WILLY. Bernard is not well liked, is he?

BIFF. He's liked, but he's not well liked.

HAPPY. That's right, Pop.

WILLY. That's just what I mean. Bernard can get the best marks in school, y'understand, but when he gets out in the business world, y'understand, you are going to be five times ahead of him. That's why I thank Almighty God you're both built like Adonises. Because the man who makes an appearance in the business world, the man who creates personal interest, is the man who gets ahead. Be liked and you will never want. You take me, for instance. I never have to wait in line to see a buyer. "Willy Loman is here!" That's all they have to know, and I go right through.

BIFF. Did you knock them dead, Pop?

WILLY. Knocked 'em cold in Providence, slaughtered 'em in Boston.

HAPPY [*on his back, pedaling again*]. I'm losing weight, you notice, Pop?

[LINDA *enters, as of old, a ribbon in her hair, carrying a basket of washing.*]

LINDA [*with youthful energy*]. Hello, dear!

WILLY. Sweetheart!

LINDA. How'd the Chevvy run?

WILLY. Chevrolet, Linda, is the greatest car ever built. [*To the boys.*] Since when did you let your mother carry wash up the stairs?

BIFF. Grab hold there, boy!

HAPPY. Where to, Mom?

LINDA. Hang them up on the line. And you better go down to your friends, Biff. The cellar is full of boys. They don't know what to do with themselves.

BIFF. Ah, when Pop comes home they can wait!

WILLY [*laughs appreciatively*]. You better go down and tell them what to do, Biff.

BIFF. I think I'll have them sweep out the furnace room.

WILLY. Good work, Biff.

BIFF [*goes through wall-line of kitchen to doorway at back and calls down*]. Fellas! Everybody sweep out the furnace room! I'll be right down!

VOICES. All right! Okay, Biff.

BIFF. George and Sam and Frank, come out back! We're hangin' up the wash! Come on, Hap, on the double! [*He and* HAPPY *carry out the basket.*]

LINDA. The way they obey him!

WILLY. Well, that's training, the training. I'm tellin' you, I was sellin' thousands and thousands, but I had to come home.

LINDA. Oh, the whole block'll be at that game. Did you sell anything?

WILLY. I did five hundred gross in Providence and seven hundred gross in Boston.

LINDA. No! Wait a minute, I've got a pencil. [*She pulls pencil and paper out of her apron pocket.*] That makes your commission. . . . Two hundred—my God! Two hundred and twelve dollars!

WILLY. Well, I didn't figure it yet, but . . .

LINDA. How much did you do?

WILLY. Well, I—I did—about a hundred and eighty gross in Providence. Well, no—it came to—roughly two hundred gross on the whole trip.

LINDA [*without hesitation*]. Two hundred gross. That's . . . [*She figures.*]

WILLY. The trouble was that three of the stores were half-closed for inventory in Boston. Otherwise I woulda broke records.

LINDA. Well, it makes seventy dollars and some pennies. That's very good.

WILLY. What do we owe?

LINDA. Well, on the first there's sixteen dollars on the refrigerator—

WILLY. Why sixteen?

LINDA. Well, the fan belt broke, so it was a dollar eighty.

WILLY. But it's brand new.

LINDA. Well, the man said that's the way it is. Till they work themselves in, y'know.

[*They move through the wall-line into the kitchen.*]

WILLY. I hope we didn't get stuck on that machine.

LINDA. They got the biggest ads of any of them!

WILLY. I know, it's a fine machine. What else?

LINDA. Well, there's nine-sixty for the washing-machine. And for the vacuum cleaner there's three and a half due on the fifteenth. Then the roof, you got twenty-one dollars remaining.

WILLY. It don't leak, does it?

LINDA. No, they did a wonderful job. Then you owe Frank for the carburetor.

WILLY. I'm not going to pay that man! That goddam Chevrolet, they ought to prohibit the manufacture of that car!

LINDA. Well, you owe him three and a half. And odds and ends, comes to around a hundred and twenty dollars by the fifteenth.

WILLY. A hundred and twenty dollars! My God, if business don't pick up I don't know what I'm gonna do!

LINDA. Well, next week you'll do better.

WILLY. Oh, I'll knock 'em dead next week. I'll go to Hartford. I'm very well liked in Hartford. You know, the trouble is, Linda, people don't seem to take to me.

[*They move on to the forestage.*]

LINDA. Oh, don't be foolish.

WILLY. I know it when I walk in. They seem to laugh at me.

LINDA. Why? Why would they laugh at you? Don't talk that way, Willy.

[WILLY *moves to the edge of the stage.* LINDA *goes into the kitchen and starts to darn stockings.*]

WILLY. I don't know the reason for it, but they just pass me by. I'm not noticed.

LINDA. But you're doing wonderful, dear. You're making seventy to a hundred dollars a week.

WILLY. But I gotta be at it ten, twelve hours a day. Other men—I don't know—they do it easier. I don't know why—I can't stop myself—I talk too much. A man oughta come in with a few words. One thing about Charley. He's a man of few words, and they respect him.

LINDA. You don't talk too much, you're just lively.

WILLY [*smiling*]. Well, I figure, what the hell, life is short, a couple of jokes. [*To himself.*] I joke too much! [*The smile goes.*]

LINDA. Why? You're—

WILLY. I'm fat. I'm—very foolish to look at, Linda. I didn't tell you, but Christmas-time I happened to be calling on F. H. Stewarts, and a salesman I know, as I was going in to see the buyer I heard him say something about—walrus. And I—I cracked him right across the face. I won't take that. I simply will not take that. But they laugh at me. I know that.

LINDA. Darling . . .

WILLY. I gotta overcome it. I know I gotta overcome it. I'm not dressing to advantage, maybe.

LINDA. Willy, darling, you're the handsomest man in the world—

WILLY. Oh, no, Linda.

LINDA. To me you are. [*Slight pause.*] The handsomest.

[*From the darkness is heard the laughter of a woman.* WILLY *doesn't turn to it, but it continues through* LINDA's *lines.*]

LINDA. And the boys, Willy. Few men are idolized by their children the way you are.

[*Music is heard as behind a scrim, to the left of the house, the* WOMAN, *dimly seen, is dressing.*]

WILLY [*with great feeling*]. You're the best there is, Linda, you're a pal, you know that? On the road—on the road I want to grab you sometimes and just kiss the life outa you.

[*The laughter is loud now, and he moves into a brightening area at the left, where the* WOMAN *has come from behind the scrim and is standing, putting on her hat, looking into a "mirror," and laughing.*]

WILLY. 'Cause I get so lonely—especially when business is bad and there's nobody to talk to. I get the feeling that I'll never sell anything again, that I won't make a living for you, or a business, a business for the boys. [*He talks through the* WOMAN'S *subsiding laughter. The* WOMAN *primps at the "mirror."*] There's so much I want to make for—

THE WOMAN. Me? You didn't make me, Willy. I picked you.

WILLY [*pleased*]. You picked me?

THE WOMAN [*who is quite proper-looking, Willy's age*]. I did. I've been sitting at that desk watching all the salesmen go by, day in, day out. But you've got such a sense of humor, and we do have such a good time together, don't we?

WILLY. Sure, sure. [*He takes her in his arms.*] Why do you have to go now?

THE WOMAN. It's two o'clock . . .

WILLY. No, come on in! [*He pulls her.*]

THE WOMAN. . . . my sisters'll be scandalized. When'll you be back?

WILLY. Oh, two weeks about. Will you come up again?

THE WOMAN. Sure thing. You do make me laugh. It's good for me. [*She squeezes his arm, kisses him.*] And I think you're a wonderful man.

WILLY. You picked me, heh?

THE WOMAN. Sure. Because you're so sweet. And such a kidder.

WILLY. Well, I'll see you next time I'm in Boston.

THE WOMAN. I'll put you right through to the buyers.

WILLY [*slapping her bottom*]. Right. Well, bottoms up!

THE WOMAN [*slaps him gently and laughs*]. You just kill me, Willy. [*He suddenly grabs her and kisses her roughly.*] You kill me. And thanks for the stockings. I love a lot of stockings. Well, good night.

WILLY. Good night. And keep your pores open!

THE WOMAN. Oh, Willy!

[*The* WOMAN *bursts out laughing, and* LINDA'S *laughter blends in The* WOMAN *dis-*appears into the dark. Now the area at the kitchen table brightens.* LINDA *is sitting where she was at the kitchen table, but now is mending a pair of her silk stockings.*]

LINDA. You are, Willy. The handsomest man. You've got no reason to feel that—

WILLY [*coming out of the* WOMAN'S *dimming area and going over to* LINDA]. I'll make it all up to you, Linda, I'll—

LINDA. There's nothing to make up, dear. You're doing fine, better than—

WILLY [*noticing her mending*]. What's that?

LINDA. Just mending my stockings. They're so expensive—

WILLY [*angrily taking them from her*]. I won't have you mending stockings in this house! Now throw them out!

[LINDA *puts the stockings in her pocket.*]

BERNARD [*entering on the run*]. Where is he? If he doesn't study!

WILLY [*moving to the forestage, with great agitation*]. You'll give him the answers!

BERNARD. I do, but I can't on a Regents! That's a state exam! They're liable to arrest me!

WILLY. Where is he? I'll whip him, I'll whip him!

LINDA. And he'd better give back that football, Willy, it's not nice.

WILLY. Biff! Where is he? Why is he taking everything?

LINDA. He's too rough with the girls, Willy. All the mothers are afraid of him!

WILLY. I'll whip him!

BERNARD. He's driving the car without a license!

[*The* WOMAN'S *laugh is heard.*]

WILLY. Shut up!

LINDA. All the mothers—

WILLY. Shut up!

BERNARD [*backing quietly away and out*]. Mr. Birnbaum says he's stuck up.

WILLY. Get outa here!

BERNARD. If he doesn't buckle down he'll flunk math! [*He goes off.*]

LINDA. He's right, Willy, you've gotta—

WILLY [*exploding at her*]. There's nothing the matter with him! You want him to be a worm like Bernard? He's got spirit, personality . . .

[*As he speaks* Linda, *almost in tears, exits into the livingroom.* Willy *is alone in the kitchen, writing and staring. The leaves are gone. It is night again, and the apartment houses look down from behind.*]

Willy. Loaded with it. Loaded! What is he stealing? He's giving it back, isn't he? Why is he stealing? What did I tell him? I never in my life told him anything but decent things.

[Happy *in pajamas has come down the stairs;* Willy *suddenly becomes aware of* Happy's *presence.*]

Happy. Let's go now, come on.

Willy [*sitting down at the kitchen table*]. Huh! Why did she have to wax the floors herself? Everytime she waxes the floors she keels over. She knows that!

Happy. Shh! Take it easy. What brought you back tonight?

Willy. I got an awful scare. Nearly hit a kid in Yonkers. God! Why didn't I go to Alaska with my brother Ben that time! Ben! That man was a genius, that man was success incarnate! What a mistake! He begged me to go.

Happy. Well, there's no use in—

Willy. You guys! There was a man started with the clothes on his back and ended up with diamond mines!

Happy. Boy, someday I'd like to know how he did it.

Willy. What's the mystery? The man knew what he wanted and went out and got it! Walked into a jungle, and comes out, the age of twenty-one, and he's rich! The world is an oyster, but you don't crack it open on a mattress!

Happy. Pop, I told you I'm gonna retire you for life.

Willy. You'll retire me for life on seventy goddam dollars a week? And your women and your car and your apartment, and you'll retire me for life! Christ's sake, I couldn't get past Yonkers today! Where are you guys, where are you? The woods are burning! I can't drive a car!

[Charley *has appeared in the doorway. He is a large man, slow of speech, laconic, immovable. In all he says, despite what he says, there is pity, and now, trepidation. He has a robe over pajamas, slippers on his feet. He enters the kitchen.*]

Charley. Everything all right?

Happy. Yeah, Charley, everything's . . .

Willy. What's the matter?

Charley. I heard some noise. I thought something happened. Can't we do something about the walls? You sneeze in here, and in my house hats blow off.

Happy. Let's go to bed, Dad. Come on.

[Charley *signals to* Happy *to go.*]

Willy. You go ahead, I'm not tired at the moment.

Happy [*to* Willy]. Take it easy, huh? [*He exits.*]

Willy. What are you doin' up?

Charley [*sitting down at the kitchen table opposite* Willy]. Couldn't sleep good. I had a heartburn.

Willy. Well, you don't know how to eat.

Charley. I eat with my mouth.

Willy. No, you're ignorant. You gotta know about vitamins and things like that.

Charley. Come on, let's shoot. Tire you out a little.

Willy [*hesitantly*]. All right. You got cards?

Charley [*taking a deck from his pocket*]. Yeah, I got them. Someplace. What is it with those vitamins?

Willy [*dealing*]. They build up your bones. Chemistry.

Charley. Yeah, but there's no bones in a heartburn.

Willy. What are you talkin' about? Do you know the first thing about it?

Charley. Don't get insulted.

Willy. Don't talk about something you don't know anything about.

[*They are playing. Pause.*]

Charley. What're you doin' home?

Willy. A little trouble with the car.

Charley. Oh. [*Pause.*] I'd like to take a trip to California.

Willy. Don't say.

Charley. You want a job?

WILLY. I got a job, I told you that. [*After a slight pause.*] What the hell are you offering me a job for?

CHARLEY. Don't get insulted.

5   WILLY. Don't insult me.

CHARLEY. I don't see no sense in it. You don't have to go on this way.

WILLY. I got a good job. [*Slight pause.*] What do you keep comin' in here for?

10   CHARLEY. You want me to go?

WILLY [*after a pause, withering*]. I can't understand it. He's going back to Texas again. What the hell is that?

CHARLEY. Let him go.

15   WILLY. I got nothin' to give him, Charley, I'm clean, I'm clean.

CHARLEY. He won't starve. None of them starve. Forget about him.

WILLY. Then what have I got to remember?

20   CHARLEY. You take it too hard. To hell with it. When a deposit bottle is broken you don't get your nickel back.

WILLY. That's easy enough for you to say.

CHARLEY. That ain't easy for me to say.

25   WILLY. Did you see the ceiling I put up in the living room?

CHARLEY. Yeah, that's a piece of work. To put up a ceiling is a mystery to me. How do you do it?

30   WILLY. What's the difference?

CHARLEY. Well, talk about it.

WILLY. You gonna put up a ceiling?

CHARLEY. How could I put up a ceiling?

WILLY. Then what the hell are you bother-

35   ing me for?

CHARLEY. You're insulted again.

WILLY. A man who can't handle tools is not a man. You're disgusting.

CHARLEY. Don't call me disgusting, Willy.

40   [UNCLE BEN, *carrying a valise and an umbrella, enters the forestage from around the right corner of the house. He is a stolid man, in his sixties, with a mustache and an authoritative air. He is utterly certain of his destiny,*

45   *and there is an aura of far places about him. He enters exactly as* WILLY *speaks.*]

WILLY. I'm getting awfully tired, Ben.

[BEN's music is heard. BEN *looks around at everything.*]

CHARLEY. Good, keep playing; you'll sleep   50 better. Did you call me Ben?

[BEN *looks at his watch.*]

WILLY. That's funny. For a second there you reminded me of my brother Ben.

BEN. I only have a few minutes. [*He strolls,*   55 *inspecting the place.* WILLY *and* CHARLEY *continue playing.*]

CHARLEY. You never heard from him again, heh? Since that time?

WILLY. Didn't Linda tell you? Couple of   60 weeks ago we got a letter from his wife in Africa. He died.

CHARLEY. That so.

BEN [*chuckling*]. So this is Brooklyn, eh?

CHARLEY. Maybe you're in for some of his   65 money.

WILLY. Naa, he had seven sons. There's just one opportunity I had with that man . . .

BEN. I must take a train, William. There are several properties I'm looking at in Alaska.   70

WILLY. Sure, sure! If I'd gone with him to Alaska that time, everything would've been totally different.

CHARLEY. Go on, you'd froze to death up there.   75

WILLY. What're you talking about?

BEN. Opportunity is tremendous in Alaska, William. Surprised you're not up there.

WILLY. Sure, tremendous.

CHARLEY. Heh?   80

WILLY. There was the only man I ever met who knew the answers.

CHARLEY. Who?

BEN. How are you all?

WILLY [*taking a pot, smiling*]. Fine, fine.   85

CHARLEY. Pretty sharp tonight.

BEN. Is Mother living with you?

WILLY. No, she died a long time ago.

CHARLEY. Who?

BEN. That's too bad. Fine specimen of a lady,   90 Mother.

WILLY [*to* CHARLEY]. Heh?

BEN. I'd hoped to see the old girl.

CHARLEY. Who died?

BEN. Heard anything from Father, have you?

WILLY [*unnerved*]. What do you mean, who died?

CHARLEY [*taking a pot*]. What're you talkin'
5 about?

BEN [*looking at his watch*]. William, it's half past eight!

WILLY [*as though to dispel his confusion he angrily stops* CHARLEY's *hand*]. That's my
10 build!

CHARLEY. I put the ace—

WILLY. If you don't know how to play the game I'm not gonna throw my money away on you!

15 CHARLEY [*rising*]. It was my ace, for God's sake!

WILLY. I'm through, I'm through!

BEN. When did Mother die?

WILLY. Long ago. Since the beginning you
20 never knew how to play cards.

CHARLEY [*picks up the cards and goes to the door*]. All right! Next time I'll bring a deck with five aces.

WILLY. I don't play that kind of game!

25 CHARLEY [*turning to him*]. You ought to be ashamed of yourself!

WILLY. Yeah?

CHARLEY. Yeah! [*He goes out.*]

WILLY [*slamming the door after him*]. Ig-
30 noramus!

BEN [*as* WILLY *comes toward him through the wall-line of the kitchen*]. So you're William.

WILLY [*shaking* BEN's *hand*]. Ben! I've been waiting for you so long! What's the answer?
35 How did you do it?

BEN. Oh, there's a story in that.

[LINDA *enters the forestage, as of old, carrying the wash basket.*]

LINDA. Is this Ben?

40 BEN [*gallantly*]. How do you do, my dear?

LINDA. Where've you been all these years? Willy's always wondered why you—

WILLY [*pulling* BEN *away from her impatiently*]. Where is Dad? Didn't you follow
45 him? How did you get started?

BEN. Well, I don't know how much you remember.

WILLY. Well, I was just a baby, of course, only three or four years old—

BEN. Three years and eleven months.   50

WILLY. What a memory, Ben!

BEN. I have many enterprises, William, and I have never kept books.

WILLY. I remember I was sitting under the wagon in—was it Nebraska?   55

BEN. It was South Dakota, and I gave you a bunch of wild flowers.

WILLY. I remember you walking away down some open road.

BEN [*laughing*]. I was going to find Father   60
in Alaska.

WILLY. Where is he?

BEN. At that age I had a very faulty view of geography, William. I discovered after a few days that I was heading due south, so instead   65
of Alaska, I ended up in Africa.

LINDA. Africa!

WILLY. The Gold Coast!

BEN. Principally diamond mines.

LINDA. Diamond mines!   70

BEN. Yes, my dear. But I've only a few minutes—

WILLY. No! Boys! Boys! [YOUNG BIFF *and* HAPPY *appear.*] Listen to this. This is your Uncle Ben, a great man! Tell my boys, Ben!   75

BEN. Why boys, when I was seventeen I walked into the jungle, and when I was twenty-one I walked out. [*He laughs.*] And by God I was rich.

WILLY [*to the boys*]. You see what I been   80
talking about? The greatest things can happen!

BEN [*glancing at his watch*]. I have an appointment in Ketchikan Tuesday week.

WILLY. No, Ben! Please tell about Dad. I   85
want my boys to hear. I want them to know the kind of stock they spring from. All I remember is a man with a big beard, and I was in Mamma's lap, sitting around a fire, and some kind of high music.   90

BEN. His flute. He played the flute.

WILLY. Sure, the flute, that's right!

[*New music is heard, a high, rollicking tune.*]

BEN. Father was a very great and a very

wild-hearted man. We would start in Boston, and he'd toss the whole family into the wagon, and then he'd drive the team right across the country; through Ohio, and Indiana, Michigan, Illinois, and all the Western states. And we'd stop in the towns and sell the flutes that he'd made on the way. Great inventor, Father. With one gadget he made more in a week than a man like you could make in a lifetime.

WILLY. That's just the way I'm bringing them up, Ben—rugged, well liked, all-around.

BEN. Yeah? [*To* BIFF.] Hit that, boy—hard as you can. [*He pounds his stomach.*]

BIFF. Oh, no, sir!

BEN [*taking boxing stance*]. Come on, get to me! [*He laughs.*]

WILLY. Go to it, Biff! Go ahead, show him!

BIFF. Okay! [*He cocks his fists and starts in.*]

LINDA [*to* WILLY]. Why must he fight, dear?

BEN [*sparring with* BIFF]. Good boy! Good boy!

WILLY. How's that, Ben, heh?

HAPPY. Give him the left, Biff!

LINDA. Why are you fighting?

BEN. Good boy! [*Suddenly comes in, trips* BIFF, *and stands over him, the point of his umbrella poised over* BIFF's *eye.*]

LINDA. Look out, Biff!

BIFF. Gee!

BEN [*patting* BIFF's *knee*]. Never fight fair with a stranger, boy. You'll never get out of the jungle that way. [*Taking* LINDA's *hand and bowing.*] It was an honor and a pleasure to meet you, Linda.

LINDA [*withdrawing her hand coldly, frightened*]. Have a nice—trip.

BEN [*to* WILLY]. And good luck with your— what do you do?

WILLY. Selling.

BEN. Yes. Well . . . [*He raises his hand in farewell to all.*]

WILLY. No, Ben, I don't want you to think . . . [*He takes* BEN's *arm to show him.*] It's Brooklyn, I know, but we hunt too.

BEN. Really, now.

WILLY. Oh, sure, there's snakes and rabbits and—that's why I moved out here. Why, Biff can fell any one of these trees in no time! Boys! Go right over to where they're building the apartment house and get some sand. We're gonna rebuild the entire front stoop right now! Watch this, Ben!

BIFF. Yes, sir! On the double, Hap!

HAPPY [*as he and* BIFF *run off*]. I lost weight, Pop, you notice?

[CHARLEY *enters in knickers, even before the boys are gone.*]

CHARLEY. Listen, if they steal any more from that building the watchman'll put the cops on them!

LINDA [*to* WILLY]. Don't let Biff . . .

[BEN *laughs lustily.*]

WILLY. You shoulda seen the lumber they brought home last week. At least a dozen six-by-tens worth all kinds a money.

CHARLEY. Listen, if that watchman—

WILLY. I gave them hell, understand. But I got a couple of fearless characters there.

CHARLEY. Willy, the jails are full of fearless characters.

BEN [*clapping* WILLY *on the back, with a laugh at* CHARLEY]. And the stock exchange, friend!

WILLY [*joining in* BEN's *laughter*]. Where are the rest of your pants?

CHARLEY. My wife bought them.

WILLY. Now all you need is a golf club and you can go upstairs and go to sleep. [*To* BEN.] Great athlete! Between him and his son Bernard they can't hammer a nail!

BERNARD [*rushing in*]. The watchman's chasing Biff!

WILLY [*angrily*]. Shut up! He's not stealing anything!

LINDA [*alarmed, hurrying off left*]. Where is he? Biff, dear!

[*She exits.*]

WILLY [*moving toward the left, away from* BEN]. There's nothing wrong. What's the matter with you?

BEN. Nervy boy. Good!

WILLY [*laughing*]. Oh, nerves of iron, that Biff!

CHARLEY. Don't know what it is. My New England man comes back and he's bleedin', they murdered him up there.

WILLY. It's contacts, Charley, I got impor-5 tant contacts!

CHARLEY [*sarcastically*]. Glad to hear it, Willy. Come in later, we'll shoot a little casino. I'll take some of your Portland money. [*He laughs at* WILLY *and exits.*]

10 WILLY [*turning to* BEN]. Business is bad, it's murderous. But not for me, of course.

BEN. I'll stop by on my way back to Africa.

WILLY [*longingly*]. Can't you stay a few days? You're just what I need, Ben, because I
15 —I have a fine position here, but I—well, Dad left when I was such a baby and I never had a chance to talk to him and I still feel—kind of temporary about myself.

BEN. I'll be late for my train.

20 [*They are at opposite ends of the stage.*]

WILLY. Ben, my boys—can't we talk? They'd go into the jaws of hell for me, see, but I—

BEN. William, you're being first-rate with your boys. Outstanding, manly chaps!

25 WILLY [*hanging on to his words*]. Oh, Ben, that's good to hear! Because sometimes I'm afraid that I'm not teaching them the right kind of—Ben, how should I teach them?

BEN [*giving great weight to each word, and
30 with a certain vicious audacity*]. William, when I walked into the jungle, I was seventeen. When I walked out I was twenty-one. And, by God, I was rich! [*He goes off into darkness around the right corner of the house.*]

35 WILLY. . . . was rich! That's just the spirit I want to imbue them with! To walk into a jungle! I was right! I was right! I was right!

[BEN *is gone, but* WILLY *is still speaking to him as* LINDA, *in nightgown and robe, enters
40 the kitchen, glances around for* WILLY, *then goes to the door of the house, looks out and sees him. Comes down to his left. He looks at her.*]

LINDA. Willy, dear? Willy?

45 WILLY. I was right!

LINDA. Did you have some cheese? [*He can't answer.*] It's very late, darling. Come to bed, heh?

WILLY [*looking straight up*]. Gotta break your neck to see a star in this yard.

LINDA. You coming in? 50

WILLY. Whatever happened to that diamond watch fob? Remember? When Ben came back from Africa that time? Didn't he give me a watch fob with a diamond in it?

LINDA. You pawned it, dear. Twelve, thir-55 teen years ago. For Biff's radio correspondence course.

WILLY. Gee, that was a beautiful thing. I'll take a walk.

LINDA. But you're in your slippers. 60

WILLY [*starting to go around the house at the left*]. I was right! I was! [*Half to* LINDA, *as he goes, shaking his head.*] What a man! There was a man worth talking to. I was right!

LINDA [*calling after* WILLY]. But your slip-65 pers, Willy!

[WILLY *is almost gone when* BIFF, *in his pajamas, comes down the stairs and enters the kitchen.*]

BIFF. What is he doing out there? 70

LINDA. Sh!

BIFF. God Almighty, Mom, how long has he been doing this?

LINDA. Don't, he'll hear you.

BIFF. What the hell is the matter with him? 75

LINDA. It'll pass by morning.

BIFF. Shouldn't we do anything?

LINDA. Oh, my dear, you should do a lot of things, but there's nothing to do, so go to sleep. 80

[HAPPY *comes down the stairs and sits on the steps.*]

HAPPY. I never heard him so loud, Mom.

LINDA. Well, come around more often; you'll hear him. 85

[*She sits down at the table and mends the lining of* WILLY's *jacket.*]

BIFF. Why didn't you ever write me about this, Mom?

LINDA. How would I write to you? For over 90 three months you had no address.

BIFF. I was on the move. But you know I thought of you all the time. You know that, don't you, pal?

LINDA. I know, dear, I know. But he likes to have a letter. Just to know that there's still a possibility for better things.

BIFF. He's not like this all the time, is he?

5 LINDA. It's when you come home he's always the worst.

BIFF. When I come home?

LINDA. When you write you're coming, he's all smiles, and talks about the future, and—
10 he's just wonderful. And then the closer you seem to come, the more shaky he gets, and then, by the time you get here, he's arguing, and he seems angry at you. I think it's just that maybe he can't bring himself to—to open up
15 to you. Why are you so hateful to each other? Why is that?

BIFF [evasively]. I'm not hateful, Mom.

LINDA. But you no sooner come in the door than you're fighting!

20 BIFF. I don't know why, I mean to change. I'm tryin', Mom; you understand?

LINDA. Are you home to stay now?

BIFF. I don't know. I want to look around, see what's doin'.

25 LINDA. Biff, you can't look around all your life, can you?

BIFF. I just can't take hold, Mom. I can't take hold of some kind of a life.

LINDA. Biff, a man is not a bird, to come and
30 go with the springtime.

BIFF. Your hair. . . [He touches her hair.] Your hair got so gray.

LINDA. Oh, it's been gray since you were in high school. I just stopped dyeing it, that's
35 all.

BIFF. Dye it again, will ya? I don't want my pal looking old. [He smiles.]

LINDA. You're such a boy! You think you can go away for a year and. . . . You've got to
40 get it into your head now that one day you'll knock on this door and there'll be strange people here—

BIFF. What are you talking about? You're not even sixty, Mom.

45 LINDA. But what about your father?

BIFF [lamely]. Well, I meant him too.

HAPPY. He admires Pop.

LINDA. Biff, dear, if you don't have any feel-ing for him, then you can't have any feeling for me.

50 BIFF. Sure I can, Mom.

LINDA. No. You can't just come to see me, because I love him. [With a threat, but only a threat, of tears.] He's the dearest man in the world to me, and I won't have anyone making
55 him feel unwanted and low and blue. You've got to make up your mind now, darling, there's no leeway any more. Either he's your father and you pay him that respect, or else you're not to come here. I know he's not easy to get
60 along with—nobody knows that better than me—but . . .

WILLY [from the left, with a laugh]. Hey, hey, Biffo!

BIFF [starting to go out after WILLY]. What
65 the hell is the matter with him? [HAPPY stops him.]

LINDA. Don't—don't go near him!

BIFF. Stop making excuses for him! He al-ways, always wiped the floor with you. Never
70 had an ounce of respect for you.

HAPPY. He's always had respect for—

BIFF. What the hell do you know about it?

HAPPY [surlily]. Just don't call him crazy!

BIFF. He's got no character—Charley
75 wouldn't do this. Not in his own house—spewing out that vomit from his mind.

HAPPY. Charley never had to cope with what he's got to.

BIFF. People are worse off than Willy Loman.
80 Believe me, I've seen them!

LINDA. Then make Charley your father, Biff. You can't do that, can you? I don't say he's a great man. Willy Loman never made a lot of money. His name was never in the paper. He's
85 not the finest character that ever lived. But he's a human being, and a terrible thing is happen-ing to him. So attention must be paid. He's not to be allowed to fall into his grave like an old dog. Attention, attention must be finally paid
90 to such a person. You called him crazy—

BIFF. I didn't mean—

LINDA. No, a lot of people think he's lost his —balance. But you don't have to be very smart to know what his trouble is. The man is ex-
95 hausted.

HAPPY. Sure!

LINDA. A small man can be just as exhausted as a great man. He works for a company thirty-six years this March, opens up unheard-of territories to their trademark, and now in his old age they take his salary away.

HAPPY [*indignantly*]. I didn't know that, Mom.

LINDA. You never asked, my dear! Now that you get your spending money someplace else you don't trouble your mind with him.

HAPPY. But I gave you money last—

LINDA. Christmas-time, fifty dollars! To fix the hot water it cost ninety-seven fifty! For five weeks he's been on straight commission, like a beginner, an unknown!

BIFF. Those ungrateful bastards!

LINDA. Are they any worse than his sons? When he brought them business, when he was young, they were glad to see him. But now his old friends, the old buyers that loved him so and always found some order to hand him in a pinch—they're all dead, retired. He used to be able to make six, seven calls a day in Boston. Now he takes his valises out of the car and puts them back and takes them out again and he's exhausted. Instead of walking he talks now. He drives seven hundred miles, and when he gets there no one knows him any more, no one welcomes him. And what goes through a man's mind, driving seven hundred miles home without having earned a cent? Why shouldn't he talk to himself? Why? When he has to go to Charley and borrow fifty dollars a week and pretend to me that it's his pay? How long can that go on? How long? You see what I'm sitting here and waiting for? And you tell me he has no character? The man who never worked a day but for your benefit? When does he get the medal for that? Is this his reward—to turn around at the age of sixty-three and find his sons, who he loved better than his life, one a philandering bum—

HAPPY. Mom!

LINDA. That's all you are, my baby! [*To* BIFF.] And you! What happened to the love you had for him? You were such pals! How you used to talk to him on the phone every night!

How lonely he was till he could come home to you!

BIFF. All right, Mom. I'll live here in my room, and I'll get a job. I'll keep away from him, that's all.

LINDA. No, Biff. You can't stay here and fight all the time.

BIFF. He threw me out of this house, remember that.

LINDA. Why did he do that? I never knew why.

BIFF. Because I know he's a fake and he doesn't like anybody around who knows!

LINDA. Why a fake? In what way? What do you mean?

BIFF. Just don't lay it all at my feet. It's between me and him—that's all I have to say. I'll chip in from now on. He'll settle for half my pay check. He'll be all right. I'm going to bed. [*He starts for the stairs.*]

LINDA. He won't be all right.

BIFF [*turning on the stairs, furiously*]. I hate this city and I'll stay here. Now what do you want?

LINDA. He's dying, Biff.

[HAPPY *turns quickly to her, shocked.*]

BIFF [*after a pause*]. Why is he dying?

LINDA. He's been trying to kill himself.

BIFF [*with great horror*]. How?

LINDA. I live from day to day.

BIFF. What're you talking about?

LINDA. Remember I wrote you that he smashed up the car again? In February?

BIFF. Well?

LINDA. The insurance inspector came. He said that they have evidence. That all these accidents in the last year—weren't—weren't—accidents.

HAPPY. How can they tell that? That's a lie.

LINDA. It seems there's a woman . . . [*she takes a breath as*]

BIFF [*sharply but contained*]. }What woman?

LINDA [*simultaneously*]. } . . . and this woman . . .

LINDA. What?

BIFF. Nothing. Go ahead.

LINDA. What did you say?

BIFF. Nothing. I just said what woman?

HAPPY. What about her?

LINDA. Well, it seems she was walking down the road and saw his car. She says that he wasn't driving fast at all, and that he didn't skid. She says he came to that little bridge, and then deliberately smashed into the railing, and it was only the shallowness of the water that saved him.

BIFF. Oh, no, he probably just fell asleep again.

LINDA. I don't think he fell asleep.

BIFF. Why not?

LINDA. Last month. . . . [*With great difficulty.*] Oh, boys, it's so hard to say a thing like this! He's just a big stupid man to you, but I tell you there's more good in him than in many other people. [*She chokes, wipes her eyes.*] I was looking for a fuse. The lights blew out, and I went down the cellar. And behind the fuse-box—it happened to fall out—was a length of rubber pipe—just short.

HAPPY. No kidding?

LINDA. There's a little attachment on the end of it. I knew right away. And sure enough, on the bottom of the water heater there's a new little nipple on the gas pipe.

HAPPY [*angrily*]. That—jerk.

BIFF. Did you have it taken off?

LINDA. I'm—I'm ashamed to. How can I mention it to him? Every day I go down and take away that little rubber pipe. But, when he comes home, I put it back where it was. How can I insult him that way? I don't know what to do. I live from day to day, boys. I tell you, I know every thought in his mind. It sounds so old-fashioned and silly, but I tell you he put his whole life into you and you've turned your backs on him. [*She is bent over in the chair, weeping, her face in her hands.*] Biff, I swear to God! Biff, his life is in your hands!

HAPPY [*to* BIFF]. How do you like that damned fool!

BIFF [*kissing her*]. All right, pal, all right. It's all settled now. I've been remiss. I know that, Mom. But now I'll stay, and I swear to you, I'll apply myself. [*Kneeling in front of her, in a fever of self-reproach.*] It's just—you see, Mom, I don't fit in business. Not that I won't try. I'll try, and I'll make good.

HAPPY. Sure you will. The trouble with you in business was you never tried to please people.

BIFF. I know, I—

HAPPY. Like when you worked for Harrison's. Bob Harrison said you were tops, and then you go and do some damn fool thing like whistling whole songs in the elevator like a comedian.

BIFF [*against* HAPPY]. So what? I like to whistle sometimes.

HAPPY. You don't raise a guy to a responsible job who whistles in the elevator!

LINDA. Well, don't argue about it now.

HAPPY. Like when you'd go off and swim in the middle of the day instead of taking the line around.

BIFF [*his resentment rising*]. Well, don't you run off? You take off sometimes, don't you? On a nice summer day?

HAPPY. Yeah, but I cover myself!

LINDA. Boys!

HAPPY. If I'm going to take a fade the boss can call any number where I'm supposed to be and they'll swear to him that I just left. I'll tell you something that I hate to say, Biff, but in the business world some of them think you're crazy.

BIFF [*angered*]. Screw the business world!

HAPPY. All right, screw it! Great, but cover yourself!

LINDA: Hap, Hap!

BIFF. I don't care what they think! They've laughed at Dad for years, and you know why? Because we don't belong in this nuthouse of a city! We should be mixing cement on some open plain, or—or carpenters. A carpenter is allowed to whistle!

[WILLY *walks in from the entrance of the house, at left.*]

WILLY. Even your grandfather was better than a carpenter.

[*Pause. They watch him.*] You never grew up. Bernard does not whistle in the elevator, I assure you.

BIFF [*as though to laugh* WILLY *out of it*]. Yeah, but you do, Pop.

WILLY. I never in my life whistled in an

elevator! And who in the business world thinks I'm crazy?

BIFF. I didn't mean it like that, Pop. Now don't make a whole thing out of it, will ya?

WILLY. Go back to the West! Be a carpenter, a cowboy, enjoy yourself!

LINDA. Willy, he was just saying—

WILLY. I heard what he said!

HAPPY [*trying to quiet* WILLY]. Hey, Pop, come on now . . .

WILLY [*continuing over* HAPPY'*s line*]. They laugh at me, heh? Go to Filene's, go to the Hub, go to Slattery's, Boston. Call out the name Willy Loman and see what happens! Big shot!

BIFF. All right, Pop.

WILLY. Big!

BIFF. All right!

WILLY. Why do you always insult me?

BIFF. I didn't say a word. [*To* LINDA.] Did I say a word?

LINDA. He didn't say anything, Willy.

WILLY [*going to the doorway of the living-room*]. All right, good night, good night.

LINDA. Willy, dear, he just decided . . .

WILLY [*to* BIFF]. If you get tired hanging around tomorrow, paint the ceiling I put up in the living-room.

BIFF. I'm leaving early tomorrow.

HAPPY. He's going to see Bill Oliver, Pop.

WILLY [*interestedly*]. Oliver? For what?

BIFF [*with reserve, but trying, trying*]. He always said he'd stake me. I'd like to go into business, so maybe I can take him up on it.

LINDA. Isn't that wonderful?

WILLY. Don't interrupt. What's wonderful about it? There's fifty men in the City of New York who'd stake him. [*To* BIFF.] Sporting goods?

BIFF. I guess so. I know something about it and—

WILLY. He knows something about it! You know sporting goods better than Spalding, for God's sake! How much is he giving you?

BIFF. I don't know. I didn't even see him yet, but—

WILLY. Then what're you talkin' about?

BIFF [*getting angry*]. Well, all I said was I'm gonna see him, that's all!

WILLY [*turning away*]. Ah, you're counting your chickens again.

BIFF [*starting left for the stairs*]. Oh, Jesus, I'm going to sleep!

WILLY [*calling after him*]. Don't curse in this house!

BIFF [*turning*]. Since when did you get so clean?

HAPPY [*trying to stop them*]. Wait a . . .

WILLY. Don't use that language to me! I won't have it!

HAPPY [*grabbing* BIFF, *shouts*]. Wait a minute! I got an idea. I got a feasible idea. Come here, Biff, let's talk this over now, let's talk some sense here. When I was down in Florida last time, I thought of a great idea to sell sporting goods. It just came back to me. You and I, Biff—we have a line, the Loman Line. We train a couple of weeks, and put on a couple of exhibitions, see?

WILLY. That's an idea!

HAPPY. Wait! We form two basketball teams, see? Two water-polo teams. We play each other. It's a million dollars' worth of publicity. Two brothers, see? The Loman Brothers. Displays in the Royal Palms—all the hotels. And banners over the ring and the basketball court: "Loman Brothers." Baby, we could sell sporting goods!

WILLY. That is a one-million-dollar idea!

LINDA. Marvellous!

BIFF. I'm in great shape as far as that's concerned.

HAPPY. And the beauty of it is, Biff, it wouldn't be like a business. We'd be out playin' ball again . . .

BIFF [*enthused*]. Yeah, that's . . .

WILLY. Million-dollar . . .

HAPPY. And you wouldn't get fed up with it, Biff. It'd be the family again. There'd be the old honor, and comradeship, and if you wanted to go off for a swim or somethin'— well you'd do it! Without some smart cooky gettin' up ahead of you!

WILLY. Lick the world! You guys together could absolutely lick the civilized world.

BIFF. I'll see Oliver tomorrow. Hap, if we could work that out . . .

LINDA. Maybe things are beginning to—

WILLY [wildly enthused, to LINDA]. Stop interrupting! [To BIFF.] But don't wear sports jacket and slacks when you see Oliver.

BIFF. No, I'll—

WILLY. A business suit, and talk as little as possible, and don't crack any jokes.

BIFF. He did like me. Always liked me.

LINDA. He loved you!

WILLY [to LINDA]. Will you stop! [To BIFF.] Walk in very serious. You are not applying for a boy's job. Money is to pass. Be quiet, fine, and serious. Everybody likes a kidder, but nobody lends him money.

HAPPY. I'll try to get some myself, Biff. I'm sure I can.

WILLY. I see great things for you kids, I think your troubles are over. But remember, start big and you'll end big. Ask for fifteen. How much you gonna ask for?

BIFF. Gee, I don't know—

WILLY. And don't say "Gee." "Gee" is a boy's word. A man walking in for fifteen thousand dollars does not say "Gee"!

BIFF. Ten, I think, would be top though.

WILLY. Don't be so modest. You always started too low. Walk in with a big laugh. Don't look worried. Start off with a couple of your good stories to lighten things up. It's not what you say, it's how you say it—because personality always wins the day.

LINDA. Oliver always thought the highest of him—

WILLY. Will you let me talk?

BIFF. Don't yell at her, Pop, will ya?

WILLY [angrily]. I was talking, wasn't I?

BIFF. I don't like you yelling at her all the time, and I'm tellin' you, that's all.

WILLY. What're you, takin' over this house?

LINDA. Willy—

WILLY [turning on her]. Don't take his side all the time, goddammit!

BIFF [furiously]. Stop yelling at her!

WILLY [suddenly pulling on his cheek, beaten down, guilt ridden]. Give my best to Bill Oliver—he may remember me. [He exits through the living-room doorway.]

LINDA [her voice subdued]. What'd you have to start that for? [BIFF turns away.] You see how sweet he was as soon as you talked hope-fully? [She goes over to BIFF.] Come up and say good night to him. Don't let him go to bed that way.

HAPPY. Come on, Biff, let's buck him up.

LINDA. Please, dear. Just say good night. It takes so little to make him happy. Come. [She goes through the living-room doorway, calling upstairs from within the living-room.] Your pajamas are hanging in the bathroom, Willy!

HAPPY [looking toward where LINDA went out]. What a woman! They broke the mold when they made her. You know that, Biff?

BIFF. He's off salary. My God, working on commission!

HAPPY. Well, let's face it: he's no hot-shot selling man. Except that sometimes, you have to admit, he's a sweet personality.

BIFF [deciding]. Lend me ten bucks, will ya? I want to buy some new ties.

HAPPY. I'll take you to a place I know. Beautiful stuff. Wear one of my striped shirts tomorrow.

BIFF. She got gray. Mom got awful old. Gee. I'm gonna go in to Oliver tomorrow and knock him for a—

HAPPY. Come on up. Tell that to Dad. Let's give him a whirl. Come on.

BIFF [steamed up]. You know, with ten thousand bucks, boy!

HAPPY [as they go into the living-room]. That's the talk, Biff, that's the first time I've heard the old confidence out of you! [From within the living-room, fading off.] You're gonna live with me, kid, and any babe you want just say the word. . . . [The last lines are hardly heard. They are mounting the stairs to their parents' bedroom.]

LINDA [entering her bedroom and addressing WILLY, who is in the bathroom. She is straightening the bed for him]. Can you do anything about the shower? It drips.

WILLY [from the bedroom]. All of a sudden everything falls to pieces! Goddam plumbing, oughta be sued, those people. I hardly finished putting it in and the thing. . . . [His words rumble off.]

LINDA. I'm just wondering if Oliver will remember him. You think he might?

WILLY [coming out of the bathroom in his

pajamas]. Remember him? What's the matter with you, you crazy? If he'd've stayed with Oliver he'd be on top by now! Wait'll Oliver gets a look at him. You don't know the average
5 caliber any more. The average young man to-day—[*he is getting into bed*]—is got a caliber of zero. Greatest thing in the world for him was to bum around.

[BIFF *and* HAPPY *enter the bedroom. Slight*
10 *pause.*]

WILLY [*stops short, looking at* BIFF]. Glad to hear it, boy.

HAPPY. He wanted to say goodnight to you, sport.

15 WILLY [*to* BIFF]. Yeah. Knock him dead, boy. What'd you want to tell me?

BIFF. Just take it easy, Pop. Good night. [*He turns to go.*]

WILLY [*unable to resist*]. And if anything
20 falls off the desk while you're talking to him —like a package or something—don't you pick it up. They have office boys for that.

LINDA. I'll make a big breakfast—

WILLY. Will you let me finish? [*To* BIFF.]
25 Tell him you were in the business in the West. Not farm work.

BIFF. All right, Dad.

LINDA. I think everything—

WILLY [*going right through her speech*].
30 And don't undersell yourself. No less than fifteen thousand dollars.

BIFF [*unable to bear him*]. Okay. Good night, Mom. [*He starts moving.*]

WILLY. Because you got a greatness in you,
35 Biff, remember that. You got all kinds a great-ness. . . . [*He lies back, exhausted.* BIFF *walks out.*]

LINDA [*calling after* BIFF]. Sleep well, dar-ling!

40 HAPPY. I'm gonna get married, Mom. I wanted to tell you.

LINDA. Go to sleep, dear.

HAPPY [*going*]. I just wanted to tell you.

WILLY. Keep up the good work. [HAPPY
45 *exits.*] God . . . remember that Ebbets Field°

Ebbets Field a well-known sports stadium in Brook-lyn named after Charles Hercules Ebbets (1859-1925). It was dismantled in 1960.

game? The championship of the city?

LINDA. Just rest. Should I sing to you?

WILLY. Yeah. Sing to me. [LINDA *hums a soft lullaby.*] When that team came out—he was the tallest, remember?
50

LINDA. Oh, yes. And in gold.

[BIFF *enters the darkened kitchen, takes a cigarette, and leaves the house. He comes downstage into a golden pool of light. He smokes, staring at the night.*]
55

WILLY. Like a young god. Hercules—some-thing like that. And the sun, the sun all around him. Remember how he waved to me? Right up from the field, with the representatives of three colleges standing by? And the buyers I
60 brought, and the cheers when he came out— Loman, Loman, Loman! God Almighty, he'll be great yet. A star like that, magnificent, can never really fade away!

[*The light on* WILLY *is fading. The gas
65 heater begins to glow through the kitchen wall, near the stairs, a blue flame beneath red coils.*]

LINDA [*timidly*]. Willy dear, what has he got against you?
70

WILLY. I'm so tired. Don't talk any more.

[BIFF *slowly returns to the kitchen. He stops, stares toward the heater.*]

LINDA. Will you ask Howard to let you work in New York?
75

WILLY. First thing in the morning. Every-thing'll be all right.

[BIFF *reaches behind the heater and draws out a length of rubber tubing. He is horrified and turns his head toward* WILLY's *room, still
80 dimly lit, from which the strains of* LINDA's *desperate but monotonous humming rise.*]

WILLY [*staring through the window into the moonlight*]. Gee, look at the moon moving be-tween the buildings!
85

[BIFF *wraps the tubing around his hand and quickly goes up the stairs.*]

Curtain

ACT II

[*Music is heard, gay and bright. The curtain rises as the music fades away.*]

[WILLY, *in his shirt sleeves, is sitting at the* 90

kitchen table, sipping coffee, his hat in his lap.
LINDA *is filling his cup when she can.*]

WILLY. Wonderful coffee. Meal in itself.

LINDA. Can I make you some eggs?

5   WILLY. No. Take a breath.

LINDA. You look so rested, dear.

WILLY. I slept like a dead one. First time in months. Imagine, sleeping till ten on a Tuesday morning. Boys left nice and early, heh?

10   LINDA. They were out of here by eight o'clock.

WILLY. Good work!

LINDA. It was so thrilling to see them leaving together. I can't get over the shaving lotion in

15   this house!

WILLY [*smiling*]. Mmm—

LINDA. Biff was very changed this morning. His whole attitude seemed to be hopeful. He couldn't wait to get downtown to see Oliver.

20   WILLY. He's heading for a change. There's no question, there simply are certain men that take longer to get—solidified. How did he dress?

LINDA. His blue suit. He's so handsome in

25   that suit. He could be a—anything in that suit!

[WILLY *gets up from the table.* LINDA *holds his jacket for him.*]

WILLY. There's no question, no question at

30   all. Gee, on the way home tonight I'd like to buy some seeds.

LINDA [*laughing*]. That'd be wonderful. But not enough sun gets back there. Nothing'll grow any more.

35   WILLY. You wait, kid, before it's all over we're gonna get a little place out in the country, and I'll raise some vegetables, a couple of chickens . . .

LINDA. You'll do it yet, dear.

40   [WILLY *walks out of his jacket.* LINDA *follows him.*]

WILLY. And they'll get married, and come for a weekend. I'd build a little guest house. 'Cause I got so many fine tools, all I'd need

45   would be a little lumber and some peace of mind.

LINDA [*joyfully*]. I sewed the lining . . .

WILLY. I could build two guest houses, so they'd both come. Did he decide how much he's going to ask Oliver for?   50

LINDA [*getting him into the jacket*]. He didn't mention it, but I imagine ten or fifteen thousand. You going to talk to Howard today?

WILLY. Yeah. I'll put it to him straight and simple. He'll just have to take me off the road.   55

LINDA. And Willy, don't forget to ask for a little advance, because we've got the insurance premium. It's the grace period now.

WILLY. That's a hundred . . .?

LINDA. A hundred and eight, sixty-eight.   60
Because we're a little short again.

WILLY. Why are we short?

LINDA. Well, you had the motor job on the car . . .

WILLY. That goddam Studebaker!   65

LINDA. And you got one more payment on the refrigerator . . .

WILLY. But it just broke again!

LINDA. Well, it's old, dear.

WILLY. I told you we should've bought a   70
well-advertised machine. Charley bought a General Electric and it's twenty years old and it's still good, that son-of-a-bitch.

LINDA. But, Willy—

WILLY. Whoever heard of a Hastings re-   75
frigerator? Once in my life I would like to own something outright before it's broken! I'm always in a race with the junkyard! I just finished paying for the car and it's on its last legs. The refrigerator consumes belts like a   80
goddam maniac. They time those things. They time them so when you finally paid for them, they're used up.

LINDA [*buttoning up his jacket as he unbuttons it*]. All told, about two hundred dollars   85
would carry us, dear. But that includes the last payment on the mortgage. After this payment, Willy, the house belongs to us.

WILLY. It's twenty-five years!

LINDA. Biff was nine years old when we   90
bought it.

WILLY. Well, that's a great thing. To weather a twenty-five-year mortgage is—

LINDA. It's an accomplishment.

WILLY. All the cement, the lumber, the re-construction I put in this house! There ain't a crack to be found in it any more.

LINDA. Well, it served its purpose.

WILLY. What purpose? Some stranger'll come along, move in, and that's that. If only Biff would take this house, and raise a family. . . . [*He starts to go.*] Good-bye, I'm late.

LINDA [*suddenly remembering*]. Oh, I forgot! You're supposed to meet them for dinner.

WILLY. Me?

LINDA. At Frank's Chop House on Forty-eighth near Sixth Avenue.

WILLY. Is that so! How about you?

LINDA. No, just the three of you. They're gonna blow you to a big meal!

WILLY. Don't say! Who thought of that?

LINDA. Biff came to me this morning, Willy, and he said, "Tell Dad, we want to blow him to a big meal." Be there six o'clock. You and your two boys are going to have dinner.

WILLY. Gee whiz! That's really somethin'. I'm gonna knock Howard for a loop, kid. I'll get an advance, and I'll come home with a New York job. Goddammit, now I'm gonna do it!

LINDA. Oh, that's the spirit, Willy!

WILLY. I will never get behind a wheel the rest of my life!

LINDA. It's changing, Willy, I can feel it changing!

WILLY. Beyond a question. G'bye, I'm late. [*He starts to go again.*]

LINDA [*calling after him as she runs to the kitchen table for a handkerchief*]. You got your glasses?

WILLY [*feels for them, then comes back in*]. Yeah, yeah, got my glasses.

LINDA [*giving him the handkerchief*]. And a handkerchief.

WILLY. Yeah, handkerchief.

LINDA. And your saccharine?

WILLY. Yeah, my saccharine.

LINDA. Be careful on the subway stairs.

[*She kisses him, and a silk stocking is seen hanging from her hand. WILLY notices it.*]

WILLY. Will you stop mending stockings?

At least while I'm in the house. It gets me nervous. I can't tell you. Please.

[LINDA *hides the stocking in her hand as she follows* WILLY *across the forestage in front of the house.*]

LINDA. Remember, Frank's Chop House.

WILLY [*passing the apron*]. Maybe beets would grow out there.

LINDA [*laughing*]. But you tried so many times.

WILLY. Yeah. Well, don't work hard today. [*He disappears around the right corner of the house.*]

LINDA. Be careful!

[*As* WILLY *vanishes,* LINDA *waves to him. Suddenly the phone rings. She runs across the stage and into the kitchen and lifts it.*]

LINDA. Hello? Oh, Biff! I'm so glad you called, I just. . . . Yes, sure, I just told him. Yes, he'll be there for dinner at six o'clock, I didn't forget. Listen, I was just dying to tell you. You know that little rubber pipe I told you about? That he connected to the gas heater? I finally decided to go down the cellar this morning and take it away and destroy it. But it's gone! Imagine! He took it away himself, it isn't there! [*She listens.*] When? Oh, then you took it. Oh—nothing, it's just that I'd hoped he'd taken it away himself. Oh, I'm not worried, darling, because this morning he left in such high spirits, it was like the old days! I'm not afraid any more. Did Mr. Oliver see you? . . . Well, you wait there then. And make a nice impression on him, darling. Just don't perspire too much before you see him. And have a nice time with Dad. He may have big news too! . . . That's right, a New York job. And be sweet to him tonight, dear. Be loving to him. Because he's only a little boat looking for a harbor. [*She is trembling with sorrow and joy.*] Oh, that's wonderful, Biff, you'll save his life. Thanks, darling. Just put your arms around him when he comes into the restaurant. Give him a smile. That's the boy. . . . Good-bye, dear. . . . You got your comb? . . . That's fine. Good-bye, Biff dear.

[*In the middle of her speech,* HOWARD WAG-

NER, *thirty-six, wheels in a small typewriter table on which is a wire-recording machine and proceeds to plug it in. This is on the left forestage. Light slowly fades on* LINDA *as it rises on* HOWARD. HOWARD *is intent on threading the machine and only glances over his shoulder as* WILLY *appears.*]

WILLY. Pst! Pst!

HOWARD. Hello, Willy, come in.

WILLY. Like to have a talk with you, Howard.

HOWARD. Sorry to keep you waiting. I'll be with you in a minute.

WILLY. What's that, Howard?

HOWARD. Didn't you ever see one of these? Wire recorder.

WILLY. Oh. Can we talk a minute?

HOWARD. Records things. Just got delivery yesterday. Been driving me crazy, the most terrific machine I ever saw in my life. I was up all night with it.

WILLY. What do you do with it?

HOWARD. I bought it for dictation, but you can do anything with it. Listen to this. I had it home last night. Listen to what I picked up. The first one is my daughter. Get this. [*He flicks the switch and "Roll out the Barrel" is heard being whistled.*] Listen to that kid whistle.

WILLY. That is lifelike, isn't it?

HOWARD. Seven years old. Get that tone.

WILLY. Ts, ts. Like to ask a little favor if you . . .

[*The whistling breaks off, and the voice of* HOWARD's *daughter is heard.*]

HIS DAUGHTER. "Now you, Daddy."

HOWARD. She's crazy for me! [*Again the same song is whistled.*] That's me! Ha! [*He winks.*]

WILLY. You're very good!

[*The whistling breaks off again. The machine runs silent for a moment.*]

HOWARD. Sh! Get this now, this is my son.

HIS SON. "The capital of Alabama is Montgomery; the capital of Arizona is Phoenix; the capital of Arkansas is Little Rock; the capital of California is Sacramento . . ." [*and on, and on.*]

HOWARD [*holding up five fingers*]. Five years old, Willy!

WILLY. He'll make an announcer some day!

HIS SON [*continuing*]. "The capital . . ."

HOWARD. Get that—alphabetical order! [*The machine breaks off suddenly.*] Wait a minute. The maid kicked the plug out.

WILLY. It certainly is a—

HOWARD. Sh, for God's sake!

HIS SON. "It's nine o'clock, Bulova watch time. So I have to go to sleep."

WILLY. That really is—

HOWARD. Wait a minute! The next is my wife.

[*They wait.*]

HOWARD'S VOICE. "Go on, say something." [*Pause.*] "Well, you gonna talk?"

HIS WIFE. "I can't think of anything."

HOWARD'S VOICE. "Well, talk—it's turning."

HIS WIFE [*shyly, beaten*]. "Hello." [*Silence.*] "Oh, Howard, I can't talk into this . . ."

HOWARD [*snapping the machine off*]. That was my wife.

WILLY. That is a wonderful machine. Can we—

HOWARD. I tell you, Willy, I'm gonna take my camera, and my bandsaw, and all my hobbies, and out they go. This is the most fascinating relaxation I ever found.

WILLY. I think I'll get one myself.

HOWARD. Sure, they're only a hundred and a half. You can't do without it. Supposing you wanna hear Jack Benny, see? But you can't be at home at that hour. So you tell the maid to turn the radio on when Jack Benny comes on, and this automatically goes on with the radio . . .

WILLY. And when you come home you . . .

HOWARD. You can come home twelve o'clock, one o'clock, any time you like, and you get yourself a Coke and sit yourself down, throw the switch, and there's Jack Benny's program in the middle of the night!

WILLY. I'm definitely going to get one. Because lots of time I'm on the road, and I think to myself, what I must be missing on the radio!

HOWARD. Don't you have a radio in the car?

WILLY. Well, yeah, but who ever thinks of turning it on?

HOWARD. Say, aren't you supposed to be in Boston?

WILLY. That's what I want to talk to you about, Howard. You got a minute? [*He draws a chair in from the wing.*]

HOWARD. What happened? What're you doing here?

WILLY. Well . . .

HOWARD. You didn't crack up again, did you?

WILLY. Oh, no. No . . .

HOWARD. Geez, you had me worried there for a minute. What's the trouble?

WILLY. Well, tell you the truth, Howard. I've come to the decision that I'd rather not travel any more.

HOWARD. Not travel! Well, what'll you do?

WILLY. Remember, Christmas-time, when you had the party here? You said you'd try to think of some spot for me here in town.

HOWARD. With us?

WILLY. Well, sure.

HOWARD. Oh, yeah, yeah. I remember. Well, I couldn't think of anything for you, Willy.

WILLY. I tell ya, Howard. The kids are grown up, y'know. I don't need much any more. If I could take home—well, sixty-five dollars a week, I could swing it.

HOWARD. Yeah, but Willy, see I—

WILLY. I tell ya why, Howard. Speaking frankly and between the two of us, y'know— I'm just a little tired.

HOWARD. Oh, I could understand that, Willy. But you're a road man, Willy, and we do a road business. We've only got a half-dozen salesmen on the floor here.

WILLY. God knows, Howard, I never asked a favor of any man. But I was with the firm when your father used to carry you in here in his arms.

HOWARD. I know that, Willy, but—

WILLY. Your father came to me the day you were born and asked me what I thought of the name of Howard, may he rest in peace.

HOWARD. I appreciate that, Willy, but there is no spot here for you. If I had a spot I'd slam you right in, but I just don't have a single solitary spot.

[*He looks for his lighter,* WILLY *has picked it up and gives it to him. Pause.*]

WILLY [*with increasing anger*]. Howard, all I need to set my table is fifty dollars a week.

HOWARD. But where am I going to put you, kid?

WILLY. Look, it isn't a question of whether I can sell merchandise, is it?

HOWARD. No, but it's a business, kid, and everybody's gotta pull his own weight.

WILLY [*desperately*]. Just let me tell you a story, Howard—

HOWARD. 'Cause you gotta admit, business is business.

WILLY [*angrily*]. Business is definitely business, but just listen for a minute. You don't understand this. When I was a boy—eighteen, nineteen—I was already on the road. And there was a question in my mind as to whether selling had a future for me. Because in those days I had a yearning to go to Alaska. See, there were three gold strikes in one month in Alaska, and I felt like going out. Just for the ride, you might say.

HOWARD [*barely interested*]. Don't say.

WILLY. Oh, yeah, my father lived many years in Alaska. He was an adventurous man. We've got quite a little streak of self-reliance in our family. I thought I'd go out with my older brother and try to locate him, and maybe settle in the North with the old man. And I was almost decided to go, when I met a salesman in the Parker House. His name was Dave Singleman. And he was eighty-four years old, and he'd drummed merchandise in thirty-one states. And old Dave, he'd go up to his room, y'understand, put on his green velvet slippers —I'll never forget—and pick up his phone and call the buyers, and without ever leaving his room, at the age of eighty-four, he made his living. And when I saw that, I realized that selling was the greatest career a man could want. 'Cause what could be more satisfying

than to be able to go, at the age of eighty-four, into twenty or thirty different cities, and pick up a phone, and be remembered and loved and helped by so many different people? Do you
5 know? when he died—and by the way he died the death of a salesman, in his green velvet slippers in the smoker of the New York, New Haven, and Hartford, going into Boston—when he died, hundreds of salesmen and buyers were
10 at his funeral. Things were said on a lotta trains for months after that. [*He stands up. HOWARD has not looked at him.*] In those days there was personality in it, Howard. There was respect, and comradeship, and gratitude in it.
15 Today, it's all cut and dried, and there's no chance for bringing friendship to bear—or personality. You see what I mean? They don't know me any more.

HOWARD [*moving away, toward the right*].
20 That's just the thing, Willy.

WILLY. If I had forty dollars a week—that's all I'd need. Forty dollars, Howard.

HOWARD. Kid, I can't take blood from a stone, I—

25 WILLY [*desperation is on him now*]. Howard, the year Al Smith° was nominated, your father came to me and—

HOWARD [*starting to go off*]. I've got to see some people, kid.

30 WILLY [*stopping him*]. I'm talking about your father! There were promises made across this desk! You mustn't tell me you've got people to see—I put thirty-four years into this firm, Howard, and now I can't pay my in-
35 surance! You can't eat the orange and throw the peel away—a man is not a piece of fruit! [*After a pause.*] Now pay attention. Your father—in 1928 I had a big year. I averaged a hundred and seventy dollars a week in com-
40 missions.

HOWARD [*impatiently*]. Now, Willy, you never averaged—

WILLY [*banging his hand on the desk*]. I averaged a hundred and seventy dollars a week

Al Smith Alfred E. Smith (1873-1944), the Democratic nominee for President in 1928, was defeated by Herbert Hoover

in the year of 1928! And your father came to 45 me—or rather, I was in the office here—it was right over this desk—and he put his hand on my shoulder—

HOWARD [*getting up*]. You'll have to excuse me, Willy, I gotta see some people. Pull your- 50 self together. [*Going out.*] I'll be back in a little while.

[*On* HOWARD's *exit, the light on his chair grows very bright and strange.*]

WILLY. Pull myself together! What the hell 55 did I say to him? My God, I was yelling at him! How could I! [WILLY *breaks off, staring at the light, which occupies the chair, animating it. He approaches this chair, standing across the desk from it.*] Frank, Frank, don't you remem- 60 ber what you told me that time? How you put your hand on my shoulder, and Frank. . . . [*He leans on the desk and as he speaks the dead man's name he accidentally switches on the recorder, and instantly—*] 65

HOWARD's SON. ". . . of New York is Albany. The capital of Ohio is Cincinnati, the capital of Rhode Island is . . ." [*the recitation continues.*]

WILLY [*leaping away with fright, shouting*]. 70 Ha! Howard! Howard! Howard!

HOWARD [*rushing in*]. What happened?

WILLY [*pointing at the machine, which continues nasally, childishly, with capital cities*]. Shut it off! Shut it off! 75

HOWARD [*pulling the plug out*]. Look, Willy . . .

WILLY [*pressing his hands to his eyes*]. I gotta get myself some coffee. I'll get some coffee . . . 80

[WILLY *starts to walk out.* HOWARD *stops him.*]

HOWARD [*rolling up the cord*]. Willy, look . . .

WILLY. I'll go to Boston. 85

HOWARD. Willy, you can't go to Boston for us.

WILLY. Why can't I go?

HOWARD. I don't want you to represent us. I've been meaning to tell you for a long time 90 now.

WILLY. Howard, are you firing me?

HOWARD. I think you need a good long rest, Willy.

WILLY. Howard—

HOWARD. And when you feel better, come
5 back, and we'll see if we can work something out.

WILLY. But I gotta earn money, Howard. I'm in no position to—

HOWARD. Where are your sons? Why don't
10 your sons give you a hand?

WILLY. They're working on a very big deal.

HOWARD. This is no time for false pride, Willy. You go to your sons and you tell them that you're tired. You've got two great boys,
15 haven't you?

WILLY. Oh, no question, no question, but in the meantime . . .

HOWARD. Then that's that, heh?

WILLY. All right, I'll go to Boston tomorrow.
20 HOWARD. No, no.

WILLY. I can't throw myself on my sons. I'm not a cripple!

HOWARD. Look, kid, I'm busy this morning.

WILLY [*grasping* HOWARD's *arm*]. Howard,
25 you've got to let me go to Boston!

HOWARD [*hard, keeping himself under control*]. I've got a line of people to see this morning. Sit down, take five minutes, and pull yourself together, and then go home, will ya? I
30 need the office, Willy. [*He starts to go, turns, remembering the recorder, starts to push off the table holding the recorder.*] Oh, yeah. Whenever you can this week, stop by and drop off the samples. You'll feel better, Willy, and
35 then come back and we'll talk. Pull yourself together, kid, there's people outside.

[HOWARD *exits, pushing the table off left.* WILLY *stares into space, exhausted. Now the music is heard—*BEN's *music—first distantly,*
40 *then closer, closer. As* WILLY *speaks,* BEN *enters from the right. He carries valise and umbrella.*]

WILLY. Oh, Ben, how did you do it? What is the answer? Did you wind up the Alaska deal already?

45 BEN. Doesn't take much time if you know what you're doing. Just a short business trip. Boarding ship in an hour. Wanted to say goodbye.

WILLY. Ben, I've got to talk to you.

BEN [*glancing at his watch*]. Haven't the 50 time, William.

WILLY [*crossing the apron to* BEN]. Ben, nothing's working out. I don't know what to do.

BEN. Now, look here, William. I've bought timberland in Alaska and I need a man to look 55 after things for me.

WILLY. God, timberland! Me and my boys in those grand outdoors!

BEN. You've a new continent at your doorstep, William. Get out of these cities, they're 60 full of talk and time payments and courts of law. Screw on your fists and you can fight for a fortune up there.

WILLY. Yes, yes! Linda, Linda!

[LINDA *enters as of old, with the wash.*] 65

LINDA. Oh, you're back?

BEN. I haven't much time.

WILLY. No, wait! Linda, he's got a proposition for me in Alaska.

LINDA. But you've got— [*To* BEN.] He's got 70 a beautiful job here.

WILLY. But in Alaska, kid, I could—

LINDA. You're doing well enough, Willy!

BEN [*to* LINDA]. Enough for what, my dear?

LINDA [*frightened of* BEN *and angry at him*]. 75 Don't say those things to him! Enough to be happy right here, right now. [*To* WILLY, *while* BEN *laughs.*] Why must everybody conquer the world? You're well liked, and the boys love you, and someday—[*to* BEN]—why, old 80 man Wagner told him just the other day that if he keeps it up he'll be a member of the firm, didn't he, Willy?

WILLY. Sure, sure. I am building something with this firm, Ben, and if a man is building 85 something he must be on the right track, mustn't he?

BEN. What are you building? Lay your hand on it. Where is it?

WILLY [*hesitantly*]. That's true, Linda, 90 there's nothing.

LINDA. Why? [*To* BEN.] There's a man eighty-four years old—

WILLY. That's right, Ben, that's right. When I look at that man I say, what is there to worry 95 about?

BEN. Bah!

WILLY. It's true, Ben. All he has to do is go into any city, pick up the phone, and he's making his living and you know why?

5 BEN [*picking up his valise*]. I've got to go.

WILLY [*holding* BEN *back*]. Look at this boy!

[BIFF, *in his high-school sweater, enters carrying suitcase.* HAPPY *carries* BIFF's *shoulder guards, gold helmet, and football pants.*]

10 WILLY. Without a penny to his name, three great universities are begging for him, and from there the sky's the limit, because it's not what you do, Ben. It's who you know and the smile on your face! It's contacts, Ben, contacts!

15 The whole wealth of Alaska passes over the lunch table at the Commodore Hotel, and that's the wonder, the wonder of this country, that a man can end with diamonds here on the basis of being liked! [*He turns to* BIFF.] And that's

20 why when you get out on that field today it's important. Because thousands of people will be rooting for you and loving you. [*To* BEN, *who has again begun to leave.*] And Ben! when he walks into a business office his name will

25 sound out like a bell and all the doors will open to him! I've seen it, Ben, I've seen it a thousand times! You can't feel it with your hand like timber, but it's there!

BEN. Good-bye, William.

30 WILLY. Ben, am I right? Don't you think I'm right? I value your advice.

BEN. There's a new continent at your doorstep, William. You could walk out rich. Rich! [*He is gone.*]

35 WILLY. We'll do it here, Ben! You hear me? We're gonna do it here!

[*Young* BERNARD *rushes in. The gay music of the boys is heard.*]

BERNARD. Oh, gee, I was afraid you left

40 already!

WILLY. Why? What time is it?

BERNARD. It's half past one!

WILLY. Well, come on, everybody! Ebbets Field next stop! Where's the pennants? [*He*

45 *rushes through the wall-line of the kitchen and out into the living room.*]

LINDA [*to* BIFF]. Did you pack fresh underwear?

BIFF [*who has been limbering up*]. I want

to go! 50

BERNARD. Biff, I'm carrying your helmet, ain't I?

HAPPY. No, I'm carrying the helmet.

BERNARD. Oh, Biff, you promised me.

HAPPY. I'm carrying the helmet. 55

BERNARD. How am I going to get in the locker room?

LINDA. Let him carry the shoulder guards. [*She puts her coat and hat on in the kitchen.*]

BERNARD. Can I, Biff? 'Cause I told every- 60 body I'm going to be in the locker room.

HAPPY. In Ebbets Field it's the clubhouse.

BERNARD. I meant the clubhouse. Biff!

HAPPY. Biff!

BIFF [*grandly, after a slight pause*]. Let him 65 carry the shoulder guards.

HAPPY [*as he gives* BERNARD *the shoulder guards*]. Stay close to us now.

[WILLY *rushes in with the pennants.*]

WILLY [*handing them out*]. Everybody wave 70 when Biff comes out on the field. [HAPPY *and* BERNARD *run off.*] You set now, boys?

[*The music has died away.*]

BIFF. Ready to go, Pop. Every muscle is ready. 75

WILLY [*at the edge of the apron*]. You realize what this means?

BIFF. That's right, Pop.

WILLY [*feeling* BIFF's *muscles*]. You're coming home this afternoon captain of the All- 80 Scholastic Championship Team of the City of New York.

BIFF. I got it, Pop. And remember, pal, when I take off my helmet, that touchdown is for you. 85

WILLY. Let's go! [*He is starting out, with his arm around* BIFF, *when* CHARLEY *enters, as of old, in knickers.*] I got no room for you, Charley.

CHARLEY. Room? For what? 90

WILLY. In the car.

CHARLEY. You goin' for a ride? I wanted to shoot some casino.

WILLY [*furiously*]. Casino! [*Incredulously.*] Don't you realize what today is? 95

LINDA. Oh, he knows, Willy. He's just kidding you.

WILLY. That's nothing to kid about!

CHARLEY. No, Linda, what's goin' on?

LINDA. He's playing in Ebbets Field.

CHARLEY. Baseball in this weather?

WILLY. Don't talk to him. Come on, come
on! [*He is pushing them out.*]

CHARLEY. Wait a minute, didn't you hear
the news?

WILLY. What?

CHARLEY. Don't you listen to the radio?
Ebbets Field just blew up.

WILLY. You go to hell! [CHARLEY *laughs.
Pushing them out.*] Come on, come on! We're
late.

CHARLEY [*as they go*]. Knock a homer, Biff,
knock a homer!

WILLY [*the last to leave, turning to* CHAR-
LEY]. I don't think that was funny, Charley.
This is the greatest day of his life.

CHARLEY. Willy, when are you going to grow
up?

WILLY. Yeah, heh? When this game is over,
Charley, you'll be laughing out of the other
side of your face. They'll be calling him
another Red Grange.° Twenty-five thousand a
year.

CHARLEY [*kidding*]. Is that so?

WILLY. Yeah, that's so.

CHARLEY. Well, then, I'm sorry, Willy. But
tell me something.

WILLY. What?

CHARLEY. Who is Red Grange?

WILLY. Put up your hands. Goddam you, put
up your hands!

[CHARLEY, *chuckling, shakes his head and
walks away, around the left corner of the
stage.* WILLY *follows him. The music rises to a
mocking frenzy.*]

WILLY. Who the hell do you think you are,
better than everybody else? You don't know
everything, you big, ignorant, stupid. . . . Put
up your hands!

[*Light rises, on the right side of the forestage, on a small table in the reception room of*
CHARLEY's *office. Traffic sounds are heard.*

Red Grange Harold Edward Grange, University of
Illinois All-American halfback and quarterback, 1923-
1925

BERNARD, *now mature, sits whistling to himself. A pair of tennis rackets and an overnight
bag are on the floor beside him.*]

WILLY [*offstage*]. What are you walking
away for? Don't walk away! If you're going
to say something say it to my face! I know you
laugh at me behind my back. You'll laugh out
of the other side of your goddam face after
this game. Touchdown! Touchdown! Eighty
thousand people! Touchdown! Right between
the goal posts.

[BERNARD *is a quiet, earnest, but self-assured
young man.* WILLY's *voice is coming from
right upstage now.* BERNARD *lowers his feet off
the table and listens.* JENNY, *his father's secretary, enters.*]

JENNY [*distressed*]. Say, Bernard, will you go
out in the hall?

BERNARD. What is that noise? Who is it?

JENNY. Mr. Loman. He just got off the elevator.

BERNARD [*getting up*]. Who's he arguing
with?

JENNY. Nobody. There's nobody with him. I
can't deal with him any more, and your father
gets all upset everytime he comes. I've got a
lot of typing to do, and your father's waiting
to sign it. Will you see him?

WILLY [*entering*]. Touchdown! Touch— [*He
sees* JENNY.] Jenny, Jenny, good to see you.
How're ya? Workin'? Or still honest?

JENNY. Fine. How've you been feeling?

WILLY. Not much any more, Jenny. Ha, ha!
[*He is surprised to see the rackets.*]

BERNARD. Hello, Uncle Willy.

WILLY [*almost shocked*]. Bernard! Well,
look who's here!

[*He comes quickly, guiltily, to* BERNARD *and
warmly shakes his hand.*]

BERNARD. How are you? Good to see you.

WILLY. What are you doing here?

BERNARD. Oh, just stopped by to see Pop.
Get off my feet till my train leaves. I'm going
to Washington in a few minutes.

WILLY. Is he in?

BERNARD. Yes, he's in his office with the
accountant. Sit down.

WILLY [*sitting down*]. What're you going to
do in Washington?

BERNARD. Oh, just a case I've got there, Willy.

WILLY. That so? [*Indicating the rackets.*] You going to play tennis there?

5 BERNARD. I'm staying with a friend who's got a court.

WILLY. Don't say. His own tennis court. Must be fine people I bet.

BERNARD. They are, very nice. Dad tells me 10 Biff's in town.

WILLY [*with a big smile*]. Yeah, Biff's in. Working on a very big deal, Bernard.

BERNARD. What's Biff doing?

WILLY. Well, he's doing very big things in 15 the West. But he decided to establish himself here. Very big. We're having dinner. Did I hear your wife had a boy?

BERNARD. That's right. Our second.

WILLY. Two boys! What do you know!

20 BERNARD. What kind of deal has Biff got?

WILLY. Well, Bill Oliver—very big sporting-goods man—he wants Biff very badly. Called him in from the West. Long distance, *carte blanche*, special deliveries. Your friends have 25 their own private tennis court?

BERNARD. You still with the old firm, Willy?

WILLY [*after a pause*]. I'm—I'm overjoyed to see how you made the grade, Bernard, over-joyed. It's an encouraging thing to see a young 30 man really—really— Looks very good for Biff —very— [*He breaks off, then*] Bernard— [*He is so full of emotion, he breaks off again.*]

BERNARD. What is it, Willy?

WILLY [*small and alone*]. What—what's the 35 secret?

BERNARD. What secret?

WILLY. How—how did you? Why didn't he ever catch on?

BERNARD. I wouldn't know that, Willy.

40 WILLY [*confidentially, desperately*]. You were his friend, his boyhood friend. There's something I don't understand about it. His life ended after that Ebbets Field game. From the age of seventeen nothing good ever happened 45 to him.

BERNARD. He never trained himself for any-thing.

WILLY. But he did, he did. After high school

he took so many correspondence courses. Radio mechanics; television; God knows what, and 50 never made the slightest mark.

BERNARD [*taking off his glasses*]. Willy, do you want to talk candidly?

WILLY [*rising, faces* BERNARD]. I regard you as a very brilliant man, Bernard. I value your 55 advice.

BERNARD. Oh, the hell with the advice, Willy. I couldn't advise you. There's just one thing I've always wanted to ask you. When he was supposed to graduate, and the math teacher 60 flunked him—

WILLY. Oh, that son-of-a-bitch ruined his life.

BERNARD. Yeah, but, Willy, all he had to do was to go to summer school and make up that 65 subject.

WILLY. That's right, that's right.

BERNARD. Did you tell him not to go to sum-mer school?

WILLY. Me? I begged him to go. I ordered 70 him to go!

BERNARD. Then why wouldn't he go?

WILLY. Why? Why? Bernard, that question has been trailing me like a ghost for the last fifteen years. He flunked the subject, and laid 75 down and died like a hammer hit him!

BERNARD. Take it easy, kid.

WILLY. Let me talk to you—I got nobody to talk to. Bernard, Bernard, was it my fault? Y'see? It keeps going around in my mind, 80 maybe I did something to him. I got nothing to give him.

BERNARD. Don't take it so hard.

WILLY. Why did he lay down? What is the story there? You were his friend! 85

BERNARD. Willy, I remember, it was June, and our grades came out. And he'd flunked math.

WILLY. That son-of-a-bitch!

BERNARD. No, it wasn't right then. Biff just 90 got very angry, I remember, and he was ready to enroll in summer school.

WILLY [*surprised*]. He was?

BERNARD. He wasn't beaten by it at all. But then, Willy, he disappeared from the block for 95 almost a month. And I got the idea that he'd gone up to New England to see you. Did he have a talk with you then?

[WILLY *stares in silence.*]

BERNARD. Willy?

5   WILLY [*with a strong edge of resentment in his voice*]. Yeah, he came to Boston. What about it?

BERNARD. Well, just that when he came back —I'll never forget this, it always mystifies me.
10 Because I'd thought so well of Biff, even though he'd always taken advantage of me. I loved him, Willy, y'know? And he came back after that month and took his sneakers—remember those sneakers with "University of
15 Virginia" printed on them? He was so proud of those, wore them every day. And he took them down in the cellar, and burned them up in the furnace. We had a fist fight. It lasted at least half an hour. Just the two of us, punching
20 each other down the cellar, and crying right through it. I've often thought of how strange it was that I knew he'd given up his life. What happened in Boston, Willy?

[WILLY *looks at him as at an intruder.*]

25   BERNARD. I just bring it up because you asked me.

WILLY [*angrily*]. Nothing. What do you mean, "What happened?" What's that got to do with anything?

30   BERNARD. Well, don't get sore.

WILLY. What are you trying to do, blame it on me? If a boy lays down is that my fault?

BERNARD. Now, Willy, don't get—

WILLY. Well, don't—don't talk to me that
35 way! What does that mean, "What happened?"

[CHARLEY *enters. He is in his vest, and he carries a bottle of bourbon.*]

CHARLEY. Hey, you're going to miss that
40 train. [*He waves the bottle.*]

BERNARD. Yeah, I'm going. [*He takes the bottle.*] Thanks, Pop. [*He picks up his rackets and bag.*] Good-bye, Willy, and don't worry about it. You know, "if at first you don't suc-
45 ceed . . ."

WILLY. Yes, I believe in that.

BERNARD. But sometimes, Willy, it's better for a man just to walk away.

WILLY. Walk away?

BERNARD. That's right.
50

WILLY. But if you can't walk away?

BERNARD [*after a slight pause*]. I guess that's when it's tough. [*Extending his hand.*] Good-bye, Willy.

WILLY [*shaking* BERNARD'S *hand*]. Good- 55
bye, boy.

CHARLEY [*an arm on* BERNARD'S *shoulder*]. How do you like this kid? Gonna argue a case in front of the Supreme Court.

BERNARD [*protesting*]. Pop! 60

WILLY [*genuinely shocked, pained, and happy*]. No! The Supreme Court!

BERNARD. I gotta run. 'Bye, Dad!

CHARLEY. Knock 'em dead, Bernard!

[BERNARD *goes off.*] 65

WILLY [*as* CHARLEY *takes out his wallet*]. The Supreme Court! And he didn't even mention it!

CHARLEY [*counting out money on the desk*]. He don't have to—he's gonna do it. 70

WILLY. And you never told him what to do, did you? You never took any interest in him.

CHARLEY. My salvation is that I never took any interest in anything. There's some money —fifty dollars. I got an accountant inside. 75

WILLY. Charley, look. . . . [*With difficulty.*] I got my insurance to pay. If you can manage it—I need a hundred and ten dollars.

[CHARLEY *doesn't reply for a moment, merely stops moving.*] 80

WILLY. I'd draw it from my bank but Linda would know, and I . . .

CHARLEY. Sit down, Willy.

WILLY [*moving toward the chair*]. I'm keeping an account of everything, remember. I'll 85
pay every penny back. [*He sits.*]

CHARLEY. Now listen to me, Willy.

WILLY. I want you to know I appreciate . . .

CHARLEY [*sitting down on the table*]. Willy, what're you doin'? What the hell is goin' on in 90
your head?

WILLY. Why? I'm simply . . .

CHARLEY. I offered you a job. You can make fifty dollars a week. And I won't send you on the road. 95

WILLY. I've got a job.

CHARLEY. Without pay? What kind of a job is a job without pay? [*He rises.*] Now, look, kid, enough is enough. I'm no genius but I know when I'm being insulted.

5 WILLY. Insulted?

CHARLEY. Why don't you want to work for me?

WILLY. What's the matter with you? I've got a job.

10 CHARLEY. Then what're you walkin' in here every week for?

WILLY [*getting up*]. Well, if you don't want me to walk in here—

CHARLEY. I am offering you a job.

15 WILLY. I don't want your goddam job!

CHARLEY. When the hell are you going to grow up?

WILLY [*furiously*]. You big ignoramus, if you say that to me again I'll rap you one! I

20 don't care how big you are! [*He's ready to fight.*]

[*Pause.*]

CHARLEY [*kindly, going to him*]. How much do you need, Willy?

25 WILLY. Charley, I'm strapped, I'm strapped. I don't know what to do. I was just fired.

CHARLEY. Howard fired you?

WILLY. That snotnose. Imagine that? I named him. I named him Howard.

30 CHARLEY. Willy, when're you gonna realize that them things don't mean anything? You named him Howard, but you can't sell that. The only thing you got in this world is what you can sell. And the funny thing is that you're

35 a salesman, and you don't know that.

WILLY. I've always tried to think otherwise, I guess. I always felt that if a man was impressive, and well liked, that nothing—

CHARLEY. Why must everybody like you?

40 Who liked J. P. Morgan?° Was he impressive? In a Turkish bath he'd look like a butcher. But with his pockets on he was very well liked. Now listen, Willy, I know you don't like me, and nobody can say I'm in love with you, but

45 I'll give you a job because—just for the hell

J. P. Morgan John Pierpont Morgan (1887-1943), famous New York banker and financier

of it, put it that way. Now what do you say?

WILLY. I—I just can't work for you, Charley.

CHARLEY. What're you, jealous of me?

WILLY. I can't work for you, that's all, don't ask me why. 50

CHARLEY [*angered, takes out more bills*]. You been jealous of me all your life, you damned fool! Here, pay your insurance. [*He puts the money in* WILLY's *hand.*]

WILLY. I'm keeping strict accounts. 55

CHARLEY. I've got some work to do. Take care of yourself. And pay your insurance.

WILLY [*moving to the right*]. Funny, y'know? After all the highways, and the trains and the appointments, and the years, you end 60 up worth more dead than alive.

CHARLEY. Willy, nobody's worth nothin' dead. [*After a slight pause.*] Did you hear what I said?

[WILLY *stands still, dreaming.*] 65

CHARLEY. Willy!

WILLY. Apologize to Bernard for me when you see him. I didn't mean to argue with him. He's a fine boy. They're all fine boys, and they'll end up big—all of them. Someday 70 they'll all play tennis together. Wish me luck, Charley. He saw Bill Oliver today.

CHARLEY. Good luck.

WILLY [*on the verge of tears*]. Charley, you're the only friend I got. Isn't that a re- 75 markable thing? [*He goes out.*]

CHARLEY. Jesus!

[CHARLEY *stares after him a moment and follows. All light blacks out. Suddenly raucous music is heard, and a red glow rises behind the* 80 *screen at right.* STANLEY, *a young waiter, appears, carrying a table, followed by* HAPPY, *who is carrying two chairs.*]

STANLEY [*putting the table down*]. That's all right, Mr. Loman, I can handle it myself. [*He* 85 *turns and takes the chairs from* HAPPY *and places them at the table.*]

HAPPY [*glancing around*]. Oh, this is better.

STANLEY. Sure, in the front there you're in the middle of all kinds a noise. Whenever you 90 got a party, Mr. Loman, you just tell me and I'll put you back here. Y'know, there's a lotta people they don't like it private, because when

they go out they like to see a lotta action around them because they're sick and tired to stay in the house by theirself. But I know you, you ain't from Hackensack. You know what
5 I mean?

HAPPY [*sitting down*]. So how's it coming, Stanley?

STANLEY. Ah, it's a dog's life. I only wish during the war they'd took me in the Army.
10 I coulda been dead by now.

HAPPY. My brother's back, Stanley.

STANLEY. Oh, he come back, heh? From the Far West.

HAPPY. Yeah, big cattle man, my brother, so
15 treat him right. And my father's coming too.

STANLEY. Oh, your father too!

HAPPY. You got a couple of nice lobsters?

STANLEY. Hundred per cent, big.

HAPPY. I want them with the claws.
20 STANLEY. Don't worry, I don't give you no mice. [HAPPY *laughs*.] How about some wine? It'll put a head on the meal.

HAPPY. No. You remember, Stanley, that recipe I brought you from overseas? With the
25 champagne in it?

STANLEY. Oh, yeah, sure. I still got it tacked up yet in the kitchen. But that'll have to cost a buck apiece anyways.

HAPPY. That's all right.
30 STANLEY. What'd you, hit a number or somethin'?

HAPPY. No, it's a little celebration. My brother is—I think he pulled off a big deal today. I think we're going into business to-
35 gether.

STANLEY. Great! That's the best for you. Because a family business, you know what I mean?—that's the best.

HAPPY. That's what I think.
40 STANLEY. 'Cause what's the difference? Somebody steals? It's in the family. Know what I mean? [*Sotto voce.*] Like this bartender here. The boss is goin' crazy what kinda leak he's got in the cash register. You put it in but
45 it don't come out.

HAPPY [*raising his head*]. Sh!

STANLEY. What?

HAPPY. You notice I wasn't lookin' right or

left, was I?
STANLEY. No.   50
HAPPY. And my eyes are closed.
STANLEY. So what's the—?
HAPPY. Strudel's comin'.
STANLEY [*catching on, looks around*]. Ah, no, there's no—   55
[*He breaks off as a furred, lavishly dressed girl enters and sits at the next table. Both follow her with their eyes.*]
STANLEY. Geez, how'd ya know?
HAPPY. I got radar or something. [*Staring* 60 *directly at her profile.*] Oooooooo . . . Stanley.
STANLEY. I think that's for you, Mr. Loman.
HAPPY. Look at that mouth. Oh, God. And the binoculars.
STANLEY. Geez, you got a life, Mr. Loman.   65
HAPPY. Wait on her.
STANLEY [*going to the girl's table*]. Would you like a menu, ma'am?
GIRL. I'm expecting someone, but I'd like a—
HAPPY. Why don't you bring her—excuse 70 me, miss, do you mind? I sell champagne, and I'd like you to try my brand. Bring her a champagne, Stanley.
GIRL. That's awfully nice of you.
HAPPY. Don't mention it. It's all company 75 money. [*He laughs.*]
GIRL. That's a charming product to be selling, isn't it?
HAPPY. Oh, gets to be like everything else. Selling is selling, y'know.   80
GIRL. I suppose.
HAPPY. You don't happen to sell, do you?
GIRL. No, I don't sell.
HAPPY. Would you object to a compliment from a stranger? You ought to be on a mag- 85 azine cover.
GIRL [*looking at him a little archly*]. I have been.
[STANLEY *comes in with a glass of champagne.*]   90
HAPPY. What'd I say before, Stanley? You see? She's a cover girl.
STANLEY. Oh, I could see, I could see.
HAPPY [*to the* GIRL]. What magazine?
GIRL. Oh, a lot of them. [*She takes the* 95 *drink.*] Thank you.

HAPPY. You know what they say in France, don't you? "Champagne is the drink of the complexion"—Hya, Biff!

[BIFF *has entered and sits with* HAPPY.]

5 BIFF. Hello, kid. Sorry I'm late.

HAPPY. I just got here. Uh, Miss—?

GIRL. Forsythe.

HAPPY. Miss Forsythe, this is my brother.

BIFF. Is Dad here?

10 HAPPY. His name is Biff. You might've heard of him. Great football player.

GIRL. Really? What team?

HAPPY. Are you familiar with football?

GIRL. No, I'm afraid I'm not.

15 HAPPY. Biff is quarterback with the New York Giants.

GIRL. Well, that is nice, isn't it? [*She drinks.*]

HAPPY. Good health.

20 GIRL. I'm happy to meet you.

HAPPY. That's my name. Hap. It's really Harold, but at West Point they called me Happy.

GIRL [*now really impressed*]. Oh, I see. How 25 do you do? [*She turns her profile.*]

BIFF. Isn't Dad coming?

HAPPY. You want her?

BIFF. Oh, I could never make that.

HAPPY. I remember the time that idea would 30 never come into your head. Where's the old confidence, Biff?

BIFF. I just saw Oliver—

HAPPY. Wait a minute. I've got to see that old confidence again. Do you want her? She's 35 on call.

BIFF. Oh, no. [*He turns to look at the* GIRL.]

HAPPY. I'm telling you. Watch this. [*Turning to the* GIRL.] Honey? [*She turns to him.*] Are you busy?

40 GIRL. Well, I am . . . but I could make a phone call.

HAPPY. Do that, will you, honey? And see if you can get a friend. We'll be here for a while. Biff is one of the greatest football players in 45 the country.

GIRL [*standing up*]. Well, I'm certainly happy to meet you.

HAPPY. Come back soon.

GIRL. I'll try.

HAPPY. Don't try, honey, try hard. 50

[*The* GIRL *exits.* STANLEY *follows, shaking his head in bewildered admiration.*]

HAPPY. Isn't that a shame now? A beautiful girl like that? That's why I can't get married. There's not a good woman in a thousand. New 55 York is loaded with them, kid!

BIFF. Hap, look—

HAPPY. I told you she was on call!

BIFF [*strangely unnerved*]. Cut it out, will ya? I want to say something to you. 60

HAPPY. Did you see Oliver?

BIFF. I saw him all right. Now look, I want to tell Dad a couple of things and I want you to help me.

HAPPY. What? Is he going to back you? 65

BIFF. Are you crazy? You're out of your goddam head, you know that?

HAPPY. Why? What happened?

BIFF [*breathlessly*]. I did a terrible thing today, Hap. It's been the strangest day I ever 70 went through. I'm all numb, I swear.

HAPPY. You mean he wouldn't see you?

BIFF. Well, I waited six hours for him, see? All day. Kept sending my name in. Even tried to date his secretary so she'd get me to him, 75 but no soap.

HAPPY. Because you're not showin' the old confidence, Biff. He remembered you, didn't he?

BIFF [*stopping* HAPPY *with a gesture*]. 80 Finally, about five o'clock, he comes out. Didn't remember who I was or anything. I felt like such an idiot, Hap.

HAPPY. Did you tell him my Florida idea?

BIFF. He walked away. I saw him for one 85 minute. I got so mad I could've torn the walls down! How the hell did I ever get the idea I was a salesmen there? I even believed myself that I'd been a salesman for him! And then he gave me one look and—I realized what a 90 ridiculous lie my whole life has been. We've been talking in a dream for fifteen years. I was a shipping clerk.

HAPPY. What'd you do?

BIFF [*with great tension and wonder*]. Well, 95 he left, see. And the secretary went out. I was all alone in the waiting-room. I don't know what came over me, Hap. The next thing I know I'm in his office—panelled walls, everything. I can't explain it. I—Hap, I took his fountain pen.

HAPPY. Geez, did he catch you?

BIFF. I ran out. I ran down all eleven flights. I ran and ran and ran.

HAPPY. That was an awful dumb—what'd you do that for?

BIFF [*agonized*]. I don't know, I just—wanted to take something, I don't know. You gotta help me, Hap, I'm gonna tell Pop.

HAPPY. You crazy? What for?

BIFF. Hap, he's got to understand that I'm not the man somebody lends that kind of money to. He thinks I've been spiting him all these years and it's eating him up.

HAPPY. That's just it. You tell him something nice.

BIFF. I can't.

HAPPY. Say you got a lunch date with Oliver tomorrow.

BIFF. So what do I do tomorrow?

HAPPY. You leave the house tomorrow and come back at night and say Oliver is thinking it over. And he thinks it over for a couple of weeks, and gradually it fades away and nobody's the worse.

BIFF. But it'll go on for ever!

HAPPY. Dad is never so happy as when he's looking forward to something!

[WILLY *enters.*]

HAPPY. Hello, scout!

WILLY. Gee, I haven't been here in years!

[STANLEY *has followed* WILLY *in and sets a chair for him.* STANLEY *starts off, but* HAPPY *stops him.*]

HAPPY. Stanley!

[STANLEY *stands by, waiting for an order.*]

BIFF [*going to* WILLY *with guilt, as to an invalid*]. Sit down, Pop. You want a drink?

WILLY. Sure, I don't mind.

BIFF. Let's get a load on.

WILLY. You look worried.

BIFF. N-no. [*To* STANLEY.] Scotch all around. Make it doubles.

STANLEY. Doubles, right. [*He goes.*]

WILLY. You had a couple already, didn't you?

BIFF. Just a couple, yeah.

WILLY. Well, what happened, boy? [*Nodding affirmatively, with a smile.*] Everything go all right?

BIFF [*takes a breath, then reaches out and grasps* WILLY's *hand*]. Pal . . . [*he is smiling bravely, and* WILLY *is smiling too*] I had an experience today.

HAPPY. Terrific, Pop.

WILLY. That so? What happened?

BIFF [*high, slightly alcoholic, above the earth*]. I'm going to tell you everything from first to last. It's been a strange day. [*Silence. He looks around, composes himself as best he can, but his breath keeps breaking the rhythm of his voice.*] I had to wait quite a while for him, and—

WILLY. Oliver?

BIFF. Yeah, Oliver. All day, as a matter of cold fact. And a lot of—instances—facts, Pop, facts about my life came back to me. Who was it, Pop? Who ever said I was a salesman with Oliver?

WILLY. Well, you were.

BIFF. No, Dad, I was a shipping clerk.

WILLY. But you were practically—

BIFF [*with determination*]. Dad, I don't know who said it first, but I was never a salesman for Bill Oliver.

WILLY. What're you talking about?

BIFF. Let's hold on to the facts tonight, Pop. We're not going to get anywhere bullin' around. I was a shipping clerk.

WILLY [*angrily*]. All right, now listen to me—

BIFF. Why don't you let me finish?

WILLY. I'm not interested in stories about the past or any crap of that kind because the woods are burning, boys, you understand? There's a big blaze going on all around. I was fired today.

BIFF [*shocked*]. How could you be?

WILLY. I was fired, and I'm looking for a little good news to tell your mother, because the woman has waited and the woman has suffered. The gist of it is that I haven't got a story left in my head, Biff. So don't give me a lecture about facts and aspects. I am not interested. Now what've you got to say to me?

[STANLEY *enters with three drinks. They wait*
5 *until he leaves.*]

WILLY. Did you see Oliver?

BIFF. Jesus, Dad!

WILLY. You mean you didn't go up there?

HAPPY. Sure he went up there.

10 BIFF. I did. I—saw him. How could they fire you?

WILLY [*on the edge of his chair*]. What kind of a welcome did he give you?

BIFF. He won't even let you work on com-
15 mission?

WILLY. I'm out! [*Driving.*] So tell me, he gave you a warm welcome?

HAPPY. Sure, Pop, sure!

BIFF [*driven*]. Well, it was kind of—

20 WILLY. I was wondering if he'd remember you. [*To* HAPPY.] Imagine, man doesn't see him for ten, twelve years and gives him that kind of a welcome!

HAPPY. Damn right!

25 BIFF [*trying to return to the offensive*]. Pop, look—

WILLY. You know why he remembered you, don't you? Because you impressed him in those days.

30 BIFF. Let's talk quietly and get this down to the facts, huh?

WILLY [*as though* BIFF *had been interrupting*]. Well, what happened? It's great news, Biff. Did he take you into his office or'd you
35 talk in the waiting-room?

BIFF. Well, he came in, see, and—

WILLY [*with a big smile*]. What'd he say? Betcha he threw his arm around you.

BIFF. Well, he kinda—

40 WILLY. He's a fine man. [*To* HAPPY.] Very hard man to see, y'know.

HAPPY [*agreeing*]. Oh, I know.

WILLY [*to* BIFF]. Is that where you had the drinks?

45 BIFF. Yeah, he gave me a couple of—no, no!

HAPPY [*cutting in*]. He told him my Florida idea.

WILLY. Don't interrupt. [*To* BIFF.] How'd

he react to the Florida idea?

BIFF. Dad, will you give me a minute to ex- 50
plain?

WILLY. I've been waiting for you to explain since I sat down here! What happened? He took you into his office and what?

BIFF. Well—I talked. And—and he listened, 55
see.

WILLY. Famous for the way he listens, y'know. What was his answer?

BIFF. His answer was— [*He breaks off, suddenly angry.*] Dad, you're not letting me tell 60
you what I want to tell you!

WILLY [*accusing, angered*]. You didn't see him, did you?

BIFF. I did see him!

WILLY. What'd you insult him or some- 65
thing? You insulted him, didn't you?

BIFF. Listen, will you let me out of it, will you just let me out of it!

HAPPY. What the hell!

WILLY. Tell me what happened! 70

BIFF [*to* HAPPY]. I can't talk to him!

[*A single trumpet note jars the ear. The light of green leaves stains the house, which holds the air of night and a dream.* YOUNG BERNARD *enters and knocks on the door of the* 75
house.]

YOUNG BERNARD [*frantically*]. Mrs. Loman, Mrs. Loman!

HAPPY. Tell him what happened!

BIFF [*to* HAPPY]. Shut up and leave me 80
alone!

WILLY. No, no! You had to go and flunk math!

BIFF. What math? What're you talking about? 85

YOUNG BERNARD. Mrs. Loman, Mrs. Loman!

[LINDA *appears in the house, as of old.*]

WILLY [*wildly*]. Math, math, math!

BIFF. Take it easy, Pop!

YOUNG BERNARD. Mrs. Loman! 90

WILLY [*furiously*]. If you hadn't flunked you'd've been set by now!

BIFF. Now look, I'm gonna tell you what happened, and you're going to listen to me.

YOUNG BERNARD. Mrs. Loman! 95

BIFF. I waited six hours—

HAPPY. What the hell are you saying?

BIFF. I kept sending in my name but he wouldn't see me. So finally he. . . . [*He continues unheard as light fades low on the restaurant.*]

YOUNG BERNARD. Biff flunked math!

LINDA. No!

YOUNG BERNARD. Birnbaum flunked him! They won't graduate him!

LINDA. But they have to. He's gotta go to the university. Where is he? Biff! Biff!

YOUNG BERNARD. No, he left. He went to Grand Central.

LINDA. Grand— You mean he went to Boston!

YOUNG BERNARD. Is Uncle Willy in Boston?

LINDA. Oh, maybe Willy can talk to the teacher. Oh, the poor, poor boy!

[*Light on house area snaps out.*]

BIFF [*at the table, now audible, holding up a gold fountain pen*]. . . . so I'm washed up with Oliver, you understand? Are you listening to me?

WILLY [*at a loss*]. Yeah, sure. If you hadn't flunked—

BIFF. Flunked what? What're you talking about?

WILLY. Don't blame everything on me! I didn't flunk math—you did! What pen?

HAPPY. That was awful dumb, Biff, a pen like that is worth—

WILLY [*seeing the pen for the first time*]. You took Oliver's pen?

BIFF [*weakening*]. Dad, I just explained it to you.

WILLY. You stole Bill Oliver's fountain pen!

BIFF. I didn't exactly steal it! That's just what I've been explaining to you!

HAPPY. He had it in his hand and just then Oliver walked in, so he got nervous and stuck it in his pocket!

WILLY. My God, Biff!

BIFF. I never intended to do it, Dad!

OPERATOR'S VOICE. Standish Arms, good evening!

WILLY [*shouting*]. I'm not in my room!

BIFF [*frightened*]. Dad, what's the matter? [*He and HAPPY stand up.*]

OPERATOR. Ringing Mr. Loman for you!

WILLY. I'm not there, stop it!

BIFF [*horrified, gets down on one knee before WILLY*]. Dad, I'll make good, I'll make good. [*WILLY tries to get to his feet. BIFF holds him down.*] Sit down now.

WILLY. No, you're no good, you're no good for anything.

BIFF. I am, Dad, I'll find something else, you understand? Now don't worry about anything. [*He holds up WILLY's face.*] Talk to me, Dad.

OPERATOR. Mr. Loman does not answer. Shall I page him?

WILLY [*attempting to stand, as though to rush and silence the OPERATOR*]. No, no, no!

HAPPY. He'll strike something, Pop.

WILLY. No, no . . .

BIFF [*desperately, standing over WILLY*]. Pop, listen! Listen to me! I'm telling you something good. Oliver talked to his partner about the Florida idea. You listening? He—he talked to his partner, and he came to me . . . I'm going to be all right, you hear? Dad, listen to me, he said it was just a question of the amount!

WILLY. Then you . . . got it?

HAPPY. He's gonna be terrific, Pop!

WILLY [*trying to stand*]. Then you got it, haven't you? You got it! You got it!

BIFF [*agonized, holds WILLY down*]. No, no. Look, Pop. I'm supposed to have lunch with them tomorrow. I'm just telling you this so you'll know that I can still make an impression, Pop. And I'll make good somewhere, but I can't go tomorrow, see?

WILLY. Why not? You simply—

BIFF. But the pen, Pop!

WILLY. You give it to him and tell him it was an oversight!

HAPPY. Sure, have lunch tomorrow!

BIFF. I can't say that—

WILLY. You were doing a crossword puzzle and accidentally used his pen!

BIFF. Listen, kid, I took those balls years ago, now I walk in with his fountain pen? That clinches it, don't you see? I can't face him like that! I'll try elsewhere.

PAGE'S VOICE. Paging Mr. Loman!

WILLY. Don't you want to be anything?

BIFF. Pop, how can I go back?

WILLY. You don't want to be anything, is that what's behind it?

5 BIFF [*now angry at* WILLY *for not crediting his sympathy*]. Don't take it that way! You think it was easy walking into that office after what I'd done to him? A team of horses couldn't have dragged me back to Bill Oliver!

10 WILLY. Then why'd you go?

BIFF. Why did I go? Why did I go? Look at you! Look at what's become of you!

[*Off left, the* WOMAN *laughs.*]

WILLY. Biff, you're going to go to that lunch
15 tomorrow, or—

BIFF. I can't go. I've got no appointment!

HAPPY. Biff, for . . . !

WILLY. Are you spiting me?

BIFF. Don't take it that way! Goddammit!

20 WILLY [*strikes* BIFF *and falters away from the table*]. You rotten little louse! Are you spiting me?

THE WOMAN. Someone's at the door, Willy!

BIFF. I'm no good, can't you see what I am?

25 HAPPY [*separating them*]. Hey, you're in a restaurant! Now cut it out, both of you! [*The girls enter.*] Hello, girls, sit down.

[*The* WOMAN *laughs, off left.*]

MISS FORSYTHE. I guess we might as well.
30 This is Letta.

THE WOMAN. Willy, are you going to wake up?

BIFF [*ignoring* WILLY]. How're ya, miss, sit down. What do you drink?

35 MISS FORSYTHE. Letta might not be able to stay long.

LETTA. I gotta get up very early tomorrow. I got jury duty. I'm so excited! Were you fellows ever on a jury?

40 BIFF. No, but I been in front of them! [*The girls laugh.*] This is my father.

LETTA. Isn't he cute? Sit down with us, Pop.

HAPPY. Sit him down, Biff!

BIFF [*going to him*]. Come on, slugger, drink
45 us under the table. To hell with it! Come on, sit down, pal.

[*On* BIFF's *last insistence,* WILLY *is about to sit.*]

THE WOMAN [*now urgently*]. Willy, are you going to answer the door!
50

[*The* WOMAN's *call pulls* WILLY *back. He starts right, befuddled.*]

BIFF. Hey, where are you going?

WILLY. Open the door.

BIFF. The door?
55

WILLY. The washroom . . . the door . . . where's the door?

BIFF [*leading* WILLY *to the left*]. Just go straight down.

[WILLY *moves left.*]
60

THE WOMAN. Willy, Willy, are you going to get up, get up, get up, get up?

[WILLY *exits left.*]

LETTA. I think it's sweet you bring your daddy along.
65

MISS FORSYTHE. Oh, he isn't really your father!

BIFF [*at left, turning to her resentfully*]. Miss Forsythe, you've just seen a prince walk by. A fine, troubled prince. A hardworking, unap-
70 preciated prince. A pal, you understand? A good companion. Always for his boys.

LETTA. That's so sweet.

HAPPY. Well, girls, what's the program? We're wasting time. Come on, Biff. Gather
75 round. Where would you like to go?

BIFF. Why don't you do something for him?

HAPPY. Me!

BIFF. Don't you give a damn for him, Hap?

HAPPY. What're you talking about? I'm the
80 one who—

BIFF. I sense it, you don't give a good goddam about him.

[*He takes the rolled-up hose from his pocket and puts it on the table in front of* HAPPY.]
85 Look what I found in the cellar, for Christ's sake. How can you bear to let it go on?

HAPPY. Me? Who goes away? Who runs off and—

BIFF. Yeah, but he doesn't mean anything to
90 you. You could help him—I can't. Don't you understand what I'm talking about? He's going to kill himself, don't you know that?

HAPPY. Don't I know it! Me!

BIFF. Hap, help him! Jesus . . . help him. . . .
95 Help me, help me, I can't bear to look at his

face! [*Ready to weep, he hurries out, up right.*]

HAPPY [*starting after him*]. Where are you going?

MISS FORSYTHE. What's he so mad about?

HAPPY. Come on, girls, we'll catch up with him.

MISS FORSYTHE [*as* HAPPY *pushes her out*]. Say, I don't like that temper of his!

HAPPY. He's just a little overstrung, he'll be all right!

WILLY [*off left, as the* WOMAN *laughs*]. Don't answer! Don't answer!

LETTA. Don't you want to tell your father—

HAPPY. No, that's not my father. He's just a guy. Come on, we'll catch Biff, and honey, we're going to paint this town! Stanley, where's the check! Hey, Stanley!

[*They exit.* STANLEY *looks toward left.*]

STANLEY [*calling to* HAPPY *indignantly*]. Mr. Loman! Mr. Loman!

[STANLEY *picks up a chair and follows them off. Knocking is heard off left. The* WOMAN *enters, laughing.* WILLY *follows her. She is in a black slip; he is buttoning his shirt. Raw, sensuous music accompanies their speech.*]

WILLY. Will you stop laughing? Will you stop?

THE WOMAN. Aren't you going to answer the door? He'll wake the whole hotel.

WILLY. I'm not expecting anybody.

THE WOMAN. Whyn't you have another drink, honey, and stop being so damn self-centered?

WILLY. I'm so lonely.

THE WOMAN. You know you ruined me, Willy? From now on, whenever you come to the office, I'll see that you go right through to the buyers. No waiting at my desk any more, Willy. You ruined me.

WILLY. That's nice of you to say that.

THE WOMAN. Gee, you are self-centered! Why so sad? You are the saddest, self-centeredest soul I ever did see-saw. [*She laughs. He kisses her.*] Come on inside, drummer boy. It's silly to be dressing in the middle of the night. [*As knocking is heard.*] Aren't you going to answer the door?

WILLY. They're knocking on the wrong door.

THE WOMAN. But I felt the knocking. And he heard us talking in here. Maybe the hotel's on fire!

WILLY [*his terror rising*]. It's a mistake.

THE WOMAN. Then tell him to go away!

WILLY. There's nobody there.

THE WOMAN. It's getting on my nerves, Willy. There's somebody standing out there and it's getting on my nerves!

WILLY [*pushing her away from him*]. All right, stay in the bathroom here, and don't come out. I think there's a law in Massachusetts about it, so don't come out. It may be that new room clerk. He looked very mean. So don't come out. It's a mistake, there's no fire.

[*The knocking is heard again. He takes a few steps away from her, and she vanishes into the wing. The light follows him, and now he is facing* YOUNG BIFF, *who carries a suitcase.* BIFF *steps toward him. The music is gone.*]

BIFF. Why didn't you answer?

WILLY. Biff! What are you doing in Boston?

BIFF. Why didn't you answer! I've been knocking for five minutes, I called you on the phone—

WILLY. I just heard you. I was in the bathroom and had the door shut. Did anything happen home?

BIFF. Dad—I let you down.

WILLY. What do you mean?

BIFF. Dad . . .

WILLY. Biffo, what's this about? [*Putting his arm around* BIFF.] Come on, let's go downstairs and get you a malted.

BIFF. Dad, I flunked math.

WILLY. Not for the term?

BIFF. The term. I haven't got enough credits to graduate.

WILLY. You mean to say Bernard wouldn't give you the answers?

BIFF. He did, he tried, but I only got a sixty-one.

WILLY. And they wouldn't give you four points?

BIFF. Birnbaum refused absolutely. I begged

him, Pop, but he won't give me those points.
You gotta talk to him before they close the
school. Because if he saw the kind of man you
are, and you just talked to him in your way,
5 I'm sure he'd come through for me. The class
came right before practice, see, and I didn't
go enough. Would you talk to him? He'd like
you, Pop. You know the way you could talk.

WILLY. You're on. We'll drive right back.

10 BIFF. Oh, Dad, good work! I'm sure he'll
change it for you!

WILLY. Go downstairs and tell the clerk I'm
checkin' out. Go right down.

BIFF. Yes, sir! See, the reason he hates me,
15 Pop—one day he was late for class so I got up
at the blackboard and imitated him. I crossed
my eyes and talked with a lithp.

WILLY [laughing]. You did? The kids like
it?

20 BIFF. They nearly died laughing!

WILLY. Yeah? What'd you do?

BIFF. The thquare root of thixthy twee is . . .
[WILLY bursts out laughing; BIFF joins him].
And in the middle of it he walked in!

25 [WILLY laughs and the WOMAN joins in offstage.]

WILLY [without hesitation]. Hurry downstairs and—

BIFF. Somebody in there?

30 WILLY. No, that was next door.

[The WOMAN laughs offstage.]

BIFF. Somebody got in your bathroom!

WILLY. No, it's the next room, there's a
party—

35 THE WOMAN [enters, laughing. She lisps
this]. Can I come in? There's something in the
bathtub, Willy, and it's moving!

[WILLY looks at BIFF, who is staring open-
mouthed and horrified at the WOMAN.]

40 WILLY. Ah—you better go back to your
room. They must be finished painting by now.
They're painting her room so I let her take a
shower here. Go back, go back. . . . [He pushes
her.]

45 THE WOMAN [resisting]. But I've got to get
dressed, Willy, I can't—

WILLY. Get out of here! Go back, go back.
. . . [Suddenly striving for the ordinary.] This

is Miss Francis, Biff, she's a buyer. They're
painting her room. Go back, Miss Francis, go 50
back . . .

THE WOMAN. But my clothes, I can't go out
naked in the hall!

WILLY [pushing her offstage]. Get outa here!
Go back, go back! 55

[BIFF slowly sits down on his suitcase as the
argument continues offstage.]

THE WOMAN. Where's my stockings? You
promised me stockings, Willy!

WILLY. I have no stockings here! 60

THE WOMAN. You had two boxes of size
nine sheers for me, and I want them!

WILLY. Here, for God's sake, will you get
outa here!

THE WOMAN [enters holding a box of stock- 65
ings]. I just hope there's nobody in the hall.
That's all I hope. [To BIFF.] Are you football
or baseball?

BIFF. Football.

THE WOMAN [angry, humiliated]. That's me 70
too. G'night.

[She snatches her clothes from WILLY and
walks out.]

WILLY [after a pause]. Well, better get going. I want to get to the school first thing in 75
the morning. Get my suits out of the closet.
I'll get my valise. [BIFF doesn't move.] What's
the matter? [BIFF remains motionless, tears
falling.] She's a buyer. Buys for J. H. Simmons.
She lives down the hall—they're painting. You 80
don't imagine— [He breaks off. After a pause.]
Now listen, pal, she's just a buyer. She sees
merchandise in her room and they have to
keep it looking just so. . . . [Pause. Assuming
command.] All right, get my suits. [BIFF 85
doesn't move.] Now stop crying and do as I
say. I gave you an order. Biff, I gave you an
order! Is that what you do when I give you an
order? How dare you cry? [Putting his arm
around BIFF.] Now look, Biff, when you grow 90
up you'll understand about these things. You
mustn't—you mustn't over-emphasize a thing
like this. I'll see Birnbaum first thing in the
morning.

BIFF. Never mind. 95

WILLY [getting down beside BIFF]. Never

mind! He's going to give you those points. I'll
see to it.

BIFF. He wouldn't listen to you.

WILLY. He certainly will listen to me. You
5 need those points for the U. of Virginia.

BIFF. I'm not going there.

WILLY. Heh? If I can't get him to change
that mark you'll make it up in summer school.
You've got all summer to—

10 BIFF [*his weeping breaking from him*].
Dad . . .

WILLY [*infected by it*]. Oh, my boy . . .

BIFF. Dad . . .

WILLY. She's nothing to me, Biff. I was
15 lonely, I was terribly lonely.

BIFF. You—you gave her Mama's stockings!
[*His tears break through and he rises to go.*]

WILLY [*grabbing for BIFF*]. I gave you an
order!

20 BIFF. Don't touch me, you—liar!

WILLY. Apologize for that!

BIFF. You fake! You phony little fake! You
fake! [*Overcome he turns quickly and weeping
fully goes out with his suitcase. WILLY is left
25 on the floor on his knees.*]

WILLY. I gave you an order! Biff, come back
here or I'll beat you! Come back here! I'll
whip you!

[*STANLEY comes quickly in from the right
30 and stands in front of WILLY.*]

WILLY [*shouts at STANLEY*]. I gave you an
order . . .

STANLEY. Hey, let's pick it up, pick it up, Mr.
Loman. [*He helps WILLY to his feet.*] Your
35 boys left with the chippies. They said they'll
see you home.

[*A second waiter watches some distance
away.*]

WILLY. But we were supposed to have din-
40 ner together.

[*Music is heard, WILLY's theme.*]

STANLEY. Can you make it?

WILLY. I'll—sure, I can make it. [*Suddenly
concerned about his clothes.*] Do I—I look
45 all right?

STANLEY. Sure, you look all right. [*He flicks
a speck off WILLY's lapel.*]

WILLY. Here—here's a dollar.

STANLEY. Oh, your son paid me. It's all right.

WILLY [*putting it in STANLEY's hand*]. No, 50
take it. You're a good boy.

STANLEY. Oh, no, you don't have to . . .

WILLY. Here—here's some more. I don't need
it any more. [*After a slight pause.*] Tell me—
is there a seed store in the neighborhood? 55

STANLEY. Seeds? You mean like to plant?

[*As WILLY turns, STANLEY slips the money
back into his jacket pocket.*]

WILLY. Yes. Carrots, peas . . .

STANLEY. Well, there's hardware stores on 60
Sixth Avenue, but it may be too late now.

WILLY [*anxiously*]. Oh, I'd better hurry. I've
got to get some seeds. [*He starts off to the
right.*] I've got to get some seeds, right away.
Nothing's planted. I don't have a thing in the 65
ground.

[*WILLY hurries out as the light goes down.
STANLEY moves over to the right after him,
watches him off. The other waiter has been
staring at WILLY.*] 70

STANLEY [*to the waiter*]. Well, whatta you
looking at?

[*The waiter picks up the chairs and moves
off right. STANLEY takes the table and follows
him. The light fades on this area. There is a 75
long pause, the sound of the flute coming over.
The light gradually rises on the kitchen, which
is empty. HAPPY appears at the door of the
house, followed by BIFF. HAPPY is carrying a
large bunch of long-stemmed roses. He enters 80
the kitchen, looks around for LINDA. Not seeing
her, he turns to BIFF, who is just outside the
house door, and makes a gesture with his
hands, indicating "Not here, I guess." He looks
into the living-room and freezes. Inside, LINDA, 85
unseen, is seated, WILLY's coat on her lap. She
rises ominously and quietly and moves toward
HAPPY, who backs up into the kitchen, afraid.*]

HAPPY. Hey, what're you doing up? [*LINDA
says nothing but moves toward him im- 90
placably.*] Where's Pop? [*He keeps backing to
the right, and now LINDA is in full view in the
doorway to the living-room.*] Is he sleeping?

LINDA. Where were you?

HAPPY [*trying to laugh it off*]. We met two 95
girls, Mom, very fine types. Here, we brought

you some flowers. [*Offering them to her.*] Put them in your room, Ma.

[*She knocks them to the floor at* BIFF's *feet. He has now come inside and closed the door behind him. She stares at* BIFF, *silent.*]

HAPPY. Now what'd you do that for? Mom, I want you to have some flowers—

LINDA [*cutting* HAPPY *off, violently to* BIFF]. Don't you care whether he lives or dies?

HAPPY [*going to the stairs*]. Come upstairs, Biff.

BIFF [*with a flare of disgust, to* HAPPY]. Go away from me! [*To* LINDA.] What do you mean, lives or dies? Nobody's dying around here, pal.

LINDA. Get out of my sight! Get out of here!

BIFF. I wanna see the boss.

LINDA. You're not going near him!

BIFF. Where is he? [*He moves into the living-room and* LINDA *follows.*]

LINDA [*shouting after* BIFF]. You invite him to dinner. He looks forward to it all day— [BIFF *appears in his parents' bedroom, looks around, and exits*]—and then you desert him there. There's no stranger you'd do that to!

HAPPY. Why? He had a swell time with us. Listen, when I—[LINDA *comes back into the kitchen*]—desert him I hope I don't outlive the day!

LINDA. Get out of here!

HAPPY. Now look, Mom . . .

LINDA. Did you have to go to women tonight? You and your lousy rotten whores!

[BIFF *re-enters the kitchen.*]

HAPPY. Mom, all we did was follow Biff around trying to cheer him up! [*To* BIFF.] Boy, what a night you gave me!

LINDA. Get out of here, both of you, and don't come back! I don't want you tormenting him any more. Go on now, get your things together! [*To* BIFF.] You can sleep in his apartment. [*She starts to pick up the flowers and stops herself.*] Pick up this stuff, I'm not your maid any more. Pick it up, you bum, you!

[HAPPY *turns his back to her in refusal.* BIFF *slowly moves over and gets down on his knees, picking up the flowers.*]

LINDA. You're a pair of animals! Not one, not another living soul would have had the cruelty to walk out on that man in a restaurant!

BIFF [*not looking at her*]. Is that what he said?

LINDA. He didn't have to say anything. He was so humiliated he nearly limped when he came in.

HAPPY. But, Mom, he had a great time with us—

BIFF [*cutting him off violently*]. Shut up!

[*Without another word,* HAPPY *goes upstairs.*]

LINDA. You! You didn't even go in to see if he was all right!

BIFF [*still on the floor in front of* LINDA, *the flowers in his hand; with self-loathing*]. No. Didn't. Didn't do a damned thing. How do you like that, heh? Left him babbling in a toilet.

LINDA. You louse. You . . .

BIFF. Now you hit it on the nose! [*He gets up, throws the flowers in the wastebasket.*] The scum of the earth, and you're looking at him!

LINDA. Get out of here!

BIFF. I gotta talk to the boss, Mom. Where is he?

LINDA. You're not going near him. Get out of this house!

BIFF [*with absolute assurance, determination*]. No. We're gonna have an abrupt conversation, him and me.

LINDA. You're not talking to him!

[*Hammering is heard from outside the house, off right.* BIFF *turns toward the noise.*]

LINDA [*suddenly pleading*]. Will you please leave him alone?

BIFF. What's he doing out there?

LINDA. He's planting the garden!

BIFF [*quietly*]. Now? Oh, my God!

[BIFF *moves outside,* LINDA *following. The light dies down on them and comes up on the center of the apron as* WILLY *walks into it. He is carrying a flashlight, a hoe, and a handful of seed packets. He raps the top of the hoe sharply to fix it firmly, and then moves to the left, measuring off the distance with his foot. He holds the flashlight to look at the seed packets, reading off the instructions. He is in the blue of night.*]

5   WILLY. Carrots . . . quarter-inch apart. Rows . . . one-foot rows. [*He measures it off.*] One foot. [*He puts down a package and measures off.*] Beets. [*He puts down another package and measures again.*] Lettuce. [*He reads the*

10 *package, puts it down.*] One foot— [*He breaks off as* BEN *appears at the right and moves slowly down to him.*] What a proposition, ts, ts. Terrific, terrific. 'Cause she's suffered, Ben, the woman has suffered. You understand me?

15 A man can't go out the way he came in, Ben, a man has got to add up to something. You can't, you can't— [BEN *moves toward him as though to interrupt.*] You gotta consider, now. Don't answer so quick. Remember, it's a

20 guaranteed twenty-thousand-dollar proposition. Now look, Ben, I want you to go through the ins and outs of this thing with me. I've got nobody to talk to, Ben, and the woman has suffered, you hear me?

25   BEN [*standing still, considering*]. What's the proposition?

WILLY. It's twenty thousand dollars on the barrelhead. Guaranteed, gilt-edged, you understand?

30   BEN. You don't want to make a fool of yourself. They might not honor the policy.

WILLY. How can they dare refuse? Didn't I work like a coolie to meet every premium on the nose? And now they don't pay off! Impos-

35 sible!

BEN. It's called a cowardly thing, William.

WILLY. Why? Does it take more guts to stand here the rest of my life ringing up a zero?

40   BEN [*yielding*]. That's a point, William. [*He moves, thinking, turns.*] And twenty thousand —that *is* something one can feel with the hand, it is there.

WILLY [*now assured, with rising power*]. Oh,

45 Ben, that's the whole beauty of it! I see it like a diamond, shining in the dark, hard and rough, that I can pick up and touch in my

hand. Not like—like an appointment! This would not be another damned-fool appoint-

50 ment, Ben, and it changes all the aspects. Because he thinks I'm nothing, see, and so he spites me. But the funeral— [*Straightening up.*] Ben, that funeral will be massive! They'll come from Maine, Massachusetts, Vermont,

55 New Hampshire! All the old-timers with the strange license plates—that boy will be thunderstruck, Ben, because he never realized—I am known! Rhode Island, New York, New Jersey—I am known, Ben, and he'll see it with

60 his eyes once and for all. He'll see what I am, Ben! He's in for a shock, that boy!

BEN [*coming down to the edge of the garden*]. He'll call you a coward.

WILLY [*suddenly fearful*]. No, that would be terrible.

65

BEN. Yes. And a damned fool.

WILLY. No, no, he mustn't, I won't have that! [*He is broken and desperate.*]

BEN. He'll hate you, William.

[*The gay music of the boys is heard.*]

70

WILLY. Oh, Ben, how do we get back to all the great times? Used to be so full of light, and comradeship, the sleigh-riding in winter, and the ruddiness on his cheeks. And always some kind of good news coming up, always

75 something nice coming up ahead. And never even let me carry the valises in the house, and simonizing, simonizing that little red car! Why, can't I give him something and not have him hate me?

80

BEN. Let me think about it. [*He glances at his watch.*] I still have a little time. Remarkable proposition, but you've got to be sure you're not making a fool of yourself.

[BEN *drifts off upstage and goes out of sight.*

85 BIFF *comes down from the left.*]

WILLY [*suddenly conscious of* BIFF, *turns and looks up at him, then begins picking up the packages of seeds in confusion*]. Where the hell is that seed? [*Indignantly.*] You can't

90 see nothing out here! They boxed in the whole goddam neighborhood!

BIFF. There are people all around here. Don't you realize that?

WILLY. I'm busy. Don't bother me.

BIFF [taking the hoe from WILLY]. I'm saying good-bye to you, POP. [WILLY looks at him, silent, unable to move.] I'm not coming back
5 any more.

WILLY. You're not going to see Oliver tomorrow?

BIFF. I've got no appointment, Dad.

WILLY. He put his arm around you, and
10 you've got no appointment?

BIFF. Pop, get this now, will you? Everytime I've left it's been a fight that sent me out of here. Today I realized something about myself and I tried to explain it to you and I—
15 I think I'm just not smart enough to make any sense out of it for you. To hell with whose fault it is or anything like that. [He takes WILLY's arm.] Let's just wrap it up, heh? Come on in, we'll tell Mom. [He gently tries to pull
20 WILLY to left.]

WILLY [frozen, immobile, with guilt in his voice]. No, I don't want to see her.

BIFF. Come on! [He pulls again, and WILLY tries to pull away.]

25 WILLY [highly nervous]. No, no, I don't want to see her.

BIFF [tries to look into WILLY's face, as if to find the answer there]. Why don't you want to see her?

30 WILLY [more harshly now]. Don't bother me, will you?

BIFF. What do you mean, you don't want to see her? You don't want them calling you yellow, do you? This isn't your fault; it's me,
35 I'm a bum. Now come inside! [WILLY strains to get away.] Did you hear what I said to you?

[WILLY pulls away and quickly goes by himself into the house. BIFF follows.]

LINDA [to WILLY]. Did you plant, dear?

40 BIFF [at the door, to LINDA]. All right, we had it out. I'm going and I'm not writing any more.

LINDA [going to WILLY in the kitchen]. I think that's the best way, dear. 'Cause there's
45 no use drawing it out, you'll just never get along.

[WILLY doesn't respond.]

BIFF. People ask where I am and what I'm doing, you don't know, and you don't care. That way it'll be off your mind and you can 50 start brightening up again. All right? That clears it, doesn't it? [WILLY is silent, and BIFF goes to him.] You gonna wish me luck, scout! [He extends his hand.] What do you say?

LINDA. Shake his hand, Willy. 55

WILLY [turning to her, seething with hurt]. There's no necessity to mention the pen at all, y'know.

BIFF [gently]. I've got no appointment, Dad.

WILLY [erupting fiercely]. He put his arm 60 around . . .?

BIFF. Dad, you're never going to see what I am, so what's the use of arguing? If I strike oil I'll send you a check. Meantime forget I'm alive. 65

WILLY [to LINDA]. Spite, see?

BIFF. Shake hands, Dad.

WILLY. Not my hand.

BIFF. I was hoping not to go this way.

WILLY. Well, this is the way you're going. 70 Good-bye.

[BIFF looks at him a moment, then turns sharply and goes to the stairs.]

WILLY [stops him with]. May you rot in hell if you leave this house! 75

BIFF [turning]. Exactly what is it that you want from me?

WILLY. I want you to know, on the train, in the mountains, in the valleys, wherever you go, that you cut down your life for spite! 80

BIFF. No, no.

WILLY. Spite, spite, is the word of your undoing! And when you're down and out, remember what did it. When you're rotting somewhere beside the railroad tracks, remem- 85 ber, and don't you dare blame it on me!

BIFF. I'm not blaming it on you!

WILLY. I won't take the rap for this, you hear?

[HAPPY comes down the stairs and stands on 90 the bottom step, watching.]

BIFF. That's just what I'm telling you!

WILLY [sinking into a chair at the table, with full accusation]. You're trying to put a knife in me—don't think I don't know what you're doing!

BIFF. All right, phony! Then let's lay it on the line. [*He whips the rubber tube out of his pocket and puts it on the table.*]

HAPPY. You crazy—

LINDA. Biff! [*She moves to grab the hose, but BIFF holds it down with his hand.*]

BIFF. Leave it there! Don't move it!

WILLY [*not looking at it*]. What is that?

BIFF. You know goddam well what that is.

WILLY [*caged, wanting to escape*]. I never saw that.

BIFF. You saw it. The mice didn't bring it into the cellar! What is this supposed to do, make a hero out of you? This supposed to make me sorry for you?

WILLY. Never heard of it.

BIFF. There'll be no pity for you, you hear it? No pity!

WILLY [*to LINDA*]. You hear the spite!

BIFF. No, you're going to hear the truth—what you are and what I am!

LINDA. Stop it!

WILLY. Spite!

HAPPY [*coming down toward BIFF*]. You cut it now!

BIFF [*to HAPPY*]. The man don't know who we are! The man is gonna know! [*To WILLY.*] We never told the truth for ten minutes in this house!

HAPPY. We always told the truth!

BIFF [*turning on him*]. You big blow, are you the assistant buyer? You're one of the two assistants to the assistant, aren't you?

HAPPY. Well, I'm practically—

BIFF. You're practically full of it! We all are! And I'm through with it. [*To WILLY.*] Now hear this, Willy, this is me.

WILLY. I know you!

BIFF. You know why I had no address for three months? I stole a suit in Kansas City and I was in jail. [*To LINDA, who is sobbing.*] Stop crying. I'm through with it.

[*LINDA turns away from them, her hands covering her face.*]

WILLY. I suppose that's my fault!

BIFF. I stole myself out of every good job since high school!

WILLY. And whose fault is that?

BIFF. And I never got anywhere because you blew me so full of hot air I could never stand taking orders from anybody! That's whose fault it is!

WILLY. I hear that!

LINDA. Don't, Biff!

BIFF. It's goddam time you heard that! I had to be boss big shot in two weeks, and I'm through with it!

WILLY. Then hang yourself! For spite, hang yourself!

BIFF. No! Nobody's hanging himself, Willy! I ran down eleven flights with a pen in my hand today. And suddenly I stopped, you hear me? And in the middle of that office building, do you hear this? I stopped in the middle of that building and I saw—the sky. I saw the things that I love in this world. The work and the food and time to sit and smoke. And I looked at the pen and said to myself, what the hell am I grabbing this for? Why am I trying to become what I don't want to be? What am I doing in an office, making a contemptuous, begging fool of myself, when all I want is out there, waiting for me the minute I say I know who I am! Why can't I say that, Willy? [*He tries to make WILLY face him, but WILLY pulls away and moves to the left.*]

WILLY [*with hatred, threateningly*]. The door of your life is wide open!

BIFF. Pop! I'm a dime a dozen, and so are you!

WILLY [*turning on him now in an uncontrolled outburst*]. I am not a dime a dozen! I am Willy Loman, and you are Biff Loman!

[*BIFF starts for WILLY, but is blocked by HAPPY. In his fury, BIFF seems on the verge of attacking his father.*]

BIFF. I am not a leader of men, Willy, and neither are you. You were never anything but a hard-working drummer who landed in the ash-can like all the rest of them! I'm one dollar an hour, Willy! I tried seven states and couldn't raise it. A buck an hour! Do you gather my meaning? I'm not bringing home any prizes any more, and you're going to stop waiting for me to bring them home!

WILLY [directly to BIFF]. You vengeful, spite-
5 ful mutt!

[BIFF breaks from HAPPY. WILLY, in fright, starts up the stair. BIFF grabs him.]

BIFF [at the peak of his fury]. Pop, I'm noth-ing! I'm nothing, Pop. Can't you understand
10 that? There's no spite in it any more. I'm just what I am, that's all.

[BIFF's fury has spent itself, and he breaks down, sobbing, holding on to WILLY, who dumbly fumbles for BIFF's face.]
15 WILLY [astonished]. What're you doing? What're you doing? [To LINDA.] Why is he crying?

BIFF [crying, broken]. Will you let me go, for Christ's sake? Will you take that phony
20 dream and burn it before something happens? [Struggling to contain himself, he pulls away and moves to the stairs.] I'll go in the morn-ing. Put him—put him to bed. [Exhausted, BIFF moves up the stairs to his room.]
25 WILLY [after a long pause, astonished, elevated]. Isn't that—isn't that remarkable? Biff—he likes me!

LINDA. He loves you, Willy!

HAPPY [deeply moved]. Always did, Pop.
30 WILLY. Oh, Biff! [Staring wildly.] He cried! Cried to me. [He is choking with his love, and now cries out his promise.] That boy—that boy is going to be magnificent!

[BEN appears in the light just outside the
35 kitchen.]

BEN. Yes, outstanding, with twenty thousand behind him.

LINDA [sensing the racing of his mind, fear-fully, carefully]. Now come to bed, Willy. It's
40 all settled now.

WILLY [finding it difficult not to rush out of the house]. Yes, we'll sleep. Come on. Go to sleep, Hap.

BEN. And it does take a great kind of a man
45 to crack the jungle.

[In accents of dread, BEN's idyllic music starts up.]

HAPPY [his arm around LINDA]. I'm getting married, Pop, don't forget it. I'm changing everything. I'm gonna run that department be- 50
fore the year is up. You'll see, Mom. [He kisses her.]

BEN. The jungle is dark but full of diamonds, Willy.

[WILLY turns, moves, listening to BEN.] 55

LINDA. Be good. You're both good boys, just act that way, that's all.

HAPPY. 'Night, Pop. [He goes upstairs.]

LINDA [to WILLY]. Come, dear.

BEN [with greater force]. One must go in to 60
fetch a diamond out.

WILLY [to LINDA, as he moves slowly along the edge of the kitchen, toward the door]. I just want to get settled down, Linda. Let me sit alone for a little. 65

LINDA [almost uttering her fear]. I want you upstairs.

WILLY [taking her in his arms]. In a few minutes, Linda. I couldn't sleep right now. Go on, you look awful tired. [He kisses her.] 70

BEN. Not like an appointment at all. A diamond is rough and hard to the touch.

WILLY. Go on now. I'll be right up.

LINDA. I think this is the only way, Willy.

WILLY. Sure, it's the best thing. 75

BEN. Best thing!

WILLY. The only way. Everything is gonna be—go on, kid, get to bed. You look so tired.

LINDA. Come right up.

WILLY. Two minutes. 80

[LINDA goes into the living-room, then re-appears in her bedroom. WILLY moves just out-side the kitchen door.]

WILLY. Loves me. [Wonderingly.] Always loved me. Isn't that a remarkable thing? Ben, 85
he'll worship me for it!

BEN [with promise]. It's dark there, but full of diamonds.

WILLY. Can you imagine that magnificence with twenty thousand dollars in his pocket? 90

LINDA [calling from her room]. Willy! Come up!

WILLY [calling into the kitchen]. Yes! Yes. Coming! It's very smart, you realize that, don't you, sweetheart? Even Ben sees it. I gotta go, baby. 'Bye! 'Bye! [*Going over to* BEN, *almost dancing.*] Imagine? When the mail comes he'll be ahead of Bernard again!

5 BEN. A perfect proposition all around.

WILLY. Did you see how he cried to me? Oh, if I could kiss him, Ben!

BEN. Time, William, time!

WILLY. Oh, Ben, I always knew one way or
10 another we were gonna make it, Biff and I!

BEN [*looking at his watch*]. The boat. We'll be late. [*He moves slowly off into the darkness.*]

WILLY [*elegiacally, turning to the house*].
15 Now when you kick off, boy, I want a seventy-yard boot, and get right down the field under the ball, and when you hit, hit low and hit hard, because it's important, boy. [*He swings around and faces the audience.*] There's all
20 kinds of important people in the stands, and the first thing you know . . . . [*Suddenly realizing he is alone.*] Ben! Ben, where do I . . .? [*He makes a sudden movement of search.*] Ben, how do I . . .?

25 LINDA [*calling*]. Willy, you coming up?

WILLY [*uttering a gasp of fear, whirling about as if to quiet her*]. Sh! [*He turns around as if to find his way; sounds, faces, voices, seem to be swarming in upon him and he flicks at
30 them, crying,*] "Sh! Sh!" [*Suddenly music, faint and high, stops him. It rises in intensity, almost to an unbearable scream. He goes up and down on his toes, and rushes off around the house.*] Shhh!

35 LINDA. Willy?

[*There is no answer.* LINDA *waits.* BIFF *gets up off his bed. He is still in his clothes.* HAPPY *sits up.* BIFF *stands listening.*]

LINDA [*with real fear*]. Willy, answer me!
40 Willy!

[*There is the sound of a car starting and moving away at full speed.*]

LINDA. No!

BIFF [*rushing down the stairs*]. Pop!

45 [*As the car speeds off, the music crashes down in a frenzy of sound, which becomes the soft pulsation of a single 'cello string.* BIFF slowly returns to his bedroom. He and HAPPY gravely don their jackets. LINDA slowly walks out of her room. The music has developed into
50 a dead march. The leaves of day are appearing over everything.* CHARLEY *and* BERNARD, somberly dressed, appear and knock on the kitchen door.* BIFF *and* HAPPY *slowly descend the stairs to the kitchen as* CHARLEY *and* BER-
55 NARD *enter. All stop a moment when* LINDA, *in clothes of mourning, bearing a little bunch of roses, comes through the draped doorway into the kitchen. She goes to* CHARLEY *and takes his arm. Now all move toward the aud-
60 ience, through the wall-line of the kitchen. At the limit of the apron,* LINDA *lays down the flowers, kneels, and sits back on her heels. All stare down at the grave.*]

REQUIEM

CHARLEY. It's getting dark, Linda. 65

[LINDA *doesn't react. She stares at the grave.*]

BIFF. How about it, Mom? Better get some rest, heh? They'll be closing the gate soon.

[LINDA *makes no move. Pause.*] 70

HAPPY [*deeply angered*]. He had no right to do that. There was no necessity for it. We would've helped him.

CHARLEY [*grunting*]. Hmmm.

BIFF. Come along, Mom. 75

LINDA. Why didn't anybody come?

CHARLEY. It was a very nice funeral.

LINDA. But where are all the people he knew? Maybe they blame him.

CHARLEY. Naa. It's a rough world, Linda. 80
They wouldn't blame him.

LINDA. I can't understand it. At this time especially. First time in thirty-five years we were just about free and clear. He only needed a little salary. He was even finished with the 85
dentist.

CHARLEY. No man only needs a little salary.

LINDA. I can't understand it.

BIFF. There were a lot of nice days. When he'd come home from a trip; or on Sundays, 90
making the stoop; finishing the cellar; putting

on the new porch; when he built the extra bathroom; and put up the garage. You know something, Charley, there's more of him in that front stoop than in all the sales he ever made.

CHARLEY. Yeah. He was a happy man with a batch of cement.

LINDA. He was so wonderful with his hands.

BIFF. He had the wrong dreams. All, all, wrong.

HAPPY [*almost ready to fight* BIFF]. Don't say that!

BIFF. He never knew who he was.

CHARLEY [*stopping* HAPPY'S *movement and reply. To* BIFF]. Nobody dast blame this man. You don't understand; Willy was a salesman. And for a salesman, there is no rock bottom to the life. He don't put a bolt to a nut, he don't tell you the law or give you medicine. He's a man way out there in the blue, riding on a smile and a shoeshine. And when they start not smiling back—that's an earthquake. And then you get yourself a couple of spots on your hat, and you're finished. Nobody dast blame this man. A salesman is got to dream, boy. It comes with the territory.

BIFF. Charley, the man didn't know who he was.

HAPPY [*infuriated*]. Don't say that!

BIFF. Why don't you come with me, Happy?

HAPPY. I'm not licked that easily. I'm staying right in this city, and I'm gonna beat this racket! [*He looks at* BIFF, *his chin set.*] The Loman Brothers!

BIFF. I know who I am, kid.

HAPPY. All right, boy. I'm gonna show you and everybody else that Willy Loman did not die in vain. He had a good dream. It's the only dream you can have—to come out number-one man. He fought it out here, and this is where I'm gonna win it for him.

BIFF [*with a hopeless glance at* HAPPY, *bends toward his mother*]. Let's go, Mom.

LINDA. I'll be with you in a minute. Go on, Charley. [*He hesitates.*] I want to, just for a minute. I never had a chance to say good-bye.

[CHARLEY *moves away, followed by* HAPPY. BIFF *remains a slight distance up and left of* LINDA. *She sits there, summoning herself. The flute begins, not far away, playing behind her speech.*]

LINDA. Forgive me, dear. I can't cry. I don't know what it is, but I can't cry. I don't understand it. Why did you ever do that? Help me, Willy, I can't cry. It seems to me that you're just on another trip. I keep expecting you. Willy, dear, I can't cry. Why did you do it? I search and search and I search, and I can't understand it, Willy. I made the last payment on the house today. Today, dear. And there'll be nobody home. [*A sob rises in her throat.*] We're free and clear. [*Sobbing more fully, released.*] We're free. [BIFF *comes slowly toward her.*] We're free . . . we're free . . .

[BIFF *lifts her to her feet and moves out up right with her in his arms.* LINDA *sobs quietly.* BERNARD *and* CHARLEY *come together and follow them, followed by* HAPPY. *Only the music of the flute is left on the darkening stage as over the house the hard towers of the apartment buildings rise into sharp focus.*]

Curtain

Samuel Beckett

1906–

All That Fall

1957

Act Without Words I

1957

It is commonly said that Samuel Beckett contemplates the human condition without hope and without faith, representing life as futile and man as impotent. It would be nothing new for a dramatist to ponder how life may be sustained without the support of hope and faith. That vision has entered into the terror and dignity of great tragic drama, whether Sophoclean or Shakespearean. Nor does comedy refuse to recognize some ultimate absurdity in human predicaments. When at the end of *Juno and the Paycock* the two befuddled derelicts judge the whole world to be "in a terrible state o' chassis," the scene mingles the pathetic and the ludicrous.

Beckett's is a special kind of drama that fuses and also reanimates the traditional comic and tragic modes. His perspective embraces contraries. Whatever appears tragic, spiritual, or even merely decorous in human behavior is seen to be toppling into the rankest commonplace; whatever seems grossly physical, or grotesque has a tone of spiritual desolation, a dying echo of tragic suffering. His most characteristic effect is a sudden and ludicrous deflation or exposure of pretentions (an effect properly known as *bathos).* However, he also sometimes reverses the process, investing the most ordinary event or object with comic nobility. No sentiment is too lofty to be shot down, no fact too mean to be oddly significant.

In *All That Fall* Mrs. Rooney's ejaculations inspired by the death of a hen illustrate Beckett's characteristic manner. Her eulogy, mingling the vulgar and the sentimental, is of course ridiculously inflated:

What a death! One minute picking happy at the dung, on the road, in the sun, with now and then a dust bath, and then—bang!— all her troubles over. [*Pause.*] All the laying and the hatching. [*Pause.*] Just one great squawk and then . . . peace. [*Pause.*] They would have slit her weasand in any case. [*Pause.*]

Absurd. Yet in full context Mrs. Rooney's words are neither purely sentimental nor merely vulgar. The theme of the play is a commonplace, that in the midst of life we are in death. Realized most obviously in the accidental death of a child, it reverberates throughout. At the beginning and the end are allusions to Schubert's "Death and the Maiden," a song in which Death whispers amorously to a dying girl. And there are scores of other similar allusions—for example, to hymns and biblical texts conventionally associated with funerals, and to the death of Mrs. Rooney's daughter. The flow of time itself, although spanning literally only an hour of a June day, is toward the fall and winter. Given such orchestration of the theme of death, in every key from inanity to horror, Mrs. Rooney's eulogy on a dead hen contributes its odd hilarious solemnity to the changes rung on the title, *All That Fall.*

That the play was written for radio does not limit its dramatic force. It exploits in addition to verbal meaning the imagined scenes and gestures that sounds powerfully suggest—bird calls, train noises, shuffling feet—and, especially, the pauses, hundreds of momentary silences that feed the imagination. Because its language is both bizarre and exact, punctuated by fertile silences, *All That Fall* possesses an outlandish realism. Because it excites the imagination, the whole conveys not a depressing weight of philosophic despair, but an impression of extraordinary and sometimes outrageous liveliness.

Act Without Words, consisting only of stage directions, as purely represents the visual and gestural elements of drama as *All That Fall* represents the auditory. From one viewpoint the "mime" describes a series of sadistically inflicted frustrations; from another it describes a clown's meticulous parody of self-pity. Characteristically, Beckett excludes neither viewpoint. The combination provokes a double vision achieved with economy and verve. Although without much hope or faith, Beckett brings to the drama a renovation of words and actions through a form and style both traditional and new.

All That Fall

A Play for Radio

BECKETT

CHARACTERS

MRS. ROONEY (MADDY)   *a lady in her seventies*
CHRISTY   *a carter*
MR. TYLER   *a retired bill-broker*
MR. SLOCUM   *Clerk of the Racecourse*
TOMMY   *a porter*
MR. BARRELL   *a station-master*
MISS FITT   *a lady in her thirties*
A FEMALE VOICE
DOLLY   *a small girl*
MR. ROONEY (DAN)   *husband of* MRS. ROONEY, *blind*
JERRY   *a small boy*

[*Rural sounds. Sheep, bird, cow, cock, severally, then together. Silence.* MRS. ROONEY *advances along country road towards railway station. Sound of her dragging feet. Music faint from house by way. "Death and the Maiden."* 5
The steps slow down, stop.]
    MRS. ROONEY. Poor woman. All alone in that ruinous old house.
    [*Music louder. Silence but for music playing. The steps resume. Music dies.* MRS. 10
ROONEY *murmurs, melody. Her murmur dies. Sound of approaching cartwheels. The cart stops. The steps slow down, stop.*]
    MRS. ROONEY. Is that you, Christy?
    CHRISTY. It is, Ma'am. 15

MRS. ROONEY. I thought the hinny was familiar. How is your poor wife?

CHRISTY. No better, Ma'am.

MRS. ROONEY. Your daughter then?

5 CHRISTY. No worse, Ma'am.

[*Silence.*]

MRS. ROONEY. Why do you halt? [*Pause.*] But why do I halt?

[*Silence.*]

10 CHRISTY. Nice day for the races, Ma'am.

MRS. ROONEY. No doubt it is. [*Pause.*] But will it hold up? [*Pause. With emotion.*] Will it hold up?

[*Silence.*]

15 CHRISTY. I suppose you wouldn't—

MRS. ROONEY. Hist! [*Pause.*] Surely to goodness that cannot be the up mail I hear already.

[*Silence. The hinny neighs. Silence.*]

CHRISTY. Damn the mail.

20 MRS. ROONEY. Oh thank God for that! I could have sworn I heard it, thundering up the track in the far distance. [*Pause.*] So hinnies whinny. Well, it is not surprising.

CHRISTY. I suppose you wouldn't be in need 25 of a small load of dung?

MRS. ROONEY. Dung? What class of dung?

CHRISTY. Stydung.

MRS. ROONEY. Stydung . . . I like your frankness, Christy. [*Pause.*] I'll ask the master. 30 [*Pause.*] Christy.

CHRISTY. Yes, Ma'am.

MRS. ROONEY. Do you find anything . . . bizarre about my way of speaking? [*Pause.*] I do not mean the voice. [*Pause.*] No, I mean 35 the words. [*Pause. More to herself.*] I use none but the simplest words, I hope, and yet I sometimes find my way of speaking very . . . bizarre. [*Pause.*] Mercy! What was that?

CHRISTY. Never mind her, Ma'am, she's very 40 fresh in herself today.

[*Silence.*]

MRS. ROONEY. Dung? What would we want with dung, at our time of life? [*Pause.*] Why are you on your feet down on the road? Why 45 do you not climb up on the crest of your manure and let yourself be carried along? Is it that you have no head for heights?

[*Silence.*]

CHRISTY [*to the hinny*]. Yep! [*Pause. Louder.*]

Yep wiyya to hell owwa that! 50

[*Silence.*]

MRS. ROONEY. She does not move a muscle. [*Pause.*] I too should be getting along, if I do not wish to arrive late at the station. [*Pause.*] But a moment ago she neighed and pawed the 55 ground. And now she refuses to advance. Give her a good welt on the rump. [*Sound of welt. Pause.*] Harder! [*Sound of welt. Pause.*] Well! If someone were to do that for me I should not dally. [*Pause.*] How she gazes at me to be 60 sure, with her great moist cleg-tormented° eyes! Perhaps if I were to move on, down the road, out of her field of vision . . . . [*Sound of welt.*] No, no, enough! Take her by the snaffle and pull her eyes away from me. Oh this is 65 awful! [*She moves on. Sound of her dragging feet.*] What have I done to deserve all this, what, what? [*Dragging feet.*] So long ago . . . . No! No! [*Dragging feet. Quotes.*] "Sigh out a something something tale of things, Done long 70 ago and ill done." [*She halts.*] How can I go on, I cannot. Oh let me just flop down flat on the road like a big fat jelly out of a bowl and never move again! A great big slop thick with grit and dust and flies, they would have to 75 scoop me up with a shovel. [*Pause.*] Heavens, there is that up mail again, what will become of me! [*The dragging steps resume.*] Oh I am just a hysterical old hag, I know, destroyed with sorrow and pining and gentility and 80 church-going and fat and rheumatism and childlessness. [*Pause. Brokenly.*] Minnie! Little Minnie! [*Pause.*] Love, that is all I asked, a little love, daily, twice daily, fifty years of twice daily love like a Paris horse-butcher's 85 regular, what normal woman wants affection? A peck on the jaw at morning, near the ear, and another at evening, peck, peck, till you grow whiskers on you. There is that lovely laburnum again. 90

[*Dragging feet. Sound of bicycle-bell. It is old MR. TYLER coming up behind her on his bicycle, on his way to the station. Squeak of brakes. He slows down and rides abreast of her.*] 95

MR. TYLER. Mrs. Rooney! Pardon me if I do

cleg-tormented tormented by horseflies.

not doff my cap, I'd fall off. Divine day for the meeting.

MRS. ROONEY. Oh, Mr. Tyler, you startled the life out of me stealing up behind me like that like a deer-stalker! Oh!

MR. TYLER [*playfully*]. I rang my bell, Mrs. Rooney, the moment I sighted you I started tinkling my bell, now don't you deny it.

MRS. ROONEY. Your bell is one thing, Mr. Tyler, and you are another. What news of your poor daughter?

MR. TYLER. Fair, fair. They removed everything, you know, the whole . . . er . . . bag of tricks. Now I am grandchildless.

[*Dragging feet.*]

MRS. ROONEY. Gracious how you wobble! Dismount, for mercy's sake, or ride on.

MR. TYLER. Perhaps if I were to lay my hand lightly on your shoulder, Mrs. Rooney, how would that be? [*Pause.*] Would you permit that?

MRS. ROONEY. No, Mr. Rooney, Mr. Tyler I mean, I am tired of light old hands on my shoulders and other senseless places, sick and tired of them. Heavens, here comes Connolly's van! [*She halts. Sound of motor-van. It approaches, passes with thunderous rattle, recedes.*] Are you all right, Mr. Tyler? [*Pause.*] Where is he? [*Pause.*] Ah there you are! [*The dragging steps resume.*] That was a narrow squeak.

MR. TYLER. I alit in the nick of time.

MRS. ROONEY. It is suicide to be abroad. But what is it to be at home, Mr. Tyler, what is it to be at home? A lingering dissolution. Now we are white with dust from head to foot. I beg your pardon?

MR. TYLER. Nothing, Mrs. Rooney, nothing, I was merely cursing, under my breath, God and man, under my breath, and the wet Saturday afternoon of my conception. My back tire has gone down again. I pumped it hard as iron before I set out. And now I am on the rim.

MRS. ROONEY. Oh what a shame!

MR. TYLER. Now if it were the front I should not so much mind. But the back. The back! The chain! The oil! The grease! The hub! The brakes! The gear! No! It is too much!

[*Dragging steps.*]

MRS. ROONEY. Are we very late, Mr. Tyler? I have not the courage to look at my watch.

MR. TYLER [*bitterly*]. Late! I on my bicycle as I bowled along was already late. Now therefore we are doubly late, trebly, quadrupedly late. Would I had shot by you, without a word.

[*Dragging feet.*]

MRS. ROONEY. Whom are you meeting, Mr. Tyler?

MR. TYLER. Hardy. [*Pause.*] We used to climb together. [*Pause.*] I saved his life once. [*Pause.*] I have not forgotten it.

[*Dragging feet. They stop.*]

MRS. ROONEY. Let us halt a moment and let this vile dust fall back upon the viler worms.

[*Silence. Rural sounds.*]

MR. TYLER. What sky! What light! Ah in spite of all it is a blessed thing to be alive in such weather, and out of hospital.

MRS. ROONEY. Alive?

MR. TYLER. Well half alive shall we say?

MRS. ROONEY. Speak for yourself, Mr. Tyler. I am not half alive nor anything approaching it. [*Pause.*] What are we standing here for? This dust will not settle in our time. And when it does some great roaring machine will come and whirl it all skyhigh again.

MR. TYLER. Well, shall we be getting along in that case?

MRS. ROONEY. No.

MR. TYLER. Come, Mrs. Rooney—

MRS. ROONEY. Go, Mr. Tyler, go on and leave me, listening to the cooing of the ring-doves. [*Cooing.*] If you see my poor blind Dan tell him I was on my way to meet him when it all came over me again, like a flood. Say to him, Your poor wife, she told me to tell you it all came flooding over her again and . . . [*the voice breaks*] . . . she simply went back home . . . straight back home . . .

MR. TYLER. Come, Mrs. Rooney, come, the mail has not yet gone up, just take my free arm and we'll be there with time and to spare.

MRS. ROONEY [*sobbing*]. What? What's all this now? [*Calmer.*] Can't you see I'm in trouble? [*With anger.*] Have you no respect for misery? [*Sobbing.*] Minnie! Little Minnie!

MR. TYLER. Come, Mrs. Rooney, come, the mail has not yet gone up, just take my free arm and we'll be there with time and to spare.

MRS. ROONEY [*brokenly*]. In her forties now she'd be, I don't know, fifty, girding up her lovely little loins, getting ready for the change . . .

MR. TYLER. Come, Mrs. Rooney, come, the mail—

MRS. ROONEY [*exploding*]. Will you get along with you, Mr. Rooney, Mr. Tyler I mean, will you get along with you now and cease molesting me? What kind of a country is this where a woman can't weep her heart out on the highways and byways without being tormented by retired bill-brokers! [MR. TYLER *prepares to mount his bicycle.*] Heavens you're not going to ride her flat! [MR. TYLER *mounts.*] You'll tear your tube to ribbons! [MR. TYLER *rides off. Receding sound of bumping bicycle. Silence. Cooing.*] Venus birds! Billing in the woods all the long summer long. [*Pause.*] Oh cursed corset! If I could let it out, without indecent exposure. Mr. Tyler! Mr. Tyler! Come back and unlace me behind the hedge! [*She laughs wildly, ceases.*] What's wrong with me, what's wrong with me, never tranquil, seething out of my dirty old pelt, out of my skull, oh to be in atoms, in atoms! [*Frenziedly.*] ATOMS! [*Silence. Cooing. Faintly.*] Jesus! [*Pause.*] Jesus!

[*Sound of car coming up behind her. It slows down and draws up beside her, engine running. It is* MR. SLOCUM, *the Clerk of the Racecourse.*]

MR. SLOCUM. Is anything wrong, Mrs. Rooney? You are bent all double. Have you a pain in the stomach?

[*Silence.* MRS. ROONEY *laughs wildly. Finally.*]

MRS. ROONEY. Well if it isn't my old admirer the Clerk of the Course, in his limousine.

MR. SLOCUM. May I offer you a lift, Mrs. Rooney? Are you going in my direction?

MRS. ROONEY. I am, Mr. Slocum, we all are. [*Pause.*] How is your poor mother?

MR. SLOCUM. Thank you, she is fairly comfortable. We manage to keep her out of pain. That is the great thing, Mrs. Rooney, is it not?

MRS. ROONEY. Yes, indeed, Mr. Slocum, that is the great thing, I don't know how you do it. [*Pause. She slaps her cheek violently.*] Ah these wasps!

MR. SLOCUM [*coolly*]. May I then offer you a seat, Madam?

MRS. ROONEY [*with exaggerated enthusiasm*]. Oh that would be heavenly, Mr. Slocum, just simply heavenly. [*Dubiously.*] But would I ever get in, you look very high off the ground today, these new balloon tires I presume. [*Sound of door opening and* MRS. ROONEY *trying to get in.*] Does this roof never come off? No? [*Efforts of* MRS. ROONEY.] No . . . I'll never do it . . . you'll have to get down, Mr. Slocum, and help me from the rear. [*Pause.*] What was that? [*Pause. Aggrieved.*] This is all your suggestion, Mr. Slocum, not mine. Drive on, Sir, drive on.

MR. SLOCUM [*switching off the engine*]. I'm coming, Mrs. Rooney, I'm coming, give me time, I'm as stiff as yourself.

[*Sound of* MR. SLOCUM *extracting himself from driver's seat.*]

MRS. ROONEY. Stiff! Well I like that! And me heaving all over back and front. [*To herself.*] The dry old reprobate!

MR. SLOCUM [*in position behind her*]. Now, Mrs. Rooney, how shall we do this?

MRS. ROONEY. As if I were a bale, Mr. Slocum, don't be afraid. [*Pause. Sounds of effort.*] That's the way! [*Effort.*] Lower! [*Effort.*] Wait! [*Pause.*] No, don't let go! [*Pause.*] Suppose I do get up, will I ever get down?

MR. SLOCUM [*breathing hard*]. You'll get down, Mrs. Rooney, you'll get down. We may not get you up, but I warrant you we'll get you down.

[*He resumes his efforts. Sound of these.*]

MRS. ROONEY. Oh! . . . Lower! . . . Don't be afraid! . . . We're past the age when . . . There! . . . Now! . . . Get your shoulder under it . . . Oh! . . . [*Giggles.*] Oh glory! . . . Up! Up! . . . Ah! . . . I'm in! [*Panting of* MR. SLOCUM. *He slams the door. In a scream.*] My frock! You've nipped my frock! [MR. SLOCUM *opens the door.* MRS. ROONEY *frees her frock.* MR. SLOCUM

SAMUEL BECKETT

slams the door. His violent unintelligible mut-
tering as he walks round to the other door.
Tearfully.] My nice frock! Look what you've
done to my nice frock! [Mr. Slocum *gets into*
5 *his seat, slams driver's door, presses starter.*
The engine does not start. He releases starter.]
What will Dan say when he sees me?

Mr. Slocum. Has he then recovered his
sight?

10 Mrs. Rooney. No, I mean when he knows,
what will he say when he feels the hole? [Mr.
Slocum *presses starter. As before. Silence.*]
What are you doing, Mr. Slocum?

Mr. Slocum. Gazing straight before me,
15 Mrs. Rooney, through the windscreen, into the
void.

Mrs. Rooney. Start her up, I beseech you,
and let us be off. This is awful!

Mr. Slocum [*dreamily*]. All morning she
20 went like a dream and now she is dead. That
is what you get for a good deed. [*Pause. Hope-*
fully.] Perhaps if I were to to choke her. [*He*
does so, presses the starter. The engine roars.
Roaring to make himself heard.] She was get-
25 ting too much air!

[*He throttles down, grinds in his first gear,*
moves off, changes up in a grinding of gears.]
Mrs. Rooney [*in anguish*]. Mind the hen!
[*Scream of brakes. Squawk of hen.*] Oh,
30 mother, you have squashed her, drive on,
drive on! [*The car accelerates. Pause.*] What a
death! One minute picking happy at the dung,
on the road, in the sun, with now and then a
dust bath, and then—bang!—all her troubles
35 over. [*Pause.*] All the laying and the hatching.
[*Pause.*] Just one great squawk and then . . .
peace. [*Pause.*] They would have slit her
weasand in any case. [*Pause.*] Here we are, let
me down. [*The car slows down, stops, engine*
40 *running. Mr. Slocum blows his horn. Pause.*
Louder. Pause.] What are you up to now, Mr.
Slocum? We are at a standstill, all danger is
past and you blow your horn. Now if instead
of blowing it now you had blown it at that
45 unfortunate—

[*Horn violently. Tommy the porter appears*
at top of station steps.]
Mr. Slocum [*calling*]. Will you come down,

Tommy, and help this lady out, she's stuck.
[Tommy *descends the steps.*] Open the door, 50
Tommy, and ease her out.

[Tommy *opens the door.*]

Tommy. Certainly, sir. Nice day for the
races, sir. What would you fancy for—

Mrs. Rooney. Don't mind me. Don't take 55
any notice of me. I do not exist. The fact is
well known.

Mr. Slocum. Do as you're asked, Tommy,
for the love of God.

Tommy. Yessir. Now, Mrs. Rooney. 60

[*He starts pulling her out.*]

Mrs. Rooney. Wait, Tommy, wait now,
don't bustle me, just let me wheel round and
get my feet to the ground. [*Her efforts to*
achieve this.] Now. 65

Tommy [*pulling her out*]. Mind your feather,
Ma'am. [*Sounds of effort.*] Easy now, easy.

Mrs. Rooney. Wait, for God's sake, you'll
have me beheaded.

Tommy. Crouch down, Mrs. Rooney, crouch 70
down, and get your head in the open.

Mrs. Rooney. Crouch down! At my time of
life! This is lunacy!

Tommy. Press her down, sir.

[*Sounds of combined efforts.*] 75

Mrs. Rooney. Pity!

Tommy. Now! She's coming! Straighten up,
Ma'am! There!

[Mr. Slocum *slams the door.*]

Mrs. Rooney. Am I out? 80

[*The voice of* Mr. Barrell, *the station-*
master, raised in anger.]

Mr. Barrell. Tommy! Tommy! Where the
hell is he?

[Mr. Slocum *grinds in his gear.*] 85

Tommy [*hurriedly*]. You wouldn't have
something for the Ladies Plate, sir. I was given
Flash Harry.

Mr. Slocum [*scornfully*]. Flash Harry! That
carthorse! 90

Mr. Barrell [*at top of steps, roaring*].
Tommy! Blast your bleeding bloody— [*He sees*
Mrs. Rooney]. Oh, Mrs. Rooney . . . . [Mr.
Slocum *drives away in a grinding of gears.*]
Who's that crucifying his gearbox, Tommy? 95

Tommy. Old Cissy Slocum.

MRS. ROONEY. Cissy Slocum! That's a nice way to refer to your betters. Cissy Slocum! And you an orphan!

MR. BARRELL [*angrily to* TOMMY]. What are you doing stravaging down here on the public road? This is no place for you at all! Nip up there on the platform now and whip out the truck! Won't the twelve-thirty be on top of us before we can turn round?

TOMMY [*bitterly*]. And that's the thanks you get for a Christian act.

MR. BARRELL [*violently*]. Get on with you now before I report you! [*Slow feet of* TOMMY *climbing steps.*] Do you want me to come down to you with the shovel? [*The feet quicken, recede, cease.*] Ah God forgive me, it's a hard life. [*Pause.*] Well, Mrs. Rooney, it's nice to see you up and about again. You were laid up there a long time.

MRS. ROONEY. Not long enough, Mr. Barrell. [*Pause.*] Would I were still in bed, Mr. Barrell. [*Pause.*] Would I were lying stretched out in my comfortable bed, Mr. Barrell, just wasting slowly, painlessly away, keeping up my strength with arrowroot and calves-foot jelly, till in the end you wouldn't see me under the blankets any more than a board. [*Pause.*] Oh no coughing or spitting or bleeding or vomiting, just drifting gently down into the higher life, and remembering, remembering . . . [*the voice breaks*] . . . all the silly unhappiness . . . as though . . . it had never happened . . . What did I do with that handkerchief? [*Sound of handkerchief loudly applied.*] How long have you been master of this station now, Mr. Barrell?

MR. BARRELL. Don't ask me, Mrs. Rooney, don't ask me.

MRS. ROONEY. You stepped into your father's shoes, I believe, when he took them off.

MR. BARRELL. Poor Pappy! [*Reverent pause.*] He didn't live long to enjoy his ease.

MRS. ROONEY. I remember him clearly. A small ferrety purple-faced widower, deaf as a doornail, very testy and snappy. [*Pause.*] I suppose you'll be retiring soon yourself, Mr. Barrell, and growing your roses. [*Pause.*] Did I understand you to say the twelve-thirty would soon be upon us?

MR. BARRELL. Those were my words.

MRS. ROONEY. But according to my watch which is more or less right—or was—by the eight o'clock news the time is now coming up to twelve . . . [*pause as she consults her watch*] . . . thirty-six. [*Pause.*] And yet upon the other hand the up mail has not yet gone through. [*Pause.*] Or has it sped by unbeknown to me? [*Pause.*] For there was a moment there, I remember now, I was so plunged in sorrow I wouldn't have heard a steam roller go over me. [*Pause.* MR. BARRELL *turns to go.*] Don't go, Mr. Barrell! [MR. BARRELL *goes. Loud.*] Mr. Barrell! [*Pause. Louder.*] Mr. Barrell!

[MR. BARRELL *comes back.*]

MR. BARRELL [*testily*]. What is it, Mrs. Rooney, I have my work to do.

[*Silence. Sound of wind.*]

MRS. ROONEY. The wind is getting up. [*Pause. Wind.*] The best of the day is over. [*Pause. Wind. Dreamily.*] Soon the rain will begin to fall and go on falling, all afternoon. [MR. BARRELL *goes.*] Then at evening the clouds will part, the setting sun will shine an instant, then sink, behind the hills. [*She realizes* MR. BARRELL *has gone.*] Mr. Barrell! Mr. Barrell! [*Silence.*] I estrange them all. They come towards me, uninvited, bygones bygones, full of kindness, anxious to help . . . [*the voice breaks*] . . . genuinely pleased . . . to see me again . . . looking so well . . . . [*Handkerchief.*] A few simple words . . . from my heart . . . and I am all alone . . . once more . . . . [*Handkerchief. Vehemently.*] I should not be out at all! I should never leave the grounds! [*Pause.*] Oh there is that Fitt woman, I wonder will she bow to me. [*Sound of* MISS FITT *approaching, humming a hymn. She starts climbing the steps.*] Miss Fitt! [MISS FITT *halts, stops humming.*] Am I then invisible, Miss Fitt? Is this cretonne so becoming to me that I merge into the masonry? [MISS FITT *descends a step.*] That is right, Miss Fitt, look closely and you will finally distinguish a once female shape.

MISS FITT. Mrs. Rooney! I saw you, but I did not know you.

MRS. ROONEY. Last Sunday we worshipped

together. We knelt side by side at the same altar. We drank from the same chalice. Have I so changed since then?

Miss Fitt [*shocked*]. Oh but in church, Mrs. Rooney, in church I am alone with my Maker. Are not you? [*Pause.*] Why even the sexton himself, you know, when he takes up the collection, knows it is useless to pause before me. I simply do not see the plate, or bag, whatever it is they use, how could I? [*Pause.*] Why even when all is over and I go out into the sweet fresh air, why even then for the first furlong or so I stumble in a kind of daze as you might say, oblivious to my co-religionists. And they are very kind I must admit—the vast majority —very kind and understanding. They know me now and take no umbrage. There she goes, they say, there goes the dark Miss Fitt, alone with her Maker, take no notice of her. And they step down off the path to avoid my running into them. [*Pause.*] Ah yes, I am distray, very distray, even on week-days. Ask Mother, if you do not believe me. Hetty, she says, when I start eating my doily instead of the thin bread and butter, Hetty, how can you be so distray? [*Sighs.*] I suppose the truth is I am not there, Mrs. Rooney, just not really there at all. I see, hear, smell, and so on, I go through the usual motions, but my heart is not in it, Mrs. Rooney, but heart is in none of it. Left to myself, with no one to check me, I would soon be flown . . . home. [*Pause.*] So if you think I cut you just now, Mrs. Rooney, you do me an injustice. All I saw was a big pale blur, just another big pale blur. [*Pause.*] Is anything amiss, Mrs. Rooney, you do not look normal somehow. So bowed and bent.

Mrs. Rooney [*ruefully*]. Maddy Rooney, née Dunne, the big pale blur. [*Pause.*] You have piercing sight, Miss Fitt, if you only knew it, literally piercing.

[*Pause.*]

Miss Fitt. Well . . . is there anything I can do, now that I am here?

Mrs. Rooney. If you would help me up the face of this cliff, Miss Fitt, I have little doubt your Maker would requite you, if no one else.

Miss Fitt. Now, now, Mrs. Rooney, don't put your teeth in me. Requite! I make these sacrifices for nothing—or not at all. [*Pause. Sound of her descending steps.*] I take it you want to lean on me, Mrs. Rooney.

Mrs. Rooney. I asked Mr. Barrell to give me his arm, just give me his arm. [*Pause.*] He turned on his heel and strode away.

Miss Fitt. Is it my arm you want then? [*Pause. Impatiently.*] Is it my arm you want, Mrs. Rooney, or what is it?

Mrs. Rooney [*exploding*]. Your arm! Any arm! A helping hand! For five seconds! Christ what a planet!

Miss Fitt. Really. . . . Do you know what it is, Mrs. Rooney, I do not think it is wise of you to be going about at all.

Mrs. Rooney [*violently*]. Come down here, Miss Fitt, and give me your arm, before I scream down the parish!

[*Pause. Wind. Sound of* Miss Fitt *descending last steps.*]

Miss Fitt [*resignedly*]. Well, I suppose it is the Protestant thing to do.

Mrs. Rooney. Pismires do it for one another. [*Pause.*] I have seen slugs do it. [Miss Fitt *proffers her arm.*] No, the other side, my dear, if it's all the same to you, I'm left-handed on top of everything else. [*She takes* Miss Fitt's *right arm.*] Heavens, child, you're just a bag of bones, you need building up. [*Sound of her toiling up steps on* Miss Fitt's *arm.*] This is worse than the Matterhorn, were you ever up the Matterhorn, Miss Fitt, great honeymoon resort. [*Sound of toiling.*] Why don't they have a handrail? [*Panting.*] Wait till I get some air. [*Pause.*] Don't let me go! [Miss Fitt *hums her hymn.° After a moment* Mrs. Rooney *joins in with the words.*] . . . the encircling gloo-oom . . . [Miss Fitt *stops humming*] . . . tum tum me on. [*Forte.*] The night is dark and I am far from ho-ome, tum tum—

Miss Fitt [*hysterically*]. Stop it, Mrs. Rooney, stop it, or I'll drop you!

Mrs. Rooney. Wasn't it that they sung on the *Lusitania?* Or Rock of Ages? Most touching it must have been. Or was it the *Titanic?*

her hymn   John Henry Newman's "Lead, Kindly Light"

[*Attracted by the noise a group, including* MR. TYLER, MR. BARRELL, *and* TOMMY, *gathers at top of steps.*]

MR. BARRELL. What the—

[*Silence.*]

MR. TYLER. Lovely day for the fixture.

[*Loud titter from* TOMMY *cut short by* MR. BARRELL *with back-handed blow in the stomach. Appropriate noise from* TOMMY.]

FEMALE VOICE [*shrill*]. Oh look, Dolly, look!

DOLLY. What, Mamma?

FEMALE VOICE. They are stuck! [*Cackling laugh.*] They are stuck!

MRS. ROONEY. Now we are the laughing-stock of the twenty-six counties. Or is it thirty-six?

MR. TYLER. That is a nice way to treat your defenseless subordinates, Mr. Barrell, hitting them without warning in the pit of the stomach.

MISS FITT. Has anybody seen my mother?

MR. BARRELL. Who is that?

TOMMY. The dark Miss Fitt.

MR. BARRELL. Where is her face?

MRS. ROONEY. Now, deary, I am ready if you are. [*They toil up remaining steps.*] Stand back, you cads!

[*Shuffle of feet.*]

FEMALE VOICE. Mind yourself, Dolly!

MRS. ROONEY. Thank you, Miss Fitt, thank you, that will do, just prop me up against the wall like a roll of tarpaulin and that will be all, for the moment. [*Pause.*] I am sorry for all this ramdam,° Miss Fitt, had I known you were looking for your mother I should not have importuned you, I know what it is.

MR. TYLER [*in marvelling aside*]. Ramdam!

FEMALE VOICE. Come, Dolly darling, let us take up our stand before the first class smokers. Give me your hand and hold me tight, one can be sucked under.

MR. TYLER. You have lost your mother, Miss Fitt?

MISS FITT. Good morning, Mr. Tyler.

MR. TYLER. Good morning, Miss Fitt.

MR. BARRELL. Good morning, Miss Fitt.

ramdam rumpus or rampage

MISS FITT. Good morning, Mr. Barrell.

MR. TYLER. You have lost your mother, Miss Fitt?

MISS FITT. She said she would be on the last train.

MRS. ROONEY. Do not imagine, because I am silent, that I am not present, and alive, to all that is going on.

MR. TYLER [*to* MISS FITT]. When you say the last train—

MRS. ROONEY. Do not flatter yourselves for one moment, because I hold aloof, that my sufferings have ceased. No. The entire scene, the hills, the plain, the racecourse with its miles and miles of white rails and three red stands, the pretty little wayside station, even you yourselves, yes, I mean it, and over all the clouding blue, I see it all, I stand here and see it all with eyes . . . [*the voice breaks*] . . . through eyes . . . oh if you had my eyes . . . you would understand . . . the things they have seen . . . and not looked away . . . this is nothing . . . nothing . . . what did I do with the handkerchief?

[*Pause.*]

MR. TYLER [*to* MISS FITT]. When you say the last train—[MRS. ROONEY *blows her nose violently and long*]—when you say the last train, Miss Fitt, I take it you mean the twelve-thirty.

MISS FITT. What else could I mean, Mr. Tyler, what else could I *conceivably* mean?

MR. TYLER. Then you have no cause for anxiety, Miss Fitt, for the twelve-thirty has not yet arrived. Look. [MISS FITT *looks.*] No, up the line. [MISS FITT *looks. Patiently.*] No, Miss Fitt, follow the direction of my index. [MISS FITT *looks.*] There. You see now. The signal. At the bawdy hour of nine. [*In rueful afterthought.*] Or three alas! [MR. BARRELL *stifles a guffaw.*] Thank you, Mr. Barrell.

MISS FITT. But the time is now getting on for—

MR. TYLER [*patiently*]. We all know, Miss Fitt, we all know only too well what the time is now getting on for, and yet the cruel fact remains that the twelve-thirty has not yet arrived.

MISS FITT. Not an accident, I trust! [*Pause.*] Do not tell me she has left the track! [*Pause.*] Oh darling mother! With the fresh sole for lunch!

[*Loud titter from* TOMMY, *checked as before by* MR. BARRELL.]

MR. BARRELL. That's enough old guff out of you. Nip up to the box now and see has Mr. Case anything for me.

[TOMMY *goes.*]

MRS. ROONEY. Poor Dan!

MISS FITT [*in anguish*]. What terrible thing has happened?

MR. TYLER. Now now, Miss Fitt, do not—

MRS. ROONEY [*with vehement sadness*]. Poor Dan!

MR. TYLER. Now now, Miss Fitt, do not give way . . . to despair, all will come right . . . in the end. [*Aside to* MR. BARRELL.] What *is* the situation, Mr. Barrell? Not a collision surely?

MRS. ROONEY [*enthusiastically*]. A collision! Oh that would be wonderful!

MISS FITT [*horrified*]. A collision! I knew it!

MR. TYLER. Come, Miss Fitt, let us move a little up the platform.

MRS. ROONEY. Yes, let us all do that. [*Pause.*] No? [*Pause.*] You have changed your mind? [*Pause.*] I quite agree, we are better here, in the shadow of the waiting-room.

MR. BARRELL. Excuse me a moment.

MRS. ROONEY. Before you slink away, Mr. Barrell, please, a statement of some kind, I insist. Even the slowest train on this brief line is not ten minutes and more behind its scheduled time without good cause, one imagines. [*Pause.*] We all know your station is the best kept of the entire network, but there are times when that is not enough, just not enough. [*Pause.*] Now, Mr. Barrell, leave off chewing your whiskers, we are waiting to hear from you—we the unfortunate ticket-holders' nearest if not dearest.

[*Pause.*]

MR. TYLER [*reasonably*]. I do think we are owed some kind of explanation, Mr. Barrell, if only to set our minds at rest.

MR. BARRELL. I know nothing. All I know is there has been a hitch. All traffic is retarded.

MRS. ROONEY [*derisively*]. Retarded! A hitch! Ah these celibates! Here we are eating our hearts out with anxiety for our loved ones and he calls that a hitch! Those of us like myself with heart and kidney trouble may collapse at any moment and he calls that a hitch! In our ovens the Saturday roast is burning to a shrivel and he calls that—

MR. TYLER. Here comes Tommy, running! I am glad I have been spared to see this.

TOMMY [*excitedly, in the distance*]. She's coming. [*Pause. Nearer.*] She's at the level-crossing!

[*Immediately exaggerated station sounds. Falling signals. Bells. Whistles. Crescendo of train whistle approaching. Sound of train rushing through station.*]

MRS. ROONEY [*above rush of train*]. The up mail! The up mail! [*The up mail recedes, the down train approaches, enters the station, pulls up with great hissing of steam and clashing of couplings. Noise of passengers descending, doors banging,* MR. BARRELL *shouting "Boghill! Boghill!", etc. Piercingly.*] Dan! . . . Are you all right? . . . Where is he? . . . Dan! . . . Did you see my husband? . . . Dan! . . . [*Noise of station emptying. Guard's whistle. Train departing, receding. Silence.*] He isn't on it! The misery I have endured, to get here, and he isn't on it! . . . Mr. Barrell! . . . Was he not on it? [*Pause.*] Is anything the matter, you look as if you had seen a ghost. [*Pause.*] Tommy! . . . Did you see the master?

TOMMY. He'll be along, Ma'am, Jerry is minding him.

[MR. ROONEY *suddenly appears on platform, advancing on small boy* JERRY's *arm. He is blind, thumps the ground with his stick and pants incessantly.*]

MRS. ROONEY. Oh, Dan! There you are! [*Her dragging feet as she hastens towards him. She reaches him. They halt.*] Where in the world were you?

MR. ROONEY [*coolly*]. Maddy.

MRS. ROONEY. Where were you all this time?

MR. ROONEY. In the men's.

MRS. ROONEY. Kiss me!

MR. ROONEY. Kiss you? In public? On the platform? Before the boy? Have you taken leave of your senses?

MRS. ROONEY. Jerry wouldn't mind. Would you, Jerry?

JERRY. No, Ma'am.

MRS. ROONEY. How is your poor father?

JERRY. They took him away, Ma'am.

MRS. ROONEY. Then you are all alone?

JERRY. Yes, Ma'am.

MR. ROONEY. Why are you here? You did not notify me.

MRS. ROONEY. I wanted to give you a surprise. For your birthday.

MR. ROONEY. My birthday?

MRS. ROONEY. Don't you remember? I wished you your happy returns in the bathroom.

MR. ROONEY. I did not hear you.

MRS. ROONEY. But I gave you a tie! You have it on!

[*Pause.*]

MR. ROONEY. How old am I now?

MRS. ROONEY. Now never mind about that. Come.

MR. ROONEY. Why did you not cancel the boy? Now we shall have to give him a penny.

MRS. ROONEY [*miserably*]. I forgot! I had such a time getting here! Such horrid nasty people! [*Pause. Pleading.*] Be nice to me, Dan, be nice to me today!

MR. ROONEY. Give the boy a penny.

MRS. ROONEY. Here are two halfpennies, Jerry. Run along now and buy yourself a nice gobstopper.

JERRY. Yes, Ma'am.

MR. ROONEY. Come for me on Monday, if I am still alive.

JERRY. Yessir.

[*He runs off.*]

MR. ROONEY. We could have saved sixpence. We have saved fivepence. [*Pause.*] But at what cost?

[*They move off along platform arm in arm. Dragging feet, panting, thudding stick.*]

MRS. ROONEY. Are you not well?

[*They halt, on* MR. ROONEY's *initiative.*]

MR. ROONEY. Once and for all, do not ask me to speak and move at the same time. I shall not say this in this life again.

[*They move off. Dragging feet, etc. They halt at top of steps.*]

MRS. ROONEY. Are you not—

MR. ROONEY. Let us get this precipice over.

MRS. ROONEY. Put your arm around me.

MR. ROONEY. Have you been drinking again? [*Pause.*] You are quivering like a blanc-mange. [*Pause.*] Are you in a condition to lead me? [*Pause.*] We shall fall into the ditch.

MRS. ROONEY. Oh, Dan! It will be like old times!

MR. ROONEY. Pull yourself together or I shall send Tommy for the cab. Then instead of having saved sixpence, no, fivepence, we shall have lost . . . [*calculating mumble*] . . . two and three less six one and no plus one one and no plus three one and nine and one ten and three two and one . . . [*normal voice*] two and one, we shall be the poorer to the tune of two and one. [*Pause.*] Curse that sun, it has gone in. What is the day doing?

[*Wind.*]

MRS. ROONEY. Shrouding, shrouding, the best of it is past. [*Pause.*] Soon the first great drops will fall splashing in the dust.

MR. ROONEY. And yet the glass was firm. [*Pause.*] Let us hasten home and sit before the fire. We shall draw the blinds. You will read to me. I think Effie is going to commit adultery with the Major. [*Brief drag of feet.*] Wait! [*Feet cease. Stick tapping at steps.*] I have been up and down these steps five thousand times and still I do not know how many there are. When I think there are six there are four or five or seven or eight and when I remember there are five there are three or four or six or seven and when finally I realize there are seven there are five or six or eight or nine. Sometimes I wonder if they do not change them in the night. [*Pause. Irritably.*] Well? How many do you make them today?

MRS. ROONEY. Do not ask me to count, Dan, not now.

MR. ROONEY. Not count! One of the few satisfactions in life!

MRS. ROONEY. Not steps, Dan, please, I always get them wrong. Then you might fall on your wound and I would have that on my manure-heap on top of everything else. No, just cling to me and all will be well.

5 [*Confused noise of their descent. Panting, stumbling, ejaculations, curses. Silence.*]

Mr. Rooney. Well! That is what you call well!

Mrs. Rooney. We are down. And little the 10 worse. [*Silence. A donkey brays. Silence.*] That was a true donkey. Its father and mother were donkeys.

[*Silence.*]

Mr. Rooney. Do you know what it is, I 15 think I shall retire.

Mrs. Rooney [*appalled*]. Retire! And live at home? On your grant!

Mr. Rooney. Never tread these cursed steps again. Trudge this hellish road for the last 20 time. Sit at home on the remnants of my bottom counting the hours—till the next meal. [*Pause.*] The very thought puts life in me! Forward, before it dies!

[*They move on. Dragging feet, panting, thud-* 25 *ding stick.*]

Mrs. Rooney. Now mind, here is the path ... Up! ... Well done! Now we are in safety and a straight run home.

Mr. Rooney [*without halting, between* 30 *gasps*]. A straight ... run! ... She calls that ... a straight ... run! ...

Mrs. Rooney. Hush! Do not speak as you go along, you know it is not good for your coronary. [*Dragging steps, etc.*] Just concen-35 trate on putting one foot before the next or whatever the expression is. [*Dragging feet, etc.*] That is the way, now we are doing nicely. [*Dragging feet, etc. They suddenly halt, on* Mrs. Rooney's *initiative.*] Heavens! I knew 40 there was something! With all the excitement! I forgot!

Mr. Rooney [*quietly*]. Good God.

Mrs. Rooney. But you must know, Dan, of course, you were on it. Whatever happened? 45 Tell me!

Mr. Rooney. I have never known anything to happen.

Mrs. Rooney. But you must—

Mr. Rooney [*violently*]. All this stopping and starting again is devilish, devilish! I get 50 a little way on me and begin to be carried along when suddenly you stop dead! Two hundred pounds of unhealthy fat! What possessed you to come out at all? Let go of me!

Mrs. Rooney [*in great agitation*]. No, I 55 must know, we won't stir from here till you tell me. Fifteen minutes late! On a thirty-minute run! It's unheard of!

Mr. Rooney. I know nothing. Let go of me before I shake you off. 60

Mrs. Rooney. But you must know! You were on it! Was it at the terminus? Did you leave on time? Or was it on the line? [*Pause.*] Did something happen on the line? [*Pause.*] Dan! [*Brokenly.*] Why won't you tell me! 65

[*Silence. They move off. Dragging feet, etc. They halt. Pause.*]

Mr. Rooney. Poor Maddy! [*Pause. Children's cries.*] What was that?

[*Pause for* Mrs. Rooney *to ascertain.*] 70

Mrs. Rooney. The Lynch twins jeering at us. [*Cries.*]

Mr. Rooney. Will they pelt us with mud today, do you suppose?

[*Cries.*] 75

Mrs. Rooney. Let us turn and face them. [*Cries. They turn. Silence.*] Threaten them with your stick. [*Silence.*] They have run away.

[*Pause.*] 80

Mr. Rooney. Did you ever wish to kill a child? [*Pause.*] Nip some young doom in the bud. [*Pause.*] Many a time at night, in winter, on the black road home, I nearly attacked the boy. [*Pause.*] Poor Jerry! [*Pause.*] What res- 85 trained me then? [*Pause.*] Not fear of man. [*Pause.*] Shall we go on backwards now a little?

Mrs. Rooney. Backwards?

Mr. Rooney. Yes. Or you forwards and I 90 backwards. The perfect pair. Like Dante's damned, with their faces arsy-versy. Our tears will water our bottoms.

Mrs. Rooney. What is the matter, Dan? Are you not well? 95

Mr. Rooney. Well! Did you ever know me

to be well? The day you met me I should have been in bed. The day you proposed to me the doctors gave me up. You knew that, did you not? The night you married me they came for me with an ambulance. You have not forgotten that, I suppose? [*Pause.*] No, I cannot be said to be well. But I am no worse. Indeed I am better than I was. The loss of my sight was a great fillip. If I could go deaf and dumb I think I might pant on to be a hundred. Or have I done so? [*Pause.*] Was I a hundred today? [*Pause.*] Am I a hundred, Maddy?

[*Silence.*]

Mrs. Rooney. All is still. No living soul in sight. There is no one to ask. The world is feeding. The wind—[*brief wind*]—scarcely stirs the leaves and the birds—[*brief chirp*]—are tired singing. The cows—[*brief moo*]—and sheep—[*brief baa*]—ruminate in silence. The dogs—[*brief bark*]—are hushed and the hens —[*brief cackle*]—sprawl torpid in the dust. We are alone. There is no one to ask.

[*Silence.*]

Mr. Rooney [*clearing his throat, narrative tone*]. We drew out on the tick of time, I can vouch for that. I was—

Mrs. Rooney. How can you vouch for it?

Mr. Rooney [*normal tone, angrily*]. I can vouch for it, I tell you! Do you want my relation or don't you? [*Pause. Narrative tone.*] On the tick of time. I had the compartment to myself, as usual. At least I hope so, for I made no attempt to restrain myself. My mind— [*Normal tone.*] But why do we not sit down somewhere? Are we afraid we should never rise again?

Mrs. Rooney. Sit down on what?

Mr. Rooney. On a bench, for example.

Mrs. Rooney. There is no bench.

Mr. Rooney. Then on a bank, let us sink down upon a bank.

Mrs. Rooney. There is no bank.

Mr. Rooney. Then we cannot. [*Pause.*] I dream of other roads, in other lands. Of another home, another—[*he hesitates*]—another home. [*Pause.*] What was I trying to say?

Mrs. Rooney. Something about your mind.

Mr. Rooney [*startled*]. My mind? Are you

sure? [*Pause. Incredulous.*] My mind? . . . [*Pause.*] Ah yes. [*Narrative tone.*] Alone in the compartment my mind began to work, as so often after office hours, on the way home, in the train, to the lilt of the bogeys. Your season-ticket, I said, costs you twelve pounds a year and you earn, on an average, seven and six a day, that is to say barely enough to keep you alive and twitching with the help of food, drink, tobacco and periodicals until you finally reach home and fall into bed. Add to this—or subtract from it—rent, stationery, various subscriptions, tramfares to and fro, light and heat, permits and licences, hairtrims and shaves, tips to escorts, upkeep of premises and appearances, and a thousand unspecifiable sundries, and it is clear that by lying at home in bed, day and night, winter and summer, with a change of pyjamas once a fortnight, you would add very considerably to your income. Business, I said— [*A cry. Pause. Again. Normal tone.*] Did I hear a cry?

Mrs. Rooney. Mrs. Tully I fancy. Her poor husband is in constant pain and beats her unmercifully.

[*Silence.*]

Mr. Rooney. That was a short knock. [*Pause.*] What was I trying to get at?

Mrs. Rooney. Business.

Mr. Rooney. Ah yes, business. [*Narrative tone.*] Business, old man, I said, retire from business, it has retired from you. [*Normal tone.*] One has these moments of lucidity.

Mrs. Rooney. I feel very cold and weak.

Mr. Rooney [*narrative tone*]. On the other hand, I said, there are the horrors of home life, the dusting, sweeping, airing, scrubbing, waxing, waning, washing, mangling, drying, mowing, clipping, raking, rolling, scuffling, shovelling, grinding, tearing, pounding, banging and slamming. And the brats, the happy little healthy little howling neighbour's brats. Of all this and much more the week-end, the Saturday intermission and then the day of rest, have given you some idea. But what must it be like on a working-day? A Wednesday? A Friday! What must it be like on a Friday! And I fell to thinking of my silent, backstreet,

basement office, with its obliterated plate, rest-couch and velvet hangings, and what it means to be buried there alive, if only from ten to five, with convenient to the one hand a bottle
5 of light pale ale and to the other a long ice-cold fillet of hake. Nothing, I said, not even fully certified death, can ever take the place of that. It was then I noticed we were at a standstill. [*Pause. Normal tone. Irritably.*] Why are you
10 hanging out of me like that? Have you swooned away?

MRS. ROONEY. I feel very cold and faint. The wind—[*whistling wind*]—is whistling through my summer frock as if I had nothing on
15 over my bloomers. I have had no solid food since my elevenses.°

MR. ROONEY. You have ceased to care. I speak—and you listen to the wind.

MRS. ROONEY. No no, I am agog, tell me all,
20 we shall press on and never pause, never pause, till we come safe to haven.

[*Pause.*]

MR. ROONEY. Never pause . . . safe to haven. . . . Do you know, Maddy, sometimes one
25 would think you were struggling with a dead language.

MRS. ROONEY. Yes indeed, Dan, I know full well what you mean, I often have that feeling, it is unspeakably excruciating.

30 MR. ROONEY. I confess I have it sometimes myself, when I happen to overhear what I am saying.

MRS. ROONEY. Well, you know, it will be dead in time, just like our own poor dear
35 Gaelic, there is that to be said.

[*Urgent baa.*]

MR. ROONEY [*startled*]. Good God!

MRS. ROONEY. Oh the pretty little woolly lamb, crying to suck its mother! Theirs has
40 not changed, since Arcady.

[*Pause.*]

MR. ROONEY. Where was I in my composition?

MRS. ROONEY. At a standstill.

45 MR. ROONEY. Ah yes. [*Clears his throat. Narrative tone.*] I concluded naturally that we

elevenses a light midmorning meal

had entered a station and would soon be on our way again, and I sat on, without misgiving. Not a sound. Things are very dull to-
50 day, I said, nobody getting down, nobody getting on. Then as time flew by and nothing happened I realized my error. We had not entered a station.

MRS. ROONEY. Did you not spring up and
55 poke your head out of the window?

MR. ROONEY. What good would that have done me?

MRS. ROONEY. Why to call out to be told what was amiss.

60 MR. ROONEY. I did not care what was amiss. No, I just sat on, saying, If this train were never to move again I should not greatly mind. Then gradually a—how shall I say—a growing desire to—er—you know—welled up within
65 me. Nervous probably. In fact now I am sure. You know, the feeling of being confined.

MRS. ROONEY. Yes yes, I have been through that.

MR. ROONEY. If we sit here much longer, I
70 said, I really do not know what I shall do. I got up and paced to and fro between the seats, like a caged beast.

MRS. ROONEY. That is a help sometimes.

MR. ROONEY. After what seemed an eternity
75 we simply moved off. And the next thing was Barrell bawling the abhorred name. I got down and Jerry led me to the men's, or Fir as they call it now, from Vir Viris I suppose, the V becoming F, in accordance with Grimm's Law.
80 [*Pause.*] The rest you know. [*Pause.*] You say nothing? [*Pause.*] Say something, Maddy. Say you believe me.

MRS. ROONEY. I remember once attending a lecture by one of these new mind doctors, I
85 forget what you call them. He spoke—

MR. ROONEY. A lunatic specialist?

MRS. ROONEY. No no, just the troubled mind. I was hoping he might shed a little light on my lifelong preoccupation with horses' but-
90 tocks.

MR. ROONEY. A neurologist.

MRS. ROONEY. No no, just mental distress, the name will come back to me in the night. I remember his telling us the story of a little girl, very strange and unhappy in her ways, and how he treated her unsuccessfully over a period of years and was finally obliged to give up the case. He could find nothing wrong with her, he said. The only thing wrong with her as far as he could see was that she was dying. And she did in fact die, shortly after he washed his hands of her.

MR. ROONEY. Well? What is there so wonderful about that?

MRS. ROONEY. No, it was just something he said, and the way he said it, that have haunted me ever since.

MR. ROONEY. You lie awake at night, tossing to and fro and brooding on it.

MRS. ROONEY. On it and other . . . wretchedness. [*Pause.*] When he had done with the little girl he stood there motionless for some time, quite two minutes I should say, looking down at his table. Then he suddenly raised his head and exclaimed, as if he had had a revelation, The trouble with her was she had never been really born! [*Pause.*] He spoke throughout without notes. [*Pause.*] I left before the end.

MR. ROONEY. Nothing about your buttocks? [MRS. ROONEY *weeps. In affectionate remonstrance.*] Maddy!

MRS. ROONEY. There is nothing to be done for those people!

MR. ROONEY. For which is there? [*Pause.*] That does not sound right somehow. [*Pause.*] What way am I facing?

MRS. ROONEY. What?

MR. ROONEY. I have forgotten what way I am facing.

MRS. ROONEY. You have turned aside and are bowed down over the ditch.

MR. ROONEY. There is a dead dog down there.

MRS. ROONEY. No no, just the rotting leaves.

MR. ROONEY. In June? Rotting leaves in June?

MRS. ROONEY. Yes, dear, from last year, and from the year before last, and from the year before that again. [*Silence. Rainy wind. They move on. Dragging steps, etc.*] There is that lovely laburnum again. Poor thing, it is losing all its tassels. [*Dragging steps, etc.*] There are the first drops. [*Rain. Dragging feet, etc.*] Golden drizzle. [*Dragging steps, etc.*] Do not mind me, dear, I am just talking to myself. [*Rain heavier. Dragging steps, etc.*] Can hinnies procreate, I wonder?

[*They halt.*]

MR. ROONEY. Say that again.

MRS. ROONEY. Come on, dear, don't mind me, we are getting drenched.

MR. ROONEY [*forcibly*]. Can what what?

MRS. ROONEY. Hinnies procreate. [*Silence.*] You know, hinnies, or jinnies, aren't they barren, or sterile, or whatever it is? [*Pause.*] It wasn't an ass's colt° at all, you know, I asked the Regius Professor.

[*Pause.*]

MR. ROONEY. He should know.

MRS. ROONEY. Yes, it was a hinny, he rode into Jerusalem or wherever it was on a hinny. [*Pause.*] That must mean something. [*Pause.*] It's like the sparrows, than many of which we are of more value, they weren't sparrows at all.

MR. ROONEY. Than many of which! . . . You exaggerate, Maddy.

MRS. ROONEY [*with emotion*]. They weren't sparrows at all!

MR. ROONEY. Does that put our price up?

[*Silence. They move on. Wind and rain. Dragging feet, etc. They halt.*]

MRS. ROONEY. Do you want some dung? [*Silence. They move on. Wind and rain, etc. They halt.*] Why do you stop? Do you want to say something?

MR. ROONEY. No.

MRS. ROONEY. Then why do you stop?

MR. ROONEY. It is easier.

MRS. ROONEY. Are you very wet?

MR. ROONEY. To the buff.

MRS. ROONEY. The buff?

MR. ROONEY. The buff. From buffalo.

MRS. ROONEY. We shall hang up all our things in the hot-cupboard and get into our dressing-gowns. [*Pause.*] Put your arm round me. [*Pause.*] Be nice to me! [*Pause. Gratefully.*] Ah, Dan! [*They move on. Wind and*

---

an ass's colt on which Jesus rode into Jerusalem on Palm Sunday; see Matthew 21:2–8.

SAMUEL BECKETT

rain. *Dragging feet, etc. Faintly same music as before. They halt. Music clearer. Silence but for music playing. Music dies.*] All day the same old record. All alone in that great empty
5 house. She must be a very old woman now.

MR. ROONEY [*indistinctly*]. Death and the Maiden.

[*Silence.*]

MRS. ROONEY. You are crying. [*Pause.*] Are
10 you crying?

MR. ROONEY [*violently*]. Yes! [*They move on. Wind and rain. Dragging feet, etc. They halt. They move on. Wind and rain. Dragging feet, etc. They halt.*] Who is the preacher to-
15 morrow? The incumbent?

MRS. ROONEY. No.

MR. ROONEY. Thank God for that. Who?

MRS. ROONEY. Hardy.

MR. ROONEY. "How to be Happy though
20 Married"?

MRS. ROONEY. No no, he died, you remember. No connexion.

MR. ROONEY. Has he announced his text?

MRS. ROONEY. "The Lord upholdeth all that
25 fall and raiseth up all those that be bowed down." [*Silence. They join in wild laughter. They move on. Wind and rain. Dragging feet, etc.*] Hold me tighter, Dan! [*Pause.*] Oh yes!

[*They halt.*]
30 MR. ROONEY. I hear something behind us.

[*Pause.*]

MRS. ROONEY. It looks like Jerry. [*Pause.*] It is Jerry.

[*Sound of* JERRY'S *running steps approach-*
35 *ing. He halts beside them, panting.*]

JERRY [*panting*]. You dropped—

MRS. ROONEY. Take your time, my little man, you will burst a blood-vessel.

JERRY [*panting*]. You dropped something,
40 sir. Mr. Barrell told me to run after you.

MRS. ROONEY. Show. [*She takes the object.*] What is it? [*She examines it.*] What is this thing, Dan?

MR. ROONEY. Perhaps it is not mine at all.
45 JERRY. Mr. Barrell said it was, sir.

MRS. ROONEY. It looks like a kind of ball. And yet it is not a ball.

MR. ROONEY. Give it to me.

MRS. ROONEY [*giving it*]. What *is* it, Dan?

MR. ROONEY. It is a thing I carry about with 50 me.

MRS. ROONEY. Yes, but what—

MR. ROONEY [*violently*]. It is a thing I carry about with me!

[*Silence.* MRS. ROONEY *looks for a penny.*] 55

MRS. ROONEY. I have no small money. Have you?

MR. ROONEY. I have none of any kind.

MRS. ROONEY. We are out of change, Jerry. Remind Mr. Rooney on Monday and he will 60 give you a penny for your pains.

JERRY. Yes, Ma'am.

MR. ROONEY. If I am alive.

JERRY. Yessir.

[JERRY *starts running back towards the* 65 *station.*]

MRS. ROONEY. Jerry! [JERRY *halts.*] Did you hear what the hitch was? [*Pause.*] Did you hear what kept the train so late?

MR. ROONEY. How would he have heard? 70 Come on.

MRS. ROONEY. What was it, Jerry?

JERRY. It was a—

MR. ROONEY. Leave the boy alone, he knows nothing! Come on! 75

MRS. ROONEY. What was it, Jerry?

JERRY. It was a little child, Ma'am.

[MR. ROONEY *groans.*]

MRS. ROONEY. What do you mean, it was a little child? 80

JERRY. It was a little child fell out of the carriage, Ma'am. [*Pause.*] On to the line, Ma'am. [*Pause.*] Under the wheels, Ma'am.

[*Silence.* JERRY *runs off. His steps die away. Tempest of wind and rain. It abates. They* 85 *move on. Dragging steps, etc. They halt. Tempest of wind and rain.*]

End

Act Without Words I

A Mime for One Player

BECKETT

Translated from the French by the Author

Desert. Dazzling light.

The man is flung backwards on stage from right wing. He falls, gets up immediately, dusts himself, turns aside, reflects.

5   Whistle from right wing.

He reflects, goes out right.

Immediately flung back on stage he falls, gets up immediately, dusts himself, turns aside, reflects.

10 Whistle from left wing.

He reflects, goes out left.

Immediately flung back on stage he falls, gets up immediately dusts himself, turns aside, reflects.

15 Whistle from left wing.

He reflects, goes towards left wing, hesitates, thinks better of it, halts, turns aside, reflects.

A little tree descends from flies, lands. It
20 has a single bough some three yards from ground and at its summit a meager tuft of palms casting at its foot a circle of shadow.

He continues to reflect.

Whistle from above.

25 He turns, sees tree, reflects, goes to it, sits down in its shadow, looks at his hands.

A pair of tailor's scissors descends from flies,

comes to rest before tree, a yard from ground.

He continues to look at his hands.

Whistle from above.   30

He looks up, sees scissors, takes them and starts to trim his nails.

The palms close like a parasol, the shadow disappears.

He drops scissors, reflects.   35

A tiny carafe, to which is attached a huge label inscribed WATER, descends from flies, comes to rest some three yards from ground.

He continues to reflect.

Whistle from above.   40

He looks up, sees carafe, reflects, gets up, goes and stands under it, tries in vain to reach it, renounces, turns aside, reflects.

A big cube descends from flies, lands.

He continues to reflect.   45

Whistle from above.

He turns, sees cube, looks at it, at carafe, reflects, goes to cube, takes it up, carries it over and sets it down under carafe, tests its stability, gets up on it, tries in vain to reach 50
carafe, renounces, gets down, carries cube back to its place, turns aside, reflects.

A second smaller cube descends from flies, lands.

He continues to reflect.   55

Whistle from above.

He turns, sees second cube, looks at it, at carafe, goes to second cube, takes it up, carries it over and sets it down under carafe, tests its stability, gets up on it, tries in vain to reach 60
carafe, renounces, gets down, takes up second cube to carry it back to its place, hesitates, thinks better of it, sets it down, goes to big cube, takes it up, carries it over and puts it on small one, tests their stability, gets up on them, 65
the cubes collapse, he falls, gets up immediately, brushes himself, reflects.

He takes up small cube, puts it on big one, tests their stability, gets up on them and is about to reach carafe when it is pulled up a   70
little way and comes to rest beyond his reach.

He gets down, reflects, carries cubes back to their place, one by one, turns aside, reflects.

A third still smaller cube descends from flies, lands.   75

SAMUEL BECKETT

He continues to reflect.

Whistle from above.

He turns, sees third cube, looks at it, reflects, turns aside, reflects.

5 The third cube is pulled up and disappears in flies.

Beside carafe a rope descends from flies, with knots to facilitate ascent.

He continues to reflect.

10 Whistle from above.

He turns, sees rope, reflects, goes to it, climbs up it and is about to reach carafe when rope is let out and deposits him back on ground.

15 He reflects, looks around for scissors, sees them, goes and picks them up, returns to rope and starts to cut it with scissors.

The rope is pulled up, lifts him off ground, he hangs on, succeeds in cutting rope, falls
20 back on ground, drops scissors, falls, gets up again immediately, brushes himself, reflects.

The rope is pulled up quickly and disappears in flies.

With length of rope in his possession he
25 makes a lasso with which he tries to lasso carafe.

The carafe is pulled up quickly and disappears in flies.

He turns aside, reflects.

30 He goes with lasso in his hand to tree, looks at bough, turns and looks at cubes, looks again at bough, drops lasso, goes to cubes, takes up small one, carries it over and sets it down under bough, goes back for big one,
35 takes it up and carries it over under bough, makes to put it on small one, hesitates, thinks better of it, sets it down, takes up small one and puts it on big one, tests their stability, turns aside and stoops to pick up lasso.

40 The bough folds down against trunk.

He straightens up with lasso in his hand, turns and sees what has happened.

He drops lasso, turns aside, reflects.

He carries back cubes to their place, one by
45 one, goes back for lasso, carries it over to cubes and lays it in a neat coil on small one.

He turns aside, reflects.

Whistle from right wing.

He reflects, goes out right.

Immediately flung back on stage he falls, 50
gets up immediately, brushes himself, turns aside, reflects.

Whistle from left wing.

He does not move.

He looks at his hands, looks around for 55
scissors, sees them, goes and picks them up, starts to trim his nails, stops, reflects, runs his finger along blade of scissors, goes and lays them on small cube, turns aside, opens his collar, frees his neck and fingers it. 60

The small cube is pulled up and disappears in flies, carrying away rope and scissors.

He turns to take scissors, sees what has happened.

He turns aside, reflects. 65

He goes and sits down on big cube.

The big cube is pulled from under him. He falls. The big cube is pulled up and disappears in flies.

He remains lying on his side, his face to- 70
wards auditorium, staring before him.

The carafe descends from flies and comes to rest a few feet from his body.

He does not move.

Whistle from above. 75

He does not move.

The carafe descends further, dangles and plays about his face.

He does not move.

The carafe is pulled up and disappears in 80
flies.

The bough returns to horizontal, the palms open, the shadow returns.

Whistle from above.

He does not move. 85

The tree is pulled up and disappears in flies.

He looks at his hands.

End

Ossie Davis

1917–

Purlie Victorious

1961

In his sunny and exuberant *Purlie Victorious*, the black playwright and actor Ossie Davis celebrates the demise of Southern white supremacy. This he lays to rest in the person of Stonewall Jackson Cotchipee, the "Ol' Cap'n," owner of a peon plantation in South Georgia. Outwitted by Purlie Judson and his followers, the Cap'n departs this life in an apoplectic rage and is turned into a piece of statuary before our eyes: "The first man I ever seen," says Purlie's brother Gitlow, "to drop dead standing up." His obsequies, which are respectably ceremonious although by no means sorrowful, are performed by the Reverend Purlie in Big Bethel Church— duly renamed the Church of the New Freedom. The note of exultation in the last scene is anticipated in the first act, where the Cap'n, melting at Gitlow's renditions of Stephen Foster, exclaims, "I live for the day you'll sing that thing over my grave." And Gitlow murmurs, "Me, too, Ol' Cap'n, me, too!"—his voice "rising to a slow, gentle, yet triumphant crescendo."

The thematic import of such scenes needs no explication, and obviously their mode is racy and uninhibited comedy laced with fantasy. The play as a whole is rarely as fantastic as this, but it is never very realistic. The characters, tending toward the stereotypical, have descriptive or suggestive names, as in the tradition of Jonsonian comedy. The name that the Reverend Purlie Victorious carries like a banner attests his aspirations toward the pearly gates of heaven and promises his ultimate success. The servile Gitlow, Purlie's foil, bears in his name the stigma of his self-abasement. The name of Charlie Cotchipee's nurse, Idella, suggests in anagram the ideal (of universal good will) that she has successfully cultivated in young Charlie. Charlie, of course, is black patois for the white man, as in James Baldwin's play *Blues for Mister Charlie*. And possibly (because *lutea* in Latin means "woman of golden hue" and the stem *lute* appears in English) the romantic heroine Lutiebelle has a name appropriate to her golden-brown beauty.

Inhabiting the mythical Cotchipee County, Georgia, these and the other persons of the drama speak in an idiom that is at once vivid and mannered—identifiably ethnic and regional, yet having the universal appeal of wit. For example, Aunt Missy, Purlie's gracious sister-in-law (who becomes a termagant only to perform deeds of necessity and mercy), doubts whether Lutiebelle can be passed off as the strikingly dissimilar Cousin Bee: Bee had been "lean, loose, and leggy," with eyes "sort of fickle to one another"; Lutiebelle's head, moreover, "ain't nearly as built like a rutabaga as Bee's own was." To which Purlie objects, "White folks can't tell one of us from another by the head!" Purlie himself, who is capable of biblical and Shakespearean eloquence, can devastate Gitlow with quick irony: "If slavery ever comes back I want to be your agent." Gitlow can defend himself as nimbly: "What's wrong with running? It emancipated more people than Abe Lincoln ever did."

This dialogue is as sparkling as any we can find in drawing-room comedy, and it often has a clear satiric point. But the satire is rarely malicious. Davis, when creating the role of Purlie on stage, said, "We've got to play these people with wit and especially with love." He has written that love into every character that is credibly lovable, and forebearance into the rest—imparting an irrepressible verve even to the groveling Gitlow and the wretched old bigot Cap'n Cotchipee. Davis claims, through Purlie, a "laughing kindness" as a part of his racial inheritance. When the bumbling but good-hearted Charlie Cotchipee, a model of unheroic courage, foils his father's designs on Big Bethel and is welcomed into the exultant brotherhood of that church, the laughing and the kindness become one.

Purlie Victorious

DAVIS

CHARACTERS

THE REVEREND PURLIE JUDSON   *Pastor of Big Bethel Church*
LUTIEBELLE JENKINS   *a girl from Alabama*
MISSY JUDSON   *Gitlow's wife*
GITLOW JUDSON   *Purlie's brother; tenant on the Cotchipee farm*
CHARLIE COTCHIPEE   *son of Cap'n Cotchipee*
IDELLA LANDY   *Charlie's childhood nurse*
(OL' CAP'N) STONEWALL JACKSON COTCHIPEE   *owner of a Georgia peon farm*
SHERIFF OF COTCHIPEE COUNTY
DEPUTY
PALLBEARERS FOR CAP'N COTCHIPEE

SCENE. *Cotchipee County, Georgia.*

ACT I

Scene i

[SCENE. *The setting is the plain and simple interior of an antiquated, run-down farmhouse such as Negro sharecroppers still live in, in South Georgia. Threadbare but warm-hearted,* 5 *shabby but clean. In the Center is a large, rough-hewn table with three homemade chairs and a small bench. This table is the center of all family activities. The main entrance is a door in the Upstage Right corner, which leads* 10 *in from a rickety porch which we cannot see. There is a small archway in the opposite corner, with some long strips of gunny-sacking hanging down to serve as a door, which leads off to the kitchen. In the center of the Right wall is a window that is wooden, which opens outward* 15

Reprinted by permission of Ossie Davis.

*on hinges. Downstage Right is a small door
leading off to a bedroom, and opposite, Downstage Left, another door leads out into the backyard, and on into the cotton fields beyond.*
5 *There is also a smaller table and a cupboard
against the wall. An old dresser stands against
the Right wall, between the window and the
Downstage door. There is a shelf on the Left
wall with a pail of drinking water, and a large
10 tin dipper. Various cooking utensils, and items
like salt and pepper are scattered about in
appropriate places.*]

[AT RISE. *The curtain rises on a stage in
semi-darkness. After a moment, when the*
15 *lights have come up, the door in the Up Right
corner bursts open:* Enter PURLIE JUDSON.
PURLIE JUDSON *is tall, restless, and commanding.
In his middle or late thirties, he wears a wide-
brim, ministerial black hat, a string tie, and a*
20 *claw-hammer coat,° which, though far from
new, does not fit him too badly. His arms are
loaded with large boxes and parcels, which
must have come fresh from a department store.*
PURLIE *is a man consumed with that divine*
25 *impatience, without which nothing truly good,
or truly bad, or even truly ridiculous, is ever
accomplished in this world—with rhetoric and
flourish to match.*]

PURLIE [*calling out loudly*]. Missy! [*No*
30 *answer.*] Gitlow!—It's me—Purlie Victorious!
[*Still no answer.* PURLIE *empties his overloaded
arms, with obvious relief, on top of the big
Center table. He stands, mops his brow, and
blows.*] Nobody home it seems. [*This last he*
35 *says to someone he assumes has come in with
him. When there is no answer he hurries to the
door through which he entered.*] Come on—
come on in!

[*Enter* LUTIEBELLE JENKINS, *slowly, as if be-*
40 *mused. Young, eager, well-built: though we
cannot tell it at the moment. Clearly a girl from
the backwoods, she carries a suitcase tied up
with a rope in one hand, and a greasy shoebox
with what's left of her lunch, together with an*
45 *out-moded, out-sized handbag, in the other.
Obviously she has traveled a great distance,*

*but she still manages to look fresh and healthy.
Her hat is a horror with feathers, but she wears
it like a banner. Her shoes are flat-heeled and
plain white, such as a good servant girl in the* 50
*white folks' kitchen who knows her place is
absolutely bound to wear. Her fall coat is
dowdy, but well-intentioned with a stingy strip
of rabbit fur around the neck.* LUTIEBELLE *is like
thousands of Negro girls you might know.* 55
*Eager, desirous—even anxious, keenly in search
for life and for love, trembling on the brink of
self-confident and vigorous young womanhood
—but afraid to take the final leap: because no
one has ever told her it is no longer necessary* 60
*to be white in order to be virtuous, charming,
or beautiful.*]

LUTIEBELLE [*looking around as if at a museum
of great importance*]. Nobody home it seems.

PURLIE [*annoyed to find himself so exactly* 65
*echoed, looks at her sharply. He takes his watch
from his vest pocket, where he wears it on a
chain*]. Cotton-picking time in Georgia it's
against the law to be home. Come in—unload
yourself. [*Crosses and looks out into the* 70
kitchen. LUTIEBELLE *is so enthralled, she still
stands with all her bags and parcels in her
arm.*] Set your suitcase down.

LUTIEBELLE. What?

PURLIE. It's making you lopsided. 75

LUTIEBELLE [*snapping out of it*]. It is? I didn't
even notice. [*Sets suitcase, lunch box, and
parcels down.*]

PURLIE [*studies her for a moment; goes and
gently takes off her hat*]. Tired? 80

LUTIEBELLE. Not stepping high as I am!

PURLIE [*takes the rest of her things and sets
them on the table*]. Hungry?

LUTIEBELLE. No, sir. But there's still some of
my lunch left if you— 85

PURLIE [*quickly*]. No, thank you. Two ham-
hock sandwiches in one day is my limit. [*Sits
down and fans himself with his hat.*] Sorry I
had to walk you so far so fast.

LUTIEBELLE [*dreamily*]. Oh, I didn't mind, sir. 90
Walking's good for you, Miz Emmylou sez—

PURLIE. Miz Emmylou can afford to say that:
Miz Emmylou got a car. While all the transportation we got in the world is tied up in

---

claw-hammer coat dress coat

second-hand shoe leather. But never mind, my
sister, never-you-mind! [*Rises, almost as if to
dance, exaltation glowing in his eyes.*] And
toll the bell, Big Bethel—toll that big, black,
5 fat and sassy liberty bell! Tell Freedom the
bridegroom cometh; the day of her deliverance
is now at hand! [PURLIE *catches sight of* MISSY
through door Down Left.] Oh, there she is.
[*Crosses to door and calls out.*] Missy!—Oh,
10 Missy!

MISSY [*from a distance*]. Yes-s-s-s!
PURLIE. It's me!—Purlie!
MISSY. Purlie Victorious?
PURLIE. Yes. Put that battling stick° down
15 and come on in here!
MISSY. All right!
PURLIE [*crosses hurriedly back to above table
at Center*]. That's Missy, my sister-in-law I
was telling you about. [*Clears the table of
20 everything but one of the large cartons, which
he proceeds to open.*]
LUTIEBELLE [*not hearing him. Still awe-struck
to be in the very house, in perhaps the very
same room that* PURLIE *might have been born
25 in*]. So this is the house where you was born
and bred at.
PURLIE. Yep! Better'n being born outdoors.
LUTIEBELLE. What a lovely background for
your homelife.
30 PURLIE. I wouldn't give it to my dog to raise
fleas in!
LUTIEBELLE. So clean—and nice—and warm-
hearted!
PURLIE. The first chance I get I'ma burn the
35 damn thing down!
LUTIEBELLE. But—Reb'n° Purlie!—It's yours,
and that's what counts. Like Miz Emmylou
sez—
PURLIE. Come here! [*Pulls her across to the
40 window, flings it open.*] You see that big white
house, perched on top of that hill with them
two windows looking right down at us like two
eyeballs: that's where Ol' Cap'n lives.

battling stick paddle for beating clothes during washing
Reb'n Reverend

LUTIEBELLE. Ol' Cap'n?
PURLIE. Stonewall Jackson Cotchipee. He 45
owns this dump, not me.
LUTIEBELLE. Oh—
PURLIE. And that ain't all: hill and dale, field
and farm, truck and tractor, horse and mule,
bird and bee and bush and tree—and cotton!— 50
cotton by boll and by bale—every bit o' cotton
you see in this country!—Everything and
everybody he owns!
LUTIEBELLE. Everybody? You mean he owns
people? 55
PURLIE [*bridling his impatience*]. Well—
look!—ain't a man, woman or child working
in this valley that ain't in debt to that ol'
bastard!—[*catches himself*] bustard!—[*this
still won't do*] buzzard!—And that includes 60
Gitlow and Missy—everybody—except me.—
LUTIEBELLE. But folks can't own people no
more, Reb'n Purlie. Miz Emmylou sez that—
PURLIE [*verging on explosion*]. You ain't
working for Miz Emmylou no more, you're 65
working for me—Purlie Victorious. Freedom
is my business, and I say that ol' man runs this
plantation on debt: the longer you work for
Ol' Cap'n Cotchipee, the more you owe at the
commissary; and if you don't pay up, you can't 70
leave. And I don't give a damn what Miz
Emmylou nor nobody else sez—that's slavery!
LUTIEBELLE. I'm sorry, Reb'n Purlie—
PURLIE. Don't apologize, wait!—Just wait!—
'til I get my church;—wait 'till I buy Big Bethel 75
back— [*Crosses to window and looks out.*]
Wait 'till I stand once again in the pulpit of
Grandpaw Kinkaid, and call upon my people—
and talk to my people— About Ol' Cap'n, that
miserable son-of-a— 80
LUTIEBELLE [*just in time to save him*]. Wait—!
PURLIE. Wait, I say! And we'll see who's
gonna dominize this valley!—him or me!
[*Turns and sees* MISSY *through door Down
Left.*] Missy—! 85
[*Enter* MISSY, *ageless, benign, and smiling.
She wears a ragged old straw hat, a big house
apron over her faded gingham, and low-cut,
dragged-out tennis shoes on her feet. She is
strong and of good cheer—of a certain shrewd- 90

ness, yet full of the desire to believe. Her eyes light on LUTIEBELLE, *and her arms go up and outward automatically.*]

MISSY. Purlie!

5 PURLIE [*thinks she is reaching for him*]. Missy!

MISSY [*ignoring him, clutching* LUTIEBELLE, *laughing and crying*]. Well—well—well!

PURLIE [*breaking the stranglehold*]. For 10 God's sake, Missy, don't choke her to death!

MISSY. All my life—all my life I been praying for me a daughter just like you. My prayers is been answered at last. Welcome to our home, whoever you is!

15 LUTIEBELLE [*deeply moved*]. Thank you, ma'am.°

MISSY. "M'am—m'am." Listen to the child, Purlie. Everybody down here calls me Aunt Missy, and I'd be much obliged if you would, 20 too.

LUTIEBELLE. It would make me very glad to do so—Aunt Missy.

MISSY. Uhmmmmmm! Pretty as a pan of buttermilk biscuits. Where on earth did you 25 find her, Purlie? [PURLIE *starts to answer.*] Let me take your things—now, you just make yourself at home— Are you hungry?

LUTIEBELLE. No, ma'am, but cheap as water is, I sure ain't got no business being this 30 thirsty!

MISSY [*starts forward*]. I'll get some for you—

PURLIE [*intercepts her; directs* LUTIEBELLE]. There's the dipper. And right out yonder by 35 the fence just this side of that great big live oak tree you'll find the well—sweetest water in Cotchipee county.

LUTIEBELLE. Thank you, Reb'n Purlie. I'm very much obliged. [*Takes dipper from water 40 pail and exits Down Left.*]

MISSY. Reb'n who?

PURLIE [*looking off after* LUTIEBELLE]. Perfection—absolute Ethiopian perfect. Hah, Missy?

MISSY [*looking off after* LUTIEBELLE]. Oh, I 45 don't know about that.

PURLIE. What you mean you don't know? This girl looks more like Cousin Bee than Cousin Bee ever did.

MISSY. No resemblance to me. 50

PURLIE. Don't be ridiculous; she's the spitting image—°

MISSY. No resemblance whatsoever!

PURLIE. I ought to know how my own cousin looked— 55

MISSY. But I was the last one to see her alive—

PURLIE. Twins, if not closer!

MISSY. Are you crazy? Bee was more lean, loose, and leggy— 60

PURLIE. Maybe so, but this girl makes it up in—

MISSY. With no chin to speak of—her eyes: sort of fickle one to another—

PURLIE. I know, but even so— 65

MISSY [*pointing off in* LUTIEBELLE'S *direction*]. Look at her head—it ain't nearly as built like a rutabaga as Bee's own was!

PURLIE [*exasperated*]. What's the difference! White folks can't tell one of us from another 70 by the head!

MISSY. Twenty years ago it was, Purlie, Ol' Cap'n laid bull whip to your natural behind—

PURLIE. Twenty years ago I swore I'd see his soul in hell! 75

MISSY. And I don't think you come full back to your senses yet— That ol' man ain't no fool!

PURLIE. That makes it one "no fool" against another.

MISSY. He's dangerous, Purlie. We could get 80 killed if that old man was to find out what we was trying to do to get that church back.

PURLIE. How can he find out? Missy, how many times must I tell you, if it's one thing I am foolproof in it's white folks' psychology. 85

MISSY. That's exactly what I'm afraid of.

PURLIE. Freedom, Missy, that's what Big Bethel means. For you, me and Gitlow. And we

---

ma'am lengthened for emphasis; Missy uses the commoner monosyllable *m'am*

spitting image identical likeness (derived by folk etymology from "spit and image")

can buy it for five hundred dollars, Missy. Freedom!—You want it, or don't you?

MISSY. Of course I want it, but— After all, Purlie, that rich ol' lady didn't exactly leave that $500 to us.

PURLIE. She left it to Aunt Henrietta—

MISSY. Aunt Henrietta is dead—

PURLIE. Exactly—

MISSY. And Henrietta's daughter Cousin Bee is dead, too.

PURLIE. Which makes us next in line to inherit the money by law!

MISSY. All right, then, why don't we just go on up that hill man-to-man and tell Ol' Cap'n we want our money?

PURLIE. Missy! You have been black as long as I have—

MISSY [not above having her own little joke]. Hell, boy, we could make him give it to us.

PURLIE. Make him—how? He's a white man, Missy. What you plan to do, sue him?

MISSY [drops her teasing; thinks seriously for a moment]. After all, it is our money. And it was our church.

PURLIE. And can you think of a better way to get it back than that girl out there?

MISSY. But you think it'll work, Purlie? You really think she can fool Ol' Cap'n?

PURLIE. He'll never know what hit him.

MISSY. Maybe—but there's still the question of Gitlow.

PURLIE. What about Gitlow?

MISSY. Gitlow has changed his mind.

PURLIE. Then you'll have to change it back.

GITLOW [offstage]. Help, Missy; help, Missy; help, Missy; help, Missy! [GITLOW runs on.]

MISSY. What the devil's the matter this time?

GITLOW. There I was, Missy, picking in the high cotton, twice as fast as the human eye could see. All of a sudden I missed a boll and it fell—it fell on the ground, Missy! I stooped as fast as I could to pick it up and—[he stoops to illustrate. There is a loud tearing of cloth] ripped the seat of my britches. There I was, Missy, exposed from stem to stern.

MISSY. What's so awful about that? It's only cotton.

GITLOW. But cotton is white, Missy. We must maintain respect. Bring me my Sunday School britches.

MISSY. What!

GITLOW. Ol' Cap'n is coming down into the cotton patch today, and I know you want your Gitlow to look his level best. [MISSY starts to answer.] Hurry, Missy, hurry! [GITLOW hurries her off.]

PURLIE. Gitlow—have I got the girl!

GITLOW. Is that so—what girl?

PURLIE [taking him to the door]. See? There she is! Well?

GITLOW. Well what?

PURLIE. What do you think?

GITLOW. Nope; she'll never do.

PURLIE. What you mean, she'll never do?

GITLOW. My advice to you is to take that girl back to Florida as fast as you can!

PURLIE. I can't take her back to Florida.

GITLOW. Why can't you take her to Florida?

PURLIE. 'Cause she comes from Alabama. Gitlow, look at her: she's just the size—just the type—just the style.

GITLOW. And just the girl to get us all in jail. The answer is no! [Crosses to kitchen door.] MISSY! [Back to PURLIE.] Girl or no girl, I ain't getting mixed up in no more of your nightmares—I got my own. Dammit, Missy, I said let's go!

MISSY [entering with trousers]. You want me to take my bat to you again?

GITLOW. No, Missy, control yourself. It's just that every second Gitlow's off the firing line-up, seven pounds of Ol' Cap'n's cotton don't git gotten. [Snatches pants from MISSY, but is in too much of a hurry to put them on—starts off.]

PURLIE. Wait a minute, Gitlow. . . . Wait! [GITLOW is off in a flash.] Missy! Stop him!

MISSY. He ain't as easy to stop as he used to be. Especially now Ol' Cap'n's made him Deputy-For-The Colored.

PURLIE. Deputy-For-The-Colored? What the devil is that?

MISSY. Who knows? All I know is Gitlow's changed his mind.

PURLIE. But Gitlow can't change his mind!

MISSY. Oh, it's easy enough when you ain't

got much to start with. I warned you. You don't know how shifty ol' Git can git. He's the hardest man to convince and keep convinced I ever seen in my life.

5   PURLIE. Missy, you've got to make him go up that hill, he's got to identify this girl— Ol' Cap'n won't believe nobody else.

   MISSY. I know—

   PURLIE. He's got to swear before Ol' Cap'n
10 that this girl is the real Cousin Bee—

   MISSY. I know.

   PURLIE. Missy, you're the only person in this world ol' Git'll really listen to.

   MISSY. I know.

15   PURLIE. And what if you do have to hit him a time or two—it's for his own good!

   MISSY. I know.

   PURLIE. He'll recover from it, Missy. He always does—

20   MISSY. I know.

   PURLIE. Freedom, Missy—Big Bethel; for you; me; and Gitlow—!

   MISSY. Freedom—and a little something left over—that's all I ever wanted all my life.
25 [*Looks out into the yard.*] She do look a little somewhat like Cousin Bee—about the feet!

   PURLIE. Of course she does—

   MISSY. I won't guarantee nothing, Purlie— but I'll try.

30   PURLIE [*grabbing her and dancing her around*]. Everytime I see you, Missy, you get prettier by the pound!

   [LUTIEBELLE *enters.* MISSY *sees her.*]

   MISSY. Stop it, Purlie, stop it! Stop it. Quit
35 cutting the fool in front of company!

   PURLIE [*sees* LUTIEBELLE, *crosses to her, grabs her about the waist and swings her around too*].

How wondrous are the daughters of my
                       [people,
40 Yet knoweth not the glories of themselves!

   [*Spins her around for* MISSY'S *inspection. She does look better with her coat off, in her immaculate blue and white maid's uniform.*]

Where do you suppose I found her, Missy—
45 This Ibo prize—this Zulu° Pearl—

This long lost lily of the black Mandingo— Kikuyu maid, beneath whose brown embrace Hot suns of Africa are burning still:
                     [where—where?

A drudge; a serving wench; a feudal   50
                    [fetch-pot:

A common scullion in the white man's
                    [kitchen.

Drowned is her youth in thankless Southern
                 [dishpans; 55

Her beauty spilt for Dixiecratic pigs!

This brown-skinned grape! this wine of
                 [Negro vintage—

   MISSY [*interrupting*]. I know all that, Purlie, but what's her name?   60

   [PURLIE *looks at* LUTIEBELLE *and turns abruptly away.*]

   LUTIEBELLE. I don't think he likes my name so much; it's Lutiebelle, ma'am—Lutiebelle Gussiemae Jenkins!   65

   MISSY [*gushing with motherly reassurance*]. Lutiebelle Gussiemae Jenkins! My, that's nice.

   PURLIE. Nice! It's an insult to the Negro people!

   MISSY. Purlie, behave yourself!   70

   PURLIE. A previous condition of servitude, a badge of inferiority, and I refuse to have it in my organization—change it!

   MISSY. You want me to box your mouth for you!   75

   PURLIE. Lutiebelle Gussiemae Jenkins! What does it mean in Swahili? Cheap labor!

   LUTIEBELLE. Swahili?

   PURLIE. One of the thirteen silver tongues of Africa: Swahili, Bushengo, Ashanti, Baganda, 80 Herero, Yoruba, Bambora, Mpongwe, Swahili:° a language of moons, of velvet drums; hot days of rivers, red-splashed, and bird-song bright!, black fingers in rice white at sunset red!—ten thousand Queens of Sheba—° 85

   MISSY [*having to interrupt*]. Just where did Purlie find you, honey?

Ibo . . . Zulu African tribes, more of which are named below

Swahili . . . Swahili a list of African languages (pieced out by Purlie's imagination)

Queens of Sheba regal black women. The Queen of Sheba (in tradition although not in history) was an Ethiopian queen and Solomon's favorite wife

LUTIEBELLE. It was in Dothan, Alabama, last Sunday, Aunt Missy, right in the junior choir!

MISSY. The junior choir—my, my, my!

PURLIE [still carried away].

5 Behold! I said, this dark and holy vessel,
In whom should burn that golden nut-
[brown joy
Which Negro womanhood was meant to be.
Ten thousand queens, ten thousand Queens
10 [of Sheba:
[Pointing at LUTIEBELLE.]
Ethiopia herself—in all her beauteous
[wonder,
Come to restore the ancient thrones of Cush!

15 MISSY. Great Gawdamighty, Purlie, I can't hear myself think—!

LUTIEBELLE. That's just what I said last Sunday, Aunt Missy, when Reb'n Purlie started preaching that thing in the pulpit.

20 MISSY. Preaching it!?

LUTIEBELLE. Lord, Aunt Missy, I shouted clear down to the Mourners' Bench.°

MISSY [to PURLIE]. But last time you was a professor of Negro Philosophy.

25 PURLIE. I told you, Missy: my intention is to buy Big Bethel back; to reclaim the ancient pulpit of Grandpaw Kincaid, and preach freedom in the cotton patch—I told you!

MISSY. Maybe you did, Purlie, maybe you
30 did. You got yourself a license?

PURLIE. Naw!—but—

MISSY [looking him over]. Purlie Victorious Judson: Self-made minister of the gospel—claw-hammer coattail, shoe-string tie and all.

35 PURLIE [quietly but firmly holding his ground]. How else can you lead the Negro people?

MISSY. Is that what you got in your mind: leading the Negro people?

40 PURLIE. Who else is they got?

MISSY. God help the race.

LUTIEBELLE. It was a sermon, I mean, Aunt Missy, the likes of which has never been heard before.

45 MISSY. Oh, I bet that. Tell me about it, son. What did you preach?

Mourners' Bench   front bench for the penitential

PURLIE. I preached the New Baptism of Freedom for all mankind, according to the Declaration of Independence, taking as my text the Constitution of the United States of America, 50 Amendments First through Fifteenth, which readeth as follow: "Congress shall make no law—"

MISSY. Enough—that's enough, son—I'm converted. But it is confusing, all the changes 55 you keep going through. [To LUTIEBELLE.] Honey, every time I see Purlie he's somebody else.

PURLIE. Not any more, Missy; and if I'm lying may the good Lord put me down in the 60 book of bad names: Purlie is put forever!

MISSY. Yes. But will he stay put forever?

PURLIE. There is in every man a finger of iron that points him what he must and must not do— 65

MISSY. And your finger points up the hill to that five hundred dollars with which you'll buy Big Bethel back, preach freedom in the cotton patch, and live happily ever after!

PURLIE. The soul-consuming passion of my 70 life! [Draws out watch.] It's 2:15, Missy, and Gitlow's waiting. Missy, I suggest you get a move on.

MISSY. I already got a move on. Had it since four o'clock this morning! 75

PURLIE. Time, Missy—exactly what the colored man in this country ain't got, and you're wasting it!

MISSY [looks at PURLIE, and decides not to strike him dead]. Purlie, would you mind 80 stepping out into the cotton patch and telling your brother Gitlow I'd like a few words with him? [PURLIE, overjoyed, leaps at MISSY as if to hug and dance her around again, but she is too fast.] Do like I tell you now—go on! 85 [PURLIE exits singing. MISSY turns to LUTIEBELLE to begin the important task of sizing her up.] Besides, it wouldn't be hospitable not to set and visit a spell with our distinguished guest over from Dothan, Alabama. 90

LUTIEBELLE [this is the first time she has been called anything of importance by anybody]. Thank you, ma'am.

MISSY. Now. Let's you and me just set back

and enjoy a piece of my potato pie. You like potato pie, don't you?

LUTIEBELLE. Oh, yes ma'am, I like it very much.

5   MISSY. And get real acquainted. [*Offers her a saucer with a slice of pie on it.*]

LUTIEBELLE. I'm ever so much obliged. My, this looks nice! Uhm, uhn, uhn!

MISSY [*takes a slice for herself and sits 10 down*]. You know—ever since that ol' man—[*indicates up the hill*] took after Purlie so unmerciful with that bull whip twenty years ago—he fidgets! Always on the go; rattling around from place to place all over the country: one 15 step ahead of the white folks—something about Purlie always did irritate the white folks.

LUTIEBELLE. Is that the truth!

MISSY. Oh, my yes. Finally wound up being locked up a time or two for safe-keeping— 20 [LUTIEBELLE *parts with a loud, sympathetic grunt. Changing her tack a bit.*] Always kept up his schooling, though. In fact that boy's got one of the best second-hand educations in this country.

25   LUTIEBELLE [*brightening considerably*]. Is that a fact!

MISSY. Used to read everything he could get his hands on.

LUTIEBELLE. He did? Ain't that wonderful!

30   MISSY. Till one day he finally got tired, and throwed all his books to the hogs—not enough "Negro" in them, he said. After that he puttered around with first one thing then another. Remember that big bus boycott they had in 35 Montgomery? Well, we don't travel by bus in the cotton patch, so Purlie boycotted mules!

LUTIEBELLE. You don't say so?

MISSY. Another time he invented a secret language, that Negroes could understand but 40 white folks couldn't.

LUTIEBELLE. Oh, my goodness gracious!

MISSY. He sent it C.O.D. to the NAACP but they never answered his letter.

LUTIEBELLE. Oh, they will, Aunt Missy; you 45 can just bet your life they will.

MISSY. I don't mind it so much. Great leaders are bound to pop up from time to time 'mongst our people—in fact we sort of look forward to it. But Purlie's in such a hurry I'm afraid he'll lose his mind. 50

LUTIEBELLE. Lose his mind—no! Oh, no!

MISSY. That is unless you and me can do something about it.

LUTIEBELLE. You and me? Do what, Aunt Missy? You tell me—I'll do anything! 55

MISSY [*having found all she needs to know*]. Well, now; ain't nothing ever all that peculiar about a man a good wife—and a family—and some steady home cooking won't cure. Don't you think so? 60

LUTIEBELLE [*immensely relieved*]. Oh, yes, Aunt Missy, yes. [*But still not getting* MISSY'S *intent.*] You'd be surprised how many tall, good-looking, great big, ol' handsome looking mens—just like Reb'n Purlie—walking around, 65 starving theyselves to death! Oh, I just wish I had one to aim my pot at!

MISSY. Well, Purlie Judson is the uncrowned appetite of the age.

LUTIEBELLE. He is! What's his favorite? 70

MISSY. Anything! Anything a fine-looking, strong and healthy—girl like you could put on the table.

LUTIEBELLE. Like me? Like ME! Oh, Aunt Missy—! 75

MISSY [PURLIE'S *future is settled*]. Honey, I mind once at the Sunday School picnic Purlie et a whole sack o' pullets!

LUTIEBELLE. Oh, I just knowed there was something—something—just reeks about that 80 man. He puts me in the mind of all the good things I ever had in my life. Picnics, fish-fries, corn-shuckings, and love-feasts, and gospel-singings—picking huckleberries, roasting groundpeas, quilting-bee parties and bar- 85 becues; that certain kind of—welcome—you can't get nowhere else in all this world. Aunt Missy, life is so good to us—sometimes!

MISSY. Oh, child, being colored can be a lotta fun when ain't nobody looking. 90

LUTIEBELLE. Ain't it the truth! I always said I'd never pass for white, no matter how much they offered me, unless the things I love could pass, too.

MISSY. Ain't it the beautiful truth! 95
[PURLIE *enters again; agitated.*]

PURLIE. Missy—Gitlow says if you want him come and get him!

MISSY [*rises, crosses to door Down Left; looks out*]. Lawd, that man do take his cotton picking seriously. [*Comes back to* LUTIEBELLE *and takes her saucer.*] Did you get enough to eat, honey?

LUTIEBELLE. Indeed I did. And Aunt Missy, I haven't had potato pie like that since the senior choir give—

MISSY [*still ignoring him*]. That's where I met Gitlow, you know. On the senior choir.

LUTIEBELLE. Aunt Missy! I didn't know you could sing!

MISSY. Like a brown-skin nightingale. Well, it was a Sunday afternoon—Big Bethel had just been—

PURLIE. Dammit, Missy! The white man is five hundred years ahead of us in this country, and we ain't gonna ever gonna catch up with him sitting around on our non-Caucasian rumps talking about the senior choir!

MISSY [*starts to bridle at this sudden display of passion, but changes her mind*]. Right this way, honey. [*Heads for door Down Right.*] Where Cousin Bee used to sleep at.

LUTIEBELLE. Yes, ma'am. [*Starts to follow* MISSY.]

PURLIE [*stopping her*]. Wait a minute—don't forget your clothes! [*Gives her a large carton.*]

MISSY. It ain't much, the roof leaks, and you can get as much September inside as you can outside any time; but I try to keep it clean.

PURLIE. Cousin Bee was known for her clothes!

MISSY. Stop nagging, Purlie— [*To* LUTIE- BELLE.] There's plenty to eat in the kitchen.

LUTIEBELLE. Thank you, Aunt Missy. [*Exits Down Right.*]

PURLIE [*following after her*]. And hurry! We want to leave as soon as Missy gets Gitlow in from the cotton patch!

MISSY [*blocking his path*]. Mr. Preacher— [*She pulls him out of earshot.*] If we do pull this thing off—[*studying him a moment*] what do you plan to do with her after that?—send her back where she came from?

PURLIE. Dothan, Alabama? Never! Missy, there° a million things I can do with a girl like that, right here in Big Bethel!

MISSY. Yeah! Just make sure they're all legitimate. Anyway, marriage is still cheap, and we can always use another cook in the family! [*PURLIE hasn't the slightest idea what* MISSY *is talking about.*]

LUTIEBELLE [*from Offstage*]. Aunt Missy.

MISSY. Yes, honey.

LUTIEBELLE [*Offstage*]. Whose picture is this on the dresser?

MISSY. Why, that's Cousin Bee.

LUTIEBELLE [*a moment's silence. Then she enters hastily, carrying a large photograph in her hand*]. Cousin Bee!

MISSY. Yes, poor thing. She's the one the whole thing is all about.

LUTIEBELLE [*the edge of panic*]. Cousin Bee — Oh, my!—Oh, my goodness! My goodness gracious!

MISSY. What's the matter?

LUTIEBELLE. But she's pretty—she's so pretty!

MISSY [*takes photograph; looks at it tenderly*]. Yes—she was pretty. I guess they took this shortly before she died.

LUTIEBELLE. And you mean—you want me to look like her?

PURLIE. That's the idea. Now go and get into your clothes. [*Starts to push her off.*]

MISSY. They sent it down to us from the college. Don't she look smart? I'll bet she was a good student when she was living.

LUTIEBELLE [*evading* PURLIE]. Good student!

MISSY. Yes. One more year and she'd have finished.

LUTIEBELLE. Oh, my gracious Lawd have mercy upon my poor soul!

PURLIE [*not appreciating her distress or its causes*]. Awake, awake! Put on thy strength, O, Zion—put on thy beautiful garments. [*Hurries her Offstage.*] And hurry! [*Turning to* MISSY.] Missy, Big Bethel and Gitlow is waiting. Grandpaw Kincaid gave his life. [*Gently places the bat into her hand.*] It is a far greater

---

there elision of *there are*

thing you do now, than you've ever done be-
fore°—and Gitlow ain't never got his head
knocked off in a better cause. [Missy *nods her
head in sad agreement, and accepts the bat.*
5 PURLIE *helps her to the door Down Left, where
she exits, a most reluctant executioner.* PURLIE
*stands and watches her off from the depth of
his satisfaction. The door Down Right eases
open, and* LUTIEBELLE, *her suitcase, handbag,*
10 *fall coat and lunch box firmly in hand, tries to
sneak out the front door.* PURLIE *hears her, and
turns just in time.*] Where do you think you're
going?

LUTIEBELLE. Did you see that, Reb'n Purlie?
15 [*Indicating bedroom from which she just
came.*] Did you see all them beautiful clothes
—slips, hats, shoes, stockings? I mean nylon
stockings like Miz Emmylou wears—and a
dress, like even Miz Emmylou don't wear. Did
20 you look at what was in that big box?

PURLIE. Of course I looked at what was in
that big box—I bought it—all of it—for you.

LUTIEBELLE. For me!

PURLIE. Of course! I told you! And as soon
25 as we finish you can have it!

LUTIEBELLE. Reb'n Purlie, I'm a good girl. I
ain't never done nothing in all this world,
white, colored or otherwise, to hurt nobody!

PURLIE. I know that.

30 LUTIEBELLE. I work hard; I mop, I scrub, I
iron; I'm clean and polite, and I know how to
get along with white folks' children better'n
they do. I pay my church dues every second
and fourth Sunday the Lawd sends; and I can
35 cook catfish—and hushpuppies°—You like
hushpuppies, don't you, Reb'n Purlie?

PURLIE. I love hushpuppies!

LUTIEBELLE. Hushpuppies—and corn dodgers;
I can cook you a corn dodger would give you
40 the swimming in the head!

PURLIE. I'm sure you can, but—

LUTIEBELLE. But I ain't never been in a mess
like this in all my life!

PURLIE. Mess—what mess?

LUTIEBELLE. You mean go up that hill, in all 45
them pretty clothes, and pretend—in front of
white folks—that—that I'm your Cousin Bee—
somebody I ain't never seen or heard of before
in my whole life!

PURLIE. Why not? Some of the best pretend- 50
ing in the world is done in front of white folks.

LUTIEBELLE. But Reb'n Purlie, I didn't know
your Cousin Bee was a student at the college;
I thought she worked there!

PURLIE. But I told you on the train— 55

LUTIEBELLE. Don't do no good to tell ME
nothing, Reb'n Purlie! I never listen. Ask Miz
Emmylou and 'em, they'll tell you I never listen.
I didn't know it was a college lady you wanted
me to make like. I thought it was for a sleep- 60
in° like me. I thought all that stuff you bought
in them boxes was stuff for maids and cooks
and— Why, I ain't never even been near a
college!

PURLIE. So what? College ain't so much 65
where you been as how you talk when you get
back. Anybody can do it; look at me.

LUTIEBELLE. Nawsir, I think you better look
at me like Miz Emmylou sez—

PURLIE [*taking her by the shoulders, tender-* 70
ly]. Calm down—just take it easy, and calm
down. [*She subsides a little, her chills banished
by the warmth of him.*] Now—don't tell me,
after all that big talking you done on the train
about white folks, you're scared. 75

LUTIEBELLE. Talking big is easy—from the
proper distance.

PURLIE. Why—don't you believe in yourself?

LUTIEBELLE. Some.

PURLIE. Don't you believe in your own race 80
of people?

LUTIEBELLE. Oh, yessir—a little.

PURLIE. Don't you believe the black man is
coming to power some day?

LUTIEBELLE. Almost. 85

PURLIE. Ten thousand Queens of Sheba!

Awake . . . done before Purlie recalls rhetorical passages from Old Testament poetry and from Dickens's
Tale of Two Cities
hushpuppies like corn dodgers (below), a fried dough
of cornmeal

sleep-in maid

What kind of a Negro are you! Where's your race pride?

LUTIEBELLE. Oh, I'm a great one for race pride, sir, believe me—it's just that I don't need it much in my line of work! Miz Emmylou sez—

PURLIE. Damn Miz Emmylou! Does her blond hair and blue eyes make her any more of a woman in the sight of her men folks than your black hair and brown eyes in mine?

LUTIEBELLE. No, sir!

PURLIE. Is her lily-white skin any more money-under-the-mattress than your fine fair brown? And if so, why does she spend half her life at the beach trying to get a sun tan?

LUTIEBELLE. I never thought of that!

PURLIE. There's a whole lotta things about the Negro question you ain't thought of! The South is split like a fat man's underwear; and somebody beside the Supreme Court has got to make a stand for the everlasting glory of our people!

LUTIEBELLE. Yessir.

PURLIE. Snatch Freedom from the jaws of force and filibuster!

LUTIEBELLE. Amen to that!

PURLIE. Put thunder in the Senate—!

LUTIEBELLE. Yes, Lawd!

PURLIE. And righteous indignation back in the halls of Congress!

LUTIEBELLE. Ain't it the truth!

PURLIE. Make Civil Rights from Civil Wrongs; and bring that ol' Civil War to a fair and a just conclusion!

LUTIEBELLE. Help him, Lawd!

PURLIE. Remind this white and wicked world there ain't been more'n a dime's worth of difference twixt one man and another'n, irregardless of race, gender, creed, or color—since God Himself Almighty set the first batch out to dry before the chimneys of Zion got hot! The eyes and ears of the world is on Big Bethel!

LUTIEBELLE. Amen and hallelujah!

PURLIE. And whose side are you fighting on this evening, sister?

LUTIEBELLE. Great Gawdamighty, Reb'n Purlie, on the Lawd's side! But Miss Emmylou sez—

PURLIE [blowing up]. This is outrageous— this is a catastrophe! You're a disgrace to the Negro profession!

LUTIEBELLE. That's just what she said all right —her exactly words.

PURLIE. Who's responsible for this? Where's your Maw and Paw at?

LUTIEBELLE. I reckon I ain't rightly got no Maw and Paw, wherever they at.

PURLIE. What!

LUTIEBELLE. And nobody else that I knows of. You see, sir—I been on the go from one white folks' kitchen to another since before I can remember. How I got there in the first place —whatever became of my Maw and Paw, and my kinfolks—even what my real name is—nobody is ever rightly said.

PURLIE [genuinely touched]. Oh! A motherless child—

LUTIEBELLE. That's what Miz Emmylou always sez—

PURLIE. But—who cared for you—like a mother? Who brung you up—who raised you?

LUTIEBELLE. Nobody in particular—just whoever happened to be in charge of the kitchen that day.

PURLIE. That explains the whole thing—no wonder; you've missed the most important part of being somebody.

LUTIEBELLE. I have? What part is that?

PURLIE. Love—being appreciated, and sought out, and looked after; being fought to the bitter end over even.

LUTIEBELLE. Oh, I have missed that, Reb'n Purlie, I really have. Take mens—all my life they never looked at me the way other girls get looked at!

PURLIE. That's not so. The very first time I saw you—right up there in the junior choir— I give you that look!

LUTIEBELLE [turning to him in absolute ecstasy]. You did! Oh, I thought so!—I prayed so. All through your sermon I thought I would faint from hoping so hard so. Oh, Reb'n Purlie —I think that's the finest look a person could ever give a person— Oh, Reb'n Purlie! [She closes her eyes and points her lips at him.]

PURLIE [starts to kiss her, but draws back shyly]. Lutiebelle—

LUTIEBELLE [*dreamily, her eyes still closed*]. Yes, Reb'n Purlie—

PURLIE. There's something I want to ask you—something I never—in all my life—thought
5 I'd be asking a woman— Would you—I don't know exactly how to say it—would you—

LUTIEBELLE. Yes, Reb'n Purlie?

PURLIE. Would you be my disciple?

LUTIEBELLE [*rushing into his arms*]. Oh, yes,
10 Reb'n Purlie, yes!

[*They start to kiss, but are interrupted by a NOISE coming from Offstage.*]

GITLOW [*Offstage; in the extremity of death*]. No, Missy. No—no!—NO!—

15 [*This last plea is choked off by the sound of some solid object brought smartly into contact with sudden flesh. "CLUNK!"* PURLIE *and* LUTIEBELLE *stand looking off Left, frozen for the moment.*]

20 LUTIEBELLE [*finally daring to speak*]. Oh, my lawd, Reb'n Purlie, what happened?

PURLIE. Gitlow has changed his mind. [*Grabs her and swings her around bodily.*] Toll the bell, Big Bethel!—toll that big, fat, black and
25 sassy liberty bell. Tell Freedom— [LUTIEBELLE *suddenly leaps from the floor into his arms and plants her lips squarely on his. When finally he can come up for air.*] Tell Freedom—tell Freedom—WOW!

Scene ii

30 [TIME. *It is a little later the same afternoon.*]

[SCENE. *We are now in the little business office off from the commissary, where all the inhabitants of Cotchipee Valley buy food, clothing, and supplies. In the back a traveler
35 has been drawn with just enough of an opening left to serve as the door to the main part of the store. On Stage Left and on Stage Right are simulated shelves where various items of reserve stock are kept: A wash tub, an axe, sacks
40 of peas, and flour; bolts of gingham and calico, etc. Downstage Right is a small desk, on which an ancient typewriter, and an adding machine, with various papers and necessary books and records of commerce are placed. There is
45 a small chair at this desk. Downstage Left is a table, with a large cash register, that has a*

functioning drawer. Below this is an entrance from the street.]

[AT RISE. *As the CURTAIN rises, a young
50 white* MAN *of 25 or 30, but still gawky, awkward, and adolescent in outlook and behavior, is sitting on a high stool Downstage Right Center. His face is held in the hands of* IDELLA, *a Negro cook and woman of all work, who has been in the family since time immemorial. She
55 is the only mother* CHARLIE, *who is very much oversized even for his age, has ever known.* IDELLA *is as little as she is old and as tough as she is tiny, and is busily applying medication to* CHARLIE's *black eye.*]
60

CHARLIE. Ow, Idella, ow!—Ow!

IDELLA. Hold still, boy.

CHARLIE. But it hurts, Idella.

IDELLA. I know it hurts. Whoever done this to you musta meant to knock your natural
65 brains out.

CHARLIE. I already told you who done it—OW!

IDELLA. Charlie Cotchipee, if you don't hold still and let me put this hot poultice on your
70 eye, you better! [CHARLIE *subsides and meekly accepts her ministrations.*] First the milking, then the breakfast, then the dishes, then the washing, then the scrubbing, then the lunch time, next the dishes, then the ironing—and
75 now; just where the picking and plucking for supper ought to be—you!

CHARLIE. You didn't tell Paw?

IDELLA. Of course I didn't—but the sheriff did.
80

CHARLIE [*leaping up*]. The sheriff!

IDELLA [*pushing him back down*]. Him and the deputy come to the house less than a hour ago.

CHARLIE [*leaping up again*]. Are they coming
85 over here?

IDELLA. Of course they're coming over here—sooner or later.

CHARLIE. But what will I do, Idella, what will I say?
90

IDELLA [*pushing him down.* CHARLIE *subsides*]. "He that keepeth his mouth keepeth his life—"

CHARLIE. Did they ask for me?

IDELLA. Of course they asked for you.

CHARLIE. What did they say?

IDELLA. I couldn't hear too well; your father took them into the study and locked the door behind them.

CHARLIE. Maybe it was about something else.

IDELLA. It was about YOU: that much I could hear! Charlie—you want to get us both killed?

CHARLIE. I'm sorry, Idella, but—

IDELLA [overriding; finishing proverb she had begun]. "But he that openeth wide his lips shall have destruction!"

CHARLIE. But it was you who said it was the law of the land—

IDELLA. I know I did—

CHARLIE. It was you who said it's got to be obeyed—

IDELLA. I know it was me, but—

CHARLIE. It was you who said everybody had to stand up and take a stand against—

IDELLA. I know it was me, dammit! But I didn't say take a stand in no barroom!

CHARLIE. Ben started it, not me. And you always said never to take low talk from the likes of him!

IDELLA. Not so loud; they may be out there in the commissary! [Goes quickly to door Up Center and peers out; satisfied no one has overheard them she crosses back down to CHARLIE.] Look, boy, everybody down here don't feel as friendly towards the Supreme Court as you and me do—you big enough to know that! And don't you ever go outta here and pull a fool trick like you done last night again and not let me know about it in advance. You hear me!

CHARLIE. I'm sorry.

IDELLA. When you didn't come to breakfast this morning, and I went upstairs looking for you, and you just setting there, looking at me with your big eyes, and I seen that they had done hurt you—my, my, my! Whatever happens to you happens to me—you big enough to know that!

CHARLIE. I didn't mean to make trouble, Idella.

IDELLA. I know that, son, I know it. [Makes final adjustments to the poultice.] Now. No matter what happens when they do come I'll be right behind you. Keep your nerves calm and your mouth shut. Understand?

CHARLIE. Yes.

IDELLA. And as soon as you get a free minute come over to the house and let me put another hot poultice on that eye.

CHARLIE. Thank you, I'm very much obliged to you. Idella—

IDELLA. What is it, son?

CHARLIE. Sometimes I think I ought to run away from home.

IDELLA. I know, but you already tried that, honey.

CHARLIE. Sometimes I think I ought to run away from home—again!

[OL' CAP'N has entered from the Commissary just in time to hear this last remark.]

OL' CAP'N. Why don't you, boy—why don't you? [OL' CAP'N COTCHIPEE is aged and withered a bit, but by no means infirm. Dressed in traditional southern linen, the wide hat, the shoestring tie, the long coat, the twirling moustache of the Ol' Southern Colonel. In his left hand he carries a cane, and in his right a coiled bull whip: his last line of defense. He stops long enough to establish the fact that he means business, threatens them both with a mean cantankerous eye, then hangs his whip —the definitive answer to all who might foolishly question his Confederate power and glory —upon a peg. CHARLIE freezes at the sound of his voice IDELLA tenses but keeps working on CHARLIE's eye. OL' CAP'N crosses down, rudely pushes her hand aside, lifts up CHARLIE's chin so that he may examine the damage, shakes his head in disgust.] You don't know, boy, what a strong stomach it takes to stomach you. Just look at you, sitting there—all slopped over like something the horses dropped; steam, stink and all!

IDELLA. Don't you dare talk like that to this child!

OL' CAP'N [this stops him—momentarily]. When I think of his grandpaw, God rest his Confederate soul, hero of the battle of Chica-

mauga— [*It's too much.*] Get outta my sight!
[CHARLIE *gets up to leave.*] Not you—you!
[*Indicates* IDELLA. *She gathers up her things in
silence and starts to leave.*] Wait a minute—
5 [IDELLA *stops.*] You been closer to this boy than
I have, even before his ma died—ain't a
thought ever entered his head you didn't know
'bout it first. You got anything to do with what
my boy's been thinking lately?

10 IDELLA. I didn't know he had been thinking
lately.

OL' CAP'N. Don't play with me, Idella—and
you know what I mean! Who's been putting
these integrationary ideas in my boy's head?
15 Was it you— I'm asking you a question, dammit! Was it you?

IDELLA. Why don't you ask him?

OL' CAP'N [*snorts*]. Ask him! ASK HIM! He
ain't gonna say a word unless you tell him to,
20 and you know it. I'm asking you again, Idella
Landy, have you been talking integration to
my boy!?

IDELLA. I can't rightly answer you any more
on that than he did.

25 OL' CAP'N. By God, you will answer me. I'll
make you stand right there—right there!—all
day and all night long, till you do answer me!

IDELLA. That's just fine.

OL' CAP'N. What's that! What's that you
30 say?

IDELLA. I mean I ain't got nothing else to do
—supper's on the stove; rice is ready, okra's
fried, turnip's simmered, biscuits' baked, and
stew is stewed. In fact them lemon pies you
35 wanted special for supper are in the oven right
now, just getting ready to burn—

OL' CAP'N. Get outta here!

IDELLA. Oh—no hurry, Ol' Cap'n—

OL' CAP'N. Get the hell out of here! [IDELLA
40 *deliberately takes all the time in the world to
pick up her things. Following her around trying to make his point.*] I'm warning both of
you; that little lick over the eye is a small
skimption° compared to what I'm gonna do.
45 [IDELLA *pretends not to listen.*] I won't stop till

skimption   minuscule part

I get to the bottom of this! [IDELLA *still ignores
him.*] Get outta here, Idella Landy, before I
take my cane and— [*He raises his cane but
IDELLA insists on moving at her own pace to
exit Down Left.*] And save me some buttermilk   50
to go with them lemon pies, you hear me!
[*Turns to* CHARLIE; *not knowing how to
approach him.*] The sheriff was here this
morning.

CHARLIE. Yessir.   55

OL' CAP'N. Is that all you got to say to me:
"Yessir"?

CHARLIE. Yessir.

OL' CAP'N. You are a disgrace to the southland!   60

CHARLIE. Yessir.

OL' CAP'N. Shut up! I could kill you, boy,
you understand that? Kill you with my own
two hands!

CHARLIE. Yessir.   65

OL' CAP'N. Shut up! I could beat you to death
with that bull whip—put my pistol to your
good-for-nothing head—my own flesh and
blood—and blow your blasted brains all over
this valley! [*Fighting to retain his control.*] If   70
—if you wasn't the last living drop of Cotchipee blood in Cotchipee County, I'd—I'd—

CHARLIE. Yessir. [*This is too much.* OL' CAP'N
snatches CHARLIE *to his feet. But* CHARLIE *does
not resist.*]   75

OL' CAP'N. You trying to get non-violent
with me, boy? [CHARLIE *does not answer, just
dangles there.*]

CHARLIE [*finally*]. I'm ready with the books,
sir—that is—whenever you're ready.   80

OL' CAP'N [*flinging* CHARLIE *into a chair*].
Thank you—thank you! What with your Yan-
kee propaganda, your barroom brawls, and all
your other non-Confederate activities, I didn't
think you had the time.   85

CHARLIE [*picks up account book; reads*].
"Cotton report. Fifteen bales picked yesterday
and sent to the cotton gin; bringing our total
to 357 bales to date."

OL' CAP'N [*impressed*]. Three hundred and   90
fifty-seven—boy, that's some picking. Who's
ahead?

CHARLIE. Gitlow Judson, with seventeen bales up to now.

OL' CAP'N. Gitlow Judson; well I'll be damned; did you ever see a cotton-pickinger darky in your whole life?!

CHARLIE. Commissary report—

OL' CAP'N. Did you ever look down into the valley and watch ol' Git a-picking his way through that cotton patch? Holy Saint Mother's Day! I'll bet you—

CHARLIE. Commissary report!

OL' CAP'N. All right!—commissary report.

CHARLIE. Yessir—well, first, sir, there's been some complaints: the flour is spoiled, the beans are rotten, and the meat is tainted.

OL' CAP'N. Cut the price on it.

CHARLIE. But it's also a little wormy—

OL' CAP'N. Then sell it to the Negras— Is something wrong?

CHARLIE. No, sir—I mean, sir . . . , we can't go on doing that, sir.

OL' CAP'N. Why not? It's traditional.

CHARLIE. Yessir, but times are changing— all this debt— [Indicates book.] According to this book every family in this valley owes money they'll never be able to pay back.

OL' CAP'N. Of course—it's the only way to keep 'em working. Didn't they teach you nothin' at school?

CHARLIE. We're cheating them—and they know we're cheating them. How long do you expect them to stand for it?

OL' CAP'N. As long as they're Negras—

CHARLIE. How long before they start a-rearing up on their hind legs, and saying: "Enough, white folks—now that's enough! Either you start treating me like I'm somebody in this world, or I'll blow your brains out"?

OL' CAP'N [shaken to the core]. Stop it— stop it! You're tampering with the economic foundation of the Southland! Are you trying to ruin me? One more word like that and I'll kill—I'll shoot— [CHARLIE attempts to answer.] Shut up! One more word and I'll—I'll fling myself on your Maw's grave and die of apoplexy. I'll—! I'll—! Shut up, do you hear me? Shut up! [Enter GITLOW, hat in hand, grin on face, more obsequious today than ever.] Now what the hell you want?

GITLOW [taken aback]. Nothing, sir, nothing! —That is—Missy, my ol' 'oman—well, suh, to git to the truth of the matter, I got a little business—

OL' CAP'N. Negras ain't got no business. And if you don't get the hell back into that cotton patch you better. Git, I said! [GITLOW starts to beat a hasty retreat.] Oh, no—don't go. Uncle Gitlow—good ol' faithful ol' Gitlow. Don't go—don't go.

GITLOW [not quite sure]. Well—you're the boss, boss.

OL' CAP'N [shoving a cigar into GITLOW'S mouth]. Just the other day, I was talking to the Senator about you— What's that great big knot on your head?

GITLOW. Missy—I mean, a mosquito!

OL' CAP'N [in all seriousness, examining the bump]. Uh! Musta been wearin' brass knucks.° —And he was telling me, the Senator was, how hard it was—impossible, he said, to find the old-fashioned, solid, hard-earned, Uncle Tom type Negra nowadays. I laughed in his face.

GITLOW. Yassuh. By the grace of God, there's still a few of us left.

OL' CAP'N. I told him how you and me growed up together. Had the same mammy— my mammy was your mother.

GITLOW. Yessir! Bosom buddies!

OL' CAP'N. And how you used to sing that favorite ol' speritual of mine: [Sings.] "I'm a-coming . . . I'm a-coming, For my head is bending low," [GITLOW joins in on harmony] "I hear the gentle voices calling, Ol' Black Joe. . . ." [This proves too much for CHARLIE; he starts out.] Where you going?

CHARLIE. Maybe they need me in the front of the store.

OL' CAP'N. Come back here! [CHARLIE returns.] Turn around—show Gitlow that eye. [CHARLIE reluctantly exposes black eye to view.]

brass knucks brass knuckles; metal fitted across the knuckles for fighting

GITLOW. Gret Gawdamighty, somebody done cold cocked° this child! Who hit Mr. Charlie, tell Uncle Gitlow who hit you? [CHARLIE *does not answer*.]

5 OL' CAP'N. Would you believe it? All of a sudden he can't say a word. And just last night, the boys was telling me, this son of mine made hisself a full-fledged speech.

GITLOW. You don't say.

10 OL' CAP'N. All about Negras—NeGROES he called 'em—four years of college, and he still can't say the word right—seems he's quite a specialist on the subject.

GITLOW. Well, shut my hard-luck mouth!

15 OL' CAP'N. Yessireebob. Told the boys over at Ben's bar in town, that he was all for mixing the races together.

GITLOW. You go on 'way from hyeah!

OL' CAP'N. Said white children and darky 20 children ought to go the same schoolhouse together!

GITLOW. Tell me the truth, Ol' Cap'n!

OL' CAP'N. Got hisself so worked up some of 'em had to cool him down with a co-cola bottle!

25 GITLOW. Tell me the truth—again!

CHARLIE. That wasn't what I said!

OL' CAP'N. You calling me a liar, boy?

CHARLIE. No, sir, but I just said, that since it was the law of the land—

30 OL' CAP'N. It is not the law of the land no sucha thing!

CHARLIE. I didn't think it would do any harm if they went to school together—that's all.

OL' CAP'N. That's all—that's enough!

35 CHARLIE. They do it up North—

OL' CAP'N. This is down South. Down here they'll go to school together over me and Gitlow's dead body. Right, Git?!

GITLOW. Er, you the boss, boss!

40 CHARLIE. But this is the law of the—

OL' CAP'N. Never mind the law! Boy—look! You like Gitlow, you trust him, you always did —didn't you?

CHARLIE. Yessir.

45 OL' CAP'N. And Gitlow here, would cut off his right arm for you if you was to ask him. Wouldn't you, Git?

GITLOW [*gulping*]. You the boss, boss.

OL' CAP'N. Now Gitlow ain't nothing if he ain't a Negra!—Ain't you, Git? 50

GITLOW. Oh—two-three hundred percent, I calculate.

OL' CAP'N. Now, if you really want to know what the Negra thinks about this here integration and all lacka-that,° don't ask the Supreme 55 Court—ask Gitlow. Go ahead—ask him!

CHARLIE. I don't need to ask him.

OL' CAP'N. Then I'll ask him. Raise your right hand, Git. You solemnly swear to tell the truth, whole truth, nothing else but, so help 60 you God?

GITLOW [*raising hand*]. I do.

OL' CAP'N. Gitlow Judson, as God is your judge and maker, do you believe in your heart that God intended white folks and Negra 65 children to go to school together?

GITLOW. Nawsuh, I do not!

OL' CAP'N. Do you, so help you God, think that white folks and black should mix and 'sociate in street cars, buses, and railroad 70 stations, in any way, shape, form, or fashion?

GITLOW. Absolutely not!

OL' CAP'N. And is it not your considered opinion, God strike you dead if you lie, that all my Negras are happy with things in the 75 Southland just the way they are?

GITLOW. Indeed I do!

OL' CAP'N. Do you think ary° single darky on my place would ever think of changing a single thing about the South, and to hell with 80 the Supreme Court as God is your judge and maker?

GITLOW. As God is my judge and maker and you are my boss, I do not!

OL' CAP'N [*turning in triumph to* CHARLIE]. 85 The voice of the Negra himself! What more proof do you want!

CHARLIE. I don't care whose voice it is—it's

---

cold cocked knocked unconscious ("cold")

all lacka-that all such things; "every like (counterpart) of that"

ary e'er a; i.e., any

still the law of the land, and I intend to obey it!

OL' CAP'N [*losing control*]. Get outta my
face, boy—get outta my face, before I kill you!
Before I—

5   [CHARLIE *escapes into the commissary.* OL'
CAP'N *collapses.*]

GITLOW. Easy, Ol' Cap'n, easy, suh, easy!
[OL' CAP'N *gives out a groan.* GITLOW *goes to
shelf and comes back with a small bottle and*
10 *a small box.*] Some aspirins, suh . . . , some
asaphoetida? [PURLIE *and* LUTIEBELLE *appear at
door Left.*] Not now—later—later! [*Holds bottle to* OL' CAP'N's *nose.*]

OL' CAP'N. Gitlow—Gitlow!

15   GITLOW. Yassuh, Ol' Cap'n—Gitlow is here,
suh; right here!

OL' CAP'N. Quick, ol' friend—my heart. It's
—quick! A few passels,° if you please—of that
ol' spiritual.

20   GITLOW [*sings most tenderly*]. "Gone are the
days, when my heart was young and gay . . . "

OL' CAP'N. I can't tell you, Gitlow—how
much it eases the pain— [GITLOW *and* OL'
CAP'N *sing a phrase together.*] Why can't he
25 see what they're doing to the Southland, Gitlow? Why can't he see it, like you and me? If
there's one responsibility you got, boy, above
all others, I said to him, it's these Negras—your
Negras, boy. Good, honest, hard-working cot-
30 ton choppers. If you keep after 'em.

GITLOW. Yes, Lawd. [*Continues to sing.*]

OL' CAP'N. Something between you and them
no Supreme Court in the world can understand
—and wasn't for me they'd starve to death.
35 What's gonna become of 'em, boy, after I'm
gone—?

GITLOW. Dass a good question, Lawd—you
answer him. [*Continues to sing.*]

OL' CAP'N. They belong to you, boy—to you,
40 evah one of 'em! My ol' Confederate father
told me on his deathbed: feed the Negras first
—after the horses and cattle—and I've done
it evah time! [*By now* OL' CAP'N *is sheltered in*
GITLOW's *arms. The* LIGHTS *begin slowly to*
45 *fade away.* GITLOW *sings a little more.*] Ah,

passels portions ("parcels")

Gitlow ol' friend—something, absolutely sacred
'bout that speritual—I live for the day you'll
sing that thing over my grave.

GITLOW. Me, too, Ol' Cap'n, me, too! [GIT-
LOW's *voice rises to a slow, gentle, yet trium-* 50
phant crescendo, as our LIGHTS *fade away.*]

Blackout

Curtain

ACT II

Scene i

[TIME. *A short while later.*]

[SCENE. *The scene is the same: the little commissary office.*]

[AT RISE. *The Stage is empty. After a moment* 55
GITLOW *hurries in from the commissary proper,
crosses down to the little back door and opens
it.*]

PURLIE [*entering hurriedly*]. What took you
so long? 60

GITLOW. S-sh! Not so loud! He's right out
there in the commissary! [PURLIE *crosses over
and looks out into the commissary, then crosses
back to the little back door and holds out his
hands.* LUTIEBELLE *enters. She is dressed in what* 65
*would be collegiate style. She is still full of awe
and wonder, and—this time—of fear, which
she is struggling to keep under cover.*] Ain't
she gonna carry no school books?

PURLIE. What are they doing out there? 70

GITLOW. The watermelon books don't
balance.

PURLIE. What!

GITLOW. One of our melons is in shortage!

PURLIE. You tell him about Lutiebelle—I 75
mean, about Cousin Bee?

GITLOW. I didn't have time. Besides, I wanted
you to have one more chance to get out of here
alive!

PURLIE. What's the matter with you!? Don't 80
five hundred dollars of your own lawful money
mean nothing to you? Ain't you got no head
for business?

GITLOW. No! The head I got is for safekeep-
ing, and—besides—[PURLIE *lifts* OL' CAP'N's 85

bull whip down from its peg] don't touch that thing, Purlie! [GITLOW *races over, snatches it from him, replaces it, and pats it soothingly into place, while at the same time looking to see*

5 *if OL' CAP'N is coming—and all in one continuous move.*]

PURLIE. Why not? It touched me!

GITLOW [*aghast*]. Man, ain't nothing sacred to you!?

10 OL' CAP'N [*calling from Off in the commissary*]. Gitlow, come in here!

GITLOW [*racing off*]. Coming, Ol' Cap'n, coming!

OL' CAP'N [*Offstage*]. Now! We are going

15 to cross-examine these watermelons one more time—one watermelon—

GITLOW [*Offstage*]. One watermelon!

CHARLIE [*Offstage*]. One watermelon!

OL' CAP'N. Two watermelons—

20 GITLOW. Two watermelons—

CHARLIE. Two watermelons—

[*The sound of the watermelon count-down continues in the background.* PURLIE, *finding he's got a moment, comes over to reassure*

25 LUTIEBELLE.]

PURLIE. Whatever you do, don't panic!

LUTIEBELLE [*repeating after him: almost in hypnotic rote*]. Whatever you do, don't panic!

PURLIE. Just walk like I taught you to walk,

30 and talk like I taught you to talk—

LUTIEBELLE. Taught like I walked you to—

PURLIE [*shaking her shoulders*]. Lutiebelle!

LUTIEBELLE. Yes, Reb'n Purlie!

PURLIE. Wake up!

35 LUTIEBELLE. Oh my goodness, Reb'n Purlie— was I sleep?

PURLIE. Alert!

LUTIEBELLE. Alert!—

PURLIE. Wide awake!—

40 LUTIEBELLE. Wide awake!—

PURLIE. Up on your toes!

LUTIEBELLE [*starting to rise on toes*]. Up on your—

PURLIE. No. No, that's just a figure of speech.

45 Now! You remember what I told you—?

LUTIEBELLE. No, sir. Can't say I do, sir.

PURLIE. Well—first: chit-chat—small-talk!

LUTIEBELLE. Yessir—how small?

PURLIE. Pass the time of day—you remem-

50 ber? The first thing I taught you on the train?

LUTIEBELLE. On the train— Oh! "Delighted to remake your acquaintance, I am sure."

PURLIE. That's it—that's it exactly! Now. Suppose he was to say to you: [PURLIE *imitates*

55 OL' CAP'N.] "I bet you don't remember when you wasn't kneehigh to a grasshopper and Ol' Cap'n took you by the hand, and led you down on your first trip to the cotton patch?"

LUTIEBELLE. Just like you told me on the

60 train?

PURLIE. Yes!

LUTIEBELLE. "I must confess—that much of my past life is vague and hazy."

PURLIE [*imitating*]. Doggone my hide—

65 you're the cutest li'l ol' piece of brown skin sugar I ever did see!

LUTIEBELLE. Oh, thank you, Reb'n Purlie!

PURLIE. I ain't exactly me, saying that—it's Ol' Cap'n. [*Continues imitation.*] And this is

70 my land, and my cotton patch, and my commissary, and my bull whip—still here, just like you left us. And what might be your name, li'l gal?

LUTIEBELLE [*warming to the game*]. Beatrice

75 Judson, sir.

PURLIE. And what is your daddy's name, li'l gal?

LUTIEBELLE. Horace Judson, sir.

PURLIE. And what did they teach you up in

80 that college, li'l gal?

LUTIEBELLE. It was my major education, Ol' Cap'n—

PURLIE. You mean you majored in education. [*Resumes imitation.*] Well—nothing wrong

85 with Negras getting an education, I always say — But then again, ain't nothing right with it, either. Cousin Bee—heh, heh, heh—you don't mind if I call you Cousin Bee, do you, honey?

LUTIEBELLE. Oh, sir, I'd be delighted!

90 PURLIE. Don't! Don't be delighted until he puts the money in your hands. [*Resumes imitation.*] And where did you say your Maw worked at?

LUTIEBELLE. In North Carolina.

PURLIE. Where is your maw at now?

LUTIEBELLE. She's at the cemetery: she died.

PURLIE. And how much is the inheritance?

LUTIEBELLE. Five hundred dollars for the next
5 of kin.

PURLIE [delighted at her progress]. Wonderful, just—just—wonderful! [Enjoying his own
imitation now.] [OL' CAP'N enters from the
commissary, followed by GITLOW. LUTIEBELLE
10 sees OL' CAP'N, but PURLIE is so wrapped up
in his own performance he does not.] Say, maybe you could teach a old dog like me some new
tricks. [He tries to get a rise out of LUTIEBELLE
but she is frozen in terror. OL' CAP'N becomes
15 aware of PURLIE's presence, and approaches.]
By swickery—a gal like you could doggone
well change a joker's luck° if she had a mind
to—see what I mean? [PURLIE hunches what he
expects to be an invisible GITLOW in the ribs.
20 His blow lands upon OL' CAP'N with such force,
he falls into a pile of sacks of chicken feed.]

OL' CAP'N [sputtering]. What! What in the
name of— [GITLOW and PURLIE scramble to
help him to his feet.]
25 PURLIE. My compliments, sir—are only exceeded by my humblest apologies. And allow
me, if you please, to present my Aunt Henrietta's daughter, whom you remember so well;
Beatrice Judson—or as we call her—Cousin
30 Bee.

OL' CAP'N [he is so taken by what he sees
he forgets his anger]. Well I'll be switched!

PURLIE. Come, Cousin Bee. Say "howdo" to
the man.
35 LUTIEBELLE. How do to the man. I mean—
[Takes time to correct herself, then.] Delighted
to remake your acquaintance, I'm sure.

OL' CAP'N. What's that? What's that she's
saying?
40 PURLIE. College, sir.

OL' CAP'N. College?

PURLIE. That's all she ever talks.

OL' CAP'N. You mean Henrietta's little ol'

could . . . change . . . luck i.e., might well be sought
out for intimacies: in gamblers' superstition, intercourse with a black woman restores good luck

button-eyed pickaninny was in college? Well
bust my eyes wide open! Just LOOK at that! 45
[Gets closer, but she edges away.] You remember me, honey. I'm still the Ol' Cap'n round
here.

LUTIEBELLE. Oh, sir, it would not be the same
without you being the Ol' Cap'n around here. 50

OL' CAP'N. You don't say! Say, I'll bet you
don't remember a long time ago when—

LUTIEBELLE. When I wasn't but knee high to
a hoppergrass, and you took me by the hand,
and led me on my very first trip to the cotton 55
patch.

OL' CAP'N [ecstatic]. You mean you remember that!

LUTIEBELLE. Alert, wide awake, and up on my
toes—if you please, sir! [Rises up on her toes.] 60

OL' CAP'N [moving in]. Doggone my hide.
You're the cutest li'l ol' piece of brown sugar
I ever did see—

LUTIEBELLE [escaping]. And this is your land,
and your cotton patch, and your commissary, 65
and your bull whip—

OL' CAP'N. What's that?

LUTIEBELLE. Just a figure of speech or two—

OL' CAP'N. Well, Beatrice—you wouldn't
mind if Ol' Cap'n was to call you Cousin Bee? 70

LUTIEBELLE. Oh, positively not, not!—since
my mother's name was Henrietta Judson; my
father's name was Horace Judson—

OL' CAP'N. But most of all, I remember that
little ol' dog of yours—"Spicey," wasn't it? 75

LUTIEBELLE. Oh, we wasn't much for eating
dogs, sir—

OL' CAP'N. No, no! Spicey was the name—
wasn't it?

[LUTIEBELLE looking to PURLIE for help, but 80
PURLIE cannot help. He looks to GITLOW, who
also cannot remember.]

LUTIEBELLE. You, er, really think we really
called him "Spicey"?

OL' CAP'N. Not him—her! 85

PURLIE. HER!

LUTIEBELLE. Oh, her! Her! I am most happy
to recollect that I do.

OL' CAP'N. You do! You don't say you do!

LUTIEBELLE. I did, as I recall it, have a fond 90

remembrance of you and "Spicey," since you-all went so well together—and at the same time!

OL' CAP'N. You do? Well hush my mouth, eh, Git?

GITLOW. Hush your mouth indeed, sir.

LUTIEBELLE. Co'se,° soon it is my sworn and true confession that I disremembers so many things out of my early pastime that mostly you are haze and vaguey!

OL' CAP'N. Oh, am I now!

LUTIEBELLE. Oh, yes, and sir—indeedy.

OL' CAP'N. Doggone my hide, eh, Git?

GITLOW. Doggone your hide indeed, suh.

LUTIEBELLE. You see of coursely I have spount—

PURLIE. Spent—

LUTIEBELLE. Spunt so much of my time among the college that hardly all of my ancient maidenhead—

PURLIE. Hood.

LUTIEBELLE. Is a thing of the past!

OL' CAP'N. You don't say!

LUTIEBELLE. But yes, and most precisely.

OL' CAP'N. Tell me, Li'l Bee—what did they teach you up at that college?

LUTIEBELLE. Well, mostly they taught me an education, but in between I learned a lot, too.

OL' CAP'N. Is that a fact?

LUTIEBELLE. Reading, writing, 'rithmetic—oh, my Lord—just sitting out on the rectangular every evening after four o' clock home work and you have your regular headache—

OL' CAP'N. You know something, I been after these Negras down here for years: Go to school, I'd say, first chance you get—take a coupla courses in advanced cotton picking. But you think they'd listen to me? No sireebob. By swickety! A gal like you could doggone well change a joker's luck if she was a mind to. [*Gives* GITLOW *a broad wink and digs him in his ribs.* GITLOW *almost falls.*] See what I mean?

LUTIEBELLE. Oh, most indo I deed.

OL' CAP'N. Look—anything! Ask me anything! Whatever you want—name it and it's

Co'se of course

yours!

LUTIEBELLE. You mean—really, really, really?

OL' CAP'N. Ain't a man in Cotchipee County can beat my time when I see something I want —name it! [*Indicates with a sweep the contents of the commissary.*] Some roasted peanuts; a bottle of soda water; a piece of pepmint candy?

LUTIEBELLE. Thank you, sir, but if it's all the same to you I'd rather have my money.

OL' CAP'N [*as if shot*]. Your WHAT!

LUTIEBELLE [*frightened but determined to forge ahead under her own steam*]. Now I'm gonna tell you like it was, Your Honor: You see, Reb'n Purlie and Uncle Gitlow has one aunty between them, name of Harrietta—

PURLIE. Henrietta!

LUTIEBELLE. Henrietta—who used to cook for this rich ol' white lady up in North Carolina years ago; and last year this ol' lady died—brain tumor—

PURLIE. Bright's disease!

LUTIEBELLE. Bright's disease—leaving five hundred dollars to every servant who had ever worked on her place, including Henrietta. But Henrietta had already died, herself: largely from smallpox—

PURLIE. No!

LUTIEBELLE. Smally from large pox?

PURLIE. Influenza!

LUTIEBELLE. Influenza—and since Henrietta's husband Harris—

PURLIE. Horace!

LUTIEBELLE. Horace—was already dead from heart trouble—

PURLIE. Gunshot wounds!—

LUTIEBELLE [*exploding*]. His heart stopped beating, didn't it?!

PURLIE. Yes, but—

LUTIEBELLE. Precisely, Reb'n Purlie, precisely! [*Turning back to* OL' CAP'N.] Since, therefore and where-in-as Cousin Bee, her daughter, was first-in-line-for-next-of-kinfolks, the five hundred dollars left in your care and keep by Aunt Henrietta, and which you have been saving just for me all these lonesome years—

OL' CAP'N. I ain't been saving no damn sucha thing!

PURLIE [*stepping swiftly into the breach*]. Oh, come out from behind your modesty, sir!

OL' CAP'N. What!

5 PURLIE. Your kindness, sir; your thoughtfulness, sir; your unflagging consideration for the welfare of your darkies, sir: have rung like the clean clear call of the clarion from Maine to Mexico. Your constant love for them is both hallmark and high water of the true gentility 10 of the dear old South.

OL' CAP'N. Gitlow, Gitlow—go get Charlie, I want him to hear this. [GITLOW *exits Upstage Center.*] Go on, boy, go on!

PURLIE. And as for your faithful ol' darkies 15 themselves, sir—why, down in the quarters, sir, your name stands second only to God Himself Almighty.

OL' CAP'N. You don't mean to tell me!

PURLIE. Therefore, as a humble token of their 20 high esteem and their deep and abiding affection, especially for saving that five hundred dollar inheritance for Cousin Bee, they have asked me to present to you . . . this plaque! [PURLIE *unveils a "sheepskin scroll" from his in-* 25 *side coat pocket.* OL' CAP'N *reaches for it, but* PURLIE *draws it away.* CHARLIE *appears in the doorway Upstage Center followed by* GITLOW.] Which bears the following citation to wit, and I quote: "Whereas Ol' Cap'n has kindly allow- 30 ed us to remain on his land, and pick his cotton, and tend his cattle, and drive his mules, and whereas Ol' Cap'n still lets us have our hominy grits and fat back on credit and whereas Ol' Cap'n never resorts to bull whip except as a 35 blessing and a benediction, therefore be it resolved, that Ol' Cap'n Cotchipee be cited as the best friend the Negro has ever had, and officially proclaimed Great White Father of the Year!"

40 OL' CAP'N [*stunned*]. I can't believe it—I can't believe it! [*Sees* CHARLIE.] Charlie, boy—did you hear it? Did you hear it, Charlie, my boy—GREAT WHITE FATHER OF THE YEAR!

45 PURLIE [*like a professional undertaker*]. Let me be the first to congratulate you, sir. [*They shake hands solemnly.*]

OL' CAP'N. Thank you, Purlie.

LUTIEBELLE. And me. [*They shake hands solemnly.*] 50

OL' CAP'N. Thank you, Cousin Bee.

GITLOW. And me, too, Ol' Cap'n.

OL' CAP'N [*on the verge of tears, as they shake hands*]. Gitlow—Gitlow. I know this is some of your doings—my old friend. [*He turns* 55 *expectantly to* CHARLIE.] Well, boy—[CHARLIE *is trapped*] ain't you gonna congratulate your father?

CHARLIE. Yessir. [*Shakes his hand.*]

OL' CAP'N. This—is the happiest day of my 60 life. My darkies—my Negras—my own—[*Chokes up; unable to continue.*]

PURLIE. Hear, hear!

GITLOW AND LUTIEBELLE. Hear, hear!

[CHARLIE *tries to sneak off again, but* OL' 65 CAP'N *sees him.*]

OL' CAP'N. I am just too overcome to talk. Come back here, boy. [CHARLIE *comes back and stands in intense discomfort.*] Silent—speechless—dumb, my friends. Never in all the 70 glorious, hoary and ancient annals of all Dixie—never before— [*Chokes up with tears; blows nose with big red handkerchief, and pulls himself together.*] My friends, in the holy scripture—and I could cite you chapter and verse if I 75 was a mind to— "In the beginning God created white folks and He created black folks," and in the name of all that's white and holy, let's keep it that way. And to hell with Abraham Lincoln and Martin Luther King! 80

PURLIE. I am moved, Ol' Cap'n—

GITLOW AND LUTIEBELLE. Uhn!

PURLIE. Moved beyond my jurisdiction; as for example, I have upon my person a certificate of legal tender duly affixed and so nota- 85 rized to said itemized effect—[*hands over an official-looking document*] a writ of Habeas Corpus.

OL' CAP'N [*taking the document*]. Habeas who? 90

PURLIE. Habeas Corpus. It means I can have the body.

OL' CAP'N. Body—what body?

PURLIE. The body of the cash—the five hundred dollars—that they sent you to hold 95 in trust for Cousin Bee.

OL' CAP'N [*pauses to study the eager faces in the room; then*]. Charlie—

CHARLIE. Yessir.

OL' CAP'N. Bring me—five hundred dollars —will you? [CHARLIE *starts for safe.*] No, no, no—not that old stuff. Fresh money, clean money out of my private stock out back. Nothin's too good for my Negras.

CHARLIE. Yessir—yessir! [*Starts out, stops.*] And Paw?

OL' CAP'N. Yes, son?

CHARLIE. All I got to say is "Yessir!" [*Crosses to cash register.*]

OL' CAP'N. Just wait—wait till I tell the Senator: "Great White Father of the Year."

CHARLIE [*returns with roll of bills which he hands to his father*]. Here you are, Paw.

OL' CAP'N. Thank you, boy.

[*Enter* IDELLA, *followed by the* SHERIFF *and the* DEPUTY.]

IDELLA. Here everybody is, back in the office.

OL' CAP'N [*overjoyed to see them*]. Just in time, Sheriff, for the greatest day of my life. Gentlemen—something has happened here today, between me and my Negras, makes me proud to call myself a Confederate: I have just been named Great White Father of the Year. [*To* PURLIE.] Right?

PURLIE. Right. And now if you'll just —

SHERIFF AND DEPUTY. Great White Father of the Year! Congratulations! [*They shake his hands warmly.*]

OL' CAP'N. True, there are places in this world where the darky is rebellious, running hog wild, rising up and sitting down where he ain't wanted, acting sassy in jail, getting plumb out of hand, totally forgetting his place and his manners—but not in Cotchipee County! [*To* PURLIE.] Right?

PURLIE. Right! And now perhaps we could get back to the business at hand.

OL' CAP'N [*finishing his count*]. All right— five hundred dollars. [PURLIE *impulsively reaches for the money, but* OL' CAP'N *snatches it back.*] Just a moment. There's still one small formality: a receipt.

PURLIE. A receipt? All right, I'll—

OL' CAP'N. Not you—You! [*Thrusts a printed form toward* LUTIEBELLE.] . . . just for the record. [*Offers her a fountain pen.*] Sign here. Your full and legal name—right here on the dotted line.

PURLIE [*reaching for the pen*]. I'll do it—I have her power of attorney.

LUTIEBELLE [*beating* PURLIE *to the pen*]. It's all right, Reb'n Purlie, I can write. [*Takes pen and signs paper with a flourish.*]

OL' CAP'N [*takes up paper and reads the signature*]. Sheriff, I want this woman arrested!

PURLIE. Arrested?! For what?

OL' CAP'N. She came into my presence, together with him—[*indicates* PURLIE] and with him—[*indicates* GITLOW]. And they all swore to me that she is Beatrice Judson.

PURLIE. She IS Beatrice Judson!

OL' CAP'N [*pouncing*]. Then how come she to sign her name: Lutiebelle Gussiemae Jenkins!

PURLIE. Uhn-uhn!

GITLOW. Uhn-uhn!

LUTIEBELLE. Uhn-uhn!

GITLOW [*starting off suddenly*]. Is somebody calling my name out there—

OL' CAP'N. Come back here, Gitlow— [GITLOW *halts in his tracks.*] You'll go out of that door when the Sheriff takes you out. And that goes for all of you. [*The* SHERIFF *starts forward.*] Just a minute, Sheriff. Before you take 'em away there's something I've got to do. [*Crosses to where the whip is hung.*]

GITLOW [*horrified at the thought of the whip*]. I'll make it up to you in cotton, Ol' Cap'n—

OL' CAP'N. Shut up, Gitlow. [*Takes whip down, and starts to uncoil it.*] Something I started twenty years ago with this bull whip— [*Fastening his eyes on* PURLIE.] Something I intend to finish.

GITLOW [*drops to his knees and begins to sing*]. "Gone are the days—"

OL' CAP'N [*turning to* GITLOW]. Dammit! I told you to shut up! [*Then back to* PURLIE.] I'm gonna teach you to try to make a damn fool outta white folks; all right, boy, drop them britches.

PURLIE. The hell you preach!

OL' CAP'N. What's that you said?

LUTIEBELLE. He said, 'The hell you preach!''

CHARLIE. Paw, wait, listen—!

OL' CAP'N. I thought I told you to shut up!
5 [*Back to* PURLIE.] Boy, I'm gonna teach you to mind what I say!

[PURLIE *doesn't move.* OL' CAP'N *takes a vicious cut at him with the bull whip, and* PURLIE, *leaping back to get out of the way, falls*
10 *into the arms of the* SHERIFF.]

SHERIFF. I distinctly heard that gentleman order you to drop your britches. [*Spins* PURLIE *around, sets him up, and swings with all his might.* PURLIE *easily ducks and dances away.*]

15 DEPUTY. Save a little taste for me, Sheriff!

[*The* SHERIFF *swings again; and again,* PUR-LIE *dances away. He swings still again, but to no avail.*]

SHERIFF [*aggravated*]. Hold still, dammit!
20 [*Swings again, and once more* PURLIE *ducks away.*] Confound it, boy! You trying to make me hurt myself?

DEPUTY. What's the matter, Sheriff—can't you find him?! [*Laughs.*]

25 SHERIFF [*desperate*]. Now, you listen to me, boy! Either you stand up like a man, so I can knock you down, or—

LUTIEBELLE [*stepping between the* SHERIFF *and* PURLIE]. Don't you dare!

30 SHERIFF. What!

LUTIEBELLE. Insultin' Reb'n Purlie, and him a man of the cloth! [*Grabs his gun arm and bites it.*]

SHERIFF. Owwww! [*She kicks him in the*
35 *shin.*] Owwwwwww!

[*The* DEPUTY *charges in to the rescue. He attempts to grab* LUTIEBELLE, *but she eludes him and steps down hard on his corns.*]

DEPUTY. Owwwwwwwwww!

40 PURLIE [*going for the* DEPUTY]. Keep your hands off her, you hypothetical baboon, keep your hands OFF her! [*Grabs the* DEPUTY, *spins him around and knocks him across the room; starts to follow, but the* SHERIFF *grabs him and*
45 *pins his arms behind him.*]

CHARLIE [*breaks loose from* IDELLA, *snatching at the* SHERIFF]. You let him go, dammit, let him go! [*With one arm the* SHERIFF *pushes* CHARLIE *away.*]

SHERIFF [*still holding* PURLIE'S *arms pinned* 50 *back*]. All right, Dep, he's all yours. Throw him your fast ball—high, tight and inside!

DEPUTY. Glad to oblige you, Sheriff! [*He draws back like a big league baseball pitcher.*]

CHARLIE [*rushing into the breach*]. Stop! 55 Stop—stop in the name of the— [*The* DEPUTY *swings from the floor,* PURLIE *ducks and rolls his head sharply to one side.* CHARLIE *runs full into the force of the blow. Collapsing heavily.*] Idella—aaaaaaa! 60

OL' CAP'N [*rushing to him*]. Charlie—!

IDELLA. Charlie—!

[PURLIE, *taking advantage of the confusion, snatches* LUTIEBELLE *by the arms and dashes with her out the back door.*] 65

OL' CAP'N. After them, you idiots, after them!

SHERIFF [*to the* DEPUTY]. After them, you idiot! [*They both run off after* PURLIE *and* LUTIEBELLE.] 70

[OL' CAP'N *and* IDELLA *are kneeling beside the prostrate* CHARLIE. GITLOW, *after a moment, comes into the picture.*]

OL' CAP'N. His eyes, Idella, his eyes! Where are his eyes? 75

IDELLA. Gitlow, fetch me the asaphoetida, Ol' Cap'n, you rub his hands.

GITLOW. Yes'm.

IDELLA [*slapping his face*]. Charlie, honey, wake up—wake up! It's me, Idella. 80

[OL' CAP'N *is too disorganized to be of any assistance.* GITLOW *has returned with a bottle which he hands to* IDELLA. *He then kneels and starts rubbing* CHARLIE'S *hands.*]

GITLOW. Mr. Charlie, wake up— 85

[*With* GITLOW *and* IDELLA'S *help,* CHARLIE *slowly rises to his feet. Still unsteady, his eyes glazed and vacant.*]

OL' CAP'N [*snapping his fingers in front of his eyes*]. It's me, Charlie, me— It's your 90 daddy, boy! Speak to me—talk to me—say something to me!

CHARLIE [*snaps suddenly into speech—but still out on his feet*]. Fourscore and seven years ago, our fathers brought forth— 95

OL' CAP'N. Shut up!

Curtain

Scene ii

[TIME. *Two days later.*]

[SCENE. *Back at the shack, outside in the yard area.*]

[AT RISE. MISSY *is discovered, busy working on some potted plants. She is preoccupied, but we feel some restlessness, some anticipation in the manner in which she works.* PURLIE *enters.*]

PURLIE [*the great prophet intones his sorrows*]. Toll the bell—Big Bethel; toll the big, black, ex-liberty bell; tell Freedom there's death in the family.

MISSY. Purlie—

PURLIE. All these wings and they still won't let me fly!

MISSY. Where you been these last two days, Purlie? We been lookin' for you. All this plotting and planning—risking your dad-blasted neck like a crazy man! And for what—FOR WHAT! [IDELLA *enters.*] Oh, come in, Miz Idella.

IDELLA. Is anybody here seen Charlie Cotchipee this morning?

MISSY. No, we haven't.

PURLIE. Is something wrong, Miz Idella?

IDELLA. He left home this morning right after breakfast—here it is after lunch and I ain't seen him since. I can't find Charlie—first time in forty-five years I been working up there in that house I ever misplaced anything! You don't suppose he'd run away from home and not take me—?

MISSY. Oh, no, Miz Idella! Not li'l Charlie Cotchipee.

IDELLA. Well, I guess I'd better be getting back. If you should see him—

MISSY. Miz Idella, we all want to thank you for keeping Purlie out of jail so kindly. [*Hands her flowers.*]

IDELLA. Oh, that was nothing; I just told that ol' man if he didn't stop all that foolishness about chain gangs and stuff, I would resign from his kitchen and take Charlie right along with me! But now I've lost Charlie. First time in forty-five years I ever misplaced anything! [*She exits.*]

MISSY [*turns to* PURLIE]. Don't you know there's something more important in this world than having that broken down ol' ex-church of a barn to preach in?

PURLIE. Yeah—like what?

MISSY. Like asking Lutiebelle to marry you.

PURLIE. Asking Lutiebelle to marry me?

MISSY. She worships the ground you walk on. Talks about you all the time. You two could get married, settle down, like you ought to, and raise the cutest little ol' family you ever did see. And she's a cookin', po' child—she left you some of her special fritters.

PURLIE. Freedom, Missy, not fritters. The crying need of this Negro day and age is not grits, but greatness; not cornbread but courage; not fat-back, but fight-back; Big Bethel is my Bethel; it belongs to me and to my people; and I intend to have it back if I have to pay for it in blood!

MISSY. All right—come on in and I'll fix you some dinner.

GITLOW [*enters front door, singing*]. "I'm comin', I'm comin'—"

MISSY [*entering house*]. Not so loud, Gitlow. You want to wake up the mule?

GITLOW. Not on his day off. "For my head is bendin' low—" [GITLOW *sits, unfolds comic section and reads.*]

MISSY. Where's Lutiebelle, Gitlow?

GITLOW. "The history of the War Between the States will be continued next week." That sure is a good story—I wonder how that's gonna come out?

MISSY. Grown man, deacon in the church, reading the funny-paper. And your shirt. You sneaked outta here this morning in your clean white shirt, after I told you time and time again I was saving it!

GITLOW. Saving it for what?

MISSY. It's the only decent thing you got to get buried in! [*Exits side door.*]

GITLOW. Don't you know that arrangements for my funeral has been taken over by the white folks? [*To* PURLIE.] Besides, I got the money!

PURLIE. What kinda money?

GITLOW. The five hundred dollar kinda money.

PURLIE. Five hundred dollars! You mean Ol' Cap'n give the money to you?

GITLOW. "Gitlow," he said "Ain't another man in this valley, black, white, or otherwise, I would trust to defend and protect me from the N double ACP but you."

5 PURLIE. Is that a fact?

GITLOW. Well, now. Whatever become of you? All them gretgawdamighty plans your mouth runneth over—all that white folks' psychology?

10 PURLIE. Gitlow! Er, Deacon Gitlow—Big Bethel is waiting!

GITLOW. So you're the good-for-nothing, raggedy ass high falute 'round here that goes for who-tied-the-bear!

15 PURLIE. Naw, Git, man—ain't nothing to me.

GITLOW. Always so high and mighty—can't nobody on earth handle white folks but you—don't pay no 'tention to Gitlow; naw—he's a Tom. Tease him—low-rate him—laugh at ol'

20 Gitlow; he ain't nothing but a fool!

PURLIE. Aw, Git, man, you got me wrong. I didn't mean nothing like that!

GITLOW. Who's the fool now, my boy—who's the fool now?

25 PURLIE. Er—I'm the fool, Gitlow.

GITLOW. Aw, man, you can talk plainer than that.

PURLIE. I'm the fool, Gitlow.

GITLOW. Uh-huh! Now go over to that win-

30 dow, open it wide as it will go and say it so everybody in this whole damn valley can hear you! Go on! Go on, man—I ain't got all day!

PURLIE [goes to window]. I'm the fool, Git-

35 low!

GITLOW. Nice. Now beg me!

PURLIE. What!

GITLOW. I said if you want to see the money, beg me! Do it like you do white folks.

40 PURLIE. I'd rather die and go to hell in a pair gasoline drawers— [GITLOW starts to put money away.] No, wait. Holy mackerel, dere, Massa Gitlow—hee, hee, hee. Hey! Boss, could I possible have a look at that there five hun-

45 dred dollars dere, suh? Hyuh, hyuh, hyuh!

GITLOW. Man, you sure got style! You know together you and me could make the big time! [PURLIE reaches for money.] Come in and see

me during office hours! As Deputy-For-The-Colored, I guess I'll just sort of step outside 50 for a minute and let that low September sun shine down on a joker as rich as he is black!

PURLIE. Gitlow—Gitlow! [GITLOW starts for side door.] If slavery ever comes back I want to be your agent! 55

GITLOW. Now that was a snaggy-toothed, poverty-struck remark if I ever heard one.

MISSY [enters side door]. Youall wash your hands and git ready—Gitlow! Where's Lutie-belle? 60

GITLOW [evasive]. She didn't get back yet.

MISSY. We know she didn't get back yet.

PURLIE. Where is Lutiebelle, Gitlow?

GITLOW. What I mean is—on our way home from church, we stopped by Ol' Cap'n's awhile, 65 and he asked me to leave her there to help with the Sunday dinner.

PURLIE. And you left her!

MISSY. With that frisky ol' man?

GITLOW. For goodness' sakes, she's only 70 waiting on table.

PURLIE. The woman I love don't wait on table for nobody, especially Ol' Cap'n; I know that scoun'. I'm going and get her!

GITLOW. Wait a minute—you can't get her 75 right now!

PURLIE [studying him]. What you mean, I can't get her right now?

GITLOW. Not right this minute—that'll spoil everything. Ol' Cap'n wouldn't like it. 80

MISSY. How low can you git, Gitlow!

GITLOW. I mean she's got to stay and bring us the five hundred dollars.

MISSY. What five hundred dollars?

PURLIE. I thought you already had the 85 money?

GITLOW. Well, not exactly. But he promised me faithful to send it down by Lutiebelle.

PURLIE. I'm going and get Lutiebelle—

GITLOW. Wait a minute, wait a minute; you 90 want to buy Big Bethel back or don't you?

PURLIE [a glimmering of truth]. I hope I mis-understand you!

GITLOW. You said it yourself: It is meet that the daughters of Zion should sacrifice them- 95 selves for the cause.

PURLIE [*grabbing up* MISSY'S *bat*]. Gitlow, I'll kill you—!

GITLOW. Wait a minute, wait a minute, wait a MINUTE!

5 [*The door opens suddenly, and there stands* LUTIEBELLE. *She, too, has on her Sunday best, but it is disheveled. She has a work apron over her dress, with her hat completely askew, the once proud feather now hanging over her face.* 10 *In her hands she still clutches a rolling pin.*]

MISSY. Lutiebelle—Lutiebelle, honey!

LUTIEBELLE. I think I am going to faint. [*She starts to collapse, and they rush toward her to help; but suddenly she straightens up and* 15 *waves them off.*] No, I ain't, either—I'm too mad! [*She shudders in recollection.*] I was never so insulted in all my dad-blamed life!

PURLIE. Lutiebelle!

LUTIEBELLE. Oh, excuse me, Reb'n Purlie—I 20 know I look a mess, but—

MISSY. What happened up there?

LUTIEBELLE [*boiling again*]. I'm a maid first class, Aunt Missy, and I'm proud of it!

MISSY. Of course you are.

25 LUTIEBELLE. I ain't had no complaints to speak of since first I stepped into the white folks' kitchen. I'm clean; I'm honest, and I work hard —but one thing: I don't stand for no stuff from them white folks.

30 PURLIE. Of course you don't. You don't have to—

LUTIEBELLE. I mean, I KNOW my job, and I DO my job—and the next ol' sweaty, ol' grimey, ol' drunkeny man puts his hands on 35 me—so much as touch like he got no business doing—God grant me strength to kill him! Excuse me, Reb'n Purlie.

GITLOW. Well, Ol' Cap'n do get playful at times. Did he send the money?

40 LUTIEBELLE. Money! What money? There ain't none!

GITLOW. What! Naw, naw! He wouldn't do that to me—not to good ol', faithful ol' Gitlow, nawsir!

45 LUTIEBELLE. The whole thing was a trick— to get you out of the house—

GITLOW. Not to ME he didn't!

LUTIEBELLE. So he could—sneak up behind me in the pantry!

MISSY. What I tell you!—what I tell you! 50

LUTIEBELLE. I knowed the minute I—Come grabbing on me, Reb'n Purlie; come grabbing his dirty ol' hands on me!

PURLIE. He did!

LUTIEBELLE. And twisting me around, and— 55 and pinching me, Reb'n Purlie!

PURLIE. Pinching you—where? Where?

LUTIEBELLE. Must I, Reb'n Purlie—?

PURLIE. I demand to know—where did he pinch you! 60

[LUTIEBELLE *diffidently locates a spot on her left cheek. They all examine it anxiously.*]

MISSY. That's him all right!

GITLOW. Aw, Missy—

MISSY. I'd know them fingerprints anywhere! 65

LUTIEBELLE. Right in the pantry—and then he, he— Oh, Reb'n Purlie, I'm so ashamed!

PURLIE. What did he do? Tell me, woman, tell me: what did he do? WHAT DID HE DO?

LUTIEBELLE. He kissed me! 70

PURLIE AND MISSY. No!

LUTIEBELLE. He kissed me—right here.

MISSY [*squinting, it is a very small spot indeed*]. Right where? [LUTIEBELLE *is so broken up, she can only point to her other cheek.*] 75

GITLOW. Aw, for Pete's sakes.

PURLIE [*almost out of control*]. He kissed my woman, Gitlow—he kissed the woman I love!

GITLOW. So what!

PURLIE. So what do you mean, "So what"? 80 No man kisses the woman I love and lives! [GITLOW *laughs.*] Go ahead, laugh! Laugh. Let's have one last look at your teeth before I knock 'em down your throat!

GITLOW. Aw, man, git off my nerves. 85

PURLIE. I'm going up that hill, and I'm gonna call that buzzardly ol' bastard out, and I wouldn't be surprised if I didn't beat him until he died.

LUTIEBELLE [*suddenly not so sure*]. Reb'n 90 Purlie—

GITLOW [*also wondering about* PURLIE]. Now looka here, Purlie—don't you be no fool, boy —you still in Georgia. If you just got to defend the honor of the woman you love, do it some- 95 where else.

PURLIE. Kissing my woman—kissing my woman! [*Runs to window, flings it open and shouts out.*] Man, I'll break your neck off!

LUTIEBELLE [*helping* GITLOW *and* MISSY *to*
5 *wrestle* PURLIE *away from the window*]. Please, Reb'n Purlie!

PURLIE [*breaks away and goes to window and shouts again*]. I'll stomp your eyeballs in!

LUTIEBELLE [*they snatch him from the win-*
10 *dow again*]. Don't, Reb'n Purlie—oh my goodness!—

PURLIE [*breaks away still again and shouts from window*]. I'll snatch your right arm outta the socket, and beat the rest of you to death!

15 LUTIEBELLE [*this time they get him away, and close the window*]. Don't talk like that, Rebn' Purlie!

MISSY [*standing at the window, arms wide-spread to block him*]. Have you gone crazy?

20 GITLOW [*still struggling with* PURLIE]. You go up that hill tonight, boy, and they'll kill you!

PURLIE. Let 'em kill me, it won't be the first time.

LUTIEBELLE. Aunt Missy, stop him—

25 GITLOW. Listen, boy! This is your Deputy-For-The-Colored telling you you ain't gonna leave this house, and that's an order!

PURLIE. You try and stop me!

GITLOW. Good gracious a life, what's the
30 matter with you? The man only kissed your woman.

PURLIE. Yeah! And what you suppose he'd a done to me if I'd a kissed his? [*The one question too obvious to answer.*] And that's
35 exactly what I'm gonna do to him!

LUTIEBELLE. Please, Reb'n Purlie. I beg you on bended knees. [*She throws her arms around him.*]

PURLIE [*holds her close*]. For the glory and
40 honor of the Negro National Anthem; for the glory and honor of brown-skin Negro woman-hood; for the glory and honor of—[LUTIEBELLE *suddenly kisses him big and hard*]—for LUTIE-BELLE! [*His emotions explode him out of the*
45 *door which slams shut behind him.*]

GITLOW [*singing*]. "I hear them gentle blood-hounds callin'—Old Black Joe." . . .

[LUTIEBELLE *finds the deepest spot in* MISSY's *shoulder to bury her head and cry, as:*]

Curtain

ACT III

Scene i

[SCENE. *The shack.*]
[TIME. *Later that same night.*]
[AT RISE. *There is light only from a KERO-* 50
SENE LAMP turned down low. The air of Sunday is gone from the room. The tablecloth has been changed, and things are as they were before. LUTIEBELLE *enters Down Right.*]

LUTIEBELLE. Is it him, Aunt Missy, is it him? 55
MISSY. No, honey, not yet.

LUTIEBELLE. Oh, I could have sworn I thought it was him. What time is it?

MISSY. About four in the morning from the sound of the birds. Now, why ain't you sleep 60 after all that hot toddy I give you?

LUTIEBELLE. I can't sleep. The strangest thing. I keep hearing bells—

MISSY. Bells?

LUTIEBELLE. Wedding bells. Ain't that funny? 65 Oh, Lord, please don't let him be hurt bad, please! Where can he be, Aunt Missy?

MISSY. Now don't you worry 'bout Purlie. My! You put on your pretty pink dress!

LUTIEBELLE. Yes, ma'am. It's the only thing 70 I got fitting to propose in.

MISSY. Oh?

LUTIEBELLE. I thought, to sort of show my gratitude, I'd offer him my hand in matrimony—it's all I've got. 75

MISSY. It's a nice hand, and a nice dress—just right for matrimony.

LUTIEBELLE. You really think so, Aunt Missy: really, really, really?

MISSY. I know so, and wherever Reb'n Purlie 80 is this morning, you can bet your bottom dollar he knows it, too.

LUTIEBELLE. Ten thousand Queens of Sheba! Aunt Missy—

MISSY. Yes— 85

LUTIEBELLE [*letting it out in a gush*]. I wanted him to get mad; I wanted him to tear out up that hill; I wanted him to punch that sweaty ol' buzzard in his gizzard— You think I was wrong?

MISSY. I should say not!

LUTIEBELLE. Course I coulda punched him myself, I reckon.

MISSY. Why should you? Why shouldn't our men folks defend our honor with the white folks once in a while? They ain't got nothing else to do.

LUTIEBELLE. You really, really, really think so?

MISSY [*shrugs*]. Ten thousand Queens of Sheba—

LUTIEBELLE. Oh, my goodness, when he walks through that door, I'm just gonna—

[*Door Down Left suddenly swings open to reveal* GITLOW.]

GITLOW [*entering*]. Well, well, Lutiebelle.

LUTIEBELLE. Did you find him, Uncle Git?

MISSY. Don't depend on Gitlow for nothing, honey— [*Exits to kitchen.*]

LUTIEBELLE. Where can he be, Uncle Gitlow, where can he be?

GITLOW. Oh—good wind like this on his tail oughta put him somewhere above Macon long 'bout now, if his shoes hold out!

LUTIEBELLE. You mean—running!

GITLOW. What's wrong with running? It emancipated more people than Abe Lincoln ever did.

LUTIEBELLE. How dare you! The finest, bravest man—

GITLOW. The finer they come, the braver they be, the deader these white folks gonna kill 'em when they catch 'em!

MISSY [*entering from the kitchen*]. Gitlow, I'll skin you!

GITLOW. All that talk about calling that man out, and whipping him—

MISSY. The man is duty-bound to defend the honor of the woman he loves, and any woman worth her salt will tell you so.

LUTIEBELLE. Love can make you do things you really can't do—can't it, Aunt Missy?

GITLOW. Look. That man's got the president, the governor, the courthouse, and both houses of the Congress—on his side!

MISSY. Purlie Judson is a man the Negro woman can depend on!

LUTIEBELLE. An honor to his race, and a credit to his people!

GITLOW [*not to be sidetracked*]. The army, the navy, the marines; the sheriff, the judge, the jury, the police, the F.B.I.—all on his side. Not to mention a pair of brass knucks and the hungriest dogs this side of hell! Surely youall don't expect that po' boy to go up against all that caucasiatic° power empty-handed!

MISSY. O, ye of little faith!

LUTIEBELLE. Didn't my Lord deliver Daniel?

GITLOW. Of course he did—but lions is one thing and white folks is another!

MISSY. Where there's a will there's a woman—

LUTIEBELLE. And where there's a woman there's a way!

GITLOW [*exasperated*]. Great Gawdamighty! All right—go ahead and have it your way. But I'll lay you six bits 'gainst half my seat on the heavenly choir, Purlie ain't been up that hill. And the minute he walks in that door—if he ever shows up again around here—I'm gonna prove it! Oh, damn—I can make better time out there talkin' to that mule.

MISSY. Why not—it's one jackass to another.

[GITLOW *exits to the kitchen.* MISSY *and* LUTIEBELLE *look at each other, both determined not to give way to the very real fright they feel. There is a long, uncomfortable pause.*]

LUTIEBELLE. It sure is a lovely year—for this time of morning, I mean. [*There is a pause.*] I can't tell you how much all this fresh air, wine-smoke, and apple-bite reminds me of Alabama.

MISSY. Oh, yes—Ol' Georgia can sure smile pretty when she's of a mind to—

PURLIE [*bursts in*]. "Arise and shine for thy light has come."°

MISSY. Purlie—Purlie Victorious! [*They embrace.*]

---

caucasiatic white ("Caucasian")
has come Purlie remembers Isaiah 60:1 and (below) Psalm 85:10

LUTIEBELLE. Oh, you Reb'n Purlie you!

PURLIE. "Truth and Mercy are met together, Righteousness and Peace have kissed each other!" [*They embrace.*]

5 MISSY. Let me look at you—behold the man! —knee-deep in shining glory. Great day the righteous marching! What happened to you?

PURLIE. Mine enemy hath been destroyed!

MISSY. What!

10 PURLIE. I told that ol' man twenty years ago, Missy, that over his dead body, Big Bethel would rise again!

MISSY. Purlie—! You mean you done—

PURLIE. "Have I any pleasure that the wicked 15 should die, saith the Lord, and not turn from his ways and live?" Lutiebelle, put on your hat and coat, and hurry!

LUTIEBELLE. Yessir!

PURLIE. Missy, throw us some breakfast into 20 a paper sack, and quick!

MISSY. Yessir!

PURLIE. Gitlow, I'm calling on you and your fellow mule to write a new page in the annals of Negro History Week.

25 GITLOW [*entering*]. Well, if it ain't ol' little black riding hood, dere! How was the mean ol' peckerwolf tonight, dere, kingfish?°

MISSY. Tell him, Purlie boy, what you told us: how you sashayed° up that hill with force 30 and fistfight!

GITLOW. Hallelujah!

MISSY. How you fit Ol' Cap'n to a halt and a stand-still!

GITLOW. Talk that talk!

35 MISSY. And left him laying in a pool of his own Confederate blood!

GITLOW. For Pete sakes, Missy—quit lying!

MISSY. Don't you dare call Purlie Judson a liar!

40 LUTIEBELLE. No man calls Reb'n Purlie a liar and lives!

GITLOW. What's the matter with you people?

Purlie ain't been up that hill; Purlie ain't seen Ol' Cap'n; Purlie ain't done doodley squat!° And all that gabble about leaving somebody 45 in a pool of his own Confederate blood ain't what the bull left in the barnyard!

PURLIE. Five hundred dollars says it is! [*Draws roll of bills from his pocket, for all to see.*] 50

ALL. Five hundred dollars!

PURLIE. In cool September cash!

GITLOW. Money! [*Lunges forward, but PURLIE slaps his hand.*]

PURLIE. And that ain't all I got— [*Opens bag* 55 *he has brought. They look in.*]

GITLOW [*almost choking in awe*]. Oh, my goodness, Missy—great day in the morning time—Missy—Missy!

MISSY [*also impressed*]. Gitlow, that's *it!* .. 60

GITLOW. That's *it*, Missy—that's *it!*

MISSY. Of course that's *it!*—ain't nothing in the world but *it!* [PURLIE *slowly pulls out* OL' CAP'N'S *bull whip.*]

GITLOW. Ain't but one way—one way in all 65 this world—for nobody to get that bull whip off'n Ol' Cap'n!

MISSY. And that's off'n his dead body!

GITLOW. And that's the everlovin' truth, so help me. 70

PURLIE. Here, take it—and burn it in a public place. Lutiebelle—

LUTIEBELLE. Yes, Reb'n Purlie.

PURLIE. This money belongs to the Negro people— 75

GITLOW. Reb'n Purlie, my boy, I apologize from the bottom of my knees. [*Kneels and starts to sing.*] "Gone are the days—"

MISSY [*snatching him to his feet*]. Get up and shut up! 80

PURLIE [*deliberately continuing to* LUTIEBELLE]. Take it, and wear it next to your heart.

LUTIEBELLE [*very conscious of the great charge laid upon her, turns her back to* GITLOW *and hides the money in her bosom*]. Until death 85 us do part.

MISSY [*to* GITLOW]. If I ever catch you with

---

peckerwolf . . . kingfish *pecker* (an obscene appellation) is combined with *wolf* (a predator); a kingfish is a "top dog"

sashayed went (with implications of a singular gait); a term derived from square dancing

doodley squat anything whatsoever (with a scatological suggestion)

that song in your mouth again I'll choke you with it!

PURLIE. And go wake up the mule. We due in Waycross to buy Big Bethel.

GITLOW. I'm going, I'm going. [*Starts, but can't tear himself away.*] Cash—five hundred dollars in cash. And a bull whip, from Ol' Cap'n Cotchipee himself— Man, I'd give a pretty piece of puddin' to know how you did it!

MISSY. You go and wake up that mule! [*Turning back to* PURLIE.] Me, too! How did you do it, Purlie?

LUTIEBELLE. What happened when you first got there?

PURLIE [*almost laughing*]. Now wait a minute —don't rush me!

MISSY. That's what I say: don't rush him— let the man talk!

PURLIE. Talk! Missy, I told you. I haven't got time—

GITLOW. That's all right, Purlie, we'll listen in a hurry.

LUTIEBELLE. What happened when you called him out and whipped him?

PURLIE. I didn't call him out and whip him!

GITLOW What!

MISSY. You didn't!

LUTIEBELLE. Reb'n Purlie—?

PURLIE. I mean, I did call him out—!

LUTIEBELLE [*in ecstatic relief*]. Oh— You did call him out!

PURLIE. Yeah—but he didn't come.

ALL. What!

PURLIE. So—er—I went in to get him!

ALL. You did! Sure enough! What happened then?

PURLIE [*still seeking escape*]. Well, like I told you—

LUTIEBELLE. Tell us, Reb'n Purlie—please!

PURLIE [*no escape*]. Well—here was me; and there was him—twisted and bent like a pretzel! Face twitchified like a pan of worms; eyes bugging out; sweat dreening down like rain; tongue plumb clove to the roof of his mouth! [*He looks to his audience, and is impelled to go on.*] Well—this thief! This murderer; this adulterer—this oppressor of all my people, just a sitting there: Stonewall Jackson Cotchipee,

just a sitting there. [*Begins to respond to his own fantasy.*] "Go to, rich man, weep and howl, for your sorrows shall come upon you." And-a "Wherefore abhor yourself, and repent Ye in sackcloth and ashes!" cause ol' Purlie is done come to get you!

LUTIEBELLE [*swept away*]. Oh, my Lawd!

MISSY. What he do, Purlie—what he do!?

PURLIE. Fell down on bended knees and cried like a baby!

MISSY. Ol' Cap'n Cotchipee on his knees!?

GITLOW. Great day in the morning time!

PURLIE [*warming to the task*]. Don't beg me, white folks, it's too late. "Mercy?" What do you know about mercy?! Did you have mercy on Ol' Uncle Tubb when he asked you not to cheat him out of his money so hard, and you knocked him deaf in his left ear?—Did you have mercy on Lolly's boy when he sassed you back, and you took and dipped his head in a bucket of syrup! And twenty years ago when little Purlie, black and manly as he could be, stood naked before you and your bull whip and pleaded with tears in his li'l ol' eyes, did you have mercy!?

GITLOW. Naw!

PURLIE. —And I'll not have mercy now!

ALL. Amen! Help him, Lawd! Preach it, boy, preach it! [*Etc.*]

PURLIE. Vengeance is mine saith the Lord! [*Hallelujah!*] Ye serpents; ye vipers; ye low-down sons of—! [*Amen!*] How can ye escape the damnation of hell!

MISSY. Throw it at him, boy!

PURLIE. And then, bless my soul, I looked up—up from the blazing depths of my righteous indignation! And I saw tears spill over from his eyeballs; and I heard the heart-be-clutching anguish of his outcry! His hands was both a-tremble; and slobber a-dribblin' down his lips!

GITLOW. Oh, my Lawd!

PURLIE. And he whined and whimpered like a ol' hound dog don't want you to kick him no more!

LUTIEBELLE. Great goodness a mighty!

PURLIE. And I commenced to ponder the meaning of this evil thing that groveled be-

neath my footstool—this no-good lump of
nobody!—not fit to dwell on this earth beside
the children of the blessed—an abomination to
the Almighty and stench in the nostrils of his
5 people! And yet— [*Pause for effect.*] And yet
—a man! A weak man; a scared man; a pitiful
man; like the whole Southland bogged down
in sin and segregation crawling on his knees
before my judgment seat—but still a MAN!
10 GITLOW. A man, Lawd!
PURLIE. He, too, like all the South, was one
of God's creatures—
MISSY. Yes, Lawd!
PURLIE. He, too, like all the South, could
15 never be beyond the reach of love, hope, and
redemption.
LUTIEBELLE. Amen!
PURLIE. Somewhere for him—even for him,
some father's heart was broken, some mother's
20 tears undried.
GITLOW. Dry 'em, Lawd!
PURLIE. I am my brother's keeper!
ALL. Yes, Lawd.
PURLIE. And thinking on these things, I
25 found myself to pause, and stumble in my great
resolve—and sorrow squeezed all fury from
my heart—and pity plucked all hatred from
my soul—and the racing feet of an avenging
anger slowed down to a halt and a standstill—
30 and the big, black, and burly fist of my strong
correction—raised on high like a stroke of
God's own lightning—fell useless by my side.
The book say, "Love one another."
MISSY. Love one another!
35 PURLIE. The book say, "Comfort ye one
another."
LUTIEBELLE. Comfort ye one another.
PURLIE. The book say, "Forgive ye one
another."
40 GITLOW. Forgive Ol' Cap'n, Lawd.
PURLIE. Slowly I turned away—to leave this
lump of human mess and misery to the infinite
darkness of a hell for white folks only, when
suddenly—
45 MISSY. Suddenly, Lawd.
PURLIE. Suddenly I put on my brakes—Purlie
Victorious Judson stopped dead in his tracks
—and stood stark still, and planted his feet,

and rared° back, asked himself and all the
powers-that-be some mighty important ques- 50
tions.
LUTIEBELLE. Yes, he did, Lawd.
MISSY. And that is the truth!
PURLIE. How come—I asked myself, it's al-
ways the colored folks got to do all the for- 55
giving?
GITLOW. Man, you mighty right!
PURLIE. How come the only cheek gits turned
in this country is the Negro cheek!
MISSY. Preach to me, boy! 60
PURLIE. What was this, this—man—Ol'
Cap'n Cotchipee—that in spite of all his sins
and evils, he still had dominion over me?
LUTIEBELLE. Ain't that the truth!
PURLIE. God made us all equal—God made 65
us all brothers—
ALL. Amen, amen.
PURLIE. "And hath made of one blood all
nations of men for to dwell on the face of the
earth."—Who changed all that!? 70
GITLOW [*furious*]. Who changed it, he said.
PURLIE. Who took it and twisted it around!
MISSY [*furious*]. Who was it, he said!
LUTIEBELLE [*furious*]. And where's that scoun'
hiding?! 75
PURLIE. So that the Declarator of Indepen-
dence himself might seem to be a liar?
GITLOW. Who, that's what I want to know,
who?
PURLIE. That a man the color of his face— 80
[*pointing up Cotchipee Hill*] could live by the
sweat of a man the color of mine!
LUTIEBELLE. Work with him, Lawd, work
with him!
PURLIE. —Could live away up there in his 85
fine, white mansion, and us down here in a
shack not fitting to house the fleas upon his
dogs!
GITLOW. Nothing but fleas!
PURLIE. —Could wax hisself fat on the fat of 90
the land; steaks, rice, chicken, roastineers,°
sweet potato pies, hot buttered biscuits and
cane syrup anytime he felt like it and never

rared reared
roastineers ears of roasting corn

hit a lick at a snake! And us got to everyday git-up-and-git-with-it, sunup-to-sundown, on fatback and cornmeal hoecakes—and don't wind up owning enough ground to get buried
5 standing up in!

MISSY. Do, Lawd!

PURLIE. —And horses and cadillacs, bull whips and bourbon, and two for 'leven dollar seegars—and our fine young men to serve at
10 his table; and our fine young women to serve in his bed!

LUTIEBELLE. Help him, Lawd.

PURLIE. Who made it like this—who put the white man on top?

15 GITLOW. That's what I wants to know!

PURLIE. Surely not the Lord of Israel who is a just God!

MISSY. Hah, Lawd!

PURLIE. And no respecter of persons! Who
20 proved in the American Revolution that all men are created equal!

GITLOW. Man, I was there when he proved it!

PURLIE. Endowed with Civil Rights and First Class Citizenship, Ku Klux Klan, White Cit-
25 izens Council notwithstanding!

MISSY. Oh, yes, he did!

PURLIE. And when my mind commenced to commemorate and to reconsider all these things—

30 GITLOW. Watch him, Lawd!

PURLIE. And I thought of the black mother in bondage—[*yes*] and I thought of the black father in prison—[*ha, Lawd!*] And of Momma herself—Missy can tell how pretty she was—

35 MISSY. Indeed I can!

PURLIE. How she died outdoors on a dirty sheet 'cause the hospital doors said—"For white folks only." And of Papa, God rest his soul—who brought her tender loving body
40 back home—and laid her to sleep in the grave-yard—and cried himself to death among his children!

MISSY [*crying*]. Purlie, Purlie—

PURLIE [*really carried away*]. Then did the
45 wrath of a righteous God possess me; and the strength of the host and of ten thousand swept into my good right arm—and I arose and I smote Ol' Cap'n a mighty blow! And the wind

from my fist ripped the curtains from the eastern walls—and I felt the weight of his ol' 50 bull whip nestling in my hands—and the fury of a good Gawd-almighty was within me; and I beat him—I whipped him—and I flogged him —and I cut him—I destroyed him!

[IDELLA *enters.*] 55

GITLOW. Great day and the righteous marching— Whoeeeee! Man, I ain't been stirred that deep since the tree caught fire on a possum hunt and the dogs pushed Papa in the pot.

MISSY. Idella, you shoulda heard him! 60

IDELLA. I did hear him—all the way across the valley. I thought he was calling hogs. Well, anyway: all hell is broke loose at the big house. Purlie, you better get outta here. Ol' Cap'n is on the phone to the sheriff. 65

MISSY. Ol' Cap'n Cotchipee is dead.

IDELLA. The hell you preach.

ALL. What!

IDELLA. Ol' Cap'n ain't no more dead than I am. 70

LUTIEBELLE. That's a mighty tacky thing to say about your ex-fellow man.

MISSY. Mighty tacky.

LUTIEBELLE. Reb'n Purlie just got through preaching 'bout it. How he marched up Cot- 75 chipee hill—

GITLOW [*showing the bull whip*]. And took Ol' Cap'n by the bull whip—

MISSY. And beat that ol' buzzard to death!

IDELLA. That is the biggest lie since the devil 80 learned to talk!

LUTIEBELLE. I am not leaving this room till somebody apologizes to Reb'n Purlie V. Jud-son, the gentleman of my intended.

IDELLA. Purlie Judson! Are you gonna stand 85 there sitting on your behind, and preach these people into believing you spent the night up at the big house whipping Ol' Cap'n to death when all the time you was breaking into the commissary! 90

MISSY. Breaking into the commissary!

GITLOW. Something is rotten in the cotton!

PURLIE. It's all right, Miz Idella—I'll take it from there—

MISSY. It is not all right—! 95

PURLIE. While it is true that, maybe, I did

not go up that hill just word for word, and call
that ol' man out, and beat him to death so
much on the dotted line—!

MISSY [*snatching up the paper bag*]. I'm
5 goin' to take back my lunch!

PURLIE. Missy! Wait a minute!

LUTIEBELLE. You know what, Aunt Missy?

MISSY. Yes, honey?

LUTIEBELLE. Sometimes I just wish I could
10 drop dead for a while!

PURLIE. Wait, Lutiebelle, give me a chance
to—

LUTIEBELLE. Here's your money!—[*Puts roll
into PURLIE's hand.*] And that goes for every
15 other great big ol' handsome man in the whole
world!

PURLIE. What you want me to do? Go up
that hill by myself and get my brains knocked
out?

20 MISSY. It's little enough for the woman you
love!

LUTIEBELLE. Why'd you have to preach all
them wonderful things that wasn't so?

GITLOW. And why'd you have to go and
25 change your mind?

PURLIE. I didn't mean for them not to be
so: it was a—a parable! A prophecy! Believe
me! I ain't never in all my life told a lie I didn't
mean to make come true, some day! Lutie-
30 belle—!

IDELLA. Purlie: unless you want to give heart-
break a headache, you better run!

PURLIE. Run—run for what!

MISSY. You want Ol' Cap'n to catch you
35 here?!

PURLIE. Confound Ol' Cap'n! Dad-blast Ol'
Cap'n! Damn, damn, damn, and double-damn
Ol' Cap'n!

[*The front door swings open and in walks
40 Ol' CAP'N steaming with anger.*]

OL' CAP'N [*controlling himself with great
difficulty*]. Somebody—I say somebody—is
calling my name!

GITLOW. Ol' Cap'n, you just in time to settle
45 a argument: is Rudolph Valentino° still dead?

Rudolph Valentino a romantic hero of the silent
screen

OL' CAP'N. Shut up!

GITLOW [*to MISSY*]. See—I told you.

OL' CAP'N. One thing I have not allowed in
my cotton patch since am-I-born-to-die! And
that's stealin'! Somebody broke into my com- 50
missary tonight—took two cans of sardines, a
box of soda crackers, my bull whip!—[*Picks
up whip from table.*] And five hundred dollars
in cash. And, boy—[*walking over to PURLIE*]
I want it back! 55

LUTIEBELLE. Stealing ain't all that black and
white.

MISSY. And we certainly wasn't the ones that
started it!

GITLOW. Who stole me from Africa in the 60
first place?

LUTIEBELLE. Who kept me in slavery from
1619 to 1863, working me to the bone without
no social security?

PURLIE. And tonight—just because I went up 65
that hill, and disembezzled my own inheritance
that you stole from me—!

OL' CAP'N [*livid*]. I have had a belly full of
your black African sass—!

[*The door bursts open again; this time it is* 70
the SHERIFF who comes in with pistol drawn.]

SHERIFF. All right, everybody, drop that gun!

PURLIE. Drop what gun?

OL' CAP'N. So there you are, you idiot—
what kept you so long? 75

SHERIFF. Like you told us to do on the phone,
suh, we was taking a good, long, slow snoop
'round and 'bout the commissary looking for
clues! And dog-gone if one didn't, just a short
while ago, stumble smack into our hands! 80

OL' CAP'N. What!

SHERIFF. We caught the culprit red-handed
—bring in the prisoner, Dep!

DEPUTY. Glad to oblige you, Sheriff.

[*Enter DEPUTY, dragging CHARLIE, who has* 85
his hands cuffed behind him; wears heavy leg
shackles and has a large white gag stuck into
his mouth.]

SHERIFF. Southern justice strikes again!

OL' CAP'N. Charlie!—oh, no! 90

IDELLA. Charlie, my baby!

OL' CAP'N. Release him, you idiots! Release
him at once! [*EVERYBODY pitches in to set*

CHARLIE *free.*] What have they done to you, my boy?

IDELLA. What have they done to you!

CHARLIE [*free from the gag*]. Hello, Paw—
5 Idella—Purlie—

OL' CAP'N. I'll have your thick, stupid necks for this!

SHERIFF. It was you give the orders, suh!

OL' CAP'N. Not my son, you idiot!

10 DEPUTY. It was him broke into the commissary.

OL' CAP'N. What!

SHERIFF. It was him stole the five hundred dollars—he confessed!

OL' CAP'N. Steal? A Cotchipee? Suh, that is
15 biologically impossible! [*To* CHARLIE.] Charlie, my boy. Tell them the truth—tell them who stole the money. It was Purlie, wasn't it boy?

CHARLIE. Well, as a matter of fact, Paw—it was mostly me that broke in and took the
20 money, I'd say. In fact it WAS me!

OL' CAP'N. No!

CHARLIE. It was the only thing I could do to save your life, Paw.

OL' CAP'N. Save my life! Idella, he's delir-
25 ious—!

CHARLIE. When Purlie come up that hill after you last night, I seen him, and lucky for you I did. The look he had on his face against you was not a Christian thing to behold! It was
30 terrible! I had to get into that commissary, right then and there, open that safe, and pay him his inheritance—even then I had to beg him to spare your life!

OL' CAP'N [*to* PURLIE]. You spare my life,
35 boy? How dare you? [*To* CHARLIE.] Charlie, my son, I know you never recovered from the shock of losing your mother—almost before you were born. But don't worry—it was Purlie who stole that money and I'm going to prove
40 it. [*Starts to take out gun.* GITLOW *grabs gun.*] Gitlow, my old friend, arrest this boy, Gitlow! As Deputy-For-The-Colored—I order you to arrest this boy for stealing!

GITLOW [*with a brand new meaning*]. "Gone
45 are the days—" [*Still twirls pistol safely out of* OL' CAP'N's *reach.*]

PURLIE. "Stealin'," is it? Well, I'm gonna really give you something to arrest me for.

[*Snatches bull whip.*]

OL' CAP'N. Have a care, boy: I'm still a white 50 man.

PURLIE. Congratulations! Twenty years ago, I told you this bull whip was gonna change hands one of these days!

MISSY. Purlie, wait—! 55

PURLIE. Stay out of my struggle for power!

MISSY. You can't do wrong just because it's right!

GITLOW. Never kick a man when he's down except in self-defense! 60

LUTIEBELLE. And no matter what, you are and always will be—the hero of Cotchipee Hill.

PURLIE. Am I?

LUTIEBELLE. Ten thousand queens!

PURLIE. I bow to the will of the Negro people. 65
[*Throws whip away. Back to* OL' CAP'N.] But one thing, Ol' Cap'n, I am released of you— the entire Negro people is released of you! No more shouting hallelujah! every time you sneeze, nor jumping jackass every time you 70 whistle "Dixie"! We gonna love you if you let us and laugh as we leave if you don't. We want our cut of the Constitution, and we want it now: and not with no teaspoon, white folks— throw it at us with a shovel! 75

OL' CAP'N. Charlie, my boy—my own, lily- white, Anglo-Saxon, semi-Confederate son. I know you never recovered from the shock of losing your mother almost before you were born. But don't worry: there is still time to 80 take these insolent, messy cotton-picking in- grates down a peg—and prove by word and deed that God is still a white man. Tell 'em! Boy, tell 'em!

CHARLIE. Tell 'em what, Paw? 85

OL' CAP'N. Tell 'em what you and me have done together. Nobody here would believe me. Tell 'em how you went to Waycross, Saturday night, in my name—

CHARLIE. Yes, sir—I did. 90

OL' CAP'N. Tell 'em how you spoke to Ol' Man Pelham in my name—

CHARLIE. Yes, sir—I spoke to him.

OL' CAP'N. And paid him cash for that ol' barn they used to call Big Bethel! 95

CHARLIE. Yes, sir; that's what I did, all right.

OL' CAP'N. And to register the deed in the courthouse in my name—

CHARLIE. Yes, sir, that's exactly what you told me to do—

5 OL' CAP'N. Then—ain't but one thing left to do with that ramshackle dungsoaked monstrosity—that's burn the damn thing down. [*Laughs aloud in his triumph.*]

CHARLIE. But Paw—

10 OL' CAP'N. First thing, though—let me see the deed: I wouldn't want to destroy nothing that didn't—legally—belong to me [*Snatches deed from* CHARLIE's *hand. Begins to mumble as he reads it.*]

15 IDELLA. Twenty years of being more than a mother to you!

CHARLIE. Wait, Idella, wait. I did go to Waycross, like Paw said; I did buy the barn—excuse me Purlie: the church—like he said; and I registered the deed at the courthouse like he told me—but not in Paw's name—

20

OL' CAP'N [*startled by something he sees on the deed*]. What's this?

CHARLIE [*to* IDELLA]. I registered the deed in the name of—

25

OL' CAP'N [*reading, incredulous*]. "Purlie Victorious Judson—" No!

IDELLA. PURLIE VICTORIOUS Judson?

OL' CAP'N [*choking on the words*]. Purlie Victorious Judsssss—aaaarrrrgggghhhhh! [*The horror of it strikes him absolutely still.*]

30

CHARLIE [*taking the deed from* OL' CAP'N's *limp hand*]. It was the only thing I could do to save your life. [*Offering deed to* PURLIE.] Well, Purlie, here it is.

35

PURLIE [*counting out the five hundred dollars*]. You did a good job, Charlie—I'm much obliged!

CHARLIE [*refuses money; still holds out deed to* PURLIE]. Thank you, Purlie, but—

40

PURLIE. Big Bethel is my Bethel, Charlie: it's my responsibility. Go on, take it.

CHARLIE. No, no! I couldn't take your money, Purlie—

45 IDELLA. Don't be a fool, boy—business is business. [*She takes the deed from* CHARLIE *and gives it to* PURLIE, *while at the same time taking the money from* PURLIE.]

CHARLIE. Idella—I can't do that!

IDELLA. I can! I'll keep it for you. 50

CHARLIE. Well—all right. But only, if—if—

IDELLA. Only if what?

CHARLIE [*to* PURLIE]. Would you let me be a member of your church?

MISSY. You? 55

GITLOW. Li'l Charlie Cotchipee!

LUTIEBELLE. A member of Big Bethel?

CHARLIE. May I? That is—that is, if you don't mind—as soon as you get it started?

PURLIE. Man, we're already started: the doors 60 of Big Bethel, Church of the New Freedom for all Mankind, are hereby declared "Open for business!"

GITLOW. Brother Pastor, I move we accept Brother Charlie Cotchipee as our first candidate 65 for membership to Big Bethel on a integrated basis—

MISSY. I second that motion!

PURLIE. You have heard the motion. Are you ready for the question? 70

ALL [*except* OL' CAP'N]. Question!

PURLIE. Those in favor will signify by saying "Aye." [EVERYBODY, *except* OL' CAP'N, *crowds around* CHARLIE, *saying "Aye" over and over, in such a crescendo of welcome that* PURLIE 75 *has to ride over the noise.*] Those opposed? [*Looks at* OL' CAP'N, *who is still standing, as if frozen, as we last saw him. He does not answer.*] Those opposed will signify by saying— 80

[*He stops . . . all eyes focus on* OL' CAP'N *now, still standing in quiet, frozen-like immobility. There is a moment of silence, an unspoken suspicion in everybody's face. Finally,* GITLOW *goes over and touches* OL' CAP'N, *still* 85 *standing rigid. Still he does not move.* GITLOW *feels his pulse, listens to his heart, and lifts up his eyelids. Nothing.*]

GITLOW. The first man I ever seen in all this world to drop dead standing up! 90

Blackout

Epilogue

[TIME. *Immediately following.*]

[SCENE. *We are at Big Bethel at funeral services for* OL' CAP'N.]

[AT RISE. *We cannot see the coffin. We hear*

the ringing of the CHURCH BELL as we come out of the blackout. PURLIE *is in the pulpit.*]

PURLIE. And toll the bell, Big Bethel, toll the bell! Dearly beloved, recently bereaved, and friends, we welcome you to Big Bethel, Church of the New Freedom: part Baptist; part Methodist; part Catholic—with the merriness of Christmas and the happiness of Hanukkah; and to the first integrated funeral in the sovereign, segregated state of Georgia. Let there be no merriments in these buryments! Though you are dead, Ol' Cap'n—and in hell, I suspect—as post-mortal guest of honor at our expense, it is not too late to repent. We still need togetherness; we still need each-otherness —with faith in the futureness of our cause. Let us, therefore, stifle the rifle of conflict, shatter the scatter of discord, smuggle the struggle, tickle the pickle, and grapple the apple of peace!

GITLOW. This funeral has been brought to you as a public service.

PURLIE. Take up his bones. For he who was my skin's enemy, was brave enough to die standing for what he believed. . . . And it is the wish of his family—and his friends—that he be buried likewise— [*The* PALLBEARERS *enter, carrying* OL' CAP'N's *ornate coffin just as he would have wished: standing up! It is draped in a Confederate flag; and his hat, his bull whip, and his pistol, have been fastened to the lid in appropriate places.*] Gently, gently. Put kindness in your fingers. He was a man— despite his own example. Take up his bones. [*The* PALLBEARERS *slowly carry the upright coffin across the stage.*] Tonight, my friends— I find in being black a thing of beauty: a joy, a strength, a secret cup of gladness; a native land in neither time nor place—a native land in every Negro face! Be loyal to yourselves: your skin, your hair; your lips, your southern speech, your laughing kindness—are Negro kingdoms, vast as any other! Accept in full the sweetness of your blackness—not wishing to be red, or white, or yellow: or any other race, or face but this. Farewell, my deep and Africanic brothers! Be brave, keep freedom in the family, do what you can for the white folks, and write me in care of the post office.

Now, may the Constitution of the United States go with you; the Declaration of Independence stand by you; the Bill of Rights protect you; and the State Commission Against Discrimination keep the eyes of the law upon you, henceforth, now and forever. Amen.

Curtain

Imamu Amiri Baraka

(LeRoi Jones)

1934–

The Toilet

1964

The Toilet, a spare but powerful episode drawn from urban life, deals with an unresolved personal and communal dilemma. It offers no catharsis, only—perhaps—an insight into what it is to live as these persons live, to pay the price they and society pay.

The stinking boys' john of an inner-city high school provides the setting. The language is that of the graffiti scrawled on privy walls. The action is violent. One of the characters is white, one is Puerto Rican, nine are black. The blacks constitute an unruly, unstable gang precariously dominated by the intelligent, manic, and sensitive Foots. Foots's receipt of a love letter from the Puerto Rican boy Karolis gives the plot its impetus, for by the gang's code such an "insult" mandates a fight.

Neither Karolis, who is being pursued in the school's upper hallways, nor Foots, who is being held in class, appears until midway in the play. The audience does not learn at first exactly what is to happen; it never learns exactly why. What it sees is the gathering of the gang. What it experiences is a mounting, ever more sickening suspense as it anticipates the confrontation and violence to come.

Ora opens the play spraying urine over the seat of a commode. He and Love trade insults about their mothers. Hines and Holmes jeer at Love for "pulling his whatchamacallit." Love and Hines grab Holmes and threaten to put "this little bastard's head in the goddam urinal!" Holmes taunts Love with his mother's promiscuity and receives a blow in return. Love and Ora momentarily square off. Ora punches Farrell in the stomach. In thought, word, gesture, and deed, the gang is dominated by violence.

Violence is not all. Some of the exchange is good humored, much of it witty. Natural exuberance manifests itself in a series of simulated basketball skirmishes. George has a sense of decency. Hines and Love are friends. Foots, when he enters, shows intelligence and a hint of compassion. Although it offers its members only a kind of half-life, the gang's very existence testifies to a natural longing for community. And the gang's code, although only a stunted adolescent chivalry, expresses a felt need for moral standards. Yet as the play rhythmically alternates its exhibition of vital and liberating impulses with those that are brutal and destructive, the audience comes to realize that in every instance the latter triumph. Every momentary affirmation of humanity yields before the violence that is in all of them and in Ora most of all.

For if Foots is the gang's leader, Ora is its evil genius. His brutality provokes the violence smoldering in each—a violence generated, one infers, by self-contempt and desperation. Out of this violence they brutalize each other. To this, dominated by Ora, they sacrifice Foots. To this they surrender as they join Ora in savaging Karolis. Under the pressure of this they abandon themselves.

With wordless pathos the ending of the play underscores the high human price they pay for such impoverished communal identity as their brutality brings them. Foots and Karolis lie unconscious on the floor. The others leave, "all making noise, laughing, cursing." Then—until the convulsive conclusion the stage action progressing more slowly than the words that describe it —Foots comes to, rises, and leaves. As time passes Karolis painfully regains consciousness and struggles to rise. At length he manages to crawl to a commode and pull himself up; then he falls backward. And then Foots comes cautiously back in and runs to Karolis' body to cradle his head in his arms and weep.

The Toilet

BARAKA

CHARACTERS

ORA [Big Shot] *Short, ugly, crude, loud.*
WILLIE LOVE *Tall, thin. Should have been sensitive. Smiles.*
HINES *Big, husky, garrulous. He and Love are closest friends.*
JOHNNY BOY HOLMES *Short, curly hair. Bright, fast, likable.*
PERRY *Tall, dark, somber, cynical.*
GEORGE DAVIS *Tall, thin, crudely elegant. Judicious.*
SKIPPY *Quick. Rather stupid but interested. Someone to be trusted.*
KNOWLES *Large and ridiculous. A grinning ape.*
DONALD FARRELL *Tall, thin, blonde, awkward, soft.*
FOOTS [Ray] *Short, intelligent, manic. Possessor of a threatened empire.*
KAROLIS *Medium height. Very skinny and not essentially attractive except when he speaks.*

The scene is a large bare toilet built of gray rough cement. There are urinals along one wall and a partition separating them from the commodes which are along the same wall. The toilet must resemble the impersonal ugliness 5 *of a school toilet or a latrine of some institution. A few rolls of toilet paper are spread out on the floor, wet through. The actors should give the impression frequently that the place smells.* 10

[ORA *breaks through the door grinning, then*

giggling. Looks around the bleak place, walks around, then with one hand on his hip takes out his joint and pees, still grinning, into one of the commodes, spraying urine over the seat.]

LOVE [*sticking his head through the door*]. Big Shot! Hey, Big Shot! These guys say come and help them.

ORA [*zipping his fly and wiping the one hand on the back of his pants*]. Yeh? [*Turning to* LOVE.] Yeh? They got him, huh?

LOVE [*pushing door open so his arm is straight*]. Naw, they don't have him yet. He's on the second floor, running back and forth and hiding in empty rooms. But Knowles said for you to come help.

ORA [*flushing all the commodes and urinals in the row as he walks past*]. Sheet! I'll catch that bastid in a second. [*Ducks under* LOVE's *arm to go out.*] Why the hell don't you get up there. You supposed to be faster than me.

LOVE. I'm s'posed to stay here and keep the place clear. [*Making a face.*] Damn. This place smells like hell.

ORA [*without turning around*]. Yeh [*giggling*], this must be your momma's house.

LOVE [*slipping inside the door and holding it against* ORA]. Shit. At least I got one.

ORA [*thumps against the door, not really angry*]. Bastid!

[LOVE *waits a few seconds, then pulls the door open slightly. Then lets it shut and walks to a closed commode and noticing it's wet wipes it with some of the strewn toilet paper. He sits down and stretches his legs. Then gets up and opens the commode to pee. There are voices outside and then the door swings open and* HINES *and* HOLMES *come in.*]

HINES. Hey, Willie.

LOVE [*still peeing*]. What you want? [*Comes out, zipping his pants.*]

HINES [*to* HOLMES]. Man, this cat's in here pulling his whatchamacallit.

HOLMES [*to* LOVE]. Yeh. Damn, Love, why don't you go get Gloria to do that stuff for you.

LOVE. She-et. [*Grinning.*] Huh. I sure don't need your ol' lady to be pullin' on my joint.

[*Laughs.* HOLMES *begins to spar with him.*]

HINES. They didn't even catch that skinny nose punk yet.

LOVE. No? Why in hell not?

HOLMES. He's still running up and down the damn halls. I should go up there and drag that sonofabitch down.

[HOLMES *and* HINES *begin to pee also in the commodes.* LOVE *pulls open the door a small bit and looks out.*]

LOVE. Shit. Boy, all you slow ass cats. I'd catch that little skinny paddy boy in a second. Where's that little popeyed Foots?

HINES. Damn if I know. I think he's still in Miss Powell's class. You know if he missed her class she'd beat his head, and then get his ol' lady to beat his head again.

HOLMES. Shit. Skippy should've got hold of that damn Karolis by now. He ain't fast worth a bitch.

LOVE. Yeh, but he's so goddamned scary he might just jump out a goddamn window.

[HOLMES *finishes peeing and starts pushing* LOVE *and they begin to spar around.* HOLMES *is very funny, making boxer-like sounds and brushing his nose continuously with his thumbs.* LOVE *just stands straight with his left hand stiff and stabbing it out toward* HOLMES' *face.* HINES *finishes and gets in the action too. Both he and* HOLMES *are against* LOVE, *who starts to laugh and curse good naturedly.*]

LOVE. Two a' you bastids, huh? I'll take you both. [*He starts kicking at them.*]

HINES. Boy, if you kick me, you'll die just like that . . . with your skinny ass leg up. They'll have to build you a special coffin with a part for your leg.

HOLMES [*backing away, and then turning on* HINES. *Laughing*]. Let's get this sum'bitch, Willie.

HINES [*backing away, now kicking and swinging . . . but just timing blows so they won't strike anyone*]. Goddamn, Johnny Boy, you a crooked muthafucka. You cats think you can mess with the kid?

[*The two spar against* HINES *and then* LOVE *turns against* HOLMES.]

Love. Let's get this little assed cat.

[Holmes *kicks at them, then jumps up on the commodes in order to defend himself more "heroically."*]

Holmes. I'm gonna get your ass, Willie. I'm just trying to help you out and you gonna play wise. Ya' bastid.

Hines. Listen to that cat. [*Runs after Holmes.*] I'm gonna put your damn head in one of those damn urinals.

[*He and* Love *finally grab* Holmes *and he begins struggling with them in earnest.*]

Let's put this little bastard's head in the goddamn urinal!

Holmes. You bastids! Let me go! I'm gonna cut somebody. Bastids!

[*The door opens and* Ora *comes in. His shirt is torn. But he rushes over laughing and starts punching everyone, even* Holmes.]

Hines. Goddamn it, Big Shot, get the hell out of here.

Holmes. Get 'em, Big Shot.

Ora [*punches* Holmes *who's still being held by* Love]. I'm gonna punch you, you prick. Hold the cocksucker, Love.

Love [*releasing* Holmes *immediately*]. I ain't gonna hold him so you can punch him.

[Ora *and* Holmes *square off, both laughing and faking professional demeanor.*]

Love. Hey, Big Shot, what happened to your shirt?

Ora [*putting his hands down and handling the torn part of his shirt*]. That muthafuckin' Karolis ripped it.

[*The other three yowl.* Hines *puts his fingers to the hole as if to tear it again.*]

Get outta here you black ass bastid. [*He squares off at* Hines, *then pushes him away.*] That paddy bastid! I had the cocksucker around the waist, and then he rips my shirt and scratches me. [*He holds up his wounded hand.*]

Hines. You let him get away?

Ora. No, hell. I punched the bastid right in his lip. But he was making so much noise we thought somebody'd come out and see us so Knowles and Skippy took him in the broom closet and I cut down the stairs. The stupid bastid was screaming and biting right outside of ol' lady Powell's room.

Holmes. Did anybody come outta there?

Ora. You think I was gonna stay around and see? She and Miss Golden after me anyway.

Love. Did you see Foots in there?

Ora [*going to the door and peering out*]. Yeh. And George Davis and Perry are in there too. [*He pushes door open and leans all the way out.*]

Hines. Shit. They're never gonna bring that sonofabitch down here. We ain't got all day.

Ora [*letting the door shut*]. Yeh, Perry and Foots and them ought to be down here in a few minutes. It's almost 3:00 now.

Love [*pretending he has a basketball in his hands, he pretends to dribble and lunges forward simulating a fake at* Hines, *then he sweeps past* Hines *and leaps in the air as if making a layup shot*]. Peed on you, just then, buddy.

Hines. Sheet, Man, you what you call a self-checker. I don't even have to block that shot. I just take it off the back-board like this. [*He spins around and leaps up at the imaginary basket and scoops the imaginary ball off, landing and shaking his head as if to shake off imaginary defenders.*] Another rebound! [*Makes motion of long pass down toward opposite "court."*] Now, the fast break. [*He moves in position for his own pass, receives it, makes one long stepping dribble and leaps as if dunking the ball in the basket.*] Two!

Holmes. Boy, you guys sure play a lot of ball . . . off the court.

Ora [*opening the door again*]. No shootin' cocksuckas.

Love [*still whirling and leaping as if he is making successful hook shots from an imaginary foul line*]. Hey, what we gonna do to this cat when he gets here?

Ora [*leaning back in from the door though keeping it open with his fingers*]. Damn, Love. You a stupid bastid. [*Peeks out door.*] We gonna kick that little frail bastid's ass.

Hines. In fact, you the one gonna do it, Willie.

HOLMES. Yeh, Love. [*Blocking one of* LOVE's *"shots."*]

LOVE. Shit. Karolis never bothered me. [*Faking* HOLMES *and swinging to shoot from the other side.*]

ORA [*looking back in and letting the door swing shut*]. Damn, Willie [*in mocking seriousness*], Karolis is always telling everybody how he bangs the hell out of Caroline, every chance he gets. [*Begins to giggle.*]

HOLMES. Is that your mother's name, Love, Caroline?

HINES [*busy trying to lift a back window to look out on the yard*]. What you mean, Johnny Boy, is that his mother's name? You the one told me.

LOVE [*swinging around as if to shoot again he suddenly punches* HOLMES *on the shoulder.* HOLMES *lets out a yelp of pain*]. Uhhuh . . . I told you about messin' with me.

HOLMES [*holding his shoulder*]. Shit. Why didn't you hit Big Shot, you bastard? He brought the shit up.

ORA [*has the door propped open again*]. Shit. That narrow head bastid know better than to fuck with me. [*He peers out the door and as he does* LOVE *gestures as if to hit him in the back.*]

HOLMES [*to* LOVE]. You scared ass bastard. Why don't you do it?

ORA [*turning around and throwing up his hands to defend himself*]. Yeh, I wish you would, you bullet head sonofabitch.

[HOLMES *goes and sits on a radiator next to* HINES.]

LOVE. Man, nobody's thinking about you, Big Shot. [*He goes to pee.*]

ORA [*pulling the door open again*]. Here come Perry and them.

HOLMES [*jumping off the radiator still holding his shoulder*]. Perry and who else?

ORA. George Davis and Donald Farrell.

HINES. Donald Farrell? What the hell's he doin' down here? Where the hell is Foots?

LOVE. Yeh, what the hell is Perry doing bringing Farrell down here with 'em? Shit.

[ORA *pulls the door open, and* PERRY, DAVIS, *and* FARRELL *come in.*]

PERRY. Hey, what's happening?

HOLMES. Shit. I should ask you. Where's Foots?

GEORGE. He had to stay upstairs for awhile. Powell wanted to talk to him . . . or something.

ORA [*to* F   ]. Man, whatta you want down here? Nobody asked you to come.

GEORGE. I told him he could come. Why not?

ORA. Whatta you mean, why not? You know goddamn well, why not. Silly sumbitch!

PERRY. Ah, Big Shot, why don't you be cool for a change, huh?

GEORGE. Yeh, man, Big Shot. Donald's not going to hurt anything.

ORA. No? [*Taking out a much-smoked cigarette butt.*] Maybe you don't think so . . . but I do.

GEORGE. Oh, man, shit.

FARRELL. Why don't you want me here, Big Shot?

ORA [*glaring at* FARRELL]. Man, don't be asking me questions.

FARRELL. Don't ask you questions? Why the hell not?

ORA [*menacingly at* FARRELL]. Cause I said so, that's why. You don't like it, muthafucka?

PERRY [*stepping between them*]. Goddamn it, Big Shot, why don't you sit your ass down for awhile and shut the hell up?

ORA [*turning to* PERRY]. You gonna make me, muthafucka?

PERRY [*stepping to face* ORA]. I can. And you better believe it, Baby!

ORA. Shit. [*Disparagingly. Moving away from* FARRELL *and back to the center of the room.*] Well you damn sure got your chance right now, you black sonofabitch.

GEORGE [*moves between* PERRY *and* ORA]. Oh, goddamnit why don't both you guys sit down. You too, Donald.

[FARRELL *moves to sit on a radiator beside* HOLMES *and* HINES.]

Ora, you wrong, man, and you know it.

ORA. How come I'm wrong, huh? You know goddamn well that skinny cocksucka over there [*at* FARRELL] ain't got no business down here. He ain't gonna do a damn thing but stand around and look.

LOVE [*laughing*]. That's all I'm gonna do.

HINES [*hunching* HOLMES *with his elbow*]. Yeh, but that's okay for you, Willie. You so black, if you stand still nobody'll know you're standing there anyway.

[*All laugh.* ORA *takes the opportunity to go to the door and crack it open.*]

PERRY. Where's the rest of those guys?

HINES. I guess they must still be upstairs in that broom closet.

PERRY. Broom closet?

[*He and* DAVIS *lean against one of the walls and begin to smoke.*]

HINES. Yeh, Knowles and Skippy got Karolis upstairs in a broom closet waiting till everybody leaves the floor I guess.

FARRELL. Jimmy Karolis?

HOLMES. Yeah, that's who we're waiting for. [*Giggles.*]

FARRELL. What the hell's gonna happen then?

ORA [*turning from door*]. Man, what the hell you care, huh? Pee-the-bed-muthafucka!

HINES. Damn, George!

GEORGE. Damn, what?

HINES. Seems to me like Big Shot's right. You bring this cat down here and he doesn't even know what's happening.

ORA. You goddamn real I'm right. Simple ass cats.

FARRELL. What're you guys gonna gang Jimmy Karolis?

ORA. We gonna break that muthafucka's back.

FARRELL. For what?

ORA. Look man, why don't you shut up and get the hell out of here, huh?

FARRELL. You mean all you guys're gonna jump on Karolis?

ORA [*walking over to* FARRELL *and grabbing him by the shirt*]. You gonna stick up for him?

[FARRELL *tries to push Ora's hands from his shirt, and though he is much taller than* ORA, ORA *pulls him from his seat.*]

FARRELL. Goddamn it, Ora, why don't you cut the shit?

GEORGE. Yeh, Ora, cut it out.

PERRY. Goddamn; that cat's always going for bad.

[GEORGE *comes over to restrain* ORA, *but* ORA *succeeds in punching* FARRELL *in the stomach.* FARRELL *clutches his stomach and sinks to the floor groaning.*]

PERRY [*to* ORA]. You bastard.

[ORA *swings around to confront him.*]

ORA. You come on too, if you want to, you black sonofabitch!

[GEORGE *pushes them apart again and his push sends* ORA *rattling heavily against the door.*]

Goddamnit, George, why don't you stay the fuck out of this?

GEORGE. Because there wasn't a goddamn reason in the world for you to hit Donald like that. [*Going to help* FARRELL *up.*] Damn, Ora, you're a wrong sonofabitch, you know that?

FARRELL [*still doubled up and holding his stomach. He pulls his arm back when* GEORGE *tries to help him up*]. No, man! Lemme stay here. [*Still groaning.*] Ora, you dirty cocksucker.

ORA. Boy, you better shut up before I stomp mudholes in your pissy ass.

[*The door is suddenly pushed open and* KNOWLES *and* SKIPPY *come in holding* KAROLIS *by the arms.* KAROLIS' *head is hanging, and he is crying softly and blood is on his shirt and face. His hair is mussed and standing all over his head.*]

LOVE. Ga-uh damn! What'd you cats do?

KNOWLES [*giggling stupidly*]. Love, now what the hell does it look like we did? Broke this muthafucka's jaw.

HINES. Damn. I thought we were just bringing the cat down here to fight Foots. I didn't know you guys were gonna break his head first.

SKIPPY. Well, he didn't wanna come. We had to persuade him.

KNOWLES. Shit, Skippy, whatta you mean "we"? I did all the persuading.

ORA. Aw, shit, Knowles. I bloodied the cat's lip. You trying to take all the credit.

SKIPPY. Yeh, Knowles. You didn't hit the

cat but once, and that was on the goddamn shoulder.

[*Letting* KNOWLES *drag* KAROLIS *into a corner where he lets him drop.*]

5   You know what this cat was doing all the time we was in that goddamn broom closet? Tellin' jokes. [*Laughs.*] They must not a been funny either. Karolis didn't laugh once.

KNOWLES. What should I do with this guy. 10 I gotta drag him everywhere.

ORA. Drop him in that goddamn corner. [*Walks over to corner and nudges* KAROLIS *with his foot.*] Hey, muthafucka. Hey! Why don't you straighten up?

15   SKIPPY [*noticing* FARRELL, *who is still crumpled in an opposite corner, but stirring*]. Damn! What the hell happened to Donald?

PERRY. That goddamn Big Shot had to show how bad he was.

20   ORA [*laughing paradoxically*]. He called me a nigger.

[*All laugh.*]

LOVE. Well, what the hell are you? Wha's the matter, you shamed of your people?

25   ORA. Fuck you! [*He still stands over* KAROLIS, *nudging him with his foot.*] Hey, man, get up! [*Laughs.*]

HINES. Damn, Ora. Why don't you leave the cat alone?

30   ORA [*bending over as if to talk in* KAROLIS' *ear*]. Hey, baby, why don't you get up? I gotta nice fat sausage here for you.

GEORGE. Goddamn, Big Shot . . . You really a wrong sonofabitch!

35   ORA. Look man. [*Now kneeling over the slumped figure.*] If you want to get in on this you line up behind me. I don't give a shit what you got to say.

LOVE. Man, George, leave the cat alone. You 40 know that's his stick. That's what he does [*laughing*] for his kicks . . . rub up against half-dead white boys.

[*All laugh.*]

ORA [*looking over his shoulder . . . grud-* 45 *gingly having to smile too*]. I'd rub up against your momma too. [*Leaning back to* KAROLIS.] Come on, baby . . . I got this fat ass sa-zeech for you!

LOVE. Ora, you mad cause you don't have a momma of your own to rub up against.   50

[*All laugh.*]

ORA [*turns again, this time less amused*]. Fuck you, you bony head sonofabitch. As long as I can rub against your momma . . . or your fatha' [*laughs at his invention*] I'm doin' al- 55 right.

[*Door is pushed open suddenly and* FOOTS *comes in. He is nervous but keeps it hidden by a natural glibness and a sharp sense of what each boy in the room expects, singularly, from* 60 *him. He is the weakest physically and smallest of the bunch, but he is undoubtedly their leader. When* FOOTS *comes in* KAROLIS *looks up quickly, then slumps again.*]

HINES. Man, where the hell you been?   65

FOOTS. That goddamn Van Ness had me in his office. He said I'm a credit to my race. [*Laughs and all follow.*] He said I'm smart-as-a-whip [*imitating Van Ness*] and should help him to keep all you unsavory [*again imitating*] 70 elements in line.

[*All laugh again.*]

LOVE. Yeh? What's he talking about?

FOOTS. Well, he seems to think that you guys . . . particularly that goddamn Big Shot 75 and Knowles, are not good influences in this joint.

PERRY. Boy, you can say that again. Nutty muthafuckas!

ORA [*to* PERRY]. Fuck you, tar baby!   80

FOOTS. Well, I'm supposed to make sure that you guys don't do anything bad to anybody. Especially to James Karolis. [*Laughing.*]

GEORGE. Oh yeh? He know about that?

FOOTS. Yeh, somebody told him Knowles 85 said he was gonna kick Karolis' ass. [*Seeing* KAROLIS *in the corner for the first time. His first reaction is horror and disgust . . . but he keeps it controlled as is his style, and merely half-whistles.*] Goddamn! What the fuck hap- 90 pened to him? [*He goes over to* KAROLIS *and kneels near him, threatening to stay too long. He controls the impulse and gets up and walks back to where he was. He is talking through-*

out his action.] Damn! What'd you guys do, kill the cat?

PERRY. Heavy handed Big Shot again.

FOOTS [*looks at* ORA *quickly with disgust but softens it immediately to comic disdain*]. What the hell you hit him with, Ora, a goddamn train?

ORA [*happy at the notice of his destruction*]. No, man, I just bopped him in the mouth with the back of my hand.

FOOTS. Ga-uhd damn! You a rough ass cat, Shot. He sure don't look like he's in any way to fight anybody.

ORA [*laughing*]. No, but he might be able to suck you off. Hee, hee.

LOVE. Shit. You the one that look like you want that, Big Shot.

FOOTS. Oh, shit. There wasn't any need of bringing the cat down here if you guys were gonna fuck him up before I got here. He was supposed to fight me. [*Almost angry.*]

HINES. Yeh, that's what I thought. You shouldn't of sent Ora and Knowles up after him then.

FOOTS. The only person I asked to go up was Skippy.

SKIPPY. Well, the sonofabitch wouldn't come . . . So, I got Super-duck over there to help me. I didn't ask Ora to come. Knowles did.

KNOWLES. Oh, man, the cat's here. Get him up on his feet [*laughs*] then knock him down. That's all. That don't seem like no big problem to me. [*Through most of the action* KNOWLES *is drumming on the walls or the window or the door or the floor, in a kind of drum and bugle corps beat . . . also supplying the bugle parts vocally.*]

LOVE. Man, Knowles, why don't you stop being a goddamn Elk all the time. Damn. That cat's always drumming on something. Why don't you get a goddamn drum?

KNOWLES. I'm going to drum on your bony head in a little while if you don't shut up.

FOOTS. Well, I don't see any reason to keep all this shit up. Just pour water on the cat and let's get outta here.

ORA. What? You mean you made us go through all this bullshit for nothing?

FOOTS. Well, what the hell am I gonna do, beat on the guy while he's sprawled on the floor. Damn, Ora, you're a pretty lousy sonofabitch.

HINES. Man, Big Shot'd stomp anybody in any damn condition. He likes it when they're knocked out first, especially.

FOOTS. I'm pushed! There's no reason to stay here. I can't fight the guy like he is.

FARRELL [*who has pushed himself up and is leaning against the wall*]. I sure am glad somebody's got some sense here.

FOOTS [*seeing* FARRELL *for the first time*]. What the hell you doing here? Who asked you to come here, huh? [*Embarrassed and angry.*]

ORA. That stupid ass Perry brought him.

PERRY. That's right. I just thought there was gonna be a fight. I didn't know you guys were gonna lynch anybody.

FOOTS. Lynch, your ass. Look, Donald, why don't you leave, huh? Nobody needs you here.

FARRELL [*slowly*]. Yeh, okay, Ray. But I just want to know why you're gonna beat up on Jimmy like this. What the hell did he do to you?

FOOTS [*almost indignantly*]. None of your goddamn business, Farrell. Just leave!

ORA. Yeh, man. I should've thrown your ass out when you first come in here. Pee-the-bed sonofabitch.

FARRELL. O.K. [*Stands up, still lightly holding his stomach.*] O.K. But I want to take Jimmy out of here with me. He can't fight anybody.

ORA. Man, you better shut your goddamn mouth and get outta here!

FOOTS. Look, Donald, just leave, that's all. You hear? [*Turns his back on* FARRELL *and walks toward* KAROLIS, *then thinking better of it turns toward* FARRELL *again.*]

FARRELL. Ray! You're not gonna beat the guy up when he's like that are you?

FOOTS. I don't need you to tell me what to do. [*He goes over and pulls the door open slightly.*] Just get out of here . . . now!

FARRELL [*takes a step then looks toward*

KAROLIS]. But look at him, he can't do anything. [*To* FOOTS.] Why do you want to do this?

FOOTS. Goddamn it, get out!

FARRELL. That's no answer.

FOOTS. Man, I'll punch you in the belly myself.

FARRELL. Shit. [*Disparagingly . . . which makes* FOOTS *madder.*]

FOOTS [*in low horrible voice*]. Goddamnit. You better get the fuck outta here, right now!

FARRELL. Nobody's gonna tell me why? [*He starts to move for the door.*]

PERRY. Look, Donald, you better cool it, Buddy. You heard about that letter didn't you?

FARRELL. Letter? What letter?

FOOTS. Man, I told you to leave. I'm not gonna tell you again.

PERRY [*laughing*]. The letter Karolis sent Foots telling him he thought he was "beautiful" . . . and that he wanted to blow him.

[*All giggle.*]

FARRELL [*turning sharply toward* FOOTS]. A letter?

ORA [*rushing at* FARRELL *from the side and punching him*]. Goddamn it! Didn't you hear somebody say leave, pee ass?

FOOTS [*pushing between* FARRELL *and* ORA]. Cut it out, Ora!

FARRELL [*hurt again and slumping.* ORA *tries to hit him again and the punch is blocked by* FOOTS *who glares savagely at* ORA]. A letter? [*Groaning.*] Oh, Ray, come on. Why don't you come off it? [*He is looking up at* FOOTS.]

ORA [*leaps around* FOOTS *and pushes* FARRELL *into the door*]. Get out of here you dumb bastid!

[KNOWLES *pulls the door open and shoves* FARRELL *through it.*]

Goddamn, what a stupid punk. [*He laughs, as do some of the others.*]

FOOTS [*stares at the closed door for a second, then he turns slowly to the others*]. Look, let's get out of here. This stuff is finished.

KAROLIS [*has brought his head up during the preceding scuffle, and has been staring at* FOOTS. *As* FOOTS *and the others look over to-*ward him, he speaks very softly, but firmly*]. No. Nobody has to leave. I'll fight you, Ray. [*He begins to pull himself up. He is unsteady on his feet, but determined to get up . . . and to fight.*] I want to fight you.

[FOOTS *is startled and his eyes widen momentarily, but he suppresses it.*]

HINES. Damn. Some guys don't know when they're well off.

ORA. Yeh. You little skinny muthafucka. You should've kept your mouth shut, and played dead.

KNOWLES. Goddamn. You mean that sonofabitch wasn' dead? Shit, Big Shot, you must hit like a girl.

ORA [*to* KNOWLES]. Yeh? Well, let me hit you, you bastid.

KNOWLES [*disparagingly*]. Shit.

KAROLIS [*pushing himself off the wall slightly and wiping his face with his sleeve*]. No, Ray. Don't have them leave. I want to fight you.

FOOTS [*very silent and stiff, not wanting to be pushed*]. Oh? [*Slowly.*] Well, that's damn fine with me.

ORA [*going behind* KAROLIS *and pushing him toward* FOOTS]. You wanna fight? Well, go ahead, dick licker. [*Howls.*]

HINES. Yeh, get it on, fellas.

HOLMES. Karolis must be bad. [*Laughs.*]

GEORGE. Man [*to* KAROLIS], you sure you want to get in this? You look kinda shaky to me.

SKIPPY. Man, just sit down and watch. This might be good.

KAROLIS. Yes, Ray, I want to fight you, now. I want to kill you. [*His voice is still soft and terrible. The word "kill" is almost spit out.* FOOTS *does not move. He turns his head slightly to look* KAROLIS *in the eye, but he is motionless otherwise.*]

ORA. Goddamn it, fight!

[*He pushes* KAROLIS *again. This time* KAROLIS *almost bumps* FOOTS *and* FOOTS *throws up his hands and pushes him away.*]

FOOTS. Goddamn you! Goddamn you! [*His body moves from being completely immobile to an angry snarling figure.*] You bastard! [*The others become animated, clapping their hands, shouting, whistling, and moving around as if they were also fighting.*]

5 KAROLIS. No, Ray. I want to fight you. [*He is moving around now, but his hands are still held tightly and awkwardly at his sides.*] I want to fight you.

FOOTS [*moving around with his hands up to
10 fight. They both move around each other and FOOTS seems to get momentarily, a change of heart*]. Look now, Karolis . . . you're just gonna get your head blocked.

KAROLIS [*as if he didn't hear*]. No. You have
15 to fight me. I sent you a note, remember. That note saying I loved you. [*The others howl at this.*] The note saying you were beautiful. [*Tries to smile.*] You remember that note, Ray?

FOOTS. Goddamn it, if you're going to fight,
20 fight you cocksucker!

KAROLIS. Yeh. That's what I'm going to do Ray. I'm going to fight you. We're here to fight. About that note, right? The one that said I wanted to take you into my mouth.

25 [*FOOTS lunges at KAROLIS and misses.*]
Did I call you Ray in that letter . . . or Foots? [*Trying to laugh.*] Foots! [*Shouts.*] I'm going to break your fucking neck. That's right. That's who I want to kill. Foots!

30 ORA [*pushing KAROLIS into FOOTS*]. Fight, you goddamn sissy-punk bastid!

FOOTS [*slaps KAROLIS with his open hand*]. You crazy bastard!

KAROLIS [*backing up . . . wanting to talk but
35 still moving as if to fight*]. Are you Ray or Foots, huh?

[*The crowd begins to move forward to cut down the area of the match so that the two fighters will have to make contact.*]

40 HINES. Hit the sonofabitch, Foots!

FOOTS. Fight, you bastard!

KAROLIS. Yeh! That's why we're here, huh? I'll fight you, Foots! [*Spits the name.*] I'll fight you. Right here in this same place where you
45 said your name was Ray. [*Screaming. He lunges at FOOTS and manages to grab him in a choke hold.*] Ray, you said your name was. You said Ray. Right here in this filthy toilet.

You said Ray. [*He is choking FOOTS and
50 screaming. FOOTS struggles and is punching KAROLIS in the back and stomach, but he cannot get out of the hold.*] You put your hand on me and said Ray!

SKIPPY. Goddamn, that bastid is choking
55 the shit out of Foots.

[*The two still struggle, with KAROLIS continuing to have the advantage.*]

HINES. That fuck is trying to kill Foots!
HOLMES. Goddamn it!

60 ORA [*suddenly leaping on Karolis' back, puts the same choke hold on him*]. You cocksucka . . . how's that feel, huh? [*He pulls KAROLIS off of FOOTS who falls to his knes.*] Huh?

65 KNOWLES. Let's kick this cocksucka's ass real good.

[*He rushes up to help ORA, and the whole of the crowd surges into the center punching the fallen KAROLIS in the face. KNOWLES is
70 screaming with laughter.*]

KAROLIS. No, no, his name is Ray, not Foots. You stupid bastards. I love somebody you don't even know.

[*He is dragged to the floor. The crowd is
75 kicking and cursing him. ORA in the center punching the fallen KAROLIS in the face. KNOWLES is screaming with laughter.*

[*FOOTS is now on his hands and knees but his head hangs limply and he is unaware of
80 what is happening. He slumps again.*]

[*They have beaten KAROLIS enough. KAROLIS is spread in the center of the floor and is unmoving. ORA drapes some of the wet toilet paper across his body and face.*]

85 ORA. Let's stick the sonofabitch's head in the damn toilet.

PERRY. Oh, man, fuck you. The cat's completely out. What more can you do to him?

GEORGE. Yeh, let's get Foots, and get outta
90 here before somebody comes in.

ORA. Yeh. Hee, hee. Look at ol' Foots. That fuckin' paddy boy almost kilt him.

LOVE. Yeh. [*Laughing.*] I told you Karolis was probably bad!

95 [*All laugh.*]
KNOWLES. Nutty sonofabitch.

Love [*picking up* Foots, *helped by* Hines *and* Holmes]. Hey, big eye! Get the hell up.

Ora [*takes a paper cup and dips it in the commode and throws it in Foots' face*]. Yeh,
5 get up, bad ass. [*Laughs.*]

[*They all leave, as* Foots *begins to come to. All making noise, laughing, cursing.* Foots *follows them.*° Karolis *lies as before in the center of the room, motionless.*

10 [*After a minute or so* Karolis *moves his hand. Then his head moves and he tries to look up. He draws his legs up under him and pushes his head off the floor. Finally he manages to get to his hands and knees. He crawls over to*
15 *one of the commodes, pulls himself up, then falls backward awkwardly and heavily. At this point, the door is pushed open slightly, then it opens completely and* Foots *comes in. He stares at* Karolis' *body for a second, looks*
20 *quickly over his shoulder, then runs and kneels before the body, weeping and cradling the head in his arms.*]

End

Foots . . . them this sentence has been inserted by the editors